New Zealand

Carolyn Bain

George Dunford, Korina Miller, Sally O'Brier , Charles Rawlings-Way

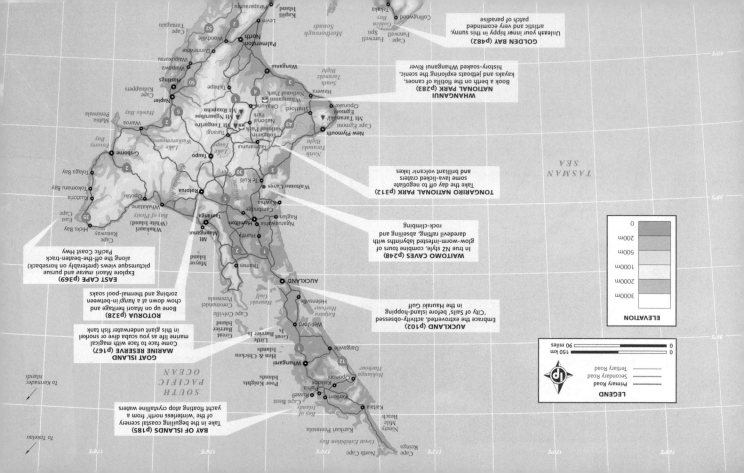

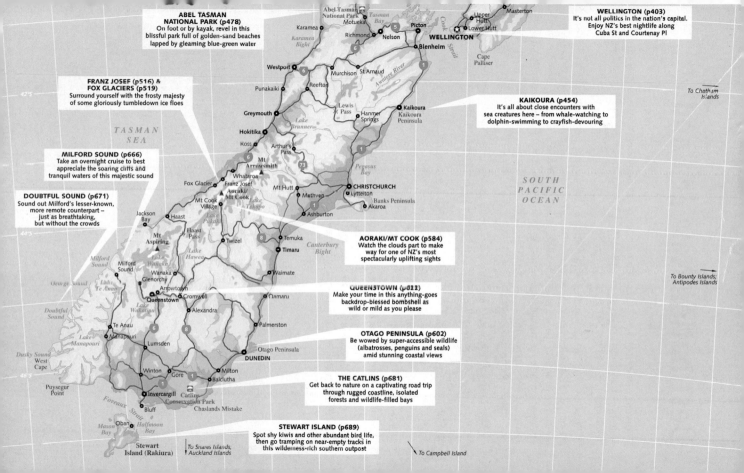

ABEL TASMAN NATIONAL PARK (p478)
On foot or by kayak, revel in this blissful park full of golden-sand beaches lapped by gleaming blue-green water

WELLINGTON (p403)
It's not all politics in the nation's capital. Enjoy NZ's best nightlife along Cuba St and Courtenay Pl

FRANZ JOSEF (p516) & FOX GLACIERS (p519)
Surround yourself with the frosty majesty of some gloriously tumbledown ice floes

KAIKOURA (p454)
It's all about close encounters with sea creatures here – from whale-watching to dolphin-swimming to crayfish-devouring

MILFORD SOUND (p666)
Take an overnight cruise to best appreciate the soaring cliffs and tranquil waters of this majestic sound

DOUBTFUL SOUND (p671)
Sound out Milford's lesser-known, more remote counterpart – just as breathtaking, but without the crowds

AORAKI/MT COOK (p584)
Watch the clouds part to make way for one of NZ's most spectacularly uplifting sights

QUEENSTOWN (p622)
Make your time in this anything-goes backdrop-blessed bombshell as wild or mild as you please

OTAGO PENINSULA (p602)
Be wowed by super-accessible wildlife (albatrosses, penguins and seals) amid stunning coastal views

THE CATLINS (p681)
Get back to nature on a captivating road trip through rugged coastline, isolated forests and wildlife-filled bays

STEWART ISLAND (p689)
Spot shy kiwis and other abundant bird life, then go tramping on near-empty tracks in this wilderness-rich southern outpost

TASMAN SEA

SOUTH PACIFIC OCEAN

To Chatham Islands

To Bounty Islands; Antipodes Islands

To Campbell Island

To Snares Islands; Auckland Islands

Destination New Zealand

The world's biggest film set is also the world's must-visit destination for the umpteenth year in a row – no wonder the locals are smiling. They've long known they live in paradise, and now everyone else does too.

In recent years New Zealand has been punching well above its weight and demanding to be noticed. Its movies, music, wine, progressive politics and clean green image have been kicking goals around the world, and people are paying attention in ways the country never dreamed possible. This small, remote nation, with a population of only four million, now hosts 2.4 million international visitors each year. And you'd be hard-pressed to find one that has left NZ's shores disappointed.

Why is that? Well, it's undoubtedly got something to do with the vast, empty landscapes. Words simply cannot do justice to this country's outlandishly beautiful scenery, but a pretty backdrop is not all that NZ has going for it. Genuinely friendly locals go out of their way to ensure visitors feel welcome. There's a vibrant Maori culture too, for this is a country that recognises and respects its indigenous people. And everyone rejoices in and treasures their magnificent natural surrounds. It's no surprise, then, to discover that visitors regard the world as a kinder, safer and softer place down here.

Have no doubt, you're in for the trip of a lifetime. When it's over, you'll take home memories of superb hospitality, first-class food and wine, and a smorgasbord of outdoor activities, as mild or as mad as you wished them to be. And there'll be no forgetting the natural beauty that left you breathless. One trip will not be enough.

RUTH EASTHAM & MAX PAOLI

National Parks

GARETH McCORMACK

The vast, remote Doubtful Sound (p671) is a highlight of Fiordland National Park

DAVID WALL

Mighty Aoraki/Mt Cook (p583) is the highest peak in Australasia

OTHER HIGHLIGHTS

- Shiver with awe at Fox (p519) and Franz Josef (p516) Glaciers in Westland Tai Poutini National Park
- Take a walk on the wild side on the Lake Waikaremoana Track (p384), in Te Urewera National Park

Overleaf: A woman takes part in a Maori performance on Regatta Day, Ngaruawahia (p232)

DAVID WALL

DAVID WALL

Misty, moody Westland Tai Poutini National Park (p514) is not be missed

Abel Tasman National Park (p478) is a popular spot for coastal walks

GARETH McCORMACK

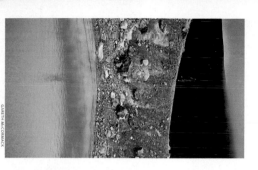

Circe the volcanic crater at Emerald Lakes, Tongariro National Park (p312)

GARETH McCORMACK

Tramp your way through soft snow at Mt Aspiring National Park (p647)

ANDREW PEACOCK

Islands & Beaches

Cruise the clear waters of the Bay of Islands (p185)
CHRISTOPHER GROENHOUT

Swim between the flags at St Clair Beach (p595), Dunedin
DAVID WALL

OTHER HIGHLIGHTS

- Experience the rugged and remote atmosphere of Stewart Island (p689), only 40km from the South Island
- Surfers can scout out brilliant breaks along the North Island's Surf Highway 45 (p271)
- Get away from it all in the islands of the Hauraki Gulf (p147), near Auckland

Traverse the flat, brown sands of Himatangi beach (p292), south of Palmerston North

RUTH EASTHAM & MAX PAOL

Sun yourself with the sea lions at Victory Beach (p604), Otago Peninsula

Spectacular Goat Island beach (p167) was the country's first marine reserve

Catch the perfect wave at Manu Bay (p237), Raglan, location of classic film *The Endless Summer*

City & Cultural Life

Deco delights abound in Napier (p386)

JOHN HAY

DAVID WALL

Immerse yourself in Maori culture on Regatta Day at Ngaruawahia (p232), near Hamilton

OTHER HIGHLIGHTS

- Stroll, tram, punt and dine your way around charming Christchurch (p527)
- Browse the eclectic little boutiques (p140) in Auckland's city centre and the art and craft shops in Devonport (p113)
- Experience the whacky and wonderful World of WearableArt & Collectable Cars Museum (p466) in Nelson

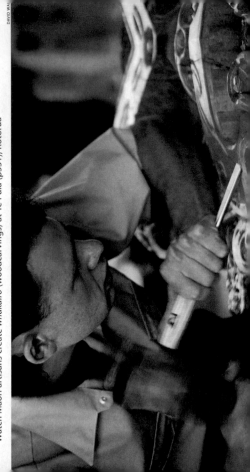

DAVID WALL

Watch Maori artisans create *whakairo* (woodcarvings) at Te Puia (p331), Rotorua

Tiered bungalows and villas line the hills of Wellington (p403)

PAUL KENNEDY

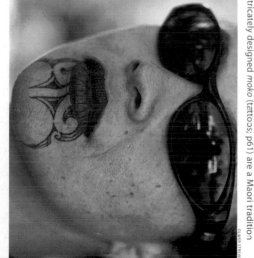

Intricately designed moko (tattoos; p61) are a Maori tradition

OLIVER STREWE

Caffeine aficionados will enjoy atmospheric Cafe L'Affare (p420), Wellington

DAVID WALL

Food & Drink

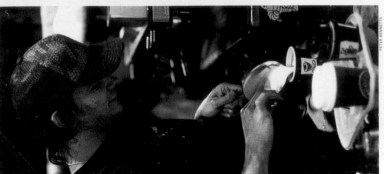

Feed your coffee addiction in hip Vulcan Lane (p133), Auckland

Gather your culinary courage to try a hare testicle at the Wildfoods Festival (p510), Hokitika

OTHER HIGHLIGHTS

- Tuck into a Maori *hangi* (p98), a meal of vegetables and meat cooked underground over hot river stones
- Whitebait (p498) is a West Coast speciality, best gobbled down in fried patties with mint sauce
- Savour the sugar buzz from pavlova topped with Kiwi fruit (p96), an iconic New Zealand dessert

Witness the pinot noir ageing to perfection at Gibbston Valley's wine cave (p632), near Queenstown

Contents

The Authors 17

Getting Started 20

Itineraries 24

Snapshot 29

History 31

The Culture 40

Maori Culture 54

Environment 62

New Zealand Outdoors 69

Food & Drink 93

Auckland Region 101
AUCKLAND 102
History 102
Orientation 103
Information 105
Sights 108
Activities 115
Walking Tour 117
Auckland for Children 118
Tours 118
Festivals & Events 119
Sleeping 119
Eating 133
Drinking 137
Entertainment 138
Shopping 140
Getting There & Away 141
Getting Around 142
AROUND AUCKLAND 144
Regional Parks 144

West of Auckland 144
HAURAKI GULF ISLANDS 147
Rangitoto & Motutapu Islands 147
Waiheke Island 149
Great Barrier Island 154
Tiritiri Matangi Island 159
Motuihe Island 159
Other Islands 159

Northland & the Bay of Islands 160
NORTH OF AUCKLAND 161
Whangaparaoa Peninsula 162
Orewa 163
Around Orewa 164
Puhoi 164
Warkworth 164
Kawau Island 165
Warkworth to Leigh 166
Leigh 166
Goat Island Beach 167
Leigh to Waipu 167
Waipu & Bream Bay 168
KAURI COAST 168
Puketi & Omahuta Forests 176
THE FAR NORTH 177
Kaitaia 177
Around Kaitaia 178
Cape Reinga & Ninety Mile Beach 179
Karikari Peninsula 181
Matakohe 169
Dargaville 169
Around Dargaville 171
Dargaville to Hokianga 172
HOKIANGA 173
Omapere & Opononi 174
Rawene 175
Kohukohu 176
Mitimiti 176
Doubtless Bay 181
Doubtless Bay to Bay of Islands 183
BAY OF ISLANDS 185
Pewhairangi 189
Paihia & Waitangi 189
Russell 193
Kerikeri 196
BAY OF ISLANDS TO WHANGAREI 199

Russell Road 200
Tutukaka Coast &
Poor Knights Islands 200
Whangarei 201
Around Whangarei 205

Coromandel
Region 206
COROMANDEL
PENINSULA 207
Thames 209
Coromandel Forest Park 212
Thames to Coromandel
Town 212
Coromandel Town 213
Far North Coromandel 215
Coromandel Town to
Whitianga 216
Whitianga 217
Around Whitianga 219
Hahei 220
Around Hahei 221
Hot Water Beach 221
Tairua 221
Around Tairua 223
Opoutere Beach 223
Whangamata 223
Waihi 224
Waihi Beach 225
HAURAKI REGION 225
Miranda 226
Paeroa 226
Te Aroha 227

Waikato &
the King Country 229
WAIKATO 230
Auckland to Hamilton 230
Hamilton 232
Waingaro Hot Springs 237
Raglan 237
Around Raglan 240
Raglan to Kawhia 240
Kawhia 241
Te Awamutu 242
Around Te Awamutu 243
Cambridge 243
Lake Karapiro 245
Matamata 245
Tirau 246
THE KING COUNTRY 246
Otorohanga 247
Waitomo 248

Marokopa Road 200
Te Kuiti 200
Te Kuiti to Mokau 201
Taumarunui 205

Taranaki 257
New Plymouth 258
Around New Plymouth 267
Mt Taranaki (Mt Egmont) 267
Around Mt Taranaki 270
Surf Highway 45 271

Wanganui &
Palmerston North 274
WANGANUI REGION 275
Wanganui 277
Whanganui National
Park & River Road 283
PALMERSTON NORTH 286
South of Palmerston
North 292

Taupo & the
Central Plateau 293
LAKE TAUPO REGION 294
Taupo 294
Around Taupo 305
Turangi 309
TONGARIRO & AROUND 312
Tongariro National Park 312
National Park 320
Ohakune 322
Lake Rotokura 326
Waiouru 326

Rotorua &
the Bay of Plenty 327
ROTORUA 328
History 328
Orientation 329
Information 329
Sights 330
Activities 334
Walking Tour 337
Rotorua for Children 338
Tours 338
Sleeping 338
Eating 341
Drinking 342
Entertainment 342
Shopping 342

Getting There & Away 343
Getting Around 343
AROUND ROTORUA 344
North of Rotorua 344
Northeast of Rotorua 346
Southeast of Rotorua 346
South of Rotorua 347
WESTERN BAY OF
PLENTY 347
Tauranga 348
Mt Maunganui 354
Around Tauranga 357
EASTERN BAY OF
PLENTY 360
Whakatane 360
Ohope Beach 364
Motuhora (Whale Island) 364
Whakaari (White Island) 364
Whakatane to Rotorua 365
Opotiki 365

The East Coast 368
EAST CAPE 369
Opotiki to East Cape 371
Raukumara & Waioeka 373
East Cape to Gisborne 373
POVERTY BAY 375
Gisborne 375
Gisborne to Wairoa 382
HAWKES BAY 382
Wairoa 383
Te Urewera National Park 383
Wairoa to Napier 386
Napier 386
Hastings 394
Havelock North 397
Around Hawkes Bay 398

Wellington Region 402
WELLINGTON 403
History 404
Orientation 405
Information 408
Sights 408
Activities 413
Walking Tour 413
Wellington for Children 414
Tours 414
Festivals & Events 415
Sleeping 416
Eating 418
Drinking 421
Entertainment 422

Shopping 423
Getting There & Away 424
Getting Around 425
HUTT VALLEY 427
KAPITI COAST 427
Paekakariki 428
Paraparaumu 429
Kapiti Island 430
Waikanae 430
Otaki 430
THE WAIRARAPA 431
Greytown 432
Martinborough 432
Wairarapa Coast 434
Masterton 434
Forest Parks 435
Mt Bruce 435

Marlborough & Nelson 436
MARLBOROUGH REGION 437
Picton 438
Marlborough Sounds 443
Havelock 447
Blenheim 449
Renwick 451
Kaikoura 454
NELSON REGION 461
Nelson 461
Nelson Lakes National Park 471
Nelson to Motueka 473
Motueka 474
Motueka to Abel Tasman 477
Abel Tasman National Park 473
GOLDEN BAY 482
State Highway 60 to Takaka 482
Takaka 483
Pohara 485
Collingwood 485
Farewell Spit & Around 486
Kahurangi National Park 487

The West Coast 489
Murchison 490
Buller Gorge 492
Westport 493
Around Westport 496
Westport to Karamea 497
Karamea 497
Westport to Greymouth 499
Grey Valley 501
Greymouth 503

Around Greymouth 507
Hokitika 508
Around Hokitika 512
Hokitika to Westland Tai Poutini National Park 512
Westland Tai Poutini National Park 514
South to Haast 522
Haast Region 523
Haast Pass 525

Christchurch & Canterbury 526
CHRISTCHURCH 527
History 527
Orientation 529
Information 529
Sights 531
Activities 536
Walking Tour 537
Christchurch for Children 538
Tours 539
Festivals & Events 539
Sleeping 539
Eating 551
Drinking 553
Entertainment 553
Shopping 555
Getting There & Away 555
Getting Around 556
AROUND CHRISTCHURCH 557
Lyttelton 557
Banks Peninsula 559
NORTH CANTERBURY 564
Hanmer Springs 564
Lewis Pass Highway 567
CENTRAL CANTERBURY 568
Craigieburn Forest Park 568
Arthur's Pass 569
Methven 571
Mt Somers 573
SOUTH CANTERBURY 574
Timaru 574
To Mackenzie Country 576
Mackenzie Country 578
Aoraki/Mt Cook National Park 583

Dunedin & Otago 589
DUNEDIN & THE OTAGO PENINSULA 590
Dunedin 590
Otago Peninsula 602

CENTRAL OTAGO 606
Cromwell 606
Clyde 607
Alexandra 608
Alexandra to Palmerston 609
Alexandra to Dunedin 611
Clutha District 613
NORTH OTAGO 613
Oamaru 614
Waitaki Valley 617
Oamaru to Dunedin 619

Queenstown & Wanaka 620
QUEENSTOWN REGION 621
Queenstown 622
Arrowtown 639
Around Arrowtown 642
Glenorchy 642
Lake Wakatipu Region 643
Tramps 645
WANAKA REGION 645
Wanaka 646
Makarora 653
Hawea 655
Cardrona 655

Fiordland & Southland 656
FIORDLAND 657
Te Anau 657
Te Anau to Milford 664
Milford Sound 666
Manapouri 670
Doubtful Sound 671
Southern Scenic Route 672
CENTRAL SOUTHLAND 674
Invercargill 674
Bluff 679
Invercargill to Dunedin 680
THE CATLINS 681
Invercargill to Papatowai 684
Papatowai to Balclutha 685

Stewart Island & Outer Islands 688
STEWART ISLAND 689
CHATHAM ISLANDS 696
OTHER ISLANDS 700
Subantarctic Islands 700
The Kermadecs 701
Tokelau 701

Directory 702

Accommodation	702
Activities	706
Business Hours	706
Children	706
Climate Charts	707
Customs	708
Dangers & Annoyances	708
Disabled Travellers	709
Discount Cards	709
Embassies & Consulates	709
Festivals & Events	710
Food	710
Gay & Lesbian Travellers	711
Holidays	711
Insurance	712
Internet Access	712
Legal Matters	713
Maps	713
Money	714
Post	715
Shopping	716
Telephone	717
Time	718
Tourist Information	719
Visas	719
Women Travellers	720
Work	720

Transport 722

GETTING THERE & AWAY	**722**
Entering the Country	722
Air	722
Sea	725
GETTING AROUND	**726**
Air	726
Bicycle	726
Boat	728
Bus	728
Car & Motorcycle	731
Hitching	735
Local Transport	736
Train	736

Health 737

BEFORE YOU GO	**737**
Insurance	737
Recommended Vaccinations	737
Medical Checklist	737
Internet Resources	738

IN TRANSIT	**738**
Deep Vein Thrombosis (DVT)	738
Jet Lag & Motion Sickness	738
IN NEW ZEALAND	**738**
Availability & Cost of Health Care	738
Infectious Diseases	739
Travellers' Diarrhoea	739
Environmental Hazards	739

Language 741

Glossary 744

Behind the Scenes 747

Index 754

World Time Zones 770

Map Legend 772

Regional Map Contents

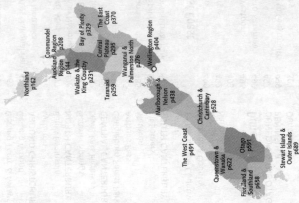

Northland p162

Auckland Region p144

Coromandel Region p208

Waikato & the King Country p231

Bay of Plenty p329

The East Coast p370

Central Plateau p295

Taranaki p259

Wanganui & Palmerston North p276

Wellington Region p404

Marlborough & Nelson p438

The West Coast p491

Christchurch & Canterbury p528

Otago p591

Queenstown & Wanaka p528

Fiordland & Southland p658

Stewart Island & Outer Islands p689

The Authors

CAROLYN BAIN
Coordinating Author, Wellington, Marlborough & Nelson, Canterbury

Melbourne-based Carolyn polished her best jandals for a trip across the Tasman to get reacquainted with the neighbours, after last covering New Zealand for Lonely Planet four years ago. A lot has changed in the Land of the Long White Cloud since she first visited more than a decade ago (Who knew they could make such amazing movies? Such fine wines?), and she's happy that so many people are now discovering the country's charms. Thankfully, some of her favourite things about NZ have remained the same: the friendliness of the locals, the sheer beauty of the landscape, the sweet mangling of the vowels...

Golden Bay○
Abel Tasman NP○
Motueka ○○Nelson
Nelson Lakes NP○

The Coordinating Author's Favourite Trip

I hadn't visited the top of the South Island before, and I wondered if it could really be as beautiful (and as sunny) as the brochures made out. Nelson Lakes National Park (p471) took me by surprise: I hadn't expected glacial lakes and snow-capped mountains in a region renowned for its coastline. I got my fill of galleries, markets and cafés in Ne son (p461), easily one of NZ's most liveable cities, then in Motueka (p474) plucked up the courage to go skydiving and was rewarded with magnificent views from a heart-stopping 12,000ft. After recovering from the adrenaline rush in Abel Tasman National Park (p478) – every bit as stunning as the brochures promised – it was up over the hill to explore Golden Bay (p482), which felt off-the-beaten-track and divinely chilled-out. And the sun shone the entire time.

GEORGE DUNFORD
Taranaki, Central Plateau, Bay of Plenty

Raised singing 'Pokarekare Ana' anc crossing the Tasman irregularly, George relished the chance to get back amongst the Swine lager and geothermal uncertainty of Aotearoa. To keep th ngs interesting the packed his mum and a friend for the journey. When he's not complaining to his travel companions, George is writing for *Australian Traveller Magazine*, *The Age Cheap Eats Guide*, the *Big Issue* and a couple of Lonely Planet guidebooks.

LONELY PLANET AUTHORS

Why is our travel information the best in the world? I''s simple: our authors are independen', dedicated travellers. They don't research using just the Internet or phone, and they don't take freebies in exchange for positive coverage. They trave w dely, to all the popular spots and off the beaten track. They personally visit thousands of hotels, restaurants, cafés, bars, galleries, palaces, museums and m>re – and they take pride in getting all the details right, and telling it how it is. For more, see the authors section on www.onelyplanet.com.

KORINA MILLER

Otago, Queenstown & Wanaka, Southland, Stewart Island

Korina grew up on Vancouver Island and was lucky enough to have parents who carted her around North America on a number of occasions, leaving her with a well-developed sense of wanderlust. At 18 she left home with her backpack and has been roaming the world ever since. In 2002, her love of the sea and mountains took her to NZ's South Island for the better part of a year, and she was thrilled to return there to work on this book. Korina has a degree in Communications, an MA in Migration Studies and has been writing for Lonely Planet since the late '90s. She lives in England…for the moment.

SALLY O'BRIEN

Auckland, Northland, Coromandel, Waikato & the King Country

Sally was pleasantly surprised to discover that on this, her third trip to NZ, stories of the great Rotorua jetboating incident of the 1970s (in which her family experienced lunch in reverse) and the great Mt Hutt skiing fiasco of the 1980s (in which her ski jacket become entangled with the chairlift) had long since died down. What a forgiving, tolerant and warm-hearted land. To celebrate, she fulfilled a lifelong dream of wearing a garish jumpsuit and hurling herself out of a plane. Next time, she's going to get a dolphin to join her in the caves at Waitomo.

CHARLES RAWLINGS-WAY

Wanganui & Palmerston North, East Coast, West Coast

A slow Houdini, Charles has spent decades trying to escape from large islands. England and Tasmania failed to contain him; NZ was the next challenge. Aotearoa first strummed a curious chord in Charles when a wandering uncle returned with a faux-greenstone *tiki* in 1981; he wore it with pride until he saw the NZ cricket team's beige uniforms in 1982. Driving 5128 Kiwi kilometres on this trip has helped him forgive – he's once again smitten with the country's phantasmal landscapes, disarming locals and determination to sculpt its own political and cultural destiny.

CONTRIBUTING AUTHORS

Professor James Belich wrote the History chapter (p31). James is one of NZ's pre-eminent historians and the award-winning author of *The New Zealand Wars*, *Making Peoples* and *Paradise Reforged*. He has also worked in TV – *NZ Wars* was screened in NZ in 1998.

Julie Biuso wrote the Food & Drink chapter (p93). After a successful stint teaching at the prestigious London School of Cordon Bleu, and setting up and running the franchised school in NZ, Julie chucked in the toque to take up the pen and set off on a hedonistic life of eating, drinking, travelling and writing, hoping someone would pay for it. She has been, and still is, food editor at a number of NZ magazines and newspapers. She has written 13 food books, is a regular on TV and radio and runs a website (www.juliebiuso.com). For relaxation she strokes her cat while watching her goldfish swimming in his bowl.

Getting Started

Russell Brown wrote the Culture chapter (p40). Russell is one of NZ's most prolific journalists. He is the host of *Mediawatch*, a weekly media commentary show on National Radio, and has written the weekly computers column in the *New Zealand Listener* since its inception. He also writes columns for NZ's leading business magazine, *Unlimited*, and the music magazine *Real Groove*. And when he's not doing any of that he's mentoring at Auckland radio station 95bFM, and tending to the award-winning website http://publicaddress.net, where his popular weblog, *Hard News*, is hosted. He lives in Auckland's Pt Chevalier with his family and likes playing and watching sport, cooking, listening to music and drinking wine in moderation.

Tony Horwitz wrote the Captain James Cook boxed text (p33) in the History chapter. Tony is a Pulitzer-winning reporter and nonfiction author. His fascination with James Cook, and with travel, took him around NZ, Australia and the Pacific while researching *Blue Latitudes* (alternatively titled *Into the Blue*), part biography of Cook and part travelogue.

Errol Hunt is a Kiwi of Scots (MacKinven) and Maori (Ngapuhi) descent, hailing from Whakatane in the Bay of Plenty. After flirting with the public service in NZ and magneto-hydrodynamic physics in Australia, Errol dropped any pretence at being interested in science and joined Lonely Planet. He has written extensively on NZ and the Pacific but has spent most of his time as Lonely Planet as the commissioning editor for guidebooks to Australia, NZ and the Pacific. Errol wrote the Maori Culture chapter (p54), the boxed texts on the Land Wars (p35) and *Lord of the Rings* (p49), and the Maori NZ boxes.

Josh Kronfeld wrote the Surfing in New Zealand boxed text (p78) in the New Zealand Outdoors chapter. Josh is an ex-All Black flanker, whose passion for surfing NZ's beaches is legendary and who found travelling for rugby a way to surf other great breaks around the world.

Dr David Millar wrote the Health chapter (p737). David is a travel-medicine specialist, diving doctor and lecturer in wilderness medicine. He is currently a medical director with the Travel Doctor in Auckland.

Nandor Tanczos MP wrote the Environmental Issues in Aotearoa New Zealand boxed text (p63). NZ's first Rastafarian Member of Parliament (NZ Greens Party), and the first to enter Parliament in dreadlocks and a hemp suit, he's also the Greens' spokesperson on constitutional issues and the environment.

Vaughan Yarwood wrote the Environment chapter (p62). Vaughan is an Auckland-based writer whose most recent book, *The History Makers: Adventures in New Zealand Biography*, is published by Random House. Earlier work includes *The Best of New Zealand*, a collection of essays on NZ life and culture by prominent Kiwis, which he edited, and the regional history *Between Coasts: from Kaipara to Kawau*. He has written widely for NZ and international publications and is the former associate editor of *New Zealand Geographic*, for which he continues to write. International assignments have taken him to many countries in Europe, Asia and the Pacific. Having travelled to Antarctica to research a book on polar exploration, he is now completing a project on iconic NZ arms.

Thanks also for the contributions from **Sir Ian McKellen** (Sandflies boxed text, p708) and **Joe Bennett** (p66).

Getting Started

How do you envisage your New Zealand trip? It's worth giving the question some serious thought in your holiday planning. Do you have three weeks to explore all corners, or six months? A preference for taking in the scenery from a bus while someone else navigates the highways, or hiring a car to enable you to set your own agenda (or a campervan to allow you to take your home wherever you go)? Have you made a shopping list of gravity-defying activities you plan to undertake before partying the nights away with fellow backpackers? Might you consider stopping to replenish funds with some fruit-picking or other money-earner? Are you hoping for spiritual awakening in some wide open spaces, with walking and bush camping high on your agenda? Or in your mind's eye, is NZ all about staying in luxury accommodation and getting acquainted with the finest local wines and produce? Perhaps a combination of all of the above?

All things are possible here. The relative ease of travel in NZ and its established network of all-budgets accommodation and organised activities make this country easy to explore. That said, look beyond the idyllic, hassle-free persona pushed by tourism brochures or you'll end up taking NZ's idiosyncratic people and landscapes for granted.

There's a lot to see and do, so think about your priorities and allow enough time to achieve them. But don't forget to also factor some space into your itinerary for those serendipitous moments that can really make your trip.

WHEN TO GO

The warmer months between November and April are the catalyst for outdoor exploration and this is the official high season, with the slightly cooler and less tourist-trafficked months of October/November and April/May among the best times to visit. Summer (December to February) is also when Kiwis lift their spirits with numerous food and wine festivals, concerts and sports events. If you're a snow bunny, visit when the white stuff is thick on the ground over winter (June to August), the high season in skiing areas – but note that if you visit in winter, some areas popular with warm-weather travellers (eg beachside towns) will be in semi-hibernation.

NZ is in the Roaring Forties and so has a prevailing wind blowing over it from west to east year-round, ranging from gentle breezes to the odd

See Climate Charts (p707) for more information.

DON'T LEAVE HOME WITHOUT...

- Double-checking the visa situation (see p719)
- A travel-insurance policy specifically covering you for any planned high-risk activities (see p712)
- Insect repellent to dissuade sandflies from dropping by for lunch (see p708)
- The ability to get excited over any game of rugby (p45)
- Packing a range of clothing to suit the changeability of the weather (p707)
- A hearty appetite for sampling the fine local food and wine (p93)
- Your mobile phone (p718) – handy for driving in remote areas and booking restaurants and accommodation while in transit

raging gale. On both main islands it gets wetter in the west than in the east because the mountains block the moisture-laden winds blowing in from the Tasman Sea. It's usually a few degrees cooler on the South Island than the North Island. When concocting your travel plans, remember that NZ has a maritime climate, meaning the weather can change very quickly – anyone tramping at high altitudes must be fully prepared for this climatic unpredictability.

If you're serious about having a holiday – as opposed to engaging in modern-day gladiatorial contests with flotillas of campervans, queues of highly strung parents and inexhaustible platoons of children for the right to stay and eat in your accommodation and restaurant of choice – then try not to visit key sites during local school holidays (particularly mid-December to early February) and public holidays (p711).

COSTS & MONEY

In recent years the NZ dollar has gained some ground against stronger international currencies such as the greenback, and the country's growing tourist popularity has seen many prices rise in line with demand. However, if you're visiting from Europe or North America it's still a fairly economical destination – unless you throw yourself out of a plane or cling to a jetboat every day of your trip, that is. In fact, the cost of activities figures prominently in the expense of every visit, and it helps to decide in advance what you'd prefer to spend your money on. Travellers who intend being very active should consider staying in cheaper accommodation to help finance their exertions, while more sedentary types who prefer sitting in front of a meal to dangling at the end of a bungy cord should limit their organised activities. Gastronomes will find that food is surprisingly pricey – cooked breakfasts at smart cafés average around $15, while main dishes at top-end restaurants cost upwards of $30.

If you do a fair amount of sightseeing, eat out once or twice a day and stay in the least expensive motels or B&Bs, you should budget at least $120 to $150 per day (per person travelling as a pair), not including car hire or extra activities. Packing kids into your suitcases obviously means greater expense, but museums, cinemas and tour and activity organisers usually offer reasonable discounts for children, and there are plenty of open-air attractions available free of charge.

At the low-cost end, if you camp or stay in hostels, cook your own meals, restrain your urge for entertainment, tackle attractions independently and travel around on a bus pass, you could probably eke out an existence on $65 per day. But if you want to enjoy the occasional

HOW MUCH?

Cup of decent coffee $3-3.50

Movie ticket $12-14

Dorm bed $19-28

Motel room $90-140

Magnificent scenery free

See also the Lonely Planet Index, inside front cover.

TOP TENS

Must-See Movies

Spending an evening or three reeling off some classic NZ films doesn't just reward you with advance screenings of some much-publicised scenery. It also allows you to dig past the country's distractingly grand surface and get right under its skin to an often-bleak mysticism that's been well captured on celluloid. See p49 for some reviews of these and other locally produced films.

- *The Lord of the Rings* trilogy (2001–03) Director: Peter Jackson
- *Once Were Warriors* (1994) Director: Lee Tamahori
- *The Piano* (1993) Director: Jane Campion
- *Whale Rider* (2002) Director: Niki Caro
- *King Kong* (2005) Director: Peter Jackson
- *In My Father's Den* (2004) Director: Brad McGann
- *An Angel at My Table* (1990) Director: Jane Campion
- *The Chronicles of Narnia: The Lion, the Witch and the Wardrobe* (2005) Director: Andrew Adamson
- *Heavenly Creatures* (1994) Director: Peter Jackson
- *Rain* (2001) Director: Christine Jeffs

Top Reads

Be it through escapist plots, multilayered fiction, reinvented realities or character-driven social commentary, the significant body of Kiwi literature presents an opportunity to learn much about the islands. NZ's unsettled history, its burgeoning cultural awareness and the physical power of the landscape go well beyond a camera lens. See p48 for some reviews of these and other NZ books.

- *Whale Rider* (1987) Witi Ihimaera
- *Hibiscus Coast* (2005) Paula Morris
- *The Book of Fame* (2000) Lloyd Jones
- *Bone People* (1988) Keri Hulme
- *The Vintner's Luck* (2000) Elizabeth Knox
- *The Carpathians* (1988) Janet Frame
- *Tu* (2004) Patricia Grace
- *Mansfield* (2004) CK Stead
- *Loving Ways* (1996) Maurice Gee
- *In a Fishbone Church* (1998) Catherine Chidgey

Festive Events

Kiwis love an excuse to party, and travellers who wish to join in the fun might like to plan their travels around the food/wine/arts events that best tickle their fancy. Here are some of our favourite excuses – quirky and traditional – to get festive. See also the Directory (p710) and the Festivals & Events sections in destination chapters.

- World Buskers Festival – Christchurch, January (p539)
- Harvest Hawkes Bay – Hawkes Bay, February (p710)
- New Zealand Festival – Wellington, February to March every two years (p415)
- Pasifika Festival – Auckland, March (p119)
- Wildfoods Festival – Hokitika, March (p510)
- New Zealand Gold Guitar Awards – Gore, June (p681)
- Carrot Festival – Ohakune, July (see the boxed text, p322)
- Queenstown Winter Festival – Queenstown, July (p632)
- New Zealand International Film Festivals – nationwide, July to November (p710)
- World of WearableArt Award Show – Wellington, September (p416)

restaurant-cooked meal and sip of beer or wine, then $90 per day is far more realistic. Staying in places for longer periods and/or travelling in a group will help lower your costs.

TRAVEL LITERATURE

In the past there has been a noticeable dearth of dedicated travel literature on NZ, but that is slowly changing, given NZ's bright, shiny place on the world tourism stage. The country's ability to inspire its explorers is obvious in most published accounts of local wanderings.

Lyttelton-based Joe Bennett, a wry, dog-loving Englishman-in-New-Zealand, writes a popular column syndicated to newspapers throughout NZ, and these columns are published annually in book form (*Dogmatic*, the latest collection, was published in November 2005). *A Land of Two Halves* (2004) is Joe's tale of hitchhiking around the country in an attempt to understand just what it is that has kept him in NZ for 15 years. The result is a fabulous travelogue, full of pithy descriptions, perceptive observations and witty anecdotes.

When another Brit, Polly Evans, reads that the traditional Kiwi bloke is becoming an endangered species, she decides to travel to NZ in search of this dying breed – the result is *Kiwis Might Fly: Around New Zealand on Two Wheels* (2004). Evans does her book no favours by writing pitifully of her decision to travel the length of the country by motorcycle (on a powerful machine and with no motorbiking experience, mind you). When the book's focus is on the places Evans visits and the people she meets, the writing is a good deal more enjoyable.

The cheesy intro and need for a good fact-checker (NZ's population is four million, not three, the Marlboro Sounds are in fact the Marlborough Sounds) didn't leave too favourable an impression, but *Staying from the Flock: Travels in New Zealand* (2005) by Alexander Elder isn't too bad a read. It's aimed at the reader who knows nothing about the country and involves the New York author, an 'ageing baby boomer' (his description) and frequent visitor to NZ, travelling from south to north over two months. En route he chronicles his daily experiences sightseeing, staying in farmstays and drinking plenty of local wine.

INTERNET RESOURCES

Destination New Zealand (www.destination-nz.com) Resourceful site with an excellent listing of websites.

Lonely Planet (www.lonelyplanet.com) Get started with summaries on NZ and travellers trading info on the Thorn Tree.

New Zealand Tourism Online (www.tourism.net.nz) A huge commercial site with over 10,000 tourism listings and plenty of useful information.

Pure New Zealand (www.newzealand.com) As you'd expect, NZ's official tourism site has comprehensive info for visitors.

Stuff (www.stuff.co.nz) Pages of NZ news, though all of it sourced from Fairfax New Zealand publications.

Te Puna Web Directory (http://webdirectory.natlib.govt.nz) Exhaustive directory of domestic websites, maintained by the National Library of New Zealand.

Itineraries

CLASSIC ROUTES

TOP TO BOTTOM   Four to Six Weeks / Auckland to Christchurch

First-time visitors to the country no doubt wish to take in NZ's tourist icons, and who are we to argue? After cruising inner-city **Auckland** (p102) and her lovely harbours, follow SH1 north to the glorious, winterless **Bay of Islands** (p185) to juggle surfboards, kayaks and scuba gear. South of Auckland, hold your nose and head for the gush and bubble of **Rotorua** (p294). Continue south to hook a trout at **Lake Taupo** (p294), then admire the triple-peaked wilderness of **Tongariro National Park** (p312) before making a beeline for the Beehive in café-lovin' **Wellington** (p403).

After navigating Cook Strait, hug the east coast on SH1 to whale-watching **Kaikoura** (p454) and cathedral-centred **Christchurch** (p527). Situated further south is the faunal sanctuary of the **Otago Peninsula** (p602) and the Victorian façades of coffee-fuelled, student-filled **Dunedin** (p590). Mix-and-match highways across the island to reach **Te Anau** (p657) for the beguiling side-road to **Milford Sound** (p631), then backtrack to SH6 and head north into the frenzy of **Queenstown** (p622). Swap SH6 for SH8 for an eyeful of the Cloud Piercer, **Aoraki/Mt Cook** (p583), before veering east to rejoin the coast road to Christchurch.

Join the main-attraction dots on a city-sampling, surf-riding, wildlife-watching and mountain-spotting tour of the country. Take your time on this well-travelled road to switch to holiday mode, get back to nature and savour the pleasures of dual-island travel.

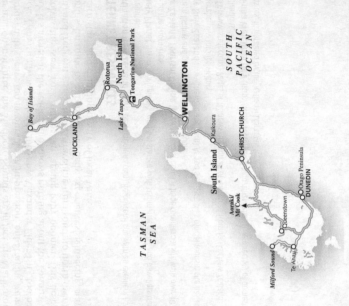

SOUTHERN EXPOSURE

One Month / Christchurch to Christchurch

The mountainous, unhurried South Island affords a popular and visually inspiring circuit.

From the manicured charms of **Christchurch** (p527) travel north up the east coast to the marvellous marine life of **Kaikoura** (p454), and make a date with a dolphin or whale in local waters. From there it's onto the grape-wreathed vineyards around **Blenheim** (p449) and the secret-coved delights of the **Marlborough Sounds** (p443). Swing by sunny, crafty **Nelson** (p461), then board a kayak for exploration of the stunning bays of **Abel Tasman National Park** (p478). From here, traverse formidable **Buller Gorge** (p452) to reach the rugged west coast at **Westport** (p493). Heading south on SH6 are the strikingly layered rocks of **Punakaiki** (p499), the greenstone-polishing town of **Hokitika** (p508) and the magnificent icy juggernauts of **Franz Josef Glacier** (p516) and **Fox Glacier** (p519). Further south, over the Haast Pass, are the perpetually active towns of **Wanaka** (p646) and **Queenstown** (p622), where you can go nuts on adrenaline activities, or just take in the remarkable Remarkables.

After heading south, detour off SH6 to **Te Anau** (p657) and then on to the divine **Milford Sound** (p631). Backtrack via Te Anau to **Manapouri** (p670) to access the fantastically remote **Doubtful Sound** (p671) – now you can join the debate on just which sound is better. Doubling back, the road south ends at **Invercargill** (p674), but a secondary road skirts the captivating coastal ecology of **The Catlins** (p681). Rejoin SH1 and forge north to Scottish-bred **Dunedin** (p590), and the stately limestone of penguin-friendly **Oamaru** (p614) before ducking inland on SH83 towards awesome **Aoraki/Mt Cook** (p583). Continue past the turquoise brilliance of **Lake Tekapo** (p578) back to Christchurch.

Feast your eyes and focus your camera on mountain highs, valley lows, icy vistas and indomitable wilderness on this journey around the deep south. Get active on a kayak, dangle from a bungy cord, cruise a sound and drink in the beauty around every turn.

ROADS LESS TRAVELLED

DUE NORTH

One Month / Auckland to Wellington

A full exploration of the volcanic, river-swept North Island doesn't always occur to visitors, who leapfrog large swaths of terrain between prominent features like the Bay of Islands and Rotorua. But a circumnavigation of this island's secluded beaches and secret forests won't disappoint.

Start by island-hopping out of **Auckland** (p102) to arty, vineyard-laden **Waiheke Island** (p149) or volcanic **Rangitoto Island** (p147). After winding up back in Auckland, head for a snorkel off **Goat Island Beach** (p167). Continue on to the iconic **Bay of Islands** (p185) to take to the waters, peruse the historic confines of **Russell** (p193) and to see where a landmark treaty was signed at **Waitangi** (p189). After sprawling on the gorgeous sands of **Matai Bay** (p181), swing north to the desolate **Ninety Mile Beach** (p179). Snake back through Auckland and head east to roam the splendidly forested **Coromandel Peninsula** (p207) from your base of a beachside bach. From here, follow SH26 to the equine paradise of **Cambridge** (p243) before heading to **Rotorua** (p328).

Take SH30 to the underground karst (limestone) glory of **Waitomo Caves** (p248), then SH3 to the dormant cone of **Mt Taranaki/Egmont** (p267). Further south, detour up the **Whanganui River Rd** (p283) before trundling north via the volcanoes of **Tongariro National Park** (p312). After a walk in the park head to **Taupo** (p294) for some fishing. The SH5 visits **Napier** (p386), with its roaring-'30s wardrobe and gourmet pleasures, while SH2 takes in the wine-happy **Wairarapa region** (p431) before ending in arts-rich **Wellington** (p403).

Hot springs, mud baths, variegated volcanic lakes, untramped native forests and tracts of sand with nary a footprint in sight will be encountered as you head north then south on this diverse trail. But there's plenty of sophisticated city action too, from the City of Sails to the windy capital.

ALMOST ALL TO YOURSELF   One to Two Months / Auckland to Christchurch

Journey to the ends of NZ earth and experience locales far removed from manmade bustle on this all-points-of-the-compass tour.

Head north from **Auckland** (p102) to tiny **Tutukaka** (p200) for a visit to the fish-rich waters and rocky underwater labyrinths of the **Poor Knights Islands** (p200). Beyond the **Bay of Islands** (p185) is rugged Aupouri Peninsula, at the tip of which is **Cape Reinga** (p179), wrapped in solitude and Maori legend.

Venture back south past Auckland and through **Rotorua** (p328) and the lush greenery of **Te Urewera National Park** (p383) to the wilderness-choked ranges of **East Cape** (p369). Follow SH2 south to Woodville before heading coastal to SH1, and take in the peaceful **Kapiti Coast** (p427) and an offshore trip to mystical **Kapiti Island** (p430). Hop across Cook Strait to pretty **Picton** (p438), then lose yourself in the waterways of **Marlborough Sounds** (p443).

Detour to the west, past the artful environs of **Nelson** (p461), to the ecofriendly and choicely chilled **Golden Bay** (p482) and enormous, species-dense **Kahurangi National Park** (p487). Travel southwest, where a memorable road north of **Westport** (p493) accesses the fabulous caverns of **Oparara Basin** (p497). Southbound, divert to the superb inland extremity of **Arthur's Pass National Park** (p569), and don't miss a voyage on utterly isolated **Doubtful Sound** (p671), accessible from **Manapouri** (p670). Ferry yourself to paradisal **Stewart Island** (p689), then sojourn in the peacefully overgrown **Catlins** (p681).

Detour north on SH8 through Central Otago, passing through some gold rush–era towns en route to mountain-biking **Alexandra** (p608), cute **Clyde** (p607) and gliding-perfect **Omarama** (p618). Journey back to the east coast through the **Waitaki Valley** (p617) on SH83, then it's a quick trip south to mellow **Oamaru** (p614) before heading north to **Christchurch** (p527).

It's hard to find less-travelled paths in NZ nowadays, but this varied route from the country's northernmost fingernail to its detached southern toe takes in plenty of minimally touristed landscapes. If you time things well, you may just feel you've got a little slice of heaven all to yourself.

TAILORED TRIPS

FINE WINES

If your palate has a fine appreciation of fermented grape juice, or you want to make an impressive splash in a spittoon with connoisseur friends back home, then consider an intoxicating tour of some of NZ's 450-odd vineyards.

On the North Island there's accomplished viticulture west of **Auckland** (p144), where speciality fruit wines can be sampled, and east of the city on **Waiheke Island** (p149), where numerous wineries compete for vintage accolades. The fertile plains around **Gisborne** (p378) are devoted to chardonnay, while **Hawkes Bay** (p398) also loves its chardy but squeezes out some premier cabernet sauvignon and merlot too. **Martinborough** (p432) in the Wairarapa region creates outstanding pinot noir flavours.

The country's most notable bouquet-sniffing realm is on the South Island in **Marlborough** (p452), where crisp sauvignon blanc and fruity riesling is guzzled with wild yet refined abandon. Also barrelling down the road to commercial success are the wineries of **Central Otago** (see the boxed text, p632), specialising in fine pinots. **Nelson** (p473) and **Waipara Valley** (p564) are relatively new grape-growing regions now holding their own against the country's big guns.

GOING TO EXTREMES

This is not, as suggested by the title, an itinerary taking in NZ's gravity-defying adrenaline charges, but rather a tour 'from Cape Reinga to Bluff' – often quoted to signify the entire length of NZ (let's overlook the fact that Bluff is not actually the South Island's southernmost point – that honour goes to Slope Point in the Catlins). So, from **Cape Reinga** (p179), NZ's northernmost point, take in **Auckland** (p102), the country's largest city, being sure to visit **Sky Tower** (p108), the tallest building in the southern hemisphere. Head to **East Cape Lighthouse** (p3720) to stand on NZ's most easterly point, then get wet at **Lake Taupo** (p294) – at 606 sq km it's the largest body of water in the country. NZ's longest river (the 420km-long Waikato) originates here.

Down south, there's Australasia's highest mountain, **Aoraki/Mt Cook** (p583), lording it over the Southern Alps at 3755m. Take in **Nelson** (p461), one of the towns laying claim to sunniest spot in NZ, and call in at tiny **Ophir** (p609), near Alexandra, which reputedly has the widest temperature range of any NZ town – from -20°C in winter to 35°C in summer. There's also **Arthur's Pass** (p569), the highest-altitude town in NZ, the country's longest swingbridge at **Buller Gorge** (p492) and the world's steepest street in **Dunedin** (p590), before you finish your journey – your choice: **Bluff** (p679) or **Slope Point** (p684)?

Auckland ⊕⊕ Waiheke Island
⊕ Gisborne
⊕ Hawkes Bay
⊕ Martinborough
⊕ Marlborough
Nelson ⊕⊕
⊕ Waipara Valley
⊕ Central Otago

Cape ⊖ Reinga
⊖ East Cape
Auckland ⊖
⊖ Lake Taupo
Nelson ⊖
Buller Gorge ⊖
Arthur's Pass ⊖ ⊖ Ophir
Aoraki/ ⊖ ⊖ Dunedin
Mt Cook
Bluff ⊖⊖ Slope Point

Snapshot

You won't need to travel far to learn that politics is often the main topic of conversation among Kiwis. The small population and accessibility of politicians probably plays a large part. And the locals put their money where their mouth is too – voter turnout come election time is around 80% (the corresponding figure for US presidential elections is between 50% and 60%).

In September 2005 New Zealanders went to the polls to elect their national government, after an intriguing, closely fought election campaign that featured politicians actively out on the hustings, plus doses of reclusive religious sects, court cases involving speeding prime ministerial motorcades, much debate over the real cost of free student loans, and televised debates between no-nonsense Prime Minister Helen Clark, leader of the Labour Party, and 'gentlemanly' Don Brash, of the conservative National Party. Labour offered the electorate more of the same (cautious economic management, inclusive and progressive social policies), the Nationals offered promises of big tax cuts and played the race card, promising to restrict race-based funding and policies.

Many other parties and pollies played more than a walk-on part in the unfolding drama, thanks to New Zealand's cumbersome MMP (mixed-member proportional) electoral system. The intricacies of the electoral system (a limited form of proportional voting) meant that it took a while for a clear election winner to become evident – Labour won the most seats in parliament in a cliffhanger (50 seats to the Nationals' 48), but not enough to form a majority to govern in its own right. The country spent a month in political limbo while Helen Clark secured her third consecutive term as prime minister by forming a Labour-led centrist coalition with four minor parties. In the process, she surprised many by jilting a former political ally, the left-wing Green Party, and partnering up with the New Zealand First Party, led by a veteran of the NZ political scene, Winston Peters. Clark shocked again by appointing the outspoken Peters, well-known for his anti-immigration and protectionist policies, as minister for foreign affairs.

Since the election it's been business as usual under Clark's strong leadership, with the government retaining their pacifist, anti-nuclear policy, and continuing to oppose NZ troop involvement in Iraq and Afghanistan (unlike their neighbour across the Tasman). A record low level of unemployment and large budget surplus equate to a buoyant domestic economy. The flow-on effects of a legislated increase in the minimum wage (from $9.50 per hour to $10.25 per hour), effective from March 2006, may see prices rise for many goods and services across the country. Travellers would certainly feel this – prices for services such as accommodation have already increased in recent years in response to increased demand.

Also on the domestic front, it's hard to avoid talk of everyone's favourite pastime: real estate. National average house prices have risen an astonishing 83% since 2001, and Auckland was recently ranked as one of the world's most costly cities in terms of housing affordability (relative to income), with Christchurch and Wellington not far behind. Wage levels can't hope to keep up with escalating house prices. During our visit, it was announced that the average house price in the Queenstown-Wanaka area is $635,000.

Aside from the obvious affordability issues, it raises the question – how does a service-driven town such as Queenstown continue to function if it can't find workers (given workers can't afford the housing there)? The issue is certainly exacerbated by the fact that there are few restrictions on overseas residents buying property in NZ, and to many of them (travelling with the purchasing power of strong northern-hemisphere currencies) the asking prices still seem reasonable.

Because the tourists still keep flocking – and if they haven't already visited, then they're desperate to do so! In many surveys in the UK, NZ is the top destination people would like to travel to, confirmed by worldwide surveys conducted by Lonely Planet. Tourism continues to boom, with the *Lord of the Rings* films still contributing, and NZ's terrorist-free status no doubt also a drawcard. In 2005, close to 2.4 million visitors flocked to the country, up 50,000 on the previous year. Overall, there's been a staggering 50% growth in visitor numbers in the last six years (only 1.6 million people visited in 1999). The lion's share is made up of Australian, English and US travellers. Still, all these extra visitors put a strain on the clean green environment NZ is renowned for. The Department of Conservation has implemented a booking system for six out of its nine Great Walks, to avoid overcrowding on tracks and minimise the impact on the environment. Authorities are also investigating the possibility of limiting air access over the Milford Sound area – if they have their way, sightseeing flights will be restricted to 75 take-offs per day (flight numbers currently reach up to 240 per day, which means visitors' enjoyment of such a captivating area may well be accompanied by a soundtrack of droning engines).

Although the influence of the *Lord of the Rings* trilogy is waning, the desire to see Middle-earth come to life is still part of the allure for many visitors to NZ. The question is, though, would they now recognise the films' director, Peter Jackson, without his big glasses and bulging girth? A makeover has seen him shed the specs (thanks to laser eye surgery) and a reported 30kg. Still, it's his filmmaking prowess that remains the focus of many of his compatriots, eager to see what he tackles next (and who he woos to Wellywood). After the success of *King Kong*, Jackson's next project, together with his partner Fran Walsh, is as executive producer of *Halo* (a film based on the popular video game of the same name). It's expected to be released in mid-2007. In the meantime there's enough to keep NZ movie fans going, including the *Chronicles of Narnia* franchise. The first Narnia film was directed by Kiwi Andrew Adamson and used a number of NZ locations; the second in the series (*The Chronicles of Narnia: Prince Caspian*), with Adamson again at the helm, is due for release in 2007. There won't be quite the hype that surrounded LOTR, but we can't help but think that's a good thing!

And then of course there's the national obsession – rugby. The All Blacks are itching to redeem themselves in the 2007 World Cup in France, but in the meantime they've relished the chance to hand out hidings to old foes – in 2005 they won the annual Tri Nations cup (staged between NZ, Australia and South Africa) and happily retained the Bledisloe Cup (fought between trans-Tasman teams). In early 2006 sports fans mourned the retirement of All Blacks skipper Tana Umaga from international competition.

History James Belich

New Zealand's history is not long, but it is fast. In less than a thousand years these islands have produced two new peoples: the Polynesian Maori and European New Zealanders. The latter are often known by their Maori name, 'Pakeha' (though not all like the term). NZ shares some of its history with the rest of Polynesia, and with other European settler societies, but has unique features as well. It is the similarities that make the differences so interesting, and vice versa.

MAKING MAORI

Despite persistent myths (see the boxed text, below), there is no doubt that the first settlers of NZ were the Polynesian forebears of today's Maori. Beyond that, there are a lot of question marks. Exactly where in east Polynesia did they come from – the Cook Islands, Tahiti, the Marquesas? When did they arrive? Solid archaeological evidence points to about AD 1200, but much earlier dates have been suggested for the first human impact on the environment. Did the first settlers come in one group or several? Some evidence, such as the diverse DNA of the Polynesian rats that accompanied the first settlers, suggests multiple founding voyages. On the other hand, only rats and dogs brought by the founders have survived, not the more valuable pigs and chickens. The survival of these cherished animals would have had high priority, and their failure to be successfully introduced suggests fewer voyages. See Kawhia, p241 and the boxed text, p360 for the tales of just two of the great migratory canoes that made the voyage.

NZ seems small compared to Australia, but it is bigger than Britain, and very much bigger than other Polynesian islands. Its regions vary wildly in environment and climate. Prime sites for first settlement were warm coastal gardens for the food plants brought from Polynesia (kumara or sweet potato, gourd, yam and taro); sources of workable stone for knives and adzes; and areas with abundant big game. NZ has no native land mammals apart from a few species of bat, but 'big game' is no exaggeration: the islands were home to a dozen species of moa (a large flightless bird), the largest of which weighed up to 240kg, about twice

THE MORIORI & THEIR MYTH

One of NZ's most persistent legends is that Maoris found mainland NZ already occupied by a more peaceful and racially distinct Melanesian people, known as the Moriori, whom they exterminated. This myth has been regularly debunked by scholars since the 1920s, but somehow hangs on.

To complicate matters, there were real 'Moriori', and Maoris did treat them badly. The real Moriori were the people of the Chatham Islands, a windswept group about 900km east of the mainland. They were, however, fully Polynesian, and descended from Maoris – 'Moriori' was their version of the same word. Mainland Maoris arrived in the Chathams in 1835, as a spin-off of the Musket Wars, killing some Moriori and enslaving the rest (see the boxed text, p698). But they did not exterminate them. The mainland Moriori remain a myth.

One of NZ's foremost modern historians, James Belich has written a number of books on NZ history and hosted the TV documentary series *NZ Wars*.

similarities in language between Maori and Tahitian indicate close contact in historical times. Maori is about as similar to Tahitian as Spanish is to French, despite the 4294km separating these island groups.

the size of an ostrich. There were also other species of flightless bird and large sea mammals such as fur seals, all unaccustomed to being hunted. For people from small Pacific islands, this was like hitting the jackpot. The first settlers spread far and fast, from the top of the North Island to the bottom of the South Island within the first 100 years. High-protein diets are likely to have boosted population growth.

By about 1400, however, the big-game supply was in rapid decline. Except in the far south, fur-seal breeding colonies were hunted out, and moa were extinct or close to it. Rumours of late survivals abound, but none have been authenticated. So if you see a moa in your travels, photograph it – you have just made the greatest zoological discovery of the last 100 years. Maori economics turned from big game to small game – forest birds and rats – and from hunting to gardening and fishing. A good living could still be made, but it required detailed local knowledge, steady effort and complex communal organisation, hence the rise of the Maori tribes. Competition for resources increased, conflict did likewise, and this led to the building of increasingly sophisticated fortifications, known as pa. Vestiges of pa earthworks can still be seen around the country, on the hilltops of Auckland for example.

The Maori had no metals and no written language (and no alcoholic drinks or drugs). But their culture and spiritual life was rich and distinctive. Below Ranginui (sky father) and Papatuanuku (earth mother) were various gods of land, forest and sea, joined by deified ancestors over time. The mischievous demigod Maui was particularly important. In legend, he vanquished the sun and fished up the North Island before meeting his death between the thighs of the goddess Hine-nui-te-po in an attempt to conquer the human mortality embodied in her. Maori traditional performance art, the group singing and dancing known as kapa haka, has real power, even for modern audiences. Visual art, notably woodcarving, is something special – 'like nothing but itself', in the words of 18th-century explorer-scientist Joseph Banks.

ENTER EUROPE

NZ became an official British colony in 1840, but the first authenticated contact between Maoris and the outside world took place almost two centuries earlier in 1642, in Golden Bay at the top of the South Island. Two Dutch ships sailed from Indonesia, then named the Dutch East Indies, to search for the legendary 'Great South Land' and anything valuable it might contain. The commander, Abel Tasman, was instructed to pretend to any natives he might meet 'that you are by no means eager for precious metals, so as to leave them ignorant of the value of the same'.

When Tasman's ships anchored in the bay, local Maori came out in their canoes to make the traditional challenge: friends or foes? Misunderstanding this, the Dutch challenged back, by blowing trumpets. When a boat was lowered to take a party between the two ships, it was attacked. Four crewmen were killed. Tasman sailed away and did not come back; nor did any other European for 127 years. But the Dutch did leave a name: 'Nieuw Zeeland' or 'New Zealand'.

Contact between Maoris and Europeans was renewed in 1769, when English and French explorers arrived, under James Cook (see the boxed

1769

European contact recommences with visits by James Cook and Jean de Surville

1814

First European mission station and settlement

CAPTAIN JAMES COOK *Tony Horwitz*

If aliens ever visit earth, they may wonder what to make of the countless obelisks, faded plaques and graffiti-covered statues of a stiff, wigged figure gazing out to sea from Alaska to Australia, from NZ to North Yorkshire, from Siberia to the South Pacific. James Cook (1728–79) explored more of the earth's surface than anyone in history, and it's impossible to travel the Pacific without encountering the captain's image and his controversial legacy in the lands he opened to the West.

For a man who travelled so widely, and rose to such fame, Cook came from an extremely pinched and provincial background. The son of a day labourer in rural Yorkshire, he was born in a mud cottage, had little schooling and seemed destined for farm work – and for his family's grave plot in a village churchyard. Instead, Cook went to sea as a teenager, worked his way up from coal-ship servant to naval officer, and attracted notice for his exceptional charts of Canada. But Cook remained a little-known second lieutenant until, in 1768, the Royal Navy chose him to command a daring voyage to the South Seas.

In a converted coal ship called *Endeavour*, Cook sailed to Tahiti, then became the first European to land at NZ and the east coast of Australia. Though the ship almost sank after striking the Great Barrier Reef, and 40% of the crew died from disease and accidents, the *Endeavour* limped home in 1771 with eye-opening reports on curiosities, including exotic Tahitian dances and, from Australia, a leaping, pouched quadruped so difficult for Europeans to classify that Cook's botanist called it an 'eighty-pound mouse'.

On a return voyage (1772–75), Cook became the first navigator to pierce the Antarctic Circle and circled the globe near its southernmost latitude, demolishing the ancient myth that a vast, populous and fertile continent surrounded the South Pole. Cook also crisscrossed the Pacific from Easter Island to Melanesia, charting dozens of islands between. Though Maoris killed and cooked 10 sailors, the captain remained strikingly sympathetic to islanders. 'Notwithstanding they are cannibals,' he wrote, 'they are naturally of a good disposition'.

On Cook's final voyage (1776–79), in search of a northwest passage between the Atlantic and Pacific, he became the first European to visit Hawaii, and coasted America from Oregon to Alaska. Forced back by Arctic pack ice, Cook returned to Hawaii, where he was killed during a skirmish with islanders who had initially greeted him as a Polynesian god. In a single decade of discovery, Cook had filled in the map of the Pacific and, as one French navigator put it, 'left his successors with little to do but admire his exploits'.

Cook's legacy extends far beyond his Pacific charts, some of them so accurate that they remained in use until the 1990s. His journeys were the first true voyage- of scientific discovery, aboard ships filled with trained observers: artists, astronomers, botanists – even poets. Their observations helped lay the foundation for modern disciplines such as anthropology and museum science, and inspired Western writers and artists to romanticise the South Pacific as an innocent paradise. The plant and animal specimens Cook's men collected also revolutionised Western understanding of nature, seeding the notion of biodiversity and blazing a trail for Charles Darwin's voyage on the *Beagle*.

But Cook's travels also spurred colonisation of the Pacific, and within a few decades of his death, missionaries, whalers, traders and settlers began transforming – and often devastating – island cultures. As a result, many indigenous people now revile Cook as an imperialist villain who introduced disease, dispossession and other ills to the Pacific (hence the frequent vandalising of Cook monuments). However, as islanders revive traditional crafts and practices, from tattooing to *tapa*, they have turned to the art and writing of Cook and his men as a resource for cultural renewal. For good and ill, a Yorkshire farm boy remains the single most significant figure in the shaping of the modern Pacific.

Tony Horwitz is a Pulitzer-winning reporter and nonfiction author. In researching Blue Latitudes *(or* Into the Blue*), Tony travelled the Pacific – 'boldly going where Captain Cook has gone before'.*

text, p33) and Jean de Surville. Despite some violence, both managed to communicate with Maoris, and this time NZ's link with the outside world proved permanent. Another French expedition arrived in 1772, under Marion du Fresne, and stayed for some weeks at the Bay of Islands to rest and refit. At first, relations with Maoris were excellent, but a breach of Maori *tapu* (sacred law) led to violence. Marion and two dozen of his men were killed, and the rest retaliated by destroying a Maori *pa*, which may or may not have belonged to the offenders.

Exploration continued, motivated by science, profit and great power rivalry. Cook made two more visits between 1773 and 1777, and there were further French expeditions. Unofficial visits, by whaling ships in the north and sealing gangs in the south, began in the 1790s. The first mission station was founded in 1814, in the Bay of Islands, and was followed by dozens of others: Anglican, Methodist and Catholic. Trade in flax and timber generated small European-Maori settlements by the 1820s. Surprisingly, the most numerous category of European visitor was probably American. New England whaling ships favoured the Bay of Islands for rest and 'recreation'; 271 called there between 1833 and 1839 alone. To whalers, 'rest and recreation' meant sex and drink. Their favourite haunt, the little town of Kororareka (now Russell) was known to the missionaries as 'the hellhole of the Pacific'. New England visitors today might well have distant relatives among the local Maoris.

One or two dozen bloody clashes dot the history of Maori-European contact before 1840 but, given the number of visits, inter-racial conflict was modest. Europeans needed Maori protection, food and labour, and Maoris came to need European articles, especially muskets. Whaling stations and mission stations were linked to local Maori groups by intermarriage, which helped keep the peace. Most warfare was between Maori and Maori: the terrible intertribal 'Musket Wars' of 1818–36. Because Northland had the majority of early contact with Europe, its Ngapuhi tribe acquired muskets first. Under their great general Hongi Hika, Ngapuhi then raided south, winning bloody victories against tribes without muskets. Once they acquired muskets, these tribes saw off Ngapuhi; but also raided further south in their turn. The domino effect continued to the far south of the South Island in 1836. The missionaries claimed that the Musket Wars then tapered off through their influence, but the restoration of the balance of power through the equal distribution of muskets was probably more important.

Europe brought such things as pigs (at last) and potatoes, which benefited Maoris, while muskets and diseases had the opposite effect. The negative effects have been exaggerated, however. Europeans expected peoples like the Maori to simply fade away at contact, and some early estimates of Maori population were overly high – up to one million. Current estimates are between 85,000 and 110,000 for 1769. The Musket Wars killed perhaps 20,000, and new diseases did considerable damage too (although NZ had the natural quarantine of distance: infected Europeans usually recovered or died during the long voyage and smallpox, for example, which devastated native Americans, did not make it here). By 1840, the Maoris had been reduced to about 70,000, a decline of at least 20%. Maoris bent under the weight of European contact, but they certainly did not break.

1853–56	1861
Provincial and central elected governments established	Gold discovered in Otago

MAKING PAKEHA

By 1840, Maori tribes described local Europeans as 'their Pakeha', and valued the profit and prestige they brought. Maoris wanted more, and concluded that accepting nominal British authority was the way to get them. At the same time, the British government was overcoming its reluctance to undertake potentially expensive intervention in NZ. It too was influenced by profit and prestige, but also by humanitarian considerations. It believed, wrongly but sincerely, that Maoris could not handle the increasing scale of unofficial European contact. In 1840, the two peoples struck a deal, symbolised by the treaty first signed at Waitangi on 6 February that year. The Treaty of Waitangi now has a standing not dissimilar to that of the Constitution in the US, but is even more contested. The original problem was a discrepancy between British and Maori understandings of it. The English version promised Maoris full equality as British subjects in return for complete rights of government. The Maori version also promised that Maoris would retain their chieftainship, which implied local rights of government. The problem was not great at first, because the Maori version applied outside the small European settlements. But as those settlements grew, conflict brewed.

In 1840, there were only about 2000 Europeans in NZ, with the shanty town of Kororareka (now Russell) as the capital and biggest settlement.

LAND WARS *Errol Hunt*

Five separate major conflicts made up what are now collectively known as the New Zealand Wars (also referred to as the Land Wars or Maori Wars). Staring in Northland and moving throughout the North Island, the wars had many complex causes; but *whenua* (land), was the one common factor. In all five wars, Maoris fought both for and against the government, on whose side stood the Imperial British Army, Australians and NZ's own Armed Constabulary. Land confiscations imposed on the Maoris as punishment for involvement in these wars are still the source of conflict today, with the government struggling to finance compensation for what are now acknowledged to have been illegal seizures.

Northland war (1844–46) 'Hone Heke's War' began with the famous chopping of the flagpole at Kororareka (now Russell, p193) and 'ended' at Ruapekapeka (south of Kawakawa) – although massive concessions from the 'victorious' government towards the 'vanquished' Heke made many at the time doubt who had really won! In many ways, this was almost a civil war between rival Ngapuhi factions, with the government taking one side against the other.

First Taranaki war (1860–51) Starting with the controversial swindling of Maori land by the government at Waitara (p267), the first Taranaki war (p258) inflamed the passions of Maori across the North Island and involved many military participants from the Waikato tribes (despite being traditional enemies of the Taranaki Maoris).

Waikato war (1863–64) The largest of the five wars. Predominantly involving Maoris of the King Movement (see the boxed text, p233), the Waikato war was caused in part by what the government saw as a challenge to sovereignty. However it was land, again, that was the real reason 'or friction. Following defeats such as Rangiriri (p230), the Waikato people were pushed entirely from their own lands, south into what became known as the King Country. Massive confiscations of land followed, for which the country is still paying now.

Second Taranaki war (1865–69) Caused by Maori resistance to land confiscations stemming from the first Taranaki war, this was perhaps the war in which the Maoris came closest to victory, under the brilliant, one-eyed prophet-general Titokowaru. However, once he lost the respect of his warriors (probably through an indiscretion with the wife of one of his warriors), the war too was lost.

East Coast war (1868–72) Te Kooti's holy guerrilla war: see the boxed text, p378.

The Waitangi National Reserve (p189), where the Treaty of Waitangi was first signed in 1840, is now a tourist attraction for Kiwis and non-Kiwis alike. Each year on 6 February, Waitangi hosts treaty commemorations and protests.

Scottish influence can still be felt in NZ, particularly in the south of the South Island. NZ has more Scottish pipe bands per capita than Scotland itself.

'Kaore e mau te rongo – ake, ake!' (Peace never shall be made – never, never!)

War chief Rewi Maniapoto in response to government troops at the battle of Orakau, 1864

By 1850, six new settlements had been formed (Auckland, Wellington, New Plymouth, Nelson, Christchurch and Dunedin), with 22,000 settlers between them. About half of these had arrived under the auspices of the New Zealand Company and its associates. The company was the brainchild of Edward Gibbon Wakefield, who also influenced the settlement of South Australia. Wakefield hoped to short-circuit the barbarous frontier phase of settlement with 'instant civilisation', but his success was limited. From the 1850s, his settlers, who included a high proportion of uppermiddle-class gentlefolk, were swamped by succeeding waves of immigrants that continued to wash in until the 1880s. These people were part of the great British and Irish diaspora that also populated Australia and much of North America, but the NZ mix was distinctive. Lowland Scots settlers were more prominent in NZ than elsewhere, for example, with the possible exception of parts of Canada. NZ's Irish, even the Catholics, tended to come from the north of Ireland. NZ's English tended to come from the counties close to London. Small groups of Germans, Scandinavians and Chinese made their way in, though the last faced increasing racial prejudice from the 1880s, when the Pakeha population reached half a million.

Much of the mass immigration from the 1850s to the 1870s was assisted by the provincial and central governments, which also mounted large-scale public works schemes, especially in the 1870s under Julius Vogel. In 1876, Vogel abolished the provinces on the grounds that they were hampering his development efforts. The last imperial governor with substantial power was the talented but Machiavellian George Grey, who ended his second governorship in 1868. Thereafter, the governors (governors-general from 1917) were largely just nominal heads of state; the head of government, the premier or prime minister, had more power. The central government, originally weaker than the provincial governments, the imperial governor and the Maori tribes, eventually exceeded the power of all three.

The Maori tribes did not go down without a fight, however. Indeed, their resistance was one of the most formidable ever mounted against European expansion, comparable to that of the Sioux and Seminole in the US. The first clash took place in 1843 in the Wairau Valley, now a wine-growing district. A posse of settlers set out to enforce the myth of British control, but encountered the reality of Maori control. Twenty-two settlers were killed, including Wakefield's brother, Arthur, along with about six Maoris. In 1845, more serious fighting broke out in the Bay of Islands, where the young Ngapuhi chief, Hone Heke, challenged British sovereignty, first by cutting down the British flag at Russell, and then by sacking the town itself. Heke and his ally Kawiti baffled three British punitive expeditions, using a modern variant of the traditional pa fortification. Vestiges of these innovative earthworks can still be seen at Ruapekapeka (south of Kawakawa). Governor Grey claimed victory in the north, but few were convinced at the time. Grey had more success in the south, where he arrested the formidable Ngati Toa chief Te Rauparaha, who until then wielded great influence on both sides of Cook Strait. Pakeha were able to swamp the few Maoris living in the South Island, but the fighting of the 1840s confirmed that the North Island at that time comprised a European fringe around an independent Maori heartland.

In the 1850s, settler population and aspirations grew, and fighting broke out again in 1860. The wars burned on sporadically until 1872 over much of the North Island. In the early years, a Maori national-ist organisation, the King Movement (see the boxed text, p33), was the backbone of resistance. In later years, some remarkable prophet-generals, notably Titokowaru and Te Kooti (see the boxed text, p378), took over. Most wars were small-scale, but the Waikato War of 1863–64 was not. Up to 5000 Maori resisted an invasion mounted by 20,000 im-perial, colonial and 'friendly' Maori troops. This conflict, fought at the same time as the American Civil War, involved armoured steamships, ultramodern heavy artillery, telegraph and 10 proud British regular regi-ments. Despite the odds, the Maoris won several battles, such as that at Gate Pa, near Tauranga, in 1864. But in the end they were ground down by European numbers and resources. Maori political, though not cul-tural, independence ebbed away in the last decades of the 19th century. It finally expired when police invaded its last sanctuary, the Urerewa Mountains, in 1916.

See the Land Wars boxed text, p35, for the major areas of conflict.

WELFARE & WARFARE

From the 1850s to the 1880s, despite conflict with Maori, the Pakeha economy boomed on the back of wool exports, gold rushes and mas-sive overseas borrowing for development. The crash came in the 1880s, when NZ experienced its Long Depression. In 1890, the Liberals came to power, and stayed there until 1912, helped by a recovering economy. Their major leader was Richard John Seddon, 'King Dick', as I am usually known'. The Liberals were NZ's first organised political party, and the first of several governments to give NZ a reputation as 'the world's social laboratory'. NZ became the first country in the world to give women the vote in 1893, and introduced a long-lasting system of industrial arbitration, but this also introduced old-age pensions in 1898. The Liberals was not enough to prevent bitter industrial unrest in 1912-13. A striker was killed by police at the gold-mining town of Waihi in 1912, and riots and a gunfight took place between unionists and the forces of the law in Wellington the following year. This happened under the conservative 'Reform' government, which had replaced the Liberals in 1912. Reform remained in power until 1928, and later transformed itself into the Na-tional Party. Renewed depression struck in 1929, and the NZ experience of it was as grim as any. The derelict little farmhouses still seen in rural areas often date from this era.

In 1935, a second reforming government took office, the First Labour Government, led by Michael Joseph Savage, easily NZ's favourite Aus-tralian. This government created NZ's pioneering version of the welfare state, and also took some independent initiatives in foreign policy. For a time, it was considered the most socialist government outside Soviet Russia. But, when the chips were down in Europe in 1939, Labour had little hesitation in backing Britain.

NZ had also backed Britain in the Boer War (1899–1902) and WWI (1914–18). Indeed, in the latter conflict, NZ's contribution was quite stag-gering for a country of just over one million people about 100,000 NZ

To find out more about the New Zealand Wars, visit www.newzealand wars.co.nz

Maurice Shadbolt's Sea-son of the Jew (1987), is a semifictionalised story of bloody campaigns led by warrior Te Kooti against the British in Poverty Bay in the 1860s. Te Kooti and his followers compared themselves to the Israelites who were cast out of Egypt.

'God's own country, but the devil's own mess.'
Prime Minister Richard (King Dick) Seddon, speaking on the source of NZ's self-proclaimed nickname 'Godzone'

men served overseas, and close on 60,000 became casualties, mostly on the Western Front in France. You can count the cost in almost any little NZ town. A central square or park will contain a memorial lined with names – more for WWI than WWII. Even in WWII, however, NZ did its share of fighting: a hundred thousand or so New Zealanders fought in Europe and the Middle East, while a hundred thousand or so Americans arrived from 1942 to protect NZ from the Japanese. NZ, a peaceful-seeming country, has spent much of its history at war. In the 19th century it fought at home; in the 20th, overseas.

BETTER BRITONS?

British visitors have long found NZ hauntingly familiar. This is not simply a matter of the British and Irish origin of most Pakeha. It also stems from the tightening of NZ links with Britain from 1882, when refrigerated cargoes of food were first shipped to London. By the 1930s, 100 giant ships carried frozen meat, cheese and butter, as well as wool, on regular voyages taking about five weeks one way. The NZ economy adapted to the feeding of London, and cultural links were also enhanced. NZ children studied British history and literature, not their own. NZ's leading scientists and writers, such as Ernest Rutherford and Katherine Mansfield (see the boxed text, p412), gravitated naturally to Britain. This tight relationship has been described as 'recolonial', but it is a mistake to see NZ as an exploited colony. Average living standards in NZ were normally better than in Britain, as were the welfare and lower-level education systems. New Zealanders had access to British markets and culture, and they contributed their share to the latter as equals. The list of 'British' writers, academics, scientists, military leaders, publishers and the like who were actually New Zealanders is long. Indeed, New Zealanders, especially in war and sport, sometimes saw themselves as a superior version of the British – the Better Britons of the south. The NZ-London relationship was rather like that of the American Midwest and New York.

'Recolonial' NZ prided itself, with some justice, on its affluence, equal-ity and social harmony. But it was also conformist, even puritanical. Until the 1950s, it was technically illegal for farmers to allow their cattle to mate in fields fronting public roads, for moral reasons. The 1954 American movie, *The Wild One*, was banned until 1977. Sunday newspapers were illegal until 1969, and full Sunday trading was not allowed until 1989. Licensed restaurants hardly existed in 1960, nor did supermarkets or TV. Notoriously, from 1917 to 1967, pubs were obliged to shut at 6pm. Yet the puritanical society of Better Britons was never the whole story. Opposi-tion to Sunday trading stemmed, not so much from belief in the sanctity of the Sabbath, but from the belief that workers should have weekends too. Six o'clock closing was a standing joke in rural areas, notably the marvellously idiosyncratic region of South Island's west coast. There was always something of a Kiwi counterculture, even before imported countercultures took root from the 1960s.

There were also developments in cultural nationalism, beginning in the 1930s but really flowering from the 1970s. Writers, artists and film-makers were by no means the only people who 'came out' in that era.

Nearly 200,000 Kiwi men (67% of the NZ males aged 18 to 45) served in WWII.

Wellington-born Nancy Wake (codenamed 'The White Mouse') led a guerrilla attack against the Nazis with a 7000-strong army. She had the multiple honours of being the Gestapo's most-wanted person and being the most decorated Allied servicewoman of WWII.

1981

Springbok rugby tour divides the nation

1985

Rainbow Warrior sunk in Auckland Harbour by French government agents

COMING IN, COMING OUT

The 'recolonial' system was shaken several times after 1935, but managed to survive until 1973, when Mother England ran off and joined the Franco-German commune now known as the EU. NZ was beginning to develop alternative markets to Britain, and alternative exports to wool, meat and dairy products. Wide-bodied jet aircraft were allowing the world and NZ to visit each other on an increasing scale. NZ had only 36,000 tourists in 1960, compared with more than two million a year now. Women were beginning to penetrate first the upper reaches of the workforce and then the political sphere. Gays came out of the closet, despite vigorous efforts by moral conservatives to push them back in. University-educated youths were becoming more numerous and more assertive.

From 1945, Maoris experienced both a population explosion and massive urbanisation. In 1936, Maoris were 17% urban and 83% rural. Fifty years later, these proportions had reversed. The immigration gates, which until 1960 were pretty much labelled 'whites only', widened, first to allow in Pacific Islanders for their labour, and then to allow in (East) Asians for their money. These transitions would have generated major socioeconomic change whatever happened in politics. But most New Zealanders associate the country's recent 'Big Shift' with the politics of 1984.

In 1984, NZ's third great reforming government was elected – the Fourth Labour government, led nominally by David Lange and in fact by Roger Douglas, the Minister of Finance. This government adopted an antinuclear foreign policy, delighting the left, and a more-market economic policy, delighting the right. NZ's numerous economic controls were dismantled with breakneck speed. Social restrictions were removed almost as fast as economic ones – the pubs still closed at six, but am, not pm. Middle NZ was uneasy about the antinuclear policy, which threatened NZ's ANZUS alliance with Australia and the US. But in 1985, French spies sank the antinuclear protest ship *Rainbow Warrior* (see the boxed text, p184) in Auckland Harbour, killing one crewman. The lukewarm American condemnation of the French act brought middle NZ in behind the antinuclear policy, which became associated with national independence. Other New Zealanders were uneasy about the more-market economic policy, but failed to come up with a convincing alternative. Revelling in their new freedom, NZ investors engaged in a frenzy of speculation, and suffered even more than the rest of the world from the economic crash of 1987.

The economy remained fairly stagnant until the late 1990s, when a recovery began. In politics, a National (conservative) government replaced Labour in 1990, and introduced proportional representation in 1996. A Labour government (now technically a Labour-led coalition), led by Helen Clark, returned to office in 1999, and was re-elected in 2002 and 2005.

The early 21st century is an interesting time for NZ. Like NZ food and wine, film and literature are flowering as never before, and the new ethnic mix is creating something very special in popular music. There are continuities, however – the pub, the sports ground, the quarter-acre section, the bush, the beach and the bach – and they too are part of the present. NZ has a great culture, reason people like to come here. Realising that NZ has a great culture, and an intriguing history, as well as a great natural environment, will double the bang for your buck.

The Ministry for Culture & Heritage's history website (www.nzhistory.net.nz) is an excellent source of info on NZ history.

The Six O'Clock Swill referred to the frantic after-work drinking at pubs when men tried to drink at much as possible from 5.05pm until strict closing time at 6pm.

NZ's staunch antinuclear stance earned it the nickname The Mouse That Roared.

The Culture Russell Brown

THE NATIONAL PSYCHE

Russell Brown is one of NZ's most prolific journalists. He writes for radio and TV, covers a variety of issues for the *New Zealand Listener* and *Unlimited* magazines, and keeps a popular weblog at http://publicaddress .net. He is also the editor of *Great New Zealand Argument: Ideas About Ourselves* (Activity Press, 2005), an anthology of writing on national identity. He lives in Auckland's Pt Chevalier with his family.

'So, what do you think of New Zealand?'... That, by tradition, is the question that visitors, especially important ones, were once asked within an hour of disembarking in NZ. Sometimes they might be granted an entire day's research before being asked to pronounce, but asked they would be. The question – composed equally of great pride and creeping doubt – was symbolic of the national consciousness.

When George Bernard Shaw visited for four weeks in 1934, he was deluged with what-do-you-think-of questions from newspaper reporters the length of the country. Although he never saw fit to write a word about NZ, his answers to those newspaper questions were collected and reprinted as *What I Saw in New Zealand*. Yes, people really were that keen for vindication.

Other visitors were willing to pronounce in print, including the British Liberal MP, David Goldblatt, who came to NZ to convalesce from a heart attack in 1955, became fascinated with the place and wrote an intriguing and prescient little book called *Democracy At Ease: a New Zealand Profile*.

Goldblatt found New Zealanders a blithe people; kind, prosperous, fond of machines, frequently devoid of theory. In 'a land in which the practice of neighbourliness is most strongly developed', no-one went wanting, yet few seemed to aspire. He admired the country's education system and its newspapers, despaired of its tariffs and barriers and wondered at laws that amounted to 'the complete control of the individual by the government'.

He was far from the first visitor to muse about NZ's contradictions – the American academic Leslie Lipson, who weathered the WWII years at Wellington's Victoria University, admired NZ's 'passion for social justice' but fretted about its 'restraint on talent' and 'lack of cultural achievement'.

For the *bon vivant* Goldblatt, the attitude towards food and drink was all too telling. Apart from one visit to a clandestine European-style restaurant in Auckland, where the bottles were hidden under tables, he found only 'the plain fare and even plainer fetch and carry of the normal feeding machine of this country' and shops catering 'in the same pedestrian fashion for a people never fastidious – the same again is the order of the day'.

Thus, a people with access to some of the best fresh ingredients on earth tended to boil everything to death. A nation strewn almost its entire length with excellent microclimates for viticulture produced only fortified plonk. Material comfort was valued, but was a plain thing indeed.

It took New Zealanders a quarter of a century more to shuck 'the same dull sandwiches', and embrace a national awareness – and, as Goldblatt correctly anticipated, it took 'hazards and misfortunes' to spur the 'divine discontent' for change.

But when it did happen, it *really* happened. Modern NZ culture pivots on a few years in the early 1980s. First, the unquestioned primacy of rugby union as a source of social cohesion (which rivalled the country's commitment to the two world wars as a foundation of nation-building) was stripped away when tens of thousands of New Zealanders took to the streets to protest a tour by the South African rugby side in 1981.

They held that the politics of apartheid not only had a place in sport, they trumped it.

The country was starkly divided; there were riots in Paradise. The mark is still strong enough that most New Zealanders over 30 will recognise the simple phrase 'The Tour' or even just '1981' as referring to those events.

The tour protests both harnessed and nourished a political and cultural renaissance among the country's native people, the Maori, which had already been rolling for a decade. Three years later, that renaissance found its mark, when a reforming Labour government gave statutory teeth to the Waitangi Tribunal, an agency that has since guided a process of land return, compensation for past wrongs and interpretation of the Treaty of Waitangi – the 160-year-old compact between Maoris and the Crown – as a living document.

NZ's fondness for social experiment also came roaring back in 1984, this time to blast away the accretions of the decades since the democracy was first constructed. The bloated public sector was slashed with sweeping privatisations, regulation was removed from many sectors, trade barriers dismantled.

If there is broad agreement that the economy had to be restructured, the reforms remain controversial. The old social guarantees no longer apply: there is poverty in NZ, and South Auckland sees Third World diseases such as tuberculosis. And yet there is a dynamism about NZ that was rare in the 'golden weather' years before the reforms. NZ farmers take on the world without the massive subsidies of yore, and Wellington's inner city – once virtually closed after dark by oppressive licensing laws – now thrives with great bars and restaurants.

As with the economic reforms, the 'Treaty process' of redress and reconciliation with Maoris makes some New Zealanders uneasy more in their uncertainty about its extent than that it has happened at all. A court decision suggesting that some Maoris might have unforeseen traditional rights to stretches of the country's seabed and foreshore (not the beaches themselves, but the area from the high tide outwards) hit a particularly raw nerve. Although its basis in law proved to be shaky, the assumption had long been that access to the beach was a NZ birthright. The conservative National Party, ailing in Opposition, tapped into public unease over this new and unexpected dimension to the Treaty process, claiming the country was moving towards 'separatism' – and shot up in the opinion polls. The Labour government, spooked by the public response, passed a law that confirmed the seabed and foreshore in Crown (public) ownership but offered Maori groups the chance to explore their 'customary rights' to places they had traditionally used.

Many Maoris, feeling they had been denied due process, were angry, and a *hikoi* (march) of 15,000 protested at Parliament, amid speculation that political allegiances with Maoris were being re-drawn. The speculation was well founded: the momentum generated by the *hikoi* led directly to the formation of the Maori Party, which won four of the seven electorates reserved for Maoris in the 2005 general election (unseating a Labour MP in each) and even hinted, in the horse trading after the election, that it might back the centre-right National Party. It remains as an independent (and not necessarily left-wing) Maori voice in a Parliament controlled by a Labour-led coalition.

And yet, for all the change, key elements of the NZ identity are an unbroken thread. If it can hardly be claimed that this is a country where all are equal, fortune is still a matter of economics rather than class. If

'When Sir Edmund Hillary was offered the post of High Commissioner to India, he thought his lack of a car would disqualify him.'

David Lange, former NZ prime minister, interviewed by Ruth Ricketts in December 2003

No matter where you are in NZ, you're never more than 128km from the sea.

Kiwi inventions include the disposable syringe, the child-proof top for pill bottles and the tear-back Velcro strip.

'There is no depression in New Zealand. There are no sheep on our farms.'

There is No Depression in New Zealand by Blam Blam Blam (1981)

you are well served in a restaurant or shop, it will be out of politeness or pride in the job, rather than servility.

You might on your travels hear the phrase 'number-eight wire' and wonder what on earth it means. It's a catchphrase New Zealanders still repeat to themselves to encapsulate a national myth: that NZ's isolation and its pioneer stock created a culture in which ingenuity allowed problems to be solved and tools to be built from scratch. A NZ farmer, it was said, could solve pretty much any problem with a piece of number-eight wire (the gauge used for fencing on farms).

It's actually largely true – NZ farms are full of NZ inventions. And in a wider sense, New Zealanders have always operated best at the intersection of practicality and creativity, as designers rather than artists.

One reason big offshore film and TV producers bring their projects here – apart from the more modest costs and huge variety of locations – is that they like the can-do attitude and ability to work to a goal of NZ technical crews. Many more New Zealanders have worked as managers, roadies or chefs for famous recording artists (everyone from Led Zeppelin and U2 to Madonna) than have enjoyed the spotlight themselves.

Although the national anthem, 'God Defend New Zealand', is an appeal to the Almighty, and Parliament begins every day with prayers, New Zealanders are not a particularly pious people – far less so, according to polls, than Australians. A New Zealander is more likely to be spiritually fulfilled in the outdoors than in church. The land and sea were spiritual constants in pre-European Maori culture and they are scarcely less so today.

This can be seen in the work of a major artist, the late Colin McCahon, which can be found in the major public galleries. His paintings might seem inscrutable, even forbidding, to the visitor, but, even where Mc-Cahon lurched into Catholic mysticism or quoted screeds from the *Bible*, his spirituality was rooted in geography. His bleak, brooding landscapes evoke the sheer power of NZ's terrain.

But McCahon's work is also riven with doubt. And culturally speaking, doubt is what separates New Zealanders from the Australians, makes them less likely to wave the flag, less confident, but also more subtle, more measured and in some ways more interesting.

NZ's cultural development was stultified for decades by the way it was walled off from the outside world. That is no longer the case. New cultures are flowing in and becoming established. Born and bred Kiwis – always great travellers, but now more inclined to return to the nest – adopt the best of what they see elsewhere. A 54-page feature in *Time* magazine in 2003 hailed what the magazine saw as a new determination among New Zealanders to seek their destinies at home rather than abroad. Perhaps Lipson's 'restraint on talent' has finally eased.

So what, as diversity grows, will remain central to the NZ cultural identity? It's instructive here to look at a failed project. Eddie Rayner, a former member of NZ's most celebrated pop group, Split Enz, led a project several years ago to devise a new national anthem to replace 'God Defend New Zealand', which is not greatly loved by New Zealanders. The song, 'This Land', was written and recorded, but did not displace the incumbent. It's pretty hard to change anthems.

And yet Rayner's explanation of the new song's theme still resonates. He and his collaborators had looked at ideas of culture, race, patriotism and history – all of them were not quite right. The one thing, they decided, on which everyone could agree, and which united all New Zealanders, was the land. And it seems likely that for future New Zealanders, it will be a defining belief that it is the land – moody, beautiful, endlessly varied – to which they belong, rather than the reverse.

LIFESTYLE

For most of its history, NZ's small population and plentiful land has seen its people live in stand-alone houses on large, green sections. And while that's still the rule, for a number of reasons it has started to change.

In Auckland, concern about suburban sprawl and poor public transport, and the gentrification of once-poor inner-city suburbs, has seen a boom in terraced housing and apartments, either in the central city or on its fringes. As immigration-fuelled population growth continues to put pressure on space, more Auckland citizens are learning to do without the birthright of a back yard.

Wellington's inner-city boom is slightly different. There, as the public service has shrunk and large companies have moved their head offices away, old office buildings and warehouses have been converted for apartment living.

At the same time, a parallel trend has seen a rush to the coastlines, and to beautiful areas such as Nelson, at the top of the South Island, where property values have rocketed and orchards have been ploughed under to make way for more housing. In the process, an icon of the Kiwi lifestyle, the bach (pronounced 'batch') – a rough beach house, often passed down through families – has begun to disappear. Many New Zealanders feel this as a loss, especially when the land goes to foreign buyers, and the fear that coastal land is getting beyond the reach of ordinary families is a significant political issue.

The growth in economic inequality in recent decades has seen a serious problem with overcrowding in a few poor urban areas, such as South Auckland. Two or three families can share a single house, with attendant public health problems. A partial return to the public housing policies that created a chunk of the country's current housing stock aims to address this problem.

Family trends, meanwhile, are similar to those in other Western countries: New Zealanders are marrying later – the median age for marriage has increased from just over 20 to about 30 years of age in the last 20 years – or not marrying at all. For those under 25 years of age, de facto unions are now more common than formal marriage, and about a third of all people between the ages of 15 and 44 who are living in partnerships are not legally married. About 20,000 couples still get married every year, and half that many get divorced.

Law changes in recent years have aimed to extend matrimonial property principles to unmarried couples, including same-sex couples. The growth in the number of sole-parent families (which tend to be poorer than two-parent households) has not been without controversy, but the majority of NZ children are still raised in the traditional family unit.

The second term of Labour-led government will be remembered for two controversial pieces of social legislation: the Prostitution Law Reform Act and the Civil Unions Act. The first legalised prostitution and made it subject to standard workplace regulation. The second created a new category of union – similar to but separate from marriage – open to both heterosexual and same-sex couples. A 'moral backlash' driven by Pentecostal churches accompanied the latter in particular, but opinion polls consistently showed a majority of the public supported the establishment of civil unions.

NZ has one book shop for every 7500 people. That's more book shops per head of population than anywhere else in the world.

The Department of Conservation (www .doc.govt.nz), or DOC as it is universally known, states its mission thus: 'To conserve NZ's natural and historic heritage for all to enjoy now and in the future.' Its site has a wealth of information on the things that make NZ what it is.

With regards to wealth, NZ sits 24th among the 30 OECD countries on a measure of GDP per head in terms of 'purchasing power parity', indicating that its people are nearly a third less affluent than those of Canada or Ireland, or roughly as wealthy as the average Spaniard.

Average weekly household income is in excess of $1000, but wealth is far less evenly spread than it was 25 years ago – some households get by on half or less of that figure.

NZ's GDP growth (still driven largely by farm incomes) outperformed that of the rest of the OECD for some time between 2000 and 2005. Despite significant balance of payments deficits, driven by a high dollar (itself fuelled by high interest rates set by the Reserve Bank to quell inflationary pressures), consumers maintained a fairly buoyant mood until 2006, when the mood began to ebb a little. The proportion of New Zealanders earning $60,000 per annum doubled from 5% to 10% between late 1999 and 2003. The wealthiest region is Wellington, where one in 25 income earners reaps more than $100,000 per annum.

NZ's geographical isolation means that young New Zealanders in particular have for some time been highly mobile – 'OE' (overseas experience) is still considered a rite of passage, but the primary destination has, in recent years, become Australia rather than Britain. In a notable development the 'brain drain' that has persisted for much of the country's history has recently been reversed, but it remains to be seen whether this trend will persist.

Although incomes are lower in NZ, returning expats seem to be attracted by the lifestyle. An international survey in 2003 named Auckland as the fifth-best city in the world for quality of life, rating the city highly for recreational opportunities and quality of housing and public services, less so for its overstretched transport system.

Much of New Zealanders' leisure time has traditionally been spent outdoors. About two-thirds of New Zealanders list walking and gardening among their leisure pursuits, around 40% enjoy swimming at some point every year, and more than a quarter go fishing. Access to beaches and wilderness areas continues to be regarded as an essential part of their heritage.

The old image of life in NZ as a cultural desert no longer applies. A recent government survey on cultural activities found that 1.2 million people, or more than a third of adult New Zealanders, had bought a book in the previous month – making reading the nation's most popular cultural activity – and about the same number had used a library or purchased recorded music, with video and DVD hire and cinema attendance not far behind.

Over the past year, just over a million people had attended a live popular music performance, and 750,000 had been to the theatre, and more than half a million had visited a *marae* (Maori meeting house). Wellingtonians' claim to be the country's most culturally active people was also borne out.

POPULATION & MULTICULTURALISM

There are just over four million resident New Zealanders, and almost one in three of them now live in the largest city, Auckland, where growth has been fuelled both by a 'drift north' that has been going on for half a century, and more recent waves of immigration. The general drift to the cities means that urban areas now account for 72% of the population.

Auckland has become easily the most multicultural centre in NZ (while, at the other end of the country, the population of the southernmost town, Bluff, is 95% European). It is effectively the capital of the South Pacific, and is home to more Pacific Islanders now than the Pacific Island nations themselves. People of Pacific Island heritage make up about 6% of the population.

Auckland has also been the prime destination for ethnic Chinese since immigration rules were relaxed in 1987. While many (east) Asian immigrants have chosen to cluster in Auckland's distant eastern suburbs, visitors are often startled by the 'Asianisation' of its central city, where thousands of Asian students reside, either studying at Auckland University, learning English, or both.

Occasional incidents involving Asians – usually Asian-on-Asian crimes such as kidnapping or driving offences – have added to disquiet about Asian immigration in some parts of the country. But recent opinion polls indicate that most Aucklanders tend to value the contribution of new migrants. Now, more than 13% of Aucklanders are Asian and 6% of these are Chinese. About 20% of Auckland Chinese were born in NZ, but considerable attention has been focused on the so-called '1.5 generation'; young Chinese born overseas but socialised (and sometimes educated) in NZ. The traditionally quiescent culture of Chinese New Zealanders has been challenged in recent years, and a dynamic group of young ethnic Asians is emerging into leadership roles not only in within their own community, but in wider NZ society.

The Maori population was somewhere between 100,000 and 200,000 at the time of first European contact 200 years ago. Disease and warfare subsequently brought the population near to collapse, but a high birth rate now sees about 15% of New Zealanders identify as Maori, and that proportion is likely to grow.

Maori is, along with English, an official language, and many Maoris believe the clear implication of the Treaty of Waitangi is one of a partnership with the Crown, representing the 80% of New Zealanders who are 'Pakeha', or of European heritage – forging a bicultural nation.

Yet somewhere within that bicultural nation, room will have to be found to accommodate the diversity, the developing multiculturalism of NZ. How will the strong claim of a cultural stake by the growing Pacific population be accommodated in coming years? The country has, over the years, absorbed and assimilated earlier waves of migrants – English, Dutch, Polynesian – but will it also do so with the more varied and, to some, exotic cultures now taking root? Will 'new' New Zealanders settle more widely, or stay in the urban north?

NZ never had an official 'white' immigration policy as Australia did, but its people for decades tended to regard it as an outpost of Britain. In the years to come, other influences – NZ's role in the Pacific, its burgeoning economic links to Asia, its offering of sanctuary to refugees – will now inevitably help shape what it is to be a New Zealander.

SPORT

New Zealanders not only watch sport, they play it; and although golf can claim more participants than any other sport, no-one doubts that the national game is rugby union. The game is interwoven with NZ's history and culture, and the national side, the All Blacks, have, even in the professional era, an almost mythical status.

The All Blacks are, however, the subject of extraordinary expectations; it frequently seems that nothing less than 100% success will satisfy the public. When the All Blacks dip out of the Rugby World Cup at semifinal stage (as they have done no fewer than three times), there is national mourning.

NZ has won more Olympic gold medals per capita than any other country.

The first referee in the world to use a whistle to halt a game was William Atack of Christchurch. He thought of this (now seemingly obvious and ubiquitous refereeing tool) in 1884.

Below top international level, the Super 14 competition with teams from Australia and South Africa offers the world's best rugby, although local purists still prefer the National Provincial Championship (NPC), which takes place later in the winter.

For all rugby's influence on the culture, don't go along to a game expecting to be caught up in an orgy of noise and cheering. Rugby crowds at Auckland's Eden Park (p139) are as restrained as their teams are cavalier, but they get noisier as you head south. Fans at Canterbury's excellent Jade Stadium (p555) are reputed to be the most one-eyed in the land.

Auckland is home to the NZ Warriors rugby league team, which plays in the Australian NRL (National Rugby League). Supporting the Warriors has become a way into the culture for South Auckland immigrant communities, and a Warriors home game at Ericsson Stadium (p139) is a noisy spectacle. The on-field action, however, is not for the faint of heart.

You need to go to the other end of the country to find the heartland of netball, the leading winter sport for women (and the one in which the national team, the Silver Ferns, perpetually vies for world supremacy with the Australians). The Invercargill-based Southern Sting (see p678) attracts a fanatical following from the local community – and repay the support by winning most of the time.

Cricket is the established summer team sport, and the State Shield (one-day) and State Championship provincial competitions take place alongside international matches involving the national side, the Black Caps, through the summer months. Wellington's Basin Reserve is the last sole-use test cricket venue in the main centres (and only a few minutes' walk from the bars and restaurants of Courtenay Pl) and New Plymouth's Pukekura Park (p261) is simply one of the prettiest cricket grounds in the world.

MEDIA

Almost all NZ cities have their own morning newspapers, sometimes coexisting with the likes of the Auckland-based *New Zealand Herald*, which cover wider regions, and they're fairly good.

The magazine market is more varied, and dominated by independent publishers. The *Listener* (like the *Herald*, owned by Australian company APN, which is in turn controlled by Irish media magnate Tony O'Reilly) is published weekly and offers TV and radio listings. Auckland's own magazine, *Metro*, is a good-looking guide to the style of the city. *Cuisine* is a sleek, popular and authoritative guide to food and wine.

Free-to-air TV is dominated by the two publicly owned Television New Zealand channels (TV One and TV2), versus the Canadian-owned TV3 and its sibling music channel C4. Regional TV struggles, but is stronger on the South Island, where Nelson's Mainland TV and Invercargill's Southland TV are part of their communities. The country's only access TV station, Triangle, reflects Auckland's cultural and ethnic diversity. The pay TV market (and with it digital broadcasting) is entirely in the hands of Sky TV, which in 2006 joined the free-to-air market by purchasing Prime TV from its Australian owners.

The two TV shows you need to know about are the nightly national soap, *Shortland Street*, a hospital drama that often does an uncanny job of anticipating the *Zeitgeist*, and the irreverent multicultural cartoon comedy *bro'Town*.

Radio Sport carries one of the true sounds of the NZ summer: cricket commentaries. The public broadcaster, Radio New Zealand, is based in

NZXsports.com (nzxsports.com) is an award-winning site that offers a way into surf and ski information, webcams and many other land- and water-based sports. Highly recommended.

Visit the *New Zealand Herald* online at www.nzherald.co.nz.

Get the scoop on independent news at www.scoop.co.nz.

Wellington; its flagship, National Radio, offers strong news and feature programming and is available nationwide.

The network of student stations, the bNet, offers an engaging and adventurous alternative (they're also the best place to hear about local gigs), and the most sophisticated of the stations, Auckland's 95bFM, is surprisingly influential.

There is also a nationwide network of *iwi* (tribal) stations, some of which, including Waikato's Radio Tainui, offer welcome respite from the commercial networks – others, such as Auckland's Mai FM, take on the national Pacific Island station Niu FM and the dance station, George FM, which can be heard in central Auckland and Queenstown.

RELIGION

Reflecting its English heritage, NZ is nominally of the Anglican-Protestant denomination, and where religion has a place in public affairs, it will be of that flavour. The Catholic church claims about 470,000 adherents to the Anglican church's 630,000.

But the number of people actively identifying with the major Christian denominations has been falling, and a 1998 survey indicated that fewer than a third of New Zealanders were 'certain' of a belief in God. Census figures show that more than a quarter of New Zealanders claim no religious affiliation. Immigrants have brought their faiths with them, but religions such as Islam and Hinduism account for less than 1% of the population.

New Pentecostal churches have grown strongly in the past decade, and churchgoing remains strong in the Pacific Island communities. Maori spirituality has historically been fused with Christianity in messianic movements such as Ratana and Ringatu, but is increasingly expressed in its own right – most notably when work on a planned motorway route in Waikato was briefly held up because a local tribe said it disturbed a *taniwha* (a kind of river dragon).

WOMEN IN NEW ZEALAND

Although NZ has prided itself on being the first country in the world, in 1893, to introduce universal suffrage, for many years the real role for women in public life was modest.

That can hardly be said now, with three of the most important roles in civil society – prime minister, governor general and chief justice – filled by women: Helen Clark, Dame Sylvia Cartwright and Dame Sian Elias respectively. The country's second-largest company, Telecom NZ, is also steered by a woman, Theresa Gattung.

Yet, even with the presence of a Ministry of Women's Affairs, some benefits have been slower to come to ordinary NZ women: paid parental leave was only instituted in 2002, for example. As in most other countries, women's wages tend to be lower than men's, although the gap is closing.

There is a very strong tradition of women's sport in NZ, and the world-champion Silver Ferns netball side and individuals such as Olympic board-sailor Barbara Kendall are household names. There is even a women's national rugby side, the Black Ferns, which labours under the same expectations as the All Blacks – the team must beat all comers, all the time – albeit with a much lower profile.

Nowhere is women's contribution to NZ stronger than in the arts and creative industries. Niki Caro, director of *Whale Rider*, is but one in a line

Stuff (www.stuff.co.nz) has news from Fairfax newspapers.

Glamorous Rotorua-born Jean Batten, known as Hine-o-te-Rangi (Daughter of the Skies), was a famous aviatrix of the 1930s. During a glittering career, she was the first pilot to make a direct flight between England and NZ.

Ministry of Women's Affairs (www.mwa.govt .nz) has lots of official content and some handy links too.

THE CULTURE •• Arts

of accomplished film-makers that includes directors Jane Campion (*The Piano*, *In the Cut*, *An Angel at My Table*), Christine Jeffs (*Rain*, *Sylvia*) and Gillian Ashurst (*Snakeskin*), Peter Jackson's longtime collaborators Fran Walsh and Philippa Boyens and top-flight costume designer Ngila Dickson, and actors Anna Paquin, Kerry Fox and Lucy (*Xena*) Lawless. In literature, Janet Frame, Fiona Kidman, Elizabeth Knox and Stephanie Johnson enjoy a stature equal to or greater than their male counterparts.

ARTS
Literature

NZ literature was dominated for a long time by an important nationalist movement that arose in the 1930s to address the challenge of defining independence from the 'mother country', Britain, whose identity had been adopted virtually by proxy until then.

Some writers who appeared then – especially the poets Allen Curnow, Denis Glover, ARD Fairburn and RAK Mason – became commanding figures in the definition of a new culture, and were still around in the 1950s to be part of what the country's most prominent historian, Keith Sinclair (himself a poet), called the time 'when the NZ intellect and imagination came alive'.

Katherine Mansfield's work began a NZ tradition in short fiction, and for years the standard was carried by novelist Janet Frame, whose dramatic life was depicted in Jane Campion's film of her autobiography, *An Angel at My Table*. A new era of international recognition began in 1985 when Keri Hulme's haunting *The Bone People* won a Booker Prize (the world is still waiting for the follow-up, *Bait*).

The centre of NZ's literary universe now is undoubtedly Bill Manhire's creative-writing course at Victoria University of Wellington, which has produced most of the country's most prominent new writers in the past decade, including novelists Catherine Chidgey, Elizabeth Knox (pick up *The Vintner's Luck*, avoid *Black Oxen*) and Emily Perkins, and playwrights and screenwriters Anthony McCarten and Duncan Sarkies. In 2003 Chidgey was named the country's best novelist under 40, and her *In a Fishbone Church* is recommended.

Manhire, a poet himself, also compiled *100 NZ Poems*, which is widely regarded as the best anthology of NZ poetry, and with Marion McLeod, *The New Zealand Short Story Collection*.

But there are also writers who, consciously or not, buck the introspective style often associated with the Manhire school. Auckland-based Chad Taylor writes tight, spare, noir fiction that is urban in character yet defiantly indigenous. His *Electric* offers a seamy view of Auckland that might surprise visitors. Also, Maori novelist Patricia Grace's *Tu* (based on the story of the legendary Maori Battalion in WWII) won the country's most prestigious book award in 2005, heading off Nigel Cox's *Tarzan Presley*, a mad fusion of NZ history and popular culture.

Much of the best (and most popular) nonfiction of recent years has concerned NZ history: Philip Temple's *A Sort of Conscience* (about the Wakefields, the family that drove the colonisation of NZ), the late Michael King's hugely popular *Penguin History of New Zealand* and James Belich's more academic *Making Peoples* are all fine works. If you want to try and understand NZ character, good places to start are *Great New Zealand Argument: Ideas About Ourselves*, which collects writing on national identity spanning 70 years, and the award-winning *At Home: A Century of New Zealand Design* by Douglas Lloyd Jenkins.

Architecture in NZ (user.chollian.net/~ucnet2001/) is a general architectural history site, with good photos and information about old churches of interest.

For info on NZ literary tourism, check out www.bookcouncil.org.nz/tourism/index.html.

Cinema

The commanding figure in NZ cinema is, without doubt, the director and screenwriter Peter Jackson, whose successful completion of the *Lord of the Rings* trilogy was not only a boon to the local industry but a significant morale boost to the country as a whole.

NEW ZEALAND'S LORD OF THE RINGS *Errol Hunt*

Peter Jackson was already a minor hero to NZ's small film industry before he directed his famous trilogy: *Lord of the Rings: Fellowship of the Ring* (2001), *Two Towers* (2002) and *The Return of the King* (2003). From his very first film, *Bad Taste* (vomit-eating aliens and exploding sheep; 1987), it was obvious that he was a unique talent. *Bad Taste* was followed by *Meet the Feebles* (muppets on acid; 1989) and an even gorier zombie movie, *Brain Dead* ('I kick ass for the Lord'; 1992). Two slightly-less-bloodstained films – *Heavenly Creatures* (1994) and *Frighteners* (1996) – preceded the *Rings* films, while of course the giant *King Kong* (2005) followed hard in the tiny hobbits' footsteps.

The effect of the three *Rings* films on NZ was unparalleled. The country embraced Jackson and his *Rings* with a passion. Wellington was renamed Middle-earth for the week of the *Fellowship* release in late 2001, a Minister for the *Rings* was named in the NZ government and Jackson was made a Comparion of the New Zealand Order of Merit for his services in the film industry. The frenzy only increased for the second and third films, especially when the world premiere (*world* premiere!) of *The Return of the King* was held in Wellington in December 2003, and of course went on to win a record 11 Oscars.

Many Kiwis contributed to the films' success; in all, about 2000 New Zealanders had full-time jobs working on the *Rings* films, and that's in addition to all the 'extras' (15,000 of them, including a few hundred NZ Army personnel pressed into armour and drafted into battle scenes for *Fellowship*). Travelling around NZ, it sometimes feels like every man and his dog had some part in the movies, or wants to tell you about a relative who did.

The effect of the *Rings* films was not only a boost to national morale: the films' effect on NZ's economy was enormous. Of the $650 million spent making the films, much stayed in NZ. The film industry has gone from strength to strength, with the filming of other Hollywood and local blockbusters here prompting Wellington's new nickname, 'Wellywood'. The effect on tourism was also massive…

Middle-earth Tourism

If you are one of those travellers inspired to come down under by the scenery of the *Rings* movies, you won't be disappointed. Jackson's decision to film here in NZ wasn't mere patriotism. Nowhere else on earth will you find such wildly varied, unspoiled landscapes.

You will doubtless recognise some places from the films. For example, Hobbiton (near Matamata; p245), Mt Doom (instantly recognisable as towering Ngauruhoe; p315) or the Misty Mountains (the South Island's Southern Alps). The visitor information centres in Wellington (p408), Twizel (p581) or Queenstown (p623) should be able to direct you to local *Rings* sites of interest. If you're serious about finding the exact spots where scenes were filmed, buy a copy of Ian Brodie's nerdtastic *The Lord of the Rings: Location Guidebook*, which includes instructions, and even GPS coordinates, for finding all the important scenes. Also check the beautiful online 'ocation guide at www.filmnz .com/midd.eearth. Private companies run *Rings* tours in Tongariro National Park (p318), Wellington (p415), Nelson (p466), Methven (p572), Queenstown (p631) and Wanaka (p650).

For fun 'rainy-weekend viewing, get a few old Jackson films cut on DVD and look for Jackson's own performances. He stars as both the chainsaw-wielding Derek and Robert the Alien in *Bad Taste*, and has cameos as the undertaker's assistant in *Brain Dead*, a derelict hobo outside a cinema in *Heavenly Creatures* and a clumsy, chain-wearing biker in *Frighteners*. In the *Rings'* films, Jackson appears as a belching hobbit outs de a pub in *Fellowship*, a stone-throwing Helms Deep defender in *Two Towers* and a captain of the Corsairs in *The Return of the King*. In *King Kong*, a slimmed-down Jackson plays one of the biplane machine gunners in the climactic end scene.

Jackson's big-budget remake of *King Kong* followed, and Jackson (and his world-leading Weta postproduction facility in Wellington) are now working on a movie version of the *Halo* video game and a film based on Alice Sebold's *The Lovely Bones*. Jackson (whose earlier works, including the shoestring splatter of *Bad Taste* and the thoroughly scabrous *Meet the Feebles*, are worth seeking out) seems set to dominate the local industry for decades yet. But he is not the only New Zealander turning out blockbusters. *Chronicles of Narnia: The Lion, the Witch and the Wardrobe* was largely filmed in NZ and directed by New Zealander Andrew Adamson, and seems set to become a major movie franchise.

Niki Caro, whose *Whale Rider* was a surprise festival hit, recently completed the Hollywood film *North Country*, featuring Charlize Theron. Close behind her are a bunch of brown and white faces behind two fine films about the multicultural Auckland experience, *Sione's Wedding* and *No. 2*, the debut of Fijian writer Toa Fraser.

Notwithstanding the scale and success of *Rings*, the status of NZ cinema remains a matter of keen debate. In his BBC-funded documentary, *Cinema of Unease*, NZ actor Sam Neill described the country's uniquely strange and dark film industry', producing bleak, haunted work. The *Listener's* film critic, Philip Matthews, offered his own characterisation, based on three celebrated local productions: 'Between (Niki Caro's) *Whale Rider*, (Christine Jeffs') *Rain* and *Lord of the Rings*, you can extract the qualities that our best films possess. Beyond slick technical accomplishment, all share a kind of land-mysticism, an innately supernatural sensibility.'

Most of the other high points of NZ cinema fall somewhere on the two men's thematic axes: the 1977 speculative political thriller *Sleeping Dogs* (starring Neill), which is credited with kick-starting local production; Geoff Murphy's vigorous 'Maori western' *Utu*; Roger Donaldson's man-on-the-edge domestic drama *Smash Palace* ('the ultimate 'unease' film', according to Matthews); Vincent Ward's haunting image of a young girl and nature, *Vigil*; the anarchic road movie *Goodbye Pork Pie*; Jane Campion's Oscar-winning *The Piano* (a tale of erotic longing that has since functioned as a postcard for its location on Karekare Beach); Lee Tamahori's graphic, jarring *Once Were Warriors*; and of course Jackson's own *Heavenly Creatures*. An industry that sometimes doubts its own existence has more than its share of overachievers.

Music

There has been music in NZ since the first human occupation, more than 800 years ago – song, dance, rhythm and melody are woven tightly into Maori culture – but it has never been stronger or more varied than it is now.

NZ music has been on a roll for the past few years, in large part because the environment has become more supportive: a voluntary local music quota agreed between the government and commercial radio broadcasters has been hugely influential. Less than a decade ago, locally produced music accounted for about 2% of commercial radio schedules – now in some cases, it's well over 20%. The perennial local heroes, the Finn brothers, of Split Enz and Crowded House, have a lot more company on the airwaves these days.

At the same time, the influence of Maori and Pacific Island artists has been growing. Contemporary Maori music is flourishing on its own terms, and several leading artists, including the very popular singersongwriter Bic Runga, have Maori heritage.

Witi Ihimaera wrote his novel *The Whale Rider* in 1987, inspired by his daughters' complaints that he took them to movies with only male heroes.

The NZ Film Archive (www.filmarchive.org .nz) is a superb online resource, lovingly curated.

Amplifier (www.amplifier .co.nz) has local music news, free and paid downloads (including video) and more.

But brown faces show up nowhere more prominently than in the country's burgeoning hip-hop scene. The country's most popular rap artists – Scribe, Savage, Tha Feelstyle, Dei Hamo and Mareko – are of Samoan heritage.

Mareko and Savage are backed by Dawn Raid, a remarkable South Auckland enterprise that encompasses a record label, a clothing factory, a community trust and even a barbershop. Clubs situated around central Auckland's Karangahape Rd (K Rd; see p139) feature the top local DJs and MCs till late.

Auckland is also home to the garage-rock scene that provided a springboard for the D4 and the Datsuns, and while those two are generally touring elsewhere, you can catch the next wave of would-bes at the Kings Arms Tavern (p139) and Karangahape Rd's Eden's Bar (p139). The same city spawned the respected drum 'n' bass (D&B) crews Concord Dawn and Bulletproof; the basement club Fu Bar (p139), in Queen St, is the best place to catch D&B.

In Wellington, it's all about groove, and no-one grooves more than Fat Freddy's Drop, a remarkable live act which merges jazzy flights of

TRY THESE FOR SIZE

Phoenix Foundation *Pegasus* (FMR) The second beguiling album from a Wellington group stacked with the sons of noted writers and poets.

Fat Freddy's Drop *Based on a True Story* (The Drop) The left-field hit of recent years. This reggae-funk-jazz fusion went multiplatinum on the strength of the group's memorable live shows.

SJD *Southern Lights* (Round Trip Mars) Sean James Donnelly's work defies classification, although it's sometimes called 'electro-folk'. It's gorgeous, anyway. Look out for the two-CD 'pick 'n' mix' version of the album, which includes remixes by the like of Kid Loco.

Pluto *Pipelines Under The Ocean* (EMI) The second album by Pluto veers from country to kraut-rock. The hypnotic 'Long White Cross', a sleeper hit on radio, is on its way to becoming a local classic.

Fly My Pretties *The Return of Fly My Pretties* (Loop) This second CD-DVD combo again catches the Wellington supergroup led by Barnaby Weir in its element; that is, on stage.

Various Artists *Rippon* (Loop) This compilation, based around the line-up for the annual festival at the beautiful Rippon vineyards in Wanaka, doubles as a handy introduction to the best local music. Includes Fly My Pretties, Pluto, Shihad, Module and new darling Hollie Smith.

Tha Feelstyle *Break It To Pieces* (FMR/Warner) The world's best Samoan-language rapper delivers an album that just oozes funky soul style.

Dave Dobbyn *Available Light* (Sony BMG) Dobbyn, who has been writing the tunes New Zealanders hum since the 1970s, gives vent to his Christian faith in the best album of his career. 'Welcome Home', a plea for tolerance, might be the most important song he's ever written.

Shihad *Love is the New Hate* (Warner Music) The thunderous (and occasionally tender) rock band briefly known as Pacifier are back to their original name and back on the form that made people love them.

Moana *Toru* (Tangata) Moana Maniapoto Jackson and her band don't just tour Europe regularly, they bring back ideas. This album fuses Maori music with the contemporary Indian and Arabic grooves she picked up at Paris's Bhudda Bar.

Goldenhorse *Out of the Moon* (Siren/EM) Intriguing, artful and eclectic pop music.

Toni Huata *Maori To* (Waahtu Creations) Huata recorded and re-interprets a clutch of traditional Maori *waiata* (songs), most written by her grandfather. Gentle and authentic.

Katchafire *Slow Burning* (Mai Music) Bob Marley's sole NZ concert in 1978 had a profound impact on many Maori musicians, and Katchafire are unabashed about their dedication to reggae, Bob-style. They're also very popular.

Bic Runga *Birds* (Sony Music) The hugely popular Maori-Malaysian singer-songwriter's latest album is sweet, mournful and hugely popular.

Savage *Moonshine* (Dawn Raid) Having emerged as the sideman to the country's biggest rapper, Scribe, livewire South Aucklander Savage has a major hit album of his own.

Loop Recordings (www
.loop.co.nz) is the sound
of groovy Wellington.
Offerings on its website
include videos and links
to its weekly LoopKast
podcast, which has more
than 30,000 subscribers
worldwide.

ART OUT THERE

Not all the best galleries are in the cities. The energetic Govett-Brewster Art Gallery (p260) – home to the legacy of sculptor and film-maker Len Lye – is worth a visit to New Plymouth in itself, and Gore's Eastern Southland Gallery (p680) has an important and growing collection of works by Ralph Hotere, Rita Angus and others.

You can listen to and buy Maori music – 'from haka to hip-hop' – at www.maorimusic.com.

improvisation with the heartbeat of dub. The group's prime movers pop up in other ventures, often on the busy Loop Recordings. The central city has two very good venues: Bodega (p423) and the Matterhorn (p421).

Flying Nun, the record label at the centre of a creative boom in the 1980s (and still a source of cult fascination for indie music buffs all over the world) is under corporate ownership now, but still releasing records by both its established artists and new acts on the scene such as the Mint Chicks.

In Dunedin, the Flying Nun label's original creative wellspring, the scruffy, arty, independent vibe is alive and well. The Arc Café (p600), the city's leading live venue, is owned and operated by an arts trust. You might also check out Records Records (p601), in a row of terraced houses just up the hill from the Octagon, which was recently sold on by owner-operator Roy Colbert, who has shaped the tastes of successive generations of local musicians. In Christchurch, home of the downbeat masters Salmonella Dub (very popular with students), the venue to check out is the Dux de Lux (p554) on the edge of the city's arts centre, which has been presenting live bands for decades.

Not all of the great music venues are located in NZ cities: indeed, some of the best are situated in beautiful country settings. The Leigh Sawmill Café (p166), in Leigh, on the east coast north of Auckland, has bands and DJs playing throughout the summer, and its dub reggae evenings are the stuff of legend. Lyttelton, Christchurch's port town, boasts the Wunderbar (p558), which hosts anything from poetry readings to drag acts. In January some good touring bills pass through the popular beach resorts.

Visual Arts

It should not be surprising that in a nation so defined by its natural environment, landscape painting constitutes the first (post-European) body of art. John Gully and Petrus van der Velden were among those to arrive and paint memorable (if sometimes overdramatised) depictions of the land. Their modern successor is Graham Sydney, whose ultra-realist depictions of the grand, wide lands of Central Otago are highly sought-after.

A little later, Charles Frederick Goldie painted a series of compelling, realist portraits of Maoris, who were feared to be a dying race. Debate over the political propriety of Goldie's work raged for years, but its value is widely accepted now: not least because the Maoris themselves generally acknowledge and value them as ancestral representations.

As was the case in literature, nationalism was a driving force in art in the 1930s and '40s, notably in the work of Toss Woollaston and Colin McCahon, whose work can be widely seen in NZ galleries, particularly Nelson's Suter Gallery (Woollaston; p463) and the Auckland Art Gallery (McCahon; p112).

Maori art has a distinctive visual style with well-developed motifs, and a few Pakeha artists have tried to incorporate and adopt it: the most

Noizyland (noizyland .com) is a bustling and literate music news and information site with many useful links.

rotable being the cool modernism of the work of Gordon Walters and the more controversial pop-art approach of Dick Frizzell's Tiki series. Leading contemporary Maori artists such as Shane Cotton and Peter Robinson are in turn worldly and (especially in Robinson's case) fond of political humour. The dean of modern Maori artists is undoubtedly Ralph Hotere, an heir to McCahon who lives and works near Dunedin. The Auckland Museum (p109) has an amazing collection of historical Maori and Pacific treasures.

For NZ museums online (including galleries), visit www.nzmuseums.co.nz.

Maori Culture Errol Hunt

MYTHOLOGY
In the Beginning...

In the beginning there was Ranginui (Sky Father) and Papatuanuku (Earth Mother), who were united. They bore many children, the most important of which were Tawhiri-matea (god of winds and storms), Tangaroa (god of the ocean), Tane-mahuta (god of the forests), Haumia-tiketike (god of wild foods), Rongo-matane (god of peace and cultivated food) and Tu-matauenga (god of war and humans).

After aeons of living in darkness, because their parents were so tightly joined together that no light came between them, the children of Ranginui and Papatuanuku could take it no longer – they wanted light! They debated what they should do and eventually decided they should separate their parents so that light could enter the world. Each tried in turn, and failed, to separate Ranginui and Papatuanuku. Finally it was Tane-mahuta's turn to try, and by pushing and straining with his shoulders to the ground and his feet to the sky, Tane finally succeeded in forcing his parents apart: light flooded into the world at last.

Because all the gods were male, a woman needed to be created in order that the earth be inhabited. After a few unsuccessful tries with immortals, Tane created the first woman, Hine-ahuone, out of soil and gave her *tihe mauriora* (breath of life). Hine-ahuone and Tane had a daughter Hine-titama (Dawn Maid), who Tane then married, thus ensuring the birth of humanity (much to the shame of Hine-titama when she eventually found out her husband and father were one and the same).

...And Then along Came Maui

A long time after the creation of the world there lived the demigod Maui, a figure who features in myths right across the Pacific, from New Zealand to the Solomon Islands to Hawai'i. Maui was a typical Polynesian hero, besting his opponents through cleverness as much as by force. He was a Pacific version of the Greeks' Prometheus or Sisyphus, America's troublemakers Coyote or Brer Rabbit, or the Norse trickster Loki. One particular story of his exploits is known in almost all Polynesian cultures. It began one day when Maui, who lived in ancient Hawaiki, went out fishing with his five brothers...

The brothers paddled their canoes far out to sea, where Maui took out his magic fish-hook (the jawbone of his sorceress grandmother), baited it with blood from his own nose, tied it to a strong rope and dropped it over the side of the canoe. Soon Maui caught an immense fish and, struggling mightily, pulled it up to the surface. This fish became the North Island of NZ, called Te Ika a Maui (The Fish of Maui) by the ancient Maori. Wellington Harbour is the fish's mouth, the Taranaki and East Coast areas are its two fins, Lake Taupo is its heart and the Northland penin-

---

MAORI NZ

For an insight into the Maori history and culture of various regions around the country, and things to do for travellers looking for a Maori experience, see boxed texts in Auckland (p103), Northland (p191), Waikato (p232), Taranaki (p260), Central Plateau (p296), the Bay of Plenty (p361), East Cape (p371), Wellington (p405) and Christchurch & the South Island (p535).

eula its tail. Mahia Peninsula in the Hawkes Bay region is Te Matau a Maui (The Fish-hook of Maui) – the magic hook with which he fished up the island.

The South Island was known as Te Waka o Maui (The Canoe of Maui) – the canoe in which he stood when he caught the fish. Kaikoura Peninsula was where Maui braced his foot while hauling up the fish, and Stewart Island was the anchor stone that held the canoe steady as he hauled in the giant fish.

No Hollywood-style hero, Maui is remembered in much of the Pacific as being particularly ugly.

TRIBAL SOCIETY

Maori society was (and to some degree, still is) tribal – Maoris refer to themselves in terms of their *iwi* (tribe), often named after an ancestor, for example, Ngati Kahungunu (descendants of the ancestor Kahungunu) or Ngapuhi (descendants of Puhi). Two or more *iwi* can be grouped into larger alliances by their descent from one *waka*, or migratory canoe. For example, the Waikato and Ngati Maniapoto tribes have traditionally been allied because of their common descent from those who arrived on the *Tainui* canoe.

Traditionally, of more relevance than the *iwi* was the *whanau* (extended family groups) and the village structure based around the *marae* (literally, the flat area in front of a meeting house, but now more often used to refer to the entire complex of buildings).

Traditional society was hierarchical, with positions of leadership largely hereditary, and almost always male. The tribes were headed by an *ariki* (supreme chief), while *hapu* (subtribes) were led by a *rangatira* (local chief). Right down at the bottom of the pecking order were the *taurekareka* (slaves) taken from opposing tribes in battle.

Tapu & Mana

Essential to Maori beliefs and society were the notions of *tapu* (complex rules of sacredness and/or prohibition) and *mana* (personal spiritual power or prestige).

Tapu applied to sacred and/or forbidden objects, such as sacred ground or a chief's possessions, and also to actions prohibited by the tribe. Its application could be temporary or permanent; canoe builders could be

Maui fishing New Zealand out of the ocean

WILHELM DITTMER, 1866-1909
LONDON, ROUTLEDGE, 1907
ALEXANDER TURNBULL LIBRARY,
WELLINGTON, NZ
REF NO PUBL-0088-049

IWI ON THE WEB

It's a sign of the incorporation of Maori society into modern NZ that one of the second-level rules of sacredness and/or prohibition) and *mana* (personal spiritual Internet domain names in NZ (the same level as other countries' .com for commercial) is .iwi, for tribal websites.

Arawa (www.tearawa.iwi.nz) Rotorua *iwi*.
Ngai Tahu (www.ngaitahu.iwi.nz) The main South Island *iwi*.
Ngapuhi (www.ngapuhi.iwi.nz) Northland *iwi* – has its main *marae* at Waitangi (p189).
Ngati Porou (www.ngatiporou.iwi.nz) East Cape – *iwi* represented in the film *Whale Rider*.

MAORI POLITICS

The Maori, like all Polynesian cultures, have always been extremely political: seemingly interminable discussions and long speeches are second nature. With a natural disposition towards politics, it's not surprising that the Maori have a prominent place in NZ politics. In this respect the Maori are by no means a downtrodden minority: they have fought for, and won, remarkably fair representation in politics when compared with other indigenous cultures around the world. (Although, of course, there are always new fights to be fought.)

Maoris entered NZ parliament early, in 1868. Modern politics probably started with the Young Maori Party at the start of the 20th century. Apirana Ngata, James Carroll (acting prime minister in 1909 and 1911) – these are names that still inspire young Maori and are taught to NZ school-kids today. Maori and Pakeha (Maori word for white or European person) alike. In the 1930s the Ratana church (see p47) entered politics, forging an alliance with the Labour Party that held the four Maori seats for Labour through most of the next 40 years. Mana Motuhake, a Maori-rights party, entered politics in the '80s, before becoming part of the short-lived Alliance party. Their successor, from 2004, was the Maori Party, under Tariana Turia and Pita Sharples, which now holds four seats and supports the current Labour minority government. New Zealand First, a party whose politics can sometimes seem a little whimsical, has been known to push both the pro-Maori and anti-Maori barrows; NZF leader Winston Peters (deputy prime minister 1996–98) is still one of the most prominent Maori politicians today.

In 1868 Maoris were given a guaranteed four seats in the 70-seat parliament – although at the time Maori formed about half of NZ's population. Their representation is more proportional now: there are seven dedicated Maori seats (of 120), but politicians of Maori descent hold another 14 of the 'general' seats. The Maori language has been spoken in parliament, with occasional controversy, since 1868.

Maori politics is extremely important in NZ. The Treaty of Waitangi (see p35) and associated land rights, as well as land claims resulting from confiscations after the Land Wars (see p35) are some of the most prominent issues. One of NZ's most divisive events – the 1981 Springbok tour (see p40) – was a measure of how strongly New Zealanders feel about race issues, and it is probably the presence of Maori here that have made it such an issue for many Pakeha New Zealanders. No government, whatever its colours, would implement Maori policies without first consulting affected Maori in *hui* (meetings) on tribal *marae*.

There's a wealth of information about NZ's Maori past and present at www.govt.nz/aboutnz.

made *tapu* in a special ceremony prior to commencing work, and war parties would be given a blood *tapu*, which was removed when they returned to their families.

Mana was possessed by chiefs (both via their ancestors and via deeds of their own) and from them it flowed through to their tribe. *Mana* could be lost – a chief captured in battle would lose his own *mana*, as well as that of his tribe. *Mana* could also be gained – the warrior who killed the first enemy in a battle would attain considerable *mana*.

Both *mana* and *tapu* are concepts very much alive in NZ today, and understood by both Maori and Pakeha (Maori for white or European) New Zealanders. It's essential, for example, that a politician or (even more importantly) an All Black captain, have *mana*. And *tapu* lands have stood in the way of even the most zealous of developers.

Whenua (Land)

Geographical features such as *maunga* (mountains) and *awa* (rivers) often delineated tribal boundaries, and were an important genealogical indicator. Some *maunga* were personified and, even today, each tribe has one or more sacred *maunga*. Tribal *whakapapa* (oral genealogies) always referred to the names of mountains, as they were an important part of the social grid.

On Pakeha settlement, the government assigned European names to many *maunga* in an almost deliberate attempt to tame the 'wilderness'. This practice was more prevalent in areas with small Maori populations (such as the South Island), while locations in heartland Maori regions like King Country, Te Urewera and Taupo have retained their original Maori names.

Land rights are one of the major issues facing Maori and the government today.

Tipuna (Ancestors)

The proper reverence for ancestors was important to the ancient Maori and, in the absence of a written language, long *whakapapa*, stretching back hundreds of years to people who arrived by *waka* from Hawaiki, were committed to memory. *Whakapapa* defined ancestral and family ties and determined everyone's place in the tribe. Maoris saw themselves not as individuals, but as part of the collective knowledge and experience of all of their ancestors.

Traditionally, the soul of the departed travelled north to Te Rerenga-Wairua (Cape Reinga; p179), where it slid down the roots of a lone pohutukawa tree (which still stands) and then rejoined the ancestral spirits in Hawaiki (simultaneously the name for the underworld and the ancestral homeland).

Marae (Tribal Home)

Strictly speaking, the *marae* is the flat area of grass in front of a *whare whakairo* (carved meeting house), but these days the term is used to describe the entire complex of buildings surrounding the meeting house – in most cases the major meeting spot for Maori in that area. A *marae* complex contains several buildings but the most important are the meeting house and the building where food is served (*whare kai*).

VISITING A MARAE

Probably the best way to gain some understanding of Maoritanga (Maori culture) is by visiting a *marae*. It's a place that is sacred to Maoris, and needs to be treated with great respect.

Maori form about 15% of the population of NZ. The largest tribe is Ngapuhi, in the north, with about 100,000 members

Indigenous New Zealand (www.indigenousnew zealand.com) is a useful gateway to Maori tourism allowing searches by region and by activity or service.

The *Maori Travelguide to the Tail of the Fish* is an excellent little guide to Auckland/Northland. If you want to see a slightly different aspect of this region, grab a copy of this guide from visitor information centres.

A welcoming ritual called *te powhiri* is followed every time visitors come onto the *marae*. The hosts and visitors exchange welcoming calls, speeches, ceremonial challenges, more speeches, songs, a few speeches, perhaps one or two speeches…you get the idea: there's a fair bit of talking involved. Once the appropriate ancestors have been praised and lineages established, the *tapu* of the visitors is deemed lifted and hosts and visitors are permitted to interact with the locals with handshakes and the *hongi* (pressing of noses).

Ah, the *hongi* – evidently a problem area for some visitors. In some parts of NZ the *hongi*, a sharing of life breath, is a single press, in others it is press, release, press. It is never a rubbing together of noses, a popular misconception. (Neither, never ever, is it a quick kiss on the nose, as was delivered by one confused Australian prime minister.)

Marae protocol varies around the country but a few things are common to all *marae*: shoes must be removed before entering the meeting house; if you receive hospitality such as food and lodging, it is customary to offer a *koha* (donation), to help towards the upkeep of the *marae*; and long, long speeches could be said to be a tradition countrywide.

Visitors to NZ are increasingly being given the opportunity to enjoy *marae* hospitality, often on one of the *marae* tours that are becoming popular. Rotorua (p332) in the Bay of Plenty probably has the most *marae* set up for tours, performances or visits. But there are other options around the country:

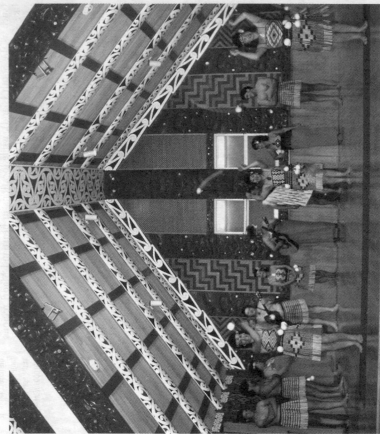

Maori dancers, Rotorua
PETER HENDRIE

Waitangi National Reserve In Northland – not an operating *marae* as such, but fascinating to visit; see p189.

Te Poho-o-Rawiri In Gisborne; see p377.

Historic Parihaka In the Taranaki; see the boxed text, p273.

Te Papa museum in Wellington – not an operating *marae* in the traditional sense; see the boxed text, p409.

Nga Hau e Wha in Christchurch; see the boxed text, p535.

In the Far North (p177), the Urewera region (p383) and around the East Cape (p369) you'll see many, many operating *marae*, but they're not usually set up for casual visitors. If someone's there, ask if you can have a look around, otherwise you'll just have to admire them from outside the gate (remember: they're private property). The Waikato region similarly holds some of NZ's most historically important *marae* – such as Turangawaewae (p232), Maketu (p241) and Te Tokanganui-o-noho (p253) – but they're not usually open for visitors.

ARTS
Waiata (Song) & Haka (Dance)

Traditionally, Maori did not keep a written history; their history was kept in long, specific and stylised songs and chants. As in many parts of the world where oral history has been practised, song and chant developed to become a magnificent art in the local culture.

The Maori arts of song and dance include some special features. The highly expressive *waiata kori* (action song) is perhaps the most beloved tradition, and a highlight of a visit to NZ could be learning some songs with members of a Maori cultural group. Usually the men perform with

Carving on top of a meeting house at Ohinemutu Maori village (p331)

KRZYSZTOF DYDYNSKI

HAKA

Haka is Maori for any form of dance, but it has come to be associated with the chant (correctly the *haka taparahi*) that traditionally preceded a battle or challenged suspicious visitors. Delivered with fierce shouting, flexing arm movements that resemble fists pummelling the side of someone's head and thunderous stamping to grind whatever is left into the dust, it is indeed a frightening sight.

Each tribe had its own *haka*, but the most famous comes from Te Rauparaha (1768–1849), a chief of the Ngati Toa tribe. He was one of the last great warrior chiefs, carving a trail of mayhem from Kapiti near Wellington to the South Island, where he oversaw several rather nasty massacres. Te Rauparaha's *haka* is said to have originated when he was fleeing from his enemies (he had more than a few). A local chief hid him in an underground kumara store, where Te Rauparaha waited in the dark, expecting to be found. When the store was opened and the sun shone in, it was not his enemies but the (hairy) local chief telling him they had gone. Te Rauparaha climbed the ladder to perform this victorious *haka*. Made famous by the All Blacks, the *haka* is as follows:

Ka mate, ka mate (It is death, it is death)
Ka ora, ka ora (It is life, it is life)
Tenei te tangata puhuruhuru (Behold the hairy man)
Nana nei i tiki mai i Whakawhiti te ra (Who caused the sun to shine)
Upane, aupane (Abreast, keep abreast)
Upane, ka aupane (The rank, hold fast)
Whiti te ra (Into the sunshine)

Sir Apirana Ngata (1874–1950) taking the lead in a *haka* on Waitangi Day

B SNOWDON, 1940, ALEXANDER TURNBULL LIBRARY, WELLINGTON, NZ, REF NO 1/2-029794-F

vigorous actions, whereas the movements of women are graceful and flowing, reflecting some of the artistic forms of Asia.

The *poi* dance is distinctive to the NZ Maori, where the dancers swing *poi* (balls tied on the end of a cord) to the rhythm of the music. The most famous *poi* dance is the *waka poi*, with the women sitting in a row as if in a canoe (in other *poi* dances the performers do their thing standing up).

Whakairo (Carving)

Woodcarving became increasingly refined after the Maori arrived in Aotearoa, and peaked in the period immediately before the arrival of Europeans. Ornate meeting houses were built, with powerful wooden carvings depicting ancestors and the relevant gods. Human figures were the central motif in such carvings, usually with enlarged head, mouth and eyes. Another prevalent feature, often seen in window lintels and along the barge boards of canoes, is the *manaia*, a 'bird-headed man' identifiable by a human-shaped head with a beak.

Beautifully carved war canoes were (and are) a source of great *mana* for a tribe and were protected by *tapu*. Built of kauri or totara, they were up to 25m in length – the bow and stern pieces were elaborately carved.

Today in Rotorua you can check out woodcarvings, see artisans at work (such as at Whakarewarewa Thermal Village, p332) and in some cases buy direct from the artists. For more information, see p716.

Maori bone carvings are another fine art form. *Tiki*, stylised human forms, are carved from *pounamu* (greenstone), or from lurid green plastic when sold in bad souvenir shops. Bone fish-hook pendants, carved in traditional Maori and modernised styles, are common (almost the badge of honour for an expat Kiwi), worn on a thong around the neck.

Paua (abalone) shell is carved into some beautiful ornaments and jewellery, as well as some impressively tacky souvenir ashtrays! It is also used as an inlay in many Maori carvings.

Moko (Tattoos)

Traditionally, the higher classes were decorated with intricate *moko* (tattoos) – women had *moko* only on their chins and lips, while high-ranking men not only had tattoos over their entire face, but also over other parts of their body (especially their buttocks). The tattoos were created using bone chisels, a mallet and blue pigment.

Maoris and Pakeha (and even visitors to NZ) now sport Maori patterns on their skin, and in Maori heartland regions such as the East Coast you might see Maori men or women with traditional full facial tattoos.

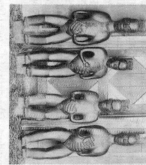

Environment   Vaughan Yarwood

Vaughan Yarwood is a historian and travel writer who is widely published in NZ and internationally. His most recent book is *The History Makers: Adventures in New Zealand Biography*.

THE LAND

New Zealand is a young country – its present shape is less than 10,000 years old. Having broken away from the supercontinent of Gondwanaland (which included Africa, Australia, Antarctica and South America) in a stately geological dance some 130 million years ago, it endured aeons of uplift and erosion, buckling and tearing, and the slow fall and rise of the sea as ice ages came and went. Straddling the boundary of two great collid-ing slabs of the earth's crust – the Pacific plate and the Indian/Australian plate – to this day NZ remains the plaything of nature's strongest forces.

The result is one of the most varied and spectacular series of landscapes in the world, ranging from snow-dusted mountains and drowned glacial valleys to rainforests, dunelands and an otherworldly volcanic plateau. It is a diversity of landforms you would expect to find across an entire con-tinent rather than a small archipelago of islands in the South Pacific.

Evidence of NZ's tumultuous past is everywhere. The South Island's mountainous spine – the 650km-long ranges of the Southern Alps – is a product of the clash of the two plates; the result of a process of rapid lift-ing that, if anything, is accelerating. Despite NZ's highest peak, Aoraki/Mt Cook (p583), losing 10m from its summit overnight in 1991 landslide, the Alps are on an express elevator that, without erosion and landslides, would see them 10 times their present height within a few million years.

On the North Island, the most impressive changes have been wrought by volcanoes. Auckland is built on an isthmus peppered by scoria cones, on many of which you can still see the earthworks of *pa* (fortified villages) built by early Maori. The city's biggest and most recent volcano, 600-year-old Rangitoto Island (p147), is just a short ferry ride from the downtown wharves. Some 300km further south, the classically shaped cone of snow-capped Mt Taranaki/Egmont (p267) overlooks tranquil dairy pastures.

But the real volcanic heartland runs through the centre of the North Island, from the restless bulk of Mt Ruapehu in Tongariro National Park (p312) northeast through the Rotorua lake district (p330) out to NZ's most active volcano, White Island (p364), in the Bay of Plenty. Called the Taupo Volcanic Zone, this great 250km-long rift valley – part of a volcano chain known as the 'Pacific Ring of Fire' – has been the seat of massive eruptions that have left their mark on the country physically and culturally.

Most spectacular were the eruptions from the volcano which created Lake Taupo (p294). Considered the world's most productive volcano in terms of the amount of material ejected, Taupo last erupted 1800 years ago in a display which was the most violent anywhere on the planet within the past 5000 years.

You can experience the aftermath of volcanic destruction on a smaller scale at Te Wairoa (the Buried Village; p346) near Rotorua on the shores of Lake Tarawera. Here, partly excavated and open to the public, lie the remains of a 19th-century Maori village overwhelmed when nearby Mt Tarawera erupted without warning. The famous Pink and White Terraces (one of several claimants to the popular title 'eighth wonder of the world') were destroyed overnight by the same upheaval.

But when Nature sweeps the board clean with one hand she often re-builds with the other: Waimangu Valley (p347), born of all that geother-mal violence, is the place to go to experience the hot earth up close and personal amid geysers, silica pans, bubbling mud pools and the world's

ENVIRONMENTAL ISSUES IN AOTEAROA NEW ZEALAND *Nandor Tanczos*

Aotearoa New Zealand is famous for having won some significant environmental battles. Since the 1980s we have seen the NZ Forest Accord (developed to protect native forest) and the end of all native logging on public land. Our national parks and reserves now cover around a third of our land area, and the first few marine reserves have been established. We are also famous for our strong antinuclear stance.

To describe ourselves as 'clean and green', however, is 100% pure fantasy. A drive in the country soon reveals that much of our land is more akin to a green desert.

The importation of European sheep and cattle grazing systems to Aotearoa New Zealand has left many hillsides with marginal productivity; they are bare of trees and prone to erosion. In many areas grazing threatens our waterways, with stock causing damage to stream and lake margins and runoff leading to nutrient overload of waterways. Regional councils and farming groups are starting to fence and plant stream banks to protect water quality but their efforts may be outstripped by the growth in dairy farming as plantation forests are converted back to dairy.

Despite increasing international and local demand for organic food, most farming in Aotearoa New Zealand relies on high levels of chemical inputs in the form of fertilisers, pesticides and herbicides. In addition, the Labour government, backed by most other political parties, has voted to end the ban on the release of genetically engineered (GE) organisms into the environment, in the face of overwhelming public opposition. However, we are still GE free and many of us are determined to keep it that way.

Our record on waste is regrettable. The parliamentary commissioner for the environment has stated that the average New Zealander generates 900kg of waste a year, which is more than the average American. Recycling facilities barely exist in some areas, although many local councils have been working with communities to combine waste reduction, job creation and reuse of reclaimed materials. Even so, some items, such as batteries, remain almost impossible to recycle, and the packaging industry has largely been left to 'self-regulate', with predicable consequences. We have just lost the last of our reusable milk bottles to plastic and Tetra Pak cartons.

Energy consumption in Aotearoa New Zealand has grown three times more than population over the last 20 years. We are one of the most inefficient users of energy in the developed world and a staggering two-thirds of our energy comes from nonrenewable resources (although most other countries use an even higher proportion of nonrenewable resources!).

Add to that the ongoing battle being fought in many communities over the disposal of sewage and toxic waste, a conflict often spearheaded by *tangata whenua* (Maori), and the 'clean and green' label begins to look seriously compromised.

We do have a number of things in our favour. Our biggest saving grace is our small population, so the cumulative effect is reduced. Also, there are many national park and reserve areas set aside to protect native ecosystems making Aotearoa New Zealand a place well worth visiting. This is a beautiful land with enormous geographical and ecological diversity. Our forests are unique and magnificent, and the bird species that evolved in response to an almost total lack of mammalian life are spectacular, although now reduced in numbers.

The responsibility of New Zealanders is to make change, not just at a personal level, but at an institutional and infrastructural level, for ecological sustainability. The responsibility of visitors to Aotearoa New Zealand is to respect our unique biodiversity, and to query and question. Every time you ask where the recycling centre is; every time you express surprise at the levels of energy use, car use and water use; every time you demand organic food at a café or restaurant, you affect the person you talk to.

Aotearoa New Zealand has the potential to be a world leader in ecological wisdom. We have a strong tradition to draw from – the careful relationship the Maori developed with the natural world over the course of many, many generations. We live at the edge of the Pacific, on the Rim of Fire, a remnant of the ancient forests of Gondwanaland. We welcome conscious travellers.

Nandor is a Member of Parliament (NZ Greens),
a high-profile campaigner on genetic engineering and a keen user of public transport.

New Zealand is one of the most spectacular places in the world to see geysers. Rotorua's short-lived Waimangu geyser, formed after the Mt Tarawera eruption, was once the world's largest, often gushing to a dizzying height of 400m. Te Whakarewarewa (p331) is a good place to see geysers today.

biggest hot spring. Or you can wander around Rotorua's Whakarewarewa Thermal Village (p332), where descendants of Maori displaced by the eruption live in the middle of steaming vents and prepare food for visitors in boiling pools.

A second by-product of movement along the tectonic plate boundary is seismic activity – earthquakes. Not for nothing has NZ been called 'the Shaky Isles'. Most quakes only rattle the glassware, but one was indirectly responsible for creating an internationally celebrated tourist attraction.…

In 1931 an earthquake measuring 7.9 on the Richter scale levelled the Hawkes Bay city of Napier (p386) causing huge damage and loss of life. Napier was rebuilt almost entirely in the then-fashionable Art Deco architectural style, and walking its streets today you can relive its brash exuberance in what has become a mecca for lovers of Art Deco (p388).

Travellers to the South Island can also see some evidence of volcanism – if the remains of the old volcanoes of Banks Peninsula (p559) weren't there to repel the sea, the vast Canterbury Plains, built from alpine sediment washed down the rivers from the Alps, would have eroded away long ago.

But in the south it is the Southern Alps themselves that dominate, dictating settlement patterns, throwing down engineering challenges and offering outstanding recreational opportunities. The island's mountainous backbone also helps shape the weather, as it stands in the path of the prevailing westerly winds which roll in, moisture-laden, from the Tasman Sea. As a result bush-clad lower slopes of the western Southern Alps are among the wettest places on earth, with an annual precipitation of some 15,000mm. Having lost its moisture, the wind then blows dry across the eastern plains towards the Pacific coast.

The North Island has a more even rainfall and is spared the temperature extremes of the South – which can plunge when a wind blows in from Antarctica. Although the important thing to remember, especially if you are tramping at high altitude, is that NZ has a maritime climate. This means weather can change with lightning speed, catching out the unprepared.

WILDLIFE

NZ may be relatively young, geologically speaking, but its plants and animals go back a long way. The tuatara, for instance, an ancient reptile unique to these islands, is a Gondwanaland survivor closely related to the dinosaurs, while many of the distinctive flightless birds (ratites) have distant African and South American cousins.

Due to its long isolation, the country is a veritable warehouse of unique and varied plants, most of which are found nowhere else. And with separation of the landmass occurring before mammals appeared on the scene, birds and insects have evolved in spectacular ways to fill the gaps.

The now extinct flightless moa, the largest of which grew to 3.5m tall and weighed over 200kg, browsed open grasslands much as cattle do today (skeletons can be seen at Auckland Museum, p109), while the smaller kiwi still ekes out a nocturnal living rummaging among forest leaf litter for insects and worms much as small mammals do elsewhere. One of the country's most ferocious-looking insects, the mouse-sized giant weta, meanwhile, has taken on a scavenging role elsewhere filled by rodents.

As one of the last places on earth to be colonised by humans, NZ was for millennia a safe laboratory for such risky evolutionary strategies, but with the arrival first of Maori and soon after of Europeans, things went downhill fast.

Many creatures, including moa and the huia, an exquisite songbird, were driven to extinction and the vast forests were cleared for their timber and to make way for agriculture. Destruction of habitat and the introduction of exotic animals and plants have taken a terrible environmental toll and New Zealanders are now fighting a rearguard battle to save what remains.

Birds & Animals

The first Polynesian settlers found little in the way of land mammals – just two species of bat – but forests, plains and coasts alive with birds. Largely lacking the bright plumage found elsewhere, NZ's birds – like its endemic plants – have an understated beauty which does not shout for attention.

Among the most musical is the bellbird, common in both native and exotic forests everywhere except Northland, though like many birds it is more likely to be heard than seen. Its call is a series of liquid bell notes, most often sounded at dawn or dusk.

The tui, another nectar eater and the country's most beautiful songbird, is a great mimic, with an inventive repertoire that includes clicks, grunts and chuckles. Notable for the white throat feathers which stand out against its dark plumage, the tui often feeds on flax flowers in suburban gardens but is most at home in densely tangled forest ('bush' to New Zealanders).

Fantails are commonly encountered on forest trails, swooping and jinking to catch insects stirred up by passing hikers, while pukeko, elegant swamp-hens with blue plumage and bright red beaks, are readily seen along wetland margins and even on the sides of roads nearby – be warned, they have little road sense.

If you spend any time in South Island high country, you are likely to come up against the fearless and inquisitive kea – an uncharacteristically drab green parrot with bright red underwings. Kea are common in the car parks of the Fox and Franz Josef Glaciers (p519 and p516), where they hang out for food scraps or tear rubber from car windscreens.

Then there is the takahe, a rare flightless bird thought extinct until a small colony was discovered in 1948, and the equally flightless kiwi, NZ's national emblem and the nickname for New Zealanders themselves.

The kiwi has a round body covered in coarse feathers, strong legs and a long, distinctive bill with nostrils at the tip for sniffing out food. It is not easy to find them in the wild, but they can be seen in simulated environments at excellent nocturnal houses. One of the best is the Otorohanga Kiwi House (p247), which also has other birds, including native falcons, moreporks (owls) and weka, as well as tuatara.

To get a feel for what the bush used to be like, take a trip to Tiritiri Matangi Island (p159), not far from Auckland. This regenerating island

B Heather and H Robertson's *Field Guide to the Birds of New Zealand* is the most comprehensive guide for bird-watchers and a model of helpfulness for anyone even casually interested in the country's remarkable bird life.

KIWI SPOTTING

The kiwi is a threatened species, and with the additional difficulty of them being nocturnal, it's only on Stewart Island (p689) that you easily see one in the wild. However, they can be observed in many artificially dark 'kiwi houses', such as:

- Whangarei Museum (p203)
- Otorohanga Kiwi House & Native Bird Park (p247)
- National Aquarium of New Zealand, Napier (p388)
- Wellington Zoo (p412)
- Southern Encounter Aquarium & Kiwi House, Christchurch (p531)
- Orana Wildlife Park, Christchurch (p536)
- Willowbank Wildlife Reserve, Christchurch (p536)
- Kiwi & Birdlife Park, Queenstown (p624)

is an open sanctuary and one of the country's most successful exercises in community-assisted conservation.

Encountering marine mammals is one of the great delights of a visit to NZ, now that well-regulated ecotourism has replaced the commercial whaling and sealing that drove many NZ species to the brink of extinction in the early 19th century. Sperm whales can be seen off the coast of Kaikoura (p454) and licensed companies offer swimming with wild dolphins in the Bay of Islands and elsewhere (p75); forget aquarium shows – sea encounters are the real thing.

Trees

No visitor to NZ (particularly Australians!) will go for long without hearing about the damage done to the bush by that bad-mannered Australian import, the brush-tailed possum. The long list of mammal pests introduced accidentally or for a variety of misguided reasons includes deer, rabbits, stoats, pigs and goats. But the most destructive by far is the possum, 70 million of which now chew through millions of tonnes of foliage a year despite the best efforts of the Department of Conservation (DOC) to control them.

Among favoured possum food are NZ's most colourful trees: the kowhai, a small-leaved tree growing to 11m, that in spring has drooping clusters of bright yellow flowers (NZ's national flower); the pohutukawa, a beautiful coastal tree of the northern North Island which bursts into vivid red flower in December, earning the nickname 'Christmas tree'; and a similar crimson-flowered tree, the rata. Rata species are found on both islands; the northern rata starts life as a climber on a host tree (that it eventually chokes).

The few remaining pockets of mature centuries-old kauri are stately emblems of former days. Their vast hammered trunks and towering, epiphyte-festooned limbs, which dwarf every other tree in the forest, are reminders of why they were sought after in colonial days for spars and building timber. The best place to see the remaining giants is Northland's Waipoua Kauri Forest (p172), home to three-quarters of the country's surviving kauri.

Now the pressure has been taken off kauri and other timber trees, including the distinctive rimu, or red pine, and the long-lived totara (favoured for Maori war canoes), by one of the country's most successful imports – *Pinus radiata*. Pine was found to thrive in NZ, growing to maturity in just 35 years, and plantation forests are now widespread through the central North Island – the southern hemisphere's biggest, Kaingaroa Forest, lies southeast of Rotorua.

You won't get far into the bush without coming across one of its most prominent features – tree ferns. NZ is a land of ferns (more than 80 species) and most easily recognised are the mamuka (black tree fern), which grows to 20m and can be seen in damp gullies throughout the country; and the 10m high ponga (silver tree fern) with its distinctive white underside. The silver fern is equally at home as part of corporate logos and on the clothing of many of the country's top sportspeople.

Pohutukawa seeds can be carried on the wind for thousands of kilometres. It is thought that in this way they eventually reached the Hawaiian Islands where, because of their intense red colour, they were declared sacred to Pele, the goddess of volcanoes.

Lifestyles of New Zealand Forest Plants, by J Dawson and R Lucas, is a beautifully photographed foray into the world of New Zealand's forests. Far from being drab and colourless, these lush treasure houses are home to ancient species dating from the time of the dinosaurs. This guidebook will have you reaching for your boots.

TOWERING KAURI

When Chaucer was born this was a sturdy young tree. When Shakespeare was born it was 300 years old. It predates most of the great cathedrals of Europe. Its trunk is sky-rocket straight and sky-rocket bulky, limbless for half its height. Ferns sprout from its crevices. Its crown is an asymmetric mess, like an inverted root system. I lean against it, give it a slap. It's like slapping a building. This is a tree out of Tolkien. It's a kauri.

Joe Bennett (A Land of Two Halves) referring to the McKinney kauri (p164) in Northland.

RESPONSIBLE TRAVEL

Toitu te whenua – care for the land. Help protect the environment by following these guidelines:

■ Treat NZ's forests and native wildlife with respect. Damaging or taking plants is illegal in most parts of the country.

■ Remove rubbish. Litter is unsightly and can encourage vermin and disease. Rather than burying or burning, carry out what you carry in.

■ In areas without toilet facilities bury toilet waste in a shallow hole away from tracks, huts, camp sites and waterways.

■ Keep streams and lakes pure by cleaning away from water sources. Drain waste water into the soil to filter out soaps and detergent. If you suspect contamination, boil water for three minutes, filter or chemically treat it before use.

■ Where possible use portable fuel stoves. Keep open fires small, use only dead wood and make sure the fire is out by dousing it with water and checking the ashes before leaving.

■ Keep to tracks where possible. Get permission before crossing private land and move carefully around livestock.

NATIONAL PARKS

A third of the country – more than five million hectares – is protected in environmentally important parks and reserves which embrace almost every conceivable landscape: from mangrove-fringed inlets in the north to the snow-topped volcanoes of the Central Plateau, and from the forested fastness of the Ureweras in the east to the Southern Alps' majestic mountains, glaciers and fiords. The 14 national parks, three maritime parks and two marine reserves, along with numerous forest parks, offer huge scope for wilderness experiences, ranging from climbing, snow skiing and mountain biking to tramping, kayaking and trout fishing.

Three places are World Heritage areas: NZ's Subantarctic Islands (p700), Tongariro National Park (p312) and Te Wahipounamu (p666), an amalgam of several national parks in southwest NZ which boast the world's finest surviving Gondwanaland plants and animals in their natural habitats.

Access to the country's wild places is relatively straightforward, though huts on walking tracks require passes and may need to be booked in advance. In practical terms, there is little difference for travellers between a national park and a forest park, though dogs are not allowed in national parks without a permit. Camping is possible in all parks, but may be restricted to dedicated camping grounds – check first. Permits are required for hunting (game birds) and licences needed for inland fishing (trout, salmon). Both can be bought online at www.fishandgame.org.nz.

The Department of Conservation website (www.doc.govt.nz) has useful information on the country's national parks, tracks and walkways. It also lists backcountry huts and camp sites.

TOP FIVE NATIONAL PARKS

Aoraki/Mt Cook (p583) Alpine landscape. Home to the wonderfully naughty *kea* and NZ's highest mountain.

Fiordland (p657) Vast untouched fiords. Waterfalls, sandflies, pristine lakes. Outstanding walks including Milford (p666) and Kepler (p660) Tracks.

Te Urewera (p383) Rugged forested hills, steeped in Maori history. Lake Waikaremoana Track (p384).

Tongariro (p312) Active volcanic wilderness. The world's fourth-oldest national park. Ski fields, rock climbing, Tongariro Northern Circuit (p315).

Abel Tasman National Park (p478) Pristine seas and gorgeous inlets. Kayaking, bushwalking, sailing, *waka* (canoe) tours.

NATIONAL PARKS

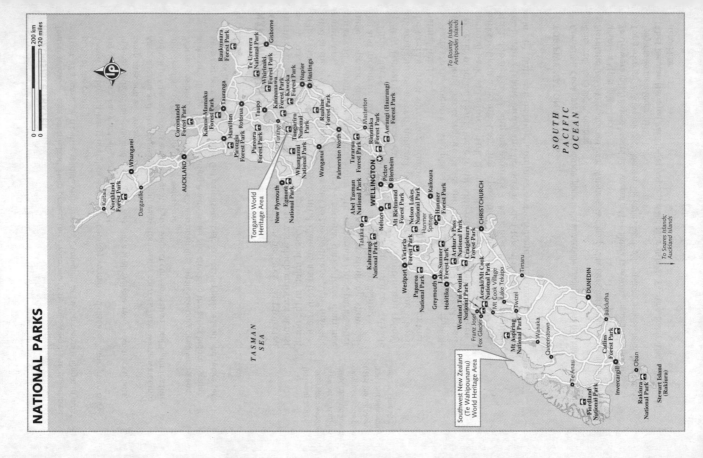

Tongariro World Heritage Area

Southwest New Zealand (Te Wahipounamu) World Heritage Area

North Island

Kaitaia
Northland Forest Park
Whangarei
Dargaville
Coromandel Forest Park
AUCKLAND
Kaimai-Mamaku Forest Park
Hamilton
Tauranga
Raukumara Forest Park
Te Urewera National Park
Whirinaki Forest Park
Gisborne
Pirongia Forest Park
Rotorua
Taupo
Kaimanawa Forest Park
Kaweka Forest Park
Napier
Hastings
Pureora Forest Park
Turangi
Tongariro National Park
Ruahine Forest Park
Whanganui National Park
Wanganui
Palmerston North
Tararua Forest Park
Masterton
Aorangi (Haurangi) Forest Park
Rimutaka Forest Park
New Plymouth
Egmont National Park

South Island

WELLINGTON
Picton
Blenheim
Abel Tasman National Park
Takaka
Nelson
Kahurangi National Park
Mt Richmond Forest Park
Nelson Lakes National Park
Kaikoura
Hanmer Springs
Hanmer Forest Park
Westport
Victoria Forest Park
Paparoa National Park
Greymouth
Lake Sumner Forest Park
Arthur's Pass National Park
Craigieburn Forest Park
CHRISTCHURCH
Hokitika
Westland Tai Poutini National Park
Franz Josef
Fox Glacier
Aoraki/Mt Cook National Park
Mt Cook Village
Lake Tekapo
Timaru
Twizel
Mt Aspiring National Park
Wanaka
Queenstown
DUNEDIN
Balclutha
Te Anau
Catlins Forest Park
Oban
Fiordland National Park
Invercargill
Rakiura National Park
Stewart Island (Rakiura)

TASMAN SEA

SOUTH PACIFIC OCEAN

To Bounty Islands; Antipodes Islands

To Snares Islands; Auckland Islands

0   200 km
0   120 miles

New Zealand Outdoors

New Zealand's outstanding natural assets will prompt even the most hard-core armchair-dweller to drag themselves outside. The country has an abundance of spacious, fresh-aired terrain, including surf-struck oceans, vast lakes and sounds, toehold-conducive mountains and trailblazed parks, the majority of which is reasonably accessible. There are also plenty of facilities and outdoor-enthused local operators to help immerse you in almost every conceivable kind of activity.

Nonthrillseekers take heart – despite NZ's reputation for extreme sports, you don't *have* to defy gravity or lose your lunch to experience the country's famed wilderness, nor do you have to rough it. Guided walks, scenic flights and cruises open up the outdoors to the soft-option-seeker. More passive activities such as fishing, golf or wine-tasting will usually involve much admiring of the spectacular surrounds, as will simply getting from Town A to Town B.

Still, there's little that's off-limits to those with energy to expend, a fact exemplified by the startling variety of ways in which Kiwis and visitors move over or through land, air and water. They jetboat, white-water sledge, raft, canoe, kayak, surf and scuba dive through the water; they bungy jump, parapente, skydive, abseil, fly and helicopter through the air; and they tramp, mountain bike, ski, horse ride, rock climb, 'zorb' and ice climb across terra firma. Beneath the surface, caving, cave rafting and exploring *tomos* (holes or cave entrances) are all undertaken.

The various adrenaline-pumping activities obviously have an element of risk, but the perception of danger is part of the thrill. Such risk is underlined in adventure sports, particularly rafting and kayaking on fast-flowing rivers. Chances of a mishap are arguably minuscule, but reassure yourself that the company you choose takes adequate safety precautions. Also make sure that you have travel insurance that fully covers you for any planned activities – for reasons why a comprehensive insurance policy is so important, including details of NZ's litigation-free approach to accidents, see p712.

Sail around Lake Wakatipu (p631), near Queenstown
DENNIS JOHNSON.

Dive down to golfball and finger sponges
JENNY & TONY ENDERBY.

AERIAL SIGHTSEEING

Small planes and helicopters circle the skies on sightseeing trips (called 'flightseeing' by the locals) all over NZ, operating from local aerodromes. It's a great way to see the country's incredible contrast in landscapes, close-ups of its spectacular mountain ranges, and the remote and otherwise little-viewed terrain deep within national-park forests and glacial valleys. Some of the most striking trips take place over the Bay of Islands, the Bay of Plenty, Tongariro National Park, Mt Taranaki, Mt Cook, the West Coast glaciers and the southern fiords.

A far more sedate way to see the countryside is from a hot-air balloon. A float above Methven snags you spectacular views of the Southern Alps and contrasting Canterbury Plains, and there are also balloon trips from Queenstown, Auckland, Hamilton and Hastings.

EXTREME (OR JUST EXTREMELY UNUSUAL) ACTIVITIES

Bungy jumping was made famous by Kiwi AJ Hackett's dive from the Eiffel Tower in 1986, after which he teamed up with NZ champion speed skier Henry van Asch to turn the endeavour into a profitable and safe commercial enterprise. The fact that an activity as patently terrifying and sanity-challenging as bungy jumping is now an everyday pursuit in NZ says a lot about how the concept of 'extreme sports' has evolved in this country. The truth is, the old days of hard-core, often-dangerous physical experimentation have more or less been replaced by safe variations on popular, well-tested themes.

A much more nerve-racking take on the bungy (but no less safe) is Auckland's **Sky Jump**, a 16-second freefall using a cable and 'fan descenders' (used by movie-industry stunt actors). At 192m it's the world's highest tower-based jump.

Another unusual above-ground activity is the **Shotover Canyon Swing**, a 109m-high rope swing (apparently the world's highest) concocted by those funsters in nearby Queenstown. There's also **Fly By Wire**, where you briefly 'fly' a cable-tethered plane at high speeds – wannabe pilots can try it in Queenstown.

At the eccentric end of the activity scale is **zorbing**, which involves rolling downhill in a transparent plastic ball – sit it out if you're prone to motion sickness, otherwise try it in Rotorua. An alternative land-based activity is **quad biking**, where you roam the countryside on four-wheel farm bikes, sniffing out mud, sand dunes and water crossings as you go. This down-and-dirty activity is found in countless places throughout the country.

NZ also offers uncommon water sports. **Cave rafting** (called 'tumu tumu toobing' and 'black-water rafting' at Waitomo, 'underworld rafting' at Westport, and 'adventure caving' at Greymouth) is technically not rafting, as it involves donning a wet suit, a lighted hard hat and a black inner tube and floating along underground rivers. It's an entertaining if not captivating diversion, particularly when you encounter glow-worms in an otherwise pitch-black cavern.

For more aquatic manoeuvring, grab a polystyrene sled or a modified boogie board, flip-pers, a wet suit and a helmet and go **river sledging** (also called 'river surfing' or 'white-water sledging'). Rivers around Queenstown and Wanaka offer this wet thrill, as does Rotorua, where there's a sizable waterfall drop on the Kaituna River. In Hawera (Taranaki), the concept has been tweaked to include 'dam dropping', where you slide down a 7m dam and proceed to sledge the Waingongoro River.

And of course it wouldn't be NZ if there wasn't a new extreme sport cropping up every couple of years. The latest is **blokarting** (and no, it's not the art of being a real bloke, although Kiwis give that a red-hot go too). Blokarting, or blokart sailing, is land-based windsurfing on small carts – created, designed and manufactured in the Bay of Plenty (see www.blokart.com). Blokarting can be sampled at Ahipara, Mt Maunganui and the Catlins (the 'fastest deck chair in the south').

BIRD-WATCHING

Twitchers have been known to flock (sorry) to NZ, because this relatively small country is home to an overwhelming number of endemic species and foreign feathered friends. Unfortunately, NZ is as (in)famous for extinct and point-of-extinction species as it is for common species.

The flightless kiwi is the species most sought after by bird-watchers. Sightings of the Stewart Island subspecies are common at all times of the year. Elsewhere, wild sightings of this increasingly rare nocturnal species are difficult, but there are quite a few kiwi enclosures (Christchurch and Auckland both have 'kiwi houses') that allow dimly lit glimpses of this shy bird. Other birds that twitchers like to sight are the royal albatross, white heron, Fiordland crested penguin, yellow-eyed penguin, Australasian gannet and wrybill.

On the Coromandel Peninsula, the Firth of Thames (particularly Miranda) is a haven for migrating birds, while the Wharekawa Wildlife Refuge at Opoutere Beach is a breeding ground of the endangered NZ dotterel. There's also a very accessible Australasian gannet colony at Muriwai, west of Auckland, and one in Hawkes Bay. There are popular trips to observe pelagic birds out of Kaikoura, and royal albatross viewing on the Otago Peninsula.

Two good guides are the newly revised *Field Guide to the Birds of New Zealand*, by Barrie Heather and Hugh Robertson, and *Birds of New Zealand: Locality Guide* by Stuart Chambers. See p65 for more information about NZ's bird life.

BUNGY JUMPING

Bungy jumping (hurtling ea-thwards from bridges with nothing between you and kingdom come but a gigantic rubber cord strapped to your limbs) has a bit of daredevil panache about it and prompts a heady adrenaline rush, but the behind-the-scenes action could hardly be more organised, with jumper safety obviously of paramount importance.

Queenstown is virtually surrounded by bungy cords, including a 43m jump off the Kawarau Bridge (which now has a bungy theatre and museum), a 47m leap from a ledge at the top of the gondola, a 102m plunge at Skippers Canyon (called the Pipeline), and the big daddy, the 134m Nevis Highwire act. Another South Island bungy jump awaits you outside Hanmer Springs, and there's a winter jump at Mt Hutt ski field.

Jumping is also done on the North Island at Taupo (45m), above the scenic Waikato River, and from Auckland Harbour Bridge (40m).

Bungy jump off the Ledge (p625) over Queenstown

DAVID WALL

If you want to know your kaka from your kea or kaki, visit the comprehensive www .nzbirds.com. Here you'll find a gallery of endemic, native and introduced birds, plus listings of twitcher-friendly guides and accommodation.

CANOEING & KAYAKING

Canoeing is especially popular on the Whanganui River on the North Island. It's also popular on northern lakes, notably Lake Taupo, as well as on many bodies of freshwater on the South Island.

Many backpacker hostels situated close to water will have kayaks for hire or free use, and loads of commercial guided trips (for those without equipment or experience) are offered on rivers and lakes throughout the country. Many trips have an eco element such as bird-watching – a good example is the beautiful Okarito Lagoon on the West Coast of the South Island.

Sea Kayaking

Highly rated sea-kayaking areas in NZ's north include the Hauraki Gulf (particularly off Waiheke and Great Barrier Islands), the Bay of Islands and Coromandel Peninsula; in the south, try the Marlborough Sounds and along the coast of Abel Tasman National Park, where this activity has become almost as big as walking. Fiordland is also a great destination, as evidenced by the number of tour operators in Te Anau, Milford, Doubtful Sounds and Manapouri arranging spectacular trips on local lakes and fiords.

CAVING

Caving opportunities abound in the honeycombed karst (limestone) regions of the islands. Auckland, Waitomo and Westport are areas where you'll find active local clubs and organised tours. One of the most spectacular caving experiences is the 100m abseil into the Lost World *tomo* (cave) near Waitomo. Local underground organisations include the **Wellington Caving Group** (http://caving.wellington.net.nz) and the **Auckland Speleo Group** (www.asg.org.nz); more can be found at www.nzcaver.org.

FISHING

Thanks to the widespread introduction of exotic rainbow trout, brown trout, quinnat salmon, Atlantic salmon, perch, char and several other fishy species, NZ has become one of the world's great recreational fisheries. The lakes and rivers of the central North Island are famous for trout fishing, especially Lake Taupo and the rivers that feed it – the town of Turangi is a top base for trout fishing in this region. The rivers and lakes of the South Island also fare well on the trout index, most notably the Mataura River (Southland) and Lake Brunner and the Arnold River (the West Coast). The rivers of Otago and Southland also have some of the best salmon fishing in the world.

Saltwater fishing is another attraction for Kiwi anglers, especially in the warmer waters surrounding the North Island, where surfcasting or fishing from boats can result in big catches of (deep breath) grey mullet, trevally, mao mao, porae, John Dory, snapper, gurnard, flounder, mackerel, hapuku (groper), tarakihi, moki and kahawai. Ninety Mile Beach (Northland) and the beaches of Hauraki Gulf are good for surfcasting. The Bay of Islands, Whangaroa, Tutukaka near Whangarei (all in Northland), Whitianga in the Coromandel, and Tuhua (Mayor Island) in the Bay of Plenty are noted big-game fishing areas.

The South Island's colder waters, especially around the Marlborough Sounds, are good for snapper, hake, hapuku, trumpeter, butterfish, ling, barracouta and blue cod. Kaikoura Peninsula is great for surfcasting.

Fishing gear can be hired in places such as Taupo and Rotorua, and at sports outlets in other main towns, but serious line-dangling enthusiasts

might want to bring their own. Rods and tackle may have to be treated by NZ quarantine officials, especially if they're made with natural materials such as cane or feathers.

A fishing permit is required to fish in inland waters. Sold at sport shops, permits cover particular regions and are available for a day, a month or a season. Local visitor information centres and **Department of Conservation** (DOC; www.doc.govt.nz) offices can provide information on fishing licences and regulations.

In terms of fishing tomes, John Kent has written the *North Island Trout Fishing Guide* and the *South Island Trout Fishing Guide*, plus various similarly themed guides. Tony Orman, a renowned NZ fisherman and author, has written *21 Great New Zealand Trout Waters*, as well as *Fishing the Wild Places of New Zealand*, which not only explains how to catch fish but also relates some of the author's fishing exploits in wilderness areas.

If you're interested in guided fishing trips, check out the website of the **New Zealand Professional Fishing Guides Association** (www.nzpfga.com).

GOLF

NZ has more golf courses per capita than any other country, and among the more than 400 courses are some spectacularly situated fairways and greens. In its biennial rankings of the world's top 100 courses, *Golf Magazine* gave gongs to two new NZ courses: Cape Kidnappers in Hawkes Bay (ranked 27th), and Kauri Cliffs in the Bay of Islands (ranked 58th). Paraparaumu, near Wellington, has made it into such rankings in the past and is regarded as one of the country's best courses.

Other popular courses include Wairakei near Taupo; Clearwater, outside Christchurch; Terrace Downs, in the high country near Methven; and Millbrook, near Queenstown.

The average green fee for an 18-hole course usually ranges from $30 to $50, though private resorts can charge a substantial amount more – at Cape Kidnappers you'll pay a hefty $300 to $400 for the privilege; Paraparaumu's green fees are a more manageable $90.

Sea kayak through Doubtful Sound (p671), Fiordland National Park
GARETH McCORMACK

Seriously fishy business is covered at www.thefishing .net.nz, a huge website covering recreational fishing in NZ, including loads of links.

www.ridenz.com links to five horse-trekking companies operating in various parts of the country, each offering different riding terrain, from mountainous high country to long sandy beaches.

HORSE RIDING

Horse riding is commonplace in NZ. Unlike some other parts of the world where beginners only get led by the nose around a paddock, here you really can get out into the countryside on farm, forest and beach rides. Rides range from one-hour jaunts (from around $50) to week-long, fully catered treks.

On the South Island, all-day adventure rides on horseback are a fine way to see the country around Kaikoura, Nelson, Mt Cook, Lake Tekapo, Hanmer Springs, Queenstown, Glenorchy, Cardrona and Dunedin. Treks are also offered alongside Paparoa National Park on the West Coast.

On the North Island, Taupo has options for wilderness horse trekking and for rides in the hills overlooking thermal regions. The Coromandel Peninsula, Waitomo, Pakiri, the Bay of Plenty and the East Cape are also good places for horse trekking.

Where to Ride In New Zealand, a pamphlet produced annually by the Hamilton-based **International League for the Protection of Horses** (ILPH; ☎ 07-849 0678; www.horsetalk.co.nz/ilph), is widely available from visitor information centres.

JETBOATING

The jetboat is a local invention, thought up by CWF Hamilton in 1957. An inboard engine sucks water into a tube in the bottom of the boat and an impeller driven by the engine blows it out of a nozzle at the stern in a high-speed stream. The boat is steered simply by directing the jet stream.

Jetboats make short work of shallow and white water because there are no propellers to damage, there's better clearance under the boat and the jet can be reversed instantly for quick braking. The jet's instant response enables these craft to execute passenger-drenching 360-degree spins almost within the length of the boat.

On the South Island, the Shotover and Kawarau Rivers near Queenstown and the Buller River near Westport are renowned jetboating waterways. The Dart River is less travelled but also good, and the Waiatoto River near Haast is a superb wilderness experience, as is the Wilkin River in Mt Aspiring National Park.

On the North Island, the Whanganui, Motu, Rangitaiki and Waikato Rivers are excellent for jetboating, and there are sprint jets at the Agrodome in Rotorua and at Waitomo. Jetboating around the Bay of Islands in Northland is also popular, particularly the trips to the Hole in the Rock.

Go jetboating (p625) on the Shotover River, Queenstown
DAVID WALL

MARINE-MAMMAL WATCHING

Kaikoura, on the northeast coast of the South Island, is NZ's nexus of marine-mammal watching. The main attraction here is whale watching, but this is dependent on weather conditions, so don't expect to just be able to rock up and head straight out on a boat for a dream encounter. The sperm whale, the largest toothed whale, is pretty much a year-round resident, and depending on the season you may also see migrating humpback whales, pilot whales, blue whales and southern right whales. Other mammals – including fur seals and dusky dolphins – are seen year-round.

Kaikoura is also an outstanding place to swim with dolphins. Pods of up to 500 playful dusky dolphins can be seen on any given day. Dolphin swimming is common elsewhere in NZ, with the animals gathering off the North Island near Whakatane, Paihia, Tauranga, and in the Hauraki Gulf, and off Akaroa on the South Island's Banks Peninsula. Seal swimming is possible in Kaikoura and in the Abel Tasman National Park.

Swimming with sharks is also possible, though with a protective cage as a chaperone; you can do it in Tutukaka and Gisborne.

New Zealand fur seal
GARETH McCORMACK

Anyone planning a cycling tour of NZ (particularly the South Island) should check out some options at www.cyclehire.co.nz.

MOUNTAIN BIKING & CYCLE TOURING

At any given time, but especially in summer, you'll come across plenty of pannier-laden tourists pedalling Kiwi highways and back roads, with one eye on the scenery and another looking out for the plentiful off-road possibilities. Most towns offer bike hire, either at backpacker hostels or specialist bike shops, but quality mountain bikes can usually be hired only in major towns or adventure-sports centres such as Queenstown, Nelson, Picton, Taupo and Rotorua. Bike service and repair shops can be found in most big settlements and some excellent cycling books are available, including Lonely Planet's *Cycling New Zealand*. The *Pedalers' Paradise* booklets by Nigel Rushton cover the North and South Islands (see www .paradise-press.co.nz). *Classic New Zealand Mountain Bike Rides* by the Kennett brothers, Paul, Simon and Jonathan, suggests a variety of short and long rides all over NZ (see www.kennett.co.nz).

For wind-in-the-hair types, various companies will take you up to the tops of mountains, hills and volcanoes (such as Mt Ruapehu, Christchurch's Port Hills, Cardrona and the Remarkables) so that you can hurtle down without the usual grunt of getting uphill beforehand. Rotorua's Redwood Grove is a noted place for mountain biking, as is the 42nd Traverse near National Park, Alexandra in Central Otago and Twizel near Mt Cook. If you're not after altitude, a popular option is to cycle the Otago Central Rail Trail between Middlemarch and Clyde.

Some of the traditional tramping tracks are open to mountain bikes, but DOC has restricted access in many cases due to track damage and the inconvenience to walkers, especially at busy times. Never cycle on walking tracks in national parks unless it's permissible (check with DOC), or risk heavy fines and the ire of hikers. The Queen Charlotte Track is a good one to bike, but part of it is closed in summer.

MOUNTAINEERING

NZ has a rich history of mountaineering and has proved an ideal training ground for greater adventures overseas – this, after all, is the home of Sir Edmund Hillary, who along with Tenzing Norgay became the first to scale Mt Everest. The Southern Alps are studded with a number of impressive peaks and offer many challenging climbs.

This very physical and highly challenging pursuit is not for the uninitiated, and the risks can be high due to fickle weather, storms, winds, extreme cold, rock falls and the like. Proper instruction and training will enable you to make common-sense decisions that will enhance your safety and get you up among those beautiful mountain peaks.

The Mt Cook region is only one of many outstanding climbing areas in the country. Others extend along the spine of the South Island from Tapuaenuku (in the Kaikoura Ranges) and the Nelson Lakes peaks in the north to the rugged southern mountains of Fiordland. Another area with possibilities for all levels of climbs is Mt Aspiring National Park, centred on the 'Matterhorn of the South', Mt Aspiring. To the south in the Forbes Mountains is Mt Earnslaw, flanked by the Rees and Dart Rivers.

The Christchurch-based **New Zealand Alpine Club** (NZAC; ☎ 03-377 7595; www.alpineclub.org.nz) gives professional information and produces the annual *NZ Alpine Journal*, the *Climber* magazine (published quarterly) and numerous other specialised publications. For those seeking to learn the necessary skills or just get climbing, there are companies in locales such as Wanaka, Mt Cook, Lake Tekapo and Fox and Franz Josef Glaciers providing expert instruction, mountaineering and ice-climbing courses and private guiding.

PARAGLIDING/PARAPENTING

Paragliding, also known as parapenting, is perhaps the easiest way for humans to achieve assisted flight. The sport involves taking to the skies in what is basically a parachute that's been modified so it glides through the air. After a half-day of instruction you should be able to do limited solo flights, and before you know it you could be taking flights at a height of 300m. One of the best places to learn the skills to operate your paraglider/parapente is at **Wanaka Paragliding** (☎ 03-443 9193; www.wanakaparagliding.co.nz).

Tandem flights, where you are strapped to an experienced paraglider, are offered all over the country. Popular tandem experiences include glides from the top of the gondola in Queenstown and from Te Mata Peak in Hawke's Bay.

ROCK CLIMBING

On the North Island, popular rock-climbing areas include the Mt Eden Quarry in Auckland, Whanganui Bay and Motuoapa in the vicinity of Lake Taupo, and Piarere near Cambridge. Wharepapa, about 20km southeast of Te Awamutu, is regarded as one of the best places in the country for climbing.

On the South Island, the Port Hills area above Christchurch has many climbs, and 100km away on the road to Arthur's Pass is Castle Hill, with great friction climbs. West of Nelson, the marble and limestone mountains of Golden Bay and Takaka Hill provide prime climbing, and north of Dunedin is Long Beach.

For more information, see the website hosted by **Climb New Zealand** (www.climb.co.nz).

SAILING

This island nation has a habit of throwing up some of the world's best mariners. There's also a good reason why Auckland is called the 'City of Sails'. If you're keen on yacht racing, try visiting the country's various sailing clubs and ask if you can help crew in local competitions. Otherwise, there are plenty of sailing operators who allow you to just laze around on deck or play a more hands-on role.

The Bay of Islands (and Whangaroa to the north), the southern lakes (Te Anau and Wakatipu) and the cities of Auckland and Nelson are good places to get some wind in your sails.

Paraglide (p628) over Queenstown

DAVID WALL

Abseil (p649) down Hospital Flat, near Wanaka

DAVID WALL

SCUBA DIVING

The Bay of Islands Maritime and Historic Park, the Hauraki Gulf Maritime Park, Great Barrier Island, Goat Island and the Marlborough Sounds Maritime Park are obvious diving locales, but there are many more deep-water possibilities around both islands. Even Invercargill, with its notoriously cold water, has a diving club.

The Poor Knights Islands, off the east coast of the North Island, are reputed to have the best diving in NZ, and the late, great Jacques Cousteau rated them among the top 10 diving spots in the world. Nearby is the diveable wreck of the Greenpeace flagship *Rainbow Warrior*. You can also submerge yourself in the Sugar Loaf Islands Marine Park, just offshore from New Plymouth.

The Marlborough Sounds have some interesting dives, including the *Mikhail Lermontov*, the largest diveable cruise-ship wreck in the world. Fiordland on the South Island is highly unusual in that the region's extremely heavy rainfall and mountain runoff leaves a layer of often peaty brown freshwater sitting on top of some of the saltwater fiords, notably

The website of Dive New Zealand (www .divenewzealand.com) is a treasure-trove of underwater information, with the lowdown on dive sites and wreck sites, plus dive operators, clubs and shops for all corners of the country.

DIVE SITES & SURF BEACHES

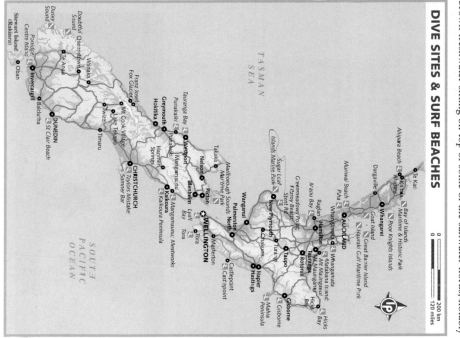

Dusky and Doubtful Sounds. The freshwater filters out light and discourages the growth of seaweed, so divers get to experience amazingly clear pseudo-deep-water conditions not far below the surface.

For more on NZ's explorable depths, pick up a copy of Lonely Planet's *Diving & Snorkeling New Zealand*, or contact the **New Zealand Underwater Association** (☎ 09-623 3252; www.nzunderwater.org.nz) in Auckland.

SURFING IN NEW ZEALAND *Josh Kronfeld*

As a surfer I feel particularly guilty in letting the reader in on a local secret – NZ has a sensational mix of quality waves perfect for beginners and experienced surfers. As long as you're willing to travel off the beaten track, you can score some great, uncrowded waves. The islands of NZ are hit with swells from all points of the compass throughout the year. So, with a little weather knowledge and a little effort, numerous options present themselves. Point breaks, reefs, rocky shelves and hollow sandy beach breaks can all be found – take your pick!

Surfing has become increasingly popular in NZ and today there are surf schools up and running at most premier surf beaches. It's worth doing a bit of pretravel research: **Surfing New Zealand** (www.surfing.co.nz) recommends a number of schools on its website. If you're on a surf holiday in NZ, consider buying a copy of the *New Zealand Surfing Guide*, by Mike Bhana.

Surf New Zealand (www.surf.co.nz) provides information on many great surf spots, but most NZ beaches hold good rideable breaks. Some of the ones I particularly enjoy:

Waikato Raglan, NZ's most famous surf break and usually the first stop for overseas surfies
Coromandel Whangamata
Bay of Plenty Mt Maunganui, now with a 250m artificial reef that creates huge waves, and Matakana Island
Taranaki Fitzroy Beach, Stent Rd and Greenmeadows Point all lie along the 'Surf Highway'
The East Coast Hicks Bay, Gisborne city beaches and Mahia Peninsula
Wellington region Beaches such as Lyall Bay, Castlepoint and Tora
Marlborough & Nelson Kaikoura Peninsula, Mangamaunu and Meatworks
Canterbury Taylors Mistake and Sumner Bar
Otago Dunedin is a good base for surfing on the South Island, with access to a number of superb breaks such as St Clair Beach
The West Coast Punakaiki and Tauranga Bay
Southland Porridge and Centre Island

New Zealand water temperatures and climate vary greatly from north to south. For comfort while surfing, wear a wet suit. In the summer on the North Island you can get away with a spring suit and boardies; on the South Island, a 2–3mm steamer. In winter on the North Island use a 2–3mm steamer, and on the South Island a 3–5mm with all the extras.

Josh is a keen surfer originally hailing from the Hawkes Bay region. While representing the All Blacks (1995–2000) he successfully juggled surfing, pop music and an international rugby career.

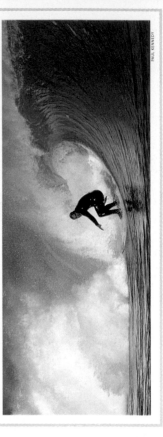

PAUL KENNEDY

SKIING & SNOWBOARDING

NZ is one of the most popular southern-hemisphere destinations for snow bunnies, with downhill (alpine), cross-country, ski touring and ski mountaineering all vigorously pursued. Heliskiing is another popular activity, where choppers are used to lift skiers to the top of long, isolated stretches of virgin snow.

Unlike Europe, America or even Australia, NZ's commercial ski areas are generally not set up as resorts with chalets, lodges or hotels. Rather, accommodation and après-ski nightlife are often in surrounding towns that connect with the main ski areas via daily shuttles.

Club ski areas are publicly accessible and usually much less crowded and cheaper than commercial ski fields, even though nonmembers pay a slightly higher fee. Many such areas have lodges you can stay at, subject to availability – winter holidays and weekends will be fully booked, but midweek you'll be OK.

The variety of resorts and conditions makes it difficult to rate the ski fields in any particular order. Some people like to be near Queenstown's party scene or the classic volcanic scenery of Mt Ruapehu, while others prefer the high slopes and quality runs of Mt Hutt, the less-crowded Rainbow Valley or the many club skiing areas.

At major ski areas, lift passes cost from $30 to $80 a day (roughly half for children and two-thirds for students). Lesson-and-lift packages are available at most resorts. Ski-equipment rental starts at around $30 a day, while daily snowboard and boots hire starts at around $45; prices decrease for multiday hire. Try to rent equipment close to where you'll be skiing, so you can easily return your gear if there's a problem with the fit.

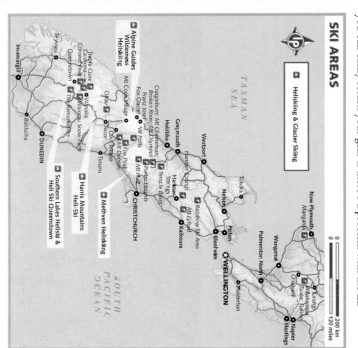

SKI AREAS

Heliskiing & Glacier Skiing

Map labels:
TASMAN SEA
SOUTH PACIFIC OCEAN

Alpine Guides Wilderness Heliskiing
Mt Cook Village
Treble Cone
Cardrona
Coronet Peak
Wanaka
Waiorau Snow Farm
The Remarkables
Queenstown
Ohau
Olympus
Mt Dobson
Fox Peak
Round Hill
Lake Tekapo
Twizel
Timaru
Craigieburn, Mt Cheeseman, Broken River, Mt Olympus, Porters Heights
Mt Hutt
Temple Basin
Arthur's Pass
Fox Glacier
Franz Josef
Hokitika
Greymouth
Westport
Hanmer Springs
Mt Lyford
Rainbow Ski Area
Nelson
Kaikoura
Hanmer Springs
CHRISTCHURCH
Harris Mountains Heli-Ski
Methven Heliskiing
Southern Lakes Heliski & Heli Ski Queenstown
Te Anau
Invercargill
Balclutha
DUNEDIN
Takaka
Picton
Blenheim
WELLINGTON
Masterton
Palmerston North
Wanganui
Napier
Hastings
Oakune
Turoa, Tukino
Whakapapa
Lirangi
New Plymouth
Mangamahu

0   200 km
0   120 miles

Snowboard at Cardrona Alpine Resort (p82)
DAVID WALL

The *NZ Ski & Snowboard Guide*, published annually by Brown Bear, is an outstanding reference for ski bunnies, detailing the country's 26 ski areas. Check it out at www.brownbear.co.nz/snow.

The ski season is generally from June to October, although it varies considerably from one ski area to another and can go as late as November.

Information centres in NZ, and the New Zealand Tourism Board (NZTB) internationally, have brochures on the various ski areas and packages, and can make bookings.

Useful snowphone services provide prerecorded information on weather, access and snow levels. Several websites (www.snow.co.nz and www.nzski.com, to name two) provide ski reports, employment opportunities, Web cams and virtual tours. The websites of various resorts (see the following listings) are also packed with up-to-date info.

North Island

The North Island is dominated by volcanic-cone skiing, with active Mt Ruapehu the premier ski area.

WHAKAPAPA & TUROA

The twin ski resorts of **Whakapapa** and **Turoa** (☎ 07-892 3738, snowphone 08-322 2182; www.mtruapehu.com; daily lift pass adult/child $72/40), on either side of Mt Ruapehu, easily form NZ's largest ski area. Lift passes are valid at both resorts.

Whakapapa, 6km above Whakapapa Village in Tongariro National Park, has 30 groomed runs. There are plenty of snowboarding possibilities, cross-country, downhill and ski touring, and the highest lift access in the country. You can drive yourself up to the slopes or take a shuttle minibus from Whakapapa Village, National Park township, Taupo or Turangi.

Smaller Turoa has a beginners' lift, snowboarding, downhill and cross-country skiing. There's no road toll or parking fee and daily ski-area transport is available from Ohakune 16km away, which has the liveliest après-ski scene in the north.

For more information on the area, see Tongariro National Park (p312).

TUKINO

Club-operated **Tukino** (☎ 0800 885 466, 06-387 6294; www.tukino.co.nz; daily lift pass adult/child $30/10) is on the eastern side of Mt Ruapehu, 50km from Turangi. It's quite remote, 14km down a gravel road from the sealed Desert Rd (State Highway 1), and you need a 4WD vehicle to get in (or make a prior arrangement to use club transport). Because access is so limited the area is uncrowded, but most runs are beginner or intermediate.

See Tongariro National Park (p312) for more info.

Ski the popular slopes of Whakapapa (above)
JENNY & TONY ENDERBY

MANGANUI SKI AREA

The **Manganui Club Ski Area** (☎ 06-759 1119, 027-280 0860; http://snow.co.nz/manganui; daily lift pass adult/child $35/20) offers volcano-slope skiing on the eastern slopes of Mt Taranaki in the Egmont National Park, 22km from Stratford. Skiing is possible off the summit; when conditions permit, it's an invigorating two-hour climb to the crater with an exhilarating 1300m descent.

For more info on the area, see Mt Taranaki/Egmont (p267).

South Island

NZ's best-known (and top-rated) skiing is on the South Island, most of it revolving around the resort towns of Queenstown and Wanaka.

CORONET PEAK

The region's oldest ski field is **Coronet Peak** (☎ 03-442 4620; www.nzski.com; daily lift pass adult/child $79/41). The season here is reliable because of a multimillion-dollar snow-making system, and the treeless slopes and good snow provide excellent skiing for all levels. The consistent gradient and the many undulations make this a snowboarder's paradise. There's night skiing on Friday and Saturday from late June to late September.

Access is from Queenstown, 18km away, and there are shuttles in the ski season. See Queenstown (p622) for details of facilities in the area.

THE REMARKABLES

The visually impressive **Remarkables Ski Area** (☎ 03-442 4615; www.nzski.com; daily lift pass adult/child $74/39) is also near Queenstown (28km away), from where shuttle buses run during the season. It has an equal smattering of beginner, intermediate and advanced runs, with chairlifts and beginners' tows; it's a family-friendly field (kids under 10 ski free). Look out for the sweeping run called Homeward Bound.

TREBLE CONE

The highest and largest of the southern lake areas, **Treble Cone** (☎ 03-443 7443; www.treblecone.com; daily lift pass adult/child $89/37) is in a spectacular location 26km from Wanaka, and has steep slopes that are best for intermediate to advanced skiers. It also has numerous natural and manmade half-pipes for snowboarding.

For info on local facilities, see Wanaka (p646).

Ski jump at Treble Cone (below)
DAVID WALL

CARDRONA

Some 34km from Wanaka, **Cardrona** (☎ 03-443 7341; www.cardrona.com; daily lift pass adult/child $71/35) has several high-capacity chairlifts, beginners' tows and extreme terrain for snowboarders. Buses run from Wanaka during the ski season, and also from Queenstown.

Cardrona has acquired a reputation for the services it offers to disabled skiers, and it was the first resort on the South Island to have an on-field crèche. In summer it attracts mountain bikers.

WAIORAU SNOW FARM

NZ's only commercial Nordic (cross-country) ski area, the **Snow Farm** (☎ 03-443 0300; www.snowfarmnz.com; daily lift pass adult/child $30/15) is 35km from Wanaka (55km from Queenstown) on the Pisa Range, high above Lake Wanaka. There are 50km of groomed trails and thousands of hectares of open rolling country for the ski tourer. Huts with facilities are dotted along the top of the Pisa Range.

SOUTH CANTERBURY REGION

The commercial ski area **Ohau** (☎ 03-438 9885; www.ohau.co.nz; daily lift pass adult/child $55/39) is located on Mt Sutton some 42km from Twizel. It has a large percentage of intermediate and advanced runs, plus excellent terrain for snowboarding, cross-country and ski touring to Lake Dumb Bell. See Lake Ohau & Ohau Forests (p583) for info on accommodation.

The 3km-wide basin at **Mt Dobson** (☎ 03-685 8039; www.dobson.co.nz; daily lift pass adult/child $52/16), a commercial ski area 26km from Fairlie, caters for learners and has a large intermediate area and terrain park. On a clear day you can see Mt Cook and the Pacific Ocean from the summit of Mt Dobson. For info on nearby facilities, see Fairlie (p578).

Fox Peak (☎ 03-684 7358; www.foxpeak.co.nz; daily lift pass adult/child $40/10) is a club ski area 36km from Fairlie in the Two Thumb Range. Fox Peak has four rope tows; there's good ski touring from the summit of Fox Peak. Accommodation is available at Fox Lodge, 3km below the ski area.

Round Hill (☎ 03-680 6977; www.roundhill.co.nz; daily lift pass adult/child $52/22) is a small field with gentle slopes catering to beginners and intermediates, about 32km from Lake Tekapo village. See Lake Tekapo (p578) for details of accommodation in the area.

MT HUTT

Mt Hutt (☎ 03-302 8811, snowphone 03-308 5074; www.nzski.com; daily lift pass adult/child $74/39) is one of NZ's highest ski areas in the southern hemisphere, as well as one of NZ's best. It's close to Methven and can be reached by bus from Christchurch (118km to the west). Ski shuttles run to/from both towns; the ski area's access road is a rough, unpaved ride and drivers should be extremely cautious when the weather is poor.

Mt Hutt has beginner, intermediate and advanced slopes, with a new six-seater chairlift, various other lifts and heliskiing to slopes further afield. The wide open faces are good for those learning to snowboard.

For info on where to stay and eat in the area, see Methven (p571).

MT POTTS

The former Erewhon club ski area, exclusive **Mt Potts** (☎ 0800 766 9228; www.mtpotts.co.nz; cat/heliskiing per day $320/650) sits above the headwaters of the Rangitata River about 75km from Methven and is one of NZ's snow-white gems. It offers NZ's only heli-accessed cat-skiing experience. The day rate of $650 gets you eight full-length heliski runs; for the lower price of $320

Skiers, Queenstown
JOHN BANAGAN

you get flown onto Mt Potts, with a snow cat transporting you to the top of the mountain for each run. Accommodation and meals are available at a lodge 8km from the ski area, with dinner, bed and breakfast (DB&B) from $89. For info on the nearby town of Mt Somers, see p573.

PORTER HEIGHTS

The closest commercial ski area to Christchurch is **Porter Heights** (☎ 03-318 4002; www.porterheights.co.nz; daily lift pass adult/child $55/32), 96km away on the Arthur's Pass road. Its Big Mama is one of the steepest runs in NZ and there's a half-pipe for snowboarders, plus good cross-country areas and ski touring out along the ridge.

For accommodation in the area, see Craigieburn Forest Park (p568).

ARTHUR'S PASS & CRAIGIEBURN REGIONS

There are five ski areas in the Arthur's Pass and Craigieburn regions.

Temple Basin (☎ 03-377 7788; www.templebasin.co.nz; daily lift pass adult/child $45/30) is a club field 4km from the Arthur's Pass township. It's a 50-minute walk uphill from the car park to the ski-area lodges. There's floodlit skiing at night and excellent back-country runs for snowboarders. For info on local facilities, see Arthur's Pass (p569).

Craigieburn (☎ 03-365 2514; www.craigieburn.co.nz; daily lift pass adult/child $50/30), centred on Hamilton Peak, is 40km from Arthur's Pass. It's one of NZ's most challenging club areas, with intermediate and advanced runs (no beginners). Not far away is **Broken River** (☎ 03-318 8713; www.brokenriver.co.nz; daily lift pass adult/child $50/30), another club field, with a 15- to 20-minute walk from the car park and a nice sense of isolation. See Craigieburn Forest Park (p568) and Arthur's Pass (p569) for details of local places to stay and eat.

Another good club area in the Craigieburn Range is family-friendly **Mt Cheeseman** (☎ 03-344 3247; www.mtcheeseman.co.nz; daily lift pass adult/child $45/24), 112km from Christchurch. The ski area, based on Mt Cockayne, is in a wide, sheltered basin.

Also in Craigieburn and difficult to find, but worth the search, is **Mt Olympus** (☎ 03-318 5840; www.mtolympus.co.nz; daily lift pass adult/child $48/28), 58km from Methven and 12km from Lake Ida. This club area has four tows that lead to intermediate and advanced runs, and there are good cross-country areas and ski-touring trails to other areas. Access by 4WD is advisable from the bottom hut.

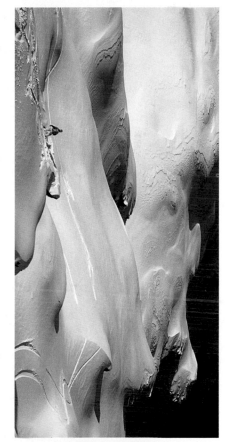

Heliski (below) at Mt Aspiring National Park
DAVID WALL

For something different, how about taking off from Wellington and skydiving into Picton? An extreme way to avoid the Interislander ferries! See p424 for details.

HANMER SPRINGS REGION

There are two ski areas near Hanmer Springs. Accommodation is on-field, or you can stay in the township (p564).

Hanmer Springs Ski Area (☎ 03-315 7233; www.skihanmer.co.nz; daily lift pass adult/child $45/20) is based on Mt St Patrick, 17km from Hanmer Springs, and has mostly intermediate and advanced runs.

Mt Lyford (☎ 03-315 6178, snowphone 03-366 1220; www.mtlyford.co.nz; daily lift pass adult/child $45/15) is about 60km from Hanmer Springs or Kaikoura, and 4km from Mt Lyford Village, where accommodation is available. There's a good mix of terrain suiting beginner, intermediate and advanced skiers and boarders.

NELSON REGION

It may come as a surprise to learn that sunny Nelson has a ski area only 100km away. St Arnaud (p471) is the closest town (32km) to **Rainbow Ski Area** (☎ 03-521 1861; www.skirainbow.co.nz; daily lift pass adult/child $45/20). It borders the Nelson Lakes National Park, with varied terrain and good cross-country ski touring.

Heliskiing

NZ's remote snow-dusted heights are tailor-made for heliskiing. From July to October, operators cover a wide off-piste area along the Southern Alps. The cost ranges from around $550 for a half-day trip (three runs), or from $750 to $950 for a full day (four to seven runs).

Some reliable heliskiing companies:

Alpine Guides Wilderness Heliskiing (☎ 03-435 1834; www.heliskiing.co.nz; Mt Cook)

Harris Mountains Heli-Ski (☎ 03-442 6722; www.heliski.co.nz; Queenstown & Wanaka)

Heli Ski Queenstown (☎ 03-442 7733; Queenstown)

Methven Heliskiing (☎ 03-302 8108; www.heliskiing.co.nz/methven/index.htm; Methven)

Southern Lakes Heliski (☎ 03-442 6222; www.southernlakesheliski.co.nz; Queenstown)

SKYDIVING

Strangely enough, ejecting yourself from a plane at high altitude and plummeting earthwards with only a few metres of cloth strapped to your back is a popular activity in NZ. There are plenty of professional operators, and at most drop zones the views on the way up (not to mention on the way down) are breathtaking.

Some operators and clubs offer static-line jumps and Accelerated Free Fall courses, but for most first-timers a tandem skydive is the way to go. After bonding with a fully-qualified instructor, you get to experience up to 45 seconds of high-speed free fall before the chute opens. The thrill is worth every dollar (specifically as much as $245/295 for a 9000/12,000ft jump).

Try tandem skydiving in the Bay of Islands, Taupo and Rotorua on the North Island, or in Motueka, Christchurch, Kaikoura, Fox Glacier, Twizel, Wanaka, Queenstown and Glenorchy on the South Island.

Tramp the volcanic
craters of Tongariro
National Park (p312)

GARETH McCORMACK®

TRAMPING

Tramping (that's Kiwi-speak for bushwalking, hiking or trekking) is a fine way to notch up first-hand experiences within NZ's natural beauty. There are thousands of kilometres of tracks, many well marked but some only a line on a map, as well as an excellent network of huts that enable trampers to avoid lugging tents and (in some cases) cooking gear. Before plodding along any track, you should get up-to-date information from the appropriate authority, usually DOC.

Tracks that receive the highest numbers of feet are the Routeburn, Milford, Tongariro Northern Circuit (and the one-day Tongariro Crossing), Kepler, Lake Waikaremoana and Abel Tasman Coastal Tracks. Most people on these tracks are from outside NZ – Kiwis are super-keen trampers, but tend to avoid the most heavily promoted tracks in favour of wilder, less-trafficked pathways gleaned from local knowledge. DOC staff can help you plan some enjoyable tramps on lesser-known tracks. Visit one of the many well-informed offices, or check out the info-loaded website, www.doc.govt.nz.

When to Go

The high season for walking is during the school summer holidays, lasting from two weeks before Christmas until the end of January; avoid it if you can. The best weather is from January to March, though most tracks can be walked enjoyably at any time from about October through to April. June and July (midwinter) is not the time to be out on the tracks, especially at altitude – some paths close in winter because of avalanche danger.

What to Bring

For an enjoyable tramp the primary considerations are your feet and shoulders. Make sure your footwear is adequate and that your pack isn't too heavy. Adequate wet-weather gear is also very important, especially on the South Island's waterlogged West Coast. And don't forget insect repellent unless you want to dance the sandfly jig in coastal areas.

If you're camping, or staying in huts where there are no stoves (eg on the Abel Tasman Coastal Track or Lake Waikaremoana Track), bring a camping stove. You can buy these, along with fuel and other camping gear, from sundry outdoor shops around NZ.

A tramper's best friend:
www.tramper.co.nz. This
is a fantastic website,
with track descriptions
and ratings by real
trampers, plus a selection
tool that can help you
choose what walk to
do according to various
criteria (length, location,
difficulty, or by specifics
such as child-friendly,
coastal, or featuring hot
pools).

RESPONSIBLE TRAMPING

To help preserve the ecology and beauty of NZ, please consider the following tips when tramping.

Rubbish

- Carry out *all* your rubbish. Make an effort to carry out rubbish left by others.

- Never bury your rubbish: digging disturbs soil and ground cover and encourages erosion. Buried rubbish will likely be dug up by animals, who may be injured or poisoned by it. It may also take years to decompose.

- Minimise waste by taking minimal packaging and no more food than you will need. Take reusable containers or stuff sacks.

- Sanitary napkins, tampons, condoms and toilet paper should be carried out despite the inconvenience. They burn and decompose poorly.

Human-Waste Disposal

- Contamination of water sources by human faeces can lead to the transmission of all sorts of nasties. Where there is a toilet, please use it. Where there is none, bury your waste. Dig a small hole 15cm deep and at least 100m from any watercourse. Cover the waste with soil and a rock. In snow, dig down to the soil.

- Ensure that these guidelines are applied to a portable toilet tent if one is being used by a large tramping party. Encourage all party members to use the site.

Washing

- Don't use detergents or toothpaste in or near watercourses, even if the products are biodegradable.

- For personal washing, use biodegradable soap and a water container (or even a lightweight, portable basin) at least 50m away from the watercourse. Disperse the waste water widely to allow the soil to filter it fully.

- Wash cooking utensils 50m from watercourses using a scourer, sand or snow instead of detergent.

Erosion

- Hillsides and mountain slopes, especially at high altitudes, are prone to erosion. Stick to existing tracks and avoid short cuts.

- If a well-used track passes through a mud patch, walk through the mud so as not to increase the size of the patch.

- Avoid removing the plant life that keeps topsoil in place.

Fires & Low-Impact Cooking

- Don't depend on open fires for cooking. The cutting of wood for fires in popular tramping areas can cause rapid deforestation. Cook on a lightweight kerosene, alcohol or Shellite (white gas) stove and avoid those powered by disposable butane gas canisters.

- In alpine areas, ensure that all members are outfitted with enough clothing so that fires are not a necessity for warmth.

- If you patronise local accommodation, select those places that do not use wood fires to heat water or cook food.

- Fires may be acceptable below the tree line in areas that get very few visitors. If you light a fire, use an existing fireplace. Don't surround fires with rocks. Use only dead, fallen wood. Remember the adage 'the bigger the fool, the bigger the fire'. Use minimal wood, just what you need for cooking. In huts, leave wood for the next person.

- Ensure that you fully extinguish a fire after use. Spread the embers and flood them with water.

Wildlife Conservation

- Do not engage in or encourage hunting. It is illegal in all parks and reserves.

- Don't buy items made from endangered species.

- Don't attempt to exterminate animals in huts. In wild places, they are likely to be protected native animals.

- Discourage the presence of wildlife by not leaving food scraps behind. Place gear out of reach and tie packs to rafters or trees.

- Do not feed the wildlife as this can lead to unbalanced populations, diseases and animals becoming dependent on hand-outs.

Camping & Walking on Private Property

- Always seek permission to camp from landowners.

Books

DOC produces very good books with detailed information on the flora and fauna, geology and history of NZ's national parks. It also publishes leaflets (each usually costing 50c to $2) outlining thousands of walking tracks throughout the country.

Lonely Planet's *Tramping in New Zealand* describes around 50 walks of various lengths and degrees of difficulty. *101 Great Tramps*, by Mark Pickering and Rodney Smith (now in its 6th edition), has suggestions for two- to six-day tramps around the country. The companion guide, *202 Great Walks: the Best Day Walks in New Zealand* by Mark Pickering, is handy for those after shorter, family-friendly excursions. *Accessible Walks*, by Anna and Andrew Jameson, is an excellent guide for trampers with a disability (and elderly walkers) to more than 100 South Island walks. There are countless books covering tramps and short walks around major cities, in varying regions and throughout the country – head for a bookshop and you're bound to find something.

Maps

Topographical maps produced by **Land Information New Zealand** (LINZ, www .linz.govt.nz) are best. Bookshops don't often have a good selection of these, but LINZ has map-sales offices in main cities and towns, and DOC offices often sell LINZ maps for tracks in their area. You may also find them in good outdoor-equipment stores. LINZ's map series induces park maps, covering national, state and forest parks; cartography for the more popular walking tracks; and the highly detailed 'Topomaps', though you may need two or three maps to cover one track.

Track Classification

Tracks are classified according to various features, including their level of difficulty. In this chapter we loosely refer to the level of difficulty as easy, medium, hard or difficult. The widely used track classification system is as follows:

Path Easy and well formed; allows for wheelchair access or constructed to 'shoe' standard (ie walking boots not required); allows for wheelchair access or constructed to 'shoe' standard. Suitable for people of all ages and fitness levels.

Walking Track Easy and well formed; constructed to 'shoe' standard. Suitable for people of most ages and fitness levels.

Tramping Track Requires skill and experience, constructed to 'boot' standard. Suitable for people of average physical fitness.

Route Requires a high degree of skill, experience and route-finding ability. Suitable for well-equipped trampers.

Track Safety

Thousands of people tramp in NZ every year without incident, but every year a few die in the mountains. Most fatalities could have been avoided if simple safety rules had been observed.

Some trails are only for the experienced and well-equipped – don't attempt such tracks if you don't fit the bill. NZ's climatic changeability subjects high-altitude walks to snow and ice even in summer so always check weather conditions before setting off.

Consult a DOC office and register your intentions before starting the longer walks and, above all, heed DOC's advice.

The Great Walks

The so-called nine Great Walks (one of which is actually a river trip) are the most popular tracks. Their beauty does indeed make them worth

Hike the Routeburn Track (p644), Lake Wakatipu

SALLY CULCH

Walk or paddle the Abel Tasman Coastal Track (p478)

DAVID WALL

experiencing, but prepare yourself for the fact that they can get quite crowded, especially over summer, when people from all over the world come to follow them.

All nine Great Walks are described in this guidebook and in Lonely Planet's *Tramping in New Zealand*, and are also detailed in pamphlets provided by DOC offices and visitor information centres.

The Great Walks:

Abel Tasman Coastal Track (p478) A three- to five-day, easy to medium, 51km walk close to beaches and bays in Abel Tasman National Park (South Island). NZ's most popular walk is inundated with people, including sea kayakers.

Heaphy Track (p487) A four- to six-day, medium to hard, 82km tramp through the forest and karst (limestone) landscape of Kahurangi National Park (South Island). The last day includes a magnificent beach walk.

Kepler Track (p660) This three- to four-day, 60km walk in Fiordland National Park (South Island) is a medium to hard tramp. It takes in lakes, rivers, gorges, glacier-carved valleys and beech forest with panoramic views.

Lake Waikaremoana Track (p384) A three- to four-day, easy to medium, 46km tramp in Te Urewera National Park (North Island), with great views of the lake and surrounding bush-clad slopes, plus good swimming opportunities.

Milford Track (p666) This four-day, 54km walk in Fiordland National Park (South Island) is one of the world's best-known. It's an easy walk through rainforest and past crystal-clear streams; it also takes in the 630m-high Sutherland Falls, NZ's highest.

Rakiura Track (p693) A three-day, 29km tramp on Stewart Island, mostly on duckboards and requiring medium fitness. The track offers copious bird life, beaches and lush bush en route, plus the chance to see kiwi in the wild.

Routeburn Track (p644) A medium, three-day, 32km walk through a huge variety of landscapes including the stunning alpine scenery of Mt Aspiring and Fiordland National Parks (South Island).

If you've got your heart set on walking the Milford, Routeburn or any other Great Walk, make sure you're familiar with the booking requirements, and get in early if you're planning to walk in summer. See the Department of Conservation website (www.doc.govt.nz) for full details.

Hike in the Darren Mountains, overlooking Milford Sound (p666)

GRANT DIXON

GREAT WALKS

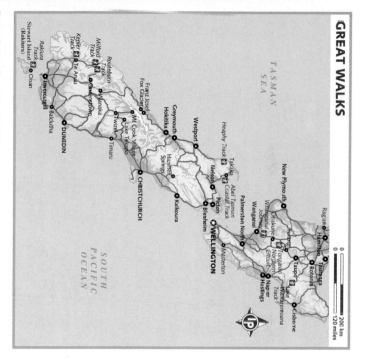

Beech tree, Kepler Track (p660), Fiordland National Park

GRANT DIXON

Tongariro Northern Circuit (p315) A four-day, medium to hard tramp through the active volcanic landscape of Tongariro National Park (North Island). Part of this tramp can be done as the one-day Tongariro Crossing (p315).

Whanganui Journey (p283) A 145km, five-day canoe or kayak trip down the Whanganui River in Whanganui National Park (North Island). There's more sitting down than walking on this great Walk.

To tramp these tracks you'll need to buy a Great Walks hut pass or camping pass before setting out, sold at DOC offices and visitor information centres in the vicinity of each walk. Hut prices vary from $10 to $40 per person per night depending on the track and the season; camping fees range from $2.50 to $15 per person per night. You can camp only at designated camping grounds; note there's no camping on the Milford Track.

In recent times, the popularity of the Great Walks has seen DOC initiate a booking system for six of the tracks, to avoid overcrowding and protect the environment. Prospective trampers must book night's in their chosen hut or campsite and specify dates when they purchase Great Walks passes. Bookings can usually be made online (www.doc.govt.nz), by email (greatwalksbooking@doc.govt.nz), or by phone, fax or in person at the DOC visitor information centre closest to the track in question. Full details are outlined on the DOC website. Note that there is no charge to do a day walk on any of the tracks – the charge is, essentially, to stay overnight.

The following applies to the Great Walks:

Lake Waikaremoana Track, Abel Tasman Coastal Track, Heaphy Track – booking required year-round

Kepler Track, Milford Track, Routeburn Track – booking required October to April

Rakiura Track, Tongariro Northern Circuit, Whanganui Journey – booking not required

Other Tracks

There are numerous tramping possibilities besides the Great Walks in all forest and national parks. Most of the following walks are *not* described in detail in this book:

NORTH ISLAND

Mt Holdsworth Circuit A medium to hard, three-day tramp in Holdsworth Forest Park, out of Masterton. The walk passes through forest and over the top of alpine Mt Holdsworth.

Ninety Mile Beach–Cape Reinga Walkway A 50km, three-day, easy beach tramp (camping only) in Northland.

Round the Mountain, Mt Taranaki/Egmont A 55km walk of four days or more in Egmont National Park, comprising medium to hard tramping through mountainous country.

Tongariro Crossing A brilliant, 18km, one-day, medium tramp through Tongariro National Park.

SOUTH ISLAND

Arthur's Pass There are many walks in Arthur's Pass National Park; most are rated difficult.

Banks Peninsula Walk A 35km, two-day (medium) or four-day (easy) walk over the hills and along the coast of Banks Peninsula, crossing private and public land near Akaroa.

Greenstone & Caples Tracks These two tracks are on stewardship land, just outside Fiordland National Park. They both meet up with the Routeburn Track and are a good way to start or finish this popular track.

Hump Ridge Track Inaugurated in 2001, this is an excellent, three-day, 53km circuit beginning and ending at Bluecliffs Beach on Te Wae Wae Bay, 20km from Tuatapere.

Inland Pack Track A 27km medium tramp in Paparoa National Park, following river valleys through the karst landscape near Punakaiki on the West Coast.

Kaikoura Coast Track A three-day, easy, 40km walk over private and public land along the spectacular coastline 50km south of Kaikoura.

Matukituki Valley Walks There are good medium-to-hard walks in the Matukituki Valley, in Mt Aspiring National Park, near Wanaka.

North-West Circuit This eight- to 12-day hard walk is one of many wilderness possibilities on Stewart Island.

Queen Charlotte Track A three- to four-day medium walk in the Marlborough Sounds affording great views of the sounds and passing many historic places. There's accommodation and water transport on this track.

Rees-Dart Track A 70km, four- to five-day hard walk in Mt Aspiring National Park, through river valleys and traversing an alpine pass.

St James Walkway This 65km, five-day medium walk in Lake Sumner Forest Park/Lewis Pass Reserve passes through excellent subalpine scenery.

Hike the challenging
Cascade Saddle (p648),
Mt Aspiring National Park
GARETH McCORMACK

Wangapeka & Leslie-Karamea Tracks The Wangapeka is a four- to five-day medium tramp along river valleys and overpasses. The Leslie-Karamea is a 90km to 100km, five- to seven-day tramp for experienced walkers only, which negotiates river valleys, gorges and passes.

Back-Country Hut & Camping Fees

DOC has a huge network of back-country huts (more than 950) in NZ's national, maritime and forest parks. There are 'serviced huts' (which have mattress-equipped bunks or sleeping platforms, water supply, heating, toilets and sometimes cooking facilities), 'standard huts' (no cooking equipment or heating) and 'basic huts' or bivvies. Back-country hut fees range from free to $35 per night for adults, paid with tickets bought in advance at any DOC office or park visitor information centre. Children under 10 can use all huts free of charge. School children aged 11 and older are charged half-price. If you plan to do a lot of tramping, DOC also sells an annual **Back-Country Hut Pass** (adult/child $90/45), applicable to all its huts bar those on the Great Walks. (On Great Walks that do not require year-round booking, regular back-country hut tickets and passes can be used to procure a bunk or camp site in the track's low season, usually from May to September.)

Depending on the category of hut, a night's stay may use one or two tickets. When you arrive at a hut, date the tickets and put them in the box provided. Accommodation is on a first-come, first-served basis.

DOC also manages 235 vehicle-accessible camping grounds – the most basic of these ('informal' sites) are free, while 'standard' and 'serviced' grounds cost between $3 and $14 per adult per night. Serviced grounds have full facilities – flush toilets, tap water, showers and picnic tables; they may also have barbecues, a kitchen and laundry. Standard grounds have toilets and water supply and perhaps barbecues and picnic tables.

Getting There & Away

Getting to and from tracks can be a real problem, except for the most popular trails, which are serviced by trampers' transport. Having a vehicle only simplifies the problem of getting to one end of the track. Otherwise you have to take public transport or hitch in, and if the track starts or ends at the terminus of a dead-end road, hitching will be difficult.

Of course, tracks that are easily accessed by public transport (such as Abel Tasman) are also the most crowded. An alternative is to arrange private transport, either with a friend or by chartering a vehicle to drop you off at one end and pick you up at the other. If you intend to leave your own vehicle at a track-head car park and return for it later, don't leave anything of value inside – thefts from cars in these isolated areas is a significant problem.

WHITE-WATER RAFTING & KAYAKING

There are almost as many white-water rafting possibilities as there are rivers in NZ, and there's no shortage of companies to take you on an exhilarating ride down some magnificently wild watercourses.

Popular raft carriers on the South Island include the Shotover and Kawarau Rivers, while the Rangitata River is considered one of the country's best. The north of the island also has great rafting possibilities, such as the Buller and Karamea Rivers; Westport and Murchison are the best bases from which to take on these river's. Other West Coast possibilities include the Arnold and Waiho Rivers.

On the North Island there are plenty of raft-worthy rivers too such as the Rangitaiki, Wairoa, Motu, Tongariro and Rangitikei. There are also the Kaituna Cascades near Rotorua – the highlight of this river is the 3m drop at Okere Falls.

Trek up Gillespie Pass (p653), Mt Aspiring National Park

GARETH McCORMACK

Kayak the rapids of Buller River (p490), near Murchison

DAVID WALL

Raft along the Buller
River (p490), near
Murchison
DAVID WALL

Rivers are graded from I to VI, with VI meaning 'unraftable'. The grading of the Shotover canyon varies from III to V+, depending on the time of year, while the Kawarau River is rated IV and the Wairoa River III to V. On the rougher stretches there's usually a minimum age limit of 12 or 13 years. All safety equipment is supplied by the operator.

Note that an excursion taking up most of a day often involves only a couple of hours on the water, with the rest of the time taken up with travel to and from the river.

White-water kayaking is popular among enthusiasts but, unlike rafting, it's a solo activity requiring skills and training. From September to April, the **New Zealand Kayak School** (☎ 03-523 9611; www.nzkayakschool.com) in Murchison offers intensive four-day courses for introductory to advanced levels from $695.

WINDSURFING & KITEBOARDING

Windsurfing has thousands of Kiwi adherents and there are plenty of lakes and other popular spots on both islands to catch the wind. Auckland harbour, Hauraki Gulf, the Bay of Islands, Oakura near New Plymouth and 'windy' Wellington are just some of the outstanding coastal locations. There are many places where you can hire boards and receive high-standard instruction. For more info on windsurfing, check out www.winzurf.co.nz/windsurf.

Kiteboarding (or kitesurfing), where a mini parachute drags you along on a surfboard, is touted as the successor to windsurfing and can be attempted at Paihia, Tauranga, Mt Maunganui, Raglan, Wellington and Nelson.

Windsurf at Otago
Harbour, Dunedin (p590)
DAVID WALL

Food & Drink Julie Biuso

Imagine a gourmet traveller hightailing it around the world, collecting the notable comestibles and culinary traditions that take their fancy, bringing it all back to New Zealand and concocting an elaborate multifaceted cuisine with the booty.

Peppered with Kiwi culinary skills and tempered by the climate and soil, this could describe NZ food in the new millennium.

We used to have 60 million cloven-hoofed woolly blankets on legs munching the lush grasslands and the dry country. Hardly any surprise then, that our national dinner was roast lamb, or more likely the longer-toothed brother, hogget.

We're still eating lamb, but something momentous has happened down on the farm, something which can't be blamed on the carnivores among us. In just over 20 years the number of sheep grown in NZ has dropped from 60 to 40 million. Who ate the other 20 million?

Deregulation hit NZ in the 1980s – which opened the farm gate to a lot more options than growing sheep and cattle. Some farmers stopped replacing animal stock and sold off their land, making way for kiwi fruit, grapevines and olive trees. It changed the look of the land and drastically altered what we put on our plates and our palates.

Shrugging off the image NZ had as a supplier of bulk frozen lamb and beef and blocks of yellow, all-purpose cheese, was not easy. But a new breed of producers and manufacturers entered the arena in the '80s and '90s with one goal in mind: excellence.

With a history of cooking rather than cuisine and eating the food of our British migrant ancestors. Kiwis have finally gone global. The past two decades have seen us embrace our unique blend of ethnic cultures and cuisines, drawing in Pacific and Asian influences and giving rise to Pacific Rim cookery.

The cultural freedom this generation enjoys has given birth to a free spirit in the kitchen, where experimentation and adaptation are now part of everyday cooking. There's a keen interest, too, in all things native and locally produced; a groundswell, if you like, of support for 'NZ Made'.

The most striking features about the food are its quality and its freshness. Prime cuts of meat from animals that graze freely outdoors, lakes of fresh milk and cream, orchards of tree-ripened fruit, fields of fresh vegetables, hundreds of vineyards producing sensational wines, all-around seas teeming with fish and skies abuzz with honey bees – no joking, this is as near to the land of milk and honey as you're likely to find.

For the visitor, it's all good news. The food and wine has never been better, and award-winning fare is easy and affordable in restaurants and cafés, in specialist stores and well-stocked supermarkets. Well-cooked fresh food is in abundance in the cities and the variety there is impressive, but it's also surprisingly easy to dine on exceptional food and wines in the proverbial 'middle of nowhere'. NZ is a culinary adventure for the hungry traveller.

STAPLES & SPECIALITIES

We're still predominately a nation of meat eaters and the quality of our meat these days is outstanding. Sheep and cattle are reared outdoors and fed entirely on grass (in fact Kiwis struggle to believe that farms could be run any other way!). The climate, the breeds and the natural diet all

Julie Biuso's food career started with a great batch of hot cross buns at the age of 10. The following year, the buns flopped and she realised she had a lot to learn – 25 years as a magazine food editor and 13 award-winning books later, she reckons she's still learning.

For an authoritative guide to food and wine, visit www.cuisine.co.nz.

combine to produce sweet-tasting lamb with particularly fine-grained meat, and beef of incomparable tenderness and flavour.

Roast lamb or hogget is a popular choice for a family meal. The classic vegetable accompaniments are roasted potatoes, kumara (sweet potato), greens and pumpkin. There's nothing quite like the sticky caramelised goo adhering to the meat, and chunks of kumara and pumpkin as you dish up a traditional Kiwi roast.

To visitors, lamb eaten in NZ can be a revelation and so much better than the distant memory of frozen NZ lamb eaten on the other side of the world. And there is something about eating food in the place it's produced.

It's still possible to catch dinner from the sea without much effort, but you don't usually *need* to – fish farms are springing up everywhere.

OUR TOP TEN EATING EXPERIENCES

Carolyn Bain

A unique, and very Kiwi, experience was a restaurant called Kai (Wellington; p420), which produces delicious 'Maori-fusion' food. The menu features a helpful glossary for those who don't know their *heihei* (chicken) from their *kuku* (mussels). Some nights you'll be serenaded by the restaurant's owner playing guitar and singing Maori songs.

Further south, I enjoyed fishy treats from Kaikoura Seafood BBQ (Kaikoura; p460) on my way to see the seals. A cheap and tasty grilled fish sandwich was perfect fuel for further exploration.

George Dunford

Discreetly hidden, yet earning great praise from locals, Bach (Taupo; p304) was a snug spot for a sophisticated meal: confit of duck with braised red cabbage and gently poached fig. The view over Lake Taupo just made everything taste sweeter.

Maketu Pies (Maketu; p360) bakes fresh pies daily that are famous throughout the region – especially the 'Kiwi-as' mint and lamb pie, which I reckon is best enjoyed on the beach.

Korina Miller

For my two top meals I've chosen a breakfast feast at Fleur's Place (Moeraki; p619), a fantastic rumble-tumble restaurant packed with character and lip-smacking seafood; and a deliciously stuffed baguette from Joe's Garage (Arrowtown; p641), eaten at one of the breathtaking southern lookout stops on the Crown Range Rd (Cardrona; p655).

Sally O'Brien

Picking two places (out of many, many meals) that stand out from my time in NZ is no mean feat, but here goes: Sahara (Paparoa; p169) is an intimate, friendly haven in a former bank building in an out-of-the-way spot in Northland – the venison and wild mushroom pie is so perfect it could be ordered as a starter, main and midnight snack; Dizengoff (Ponsonby; p136) reigns supreme for creative, nourishing breakfasts and the sort of coffee that sets you up for another big day.

Charles Rawlings-Way

At the foot of Fox Glacier on the South Island's wild West Coast, Café Nevé (Fox Glacier; p522) surprised me with a superb restaurant meal. The staff understand that local ingredients enhance the diner's (and traveller's) experience, and the menu is peppered with excellent regional seafood, venison and lamb dishes, best washed down with a cold West Coast handle of Monteith's Original Ale.

At the opposite corner of NZ, on the North Island's East Coast, it's hard to beat a takeaway hamburger from Captain Morgans (Gisborne; p381) eaten at sunset at Waikanae Beach: surfers nose their long-boards into shore, kids laugh on the sand, Norfolk Island Pines sway and murmur and everything's good in the world.

A WHIFF OF CHEESE

In a land awash with milk you'd expect a buoyant cheese industry. The inaugural cheese awards held in 1994 encouraged boutique cheesemakers to have a go at something different. Alongside the flood of Camemberts and Bries a whole host of weird and wonderful cheeses have emerged: sheep's milk, goat's milk, organic cheese, vegetarian cheeses, you name it.

When ripe, Mt Hector, a sublime goat's cheese, requires no more than a gentle squeeze of its downy white overcoat to release a rich flowing centre, reminiscent in flavour of mushrooms and garlic, salt and bubbling cream.

Brick's a real stinker. Washed-rind cheeses are treated with a mix of brine and bacteria linens which encourage a bright orangey-red bacteria on the rind. The bacteria attack the outside of the cheese and create a runny crème caramel-type of texture inside the cheese. Brick has a sticky orange-brown rind with a pungent aroma. It's very rich and unctuous, and its trace of sweet-ness is wiped clean by a spicy tang. It lingers on a smoky note. Complex in aroma and flavour, perhaps it's not the right cheese to take as a gift to a conventional dinner party (they might not let you in the door).

By law all milk in NZ must be pasteurised, robbing cheese of nature's quirks, but not with-standing this, some pretty tasty specimens are created.

The most common mussel species is the green shell. It is farmed in abundance, and famed too for its anti-inflammatory properties that have spread from folklore to fact. It's a true Kiwi icon. Such is the popularity of green shell mussels that most big supermarkets have a serve-yourself tank of them. They are often cooked on the hotplate of a barbecue until the shells open, and eaten *au naturel*. But they are also sold smoked and marinated, or served up crumbed and grilled in the half shell.

A NZ sauvignon blanc full of passionfruit, capsicum and gooseberry characters and the zing of crisp acid may be out of place on a chilly night in the northern hemisphere. But try it on a beach in NZ with the salty tang of the sea filling the nostrils, a whiff of barbecue smoke in the air, and a bowlful of plump mussels or scallops which have met the heat for just a few seconds…and you'll quickly swoon and fall in love!

Luv 'em or loathe 'em, oysters are big time here, especially the Bluff oyster, dredged around the southern tip of the South Island. From March to August oyster-lovers just can't get enough of these fat specimens. It may strike you as odd, but Bluff oysters are shucked at the source and transported around the country in pottles, or sold frozen.

Much of NZ's paua (abalone) finds its way overseas illegally, but it also appears on the menus of top-notch local seafood restaurants and seaside cafés.

NZ whitebait is a tiny threadlike fish with a deliciously sweet but delicate flavour. It features regularly on menus as whitebait fritters, and the ratio of whitebait to batter – about a quarter batter to three-quarters whitebait – is something Kiwis jump up and down about. Any more batter than that and things could turn ugly.

Other distinctive and expensive seafood offerings include the rare shellfish toheroa (a large clam that grows to around 15cm long), which is said to taste like oyster that has dined on asparagus, and crayfish, which is exported under the name of rock lobster.

And although you can't buy rainbow or brown trout, there are plenty of opportunities to fish for them, and plenty of places to stay with cooking facilities, or where the chef will cook your catch for you.

Catch this: there are more rainbow trout caught in the whopping 2kg to 3kg category) in NZ per year than everywhere else in the world combined.

Cervena (farmed deer) features on menus throughout NZ and can be purchased fresh from specialist butchers. The meat is lean and better served rare.

Kiwi fruit takes pride of place on top of the eggwhite and sugar concoction known as pavlova. The Australians have long laid claim to this sweet meringue cake, but they garnish it with kiwi fruit, too, which shows that they copied us, so we must have invented it! The pav, as it is known, is the quintessential Kiwi dessert, touted around in plastic containers to family gatherings. At its best the sugar crust cracks with a tap giving way to a mass of foamy meringue. The whole lot is sunk under a mountain of cream and a ring of kiwi fruit. Not to be missed.

A recent industry is avocado oil. The emerald green oil is redolent of artichokes and celery when you sniff it, with a hint of mushroom. It also tastes a bit like artichoke, too, with no acidity or astringency, then, at the end, a bucket-load of pure avocado flavour kicks in.

Kiwis usually start the day with cereal, fruit, yoghurt, toast, juice, and coffee or tea. Although at weekends they might make more of an effort or eat out at a café.

A city lunch, unless it's a special occasion, is eaten at the desk, on the street, in the car, or at the park without any pomp and ceremony. It's usually a bread-based meal.

Dinner takes place anytime from 6pm through to 9.30pm (many restaurants close their kitchens at 10pm).

DRINKS
Alcohol

Kiwis like to drink. Whether it's a beer after work, a glass of bubbly to celebrate a special occasion, or a glass or two of wine around the barbecue or over dinner, alcohol is part of the social culture on all levels.

It's easy to find good wine and not that much harder to find excellent wine in NZ. Good bargains can be found in supermarket wine sections,

One golden kiwi fruit contains more than double the recommended daily intake of vitamin C.

Puha (prickly sow thistle) is a popular feature of Maori cooking and grows wild in backyards and farms across the country. These leafy greens may be regarded by some as a common weed, but just try 'em boiled up with pork or mussels.

TRAVEL YOUR TASTEBUDS

There are many interesting foods to try on your travels, some unique to NZ.

Piko piko (edible fern shoots) Like a down-under version of asparagus. Nutty in flavour, they can be served up in salads and cooked dishes.

Horopito (bush pepper) Has a hot peppery bite. Made into a rub for meats, or seafood before it is smoked.

Kawakawa (bush basil) Has a subtle flavour and scent. Best for white meats and fish, or added to fresh pasta.

Kelp salt Salt flavoured with lemon, chilli or lime and is fantastic sprinkled over pan-fried, barbecued or grilled fish, and on smoked fish or seafood pasta, as well as over vegetables such as tomatoes and cooked beans. Made from hand-harvested and sun-dried kelp, it's packed full of nutrients.

Karengo (a native seaweed) Also hand-harvested and sun-dried, karengo adds the nutrients of the sea and a fresh saline flavour to dishes.

We Dare You

Marmite/Vegemite Kiwis are rather fond of the iron-rich, sticky brown yeast spread called Marmite, or the Australian equivalent called Vegemite. Spread thinly on crackers, topped with a slice or two of tomato and a sprig of parsley it makes a homespun snack, which wards off the desire for something salty and savoury. The trick is to spread it thinly – a tablespoon of either has the strength of a cup of soy sauce.

Kina A species of sea urchin plentiful around NZ coastlines, kina looks like something from outer space with its spiny exterior. It is sweetest in spring, and best eaten straight out of the water. Cut it open and scoop or suck out the contents. An acquired taste.

WINE-TOURING

Wine-touring may not seem as synonymous with NZ as it does with countries like France, Germany and Australia, but the country has nurtured some outstanding wine regions and its international reputation for quality wine continues to grow. In turn, this has fed an interest in wine-touring. There are dozens of tours available, many of which also visit food producers and places of interest.

Wineries are distributed from around Kaitaia and Kerikeri in the far north right down to Central Otago, which at a latitude of 45 degrees has some of the most southern vineyards in the world. You can cycle or drive between many of these vintage enterprises and taste at the cellar door. And many wineries are now equipped with fine cafés, restaurants, associated businesses such as cheese or preserve making, and accommodation. There are numerous operators willing to bus you around the main grape-littered regions on half- and full-day tours.

The best regions to tour are Marlborough (see the boxed text, p452), Nelson (p473), Martinborough (p432) in the Wairarapa, Hawkes Bay (p398), Gisborne (p378), Henderson (West Auckland, p144), Waiheke Island (in the Hauraki Gulf, p149) and Central Otago (see the boxed text, p632). Marlborough, Hawkes Bay and Martinborough all host big annual wine and food festivals.

but boutique wines have to be sought at wine stores or bought from the winery.

One of the best ways to get to know NZ wines, and NZ itself for that matter, is to visit wineries, which you can do independently or by taking a wine tour (see the boxed text, above).

There are still some restaurants, mainly ethnic and inexpensive, which hold a BYO (bring your own) licence, allowing diners to bring in their own wine to consume in the restaurant. You'll be charged a small fee for corkage, but will have saved yourself the usual restaurant mark-up on the wine.

While beer consumption has dropped about 30% in 30 years, there's now more choice in beer styles. Boutique breweries are popping up all over the country, and it's now considered as trendy to sip a fruity-tasting beer as it is an unoaked chardonnay or pinot gris.

Coffee

You've got to give it to the Kiwis – when they decide to do something, they do it well. Take coffee. Ten years ago most places served up 'perked' coffee, coffee that was left to stew over an element set on low, or 'drip' coffee which was kept hot for hours.

But coffee in the big cities now rivals that of NZ's nearest coffee capital, Melbourne, and it's certainly better than coffee in Italy.

Unique perhaps to NZ is the penchant for oversized bowls of latte. No self-respecting Italian would order a milky coffee after 11am, but Kiwis lap up giant bowls of the stuff day and night. And good it is, too. Practically any café that looks modern and clean will serve up a decent espresso or cappuccino.

Working as a barista is considered sexy and something the young do with a great deal of panache.

Out of the big cities they're trying hard. They've got the machines with all the bells and whistles, they just might not know how to drive them, but they'll listen up if you've good advice on how you like your cup of coffee.

CELEBRATIONS

Food and wine are celebrated throughout NZ, with many regions and cities holding festivals. It's generally a great day out, offering the visitor a chance to mingle with the locals and to sip and savour some of the

Kiwi innovator Morton Coutts revolutionised beer brewing in the 1950s with the 'continuous fermentation process', which cut the beer fermentation process from 15 weeks to less than a day. Coutts said it helped to think of yeast 'as a human being with a brain'.

Up until 1962 it was illegal for restaurants to serve alcohol. Smuggling booze into restaurants in paper bags was the done thing.

The Wildfoods Festival is held in Hokitika in March. Dare your gag reflex: deep-fried fish eyes, marinated duck tongues and hare testicles are just some of the gastronomic challenges available.

best food, wine and hospitality that particular part of the country has to offer.

The Maori *hangi* is an unusual method of cooking food in the ground over hot river stones. Potatoes, kumara, carrots, pumpkin, onion, corn, cabbage, poultry, fish and meats are thrown in together and steamed until tender, taking on some of the flavour of the earth. *Hangi* are a feature of almost any formal Maori occasion, from funerals to important meetings on the *marae* (Maori meeting house). They're also a great informal communal event: there's much exertion and nodding of wise heads as the hole is dug and food prepared, and plenty of time for sitting around talking while the stones are heated (with a few exploding stones adding moments of excitement) and while the food cooks. The Polynesian equivalent of the earth oven is the *umu*.

The most common form of entertaining and celebrating on a small scale is the backyard barbecue. Most Kiwis own a barbecue, probably gas-fired, although there is an increasing number of sophisticated outdoors kitchens-on-wheels. The NZ barbecue can either be dire – charred sausages and steak the texture of sawdust – or brilliant. With superb-quality meat and seafood it can be as simple as firing up the barbie, slapping on a few pieces of aged beef and opening a bottle of chardonnay. You may be lucky to find yourself sitting on a hay bale to eat your meal, or dining with the lapping waves at your feet. Don't turn up your nose at plastic plates and cutlery – it's the done thing here, by the river or at the beach, and the food generally outshines unimportant things like plates, knives and forks!

WHERE TO EAT & DRINK

You're spoilt for choice in the big cities, and you'll find some amazingly well-prepared fresh food all around NZ. You'll find some shockers, too, and the usual advice applies – it is a good idea to choose a clean, well-patronised place.

On the whole Auckland cafés are pavement-spilling affairs, often with cutting-edge design, lots of chrome and glass, and stylish fit-outs. Even in the chill of a winter's evening, Aucklanders sit huddled outside under huge gas lamps. To see and be seen is part of the café culture.

In Wellington and further south they're not as silly. When the southerly winds come howling in from Antarctica, people huddle around open fires in bars, cafés and restaurants. Recycled furniture and a homely welcoming feel sums up many of these unpretentious cafés.

The influences of the Pacific are as evident as those of Italy, the Mediterranean and Asia, and many restaurants and cafés seem unable to settle for one style or the other. Don't be surprised if on the same menu you find *kokoda* (raw fish marinated in lemon/lime juice and finished with coconut cream), and linguine dressed with prosciutto, parmigiano reggiano and rocket leaves.

When you make an evening reservation in a restaurant, you can pretty well rest assured that if the booking is for after 7.30pm, the table is yours for the night. If not, the restaurant will ask if you want an early or late seating. If you trawl through the courses, expect to stay two to three hours.

Quick Eats

A lot of Kiwis consume their working lunch on the go, out of a paper bag – street eating is a common sight, with pies and sandwiches of some description being the most popular. Cafés and delis offer good 'food to go' mostly based on a theme or style of cuisine. There's always plenty of vegetarian options for the lunch trade.

Bottled water is available everywhere, and there are several good local waters – no need to pay for imported 'named' bottled water unless you really want to. And of course tap water is fine to drink too.

Fish and chips is the most popular takeaway food and is usually done well. Kumara fritters and wedges are worth trying, as are scallops and paua if on offer. And if you overhear someone ordering feesh and sheeps while you're waiting for your order, don't worry, it's just an Aussie from over 'the Ditch'. Likewise, if you hear someone order a sex-pack in a booze store, it'll be another Aussie, this time ordering a six-pack of beer.

VEGETARIANS & VEGANS

Most cafés offer vegetarian food. Ethnic restaurants, particularly Indian and Middle Eastern, generally have plenty of vegetarian dishes. If you're a strict vegetarian you need to ask about the stocks and sauces to ensure that no meat or fish stocks have been used.

It's harder for vegans, but again, ethnic is the way to go.

Over 60% of NZ cheese is made from a natural rennet substitute, making it unsuitable for vegetarians.

EATING WITH KIDS

Kids in cafés are fine, especially during the day and early evening. Many places provide highchairs for toddlers, or a roped-off area for them to play.

It's another matter in fine dining establishments, which, like airlines with their business-class travel, rarely encourage patrons to bring along young children.

Check out what Auckland and Wellington restaurants have to offer at www.menus.co.nz.

THINGS TO DO IN AUCKLAND

Want to grab part of the action? If you're in Auckland, head to a supermarket. The mussel is such a part of everyday life in NZ that big tanks of green shell mussels are installed in most supermarkets. Scoop up a bagful and head over the harbour bridge, or take the ferry, to Northcote and make your way to Little Shoal Bay. Wash the mussels under the free tap and cook them on the hotplate of a pay-for barbecue, and sit on the shelly beach and look back at the bridge and the city of Auckland. It's a cracker of a view, and if you've remembered the savvie (sauvignon blanc), many of which come with a screwcap so you don't even need a corkscrew, you'll have yourself a fine repast. Nearby, Chelsea Park and Birkenhead Wharf also make good picnic spots.

Also on the North Shore, Takapuna and Cheltenham beaches (about a 12-minute drive from the CBD) are good for swimming (p116) when the tide is in. Before heading there, pick up some hot smoked salmon and bread from Seamart (p134) in Fanshawe St at the bottom of town, a bottle of sauvignon blanc, and picnic Kiwi-style with your toes in the water as you marvel at Rangitoto Island, an Auckland icon.

Take the ferry to Waiheke (a 40-minute trip), and have a casual lunch at a winery, or great fish and chips at Oneroa Fish & Chips (p153). Taste the olive oils at Rangihoua Estate, Rocky Bay.

Go on a West Auckland wine trail (p144).

THINGS TO DO OUT OF AUCKLAND

Visit the Hawkes Bay farmers market (every Sunday; p399), and the Village Growers Market (p399) on Saturdays from November to March in Havelock North, and go on a wine trail (p398).

In Kaikoura, go on a fishing boat, catch a fish and have a great chef cook it for you while you sit back and enjoy the breathtaking scenery and sample local wines.

DOS & DON'TS

■ Do take a bottle of wine, or a small gift of chocolates or flowers, if you're invited to some-one's place for a meal.

■ Do offer to bring some meat, or at least a salad, if you're invited for a barbecue.

■ Do remember the drink-driving laws (see p713). If you intend drinking more than the limit, organise a taxi (they cannot be hailed on the street) or a dial-a-driver (a twosome, one of which will drive you home in your car, followed by his or her mate in their car).

■ Do turn up on time for a restaurant reservation; if you're late you may lose your table.

■ Do ask for a corked wine (smells of dirt and cobwebs) to be replaced or return it to its source and exchange it for another.

■ Do tip for good service – it's optional, not expected, but always appreciated.

■ Don't light up a cigarette anywhere without checking first as you risk offending others, and it's now illegal to smoke in many public places (including restaurants, pubs and bars).

■ Don't belch at the table – it is considered the height of bad manners.

■ Don't tip for bad service – ever.

An exception would be ethnic restaurants, especially midrange or inexpensive Italian and Chinese. Italians seem to accept children happily in most circumstances.

There is a heritage of good Chinese cooking, usually Cantonese, in many places in NZ. It was the first foreign food many of us ate in the 1950s and '60s. Yum cha sees large Chinese families from grandma down to great-grandchildren nodding over their noodle bowls, alongside Kiwi families, the young of which amuse themselves by swinging the 'lazy Susan' tables at mind-boggling speed to see what they can deposit in their parents' laps.

HABITS & CUSTOMS

When the 19th-century migrants arrived here from Britain, they found ample fertile land at their disposal. It bred an aura of generosity as there was plenty to go around. Cooks always added 'one more for the pot' just in case an unexpected visitor turned up. The tradition continues to this day and the visitor can't help but notice the Kiwis' genuine warmth, openness and hospitality.

If you receive an invitation with the words 'bring a plate', don't turn up with an empty plate or they'll hoot with laughter. What they really want is for you to contribute some food, like a 'pot-luck' dinner. If you don't have cooking facilities, it is quite acceptable to buy something ready-made.

Auckland Region

Both a region and a thriving metropolis, Auckland (in Maori, 'Tamaki Makaurau') stretches from the Bombay Hills of the south to the Whangaparaoa Peninsula in the north and revels in a wonderful climate plus a clutch of natural and manmade attractions.

The city itself displays some greediness in nestling between not one, but two picturesque harbours – a narrow strip of land sandwiched between Waitemata and Manukau harbours. Auckland is surrounded by more sandy beaches and beautiful islands than seems entirely fair, even for a country blessed with a surfeit of glorious geography. The city proper boasts verdant parks and gardens, terraced volcanic hills where Maoris once lived in *pa* (fortified villages), a full cultural and sporting calendar, steep streets of gaily painted wooden houses and numerous opportunities to live the good life. Head west of the city if the region's vineyards, thunderous surf beaches and lush rainforest beckon.

The region seems to combine the energy of a quasi-capital (although windy Wellington down south is the actual capital) with the country's need to pack in as many outdoor and over-stimulating activities as possible. Pack the brown underpants for a full roster of daredevil leaps out of aeroplanes and off bridges, descents from towers and rock faces, shoulder-testing paddle-based activities, surfing safaris, biking adventures and dolphin swimming. The self-proclaimed 'City of Sails' presents some of the world's greatest opportunities to partake in yachting and other harbour-based pursuits, while tramping can take place on the mainland or in any of the gulf's great island escapes. All this and a full menu of multi-cultural delights (washed down with the region's wines) means that Auckland is one hell of a destination – in case the view from the flight in didn't alert you to the fact.

HIGHLIGHTS

- Getting nautical on **Waitemata Harbour** (p115)

- Visiting quirky little **boutiques** (p140) in Auckland's city centre

- Exploring Maori and other Polynesian cultures at the **Auckland Museum** (p109)

- Taking a ferry to a nearby island – volcanic **Rangitoto** (p147), vineyard-laden **Waiheke** (p149) or bird-paradise **Tiritiri Matangi** (p154)

- Perusing **Devonport** (p113) for art and craft shops, or the ultimate B&B getaway

- Jumping off **Sky Tower** (p116) or **Auckland Harbour Bridge** (p116)

- Canyoning in the **Waitakere Ranges** (p145) or surfing on the black-sand beaches of **Muriwai** (p146), **Piha** or **Karekare** (p145)

★ Piha Beach
★ Karekare Beach
★ Muriwai Beach
★ Rangitoto Island
★ Waitemata Harbour
★ Waitakere Ranges
★ Devonport
★ Auckland City
★ Waiheke Island
★ Tiritiri Matangi Island

■ TELEPHONE CODE: 09

■ www.aucklandnz.com

■ www.arc.govt.nz

cultural dining and a vibrant music scene into day and night are your thing, then Auckland is your kind of place. If relaxing and enjoying the natural beauty of one of the world's best-located harbour cities (with numerous great beaches) and plenty of walks in nearby parks appeal, then all this is possible too. Auckland makes it easy to enjoy all that's on offer, and deserves her reputation as the 'true' capital of the country.

HISTORY

Maori settlement in the Auckland area dates back at least 800 years. Initial settlements were concentrated on the coastal regions of the Hauraki Gulf islands, but gradually the fertile isthmus became settled and land was cleared for growing food. From the 17th century, tribes from outside the region challenged the local Ngati Whatua tribe for this desirable place. The locals in response built *pa* (fortified villages) on Auckland's numerous volcanic cones. But when the first Europeans arrived in the area in the 1830s they reported a land largely devoid of inhabitants. The Auckland isthmus (Tamaki Makaurau – literally, 'Tamaki Desired by Many') had largely been forsaken, either ravaged by war or the threat of it.

From early colonial times the country's administrative centre had been at Russell in Northland, but after the signing of the Treaty of Waitangi in 1840, Captain William Hobson, New Zealand's first governor, moved the capital south to Auckland because of its fine harbour (Waitemata, meaning 'Sparkling Waters'), fertile soil and more central location. Hobson named the settlement after his commanding officer George Eden (Lord Auckland). Beginning with just a few tents on a beach at Official Bay, the settlement grew quickly and soon the port was kept busy exporting the region's produce, including kauri timber. However it

AUCKLAND REGION FACTS

Eat: Breakfast at Dizengoff (p136)
Drink: Lion Red
Read: *Pavement* magazine
Listen to: Die! Die! Die!
Watch: *bro*Town, an animated comedy series about five very un-PC Auckland teenagers
Swim at: A place where dolphins are
Festival: Pasifika Festival (p119)
Tackiest tourist attraction: Sky Screamer (p116)

Climate

Summer months in the Auckland region have an average of eight days of rain, but the climate is fickle, with 'four seasons in a day' at any time of the year.

Getting There & Around

Auckland is the country's main transport hub, with an international and domestic airport, long-distance bus services and tours to all parts of the North Island and on to the South Island. There are trains to Wellington, and the local trains that service the Auckland region have been upgraded. Stagecoach provides a comprehensive bus service.

Every sort of car can be hired, and Auckland is the best place to buy or sell a cheap car. Ferries provide an escape to nearby islands.

For more information on getting to and from Auckland city see p141.

AUCKLAND

pop 1.2 million

Auckland city inspires both her inhabitants and her visitors with a staggering location, mild climate and wealth of things to see and do. If cramming cultural activities, extreme sports, business opportunities, multi-

TOP ACTIVITIES

- Leap off your choice of Auckland architecture (p116)
- Clamber up cliffs and slide down waterfalls in the luscious Waitakere Ranges (p116)
- Brave the rip (with care!) and surf at Piha (p145) or Muriwai (p146)
- Join Auckland's sailing fraternity – this is the 'City of Sails' after all (p115)
- Put a mountain bike through its paces amidst the rugged scenery of Great Barrier Island (p156)

MAORI NZ: AUCKLAND

Auckland's traditional name, Tamaki Makaurau (Tamaki Desired by Many), reflects the region's popularity in ancient times. With two magnificent harbours for food, a warm climate and plentiful hills for building defensive *pa* (fortified villages), this was an area in demand. The Ngapuhi tribe, from further north, raided the area often, most recently as part of the so-called 'Musket Wars' (p34) of the early 19th century.

The major *iwi* (tribe) of the Auckland area was the Ngati Whatua, but these days there are Maori from almost all NZ's *iwi* living here, often collectively known as Ngati Akarana, or the Auckland Tribe.

Many of Auckland's iconic hills (p114) show the sculptured trenches of Ngati Whatua *pa*. The Auckland Museum (p109) has great displays on Maori culture, as well as a daily live song-and-dance performance. You'll hear Ngati Whatua's fairly commercial Mai FM on 88.6MHz on your radio dial. Devotees of Maori history should visit Bastion Point (p114), where in 1978 the Ngati Whatua were joined by thousands of other New Zealanders in what was to become a watershed battle for land rights.

Potiki Adventures (p117) provides Maori-flavoured activities both urban and rustic.

---

lost its capital status to Wellington after just 25 years.

Since the beginning of the 20th century Auckland has been NZ's fastest-growing city and its main industrial centre. Political deals may be done in Wellington, but Auckland is the big smoke in the land of the long white cloud.

ORIENTATION

The commercial heart of the city is Queen St, which runs from the Britomart station near the waterfront up to Karangahape Rd (K Rd). On the way it passes Aotea Square, and comes within a few blocks of the landmark Sky Tower. Viaduct Harbour, west of the main waterfront area, is a dining and activity precinct.

While the central district has accommodation, restaurants and nightlife, K Rd, with its inexpensive restaurants, boisterous bars and clubs is a lively, bohemian, sometimes gritty, alternative. Parnell Rd, located just east of the city centre, is a street of renovated wooden villas converted into restaurants, cafés and boutiques, and continues to the mainstream fashion outlets in Newmarket. Just west of the city centre is Ponsonby Rd,

AUCKLAND IN...

Two Days

Breakfast in **Vulcan Lane** (p134) and take the Link bus to **Auckland Museum** (p109) for the Polynesian galleries and Maori culture show. Take the bus back into the city centre and scale the heights of **Sky Tower** (p116) to get your bearings. If you feel adventurous, take part in one of the activities based in the tower, such as Sky Jump or Vertigo Climb. Head down to **Viaduct Harbour** (p115) and book a tour of the harbour for the next day before dining and bar-hopping around the harbour (p134).

Day two, take your booked tour then return to the city to view the **Auckland Art Gallery** (p112) before boarding a ferry to **Devonport** (p113) for a walk up one or two extinct **volcanoes** (p114). Finish off with a shop in the city's cool little **boutiques** (p140). Or, take a bus to **Kelly Tarlton's Antarctic Encounter & Underwater World** (p111), followed by **kayaking** (p116) or other water sports at **Mission Bay** (p114), before dining there as the sun sets.

Four Days

Squeeze in visits to the **New Gallery** (p112) at the Auckland Art Gallery and to **Otara Markets** (p141), or learn to surf or sail (p115). Dine in **Ponsonby** (p136) then cruise around the bars, live-music venues and dance clubs in **K Rd** (p138).
Spend day four on a **Hauraki Gulf island** (p147) such as Waiheke or Rangitoto.

GREATER AUCKLAND

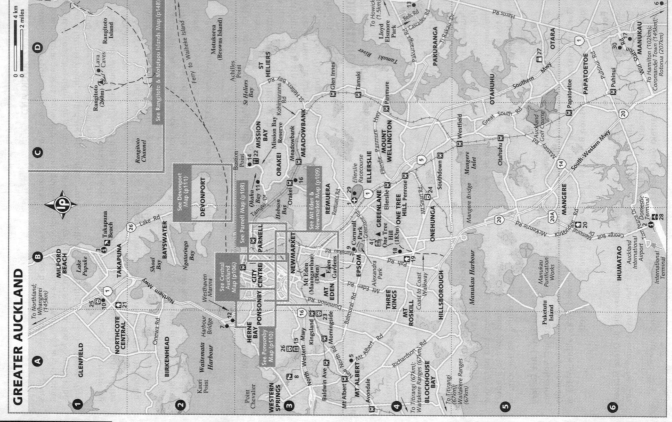

packed with a string of cafés, bars and more boutiques.

Further out, Mt Eden, Takapuna and Mission Bay are residential suburbs with restaurants, bars and cafés. Devonport, easily reached by ferry across the harbour, is a quaint waterside suburb on the southern tip of the residential North Shore, with beaches and what seems like a thousand B&Bs. Bush walks, surf beaches and wineries lie west, in the Waitakere Ranges.

The airport is 23km south of the city centre, but the airbus, shuttle minibuses and taxis can transport you to the city (see p142).

INFORMATION

Bookshops

Borders (Map p106; ☎ 09-309 3377; 291 Queen St; ☉ 10am-10pm Sun-Thu, 10am-midnight Fri-Sat) For books, music and DVDs in the Sky City Metro Centre.

Hard to Find But Worth the Effort Secondhand Bookshop (Map p111; ☎ 09-446 0300; 81a Victoria Rd, Devonport; ☉ 9.30am-5.30pm)

Whitcoulls (Map p106; ☎ 09-356 5400; 210 Queen St; ☉ 8am-6pm Mon-Thu, 8am-9pm Fri, 9am-6pm Sat, 10am-6pm Sun) Another large bookshop with good NZ, travel and fiction sections.

Women's Bookshop (Map p110; ☎ 09-376 4399; 105 Ponsonby Rd; ☉ 10am-6pm) A community resource as well as a good independent bookshop.

Emergency

Ambulance, Fire Service & Police (☎ 111)

Auckland Central Police Station (Map p106; ☎ 09-302 6400; cnr Vincent & Cook Sts)

Maps

Auckland Map Centre (Map p106; ☎ 09-309 7725; www.aucklandmapcentre.co.nz; 209 Queen St; ☉ 9am-5.30pm Mon-Fri, 10am-4pm Sat, 10am-2pm Sun)

Internet Access

Expect to pay from $2 to $4 an hour at the numerous Internet cafés, a few of which are open 24 hours.

Internet Resources

Auckland NZ (www.aucklandnz.com) Lots of tourist information.

Auckland Regional Council (www.arc.govt.nz) Information about Auckland's parks and transport.

Dine Out (www.dineout.co.nz) Locals' comments on local restaurant.

Heart of the City (www.hotcity.co.nz) Detailed, up-to-date events and attractions info.

Medical Services

Ascot Accident & Medical Clinic (Map p104; ☎ 09-520 9555, 90 Greenlane Rd E, Remuera; ☉ 24hr)

Auckland City Hospital (Map p108; ☎ 09-379 7440; Park Rd, Grafton; ☉ 24hr) This is the main accident and emergency hospital.

Travel Care Medical Centre (Map p106; ☎ 09-373 4621; Lvl 1, 125 Queen St; ☉ 9am-5.30pm Mon-Fri, 10am-5pm Sat) Specialises in health care for travellers, such as vaccinations and travel consultations.

Media

Aucklander (www.theaucklander.co.nz) A free publication available six times a week, with lots of local interest features.

New Zealand Herald (www.nzherald.co.nz) The country's biggest newspaper, with a comprehensive entertainment magazine, Time Out, on Saturdays.

Pavement A glossy, arty quarterly with a local focus and a dash of international flavour. Available in newsagents and various boutiques.

Money

There are plenty of moneychangers, banks and ATMs, especially on Queen St. For

INFORMATION		
Ascot Accident & Medical Clinic..	1	C4
Domestic Airport Visitors		
Centre..............................	2	B6
Takapuna Visitors Centre............	3	B1

SIGHTS & ACTIVITIES		
Acacia Cottage......................	4	B4
Albetton House......................	5	A4
Auckland Botanical Gardens..........	6	D6
Auckland Harbour Bridge		
Bungy Jump..........................	7	A2
Auckland Zoo........................	8	A3
Cornwall Park.......................	9	B4
Dive Centre.........................	10	B1
Fergs Kayaks........................	11	C3
Gulfwind Sailing Academy............	12	A2
Harbour Bridge Experience.......(see 7)		
Howick Historical Village...........	13	D4
Kelly Tarlton's Antarctic		
Encounter & Underwater		
World..............................	14	C3
Motel..............................	15	A3
Orakei Scuba Centre.................	16	C3
Penny Whiting Sailing..........(see 12)		
Rainbow's End Adventure		
Park...............................	17	D6
Stardome Observatory................	18	B4

SLEEPING		
Dukes Midway Lodge..................	19	B4
Jet Inn............................	20	B6
North Shore Top 10 Holiday		
Park...............................	21	B1

EATING		
Hammerheads........................	22	C3

ENTERTAINMENT		
Eden Park..........................	23	A3
Ericsson Stadium....................	24	C4
North Shore Events Centre...........	25	B1
Supertop.......................(see 24)		
Western Springs Stadium.............	26	A3

SHOPPING		
Otara Markets......................	27	D5

TRANSPORT		
Auckland International Airport......	28	B6
Ellerslie Racecourse................	29	C4
Manukau City Centre.................	30	D6

CENTRAL AUCKLAND

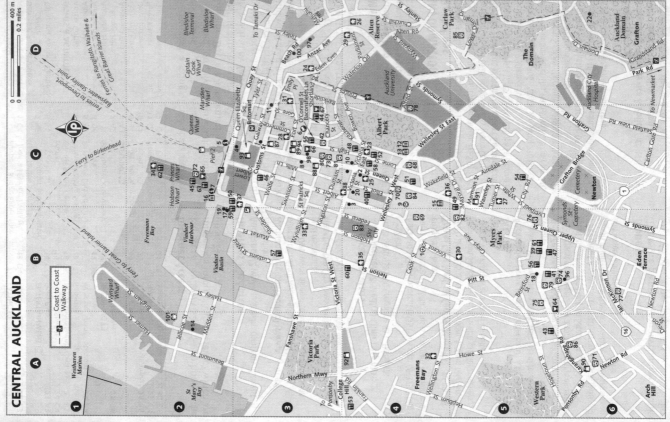

www.lonelyplanet.com

400 m
0.2 miles

Coast to Coast Walkway

INFORMATION
ASB Bank.........................(see 93)
Auckland Central Police Station....1 B4
Auckland Map Centre................2 C4
Auckland Visitors Centre.........(see 83)
Automobile Association (AA)........3 C4
Borders..........................(see 84)
Discover New Zealand...............4 C3
DOC Information Centre..............5 C3
Irish Embassy......................6 C3
NZ Visitors Centre.................7 C3
Travel Care Medical Centre.........8 C3
Wellesley St Post Office...........9 C4
Whitcoulls........................10 C4

SIGHTS & ACTIVITIES
Adventure Cycles..................11 C3
Auckland Art Gallery (Main).......12 C4
Auckland Art Gallery (New)........13 C4
Auckland Fish Market..............14 A2
Auckland Town Hall................15 C4
Dolphin & Whale Safari...........(see 17)
Fullers Cruise...................(see 4)
Great Sights.....................(see 15)
Kawau Kat Cruises.................16 B2
National Maritime Museum..........17 B2
Ocean Rafting....................(see 16)
Pride Centre......................18 B5
Pride of Auckland................(see 16)
Sail NZ...........................19 B2
Scenic Tours.....................(see 4)
Sky Jump..........................20 C4
Sky Screamer.....................(see 83)
Sky Tower.........................20 C4
Sky Tower Vertigo Climb..........(see 83)
Tepid Baths.......................21 B3
Wintergarden......................22 D6

SLEEPING
Albert Park Backpackers...........23 C4
Aspen House.......................24 D3
Auckland Central
  Backpackers.....................25 C4
Auckland City Hotel...............26 D4
Auckland International YHA.........27 C5
Base Auckland.....................28 C3
Braemar on Parliament.............29 D4
City Lodge........................30 B5
Fat Camel Hostel..................31 D3
Freeman's B&B.....................32 A4

Heritage Auckland.................33 B3
Hilton Hotel......................34 C4
Rainbow Hotel.....................35 B4
Scenic Circle Airedale
  Hotel...........................36 C4
Sebel Suites......................37 C3
Sky City Grand Hotel.............(see 83)
Surf & Snow.......................38 C4

EATING
Alleluya.........................(see 17)
Atrium on Elliot.................(see 42)
Brazil...........................(see 42)
Café Melba........................39 B5
Caluzzi...........................40 C4
City Lunchbox.....................41 B5
Euro..............................42 C3
Food Alley........................43 A5
Food for Life.....................44 C3
Foodoo............................45 C2
Kangnam Station Korean
  Restaurant......................46 C4
Kermadec Restaurant &
  Brasserie.......................47 B5
Mecca Café........................48 C4
Mentatz...........................49 C5
New World Supermarket.............50 C2
No 5 Wine Bistro..................51 C4
O'Connell St Bistro...............52 C4
Rasoi.............................53 A4
Seamart Deli & Café...............54 C5
Sheinkin..........................55 C3
Soul..............................56 B5
Toto..............................57 B3
Verona............................58 C4
White.............................59 B2
Wildfire..........................60 B4

DRINKING
Bubble Champagne..................61 B5
Bar..............................(see 52)
Gin Room.........................(see 55)
Honey............................(see 66)
Kamo.............................(see 65)
Lenin Bar.........................62 B2
Minus 5 Bar......................(see 65)
Occidental Belgian Beer
  Café............................63 C2

ENTERTAINMENT
Academy Cinema....................68 C4
Aotea Centre......................69 B4
Civic.............................70 C4
Classic Comedy Club..............(see 49)
Dogs Bollix.......................71 A6
Float.............................72 C2
Fu Bar............................73 C2
Galatos...........................74 B6
Ibiza.............................75 B5
Khuja Lounge......................76 B5
Kings Arms Tavern.................77 B6
Maidment Theatre..................78 C5
NZ Film Archives..................79 B5
Papa Jack's Voodoo Lounge.........80 C3
Rakinos...........................81 C3
Silo Theatre......................82 C3
Sky City..........................83 B4
Sky City Metro Centre.............84 C4
Sky City Theatre.................(see 83)
Sky City Village Megascreen......(see 84)
Starlight St Tennis Courts........85 D5
Urge..............................86 A6

SHOPPING
Aotea Square Market..............(see 69)
Backpackers Car Market...........(see 55)
Champions of the World............87 C3
Kathmandu.........................88 C3
Little Brother....................89 C3
Mala Brajkovic...................(see 55)
Pauanesia.........................90 A6
R&R Sport.........................91 C5
Real Groovy Records...............92 A4
Victoria Park Market..............93 A4
Westfield Downtown
  Shopping Centre.................(see 83)

TRANSPORT
Air New Zealand...................95 C3
Backpackers Car Market............96 B6
Car Rental Companies..............97 D3
Ferry Building...................(see 15)
Fullers Ferries..................(see 15)
Magic Travellers Network..........98 C3
Qantas Travel Centre..............99 C4
Sky City Coach Terminal..........(see 83)
Stray............................100 D3
Subritzky Ferry Terminal.........101 A2

White Lady........................94 C3

weekend banking visit the **ASB Bank branch** (Map p106; 9am-4.30pm Mon-Fri, 9am-4pm Sat & Sun) in the Westfield Downtown Shopping Centre.

Post

Wellesley St post office (Map p106; 7.30am-5pm Mon-Fri) Near Aotea Square. It's the place to pick up poste restante mail (ID is required).

Tourist Information

Auckland Visitors Centre (Map p106; 09-363 7182; www.aucklandnz.com; cnr Victoria & Federal Sts; 8am-8pm) in the Sky Tower Atrium and frequently busy.

Automobile Association (AA; Map p106; 09-377 4660; 99 Albert St; 9am-5pm Mon-Fri, 9am-5pm Sat) Has maps and accommodation directories.

Department of Conservation Information Centre (DOC; Map p106; 09-379 6476; www.doc.govt.nz; Ferry Bldg, 99 Quay St; 10am-5.30pm Mon-Fri, 10am-3pm Sat)

Devonport i-SITE (Map p111; 09-446 0677; www.tourismnorthshore.org.nz; 3 Victoria Rd; 8.30am-5pm) Has a list of b&bs, paid internet access and the *Old Devonport Walk* pamphlet, which guides you around the many historic buildings. For more information view www.devonport.co.nz.

Discover New Zealand Visitor Centre (Map p106; 05-307 4000; www.discovernewzealand.com; 180 Quay St; 9am-5pm)

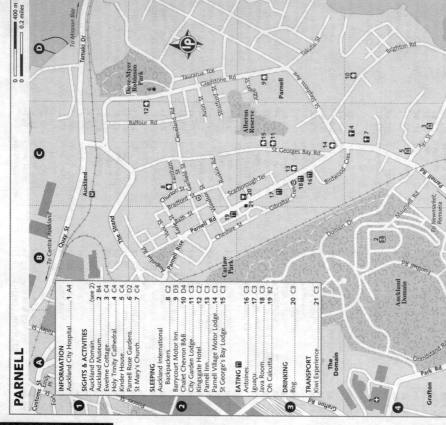

PARNELL

INFORMATION	
Auckland City Hospital..............1 A4

SIGHTS & ACTIVITIES	
Auckland Domain...................(see 2)	
Auckland Museum....................2 B4	
Ewelme Cottage.....................3 C4	
Holy Trinity Cathedral..............4 C4	
Kinder House.......................5 C4	
Parnell Rose Gardens................6 D2	
St Mary's Church...................7 C4	

SLEEPING	
Auckland International	
Backpackers.........................8 C2	
Barrycourt Motor Inn................9 D3	
Chalet Chevron B&B................10 D4	
City Garden Lodge.................11 C2	
Kingsgate Hotel...................12 C2	
Parnell Inn.......................13 C3	
Parnell Village Motor Lodge.......14 C3	
St George's Bay Lodge.............15 C3	

EATING	
Antoines.........................16 C3	
Iguaçu...........................17 C3	
Java Room........................18 C3	
Oh Calcutta......................19 B2	

DRINKING	
Bog..............................20 C3	

TRANSPORT	
Kiwi Experience..................21 C3	

Domestic Airport Visitors Centre (Map p104; ☎ 09-256 8480; ⏰ 7am–5pm) Is in the Air New Zealand section of the domestic airport, which is a short walk from the international airport.

NZ Visitors Centre (Map p106; ☎ 09-307 0612; nzvc@aucklandnz.com; 137 Quay St; ⏰ 8.30am–6pm Mon–Fri, 9am–5pm Sat & Sun) At Princes Wharf, it covers the entire country.

Takapuna Visitors Centre (Map p104; ☎ 09-486 8670; www.tourismnorthshore.org.nz; 49 Hurstmere Rd; ⏰ 8.30am–5pm Mon–Fri, 10am–3pm Sat & Sun) Covers the less touristy North Shore.

Visitors Information Centre (☎ 09-275 6467; ⏰ 1st flight–last flight) It's located on your left as you exit the customs hall. You can make free calls to Auckland accommodation providers from here.

SIGHTS
Sky Tower
The impossible to miss **Sky Tower** (Map p106; ☎ 09-363 6400; www.skycity.co.nz; cnr Federal & Victoria Sts; adult/child/backpacker/student $18/8/10/13; ⏰ 8.30am–10.30pm Sun–Thu, 8.30am–11.30pm Fri & Sat) is part of the Sky City complex, a 24-hour casino with restaurants, cafés, bars and a hotel. At 328m it is the tallest structure in the southern hemisphere and a lift takes you up to the observation decks in 40 stomach-lurching seconds; look down through the glass floor panels if you're after an extra kick with your ride. It costs $3 extra to catch the skyway lift to the ultimate viewing level. Late afternoon is a good time to go up, and the Sky Lounge sells beer, wine

and coffee, which you can sip as the sun sets. It's a great way to get your bearings when you first arrive, and boasts excellent views for up to 80km around the city. See p115 for the Sky Jump and the Sky Tower Climb.

Auckland Museum

This monumental-looking **museum** (Te Papa Whakahiku; Map p108; ☎ 09-309 0443; www.akmuseum .org.nz; admission by donation, suggest adult/child $5/free; ☑10am-5pm) sits atop a sweeping expanse of lawn that forms part of the Auckland Domain, one of Auckland's oldest parks. The museum has a comprehensive display of Pacific Island and Maori culture on the ground floor, including a magnificent 25m-

long war canoe. The 1st floor is dedicated to the natural world and has a first-class activities centre for children (plus some great life-size imitations of past giants like the moa). The 2nd floor focuses on New Zealanders at war, from the 19th century to the peace-keeping assignments of today. It also includes a nifty re-creation of Auckland shops as they would have appeared in 1866.

For many, the highlight of a visit to the museum is the performance of Maori song and dance by **Manaia** (☎ 09-306 7048; adult/ concession & child $15/12). The informal shows at 11am, noon and 1.30pm provide a good (and good-humoured) introduction to Maori culture.

MT EDEN & NEWMARKET

SIGHTS & ACTIVITIES	
Eden Gardens.........................1	C3
Highwic House.......................2	D3
Lion Breweries.......................3	C2
Olympic Swimming	
Pool...................................4	D2

SLEEPING 🏠	
Bamber House.......................5	B3
Bavaria B&B...........................6	A4
Oaklands Lodge......................7	B4

Off Broadway	
Motel...................................8	D3
Pentlands Backpackers............9	A4

EATING 🍴	
Circus Circus.........................10	B4
Footown 24-Hour	
Supermarket.........................11	A4
Frasers...............................(see 12)
Molten............................(see 12)
Mt Eden Village....................12	B4

Tea Time Café.......................13	D3
Zarbo.................................14	D2

ENTERTAINMENT 🎭	
Rialto Cinema........................15	D3

SHOPPING 🛍	
Kate Sylvester.......................16	D3
Two Double Seven Shopping	
Complex..............................17	D3
Zambesi...............................18	D2

www.lonelyplanet.com

At the time of research, major construction was taking place round the back of the museum.

It's about a 25-minute walk from Queen St through the domain to the museum, or you can catch either the Link or Explorer Bus to Parnell Rd, from where it's an easy short walk.

National Maritime Museum

This **museum** (Map p106; ☎ 0800 725 897, 09-373 0800; www.nzmaritime.org; cnr Quay & Hobson Sts; adult/student & child $12/6; ☉ 9am-6pm Oct-Apr, 9am-5pm May-Sep) is the place to learn about NZ's seafaring history. It's a well-designed, extensive display of dozens of boats, from Maori canoes and immigrant ships to jetboats, and includes the history of the America's Cup. Interesting re-creations include a tilting 19th-century steerage-class cabin and a fab '50s-era bach.

An old steamboat, *SS Puke*, is moored outside the museum and runs free 20-minute trips around the harbour on either Saturday or Sunday between 11am and 3pm. The **Ted Ashby** (adult/student & child $15/7, with museum admission $19/12), a flat-bottomed scow, operates one-hour cruises from the museum at noon and 2pm on Tuesday, Thursday, Saturday and Sunday.

Auckland Fish Market

No self-respecting city with a position like this should be without a **fish market** (Map p106;

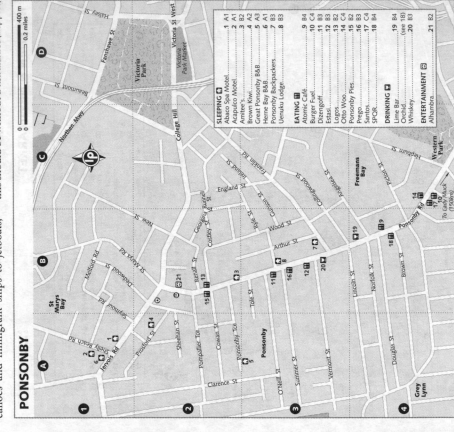

PONSONBY

SLEEPING
Abaco Spa Motel	1 A1
Acapulco Motel	2 A1
Amitee's	3 B2
Brown Kiwi	4 A2
Great Ponsonby B&B	5 A3
Herne Bay B&B	6 A1
Ponsonby Backpackers	7 B3
Uenuku Lodge	8 B3

EATING
Atomic Café	9 B4
Burger Fuel	10 C4
Dizengoff	11 B3
Estasi	12 B3
Logos	13 B2
Otto Woo	14 C4
Ponsonby Pies	15 B2
Prego	16 B3
Santos	17 C4
SPQR	18 B4

DRINKING
Lime Bar	19 B4
Orchid	(see 18)
Whiskey	20 B3

ENTERTAINMENT
Alhambra	21 B2

400 m
0.2 miles

DEVONPORT

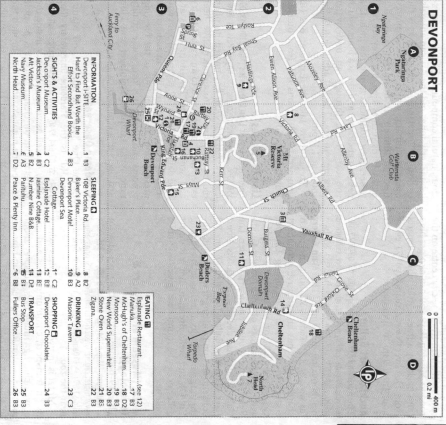

INFORMATION
Devonport i-SITE 1 B3
Hard to Find But Worth the
  Effort Secondhand Books 2 B3

SIGHTS & ACTIVITIES
Devonport Museum 3 C2
Jackson's Museum 4 B2
Mt Victoria 5 B2
Navy Museum 6 A3
North Head 7 D2

SLEEPING
108 Victoria Rd 8 B2
Baker's Place 9 A2
Devonport Motel 10 B3
Devonport Sea
  Cottage 11 C2
Esplanade Hotel 12 B3
Jasmine Cottage 13 B3
Number Nine B&B 14 D2
Parituhu 15 D2
Peace & Plenty Inn 16 B3

EATING
Esplanade Restaurant .... (see 12)
Manuka 17 B3
McHugh's of Cheltenham 18 D2
Monsoon 19 B3
New World Supermarket 20 B3
Stone Oven 21 B5
Zigana 22 B3

DRINKING
Masonic Tavern 23 C3

SHOPPING
Devonport Chocolates 24 B3

TRANSPORT
Bus Stop 25 B3
Fullers Office 26 B3

© 09-379 1490; www.aucklandfishmarket.co.nz; cnr Jellicoe & Daldy St; ☑ daily), and this one not only has a boisterous early-morning auction, but also a market and a seafood school, where you can learn how to cook either your catch or your purchase.

Kelly Tarlton's Antarctic Encounter & Underwater World

Housed in old stormwater and sewage holding tanks is this unique and beguiling **aquarium** (Map p104; © 0800 805 050, 09-528 0603; www.kellytarltons.co.nz; 23 Tamaki Dr; adult/child $26/10; ☑ 9am–6pm). A transparent tunnel runs along the centre of the aquarium, through which you travel on a conveyor belt, with the fish, including sharks and stingreys, swimming

around you. You can step off at any time to take a closer look.

The big attraction, however, is the permanent winter wonderland known as Antarctic Encounter, which includes a walkthrough a replica of Scott's 1911 Antarctic hut, and a ride aboard a heated Snow Cat through a frozen environment where a colony of King and Gentoo penguins lives at sub-zero temperatures. Displays include an Antarctic scientific base of the future and exhibits on the history of Antarctica. Needless to say, this whole experience is a fantastic adventure for adults travelling with children.

To get there take bus 74 to 76 from outside Britomart station, or the Explorer Bus (p118). It's 6km from the city centre on the road to Mission Bay. You can also get here (and back) by a free shuttle, which departs from Discover New Zealand (p107) every hour from 9am to 4pm daily.

Auckland Art Gallery

The **Auckland Art Gallery** (Map p106; ☎ 09-307 7700; www.aucklandartgallery.govt.nz; admission free, exhibitions adult/child $7/3; ☑ 10am-5pm) is housed in two neighbouring buildings. The **Main Gallery** (cnr Wellesley St E & Kitchener St), built in French chateau-style, has an extensive permanent collection of NZ art, including Charles Goldie's stark Maori portraits of a vanished age. Foreign artists of note include Guido Reni, Gainsborough and Mark Gertler. The Gallery café has a deck that overlooks Albert Park. The **New Gallery** (cnr Wellesley & Lorne Sts) concentrates on contemporary art, with intriguing works by local artists such as Seung Yul Oh and Stella Brennan. Ten private art galleries can be found near these two public galleries.

Motat (Museum of Transport & Technology)

This 19-hectare trainspotting paradise of a **museum** (Map p104; ☎ 0800 668 286, 09-815 5800; www.motat.org.nz; Great North Rd, Western Springs; adult/child $14/7; ☑ 10am-5pm) is at Western Springs near the zoo.

Motat is in two parts. Motat I has exhibits on transport, communications and energy, including vintage cars, a display about pioneer aviator Richard Pearse and the infotainment Science Centre, with hands-on displays.

Motat II features rare and historic aircraft as well as railway and military hardware. Exhibits include a V1 flying bomb and a Lancaster bomber from WWII, but pride of place goes to the huge Solent flying boat that ran a Pacific islands loop in the days of luxury flying. Electric trams run every 20 minutes from Motat I to Motat II and the zoo.

To get there, take the Explorer Bus (p118), or bus 045 from outside Britomart station.

Auckland Zoo

Although the **Auckland Zoo** (Map p104; ☎ 09-360 3800; www.aucklandzoo.co.nz; Motions Rd; adult/child $16/8; ☑ 9.30am-5.30pm) is not huge, it has spacious, natural compounds. The primate exhibit is well done, and the African animals' enclosure, Pridelands, is excellent, as is the meerkat domain, which can be explored through tunnels. A nocturnal house has native birds such as kiwi, but they are hard to see. New additions to the zoo include a penguin enclosure and the sea lions, which you can watch through an underwater viewing window. The last admission to the zoo is at 4.15pm.

To get there take the Explorer Bus (in summer; p118), or bus 045 from outside Britomart station.

Lion Breweries

Feeling thirsty? **Lion Breweries** (Map p109; ☎ 09-358 8366; www.lionzone.co.nz; 380 Khyber Pass Rd, Newmarket; adult/child $15/7.50) has turned its plain old brewery tours into an interactive 'beer experience', as opposed to an excuse to try and score free beer. Two-hour tours are held daily at 9.30am, 12.15pm and 3pm and include a history of brewing, an audiovisual presentation, a virtual tour of the brewing process and, thank the lord, some quality time spent sampling Steinlager and Lion Red beers in a replica brew house.

Stardome Observatory

In the One Tree Hill domain, off Manukau Rd, is the **Stardome Observatory** (Map p104; ☎ 09-624 1246; www.stardome.org.nz; adult/child $12/6). As well as viewing the sky inside the planetarium, on clear nights it is possible to view the night sky and stars through the courtyard telescopes. The night sky can also be viewed through a large 50cm telescope (adults per use $8). The hour-long Stardome Show in the planetarium is not dependent on Auckland's fickle weather and is usually held on Wednesday to Saturday evenings (phone the observatory or check the website for scheduled times).

Historic Buildings

The NZ Historic Places Trust owns three worthy 19th-century properties with period furnishings that give an insight into the lifestyle of wealthy pioneer families in Auckland. **Alberton House** (Map p104; ☎ 09-846 7367; 100 Mt Albert Rd; adult/child $7.50/free; ☑ 10.30am-noon & 1-4.30pm Wed-Sun) is a classic colonial-style mansion that offers detailed tours and was used as a location for some scenes in *The*

Piano. **Highwic House** (Map p109; ☎ 09-524 5729; 40 Gillies Ave; adult/child $7.50/free; ☑ 10.30am–noon & 1-4.30pm Wed-Sun) occupies a stellar hill-top position, has lush landscaped grounds and is a marvellous example of 19th-century 'Carpenter Gothic'. The exterior resembles Parnell's St Mary's Church (see below), while the inside is a nicely maintained wood-panelled museum that re-creates the interior style of 1862, despite a disconcerting Star Wars Toy Show that was on when we popped in. Entry is via Mortimer Pass.

Ewelme Cottage (Map p108; ☎ 09-379 0202; 14 Ayr St; adult/child $7.50/free; ☑ 10.30am–noon & 1-4.30pm Fri-Sun) is a storybook-like affair that was built for a clergyman in the 1860s and has been left in startlingly good condition, much as it was for the family that called it home.

Close to Ewelme Cottage is the simply restored **Kinder House** (Map p108; ☎ 09-379 4008; 2 Ayr St; adult/child $4/1; ☑ 11am-3pm Tue-Sun), which was built of volcanic stone in 1857. Designed by Frederick Thatcher, it displays the subtle but skilful watercolours and memorabilia of the Rev Dr John Kinder (1819–1903), who was the headmaster of the Church of England Grammar School. Enthusiastic and informative guided tours are provided.

St Mary's Church (Map p108; Parnell Rd; ☑ 10am-4pm Mon-Sat, 11am-4pm Sun) is a wonderful example of a wooden Gothic Revival church (1886), with a stunning burnished wooden interior and lovely stained-glass windows. It was transported to this spot from across the road in one piece back in 1982. Next door is **Holy Trinity Cathedral** (Map p108; Parnell Rd), which is worth seeing for its modern stained-glass windows. Its blue-coloured rose window, designed by English artist Carl Edwards, is particularly striking above the simple kauri altar.

In southeastern Auckland, **Howick Historical Village** (Map p104; Bells Rd, Pakuranga; adult/child $12/6; ☑ 10am-4pm) is an interesting collection of 30 restored 19th-century buildings, including a thatched sod cottage, forge, school, toy museum and chapel, with tours conducted by guides in period costume.

Devonport

Devonport is a quaint and charming suburb on the tip of Auckland's North Shore peninsula, easily reached by ferry from the centre of Auckland. One of the earliest areas of European settlement, it retains traces of a 19th-century atmosphere with many well-preserved Victorian and Edwardian buildings. Since it makes such an easy day trip from the city, it can be touristy and has lots of small shops, art and craft galleries, a couple of bookshops and plenty of cafés. There are beaches and loads of B&Bs plus magic views of the Auckland city skyline from the foreshore, especially in the evening.

There are also several museums worth a look: the **Navy Museum** (Map p111; ☎ 09-445 5186; Spring St; admission by donation; ☑ 10am-4.30pm) is a must for sea-dogs and covers the history of the NZ navy, which is based in Devonport; **Jackson's Muzeum** (Map p111; ☎ 09-446 0466; Victoria Rd), is an eccentric collection of NZ historical memorabilia and a true testament to one man's passion for collectables, sadly it was up for sale when we visited, with the owner hoping for the local council to take up the baton; and **Devonport Museum** (Map p111; ☎ 09-445 2661; 31a Vauxhall Rd; admission free; ☑ 2-4pm Sat & Sun), which chronicles Devonport's history for a select few hours each week.

The 12-minute ferry ride to Devonport departs from the Auckland Ferry Building every 30 minutes from 6.15am to 11pm (until 1am Friday and Saturday), and 7.15am to 10pm on Sunday and public holidays. The last ferries back from Devonport are at 11.30pm Monday to Thursday, 1.15am Friday and Saturday, and 10.30pm Sunday. The fare is adult/child $5.20/2.20 for a one-way ticket, $9/4.40 for an open return. The last ferries from the city to Devonport are at 11pm Monday to Thursday, 1am Friday and Saturday, and 10pm Sunday.

Buses to Devonport run regularly from outside Britomart station, but you have to pass through Takapuna and traffic can be slow. The ferry crossing is much quicker and far more enjoyable.

Fullers has ferries to Waiheke and Rangitoto Islands that call in at Devonport (Map p111).

The two volcanic cones in Devonport, Mt Victoria and North Head, were once Maori pa. **Mt Victoria** (Map p111) is the higher of the two, with a great 360-degree view and a gun emplacement at the top. It's a steep 10-minute walk to the summit from Victoria Rd. You can drive up but the gate is closed at 6.30pm in winter and 8.30pm in summer

NONE TREE HILL?

The 183m **One Tree Hill** (Map p104), or Maungakiekie (Mountain of the Kiekie Tree), is a distinctive bald hill, topped only by a huge obelisk and, until 2001, a lone Monterey pine. It was the largest and most populous of the Maori *pa* (fortified villages), supporting a population of 5000 people for many years. The terracing and dugout storage pits are still visible.

North Head (Map p111), on the other cone, is an historic reserve riddled with fortifications and old tunnels built at the end of the 19th century in response to fears of a Russian invasion that never quite eventuated. The tunnels were extended and enlarged during WWI and WWII, and some of the old guns are still here. The reserve is open to vehicles from 6am to 6pm daily and to pedestrians until 10pm. See Walking Tour (p117) for more information.

K Rd & Ponsonby

Just south of the central city area, straight up the hill from Queen St, is Karangahape Rd, known simply as **K Rd** (Map p106). In recent years artists and media companies have moved in, and the street has a growing number of nightclubs, cafés and ethnic restaurants, plus a few red-light businesses.

K Rd runs southwest to Ponsonby Rd and the fashionable suburb of **Ponsonby** (Map p110). Behind historic shopfronts, Ponsonby Rd's many restaurants, bars and cafés are abuzz with sociable chatter of caffeine fiends, fashion hints from the city's swishest sales assistants and the incessant tones of mobile phones and text messaging. It's a leafy, pretty spot and offers lots of options for tipplers and tasters.

Tamaki Drive

This scenic coastal road, lined with pohutukawa trees, which turn red at Christmas time, crosses Hobson Bay to **Orakei**, where you can hire kayaks and in-line skates at Fergs Kayaks (p116). It continues past Kelly Tarlton's Antarctic Encounter & Underwater World (p111) to **Bastion Point** (Map p104), which was occupied by members of the Ngati Whatua tribe in a 1978 land protest. The garden memorial to an early La-

bour Party prime minister, Michael Joseph Savage, has a good viewpoint.

Tamaki Drive continues to **Mission Bay** (Map p104), which has a popular beach with water sports and alfresco restaurants and bars. Further on, **St Heliers Bay** (Map p104) is smaller and more relaxed. Further east along Cliff Rd, the **Achilles Point lookout** (Map p104) has dramatic views of the city, harbour and Hauraki Gulf.

You can hire a bicycle and cycle along this route, or else take a bus (74 to 76).

Extinct Volcanoes

Auckland is punctuated by some 48 volcanoes, many of which provide parkland retreats and great views. The view from **Mt Eden** (Maungawhau; Map p109), the highest volcanic cone in the area at 196m, is superb. You can see the entire Auckland area – all the bays and the land between Manukau Harbour and Hauraki Gulf – and look 50m down into the volcano's crater. You can drive to the top or take bus 274 or 275 and then walk.

Parks & Gardens

Albert Park (Map p106) is a charming spot in the city centre to relax or have a picnic surrounded by flowerbeds and historical monuments, such as the 1899 statue of Queen Victoria.

Covering about 80 hectares, the **Auckland Domain** (Map p108), near the centre of the city, is a gloriously large public park that contains the Auckland Museum (p109), sports fields and the **Wintergarden** (Map p106; ☎ 09-379 2020; admission free; ☷ 9am–4.30pm), with its fernery, tropical house, cool house and café.

On Gladstone Rd in Parnell is the **Parnell Rose Gardens** (Map p108), which is in bloom from November to March.

The **Eden Gardens** (Map p109; ☎ 09-638 8395; 24 Omana Ave, Epsom; adult/child $5/free; ☷ 10am–4.30pm), on the slopes of Mt Eden, is a wonderful showpiece noted for camellias, rhododendrons and azaleas.

Popular for jogging, picnics and walks, **Cornwall Park** (Map p104; www.cornwallpark.co.nz) adjoins One Tree Hill on Greenlane Rd and is an extensive pastoral retreat only 6km south of the city centre. It has sports grounds, fields of grazing sheep, a visitors centre (Huia Lodge), historical **Acacia Cot-**

tage (Map p104; admission free; 7am-dusk) and a restaurant.

The 65-hectare **Auckland Botanical Gardens** (Map p104; ☎ 09-267 1457; Hill Rd; admission free; 8am-dusk) has a café and great new(ish) native plant and edible gardens, plus a hell of a lot of brides and grooms. To get there take bus 471 but it's a 20-minute walk along Hill Rd from the bus stop in South Mall, Manurewa.

ACTIVITIES

Auckland has become an adventure capital in recent years, so there's no shortage of challenging activities should walking the city's many hills fail to cut it in the excitement stakes. Look around for backpacker reductions or special offers before booking anything.

Cruises

Fullers Cruises (Map p106; ☎ 09-367 9111; www.fullers .co.nz) has lots of cruises and operates almost all the ferries that run from the Ferry Building in Quay St. Fullers runs 1½-hour harbour cruises (adult/child $30.40/15.40, includes a free return ticket to Devonport), which 'run at 1.30pm and visit a variety of sights. Ferries go to many of the nearby islands in the gulf. Rangitoto and Waiheke are easy to reach and make good day trips from Auckland.

Kawau Kat Cruises (Map p106; ☎ 0800 888 006, 09-425 8006; www.kawaukat.co.nz) also runs 1½-hour harbour cruises (adult/child $30/15), which depart at 10.30am, 1.30pm, 3pm and 5pm (the latter is one hour and $20/15 per adult/child) and tour all the harbour sights. Between Christmas and Easter boats run from Auckland to Kawau Island and on varying days of the week to Coromandel Town (adult one way $45/25, return $75/45), on the other side of the Hauraki Gulf.

Ocean Rafting (Map p106; ☎ 0800 801 193, 09-577 3194; www.oceanrafting.co.nz; Viaduct Basin) is a fast inflatable boat that whips you round the harbour or further out into the gulf. A one-hour trip out to Rangitoto costs adult/child $70/35. Based in the Viaduct Basin, bookings are essential for the Waiheke trip ($130/70).

Walking

The visitors centres and the DOC office have pamphlets on walks in and around

Auckland. DOC's *Auckland Walkways* pamphlet has a good selection of forest and coastal day walks outside the metropolitan area.

The **Coast to Coast Walkway** (16km, four hours, Map p104) is a north-south walk between the Viaduct Basin on Waitemata Harbour and Onehunga Bay on Manukau Harbour. The walk encompasses Albert Park, the university, the domain, Mt Eden, One Tree Hill and other points of interest, keeping as much as possible to reserves rather than city streets. Starting from the Viaduct Basin and heading south it's marked by yellow markers and milestones; heading north from Onehunga there are blue markers. The visitors centre has a detailed brochure and map showing the walk and describing sights along the way.

Sailing

Hey, this is the 'City of Sails' and nothing gets you closer to the heart and soul of Auckland than sailing on the harbour, plus the views are delightful.

SAIL NZL (Map p106; ☎ 0800 724 569, 09-359 5987; www.sailnewzealand.co.nz; Viaduct Basin; adult/child $125/110) This experienced and highly regarded outfit, with America's Cup yachts, has a variety of sailing tours and races on offer.

Pride of Auckland (Map p106; ☎ 09-377 4557; www.prideofauckland.com; adult/child 45min cruises $48/26, 1½hr cruises $58/32), based next to the Maritime Museum, offers sailing trips round the harbour. The 1½-hour cruise with lunch costs $68 (child $37) and a 2½-hour dinner cruise is also available for $95 (child $58).

Gulfwind Sailing Academy (Map p104; ☎ 09-521 1554; www.gulfwind.co.nz; Westhaven Marina) can provide day sailing cruises ($299 for four people), as well as personalised tuition and flexible small-group sailing courses for beginners or experienced sailors. Courses run all year, and a two-day RYA Start Sailing Learn to Sail costs $495. Westhaven Marina is a 10-minute walk from Victoria Park.

Penny Whiting Sailing (Map p104; ☎ 09-376 1322; www.pennywhiting.com; Westhaven Marina; courses $555) runs courses that consist of five three-hour practical sailing lessons. Courses run from November to March, and small-group tuition can also be arranged.

Spiderman Activities

Auckland Harbour Bridge Bungy Jump (Map p104; ☎ 09-361 2000; www.ajhackett.com; Westhaven Reserve, Curran St; 🕑 8.30am-6pm) offers a 40m leap off the bridge and a quick dip in the harbour for $85 no matter what the weather. Hours are extended in the summer months.

Sky Jump (Map p106; ☎ 0800 759 586, 09-368 1835; adult/backpacker, student & child $195/145; 🕑 10am-5.30pm) is a 192m, 16-second, 75kph base wire jump from the observation deck of the Sky Tower. It's more like a parachute jump than a bungy jump and is a rush and a half.

Sky Screamer (Map p106; ☎ 09-575 0548; www.reversebungy.com; cnr Albert St & Victoria St W; ride $35; 🕑 10.30am-10pm Sun-Thu, 10.30am-2am Fri & Sat) involves being strapped into a seat and being thrown 70m up in the air. Should you hurl, rest assured, you can get a video of it.

Harbour Bridge Experience (Map p104; ☎ 09-361 2000; www.ajhackett.co.nz; Westhaven Reserve, Curran St; climb $65) is a 1½-hour guided climb that involves climbing the arch of Auckland's big bridge. You wear a climbing suit with a harness attached to a static line. Bookings are essential, and night climbs are available upon request.

Sky Tower Vertigo Climb (Map p106; ☎ 0800 483 784, 09-368 1917; www.4vertigo.com; adult/child/backpacker & student $145/75/125) involves climbing *inside* the Sky Tower mast up to the crows nest, 80m above the observation deck – and all while wearing an orange jumpsuit. These climbs take 1½ hours.

Dolphin Swimming

Dolphin & Whale Safari (Map p106; ☎ 09-357 6032; www.dolphinsafari.co.nz; adult/child $140/100; 🕑 10.30am-4pm) has daily dolphin swimming trips departing at 11am from Viaduct Harbour. Common or bottlenose dolphins, orcas and Bryde's whales can all be seen. Swimming with dolphins is strictly controlled (eg only common dolphin can be swum with and no swimming is allowed if there are baby dolphins sleeping or feeding). Wet suits, masks, snorkels and fins are provided. If you don't see any dolphins and whales you can take another trip for free.

Canyoning

Awol Canyoning (☎ 0800 462 965, 09-834 0501; www.awoladventures.co.nz; half-/full-day $125/155) offers abseiling down waterfalls, sliding down rocks and jumping into pools in the Waitakere Ranges. Pick-up from Auckland, lunch and snacks are included in the price. The whole day trip takes from 9.30am to 5pm but the actual canyoning takes two to three hours. Night trips using headlamps can also be arranged.

Canyonz (☎ 0800 422 696, 09-815 9464; www.canyonz.co.nz; trips $145 or $225) runs canyoning trips to Blue Canyon or Sleeping God Canyon (the latter in the Coromandel Region), and offers a $30 discount if you want to do both.

Skydiving

Skydive Auckland (☎ 0800 865 867; www.skydiveauckland.com) offers a tandem skydive from 3660m (12,000ft; including a 5000ft free fall) for $250. A video costs $125 or a video and photos are $150. It all takes place at Mercer airfield, 55km south of Auckland.

Swimming

Auckland is noted for its fine and varied **beaches** (Map p144), which are dotted around the harbours and coastline. The east coast beaches along Tamaki Drive, including Mission and St Heliers Bays, are popular and can be very crowded in summer. At most east coast and harbour beaches swimming is best at high tide. Popular North Shore beaches include Cheltenham, Takapuna, Milford, and further north, Browns Bay and Long Bay. The west coast beaches such as Piha and Muriwai are great for surfing but have dangerous currents and rips (see above).

The **Tepid Baths** (Map p106; ☎ 09-379 4754; 100 Customs St; adult/child $5.50/3; 🕑 6am-9pm Mon-Fri, 7am-7pm Sat & Sun) have two undercover pools, a sauna, spa bath and steam rooms. It's a bargain, and a session in the fitness centre is $16.50.

Olympic Swimming Pool (Map p109; ☎ 09-522 4414; 77 Broadway, Newmarket; adult/child/student $6.50/4/5.50; 🕑 5.45am-10pm Mon-Fri, 7am-8pm Sat & Sun) has a spa, steam room and sauna as well as a large indoor pool. Use of the fitness centre is $20 and there's a crèche (☎ 09-522 1532) on the premises.

Parnell Saltwater Pools (☎ 09-373 3561; Judges Bay Rd; adult/child $5/3; 🕑 6am-8pm Mon-Fri, 8am-8pm Sat & Sun Nov-Apr) are outdoors, and the pools and sunbathing areas are popular in summer. Disabled access is good.

Water Sports

Fergs Kayaks (Map p104; ☎ 09-529 2230; www.fergskayaks.co.nz; 12 Tamaki Dr, Okahu Bay; 🕑 9am-6pm Mon-

Fri, 8am-6pm Sat & Sun) hires out kayaks ($10 to $18 per hour or $35 to $55 a day) and in-line skates (per hour/day $15/30). Day and night guided kayak trips are available to Devonport (8km, 4½ hours, $75) or Rangitoto Island (13km, six hours, $95).

For good, challenging surf less than 50km from the city, try Piha, Muriwai or Te Henga (Bethells Beach) on the west coast, where the water is often very rough. Most of the surfing beaches have surf clubs and lifeguards.

NZ Surf Tours (☎/fax 09-828 0426; www.newzealandsurftours.com; 1-/5-day $99/699) runs day-long surfing courses (October to June) that include transport, equipment and two surf lessons in the day. A five-day small-group course includes accommodation, transport and food.

Dive Centre (Map p104; ☎ 09-444 7698; www.divecentre.co.nz; 128 Wairau Rd, Takapuna) is a well-regarded operation with a large dive shop, PADI courses (beginner's course $499), and a 15m boat for local dive trips to Little Barrier Island ($100), Mokohinau Island ($110) and the Hen and Chickens Islands ($100 to $110).

Orakei Scuba Centre (Map p104; ☎ 09-524 2117; www.orakeidive.co.nz; 234 Orakei Rd) has a dive shop and runs PADI courses (Open Water from $479 with practice dives at the Poor Knights Islands).

Other Activities

Potiki Adventures (☎ 0800 692 3836, 021 422 773; tours $130) has Maori-style adventures that get heaps of praise and are an excellent way of getting in touch with Maori history, culture and mythology via activities such as abseiling, snorkelling and digging for shellfish. Highly recommended.

Extreme 4WD Adventures (☎ 0800 493 238; www.extreme4wd.co.nz; 1-2 drivers $122) offers driving a 4WD around a special two-hour adventure trail near Helensville behind a guiding vehicle. Training courses are also available.

4 Track Adventures (☎ 09-420 8104; www.4trackadventures.co.nz; 1hr/2hr/3hr tours $125/185/225) offers you a chance to drive a quad bike through Woodhill Forest (beach ride included on the two- and three-hour tours). Pick up from Auckland is $30 per person.

One good little outfit, **Kiwispirit** (☎ 09-476 7841; www.kiwispirit.co.nz day/trips $49 or $149), offers the choice of a day a day at Piha Beach (three departures a day) or the Coromandel Peninsula (one departure daily).

If whizzing around the harbour in a hovercraft is your thing, then **Hover NZ** (Map p106; ☎ 3800 468 371; www.hovernz.co.nz; Viaduct Harbour; rides from $40) is your operator.

Balloon Expeditions (☎ 09-416 8590; www.balloonexpeditions.co.nz; ride $250) and **Balloon Safaris** (☎ 09-415 8289; www.balloonsafaris.co.nz; ride $270) both do early morning hot-air balloon flights that take about four hours (one hour in the air) with breakfast and a bottle of bubbles.

Adventure Cycles (Map p106; ☎ 09-309 5566; 36 Customs St E; ☀ 7am-7pm) hires out road and mountain bikes ($18 to $35 a day). Cycle along Tamaki Drive to Mission Bay, or put the bike on a ferry and cycle around Devonport.

Snowplanet (☎ 09-427 0044; www.snowplanet.co.nz; 91 Small Rd, Silverdale; day pass adult/child from $59/49; ☀ 10am-10pm Sun-Thu, 10am-11pm Fri & Sat) is a winter wonderland that allows every day to be a snowy one, with indoor skiing, tobogganing and airboarding. To get there, take State Highway 1 (SH1) to 30km north of Auckland, exit at Silverdale, then follow the signs.

Amusement Parks

Apparently, you owe **Rainbow's End Adventure Park** (Map p104; ☎ 09-262 2030; www.rainbowsend.co.nz; cnr Great South & Wiri Station Rds, Manukau; super pass adult/child 4-13 yrs old $39/29; ☀ 10am-5pm) to your family. And luckily, it has enough rides (including a corkscrew roller coaster and the 'Power Surge'), shows and interactive entertainment to keep the kids happy all day, plus plenty of sugary snacks to fuel it all. Super passes allow unlimited rides while an entry-only pass is $22 at peak times.

WALKING TOUR

Start Devonport Wharf
Finish Devonport Wharf
Distance 5km
Duration Around 2½ hours

This walk affords you the experience of being reminded that this modern, bustling city has volcanic origins. Take the ferry from central Auckland to Devonport, a quiet suburb of wooden Victorian villas

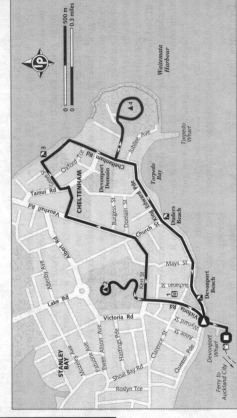

that is almost entirely surrounded by water. Head up Victoria Rd with its many well-preserved historical buildings, and browse the art and craft galleries, cafés, bookshops, antique shops and **Jackson's Muzeum** (**1**; p113). Then walk up the extinct volcanic cone **Mt Victoria** (**2**; p113), to the breathtaking panoramic viewpoint and hidden artillery on the top.

Return to Kerr St and then walk along Vauxhall Rd to sandy **Cheltenham Beach** (**3**; p116). There's a grand view of Rangitoto Island (Auckland's youngest volcano) to enjoy as you walk along the beach before turning right into Cheltenham Rd and then left to **North Head** (**4**; p114). This is another volcanic cone with extensive defence relics and coastal views from the summit. Walk down and back along King Edward Pde, with views of central Auckland, to the ferry wharf.

AUCKLAND FOR CHILDREN

Auckland is child-friendly and has plenty to keep kids entertained. **Mission Bay** has a safe beach, water-sport gear for hire and a playground in sight of a café, while **Rainbow's End Adventure Park** (p117), **Kelly Tarlton's Antarctic Encounter & Underwater World** (p111), and **Auckland Zoo** (p112) are other favourites. **Snowplanet** (p117) is a recent addition to the roster of child-friendly diversions, 30km north of Auckland.

The **Tepid Baths** (p116) has a children's pool and is open year-round. Younger kids would enjoy the **Teddy Bear's Picnic** (opposite).

TOURS

Auckland has plenty of tour operators. Three-hour bus tours will typically take you around the city centre, over the harbour bridge and out along Tamaki Drive, including stops at Mt Eden, the Auckland Museum and Parnell, for about $55.

You can spend a day touring the major Auckland attractions in the hop-on-hop-off **Explorer Bus** (☎ 0800 439 756; www.explorerbus.co.nz; adult/child $30/15). It departs daily from the Ferry Building every half-hour from 9am to 4pm from October to April and every hour from 10.30am to 4.30pm from May to September. The bus runs to Kelly Tarlton's, Mission Bay, Parnell, Auckland Museum, Sky Tower, Victoria Park Market, and back to the Ferry Building.

Scenic Tours (☎ 09-307 7880; 172 Quay St) and **Great Sights** (☎ 09-375 4700; www.greatsights.co.nz; 180 Quay St) are other major operators with city tours as well as tours to the Bay of Islands, Waitomo and Rotorua. Free hotel pick-up and drop-off is usually included with city tours.

Auckland Adventures (☎ 09-379 4545; www .aucklandadventures.co.nz; afternoon/day tours $85/120) Runs good-value tours. The afternoon one (12.45pm to 5pm) includes Muriwai gannet colony, an orchard, wineries and Mt Eden, while the day tours (9am to 5pm) can also include a hike or mountain-biking experience.

Bush & Beach (☎ 09-837 4130; www.bushand beach.co.nz) Offers a tour to the Waitakere Ranges (including hiking) and Karekare Beach for $95, among others.

Devonport Tours (☎ 09-357 6366; 2hr/3hr/dinner tours $30/55/70) Popular tours that put this neighbourhood to good use.

Fine Wine Tours (☎ /fax 09-849 4519; www.insidertouring.co.nz; 4hr tours $139) Tours the West Auckland wineries ($119) and has a deluxe harbour cruise wine tour ($400).

Geotours (☎ 09-525 3991; www.geotours.co.nz; half-/full-day tours $90/120) Offers cerebral trips led by a geologist who can explain Auckland's volcanic cones and other geological features, as well as flora and fauna.

Ports of Auckland Tours (☎ 09-367 9111; Ferry Bldg; admission free; ☑ 11am Wed) These handy 50-minute tours will get you up to speed on the life of a busy city harbour in no time. Bookings essential; tours depart from Pier 3.

Wine Trail Tours (☎ 09-630 1540; www.winetrail tours.co.nz; half-/full-day tours $95/150) Has small-group tours around the West Auckland wineries and the Waitakere Ranges as well as trips further afield to Matakana ($175). Highly recommended.

FESTIVALS & EVENTS

The visitors centre keeps a list of the many annual events held in Auckland, or view www.eventsauckland.com.

January

ASB Classic (Women) Watch some leading tennis players warm up for the Aussie Open; held early January.

Heineken Open (Men) See some famous tennis names in action as the season gets under way in Stanley St; held mid-January.

Auckland Anniversary Day Regatta The 'City of Sails' lives up to its name; held 30 January.

February

Mission Bay Jazz & Blues Streetfest New Orleans comes to the Bay as jazz and blues bands line both sides of the street as the sun sets; held early February.

Devonport Food & Wine Festival Sip and sup with the smart set at this two-day festival in mid-February.

Asia NZ Lantern Festival Three days of Asian food and culture in Albert Park to welcome the lunar New Year.

Teddy Bears Picnic Held in the Auckland Domain in mid-February, with all sorts of free entertainment aimed at children.

HERO Festival Gay-fest with events such as the Chocolate Fish Swim Meet at the Tepid Baths and the Big Gay Out; held late February.

March/April

Auckland Cup Week Try to spot the winner at the biggest horse race of the year.

Pasifika Festival Western Springs Park hosts this excellent (and giant) Polynesian party with music, dancing and food, held in early to mid-March.

Waiheke Jazz Festival The wine island is booked up months ahead for this annual music fest at Easter, although 2005's fest was cancelled, so check www.waihekejazz.co.nz beforehand.

Royal NZ Easter Show Fun for all the family with an agricultural flavour.

May/June

Oddfellows NZ International Comedy Festival Weeks-long laughfest with local and international comedians; held mid-May to early June.

NZ Boat Show One of the world's best yachting nations shows off its wares – find something to float your boat. Held in early June.

August

K Rd Fringe Arts Festival If it's to the left of centre you can revel in it in this cool multidenominational (theatre, film, art, dance, music and poetry) artfest. Runs into September.

September

Auckland Art Fair Started in 2005 and looks like a goer. Visit www.aucklandartfair.co.nz.

Air New Zealand Fashion Week Is any country (other than Australia) better qualified to show what you can do with merino wool and a sense of imagination? Find the next Karen Walker or Kate Sylvester here. Held in mid- to late September. Visit www.nzfashionweek.com.

October

Ao Tearoa Hip Hop Summit A celebration of all things hip-hop, from graffiti art to MCing and DJing. Held at Aotea Square and Auckland Town Hall, with panel discussions and workshops, plus performances.

November

Ellerslie Flower Show Five days of flowers, music and food lure crowds of visitors to Auckland and Botanical Gardens in mid-November.

December

Christmas in the Park A party so big it has to be held in the Auckland Domain.

First Night A free and alcohol-free music party in Aotea Square & Centre on 31 December.

SLEEPING

Our price listings for Auckland fall into the following accommodation categories: budget – doubles (with or without bathroom) for under $100; midrange – doubles (with bathroom) between $101 and $200; top end – doubles (with bathroom) more than $201.

Budget

Dorm prices range from $23 to $28, singles without bathrooms generally go for around $50 but can be hard to find, while doubles and twins without bathrooms usually cost $60 a night, and en suite rooms cost around $90. Prices can be a few dollars less if you have a backpacker card.

CENTRAL AUCKLAND

Hostels

Auckland has plenty of hostels in the city centre and inner suburbs, but you will still need to book ahead in summer. The city centre has the biggest hostels in town, mostly on or just off Queen St, but they can be crowded and parking is a problem. For greater ease and a more laid-back feel, try the hostels in Parnell, Mt Eden or Ponsonby.

Surf & Snow (Map p106; ☎ 09-363 8889; www.surf andsnow.co.nz; 102 Albert St; dm $23-26, s $50, d & tw $65, d/tr with bathroom $90/120) With hip décor and bright multilingual staff manning the front desk, you could be excused for thinking that this spot's going to break the budget bank, but you'd be wrong. The dorm rooms are shiny and comfy, the carpet's clean, the walls are smooth and the showers were spotless when we visited. Security (the door code changes every week) and storage facilities are good too.

Base Auckland (Map p106; ☎ 09-300 9999; www .basebackpackers.com; 16 Fort St; dm $24-28, d & tw $68, d & tw with bathroom $95) This large backpackers has a café, bar and nightclub, a reading room, a travel agency and a roof deck with a sauna and spa. Dorms have eight to 12 beds, and the cramped en suite rooms have TVs. One floor is reserved for females only.

Everything is well designed with bright colours, big windows and even big mirrors.

Fat Camel Hostel (Map p106; ☎ 09-307 0181; www .fatcamel.co.nz; 38 Fort St; dm $22-26, s, d & tw $52) The Fat Camel rather optimistically promises its guests 'two humps, guaranteed', and while this may prove impossible to provide, the keen, up-for-it young staff here certainly give the impression that they'll try as hard as they can to make sure you're happy. While you'll often feel as though you're trapped in a windowless box, you'll also relish the relatively clean kitchens and bathrooms.

Others worth considering:

Auckland International YHA (Map p106; ☎ 09-302 8200; www.stayha.com; 5 Turner St; dm $25-27, d & tw $72, d & tw with bathroom $88; [P]) The usual big well-organised YHA affair.

Albert Park Backpackers (Map p106; ☎ 09-309 0336; www.albertpark.co.nz; 27 Victoria St; dm $23-25, s/d & tw $50/60)

Hotels

Aspen House (Map p106; ☎ 09-379 6663; www.aspen house.co.nz; 62 Emily Pl; s $55, d & tw $75, r with bathroom $99; [P]) Located on a sweet, steep street a stone's throw from one of Auckland's most intriguing old parks, the Aspen has had a face-lift in recent times, and is a frequently full budget gem. And in a nice touch, it's not just the exterior that's had some work done. An additional 29 rooms have been created under the name 'Aspen Lodge' (right next door) and the original 27 rooms have had a thorough overhaul. Smart, stylish and cheap – perfect!

City Lodge (Map p106; ☎ 09-379 6183; www.city lodge.co.nz; 150 Vincent St; s/d & tw $55/75) City Lodge is a very well-run, purpose-built tower for the budget market. When we visited everything was so bright, shiny and new that we could still smell the springy carpet and the fresh paint, while tiny, stamp-sized bathrooms positively gleamed. Our tip for solo travellers is to try and score a premium single room, as they seem to utilise the space a little better. There are five disabled rooms, a fantastic industrial-style kitchen cleaned daily by housekeepers, and a comfy, modern lounge and TV room.

Auckland City Hotel (Map p106; ☎ 09-303 2463; www.aucklandcityhotel.co.nz; 131 Beach Rd; s/tr $69/99, d & tw $79-84) Stay here if you want cheap, plain and clean-enough rooms with a bathroom in a central location.

Auckland Central Backpackers (Map p106; ☎ 09-358 4877; www.gobeyond.co.nz; lvl 3, 229 Queen St; dm $25, s/d & tw $66, d & tw with bathroom $88) With more than 500 beds (and these are often full) and a veritable network of sightseeing and job-seeking contacts at one's fingertips, this place is where many young visitors to Auckland get their bearings. If you don't like a hive of activity, then you'll need to go elsewhere, as this place hums with questions about where the cheapest places to eat can be found, who's got work where, whether bungy jumping's worth it and where the cute guys/girls are. There's a bar downstairs to aid this last search.

PARNELL

Stylish Parnell is a 30-minute walk to the city centre or you can take the frequent Link bus ($1.50).

City Garden Lodge (Map p108; ☎ 09-302 0880; www.citygardenlodge.co.nz; 25 St Georges Bay Rd; dm $22-24, s $46, tw $48-58, d $58; P) Housed in a character-filled, good-boned two-storey house built for the Queen of Tonga, this friendly and well-run backpackers has a lovely garden, cruisy veranda (with hammock) and high-ceilinged rooms with solid period features. The cheaper dorm has eight beds, the others have three or four and there's a women-only dorm too. If you need privacy, a cute double room will do the trick, and if you need to unwind, indulge in some yoga on the front lawn. Delightful!

Auckland International Backpackers (Map p108; ☎ 09-358 4384; www.aibackpacker.com; 2 Churton St; dm/d & tw $22/52; □) Eat in the sunroom, the easy-going dining room or out in the small garden at this large and rambling but perfectly adequate, comfortable and friendly backpackers. Linen and towels cost extra.

MT EDEN

Mt Eden is a pleasant, quiet and leafy suburb of wooden villas that is a short bus journey from the city centre. All three of these backpackers are part of the Bamber empire.

Bamber House (Map p109; ☎ 09-623 4267; www.hostelbackpacker.com; 22 View Rd; cm $23-26, d & tw $60; P □) The original house here is a good-boned mansion of sorts, with an impressive main staircase and some nicely maintained period trimmings plus plenty of space for its 60-odd guests to stretch out. There's a stack of information and tour bookings available to combat the lethargy that often seems to strike when a hostel is this welcoming. In the newer wing of the property there are modern rooms that accommodate both dorm dwellers and guests wanting rooms of their own.

Also worth trying:

Oaklands Lodge (Map p109; ☎ 09-638 6545; www.oaklands.co.nz; 5a Oaklands Rd; cm $25-27, s $50, d & tw $65) More smart and bright accommodation near Mt Eden village.

Pentlands Backpackers (Map p109; ☎ 09-638 7031; www.pentlands.co.nz; 22 Pentland Ave; dm $23-25, s/d & tw $50/65; P) Colourful and comfortable place with small dorms and a tennis court.

PONSONBY

Uenuku Lodge (Map p110; ☎ 09-378 8990; www.uenukulodge.co.nz; 217 Ponsonby Rd; dm $24, s/d/tw $44/58/60; P) This friendly hostel looks a little flasher on the outside than it does on the inside, but one of its revamped dorm rooms is in very good condition, with lockers, sturdy bunks and floorboards. Other rooms are a little more ramshackle, but there's a decent lounge, large kitchen, good security and an outdoor area. Some of the rooms afford decent views too, and one of the share bathrooms has a bath – a rare and beautiful thing for a hostel.

Brown Kiwi (Map p110; ☎ 09-378 0191; www.brownkiwi.co.nz; 7 Prosford St; dm $24, d & tw/f $55/76; P) Like so many hostels, the outside of this old-fashioned building appeals more than the inside, although this place will certainly do as a cheap head-resting option, and an effort is made to keep it reasonably clean. Dorms have four or eight beds, and the triple rooms are set in the small, verdant garden courtyard.

Ponsonby Backpackers (Map p110; ☎ 0800 476 676, 09-360 1311; www.ponsonby-backpackers.co.nz; 2 Franklin Rd; dm/s/d & tw/f $23/40/60/85; P) Under new (and friendly) management, this place is still finding its feet and might have undergone some reworking by the time you read this. It's a little tatty in corners, although sheets are clean and some of the ceilings are high. The six-bed dorm with the 'turret' has the most atmosphere, but also smells of boy, while the double rooms are white, bright and clean and feel a little sterile. For privacy fiends, nab a whacky old-style caravan for $160 a week.

DEVONPORT

Baker's Place (Map p111; ☎ 09-445 4035; thefleafm@clear.net.nz; 30 Hastings Pde; d $65) This is a smallish, reasonably priced and fully self-contained unit in the garden and includes use of the spa pool. Excellent weekly rates can be negotiated in winter if you fancy a longer stay.

OUTER AREAS

Dukes Midway Lodge (Map p104; ☎ 09-625 4399; www.dukes.co.nz; 4 Vagus Pl, Royal Oak; d $85, unit $100, f unit $160) Dukes brings a touch of Las Vegas to suburban Auckland's Vagus Pl thanks to its rather eye-catching swimming pool, which takes the shape of a guitar. There's no reason for it to exist either, as Duke's is, in every other respect, a run-of-the-mill motor lodge. Rooms are comfortable, with OK beds, cable TV and decent bathrooms, while the quiet location (off busy Pah Rd) means you'll sleep soundly.

OTHER AREAS

Camping grounds with cabins are outside the city centre.

North Shore Top 10 Holiday Park (Map p104; ☎ 09-418 2578; www.nsmotels.co.nz; 52 Northcote Rd, Takapuna; camp sites from $25, dm/tourist flats $38/96, cabins $60-70; 🖳) An indoor pool, spa and 24-hour check-in are all available at this large Top 10 holiday park near Takapuna on North Shore, 4km north of the Harbour Bridge. It's the best in Auckland.

Midrange

Auckland has masses of motels. Costs start at around $100 for a studio double, though prices can be higher. A good area for chintz-heavy B&Bs is Devonport, which is just a 12-minute ferry ride from Queen St.

CENTRAL AUCKLAND

Heritage Auckland (Map p106; ☎ 09-379 8553; www.heritagehotels.co.nz; 35 Hobson St; superior r $199, ste $219-499; 🖳) What stands out at this hotel are the period features from when it was the high-class department store Farmers. A range of high-quality rooms and suites with smart trimmings lure business travellers, while a business centre, bar, gym, tennis court, outdoor and indoor pool, and a sauna keep them happy.

Braemar on Parliament (Map p106; ☎ 09-377 5463; www.aucklandbedandbreakfast.com; 7 Parliament St; r $150-225, ste $295) Braemar is a beautiful place to stay in the city centre with some of the most glorious historical details to have survived the city's inevitable development craze. There's a choice of three rooms and one suite for guests, although the most basic doesn't really cut it if you're after something special as it's a 'below the stairs' affair.

Freeman's B&B (Map p106; ☎ 09-376 5046; www.freemansbandb.co.nz; 65 Wellington St; s/d & tw/f $69/100/149) Freeman's is for those who can't stand to pay top dollar for the privilege of falling asleep somewhere that's not their home. Its location is eminently central, its prices firmly entrenched in the bargain basement and its standards solid. It's not

flash or particularly attractive, but it is clean, well maintained and comfortable, and you'll not want for anything basic. There's a good quiet garden too.

Rainbow Hotel (Map p106; ☎ 09-356 7272; www.rainbowhotel.co.nz; cnr Nelson & Wellesley Sts; studio $85-180) Studio apartments here are all in very good working order, and while the décor is hardly inspiring, you'll find that everything works and nothing offends. However, the smaller studios really are quite pokey, and they get pretty much no natural light (or don't even have a window); fork out for a bigger one and you'll be much more comfortable.

PARNELL

Chalet Chevron B&B (Map p108; ☎ 09-309 0290; www.chaletchevron.co.nz; 14 Brighton Rd; s $95, d & tw $150-160, f $240; 🅿) This charming B&B is in a homey building with a few mock Tudor touches and Lucy the chocolate Labrador giving it an English feel. In fact, you'll sometimes feel as though you're waking up in one of those English whodunits. Old-fashioned rooms have lovely floral wallpaper and fabrics. The best spots are Room 3 (with spiffy new bathroom) and the ground-floor twin rooms with great water views. The downstairs single rooms are comfortable but small.

Parnell Inn (Map p108; ☎ 09-358 0642; parnelin@ihug.co.nz; 320 Parnell Rd; studios $85-120; 🅿) You'll get a chipper welcome at this revamped (new-look furniture and local photography on the walls) and good-looking motel, with smaller studios on your right as you walk down the hall from reception and larger, sunnier rooms on your left; some have great harbour views (Rooms 3 and 4).

Barrycourt Motor Inn (Map p108; ☎ 0800 504 466, 09-303 3789; www.barrycourt.co.nz; 10 Gladstone Rd; lodge units $99, studios $126-252, d & tw $171-180, ste $171-342; 🅿) A mixed bag of more than a hundred motel rooms and units are available in this large, well-maintained complex with friendly multilingual staff. The lodge is spacious but old-fashioned, and the modern (north) wing starts at $171, with some fantastic harbour views. Simple, cheaper rooms with kitchenette in the south wing are a good deal. It has a restaurant-bar-café and hot spa pools.

Kingsgate Hotel (Map p108; ☎ 0800 782 548, 09-377 3619; www.millenniumhotels.com; 92 Gladstone Rd; r $110-130, ste $190; 🅿 🖳) Opposite the lovely Parnell Rose Gardens, this large hotel has smart rooms clustered in landscaped

'Tudor' or 'Colonial' (although they look the same to us) blocks, together with a restaurant and bar; an outdoor pool, hot spa pools and plenty of parking. Popular with tour groups. Bus 703 stops right outside.

Parnell Village Motor Lodge (Map p108; ☎ 09-377 1463; www.parnellmotorlodge.co.nz; 2 St Stephens Ave; studios $95-105, apt $135-150; P) An old and newer section is available in this motel where every unit is different, some have a bit of character, and all have a kitchenette. It's on a busy intersection though, so traffic noise might be a nuisance if you're a light sleeper.

MT EDEN

Bavaria B&B (Map p109; ☎ 09-638 9641; www.bavaria bandbhotel.co.nz; 83 Valley Rd; s/d $99/139; P) This clean, long-running, worn-around-the-edges B&B in a spacious villa offers big and airy, pastel-hued rooms with bathroom. There's a decent TV lounge, dining room and deck where guests can mix and mingle.

Off Broadway Motel (Map p109; ☎ 09-529 3550; www.offbroadway.co.nz; 11 Alpers Ave, Newmarket; studio $99-139, ste $185) The Off Broadway is a dandy little performer in Auckland's accommodation scene and deserves a few Stage Door Johnnies singing its praises. There are three small studios on the premises that will appeal to people seeking a decent room for less than three figures, but the larger studios are a great deal as they have a balcony and bathtub. Executive suites have separate bedrooms and represent very good value.

PONSONBY

Abaco Spa Motel (Map p110; ☎ 0800 220 066, 09-360 6850; www.abaco.co.nz; 59 Jervois Rd; r/studio/ste from $120/199/269; P) The natty Abaco has received a revamp and a half in the last couple of years and is a stylish, neutral-toned escape, a stone's throw from all the good shopping and grazing opportunities. Furnishings in the studios and suites are modern and comfortable, with plenty of fluffy white towels available for spa lovers and slick stainless steel kitchenettes (which include dish drawers and proper ovens). Room 81, on the first floor and down the back, is the best; it affords good views from its balcony.

Herne Bay B&B (Map p110; ☎ 09-360 0309; www.herne-bay.co.nz; 4 Shelly Beach Rd, Herne Bay; d $95, d with bathroom $150, apt $180) This is one of the area's most notable heritage buildings, and it not only has the looks on the exterior, it delivers the goods inside too. If you need a central, stylish B&B experience that's great value, then this is just the place to rest your weary head. Gay-friendly too.

Acapulco Motel (Map p11C; ☎ 09-376 5246; www.acapulcomotel.co.nz; 20 Shelly Beach Rd, Herne Bay; r $115-150; P) Straight out of the 1950s (and with the name to match), the Acapulco's rooms are stuck in a slightly shabby time warp that's got more character than some of the zhooshier options in this neighbourhood. Rooms are spacious indeed, Room 16 is enormous) and could be straight out of a Tarantino film. That said, service is considerate and not in the least bit violent.

DEVONPORT

Devonport has a mind-boggling range of old-fashioned B&Bs ideal for those wanting a quiet and homely place to stay that is only a 12-minute ferry ride from Queen St. Some are in restored 'villas' (lovely old weatherboard houses), while others are modern units set in gardens.

Jasmine Cottage (Map p11; ☎ 09-445 8825; www.photoalbum.co.nz/jasmine/; 23 Buchanan St; B&B cottage $110) The friendly owners, Joan and John, pamper guests who stay in the cute little courtyard hut with spotless kitchenette and a lovely garden, where you can enjoy a nice homemade breakfast. Scrupulously maintained and cute as a button.

Parituhu (Map p11; ☎ fax 09-445 6559; www.parituhu.co.nz; 3 King Edward Pde; s/d $80/100) This very good gay- and lesbian-friendly guesthouse provides a perfect base for travellers looking to have the city at their fingertips with a sense of being able to dip their toes in Auckland's most relaxing neighbourhood. The accommodation consists of one double bedroom with en suite bathroom, and both are in delightful shape. It's not a flash Edwardian-era villa that you're staying in, but it is a very homely, relaxing and welcoming place.

Number Nine B&B (Map p11; ☎ 09-445 3059; tainui@ xtra.co.nz; 9 Tainui Rd; B&B $160) You'll get a warm welcome from Christine and Pari at this cosy home that has two attractive rooms for guests. One is wildly feminine, the other a little more low-key (but with a claw-foot tub), and both are very comfortable. If you fancy a game of golf at the nearby club, you can borrow clubs here and have a round organised.

Devonport Motel (Map p11; ☎ 09-445 1010; www.devonportmotel.co.nz; 11 Buchanan St; units $130) This minimotel has just two self-contained and simple units in the back garden, but they are modern and clean and in a nice quiet location that's still close to Devonport's action (such as it may be).

Devonport Sea Cottage (Map p111; ☎ 09-445 7117; lethabys@ihug.co.nz; 3a Cambridge Tce; cottage $120) Head up the driveway here to your own self-contained cottage that holds everything you'll need for a relaxing stay near the sea (including a set of French doors onto a garden). Excellent weekly rates are also on offer in winter.

Also worth trying is **108 Victoria Road** (Map p111; ☎ 09-446 7565; 108 Victoria Rd; d $100-120; ☒).

OUTER AREAS

Jet Inn (Map p104; ☎ 09-275 4100; www.jetinn.co.nz; 63 Westney Rd; r $145-195, ste $240-295; P ☒) Jet Inn, 4km from the airport, feels like an individual business, even though many of its rooms follow the 'could be anywhere' design ethos that seems to be compulsory if you want to sleep near an airport. One option that we really liked was the 'overnighter' rooms, where you get a proper hotel room, but its dimensions mean that you're not paying for wasted space. Kick back by the pool, which resembles something from an episode of *Hawaii 5-0*.

Top End

CENTRAL AUCKLAND

Hilton Hotel (Map p106; ☎ 09-978 2000; www.hilton.co.nz; Princes Wharf, 147 Quay St; r $295-595; P ☒) Perched at the tip of Princes Wharf, this stylish luxury hotel is almost out to sea. And indeed, it's only fitting that in the 'City of Sails' the swankiest big-name hotel resembles not so much a skyscraper as a large ocean-going liner. Service is courteous and helpful without being in the least stuffy, and amenities like the well-stocked gym and a slither of modernist pool are available to all guests. Rooms are smart, with fantastic bathrooms, and every single one of them (the rooms that is) has a balcony.

Sky City Grand Hotel (Map p106; ☎ 09-363 6000; www.skycity.co.nz; cnr Victoria & Federal Sts; r $620, ste $1030; P ☒) This new place ups the Sky City stakes by being five-star and a truly smart experience. Rooms are beautifully furnished and decorated, with the sort of elaborate bed-making skills that resemble origami, and stunning floral arrangements throughout the shared spaces. Service is amongst the best in the city, with a real feel of 'your wish is my command' from the time you step up to the reception desk.

Sebel Suites (Map p106; ☎ 09-978 4000; www.mirvachotels.com.au; 85 Customs St West; ste $300-550) If you want pole position overlooking Auckland's rejuvenated Viaduct Harbour, then look no further than the Sebel Suites, 133 high-finish, super-stylish apartments with smooth service and lots of top-end details. To take full advantage of it all, you'll really need to snaffle a suite from the marina level up – why stay smack-bang on a harbour such as this and not score a water view? Ask about fantastic weekend rates.

Scenic Circle Airedale Hotel (Map p106; ☎ 09-374 1741; www.scenic-circle.co.nz; 380 Queen St; standard/superior r $225/255, ste $500) This landmark, tiled, Art Deco building in Queen St has been cleverly converted. It features plenty of old-fashioned style plus modern panache, meaning that during the week it's popular with business travellers and during the weekend it's taken over by city-break types. The spaces are sensibly planned, with room for all the necessities such as kitchenettes, but ask for the biggest possible room you can score, with natural light coming in.

PARNELL

St George's Bay Lodge (Map p108; ☎ 09-303 1050; www.stgeorge.co.nz; 43 St Georges Bay Rd; s $140-215, d $215-265, tr $275) This Edwardian-villa B&B has masses of period charm without ever succumbing to cushion overload. It keeps things elegant, attractive and comfortable, and has a prime spot on one of Parnell's most delightful streets.

PONSONBY

Great Ponsonby B&B (Map p110; ☎ 09-376 5989; www.greatpons.co.nz; 30 Ponsonby Tce; r with bathroom $210-350; P) The gregarious owners of this place weren't kidding when they labelled their B&B 'great', because it is. Guests will find it the perfect combination of Auckland's best qualities. Located a stone's throw from cool Ponsonby Rd, the B&B is a deceptively spacious weatherboard villa with lovingly maintained period features, colourful, exotic paint finishes and Pacific Island artworks. Great breakfasts too.

(Continued on page 133)

War canoe, Auckland Museum (p109)

ANDERS B. CHRQVIST

Minus 5° Bar (p138), Princes Wharf, Auckland

PETER BENNETTS

Starlight Symphony, Auckland Domain (p114)

DAVID WALL

Sky Tower (p106), Auckland

CHRIS MELLOR

DAVID WALL

Sail boats (p115), Westhaven Marina, Auckland

DAVID WALL

Oneroa Beach, Waiheke Island (p149)

JENNY JONES

Façade of the New Gallery, Auckland Art Gallery (p112)

JENNY & TONY ENDERBY

Piha Beach (p145), near Auckland

Meeting house, Waitangi National Reserve (p189), Bay of Islands

ANDERS BLOMQVIST

Waipoua Kauri Forest (p172), Northland

ANDERS BLOMQVIST

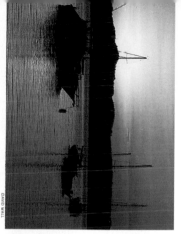

Russell (p193), Bay of Islands

DAVID WALL

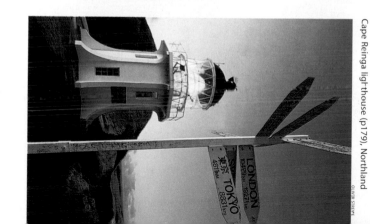

Cape Reinga lighthouse (p179), Northland

OLIVER STREWE

DAVID WALL

Hahei beach (p220), Coromandel Peninsula

OLIVER STREWE

Waitomo Caves (p248), King Country

DAVID WALL

Giant kauri, 309 Road (p216), Coromandel Peninsula

PAUL KENNEDY

Maori carving on a surfboard, Raglan (p237), Waikato

Lake Taupo, Tongariro National Park (p312)

DAVID WALL

Bayview Chateau Tongariro (p319),
Whakapapa

DAVID WALL

Lake Taupo (p294)

MICHAEL COYNE

Mt Ruapehu (p314), Tongariro National Park

RUTH EASTHAM & MAX PAOLI

DAVID WALL

Kiwi 360 (p359), Te Puke, Bay of Plenty

JOHN BANAGAN

Zorbing (p344), Rotorua

DAVID WALL

Whakaari (White Island; p364), Bay of Plenty

DAVID WALL

Champagne Pool, Waiotapu Thermal Wonderland (p347), Bay of Plenty

Hongi greeting, Te Whakarewarewa (p331), Rotorua

ANDRES BLOMQVIST

Prince of Wales' Feathers geyser (p332) at Te Whakarewarewa, Rotorua

DENNIS JOHNSON

Maori statue near Rotorua Museum of Art & History (p331)

KRZYSZTOF DYDYNSKI

Mt Maunganui (p354), Bay of Plenty

DAVID WALL

Entrance to Te Papa museum (p409), Wellington

JENNY JONES

Kapiti Coast (p427) and a distant Kapiti Island

PAUL KENNEDY

Cheap eats (p420), Wellington

PETER BENNETTS

Harbour, Wellington (p403)

DAVID

(Continued from page 124)

Amitee's (Map p110; ☎ 09-378 6325; www.amitees.com; 237 Ponsonby Rd; r $180-275, penthouse $400; P) The newish boutique option on the block is pretty Amitee's, with smart modern rooms with all the fabric trimmings and feature walls your heart desires. The penthouse is like an attic-style apartment, with a loo that might well have the best views in the building. Communal areas like the lounge/kitchen are welcoming and packed with necessities such as high-speed Internet access and a DVD player.

DEVONPORT

Peace & Plenty Inn (Map p111; ☎ 09-445 2925; www.peaceandplenty.co.nz; 6 Flagstaff Tce; B&B $325; ⏹) This perfectly located and truly wonderful five-star period house is stocked with antique furnishings and a thousand conversation pieces, plus the charming Judith, who can tell you the provenance of each and every one of them. The romantic, luxurious rooms have en suite, TV, flowers, free sherry/port and local chocolates. A delight, and easily one of the best B&Bs we've ever seen.

Esplanade Hotel (Map p111; ☎ 09-445 1291; www.esplanadehotel.co.nz; 1 Victoria Rd; r $185-225, ste $295-575) This beautiful boutique hotel takes pride of place on the corner in a 1903 heritage building, with lovingly tended period features such as supremely high ceilings and much more style than most luxury hotels in the city centre. Perfectly located, achingly romantic and with sumptuous rooms that steadfastly refuse to fall into cookie-cutter territory when it comes to décor. Excellent service too. Check for specials and deals.

EATING

Because of its size and ethnic diversity, Auckland tops the country when it comes to eating options and quality. Loads of lively Asian eateries have sprung up to cater for the numerous Asian students, offering inexpensive Japanese, Chinese and Korean staples. Cheap takeaway kebab places are also common in central Auckland. Lorne St, High St and Vulcan Lane are lined with small and smart cafés. West of the city, Ponsonby Rd is by far the best café strip, but Farrell, Mt Eden Village and Newmarket are other options if you haven't just had your hair done. Ponsonby attracts a hip, young crowd who come to drink and dine before heading off to the late-night clubs on K Rd.

The attractive Princes Wharf and Viaduct Basin waterfront area is where some of the buzziest and busiest restaurants have sprung up. This area is popular with the 'after-five' crowd and can be heaving on Friday and Saturday evenings.

Parnell has a more refined and compact eating scene, with a strip of good restaurants mingling with tasteful fashion boutiques and chichi gift shops. Along the coast, Mission Bay has a cluster of restaurants, while Devonport has a street of cafés and restaurants, and is only a short ferry ride from the city centre.

City Centre

RESTAURANTS

O'Connell St Bistro (Map p106; ☎ 09-377 1884; 3 O'Connell St; mains $29-35; ⊗ lunch Tue-Fri, dinner Mon-Sat) The delightful O'Connells is a grown-up treat, with elegant décor and truly wonderful food and wine satisfying lunchtime powerbrokers and dinnertime daters. The menu leans heavily on the duck, salmon and lamb side of things.

Toto (Map p106; ☎ 09-302 2665; 53 Nelson St; mains $24-37; ⊗ lunch Mon-Fri, dinner daily) Italian and NZ wines accompany fine modern Italian cuisine (this was the city's first such restaurant) and there are professional opera singers on Saturday and Thursday ($10 cover charge).

No 5 Wine Bistro (Map p106; ☎ 09-309 9273; 5 City Rd; mains $25-34; ⊗ dinner Mon-Sat) It's all fine dining, jus, caramelised goodies and a great wine list in this formal restaurant in a heritage building with candles, a NZ-meets-Euro menu and smooth service. It enjoys a sterling reputation among the city's better restaurants.

Mentatz (Map p106; ☎ 09-357 0960; 28 Lorne St; dishes $4-25; ⊗ lunch Mon-Fri, dinner daily) Japanese and Korean faves for homesick students dominate the long menu here, where the atmosphere is low-key and friendly and the bill ends up small. Try the spicy cold ramen noodles ($10), or some shiokara ('squid marinated in its own guts', $4) which is true to its description.

City Lunchbox (Map p106; ☎ 09-373 3787; 67 Shortland St; dinner mains $12-19; ⊗ breakfast & lunch

Mon-Fri, dinner Wed-Fri) This smart and spunky-looking lunchtime haunt also does dinner and has fab coffee. Superfat sandwiches make ideal takeaway companions. Friday is challah day, while Monday dishes up the best falafel in town.

CAFÉS

Sheinkin (Map p106; ☎ 09-303 4301; 3 Lorne St; breakfast $4.50-15.50, lunch $8-25; breakfast & lunch) Sheinkin is an airy, arty-looking space with dark wooden floors, white walls and lots of light bulbs, plus plenty of glossy reading material to accompany the perfect café latte and great eats such as feta pie.

Café Melba (Map p106; ☎ 09-377 0091; 33 Vulcan Lane; breakfast $7-17; breakfast & lunch) For breakfast try the egg, salmon or veg Benedict, or the porridge and stewed fruits in this small, old-fashioned but lively café with indoor and outdoor seating.

Mecca Café (Map p106; ☎ 09-309 6300; Vulcan Lane; meals $5-19; breakfast & lunch) Directly opposite Café Melba, it offers plenty of café staples and blessedly good coffee served French-style, in big bowls. Spanish bullfighting paintings and postcards adorn the walls, and service is sweet.

Foodoo (Map p106; ☎ 09-373 2340; 62 High St; meals $9-13; breakfast & lunch, closed Sun) Lots of delicatessen food and some more substantial offerings make a tempting display at this everything-home-cooked café and gourmet takeaway.

Seamart Deli & Café (Map p106; ☎ 09-302 8980; cnr Fanshawe St & Market Pl; 6am-6pm Mon-Sat, 7am-6pm Sun) This is a great place for fresh fish and seafood with a wide choice of sashimi, sushi and deli items to eat in or takeaway. There is lots of parking outside.

Kiwi Music Bar & Café (Map p106; ☎ 09-309 7717; 332 Queen St; regular/large pizzas $12/16; lunch Mon-Fri, dinner daily) This laid-back pizzeria and bar in Queen St plays Kiwi music only, so it's your chance to discover Scribe, Betchadupa and The Phoenix Foundation...

QUICK EATS

Food Alley (Map p106; ☎ 09-373 4917; 9 Albert St; meals $7-10; 10.30am-10pm) For authentic Asian fare, you can't beat this large, no-frills food court where nearly every meal is under $10. Come here for *bibimbap*, *roti chanai*, laksa, claypot, *okonomiyake*, Thai desserts and all your other Asian favourites.

Kangnam Station Korean Restaurant (Map p106; ☎ 09-309 1588; 329 Queen St; meals $9-20; 10.30am-2am Mon-Sat, 5pm-2am Sun) A jovial host and the chance to sample numerous Korean faves and staples make this an easy option for many homesick Korean students in town.

White Lady (Map p106; Shortland St; burgers $10-16; 7.30am-3am Mon-Thu, 24hr Fri-Sun) This long white bus has been in business here serving fast food to drunken late-night revellers since 1950. The burgers are expensive, but big and juicy. The perfect way to soak up a hangover before it hits!

Food courts in central Auckland are mostly open during shopping hours only because they're usually located in shopping centres. Westfield Downtown Shopping Centre (p141) and **Atrium on Elliot** (Map p106; Elliot St) have international food courts.

SELF-CATERING

New World supermarket (Map p106; 2 College Hill Rd; 7am-midnight) This is a monster-sized supermarket for all your food and alcohol needs. The Link bus stops very nearby.

Convenience stores are dotted around the central area and most are open 24 hours.

Viaduct Harbour & Princes Wharf

This great waterfront location is awash with some of Auckland's best restaurants and bars, most of which have outdoor areas to take advantage of the sunshine and the nautical atmosphere.

White (Map p106; ☎ 09-978 2000; Hilton Hotel, Princes Wharf; mains $37; breakfast, lunch & dinner) White is the achingly hip in-house restaurant at the swanky Hilton Hotel. It boasts stark modern décor, silky service, a star chef and some seriously great food. The crispy skin salmon is an obvious winner, but so is the $35 two-course lunchtime special.

Soul (Map p106; ☎ 09-356 7249; Viaduct Harbour; mains $15-50; lunch & dinner daily, brunch Sat & Sun) You can't come to the 'City of Sails' and not eat seafood surrounded by yachts. This modernist gastro-dome boasts an unbeatable Viaduct Harbour location and a reputation for some of the best seafood in the city. Despite its large size, it really packs them in, even at odd hours like 4pm, and the whip-smart service keeps things moving at a brisk pace. Come for the life-changing whitebait fritters and the roll-call of great local wines.

Euro (Map p106; ☎ 09-309 9866; Shed 22, Princes Wharf, mains $31-39; ☑ lunch & dinner) Euro is a thoroughly slick package of imaginative Mod-NZ cuisine, good-looking wait staff and sexy surrounds. The harbour views aren't the greatest, but the dishes are always pretty as a picture. Entrées such as Clevedon oysters with balsamic vinegar are superbly fresh and plump, and perfect with a glass of local fizz.

Kermadec Restaurant & Brasserie (Map p106; ☎ 09-309 0413; Quay St/fish &chips $19-25; ☑ lunch&dinner) This upstairs restaurant with Polynesian décor is run by one of the country's major fish companies. The restaurant and brasserie are next to each other but separate.

Wildfire (Map p106; ☎ 09-353 7595; Princes Wharf, churrasco dinner $43; ☑ lunch & dinner) This Brazilian churrasco (pronounced 'shoohasco') restaurant offers unlimited Brazilian barbecued meats, which are brought to your table, or you can settle for nicely done green-lipped mussels if you need a seafood fix. Brazilian music dominates on Saturday nights.

K Rd

K Rd is known for its late-night clubs, but cafés and plenty of inexpensive ethnic restaurants are mixed in with the fashion boutiques, tattooists and adult shops.

Verona (Map p106; ☎ 09-307 0508; 169 K Rd; dinner mains $15-25; ☑ 11am-late Mon-Sat, 3pm-late Sun) The smartest-looking place on K Rd offers mainly organic food but it's also a bar and sells deli snacks. It's a popular spot and gay-friendly.

Caluzzi (Map p106; ☎ 09-357 0778; 461 K Rd; dinner & show $50; ☑ dinner Tue-Sat) A unique restaurant and bar where three drag-queen waitresses put on a cabaret show as they serve you. Note that bookings are essential, and if you can't handle the heat, keep outta the kitchen.

Rasoi (Map p106; ☎ 09-377 7780; 211 K Rd; meals $6-15; ☑ lunch & dinner Mon-Sat) Lip-smackingly good (and delightfully cheap) vegetarian thali and South Indian food can be found here together with lassi and Indian sweets such as barfi and laddoo.

Brazil (Map p106; ☎ 09-302 2677; 256 K Rd; meals $3-16; ☑ breakfast, lunch & dinner) The unusual décor and music ('electro-industrial soundscapes') are the main attractions at this dark tunnel-like café. There's a DJ on board on Saturday afternoon.

Alleluya (Map p106; ☎ 09-377 8424; St Kevin's Arcade; meals $8-15; ☑ breakfast & lunch daily, dinner Tue-Sat) Alleluya is a very cool little café-cum-bar in the city's hippest arcade. It has moreish snacks, wines by the glass and the odd live gig.

Food for Life (Map p106; ☎ 09-300 7585; 268 K Rd; meals $6; ☑ lunch Mon-Sat, dinner Mon-Fri) This Hare Krishna vegetarian restaurant serves a bargain seven-item combination meal that may include the odd Italian animal-friendly dish as well as the usual Indian items.

Parnell

East of the city centre, Parnell Rd heads uphill and is lined with craft, gift and fashion shops as well as bars, cafés and restaurants that often have outdoor seating. It occasionally runs into twee territory, but for the most part it's a pleasant neighbourhood that rewards a ramble.

Antoines (Map p108; ☎ 09-379 8756; 333 Parnell Rd; mains $39-45; ☑ lunch Wed-Fri, dinner Mon-Sat) Antoine's is the last word in old-fashioned fine dining. Auckland-style. The French-influenced menu is inspiring stuff, while the 'nostalgic' menu features items that haven't changed since 1973. Wash it down with Dom Perignon and do your finest Mr Creosote impression while finding room for the dessert of spiced prune gnocchi ($18).

Oh Calcutta (Map p108; ☎ 09-377 9090; 151 Parnell Rd; mains $18-19; ☑ lunch & dinner) One of Auckland's best-known Indian restaurants with the usual faves (tandoori, rogan josh etc) and attractive Indian-style décor.

Iguacu (Map p108; ☎ 09-358 4804; 269 Parnell Rd; mains $19-30; ☑ lunch & dinner Mon-Fri, breakfast, lunch & dinner Sat & Sun) This always-popular, multilevel restaurant-bar complex has a relaxed atmosphere with live jazz music on occasion and hearty meat offerings on the menu.

Java Room (Map p108; ☎ 09-366 1606; 317 Parnell Rd; mains $17-24; ☑ dinner Mon-Sat) This cheery restaurant serves up Indonesian/Malaysian/Thai/Indian food and isn't afraid to get spicy. Prawn and duck dishes are perennial faves with the locals.

Mt Eden & Newmarket

Molten (Map p109; ☎ 09-638 7326; 422 Mt Eden Rd; dinner mains $27-30; ☑ lunch Mon, lunch & dinner Tue-Sat) This is easily the best newcomer on Auckland's dining scene, with an award-winning chef

(Michael Van de Elzen), glowing reviews, satisfied tummies (don't get us started on the braised pork hock)... And yes, that means you'll want to make a reservation for a late sitting, although early sittings are on a first-in, first-served basis.

Zarbo (Map p109; ☎ 09-520 2721; 24 Morrow St; salads $4-14; ✷ breakfast & lunch) This very sophisticated and capacious version of the local deli stocks gourmet provisions and does fantastic salad selections, plus there's plenty of seating for in-house feasting.

Self-caterers can forage for food and wine at the **Foodtown Supermarket** (Map p109; Valley Rd; ✷ 24hr).

Compact **Mt Eden Village** (Map p109) has good cafés, so try the following:

Frasers (Map p109; ☎ 09-630 6825; 434 Mt Eden Rd; ✷ breakfast, lunch & dinner) Packed with young and old for great scrambled-egg brunches.

Circus Circus (Map p109; ☎ 09-623 3883; 447 Mt Eden Rd; ✷ breakfast, lunch & dinner) An interesting chameleon with lively staff and comfort eats.

Tea Time Café (Map p109; ☎ 09-623 2319; 442 Mt Eden Rd; ✷ breakfast & lunch) There are more than 100 teas to drink or buy here, as well as snacks and coffee.

Ponsonby

Auckland's busiest restaurant-café-bar strip is so damn cool it has its own website (www.ponsonbyroad.co.nz). The street is well spread out and mixed with designer boutiques, plenty of hairdressers, delis and home-wares shops.

SPQR (Map p110; ☎ 09-360 1710; 150 Ponsonby Rd; pizzas $22-23, mains $27-29; ✷ noon-2am Mon-Fri, 10am-2am Sat & Sun) This ivy-covered Ponsonby Rd hot spot is well-known for good Roman-style thin, crusty pizzas (the traditional is best). If you want to go upmarket, plump for baked snapper with assorted salty trimmings. The surrounds are a stylish blend of the industrial and the chic, the lights are *low* (bring your reading glasses!) and the staff has all the smooth moves.

Estasi (Map p110; ☎ 09-361 3222; 222 Ponsonby Rd; mains $20-29; ✷ lunch & dinner) Estasi has an international menu that mixes things such as Szechwan duck and *fillet mignon* with candlelight and attractive, almost romantic décor.

Prego (Map p110; ☎ 09-376 3095; 226 Ponsonby Rd; pizzas $20-23, mains $25-31; ✷ lunch & dinner) This friendly and stylish Italian restaurant covers all the bases, with a fireplace in winter and a courtyard in summer. And on the subject of bases, the pizza is pretty damn fine, as are inventive Italian dishes such as *cinghiale* (boar) in chocolate stew on creamed polenta with sautéed silverbeet and roasted red capsicum.

Atomic Café (Map p110; ☎ 09-376 4954; 121 Ponsonby Rd; meals $7-16; ✷ breakfast, lunch & dinner) Popular and long-established, this café (with a covered garden area) offers delights such as foundation-laying Atomic porridge and powerfully good coffee.

Santos (Map p110; ☎ 09-378 8431; 114 Ponsonby Rd; meals $5-15; ✷ breakfast & lunch) A popular and buzzing café with an outdoor area, this spot offers simple healthy food, great fresh juices and fast, smiley service.

Logos (Map p110; ☎ 09-376 2433; 265 Ponsonby Rd; mains $17-19; ✷ breakfast & lunch Thu-Sun, dinner daily) If you're after vegan options, then this is the place to graze. Quirky, space age-meets-New Age décor welcomes locals and tourists alike, and the grilled mushrooms on toast are a fantastic breakfast choice.

Ponsonby Pies (Map p110; ☎ 09-361 3685; 288 Ponsonby Rd; pies around $3; ✷ 8am-6pm Mon-Fri, 8am-7pm Sat & Sun) These famous-in-NZ (and with those who stumble upon this shop) pies cost around $3 each, although you can pad out the pie with sides for $8.50. Favourites include steak and cheese, and chicken and veg. A great eat-on-the-run option.

Otto Woo (Map p110; ☎ 09-360 1989; www.ottowoo.com; 47 Ponsonby Rd; meals $6-13; ✷ lunch Mon-Fri, dinner daily) Eat in or take away at this whiter-than-white, minimalist (or should that be cubist?) Asian-style eatery that serves origi-

---

AUTHOR'S CHOICE

Dizengoff (Map p110; ☎ 09-360 0108; 256 Ponsonby Rd; breakfast around $15; ✷ breakfast & lunch daily) Great breakfasts are an essential experience in Auckland and no-one excels quite like Dizengoff. This super-stylish shoebox is blindingly white and crams in a mixed crowd of corporate and fashion types, gays, people keeping Kosher, Ponsonby denizens and visitors. Mouthwatering scrambled eggs, heart-starting coffee and mind-reading service, plus the best stack of reading material in the city if you tire of eavesdropping and people-watching.

nal, delicious fusion food in neat cardboard boxes.

Burger Fuel (Map p110; ☎ 09-378 5466; 114 Ponsonby Rd; burgers $6-12; ☒ lunch & dinner) This space-age-looking spot is the place for gourmet burgers that can be enjoyed inside or out. Try the Bastard for size and for laughs.

Devonport

Devonport has a solid range of eateries, cafés and bars, mostly along Victoria Rd.

Stone Oven (Map p111; ☎ 09-445 3185; 5 Clarence St; meals $6-17; ☒ breakfast & lunch) So damn good that on weekends you'll want to get in early or get ready to queue for the incredible breads, pastries, cakes and baked goods. Perfect for scoffing *in situ*, or away from the madding crowd.

Esplanade Restaurant (Map p111; ☎ 09-445 1291; 1 Victoria Rd; mains $29; ☒ breakfast, lunch & dinner) An unbeatable corner location in a lovely period building doesn't overwhelm the local fare of confit duck, venison or crusted salmon, all with well-executed sauces and sides. The poshest eating option on this side of the harbour.

Manuka (Map p111; ☎ 09-445 7732; 49 Victoria Rd; pizzas $19-25; ☒ 11am-late Mon-Fri, 9am-late Sat & Sun) A manuka-fired oven churns out the best pizza you'll taste on this side of the harbour. Popular with locals and everyone else who stumbles in.

Zigana (Map p111; ☎ 09-445 4151; 46 Victoria Rd; mains $17-23; ☒ breakfast, lunch & dinner) Mod-NZ dishes have a European accent at this popular eatery with good coffee and a breezy feel.

Monsoon (Map p111; ☎ 09-445 4263; 71 Victoria Rd; mains $13-18; ☒ dinner) Contemporary Thai/Malaysian food is the order of the day at this BYO joint that gets the thumbs up from locals for eat-in or takeaway escapism from the home kitchen.

McHugh's of Cheltenham (Map p111; ☎ 09-445 0305; 46 Cheltenham Rd; lunch buffet adult/child $24/12; ☒ lunch) With tranquil harbour views and a good-value lunch, McHugh's is a solid lunchtime choice, although the interior ambience is a wee bit 'function centre'.

Self-caterers can pop into the **New World** **supermarket** (Map p111; Bartley Tce), which also sells booze.

Other Areas

Along Tamaki Drive, Mission Bay has a line of restaurants, bars, fast-food outlets, ice-cream parlours and cafés. On the way is **Hammerheads** (Map p104; ☎ 09-521 4400; 19 Tamaki Dr; mains $26-43; ☒ lunch & dinner), a justifiably busy, mainly seafood restaurant with great views, a deck and plenty of parking. It's very much worth the trip, and the booking.

DRINKING

City Centre

Auckland's nightlife tends to be quiet during the week and positively funereal on Sundays, but wakes up late on Friday and Saturday when most pubs and bars are open until 1am or later.

Gin Room (Map p106; ☎ 09-377 1821; Lvl 1, 12 Vulcan Lane; ☒ 5pm-late Wed-Fri, 7pm-late Sat) All dark nooks and crannies, the Gin Room is a warm newcomer to Auckland's drinking scene. Think old-fashioned wallpaper, leopard-print boufs, chandeliers, Hotel Costes-style soundtracks and disappointingly piss-weak G&Ts but good cocktails.

Occidental Belgian Beer Café (Map p105; ☎ 09-300 6226; 6-8 Vulcan Lane; mains $13-20; ☒ 7am-3am Mon-Fri, 9am-3am Sat & Sun) Belgian beer is on tap and Belgian food (plenty of *moules* and *frites* – mussels and chips) is on the menu at this smart and popular bar located in one of the city's most attractive old buildings.

Wine Loft (Map p106; ☎ 09-379 5070; 67 Shortland St; ☒ 4pm-late Mo-Thu, 2pm-late Fri, 6pm-late Sat) Head up the stairs for a chocolate-hued, sofa-filled loft that's perfect for wine quaffing and platter sharing by an open fire (or window come summer). An eclectic list takes in wine from NZ, Australia, South America and Europe.

Honey (Map p105; ☎ 09-369 5639; 5 O'Connell St; ☒ 4pm-late) This flash-looking champagne bar with sofas sells unique Kiwi drinks such as NZ-made gin (South) and NZ-made vodka (42 Below), which can be infused with feijoa or even manuka honey. Not a bad spot to feast on eye candy.

Viaduct Harbour & Princes Wharf

Lenin Bar (Map p105; ☎ 09-377 0040; Princes Wharf; ☒ 3pm-late) This Russian-themed affair boasts lots of vodkas and DJs from Thursday to Saturday, but can seem oddly quiet on other nights. If you can't be bothered getting cold for the subzero climes of the Minus 5° Bar, then you might like to know that you can see into it from Lenin.

Minus 5° Bar (Map p106; Princes Wharf; adult/child $25/12; 2-10pm) This is an extraordinary ice bar where everything from the seats to your glass is made of ice, much like its famous counterparts in Sweden. Put on special clothing (including gloves and shoes) and sip a vodka-based drink or a juice from an edible ice glass. You can only stay inside the shimmering ice world for 30 minutes. It's more popular with out-of-towners than locals.

Bubble Champagne Bar (Map p106; 09-358 2800; Quay St; 4pm-late) This cosy, welcoming bar is resplendent in purple velvet and dozens of types of champagne.

Parnell

Parnell is more a place for dining than drinking, but there is the stone-encrusted **Bog** (Map p108; 09-377 1510; 196 Parnell Rd), which serves hearty beer-soaking food, Irish beers and has live music on Thursday, Friday and Sunday.

Ponsonby

Along Ponsonby Rd, the line between café, restaurant, bar and club gets blurred. A lot of food places also have live music or become clubs later on.

Whiskey (Map p110; 09-361 2666; 210 Ponsonby Rd; 5pm-3am) The stylish, dimly lit Whiskey is a quintessential bolthole for music-industry types. There's a long list of cocktails and spirits, and a decent 'classic rock' soundtrack.

Lime Bar (Map p110; 09-360 7167; 167 Ponsonby Rd; 4pm-2am Mon-Fri, 6pm-2am Sat) A tiny, blink-and-you-miss-it bar, which plays a decent soundtrack for getting close to the locals. Low-key atmosphere but cool and quite good fun.

Orchid (Map p110; 09-378 8186; 152b Ponsonby Rd; 5pm-2am) This gorgeous looking bar boasts a long list of alcoholic pleasures and lovely low lighting that makes the orchid-themed metallic wallpaper come to life if you imbibe enough.

Devonport

Masonic Tavern (Map p111; 09-455 0485; 29 King Edward Pde) A bewildering array of beers on tap and an authentic 'sit outside and watch the world go by' vibe make this the pick of the bunch for those after an old-fashioned pub atmosphere.

ENTERTAINMENT

The *NZ Herald* has 'The Guide' section from Monday to Friday with local what's on and entertainment features, and a larger 'Time Out' section on Saturday. *Backpacker Xpress* (free every Thursday) has what's on at some of Auckland pubs and bars. *The Fix* is a weekly brochure (also free every Thursday) with live music listings. See below for gay and lesbian venues. If you're planning on a big night along K Rd, then visit www .kroad.co.nz for a detailed list of bars and clubs.

Tickets for major events can be bought from **Ticketek** (09-307 5000; www.ticketek.co.nz), which has outlets at Aotea Centre and Sky City Atrium (among others).

Live Music

Rakinos (Map p106; 09-358 3535; 35 High St; 11am-6am Mon-Sat, 11am-3am Sun) Upstairs is this retro

GAY & LESBIAN AUCKLAND

Pride Centre (Map p106; 09-302 0590; www.pride.org.nz; K Rd) is the main contact point for the gay and lesbian community. Its premises were temporary at the time of research, so check the website.

Express is a fortnightly magazine with masses of information on the Auckland gay scene. *Up* is a monthly magazine, while *New Zealand Gay Guide* (www.gogaynewzealand.com) is a new pocket-sized booklet with listings. Log on to www.gaynz.com for news and venue listings.

Auckland hosts a HERO festival every February with two weeks of events. See p119.

Urge (Map p106; 09-307 2155; 490 K Rd; 9pm-late Thu-Sat) is the city's longest-running gay bar and club with DJs Friday and Saturday nights plus lots of cruising. **Kamo** (Map p106; 09-377 2313; 382 K Rd; mains $16-25; 10.30am-10.30pm Tue-Sun) is a gay-friendly restaurant and bar. **Flesh Bar & Nightclub** (Map p106; 09-336 1616; 17 O'Connell St; 6pm-late) is a dimly lit central lounge bar with snacks, karaoke and some handsome men. The **nightclub** (11pm-late Fri & Sat) is downstairs, usually has no cover charge and features regular drag shows by the supremely resplendent Ms Ribena.

café-bar-music venue with potent cocktails, live music and DJs. It covers a lot of bases, so it makes a great choice for either starting or ending the night.

Dogs Bollix (Map p106; ☎ 09-376 4600; cnr K & Newton Rds) This Irish pub is a live music venue at 9pm from Tuesday to Sunday but doesn't only play Irish music. Spot local musos here when they're off-duty.

Eden's Bar (Map p106; 335 K Rd) Regular live music gigs plus nights devoted to indie pop and rock. Grotty and fun.

Kings Arms Tavern (Map p106; ☎ 09-373 3240; 59 France St; ☺ 11am-late) This is one of Auckland's leading small venues for live (and local) rock bands, which play most nights. A rite of passage if you want to get into the local scene.

Galatos (Map p106; ☎ 09-303 1928; 17 Galatos St; ☺ 9pm-late Wed-Sat) Three birds with one stone: DJs, local live bands, and hip-hop in the basement.

Alhambra (Map p110; ☎ 09-373 2430; 283 Ponsonby Rd; tapas $4-5, dinner mains $13-25; ☺ 5pm-late) This local stayer has a Spanish/Moorish tinge to the décor, live jazz or blues from Wednesday to Sunday nights and some sterling city skyline views.

For big international and major local bands, the main venues include **Western Springs Stadium** (Map p104; ☎ 09-849 3807; Great North Rd, Western Springs), the **North Shore Events Centre** (Map p104; ☎ 09-443 8199; Porana Rd, Glenfield), the **Supertop** (Map p104; ☎ 09-525 0680; Maurice Rd, Penrose) and **Ericsson Stadium** (Map p104; ☎ 09-571 1699; www.ericssonstadium.co.nz; Beasley Ave, Penrose).

Nightclubs

K Rd and Ponsonby Rd are the main places to find late-night clubs, but there are a few around Vulcan Lane and the Viaduct Basin. Some clubs have a cover charge depending on the night and the event.

Fu Bar (Map p106; ☎ 09-309 3079; 166 Queen St; ☺ 10pm-late Tue-Sat) This long-running basement music club has live bands (such as popular local rockers Die! Die! Die!), DJs plus pool tables and a solid reputation for hip-hop.

Papa Jack's Voodoo Lounge (Map p106; ☎ 09-358 4847; 9 Vulcan Lane; ☺ 7pm-late Tue-Sat) This is the home of hard rock with skulls, ripped seats, a pool table, a live band on Wednesday and a DJ on Friday and Saturday.

Khuja Lounge (Map p106; ☎ 09-377 3711; 536 Queen St; cover $10; ☺ 8pm-3am Wed-Sat) Above the Westpac building, this laid-back venue offers DJs and live jazz/soul/hip-hop bands.

Ibiza (Map p106; ☎ 09-302 3354; 253 K Rd; ☺ 24hr Fri & Sat) This is a nonstop hard house and trance venue with a go hard or go home ethos that's not to everyone's taste.

Float (Map p106; ☎ 09-307 1344; Shed 19, Princes Wharf) This is a populist, mainstream night-spot choice with DJs on weekends and big screens for sports broadcasts.

Sport

Eden Park (Map p104; ☎ 09-815 5551; www.edenpark.co.nz) This is the stadium for top rugby (winter) and cricket (summer) matches. The All Blacks, the Black Caps and the Auckland Blues all play here. To get there, take the train from Britomart to Kingsland station.

Ericsson Stadium (Map p104; ☎ 09-571 1699; www.ericssonstadium.co.nz; Beasley Ave, Penrose) This stadium hosts soccer, rugby league (Warriors) and really big-name concerts.

Stanley St Tennis Courts (Map p106; ☎ 09-373 3623; 72 Stanley St) In January the women's ASB Classic is followed by the men's Heineken Open. Some famous tennis names show up to battle it out at this venue.

Theatre & Musicals

Most theatrical and major musical events can be booked through **Ticketek** (☎ 09-307 5000; www.ticketek.co.nz). Aotea Square and the buildings that surround it comprise Auckland's main arts and entertainment complex. The Edge (www.the-edge.co.nz) is the collective name given to the other venues – the Town Hall, Civic theatre and Aotea Centre.

Auckland Town Hall (Map p106; ☎ 09-309 2677; 50 Mayoral Dr) This venue hosts concert performances and is home to the NZ Symphony Orchestra and Auckland Philharmonia (www.aucklandphil.co.nz).

Aotea Centre (Map p106; ☎ 09-307 5060; 50 Mayoral Dr) This is Auckland's main venue for theatre, dance, ballet and opera. The highly regarded Auckland Theatre Company puts on a regular programme here.

Civic (Map p106; ☎ 09-309 2677; cnr Queen St & Wellesley St W) This restored grand dame of a theatre, with lavish Eastern-fantasy interior, is used by major touring productions, including opera, musicals and live theatre, as well as by the Auckland International Film Festival.

Classic Comedy Club (Map p106; ☎ 09-373 4321; www.comedy.co.nz; 321 Queen St; tickets $5-16) Auckland's top venue for comedy, with shows running Wednesday to Saturday (some 'fresh', some improvised, some professional) from around 8pm with late shows on Friday and Saturday.

Sky City (Map p106; ☎ 0800 759 2489; cnr Victoria & Hobson Sts) This is Auckland's biggest single entertainment venue. As well as restaurants, bars, the observation deck and a 700-seat theatre, it has two casinos – the huge 24-hour Sky City Casino (Level 2) and the smaller Alto Casino (Level 3), which are open 24 hours, in true casino style. Bars around the casinos offer nightly live music.

Other theatres:

Maidment Theatre (Map p106; ☎ 09-308 2383; University of Auckland, 8 Alfred St)

Silo Theatre (Map p106; ☎ 09-366 0339; www.silotheatre.co.nz; Lower Greys Ave) Specialises in youth and fringe drama.

Sky City Theatre (Map p106; ☎ 0800 759 2489, 09-363 6000; www.skycity.co.nz; cnr Victoria & Federal Sts)

Cinemas

Most cinemas offer cheaper rates on weekdays before 5pm and bargain day is all day Tuesday.

Sky City Village Megascreen (Map p106; ☎ 09-979 2401; www.villageskycity.co.nz; Lvl 3, 291 Queen St) Part of Sky City Metro, a modernistic mall that includes Borders bookshop, Starbucks, bars and a food court.

Academy Cinema (Map p106; ☎ 09-373 2761; www .academy-cinema.co.nz; 44 Lorne St; adult $11-14) In the basement of the Central City Library is the Academy, which shows independent foreign and art-house films.

Rialto Cinemas (Map p109; ☎ 09-529 2218; www .rialto.co.nz; 167 Broadway; adult $8.50-15, child $7-9) In Newmarket, and showing a bit of art-house and international, plus some mainstream fare.

NZ Film Archives (Map p106; ☎ 09-379 0688; www .filmarchive.org.nz; 300 K Rd; ☺ 11am-5pm Mon-Fri, 11am-4pm Sat) This is a wonderful resource of more than a thousand Kiwi feature films and documentaries dating from 1905, which you can watch for free on a TV screen. See p22 for some recommended Kiwi feature films.

as well as by the Auckland International Film Festival. Followers of fashion should head to High St, Chancery Lane, Newmarket, Ponsonby Rd and possibly K Rd and Victoria Park Market. An official All Black rugby shirt costs around $150. The central city area (especially Queen St) has lots of stores selling outdoor clothes and equipment.

SHOPPING

Followers of fashion should head to High St, Chancery Lane, Newmarket, Ponsonby Rd and possibly K Rd and Victoria Park Market. An official All Black rugby shirt costs around $150. The central city area (especially Queen St) has lots of stores selling outdoor clothes and equipment.

Clothing & Accessories

Mala Brajkovic (Map p106; ☎ 09-377 9001; 31 Vulcan Lane) This quirky local designer stocks interesting women's clothes that might feature silk, leather or the odd bit of ironic stonewash denim. One to watch out for.

Kate Sylvester (Map p109; ☎ 09-524 8872; 1 Teed St) One of NZ's better designers for PYTs who like to mix it up. Cute, retro-style lingerie is also on sale here.

Lady Muck (☎ 09-376 2413; 12 Ponsonby Rd) The best vintage shop in the city, with incredible period pieces from as far back as the 19th century.

Little Brother (Map p106; ☎ 09-377 6536; 5 High St) The hippest local label for men about town, with an excellent range of Flying Nun vintage design T-shirts.

Zambesi (Map p109; ☎ 09-523 1000; 2 Teed St) Hands-down, the most interesting and influential fashion label to come out of the country, and much sought after by local and international celebs.

Gifts & Souvenirs

Devonport Chocolates (Map p111; ☎ 09-445 6001; 17 Wynard St) Sells scrumptious handmade chocolates, with the dangerous promise that you can taste one free before you start your addiction.

Champions of the World (Map p106; ☎ 09-379 4937; 22 Queen St) Pick up an official All Black jersey or, even better, a Wallabies' jersey and a dirty look. Another branch is at 45 Queen St.

Pauanesia (Map p106; ☎ 09-520 6359; 35 High St) A colourful treasure trove of Polynesian-style craft and gifts.

Markets

Victoria Park Market (Map p106; ☎ 09-309 6911; 210 Victoria St W; ☺ 9am-6pm) Here you'll find mostly clothes, shoes, accessories, crafts and souvenirs but it includes a food court, cafés and a spacious pub. Cheap massages are also available. It's a 20-minute walk west from the city centre, or you can take the Link or Explorer buses.

Aotea Square Market (Map p106; Aotea Sq; ⏰ 10am-6pm Fri & Sat) It has ethnic food stalls, arts and crafts and entertainment. There's live music on Saturday from noon to 3pm.

Otara Markets (Map p104; ☎ 09-274 0830; Newbury St; ⏰ 6am-noon Sat) Held in the car park between the Manukau Polytech and the Otara town centre, this market has a real Polynesian atmosphere, and you can buy South Pacific food, music and fashions. Take bus 487 or 497 from outside Britomart station.

Music

Real Groovy Records (Map p106; ☎ 09-302 3940; 438 Queen St) This megastore of new and second-hand music also sells concert tickets and stocks DVDs, books, magazines and clothing. Bands regularly play in-store.

R&R Sport (Map p106; ☎ 09-309 6444; cnr K Rd & Grundy St) This huge shop has everything in the hiking, bicycling, skiing, surfing, camping and outdoor sports line, with some secondhand stuff.

Outdoor Gear

Kathmandu (Map p106; 151 Queen St) This local brand of outdoor gear will get you sorted for the great outdoors.

Shopping Centres

Westfield Downtown Shopping Centre (Map p106; Queen Elizabeth Sq) This shopping centre has a Flight Centre travel agency, post office, pharmacy, gift shops, Warehouse discount shop, a food court and a 24-hour Star Mart convenience store. The ASB Bank here is also open on the weekend.

Two Double Seven Shopping Complex (Map p11; ☎ 09-520 0277; Broadway) This hard-to-miss shopping centre stocks mainstream brands such as Cue, Marcs and Country Road, plus plenty of other retailers.

GETTING THERE & AWAY

Air

Auckland is the major gateway to NZ, and a hub for domestic flights. See p723 for information on international flights.

Domestic airlines operating to and from Auckland:

Air New Zealand (Map p106; ☎ 09-336 2424; www.airnewzealand.co.nz; cnr Customs & Queen Sts; ⏰ 9.30am-5pm Mon-Fri, 10am-1pm Sat)

Great Barrier Airlines (☎ 0800 900 600, 09-275 9120; www.greatbarrierairlines.co.nz; Auckland domestic terminal)

Mountain Air (☎ 09-256 7025; www.mountainair .co.nz; Auckland domestic terminal)

Origin Pacific (☎ 0800 302 302; www.originpacific .co.nz) Flies to nine local destinations from Auckland, including Wellington and Christchurch.

Qantas (Map p106; ☎ 09-357 8900; www.qantas .com.au; 191 Queen St; ⏰ 9am-5pm Mon-Fri)

Bus

The main long-distance bus company in Auckland, as for the rest of NZ, is **InterCity** (☎ 09-623 1503; www.intercitycoach.co.nz) and its travel and sightseeing arm **Newmans Coach Lines** (www.newmanscoach.co.nz). With a few exceptions, its buses go to almost all bigger towns and the main tourist areas.

There are services from Auckland to just about everywhere in NZ, which operate from the **Sky City Coach Terminal** (Map p106; ☎ 09-916 6222; 102 Hobson St, Sky City Complex).

Northliner (☎ 09-307 5873; www.northliner.co.nz) services Northland, with buses heading north from Auckland to Whangarei, the Bay of Islands and Kaitaia.

Backpacker buses operate in and from Auckland and have their main offices here:

Kiwi Experience (Map p108; ☎ 09-366 9830; www.kiwiexperience.co.nz; 195 Parnell Rd)

Magic Travellers Network (Map p106; ☎ 09-358 5600; www.magicbus.co.nz; 120 Albert St)

Stray (Map p106; ☎ 09-309 8772; www.straytravel .co.nz; 31 Beach Rd)

Car

HIRING A CAR

Auckland has countless car-hire operators and is the best city in which to hire (or buy) a vehicle for touring NZ or the city itself. Some good deals can be had for long-term hire, but be warned that cheapest is not necessarily the best.

A swag of car-rental companies (Map p106) can be found conveniently grouped together along Beach Rd opposite the old train station. The major companies (Avis, Budget, Hertz and Thrifty) are reliable, offer full insurance and have offices at the airport and all over the country. They are more expensive, but rates are often negotiable for longer hires or off-season.

If you are prepared to take limited insurance and risk losing an excess of around

$750, then the cheaper operators offer some pretty good deals. Prices vary with the season, the age of the car and length of hire. Ignore prices quoted in brochures and shop around by phone. Always read the hire agreement thoroughly before you sign.

Some of the more reputable car-hire companies (which may also hire out sleeper vans and campervans):

A2B (0800 222 929, 09-377 0824; www.a2brentals .co.nz)

Britz NZ (0800 831 900, 09-275 9090; www.britz.com)

Budget (0800 652 227, 09-375 2270; www.budget .co.nz)

Hertz (0800 654 321, 09-367 6350; www.hertz.co.nz)

Maui (0800 651 080, 09-275 3013; www.maui -rentals.com)

Omega (0800 525 210, 09-377 5573; www.omega rentals.com)

Thrifty (0800 737 070, 09-309 0111; www.thrifty.co.nz)

BUYING A CAR

For stays of two months or more, many people look at buying a car. You can buy through dealers on the buy-back scheme, at car fairs or auctions, or through ads at backpacker hostels. Before buying a car you must check that it is mechanically sound, has not been stolen, and does not have money owing on it to a finance company or bank.

Backpackers Car Market (Map p106; 09-377 7761; www.backpackerscarmarket.co.nz; 20 East St; 9.30am–5pm) can give you the lowdown on buying and selling cars in NZ. Full mechanical check with one-month guarantee and third-party insurance can be arranged. To display a car to sell there costs $65 for three days.

Buy-backs, where the dealer agrees to buy back your car for an agreed price (usually 50% of what you pay), are not a great deal, but offer a safety net if you have trouble reselling the car.

A popular way to buy a car is through the car fairs where people bring their own cars to sell them. Arrive between 8.30am and 9.30am for the best choice; car fairs are over by about noon. For a credit check quote chassis and licence-plate numbers. Mechanical inspection services, credit agencies and Auto Check details are all on hand at the following car fairs:

Ellerslie Racecourse (Map p104; 09-529 2233; www.carfair.co.nz; 9am–noon Sun) Ellerslie is near the

Greenlane roundabout. It's the largest car fair and it costs $30 to display your vehicle.

Manukau City Centre (Map p104; 09-358 5000; Manukau City Centre Car Park; 9am–1pm Sun) It costs $25 to display your car.

Motorcycle

NZ Motorcycle Rentals (09-360 7940; www.nzbike .com; 35 Crummer Rd, Ponsonby; 9am–6pm Mon-Fri, 10am–5pm Sat, 10am–3pm Sun) offers motorbike hire for $70 to $300 a day (insurance excess is $1000 upwards). Scooters cost $22 to $45 a day. Guided tours are also available.

Train

Trains arrive at and depart from **Britomart station** (Map p106; 0800 872 467; www.tranzscenic .co.nz), the largest underground diesel train station in the world, on Quay St. You can book online, or else the booking office is open from 8am to 8.30pm daily.

Only one train operates out of Auckland and goes to Wellington via Hamilton and Palmerston North. The *Overlander* runs daily, departing from Auckland at 7.25am and arriving in Wellington at 7.20pm (the return train leaves Wellington at 7.25am and arrives in Auckland at 7.20pm).

The standard Auckland–Wellington adult fare on the *Overlander* is $145 (adult with child is from $221 to $247). There are reductions of 30% and 20% off the adult fares for seniors and students respectively.

GETTING AROUND
To/From the Airport

Auckland airport (Map p104; 09-256 8899; www .auckland-airport.co.nz) is 21km south of the city centre. It has an international terminal and a domestic terminal, each with a tourist information centre. A free shuttle service operates every 20 minutes between the terminals and there's also a signposted footpath between them (about a 1km walk).

At the international terminal there's a free phone for accommodation bookings. Both terminals have left-luggage facilities, ATMs and car-rental desks, though you get better rates from companies in town.

The **AirBus** (09-375 4732; www.airbus.co.nz; adult one way/return $15/22, backpacker $13/20, child $6/12) runs every 20 or 30 minutes (from 6am to 10pm) between the international and domestic terminals and the city, stopping outside major hotels and backpacker hostels. Reservations are not required and you buy a ticket from the driver. The trip takes about one hour one way (a bit longer during rush hour).

Convenient door-to-door **shuttle minibuses** (1st person $24, each subsequent person $5) run to and from the airport. It pays to get a group together and all get off at the same place. The price increases if you want to go to an outlying suburb. Each shuttle is supposed to stay a maximum of 15 minutes, so you may be able to negotiate a lower price if one is about to leave. The main operator is **Super Shuttle** (☎ 09-306 3960).

A taxi to the airport from the city costs between $45 and $55.

Bicycle

Adventure Cycles (Map p106; ☎ 09-309 5566; 36 Customs St E; 🕑 9am–7pm) hires out road and mountain bikes ($18 to $35 a day) and carries out repairs. It also hires out touring bikes long-term, and run a buy-back scheme.

In Auckland cycling up to Mission Bay or around Devonport are both good options. The visitors centres have a useful *Bike Guide* for the Auckland region.

Boat

Fullers (Map p106; ☎ 09-367 9111; www.fullers.co.nz) operates passenger ferries between the city and Devonport, Stanley Bay, Birkenhead and Bayswater on the North Shore, the gulf islands and Half Moon Bay near Howick.

Car & Motorcycle

Parking is a problem in central Auckland, but there are plenty of car parks off Beach Rd, which is at the eastern end of Customs St. They cost around $8 for 12 hours. Most on-street parking meters (from $1 an hour) do not have to be fed money between 6pm and 8am or on Sunday. For information on car and motorcycle hiring or buying, see p141.

Public Transport

For information on public transport visit www.maxx.co.nz or call ☎ 09-366 6400.

BUS

The Auckland city bus service is primarily run by Stagecoach (☎ 09-366 6400; www.stagecoach .co.nz). There is no central bus station, but most buses leave from bus stops that are scattered around the new Britomart station (Map p106). Timetables and useful information about bus routes are on bus-stop notice boards. The Britomart Plaza has food retailers, foreign-exchange facilities and even an artist-in-residence 'booth' that is frequently mistaken for a ticket office! Downstairs are plush toilets and left-luggage lockers.

The **Link bus** (fares $1.50; 🕑 every 10–15min 6am–11.30pm Mon-Fri, 7am–11.30pm Sat & Sun) is a very handy bus service that travels clockwise and anticlockwise around a loop that includes Queen St, Sky City, Victoria Park Market, Ponsonby Rd, K Rd, Newmarket, Parnell and Britomart station.

The **City Circuit bus** (🕑 every 10min 8am–6pm) provides free transport around the inner city from Britomart station, up Queen St, past Albert Park to Auckland University and across to Sky Tower and back to Britomart.

Single-ride fares in the inner city are 50c for an adult and 30c for a child (you pay the driver when you board), but if you're travelling further afield there are fare stages from adult/child $1.50/90c to $9/5.40. A one-day pass (which includes the city centre to North Shore ferries) costs only $10, while a three-day pass costs $23, but there's no reduction for children.

The **Niterider** (☎ 09-366 6400; fares $4–6) runs from the Civic theatre (p139) on Queen St, along 10 routes between 1am and 3am on Friday and Saturday nights.

TRAIN

Tranz Metro (☎ 09-366 6400; www.rideline.co.nz; fares $1.10–5, bikes $1) runs just three routes from Britomart station: one runs west to Waitakere, while two routes run south to Pukekohe. Services are at least hourly and run from around 6am to 8pm from Monday to Saturday. A $13 Discovery Pass allows a day's travel on most bus, train and ferry services. All train carriages have wheelchair ramps.

Taxi

Auckland's many taxis usually work from ranks, but they also cruise popular areas. **Auckland Co-Op Taxis** (☎ 09-300 3000) is one of the biggest companies. Other taxi companies are listed in the *Yellow Pages*. Flagfall is $2 and then $1.75 to $2.10 per kilometre. There's a $4 toll for transport to and from the airport and cruise ships.

AROUND AUCKLAND

REGIONAL PARKS

The Auckland Regional Council (ARC) administers 21 regional parks around the Auckland region, all within 15km to 90km of the city. There are several coastal and beach parks with swimming and surfing beaches, plus bush parks, a kauri park, the Waitakere Ranges west of Auckland, the Hunua catchment southeast of Auckland and a gannet colony at Muriwai. The parks have good walking and tramping tracks, ranging from 20 minutes to several hours, and camping is allowed in a few parks.

Get an *Auckland Regional Parks* pamphlet, with a list of facilities in each park, from the Auckland visitor centre or the DOC office (p107) in the Ferry Building in Auckland. ARC has camping grounds in the regional parks, many in coastal areas. Some are accessible by vehicle, others are reached by tramping. Most tend to be *heavily* booked in summer; contact **Parksline** (☎ 09-366 2000) for information and bookings.

WEST OF AUCKLAND

Less than an hour's drive west from the city centre is the Waitakere Ranges Regional Park, which has a dramatic, rugged coastline with iron-sand beaches backed by regenerating native bush. There are some fine bush walks, surf beaches, golf courses and wineries. Obtain the *Art Out West* leaflet for information on the area's galleries and studios.

Wineries

The area west of Auckland has long been a wine-producing region, and some wineries have excellent cafés or restaurants. The free *Winemakers of Auckland* brochure gives full details and is available from visitors centres. Winery tours are available (see p118).

Soljans Winery (Map p144; ☎ 09-412 2680; 366 SH16, Kumeu; ☼ 9am-5.30pm) Tasting of up to a dozen wines is available here. Cellar tours ($10) can be booked.

Coopers Creek (Map p144; ☎ 09-412 8560; 601 SH16, Huapai; ☼ 9am-5.30pm Mon-Fri, 10.30am-5.30pm Sat & Sun) Wines to sample and buy here, as well as attractive gardens with picnicking allowed.

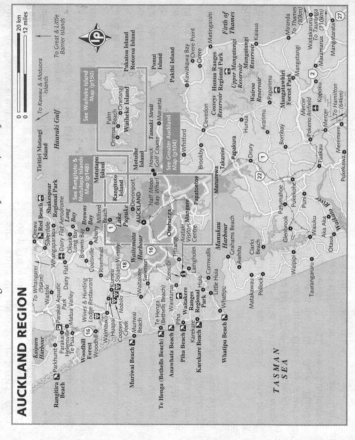

AUCKLAND REGION

Hunting Lodge (Map p144; ☎ 09-411 8259; mains $24-33; ☎ lunch & dinner Wed-Sun) The excellent restaurant at Matua Valley Wines.

Matua Valley Wines (Map p144; ☎ 09-411 8301; Waikoukou Valley Rd; ☎ 10am-5pm) This has wine tasting 3km from the main road and the restaurant, Hunting Lodge.

Nobilo (Map p144; ☎ 09-412 9148; 45 Station Rd, Huapai; ☎ 9am-5pm Mon-Fri, 10am-5pm Sat & Sun)

Waitakere Ranges

This 18,000-hectare wilderness area once supported important kauri forests, but they were logged almost to extinction in the 19th century. A few stands of ancient kauri and other mature trees, such as rimu, survive amid the regenerating rainforest, which is now protected inside the **Waitakere Ranges Regional Park**. Bordered on the west by the wildly beautiful beaches on the Tasman Sea, the park's sometimes rugged terrain with steep-sided valleys, is the most significant natural area close to Auckland and a marvellous day trip. It's popular for picnics and walks, with 250km of tracks.

SIGHTS & ACTIVITIES

Canyoning in the Waitakere Ranges is a highlight for outdoor enthusiasts. **Awol Canyoning** (☎ 0800 462 965, 09-834 0501; www.awol adventures.co.nz; half-/full day $125/155) offers abseiling down waterfalls, sliding down rocks and jumping into pools in the Waitakere Ranges. Pick-up from Auckland (if required), lunch and snacks are included in the price. The actual canyoning takes two to three hours. Night trips can also be arranged. **Canyonz** (☎ 0800 422 696, 09-815 9464; www .canyonz.co.nz; trips $145 or $225) runs canyoning trips to Blue Canyon.

The 28km SH24, also known as the **Scenic Drive**, winds its way from Titirangi to Swanson, passing numerous falls and lookouts. The **Arataki Visitors Centre** (Map p144; ☎ 09-817 4941; www.waitakereranges.org.nz; Scenic Dr; ☎ 9am-5pm) is 6km west of Titirangi along this road and is a brilliant starting point for exploring the ranges. As well as providing a host of information on the 250km of trails in the area, this impressive child-friendly centre with its Maori carvings and spectacular views is an attraction in its own right. The giant carving that greets visitors at the entrance depicts the ancestors of the Kawerau *iwi* (tribe). Inside there is a theatre showing a 20-minute video

(adult/child $2/1) on the park and its wildlife. A 1.6km nature trail opposite the centre takes visitors past labelled native species, including mature kauri. Noted walks include the Cascades/Kauri area to the north, which has three good walks, the Upper Kauri Track and the Pukemateko Track.

There are a couple of miniature train rides through the ranges but both must be booked in advance. **Waitakere Tramline Society** (☎ 09-818 4946; adult/child $10/5) runs four scenic trips every Sunday that pass through a glow-worm tunnel. Trips start from the end of Christian Rd, which runs south of Swanson station. The **Rain Forest Express** (☎ 09-302 8028; www.watercare.co.nz; 2½hr trips adult/child $25/12) departs from Jacobsons' Depot (off Scenic Drive) at 2pm on Sunday, and there's a special twilight trip at 5.30pm in summer. It runs along the 6km Nihotupu line.

SLEEPING & EATING

Fringe of Heaven (☎ 09-817 8682; www.fringeof heaven.com; 4 Otitoi Bay Rd, Titirangi; r $160-200; P) This lovely B&B gives you a beautiful king bedroom (and bathroom) with glorious views in a Frank Lloyd Wright-style house owned by friendly Bev and Julian. It's a quiet, private place and a good base for the city, the Waitakere Ranges and the airport. Very special indeed.

Nikau Club (☎ 09-814 8919; 473 Scenic Dr; mains $20-30; ☎ lunch & dinner Mon-Fri, brunch & dinner Sat & Sun) This place has a decent menu and a splendid view, plus a bar that makes this an ideal and popular place to stop. A car park, kids' play area and highchairs make this a good one for families.

Piha & Karekare Beaches

Note that swimming on these west coast beaches can be very dangerous because of strong undercurrents. Surf-lifesaving clubs patrol the main beaches in summer; always swim between the flags where lifeguards can provide help if you get into trouble.

Piha, 16km off Scenic Drive, with its beautifully rugged, iron-sand beach, has long been a favourite with Auckland holidaymakers and keen surfers, as well as with artists and alternative types. The view of the coast as you drive down on Piha Rd is quite spectacular. The distinctive **Lion Rock** (101m), which you can climb, sits just off the beach.

Surfing competitions are held in Piha in the summer and there is a horse race along the beach towards the end of summer. You can hire surfboards and wet suits, and surfing instruction is available. View www .pihasurf.co.nz for surf conditions.

There is a small general store and café, two takeaways and two basic camp sites. There is no supermarket, liquor shop, bank or petrol station.

Just five minutes down Karekare Rd, off Piha Rd, is iconic **Karekare Beach**, which is even more rugged, wild and pristine than Piha. Scenes from Jane Campion's *The Piano* were filmed there, and it's a justifiably famous stop on the 'natural wonders' pilgrimage.

SIGHTS & ACTIVITIES
Piha Surf Shop & Crafts (☎ 09-812 8896; www.piha surf.co.nz; 122 Seaview Rd) A family-run venture that sells crafts upstairs and surfboards (shaped by patriarch Mike Jolly) downstairs. Surfboards (three-hour/full day $25/35), wet suits ($5/10) and body boards ($15/25) can be hired. Private surfing lessons can also be arranged.

Lush Surf Shop (☎ 09-812 8692), next to the general store, also sells and rents surfing gear for about the same prices.

SLEEPING & EATING
Piha Domain Motor Camp (☎ 09-812 8815; 21 Seaview Rd; site per adult $10, s/d on-site caravans $25/38) Smackbang on the beach but scruffy, basic and bearing the full brunt of the weather (rain or shine). Cheap as chips that's for sure.

Piha Surf Shop Accommodation (☎ 09-812 8723; www.pihasurf.co.nz; 122 Seaview Rd; caravans per person $25-35) Each basic but charmingly tatty caravan has its own linen, TV, fridge, cooker and long-drop toilet, and all caravans share a very simple shower. This place is on the right as you head to the beach, 2km from the sand and is a great choice for surfing types.

Piha Beach Accommodation (☎ 021 969 924; www.pihabeach.co.nz; Beach Valley Rd; cabin $75, ste $130-160) This is the best-value quality accommodation you'll find in Piha, so get cracking and make a reservation. The two suites here are tight on space, but they're filled with attractive touches and smart extras such as diminutive couches, good firm beds with natty bed linen and polished floorboards. Penny-pinchers are in for a treat if they

book the Cabin, which is kitted out in 1950s Kiwiana-bach-style. Piha Beach Accommodation is gay-friendly too.

Piha Lodge (☎ 09-812 8595; www.pihalodge.co.nz; 117 Piha Rd; unit/apt $140/200; ⚡) This homestyle lodge has self-contained units with a deck, some splendid views and riotous strawberries-and-cream-style carpet. DVD players, Sky TV, a hot spa and complimentary breakfast are supplied by chatty Shirley. Book ahead, and if you fancy getting married, Shirley can do that too – she's a celebrant.

Piha Life Saving Club (☎ 09-812 8896; Lion Rock Beachfront; mains $15-21; 🕒 dinner Wed-Sun) The surfing club is a social centre with decent meals, a bar and sunsets straight off a postcard.

GETTING THERE & AWAY
The **Piha Surf Shuttle** (☎ 09-627 2644; www.surf shuttle.co.nz; one-way/same-day return $25/40) leaves Auckland at around 8.30am for Piha and returns to Auckland at 4pm daily from December to February. Booking is advisable.

Whatipu
Whatipu Beach is the most southerly beach and can be reached along Huia Rd, the last part of which is gravel. The beach has huge sandflats at low tide and lagoons that attract unusual vegetation and birds, including the endangered dotterel.

Te Henga (Bethells Beach)
Bethells Beach is reached by taking the Te Henga Rd at the northern end of Scenic Drive. It's another raw black-sand beach with surf, windswept dunes and bush walks, such as the popular one to Lake Wainamu and on to the Cascades.

Bethells Beach Cottages (☎ 09-810 9581; www .bethellsbeach.com; 267 Bethells Rd; d cottages $250-350) has two charming, self-contained cottages in a bush setting with sea and sunset views. Lovely meals can be arranged and generate as much admiration as the accommodation.

Muriwai Beach
Muriwai Beach, reached by turning off SH16 at Waimauku, is home to the **Takapu Refuge**, an Australasian gannet colony in the Muriwai Regional Park. The colony was once confined to a nearby rock stack but has now overflowed to the shore cliffs.

There's an easy walking trail to two viewing platforms, and this is a great opportunity to see (and smell) these beautiful birds at close range.

There's a **surf beach** stretching away into the distance, north of the refuge. You can go horse riding on the beach and through the bush with **Muriwai Beach Riding Centre** (☎ 09-411 8480; 1hr/2hr rides $50/70), which also runs lessons for beginners (around $60 for one hour). **Muriwai Beach Motor Camp** (☎ 09-411 9262; Motutara Rd; sites per 2 people $25) is shady, clean and on the beachfront.

Helensville
pop 2200

Less than 50km from central Auckland, this small town has a few historical buildings, a couple of antique shops, and two good accommodation options. **Helensville visitor information centre** (☎ 09-420 8060; www.helensville.co.nz; 27 Commercial Rd; 9am-5pm Mon-Fri, 1pm Sat & Sun) has details on the area.

Woodhill Mountain Bike Park (☎ 09-479 9194; admission adult/child $5/2, bike hire per hr $15-20; 7am-6pm, to 10pm Wed) has many challenging tracks around Woodhill Forest, west of Helensville.

Malolo House (☎ 09-420 7762; malolo@xtra.co.nz; 110 Commercial Rd; dm $20, d $80-90) has comfortable, refurbished accommodation that includes a communal spa bath and a lounge room with views. The dorm has six beds (bring your own sleeping bag) and some other cheapish rooms (without bathroom).

Kaipara House B&B (☎ 09-420 7462; kaiparah@ihug.co.nz; cnr SH16 & Parkhurst Rd; s $50, d & tw with bathroom $110) offers period-heavy rooms in the pink-hued house that will have most men scratching their balls as an antidote to all the flounces. Try the attractive self-contained cottages in a garden setting. There's a spa pool, and breakfast is included for the inside rooms.

Café Regent (☎ 09-420 9148; 14 Bridge St; meals $4-10; brunch, lunch & dinner Wed-Mon) in the foyer of the old Art Deco cinema, has home-cooked food, and offers a neat Saturday special of dinner ($15 at 6pm) and a movie ($10 at 8pm).

Corridor Bar (☎ 09-420 6040; 88 Commercial Rd; mains $16-31; dinner Wed-Sun) is a smart-enough bar with what passes for a view in these parts, some good main courses and a reasonable wine and cocktail list.

Parakai
pop 1100

Just 2km northwest of Helensville is **Parakai Aquatic Park** (Map p144; ☎ 09-420 8998; Parkhurst Rd; adult/child $14/8; 10am-10pm), which has a large outdoor hot-spring swimming pool and a couple of hydroslides, and is raucous on weekends with local teens. Somewhat shabby private spa pools cost an extra $4 for 30 minutes. The **camping ground** (sites per 2 people $15), next door, includes free entry to the hot pools.

HAURAKI GULF ISLANDS

The Hauraki Gulf, off Auckland, is dotted with *motu* (islands). Some are only minutes from the city and make popular day trips. Waiheke, a favourite weekend escape, and volcanic Rangitoto really should not be missed. Great Barrier, once a remote and little-visited island, still feels like a million miles from anywhere in the low season, and provides an escape from many aspects of modern life.

There are 47 islands in the Hauraki Gulf Maritime Park, administered by DOC. Some are good-sized islands, others are no more than rocks jutting out of the sea. The islands are loosely put into two categories: recreation and conservation. The recreation islands can easily be visited and their harbours are dotted with yachts in summer. The conservation islands, however, have restricted access. Special permits are required to visit some, and others cannot be visited at all as they are refuges for the preservation of rare plants and animals, especially birds.

For information on Kawau Island and Goat Island, see p165 and p167 respectively.

Information

The DOC information centre (p107) in Auckland's Ferry Building has the best information about walks and camping on the islands. The Auckland Visitors Centre (p107) is where you can find out about the more commercial aspects of the islands, such as accommodation and ferry services.

RANGITOTO & MOTUTAPU ISLANDS
pop 105

As recently as some 600 years ago, Rangitoto (260m) erupted from the sea and was

www.lonelyplanet.com

RANGITOTO & MOTUTAPU ISLANDS

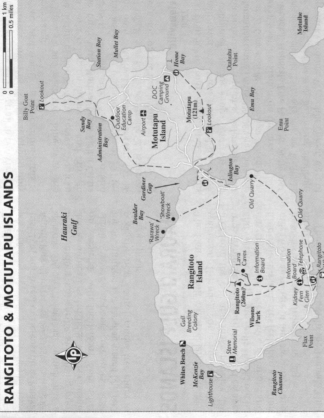

probably active for several years before settling down. It's now believed to be extinct. Maoris living on nearby Motutapu Island, to which Rangitoto is now joined by a causeway, certainly witnessed the eruptions, as human footprints have been found embedded in the ash thrown out during the course of the mountain's creation. Rangitoto (literally 'Blood Red Sky') is the largest and youngest of Auckland's volcanic cones.

Ten kilometres northeast of central Auckland, Rangitoto is a great place for a picnic. It has many pleasant walks, barbecues, a surprising amount of flora (including redflowering pohutukawa in summer) and a great view from the summit of the cone. There's an information board at the wharf with maps of the walks.

The hike from the wharf to the summit takes about an hour. Up at the top, a loop walk goes around the crater's rim. The walk to the lava caves branches off the summit walk and takes 30 minutes return. As the island's black volcanic rock can get hot in summer, you'll need good shoes and plenty of water.

Motutapu (www.motutapu.org.nz), in contrast to Rangitoto, is mainly covered in grassland, which is grazed by sheep and cattle. Archaeologically, this is a very significant island, and the traces of some 500 years of continuous human habitation are etched into its landscape.

A **DOC camping ground** (09-372 7348; adult/ child \$5/2.50) is at Home Bay on Motutapu. Facilities are basic, with only a water tap and flush toilet provided. Bring cooking equipment, as open fires are forbidden. It's a three-hour walk from Rangitoto wharf.

The **Outdoor Education Camp** (09 445 4486 www.motutapucamp.org.nz; per person/cottage/lodge \$15/ \$150/\$300) has a self-contained cottage that sleeps up to 12 people in bunk rooms, a lodge that sleeps 34 in bunk rooms and a main camp that sleeps 180 in dormitories. Pick up from Rangitoto ferry can be arranged, and kayaking, sailing, abseiling and other courses and activities are available. Bookings essential.

Fullers (09-367 9111) has the tour of the island, the **Volcanic Explorer** (adult/child \$29/15), which gives you a ride around the island in a canopied trailer, towed by a 4WD tractor, to a 900m boardwalk leading to the summit (the views are great).

Getting There & Around

The ferry trip to Rangitoto Island from Auckland's Ferry Building takes about 20 minutes. **Fullers** (☎ 09-367 9111; adult/child return $18.40/10.40) has boats leaving Auckland at 9.15am, 12.15pm and 3pm daily.

WAIHEKE ISLAND

pop 8500

Waiheke is the most visited of the gulf islands and, at 93 sq km, is one of the largest. Though only a little over half an hour by ferry from Auckland, Waiheke enjoys a relaxed pace and a fine climate; its many picturesque bays and safe beaches make it a great place to relax, and vineyards and olive groves proliferate.

The island attracts artistic types who exhibit their work in local galleries and craft shops. It is a fashionable seaside retreat that deserves more than one day. To experience Waiheke at its peaceful best, try to avoid weekends.

Waiheke has been inhabited since about AD 950 and Maori oral legends relate that one of the pioneering canoes landed on the island. Traces of an old fortified *pa* can still be seen on the headland overlooking Putiki Bay. Europeans arrived with the missionary Samuel Marsden in the early 1800s and the island was soon stripped of its kauri forest.

The biggest event on the island is the annual **Waiheke Jazz Festival** (www.waihekejazz.co.nz), which draws up to 30,000 people over the Easter weekend.

Information

Netspace (☎ 09-372 9921; Pendragon Mall; per hr $5; ⊗ 9am–6pm Mon-Sat, noon–5pm Sun) Has Internet access.

Waiheke Island visitors centre (☎ 09-372 1234; info@waiheke.co.nz; 2 Korora Rd; ⊗ 9am–5pm) In the Artworks complex in Oneroa.

Orientation

Nearly 2km from Matiatia wharf, the main village is Oneroa, which has a sandy beach below. The eastern half of the island is lightly populated and well worth exploring. There are petrol stations in Ostend and Onetangi, and Oneroa has ATMs.

Sights

The **Artworks complex** (☎ 09-372 6900; cnr Ocean View & Korora Rds; ⊗ daily) houses a library, community theatre and cinema, art and craft galleries and secondhand bookshop as well as an Indian restaurant and the visitors centre. Also part of the complex is **Whittaker's Musical Experience** (☎ 09-372 5573; adult/child $12.50/5; ⊗ 10am–4pm, closed Tue & Fri), an endearingly run collection of antique organs and instruments, which the owners play and talk about from 1pm to 2.30pm on open days.

On the road to Onetangi, next to the golf club, is the **Waiheke Island Historic Village & Museum** (☎ 09-372 2970; admission by donation; Onetangi Rd; ⊗ noon–4pm Mon, Wed, Sat & Sun) with exhibits displayed in five restored buildings.

The free *Waiheke Island Art Map* gives details of more than 30 photographers, potters, artists and jewellery designers who can be visited.

The bustling **Ostend market** (Belgium St; ⊗ 8am–1pm Sat) is held inside and outside the Ostend Hall, next to the RSA. Here you can find local produce, books and clothes, handicrafts, plants and so on.

WINERIES

Waiheke has 24 vineyards that you can visit for tasting and sales, and some of them have very good restaurants. Because of an emphasis on quality rather than quantity, the premium wine produced here is relatively expensive and nearly all the wineries charge for tastings (around $10). Some are spectacularly located and worth a visit for that reason alone. Pick up the free *Waiheke island of Wine* brochure from the visitors centre. Opening hours vary considerably.

Connells Bay (☎ 09-372 8957; www.connellsbay.co.nz; Connells Bay; adult/child $30/15; ⊗ by appointment) is an extraordinary sculpture park and a definite Waiheke highlight. It features a stellar roster of NZ artists, such as Paul Dibble, Cathryn Monro, Virginia King and Jeff Thomson. Particular highlights are the kinetic works of Phil Price, and Chris Booth's *Slip*. Admission includes a detailed and highly informative guided tour and the chance to take in some of Waiheke's most breathtaking views. See p152 for details about accommodation at this very special spot.

Te Whau (☎ 09-372 7191; www.tewhau.com; 218 Te Whau Dr; mains $28–78; ⊗ lunch Wed-Mon Oct-Easter, Sat & Sun Easter-Sep) is a spectacular place perched

www.lonelyplanet.com

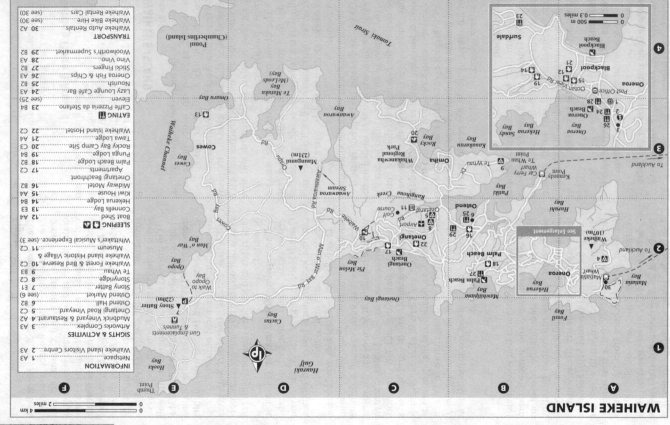

WAIHEKE ISLAND

INFORMATION
Netspace 1 A3
Waiheke Island Visitors Centre........ 2 A3

SIGHTS & ACTIVITIES
Artworks Complex 3 A3
Mudbrick Vineyard & Restaurant 4 A2
Onetangi Road Vineyard 5 C2
Ostend Hall 6 B2
Ostend Market .... (see 6)
Stony Batter 7 E1
Storyridge 8 C2
Te Whau 9 B3
Waiheke Forest & Bird Reserve..... 10 C2
Waiheke Island Historic Village &
Museum 11
Whittaker's Musical Experience.. (see 3)

SLEEPING
Boat Shed 12 A4
Connells Bay 13 E3
Hekerua Lodge 14 B4
Kiwi House 15 A4
Midway Motel 16 B2
Onetangi Beachfront
Apartments 17 C2
Palm Beach Lodge 18 B2
Punga Lodge 19 B4
Rocky Bay Camp Site 20 C3
Tawa Lodge 21 A4
Waiheke Island Hostel 22 C2

EATING
Caffe Pizzeria da Stefano 23 B4
Eleven .... (see 25)
Lazy Lounge Café Bar 24 A3
Nourish 25 B2
Oneroa Fish & Chips 26 A3
Sticki Fingers 27 B2
Vino Vino 28 A3
Woolworth's Supermarket 29 B2

TRANSPORT
Waiheke Auto Rentals 30 A2
Waiheke Bike Hire .... (see 30)
Waiheke Rental Cars .... (see 30)

on the end of Te Whau peninsula, with extraordinary views. It is open for tastings from 11am to 5pm Wednesday to Monday in summer, Saturday and Sunday in winter. The excellent restaurant menu (under the guidance of chef Craig Hill) concentrates on Pacific Rim fare.

Picturesque **Mudbrick Vineyard & Restaurant** (☎ 09-372 9050; www.mudbrick.co.nz; 126 Church Bay Rd; mains $32-38; ☑ lunch & dinner) has tours and wine tasting, plus sweeping views and a truly special dining area.

Stonyridge (☎ 09-372 8822; www.stonyridge.co.nz; 80 Onetangi Rd; mains $26-29; ☑ lunch daily Oct-Easter, Fri-Sun winter) is one of the oldest and most famous wineries on Waiheke. Tours cost $10 and include cork trees, an olive grove and tasting; they take place at 11.30am Saturday and Sunday, but daily during the peak season.

Onetangi Road Vineyard (☎ 09-372 1014; www.onetangiroad.co.nz; 82 Onetangi Rd; platters $16-18; ☑ 11am-6pm daily Dec-Mar, 11am-4pm Wed-Sun Apr-Nov) has a winery and a microbrewery. Wine tasting (four wines), beer tasting (four beers), a wine-making tour and a beer-brewing tour are available. The Baroona Dark Ale is a winner.

BEACHES

Deservedly popular beaches with good sand and swimming include **Oneroa Beach**, **Palm Beach** and the adjacent **Little Oneroa Beach**. Palm Beach is in a truly lovely little cove, and there's a long stretch of sand at Onetangi Bay, 12km from Matiatia wharf. A number of the beaches have shady pohutukawa trees. There are nudist beaches at Palm Beach and Onetangi Bay; head west just past some rocks in both cases.

Activities

Waiheke has a good system of walkways outlined in the *Waiheke Islands Walkways* pamphlet, which has detailed maps and descriptions of eight hikes that take from 1½ to three hours. It is available on the island or at the DOC office in Auckland (p107).

In Onetangi there's the **Waiheke forest & bird reserve** with several good walks. For coastal walks, a good, well-marked track leads right around the coast from Oneroa Bay to Palm Beach. It's about a two-hour walk; and at the Palm Beach end you can jump on a bus back to town. Another good coastal walk begins at the Matiatia ferry wharf.

Other walks are in the relatively undeveloped eastern part of the island. At the end of Man o' War Bay Rd there's a car park and a 1.5km walk to **Stony Batter**, where you can explore WWII tunnels and gun emplacements that were built in 1941 to defend Auckland's harbour. The walk leads through private farmland, and derives its name from the boulder-strewn fields. The tunnels are open from 9am to 3pm Thursday, Saturday and Sunday and admission costs $5. Bring a torch.

Ross Adventures (☎ 09-372 5550; www.kayakwaiheke.co.nz; Matiatia; 4hr trip $65) runs good short trips as well as overnight and all-day paddles ($125). Kayak hire starts at $15 per hour.

Kayak Company (☎ 09-372 2112; www.thekayakcompany.co.nz; half-/full-day trips $75/120) operates day and moonlight excursions. Kayak hire is $55 a day.

Flying Carpet (☎ 09-372 5621; www.flyingcarpet.co.nz; half-/full-day trips $50/110) offers outings on an ocean-going catamaran sailing boat.

Windsurfing Waiheke (☎ 09-372 6275; www.windsurfing-waiheke.co.nz; boards per hr $20-30, tuition per hr $45) operates from different beaches depending on conditions.

Tours

Fullers (☎ 09-367 9111) runs a Vineyard Explorer tour (adult $85, usually at 11am) that visits three of the island's top wineries and includes a light lunch at Stonyridge (left). There's also a 1½-hour Explorer tour (adult/child $42/21, at 10am and noon), which provides a good introduction to the lay of the land.

Waiheke Island Adventures (☎ 09-372 6127; www.waihekeislandadventures.com) runs customised tours such as one-hour scenic tours ($25), two-hour vineyard tours ($50), or Stony Batter tours ($35) in a 15-seater bus. Art and beach tours are also available.

With **Ananda Tours** (☎ 09-372 7530; www.ananda.co.nz) you can do a guided walk on the eco tour (around $65) or visit artists and their studios, or local wineries ($95 to $170). The informal minibus and 17-seater bus tours (three to four hours) can both be customised to suit your needs.

Sleeping

Waiheke has more than a hundred backpackers, B&Bs, lodges, baches or apartments for rent, costing anything from $21 to $700

AUTHOR'S CHOICE

Connells Bay (☎ 09-372 8957; www.connells bay.co.nz; Cowes Bay Rd; cottage $350) Fancy your own private art-filled retreat that combines the best of the country and the seaside and is luxurious without being glitzy? Connells Bay is the perfect place. Descend to this extraordinary property via a perilously steep driveway to the magnificent sculpture garden created by the husband-and-wife team of John and Jo Gow. The native-plant bedecked landscape is studded with innovative and often site-specific sculpture pieces by renowned artists such as Jeff Thomson, Chris Booth, Paul Dibble, Phil Price and Virginia King, and a guided two-hour walking tour through the works is included in the price. Your actual accommodation couldn't be more heavenly – a century-old weatherboard two-bedroom cottage with kauri pine floors, smart kitchen, veranda, garden and absolute water frontage. The interior is comfortable, beautiful and chic and allows you to instantly relax as soon as you cross the threshold, making this an excellent romantic escape. One of the greatest properties we've ever seen, without a doubt.

HOSTELS & CAMP SITES

Hekerua Lodge (☎ 09-372 8990; www.hekerualodge .co.nz; 11 Hekerua Rd; dm $22-30, s $38, d & tw $68, d with bathroom $100, self-contained cabin $220; ☐) This secluded hostel is one of the city's great escapes and represents the perfect chance to go native on glorious Waiheke Island. It's far from luxurious, and a bit of a pain to get to without your own car, but it's one of the most memorable hostels in the Auckland area and has a lovely, laid-back feel. Guests here seem notably more relaxed than guests at other hostels, or even hotels. There's a barbecue, stone-tiled pool, sunny deck, casual lounge area and it even has its own bush track. It's a 15-minute walk to Oneroa but buses stop nearby.

Waiheke Island Hostel (☎ 09-372 8971; www.wai heke.cjb.net; 419 Seaview Rd, Onetangi Bay; dm/s $24/36, d $54-76) This colourful associate-YHA has a large garden, helpful staff and overlooks Onetangi Beach. The dorms have only two bunk beds, linen is provided, mountain bikes can be hired and other activities can be booked commission-free. One drawback? It's a little smelly in corners.

At the far end of Gordons Rd in the Whakanewha Regional Park is **Rocky Bay camp site** (☎ 09-366 2000; site adult/child $5/3). Telephone to make a reservation and for the combination number to unlock the gate. Only drinking water and long-drop toilets are provided.

B&BS & LODGES

Kiwi House (☎ 09-372 9123; kiwihouse@clear.net.nz; 23 Kiwi St; s $45, d & tw $85, d & tw with bathroom $95) This friendly guesthouse offers pleasant decks, a shared kitchen and reasonable prices, plus a dog whose bark is worse than its bite.

Punga Lodge (☎/fax 09-372 6675; www.punga lodge.co.nz; 223 Ocean View Rd; apt $135-200) Both the colourful en suite rooms in the house and the self-contained garden units have access to decks in this very bushy setting. There's a spa pool, and prices include homemade breakfast, afternoon tea and transfers from Matiatia Wharf.

The same people who own Punga Lodge also own the very good **Tawa Lodge** (☎ 09-372 9434; tawalodge@hotmail.com; 15 Tawa St; B&B $115, apt $160, cottage $220).

a night. Prices at most places jump from mid-December to the end of January and at Easter (when you'd be lucky to get a bed anywhere without reservations).

MOTELS, APARTMENTS & RESORTS

Midway Motel (☎ 09-372 8023; waihekemidway@xtra .co.nz; 1 Whakarite Rd, Ostend; studio/1-bed unit/3-bed house $90/100/120; ☐) Units have Sky TV and kitchens but the main attraction at this reasonably priced and centrally located motel is the heated covered pool and spa.

Onetangi Beachfront Apartments (☎ 09-372 7051; www.onetangi.co.nz; 27 The Strand, Onetangi Beach; studio $150, 1- & 2-bed apt $210-245, luxury apt $350) The price variations are seasonal and quite dramatic for this smart, perfectly located accommodation with a spa and sauna, and good management.

Palm Beach Lodge (☎ 09-372 7763; www.waiheke .co.nz/palmbch.htm; 23 Tiri View Rd; 2-bed apt $280) You'll have no complaints about the huge rooms, the million-dollar views or the warm hospitality at this great place, where it seems that even the budgerigars match the décor.

Boat Shed (☎ 09-372 3242; www.boatshed.co.nz; cnr Tawa & Huia Sts; units $630-790) This scene-stealing architect-designed home has very fine views and a telescope, plus an abundance of candles, flowers, music, a log fire, a bar and a restaurant. It's pretty plush, but it does have a slightly 'stage-managed' feel that resembles a Ralph Lauren shop in parts. A lovely four-course dinner costs $90.

Eating & Drinking

The place for cafés, bars and restaurants is Oneroa's main street, but there are a few scattered around in Matiatia, Surfdale, Palm Beach, Ostend and Onetangi. Surfdale, between Oneroa and Ostend, has a restaurant-takeaway, café and a pub. For details on restaurants at wineries see p149.

Vino Vino (☎ 09-372 9888; 153 Ocean View Rd, Oneroa; dinner mains $17-25; ☒ lunch & dinner summer) One of the island's best restaurants, with a bar, deck, beautiful sea views and an emphasis on Mediterranean-style seafood, such as Coromandel mussels in crayfish bisque. Smooth service too.

Oneroa Fish & Chips (☎ 09-372 8752; 29 Waikare Rd, Oneroa; boxed meals $4-12; ☒ lunch & dinner) Hidden away between the police station and another café is this superior takeaway that also does mouthwatering burgers.

Lazy Lounge Café Bar (☎ 09-372 5732; 139 Ocean View Rd, Oneroa; snacks $5-16; ☒ breakfast, lunch & dinner) This funky laid-back place above the Rockit Gallery has indoor/outdoor areas, some of which have a 1960s feel, with worn sofas, good music, art on the walls, sea views and a great range of food from deli items to pizzas.

Caffe Pizzeria da Stefano (☎ 09-372 5309; 18 Hamilton Rd, Surfdale; pasta $14-17; ☒ dinner Tue-Sun) Stefano's is the best-smelling joint on Waiheke, and serves lovely pasta staples, wonderful pizzas and great garlic bread (plus wine by the glass) in the presence of an authentically dodgy mural.

Sticki Fingers (☎ 09-372 3068; 39 Palm Rd, Surfdale; pizza $14-20; ☒ breakfast, lunch & dinner summer) This breezy, welcoming café-restaurant-bar at Palm Beach offers an interesting pizza menu (including a vegan option) and fine coffee.

Nourish (☎ 09-372 3557; 3 Belgium St, Ostend; breakfast $5.50-18; ☒ lunch and dinner daily Oct-Apr, dinner Fri & Sat Oct-Apr) This cool modern café with outdoor seating has the best brekkie on the island (the mushrooms in balsamic cream

are reason enough to come to Waiheke) and beautiful lunch treats such as lamb shanks. Also, the coffee is fantastic.

Eleven (☎ 09-372 5611; 11 Belgium St, Ostend; mains $26-33) This is Ostend's swishest option, with a wine bar and good restaurant serving bouillabaisse and risotto for dinner. On the premises is the Rock Sports Bar, which isn't bad for a beer.

Self-caterers should head to **Woolworth's Supermarket** (102 Ostend Rd, Ostend).

Getting There & Away

Fullers (☎ 09-367 9911; adult/child return $26/13) runs frequent daily ferries between central Auckland and Matiatia Wharf. From Monday to Friday ferries operate approximately hourly from 5.20am to 11.45pm (on the hour between 9am and 5pm). On Saturday it's 6.30am to 11.45pm, and on Sunday and public holidays 7am until 9.30pm. Services take 35 minutes and a few go via Devonport.

Subritzky Line (☎ 09-300 5900; www.subritzky.co.nz/car/motorcyclereturn $113/40, adult/child return $26.50/14.50) takes cars and passengers on its route from Half Moon Bay in Pakuranga to Kennedy Point on Waiheke. The ferry runs at least every two hours between 6am and 7.30pm Monday to Friday, 6am and 7pm on Saturday and 7am and 6pm on Sunday. The journey takes 45 minutes and bookings are essential.

Getting Around

BUS

Fullers (☎ 09-366 6400) operates four bus routes on the island and all connect with the arriving and departing ferries. All buses go from Matiatia Wharf to Oneroa, then depending on the route you can get to Little Oneroa, Palm Beach, Ostend and Rocky Bay; or Blackpool, Surfdale, Ostend and Onetangi. Matiatia to Oneroa costs $1.20, Matiatia Wharf to Palm Beach costs $2.90 and an all-day bus pass is $10.

CAR & BICYCLE

The island is hilly and places to visit are spread out, and there are 12km, 25km and 70km loop bicycle routes. Mountain bikes can be hired at **Waiheke Bike Hire** (☎ 09-372 7937; Matiatia Wharf; ☒ 9am-5pm) for $20/30 per half/full day.

Waiheke Auto Rentals (☎ 09-372 8998) and **Waiheke Rental Cars** (☎ 09-372 8635), both at

Matiatia Wharf, rent out cars from $50 a day and 4WDs from $75. You must be over 21, pay 60c a kilometre, and the insurance excess (deposit) is $750. A cheaper rate applies for two-hour hires. Waiheke Rental Cars also hires out 50cc scooters ($30 for two hours, $500 excess) and motorbikes ($45 for four hours, $750 excess) neither of which have a kilometre charge.

TAXI

There are lots of car and minibus taxis. Try **Waiheke Taxis** (☎ 09-372 8038).

GREAT BARRIER ISLAND

pop 1000

Great Barrier (Aotea), 88km from the mainland, is the largest island in the gulf. It's a rugged and scenic island, resembling the Coromandel Peninsula to which it was once joined. Named by James Cook, Great Barrier Island later became a whaling, mining and logging centre, but all these industries have had their day. Most of the island is publicly owned and managed by DOC.

Great Barrier has unspoilt beaches, hot springs, old kauri dams, a forest sanctuary and a network of tramping tracks. Because there are no possums on the island, the native bush is lush. The west coast has safe sandy beaches, while the east coast beaches are good for surfing. Mountain biking, swimming, fishing, diving, boating, sea kayaking and just relaxing are other popular activities on the island.

Although easily reached from Auckland, Great Barrier seems a world – and a good many years – away. The island has no supermarket, no electricity supply (only private generators), no main drainage (only septic tanks), most roads are unsealed, and petrol costs are high. Mobile-phone reception is very limited and there are no banks, ATMs or street lights. It's a wild, untamed and very special place with its own rules, and is a definite breath of fresh air.

From around mid-December to mid-January is the peak season, so make sure you book transport, accommodation and activities well in advance.

Orientation

Tryphena is the main settlement and is 3km away from the ferry wharf at Shoal Bay. Strung out along several kilometres

of coastal road, it consists of a few dozen houses, a primary school and a handful of shops and accommodation places dotted around the harbour. From the wharf it is a couple of kilometres to Mulberry Grove, and then another 1km over the headland to Pa Beach and the Stonewall Store.

The airport and visitors centre are at Claris, a small settlement with a general store, bottle shop, laundrette, vehicle repair garage, fuel, an adventure centre and café, about 16km north of Tryphena. Whangaparapara is an old timber town and the site of the island's 19th-century whaling activities. Port Fitzroy is the other main harbour on the west coast, a one-hour drive from Tryphena (roads are unsealed beyond Claris).

Information

The free *Great Barrier Island* booklet is full of useful and up-to-date information.

Aotea Health Centre (☎ 09-429 0356; Claris) Has a full-time doctor and dentist as well as nurses. A nurse is also stationed at Port Fitzroy.

DOC office (☎ 09-429 0044; Port Fitzroy; ⏰ 8am-4.30pm Mon-Fri) Is 1km from the Port Fitzroy jetty and deals with the DOC huts, camp sites and hiking trails.

Great Barrier Island visitors centre (☎ 09-429 0033; www.greatbarrier.co.nz; Claris; ⏰ 9am-3pm Mon-Fri, 9am-1pm Sat & Sun) Is opposite the airfield and has shorter hours in winter. The staff know most of the people on the island and can help with fishing charters.

Post office (Tryphena) Located in the Outpost gift shop.

Activities

SWIMMING & SURFING

Beaches on the west coast are safe, but care needs to be taken on the surf-pounded

---

PIGEON-GRAMS

Great Barrier's first pigeon-gram service took flight in 1897, a year after an enterprising Auckland newspaper reporter had used a pigeon to file a report from the island. From small beginnings the service expanded to include a good part of the Hauraki Gulf. Shopping lists, election results, mine claims and important pieces of news winged their way across land and sea tied to the legs of the canny birds. The arrival of the telegraph in 1908 grounded the service, but the pigeon-gram stamps are now prized collector's items.

GREAT BARRIER ISLAND

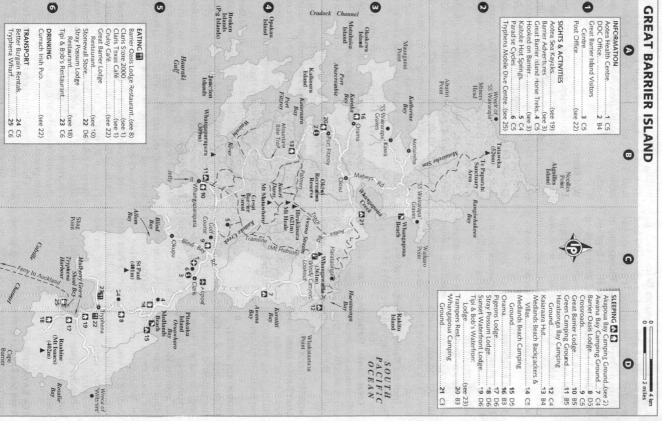

INFORMATION
Aotea Health Centre	1 C5
DOC Office	(see 3)
Great Barrier Island Visitors Centre	2 B4
Post Office	(see 22)

SIGHTS & ACTIVITIES
Aotea Sea Kayaks	(see 19)
Barrier Adventures	(see 3)
Great Barrier Island Horse Treks	4 C5
Hooked on Barrier	(see 3)
Katiote Hot Springs	5 C4
Parad se Cycles	6 C5
Tryphena Mobile Dive Centre	(see 25)

SLEEPING
Akapoua Bay Camping Ground	(see 2)
Awana Bay Camping Ground	7 C4
Barrier Oasis Lodge	8 C5
Crossroads	9 C5
Great Barrier Lodge	10 B5
Green Camping Ground	11 B5
Harataonga Bay Camping Ground	12 C4
Kaiaraara Hut	13 B4
Medlands Beach Backpackers & Villas	14 C5
Medlands Beach Camping Ground	15 D5
Orama	16 B3
Pigeons Lodge	17 D6
Stray Possum Lodge	18 D6
Sunset Waterfront Lodge	19 D6
Tipi & Bob's Waterfront Lodge	(see 23)
Trampers Rest	20 B3
Whangapoua Camping Ground	21 C3

EATING
Barrier Oasis Lodge Restaurant	(see 8)
Claris Store 2000	(see 1)
Claris Texas Café	(see 1)
Crusty Café	(see 22)
Great Barrier Lodge Restaurant	(see 10)
Stonewall Store	22 D6
Stray Possum Lodge	(see 18)

DRINKING
Currach Irish Pub	(see 22)
Tipi & Bob's Restaurant	23 C6

TRANSPORT
Better Bargain Rentals	24 C5
Tryphena Wharf	25 C6

0   2 miles
0   4 km

eastern beaches. **Medlands Beach**, with its wide sweep of white sand, is one of the best beaches on the island and is easily accessible from Tryphena. Remote **Whangapoua** in the northeast requires more effort to get to, while **Kaitoke**, **Awana Bay** and **Harataonga** on the east coast are also worth a visit.

Okiwi Bar has an excellent right-hand break, while Awana has both left- and right-hand breaks. Tryphena's bay, lined with pohutukawa, has sheltered beaches.

DIVING & FISHING

There's pinnacle diving, shipwreck diving, lots of fish and more than 33m visibility at some times of the year.

Hooked on Barrier (☎ 09-429 0417; Claris) sells and hires out diving, snorkelling, fishing, surfing and kayak (both from $35 per hour) gear. You can dive from a beach or charter a boat.

Tryphena Mobile Dive Centre (☎ 09-429 0654; Tryphena Wharf) hires out dive tanks and weight belts and fills tanks.

Great Barrier Surfcasting Safaris (☎ 09-429 0995; www.islandaccommodation.co.nz; per head $85-130) offers rockfishing trips that have all safety gear and the local knowledge of Big John.

HORSE TREKKING

Great Barrier Island Horse Treks (☎ 09-429 0274; Medlands; 1hr/2hr rides $40/80) offers guided beach riding and swimming with horses (the horses do the swimming).

MOUNTAIN BIKING

With rugged scenery and little traffic on the unsealed roads, mountain biking is a popular activity here. A good ride is from Tryphena to Whangaparapara: cycle about an hour to Medlands Beach, then cycle another hour to the hot springs, from where it's another half-hour to accommodation in Whangaparapara. Spend another day cycling through the forest up to Port Fitzroy, stopping on the way for a hike up to the kauri dams on a good, well-marked 4WD track.

Paradise Cycles (☎ 09-429 0303; Claris) hires out mountain bikes and organises cycling tours.

SEA KAYAKING

Aotea Sea Kayaks (☎ 09-429 0664; www.greatbarrier .co.nz/kayak/index.htm) runs sunset ($35), snor-

kelling ($55), and guided paddles ($85). You can even paddle right round the island, but it takes 10 days. Night paddlers experience phosphorescence on the water surface.

WALKING

Many people come here for the walks but be aware that trails are not always well signposted, although they are regularly upgraded. Be properly equipped with water and food, and be prepared for bad weather. The best tramping trails are in the Great Barrier Forest north of Whangaparapara, where there has been a great deal of reforestation.

The most spectacular short walk is from Windy Canyon to Hirakimata (Mt Hobson). **Windy Canyon**, which is only a 15-minute walk from the main Port Fitzroy–Harataonga (Aotea) road, has spectacular rock outcrops and affords great views of the island.

From Windy Canyon, an excellent trail continues for another 1½ hours through scrubby forest to **Hirakimata** (621m), the highest point on the island, with views across to the Coromandel and Auckland on a fine day. Near the top of the mountain are lush forests and a few mature kauri trees that survived the logging days. From Hirakimata it is two hours through forest to the hut closest to Port Fitzroy and then 45 minutes to Port Fitzroy itself.

Another very popular walk is the **Kaitoke Hot Springs Track**. The natural hot pools can be reached from Whangaparapara Rd (45 minutes).

A more challenging tramp is the **Tramline Track** (five hours), which starts on Aotea Rd and follows old logging tramlines to Whangaparapara Harbour. The track is hilly and in some parts the clay becomes slippery after rain.

Many other trails traverse the forest, taking between 30 minutes and five hours. Pick up a copy of DOC's fold-out *Great Barrier Island* hiking brochure ($2 donation), which has a detailed map and short descriptions of 23 hikes. It's available from the visitors centre and many accommodation places.

There is a good trampers bus service that will drop you at the start of a trail and pick you up at the other end; see p158.

OTHER ACTIVITIES

Barrier Adventures (09-429 0699; www.barrier adventures.co.nz; Claris; adult/child $49/20) offers one-hour 8WD Argo tours around the Claris area that traverse beach, wetland and volcanic terrain. Mountain bikes can also be hired to ride along special tracks, and bouldering, abseiling and even archery are available. It is near the airport.

Sleeping

There are half a dozen camp sites and backpacker hostels and more than 50 lodges, cottages and B&Bs spread around the island. Some accommodation places cater for a range of visitors from backpackers and campers to luxury-seeking honeymooners and also run restaurants and bars that are open to nonguests. Prices can be steep in summer, but rates can drop dramatically outside the peak period. Summer prices are quoted here.

CAMP SITES, HUTS & HOSTELS

There are DOC camping grounds at Harataonga Bay, Medlands Beach, Akapoua Bay, Whangapoua, The Green (Whangaparapara) and Awana Bay. Prices are adult/child $9/4.50. All have basic facilities, including water (cold showers) and chemical toilets. You need to bring your own gas cooking stove. Bookings are essential in December and January and camping is not allowed outside the camping grounds without a permit. To book, contact the DOC information office, p154.

Kaiaraara Hut (per person $10) This DOC hut in the Great Barrier Forest is a 45-minute walk from Port Fitzroy wharf. The hut sleeps up to 28 in two bunk rooms, and facilities include cold water, chemical toilets and a kitchen with a wood stove. Bring your own sleeping bag and cooking equipment. It operates on a first-come, first-served basis, but is never full. You can also camp outside for $5 (child $2.50).

Stray Possum Lodge (0800 767 785, 09-429 0109; www.straypossum.co.nz; sites per person $12, dm/d & tw/chalets $20/60/125) Nestled in the bush south of Tryphena is this popular place with its own bar and restaurant (see p158). Good dorms have six or eight beds and the chalets are self-contained and sleep up to six.

Crossroads (09-429 0889; xroads@ihug.co.nz; 1 Blind Bay Rd, Claris; dm/d/tw $25/35/60) This comfy,

low-key backpackers is 2km from the airfield and is run by lovely Kate and boisterously un-PC Bruce. Mountain bikes can be hired, and golf clubs can be borrowed free to play on the nearby nine-hole golf course.

Medlands Beach Backpackers & Villas (09-429 0320; www.medlandsbeach.com; 9 Mason Rd; dm $25, d & tw $60-80) Basic accommodation is provided at the cheaper rates. It's a five-minute walk to a beautiful beach and there's usually some water-sport equipment. The villa sleeps up to six, the chalet is for those wanting privacy.

Orama (09-429 0063; www.orama.org.nz; Karaka Bay; sites per person $10, dm $30, units $130-220;) Surrounded by hectares of bush, plenty of diverse accommodation is available at this Christian community just north of Port Fitzroy. There's a small shop, and kayaks, rowing dinghies, fishing and snorkelling gear are available. Environmental projects pursued here include protecting the endangered brown teal and kaka parrot.

Trampers Rest (09-429 0503; 244 Kaiaraara Bay Rd, Port Fitzroy; dm $25) An ideal place to recuperate from tramping, in a secluded, restful spot near Port Fitzroy. Accommodation is very simple (two beds in a hut with only an outdoor dunny), but it's a bargain.

GUESTHOUSES, LODGES & MOTELS

Great Barrier Lodge (09-429 0488; Whangaparapara Harbour; dm $80, studio units $145-165, cottage $175) This large modern place on the water's edge enjoys a glorious outlook over the inlet and is near the tramping tracks. There's a small shop, restaurant (p158) and bar, and mountain bikes and kayaks are available.

Pigeons Lodge (09-429 0437; www.pigeons lodge.co.nz; 179 Shoal Bay Rd; cottage $120, d & tw $150) On the beachfront south of Tryphena, this lovely lodge has a 2.5-acre bush setting, friendly management and good breakfasts.

Tipi & Bob's Waterfront Lodge (09-429 0550; www.waterfrontlodge.co.nz; Puriri Bay Rd, Tryphena; units $150-200) West of Tryphena, these modern units have some wonderful sea views. The complex includes a restaurant and bar (p158), taking care of almost everything.

Sunset Waterfront Lodge (09-429 0051; www .sunsetlodge.co.nz; Tryphena; studios/A-frame villas $168/208) The airy, attractive units have decks and views, and facilities include a games room and a three-hole pitch-and-putt on the lawn, plus a helipad. A small shop and café is next door.

Barrier Oasis Lodge (☎ 09-429 0021; www.barrier oasis.net; B&B d $250) This is a great choice for those seeking a little luxury and character, with three bright rooms, plus a self-contained unit, on a property that includes a vineyard and winery offering wine tasting. The restaurant here is also worth a visit (below).

Eating & Drinking

Claris Texas Café (☎ 09-429 0811; Claris Centre; ☷ 9am-3pm Mon-Fri, 9am-1pm Sat & Sun) This café is licensed, has Internet access, Atomic coffee and pretty good nachos, *panini* and other basic fare, in a suitable 'Paris, Texas' style.

Stray Possum Lodge Restaurant (☎ 09-429 0109; meals under $25) Offers pizzas and a varied takeaway-style menu in a very convivial atmosphere (especially in summer) that's fully licensed. This is also a good, casual place to stay (p157).

Tipi & Bob's Restaurant (☎ 09-429 0550; www .waterfrontlodge.co.nz; Puriri Bay Rd, Tryphena; bar menu $4-23; ☷ breakfast, lunch & dinner) This popular haunt has a very inviting deck overlooking the harbour, with fresh fish, seafood and steaks on the menu. There's a bistro menu in the bar, which has good fish and chips, and a nicer licensed restaurant on the premises.

Barrier Oasis Lodge Restaurant (☎ 09-429 0021; Tryphena; dinner $65) This is a very good place for a night of fine dining in attractive surrounds. It features a fixed-price two-course lunch or three-course dinner with fresh, local seafood (such as Clevedon oysters and whitebait fritters) a speciality.

Great Barrier Lodge Restaurant (☎ 09-429 0488; Whangaparapara Harbour; mains $18-30) The menu here is based around lamb, steak and fresh fish, and it's handled very well too. The tranquil setting and beautiful view is an added bonus.

Claris Store 2000 (☎ 09-429 0852) Near the airport, and well-stocked with groceries, bread, organic meat, pizzas and pies.

Stonewall Store (☎ 09-429 0474; Blackwell Dr, Tryphena) You'll find this store, which sells groceries, juice, coffee and bait, in Tryphena.

Cruisy Café (☎ 09-429 0997; Blackwell Dr, Tryphena) Offers great locally baked goods.

Currach Irish Pub (☎ 09-429 0211; Blackwell Dr, Tryphena; mains $12-21) This lively and child-

friendly pub has a changing menu of seafood, steak and Asian-style meals and is the island's social centre. There's also live music at the weekend in summer.

Getting There & Away
AIR

Great Barrier Airlines (☎ 0800 900 600, 09-275 9120; www.greatbarrierairlines.co.nz; adult/child one way $89/55, fly/boat deal adult/child $139/90) flies roughly three times daily to Great Barrier Island from Auckland airport and twice daily from Dairy Flat aerodrome on Portman Rd on the way to Orewa. Flights take 35 minutes. You can fly one way and take a Subritzky ferry the other or fly to Great Barrier Island from Whangarei or Whitianga.

Mountain Air (Great Barrier Express; ☎ 0800 222 123, 09-256 7025; www.mountainair.co.nz; one way adult/child $95/55, fly/boat deal adult/child $139/90) flies three or four times a day to Great Barrier Island from Auckland airport, and four times a week from Whangarei. Both trips cost the same.

BOAT

Subritzky (☎ 09-300 5900; www.subritzky.co.nz; adult/child one way $60/40, return $95/65) is the main ferry provider, usually operating daily except Monday, Wednesday and Saturday, although daily in December and January. The boats also take cars ($315 return) and run from Wynyard Wharf in Auckland to Tryphena's Shoal Bay. Ring for times of sailings, which vary.

Fullers (☎ 09-367 9111; www.fullers.co.nz; adult/child one way $50/25, return $100/50) runs seasonal services, which take about two hours, from Auckland Ferry Building to Tryphena from mid-December to the end of January, usually at the weekend and public holidays.

Getting Around

From Tryphena in the south to Port Fitzroy in the north is 47km by (mostly) unsealed road, or 40km via Whangaparapara using the walking tracks. The roads are sealed, but narrow and winding, from Tryphena to Claris. Elsewhere they are graded but quite rough.

Great Barrier Buses (☎ 09-429 0474; www.great barrierbuses.co.nz) runs five buses a day from Stray Possum Lodge to Claris via Tryphena and Medlands Beach with two services continuing on to the hot pools and White

Cliffs. It also offers an excellent trampers transport service, which can drop you off at any of the main trail heads and pick you up at the other end. A one-day pass that includes trampers transport or scheduled services is $35, a weekend pass is $45 and a three-day pass is $55.

GBI Rent-A-Car (☎ 09-429 0062; gbi.rentacar@xtra.co.nz; Mulberry Grove Bay, Tryphena & Claris) hires out a wide range of hardy vehicles, including rattling Mazda Fun Tops starting at $60 and mokes at $80. The company also hires out adventure gear.

Great Barrier Buses & Aotea Rentals (☎ 09-429 0055) has airport and wharf transfers ($12 from Claris to Tryphena) and a bus service from Tryphena to Port Fitzroy ($15), which runs daily from December to February, and from Monday to Friday the rest of the year. Tours of the island can also be arranged.

Better Bargain Rentals (☎ 09-4290092; Tryphena) has cars from $65 a day and 4WDs from $85 a day.

Many of the accommodation places will pick you up from the airport or wharf if notified in advance.

TIRITIRI MATANGI ISLAND

This magical 210-hectare and predator-free island (www.tiritirimatangi.co.nz) is home to lots of endangered native birds, including the very rare and colourful takahe. Other birds that can be seen here are the bell bird (NZ's nightingale), stitch bird, saddleback, whitehead, kakariki, kokako, little spotted kiwi, brown teal, NZ robin, fernbird and penguins. The saddleback was close to extinction with just 150 left, but now there are more than 200 on Tiritiri alone.

The island was occupied by Maoris but was sold to the Crown in 1841 and farmers came in and cut down or burnt the forest. But since 1984 hundreds of volunteers have planted 250,000 native trees and the forest cover has regenerated. An 1865 lighthouse stands on the eastern end of the island.

Gulf Harbour Ferries (☎ 0800 888 006; adult/child from Auckland $46/23, from Gulf Harbour $26/14) has fer-ries to the island from Auckland and Gulf Harbour on the Whangaparaoa Peninsula on Thursday, Saturday and Sunday. The ferries leave central Auckland at 9am and Gulf Harbour at 9.50am, and arrive back in Gulf Harbour at 4pm and Auckland at 4.50pm. A guided walk on the island is a good deal at adult/child $5/2.50.

MOTUIHE ISLAND
pop 2

Between Waiheke and Rangitoto Islands, the remote 176-hectare Motuihe Island can be enjoyed for a couple of nights at a bargain price. Regenerating bush, walking tracks and sandy beaches are features of this island, which was a prison camp during WWI and has only two permanent residents. **Camping** (☎ 09-534 5419; adult/child $5/2) is possible but the only facilities are toilets and water.

Rubens water taxis (☎ 09-422 8881) has a shuttle service on Sundays and a water taxi service that you can book any time, although the latter will cost you a maximum of $110 one way.

OTHER ISLANDS

Little Barrier, located 25km northeast of Kawau Island (see p165), is one of NZ's prime nature reserves, and the only area of NZ rainforest unaffected by humans, deer or possums. Several rare species of birds, reptiles and plants live in the varied habitats on the volcanic island. Access to the island is highly restricted and a DOC permit is required before landing can be made on this closely guarded sanctuary.

Motuora is halfway between Kawau and Tiritiri Matangi. There is a wharf and camping site on the west coast of the island, but there is no regular ferry service (you'll need your own motor boat). Get a camping permit from the **ranger** (☎ 09-492 8586; adult/child $5/2.50) on Kawau. You can also book to sleep in the **bach** ($50 that sleeps four to five. Bring your own linen and food, although cooking equipment is included.

Northland & the Bay of Islands

If you're after breathtaking coast and seascapes, then this is the place to come. Blessed with some of New Zealand's most varied and spectacular scenery, Northland is the winterless paradise that takes in the country's atmospheric wind-blasted tip at Cape Reinga. In between you'll find surf-pounded beaches, a pristine west coast, 19th-century towns on once-bustling trade harbours, wild and lush national parks, mountainous golden sand dunes, scenic peninsulas, sheltered bays, diminutive rock islands, frolicking dolphins, world-class dive sites and what seems like thousands of tour operators ready to make your stay as exciting as possible.

Spend two weeks in this aquatic adventure zone and you could enjoy a different water sport or adventure activity every day, particularly in the Bay of Islands, where a lack of experience or equipment is never a problem. But there's also a palpable sense of history here, both Maori and Pakeha: Waitangi is where the treaty between tattooed Maori chiefs and the British Crown was first signed in 1840 after a vigorous debate that still continues over 165 years later. With Maori settlement also starting in this region, Northland is 'the birthplace of the nation' and the strong Maori influence in Northland adds an extra cultural dimension to any visit.

Tree-huggers will see their arms stretched to the limit as they eye up the awesome kauri trees that once covered much of the region. A few centuries-old giant kauri can still be seen, mainly in the protected and wild Waipoua Kauri Forest on the west coast. A keen local awareness of environmental issues makes a trip to the region an added pleasure for visitors.

HIGHLIGHTS

- Having your breath taken away by the scenery and the activities of the **Bay of Islands** (p185)
- Getting dwarfed by the ancient kauri trees of **Waipoua Kauri Forest** (p172)
- Touring in a 4WD along mighty **Ninety Mile Beach** (p180) to sacred **Cape Reinga** (p179)
- Scuba diving around the **Poor Knights Islands** (p200) and the Cavalli Islands, home to the **wreck of the Rainbow Warrior** (p184), and snorkelling or diving around **Goat Island Marine Reserve** (p167)
- Uncovering a unique sense of history at **Waitangi** (p189)
- Discovering remote, pristine and perfect beaches on the east coast at **Pakiri** (p167), **Matauri Bay** (p184) and **Matai Bay** (p181)
- Stepping back in time at charming and historic **Russell** (p193), **Mangonui** (p182) and **Rawene** (p175)

- ★ Cape Reinga
- ★ Ninety Mile Beach
- ★ Matai Bay
- ★ Mangonui ★ Cavalli Islands
- ★ Matauri Bay
- Waitangi ★ Russell ★ Bay of Islands
- ★ Rawene
- ★ Waipoua
- Kauri Forest
- ★ Poor Knights Islands
- Pakiri ★ Goat Island

■ TELEPHONE CODE: 09

■ www.northlandnz.com

NORTHLAND & THE BAY OF ISLANDS FACTS

Eat: Fried oysters from the Mangonui Fish Shop (p183)

Drink: Your way through the list of chemical-free microbrews at Brauhaus Frings (p204) in Whangarei

Read: The poems of Hone Tuwhare

Listen to: The one that got away' stories in any fishing club's bar

Watch: Christmas (2003) by director Gregory King and Christmas in an NZ bathroom will never seem the same

Swim with: Dolphins

Festival: Warkworth Scarecrow Festival (p165)

Tackiest tourist attraction: Not tacky but certainly quirky is Hundertwasser's rather splendid toilet block (p199) in Kawakawa

Climate

The Northland region averages seven rainy days per month in summer but 15 in winter. Temperatures can be a degree or two warmer than Auckland, especially on the east coast.

Getting There & Around

There are two main routes – east and west – through Northland to Cape Reinga at the top of NZ, and these can be travelled as a loop.

After visiting Orewa's beach, Waiwera Hot Springs and recommended detours to Puhoi historical village, Goat Island, Pakiri Beach and Waipu, take Hwy 12 and head west of Brynderwyn. The west coast route then passes along the Kauri Coast through Matakohe, Dargaville, the beautiful Waipoua Kauri Forest and the remote and scenic Hokianga Harbour to Kaitaia and on to Cape Reinga. This chapter describes a clockwise (west coast) route, but the direction you take may depend on the prevailing weather – if it's fine in the Bay of Islands, take advantage of it and head there first.

Northliner (☎ 09-307 5873; www.northliner.co.nz) and InterCity (☎ 09-623 1503; www.intercitycoach.co.nz) are the main bus services in Northland. The Northliner runs daily from Auckland to Paihia in the Bay of Islands and on to Kaitaia. The standard fare to Paihia is $45, but backpackers and over 50s receive a 30% discount. Travel on Wednesday affords the chance to take advantage of a limited number of discounted (25%) fares. Buy a backpacker or YHA card and you are entitled to excellent-value passes. The Bay of Islands pass ($60) takes you from Auckland to Paihia and back and you can get on and off anywhere along the way. The Loop pass ($90) is similar but you go up to Paihia and across to Opononi on the southern shore of the Hokianga Harbour and down the west coast past the Waipoua Kauri Forest to Dargaville, Matakohe and back to Auckland. The Northland Freedom pass ($120) adds in Kerikeri, Mangonui (north of the Bay of Islands) and Kaitaia to the Loop Pass.

InterCity's bus service and basic prices are similar to Northliner, but backpackers receive only a 15% discount and passengers must be over 60 to receive a 20% discount.

NORTH OF AUCKLAND

While many visitors, in their haste to get to the Bay of Islands, do this trip along State Highway 1 (SH1) in just a few hours, the east coast, north of Auckland, has many delightful bays and beaches. A multilane motorway takes you as far as Orewa and the Hibiscus Coast between Whangaparaoa

TOP ACTIVITIES

- Travel NZ's longest beach by 4WD (p180)
- Dive the Poor Knights Islands to see tropical coral (p200) or pay a visit to the *Rainbow Warrior* (p187)
- See NZ's famous kauri trees at Trounson (p172) or Waipoua (p172)
- Sandboard the dunes of Hokianga (p174) or Ahipara (p179)
- For one of the best chances of seeing dolphins in NZ, hit the waves in the Bay of Islands (p187)

and Warkworth. This is a popular holiday area for Aucklanders over the Christmas season. Heading further north, the coast is less developed but no less beautiful, with diving and snorkelling opportunities at Goat Island Marine Reserve.

WHANGAPARAOA PENINSULA

The Whangaparaoa (fa-nga-pa-ro-a) Peninsula – just north of Auckland off SH1 – is a heavily developed spit of land with a sub-urban feel and the 376-hectare **Shakespear Regional Park** at its tip. Windsurfers flock to Manly Beach, boaties leave from the Weiti River and Gulf Harbour, while swimmers head to one of the peninsula's fine beaches, and walkers and mountain bikers follow the

trails around the park. Hiking trails take 1½ to 2½ hours. Many native bush birds (especially pukeko) and waders can be seen here as well as native trees such as karaka, kowhai and puriri.

Buses from Auckland run to the park (about one hour). **Stagecoach** (☎ 09-373 9118; www.stagecoach.co.nz) runs buses commencing with the numbers 89- to the park from Wyndam St in central Auckland. The one-way fare is $9 so it's best to buy a $10 day pass.

The park is just beyond the impressive Gulf Harbour Marina development, which boasts a resort golf course and country club. **Gulf Harbour Ferries** (☎ 0800 888 006; www.gulf-harbour.co.nz, www.kawaukat.co.nz) go from here to and

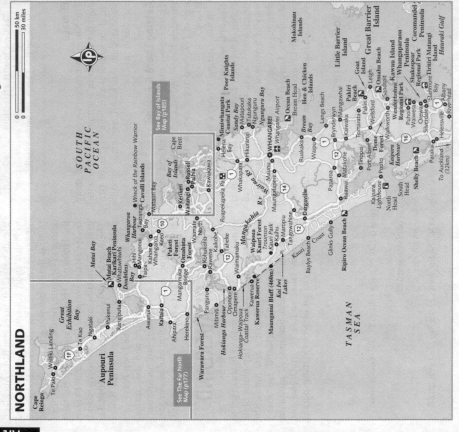

from Tiritiri Matangi Island on the regular service from central Auckland (see p159); taking this ferry is a good option for cyclists wanting to skip the boring road trip out of Auckland.

The **Whangaparaoa Steam Railway** (☎ 09-424 5018; www.rail.co.nz; 400 Whangaparaoa Rd; admission to railway & animal park plus 1 ride $6; ☑ 10am-5pm Sun Sep-Jun) is at Stanmore Bay on the main road into the peninsula. There are steam-train rides and an animal park.

OREWA

pop 4900

Just 38km north of Auckland, Orewa (www.orewa-beach.co.nz) is the main town on the Hibiscus Coast and has a 3km-long sheltered and sandy beach that is patrolled by lifeguards in the peak season (December and January). It has a dormitory suburb feel in parts, but makes a good coastal base if you still wish to remain close to Auckland.

Information

ASB (cnr Hibiscus Coast Hwy & Moana St) has ATM.

Hibiscus Coast visitor information centre (☎ 09-426 0076; 214a Hibiscus Coast Hwy; ☑ 9am-5pm Mon-Sat, 10am-4pm Sun) Next to a minigolf course; can help with fishing and horse-riding trips.

PC Time (Westpac Plaza; per hr $3; ☑ 10am-10pm Mon-Sat, to 8pm Sun) For internet access.

Post office (Florence Ave)

Sights & Activities

The **Alice Eaves Scenic Reserve**, to the north of the town, is 10 hectares of native bush with labelled trees, easy short walks, a Maori *pa* (fortified village) and a lookout, while the **Millennium Walkway** is an 8km walk that takes in part of the reserve.

Sleeping

BUDGET

Pillows Travellers Lodge (☎ 09-426 6338; www.pillows.co.nz; 412 Hibiscus Coast Hwy; dm/s/d $25/55/60) This clean and tidy backpackers has the best location with rooms around a pleasant garden as well as an outdoor spa pool, free tea and coffee, a piano and TVs in the private rooms.

Marco Polo Backpackers Inn (☎ 09-426 8455; www.marcopolo.co.nz; 2d Harmond Ave, Hatfields Beach; dm/s $22/43; d & tw $55-60) This equally clean and tidy backpackers just north of Orewa is in a peaceful spot and has bananas growing in the garden. No TV is the policy here but

there are pleasant hillside views to look at from the deck.

Puriri Park (☎ 09-426 4648; www.puriripark.com; 290 Centreway Rd; powered sites per 2 people $32, cabins $70, units $90-120; ☑) Peacocks roam around this large, well-equipped holiday park that borders Alice Eaves Scenic Reserve and has modern units with TVs, kitchens and linen. Facilities include 24-hour check-in, a café, shop and a 25m heated pool.

MIDRANGE & TOP END

Orewa Motor Lodge (☎ 09-426 4027; www.orewamotorlodge.co.nz; 290 Hibiscus Coast Hwy; units $125-165) This lodge is in a string of motels that line the main road. Quiet units here have standard features such as Sky TV, kitchens and pine décor, and there's an outdoor covered spa pool.

Beachcomber Motel (☎ 09-426 5973; www.beachcombermotel.co.nz; 246 Hibiscus Coast Hwy; units $90-150) The tidy units here have the usual midrange amenities such as Sky TV and some have spa baths and sea views. Palm trees add a lush subtropical touch, and good access to the Waiwera baths is all part of the deal.

Orewa Bach B&B (☎ 09-426 3510; grahame@xtra.co.nz; 309a Hibiscus Coast Hwy; s/d $180/200) This smart modern guesthouse opposite the shopping centre offers nicely appointed beachfront rooms with a lounge, stunning views and a sense of Pacific style.

Eating

Rock Salt (☎ 09-426 3379; 2nd fl, 350 Hibiscus Coast Hwy; mains $19-27; ☑ lunch Thu-Sun, dinner daily) This is Orewa's best restaurant, with magnificent sea views from its deck and a shmick setting. Beautifully prepared mains might include the crusted pork loin with kumara mash or a great seafood selection. All this and damn fine coffee.

Kai Zen (☎ 09-427 5633; 350 Hibiscus Coast Hwy; meals $14-19; ☑ breakfast & lunch) This café has good coffee and (despite the somewhat misleading name) an ever-changing Italian-style menu that's served in attractive décor.

Asahi (☎ 09-426 0065; 6 Bakehouse Lane; dishes $9-19; ☑ lunch Mon-Sat, dinner Tue-Sat) Asahi is a handy little option for those craving Japanese food. If you're really in need, don't go past the sushi boat, a veritable barge of titbits for a tidy $48. The *bento* boxes are recommended.

Plantation Café (☎ 09-426 5083; 226 Hibiscus Coast Hwy; meals $6-17; ☑ breakfast, lunch & dinner) At the entrance to town, this place has sea views and serves ice cream and homemade munchies, including fantastic giant sausage rolls.

New World supermarket (11 Moana Ave; 7am-10pm) Self-caterers can shop here.

Drinking

Muldoon Irish Bar & Brasserie (09-427 8000; Westpac Plaza, Moana Ave; meals $12; lunch & dinner) This bog-standard Irish theme pub has huge burgers and Ballydooly cider (from Napier) is on tap. There's live music most Fridays (8pm) and Sundays (5pm).

Getting There & Away

Stagecoach (09-373 9118; www.stagecoach.co.nz) runs buses to Orewa and the service to Waiwera goes to Wenderholme Regional Park (below) in summer. Buses leave from Wellesley St in central Auckland.

AROUND OREWA

Near Waiwera (literally 'warm water'), an unspoilt beach just 6km north of Orewa, is the **Waiwera Thermal Resort** (09-427 8000; www.waiwera.co.nz; adult/child $22/11; 9am-10pm Sun-Thu, to 10.30pm Fri & Sat). This resort boasts 19 pools, including a movie pool, 10 big slides, private spas ($30), a sauna, a sun bed, massages (one hour $95), a gym ($8) and even barbecue hire. All the pools use hot spring water from 1500m underground. An hourly bus service (bus 895) runs here from Auckland.

Just north of Waiwera is the 134-hectare **Wenderholme Regional Park**, with a diverse ecology, abundant bird life, beaches, an estuary, and fine views and walks (one to two hours). **Couldrey House** (09-528 3713; adult/child $3/1; 1-4pm Sat, Sun & public holidays), the original homestead, is now a museum. Bus 895 from Auckland goes into the park, or you can walk there from Waiwera Thermal Resort.

PUHOI

pop 450

Only 1km off the main road, Puhoi ('slow water') is a quaint village that was founded by Bohemian peasants who spoke a German dialect. Around 200 of them settled here in the 1860s and were each given 40 acres of bush.

The **Bohemian Museum** (09-422 0816; Puhoi Rd; admission by $2 donation; 1-4pm Oct-Easter) concentrates on the early days. Next door is

the village's attractive **Catholic Church**, built in 1881, which is usually open.

Puhoi River Canoe Hire (09-422 0891; www.puhoirivercanoes.co.nz; 84 Puhoi Rd; s/d kayak per hr $20/30) has been running trips on the tidal Puhoi River since 1991. Moonlight canoeing is also possible. Booking is essential.

In the **Puhoi Hotel** (09-422 0812; cnr Saleyards & Puhoi Rds; 11am-10pm) there's character and then some, with bar walls completely covered in old photos, animal heads and vintage household goods – an amazing sight. A Bohemian band plays regularly; musical instruments include a 'doodlesac' – Bohemian bagpipes.

Five hundred metres beyond the village is **Puhoi Cottage** (09-422 0604; 50 Ahuroa Rd; 9.30am-5pm Thu-Tue), which is well known for its Devonshire teas ($7) and coffees ($7.50). Just 3km further on is the **Art of Cheese Café** (09-422 0670; 275 Ahuroa Rd; platters $14-19; 9am-5pm) where the people understand that any balanced diet consists of about 90% cheese. Watch cheese being made, buy a big hunk of yellow happiness or dine on very good platters in the licensed café (there's also a kids menu and playground).

WARKWORTH

pop 2800

Just off the main highway, beside the Mahurangi River, Warkworth makes an effort to retain a village atmosphere with plenty of cafés and art-and-craft shops, although on weekends it closely resembles a satellite suburb of Auckland. A free Heritage Trail leaflet is available from the visitor information centre and features the main historical buildings.

Information

Entouch@ww (09-422 3342; Riverside Arcade, Queen St; per hr $8) Internet access available here.

Warkworth visitor information centre (09-425 9081; www.warkworth-information.co.nz; 1 Baxter St; 8.30am-5pm Mon-Fri, 9am-4pm Sat & Sun) Extremely helpful; can book boat tours along the river; located near the bus stop and the New World supermarket.

Sights & Activities

Just south of town, the 8.5-hectare **Parry Kauri Park** has a 15-minute forest boardwalk and a couple of giant old kauri, including the 800-year-old McKinney kauri. Also at the park, the small **Warkworth Museum** (09-

425 7093; www.wwmuseum.orcon.net.nz; Tudor Collins Dr; adult/child $6/1; ⏰9am-4pm) features pioneer-era exhibits.

About 5km south of Warkworth, the **Honey Centre & Café** (☎09-425 8003; www.honeycentre.co.nz; SH1; ⏰8.30am-5pm) has free honey tasting and glass-fronted hives where you can see thousands and thousands of bees at work. The shop sells all sorts of bee-related products, from honey to beeswax candles. Try the delicious manuka-honey ice creams.

Sheepworld (☎09-425 7444; www.sheepworldfarm.co.nz; adult/child ind sheep & dog show $15/7, exd show $7.50/4; ⏰9am-5pm), 4km north of Warkworth on SH1, demonstrates many aspects of NZ sheep farming and invites sniggering asides about NZ's love of sheep from those who should know better. Displays include sheep shearing and are held at 11am and 2pm daily (eel feeding is at 1.15pm), and visitors can feed sheep and lambs in the minifarm and browse the large arts-and-crafts shop, which includes wool products. There's also an adventure playground, pony rides on weekends, an ecotrail and a café.

Further north on SH1, the **Dome Forest** is a regenerating forest that was logged about 90 years ago. A walking track to the Dome summit (336m), which has great views across the Mahurangi Peninsula, leads from the car park and takes about 1½ hours return. A three-hour return walk leads beyond the Dome summit to the **Waiwhiu Kauri Grove**, a stand of about 20 mature kauri trees. The start of the walkway is some 6km north of Warkworth.

If you're in town from the last week of September to the first week of October you'd do well to check out the **Warkworth Scarecrow Festival** (www.eventswarkworth.co.nz), which is staged at Sheepworld and features some endearingly creative creations that will amuse young and old while raising money for various charities.

Sleeping & Eating

Sheepworld Caravan Park (☎09-425 9962; www.sheepworldcaravanpark.co.nz; SH1; sites per 2 people $25, caravans/cabins/chalets $45/50/80) Set on a large farm next to Sheepworld, 4km north of Warkworth, this peaceful park with friendly owners has good facilities including a spa pool. If you've ever wanted to sleep with a sheep…

Bridge House Lodge & Bar (☎09-425 8351; www.bridgehouse.co.nz; 16 Elizabeth St; dm $25, d $75-100) This lodge, next to the river, has a mix of rooms – some are rather old-fashioned and others have new bathrooms attached. Ask to see something first if you're particular about the age of your water closet. The refurbished bar and restaurant (mains $17 to $25) has a décor that seems to meld rustic and modern and dishes up trendy takes on fare such as surf 'n' turf.

Ducks Crossing Café (☎09-425 9940; Riverview Plaza, Kapanui St; meals $5-16; ⏰breakfast & lunch) Overlooking the river and the wharf is this café with a patio. It serves coffee and vegetarian and light meals.

Millstream Restaurant, Bar & Cinema (☎09-422 2292; 17 Elizabeth St; lunch mains $8-10; ⏰lunch & dinner Tue-Sun) This quirky restaurant opposite Bridge House Lodge serves Indian and Pacific rim food and has a cinema downstairs that usually shows film-festival movies. Live piano music is played on Friday.

Getting There & Away

Auckland to Warkworth takes 50 minutes on the daily **InterCity** (☎09-623 1503; www.intercitycoach.co.nz) or **Northliner** (☎09-307 5873; www.northliner.co.nz) bus and costs $20 one way.

There is no bus from Warkworth to Sandspit for Kawau Island; the only option is a taxi which costs about $20 one way. A taxi to Leigh costs around $55.

KAWAU ISLAND

pop 300

East of Warkworth is the scenic Mahurangi Peninsula and Sandspit, from where ferries depart for Kawau Island. The island's main attraction is **Mansion House** (☎09-422 8882; adult/child $4/2; ⏰10am-4pm), an impressive historic house rebuilt from an earlier structure by Sir George Grey, a former governor of NZ, who purchased the island in 1862. It was a hotel for many years before being restored and turned into a museum. Inside is a collection of Victorian memorabilia including items once owned by Sir George.

Kawau has some truly beautiful walks, starting from Mansion House and leading to beaches, the old copper mine and a lookout. The Kawau Island Historic Reserve pamphlet ($1) published by the Department of Conservation (DOC) has a map of walking tracks. The pamphlet is available from the DOC office in Auckland.

Sleeping & Eating

Moana Lodge (☎ 09-422 8831; www.sailingholiday .co.nz; North Harbour; from $150) This lovely boutique resort has delightful views and sailing excursions can be arranged as part of a package ($1020 per couple for a weekend with accommodation). Excellent meals can also be made part of the deal.

Beach House (☎ 09-422 8850; beachhouse@paradise .net.nz; Vivian Bay; ste $320-480) On the north of the island, on Kawau's only sandy beach, this upmarket place has suites and self-contained chalets. Water sports and *pétanque* are free, but lunch is extra.

Getting There & Away

Two ferry companies (Kawau Kat and Matata Cruises, see following) operate trips to Kawau from Sandspit (one hour) year-round. Car parking at Sandspit costs $8.

The **Kawau Kat** (☎ 0800 888 006, 09-425 8006; www.kawaukat.co.nz) has a 3½-hour Royal Mail Run daily at 10.30am, which stops at Mansion House and many coves, bays and inlets (per adult/child $45/15, with barbecue lunch $59/20). Check the website for details of other tours.

Matata Cruises (☎ 021960910; www.matata-cruises .co.nz) has a coffee cruise to Kawau for $30/15 per adult/child at 10am daily (returning 2pm) and a combined three-hour Mansion House lunch cruise ($45/30). From December to April there is also a 2pm sailing. Bookings are essential.

WARKWORTH TO LEIGH

Less frequented than the main highway to Whangarei is the scenic Matakana Rd route from Warkworth out to Leigh, 22km away on the east coast, and then north via Mangawhai and Waipu to Bream Bay. This route has a number of attractions including scenic beaches, wineries, craft galleries and the fantastic Goat Island Marine Reserve.

Excellent wineries along Matakana Rd include **Ascension Vineyard & Restaurant** (☎ 09-422 9601; www.ascensionvineyard.co.nz; 480 Matakana Rd; set menus $35 & $55; ☺ lunch daily, dinner long weekends & Jan), which has tours for $15 ($8 for diners) and fresh, Mediterranean-style cuisine; **Matakana Estate** (☎ 09-425 0494; 568 Matakana Rd; ☺ 10am-5pm), which discourages visits from

tour groups; and **Heron's Flight Vineyard Café** (☎ 09-422 7915; www.heronsflight.co.nz; 49 Sharps Rd; platters $18; ☺ 10am-6pm), which offers wine tastings daily from 10am to 5pm.

Morris & James Café, Bar & Tileworks (☎ 09-422 7116; www.morrisandjames.co.nz; 48 Tongue Farm Rd; meals $8-20; ☺ breakfast & lunch) has a lovely courtyard and colourful (and practical) ceramics are on sale. There are free weekday tours at 11.30am. It's just off the main road.

The first good beach, **Omaha**, is 6km off the Leigh road with a long stretch of white sand, good surf and holiday homes.

LEIGH

pop 450

The gateway to Goat Island, Leigh (www .leighbythesea.co.nz) is a small community perched above a picturesque harbour dotted with fishing boats.

Goat Island Dive (☎ 0800 348 369, 09-422 6925; www.goatislanddive.co.nz; 142a Pakiri Rd; ☺ 8am-5.30pm summer, 9am-5pm winter) has a shop in Leigh and a boat that can take you diving anywhere in the Hauraki Gulf, including wreck dives and overnight trips at any time of year. Snorkel, fin and mask hire is $15. Gear for a two-tank dive costs $90, dive trips are $70 to $310, and a shore dive with instruction is $150. Professional Association of Diving Instructors (PADI) courses (four days including four sea dives) cost $500.

Leigh Sawmill Café & Accommodation (☎ 09-422 6019; www.sawmillcafe.co.nz; 142 Pakiri Rd; dinner mains $24-28, dm/d with bathroom $25/125; ☺ lunch & dinner daily summer, Fri-Sun winter) is a funky bar, microbrewery and café (the pizzas are excellent), decorated with sawmill memorabilia, which puts on DJs and great live music. Accommodation includes backpacker rooms and separate smart (and spacious) modern units with a Japanese feel inside an old sawmill shed.

Leigh Motel (☎/fax 09-422 6179; 15 Hill St; units $105-147) has eight comfortable hillside units with kitchens and a rather impressive collection of frogs in the reception area.

Fresh local fish and homecooked food, including scotch eggs, are available at **Leigh Café Bar & Grill** (☎ 09-422 6033; 21 Hauraki Rd; meals $5-15; ☺ breakfast, lunch & dinner), and for takeaways there is **Leigh Fish & Chips** (☎ 09-422 6035; 18 Cumberland St; meals $5-10; ☺ 11am-7.30pm, closed Mon & Tue winter).

GOAT ISLAND BEACH

This is one of NZ's very special places and only 3km from Leigh. Goat Island Marine Reserve (547 hectares), the country's first marine reserve, was established here in 1978 and the sea has become a giant aquarium. Walk to the right over the rocks and you can usually see snapper (the big fish with blue dots and fins), blue maomao and stripy parore swimming around. You can snorkel or scuba dive from the black-sand beach, and there are dive areas all round Goat Island, which is just offshore. You can see colourful sponges, forests of brown seaweed, boarfish, crayfish, stingrays, and if you're very lucky, orca and bottle-nosed dolphins. Visibility is claimed to be 10m or more 75% of the time.

A glass-bottomed boat, the **Habitat Explorer** (09-422 6334; www.glassbottomboat.co.nz/adult/child $20/12), provides a great all-year on-the-hour trip around Goat Island to see the underwater life. Trips last 45 minutes and run from the beach. When the sea is too rough the boat doesn't operate; ring to check.

Snorkelling, diving gear and wet suits can be hired at **Seafriends** (09-422 6212; www.seafriends.org.nz; 7 Goat Island Rd; 10am–5pm), 1km before Goat Island beach. You can hire a mask with a lens if you are short-sighted or a buoyant wet suit if you are a poor swimmer. Seafriends also runs a saltwater aquarium, marine education centre, café and restaurant. Call ahead to see if it's open.

LEIGH TO WAIPU

Instead of driving back to Warkworth from Leigh, you can make a loop to Wellsford via Pakiri, or carry on past Pakiri along good-quality gravel roads via Tomarata to Mangawhai, where the tarseal begins again. From there you can drive on to Bream Bay and Waipu, which is only 1km from SH1.

Pakiri, 11km from Leigh, is a secret paradise with a beautiful 9km white-sand beach, sand dunes and surf. **Pakiri Beach Holiday Park** (09-422 6199; www.pakiriholidaypark.co.nz; 261 Pakiri River Rd; sites $28, cabins $50–55, cottages $110) has a shop and good units in a magical beach-front setting.

Just 6km on from Pakiri is **Pakiri Horse Riding** (09-422 6275; www.horseride-nz.co.nz; Rahuikiri Rd), which has over 100 horses with superb bush-and-beach rides ranging from one hour ($40) to all day ($190). Booking is essential. The **Stables Café** (snacks $5–12; breakfast & lunch) serves baps, panini, burgers and vegetarian food.

Another 12km on from Pakiri Horse Riding, turn left for Wellsford or turn right for Mangawhai and Waipu.

A long and winding gravel road goes to **Mangawhai** (www.mangawhai.org.nz), but the final 6km and the rest of the route to Waipu is sealed. The **Mangawhai Cliffs Walkway** (1½ to two hours one way) starts at the surf beach and affords extensive views inland and out to the Hauraki Gulf islands. Mangawhai has camping grounds, a general store, petrol station and B&Bs, plus the impossible-to-miss **Smashed Pipi Café, Bar, Restaurant & Gallery** (09-431 4847; 40 Moir Rd; dinner mains $19–27; breakfast & lunch daily, dinner Thu-Sun), which has occasional live music in the bar, vibrant ceramics in the gallery, and delicious deli food in the café.

Mangawhai Heads is the next community where facilities include the usual cluster of local amenities, such as an Internet café, a bait and tackle shop, a pharmacy and a truly great café.

Coastal Cow Backpackers (09-431 5444; coastalcow@xtra.co.nz; 299 Molesworth Dr; dm/s/d/tw $22/40/54/54) is a cheery, bright backpackers that gets rave reviews from a devoted clientele and features plenty of cow-themed decorative touches. Rooms are modern, comfy and spotless and bathrooms and the kitchen sparkle.

Milestone Cottages (09-431 4018; www.milestonecottages.co.nz; 27 Moir Pt Rd; cottages $115–225;) are wonderful award-winning themed cottages set in superb gardens with a South Pacific feel near the sea. Free videos, kayaks, croquet and pétanque are available.

THAT SINKING FEELING

The decommissioned NZ Navy Leander Class frigate, the Canterbury, is the subject of a campaign by dive-loving locals who want to see her sunk in the area (but not in the Marine Reserve) at about 28m. There's no doubt that it would make a fantastic addition to the diving opportunities in this part of the world, although things were still up in the air at the time of research. Visit the website www.divecanterbury.co.nz for further details and updates.

Mangawhai Lodge B&B (☎ 09-431 5311; www.sea viewlodge.co.nz; 4 Heather St; s/d $145/165) is a boutique B&B with a commanding position and great views, and the very comfortable, cosy rooms have access to the picture-perfect wraparound veranda.

Sail Rock Café (☎ 09-431 4051; 12a Wood St; mains $22-32; ⏱ breakfast, lunch & dinner summer) is a wonderful local eatery that takes justified pride in its salt-and-pepper squid, a dish that provokes an almost-religious experience in many a diner. All that plus charming service, great pizzas (after 5pm) and an award-winning coffee blend make this the best place to eat for miles and miles.

From Mangawhai Heads, a particularly scenic road goes over the headland to Langs Beach and then on to Waipu.

WAIPU & BREAM BAY
pop 1980

Just before Waipu is Waipu Cove, which has some accommodation. **Camp Waipu Cove** (☎ 09-432 0410; www.campwaipucove.com; Cove Rd; unpowered/powered sites per 2 people $25/28, cabins $50-100) is a large and comfortable camping ground on the beach, with the added appeal of being able to catch snapper from the rocks.

On the main road between Waipu Cove and Waipu is the **Stonehouse** (☎ 09-432 0432; stonehousewaipu@xtra.co.nz; dm loft $20, d $120), a unique Cornish-style house built of huge stone slabs in a lovely location. Guests are accommodated in separate units and can use a kayak or rowing boat to cross the saltwater lagoon and get to the beach, which has shellfish and plenty of shore birds. The backpackers loft is basic.

The **House of Memories** (☎ 09-432 0746; 36 The Centre; adult/child $5/2; Waipu; ⏱ 9.30am-4.30pm), a museum that doubles as the local information centre, tells the story of the 900 Scottish settlers who came to Waipu in six ships between 1853 and 1860 via Nova Scotia in Canada. Only 10% of locals are direct descendants, but there is a big get-together on 1 January every year when the Waipu **Highland Games** (www.highlandgames.co.nz), established in 1871, takes place in Caledonian Park.

The displays at the **Old Waipu Firehouse Art Gallery** (☎/fax 09-432 0797; 7 The Braigh; ⏱ 10am-4pm) include the well-known handpainted Waipu tiles.

Activities include surfing, fishing, boat trips and hiking to a cave with glow-worms.

Just 10 minutes' drive west of Waipu is **North River Treks** (☎ 0800 743 344, 09-432 0565; www.north river.co.nz; Helmsdale Rd; rides from $35), which offers a variety of horse rides through farmland and along rivers.

Waipu Wanderer Backpackers (☎ 09-432 0532; www.waipu.co.nz/waipuwanderers; 25 St Marys Rd; dm/ s/d $20/35/50) is a small, simple and friendly backpackers in town – a real home from home – with free fruit in season.

Waihoihoi Lodge (☎ 09-432 1234; www.waihoihoi .co.nz; 219 Massey Rd; lodge s $50-135, d & tw $95-150, studio $125) is women-only, and dinner with wine is available ($40). The separate self-contained studio is open to men and women, has a veranda and can sleep four. All prices include a Pacific breakfast. With a rural ambience 3km inland from Waipu, both options are stylish and have great views of Bream Bay. If those lovely views and a good night's sleep don't undo a few cricks, then massages and other pampering options can be arranged.

Pizza Barn 'n' Bar (☎ 09-432 1011; 2 Cove Rd small/ large pizza $10/20) has popular platters and light fare as well as hunger-assuaging pizzas that go well with cold beer.

Waipu has a bus depot and **Intercity** (☎ 09-623 1503; www.intercitycoach.co.nz) and **Northliner** (☎ 09-307 5873; www.northliner.co.nz) buses stop here on the way from Auckland to Whangarei ($15).

From Waipu it's a 38km drive north to Whangarei, or you can head south to Brynderwyn and then west to the Kauri Coast.

KAURI COAST

Unless you're a passionate fan of the kumara (sweet potato), which is the dominant vegetable of the rolling farmland, your main reason for coming here will be to marvel at the magnificent kauri forests – one of the great natural highlights of NZ.

Turn off SH1 at Brynderwyn and travel west along SH12. A must-see is the Kauri Museum (opposite) at Matakohe on the way to the west coast. From the northern end of Kaipara Harbour, extending along the west coast to Hokianga, the Kauri Coast is so-called because of the kauri timber and gum industry that flourished here in the 19th century, generating much of NZ's wealth at the time. Those massive kauri forests are all but gone now, but the Waipoua Kauri Forest (p172) has untouched kauri stands and is the best place in NZ to see these majestic trees.

Baylys Beach and Ahipara offer seaside fun and activities.

MATAKOHE
pop 400

At Matakohe, the superb **Kauri Museum** (09-431 7417; adult/child/family $12/3/25; 9am-5pm) will leave you amazed at how incredible the forests here were. There's a scale exhibit of a working pioneer sawmill, clever static displays showing the lives of kauri bushmen, tradesmen and their families (you'll never complain about hard work again), and a gallery with a huge vertical cross section of kauri. But perhaps the most fascinating aspect is the **Gum Room**, a weird and wonderful collection of kauri gum or resin, the amber substance that can be carved, sculpted and polished to a jewel-like quality. The museum shop has plenty of excellent items crafted from kauri wood and gum.

Facing the museum is the tiny **Matakohe Pioneer Church**, built in 1867 of local kauri, which served both Methodists and Anglicans, and also acted as the town hall and school for the pioneer community.

Kauri Country Eco-tours (0800 246 528, 09-431 6007; www.kauricountry.co.nz; adult/child $85/65) has a descendant of one of the area's original pioneering families who provides explanations of the history of kauri logging and an insight into conservation efforts today. You can also dig for kauri gum and meet a bullock team. The three-hour trips leave from the museum and bookings are essential.

Sleeping & Eating
Matakohe Top 10 Holiday Park (09-431 6431; www.matakohetop10.co.nz; Church Rd; sites per 2 people $28, cabins $46, units $80-90) This very friendly, helpful camp has modern amenities in very good condition, plenty of space, good views of Kaipara Harbour and is only 350m from the museum. Nonmetered showers win then extra snaps.

Petite Provence (09-431 7552; www.petite-provence.co.nz; 703c Tinopai Rd; s/d $90/130) This very attractive French-influenced B&B is a popular weekend getaway option for many Aucklanders, so it pays to book ahead. Excellent dinners can be arranged for a bargain $35 per person (wine not included).

Matakohe House (09-431 7091; 24 Church Rd; s $90, d $125-135) This lovely B&B and attached restaurant, a short walk from the museum, is built in colonial style. Rooms feature antique furnishings and open out onto a veranda. Prices include breakfast. The licensed restaurant is a good spot for a meal (open 7.30am to 5pm, and by prior arrangement for dinner).

Sahara (05-431 6833; cnr Franklin & Paparoa Valley Rds, Paparoa; mains $22-25; dinner Wed-Sun, lunch Sat & Sun) Head down to nearby Paparoa for one of the best meals you'll have in NZ. This handsome former bank building has been transformed into a stellar restaurant that serves innovative, beautifully prepared dishes made from local ingredients. Pounce on the wonderful venison and wild mushroom pie with asparagus, roasted tomatoes and *taleggio* sauce and then marvel at the more than reasonable bill.

Gumdiggers Café (09-431 7075; Church Rd; meals $5-15; breakfast & lunch) This is licensed and opposite the museum, but the food ain't great (greasy, yes) and it exudes a strong aroma of tour-bus groups.

Getting There & Away
The West Coaster bus provides a Monday to Saturday service down to Auckland ($32, three hours) and up to Dargaville, with buses continuing on to Rawene and Paihia on Tuesday, Thursday and Saturday.

DARGAVILLE
pop 4530

Dargaville probably won't hold your attention for long, unless you're obsessed with sweet potatoes. That's right, this town is the 'Kumara capital of NZ', and produces two-thirds of the country's output, necessitating an annual Kumara Festival in April. It wasn't always like this – Dargaville was founded in 1872 by a timber merchant, Joseph Dargaville, and this once-important river port thrived on the export of kauri timber and gum. As the forests were decimated, it declined and today is a quiet backwater servicing the agricultural Northern Wairoa area.

Information
Bank of NZ (05-439 3200; 72 Victoria St)
Dargaville visitor information centre (09-439 8360; www.kauricoast.co.nz; cnr Normanby & Poto Sts;

DARGAVILLE

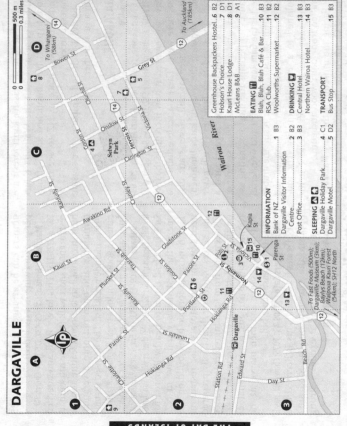

0   500 m
0   0.3 miles

To Whangarei (58km)
To Whangarei (58km)
To Auckland (185km)

Wairoa River

INFORMATION
Bank of NZ....................................1 B3
Dargaville Visitor Information
Centre..2 B2
Post Office....................................3 B3

SLEEPING
Dargaville Holiday Park................4 C1
Dargaville Motel..........................5 D2

Greenhouse Backpackers Hostel...6 B2
Hobson's Choice............................7 D1
Kauri House Lodge.........................8 D1
McLeans B&B.................................9 A1

EATING
Blah, Blah, Blah Café & Bar.......10 B3
RSA Club......................................11 B2
Woolworths Supermarket............12 B2

DRINKING
Central Hotel...............................13 B3
Northern Wairoa Hotel...............14 B3

TRANSPORT
Bus Stop......................................15 B3

To Fast Foods (500m);
Dargaville Museum (3km);
Baylys Beach (12km);
Waipoua Kauri Forest
(54km); SH12 North

8.30am-5pm Mon-Fri, 10am-4pm Sat & Sun) Helpful centre; has Internet access and can help with booking tours, buses and accommodation.
Post office (80 Victoria St)

Sights

Perched on top of a hill just out of town, the **Dargaville Museum** (☎ 09-439 7555; www.dargaville museum.co.nz; adult/child $5/1; 9am-4pm) houses pioneer artefacts plus a kauri gum-diggers display. There's also a maritime section that includes a vintage Maori canoe and the masts of the *Rainbow Warrior*, the Greenpeace flagship blown up by French agents in 1985 (see the boxed text, p184).

Tours

The **Kaipara Kat** (☎ 09-439 1400; trip $40) has an interesting catamaran tour from Dargaville to Shelly Beach and back, while a dinner cruise costs $75.

Sleeping

BUDGET

Greenhouse Backpackers Hostel (☎ 09-439 6342; fax 09-439 6327; 13 Portland St; dm/s/d/tw $20/29/46/46)
This converted 1921 schoolhouse has a reception that resembles a museum, large partitioned dorms, small new units in the back garden and a good honest atmosphere. It's a cash-only affair and office hours can be erratic.

McLeans B&B (☎ 09-439 5915; westendnursery@xtra .co.nz; 136 Hokianga Rd; s/d $40/80) Guests share a large lounge in this spacious 1934 house originally built by the local mayor. Prices include breakfast. The friendly hosts know all about the area and will take you on a daylong 4WD tour for around $110.

Dargaville Holiday Park (☎ 0800 114 441, 09-439 1011; www.kauriparks.co.nz; 10 Onslow St; sites per 2 people $24, cabins $48, units $50-85) The facilities are impressive here and it makes for a great base if you wish to explore the area, although you'll be needing to bring everything bar the kitchen sink unless you feel like forking out for it all.

MIDRANGE

Hobson's Choice (☎ 0800 158 786, 09-439 8551; hob sonschoice@xtra.co.nz; 212 Victoria St; units $100-180;)
This Spanish villa–style motel has upmar-

...ket, immaculate refurbished units and the relaxing pool area brings a splash of the tropics to Dargaville. A restaurant was under construction when we popped in.

TOP END

Kauri House Lodge (☎09-439 8082; kaurihouse@xtra.co.nz; Bowen St; s $20-275; ❄) This grand colonial homestead, built by a kauri king in 1910 and now a B&B, is packed with amazing antiques and curios and resembles a museum. It's a stately home with a snooker room, a study-library, extensive gardens and a long driveway. All rooms are en suite and prices include breakfast. Booking is essential.

Dargaville Motel (☎09-439 7734; 217 Victoria St; d $95) These clean, old-fashioned studio units with Sky TV and kitchenettes have views of the eternally muddy Wairoa River and good storage for things such as bikes. It's a very friendly place, and one room is wheelchair-accessible.

Eating & Drinking

Blah, Blah, Blah Café & Bar (☎09-439 6300; 101 Victoria St; café meals $5-16, dinner mains $18-28; ☼breakfast & lunch daily, dinner Tue-Sat) The number-one pick (that's not saying much admittedly) in Dargaville has a garden area, deli-style snacks, a global menu, salads, pizzas, curried kumara, twice-cooked duck, mulled wine (spicy and warm) and cocktails.

RSA Club (☎09-439 3164; Hokianga Rd; mains $12-19; ☼dinner Tue-Sat) Three evenings a week you can get an RSA roast of the day the way God and the Queen intended it.

Self-caterers should head to **Woolworths** supermarket (129 Victoria St; ☼7am-9pm), while locals reckon the best fish and chips is at **Fast Foods** (☎09-439 8497; 3 Murdoch St; meals $5-14; ☼lunch & dinner) on the way out of town going north (follow the signs to the museum and you'll find it easily).

Pop into either the **Central Hotel** (☎09-439 8923; cnr Victoria St & Hokianga Rd) or the **Northern Wairoa Hotel** (☎09-439 8923; cnr Victoria St & Edward Sts) if you feel like a handle of something cold in a refreshingly honest NZ pub environment.

Getting There & Away

The bus stop is on Kapia St. **Main Coachlines** (☎09-278 8070; www.maincoachline.co.nz) runs a bus to and from Auckland via Matakohe (book for this leg) from Monday to Friday and Sunday ($39, three hours).

AROUND DARGAVILLE

Baylys Beach

Baylys Beach, 12km from Dargaville off SH12, lies on the 100km-long Ripiro Ocean Beach, and this stretch of surf-pounded coast has been the site of many shipwrecks. Ripiro Ocean Beach is a gazetted highway and you can drive along its hard sand at low tide, although it is primarily for 4WD vehicles. Several tour companies run tours along it. Ripiro is NZ's longest drivable beach and less crowded than Ninety Mile Beach further north. Ask locals about conditions before venturing out onto the sand. Quad bikes can be hired at the holiday park.

A taxi to Baylys Beach from Dargaville should cost aro and $25.

SLEEPING & EATING

Hunky Dory Travellers Accommodation (☎09-439 0922; ayndith@paradise.net.nz; 29 Kelly St; dm per night/week $20/90) This bright and breezy, intimate backpackers with helpful owners has a creative vibe, colourful décor and a deck. It's a good chill-out spot.

Baylys Beach Holiday Park (☎/fax 09-439 6349; www.baylysbeach.co.nz; 22 Seaview Rd; unpowered/powered sites per 2 people $24/26, caravan $42, cabins $40-60, motel $80-95, cottage $100) This place has good management and facilities, and quad bikes for hire; $60 for the first half-hour, $45 for subsequent tours. Ride motorbikes on the beach to view volcanic Maunganui Bluff (460m), but the hike up and down it takes five hours. Also available are 4WD van trips ($60 per person, 5½ hours) and fishing trips ($60 a day).

Funky Fish Café & Bar (☎09-439 8883; 34 Seaview Rd; mains $17-28; ☼lunch & dinner) Brightly decorated with murals and mosaics, this very popular restaurant café and bar has a wide-ranging menu (although fish dishes are the standouts) and bookings are advisable in summer. People drive from far and wide in this part of the world to eat here.

Sharky's (☎09-439 4549; 1 Seaview Rd; meals $5-21; ☼breakfast, lunch & dinner) Quick snacks and all-day breakfasts are the order of the day at this handy bottle shop-cum-general store.

Pouto & Kaipara Lighthouse

Various 'sand buses' do tours 71km along the beach to the remote Kaipara Lighthouse (built with kauri in 1884) at Pouto Point. You go down along the sand and back along the inland road, which is sealed for 30km south of Dargaville but gravel the rest of the way. If you have a 2WD stick to the inland road. Pouto (po-to) has a hostel and a luxury lodge for those who enjoy staying in wild and remote places. Quad-bike rides are available from Pouto to the lighthouse, which you can climb up. Fishing from the beach is a popular and rewarding activity.

Lighthouse Lodge B&B (☎ 09-439 5150; www .lighthouse-lodge.co.nz; d $190-210, ste $350-450) is an architect-designed contemporary building in a remote spot, with light and stylish rooms with verandas that have great sea views. There's Sky TV, a bar and dining room (three-course dinner $40).

DARGAVILLE TO HOKIANGA

The highlights of the Kauri Coast are the lakes and forests north of Dargaville – apart from several massive kauri trees, there are other walks in Waipoua Kauri Forest and the smaller reserves. Get the DOC brochure *Waipoua & Trounson Kauri Forests* ($1) from the Dargaville visitor information centre. If you're planning to overnight along here, bring your own food as there are few stores or restaurants between Dargaville and Opononi, and no ATMs until Kaitaia.

Kai Iwi Lakes

Only 34km north of Dargaville, and 12km off the highway, are three beautiful freshwater lakes that are close together. The largest, Taharoa, has blue-coloured water fringed with sandy patches and pine trees. Lake Waikere is popular with water skiers while Lake Kai Iwi is relatively untouched. A half-hour walk takes you from the lakes to the coast and it's another two hours to reach the base of Maunganui Bluff. There's also trout fishing and a mountain-bike trail.

Willowdale (☎ 09-439 4645; www.willowdale.co.nz; 115 Kai Iwi Lakes Rd; B&B d & tw $132) is a homestead-style house, which has pretty rooms with bathroom and a self-contained cottage that sleeps up to eight. Meals are available ($40 for two courses and a glass of wine or beer).

Trounson Kauri Park

The 450-hectare Trounson Kauri Park, 40km north of Dargaville (turn off the highway at Kaihu), has an easy half-hour walk

leading from the parking and picnic area by the road. It passes through a beautiful forest with streams and some fine kauri stands, a couple of fallen kauri trees and the Four Sisters – two trees each with two trunks. There's a ranger station and camping grounds.

Guided night-time **nature walks** (adult/child $15/9), organised by the Kauri Coast Top 10 Holiday Park, explain the flora and nocturnal wildlife that thrives here. This is a rare chance to see a kiwi in the wild. Trounson has a predator-eradication programme and has become a mainland refuge for threatened native bird species, so you should at least hear a morepork (a native owl) or a brown kiwi.

SLEEPING

Kauri Coast Top 10 Holiday Park (☎/fax 0800 807 200, 09-439 0621; www.kauricoasttop10.co.nz; sites per 2 people $28, units $45-80) Just 2km from the main road and before Trounson Kauri Park car park, this attractive riverside camping ground has good facilities, a small shop and organises night safaris (see preceding), horse rides, fishing and quad-bike trips.

Kaihu Farm Hostel (☎ 09-439 4004; kaihufam@ clear.net.nz; SH2; dm/s/d/tw $21/38/50/50) A cosy and well-kept farm-based hostel, 2km north of the Trounson turn-off, this place has farm produce for sale, a bush walk with glow-worms and a no-TV policy. The hosts can provide low-cost meals and transport to local attractions (for a small fee).

Waipoua Kauri Forest

The highlight of the west coast, this superb forest sanctuary – proclaimed in 1952 after much public pressure and antagonism towards continued milling – is the largest remnant of the once-extensive kauri forests of northern NZ.

The road through the jungly forest stretches for 18km and passes some huge kauri trees – a fully grown kauri can reach 60m in height and have a trunk 5m in diameter. Just after you enter the park, turn off to the forest lookout, which offers a spectacular view, and the short Toatoa viewpoint walk is just 1km away. Back on the main road is a picnic spot and some youthful kauri trees (called rickers). A little further north, the **park visitor information centre** (☎ 09-439 3011; ☼ 8.30am-4pm winter, 8.30am-5pm summer) has information and interpretive displays on kauri

WAIPOUA KAURI FOREST

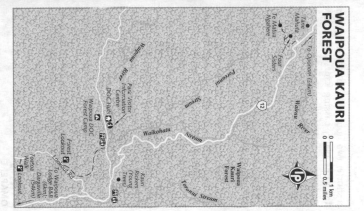

trees, the gum industry, native birds and other wildlife.

From the visitor information centre, the highway winds through this lush forest of ferns and native trees for about 8km before the signposted turn-off to the kauri walks, where several giant trees are easily reached. The car park here is guarded – theft from cars has been a problem – and a $2 donation pays for the protection service.

Te Matua Ngahere ('The Father of the Forest') has a trunk over 5m in diameter, believed to be the widest girth of any kauri tree in NZ, and could be the oldest in NZ (probably 2000 years old). This massive tree, a 20-minute walk from the car park, has to be seen to be believed. It presides over a clearing surrounded by mature trees that look like matchsticks in comparison. Close by are the **Four Sisters** (not to be confused with the kauri siblings of the same name in Trounson Kauri Park), a graceful stand of four tall trees clumped together.

Unfortunately, the large **Yakas Track** is closed for the foreseeable future (at least until 2010).

Further north up the highway is **Tane Mahuta**, named for the Maori god of the forests. It's the largest kauri tree in NZ, standing close to the road and estimated to be between 1200 and 2000 years old. At 51m, it's much taller than Te Matua Ngahere but doesn't have the same impressive girth.

SLEEPING

Waipoua DOC Forest Camp (☎ 09-439 3011; sites & cabins per person $10) This camping ground is situated in the heart of the forest, next to the Waipoua River and just past the visitor information centre. There are spacious but spartan cabins, plus sites for camping and caravans. Bring your own bedding (BYOB) and book ahead for cabins in summer. There are hot showers, flush toilets and a separate kitchen and it's on a first-come, first-served basis. InterCity (☎ 09-913 6100) buses stop here on the way to Dargaville (one hour) and Omapere (50 minutes).

Waipoua Lodge B&B (☎ 09-439 0422; www.waipoualodge.co.nz $490-540) This fine old villa, run by hosts who work hard to please their guests, is on the highway at the southern edge of the forest, 48km north of Dargaville. The four luxurious apartments with imaginative décor were originally the stables, the woolshed and the calf-rearing pen! Prices include breakfast. Dinner is available at the lodge restaurant.

HOKIANGA

North of the Kauri Coast, the road winds down to Hokianga Harbour and the tiny twin towns of Omapere and Opononi. Hokianga is a 'Kiwi Outback' area with little development, and the harbour is unspoilt and beautiful. It's a good place to take time out to relax for a while, as plenty of alternative lifestylers have discovered. As you come up over the hill from the south, the lookout point on **Pakia Hill** has a spectacular view of the harbour and the golden sand dunes.

Further down the hill, 2km west of Omapere, Signal Station Rd leads out to **Arai-Te-Uru Recreation Reserve**, on the South Head of Hokianga Harbour. It's about a 30-minute walk from Omapere or, if you're driving, a five-minute walk from the car park to Signal Station Point. This looks over the harbour entrance, the massive sand dunes of North Head and the turbulent confluence of the harbour and the open sea. There's a swimming beach, and it's also the northern end of the superb Hokianga–Waipoua Coastal Track (see below). But be wary – theft from cars is a problem.

OMAPERE & OPONONI
pop 630
These two tranquil settlements, on the southern shore of Hokianga Harbour, more or less run into one another.

Information
The very helpful **Hokianga visitor information centre** (☎ 09-405 8869; hokiangainfo@xtra.co.nz; SH12, Omapere; ☺ 8.30am–5pm) has Internet access.

Sights
Located in the same building as the visitor information centre is a tiny local **museum** (☎ 09-405 8869; SH12, Omapere; admission by donation; ☺ 9.30am–4.30pm), which tells the story of the hippie invasion of the 1970s and of 'Opo', a wild dolphin that played with children and learned to do tricks with beach balls back in the 1950s. Opo became a national celebrity but died of unknown causes a year after his arrival.

Activities
WALKING
The **Hokianga–Waipoua Coastal Track** leads south along the coast from South Head, at the entrance of Hokianga Harbour. It's four hours to the Waimamaku Beach exit, six hours to the Kawerua exit and 12 hours to the Kerr Rd exit. Or you can continue the entire 16 hours (allow about three days) to Kai Iwi Lakes. Pick up a brochure from any local visitor information centre or DOC office. Hikers must carry all their own water and food, and cross the major rivers two hours either side of low tide.

From Cemetery Rd on the eastern outskirts of Opononi, a half-hour climb leads up **Mt Whiria**, a *pa* site with a splendid view of the harbour.

Two kilometres east of Opononi, Waiotemarama Gorge Rd turns south for 6km to the **Waiotemarama bush track**, which climbs Mt Hauturu (680m). It's a four-hour walk to the summit (six hours return), but there's a shorter two-hour loop walk starting from the same place, passing kauri trees and a picturesque waterfall.

The **Six Foot Track** at the end of Mountain Rd (near Okopako Lodge; see opposite) gives access to many Waima Range walks.

OTHER ACTIVITIES
Hokianga Express (☎ 021 405 872; adult/child $20/10) is a fast boat that leaves from Opononi jetty and takes you across the harbour to the large golden sand dunes. You can **sandboard** down a 30m slope as often as you like and even skim over the water. The price includes hire of a sandboard and a return boat ride. Trips leave every hour.

Okopako Horse Trekking (☎ 09-405 8815) at Okopako Lodge (opposite) has two-hour horse treks ($45) and longer rides through the bush of the Waima Range.

Footprints – Waipoua (☎ 09-405 8737; www.omapere.co.nz; tours around $65) is a highly regarded outfit operating fascinating tours of the Waipoua Forest at twilight from the Copthorne Hotel & Resort (below). An essential experience if you have the time.

Sleeping
OMAPERE
Globe Trekkers Backpackers' Lodge (☎ 09-405 8183; www.globetrekkerslodge.com; SH12; dm/d/tw $20/50/50) This considerate, home-style lodge is ideally placed to put you in touch with myriad local activities, or to just relax and unwind in casual style.

Copthorne Hotel & Resort (☎ 09-405 8737; www.omapere.co.nz; SH12; units $85–135; ☒) Lovely harbourside units are available here with a choice restaurant and bar and pretty garden surrounds.

Hokianga Haven (☎ 09-405 8285; www.hokianga haven.co.nz; 226 SH12; r $130–180) This modern house with original Kiwi art on the walls offers exceptional accommodation on the harbour's edge and glorious views of the sand dunes. The room has private facilities and there is a hot tub, plus alternative healing therapies can be arranged. Prices include breakfast.

OPONONI
House of Harmony (☎ 09-405 8778; www.houseofharmony.co.nz; SH12; sites per 2 people $28, dm/d/tw $20/44/44) This cosy and friendly backpackers with good facilities has blue-and-white-

painted quarters and a veranda. It's near the jetty and haircuts are available too.

Okopako Lodge (☎/fax 09-405 8815; 140 Mountain Rd; unpowered/powered sites per 2 people $20/34, dm/s/tw/d $29/35/44/50) High up in the bush 5km east of Opononi and 2km down a reasonable gravel road, this comfortable YHA associate offers horse trekking, hiking (the Six Foot Track begins here) and seasonal farm activities. Breakfast ($10) and dinner ($17) are available as well as pick-ups from the main road where buses can drop you off.

Opononi Lighthouse Motel (☎ 09-405 8824; www.lighthousemotel.co.nz; SH12; units $80-160) This refurbished (new beds, fresh paint, springy carpet) motel has very comfortable harbourside units with kitchens and decks, plus sand-dune views.

Eating

Harbourmaster's Restaurant (☎ 09-405 8826; breakfast, lunch & dinner) This very good hotel restaurant at the Copthorne Hotel and Resort has a deck, great harbour views and wonderful fresh local crayfish on the menu. A casual bistro is also on the premises and does good light meals.

Opononi Resort Hotel (☎ 09-405 8858; SH12; bistro meals $14-24; breakfast, lunch & dinner) This is the centre of Opononi's social life; the pleasant restaurant has a terrace and serves bistro meals while the bar serves bar meals and takeaways and has live music some Saturdays.

Getting There & Away

InterCity/West Coaster (☎ 09-913 6100) buses stop off at Omapere and Opononi from Paihia on Monday, Wednesday and Friday and from Dargaville on Tuesday, Thursday and Saturday. It's a two-hour trip from Paihia to Omapere, and one hour and 50 minutes from Dargaville to Omapere.

RAWENE

pop 515

Rawene (www.rawene.co.nz) is a special little settlement from where a car ferry crosses Hokianga Harbour to Kohukohu. There is a surprising number of historic buildings, including six churches, from the time when kauri timber and gum was exported from here and the harbour was a lot busier than

---

BOTTOM OF THE HARBOUR

Once-busy Hokianga Harbour saw a roaring shipping trade until its decline, but one out-of-sight vestige from these days remains: empty ships from across the Tasman Sea were frequently loaded with ballast that consisted of blocks of sandstone from Sydney, Australia, and tonnes of the stuff remains on the bottom of the harbour to this day.

---

it is nowadays. There is a heritage trail with information boards, and you can get petrol here.

Walk along the harbour front to see around **Clendon House** (☎ 09-405 7874; adult/child $5/free; 10am-4pm Sat-Mon Nov-Apr), which was built in the bustling 1860s by James Clendon, a trader, shipowner and magistrate. A little further on are some mangroves with a short **mangrove boardwalk**.

Hokianga Blue Kayak Hire (☎ 09-405 7675; www.hokiangablue.co.nz; Pamell St) runs guided tours from $65 to $495 per person and hires out kayaks (per person half-/full day $30/45). Motorcycle tours and accommodation can also be arranged.

Rawene Motor Camp (☎ 09-405 7720; 1 Marmon St; unpowered/powered sites per 2 people $20/22, dm/d $16/44) is a nicely managed caravan park that has been revived after a bad turn and is once again worth staying at. The grounds are verdant, the cabins are simple but super tidy and a lot of effort is being made with the upkeep. Two of the cabins have disabled access.

To stay at the **Postmaster's Lodgings** (☎ 09-405 7676; fax 09-405 7473; 3 Parnell St; r with bathroom $85-125), which has a lounge and kitchenette, contact the gentleman at the Ferry House. Rooms are high-ceilinged and very comfortable, with lots of kauri pine and an old-fashioned feel that's never twee.

Old Lane's Store Homestay (☎ 09-405 7554; 9 Clendon Esplanade; s/d $90/115) is an attractive self-contained apartment with its own parking and courtyard. Prices include breakfast.

You can eat on a deck over the water at the excellent **Boatshed Café** (☎ 09-405 7728; 8 Clendon Esplanade; lunch mains $6-14; breakfast & lunch), a cute deli-style café with art on the walls and heart-warming food and service.

Ferry House (☎ 09-405 7676; 1 Parnell St; dinner mains $20-30; ☉ lunch & dinner Tue-Sun) offers a memorable dining experience, with convivial hosts and surroundings that seem to include a thousand conversation pieces, plus a lot of books. It's opposite the ferry.

Masonic Hotel (☎ 09-405 7822; Parnell St) is the local pub, with occasional live country-and-western music shows.

If you opt to continue on the main highway, heading towards the Bay of Islands, you'll pass through **Kaikohe**, a centre for the Ngapuhi tribe and the scene of bloody battles during the Northland Land War (1844–46). Hone Heke eventually settled in Kaikohe and died there in 1850.

Getting There & Away

The **car ferry** (☎ 09-405 2602; car & driver one-way/return $14/19, passenger $2/4) operates hourly from 7.30am to 7.30pm. You can buy your ticket for this 15-minute ride on board. It runs more frequently if necessary so there shouldn't be a queue, and usually leaves Rawene on the half-hour. The **InterCity** (☎ 09-9136100) bus stops outside the Wharf House on its way to Paihia and Omapere.

KOHUKOHU
pop 220

Once Kohukohu, 4km from the ferry, was a busy town (it was at the heart of the kauri industry) with a sawmill, a shipyard, two newspapers and banks. These days it's a very quiet backwater on the north side of Hokianga Harbour. There are a number of historic kauri villas over 100 years old and other fine buildings including the Masonic Lodge, the Anglican Church and an old school, but you have to detour off the main road to see them. Some buildings are derelict.

Kohukohu Tree House (☎ 09-405 5855; www.tree house.co.nz; sites per 2 people $30, dm/s/d/tw $21/40/56/56) is a fantastic place with friendly, helpful hosts and brightly painted little cottages set among exotic fruit and nut trees. This quiet retreat is 2km from the ferry terminus (turn sharp left as you come off the ferry). You can sleep in an old school bus (per single/double $26/42), play volleyball in the macadamia orchard or just relax. Pick-ups are offered from the ferry. Very special indeed.

Waterline Café (☎ 09-405 5552; meals $5-16; ☉ 10am-5.30pm Tue-Sun, till late Fri, closed Jul-Sep), at the waterfront, is an excellent café and bar with interesting pizzas and ever-changing blackboard offerings that lean toward the Mod-NZ side of things.

Palace Flophouse & Grill (☎ 09-405 5858; burgers $5.50-8; ☉ lunch & dinner Tue-Sun) is a fast-food restaurant serving great burgers, including vegetarian and fish varieties.

MITIMITI

About 40km west of Kohukohu, via Panguru on a rugged, wild stretch of coast, is the tiny isolated Maori settlement of Mitimiti, which consists of only 30 families and not even a shop. The last 20km of the road is gravel.

Stay at **Manaia Lodge** (☎ 09-409 5347; mitimiti@ xtra.co.nz; West Coast Rd; cottage $130) to experience life in a remote Maori community. You can take the owner's flexible Maori culture tour (two hours, $30) that includes a *marae* (meeting house) visit, go on wilderness walks in Warawara Forest (NZ's second-largest kauri forest), fish off the rocks or try dragnetting. You'll need to self-cater and the cottage accommodates four people maximum.

PUKETI & OMAHUTA FORESTS

North of Kaikohe, the Puketi and Omahuta Forests consist of one large forest area with kauri groves and other native trees, camping and picnic areas, streams and pools. Kauri milling in Puketi was stopped some years back to protect not only the kauri trees but also the rare kokako bird. It seems that the kokako here have their own dialect and won't breed with kokako from other areas.

The two forests are reached by several entrances and contain a network of walking tracks varying in length from 15 minutes (the wheelchair-accessible Manginangina kauri walk) to two hours (the 2.6km Waihoanga Gorge kauri loop walk) and two days (the 20km Waipapa River track). A pamphlet ($1) detailing the tracks and features of the forests is available from any DOC office. Camping is permitted and there is a **camping ground** (☎ 09-403 9005; adult/child $7/3.50) at Puketi Recreation Area on Waiare Rd, 28km north of Kaikohe. It has hot showers, a kitchen with a stove and fridge, and composting toilets.

THE FAR NORTH

KAITAIA

pop 5630

The highlight of no-one's trip to NZ, Kaitaia (www.kaitaia.com) is mainly the jumping-off point for trips up Ninety Mile Beach to Cape Reinga. In the museum you'll see a welcome sign in three languages – welcome (English), *haere mai* (Maori) and *dobro došli* (Dalmatian) – as both Maoris and Dalmatians live in the area. Both groups are culturally active, with a Maori *marae* and the Dalmatian Cultural Club the focus of local activities. On a depressing note, theft from cars is a *big* problem here, meaning that

leaving anything (even in the locked boot) of your vehicle is close enough to saying you don't want it anymore. Or the car, for that matter.

On a more positive note, each year in March a special marathon, the **Te Houtawea Challenge**, takes place along the length of Ninety Mile Beach, celebrating the legend of Te Houtaewa. This great runner ran the length of the beach from Te Kao to Ahipara to steal kumara from the Te Rarawa people, returning with two full baskets after being angrily pursued. The marathon celebrates the return of the kumara – reconciliation for a past deed. A **Maori food festival** and *waka* (canoe) racing are also held in March.

SIGHTS & ACTIVITIES

Ancient Kauri Kingdom..................1 D3
Gumdiggers Park..........................2 D3
North Wind Lodge Backpackers.....7 C2
Marty's Pack or Paddle................3 C2
Okahu Estate Winery...................4 D4

SLEEPING

Houhora Lodge & Homestay.........5 C3
Kapowairua Camping Site.............6 C1
Pukenui Farm Backpackers............8 C3
Rarawa Beach Camp Site..............9 C2
Tapotupotu Bay Camp Site..........10 B1
Wagener Holiday Park &
 Backpackers..............................11 D3
Waitiki Landing Complex.............12 B1

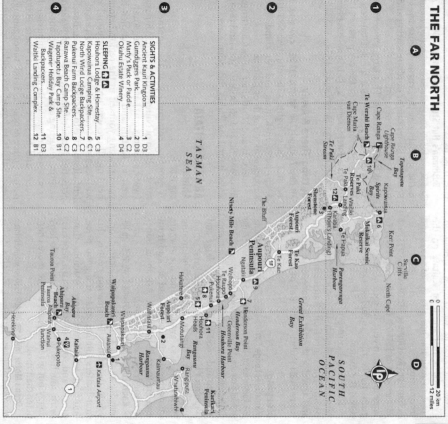

Information

ATMS are rare up north, but the Bank of New Zealand (108 Commerce St) has one.

Far North visitor information centre (☎ 09-408 0879; www.topofnz.co.nz; Jaycee Park, South Rd; ☒ 8.30am–5pm) Has Internet access and information on Kaitaia and the region, and books accommodation, tours and activities.

Post office (104 Commerce St)

Vodafone (84 Commerce St; 30 min $5) Internet access.

Sights & Activities

The **Far North Regional Museum** (☎ 09-408 1403; 6 South Rd; adult/child $4/1; ☒ 10am–4pm Mon–Fri) has among its eclectic bag of exhibits a giant moa skeleton and a 1769 anchor.

Okahu Estate Winery (Map p177; ☎ 09-408 2066; www.okahuestate.co.nz; cnr Okahu & Pukepoto Rds; ☒ 10am–5pm), just south of Kaitaia on the road to Ahipara, has a range of wines and free tasting.

Harrisons Reef Runner (☎ 09-408 1033; 123 North Rd; tours adult/child $35/25) is a Unimog 4WD (a large all-terrain vehicle) tour of the Ahipara gum fields that includes sandboarding down the dunes.

Kaitaia is a centre for popular tours up Ninety Mile Beach to Cape Reinga (see p180). The tours from Kaitaia are cheaper and travel a shorter distance than similar tours from Paihia in the Bay of Islands.

Sleeping

Mainstreet Lodge (☎ 09-408 1275; www.tall-tale.co.nz; 235 Commerce St; sites per 2 people $30, dm $30-32, dm without bathroom $25-28, s with/without bathroom $60/50, d & tw with/without bathroom $64/56) There's plenty of space and good facilities in this large and popular YHA-associate backpackers, which also has some simple rooms with bathroom. Parking is also available and the owners know the area inside-out and back-to-front and are incredibly helpful. Ask about bone-carving lessons with Peter.

Kauri Lodge Motel (☎ 09-408 1190; 15 South Rd; units $80-90; ☒) Conveniently located opposite the visitor information centre, this motel offers kitchen units at a good price, some of which are more spacious than others, and some of which retain very cool retro touches that the owners think give the place a little more daggy but give the place a little more character than most.

Orana Motor Inn (☎ 09-408 1510; oranamotorinn@xtra.co.nz; 238 Commerce St; r $90-100; ☒) This 1970s-era motel looks like a Pizza Hut franchise on the outside and has one of the most lugubrious reception areas in the country. Rooms are OK though.

Vineyard Cottage (☎ 09-408 2066; www.okahuestate.co.nz; cnr Okahu & Pukepoto Rds; d $180) This lovely, charming self-contained cottage is nestled among the Shiraz vines of Okahu Estate on the road to Ahipara. The room comes with a free bottle of wine.

Eating & Drinking

Beachcomber (☎ 09-408 2010; 222 Commerce St; mains $14-28; ☒ lunch Mon-Fri, dinner Mon-Sat) Easily the best place to eat in town, with delightful service, a wide-ranging menu and a well-stocked salad bar. You won't want to eat anywhere else, trust us.

Bushman's Hut Steakhouse (☎ 09-408 4320; 7 Bank St; mains $20-28; ☒ dinner) Barbecued meat is the speciality at this rustic licensed restaurant with indoor or outdoor seating and not a vegetarian in sight.

Pak N Save (West Lane) This large supermarket is the cheapest place for self-caterers. Don't leave valuables in the car park.

Kaitaia Hotel (Commerce St) This hotel has been quenching large thirsts since 1839.

Getting There & Away

Air New Zealand (24hr ☎ 0800 737 000; www.airnz.co.nz) has daily flights (50 minutes. $85 to $225) between Kaitaia and Auckland. The airport is 6km north of Kaitaia.

InterCity and Northliner buses leave from Blencowe St, and go daily to Auckland ($68, seven hours) via Paihia and Whangarei.

AROUND KAITAIA

Ahipara
pop 1000

A growing community at the southernmost section of Ninety Mile Beach, Ahipara (www.ahipara.co.nz) is only 14km southwest of Kaitaia and a far nicer choice if you're basing yourself in the region before heading all the way up north. It's popular with locals and visitors and makes an excellent alternative to staying at Kaitaia. Beach activities include fishing, blokarting (sand yachting), surfing and horse riding, but the area is also known for its mountainous sand dunes and massive gum field where 2000 people once worked. Sand tobogganing, beach safaris and quad-bike rides are popular activities on the dunes above Ahipara and further around the Tauroa Peninsula.

Ahipara Adventure Centre (☎ 09-409 2055; www.ahipara.co.nz/adventurecenter/main.html; 15 Takahe St; ☑ 9am-5pm) can book you on daylong Cape Reinga bus tours including a barge trip (adult/child $55/35) plus it hires out sandboards, and mountain bikes, kayaks, blokarts, quad bikes and surfboards. Blokarts cost $25 for the first half-hour (including instruction) and $20 for subsequent half-hours.

Tuatua Tours (☎ 09-409 4875; www.tuatuatours.co.nz; Ahipara Rd; 2hr ride $120) gets great word of mouth and offers both reef and dune rider tours (cheaper if you're part of a double) and gum fields safaris. Bookings are essential.

On the beachfront is a superb kauri house, the friendly **Endless Summer Lodge** (☎ 09-409 4181; www.endlesssummer.co.nz; 245 Foreshore Rd; dm $20, d &tw $50-56), which has been beautifully restored with natural wood décor. Free boogie boards are available, surfboards can be hired for $20 a day and surfing instruction is usually available. Booking is advised.

Beachfront (☎ 09-409 4007; www.beachfront.net.nz; 14 Kotare St; studio/apt $150/200) is a relatively new upmarket option with absolute beach frontage and a remarkable sense of escape. Breakfasts and dinners can be provided by arrangement (and a price), and good low-season rates are available.

Fortunately for locals and tourists alike, the **Ninety Mile Café** (☎ 09-409 2010; 22 Reef View Rd; mains $8-85; ☑ breakfast, lunch & dinner summer) provides delightful food (the seafood is a particular strength), with great views and friendly service. Call ahead in the low season, as hours may vary.

Gumdiggers Park

This **park** (Map p177; ☎ 09-406 7166; www.gumdiggerspark.co.nz; Heath Rd; adult/child $8/4; ☑ 9am-5pm) is 35km north of Kaitaia and 3km off the highway. It has a maze of footpaths around a major gum-digging site and an original gum-digger's hut, evidence of ancient buried swamp-kauri forests and shafts and holes from where kauri resin or gum was extracted. It was a hard life for the workers, who used jute sacks for their tents, bedding and clothing. This major Northland industry ran from the 1870s to the 1920s. In 1900, some 7000 gum-diggers in gumboots were digging holes all over Northland looking for buried kauri gum treasure. The gum was used in making varnish, linoleum and other products. The park has a small gift shop. If the site is unattended you can wander around on your own.

Ancient Kauri Kingdom

The impressive (if very touristy) **Ancient Kauri Kingdom** (Map p177; ☎ 09-406 7172; Far North Rd; ☑ 9am-5pm) is a workshop, café and gallery on the highway at Awanui and is well worth a visit. Here 50,000-year-old kauri stumps, which have been dragged up from swamps, are fashioned into furniture and woodcraft products, with some superb, eye-catching results. A huge upright kauri log has a spiral staircase carved into it that takes you to the mezzanine level.

CAPE REINGA & NINETY MILE BEACH

At the top of the long Aupouri Peninsula, Cape Reinga (116km by road from Kaitaia) is almost at the northern tip of NZ. Standing at the windswept Cape Reinga lighthouse and looking out over the endless ocean has a real end-of-the-world feel to it. The lighthouse is still in use, and directly below it is where the waters of the Tasman Sea and Pacific Ocean meet, generating waves up to 10m high in stormy weather. Still visible on the very tip of Cape Reinga is the 800-year-old pohutukawa tree whose roots hide the entrance to the mythical Maori Underworld; see p57. This point is known in Maori legend as Te Rerenga-Wairua, where the spirits of the dead depart the earth. Show respect for local traditions by refraining from eating or drinking here – posting a letter from what must surely be NZ's most remote mailbox is OK though.

Sights & Activities

From Cape Reinga you can walk along Te Werahi Beach to **Cape Maria van Diemen**, which takes about five hours return. Beautiful **Tapotupotu Bay** is a two-hour walk east of Cape Reinga car park, via Sandy Bay and the cliffs. From Tapotupotu Bay it is about an eight-hour walk to **Kapowairua** at the eastern end of Spirits Bay. Both Tapotupotu Bay and Kapowairua have basic camping grounds (see p181) and there is road access.

The **Aupouri Peninsula** is known to the Maori as Te Hiku o te Ika a Maui (The Tail of Maui's Fish) from the creation legend that tells of how Maui hauled a great fish from the sea, which became the North Island. The peninsula is a rugged, desolate landscape dominated by high sand dunes and flanked by Ninety Mile Beach – if it was metricated to Ninety Kilometre Beach the name would be more accurate.

The **Aupouri Forest**, about 75km long and 5km wide, covers two-thirds of the western side of the peninsula. Kauri forest used to cover the area but now it's mostly pine and planted for commercial timber.

Te Paki Reserves are public land with free access; just leave the gates as you found them and don't disturb the animals. There are about 7 sq km of giant sand dunes on either side of where Te Paki Stream meets the sea. A stop to take flying leaps off the dunes or toboggan down them is a highlight of locally operated tours.

Bus tours (see Tours, following) travel along the hard sands of **Ninety Mile Beach** on their way from Kaitaia or Paihia to Cape Reinga, or vice versa, depending on the tides. Private vehicles can also do the beach trip but all hire-car agreements prohibit driving on the beach. The usual access point for vehicles is Waipapakauri, just north of Kaitaia. The beach 'road' is only for the well prepared with rugged vehicles. Cars have hit soft sand before now and been swallowed by the tides – you may see the roof of an unfortunate vehicle poking through the sands. Check tide times before setting out, avoid it 2½ hours either side of high tide – and watch out for 'quicksand' on Te Paki Stream (keep moving).

Tours

Bus tours go to Cape Reinga from Kaitaia, Mangonui on Doubtless Bay (north of the Bay of Islands), and the Bay of Islands. It makes sense to take the tour from Kaitaia or Doubtless Bay since they are much closer to Cape Reinga and offer a cheaper deal.

Fullers, Kings Tours, Dune-Rider 4X4, Northern Exposure and Awesome Adventures operate long day trips from the Bay of Islands (see p188).

Far North Outback Adventure (☎ 09-408 0927; www.farnorthtours.co.nz) Runs small-group, flexible, daylong tours from Kaitaia for around $400 per person (minimum two people) including lunch. As well as Cape Reinga, you can visit remote areas such as Great Exhibition Bay and Tauroa Point.

Harrison's Cape Runner (☎ 0800 227 373, 09-408 1033; 123 North Rd; adult/child $40/20) Has 19- to 45-seater buses for day trips that take in the main features of the cape as well as sand tobogganing; includes picnic lunch.

Marty's Pack or Paddle (Map p177; ☎ 09-409 8445; www.packorpaddle.co.nz; ½-/full-day 4WD trips $75/135) At Thom's Landing, offers combined sea kayaking and fishing trips around the superb Parengarenga Harbour. Try the full moon kayaking tour ($150) for something that's both special and different.

Paradise Connexion (☎ 0800 494 392, 09-406 0460; www.paradisenz.co.nz; adult/child $65/35) Operates from Mangonui on Doubtless Bay. Also available are personalised 4WD VIP tours (including a seafood lunch and a bottle of wine) for $350 per vehicle (with tour guide, minimum two people).

Sand Safaris (☎ 09-408 1778; www.sandsafaris.co.nz; 221 Commerce St, Kaitaia; adult/child $55/29) A family-owned operation in Kaitaia running 28- and 31-seater buses up to Cape Reinga including a picnic lunch and a guided tour of Gumdiggers Park.

Sleeping & Eating

FAR FAR NORTH

Waitiki Landing Complex (Map p177; ☎ /fax 09-409 7508; unpowered/powered sites per 2 people $14/18, dm/cabins $20/55) This accommodation, 21km south of Cape Reinga, is the northernmost in NZ and the road north is gravel. There is a camp kitchen, laundrette and hot showers ($1). Waitiki Landing is also the last stop for fuel (and they don't even take this opportunity to rob you blind!), and has a shop, liquor store and a restaurant that does reasonable pizzas and ostrich burgers. Sandboard hire is $10 for four hours ($50 bond). Trips to Cape Reinga, Te Paki sandboarding, scenic flights, kayaking, fishing and tours to the white silica sand across Parengarenga Harbour can all be arranged. Drop-offs and pick-ups for hiking trips are possible – for example the three-day hike from Te Paki Stream to Spirits Bay.

North Wind Lodge Backpackers (Map p177; ☎ 09-409 8515; www.northwind.co.nz; Otaipango Rd, Henderson Bay; dm/tw/d $18/40/54) This unusual, homely retreat with turrets is by the ocean, 6km down an unsealed road on the peninsula's east side. It is spacious and modern, every room has its own bathroom and it's near a great stretch of beach. Boogie boards and sandboards are available to guests.

There are several DOC camping grounds in the Cape Reinga area. The **Kapowairua**

camp site (Map p177; adult/child $7/3.50), on Spirits Bay, has cold water and limited toilet facilities, and the **Tapotupotu Bay camp site** (Map p177; adult/child $7/3.50) has toilets and showers; neither has electricity. Both bays have mosquitoes and biting sandflies, so come prepared with repellent. The **Rarawa Beach camp site** (Map p177; adult/child $7/3.50), at the end of Rarawa Beach Rd, 3km north of Ngataki or 10km south of Te Kao, has water and toilet facilities only (no prior bookings, no open fires; open September to April).

PUKENUI

This village, on the highway about 45km north of Kaitaia, is situated on the Houhora Harbour and has the usual smattering of shops, a café and a bar. Boats for fishing and cruising can be hired and there are a couple of budget places to stay.

Pukenui Lodge Motel & Youth Hostel (09-409 8837; www.pukenuilodge.co.nz; dm/d/tw $18/45/45, units $70-120;) This clean, welcoming YHA-associate backpackers is in a historic house, built in 1891, and has spotless, pleasant rooms, some of which overlook Houhora Harbour. Motel guests can also access a spa pool.

Pukenui Farm Backpackers (Map p177; 09-409 7863; farmbackpackers@xtra.co.nz; Lamb Rd; sites per 2 people $18, dm/d $18/40) Just 2km down the mostly unsealed Lamb Rd is this modern, comfortable cottage with a veranda from which you see memorable sunsets. The owners will pick you up from the Pukenui shops, and guests can take part in farm activities.

Pukenui Holiday Park (09-409 8803; www.north land-camping.co.nz; 34 Lamb Rd; unpowered/powered sites per 2 people $24, cabins $50-65) Take an un-metered hot shower after a hard day's touring around the Cape then relax among the bushland at this welcoming, good-value caravan park.

Houhora Lodge & Homestay (Map p177; 09-409 7884; www.topstay.co.nz; 3994 Far North Rd; s/d B&B $100/160) Rooms in this stylish architect-designed home, 2km south of the Pukenui village shops, have en suite or private facilities. It's an airy, attractive place and an ideal spot for a quiet escape, with a deck that's just begging for someone to kick back on it after making good use of the wood-fired pizza oven.

AROUND PUKENUI

Wagener Holiday Park & Backpackers (Map p177; 09-409 8564; www.northlandholiday.co.nz; Houhora Heads; unpowered/powered sites per 2 people $20/24, dm, s & d per person $18) Kayaks, mountain bikes, surfboards and fishing gear can be hired at this beautiful waterfront spot at Houhora Heads, 2km off the main road. The complex includes a café, free local museum and the 15-room Subritzky Homestead (09-409 8564; tours adult/child $15/7.50), an 1862 homestead constructed of local swamp kauri set in a pretty garden. It's undergoing restoration work to the tune of over $600,000 and is fragile, so you'll need to call ahead and book if you want a visit.

KARIKARI PENINSULA

Karikari Peninsula forms the northwestern end of Doubtless Bay. Roads are mostly sealed and sandy beaches along the peninsula face all directions. There are plenty of holiday homes as well as a luxury golf club and winery but few facilities in this out-of-the-way area.

Rangiputa has lovely white-sand beaches that are easy to reach. A turn-off on the road to Rangiputa takes you to remote **Puheke Beach** with white sand dunes and long, lonely windswept beaches. On the east coast of the peninsula, **Matai Bay** (21km from the turn-off), with its tiny 'twin coves', is the loveliest of the beaches. There is a large **DOC camping ground** (09-408 6014; adult/child $8/4) with chemical toilets and cold water.

Just 1km along the road up the peninsula is the aptly named **Rockhouse** (09-406 7151; rochouselan@clearnet.nz; dm $25), which has unusual but very comfortable en suite accommodation (think Fred Flintstone meets Hundertwasser) and a laid-back, friendly host. Prices include breakfast. Meals ($20) can be served by arrangement, making this a great budget getaway.

Whatuwhiwhi Top 10 Holiday Park (09-408 7202; www.whatuwhiwhitop10.co.nz; Whatuwhiwhi Rd; unpowered/powered sites per 2 people $28/32, cabins $50-110, units $75-220) has a great location that overlooks a beach, nicely maintained facilities, efficient management and a little shop plus kayaks for hire.

DOUBTLESS BAY

The bay gets its unusual name from an entry in Captain Cook's logbook, where he wrote that the body of water was 'doubtless a bay'. Lying east of the Karikari Peninsula, Doubtless Bay has picturesque coves and beaches. The whole area is great for fishing and shellfishing, boating, swimming and other water sports.

The main centre, **Mangonui** (its name means 'Great Shark'), is a fishing port and has a line of well-labelled historical buildings along the waterfront that were constructed in the days when it used to be a centre of the whaling industry (1792–1850) and exported flax, kauri wood and gum. Nowadays the buildings are tourist-oriented with cafés, gift shops and accommodation. Stretching west along the bay are the beach resorts of Coopers Beach, Cable Bay and Taipa.

Information

Doubtless Bay visitor information centre
(09-406 2046; www.doubtlessbay.com; Waterfront Rd; 8am–6pm summer) Helpful volunteers; can arrange fishing trips.

Post office (Beach Rd)

Sights & Activities

Mr Roosevelt (09-406 1554; www.sailingchartersnz.co.nz; Mill Bay; per person $75) offers one-day sailing trips on a 12m boat (the aforementioned *Mr Roosevelt*), or overnight cruises further afield for $150 per person (overnight cruises maximum four or six people).

From Mangonui, **Paradise Connexion** (0800 494 392, 09-406 0460; www.paradisenz.co.nz; adult/child $65/35) operates 4WD bus tours up Ninety Mile Beach to Cape Reinga. Also available are personalised 4WD VIP tours (including a seafood lunch and a bottle of wine) for $350 per vehicle (minimum two people).

A free **Heritage Trail** brochure is a guide to a 3km walk around 18 of the historical buildings in the village. Other walks are to attractive **Mill Bay**, west of Mangonui and **Rangikapiti Pa Historic Reserve**, with ancient Maori terracing and a spectacular view of Doubtless Bay. A walkway runs from Mill Bay to the top of the *pa*.

At Hihi, a 15km drive east of Mangonui, is **Butler Point**. A guided tour around the small **whaling museum** (09-406 0006; www.butlerpoint.co.nz; adult/child $12/2), an 1843 homestead furnished in the Victorian style, and the gardens is worthwhile. Captain Butler, who built the homestead, left Dorset in England when he was 14 years old and at 24 was

captain of a whaling ship. He settled down here in 1839, had 13 children and became a trader, farmer, magistrate and member of parliament. You must telephone to arrange a visit.

Swamp Palace Cinema (09-408 7040; Oruru) shows films regularly but is 7km inland off the main road.

BEACHES

The first beach west of Mangonui is **Coopers Beach**, a fine sweep of sand lined with pohutukawa trees. Coopers Beach is quite developed and has a small shopping centre that includes a shop with diving and fishing gear and a quality restaurant. The next bay along is the less developed **Cable Bay**, and across the river is **Taipa**, another popular summer destination, which has a fine beach, a harbour where the Taipa River meets the sea, and several motels and motor camps.

Sleeping

BUDGET

Mangonui Hotel (09-406 0003; Waterfront Rd; dm $25, s/d without bathroom $40, d with bathroom $80) Rooms in this fine 1905 heritage building are upstairs and pretty comfortable with doors onto the veranda and splendid harbour views (from Nos 10, 12 and 15). Downstairs is a pub and Angie's dining room.

Old Oak Inn (09-406 0665; 66 Waterfront Rd; dm with/without bathroom $25/20, r without bathroom $45-80, d with bathroom $130) This inn is in an 1861 kauri building with a backpacker section and comfy but worn accommodation up a very narrow flight of stairs with decent en suite rooms. The pub has seafaring décor and offers bistro meals, and the building is reputedly haunted by a female ghost, which may well be part of its roughish charm.

MIDRANGE

Mangonui Motel (09-406 0346; www.mangonuimotel.co.nz; 1 Colonel Mould Dr; r $95-175) Stay at this spruce motel, which has six one-bedroom apartments and an elevated position, meaning that glorious views are on offer for every guest. It's a quick walk to the Mangonui Fish Shop, which is reason enough to stay.

Driftwood Lodge (09-406 0418; www.driftwoodlodge.co.nz; SH10, Cable Bay; r $95-210) Head along State Highway 10 (SH10) to discover this absolute beachfront gem, where seven rooms can sleep a number of people. It's an ideal spot for keen fishers and a truly relaxing part of the world.

Waterfront Apartments (☎ 09-406 0347; www mangonuiwaterfront.co.nz; Waterfront Rd; apt $130-150) These gaily painted, colourful apartments on the waterfront have loads of charm and character and each one is different and attractive; try to book Rua or Tahi. They're excellent value for money too.

Esquire Motel (☎ 09-406 0451; esquiremotel@ hotmail.com; 76 Waterfront Rd; 1-bedroom units $120-150) With tidy, nifty little units on offer and a lobby devoted to collectable items of the King, this is just the spot for devotees of Elvis Presley to kick back and look at the bay. Insert your own 'Elvis has left the building' gag here.

TOP END

Taipa Bay Resort (☎ 09-406 0656; www.taipabay.co nz; 22 Taipa Point Rd; studios $175-195, 1-bedroom apt $215-285; ☒) Pricing is seasonal at these immaculate modern holiday units on the sandy beach at Taipa (which means that prices really plummet in the low season). Tennis, table tennis, croquet, volleyball and pétanque are all available and there is a spa pool and a restaurant which is open for breakfast, lunch and dinner.

Eating

Mangonui Fish Shop (☎ 09-406 0478; Waterfront Rd; meals $5-50; ☒ breakfast, lunch & dinner) You can eat outdoors over the water in this licensed and deservedly famous fish-and-chip shop, which also sells smoked fish, seafood salads, raw fish and cooked crayfish. Grab a handful of plump fried oysters, a cold beer and all's right with the world.

Galley Cafe (☎ 09-406 1233; 118 Waterfront Rd; lunch mains $14-15; ☒ breakfast, lunch & dinner) This lovely-looking and friendly café serves imaginative Mod-NZ dishes in an elegantly rustic atmosphere – and the prices are more than reasonable.

Waterfront Café (☎ 09-406 0850; Waterfront Rd; mains $12-28; ☒ breakfast, lunch & dinner) This café has fresh fish, seafood laksa, whitebait (when in season) and plenty more.

Mangonui Hotel (☎ 09-406 0003; Waterfront Rd; mains $11-22; ☒ lunch & dinner) This unpretentious pub restaurant has an ever-changing but good-deal menu that includes T-bone s-eaks that warrant their own postcode, scallops and flounder.

For self-caterers there's a **Four Square supermarket** (Waterfront Rd) next to the post office.

Getting There & Away

InterCity (☎ 09-623 1503; www.intercitycoach.co.nz) and **Northliner** (☎ 09-307 5873; www.northliner. co.nz) buses stop at Wilton's BP Garage on Waterfront Rd. It's 40 minutes to Kaitaia ($15) and one hour to Kerikeri ($18).

DOUBTLESS BAY TO BAY OF ISLANDS

From Mangonui it's about 44km to Kerikeri via the main highway (SH10), but about halfway along you can make a worthwhile scenic detour to busy Whangaroa Harbour and on to the very picturesque Matauri Bay (a mini Bay of Islands) before rejoining the highway.

Whangaroa Harbour

The small fishing village of Whangaroa is 6km off the main road and calls itself the 'Marlin Capital of New Zealand', meaning it's a popular place to dislocate your shoulder while trying to land a Lee Marvin–sized monster. **Boyd Gallery** (☎ 09-405 0230; Whangaroa Rd; ☒ 8am-7pm) is the general store but also acts as a tourist information office.

For **game-fishing** (November to May), particularly for marlin, there are plenty of charter boats and prices start at around $900 a day.

Contact the owner of **Whangaroa Harbour Retreat** (☎ /fax 09-405 0306; http://whangaroa.tri pod.com) for dive equipment hire and dive trips around the Cavalli Islands (including the wreck of the Rainbow Warrior); or for crayfish (maximum six) or scallops (maximum 20).

Snow Cloud (☎ 09-405 1663;www.snowcloud.co.nz day trips adult/child $80/45), an 11.2m yacht, makes day trips to the Cavalli Islands, where there are excellent beaches, diving spots, snorkelling opportunities and walks. Yacht charters can also be arranged.

An excellent 30-minute **hike** starts from the car park at the end of Hospital Rd and goes up **St Paul's Rock** (213m), which dominates the village. During the last part you have to use a wire cable to pull yourself up, but the views from the top make it worth the effort.

The Wairakau track north to Pekapeka Bay begins near the church hall on Campbell Rd in Totara North on the other side of the bay. The two-hour hike passes through farmland, hills and shoreline before arriving at DOC's **Lane Cove Hut** (09-403 9005; per person $12), which is a hut with 16 beds, cold showers and composting toilets. You need to bring your own cooker and no camping is permitted.

Up the hill in Whangaroa, the sun-filled (hence the name) **Sunseeker Lodge** (09-405 0496; www.sunseekerlodge.co.nz; Old Hospital Rd; dm $25, d & tw $60, units $100) has friendly staff, a spa bath with a jaw-dropping view, hires out kayaks and will pick you up from Kaeo on SH10. **Whangaroa Motel** (/fax 09-405 0022; whangaroamotel@xtra.co.nz; Church St; d $90-125) is up the hill and the owner runs fishing trips, if you can tear yourself away from the views.

On the main road north of the turn-off to Whangaroa, **Kahoe Farm Hostel** (09-405

1804; www.kahoefarms.co.nz; dm/s/d/tw $23/43/56) is a beautiful place with a great reputation and serves up excellent Italian-style homemade pizzas, seafood risottos and pasta and has kayaks ($40 for the day).

Visitors are welcome to the bar and dinning room of the **Whangaroa Big Gamefish Club** (09-405 0399; 4.30-11pm daily Oct-Apr, Thu-Sun May-Sep).

Tauranga & Matauri Bays

For a drive passing beautiful bays and beaches, head back out of Whangaroa and turn east towards Tauranga Bay and Te Ngaire. The highlight is Matauri Bay, with the 17 Cavalli Islands scattered offshore and a sandy beach with surf. On top of the far headland is a monument to the *Rainbow*

THE BOMBING OF THE RAINBOW WARRIOR

In 1985, a tragic, explosive event in Auckland Harbour made world headlines and put NZ on the map. The Greenpeace flagship *Rainbow Warrior* lay anchored in Auckland Harbour, preparing to sail to Moruroa near Tahiti to protest against French nuclear testing. But it never left Auckland because French saboteurs, in the employ of the French government, attached explosives to the side of the ship and sank her, killing a green campaigner, Fernando Pereira.

It took some time to find out exactly what had happened, but two of the saboteurs were captured, tried and found guilty, although the others have never been brought to justice.

The incident caused an uproar in France – not because the French government had conducted a deliberate and lethal act of terrorism on the soil of a friendly nation, but because the French secret service had bungled the operation and been caught. The French used all their political and economic might to force NZ to release the two saboteurs, and in a farcical turn of events the agents were imprisoned on a French Pacific island as if they had won a trip to Club Med. Within two years, and well before the end of their sentence, they returned to France to receive a hero's welcome.

Northland was the stage for this deadly mission involving several secret service agents. Explosives for the sabotage were delivered by a yacht (which had picked them up from a submarine) from Parengarenga Harbour in the Far North. They were driven to Auckland in a Kombi van by French agents posing as tourists. Bang! An innocent man dead, and international outrage – NZ was in the news.

The skeletal remains of the *Rainbow Warrior* were taken to the waters of Northland's beautiful Cavalli Islands, where it can now be explored by divers. The masts of this oceanic crusader were bought by the museum in Dargaville, where they are displayed outside. The memory of the Portuguese photographer and campaigner who died endures in a peaceful bird hide in Thames. A haunting memorial to the once-proud boat sits atop a Maori *pa* site at Matauri Bay, north of the Bay of Islands.

Attention again focused on the *Rainbow Warrior* in 1995. Ten years after the sinking the French announced they were resuming nuclear testing in the Pacific, and Greenpeace's new flagship bearing the name of its ill-fated predecessor set sail for the Moruroa test site. It entered the exclusion zone only to be stormed by French marines.

In 2005, the 20th anniversary of the bombing was commemorated in Auckland (with a tribute concert taking place at St James' Theatre), Paris (with a gathering of 500 people), and at the site of the original *Rainbow Warrior* (joined above the depths by the new ship of the same name). You can find out more about the story at www.rainbow-warrior.org.nz.

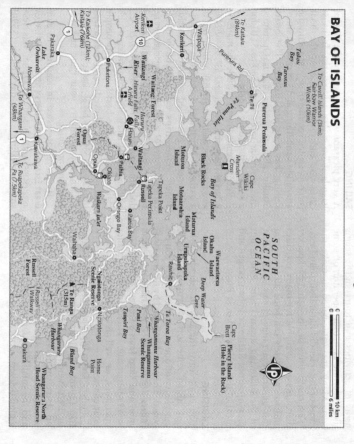

Warrior, the ship that was deliberately sunk off one of the islands and is a popular dive site. See the boxed text, opposite for more on the *Rainbow Warrior* story. Matauri Bay is about 25km from Whangaroa and it's another 18km back to SH10.

Based on the coast past Tauranga Bay, **Northland Sea Kayaking** (☎ 09-405 0381; www.north landseakayaking.co.nz; half-/full-day tours $60/80) offers kayak tours to explore this magical coastline of bays, sea caves and islands. Accommodation is available for $20 extra per person and pick-up from Kaeo can be arranged.

There is accommodation at **Tauranga Bay Holiday Park** (☎ 09-405 0436; www.taurangabay.co.nz; unpowered/powered sites per 2 people $22/26, cabins $50-70), which is on the picturesque, sandy beach, but the park lacks trees and bears the brunt of the weather, rain or shine.

Also on a great beach is **Matauri Bay Holiday Park** (☎ 05-405 0525; www.matauribay.co.nz; unpowered/ powered sites per 2 people $24/27, on-site caravans d $50). There is a shop with a liquor licence and a petrol station on the site.

At the end of the beach road at Matauri Bay, **Oceans Holiday Village** (☎ 09-405 0417; www

matauribay.co.nz/oceans; d $150, units $170) has cute cottages on its own little cove beach. Facilities include a bar and licensed restaurant, and kayaks and dinghies are available.

BAY OF ISLANDS

The footage that first made you want to come to NZ no doubt featured lingering shots of the Bay of Islands. When prospective visitors aren't fantasising about the South Island's glaciers, mountains and skiing, they're envisioning lazy, sun-filled days on a yacht floating atop crystalline waters. Long famed for its stunning coastal scenery, the Bay of Islands is one of NZ's most worthy attractions, punctuated by dozens of coves and filled with clear waters ranging in hue from turquoise to deep blue. Although a hugely popular tourist and sailing destination, the 150 or so islands have thankfully escaped development; townships are all on the mainland.

The Bay of Islands is also of enormous historical significance. As the site of NZ's first permanent English settlement, it is the birthplace of European colonisation. It was here that the Treaty of Waitangi was drawn up and first signed by 46 Maori chiefs in 1840; the treaty remains the linchpin of race relations in NZ today (see p35).

Paihia is the hub of the Bay of Islands. Though only a small town, its population swells dramatically in summer and it has all the trappings of a thriving tourist centre. Waitangi National Reserve, with its historic Treaty House, is within walking distance.

Only a short passenger-ferry ride away, Russell has all the charm and character that Paihia often lacks. Though also a popular side trip for Bay of Islands tourists, historic Russell is a smaller, sleepier town with many fine old buildings and a delightful waterfront.

To the north Kerikeri, famous for its orchards and outdoor cafés, is much less touristy, but still has a few attractions and a great deal of history.

Activities & Tours

The Bay of Islands has a mind-boggling array of activities and tours and it seems like everyone is a tour operator of some sort. Many are water-based to make the most of the splendid natural surroundings. It's a competitive business and backpacker discounts are available for many activities and tours. Hostels can book all tours and can generally arrange cheap deals. Most of the following depart from Paihia, but pick-ups from Kerikeri can be arranged and most of the cruises call in at Russell.

CRUISING

You can't leave the Bay of Islands without taking some sort of cruise and there are plenty of operators keen to get you on board. They are dominated by the 'big two': **Fullers** (☎ 09-402 7421; www.fullers-bay-of-islands .co.nz) and **Kings Tours & Cruises** (☎ 09-402 8288; www.kings-tours.co.nz). There are also smaller operators, as well as sailing and fishing boat charters.

Fullers' **Cream Trip** (adult/child $90/45) is a day trip (10am to 4.15pm) that started back in 1920 when one Captain Lane picked up dairy products from the many farms around the bay. As more roads were built and the small dairy farms closed, it became a mail delivery service. It is now part of the 'Supercruise', which incorporates the Hole in the Rock off Cape Brett, passing through it if conditions are right, and a one-hour stopover on Urupukapuka Island where Westerns writer Zane Grey went big-game fishing, and a tourist submarine, the **Nautilus** (adult/child $10/5), is submerged.

Other Fullers' cruises include the **Hole in the Rock** (adult/child $70/35), with a stopover on Urupukapuka Island. The tour lasts four hours with one hour on the island.

Kings has a **Day in the Bay cruise** (adult/child $95/50), which combines the Cream Trip route and the Hole in the Rock with dolphin swimming.

JETBOATING

Also very popular are the high-speed Hole in the Rock trips on board a jetboat – good fun and handy if you're short on time. Put on the waterproof gear provided and fasten your seatbelts! **Excitor** (☎ 09-402 7020; www.excitor.co.nz; adult/child $72/36) and **Mack Attack** (☎ 0800 622 528, 09-402 8180; www.mackattack.co.nz; adult/child $68/34) have regular 1½-hour trips.

SAILING

A very pleasant way to explore the Bay of Islands is on a day sailing trip. In most cases you can either help crew the boat (no experience required), or just spend the afternoon sunbathing and swimming, snorkelling, kayaking and fishing. The boats usually call in at various islands. Operators charge similar rates: about $80 to $110 for a full day, including lunch.

Recommended boats include the majestic **R Tucker Thompson** (☎ 0800 882 537, 09-402 8430; www.tucker.co.nz; adult/child $110/55), which offers a barbecue lunch and a cruise on a classic schooner that has sailed around the world. Other, longer trips can also be booked: **Carino** (☎ 09-402 8040; www.sailingdolphins.co.nz; adult/child $80/45), which combines sailing and dolphin swimming; **Phantom** (☎ 0800 224 421; adult/child $90/45), a fast 50ft ocean racer, which claims to offer the best lunch (10 people maximum, BYO allowed); and **She's a Lady** (☎ 0800 724 584; www.bay-of-islands.com; adult $85), on which you can try your hand at kneeboarding or tubing.

If you're interested in learning to sail, **Great Escape Yacht Charters** (☎ 09-402 7143; www .greatescape.co.nz), based in Opua, has lessons, including a five-day course ($590) with training for two days after which you are on your own. Two-day courses cost $295. Yachts can be hired for $100 to $390 a day.

OVERNIGHT CRUISES

The cheapest way to spend a possibly romantic night on the water is aboard the **Rock** (0800 762 527; www.rocktheboat.co.nz; 24hr cruises $148), an unlikely-looking vessel set up for backpackers. A double room costs an extra $15 per person. The Rock was a vehicle ferry in a former life but now it's a comfortable floating hostel with four-bed dorms, twin and double rooms, and (of course) a bar. The cruise departs at about 5pm and includes an excellent barbecue and seafood dinner with live music, then a full day spent cruising around and visiting islands, fishing, kayaking, snorkelling and swimming.

Ecocruz (0800 432 6278; www.ecocruz.co.nz; cruises dm/d $495/575) is a highly recommended three-day/two-night sailing cruise with an emphasis on marine wildlife and environment, aboard the 72ft ocean-going yacht *Manawanui*. The cost includes accommodation, all meals and activities that include fishing, kayaking and snorkelling.

DOLPHIN SWIMMING

These trips operate all year and you get to cruise around the islands as well as watch and swim with the dolphins. They have a high success rate, and operators generally offer a free trip if dolphins are not sighted. Dolphin swims are subject to weather and sea conditions, with restrictions if the dolphins have young. As well as encountering bottlenose and common dolphins, whales, orcas and penguins may be seen. With all operators a portion of the cost goes towards marine research, via DOC.

Dolphin Discoveries (09-402 8234; www.dolphinz.co.nz; adult/child $99/59) was the first to do dolphin-swimming trips in the bay, in 1991. Trips last about 3½ hours and all equipment is provided.

Dolphin Adventures (09-402 6985; www.awesomenz.com; per person $105) has similar trips with an option to spend time on Urupukapuka Island.

Kings Cruises (09-402 8288; www.dolphincruises .co.nz; adult/child $95/50) runs dolphin-swimming trips daily that include boom netting.

SEA KAYAKING

There are plenty of opportunities for kayaking around the bay, either on a guided tour or by renting a kayak and going it alone.

Coastal Kayakers (Map p190; 09-402 8105; www .coastalkayakers.co.nz; Te Karuwha Pde) runs a guided tour (half-/full day per person $55/$75), and a two-day budget harbour wilderness tour is $130. A minimum of two people is required. Kayaks can be rented (half-/full day $30/40).

New Zealand Sea Kayak Adventures (09-402 8596; www.seakayakingadventures.com; 3-/6-day trips $450/901) runs kayaking and camping trips in the Bay of Islands and the outer northeast coast.

Island Kayaks (Map p190; 09-402 6078; www .islandkayaking.co.nz; Marsden Rd, Paihia; s/d kayak tours $55/110) operates from Bay Beach Hire in Paihia.

SCUBA DIVING

The Bay of Islands offers some fine subtropical diving and local operators all go out to the wreck of the *Rainbow Warrior* off the Cavalli Islands, about an hour from Paihia by boat.

Dive North (09-402 7079; www.divenorth.co.nz) also has trips to the *Rainbow Warrior* and other popular dive sites such as Deep Water Cove and Cape Brett. A good 'discover scuba' course starts at $180 (for one dive), or there's a similar two-dive option for $250.

Paihia Dive (Map p190; 09-402 7551; www.dive nz.com; Williams Rd, Paihia) offers *Rainbow Warrior* dive trips ($195 for two dives including gear) or you can do two adventure dives in the Bay of Islands for the same price.

SURFING

New Zealand Surf & Snow Tours (05-828 0426; www.newzealandsurftours.com; tours $699), based in Auckland, runs a five-day surfing tour at surf beaches near the Bay of Islands (among others in Northland) and includes meals, transport, surfboards, wet suits and lessons.

OTHER ACTIVITIES

The Bay of Islands is noted for its **fishing** and charter boats can be booked at the Maritime Building in Paihia (see p189) or at Russell wharf.

Skydive Bay of Islands Skydive (0800 427 593, 09-402 6744) operates from the Haruru Falls airport. A tandem skydive to 12,000ft costs

$260, a DVD of it is $150, and a DVD and digital photograph costs $175.

Bay Beach Hire (Map p190; ☎ 09-402 6078; www .baybeachhire.co.nz; Marsden Rd, Paihia; ⏱ 9am-5.30pm) hires out just about everything: kayaks (from $10 per hour), small sailing catamarans ($40 per hour), mountain bikes ($20 half-day), boogie boards, fishing rods, wet suits and snorkelling gear. Guided kayak tours and overnight kayak tours are available. Bay Beach Hire also runs **Flying Kiwi Parasail** (☎ 09-402 6078; www.parasail-nz.co.nz; trips $70-85), which organises one-hour parasailing trips leaving from Paihia wharf hourly during summer.

Salt Air (☎ 09-402 8338; www.saltair.co.nz) has scenic flights ranging from a one-hour discovery tour of the Bay of Islands (per person $175) to a five-hour flight-and-4WD tour to Cape Reinga and Ninety Mile Beach ($345). Helicopter flights out to the Hole in the Rock and Cape Brett cost $170.

CAPE REINGA TOURS

It's cheaper and easier to do trips to Cape Reinga and Ninety Mile Beach from Kaitaia or Doubtless Bay if you're heading up that way (see p180). However, if you're short on time, it's possible to do a long day trip (10 to 12 hours) from the Bay of Islands with several operators. They're all pretty similar bus tours, driving one way along Ninety Mile Beach, with visits to Puketi forest, sandboarding on the dunes and other places on the way, but check the stops and whether lunch is included.

Awesome Adventures (Map p190; ☎ 09-402 6985; www.awesomenz.co.nz; Maritime Bldg, Paihia; trips $99) has backpacker-oriented trips with sandboarding on the 85m dunes, swimming at Tapotupotu Bay and a visit to Puketi kauri forest.

Dune-Rider 4X4 (☎ 09-402 8681;www.dunerider.co .nz; adult/child $95/50) is popular among backpackers and younger travellers. The smaller group trips (20-seater buses) make plenty of stops for sandboarding and swimming.

Northern Exposure (☎ 0800 573 875, 09-402 8644; trips $92) also aims its trips at backpackers; for instance, no children are allowed.

Fullers (☎ 09-402 7421; adult/child $99/50, trips with BBQ lunch $118/69) has all-day trips departing from Paihia and Kerikeri.

Kings Tours (☎ 0800 222 979, 09-402 8288; adult/ child $95/48) has coach tours (no lunch).

Festivals & Events

Tall Ship Race This takes place in Russell in January.
Waitangi Day Various ceremonial events at Waitangi on 6 February.
Country Music Festival This is held the second weekend in May.
Jazz & Blues Festival Held the second weekend in August.
Weekend Coastal Classic Held during Labour Weekend in October; this is NZ's largest yacht race, from Auckland to the Bay of Islands.
Wine & Food Festival This popular festival is held in early November in Waimate.

Bay of Islands for Children

This area is one of the most family-friendly in NZ, with plenty of tour operators, squeal-worthy activities and chip-laden children's menus, plus a lot of stunning scenery that will fire up young imaginations. Popular activities with the young include the **Paihia Duck** (left), the **Nautilus submarine** (p186) at Urupukapuka Island and a spot of **jetboating** (p186) for those with staunch stomachs. Kids will find the incredible war canoe, cultural performance and night-time sound and light show at **Waitangi** (opposite) as fascinating as adults do.

Getting There & Away

All buses serving Paihia arrive at and depart from the Maritime Building by the wharf. **InterCity** (☎ 09-623 1503; www.intercitycoach.co.nz) and **Northliner** (☎ 09-307 5873; www.northliner.co .nz) have buses daily from Auckland to the Bay of Islands, via Whangarei. Paihia to Kerikeri ($11) takes 20 minutes, Paihia to Kaitaia ($32) takes two hours and 40 minutes, and Paihia to Auckland ($47) takes four hours.

Getting Around

Passenger ferries connect Paihia with Russell, running from around 7am to 7pm (to 10pm from October to June). Ferries operate on average every 20 minutes from Russell to Paihia in summer. The adult/child one-way fare is $5/2.50.

To get to Russell with your car, you have to drive down to Opua and cross to Okiato

Point using the car ferry (see p196) or drive another 40km along mainly gravel roads via Waihaha.

There's also a **fast ferry** (☎ 09-402 8288; one way/return $5/9; every 25min 8.30am-late summer, 8.30am-5.30pm winter) operated by Kings. Buy tickets on board.

Xmas Goose Island Shuttle (☎ 0800 3878 9276, 09-402 7578; www.islandshuttle.co.nz) is a shuttle service perfect for getting around the bay islands if you're in a group of four or more. It does trips to various islands and coves and can organise activities too. **Kiwi Ecotours water taxi** (☎ 09-403 8823) is a reliable service too. For bicycle hire visit **Bay Beach Hire** (Map p190; ☎ 09-402 6078; Marsden Rd) in Paihia.

PEWHAIRANGI

This park consists of 40 separate areas that extend from Whangamumu Harbour in the south to Whangaroa in the north. Diverse hikes cover islands, *pa* sites and some spectacular scenery. The **DOC Pewhairangi Bay of Islands visitor information centre** (Map p194; ☎ 09-403 9005; www.doc.govt.nz; The Strand; 9am-5pm) in Russell can provide information. The Cape Brett hike (p200) is famous.

Camping (per adult/child $8/2) is permitted at two other bays on **Urupukapuka Island**. Cable and Urupukapuka Bays have water supplies, cold showers and composting toilets but you need to bring food, a stove and fuel.

It's hard to imagine a more idyllic setting than **Zane Grey's Restaurant & Bar** (☎ 09-403 7009; www.zanegrey.co.nz; The Strand; mains $15-20; breakfast, lunch & dinner) at Otehei Bay, which also provides **accommodation** (sites per 2 people $24-30, dm $20, d cabins with/without bathroom $60/30, cottage $85). There's a small store and craft shop and kayaks can be hired (per hour single/double $10/18). Hikes on the island range up to five hours.

To get to Urupukapuka Island, take a **water taxi** (☎ 09-403 8823), the Xmas Goose shuttle or a Fullers tour boat, get off at Otehei Bay and arrange to catch the boat back on the day you want to return.

PAIHIA & WAITANGI
pop 7250

Paihia has a very pretty setting and is a modern-day tourist town par excellence, with countless activity and accommodation options. Paihia was first settled by Euro-peans as a mission station in 1823 with the arrival of Reverend Henry Williams.

Adjoining Paihia, the site of the historic signing on 6 February 1840 of the treaty between mainly local Maori chiefs and the representatives of Queen Victoria's government. The treaty then toured the country and many other chiefs added their signatures or marks.

Information

Bay of Islands visitor information centre (☎ 09-402 7345; visitorinfo@mdc.govt.nz; Marsden Rd; 8am-5pm winter, to late in summer) Near the ferry launch and terminal.

Maritime Building (Marsden Rd; per hr $6) Next to the visitor information centre; Fullers, Kings, Awesome Adventures and other tour and activity companies have offices here and buses stop outside; has Internet access.

Boots Off Travellers Centre (☎ 09-402 6632; Selwyn Rd; per hr $9) Has Internet access.

Medical Centre (☎ 09-402 8407; Selwyn Rd) Can give dive physicals.

Post office (2 Williams Rd)

Sights & Activities
WAITANGI NATIONAL RESERVE

A visit to the **Waitangi National Reserve** (☎ 09-402 7437; www.waitangi.net.nz; admission $10; 9am-6pm) is definitely a must for every itinerary. The **Waitangi visitor information centre** (9am-6pm) here shows an interesting 15-minute audiovisual that is played every half-hour from 9am. The centre also has a gallery of portraits, Maori weaponry and a gift shop.

A 30-minute **He Toho** (cultural performance; admission $12) takes place at 11.30am and 12.30pm and includes *poi* (a women's formation dance that involves singing and manipulating a ball of woven flax), the *haka* (war dance), songs and dances. A **Maori guided tour** (adult/child $20/5) is available at 10.30am and 1pm. A **garden tour** (per person $12) takes 20 minutes, at 11.30am Monday to Friday, takes 20 minutes. Finally a 1½-hour **sound & light show** (www.culturenorth.co.nz; admission $45), which includes live performers, takes place at 8pm Monday, Wednesday, Thursday and Saturday from October to April. Pick-ups from Paihia are available.

Waitangi is full of cultural icons – the colonial-style Treaty House with its garden and lawns transplanted from a faraway land, the surrounding native bush full of native birds, the spiritual *whare* and the three flags (the UK, NZ

www.lonelyplanet.com

PAIHIA & WAITANGI

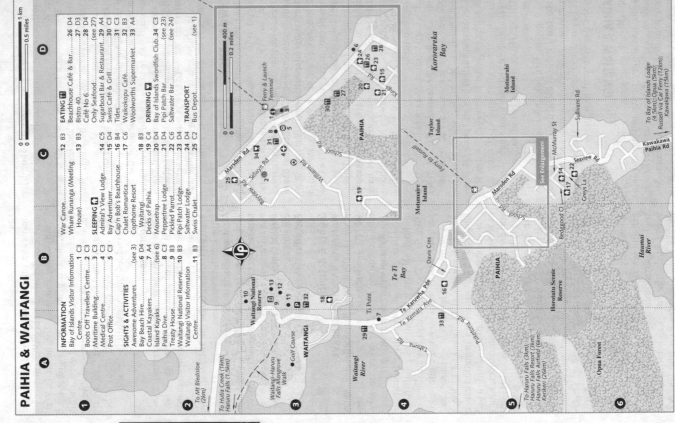

INFORMATION
Bay of Islands Visitor Information Centre..................1	C3
Boots Off Travellers Centre......2	C3
Maritime Building.....................3	C3
Medical Centre..........................4	C3
Post Office................................5	C3

SIGHTS & ACTIVITIES
Awesome Adventures............(see 3)	
Bay Beach Hire.........................6	D4
Coastal Kayakers...................7	A4
Island Kayaks.....................(see 6)	
Paihia Dive...............................8	C3
Treaty House............................9	B3
Waitangi National Reserve.....10	B3
Waitangi Visitor Information Centre.....................11	B3

SLEEPING
Admiral's View Lodge..............14	C5
Bay Adventurer.......................15	D4
Cap'n Bob's Beachhouse.........16	B4
Chalet Romantica....................17	C6
Copthorne Resort Waitangi......18	B3
Decks of Paihia......................19	C4
Mousetrap..............................20	D4
Peppertree Lodge...................21	C6
Pickled Parrot.........................22	C6
Pipi Patch Lodge....................23	D4
Saltwater Lodge....................24	D4
Swiss Chalet..........................25	C2

War Canoe..............................12 | B3 |
Whare Runanga (Meeting House).....................13 | B3 |

EATING 🍴
Beachhouse Café & Bar..........26	D4
Bistro 40................................27	D3
Café No 6...............................28	D4
Only Seafood....................(see 27)	
Sugarboat Bar & Restaurant...29	A4
Swiss Café & Grill...................30	C3
Tides.......................................31	C3
Waikokopu Café.....................32	B3
Woolworths Supermarket.......33	A4

DRINKING
Bay of Islands Swordfish Club 34	C3
Pipi Patch Bar...................(see 23)	
Saltwater Bar...................(see 24)	

TRANSPORT
Bus Depot........................(see 1)	

and Maori flags), and the hillside views of a still-beautiful land.

The **Treaty House**, the centrepiece of the impressive grounds, has special significance in NZ's history. Built in 1832 as the four-room home of British resident James Busby, eight years later it was the setting for the signing of the Treaty of Waitangi. The house, with its gardens and beautiful lawn running down to the bay, was restored in 1989 and is preserved as a memorial and museum. Inside are photographs and displays, including a facsimile copy of the original treaty.

Just across the lawn, the magnificently detailed Maori **whare runanga** (meeting house) was completed in 1940 to mark the centenary of the treaty. The fine carvings represent the major Maori tribes and a 15-minute audiovisual uses legends, songs and stories to explain the carvings and summon up a Polynesian world of all-powerful chiefs and dreaded gods.

Near the cove is a 35m **war canoe** – the Maori canoe *Ngatokimatawhaorua* – named after the canoe in which the legendary Polynesian navigator Kupe discovered NZ. It too was built for the centenary, and a photographic exhibit details how the canoe was made from two gigantic kauri logs.

Beyond the Treaty House a gravel road climbs Mt Bledisloe, from where there are commanding views. Beginning from the visitors car park, a **walking track** takes off through the reserve, passing through the mangrove forest (over a boardwalk) around Hutia Creek and on to Haruru Falls. The walk to the falls takes about 1½ hours each way.

WALKING

Just behind Paihia is **Opua Forest**, a regenerating forest with a small stand of kauri trees and a number of walking tracks with walks ranging from 10 minutes to three hours.

HARURU FALLS

A few kilometres upstream from Waitangi Falls, which are lit up at night and are accessible by road or via the walkway through Waitangi National Reserve. At the foot of the falls there's good swimming and several holiday parks (see Haruru Falls Resort, p192).

MAORI NZ: NORTHLAND

The Northland region, known to Maori as Te Tai Tokerau, has a long and proud Maori history and today has one of the country's highest percentages of Maori. Along with the East Coast, it's one place you'll commonly hear Maori being spoken. In mythology the region is known as the tail of the fish of Maui (see the legend, p54). Maori sites of particular significance include the Waitangi National Reserve (p189), Cape Reinga (p179) and Tane Mahuta (p173).

But there are many, many more... For more information, grab a copy of the *Maori Travelguide to the Tail of the Fish* from visitor information centres, or visit Tai Tokerau Tourism (www.taitokerau.co.nz).

There are lookouts up graded tracks from the access roads and a few large trees have escaped axe and fire, including some big kauri trees. If you walk up from School Rd for about 20 minutes, you'll find a couple of good lookouts. Pamphlets with details on all the Opua Forest walks are published by DOC (available for around $1 at the DOC office in Russell (see p194). You can also drive into the forest by taking the Oromahoe Rd west from Opua.

Sleeping

BUDGET

Paihia has the greatest concentration and arguably the highest standard of backpacker hostels in Northland and some offer midrange accommodation too; all make discount bookings for activities and most are on Kings Rd, Paihia's 'backpackers row'.

Saltwater Lodge (☎ 0800 002 266; ☎ 09-402 7075; www.saltwaterlodge.co.nz; 14 Kings Rd; dm $25, d & tw $100-130) This is an excellent, large, purpose-built backpackers. All rooms are en suite, with bedding and lockers, and dorms have four to six beds. There are large balconies (although the view was in the process of getting built out when we visited), a lift for the disabled, a bar (see p193), all the usual facilities and free bicycles, movies and tennis racquets. A special feature is the gym, which has a variety of weights.

Bay Adventurer (☎ 09-402 5162; www.bayadventurer.co.nz; 28 Kings Rd; cm $25, d without bathroom $75, studio $125, 2-bedroom apt $185; 🛏) The Bay Adventurer has cheerful new management and large comfy rooms. There's a spa pool, access to tennis courts, a women-only dorm and a sunbed if you need to work on your tan. Good, very clean shared areas plus free bikes and social summer barbecues ($10) make this a great choice.

Cap'n Bob's Beachhouse (☎ 09-402 8668; capn bobs@xtra.co.nz; 44 Davis Cres; dm $24, d & tw $56-72) This small but stylish backpackers is a spotless home-away-from-home with a hardworking owner, views from the veranda and more than a touch of charm.

Mousetrap (☎ 09-402 8182; www.mousetrap.co .nz; 11 Kings Rd; dm $21-23, s/d/tw $45/56/56) There are plenty of small chill-out areas in this nautical-themed, natural-wood décor hostel where a mixed bag of rooms have good features. Bikes are free in winter, cheap in summer and there's *pétanque* out the front.

Pickled Parrot (☎ 0508 727 768, 09-402 6222; www .pickledparrot.co.nz; Greys Lane; sites per 2 people $32, dm $22-24, r $60) Surrounded by flame and banana trees, this friendly, well-maintained backpackers' stalwart has cute cabins and a good vibe. The parrot nips.

Peppertree Lodge (☎ 09-402 6122; www.pepper tree.co.nz; 15 Kings Rd; dm $23-25, d & tw $69, unit $85) Simple, tidy rooms with high ceilings are on offer here, plus there's a stash of bikes, tennis racquets, kayaks and two barbecues for guests' use, making this a nice low-key choice. Single-sex dorms are available.

Pipi Patch Lodge (☎ 09-402 7111; www.pipi-patch .co.nz; 18 Kings Rd; dm $23, d & tw with/without bathroom $82/62; ☒) Popular with tour groups, this backpackers has eight-bed dorms (which are en suite with a sink and a fridge), a spa and the world's tiniest swimming pool. It's a party place with a bar (see opposite).

MIDRANGE
Chalet Romantica (☎ 09-402 8270; chalet-romantica@ xtra.co.nz; 1 Bedgood Cl; d $115-165, apt $115-225; ☒) This spacious Swiss-style chalet has pretty rooms with colourful furnishings and some beautiful views over the bay. It's run by the redoubtable team of Inge and Edi, who also own the Swiss Café & Grill (see the boxed text, opposite). Edi also has a yacht that can be chartered ($500/1100 per day/overnight).

Swiss Chalet (☎ 09-402 7615; www.swisschalet .co.nz; 3 Bayview Rd; studios $85-200, 1- & 2-bedroom units $145-250) This Swiss-style motel has a spa, Sky TV and good clean rooms with

balconies. There's a slight (Swiss) cheese factor, but you can't accuse it of looking anonymous...

Admiral's View Lodge (☎ 09-402 6236; www.ad miralsviewlodge.co.nz; 2 McMurray St; studios $115-245, apt $275) This good lodge offers natty, smart-looking units with balconies just begging for a sunset gin and tonic, although the welcome could be a little less harried.

Haruru Falls Resort (☎ 0800 757 525, 09-402 7525; www.harurufalls.co.nz; Old Wharf Rd; powered & unpowered sites $30, d/units/apt/ste $120/140/200/240; ☒) This family-friendly resort has reasonable and various accommodation options to suit a range of budgets. It also has a bar, restaurant and a view of the Haruru Falls, which is lit up at night. Fishing and diving trips can be arranged.

TOP END
Bay of Islands Lodge (☎ 09-402 6075; www.bayof islandslodge.co.nz; SH1, Port Opua; d $580; ☒) This luxurious retreat affords some of the most glorious views in the area and resembles a modern work of art. Situated south of Paihia, it's spacious, private, has a fantastic pool with an infinity lip and makes a strong case for a life lived without neighbours or kids. A smart wheelchair-accessible room is also available.

Decks of Paihia (☎ 09-402 6146; www.decksofpai hia.com; 69 School Rd; d $230) This new place offers light, modern bedrooms, a smart kitchen area, granite bathrooms and a big deck with great bay views. Low-season rates are very attractive.

Copthorne Resort Waitangi (☎ 09-402 7411; www.copthornebayofislands.co.nz; Tau Henare Dr; r $130-300; ☒) This sprawling chain compound has innocuous but comfortable rooms set amid nice grounds and the usual big-name facilities for guests. It's a stone's throw from the Treaty grounds and open to low-season price deals.

Eating
RESTAURANTS
Sugarboat Bar & Restaurant (☎ 09-402 7018; mains $29; ☒ dinner) This is certainly the most eye-catching dining option in the area, as it's aboard an old sailing boat. Service and décor are both smart, and Mod-NZ dishes reveal a great amount of care and flair.

Bistro 40 (☎ 09-402 7444; 40 Marsden Rd; mains $29-30; ☒ dinner) One of the area's best-known

Swiss Café & Grill (09-402 6701; 48 Marsden Rd; mains $18-25; dinner) This unpretentious but excellent European-style restaurant on the waterfront has indoor and outdoor options, and candles add a romantic touch. The wide-ranging and eclectic menu includes vegetable curry, nicely prepared fish dishes and wonderful Swiss comfort food such as homemade strudel. Inge, the charming owner, ensures every diner leaves with a smile, making this a very popular choice throughout the year.

restaurants, this reservations-essential joint does lovely seafood mains such as seared yellow-fin tuna with roasted langoustines, caramelised aubergine and tomato chilli jam – and all in effortless style.

Only Seafood (09-402 6066; upstairs, 40 Marsden Rd; mains $25-30; dinner) This is an excellent place to go for local seafood, including fish, mussels, oysters and scallops, and you certainly can't say that the name equivocates.

Tides (09-402 7557; Williams Rd; lunch mains $10-19; breakfast, lunch & dinner) Tides provides reasonable meals with daily seafood specials in a slightly ad hoc manner that doesn't seem to deter visitors.

CAFÉS & QUICK EATS

Beachhouse Café & Bar (09-402 7479; 16 Kings Rd; burgers $7-12; breakfast, lunch & dinner, bar till 1am) This lively place decorated with loads of photographs and leis has lovely fresh juices, gourmet burgers, all-day breakfasts, big beer glasses, and a DJ (Friday) live music (Saturday), and a jam session (Sunday).

Café No 6 (09-402 6797; 6 Marsden Rd; mains $11-22; breakfast, lunch & dinner summer) An informal café that serves mainly Mediterranean food, including tapas and ciabatta bread, but occasionally Bavarian meatballs sneak onto the menu. It closes for most of the winter.

Waikokopu Café (09-402 6275; Treaty Ground, Waitangi; lunch mains $16; breakfast & lunch year-round, dinner summer) This good café near the Waitangi visitor information centre offers wholesome snacks and light meals for day and more substantial fare at night.

Self-caterers can buy supplies at **Woolworths supermarket** (6 Puketona Rd; 7am-10pm).

Drinking & Entertainment

There are literally dozens of places along Marsden Rd and Kings Rd in which to enjoy a drink and a dance, so don't feel hemmed in by our list.

Bay of Islands Swordfish Club (09-402 7773; Marsden Rd; 4pm-1am) There are great views, cold beer and tall tales at this club bar that welcomes visitors and feeds them at very sensible prices.

PipiPatch Bar (09-402 7111; 18 Kings Rd; 5pm-midnight) This bar, at Pipi Patch Lodge, has a DJ on weekends, good-natured competitions with some great activities-based prizes, and other backpacker fun and games.

Saltwater Bar (09-402 7783; 14 Kings Rd; noon-1am) This bar, at Saltwater Lodge, serves OK pizzas and has karaoke, bar games and quizzes, plus the odd pole-dancing extravaganza.

RUSSELL

pop 1140

Historic Russell is directly across the bay from Paihia but may as well be a world away in terms of style. It was originally a fortified Maori settlement that spread over the entire valley, then known as Kororareka (Sweet Penguin). It's a peaceful and pretty little place, which frequently calls itself 'romantic' in promotional material, and the town's waterfront is lined with stately colonial buildings and pohutukawa trees.

Russell's early European history was turbulent. In 1830 it was the scene of the so-called War of the Girls, when two pairs of Maori girls (one pair from the northern Bay of Islands and one pair from the south) were vying for the wealth and attention of a whaling captain called Brind. The rivalry resulted in verbal abuse and fighting when they happened to meet on the beach. This minor conflict quickly escalated as family members rallied around to meet on the beach. This insult and harm done to their respective relatives. Hundreds were killed and injured over a two-week period before missionaries managed to broker a peace settlement.

In 1845, during the Northland Land War, government soldiers and marines garrisoned the town after the Ngapuhi leader Hone Heke threatened to chop down the flagstaff, a symbol of Pakeha authority, for the fourth time – he had already chopped it down three times. On 11 March 1845 the Ngapuhi staged a diversionary siege of Russell. It was a great tactical success, with Chief Kawiti attacking from the south and another Ngapuhi war party attacking from Long Beach. While the troops rushed off to protect the township, Hone Heke felled the hated symbol of European authority on Maiki (Flagstaff Hill) for the fourth and final time. The Pakeha were forced to evacuate to ships lying at anchor off the settlement. The captain of HMS *Hazard* was wounded severely in the battle and his replacement ordered the ships' cannons to be fired on the town and most of the buildings were razed.

In its early days Russell was a magnet for rough elements such as fleeing convicts, whalers, prostitutes and drunk sailors. Charles Darwin described it in 1835 as full of 'the refuse of society' and it also picked up the chirpy nickname 'hellhole of the Pacific'. Sadly, all good things must come to an end, and the town is now a bastion of cafés, gift shops and B&Bs.

Most Bay of Islands' water-based tours pick up from here, so Russell is certainly a good alternative base.

Information

DOC Pewhairangi Bay of Islands visitor information centre (☎ 09-403 9005; www.doc.govt.nz; The Strand; ☉ 9am-4.30pm Mar-Sep, 9am-5pm Oct-Apr) Excellent centre; has information on Pewhairangi, a park consisting of 40 separate areas – see p189.

Innovation (☎ 09-403 8843; Traders Mall) Internet access.

Medical Centre (☎ 09-403 7690l Church St)

Russell visitor information centre (☎ 09-403 8020; www.russell-information.co.nz; ☉ 8.30am-5pm Mar-Sep, 7.30am-9pm Oct-Apr) On the pier where the passenger ferry from Paihia docks.

Sights & Activities

The small but modern **Russell Museum** (☎ 09-403 7701; 2 York St; adult/child $5/1; ☉ 10am-4pm) has a fine 1:5 scale model of Captain Cook's *Endeavour* and a 7kg crayfish as well as Maori and Pakeha relics and a 10-minute history video. Captain Cook visited the Bay of Islands for a week in 1769.

Russell lays claim to some of NZ's oldest buildings, including **Christ Church** (1847), NZ's oldest church; it's scarred with musket and cannonball holes, and has an interesting

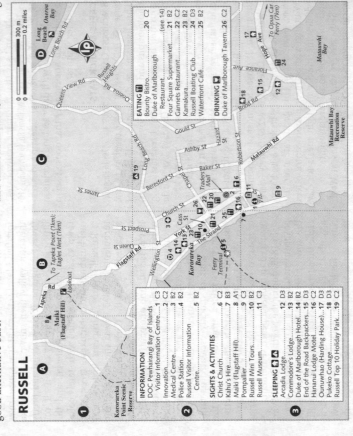

graveyard, Charles Darwin made a donation towards the cost of its construction.

Pompallier (☎ 09-403 9015; tours adult/child $7.50/ free; ☑ 10am-5pm Dec-Feb & school holidays, 5 tours a day Mar-Nov) was a rammed-earth construction built in 1842 to house the Roman Catholic mission's printing press, which printed a staggering 40,000 books in Maori (take the brilliant guided tour to discover just why this figure is so mind-boggling). In the 1870s it was converted into a private home but it has been restored to its original state. It's the last remaining building of the Roman Catholic mission in the Western Pacific, so is worth a visit.

Overlooking Russell is **Maiki** (Flagstaff Hill), where Hone Heke chopped down the flagpole four times. The view is well worth the effort of the climb. By car take Tapeka Rd or if on foot, take the track west from the boat ramp along the beach at low tide, or up Wellington St at high tide.

In good weather **Kahu's Hire** on the Strand rents kayaks or dinghies for around $12 an hour.

About 1.5km behind Russell and an easy walk or cycle is **Long Beach** (Oneroa Bay Beach). Turn left (facing the sea) to visit Donkey Bay, a small cove that is an unofficial nudist beach.

Tours

Russell Mini Tours (☎ 09-403 7866; adult/child $17/8) departs from the Fullers office, which fronts Russell Wharf, six times daily on the hour from 10am (not at noon) and visits local sites of interest.

Many of the cruises out of Paihia pick up passengers at Russell about 15 minutes after their Paihia departure.

Sleeping
BUDGET

Pukeko Cottage (☎ 09-403 8498; www.pukekocottage backpackers.co.nz; 14 Brind Rd; dm/d $25/50) This is a minihostel (it only sleeps a maximum of seven people) that's more like a homestay, where you can chat with the artistic owner over a cup of tea or take in glorious sunset views in lush surrounds.

End of the Road Backpackers (☎ 09-403 8827; 24 Brind Rd; dm/d/tw $20/45/45) This is a homely and comfy cottage with views over the marina, and the dorm has just two bunk beds and sleeps four all up, meaning that it's

often fully booked. Come for a night and you might want to stay a week.

Russell Top 10 Holiday Park (☎ 09-403 7826; www.russelltop10.co.nz; Long Beach Rd; sites per 2 people $30-34, cabins $69, 2-bedroom units $195) This park has a small store, good facilities, an attractive setting and tidy forest green cabins and nice units. Showers are clean, but metered.

MIDRANGE

Commodore's Lodge (☎ 09-403 7899; www.commo doreslodgemotel.co.nz; 28 The Strand; units $130-250; ☑) Spacious, nicely presented units are the order of the day here, with the added appeal of some fine sunset-watching opportunities and a really nice pool.

Hananui Lodge Motel (☎ 09-403 7875; www.hana nui.co.nz; The Strand; units $145-210) This trim white building in the centre of town is managed by a couple who really know how to keep things clean. Units are simple, neat and nice, but for a bit of extra flash, get one of the smarter waterfront units that have recently been redecorated. Wheelchair access is possible.

TOP END

Duke of Marlborough Hotel (☎ 09-403 7829; www .theduke.co.nz; 35 The Strand; d $195-450) This fine hotel, situated right on the waterfront, has real old-fashioned charm and the sun-filled rooms are in great condition. The harbour-facing rooms are the best (and, as is always the case, the most expensive). Prices include breakfast.

Ounuwhao (Harding House; ☎ 09-403 7310; ounuwh ao@bay-of-islands.co.nz; 16 Hope Ave; s $135-170, d $185-250)

AUTHOR'S CHOICE

Arcadia Lodge (☎ 09-403 7756; 10 Florance Ave; d $125-275) This beautiful 1890 house on a hill is being lovingly restored by the talented and tasteful Brad and David and no stone has been left unturned – literally (ask to see the house's old whale-vertebra foundations!). Stylish, characterful rooms have wonderful bed linen and interesting pieces throughout, while the food is probably the best you'll eat in the town – it's not only organic, it's delicious. Enjoy the homemade muesli while taking in a tranquil bay view.

This beautiful 1894 period house, where the owner's wonderful quilts are an outstanding decorative feature, is 1km from town. Prices include a gourmet breakfast. There's also a large self-contained cottage out the back if you want extra privacy.

Eagles Nest (☎ 09-403 8333; www.eaglesnest.co.nz; 60 Tapeka Rd; villas $1800-3500) This may well be the most expensive and luxurious accommodation in the country, but it offers unparalleled views, beautiful modern architecture, privacy and amenities (such as personal chefs and Porsches at your disposal) and a full roster of New Age blandishments. Don't even think about popping in for a stickybeak – it's hard to find and security is strict. The jewel in the crown is the massive Sanandaloka villa, where the phrase 'If you have to ask, you can't afford it' comes into its own. We asked – $150,000 a week.

Eating & Drinking

Kamakura (☎ 09-402 7771; The Strand; lunch mains $8-22; lunch & dinner) This restaurant is the most fashion-conscious option in town, with a bright and breezy beachhouse feel that takes advantage of its waterfront position. Service can be a little harried, the list of wines by the glass is overpriced, but the modern, nicely prepared food is worth any wait.

Gannets Restaurant (☎ 09-403 7990; cnr York & Chapel Sts; mains $20-32; dinner Tue-Sun) The red snapper in curry invariably gets a mention when locals talk about this restaurant, and with good reason.

Duke of Marlborough Restaurant (☎ 09-403 7829; 35 The Strand; dinner mains $25-32; lunch & dinner) The grand old Duke has period charm with a veranda, although no-one's really coming here for the food anymore. Try the bistro if you're after all-day dining at a lower price.

Duke of Marlborough Tavern (☎ 09-403 7851; York St) This relaxing, comfortable bar has live music on occasion and a wonderful open fireplace in winter. It's a good spot to unwind in a traditional atmosphere.

There's a **Four Square supermarket** (The Strand) in town.

Easy, cheap dining options include the following:

Bounty Bistro (☎ 09-403 8870; York St; mains $15-25; lunch & dinner) Owned by a descendant of the Bounty mutiny. Great fish and chips.

Russell Boating Club (☎ 09-403 8231; Matauwhi Bay; meals under $25; dinner) The roast pork is excellent.

Waterfront Café (☎ 09-403 7589; The Strand; breakfast & lunch, closed Mon winter) Big breakfast and friendly service.

Getting There & Around

From Paihia, the quickest and easiest way to reach Russell is on the regular **passenger ferry** (adult/child one way $5/2.50). It runs from 7.20am to 7.30pm (until 10.30pm October to May), generally every 20 minutes. Buy your tickets on board. Return fares are $9/4.50 per adult/child.

The **car ferry** (one way/return vehicle & driver $9/17, motorcycle & rider $4/7, additional passenger $1/2) runs every 10 minutes or so from Opua (about 8km from Russell) to Okiato Point, between 6.50am and 10pm. Buy your tickets on board.

KERIKERI

pop 5000

At the northern end of the Bay of Islands, Kerikeri has historical and natural attractions as well as a relaxed feel with its citrus orchards and café culture. Kerikeri means 'to dig', and the Maori grew kumara here before the Pakeha arrived; its fertile soils now produce kiwi fruit and oranges as well as vegetables. Picking and pruning go on virtually all year, and attract workers at wage rates that are around $9 an hour.

Information

DOC (☎ 09-407 8474; 34 Landing Rd) Hiking information and brochures available here.

Kerikeri visitor information centre (☎ 09-407 9297; www.kerikeri.co.nz; Cobham Rd; 9am–5pm Mon-Fri, 10am–noon Sat) Part of the new library complex, which has Internet access.

Post office (6 Hobson Ave) Opposite the cinema.

Sights & Activities

The **Stone Store** (☎ 09-407 9236; adult/child $3.50/ free, incl Mission House $7.50/free; 10am–5pm Nov-Apr, to 4pm May-Oct), on the banks of the Kerikeri River, was built between 1832 and 1836 and is the oldest stone building in NZ. It's full of the type of goods that used to be bartered in the store, including muskets and blankets, as well as diaries and other relics of missionary endeavour. At one time a blanket was worth a pig but a musket cost eight or 10 pigs (or blankets). The role of missionaries in arming northern Maoris with muskets is still a controversial topic.

KERIKERI

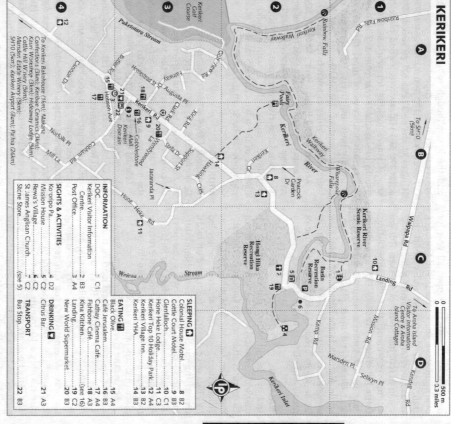

INFORMATION
DOC.................................C1
Kerikeri Visitor Information
Centre..........................**2** B3
Post Office.........................A4

SIGHTS & ACTIVITIES
Ko oripo Pa........................C1
Mission House...................**3** D2
Rewa's Village..................**5** C2
St James Anglican Church...........C2
Stone Store.....................(see 5)

SLEEPING
Colonial House Motel............**8** B2
Cottage Court Motel.............**9** B3
Glenfalloch.....................**10** C1
Hone Heke Lodge.................**11** C3
Kerikeri Top 10 Holiday Park....**12** A4
Kerikeri Village Inn............**13** B3
Kerikeri YHA....................**14** B3

EATING
Black Olive.....................**15** A4
Café Jerusalem..................**16** B3
Cathay Cinema Cafe..............**17** A4
Fishbone Café...................**18** A4
Kina Kitchen....................(see 16)
Landing.........................**19** C2
New World Supermarket...........**20** C2

DRINKING
Citrus Bar......................**21** A3

TRANSPORT
Bus Stop........................**22** B3

Adjacent to the Stone Store, the **Mission House** (adult/child $5/free, incl Stone Store $7.50/free; 10am-4pm) is even older – erected in 1822 by Reverend Butler. It's the country's oldest wooden building and contains some original fittings and chattels and is a must-see.

At the time of writing this area was campaigning for recognition as a Unesco World Heritage Site and there were plans for the small one-lane bridge to be closed (flooding and pollution is a serious threat here), with construction of a new road bypassing the fragile site. Hopefully this will have taken place by mid-2007.

Just across the river from the Stone Store, **Rewa's Village** (☎ 09-407 6454; adult/child $3/50c; 9am-5pm summer, 10am-4pm winter) has a video,

a mock-up of a pre-European Maori village, and information boards on plants that were used by Māoris. By all accounts some food plants like fern roots did not taste good.

Aroha Island visitor information centre (☎ 09-407 5243; www.arohaa.net.nz; Aroha Island; admission free; 9.30am-5.30pm Tue-Sun Sep-mid-Jun) is located on a tiny 5-hectare island, 12km northeast of Kerikeri. It is reached via a permanent causeway through mangrove bushes. The visitor information centre has environmental displays and currently a few adult North Island brown kiwis live on the island along with lots of other birds such as fantails and tui. Kayaks can be rented ($25 for two hours) and fascinating **guided tours** (per person $60) at dusk can be booked a few days ahead The island is open all year for overnight stays; see Aroha Island Cottages, right. Do the right thing and support this valuable resource by making a donation.

On SH10, just south of Kerikeri Rd, are a couple of wineries that offer wine tasting. **Cottle Hill Winery** (☎ 09-407 5203; www.cottlehill .co.nz; ☼ 10am–5pm) is a boutique winery that sells cheese and meat platters for lunch, while **Marsden Estate Winery** (☎ 09-407 9398; www.marsdenestate.co.nz; Wiroa Rd; ☼ 10am–5pm daily Sep–Jun, to 4pm Tue–Sun Jul & Aug) offers a range of meals and platters on its deck.

WALKING

Just up the hill behind the Stone Store is a marked historical walk, which takes about 10 minutes and leads to **Kororipo Pa**, the fortress of the famous Ngapuhi chief Hongi Hika. Huge Ngapuhi warfaring parties led by Hika once departed from here on raids, terrorising much of the North Island during the so-called Musket Wars (see p34). The walk finally emerges near the St James Anglican Church, a small wooden structure that was built in 1878 and was the birthplace of Christianity in NZ.

Across the river from the Stone Store is a scenic reserve with several marked tracks. There's a 4km Kerikeri River track leading to the 27m **Rainbow Falls**, passing by the Wharepoke Falls and the Fairy Pools along the way. Alternatively, you can reach the Rainbow Falls from Waipapa Rd, in which case it's only a 10-minute walk to the falls. The Fairy Pools are great for swimming and picnics and can be reached from the dirt road beside the Kerikeri YHA, if you're not up to the hike along the river.

Sleeping

BUDGET

Kerikeri YHA (☎ 09-407 9391; yha.kerikeri@yha.org.nz; 144 Kerikeri Rd; dm/d/tw $25/54/54) This very good hostel has quite a bit of character, a tranquil setting with a large garden leading down to the river, and you might see a kingfisher on the volleyball net.

Hone Heke Lodge (☎ 09-407 8170; www.honehek .co.nz; 65 Hone Heke Rd; dm $20, d & tw without bathroom $50, with bathroom $50-65; ☐) Hone Heke has a line of single-storey units that caters mainly to those working in local orchards. Weekly rates are available and recreation areas are good, with volleyball, pool tables, barbecues and the like, although some of the living areas can seem a bit ropey.

Hideaway Lodge (☎ 0800 562 746, 09-407 9773; 111 Wiroa Rd; sites per 2 people $26, per week dm $94, d $184-194; ☐) Hideaway is a good place to stay if you're looking for work as there's usually lots available year-round. The lodge is spacious with two of most things and is usually busy and lively. It's 5km out of Kerikeri, west of the SH10 junction, but there are free rides to town twice a day.

Kerikeri Top 10 Holiday Park (☎ 09-407 9326; www.aranga.co.nz; Kerikeri Rd; unpowered/powered sites per 2 people $22/24, cabins/units/motel r $58/110/120) This is a large riverside camping ground with good facilities that is within walking distance of the town centre. Seasonal picking work can be arranged here.

MIDRANGE

Glenfalloch (☎ 09-407 5471; glenfall@ihug.co.nz; 48 Landing Rd; s/d $90/115; ☐) This relaxing homestay B&B with a beautiful garden and a tennis court is 500m north of the Stone Store. Rooms have en suite or private facilities and the hosts go out of their way to please.

Colonial House Motel (☎ 09-407 9106; www.colonialhousemotel.co.nz; 178 Kerikeri Rd; units $125-195; ☐) The Colonial was recently taken over and gradual improvements are taking place. It's a well-run joint, with good rooms and nice winter discounts.

Aroha Island Cottages (☎ 09-407 5243; www.aroha.net.nz; Aroha Island; unpowered sites per 2 people $26, powered sites per 2 people $28-30, cottages d $110) The modern, self-contained cottages on this small kiwi island with a causeway sleep up to 10.

Cottle Court Motel (☎ 09-407 8867; cottlecourt@ xtra.co.nz; Kerikeri Rd; d $130; ☐) The plus point here is that it's in the middle of town, plus it's a friendly, neat and tidy sort of place where nothing untoward ever happens. Solid and respectable.

TOP END

Kerikeri Village Inn (☎ 09-407 4666; www.kerikerivillageinn.co.nz; 165 Kerikeri Rd; d $145-235) This stylish B&B, decorated with a cool hacienda feel and attractive furnishings, has en suite rooms and a communal lounge. Prices include a gourmet breakfast.

Eating & Drinking

With its orange orchards, palm trees and basketed blooms hanging from the awnings of the main street and indoor/outdoor café/restaurant/bars, Kerikeri sometimes exudes a relaxed Mediterranean atmosphere (especially during the spring and summer) and is the café capital of the North.

Café Jerusalem (09-407 1001; Cobblestone Mall; mains $13-21; lunch Mon-Fri, dinner Mon-Sat) Enjoy the authentic Middle Eastern food such as *schwarma*, falafel and baklava, which you can eat in or take away. It all comes with a smile and a social vibe. It has a sister operation on the main backpackers' party street in Paihia.

Kerikeri Bakehouse (09-407 7266; 324 Kerikeri Rd; breakfast & lunch) This wonderful barn of a place has a huge range of popular café-style snacks and the best pies in Northland.

Cathay Cinema Café (Hobson Ave; dinner & movie $25) Treat yourself to dinner and a movie at this cute local cinema, where the bargain combo deal might include a tasty Indian-style curry with the latest release.

Fishbone Café (09-407 6065; 88 Kerikeri Rd; breakfast & lunch, sometimes dinner) The popular Fishbone specialises in coffee but also serves imaginative food with an Italian/Kiwi twist.

Black Olive (dinner Tue-Sun) This place serves up popular pasta and pizza takeaways or you can sit down and eat in the back if you need to escape your accommodation.

Kina Kitchen (09-407 7669; Cobblestone Mall; mains $21-30; lunch & dinner) Definitely one of the better eateries in Kerikeri, with an imaginative range of mains and a convivial atmosphere. A nice spot for a drink too.

Landing (09-407 8479; Stone Store Basin; dinner mains $25-29; lunch & dinner) Lovely views of the basin from this homestead-style building are the main reason for coming here, although the food's perfectly good too, with a couple of vegetarian options but mostly meat dishes.

Citrus Bar (09-407 1050; Kerikeri Rd; pizzas $14-24; 10am-late) Citrus is probably the most popular nightspot in town, with live bands or a DJ on Friday night, plus the odd foam party and stripper. The bistro menu includes top-heavy pizza and nachos.

The **New World supermarket** (99 Kerikeri Rd) has everything self-caterers might need.

Shopping

Pick up the brochure from the information centre on the **Art & Craft Trail**, which covers many art, furniture, wool and pottery outlets.

On the road into Kerikeri from the south are orchards, fruit stalls and a cluster of shops: colourful crockery at **Keriblue Ceramics** (09-407 4634; 560 Kerikeri Rd); delicious handmade-on-the-premises finger-lickin' chocolate at **Makana Confections** (09-407 6800; www.makara.co.nz), and kauri products at **Kauri Workshop** (09-407 9196).

Getting There & Away

Air New Zealand (24hr 0800 737 000; www.airnz.co.nz) operates about five flights daily ($85 to $275) from Auckland to Kerikeri.

The InterCity and Northliner buses arrive at and leave from a stop in Cobham Rd, opposite the new library and visitor information centre, Kerikeri to Mangonui ($18) takes an hour, and Kerikeri to Auckland ($47) takes five hours.

BAY OF ISLANDS TO WHANGAREI

On the way to Whangarei there are two scenic detour routes: the back road from Russell to SH1, and the drive out to Tutukaka from Hikurangi on SH1, which loops around to Whangarei. Out to sea are the Poor Knights Islands, a world-class marine reserve and a paradise for scuba divers.

HUNDERTWASSER'S LOO

Kawakawa is just an ordinary Kiwi outback town, located just off SH1 south of Paihia, but the public toilets (60 Gillies St) were designed by Austrian-born artist and ecoarchitect, Friedensreich Hundertwasser. He lived near Kawakawa in an isolated house without electricity from 1973 until his death in 2000.

The most photographed toilets in NZ are typical Hundertwasser – lots of wavy lines, decorated with ceramic mosaics and brightly coloured bottles, and with grass and plants on the roof. Other examples of his work can be seen in cities as far apart as Vienna and Osaka. The café opposite was another of his designs, and inside are books and photographs of his work.

RUSSELL ROAD

The back road from Russell skirts around the coast before joining SH1 at Whakapara. The scenic road is long, unsealed and rough for most of the way – strictly for those with their own transport, plenty of time and a desire to get off the beaten track.

From Russell, the road starts near Orongo Bay and skirts along the Waikare Inlet before reaching the Waikare Rd to Waihaha. This turn-off eventually leads back to the highway and Paihia. It's about a 90-minute drive from Russell.

Continuing along Russell Rd past the Waihaha turn-off, there's access to the **Ngaiotonga Scenic Reserve**, which conserves the mixed forest that once prevailed throughout Northland. There are two short walks – the 20-minute **Kauri Grove Nature Walk** and the 10-minute **Twin Bole Kauri Walk**.

Closer to the Rawhiti turn-off, a shorter one-hour walk leads through Maori land and over the headland to Whangamumu Harbour. At the main beach on the harbour, the **Whangamumu Scenic Reserve** has camping. There are over 40 prehistoric sites on the peninsula and the remains of an unusual whaling station. A net, fastened between the mainland and Net Rock, was used to ensnare or slow down whales so the harpooners could get an easy shot in.

Further north is the turn-off to isolated **Rawhiti**, a small Ngapuhi settlement where life still revolves around the *marae*. Rawhiti is also the starting point for the trek to **Cape**

Brett, a hard 7½-hour, 20km walk to the top of the peninsula, where overnight stays are possible in the Cape Brett Hut. The hike costs $30 on top of the cost of the hut ($12 per adult per night). You can book the hut and get information on the walk at the DOC Pewhairangi Bay of Islands visitor information centre in Russell (see p194).

Further south, another side road leads to the **Whangaruru North Head Scenic Reserve**, which has beaches, camping grounds, walks and fine coastal scenery in a farmland park setting.

At Helena Bay, Russell Rd returns to tarseal and leads back to SH1. About 8km from Helena Bay along a rough, winding side road is the Mimiwhangata Coastal Park (p205). This is a truly scenic part of the coastline, with coastal dunes, pohutukawa trees, jutting headlands and picturesque beaches.

TUTUKAKA COAST & POOR KNIGHTS ISLANDS

At Hikurangi on SH1 you can turn off for the winding scenic but still sealed road to Whangarei via the Tutukaka Coast. After 25km you reach **Sandy Bay**, a small surf beach, followed by a succession of idyllic bays where you can surf, swim, walk, relax or fish.

Another 11km on from Sandy Bay is fun **Tutukaka**, which is 26km northeast of Whangarei. The marina is a hive of activity with yachts, dive boats and game-fishing boats moored together. It is the base for diving trips that run all year to the Poor

WORLD-CLASS DIVING AT THE POOR KNIGHTS ISLANDS

This marine reserve, 24km off Northland's east coast near Tutukaka, was established in 1981. It is reputed to have the best scuba diving in NZ and has been rated as one of the world's top 10 diving spots.

The islands are bathed in a subtropical current from the Coral Sea, so varieties of tropical and subtropical fish not seen in other coastal waters are observed here. The waters are clear, with no sediment or pollution problems. The 40m to 60m underwater cliffs drop steeply to the sandy bottom, and are a labyrinth of archways, caves, tunnels and fissures that attract a wide variety of sponges and colourful underwater vegetation. Manta rays are common.

The two main volcanic islands, Tawhiti Rahi and Aorangi, were once home to members of the Ngai Wai tribe but, since a raiding-party massacre in the early 1800s the islands have been *tapu* (forbidden). Even today no-one is allowed to set foot on the islands, in order to protect their pristine environment. Not only do tuatara and Butler's shearwater breed there, but there are unique species of fauna and flora, such as the Poor Knights red lily.

Dive trips can be organised from Whangarei or Tutukaka and cater for first-timers and experts. A comprehensive diving guide with excellent photographs is *Poor Knights Wonderland* by Glen Edney, available from local dive shops.

Knights Islands, 24km offshore. You can organise diving trips to the islands from Whangarei or Tutukaka.

Dive! Tutukaka (☎ 0800 288 882, 09-434 3867; www.diving.co.nz; ☺ 8am-5pm) is the main operator in this hamlet. Diving here is unique and world-class; see the boxed text, opposite. You can also explore two navy ships, the *Tui* and the *Waikato*, that were sunk on purpose outside the reserve for recreational diving. A five-day PADI open-water course is $600 (medical certificate required). Tutukaka is a good place for first-time divers, too, with plenty of experienced instructors around.

Another very experienced operator is **Pacific Hideaway Charters** (☎ 09-434 3762; www.divenz.co.nz; day trip with 2 dives & equipment $185) which runs a large catamaran boat and will pick you up from Whangarei where the owner lives.

The owner of **Knight Diver Tours** (www.poorknights.co.nz; day trip with 2 dives & equipment $180) has dived the Poor Knights over 10,000 times but still comes back for more!

Oceanblue Adventures (☎ 09-434 0459; www.oceanblue.co.nz; customised day trips per person $190), run by Glen and Tiana Edney, specialises in overnight trips (one to four nights) for experienced divers, including night dives. Six is the maximum number taken.

Another small operator is **Yukon Dive** (☎ 021 261779; www.yukon.co.nz), which takes groups of four to eight. It also offers fishing trips.

Delray Charters (☎ 09-434 3028; delray@ihug.co.nz) has a 45ft boat for cruising, game-fishing or bottom fishing.

Shuttle buses depart from Whangarei at 7.10am and 3pm and leave Tutukaka Marina at 8.15am and 4.15pm. In summer the shuttle also runs from Whangarei to Paihia at 5.30pm and leaves Paihia for Whangarei at 7.30pm.

Three kilometres north of Tutukaka Marina is **Tutukaka Wild** (☎ 09-434 3423; Matapouri Rd; zoo adult/child $7/5; ☺ 10am-4pm), which has many different animals including alpacas, llamas, ostriches, emus, donkeys, miniature horses and birds, along with arts and crafts and a café. There are also activities such as the luge, kayaking and outdoor wall climbing.

Sleeping

Tutukaka Holiday Park (☎ 09-434 3938; www.tuttuka-holidaypark.co.nz; Matapouri Rd; sites per 2 people $24, d/w/cabins $20/50) This park has modern, freshly painted facilities and is near the marina. Communal areas are in good condition and management's helpful. Look for the giant marlin at the gate.

Bluewater Cottage (☎ 09-434 3423; www.bluewaterparadise.co.nz; Matapouri Rd; d $135) These attractive, self-contained, open-plan cottages with indoor/outdoor flow can sleep six. The cottages enjoy sea views from an evergreen hillside 3km north of Tutukaka marina.

Oceans (☎ 09-470 2000; www.oceanshotel.co.nz; Marina Dr; r $225, apt $325-535) This high-rise (for Tutukaka) hotel sticks out like a sore thumb but it does offer swanky modern rooms from that look like they've leapt from the pages of a design mag. A flash restaurant and bar are on the premises too.

Eating & Drinking

Tutukaka has some great eateries and easy-going drinking options on the marina.

Schnappa Rock Café (☎ 09-434 3774; dinner mains $15-28; ☺ lunch & dinner bar till late) This is a great and relaxed café-restaurant/bar where top NZ bands play on summer weekends and the atmosphere is perfect for unwinding.

Marina Pizzeria (☎ 09-434 3166; large pizzas $15-22; ☺ breakfast, lunch & dinner Thu-Sun) Further along the harbour, this is an excellent take-away and eatery where everything is home-made – the bread, the pasta, the pizza and the ice cream. The pizzas have perfect thin crusts and plenty of topping options.

Whangarei Deep Sea Anglers Club (☎ 09-434 3818; Marina Rd, Tutukaka; mains $18-22; ☺ 4pm-late winter, noon-late summer) This venue plays host to the nicely named Moocha's, where standard NZ eats and a good children's menu mingle with a lot of stuffed and mounted big fish and garrulous locals.

WHANGAREI

pop 45,800

Whangarei is the major city in Northland and is pleasant enough to serve as a base for the immediate area, with an equable climate, parks and walks, and plenty of eating and sleeping options. The main local attractions are definitely in the surrounding area, though. Whangarei Heads with its attractive beaches and scenery, and diving around the Poor Knights Islands.

Information

Automobile Association (AA; ☎ 09-438 4848; cnr Robert & John Sts) Has maps and advice.

www.lonelyplanet.com

WHANGAREI

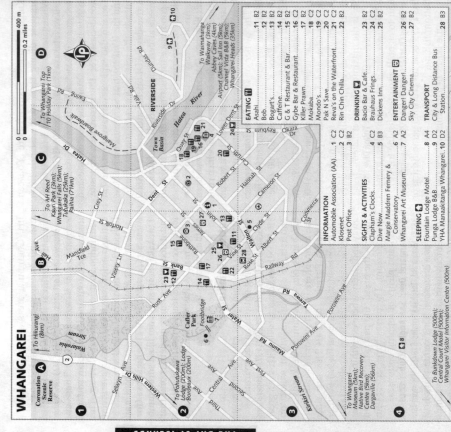

INFORMATION

Automobile Association (AA)....	1	C2
Klosenet..........................	2	C2
Post Office........................	3	B2

SIGHTS & ACTIVITIES

Clapham's Clocks...............	4	C2
Dive Now.........................	5	B3
Margie Madden Fernery &		
Conservatory.................	6	A2
Whangarei Art Museum........	7	A2

SLEEPING

Fountain Lodge Motel...........	8	A4
Punga Lodge B&B...............	9	D2
YHA Manaakitanga Whangarei.	10	D2

EATING

Asahi...............................	11	B2
Bob.................................	12	B2
Bogart's...........................	13	B2
Caffeine...........................	14	B2
G & T Restaurant & Bar........	15	B2
Gybe Bar & Restaurant.........	16	B2
Killer Prawn......................	17	B2
Mokaba...........................	18	C2
Mondo's..........................	19	C2
Pak 'N Save.......................	20	C2
Reva's on the Waterfront......	21	C2
Rin Chin Chilla...................	22	B2

DRINKING

Bacio Bar & Cafe................	23	B2
Brauhaus Frings.................	24	C2
Dickens Inn.......................	25	B2

ENTERTAINMENT

| Danger! Danger!................. | 26 | B2 |
| Sky City Cinema................. | 27 | B2 |

TRANSPORT

| City & Long Distance Bus | | |
| Station.......................... | 28 | B3 |

Klosenet (34 John St; per hr $4) Has speedy Internet access.

Post office (16-20 Rathbone St) Conveniently located.

Whangarei visitor information centre (09-438 1079; www.whangareinz.org.nz; 92 Otaika Rd/SH1; 8.30am–5pm Mon–Fri, 9.30am–4.30pm Sat & Sun) At Tarewa Park to the south of the city; there's a café in the same building.

Sights & Activities

Margie Madden Fernery & Conservatory (09-430 4200; First Ave; admission free; 10am–4pm) has one of the best displays of native ferns in NZ. Each fern adapts to a different degree of shade. Next door are tropical plants and cacti in a heated conservatory. Nearby is **Whangarei Art Museum** (09-430 4240; www.whan-

gareiartmuseum.co.nz; admission by donation; 10am–4pm Tue–Fri, noon–4pm Sat & Sun), which showcases Northland arts and crafts. In front of the art gallery is a rose garden and alongside is delightful little **Cafler Park**, which spans Waiarohia Stream.

The **Town Basin** is a busy harbour full of yachts and fishing boats and a slightly twee collection of fine cafés, restaurants, art and craft shops and a bicycle-hire kiosk. **Clapham's Clocks** (09-438 3993; Town Basin; adult/child $8/4; 9am–5pm) has a mind-boggling 1300 timepieces inside, ticking and gonging away.

West of Whangarei, 5km out on the road to Dargaville at Maunu, is the **Whangarei Museum** (09-438 9630; www.whangareimuseum.co.nz; 4 SH14; 10am–4pm). The museum includes a kiwi house (adult/child $5/2.50), the 1885 Clarke Homestead and the Exhibition Centre Museum, which houses European relics and an impressive collection of Maori artefacts, including superb feather cloaks.

Beside the museum is the Native Bird Recovery Centre (☎ 09-438 1457; www.whangareinativebird recovery.org.nz; admission by donation; ☑ 10.30am-4pm Mon-Fri), which nurses sick and injured birds back to health.

The 26m-high Whangarei Falls, 5km north of town, are very photogenic, with water cascading over the edge of an old basalt lava flow. The falls can be reached on the Tikipunga bus (Monday to Friday only). Buses leave from the city bus station.

The AH Reed Kauri Park, northeast of the city, has short walks including a cleverly designed boardwalk high up in the treetops. Southeast of Whangarei, the Waimahanga Walkway in Onerahi is an easy walk along an old railway embankment. It takes two hours and passes through mangrove swamps and over a 300m-long timber truss harbour bridge. The free Whangarei Walks, available from the information centre, describes more walks.

Abbey Caves is an undeveloped network of limestone caves full of glow-worms and formations just off Abbey Caves Rd, about 4km east of town. It's possible to visit them alone for free (take a torch and wear strong shoes), but you'll get further with a guided tour. Bunkdown Lodge (below) organises cave tours.

Whangarei is a popular centre for diving and fishing, mostly organised out of Tutukaka; see p200. If you want to organise your trip from here, though, pop into Dive Now (☎ 09-438 1075; www.divenow.co.nz; 41 Clyde St).

Sleeping
BUDGET
Bunkdown Lodge (☎ 09-438 8886; www.bunkdown lodge.co.nz; 23 Otaika Rd/SH1; dm $20-22, d & tw $48-50) There's a slightly worn, but very homely atmosphere in this just-south-of-town backpackers with an aviary and Kiwiana garden. Big lounges and board games aid socialising. The lodge runs Abbey Caves tours ($40) and bookings are taken for Bushwacka Experience tours. Pick-ups are available from the bus station.

YHA Manaakitanga Whangarei (☎ 09-438 8954; yha.whangarei@yha.org.nz; 52 Punga Grove Ave; dm/d/tw $24/54/54) This small, easy-going hostel with the tongue twister of a name is up a hill just a short walk from the town centre. The manager does a free walk to a nearby cave and glow-worms and the atmosphere is social but not rowdy.

Punga Lodge B&B (☎ 09-438 3879; 9 Punga Grove; s/d $50/70) Centrally located, this B&B is a regular suburban home with a sense of privacy and space.

Whangarei Top 10 Holiday Park (☎ 09-437 6856; www.whangareitop10.co.nz; 24 Mair St; sites per 2 people $26, cabins $55, units $8c-95) This holiday park has a better-than-average set of cabins and a variety of bush walks start from here.

MIDRANGE
Pohutukawa Lodge (☎ 0800 200 355, 09-430 8634; www.pohutukawalodge.co.nz; 362 Western Hills Dr; units $100-160) Just west of town, this straightforward, nicely furnished place has 14 units with well-kept facilities and ample parking.

Channel Vista B&B (☎ 09-436 5529; bnbwhangarei .co.nz; 254 Beach Rd, Onerahi; s/d $100/160) This upmarket beachside accommodation (with nifty views) east of town is self-contained or in-house. Bedrooms are a little sparse-looking, but they are spotless and in good working order. A cooked brekkie is all part of the deal.

Fountain Lodge Motel (☎ 0800 999 944, 09-438 3532; www.fountainlodgemotel.co.nz; 17 Tarewa Rd; units $90-135) The hosts n this salmon-pink compound are friendly, the prices are reasonable and it's clean, although rooms can be somewhat dark and a little drab in parts.

Central Court Motel (☎ 09-438 4574; www.central courtmotel.co.nz; 54 Otaika Rd/SH1; s $60-80, d $65-90) Just south of town, this motel is a good deal at this price with a spa. Finnish sauna and Sky TV. It's built in classic motel-on-approach-road style.

TOP END
Lodge Bordeaux (☎ 09-438 0404; www.lodgebor deaux.co.nz; 361 Western Hills Dr; units $175-250; ☑) This newbie is supersmart, with beautiful, tasteful units with stellar kitchens and bathrooms, private balconies and plenty of excellent wines available to guests.

Sail Inn (☎ 09-43€2356; sailinn@xtra.co.nz; 148 Beach Rd, Onerahi; d & tw $195) East of town with jaw-dropping harbour views and very attractive rooms, this is high-quality accommodation.

Breakfast on the sun-drenched deck is a particular highlight of a stay here.

Eating

TOWN CENTRE

Bob (☎ 09-438 0881; 29 Bank St; lunch dishes $5-22; ☑ breakfast & lunch year-round, dinner summer) Bob is the coolest of Whangarei's cafés, with an arty, industrial feel and the fluffiest scrambled eggs and best bread in town. Flick through glossy mags while nodding your head to the great music in the background and unwind in style.

Caffeine (☎ 09-438 6925; 4 Water St; meals $14-15; ☑ breakfast & lunch) There's no doubting what the regulars are here for – good coffee. Big bowls hold commendable café lattes, and a free chocolate on the side never hurts. Nice brekkies and café snacks too.

Bogart's (☎ 09-438 3088; cnr Cameron & Walton Sts; mains $22-29; ☑ dinner daily & lunch Fri) This place does a mean seafood chowder packed with fishy goodness. Other dishes aren't quite as worthy, although overall the effect is a very pleasant one.

Asahi (☎ 09-430 3005; cnr Vine & Quality Sts; dishes $10-19; ☑ dinner Mon-Sat) This is an attractive, lantern-bedecked haunt with a comprehensive menu of Japanese and Korean dishes and chipper waitstaff who aren't in the least bit fazed by people ordering via the finger-pointing technique.

Killer Prawn (☎ 09-430 3333; 28 Bank St; mains $30-38; ☑ lunch & dinner Mon-Sat) Worth a visit for the name alone, and to stickybeak at the pics of the nearly famous (wasn't Matt Lattani married to Olivia Newton-John?) going nuts and getting sticky fingers for the famous garlic prawns.

G & T Restaurant & Bar (☎ 09-438 0999; 15a Rathbone St; mains $15-32; ☑ breakfast & lunch daily, dinner Mon-Sat) This restaurant has a varied menu, but you'd do well to snaffle a serve of whitebait fritters if they're in season.

Rin Chin Chilla (☎ 09-438 5882; 6 Vine St; meals $7-14; ☑ lunch & dinner) Cheap and cheerful Middle Eastern munchies keep hunger pangs at bay at this good standby eatery.

There's a **Pak N Save** (Carruth St) supermarket for self-caterers.

TOWN BASIN

Mokaba (☎ 09-438 7557; Town Basin; meals $6-16; ☑ breakfast, lunch & afternoon tea) Mokaba offers a relatively upmarket experience and a good

stash of outdoor seating. The muffins are highly recommended and the atmosphere on weekends infectious.

Mondo's (☎ 09-430 0467; Town Basin; meals $6-15; ☑ breakfast & lunch) The menu on the megaboard has masses of deli snacks and week-end brunch items and attracts the masses (and their gregarious kids).

Gybe Bar & Restaurant (☎ 0800 346 336; Town Basin; dinner mains $14-39; ☑ breakfast, lunch & dinner) This slick-looking establishment also offers hearty all-day breakfasts and has an upmarket feel, although it would have been nice to get the appropriate cutlery for the dozen oysters we ordered (which were nevertheless good).

Reva's on the Waterfront (☎ 09-438 8969; Town Basin; lunch mains $15-26; ☑ lunch & dinner) This long-running casual restaurant serves pizzas, seafood and a global menu and has live music at the weekends. It sits right on the water overlooking the harbour.

Drinking & Entertainment

Brauhaus Frings (☎ 09-438 4664; www.frings.co.nz; 104 Dent St; ☑ 9am-late) This popular microbrewery has a range of great chemical-free beers, a lovely beer garden and board games for patrons to play. Very good food is also on offer, and it matches the beers well.

Bacio Bar & Café (☎ 09-430 0446; 31 Bank St; ☑ lunch & dinner Mon-Sat, bar till late) This relatively sleek, modern-looking bar is a good place to nurse a drink or two and catch a game on the big screen.

Dickens Inn (☎ 09-430 0406; cnr Cameron & Quality Sts) This English-style pub has the usual suspects on tap and an easy-going feel. It also serves decent food (including a children's menu) all day.

Danger! Danger! (☎ 09-459 7461; 37 Vine St; ☑ 10.30am-very late) This popular and populist wood-clad barn has plenty of food, but more importantly, drink, for excitable locals who come to socialise. It's a nightclub of sorts later in the evenings.

Sky City Cinema (☎ 09-438 8550) Shows the latest mainstream movies.

Getting There & Around

AIR

Air New Zealand (24hr ☎ 0800 737 000; www.airnz .co.nz) operates four to six flights a day (35 minutes, $75 to $165) between Auckland and Whangarei. **Great Barrier Airlines** (☎ 0800

900 600, 09-275 9120; www.greatbarrierairlines.co.nz; one way adult/child $100/65) flies twice a week between Whangarei and Great Barrier Island. **Mountain Air** (☎ 0800 222 123, 09-256 7025; www .mountainair.co.nz; one way adult/child $95/55) flies between Whangarei and Great Barrier four times a week. The airport is at Onerahi, to the east of the town centre.

The **Whangarei Airport Shuttle** (☎ 09-437 0666) has a door-to-door service for around $12.

BUS

The **City & Long Distance Bus Station** (☎ 09-438 2653) is on Rose St. InterCity has daily buses between Auckland and Whangarei ($36, two hours and 50 minutes), which continue north to Paihia ($23, 1½ hours from Whangarei). **Main Coachlines** (☎ 09-278 8070) runs a bus daily to and from Auckland (one way $30).

There is a local city bus service – a useful one can take you to Whangarei Falls.

AROUND WHANGAREI
Mimiwhangata Coastal Park

This park is 48km from Whangarei and 52km from Russell and can be reached via a gravel road from Helena Bay on the old Russell Rd. Accommodation can be booked with the **park's managers** (☎ 09-433

6554; cmoretti@doc.govt.nz; There is a luxurious lodge ($500 to $2000 per week) run by DOC, and a simpler but comfortable cottage ($350 to $1500 per week); both sleep eight people. There's also a beachhouse, which sleeps seven and costs the same as the cottage. Self-contained accommodation must be booked for one week minimum, but camping ($12 per person; the only facilities are water and toilets) is available at secluded Waikahoa Bay, where there are cliffs and dunes and great hiking trails.

Whangarei Heads

From Whangarei, Heads Rd winds its way past picturesque coves and bays to the heads at the harbour entrance 35km away. This drive (there is no bus) passes small settlements and there are great views from the top of 419m **Mt Manaia**, a sheer rock outcrop above McLeod Bay, but it is a lung- and leg-busting 1½-hour climb.

From Woolshed Bay it is a 30-minute walk over the headland to the delightful beach at **Smugglers Bay**. You can also drive on to **Ocean Beach**.

A detour from Parua Bay takes you to glorious **Pataua**, a small settlement that lies on a shallow inlet. A pedestrian footbridge crosses the inlet to a surf beach.

Coromandel Region

By and large, life in the Coromandel region is blissfully quiet, except from Christmas to February when local holidaymakers and their much-needed cash flood the peninsula. It's a great, quintessential getaway spot, with an old-fashioned holiday feel and plenty of opportunities to get back to basics. After all, some of the more remote communities in these parts are still accessed by gravel roads, and an aura of rugged individualism hangs like mist over this compact and special region.

The spine of the Coromandel Peninsula is densely forested and mountainous, crisscrossed with hiking trails, around which narrow roads wind along the attractive, rough-hewn coastline. The historical gold-mining towns of Thames and Coromandel Town on the west coast retain a pioneer atmosphere, and the whole area attracts city dropouts who have exchanged their stressful jobs for 10-hectare properties with sea views.

The east coast has rapidly expanding patches of holiday homes around some beaches but most of the coast, particularly in the north, is much as it was when Captain Cook sailed by in the late 18th century. Whitianga and nearby Hahei are a mini Bay of Islands with plenty of activities in, on and below the water and lots of baches – those most authentic NZ shelters.

The star ecological attraction is the top bird-watching site at Miranda, southwest of the peninsula, where sharp-eyed waders feast on the tidal mud-flat banquet of worms and shellfish. Further east at Karangahake Gorge, rusting 19th-century relics of the gold-rush era can be seen while you're tramping through evocative scenery.

HIGHLIGHTS

- Getting wet while boating, scuba diving, snorkelling, kayaking and fishing around **Whitianga** (p217) and **Cathedral Cove** (p220)
- Making your own natural spa bath at stunning **Hot Water Beach** (p221)
- Hitting a high point at the **Pinnacles** (p212) and along the **Coromandel Coastal Walkway** (p216)
- Striking gold (and a sense of history) at **Karanga-hake Gorge** (p226)
- Savouring unspoilt east coast beaches at **Opito Bay** (p216) or **Opoutere** (p223) and superb surf at **Whangamata** (p223)
- Watching the birds go by on the mud flats at **Miranda** (p226)
- Trainspotting on the charming **Driving Creek Railway** (p213)

- TELEPHONE CODE: 07
- www.thecoromandel.com

Coromandel Coastal Walkway ★

Driving Creek Railway ★

Opito ★

Whitianga ★

Cathedral Cove ★

Hot Water Beach ★

Pinnacles ★

Opoutere ★

Whangamata ★

Karangahake Gorge ★

Miranda ★

COROMANDEL PENINSULA

The Coromandel Peninsula juts out into the South Pacific Ocean, bordered on the west by the Hauraki Gulf. It boasts some of the North Island's best beaches and coastal scenery and attracts alternative lifestylers wanting to escape from the city rat race and reclaim the Age of Aquarius.

Thames and Coromandel Town on the west coast are quaint, historical towns, and there are tiny settlements and rugged coastline further north. The best beaches (including the famed and fabulous Hot Water Beach) are on the east coast, which also has the main holiday resorts.

The peninsula is compact, but the narrow and winding roads mean that travel speeds are low. It's best to take your time when touring the Coromandel, and cyclists should be prepared for some narrow roads and a fair bit of heart-pounding hill climbing.

History

Maoris lived on the peninsula well before the first European settlers arrived, and the sheltered areas of the east coast supported a large population. This was one of the major moa-hunting areas of the North Island, although other subsistence practices included fishing, sealing, bird-hunting and horticulture.

The history of European colonisation of the peninsula and plains to the south is steeped in gold-mining, kauri logging and gumdigging. Gold was first discovered in New Zealand near Coromandel Town in 1852. Although this first rush was short-lived, more gold was discovered around Thames in 1867 and later in Coromandel

---

COROMANDEL REGION FACTS

Eat: Smoked mussels

Drink: Feijoa wine

Read: Anything by Michael King (he called Opoutere home from 1993 until his death in 2004)

Listen to: Soul Sax Plus

Watch: *Crooked Earth* (2000), a modern-day examination of Maori identity, starring Temuera Morrison

Swim at: Hahei (p220)

Festival: Coromandel Dive Festival (p222)

Tackiest tourist attraction: The big L&P bottles in Paeroa (p226)

Climate

Being mountainous, the region attracts more rainfall (3000mm or even 4500mm a year) than elsewhere on the east coast.

Getting There & Around

Great Barrier Airlines services the Coromandel Peninsula. It operates flights between Auckland and Whitianga, and between Great Barrier Island and Whitianga.

For bus travel, InterCity's North Island Value Pass (adult/child $150/100) starts from Auckland, includes Thames and Paeroa, and goes on to Rotorua. The Pacific Coast Hwy Pass ($200/135) departs Auckland and includes Whitianga in the Coromandel loop, before heading down to Wellington, via Rotorua, Gisborne and Napier.

Go Kiwi Shuttles operates door-to-door services. Shuttle buses run daily from Auckland city and Auckland airport to Whitianga via Thames and Tairua. Shuttle buses also go from Whitianga via Tairua, Opoutere, Whangamata, Waihi, Tauranga to Rotorua daily in summer. Services run daily in winter if there are reservations.

TOP ACTIVITIES

- Jump into a variety of marine vessels to explore the waters of Whitianga (p217)
- Hike the paths of Coromandel Forest Park to experience leafy solitude (p212)
- Join the surfy crowd in Whangamata (p223)
- Catch your own lunch: go fishing in Coromandel (p213), Whitianga (p217) or Tairua (p222)
- Enjoy thermal bathing at Hot Water Beach (p221), Waihi (p225), Miranda (p226) or Te Aroha (p227)

www.lonelyplanet.com

COROMANDEL REGION

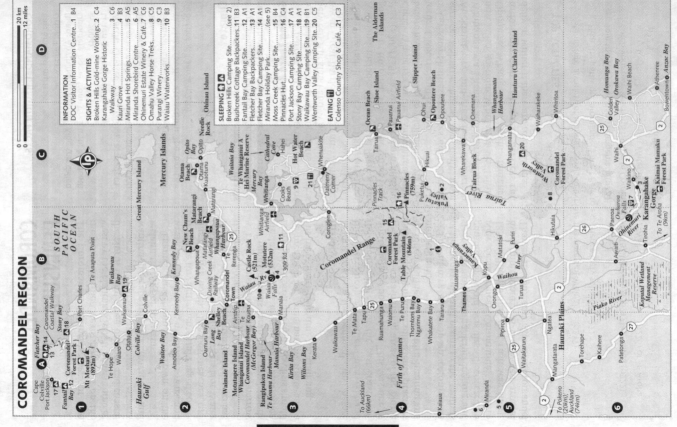

INFORMATION
DOC Visitor Information Centre...1 B4

SIGHTS & ACTIVITIES
Broken Hills Gold-mine Workings..2 C4
Karangahake Gorge Historic
  Walkway 3 C6
Kauri Grove 4 B3
Miranda Hot Springs.................5 A5
Miranda Shorebird Centre...........6 A5
Ohinemuri Estate Winery & Café..7 C6
Omahu Valley Horse Treks..........8 C5
Purangi Winery.......................9 C3
Waiau Waterworks..................10 B3

SLEEPING
Broken Hills Camping Site........11 B3
Bushcreek Cottage Backpackers...(see 2)
Fantail Bay Camping Site..........12 A1
Fletcher Bay Backpackers..........13 A1
Fletcher Bay Camping Site.........14 A1
Miranda Holiday Park..............(see 5)
Moss Creek Camping Site..........15 B4
Pinnacles Hut......................16 C4
Port Jackson Camping Site.........17 A1
Stony Bay Camping Site............18 A1
Waikawau Bay Camping Site.......19 B1
Wentworth Valley Camping Site..20 C5

EATING
Colenso Country Shop & Café...21 C3

Town, Kuaotunu and Karangahake. The peninsula is also rich in semiprecious gemstones, such as quartz, agate, amethyst and jasper. A fossick on any west coast beach can be rewarding.

Kauri logging was big business on the peninsula for more than 60 years. Allied to the timber trade was shipbuilding, which took off in 1832 when a mill was established at Mercury Bay. Things got tougher once the kauri around the coast became scarce and the loggers had to penetrate deeper into the bush for timber. Kauri dams were built that used water power to propel the huge logs to the coast. By the 1930s virtually no kauri trees remained on the peninsula and the logging industry died.

THAMES

pop 10,000

Thames is the western gateway to and the main service centre of the Coromandel, and lies on the shallow Firth of Thames. Plenty of 19th-century wooden stores, hotel pubs and houses have survived from the time when gold-mining and kauri logging made Thames a thriving and important business centre, and the town retains a historical atmosphere, with the area's most bustling main street. Nowadays it's a base for tramping or canyoning in the nearby Kauaeranga Valley.

Information

Laundromat Internet/Pohutukawa Design (740 Pollen St) Internet access while you wash your clothes.

Post office (Pollen St)

Thames visitor information centre (☎ 07-868 7284; www.thames.nf0.co.nz; 206 Pollen St; ☑ 8.30am-5pm Mon-Fri, 9am-4pm Sat & Sun) Has loads of brochures; open extended hours in summer.

United Video & Internet (456 Pollen St) For Internet access.

Sights & Activities

The **Gold Mine Experience** (☎ 07-868 8514; www .goldmine-experience.co.nz; adult/child $10/4; ☑ 10am-4pm) is a really worthwhile diversion that includes walking through a gold-mine tunnel, watching a stamping battery crush rock, learning about the history of the people of Cornish descent who worked in the mines and also panning for gold ($2 extra). The guys who run it are enthusiastic, and constant improvements and additions are made to the roster.

The **Butterfly & Orchid Garden** (☎ 07-868 8080; Victoria St; adult/child $9/4; ☑ 10am-4pm summer), north of town next to the Dickson Holiday Park, is an indoor tropical jungle full of hundreds of colourful butterflies that allows visitors to observe the beauty of nature at close range. Call for winter opening hours.

Karaka Bird Hide is a great bird-watching hide that is easily reached by a boardwalk through the mangroves just off Brown St. It overlooks the Firth of Thames, and the best viewing time is two hours either side of high tide.

The **School of Mines & Mineralogical Museum** (☎ 07-868 6227; cnr Brown & Cochrane Sts; adult/child $3.50/free; ☑ 11am-4pm Wed-Sun) has a full collection of NZ rocks, minerals and fossils, and is situated on an ancient Maori burial ground.

The local **historical museum** (☎ 07-868 8509; cnr Cochrane & Pollen Sts; adult/child $4/2; ☑ 1-4pm) has pioneer relics, rocks and old photographs of the town.

Harley Davidson Motor Cycle Rides (☎ 07-867 5661; www.harleyoursnewzealand.co.nz; Coromandel passenger tour $340) is the coolest way to tour the Coromandel. You can also hire Harley's for $385 per day. Fully inclusive tours around other regions (including the South Island) are also possible.

Eyez Open (☎ 07-868 2238; www.eyezopen.co.nz; dayhike $30) rents out bikes and also organises interesting cycling tours of the peninsula (around $75). They'll deliver bikes to your accommodation.

Paki Paki Bike Shop (☎ 07-867 9026; pakipaki@xtra .co.nz; Goldfields Shopping Centre) rents out bikes for $25 a day.

The **Saturday morning market** (☑ 9am-noon) has lots of organic produce and handicrafts. It's at the northern end of Pollen St, which is known as Grahamstown.

Young kids can enjoy a train ride on the cute-as-a-button **Thames Small Gauge Railway** (☎ 07-868 6803; tickets $1; ☑ 11am-3pm Sun), a 900m-loop small-gauge track.

Matatoki Farm Cheese (☎ 07-868 1284; www .matatokicheese.co.nz; ☑ 9am-4.30pm Mon-Fri, 10am-4.30pm Sat & Sun, closed Sun May-Oct) is an organic cheese factory and shop, located 12km from Thames, on State Highway 26 (SH26) en route to Paeroa. You can taste and buy cheeses handmade from milk produced by the farm's cows and ewes.

Omahu Valley Horse Treks (Map p208; ☎ 07-868 1289; Omahu Valley Rd), a 15-minute drive south

www.lonelyplanet.com

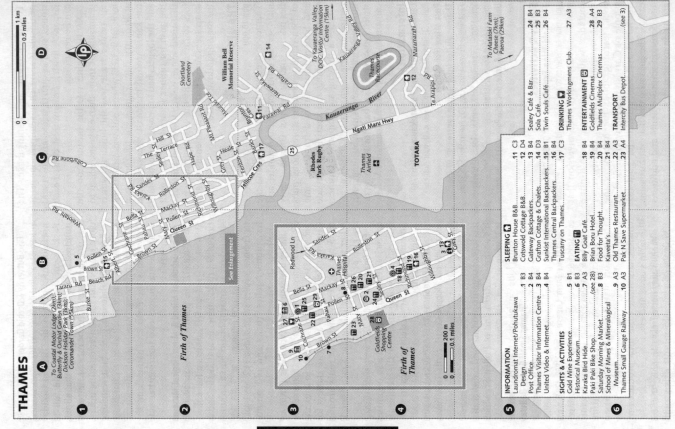

THAMES

0 1 km
0 0.5 miles

0 1 mile
0 0.5

See Enlargement

Firth of Thames

Shortland Cemetery

William Bell Memorial Reserve

To Coastal Motor Lodge (2km);
Butterfly & Orchid Garden (3km);
Dickson Holiday Park (3km);
Coromandel Town (55km)

To Matatoki Farm
Cheese (7km);
Paeroa (29km)

To Kauaeranga Valley;
DOC Visitor Information
Centre (15km)

Kauaeranga River

Ngati Maru Hwy

Rhodes Park Rugby

Thames Airfield

TOTARA

Thames Racecourse

Firth of Thames

Goldfields Shopping Centre

0 200 m
0 0.1 miles

INFORMATION
Laundromat Internet/Pohutukawa
Design..1 B3
Post Office.....................................2 B4
Thames Visitor Information Centre..3 B4
United Video & Internet................4 B4

SIGHTS & ACTIVITIES
Gold Mine Experience...................5 B1
Historical Museum.........................6 B3
Karaka Bird Hide...................(see 28)
Paki Paki Bike Shop.......................7 A3
Saturday Morning Market..............8 B3
School of Mines & Mineralogical
Museum..9 A3
Thames Small Gauge Railway.......10 A3

SLEEPING
Brunton House B&B.....................11 C3
Cotswold Cottage B&B................12 D4
Gateway Backpackers..................13 B4
Grafton Cottage & Chalets...........14 D3
Sunkist International Backpackers..15 B1
Thames Central Backpackers........16 B4
Tuscany on Thames......................17 C3

EATING
Billy Goat Café............................18 B4
Brian Boru Hotel..........................19 B4
Food for Thought.........................20 B4
Kaveeta's....................................21 B4
Old Thames Restaurant................22 A3
Pak N Save Supermarket..............23 A4

Sealey Café & Bar.......................24 B4
Sola Café....................................25 B3
Twin Souls Café...........................26 B4

DRINKING
Thames Workingmens Club..........27 A3

ENTERTAINMENT
Goldfields Cinemas......................28 A4
Thames Multiplex Cinemas...........29 B3

TRANSPORT
Intercity Bus Depot...............(see 3)

COROMANDEL REGION

of Thames, has horse treks through the surrounding area for $25 per hour.

See the Auckland Region chapter (p116) for details of canyoning trips that can be organised in the nearby Sleeping God Canyon. These trips can also be booked from Sunkist International Backpackers (below).

Sleeping

BUDGET

Gateway Backpackers (☎ 07-868 6339; 209 Mackay St; dm $20, d & tw $46, d & tw with bathroom $56) This well-located, relaxed backpackers has comfy rooms and a casual home-away-from-home feel, with plenty of simple facilities and a deck in the garden. The hard-working young owners also offer free bikes, free use of the washing machine and free tea and coffee.

Sunkist International Backpackers (☎/fax 07-868 8808; www.sunkistbackpackers.com; 506 Brown St; unpowered sites per 2 people $28, dm $19-23, d & tw $50) This character-filled, family-run heritage 1860s building has spacious dorms, spotless bathrooms and a garden, and offers free bikes, lots of information and a shuttle-bus service to the Kauaeranga Valley hikes (p212).

Dickson Holiday Park (☎ 07-868 7308; www.dicksonpark.co.nz; unpowered/powered sites per 2 people $25/26, cabins $48-69, units $90; 🖳) Situated in a calm, quiet valley, 4km north of Thames, this pleasant, well-run camping ground has a shop, free bikes and a three-hour bush hike up into the hills, which are riddled with gold-mine tunnels.

Also worth trying is **Thames Central Backpackers** (☎ 07-868 5332; www.thamescentralbackpackers.com; 330 Pollen St; dm $18-20, s $35, d & tw $44, tr $6).

MIDRANGE & TOP END

Coastal Motor Lodge (☎ 07-868 6843; www.stayatcoastal.co.nz; 608 Tararu Rd; chalets $155, garden cottages $120-160) Superior chalet-style accommodation is provided at this smart, modern and welcoming place, 2km north of Thames. It overlooks the sea and is very well looked after, making it a popular choice, especially in the summer months.

Grafton Cottage & Chalets (☎/fax 07-868 9971; www.graftoncottage.co.nz; 304 Grafton Rd; d & tw $115-205; 🖳) This is an attractive, homely choice, with self-contained or studio chalets. They come with decks and good views, plus there's an outdoor pool and a spa.

Brunton House B&B (☎ 07-868 5160; www.bruntonhouse.co.nz; 210 Parawai Rd; s/d $150/165; 🖳) This very impressive two-storey kauri villa (built in the 1870s) is encircled by verandas and has real historical charm, plus a tennis court and outdoor pool.

Cotswold Cottage B&B (☎ 07-868 6306; www.cotswoldcottage.co.nz; 46 Maramarahi Rd; s $75, d & tw $120-130) This pretty riverside villa has comfortable rooms with tidy bathrooms and helpful hosts who know the area well.

Tuscany on Thames (☎ 07-868 5099; www.tuscanyonthames.co.nz; Jellicoe Cres; units $140-160) The décor is close enough to Tuscany, although not quite there, but the good-quality units are very decent value. You're not in the centre of town, but everything is reasonably close. Light sleepers should note that traffic noise might be a problem.

Eating & Drinking

Thames has a handful of good cafés.

Sola Café (☎ 07-868 3781; 720b Pollen St; dinner mains $15-19; 🕑 breakfast & lunch daily year-round, dinner Thu-Sun Dec-Feb, rest of year) This is a brilliant vegetarian café with vegan, dairy-free and gluten-free food that includes heavenly salads. The risotto cakes are deservedly popular, and local artworks dot the walls.

Food for Thought (☎ 07-868 6065; 574 Pollen St; meals $5-15; 🕑 breakfast & lunch Mon-Sat) Fantastic pies and French toast give you ample reasons to mull over the big issues of the day with a mouth full of food at this friendly place. Good coffee too.

Twin Souls Café (☎ 07-868 5255; 578 Pollen St; meals $7-14; 🕑 breakfast & lunch Mon-Sat) Good coffee and lip-smacking snacks can be found at this cool, hard-to-define café. Breakfasts are a real highlight.

Billy Goat Café (☎ 07-868 7384; 444 Pollen St; meals $5-10; 🕑 breakfast & lunch daily Dec-Feb, Mon-Fri rest of year) Home-baked cakes as well as bagels, lasagne and salads are available at this spare-looking joint that stocks Auckland's Atomic-brand coffee.

Kaveeta's (☎ 07-838 7049; 518 Pollen St; dinner mains $12-14; 🕑 lunch & dinner) This place serves up good Indian food, pizza (including Indian-style varieties), a herby lassi, and kulfi ice cream in th s unusual and inexpensive restaurant. Kaveeta's also has a great vegetarian selection.

Old Thames Restaurant (☎ 07-868 7207; 705 Pollen St; dinner mains $25-28; 🕑 lunch Thu-Sat & dinner daily)

This masculine-looking and well-established place serves hearty NZ fare – try the local flounder or tarakihi with lemon pepper and herbs – as well as pizza.

Sealey Café & Bar (☎ 07-868 8641; 109 Sealey St; dinner mains $19-28; ⏱ breakfast, lunch & dinner) This all-day café-restaurant has an inviting courtyard out the front and some unusual and tempting combinations and salads on its menu.

Brian Boru Hotel (☎ 07-868 6523; 200 Richmond St; meals around $15; ⏱ dinner) This rough-round-the-edges boozer does a popular pizza 'n' pint deal for a bargain $12.

Thames Workingmens Club (☎ 07-868 6416; cnr Pollen & Cochrane Sts) This gold rush–era gem has a lovely exterior and a low-key, slightly grungy interior that will have you thinking the era of the six o'clock swill will never stopped.

Self-caterers might like to try **Pak N Save Supermarket** (Mary St).

Entertainment

There are two cinemas: **Thames Multiplex** (☎ 07-868 6600; 708 Pollen St) and **Goldfields Cinemas** (☎ 07-867 9100; Goldfields Shopping Centre).

Getting There & Around

Thames is the transport hub of the Coromandel. **InterCity** (Auckland ☎ 09-623 1503; www .intercitycoach.co.nz) has daily buses from Auckland to Thames ($23, two hours), from where you can continue on to Paeroa, Waihi, Tauranga and Rotorua. **Go Kiwi Shuttles** (☎ 0800 446 549, 07-866 0336; www.go-kiwi.co.nz) also has services from Auckland ($32). InterCity buses stop at the InterCity bus depot, while Go Kiwi Shuttles run door-to-door.

COROMANDEL FOREST PARK

Over 30 walks and tramps crisscross the Coromandel Forest Park, which stretches from Paeroa up to Cape Colville. The most popular hike is the 3½-hour hike up to the dramatic **Pinnacles** (759m) in the Kauaeranga Valley behind Thames. There are old kauri dams in the valley, including the Tarawaere Waterfalls, Dancing Camp, Kauaeranga Main, Moss Creek and Waterfalls Creek dams. Other outstanding hikes include the Coromandel Coastal Walkway from Fletcher Bay to Stony Bay (see p216) in the far north, and the Puketui Valley (p223) walk to old gold-mine workings.

The **Department of Conservation (DOC) visitor information centre** (Map p208; ☎ 07-867 9080; Kauaeranga Valley Rd; ⏱ 8am-4pm) has hiking information, maps and takes bookings for the Pinnacles hut. In 2004 the centre was destroyed by fire and was still under construction during research for this book, but a temporary shed was serving its purpose. The centre is 14km off the main road, and a further 9km along a gravel road is the start of the hiking trails. Sunkist International Backpackers (see p211) has transport from Thames to the hiking trails.

The **DOC Pinnacles hut** (Map p208; ☎ 07-867 9080; adult/child $15/7.50) has 80 beds, gas cookers, heaters, toilets and cold showers, and must be prebooked. Very basic DOC **camp sites** (adult/child $9/4.50) are scattered throughout Coromandel Forest Park at Fantail Bay, Port Jackson, Fletcher Bay, Stony Bay and Waikawau Bay in the north, further south at Broken Hills and Wentworth Valley, and near the Pinnacles hut at Moss Creek (see Map p208). Expect chemical toilets and few, if any, other facilities. Camp sites are on a first-come, first-served basis but Waikawau Bay requires booking (☎ 07-866 1106) over Christmas and New Year.

THAMES TO COROMANDEL TOWN

As you travel north from Thames, the narrow SH25 snakes along the coast past pretty little bays and rocky beaches. Sea birds can be seen, especially around high tide, and you can fish, look for shellfish and fossick for quartz, jasper and even gold-bearing rocks on the beaches. The landscape turns crimson when the pohutukawa (often referred to as the 'NZ Christmas tree') blooms in late December. At Wilsons Bay the road leaves the coast and climbs over several hills and valleys before dropping down to Coromandel Town, 54km from Thames. A handful of stores, motels, B&Bs and camping grounds are spread around the tiny settlements that front the bays. At Tapu, it's worth making a point of seeing the stunning **Rapaura Water Gardens** (☎ 07-868 4821; www.rapaurawatergardens.co.nz; 586 Tapu-Coroglen Rd; cottage/lodge $145/25C; garden ☑ 9am-5pm), a beautiful, harmonious marriage of water, greenery and sculpture. The accommodation here is very special too, and can easily lay claim to having the loveliest gardens in the area.

There are holiday parks with camping and cabins at regular intervals along the highway, including **Waiomu Bay Holiday Park** (☎ 07-868 2777; Waiomu Valley Rd; sites per 2 people $21, cabins $50, motel units $65-95; ☑), a very comfortable choice in Waiomu, which also has a good pool and children's playground.

About 11km north of Thames **Te Puru Coast View Lodge** (☎ 07-868 2326; www.tepurulodge .co.nz; 468 Thames Coast Rd, Te Puru; d & tw $150-175) is a swanky Mediterranean-style villa on a hill overlooking the Firth of Thames and enjoying some heavenly sunsets. All meals can be provided for guests via the very good on-site restaurant.

COROMANDEL TOWN
pop 1620

At the height of the gold rush (Charles Ring discovered the precious metal at Driving Creek, 3km north of here, in 1852), Coromandel Town boasted a population of more than 10,000. These days the town is a far sleepier proposition, but a far more attractive base than Thames, thanks to its mix of old-timers, alternative New Age types, smoked mussels (more on that later), natty cafés and decent pubs.

Information

Bank of New Zealand (BNZ; ☎ 0800 866 8865; cnr Tiki & Wharf Rds) Close to the harbour.

Coromandel Town visitor information centre (☎ 07-866 8598; www.coromandeltown.co.nz; 355 Kapanga Rd; ☑ 9am-5pm Mon-Sat, 10am-2pm Sun) Delightfully helpful; has Internet access ($6 per hour) and information on DOC hikes and camping grounds.

Police station (☎ 07-866 8777; 405 Kapanga Rd)

Post office (Kapanga Rd)

Sights & Activities

The amazing **Driving Creek Railway & Pottery** (☎/fax 07-866 8703; www.drivingcreekrailway.co.nz; 410 Driving Creek Rd; train trips adult/child $17/9) is 3km north of Coromandel Town. The unique trains run at 10.15am and 2pm (more often in summer) up steep grades, across four trestle bridges, along two spirals and a double switchback, and through two tunnels, finishing at the 'Eye-full Tower'. The hour-long trip goes up into the hills, past artworks and through an area of recently planted native trees. The owner is a well-known NZ potter and ceramics are for sale at reasonable prices.

The **Coromandel Goldfield Centre & Stamper Battery** (☎ 07-866 7933; 410 Buffalo Rd; adult/child $10/5; ☑ 10am-4pm Thu-Tue) has informative one-hour tours of this working 1899 rock-crushing plant with NZ's largest working water wheel.

The small **Coromandel Mining & Historic Museum** (☎ 07-866 7251; 900 Rings Rd; adult/child $2/50c; ☑ 1-4.30pm Sat & Sun, 10am-4pm daily summer) provides a glimpse (in terms of opening hours) of life in the golden days.

The award-winning **Waiatai Gardens** (☎ 07-866 8659; 485 Buffalo Rd; admission $5) have been created either side of a long drive. The gardens feature unusual and rare plants, native orchids, rhododendrons and native trees, plus NZ's rarest gecko.

Te Kaihau (☎ 07-868 7546; www.sailcoro.co.nz; day/overnight trips incl meals per adult $85/100, per child $30/50) is a trimaran sailing ship, fully equipped with snorkelling and fishing gear. Longer trips are possible.

Mussel Barge (☎ 07-866 7667; adult/child $35/20) offers fishing trips (such as the snapper safari) with a uniquely local flavour.

Argo Tours (☎ 07-866 7667) explores old gold workings in a mini 8WD. Two/three hours cost $55/75 per person (on the basis of a five-person tour).

Sleeping
BUDGET

Lion's Den (☎ 07-866 8157; 126 Te Tiki St; dm/s/d $20/38/44) There's a really nice, laid-back feel to this place, which is easily the town's best hostel if you're keen on an alternative lifestyle experience and the odd flashback. A tranquil garden with fish pond and wisteria vines outside and a relaxed collection of comfy rooms (dotted with African and

North American bits and bobs) make for a soothing spot to rest your bones. Breakfast and dinner are also available.

Tui Lodge (☎ 07-866 8237; tuilodge@paradise.net .nz; 60 Whangapoua Rd; dm $20, d $45, d & tw with bathroom $65) This relaxed, clean-enough and cheery backpackers has a pleasant shady garden with trees, a sauna and free bikes, fruit (when in season) and straight-up rooms.

Tidewater Tourist Park (☎ 07-866 8888; www.tide water.co.nz; 270 Tiki Rd; sites per 2 people $20, dm/d $20/55, units $95-145) Units are natty, newish and well maintained at this friendly YHA associate, which also has bicycles and kayaks for hire and a sauna.

Coromandel Town Backpackers (☎ 07-866 8327; 732 Rings Rd; dm $19, d & tw $38) This central hostel

has a shedlike ambience and small modern rooms that lack much in the way of character but certainly do the job if you're after a cheap sleep and not much more. The InterCity coach stops here.

Coromandel Motels & Holiday Park (☎ 07-866 8830; www.coromandelholidaypark.co.nz; 636 Rings Rd; unpowered/powered sites per 2 people $28/32, cabins $67-77, units $127, cottages $140; ☞) This park is welcoming, with nicely painted cabins, a swimming pool and manicured lawns and the like, but rather ordinary communal areas like kitchens and lounge rooms.

MIDRANGE
Coromandel Court Motel (☎ 07-866 8402; corocourt@ xtra.co.nz; 365 Kapanga Rd; units seasonal range $95-165)

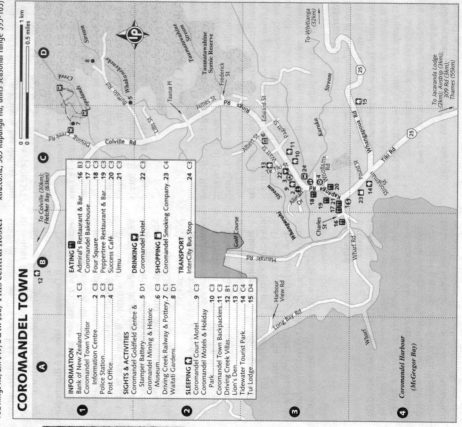

COROMANDEL TOWN

INFORMATION	
Bank of New Zealand.....................1	C3
Coromandel Town Visitor	
Information Centre.....................2	C3
Police Station...............................3	C3
Post Office....................................4	C3

SIGHTS & ACTIVITIES	
Coromandel Goldfield Centre &	
Stamper Battery.........................5	D1
Coromandel Mining & Historic	
Museum.....................................6	C3
Driving Creek Railway & Pottery....7	C1
Waitati Gardens............................8	D1

SLEEPING	
Coromandel Court Motel................9	C3
Coromandel Motels & Holiday	
Park...10	C3
Coromandel Town Backpackers....11	C3
Driving Creek Villas....................12	B1
Lion's Den..................................13	C3
Tidewater Tourist Park................14	C4
Tui Lodge..................................15	D4

EATING	
Admiral's Restaurant & Bar...........16	B3
Coromandel Bakehouse................17	C3
Four Square...............................18	C3
Peppertree Restaurant & Bar........19	C3
Success Café..............................20	C3
Umu..21	C3

DRINKING	
Coromandel Hotel.......................22	C3

SHOPPING	
Coromandel Smoking Company....23	C4

TRANSPORT	
InterCity Bus Stop......................24	C3

These spick-and-span units are spotless, smart and ideally located just behind the information centre. The owners, Raymond and Gael, go out of their way to ensure their guests are comfortable, and will even organise fishing trips for you if you fancy. Disabled access is available.

Jacaranda Lodge (☎ 07-866 8002; www.jacaranda lodge.co.nz; 3195 Tiki Rd; s $70, d $100-145) Jacaranda is a picture-book rural cottage, located south of town among 6 hectares of true NZ farmland, and it makes for an authentic bucolic retreat. Rooms are not terribly fancy, but they are comfortable and you'll sleep well.

TOP END

Driving Creek Villas (☎ 07-866 7755; www.driving creekvillas.com; 21a Colville Rd; s $175, d $195-245) This is the posh, grown-ups choice in the area, with spacious, beautiful villas and all the privacy you could hope for. Furnishings are up-to-the-minute and smart without being pr.ssy, and all seems right with the world when you're here.

Eating & Drinking

Umu (☎ 07-866 8618; 22 Wharf Rd; pizzas $16-23; ☯ breakfast, lunch & dinner) Umu has indoor and outdoor seating and serves up classy, inventive café food, including the best pizzas in the region, superb coffee and tummy-taming breakfasts.

Admiral's Restaurant & Bar (☎ 07-866 8020; upstairs, 146 Wharf Rd; dinner mains $8-25; ☯ lunch & dinner) This ripper of a pub restaurant has harbour views from the veranda, meaning you should come for dinner early in the summer months. Meals are a nice mix of traditional and modern. There is live music once a week at the somewhat flash Admiral's Sports Bar down below.

Peppertree Restaurant & Bar (☎ 07-866 8211; 31 Kapanga Rd; dinner mains $22.50-120; ☯ breakfast, lunch & dinner) The most traditional choice in town is this upmarket restaurant dominated by a large pepper tree. It has plenty of outdoor seating, making it quite a romantic spot in the summer months. The food is reassuringly old-fashioned, with dishes like trifle popping up on the dessert menu.

Success Café (☎ 07-866 7100; 104 Kapanga Rd; dinner mains $17-23; ☯ breakfast, lunch & dinner) This easygoing local eatery wins points for having a designated kids' menu, plus lots of solid, fish-themed options, such as mussel chowder or the great fisherman's brekkie.

Coromandel Bakehouse (☎ 07-868 8554; 92 Wharf Rd; snacks $3.50-7) Nip in here for a quick snack, such as a stuffed croissant to go.

Coromandel Hotel (☎ 07-866 8760; 611 Kapanga Rd) This is the local pub. Enough said.

Self-caterers can raid the **Four Square** (255 Kapanga Rd) supermarket.

Shopping

Coromandel Smoking Company (☎ 07-866 8793; 70 Tiki Rd) This shop stocks a great range of smoked fish and seafood, and the staff will smoke your catch too. Try the smoked fish pâté or the deservedly raved-about smoked mussels, which will have you wanting them for breakfast, lunch and dinner.

Getting There & Away

The **Kawau Kat** (☎ 0800 888 006; adult/child one way $75/45) boat runs between central Auckland and Coromandel Town three times a week (trips take two hours). It's a good alternative to the bus.

InterCity (☎ 09-623 1503; www.intercitycoach.co.nz) runs daily buses to and from Thames ($16, one hour 45 minutes) and Whitianga ($18, one hour 20 minutes), which stop in the centre of town, while **Go Kiwi Shuttles** (☎ 0800 446 549, 07-866 0336; www.go-kiwi.co.nz) goes door-to-door and costs $25 for each route.

FAR NORTH COROMANDEL

The road north is sealed up to the tiny settlement of **Colville** (25km north of Coromandel Town), which is home to a few alternative lifestylers. There is a Buddhist retreat; the **Colville Café** (☎ 07-866 6690; 2312 Colville Rd; ☯ breakfast & lunch Mon-Sat, dinner Sat), which has excellent cakes and very good takeaways meals; and the quaint **Colville General Store** (☎ 07-566 6805; Colville Rd; ☯ 8.30am-5pm), which sells just about everything, including organic food and petrol (take note – it's the last stop before the cape).

North of Colville, the gravel roads are narrow but in reasonable condition. Heading north along the west coast takes you to **Fletcher Bay**, but a detour over the ranges goes to **Port Charles** where there are holiday baches (cottages) on a pleasant bay beach and then on to the aptly named **Stony Bay**, which has a DOC camp site (Map p208). From Stony Bay, hiking tracks lead north to Fletcher Bay and south to Mt Moehau (892m), the peninsula's highest peak.

Following the west coast road, 12km north of Colville is Te Hope, the start of the demanding eight-hour return hike to the top of Mt Moehau that rewards you with fine views of Coromandel and the Hauraki Gulf. The road stops at **Fletcher Bay**, which is a real land's end and a magical get-away-from-it-all place with deserted beaches, forest and coastal hikes and splendid views across to Great Barrier, Little Barrier and Cuvier Islands.

The **Coromandel Coastal Walkway** is a scenic three-hour (although four hours is a distinct possibility) hike between Fletcher Bay and Stony Bay. It's a relatively easy walk with great coastal views and an ambling section across open farmland. **Strongman Coaches/ Coromandel Coastal Walkway Tours** (☎ 07-866 8175) will drive you from Coromandel Town up to Fletcher Bay and pick you up from Stony Bay three or four hours later. The cost is $85.

Mahamudra Centre (☎ 07-866 6851; www.maha mudra.org.nz; dm/s/tw $20/30/35, huts $40) is a serene Buddhist retreat that has a stupa and a yoga and meditation hall. It offers simple but comfortable accommodation in a park-like setting, located 1km south of Colville. Buddhist teachers run courses, which are open to all.

The 1260-hectare **Colville Farm** (☎ 07-866 6820; 2140 Colville Rd; unpowered/powered sites per 2 people $14, campervan sites per 2 people $18, dm/s $18/21, d & tw $42, units $70-80) has interesting accommodation, and guests can milk cows by hand and try other types of farm work. Horse-riding tours are also on offer for a reasonable rate.

On a farm property on the tip of the peninsula, remote **Fletcher Bay Backpackers** (Map p208; ☎ 07-866 6712; js.lourie@xtra.co.nz; dm $15, powered sites per 2 people $26) is a quiet, comfortable and restful 16-bed cottage. There are four dorms with two double bunks (ie four spots) in each room. It has all facilities but you must bring food as there are no shops and no meals are provided. You can also experience back-to-basics camping here (ie no access to power or hot water, and only 'sunny dunnies') for a rock-bottom $9/4.50 per adult/child.

Very basic DOC **camp sites** (adult/child $9/4.50) are at Waikawau Bay and Stony Bay on the

eastern side of the peninsula, and at Fantail Bay, Port Jackson and Fletcher Bay, which can be reached from the west coast road (see Map p208 for camp sites). There is no road between Fletcher Bay and Stony Bay.

COROMANDEL TOWN TO WHITIANGA

There are two routes from Coromandel Town southeast to Whitianga. The main road is the slightly longer SH25, which follows the coast, enjoys sea views and has short detours to pristine sandy beaches. The other route is via the mainly gravel 309 Rd, which has some fine forest walks along the way.

State Highway 25

First stop on the SH25 east of Coromandel Town is Te Rerenga, almost on the shore of Whangapoua Harbour. The road forks at the harbour, and if you detour north you can visit Whangapoua, from where you can walk along the rocky foreshore to the isolated and often deserted **New Chum's Beach** (30 minutes).

Also at Te Rerenga is the **Castle Rock Winery** (☎ 07-866 4542; units $90-135; ☼ wine-tasting 10am-6pm daily Oct-Easter, 10am-4pm Tue-Sun Easter-Oct), which produces a range of fruit wines – try the feijoa. Platter lunches, jams, pickles and organic ale are also for sale.

Continuing east you soon reach **Kuaotunu**, a quaint settlement with a delightful beach and **Black Jack Backpackers** (☎ 07-866 2988; www .black-jack.co.nz; sites per 2 people $32, dm $24, d $65-85), which is quite smart, with sunny decks and free kayaks for paddling on the river. Meals are provided by arrangement.

Heading off the highway at Kuaotunu takes you to an even more remote area where **Otama Beach** and **Opito Bay** have some of the finest stretches of sand on the east coast. At the end of Opito Bay there's a walk up to a viewpoint on the headland.

309 Road

This is the shorter route to Whitianga (45 minutes, 26km), and the well-maintained gravel road is being sealed bit by bit. The **Waiau Waterworks** (Map p208; ☎ 07-866 7191; www .waiauwaterworks.co.nz; 471 309 Rd; adult/child $10/5; ☼ 9am-5pm), 5km from SH25, is a family theme park with whimsical water-powered amusements, a flying fox and a playground.

Forest walks along the 309 Rd include a two-hour return trail to the summit of **Castle Rock** (521m) and short walks to **Waiau Falls** and to a **kauri grove** (Map p208).

Bushcreek Cottage Backpackers (Map p208; ☎ 07-866 5151; 1694 309 Rd; www.bushcreek.co.nz; sites per 2 people $24, dm $19, d & tw $44, located about 10km from Whitianga, is a lovely 150-year-old kauri cottage beside a river with swimming holes (and the chance of tepee sleeping). It's a relaxing place surrounded by bush and an organic farm. Call before showing up – the business was for sale as we went to press.

WHITIANGA
pop 3580

The legendary Polynesian explorer and seafarer Kupe is said to have landed near here in about AD 800 and the area was called Te Whitianga a Kupe (the Crossing Place of Kupe). Whitianga is the main town on Mercury Bay. It's a popular resort with a harbour and plenty of marine activities such as scuba diving and kayaking around offshore islands, and on land, bone carving and horse riding. Nearby are two famous and fantastic natural attractions, Cathedral Cove and Hot Water Beach.

Information
Medical Centre (24hr number ☎ 07-866 5911; 87 Albert St; ☑ 8.30am-5pm Mon-Fri, 9-11am Sat & Sun, winter closed Sun)

Post office (72 Albert St)

Whitianga visitor information centre (☎ 07-866 5555; www.whitianga.co.nz; 66 Albert St; ☑ 9am-5pm Mon-Fri, to 4pm Sat & Sun) Well-organised centre; has Internet access for $9 per hour.

Sights & Activities
The **museum** (☎ 07-866 0730; 12 The Esplanade; adult/child $4/50c; ☑ 10am-4pm) has local history, nature displays and an interesting video about Maori and Pakeha views on Captain Cook.

Maurice Aukett of **Bay Carving** (☎ 07-866 4021; The Esplanade; ☑ 9am-4pm), next door to the museum, will help you create a high-quality Maori-style carving using a dentist drill and sandpaper. It takes about two to three hours, costs between $40 and $80 and is recommended. **Bone Studio** (☎ 07-866 2158; www.carving.co.nz; 6b Bryce St) also offers in-depth bone-carving tuition ($80 a day).

The **Cave Cruzer** (☎ 0800 427 893, 07-866 2275; www.cavecruzer.co.nz; 1-3hr trips $40-90) is a rigid-hull inflatable boat that offers trips around the caves and islands with snorkelling, fishing, music and commentary.

The **Blue Boat** (☎ 07-866 4904; adult/child $45/10) operates a two-hour trip to Cathedral Cove at 10am and 2pm. In summer it also runs at 5pm (minimum four adults).

Ocean Wave Tours (☎ 0800 806 060, 07-866 5555; www.oceanwave.co.nz; adult/child $55/35) runs scenic boat tours at 10am, 1pm and 3.30pm. Tours take 1½ to two hours.

Seafari Glass Bottom Boat (☎ 07-867 1962; www.glassbottomboatwhitianga.co.nz; adult/child $60/35) operates tours year-round. You can see what's under the water as well as the limestone coastal scenery. Three trips a day are offered in summer; snorkelling gear is available and bookings can be made at Whitianga visitor information centre.

Banana Boat (☎ 07-866 5617) has banana-boat rides from $10, but boats only operate between Boxing Day and the end of January.

Whitianga marina is a base for **game-fishing** (particularly marlin and tuna) between January and March, and boat charters start at around $900. Up to a dozen boats also run fishing trips. Game-fishing charters can easily set you back $2400 a day, while line-fishing costs about half that.

For horse trekking, the **Twin Oaks Riding Ranch** (☎ 07-866 5388; www.twinoaksridingranch.co.nz; 2hr adult/child $35/30) is 9km north of Whitianga on the Kuaotunu Rd.

Seafari Windsurfing (☎ 07-866 0677; Brophy's Beach, 4km north of Whitianga, hires out sailboards (from $25 per hour) and kayaks (from $10 per hour) and provides windsurfing lessons (from $40). Wet suits and life jackets are free with lessons.

Highzone (☎ /fax 07-866 2113; www.highzone.co.nz; 49 Kaimarama Rd; activities $15-60) offers high adventure on a ropes course, which involves various challenges 12m above ground level, including a leap onto a trapeze. It's located 7km south of Whitianga, just off the main road. Call for times.

Sleeping
BUDGET
On The Beach Backpackers Lodge (☎ 07-866 5380; www.coromandelbackpackers.com; 46 Buffalo Beach Rd; dm $24-25, d & tw $58, d & tw with bathroom $86) This large, bright-blue painted and well-run YHA-associate has plenty of rooms and space, and

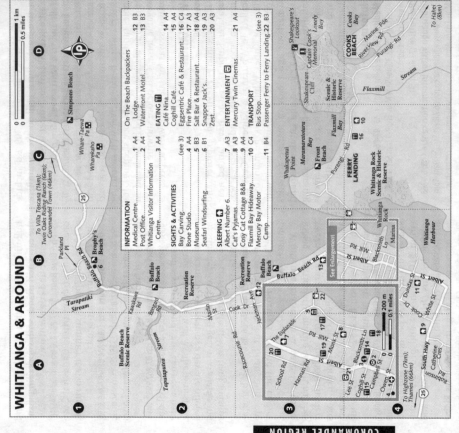

Book accommodation online at www.lonelyplanet.com

WHITIANGA & AROUND

INFORMATION
Medical Centre	1 A4
Post Office	2 A4
Whitianga Visitor Information Centre	3 A4

SIGHTS & ACTIVITIES
Bay Carving	(see 3)
Bone Studio	4 A4
Museum	5 B3
Seafari Windsurfing	6 B1

SLEEPING
Albert Number 6	7 A3
Cat's Pyjamas	8 A3
Cosy Cat Cottage B&B	9 C4
Flaxmill Bay Hideaway	10 C4
Mercury Bay Motor Camp	11 B4

EATING
On The Beach Backpackers Lodge	12 B3
Waterfront Motel	13 B3
Café Nina	14 A4
Coghill Café	15 A4
Eggsentric Café & Restaurant	16 C4
Fire Place	17 A3
Salt Bar & Restaurant	18 A4
Snapper Jack's	19 A3
Zest	20 A3

ENTERTAINMENT
Mercury Twin Cinemas	21 A4

TRANSPORT
Bus Stop	(see 3)
Passenger Ferry to Ferry Landing	22 B3

offers free kayaks, surfboards and spades (for digging a pool on Hot Water Beach) and bike hire, plus the chance to hear the waves of Mercury Bay as you drift off to sleep.

Cat's Pyjamas (07-866 4663; www.cats-pyjamas .co.nz; 4 Monk St; dm $20, sites per 2 people $24, d & tw $45, d & tw with bathroom $50) This small and bright backpackers with friendly hosts can arrange activities in the area with no hassles. It's a very quick hop, skip and jump from the town centre.

Mercury Bay Motor Camp (/fax 07-866 5579; 121 Albert St; unpowered/powered sites per 2 people $24/29, cabins $95, tourist flats $140;) This camp is small and shady with a spa, clean facilities and kayaks for hire at $10 a day. It scores

extra points for providing refuge for garden gnomes.

MIDRANGE

Cosy Cat Cottage B&B (07-866 4488; www.cosycat .co.nz; 41 South Hwy; s $55-75, d $85-105, units $90-160) This long-running place is indeed cosy and is crawling with images of cats. Run by a cat-lover who cares about her guests, this is a quaint, cheery place. If you are worried about kitty overload, the self-contained units are a little more restrained.

Albert Number 6 (07-866 0036; www.albert numbersix.co.nz; 6 Albert St; d & tw $85, tr $130) These smart modern units with colourful and stylish furnishings have no cooking facilities but there are plenty of nearby takeaways,

TOP END

Villa Toscana (☎ 07-866 2293; www.villatoscana.co.nz; Ohuka Park; d & tw Nov-Mar $720, Apr-Oct $440) Of the rash of nowhere-near-Chiantishire places that plonk the word 'Tuscany' in their names, this one actually gets away with it. Experience stylish luxury and gracious hosts at this palatial Italian-style hillside villa just north of town, with breathtaking views, a helipad, a hot spa and Italian antiques and wines. Kayaks and mountain bikes are available and the owners' game-fishing boat *Mamma Mia!* can be chartered ($900 per day).

Waterfront Motel (☎ 07-866 4498; www.waterfrontmotel.co.nz; 2 Buffalo Beach Rd; units 5225-360) This collection of holiday apartments has some sterling sunny views on offer. The apartments themselves are modern, clean, spacious and kitted out with everything you need, plus the building is very secure. Prices dive in the low season.

Eating

Café Nina (☑ breakfast, lunch & dinner Oct-Apr, breakfast & lunch May-Sep) This cool little spot, hidden from view by triffid-style foliage, is worth seeking out for barbecue breakfasts, an ever-changing lunch menu, afternoon tea and cakes, and dinner (summer only).

Coghill Café (☎ 07-866 0592; 10 Coghill St; meals $9-14; ☑ breakfast & lunch) This cool yet cosy café opens early and provides homemade snacks, giant pies, date scones, smoothies and meals like seafood chowder and pumpkin soup if you need warming up.

Snapper Jack's (☎ 07-866 5482; Albert St; meals $5-25; ☑ lunch & dinner) This popular fast-food outlet serves up fish or chicken and chips, takeaway or sit-down, and deserves at least one visit if you're hanging around town.

Salt Bar & Restaurant (☎ 07-866 5818; 1 Blacksmith Lane; mains $15-26; ☑ lunch & dinner) European and Thai dishes are served inside or on the terrace (easily the best seating in the house) overlooking the marina. The sports bar has live music and DJs on a regular basis.

Zest (☎ 07-866 5127; 5 Albert St; mains $16-26; ☑ dinner daily summer, Wed-Sun winter) Red-and-

orange-hued Zest offers a global-fusion menu and great desserts in a casually cool manner. It's a good spot to unwind.

Fire Place (☎ 07-866 4828; 9 The Esplanade; mains $21-29; ☑ lunch & dinner) The top place for pizzas and *nouvelle cuisine*, with geometric, smallish portions and delicate sauces, plus a very appealing atmosphere.

Stroll along the Esplanade for a string of popular steak and seafood restaurants that are especially appealing in the warmer months.

Entertainment

Mercury Twin Cinemas (☎ 07-866 1001; Lee St) Offers latest-release mainstream and independent films for when all the water sports start to pall.

Getting There & Around

Go Kiwi Shuttles (☎ 0800 446 549, 07-866 0336; www.go-kiwi.co.nz) has a daily shuttle bus from Whitianga to Thames ($30, 1½ hours), Coromandel Town ($25, 45 minutes) and Tairua ($20, 50 minutes). It also runs shuttle buses from Ferry Landing to Hahei and Hot Water Beach; see p220.

The InterCity (Auckland ☎ 09-623 1503) stops at the visitor information centre. Buses travel from Whitianga to Thames via Tairua ($33, 1½ hours).

Great Barrier Airlines (☎ 0800 900 600, Auckland 09-275 9120; www.greatbarrierairlines.co.nz; adult/child one way $99/65) operates flights five times a week between Auckland and Whitianga, and twice a week between Great Barrier Island and Whitianga (the cost is the same for both).

AROUND WHITIANGA

From the Narrows, on the southern end of Whitianga, a small passenger ferry crosses over to **Ferry Landing**, where there is a general store, a café, a motel and a B&B. From there you can travel by foot, bike or shuttle bus to Flaxmill Bay, Shakespeare's Lookout, Captain Cook's Memorial, Lonely Bay, Cooks Bay and further afield to Cathedral Cove, Hahei and Hot Water Beach.

The **passenger ferry** (adult one way $1.50, child or bicycle one way 80¢) takes five minutes, and runs continuously from 7am to 10.30pm in summer, and from 7am to 6.30pm, 7.30pm to 8.30pm and 9.30pm to 10.30pm in winter.

HAHEI

Hahei (www.hahei.co.nz) is a truly lovely white-sand beach with islands scattered out in the bay, and is 38km by road from Whitianga via Coroglen. The dramatic limestone coastline and small islands here make up the Te Whanganui a Hei Marine Reserve. Kayaking, snorkelling, diving and boat trips are all popular activities. It's a charming spot, and a great place to unwind for a few days, especially in the quieter months.

Sights & Activities

Just 1km north of Hahei is the car park for the 45-minute walk to the magnificent **Cathedral Cove** with its famous gigantic limestone arch. On the way you can visit the rocky cove at **Gemstone Bay**, which has an excellent snorkelling trail, and a sandy cove at **Stingray Bay**. It's a 70-minute walk along the coast from Hahei Beach to Cathedral Cove. At the southern end of Hahei Beach is a 20-minute walk up to an old Maori *pa* (fortified village), **Te Pare Point**, with splendid coastal views especially if you walk through the grass and look south.

Cathedral Cove Sea Kayaking (☎ 07-866 3877; www.seakayaktours.co.nz; 188 Hahei Beach Rd; half-day trips $70) has guided kayaking trips around the fascinating limestone arches, caves and islands in the Cathedral Cove area. The Remote Coast Tour heads the other way when conditions permit and is also highly recommended with caves, blowholes, a long tunnel and great limestone scenery. A free pick-up is available from Ferry Landing.

Hahei Explorer (☎ 07-866 3910; www.haheiexplorer.co.nz; Hahei Beach Rd; adult/child $55/35) is a rigid inflatable boat that makes daily hour-long scenic tours covering 14km.

Cathedral Cove Dive (☎ 07-866 3955; 3 Margaret Pl) has dives two or three times daily. Prices vary from $55 (own gear) to $85 (includes all gear). A Discover Scuba half-day course for first-timers is $150 and Professional Association of Diving Instructors (PADI) courses cost $500 including all the gear. Its shop in the shopping centre rents out scuba and snorkelling gear and boogie boards.

Snorkelling is best done in Gemstone Bay (on the walk to Cathedral Cove), which is a boulder beach but has a DOC snorkelling trail. You can hire snorkelling gear (including a wet suit) for about $45 a day. Big snapper, crayfish and stingrays can be seen in this protected marine reserve.

Sleeping

Hahei Holiday Resort (☎ 07-866 3889; www.haheiholidays.co.nz; Harsant Ave; unpowered sites per 2 people $26, powered sites per 2 people $28-32, cabins $45-99) Large and perfectly located on the pristine beachfront. The camping accommodation is good, but the cosy little cabins (get one with a kitchen if you can) are great for getaways.

Cathedral Cove Lodge Villas (☎ 07-866 3889; www.cathedralcove.co.nz; unit/villa $169/395) The sister business to Hahei Holiday Resort, this place will suit those travelling in a group (units sleep up to four people, villas up to six people).

Tatahi Lodge (☎ 07-866 3992; tatahi_lodge@xtra.co.nz; Grange Rd; dm $22-25, d & tw $55, studios/units/cottages $120/165/200) This tucked-away spot with lots of greenery and an alpine-chalet design is spotless and smart, plus it's next to the shops and cafés and some options have views. The dorm area is a real steal – good quality and a relaxing atmosphere.

Church (☎ 07-866 3533; www.thechurchhahei.co.nz; 87 Beach Rd; cottages $130-150) These beautifully kitted-out, self-contained timber cottages have stylish, tasteful and natural wood interiors in a photogenic garden setting. Smaller units ($110) have no kitchen but breakfast is included in the cost.

Eating

Grange Road Café (☎/fax 07-866 3502; 7 Grange Rd; dinner mains $20-30; ⏲ breakfast, lunch & dinner summer) The kitchen here turns out excellent and very different (for this part of the world) meals, such as Hungarian goulash or deep-fried tofu on soba noodles. There's a decent vegetarian selection and NZ wines and beers, as well as fresh juices. The café is open less frequently in winter. You might want to call ahead first.

Luna Café (☎ 07-866 3016; 1 Grange Rd; mains $13-26; ⏲ breakfast, lunch & dinner) This is another good restaurant-café (and BYO too) with a decent stack of well-thumbed women's weekly rags and mainly Mediterranean-style homemade food (including pretty decent pizzas). Luna is open less frequently in winter – it's best to call ahead.

Getting There & Around

If you don't have a car the easiest way to get from Whitianga to Hahei is by using the ferry

Book accommodation online at www.lonelyplanet.com

crossing at **Go Kiwi Shuttles** (☎ 0800 446 549, 07-866 0335; www.go-kiwi.co.nz) runs a bus three times daily from Ferry Landing to Cooks Beach ($6, 10 minutes), Hahei ($10, 35 minutes) and Hot Water Beach ($13, 45 minutes), with some services continuing to Dalmeny Corner on the highway for connections with buses to Auckland and Whitianga. Worth considering if you don't have your own transport is Go Kiwi's Eastern Beaches Tour, which (over four hours from Ferry Landing) takes in Cathedral Cove and Hot Water Beach (among others) for $35. You can pick up a timetable and make a booking at the Whitianga visitor information centre (p217).

HOT WATER BEACH

Just 9km south of Hahei is the famous Hot Water Beach, where thermal waters brew just below the sand in front of a rocky outcrop. You can join the crowd on the beach two hours each side of low tide, dig a hole in the sand with a spade, and then relax in your own natural spa pool as your bum gets roasted red. Spades can be hired for $4 ($20 deposit) from both the **Tarte Café**

AROUND HAHEI

On the way to Cooks Beach and Ferry Landing, taste wines made from kiwi fruit, feijoa and manuka honey at the endearingly New Age–looking **Purangi Winery** (Map p208; ☎ 07-866 3724; ☉ 10am–5pm). Excellent light meals are also available.

A little further on from Cooks Beach (which is itself 14km from Hahei) is what might well be NZ's most expensive camping option, the beautiful, exclusive (reservations essential) **Flaxmill Bay Hideaway** (Map p218; ☎ 07-866 2386; www.flaxmillbay.co.nz; 1019 Purangi Rd; unpowered/powered sites up to 6 people $85/95, cabins $95-195) and the too-cute-for-words **Eggsentric Café & Restaurant** (Map p218; ☎ 07-866 0307; 1047 Purangi Rd; dinner mains $26-29; ☉ lunch & dinner), which has an innovative menu, art seemingly everywhere, live music nightly and jam sessions on the first Sunday of the month from 3pm. A pick-up from Ferry Landing, 1.5km away, is usually possible.

The beguiling **Colenso Country Shop & Café** (Map p208; ☎ 07-866 3725; Whenuakite; snacks under $12) has myriad treats like scones, cakes and light snacks, and a sweet atmosphere. It's on the main highway to Tairua, just before the Hot Water Beach turn-off.

(☎ 07-866 3006; ☉ 9am–5pm winter, 9am–7pm summer) and the wonderful, stylish-looking **Hot Waves Café** (☎ 07-866 3887; 8 Pye Pl; meals $9-15; ☉ breakfast & lunch), which has fantastic fry-ups at breakfast and the odd dose of laid-back live music on weekends. See the boxed text (above) about the hidden dangers of swimming at this beach.

Opposite the Tarte Café, the stylish **Moko** (☎ 07-866 3367; www.moko.co.nz; 24 Pye Pl) has modernist Pacific Rim décor and an art gallery out the back, which stocks great special souvenirs of your time here.

Auntie Dawn's Place (☎ 07-866 3707; www.auntiedawn.co.nz; 15 Radar Rd; un ts $110-125) is a comfortable, spacious and homely place to stay with a big garden that includes ancient pohutukawa trees. Breakfast fixings and potent home-brewed beer are supplied. Backpacker beds are available in garden huts in summer ($25 per person).

A nice luxury-style pad, just up the road from the Tarte Café, is **Hot Water Beach B&B** (☎ 07-866 3991; www.hctwaterbedandbreakfast.co.nz; 48 Pye Pl; s/d $180/200), which has priceless views, a spa bath on the deck and attractive living quarters.

TAIRUA

pop 1566

Tairua is a small town on an estuary, with cafés, restaurants, water sports, walks and some good accommodation. Pauanui is its twin town on the other side of the harbour – Tairua is definitely the more appealing of the two.

Information

Tairua Video (☎ 07-864 8170; 228 Main Rd) Over the road from the visitor information centre; has Internet access.
Tairua visitor information centre (☎ 07-864 7575; www.tairua.info; 223 Main Rd; ☉ 9am–5pm Oct–May, 9am–4pm Jun–Sep) Superfriendly and helpful.

GETTING YOURSELF INTO HOT WATER...

Hot Water Beach has dangerous currents (also known as r ps or undertows) year-round. It's one of the four most dangerous beaches in NZ in terms of drowning numbers. Swimming t ere is not safe, so restrict your activities to burning your bum in a self-built hot-water pool in the sand.

Sights & Activities

Tairua Dive & Fishinn (☎ 07-864 8054; www.divetairua.co.nz; Paku Boat Ramp; ⏱ 8am-5pm) hires out sailboards, sailing boats, dinghies and kayaks as well as scuba, snorkel and fishing gear. The company also runs dive trips out to the Aldermen Islands (dive and full gear \$175, trip only \$95, snorkelling \$75) and PADI courses (\$475). Come December, they also run a **dive festival** – check it out at www.divefestival.co.nz.

A popular walk is the climb up **Paku**, an old *pa* site, which takes 30 minutes from the Esplanade and provides 360-degree views. If you climb Paku, legend has it that you will return in seven years.

For nature and wilderness walks in this area, **Kiwi Dundee Adventures** (☎ 07-865 8809; www.kiwidundee.co.nz) has built up quite a reputation (and a good one at that) over the years. Guide Doug Johansen has been called NZ's answer to Crocodile Dundee, and he'll lead you on informative day-long adventure walks.

Sleeping

Tairua Beach Villa Backpackers (☎ 07-864 8345; tairuabackpackers@xtra.co.nz; 200 Main Rd; unpowered sites per 2 people \$30, dm/s \$22/37, d & tw \$52) This is a fantastic backpackers in a beautiful garden setting just south of the town centre, and the gregarious owner works hard to keep everyone happy – and pulls it off. Rooms are homey and casual, while the dorm scores great views. Guests can help themselves to avocados, feijoas, eggs, fishing rods, kayaks, sailboards and bikes, and windsurfing lessons cost a paltry \$20. Note there's another business with a similar name; coming from the north you want to head over the bridge just past town.

Pinnacles Backpackers (☎ 07-864 8448; flying.dutchman.bp@xtra.co.nz; 305 Main Rd; sites per 2 people \$26, dm \$23, tw & d \$56) North of the town centre, this place has bright rooms, a balcony, a free pool table, and bikes for hire.

Dell Cote (☎ 07-864 8142; www.dellcote.co.nz; Rewarewa Valley Rd; d \$180) You'll not have a more politically correct sleep than at this excellent and interesting option, where the organic-style buildings feature all nontoxic materials, and there's fantastic bushland. If you're worried that this means it's daggy looking then fear not – this place is mighty attractive.

Pacific Harbour Lodge (☎ 07-864 8581; www.pacificharbour.co.nz; Main Rd; s \$100-180, d \$120-185) This very attractive 'island-style' resort in the town centre has great, spacious chalets with natural wood and Gauguin décor inside and a South Seas garden outside. The 20-plus years of hard work that the owners have put into the place is evident and has really paid off. The Shells restaurant is part of the complex.

Harbourview (☎ 07-864 7040; www.harbourviewlodge.co.nz; 179 Main Rd; s/d \$150/175; ▨) This immaculate guesthouse has stylish, very comfortable rooms (and excellent beds) with bathroom, a lounge area and some fine views. It's well located and exudes a sense of ease.

Eating & Drinking

Shells Restaurant & Bar (☎ 07-864 8811; Main Rd; mains \$21-29; ⏱ dinner daily Oct-Apr, Tue-Sat May-Sep) Next to the Pacific Harbour Lodge, this place offers shipshape dining with tables decorated with said shells for effect. The food is modern NZ-ish (and not all of it seafood as you might expect) and definitely recommended.

Out of the Blue Café (☎ 07-864 8987; 227 Main Rd; meals \$9-17; ⏱ breakfast & lunch) This popular meeting place serves decent coffee, breakfast, deli snacks and light meals such as a lovely smoked salad and fat sandwiches.

Tairua Landing Bar & Café (☎ 07-864 7774; 222 Main Rd; meals \$13-25; ⏱ breakfast, lunch & dinner) This good establishment offers decent snacks and meals indoors or in a pleasant outdoor area that overlooks the estuary.

Punters Café & Bar (☎ 07-864 9370; Main Rd; mains \$12-25; ⏱ lunch & dinner) This is primarily a pub-bar but it also serves snacks and highly regarded grills, and locals will no doubt tell you that a 'real chef is in the kitchen, hence the crunchy *panini* slices with dips to start.

About 2km from the town centre along the estuary is the Paku Boat Ramp, where there are a couple of restaurants. The **Upper Deck Restaurant & Bar** (☎ 07-864 7499; mains \$19-27; ⏱ dinner daily), in the grounded *SS Ngotrio*, is an almost-floating restaurant in a former Auckland steamer ferry and an atmospheric place for a meal or a drink with occasional live entertainment in summer. A children's menu makes it popular with families.

OPOUTERE BEACH

Just 4km off the main road is the car park for the 15-minute walk to the long, unspoilt and sandy Opoutere Beach, but swimming is dangerous, especially near Hikinui islet, which is close to the beach. On the sand spit is the **Wharekawa Wildlife Refuge**, a breeding ground for the endangered NZ dotterel. Lots of other birds can be seen in this unpopulated area.

Opoutere YHA (☎ 07-865 9072; www.yha.co.nz; unpowered sites per 2 people $24, dm $20-23, d & tw $54-76), located just before the car park, has good, comfortable rooms in a wonderful get-away-from-it-all bush setting that is full of birdsong. Kayaks, hot-water bottles, alarm clocks, stilts and Hula Hoops can all be borrowed. You can harvest shellfish from the beach but other food you'll need to bring with you as there are no shops here.

Slipper Island

Off the coast, the privately owned **Slipper Island** (☎ 07-864 7560; www.slipper.co.nz) has camp sites ($15 per person) in South Bay and chalet accommodation (self-contained units $1000 to $1500 per week) in Home Bay. It's a beautiful little retreat, but the problem is actually getting out there; check with the Tairua visitor information centre (p221) about boat trips to the island.

AROUND TAIRUA

Puketui Valley

Located about 12km south of Tairua is the turn-off to Puketui Valley and the historical **Broken Hills gold-mine workings** (Map p208), which are 8km from the main road along a mainly gravel road. There are short walks up to the sites of stamper batteries, but the best hike is through the 500m-long Collins Drive (mine tunnel). It takes between two and three hours return; remember to take a torch and a jacket with you. This is a wilderness area so take care and be properly prepared. Water from the river should be boiled before drinking. It's hard to imagine that two hundred miners were living in this area a century ago.

WHANGAMATA

pop 3880

Whangamata (pro¬nounced fa-nga-ma-ta) has a great 4km-long surf beach with an excellent break by the bar. It attracts a big influx of surfers and NZ family holidaymakers in December and January, but it's usually quiet the rest of the year. That said, we did notice a fair bit of construction going on around town, plus the installation of traffic lights, meaning that this town's near-perfect holiday qualities could be slowly disappearing.

Information

Bartley Internet & Graphics (☎ 07-865 8832; Port Rd) Has Internet access.

Whangamata visitor information centre (☎ 07-865 8340; www.whangamatainfo.co.nz; 616 Port Rd; ☉ 9am-5pm Mon-Sat, to 2pm Sun)

Activities

Besides surfing, kayaking, fishing (game-fishing runs from January to April), snorkelling near Hauturu (Clarke) Island, orienteering and mountain biking, there are excellent walks. The **Wentworth Falls walk** takes 1½ hours one way and starts 3km south of the town and 4km down a good gravel road.

Sleeping

DOC camping ground (☎ 07-865 7032; adult/child $9/4.50) This camping ground has toilets, hot showers and gas barbecues.

Garden Lodge (☎ 07-865 9574; www.gardenlodge .whangamata.co.nz; cnr Port Rd & Mayfair Ave; lodges $55, studios $110-130) This hard-to-miss, corner-hogging, bright-green complex is in a garden setting north of the town centre and has clean, spacious and modern accommodation to suit just about everyone. It also provides boogie boards and fishing gear.

Blake Court Motel (☎ 07-865 7958; www.blake court.co.nz; 310 Port Rd; d $140-200) The Blake Court is a good example of the NZ motel/motor inn, with reasonably attractive, superbly tidy rooms and friendly management. Little

Getting There & Away

InterCity (Auckland ☎ 09-623 1503; www.intercitycoach .co.nz) charges $17 to travel from Whitianga (one hour); while **Go Kiwi Shuttles** (☎ 0800 446 549, 07-866 0336; www.go-kiwi.co.nz) charges $20.

kitchenettes come into their own during the quiet months, when it seems hard to find an open eatery.

Copsefield B&B (☎ 07-865 9555; www.copsefield .co.nz; 1055 SH25; s/d $130/180) This peaceful country-style villa with kind hosts and en suite rooms is 8km north of Whangamata and set in attractive, lush garden with a sense of space. If you require privacy, book the cottage, which sleeps four and costs a bargain $100 a night.

Windsong (☎ 07-865 9995; www.whangamatabeach .co.nz; 305 Winifred Ave; bach $600) This perfectly positioned fibro bach has two comfortable bedrooms, a smart interior and glorious uninterrupted views that might just break your heart. Low season rates plummet to around $120 a night.

Eating & Drinking

Caffe Rossini (☎ 07-865 6117; 646 Port Rd; dinner mains $19-31; breakfast & lunch daily Oct-Apr, Fri-Mon May-Sep, dinner Thu-Tue year-round) Very good dishes, including juicy cuts of steak and the ubiquitous fish of the day (fish of the century?) – terakihi.

Oceana's (☎ 07-865 7157; 328 Ocean Rd; mains $28-31; dinner, closed Sun & Mon winter) The town's main 'sense of occasion' restaurant specialises in well-executed seafood entrées and mains and the odd venison dish. It has outdoor seating.

Vibes Café (☎ 07-865 8494; 636 Port Rd; mains $9-17; breakfast & lunch) Vibes has good espresso and hearty food (such as wholemeal spinach and feta quiche with salad) that does a good job of lining your insides after a surf.

Craig's Traditional Fish & Chips (☎ 07-865 8717; 710 Port Rd; fish meals $10; lunch Fri & Sat, dinner daily) It's worth popping into Whangamata just to get dinner from the best little fish and chipper in the Coromandel. And judging by the numbers (especially on a Friday), the secret has been well and truly out for some time. Fabulous pieces of grilled fish and fat, salted chips, with all the trimmings you could hope for (the tartare sauce is a winner), plus friendly service and a stack of trashy mags to speed up the wait. Craig's is a slice of holiday-town nostalgia – and long may it reign.

Coast (☎ 07-865 6999; 501 Port Rd; 5pm-late Mon-Sat Oct-Apr) This smart bar-cum-restaurant does a roaring trade come the summer season (it hibernates in winter).

The new monster-sized **New World** (300 Aicken St; 8am-8pm) will take care of the grocery needs of self-caterers.

Getting There & Away

Go Kiwi Shuttles (☎ 0800 446 549, 07-866 0336; www .go-kiwi.co.nz) charges $29 between Whangamata and Whitianga (1½ hours).

WAIHI
pop 4700

Gold was first discovered here in 1878 and the Martha Mine became the richest in NZ. After closing down in 1952, open-cast mining restarted in 1988. The mine is still (but only just) producing gold (it takes a ton of rock to yield 3g to 6g of gold), and it will run out some time while this book is in print. A new underground mine was being built at the time of research and big plans were afoot to turn the old one into a tourist attraction of sorts, although developments were very much in the far-off phase.

Information

Waihi visitor information centre (☎ 07-863 6715; Seddon St; 9am-5pm Oct-Apr, 9am-4.30pm May-Sep) Bend-over-backwards helpful.

Sights & Activities

Martha Gold-mine Tours (☎ 07-863 9880; tours adult/child $5/2; 10am & 1.30pm Mon-Fri) last 1½ hours (bookings essential). Find out how a mine is run and then compare it to the old days by taking the vintage-train ride to Waikino.

You can see the 200m-deep hole that is Martha Mine from a **lookout** in Moresby Ave near the Waihi visitor information centre.

The **Goldfields Vintage Train** (☎ 07-863 8251; www.goldfieldsrailway.org.nz; adult/child return $12/6) is run by volunteers. The train leaves Waihi Station, in Wrigley St, daily at 11am, 12.30pm, 1.15pm and 2.00pm. The 7km-long scenic journey takes 25 minutes. See p226 for some interesting hikes around Waikino.

Waihi Arts Centre & Museum (☎ 07-863 8386; 54 Kenny St; adult/child $5/2; 10am-4pm Mon-Fri, 1.30-4pm Sun) features displays and models of the region's gold-mining history.

Mathers Rd Mountain Bike Track

(☎ 07-863 8218; Mathers Rd; entry from $15) is a rugged cross-country track which cuts through farmland and forest and affords the odd sea view (if you can manage a glimpse).

Sleeping

Waihi Motor Camp (☎ 07-863 7654; www.waihimotor camp.co.nz; 6 Walmsley Rd; unpowered/powered sites per 2 people $24/25; dm $20, cabins $45-75, units $85) Cute cabins and well-looked-after facilities make this a nifty budget choice. The site itself is well shaded (verdant even) and close to both the beach and Karangahake Gorge.

Westwind B&B (☎ 07-863 7208; westwindgarden@xtra.co.nz; 58 Adams St; s/d $40/75) On the way to Tauranga, this guesthouse has a nice garden and good $20 dinners for guests. Breakfast is included.

Goldmine Motel (☎ 07-863 7111; fax 07-863 3084; 6 Victoria St; s/d $80/95) The pick of Waihi's motels, it's near the railway station, has relatively new facilities (with an indoor spa and air conditioning in all rooms) and a good reputation.

Eating

Farmhouse Café (☎ 07-863 7649; 14 Hazard St; mains $12-16; ☑ breakfast & lunch daily, dinner Fri & Sat) This attractive yellow café has a relaxing garden area, a blackboard menu, local wines and some gluten-free goodies.

Chambers Wine Bar & Restaurant (☎ 07-863 7474; 22 Hazard St; mains $20-27; ☑ lunch & dinner) This restaurant in a heritage building offers a fairly comprehensive dinner menu, good lunch meals and bar snacks.

Getting There & Away

Lots of buses come in and out of this transport hub, and they stop outside the BP petrol station in Rosemount Rd. **InterCity** (Auckland ☎ 09-623 1503; www.intercitycoach.co.nz) and **Go Kiwi Shuttles** (☎ 0800 446 549, 07-866 0336; www.go-kiwi.co.nz) run buses from Waihi to Whitianga ($32, two hours 10 minutes) via Whangamata. Long-distance buses and shuttles go to Tauranga and Rotorua.

WAIHI BEACH

pop 1700

Just 11km east of Waihi, the 9km-long sandy Waihi Beach is lined with holiday homes. The shopping area in Wilson Rd includes the usual line-up of holiday-town essentials (supermarket, chemist, cafés etc). There are ocean surfing beaches and sheltered harbour beaches such as beautiful Anzac Bay beyond Bowentown. A very popular 45-minute walk is north through bush to pristine Orokawa Bay, which has no road access.

Boating and game-fishing are popular, and out to sea is Tuhua (Mayor) Island with its Blue and Green crater lakes (see p357); contact **Waihi Beach Boat Charter** (☎ 07-863 5385) if you want to visit.

Another 8km south is **Athenree Hot Springs** (☎ 07-863 5600; adult/child $5.50/3.50; ☑ 10am-7.30pm) with two bubbling and clean outdoor hot pools. Stay in the **holiday park** (☎ 07-863 5600; unpowered/powered sites per 2 people $30/40, units/chalets $90/110) and entry to the hot pools is free.

There are holiday parks at Waihi Beach as well as lots of B&Bs. Turn left when you reach the sea and go to the end of the road for **Waihi Beach Top 10 Holiday Park** (☎ 07-863 5509; www.waihibeach.com; 15 Main Rd; unpowered/powered sites per 2 people $30/42.50, cabins $50-105, units $90-180) a large, clean and modern camping ground with a wide range of good accommodation. Kayaks, surfboards, boogie boards, bikes and even baby-sitters can be hired here.

Beachfront B&B (☎ 07-863 5393; mortons_garage@xtra.co.nz; 3 Shaw Rd; d $100) is true to its name, with absolute beachfront and attractive sea views. The tastefully furnished rooms have TV and the usual modest facilities.

The Porch (☎ 07-863 1330; 23 Wilson Rd; mains $20-25; ☑ breakfast, lunch & dinner) is a trendy-looking spot and the town's coolest chow-down – with slow-braised pork belly or loin of lamb with roasted veg competing for diners' affections. Dinner reservations are a good idea.

Cactus Jacks (☎ 07-863 5160; 31 Wilson Rd; mains $12-18) is a crazy BYO mélange of Tex-Mex style that serves steaks, chicken, seafood and something called the 'siesta burger' in sizable portions.

HAURAKI REGION

The big drawcards on the mainly pancake-flat Hauraki Plains are the superb bird-watching at Miranda and the hot springs at Miranda and Te Aroha. Beyond the collection of antique shops in Paeroa is the historic and scenic Karangahake Gorge, with hikes around derelict gold-mine workings.

MIRANDA

Avid bird-watchers love this area – one of the most accessible for studying waders or shore birds all year round. It is 11km from Waitakaruru and the Thames–Pokeno road, and just an hour's drive from Auckland. The vast mud flat on the western side of the Firth of Thames is teeming with aquatic worms and crustaceans, which attract thousands of Arctic-nesting shore birds over the winter; 43 species of wader have been spotted here. The two main species that can be seen are the bar-tailed godwit and the lesser or red knot, but it isn't unusual to see turnstones, sandpipers and the odd vagrant red-necked stint. Internal migrants include the pied oystercatcher and the threatened wrybill from the South Island, and banded dotterels and pied stilts from both main islands.

The **Miranda Shorebird Centre** (Map p208; ☎ 09-232 2781; www.miranda-shorebird.org.nz; 283 East Coast Rd; dm/d members $13/40, nonmembers $18/50; ☼ centre 9am-5pm) offers basic but clean accommodation with a kitchen. The centre also has displays on the bird life, hires out binoculars and sells useful $2 pamphlets on birds you can see. Nearby is a bird-watching hide and there are walks that take from half an hour to two hours.

Five kilometres south of Miranda Shorebird Centre is **Miranda Hot Springs** (Map p208; ☎ 07-867 3055; Front Miranda Rd; adult/child $10/7; ☼ 8am-9.30pm), which has a large hot-spring swimming pool, a superhot sauna pool, and private spa tubs ($7 extra).

Next door is **Miranda Holiday Park** (Map p208; ☎ 07-867 3205; www.mirandaholidaypark.co.nz; sites per 2 people $32, cabins/units $58/120), which has excellent, sparkling clean and newish units and facilities with its own hot-spring pool and floodlit tennis court.

PAEROA
pop 4000

According to the signs, 'All Roads Lead to Paeroa', not Rome, so you may as well use this as an opportunity to succumb to the town's most famous product. The town was the birthplace of Lemon & Paeroa (L&P), the soft drink that describes itself as 'World

famous in NZ' (it would appear that the town's sign-writers are either delightfully tongue-in-cheek or painfully swollen with civic pride). Two giant L&P bottles are reminders that it was produced here from 1907 until 1980 when production was moved to Auckland.

The **information centre** (☎/fax 07-862 8636; www.hauraki-dc.govt.nz; 17 Belmont Rd; ☼ 9am-5pm daily Dec-Feb, 9am-5pm Mon-Fri & 10am-3pm Sat & Sun Mar-Nov) is to the north of the town.

The small **museum** (☎ 07-862 8942; 37 Belmont Rd; adult/child $2/1; ☼ 10.30am-3pm Mon-Fri) has a splendid selection of Royal Albert porcelain and other pioneer and Maori artefacts – look in the drawers.

The town is a well-known stop on the antiques and secondhand trail, and if you're after this sort of thing you should pick up the brochure (from the information centre) that lists the businesses that cater to this market.

Casa Mexicana (☎ 07-862 8216; casa.mexicana@wave.co.nz; 71 Puke Rd; d $80), just north of town, has obliging owners, and represents very good value for money, with attractive, straightforward rooms with all the mod cons you'd expect.

Lazy Fish (☎ 07-862 2822; 56 Belmont Rd; mains $19-29; ☼ breakfast, lunch & dinner daily summer, Wed-Sun winter) is the best eating choice in town and has a tempting menu featuring international cuisine, with very good Mediterranean-style options, in the centre of town.

World Famous in NZ Café (☎ 07-862 7773; SH2; dinner mains $17-28; ☼ breakfast, lunch & dinner), opposite the information centre, serves a wide range of food, plus L&P ice cream, L&P muffins and L&P cheesecake. And, we swear, the toilets seem to be L&P scented.

Karangahake Gorge

The very worthwhile 4.5km **Karangahake Gorge Historic Walkway** (Map p208) takes 1½ hours and starts from the car park, 8km east of Paeroa. It follows the disused railway line and the Ohinemuri River to Owharoa Falls and Waikino Station, from where a veteran train runs to Waihi four times a day. The **Waikino Station Café** (☎ 07-863 8640; ☼ breakfast & lunch, snacks till 4pm) is a perfect lunch and snack stop before heading back.

A shorter walk from the car park takes only an hour and crosses two bridges before following the boulder-strewn river for

20 minutes. Then turn left over another bridge and through a long tunnel where a torch is useful but not necessary. The track then loops back to the car park and the cheery **Talisman Café** (9am-5pm).

The huge **Victoria Battery**, a five-minute walk from Waikino Station, operated from 1896 to 1952. You can see eight large kilns and other gold-mining relics.

Ohinemuri Estate Winery & Café (Map p208; ☎ 07-862 8874; Moresby St; lunch mains $9-19; winery 10am-5pm Oct-Apr, 10am-5pm Fri-Sun May-Sep) is a lovely spot with free wine tasting (and excellent meals), just off the main road at Karangahake. If you imbibe too much, snaffle a chalet-style hut and revel in the cosy atmosphere of this charming place (units $100).

TE AROHA

pop 3800

Te Aroha, 21km south of Paeroa and 55km northeast of Hamilton on SH26, is nestled at the foot of bush-clad 952m-high Mt Te Aroha (literally 'the love') and practically screams 'Tidy Town Winner'. It's a sweet spot, with friendly residents and makes a good base for the area. Another natural attraction is the town's therapeutic hot springs, which have a high soda content and have attracted splashers since the late 19th century.

Information

Te Aroha visitor information centre (☎ 07-884 8052; www.te-aroha.com; 102 Whitaker St; 9am-5pm Mon-Fri, 10am-3pm Sat & Sun) Delightfully friendly and helpful.

Sights & Activities

At the top of the domain behind the visitor information centre is the **Hot Spring Spa Pools** (☎ 07-884 8717; www.tearohapools.co.nz; 30min sessions weekday/weekend $10/15; 10am-10pm), which offers great private tubs and aromatherapy and the world's only soda spa geyser. Children are half-price and booking is recommended. Nearby is **Mokena Geyser**, which shoots 3m in the air every 40 minutes or so, but it can be temperamental.

Lower down the domain is the outdoor **Wyborn Leisure Pool** (☎ 07-884 4498; adult/child $5/3; 11am-7pm), which is heated but uses ordinary water. Next to it is the indoor **Hot Spa No 2** ($1 extra), a natural spa with hot water and bubbles rising directly from a spring. A **drinking fountain** has warm, soapy water that tastes better cold and mixed with whisky. It's good for constipation however you drink it.

The **museum** (☎ 07-884 4427; admission by donation; 11am-4pm Dec-Apr, 11am-4pm Mon-Fri & 1-4pm Sat & Sun May-Nov) is in a converted bathhouse on the domain. More interesting than most, the displays include souvenir ceramics.

Fans of quilting will definitely benefit from a visit to the **Post Office Quilt & Textile Gallery** (☎ 07-884 8222; 111 Whitaker St; 10am-4.30pm Tue-Sun), where the deft work of nimble, creative fingers is on display.

The **hiking** trails up Mt Te Aroha start at the top of the domain. It takes an hour to climb up to the **Bald Spur/Whakapipi Lookout** (350m). Then it's another 2.7km or two hours climbing to the summit.

An easier one-hour hike (4km but flat) is around the **Howarth Wetlands Reserve**, which attracts plenty of birds, and is reached from the southern part of the town.

Sleeping

Te Aroha Holiday Park (☎ 07-884 9567; marta@xtra.co.nz; 217 Stanley Rd; sites per 2 people $10, cabins $25-40;) Wake up to a bird orchestra in the large oak trees at this gym-equipped site, 3km southwest of town. The pricing options are mind-boggling, so if you feel like haggling, you may as well.

Te Aroha YHA (☎ 07-884 8739; tearoha.yha@xtra.co.nz; Miro St; dm/d $2(/45) This unusual but long-running hostel is a cosy, TV-free, three-bedroom cottage with a homely atmosphere and welcoming management. Free mountain bikes are available and a 10km mountain-bike track starts at the back door.

Te Aroha Motel (☎ 07-884 9417; tearohamotel@xtra.co.nz; 108 Whitaker St; s/d $65/85) This collection of a dozen reasonably priced, welcoming and tidy units puts you in the centre of town, and the owners leave lollies on your pillows.

Aroha Mountain Lodge B&B (☎ 07-884 8134; www.arohamountainlodge.co.nz; 5 Boundary St; s/d $115/155) This handsome, upmarket spot is a great escape destination for many Aucklanders. The new Strathern Wing is a brilliant bargain option – attractive décor, with-it management and rock-bottom rates ($80).

Eating

Banco (☎ 07-884 7574; 174 Whitaker St; mains $19-27; ⊙ lunch Tue-Sun, dinner Thu-Sun) Housed in a big, red, former bank building, this is the pick of the bunch when it comes to eating out in Te Aroha. The menu is both inventive and comforting, the décor imaginative and the service sweeter than sweet.

Ironique Café, Restaurant & Bar (☎ 07-884 8489; 159 Whitaker St; lunch mains $12, dinner mains $14-29; ⊙ lunch & dinner) This slightly retro café with décor of ironwork and totara wood serves decent food and big coffees that help to fuel a tramping session.

Getting There & Away

Turley-Murphy Buses (☎ 07-884 8208) has services from Thames to Te Aroha ($14, one hour 20 minutes) and from Te Aroha to Hamilton ($8, one hour 10 minutes).

Waikato & the King Country

Postcard-perfect rural New Zealand comes to life in this lush, well-hydrated and verdant region, where pastoral landscapes of grazing cattle, sheep, deer and horses greet you at every bend in the road. It's a pretty and bucolic vision of what could be yesteryear, or indeed, another world, so it's no surprise that Peter Jackson chose a farm here as the site to re-create the rustic paradise of Hobbiton village in his *Lord of the Rings* trilogy. The area's prosperity is the gift of the mighty 420km Waikato River, which flows from Lake Taupo to Port Waikato on the west coast. It still rolls on despite the eight hydroelectric dams that do their best to impede its flow.

The orderliness of the tamed landscape is reflected in its major city, Hamilton, the country's largest inland city and the 'capital of nice' with its careful town planning, lively student population, manicured civic attractions and caffeinated main street.

Adrenaline is the heart-starter of choice further south in Waitomo, where you can abseil underground and explore or float along dark limestone caves and tunnels decorated by starry glow-worms. At the country's top rock-climbing site at Wharepapa South you can cling to rocky cliffs by your fingertips. Surfers travel thousands of kilometres to laid-back Raglan on the west coast to ride its world-famous left-hand break, and excellent surfing instruction is available.

To visit quaint remote communities and for more of a wilderness experience, follow the little-used roads to Kawhia Harbour or Marokopa, both tiny outposts in a natural wonderland.

HIGHLIGHTS

- Getting extreme and going underground at **Waitomo** (p248)
- Experiencing your own *Endless Summer* at **Raglan** (p237)
- Taking advantage of remote beaches such as **Mokau** (p254) and **Marokopa** (p253), and the underrated hot-water beach near **Kawhia** (p241)
- Hobbit-spotting at abandoned Hobbiton, outside **Matamata** (p245)
- Horsing around in equine-crazy **Cambridge** (p243)
- Getting up close and personal with an adorable kiwi in **Otorohanga** (p247)
- Going gourmet in the laid-back, riverside city of **Hamilton** (p232), with its pretty gardens and student social life

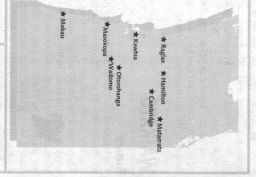

TELEPHONE CODE: 07 ■ www.waikatonz.co.nz ■ www.kingcountry.co.nz

peans' pressure to purchase Maori land for settlement. By the early 1860s the Waikato Maori had formed a 'King Movement' (see p233) and united to elect a king. In July 1863 the Europeans sent soldiers on gunboats and small craft up the Waikato River to put down what they regarded as the open rebellion of the King Movement. After almost a year of battles and skirmishes, known as the Waikato Land War, the Kingites retreated south in 1864 to what became known as the King Country. Europeans dared not venture there for several decades and even today Maori influence is stronger there than elsewhere in the country.

AUCKLAND TO HAMILTON

The trip to Hamilton by road from Auckland takes about 1½ hours and there are a few points of interest along the way. Steam-train enthusiasts can detour to the **Glenbrook Vintage Railway** (09-236 3456; adult/child $12/6; 11am-4pm Sun & public holidays Oct-Jun) for a 12km steam-train ride. To get there leave the Southern Motorway at Drury, 31km south of Auckland, and follow the yellow signs west towards Waiuku.

Cooks Landing (07-826 0004; www.cookslanding .co.nz; Paddy Rd; lunch mains $13-17; 10am-4pm daily, dinner Fri-Sun) is on State Highway 1 (SH1), 67km south of Auckland, and has free wine tasting. Buy a bottle and enjoy it with a meat, seafood or cheese platter overlooking the vineyard.

A few kilometres south at Rangiriri, on SH1, the **Rangiriri Battle Site Heritage Centre** (07-826 3663; Talbot St; 9am-3pm) has displays about this decisive battle between

---

Climate

The southern area around Taumarunui is wetter and colder than the rest of the region, which can suffer summer droughts.

Getting There & Around

Hamilton is the transport hub and Inter-City buses link the city with Auckland and south to Te Awamutu, Otorohanga, Waitomo Caves, Te Kuiti, Taumarunui, Mokau and on to New Plymouth and Wanganui. Other bus services go from Hamilton to Cambridge, Matamata, Thames, Tauranga, Rotorua and Lake Taupo.

The Waitomo Wanderer links Rotorua, Waitomo Caves and Wharepapa, a rock-climbing Mecca. Other buses run to Raglan and Kawhia.

Trains are another option but they are infrequent. Hamilton's airport has flights to domestic destinations and Australia.

WAIKATO

History

The banks of the Waikato River were planted by the Maoris in pre-European times with kumara (sweet potatoes) and other crops. There was a *pa* (Maori village) and a chief at every bend of the river. In the 1830s missionaries introduced European crops and farming methods to Waikato, and by the 1840s Maoris were trading their agricultural produce with European settlers in Auckland.

Relations between the two cultures soured during the 1850s, largely due to the Euro-

---

TOP ACTIVITIES

- Enjoy subterranean rafting and glow-worm caves at Waitomo (p250)
- Climb in the saddle in the home of champions: Cambridge (p244)
- Learn to surf in Raglan (p238)
- Scale a rock face at Wharepapa South (p243)
- Tell someone in Te Awamutu (see the boxed text, p242) that you don't think much of Split Enz...then run for your life

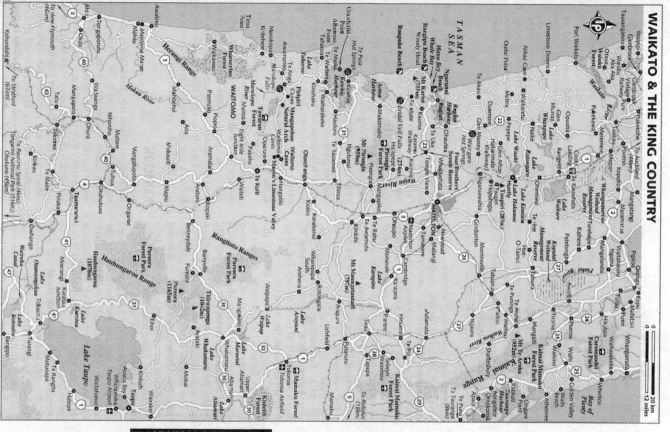

MAORI NZ: WAIKATO

The Waikato region has had a turbulent history. The area was one of the first inland regions of Aotearoa to be initially settled from distant Hawaiki, largely by the *Tainui* canoe (see p241 and p254).

The first elected leader of the Maori King Movement (opposite) was a Waikato chief, Potatau-te-wherowhero. It was to the King Country (p246) that the Waikato retreated after being defeated in war (see the boxed text, p35) by government forces in 1864.

Major *iwi* (tribes) in the region are the eponymous Waikato (see www.tainui.co.nz) and, in the King Country, the Ngati Maniapoto (www.maniapoto.iwi.nz). The current *ariki* (leader) of the Waikato, the 'Maori Queen' Te Atairangikaahu, is one of the most prominent of NZ Maori.

Reminders of the Waikato Land War can be seen at Rangiriri (p230). For an old-fashioned Biggles-style version of the story, find Errol Braithewaite's *The Needle's Eye* in a local secondhand bookshop. There are excellent Maori displays at museums in Hamilton (opposite) and Te Awamutu (p242). The home of the King Movement, Turangawaewae Marae in Ngaruawahia (below), is open to the public for Regatta Day in March.

British troops and Maori warriors. On 20 November 1863, 1500 British troops, backed by gunboats and artillery, were repulsed a number of times and lost 60 men, but overnight many of the 500 Maori defenders retreated and the remaining 180 were taken prisoner the next day. The centre has a café and the audiovisual show ($2) is worth seeing. On the other side of the road is the overgrown *pa* site where the battle took place.

Next to the heritage centre is the historic **Rangiriri Hotel** (☎ 07-826 3467; Talbot St), which has plenty of beers on tap, including Waikato Draught, the local fave.

From Rangiriri the road follows the Waikato River all the way to Hamilton. Along the way is **Huntly**, a coal-mining town with a large power station. The well-stocked **visitor information centre** (☎ 07-828 6406; SH1; ☼ 9am-5pm Mon-Fri, to 3pm Sat & Sun) is next to a café, souvenir shop and toilet block.

The **Waikato Coalfields Museum** (☎ 07-828 8128; 26 Harlock Pl, Huntly; adult/child $5/2; ☼ 10am-4pm) is large and concentrates on the local mining industry. From near here you can walk around **Lake Hakanoa** (3.6km, one hour).

South of Huntly the road passes through a range and you can see the sacred mountain Taupiri (287m) and a Maori cemetery. **Ngaruawahia**, 19km north of Hamilton on SH1, is the site of the Maori Queen's (see the boxed text, opposite) headquarters, the impressive **Turangawaewae Marae** (☎ 07-824 5189; River Rd), but visitors are only allowed inside on Regatta Day in March.

If you're fit, the top of Taupiri Mountain has excellent views (a sign on the track

explains the appropriate etiquette near graves), and the **Hakarimata Walkway** also has good views. Its northern end leads off Parker Rd, which can be reached by crossing the river at Huntly and following the Ngaruawahia–Huntly West Rd. The southern end meets the Ngaruawahia–Waingaro Rd just out of Ngaruawahia. To walk the length of the track takes up to seven hours, but shorter hikes are possible. Easier to get to if you have no transport is the three-hour return trek from Brownlee Ave, Ngaruawahia, to Hakarimata Trig (371m). The top part is fairly steep but the view is rewarding. Tracks from each access point meet at the trig.

If you detour way out west along SH22, you reach **Nikau Cave** (☎ 09-233 3199; www.nikau cave.co.nz; 1779 Waikaretu Rd; adult/child $25/15), where you can see glow-worms, limestone formations and subterranean streams in a far less crowded environment than at Waitomo. It's on a private farm and refreshments are included. Bookings are essential.

HAMILTON

pop 132,000

NZ's largest inland city, Hamilton is 129km south of Auckland and is the Waikato region's major centre. European settlement began in 1864 but the Waikato River was Hamilton's only transport and communication link with other towns until the railway arrived in 1878. Hamilton Gardens and its conservation zoo are the main attractions, but there are walks, kayak trips and cruises along the river, and a **hot-air balloon festival** (www.balloonsoverwaikato.co.nz) in April, plus the added bonus of the city's reputation for good eating. University students enliven the city during term time and theatres, cinemas, cafés, restaurants and bars crowd the city centre.

Information

The well-informed **Hamilton visitor information centre** (☎ 07-839 3580; www.waikatonz.com; cnr Bryce & Anglesea Sts; ☷ 8.30am-5pm Mon-Fri, 9am-4pm Sat, 10am-4pm Sun) is inside the Hamilton Transport Centre, which also has a café and Internet access (per hour $5). View www .hamiltonevent.co.nz for what's on locally and www.absorbed.co.nz for entertainment news.

The **post office** (35 Bryce St; ☷ 8am-5pm Mon-Fri, 9am-2pm Sat, to noon Sun) is near the visitor information centre.

Victoria Central Medical Centre (☎ 07-834 0333; 750 Victoria St; ☷ 8am-10pm) offers walk-in service, can take X-rays and sets fractures. **Anglesea Clinic** (☎ 07-858 0800; Anglesea St; ☷ 24hr) has doctors, a dentist (from 8am to 5pm) and a pharmacy (from 7.30am to 11pm).

Sights

The splendid 50-hectare **Hamilton Gardens** (☎ 07-856 3200; www.hamiltongardens.co.nz; Cobham Dr; admission free; ☷ 7.30am-sunset) is a collection of themed gardens. The rose gardens, herb and scented garden, glasshouse garden, American garden, Renaissance garden and Asian garden are well worth a look, and there is a café, restaurant and shop.

The **Waikato Museum of Art & History** (☎ 07-838 6606; www.waikatomuseum.co.nz; 1 Grantham St; admission by donation; ☷ 10am-4.30pm) has an excellent permanent collection of Tainui Maori treasures on display. They include exquisite weaving and woodcarving, which are well displayed in a darkened room. Other temporary exhibitions are held here (admission varies), as well as displays on the agricultural history of the area (keep an eye out for the ancient copy of *Mastitis Melodies*, an historic LP devoted to soothing the udders of pained cows). There is also an award-winning café here (p236).

ArtsPost (☎ 07-839 3857; 120 Victoria St; admission free; ☷ 10am-4.30pm), near the museum, is a contemporary art gallery housed in the rather grand former Post Office that mainly focuses on local artists.

Hamilton Zoo (☎ 07-838 6720; www.hamiltonzoo.co.nz; Brymer Rd; adult/child $10/5; ☷ 9am-5pm, last entry 3.30pm) has natural pens to house its 400-plus species and a programme to breed endangered species (the current star is Mtoto the white rhino) from around the world. Check with the zoo for the 'Meet the Keeper' schedule, which is an interesting way to find out more about certain animals' daily lives. The zoo itself is well laid out, with spacious grounds and a large walk-through aviary of native birds, but is 8km from the city

THE MAORI KING MOVEMENT

The King Movement stemmed from a need for greater unity and organisation of Maori tribes against the Pakeha and from a desire to have a Maori leader equivalent to the British queen when dealing with the Pakeha.

Potatau Te Wherowhero was a high chief of the Waikato tribes when he was made the first Maori king in 1858. He died in 1860 aged about 85 and was succeeded by his son, the second and most widely known Maori king, Matutaera Te Wherowhero – known as King Tawhiao – who held the position for the next 34 years until his death, and led the Waikato Maori through the Land War of 1863–64 (p35).

The King Movement was a nationalistic step for those Maoris who were unwilling to sell or otherwise lose their land to the Europeans. Based in Te Kuiti, the king and his followers continued to resist Pakeha incursions. However, after the king and the chiefs agreed to the Auckland-Wellington railway being built through their land, Europeans were allowed to enter the King Country in the 1890s.

Te Arikinui Dame Te Atairangikaahu, the present 'Maori queen', is the sixth in line of succession, and has held the position since her father, Koroki Mahuta, died in 1966. She is head of the Tainui tribal confederation, which consists of four major tribes – the Waikato, Maniapoto, Hauraki and Raukawa – who are all descended from those who arrived in NZ on the *Tainui* canoe (see p241).

Activities

MV Waipa Delta (☎ 07-854 7813; ☺ cruises Thu-Sun) is a replica of an 1876 Waikato paddle steamer and runs popular river cruises from centre – take Norton Rd then SH23 west towards Raglan, turn right at Newcastle Rd and then left onto Brymer Rd.

Memorial Park, on the river bank opposite the city centre. There are 1½-hour buffet-lunch cruises ($43), one-hour afternoon-tea cruises ($20) and evening buffet and music cruises ($59). Children are half-price and reservations are recommended.

Riverside Entertainment Centre (☎ 07-8334900; 346 Victoria St; ☺ 9am-3am Sun-Wed, to 5am Thu-Sat), a

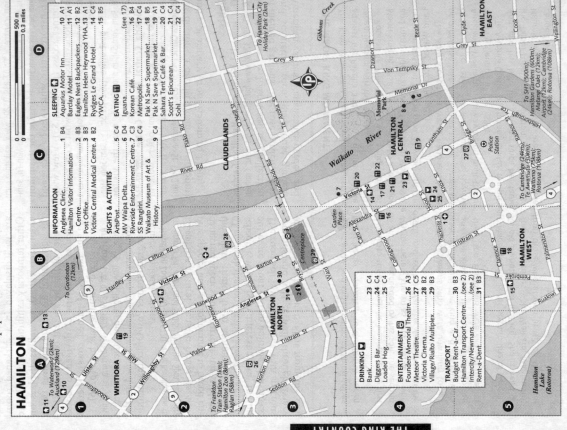

HAMILTON

INFORMATION
Anglesea Clinic............................	1 B4
Hamilton Visitor Information	
Centre...................................	2 B3
Post Office..................................	3 B3
Victoria Central Medical Centre..	4 B2

SIGHTS & ACTIVITIES
ArtsPost.....................................	5 C4
MV Waipa Delta..........................	6 D4
Riverside Entertainment Centre..	7 C3
SS Rangiriri.................................	8 C4
Waikato Museum of Art &	
History..................................	9 C4

SLEEPING
Aquarius Motor Inn.....................	10 A1
Barclay Motel.............................	11 A1
Eagles Nest Backpackers............	12 B2
Hamilton Helen Heywood YHA.13	A1
Rydges Le Grand Hotel...............	14 C4
YWCA.......................................	15 B5

EATING
Iguana..................................	(see 17)
Korean Café...............................	16 B4
Metropolis..................................	17 C4
Pak N Save Supermarket............	18 B5
Pak N Save Supermarket............	19 A1
Sahara Tent Café & Bar..............	20 C4
Scott's Epicurean......................	21 C4
Sohl...	22 C4

DRINKING
Bank...	23 C4
Diggers Bar...............................	24 C4
Loaded Hog..............................	25 C4

ENTERTAINMENT
Founders Memorial Theatre........	26 A3
Meteor Cinema..........................	27 C5
Victoria Cinema.........................	28 B2
Village/Rialto Multiplex..............	29 B3

TRANSPORT
Budget Rent-a-Car.....................	30 B3
Hamilton Transport Centre.........	(see 2)
Intercity/Newmans.....................	(see 2)
Rent-a-Dent...............................	31 B3

relatively new entertainment complex, has a Skycity casino, a few restaurants and bars, a Belgian beer café, a bowling alley and a kid-friendly entertainment den called the Megazone, plus three smoking decks.

Waterworld (☎ 07-958 5860; Garnett Ave; adult/child $4/2; ☼ 6am-9pm Mon-Fri, 7am-9pm Sat, 9am-9pm Sun; located 4km north of the city centre, has indoor and outdoor pools, water slides, a gym, spa and crèche.

Via **Kiwi Balloon Company** (☎ 07-355 1615; www.kiwiballooncompany.co.nz; per person $250), gaze over this lush countryside from the best possible vantage point – a hot-air balloon. Trips last about four hours and depart from near Hamilton, or Karapiro (by arrangement) in the morning. A champagne breakfast is part of the deal.

Bush-covered riverside walkways run along both sides of the Waikato River and provide a green belt to the city. Memorial Park is particularly attractive and embedded in the riverbank is part of **SS Rangiriri**, an iron-clad, steam-powered gunboat that saw action in the Waikato Land War.

Tours

Archer Tours (☎ 07-855 2860; www.archertours.co.nz) runs day tours to Rotorua, Waitomo, Coromandel, Auckland and Taupo for $130 to $145, and often includes lunch.

Sleeping
BUDGET

Hamilton Helen Heywood YHA (☎ 07-838 0009; yhahamil@yha.org.nz; 1190 Victoria St; dm/s/d/tw $24/35/56/56) Dorms have three to five beds and there are no en suites, but some rooms have tables, chairs and cupboards. The garden, with native tree ferns, stretches down to the river.

Eagles Nest Backpackers (☎ 07-838 2704; www.eaglesnestbackpackers.co.nz; 937 Victoria St; dm $20) With a homely common area and caring management, this new budget choice is proving popular. Rooms are small, boxlike and starkly lit, but they are very clean and the gas hot-water showers immaculate.

YWCA (☎ 07-838 2219; www.ywcahamilton.org.nz; cnr Pembroke & Clarence Sts; dm $20) This three-storey apartment block of a hostel accepts men and women and the rooms are small with shared facilities. Each floor has a kitchen and a TV and video. It has a fairly steady clientele of long-term stayers too.

Hamilton City Holiday Park (☎ 07-855 8255; www.hamiltoncityholidaypark.co.nz; 14 Ruakura Rd; sites per 2 people $24, cabins $24-45, tourist flats $55-70) A shady park with good simple cabins and well-maintained communal facilities, 2km east of town.

MIDRANGE

The road into town from Auckland is lined with dozens of midrange motels, many of them much of a muchness, but perfectly adequate.

Barclay Motel (☎ 07-838 2475; www.barclay.co.nz; 280 Ulster St; studio $120, units $140-345) Modern, nicely maintained accommodation options and professional service earn this place a good reputation with business travellers and the like. Large groups should seek out the three-bedroom unit option, which certainly has a 'your house is my house' feel.

Matangi Oaks (☎ 07-829 5765; www.matangioaks.co.nz; 634 Maychurch Rd, Matangi; s/d/tw $120/185/185) Private or en suite rooms are available in this modern, spacious house that has well-appointed rooms. Prices include full breakfast. It's 12km from Hamilton on the way to Cambridge, and cattle and crops are farmed, plus dinner can be provided.

Aquarius Motor Inn (☎ 0800 839 244, 07-839 2447; www.aquarius-motor-inn.co.nz; 230 Ulster St; studios/family units $90/125; ☒) Th·s smart, solidly furnished motel comes with Sky TV and has an indoor heated pool. It is at the city's northern end and has very good low-season rates. If you're self-catering, book a unit so you can take advantage of the kitchenettes.

TOP END

Rydges Le Grand Hotel (☎ 0800 446 187, 07-839 1994; www.rydges.com; 237 Victoria St; s&d/from $225) This 38-room boutique hotel in a heritage building is the kind of place that puts up a riotously decorated Christmas tree in September, and has stylish furnishing and bright colours in a range of rooms. Prices are often negotiable and special packages usually available. The bar (live jazz some evenings) and restaurant are like the hotel – small but smart.

Eating

The following are just a selection of the dining options, which include Indian, Chinese, Cambodian and Thai. Both the Centreplace and Downtown Plaza malls have small international food courts.

Canvas (☎ 07-839 2535; 1 Grantham St; mains $20-28; ⏰ lunch Mon-Fri, dinner Mon-Sat) The award-winning café in the Museum of Art & History has a classy menu, lovely outlook, smart ultramodern décor and is a very nice spot for unwinding after some sightseeing, or for brunch, when corned-beef hash and excellent coffee beckon.

Sahara Tent Café & Bar (☎ 07-839 3939; 237 Victoria St; mains $21-27; ⏰ lunch & dinner) Over-the-top Middle Eastern décor competes with a detailed matching menu that throws up the odd surprise, such as Tropical Mussels, which tasted far better than it sounds. Check out the rather bizarre/bazaar murals above the bar *before* you've had too much to drink.

Metropolis (☎ 07-834 2081; 211 Victoria St; mains $19-27; ⏰ 9am-midnight) A global and varied menu is offered at this casual and popular café, which covers all the bases and has a chirpy, fun atmosphere.

Sohl (☎ 07-839 1996; 236 Victoria St; mains $17-29; ⏰ dinner Mon-Sat) This nifty-looking and very popular place is an excellent choice for dinner or even just a drink or two. The food concentrates on dishes best described as Mod NZ.

Iguana (☎ 07-834 2280; 203 Victoria St; medium pizzas/mains $18/27; ⏰ 10am-late) This has a garden bar and serves up popular gourmet pizzas, and at night the cavernous space becomes a tad more romantic thanks to the addition of candlelight.

Korean Café (☎ 07-838 9100; cnr Collingwood & Alexandra Sts; mains $7-13; ⏰ lunch & dinner Mon-Sat) All the Korean favourites are here – including an eye-watering *kimchi* and some good *bulgogy*. Décor is stark and simple, and service brisk but friendly.

For picnic and other food items head to the branches of Pak N Save supermarket on Clarence St or Mill St.

Drinking

Nightspots in the Hood St area are lively on Friday and Saturday nights with live music and DJs.

Loaded Hog (☎ 07-839 2777; 27 Hood St; ⏰ 10.30am-late) This restaurant and bar with a popular outdoor deck (come summer) becomes a nightclub around 10pm, where drunken dancing gets the party started in the heart of many a local. Good, clean fun, and the food's not bad either.

Diggers Bar (☎ 07-834 2228; 17b Hood St; ⏰ 5pm-late Tue-Sun) This bar has a wealth of liquid bread on tap, booze-soaking pizzas, and live music from around 8.30pm Wednesday to Saturday.

Bank (☎ 07-839 4740; cnr Victoria & Hood Sts; ⏰ 11am-late) Inside this cream 1878 heritage building are plenty of beers on tap, a good selection of wines offered by the glass, a welcoming atmosphere and plenty of big screens to catch the latest big-ticket sporting event.

Entertainment

Village/Rialto Multiplex (☎ 07-839 2981; Centreplace Mall; adult $8.50-14.50, child $7-8.50) Located in the shopping centre, this has a total of 10 screens between two cinema businesses.

Victoria Cinema (☎ 07-838 3036; 690 Victoria St; adult $13-15) Puts on festival and other interesting films and you can sip a glass of wine or beer in the cinema.

Live theatre and concerts can be enjoyed at the **Meteor Theatre** (☎ 07-838 6603; 1 Victoria St) and **Founders Memorial Theatre** (☎ 07-838 6603; 221 Tristram St).

Getting There & Away

AIR

Freedom Air (☎ 0800 600 500; www.freedomair.com) has direct flights from Hamilton to Brisbane, Gold Coast, Melbourne and Sydney.

Air New Zealand (☎ 0800 737 000; www.airnz.co.nz; ⏰ 24hr) has three direct flights daily to and from Auckland as well as direct and connecting flights to all domestic airports (Wellington and Christchurch). The cheapest flights must be booked online.

Origin Pacific (☎ 0800 302302) has direct flights from Hamilton to Wellington, Christchurch

---

AUTHOR'S CHOICE

Scott's Epicurean (☎ 07-839 6680; 181 Victoria St; lunch mains $8-15; ⏰ breakfast & lunch) This gorgeous, airy joint features swanky leather banquettes, pressed-tin ceilings, Hamilton's best coffee and a comprehensive menu of tasty staples, such as the eternally popular *spaghetti aglio e olio* ($7.50), which is both a winner and a bargain. Service is friendly, it's fully licensed and a charming outdoor area beckons in the warmer months.

and Nelson, and connecting flights to Blenheim. Most fly daily.

BUS

All local and long-distance buses arrive at and depart from the **Hamilton Transport Centre** (☎ 07-834 3457; cnr Anglesea & Bryce Sts).

InterCity/Newmans (☎ 07-834 3457; cnr Anglesea & Bryce Sts) has an office in the transport centre. Buses run to Auckland ($24 to $27, two hours), Thames ($24, 1¾ hours), Rotorua ($27 to $38, 1¾ hours), Whakatane ($48, 3½ hours), Opotiki ($48, 4½ hours), Gisborne ($68, 6¾ hours), Taupo ($37 to $59, 2½ hours), New Plymouth ($44, 4½ hours), Wellington ($79 to $85, 8¼ hours) and Waitomo Caves ($31, two hours).

Guthreys (☎ 0800 759 999) operates services to Auckland ($24, two hours) and Rotorua ($27, 1½ hours).

Dalroy Express (☎ 0508 465 622; www.dalroytours .co.nz) operates a daily service between Auckland ($18, two hours) and Hawera ($44, 4¾ hours) via Hamilton, stopping at most towns, including New Plymouth ($35, 3½ hours) and Te Kuiti ($14, 1¾ hours). Local bus companies run regular services to nearby towns such as Raglan, Huntly, Te Awamutu, Te Aroha and Thames.

TRAIN

Hamilton is on the main rail line between Auckland and Wellington (one train a day in each direction). Trains stop at Hamilton's **Frankton train station** (☎ 07-846 8353; Queens Ave), located 1km west of the city centre. Dinsdale buses run between the Hamilton Transport Centre and near the train station ($2, every 30 minutes).

Getting Around

TO/FROM THE AIRPORT

Hamilton Airport (☎ 07-848 9027; www.hamiltonairport.co.nz) is 12km south of the city. Departure tax is $25 (for those 12 years and over). The **Super Shuttle** (☎ 07-843 7778) offers a door-to-door service into the city ($15). A taxi costs around $40.

BUS

Hamilton's city bus system, **Busline** (☎ 0800 4287 5463), operates Monday to Saturday from around 7am to 5.45pm (later on Friday). All buses pass through Hamilton Transport Centre.

CAR

Budget Rent-A-Car (☎ 07-838 3585; www.budget .co.nz; 404 Anglesea St)

Rent-a-Dent (☎ 07-839 1049; www.rentadent.co.nz; 383 Anglesea St)

WAINGARO HOT SPRINGS

A popular, easy day trip from Hamilton are the **Waingaro Hot Springs** (☎ 07-825 4761; adult/child $8/4; ☑ 9am-10pm), which have three thermal mineral pools, private spa pools, giant water slides, bumper boats, children's play areas and barbecues. Local kids are mighty enthusiastic about spending large chunks of the weekend here, soaking up the water sports. The **motel & caravan park** (☎ 07-825 4761; sites per 2 people $28, caravans/units $50/90) here offers free entry to the hot pools. To get to the springs, turn west at Ngaruawahia, 19km north of Hamilton, and travel for 23km; they are clearly signposted.

RAGLAN

pop 2700

On the coast, 48km west of Hamilton, is the small, delightful community of Raglan, named after Lord Raglan, a British officer who seriously wiped out at the charge of the Light Brigade during the Crimea War. Nearby bays are internationally famous for their waves and attract surfers from around the world, especially in summer when surfing competitions are held. Bruce Brown's classic 1964 film *The Endless Summer*, about surfers roaming the world in search of the perfect wave, features footage shot at Manu Bay, west of Raglan.

The laid-back town, with its low-key shops and friendly cafés, lies on a beautiful sheltered harbour (good for kayaking, boating and swimming). It's the sort of charming place that sees you inevitably shuffle your itinerary as you make plans to extend your stay and the time spent in your jandals.

Information

Health centre (☎ 07-825 0114; Wallis St; ☑ 9am-5pm Mon-Fri to 1pm Sat)

Post office (39 Bow St)

Raglan Video (☎ 07-825 0008; 9 Bow St; per 30min $5; ☑ 10am-8.30pm) Has Internet access.

Raglan visitor information centre (☎ 07-825 0556; www.raglan.org.nz; 4 Wallis St; ☑ 10am-3pm Mon-Fri, to 4pm Sat & Sun May-Sep, 9am-5pm daily Oct-Apr)

www.lonelyplanet.com

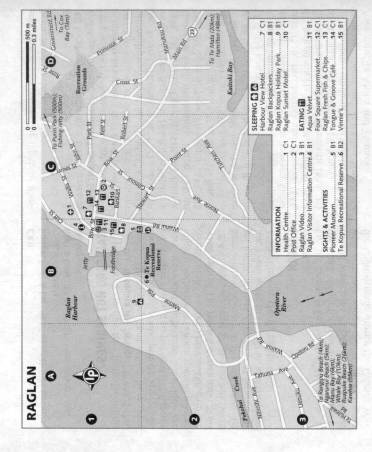

RAGLAN

500 m
0.3 miles

To Cox
Bay (1km)
To Cox Rd
Government Rd

Recreation
Grounds

Primrose St
Main Rd (23)
Namanu Rd
To Te Mata (20km);
Hamilton (48km)
Cross St
Kaitoki Bay

Rose St

Park St
Kent St
Robert St
James St
Wallis St
St John St
Bow St
Bankart
Point St
Gilmour St
Turnhen Ave
Stewart St
Norrie Ave
Wainui Rd
Cliff St

To Puriri Park (500m);
Fishing Jetty (500m)

Jetty
Footbridge
Marine Pde
Te Kopua
Recreational
Reserve

Raglan
Harbour

Opotoru
River

Wainui Rd
Opotoru Rd
Tahuna Ave
Nihinihi Ave
Pokohui Creek
Uenuku Ave
Te Hutewai Rd

To Rangipu Beach (4km);
Ngarunui Beach (5km);
Manu Bay (6km);
Whale Bay (10km);
Ruapuke Beach (26km);
Kawhia (55km)

INFORMATION
Health Centre......................1 C1
Post Office..........................2 C1
Raglan Video.......................3 B1
Raglan Visitor Information Centre 4 B1

SIGHTS & ACTIVITIES
Pioneer Museum..................5 B1
Te Kopua Recreational Reserve...6 B2

SLEEPING
Harbour View Hotel..............7 C1
Raglan Backpackers..............8 B1
Raglan Kopua Holiday Park......9 B1
Raglan Sunset Motel.............10 C1

EATING
Aqua Velvet......................11 B1
Four Square Supermarket........12 C1
Raglan Fresh Fish & Chips.......13 B1
Tongue & Groove Café...........14 C1
Vinnie's...........................15 B1

The very helpful staff members can book many activities, including surfing lessons.

Sights & Activities
PIONEER MUSEUM
Visit the small **pioneer museum** (13 Wainui Rd; admission by donation; 1-3.30pm Sat & Sun) to explore stories of local Maori and Pakeha pioneers through artefacts, photos and newspapers. Make note of the meagre opening hours, but don't kick yourself if you miss them.

BEACHES
Te Kopua Recreational Reserve, over the footbridge by the holiday park, is a safe, calm, harbour black-sand beach that is popular with families. Other beaches are at **Cox Bay**, which is reached by a walkway from Government Rd or Bayview Rd, and at **Puriri Park**, towards the end of Wallis St, which is a safe swimming spot around high tide. See p240 for details of the surfing beaches.

SURFING
Learn to catch waves with the **Raglan Surfing School** (07-825 7873; www.raglansurfingschool.co.nz;

Whale Bay; 3hr lesson $79) on soft surfboards that make it easier to stand up and stay up. All equipment is provided and instructors pride themselves on getting 95% of first-timers standing on a surfboard during their first lesson. If you're already experienced you can rent surfboards (from $15 per hour), boogie boards ($5 per hour) and wet suits ($5 per hour). The school operates from Ngarunui Beach, 7km west of Raglan, and lessons can be booked at the Raglan visitor information centre. See Whale Bay (p240) for details of the school's own accommodation in a beautiful bush setting.

Solscape (07-825 8268; www.solscape.co.nz; 611 Wainui Rd, Manu Bay; lessons $85) offers 2½-hour-long lessons from a female surfer. The company also rents out surfing equipment and kayaks and offers scuba-diving trips to Gannet Island and offers accommodation (p240).

Skyrider (07-825 7453; lessons $100) offers two-hour, one-on-one kite-surfing lessons at Rangipu Beach, 6km west of Raglan. They can be booked at the Raglan visitor information centre.

KAYAKING

Kayaks are offered free to guests at Raglan Backpackers (see the boxed text, below), which also hires out kayaks to nonguests ($5 for two hours). A 15-minute paddle (ask the owners for directions) brings you to the **Rocks**, which has limestone pinnacles and sea caves.

Tours

Raglan Scenic Tours (07-825 7805; www.raglanscenic tours.co.nz) runs good-value, good-feedback, small-group tours. It includes a one-hour to ur around Raglan for $15/10 per adult/ child and the popular three-hour Round the Mountain tour ($45/30), which includes Te Toto Gorge, Ruapuke Beach and the Bridal Veil Falls. Book at the visitor information centre.

Sleeping

Contact the visitor information centre for details of local B&Bs.

Raglan Kopua Holiday Park (07-825 8283; raglanholidaypark@xtra.co.nz; Marine Pde; sites per 2 people $22, dm/cabins/cottages/houses $20/50/65/80) This is a nicely maintained, well-managed facility situated on a sheltered, inner-harbour beach across the inlet from town. There's loads of room for games and play, making this an ideal spot for families.

Harbour View Hotel (07-825 8010; 14 Bow St; s/d/tw $60/80/80, f $95-110) This two-storey heritage

pub with verandas has largish, clean rooms without bathrooms and attractive touches thanks to kauri wood trimmings. Restaurant meals (the seafood chowder is great), a bar downstairs and live music at the weekends add to its 'social centre' atmosphere.

Raglan Sunset Motel (07-825 0050; www.raglan sunsetmotel.co.nz; 7 Bankart St; units $120-160) Twenty-two new-looking units with Sky TV and balconies that overlook a paved courtyard. It's a nice place, and good for a bit of peace and quiet.

Eating

Tongue & Groove Café (07-825 0027; 19 Bow St; dinner mains $15-26; breakfast, lunch & dinner) This fantastic café-restaurant has music, a charming atmosphere and local art on the walls, plus a lovely menu of healthy international dishes and comfy couches for wine sipping.

Aqua Velvet (07-825 8588; www.aquavelvet.net .nz; 18 Bow St; lunch dishes $5-15; lunch & dinner, closed Wed May-Nov) This airy space, dominated by the colour blue, serves up mainly organic food and a bustling, cool atmosphere. Great, generous brekkies and good coffee draw an appreciative crowd of mums and bubs, and the weekend live music draws everyone else.

Raglan Fresh Fish & Chips (07-825 8119; 33 Bow St; 11.30am-7.30pm) Choose your own fresh fish, including snapper, or if you've caught something, have it cooked for a reasonable fee.

Self-caterers should visit the **Four Square supermarket** (Bow St).

Entertainment

Both Aqua Velvet (above) and the Harbour View Hotel (left) host live music most Saturday nights, with top Kiwi bands playing in summer at the Harbour View Hotel.

Vinnie's (07-825 7273; 7 Wainui Rd; mains $18-25; breakfast, lunch & dinner Tue-Sun) Eat outside, downstairs or in the loft at this unpretentious, welcoming café-restaurant, which serves up a wide range of yummy food and drink. Takeaway is also available.

Getting There & Away

Simpson's (07-846 1975; adult/child $5.50/3.30) runs buses between Hamilton and Raglan three times daily Monday to Friday and daily on weekends (one hour).

AUTHOR'S CHOICE

Raglan Backpackers (07-825 0515; www .raglanbackpackers.co.nz; 6 Wi Neera St; dm/d/tw $21/48/48) This is an excellent, purpose-built hostel with one of the warmest welcomes you'll ever receive and a delightfully laid-back holiday-house feel. It's on the water's edge, with sea views from some rooms, and all rooms are arranged around a garden courtyard, plus there's a great lounge area and well-kept kitchen. This is one of those places where you'll find yourself asking if it's possible to stay another night. Outdoor gear such as kayaks, bikes and surfboards are available for guests (you'll pay about $20 a day for the boards though), and if that's too strenuous, then it's hard to beat lying about in a hammock with the friendly black Labrador.

AROUND RAGLAN

Four Brothers Scenic Reserve

On the road between Hamilton and Raglan, the **Karamu Walkway** goes through the reserve. A 15-minute hike up a gully covered in native bush leads to a hilltop where cows and sheep enjoy panoramic views.

Rangipu Beach

Just 6km west of Raglan, down Riria Kereopa Memorial Drive, this beach with sand dunes at the mouth of the harbour is popular with windsurfers and kite surfers.

Ngarunui Beach

Seven kilometres west of Raglan, this blacksand beach is popular with surfers. On the clifftop is the impressive club for the volunteer lifeguards who patrol part of the beach from late October until April. This is the only beach with lifeguards.

Manu Bay

Eight kilometres west of Raglan is this rocky but famous surfing beach, said to have the longest left-hand break in the world. The very long, uniform waves are created by the angle at which the ocean swell from the Tasman Sea meets the coastline.

Solscape (☎ 07-825 8268; www.solscape.co.nz; 611 Wainui Rd; sites per 2 people $24, d/md/tw/f $20/60/60/120) is a unique accommodation option perched on a hilltop (with some great views), and offers appealing units inside gaily painted railway cabooses. Scuba diving, surfing tuition, surfboard and sea-kayak hire are all available in this pleasing surfer hang-out, which also offers free pick-ups from Raglan. Highly recommended.

Whale Bay

This famous surfing spot is a couple of kilometres further west of Manu Bay.

Deep in native bush, **Karioi Outdoor Adventure Centre** (☎ 07-825 8287; 5A Whaanga Rd; www.raglan.net.nz/karioiADV; dm/d $22/66) offers basketball, a flying fox, mountain bikes, bush walks and surf lessons by Raglan Surfing School (p238). There are no en suite rooms but it has a wonderful location and good cheap meals (dinner $12) are available. **Sleeping Lady Lodging** (☎ 07-825 7873; www.sleepinglady.co.nz; lodges $120-220) has self-contained lodges nearby.

Indicators Beach House (☎ 07-825 8818; www.indicators.co.nz; d $200) is a wonderful, large and

fully equipped house that overlooks the beach (those views!) and has a deck. Woodlined, with every modern need met and sleeping up to seven (add $50 extra per person). You'll want to move in.

Ruapuke Beach

Whale Bay marks the end of the sealed road, but a gravel road continues to Ruapuke Beach, 28km from Raglan, which is dangerous for swimmers but popular with surf-casting fisherfolk. **Ruapuke Motor Camp** (☎ 07-825 6800; unpowered/powered sites per 2 people $15/19, cabins $25-30, units $40) is near the beach and has an end-of-the-world feel, making this a very good getaway spot. The gravel road continues on round Mt Karioi and rejoins the inland road at Te Mata. The journey from Raglan to Te Mata takes around an hour.

RAGLAN TO KAWHIA

The back roads between Raglan and Kawhia, 55km south on the coast, are slow and winding but scenic, enjoyable and off the beaten track. The gravel roads take at least 1½ hours of driving time, not counting stops. Traffic is light.

There are two routes between Raglan and Kawhia. From Raglan you can head west along the coast, past Ngarunui Beach, Manu Bay and Whale Bay, until the road turns inland and meets the interior road at Te Mata, 20km south of Raglan. Along this route, starting from Te Toto car park, a strenuous but scenic track goes up the western side of **Mt Karioi** (755m). It takes 2½ hours to reach a lookout point, followed by an easier hour up to the summit. From the east side, the Wairake Track is a steeper 2½-hour climb to the summit, where it meets the Te Toto Track.

The alternative route from Raglan is to head towards Hamilton and take the signposted Te Mata–Kawhia turn-off. **Magic Mountain Farmstay** (☎ 07-825 6892; www.magicmountain.co.nz; 334 Houchen Rd; s/d B&B $120/180, self-contained lodge $250) has truly stunning views and provides horse rides from $30. Turn off 4km before Te Mata and it's 4km from the main road. At the time of research the business was for sale, so call ahead.

Located just 1km past Te Mata is the turn-off to the spectacular 55m **Bridal Veil Falls**, 4km from the main road. From the car park, it's an easy 10-minute walk through mossy native bush to the top of the falls. A further 10-minute walk leads to the pool at the bottom, where it's possible to swim once you've admired the view. Unfortunately, theft from cars is a big problem here.

The road is sealed until 7km beyond Te Mata and then it's gravel until Hwy 31, the Te Awamutu–Kawhia road.

KAWHIA

pop 670

It was in Kawhia that the *Tainui* canoe – one of the ancestral canoes that arrived in Aotearoa during the 14th century from the Maori homeland, Hawaiki, thousands of kilometres away – made its final landing. Kawhia, the Maketu Marae and the burial place of the *Tainui* canoe are all sacred to the Tainui people.

The two leaders of the *Tainui* canoe – Hoturoa, the captain, and Rakataura, the *tohunga* or high priest – knew that the *Tainui*'s home was destined to be on the west coast. They searched up and down the coast, until they finally recognised their prophesied new home at Kawhia Harbour.

When they landed the canoe, they tied it to a pohutukawa tree on the shore, naming the tree Tangi te Korowhiti. Though the tree is not marked, it still grows with a few other pohutukawa trees on the shoreline between Kawhia and the Maketu Marae. At the end of its long and epic voyage, the *Tainui* canoe was dragged up onto a hill and buried. Hoturoa and Rakataura placed sacred stones at either end to mark its resting place. Hani, on higher ground, is the stone marking the bow of the canoe, and Puna, the lower stone, marks the stern.

Today, Kawhia is a sleepy little fishing port on pretty Kawhia Harbour, which is large but has a narrow entrance – Captain Cook missed it when he sailed past in 1770, naming Albatross Point on its southern side but failing to note the harbour itself. Kawhia (kar-fee-a) is quaint and quiet, except in summer when accommodation can fill up.

Kawhia has a **general store-post office** (7am–7pm) and a petrol station; fish bait is for sale near the wharf.

Sights & Activities

The **Kawhia Museum** (07-870 0161; admission free; 11am–4pm Wed-Sun Oct–Apr, noon-4pm Sat &

Sun May–Sep) is a modest but cute affair near the wharf, and serves as the visitor information centre.

Kayaks can be hired from Kawhia Beachside S-Cape (below) for about \$7.50/15 per hour per single/double. Quad bikes can be hired (two hours for \$35) from **Kawhia Camping Ground** (07-871 0863; www.kawhiacamping.co.nz; Moke St). For fishing trips contact **Dove Charters** (07-871 5854) or **Taylors Harbour Cruises** (07-871 0149), which also does a three-hour harbour tour (Gilligan's Island anyone?) aboard the *MV Kotuku* for \$30/10 per adult/child.

Six kilometres west of Kawhia, through the Tainui Kawhia Pine Forest is windswept Ocean Beach and its high, black-sand dunes. Swimming can be dangerous, but one to two hours either side of low tide you can find the **Te Puia Hot Springs** in the sand – just dig a hole for your own natural hot pool. It's a lot less crowded than Hot Water Beach (p221) near Hahei on the Coromandel. You can walk from the car park or there's a drivable track over the dunes and quad bikes can be hired.

From the wharf, a pleasant walk extends along the coast to the **Maketu Marae**, which has an impressively carved meeting house, Auaukiterangi. Through the *marae* grounds and behind the wooden fence, the two stones, Hani and Puna, mark the burial place of the *Tainui* canoe (see left). You need permission from a local elder to visit this *marae*.

Sleeping

Kawhia Beachside S-Cape (07-871 0727; www .kawhiabeachsidescape.co.nz; 225 Pouewe St; unpowered/powered sites per 2 people \$25/30, dm/cabins \$23/45, units \$95-125) Perfectly positioned on the water's edge at the entrance to Kawhia, herons, godwits, oystercatchers and royal spoonbills sometimes visit. The backpackers cabin is rudimentary, but the sites are well positioned and impressive improvements were underway when we visited.

SIGNING OFF

The last signature to the Treaty of Waitangi was added in Kawhia on 3 September 1840. A copy of the treaty can be seen in the Kawhia Museum (left), along with the rest of the town's history display.

Kawhia Motel (☎ 07-871 0865, fax 07-871 0165; cnr Jervois & Tainui Sts; s/d/tw $75/85/85) What more to say? Six nicely painted units with kitchens and comfortable amenities at a good price and a slightly retro feel.

Eating & Drinking

Annie's Café & Restaurant (☎ 07-871 0198; 146 Jervois St; meals $5-18; 9.30am-4pm, closed Mon & Tue in winter) A pleasant place in the main street, serving espresso, local flounder and chips, and great steak sammies and salad. It's licensed too.

Happy Flounder (Jervois St) Offers locally caught fish – feast on the flounder, chips and salad for around $15.

Getting There & Away

You'll need your own transport to get between Kawhia and Te Awamutu, as a bus service no longer connects the two.

TE AWAMUTU

pop 9340

Te Awamutu (which means 'The River Cut Short' since the river above this point was unsuitable for large canoes) is a service town for the local dairy-farming community. It's noted for its rose garden and is the gateway to the rock-climbing centre of Wharepapa South, 23km southeast.

Information

Te Awamutu visitor information centre (☎ 07-871 3259; www.teawamutu.co.nz; cnr Gorst Ave & SH3; 9am-4.30pm Mon-Fri, 9.30am-3pm Sat & Sun) provides information and Internet access is available at the **G Net Cafe** (☎ 07-870 3060; 59a Bank St).

> **LOCAL BOYS MADE GOOD**
>
> Te Awamutu's most famous sons are none other than Tim and Neil Finn, of Split Enz and Crowded House (see p50) fame, and the town even gets a namecheck in the Crowded House song 'Mean to Me' from the band's first album. If you want to learn a little more about their early lives in the town, you can pick up a souvenir tour booklet that lists the addresses that played a role in the boys' lives (their childhood home at 588 Teasdale St is now a rest home). The booklet, on sale at the Te Awamutu visitor information centre, costs $5.

Sights & Activities

The **Rose Garden** is next to the visitor information centre and has 2000 rose bushes with 50 varieties that usually bloom from November to April.

St John's Anglican Church is across the road from the visitor information centre (where the key is kept). It opened in 1854 and is constructed of matai and rimu. The sanctuary's stained-glass window is one of the oldest in the country. Memorials relating to the Waikato Land War can be seen here.

The **museum** (☎ 07-872 0030; www.tamuseum.org.nz; Civic Centre, 135 Roche St; admission by donation; 10am-4pm Mon-Fri, to 1pm Sat, 1-4pm Sun) has a fine collection of Maori *taonga* (treasures). Other displays tell the story of the Waikato Land War and of music heroes Tim and Neil Finn – a must for fans of Split Enz or Crowded House – who came from here.

Ask at the visitor information centre for the **Te Awamutu Heritage Trail** brochure, a 1½-hour walk that takes in old fortifications and heritage buildings.

Behind the visitor information centre and the Rose Garden is the Events Centre, which has a large **indoor pool** (☎ 07-871 2080; cnr Mahoe & Selwyn Sts; adult/child $3.50/2; 6am-9pm Mon-Fri, 8am-7pm Sat & Sun). The hydroslide is an extra $3 for adults and children. Spas and saunas are also available.

Sleeping

Road Runner Motel & Holiday Park (☎ 07-871 7420; road.runner@xtra.co.nz; 141 Bond Rd; powered/unpowered sites per 2 people $22/20, cabins $70, units s/d $70/75) This small camping ground has modern facilities and the motel units are kind of straightforward but perfectly comfortable.

Rosetown Motel (☎ 07-871 5779; rosetownmotel@hotmail.com; 844 Kihikihi Rd; d $85-115) These comfortable units have kitchens and Sky TV, and share a spa pool, making them a good little choice if you're hankering for straight-up small-town sleeps.

Albert Park Motor Lodge (☎ 07-870 2995; albert.park@xtra.co.nz; 299 Albert Park Dr; units $95-120) Another example of the reasonable, tidy and modern joint that seems to flourish in this part of the world. These units have Sky TV and some have spa baths.

Eating & Drinking

Rose & Thorn (☎ 07-871 8761; 32 Arawata St; mains $26-30) The smartest restaurant in town with a lively bar next door that has a mixed bag of live music on Thursday, Friday and Saturday nights.

Redoubt Bar & Eatery (☎ 07-871 4768; cnr Rewi & Alexandra Sts; bar meals around $12) A relaxed, natural-wood bar with cheap but potent cocktails, old photos on the walls and daily food specials.

Entertainment

Regent 3 Cinema (☎ 07-871 6678; Alexandra St; tickets adult $14) Built in 1932, this Art Deco cinema has four screens and movie memorabilia in the foyer.

Getting There & Away

InterCity (☎ 0508 353 947) buses stop at Te Awamutu, outside Stewart Law Motors in Mahoe St.

Dalroy (☎ 0508 465 622; www.dalroytours.co.nz) runs buses daily to Auckland departing at 10.35am ($24, two hours) and New Plymouth at 3.45pm, ($34, 3¾ hours). Both leave from outside the visitor information centre.

Go Bus Hodgson's (☎ 07-871 6373; adult/child $5.50/3.50) runs buses from Te Awamutu to Hamilton and back five times daily Monday to Friday. The trip takes 30 minutes. Departures are from Stuart Law Motors on Mahoe St.

AROUND TE AWAMUTU

Wharepapa South

Wharepapa South, 25km southeast of Te Awamutu, is one of the best places for rock climbing in the North Island. Froggatt Edge is a climbing mecca with more than 115 routes, but there are plenty of other world-class climbs nearby. One of the best, Whanganui Bay at Lake Taupo, is only an hour's drive away.

Staff at **Bryce's** (Wharepapa Outdoor Centre; ☎ 07-872 2533; www.rockclimb.co.nz; 1424 Owairaka Valley Rd; dm/d $20/52) have a wealth of knowledge and experience about climbing in the area – this is the place to come if you are a serious climber. There's a well-stocked shop that sells and hires out a full range of climbing gear, an indoor bouldering cave (free to guests) and a licensed café. A day's instruction costs around $365. There's accommodation available at the centre.

Castle Rock Adventure (☎ 07-872 2509; www.castlerockadventure.co.nz; 1250 Owairaka Valley Rd; dm $25-30, d & tw $80) provides a range of accommodation and lots of fun activities. The cheaper dorm has 10 beds while the more expensive one has four. A worthwhile feature is the Woolshed, which has hot showers and a small kitchen and you can sleep on a mattress on the floor for $10. Rock-climbing or abseiling instruction for half a day is $79, and you can add in the 200m flying fox off a cliff for no extra charge. Mountain bike and helmet hire is $10 an hour and there are three tracks to try out. An adventure package that covers rock climbing, abseiling, the flying fox, a two-hour mountain bike ride and a night in a dorm costs $99.

The best way to get here is on the **Waitomo Wanderer** (☎ 027 492 6336), which runs daily from Rotorua ($30, 7.45am) and Waitomo ($10, 3.45pm). Otherwise phone Castle Rock Adventure or Bryce's for a pick-up from Te Awamutu ($15).

Pirongia Forest Park

The main attraction of this park is **Mt Pirongia**, its 959m summit clearly visible from much of the Waikato region. The mountain is usually climbed from Corcoran Rd. There's a hut near the summit if you want to spend the night. Maps and information about Pirongia Forest Park are available from DOC in Hamilton. You can go horse riding on the slopes of the mountain with **Mt Pirongia Horse Treks** (☎ 07-871 9960; 394 Mangati Rd; 1hr ride $25), southwest of Pirongia.

CAMBRIDGE

pop 11,300

Cambridge is the sort of green, gabled and old-fashioned small town that will have you itching to utter the phrase 'I say old chap...', thanks to its charming rural-English atmosphere, which sees cricket played on the village green and the avenues lined with broad, shady European trees (at their best in autumn or spring). The Cambridge region is famous for the breeding and training of thoroughbred horses. You'll find the town on the Waikato River, 22km southeast of Hamilton. Nearby Lake Karapiro (p245) is the place for water sports, with local golden girls (and Olympic champions) Caroline and Georgina Evers-Swindell putting in plenty of good words for the body of water in the aim of hosting the 2010 World Rowing Championships.

Information

The **Cambridge visitor information centre** (☎ 07-823 3456; www.cambridge.net.nz; cnr Victoria & Queen Sts; ☾ 9am-5pm Mon-Fri, 10am-4pm Sat & Sun) has plenty of details on local B&Bs and farmstays.

Sights & Activities

Cambridge has a 1½-hour **heritage trail** that includes the town's historical buildings, the Waikato River and Te Koutu lake, which attracts water birds. Don't miss the interior of **St Andrew's Anglican Church** (☎ 07-827 6751; 85 Hamilton Rd). The visitor information centre has a leaflet with a map.

The delightfully musty **Cambridge Museum** (☎ 07-827 3319; Victoria St; admission by donation; ☾ 10am-4pm Mon-Sat, to 2pm Sun), housed in the former courthouse, has the usual pioneer relics and a scale model of the local Te Totara Pa before it was wiped out by Maoris from the north.

The **Cambridge Thoroughbred Lodge** (☎ 07-827 8118; www.cambridgethoroughbredlodge.co.nz; horse shows adult/child $12/5; ☾ usually 10.30am), 6km south of town on SH1, is a top-notch horse stud. The one-hour shows (known as 'NZ Horse Magic') include tea and introduce you to the world of thoroughbred horses, which put on a show. Bookings are essential.

Stud Tours (☎ 07-827 5910; www.barrylee.co.nz; tours $120) offers visits to local stud farms by a local bloodstock expert. Prices are for up to four people, which makes this a very reasonably priced and unique tour. Booking is essential, especially in January.

Cambridge Raceway (☎ 07-827 5506; www.cambridgeraceway.co.nz; Taylor St) is the venue for harness and greyhound racing three times a month. Check the website for dates and times.

Cambridge Country Store (☎ 07-827 8715; 92 Victoria St; ☾ 9am-5.30pm; 🅿), housed in a former 'wooden Gothic' church, has a wide range of mainly Kiwi-made gifts and interesting souvenirs.

Sleeping

Cambridge Motor Camp (☎ 07-827 5649; 32 Scott St; sites per 2 people $24, s/d cabins $30/40, tourist flats $80) This is a quiet, well-maintained campground with lots of green, green grass. Find it over the bridge from Cambridge town centre, which is 1.5km away.

Pamade (☎ 07-827 4916; pamade@hotmail.com; 229 Shakespeare St; s without bathroom $65, d with/without bathroom $95/80; 🅿) The rooms at this neat,

homely place are self-contained and cosily decorated. Prices include a continental breakfast. There is a hot spa as well as a pool.

Cambrian Lodge Motel (☎ 07-827 7766; www.cambrianlodge.net.nz; 63 Hamilton Rd; units $80-110; 🅿) An attractive poolside area is the main selling point of this run-of-the-mill NZ motel with simple, decent rooms that have Sky TV and an indoor spa.

Park House (☎ 07-827 6368; www.parkhouse.co.nz; 70 Queen St; s/d/tw $120/160/160; 🅿) Centrally located and overlooking the cricket green, this stately house is full of antiques, quilts and period features. Experienced hosts serve an ample breakfast in the formal dining room and add their touch of old-world charm.

Souter House (☎ 07-827 3610; www.souterhouse.co.nz; 19 Victoria St; d $120-140) Victorian-era elegance and style with nifty modern facilities such as central heating and spa baths can be found in this Victorian homestead with a veranda. It's on the main street near the town centre and also has a fine restaurant. It's wheelchair-accessible.

Cambridge Mews (☎ 07-827 7166; www.cambridgemews.co.nz; 20 Hamilton Rd; units $130-240) All the units in this boutique motel have double spa baths, kitchens and Sky TV and are immaculately maintained. It's easily one of the best choices for this neck of the woods, with rooms combining modern facilities with a few old-fashioned flourishes and a leafy setting.

A novel place to spend a couple of nights is relaxing on a houseboat on Lake Karapiro – contact Houseboat Holidays (opposite).

Eating

Victoria St has numerous cafés and eateries and is the best place to look for something that whets your appetite.

All Saints Café (☎ 07-827 7100; 92 Victoria St; ☾ breakfast & lunch) Savouries worth savouring, cakes worth diving into, plus sandwiches and speciality teas are served upstairs in the Cambridge Country Store (left). All the goodies are made in-house.

Deli on the Corner (☎ 07-827 5370; 48 Victoria St; snacks $5-8; ☾ 9am-5pm Mon-Fri, to 4pm Sat, 10am-2pm Sun) This tiny, triangular café has character and offers a touch of gourmet home cooking – try the *mezze* platter if you're on the run.

Rata (☎ 07-823 0999; 64c Victoria St; mains $19-28; ☾ 10am-3pm Sun & Mon, 9am-5pm Tue & Wed, till late Thu-Sat) This funky bar-café-restaurant has a large blackboard menu that doubles as a work of art and features lengthy items with a Mod-NZ mood predominating.

Oasis Wine Bar & Restaurant (☎ 07-827 8004; 35 Duke St; mains $20-28; ⌚ 11am-late) Stylish, modern cuisine is available here and bookings are advisable on weekends for dinner.

Souter House (☎ 07-827 3610; 19 Victoria St; mains $21-30; ⌚ dinner Mon-Sat) Enjoy elegant but relaxed charm in this smart hotel restaurant that offers the classics: venison, ostrich, salmon and, NZ must-haves, lamb and beef.

Getting There & Away

Lying on SH1, Cambridge is well connected by bus. Most long-distance buses from Hamilton to Rotorua or the Bay of Plenty stop in the town.

Cambridge Travel Lines (☎ 07-827 7363; adult/child $5/3) runs buses to and from Hamilton, twice daily (40 minutes).

LAKE KARAPIRO

Karapiro, the furthest downstream of a chain of eight hydroelectric power stations on the Waikato River, was opened in 1947. It is 30km southeast of Hamilton, 8km from Cambridge, and 3km off SH1. The 21km-long lake is popular for all kinds of aquatic sports, especially kayaking and rowing.

Drive down Gorton Rd to reach the **Boatshed Café** (☎ 07-827 8286; www.theboatshed.net.nz; 21 Amber Lane; mains $10-15; ⌚ 10am-4pm, closed mid-Jun–Jul). This popular café on the lakeside sells mainly homemade food, some of which is gluten- and dairy-free. The rowing boat of Rob Waddel (NZ's Olympic gold-medallist rower) is part of the décor – he used to practise here. Kayaks can be hired for $20/40 per half/full day. You can paddle to a couple of waterfalls in around an hour.

Houseboat Holidays (☎ 07-827 2195; www.houseboatescape.co.nz; 2 nights $600) hires out a smart houseboat (sleeps seven) on the lake. It's the perfect way to relax for a couple of days, and you can load the boat up with kayaks. Available all year, fuel will cost extra, and you can fish for trout if you have a licence and fishing gear.

At **Birches** (☎ 07-827 6556; birchesbandb@xtra.co.nz; 263 Maungatautari Rd; s/d $65/100) you can stay in a separate, charmingly decorated country-style cottage or in the house with a spa bath. There's a wide range of breakfast options, plus a tennis court.

MATAMATA

pop 7800

Famous for its thoroughbred stud farms (it seems that every business in town's advertising features a silhouette of a horse), Matamata lies 23km from Cambridge and probably wouldn't have featured so prominently on many an itinerary but for Peter Jackson's epic film trilogy *Lord of the Rings*. A nearby farm was used to create Hobbiton and thousands of the film's fans have been taking the tour to visit the setting for the Hobbit village. Just enough remains of the set for your imagination (and you'll sometimes need to use it) to fill in the holes, and the guides are full of stories about the making of the film. Other attractions in the area include tandem skydiving at the nearby airport, a pioneer village, a hot-spring resort and an attractive waterfall.

Information

The **visitor information centre** (☎ 07-888 7260; www.matamata-info.co.nz; 45 Broadway; ⌚ 8.30am-5pm Mon-Fri, 9.30am-3pm Sat & Sun) can book tickets, including the Hobbiton tour. Opposite the visitor information centre is an Internet centre.

Sights & Activities

Visit Hobbiton with **Rings Scenic Tours** (☎ 07-888 6838; www.hobbitontours.com; adult/child under 10/child 10-14 $50/free/25). The two-hour tours have proved to be so popular (over 65,000 have bought a ticket) that the number of tours each day has only increased with time. Bear in mind that reactions to the tour can be mixed, with some thinking it only suitable for die-hard LOTR fans (of which there are many). Book at the local visitor information centre.

Skydive Waikato (☎ 07-888 8763; www.freefall.co.nz; SH27) runs thrilling gravity-powered adventures, such as tandem skydiving from 7500ft, which costs $175. See the website for other options. The airfield is located 10km north of Matamata.

The **Firth Tower** (☎ 07-888 8369; Tower Rd; adult/child $5/1; ⌚ 10am-4pm Wed-Sun) was built in 1882 by Auckland businessman Josiah Firth. He acquired 56,000 acres from his friend Wiremu Tamihana, chief of the Ngati Haua. The tower was a fashionable status symbol rather than for defence as the Waikato Land War was long over by the time it was built. The concrete tower is filled with Maori and pioneer relics and around it are 10 other buildings including a pioneer schoolroom, jail, cottage and 14m-deep bricked well – hard work to dig and build. It's 3km from town.

Opal Hot Springs (☎ 07-888 8198; www.opalhot springs.com; Okauia Springs Rd; swimming pool adult/child $6/3, 30min private spas $8/4) is 2km down an access road off Tower Rd, just north of Firth Tower and 6km from Matamata. Try Ramaroa Spa, a private outdoor hot spa for a Garden of Eden experience. There's also a camping ground (below).

Carry on past Opal Pools to visit the 150m-high **Wairere Falls.**

Sleeping & Eating

Opal Hot Springs Holiday Park (☎ 07-888 8198; www.opalhotsprings.com; Okauia Springs Rd; unpowered/ powered sites per 2 people $22/24, cabins/tourist flats $40/53) Basic facilities are the order of the day here, but things are clean and free entry to the hot pools is part of the deal.

O'Reilly's Motor Inn (☎ 07-888 9126; www.oreillys .co.nz; 187 Firth St; studios $90-105, units $110-160) Attractive, neat and spacious units of varying size can be found in this Hunuera stone building on the SH27 into town from Hamilton. There are two suites with good wheelchair access.

Southern Belle B&B (☎ 07-888 5518; www.south embelle.co.nz; 101 Firth St; d $120) This very attractive B&B has three elegant bedrooms, a comfortable lounge and bathroom facilities. Up to five people can be accommodated here, at a charge of $30 per extra adult ($10 extra per child – and they are very welcome).

Workman's Café & Bar (☎ 07-888 5498; 52 Broadway; dinner mains $23-29; breakfast, lunch & dinner Tue-Sun) The menu here in this retro cafébar-restaurant lined with pictures and photos changes regularly but it has built itself a reputation that extends beyond Matamata. Definitely the pick of the bunch for a munch in Matamata – the menu is pretty meaty, and the dishes lovingly prepared.

Getting There & Away

InterCity (☎ 07-834 3457) runs (via a private operator) daily buses that link Matamata with Cambridge ($19, 30 minutes), Hamilton ($23, one hour) and Tauranga ($20, one hour).

TIRAU

pop 720

The small gift-shop town of Tirau (blessed with a name that translates as 'Many Cabbages'). 54km southeast of Hamilton at the junction of SH1 and SH5, has fallen head-over-heels in love with corrugated iron – keep your eyes peeled for the giant green grasshopper as you approach from Matamata. This material has been used to construct a giant dog and sheep, which are bigger than most buildings in town. The dog houses the **visitor information centre** (☎ 07-883 1202; www.tirauinfo.co.nz), while the sheep houses a large gift shop. Other fun corrugated-iron art around the town includes a big cheese, a pukeko and a cow pushing a shopping trolley. For something equally outlandish, visit the **Castle Pamela** (☎ 07-883 1112; adult/child $8/5; 9am-4.30pm) at the southern end of town. It houses a toy museum (those who find dolls creepy should steer clear) and is a monument of sorts to one couple's dream of sharing (or inflicting…) their mammoth-proportioned passion on a small town.

Just off SH27, 5km north of Tirau, is **Oraka Deer Park** (☎ 07-883 1382; www.oraka-deer .co.nz; 71 Bayly Rd; d & tw $180;), which offers a self-contained cottage or en suite rooms in the house with your own entrance. The farm has 700 deer and a deer shop. Venison meals may be possible, and it's ideal for children; it includes a pool, spa and tennis court.

Many **InterCity** (☎ 07-834 3457) buses pass through Tirau and link it with just about everywhere. The bus stop is outside the visitor information centre.

THE KING COUNTRY

The King Country is named after the Maori King Movement (see the boxed text, p233), which developed in the Waikato region in the late 1850s and early 1860s. When King Tawhiao and his people were forced to move from Waikato after being defeated by British troops during the Waikato Land War (1863–64), they came south to this region. Legend has it that King Tawhiao placed his top hat on a large map of NZ and declared that all the land it covered would be under his *mana*, or authority. It was only

OTOROHANGA

pop 2700

Otorohanga (often called 'Oto' by locals) is a friendly, easy-going farming community and the perfect example of the Kiwi icon that is the one-street (Maniatopo St) town that is services just such a demographic. The aforementioned street is decorated with murals and displays of other kiwiana, including the All-Blacks, sheep, Maori carvings, gumboots, Anchor butter and pavlova. You can also learn about other local icons, such as Footrot Flats, 'the good old quarter acre', No 8 wire, Marmite and Buzzy Bees, but the town's biggest attraction is definitely the kiwi and native-bird house.

Information

The useful **visitor information centre** (07-873 8951; www.otorohanga.co.nz; 57 Maniapoto St; 9am-5.30pm Mon-Fri, 10am-4pm Sat & Sun) is the AA agent, and it also sells bus, ferry and train tickets. The **post office** (39 Maniapoto St) is conveniently located on the main street.

Sights

The **Otorohanga Kiwi House & Native Bird Park** (07-873 7391; www.kiwihouse.org.nz; Alex Telfer Dr; adult/child $12/4; 9am-4.30pm) is a must-see. In the kiwi house night and day are reversed and you are guaranteed to see active kiwi in their indoor enclosure – they are usually energetically digging with their long beaks, searching for food. Other native birds, such as kaka, kea, falcon, morepork and weka, can also be seen.

A small **museum** (Kakamutu Rd; admission free; 2-4pm Sun) covers local history and **Otorohanga Sheepskins** (07-873 7799; 52 Maniapoto St) sells kiwiana souvenirs, including the adorable Buzzy Bee toy for small kids.

Sleeping

Oto-Kiwi Lodge (07-873 6022; oto-kiwi@xtra.co.nz; 1 Sangro Cres; sites per 2 people $21, dm/d/tw $20/46/46) This small but tidy backpackers, near the kiwi house, has a log fire and a deck. It's a well-ordered, easy-going spot and represents good value. Mountain bikes are for hire and kayak trips can be arranged.

Otorohanga Holiday Park (07-873 7253; www .kiwiholidaypark.co.nz; 12 Huiputea Dr; sites per 2 people $24, cabins/motel $45/85, units $60-85) The park's solid and serviceable facilities include a fitness centre. Sites are in good condition.

Mt Heslington (07-873 1873; www.ubd-online .co.nz/mtheslingtonfarmstay; 1375 SH3; s/d/tw $70/90/90) This 80-hectare farm, 12km north of Otorohanga, breeds cattle and racehorses, as well as growing vegetables and fruit. There are two rooms in a separate guest section, but only one group stays there at a time. Facilities include a pool table.

Palm Court Motel (07-873 7122; palmcourt@xtra .co.nz; cnr Clarke & Maniapoto Sts; studio/1-bedroom units $95/140) These smart and modern units are at the southern end of town and some have spa baths.

Eating

Thirsty Weta (07-873 6699; 57 Maniapoto St; meals $7-20; breakfast, lunch & dinner) The top pick in town, with good, hearty snacks (of the pizza, pasta, soup variety) and the promise of things kicking off after dinner when the wine-bar vibe takes over and the odd low-key live act attempts to kick out the jams.

Be Guiness Bar & Brasserie (07-873 8010; 91 Maniapoto St; mains $18-25; dinner Tue-Sun) There's a Serious Seafood Platter, a fabbo 1970s-style shrimp cocktail or you can take on a double challenge – the Hog Slab followed by any of the gut-busting desserts.

Regent Café & Bar (07-873 7373; 48 Maniapoto St; meals $5-11; breakfast & lunch daily, dinner Fri-Sun) A spacious self-service café that offers lots of simple staples, mostly homemade.

Self-caterers should head to the big **Woolworths** (125 Maniapoto St; 7am-8pm) at the southern end of town.

Getting There & Away

InterCity (0508 353 947) buses arrive at and depart from the visitor information centre, which sells tickets. There are regular buses to Rotorua ($34 to $49, three hours and 20 minutes) and Auckland ($36 to $48, four hours and 20 minutes) daily. The **Waitomo Shuttle** (0800 808 279) runs to Waitomo from Hamilton ($9, two hours 15 minutes, booking necessary).

Train services between Auckland and Wellington stop at Otorohanga station in the town centre.

---

after 1884 that Pakeha were allowed into the district and it still retains a powerful Maori influence, as Maoris are less outnumbered here than elsewhere.

WAITOMO

Waitomo is a must-do on the NZ adventure activities pilgrimage and justifiably so. The name Waitomo, which comes from *wai* (water) and *tomo* (hole or shaft), is only fitting; dotted throughout the countryside are numerous shafts dropping abruptly into underground cave systems and streams. There are more than 300 mapped caves in the Waitomo District and these limestone caves and accompanying limestone formations make up one of the premier attractions of the North Island. In late 2005 a fire destroyed all the buildings and decks at the entrance to the Glowworm Cave. Luckily, the caves (and the glow-worms) were not damaged and while new buildings for tourist operators and the souvenir shop are in the midst of being rebuilt, it's pretty much business as usual and you can still purchase tickets at the entrance to the cave.

Tours through the Glowworm Cave (also known as the Waitomo Cave) and the Aranui Cave have been feature attractions for decades, but in typical Kiwi fashion the list of things to do has grown and become

more daring. Now you can abseil, raft and tube through the caves, or try your hand at a number of aboveground activities such as driving a jetboat, riding a horse or quad bike, or swinging on a high-ropes course.

Information

The **visitor information centre** (☎ 07-878 7640; www.waitomocaves.com; 21 Waitomo Caves Rd; 8am-8pm Jan & Feb, to 5pm Mar-Dec) is in the Museum of Caves (opposite). It has Internet access, an ATM and bookshop, and acts as a post office and booking agent. Next door, in the general store, is **Waitomo Adventures** (☎ 0800 924 866, 07-878 7788; Waitomo Caves Rd; 7am–8pm summer, to 6pm winter).

Sights

WAITOMO CAVES

The **Glowworm Cave** had been known to the local Maoris for a long time, but the first European to explore it was an English surveyor called Fred Mace, who was shown the cave in December 1887 by Maori chief Tane Tinorau. Mace prepared an account of the expedition, a map was made and

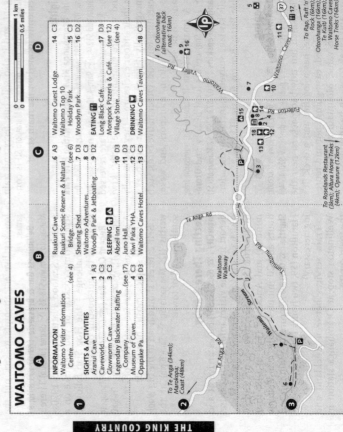

WAITOMO CAVES

INFORMATION	
Waitomo Visitor Information	
Centre...............................(see 4)	
SIGHTS & ACTIVITIES	
Aranui Cave...........................1 A3	
Caveworld..............................2 C3	
Glowworm Cave....................3 C3	
Legendary Blackwater Rafting	
Company.........................(see 17)	
Museum of Caves..................4 C3	
Opapaku Pa..........................5 D3	

| Ruakuri Cave..........................6 A3 |
| Ruakuri Scenic Reserve & Natural |
| Bridge...........................(see 6) |
| Shearing Shed........................7 D3 |
| Waitomo Adventures...............8 C3 |
| Woodlyn Park & Jetboating.....9 D2 |
| |
| **SLEEPING** |
| Abseil Inn...........................10 D3 |
| Juno Hall.............................11 D3 |
| Kiwi Paka YHA....................12 C3 |
| Waitomo Caves Hotel...........13 D3 |

| Waitomo Guest Lodge...........14 C3 |
| Waitomo Top 10 |
| Holiday Park.....................15 C3 |
| Woodlyn Park....................16 D2 |
| |
| **EATING** |
| Long Black Café...................17 D3 |
| Morepork Pizzeria & Café.....(see 12) |
| Village Store.......................(see 4) |
| |
| **DRINKING** |
| Waitomo Caves Tavern.........18 C3 |

0   1 km
0   0.5 miles

A   B   C   D

1

2

3

To Te Anga (34km); Marokopa, Coast (48km)

Te Anga Rd

Tumutumu Rd

Waitomo Walkway

Waitomo Stream

Waitomo Stream

To Roselands Restaurant (3km); Altura Horse Treks (4km); Opapure (12km)

Fullerton Rd

Waitomo Valley Rd

Waitomo Caves Rd

To Otorohanga alternative back road; 16km)

To Rap, Raft 'n' Rock (6km); Otorohanga (16km); Te Kuiti (16km); Waitomo Caves Horse Treks (16km)

photographs given to the government, and before long Tane Tinorau was operating tours of the cave. The Glowworm Cave is just a big cave with the usual assortment of stalactites and stalagmites – until you board a boat and swing off onto the river. As your eyes grow accustomed to the dark, you'll see a Milky Way of little lights surrounding you – these are the glow-worms. You can see them in other caves and other places around Waitomo, and in other parts of NZ, but the ones in this cave are something special. Conditions for their growth are just about perfect in this cave, so there is a remarkable number of them. Try to avoid the big tour groups, most of which arrive between 10.30am and 2.30pm. Photography is not allowed.

Three kilometres west from the Glow-worm Cave is the **Aranui Cave**. This cave has no river running through it and hence no glow-worms. It is a large cave with thousands of tiny 'straw' stalactites hanging from the ceiling. Various scenes in the colourful formations are pointed out and photography is permitted. It's an hour's walk to the caves or the ticket office can arrange transport.

Tickets for the two caves are sold at the entrance to the Glowworm Cave. Entry to one cave per adult/child is $30/13, or a combined two-cave ticket costs $48/22.50.

To visit the caves you'll need to take a tour. The 45-minute tours of the Glowworm Cave leave daily on the half-hour from 9am to 5pm. From late October to Easter there's also a 5.30pm tour, with more at the height of the summer season. Aranui Cave tours leave at 10am, 11am, 1pm, 2pm and 3pm, and also take about 45 minutes.

The nearby **Ruakuri Cave** is open only for group tours (see Black-Water Rafting, p250).

MUSEUM OF CAVES

This **museum** (☎ 07-878 7640; www.waitomo-museum.co.nz; 21 Waitomo Caves Rd; adult/child $5/free; ☑ 8.30am-5.30pm Mar-Dec, 8am-8pm Jan & Feb) has some excellent exhibits that explain exactly how caves are formed, the flora and fauna that thrive in them and the history of the caves and cave exploration. Displays include a cave model, fossils of extinct birds and animals that have been discovered in caves, and a cave crawl. There are also audiovisual presentations about caving, glow-worms and other natural attractions in the Waitomo area.

Free entry is generally included with various activities.

GLOW-WORM MAGIC

Glow-worms are the larvae of the fungus gnat, which looks much like a large mosquito without mouth parts. The larva glow-worms have luminescent organs that produce a soft, greenish light. Living in a sort of hammock suspended from an overhang, they weave sticky threads that trail down and catch unwary insects attracted by their lights. When an insect flies towards the light, it gets stuck in the threads and becomes paralysed – the glow-worm reels in the thread and eats the insect.

The larval stage lasts for six to nine months, depending on how much food the glow-worm gets. When the glow-worm has grown to about the size of a matchstick it goes into a pupa stage, much like a cocoon. The adult fungus gnat emerges about two weeks later.

The adult insect does not live very long because it does not have a mouth. It emerges, mates, lays eggs and dies, all within about two or three days. The sticky eggs, laid in groups of 40 or 50, hatch in about three weeks to become larval glow-worms.

Glow-worms thrive in moist, dark caves but they can survive anywhere if they have the requisites of moisture, an overhang to suspend from and insects to eat. Waitomo's famous for its glow-worms but you can see them in many other places around NZ, both in caves and outdoors.

When you come upon glow-worms, don't touch their hammocks or hanging threads, try not to make loud noises and don't shine a light right on them. In daylight their lights fade out, and if you shine a torch right on them they will dim their lights. It takes the lights a few hours to become bright again, during which time the glow-worm will catch no food. The glow-worms that shine most brightly are the hungriest.

SHEARING SHED

The **Shearing Shed** (☎ 07-878 8371; admission free; ☼ 9am-4pm) is where big fluffy Angora rabbits are sheared for an audience at 12.45pm. The store has a variety of Angora fur products.

Activities

If it's challenging underground adventures that you're after, then Waitomo, which seems so sweet and tranquil aboveground, is the place to be, with abseiling, rock climbing and cave tubing along underground rivers. You can pick and choose from a number of operators.

CAVING & ABSEILING

Spellbound (☎ 0800 773 552; www.waitomospellbound .co.nz; 3hr trip $45) is a good option if you don't want to get wet. This guided tour departs from the visitor information centre; and goes through parts of the Mangawhitikau cave system, 12km south of Waitomo.

Waitomo Adventures (☎ 0800 924 866, 07-878 7788; www.waitomo.co.nz) offers a range of cave adventures. With 100m of abseiling to get into the Lost World Cave, its Lost World trip is amazing, and you don't even need prior abseiling or caving experience. The principal trip to Lost World is an all-day one ($355). Trips run from 10.30am to 5.30pm, followed by dinner. First you abseil 100m down into the cave (accompanied by your guide), then by a combination of walking, climbing, spider-walking, inching along narrow rock ledges, wading and swimming through a subterranean river, you take a three-hour journey through a 30m-high cave to get back out, passing glow-worms, amazing rock and cave formations, waterfalls and more. The price includes lunch (underground) and dinner.

The other option is a four-hour dry trip ($225) that involves a 100m abseil into the cave, with a guide beside you on another rope. At the bottom, you walk for about an hour into the cave and exit via another vertical cavern back to the surface, without doing the underground river trip. These trips depart at 7.10am, 11.30am and 3pm but can vary.

Haggas Honking Holes is a four-hour caving trip ($165) that includes professional abseiling instruction followed by a caving trip with three abseils, rock climbing and travelling along a subterranean

river with waterfalls. Along the way you see glow-worms and a variety of cave formations – including stalactites, stalagmites, columns, flowstone (calcite deposited by a thin sheet of flowing water) and cave coral. It's a good way to see real caving action, using caving equipment and going through caverns of various sizes, from squeezing through tight, narrow passageways to traversing huge caverns.

The name of the adventure derives from a local farmer, 'Haggas', and characters in a Dr Seuss story, 'honking holers'. Trips depart at 10am and 3pm but can vary. The Gruesome Twosome combines this with the four-hour Lost World trip ($370).

'Tumu Tumu Toobing' is a more physical four-hour tubing trip ($95) for the adventurous traveller. Trips leave twice daily. If you combine the Lost World and Tumu Tumu trips it will save you $20.

St Benedict's Cavern is a three-hour trip ($100) that includes abseiling, a subterranean flying fox and 1½ hours underground in this attractive cave with straw stalagmites.

Caveworld (☎ 0800 228 396, 07-878 6577; www .caveworld.co.nz; cnr Hotel Access & Waitomo Caves Rd; rafting/caving $95/95) is on the main road in town. It operates daily 'float through' caving adventures for groups – three times daily in winter but six in summer. A good combo deal is also on offer, with black-water rafting and a night abseil costing $180.

Rap, Raft n Rock (☎ 0800 228 372; www.caveraft .com; 95 Waitomo Caves Rd; trips $99) runs a five-hour trip with small groups. It starts with abseil training, followed by a 27m abseil into a natural cave, and then involves floating along a subterranean river on an inner tube. How fast you float will depend on the season and the recent rainfall, but there are always plenty of glow-worms. After some caving you do a belayed rock climb up a stepped 20m pitch to the surface.

BLACK-WATER RAFTING

The **Legendary Black Water Rafting Company** (☎ 0800 228 464, 07-878 6219; 585 Waitomo Caves Rd; www.blackwaterrafting.co.nz), with its headquarters at the Long Black Café, runs adventures that get rave reviews. The cost of each trip includes admission into the Museum of Caves.

Black Labyrinth (three-hour trip with one hour underground, $90) involves floating on an inner tube down a subterranean river that flows through Ruakuri Cave. The high point is leaping off a small waterfall and then floating through a long, glow-worm-covered passage. The trip ends with hot showers, soup and bagels in the café. You wear a wet suit, which will keep you warm, but having something hot to eat or drink before the trip will make you feel more comfortable.

Black Abyss (five-hour trip with two to three hours underground, $175) is more adventurous and includes a 30m abseil into Ruakuri Cave and more glow-worms, tubing and cave climbing. Hot showers and snacks are included.

WALKING

The Museum of Caves has free pamphlets on various walks in the area. The walk from the Aranui Cave to the **Ruakuri Cave** is an excellent short path. From the Glowworm Cave ticket office, it's a 15-minute forest walk to a grove of California redwood trees. Also from here, the 5km, three-hour-return **Waitomo Walkway** takes off through farmland, following Waitomo Stream to the **Ruakuri Scenic Reserve**, where a 30-minute return walk passes by the river, caves and a natural limestone bridge.

At night, drive to the Ruakuri Scenic Reserve car park and walk across the bridge where glow-worms put on a magical display. Bring a torch to find your way.

OTHER ACTIVITIES

Woodlyn Park (☎ 07-878 6666; www.woodlynpark .co.nz; 1177 Waitomo Valley Rd; adult/child $18/10; ⊙ shows 1.30pm) has a rustic theatre where local entrepreneur Barry Woods puts on a one-hour farm animal show that combines history, broad humour, local critters and audience participation. The **jetboating** (7 laps $55; ⊙ 9.30am-6.30pm Nov-Apr, to 5pm May-Oct) at the park is unique because you get the chance to drive a jetboat around a figure-of-eight course instead of just being a passenger. There is also accommodation (p252).

Waitomo Caves Horse Treks (☎ 07-878 5065; wai tomocavehorsetreks@xtra.co.nz; 2hr/half-day rides $60/90) offers a variety of different rides through bush or farmland. All levels are catered for, from beginners to adrenaline riders. The stables are a 20-minute drive west of Waitomo or pick-ups can be arranged from Waitomo.

Altura Horse Treks (☎ 07-878 5278; www.altura parktreks.co.nz; 47 Fullerton Rd; 30min/1½-2hr treks $40/60 per person, has leisurely treks with interesting views and nice horses. Head south down Fullerton Rd from Waitomo Caves Rd (signposted).

Big Red (☎ 07-878 7640; www.waitomobigred.co .nz; 2hr trips $90) takes knockabout self-drive, quad-bike trips over hill and dale in this lush part of the world. Book at the visitor information centre/Waitomo Museum.

Trak n Paddle (☎ 07-957 0002; www.tracknpaddle .co.nz; tours $100-350) runs mountain biking, hiking and kayaking tours from Waitomo to Marokopa and Kawhia Harbour three times a week with small groups (maximum eight).

Caving company **Rap, Raft n Rock** (☎ 0800 228 372; www.caveraft.com) has a high-ropes course ($40), 9m above the ground. Cave rafting is also available from $99.

Sleeping

The road approaching Waitomo is lined with decent sleeping options. We've listed the ones closest to the action.

BUDGET

Kiwi Paka YHA (☎ 07-878 3395; www.kiwipaka-yha.co .nz; School Rd; dm/s/d/tw $24/54/54/56, chalets $120; P) This excellent purpose-built, Alpine-style hostel has four-bed dorms, a popular restaurant (see p252) and tidy, well-maintained facilities. Doubles and twins with bathroom and TV are also available ($75 to $90).

Juno Hall (☎ /fax 07-878 7649; junohall@junowai tomo.co.nz; 600 Waitomo Caves Rd; sites per person $10, dm $22, d & tw with/without bathroom $60/50; P) A smaller purpose-built log-cabin-style hostel with a warm welcome and an outdoor pool and tennis court. It can organise fishing, hunting and farmstays.

Waitomo Top 10 Holiday Park (☎ 07-878 7639; www.waitomopark.co.nz; sites per 2 people $30, cabins $50, tourist flats $90-105; ⊙) Opposite the museum, this spotless, modern and very well-maintained park has an outdoor pool and spa. Ask for a free torch for the Ruakuri Scenic Reserve glow-worm walk (left).

MIDRANGE

Abseil Inn (☎ 07-878 7815; abseilinn@xtra.co.nz; 709 Waitomo Caves Rd; r $130-150) A steep, steep driveway takes you to this delightful B&B with three themed rooms, great breakfasts and

Waitomo's wittiest, warmest hostess, Helen. Lovely.

Woodlyn Park (☎ 07-878 6666; www.woodlynpark.co.nz; 1177 Waitomo Valley Rd; r $100-130) You certainly won't be complaining about blandness or sameness if you stay here! Take your pick from an aeroplane (cockpit or tail room), train or Hobbit home that's better than what's left over at Matamata (p245). Bookings essential.

Waitomo Caves Hotel (☎ 07-878 8204; www.waitomocaveshotel.co.nz; School Rd; dm $30, d $70-180, f $160-180) If *The Shining* and *Fawlty Towers* had a bastard son, it would be this place. The phrase 'faded grandeur' doesn't quite cut it, but it certainly has character (and, reputedly, ghosts) and once-grand rooms (with wretched bathrooms) have generous old-world proportions and furnishings. The dorms are best avoided.

Waitomo Guest Lodge (☎ 07-878 7641; 7 Waitomo Caves Rd; s $60, d $80-90) Bags your own cosy little cabin at this central lodge with a sweet garden setting. Some lodgings may be under renovation.

Eating & Drinking

Morepork Pizzeria & Café (☎ 07-878 8395; School Rd; pizza $14-27; ☺ breakfast, lunch & dinner) Hefty, creative pizzas with perfect crispy bases are the order of the day at this pleasant eatery in the Kiwi Paka hostel that lets you BYO and has some lovely views.

Long Black Café (Waitomo Caves Rd; meals $5-14; ☺ breakfast & lunch) This spacious café, run by one of the caving companies, has pasta, salads and 'big rafting breakfasts' ($13.50), plus good coffee to fire you up for what lies ahead.

Roselands Restaurant (☎ 07-878 7611; Fullerton Rd; BBQ lunches $25; ☺ lunch) This good buffet restaurant, 3km from Waitomo, has a garden setting and is customised mostly by tour groups in coaches.

Waitomo Caves Tavern (☎ 07-878 8448; School Rd; mains $14-20) This tavern has lots of beer on tap, good-value bistro meals, kauri-pine benches and tables, and live music on weekends.

The **village store** (Waitomo Caves Rd) beside the Museum of Caves is small but has an ice-cream parlour, a bar and Internet access.

Getting There & Away

The **Waitomo Shuttle** (☎ 07-873 8279) operates up to five times daily between Waitomo and Otorohanga ($9, about 20 minutes). Bookings are essential.

InterCity/Newmans (☎ 0508 353 947) runs a daily bus service to Waitomo Caves from Auckland ($66, four hours 20 minutes) and Rotorua ($66, three hours 20 minutes).

The **Waitomo Wanderer** (☎ 027 492 6336; www.waitomotours.co.nz) operates a useful daily loop from Rotorua to Waitomo via the rock-climbing centre of Wharepapa. The bus leaves Rotorua at 7.45am, arrives at Waitomo at 10am, then departs again at 3.45pm, arriving back in Rotorua at 6pm. The cost is $40 one way.

Guthreys (☎ 0800 732 528) runs buses daily between Auckland and Waitomo ($45), departing Auckland at 7am and Waitomo at 3.45pm.

MAROKOPA ROAD

Heading west from Waitomo, you start to enter a little-visited corner of NZ. Te Anga Rd becomes Marokopa Rd, and follows a rewarding and scenic route with a couple of natural attractions worth visiting. The useful *West to Marokopa* pamphlet ($1) is produced by DOC. There are no petrol stations on the Marokopa Rd.

The **Tawarau Forest**, about 20km west of Waitomo village, has various walks outlined in the DOC pamphlet, including a one-hour walk to the Tawarau Falls from the end of Appletree Rd.

The **Mangapohue Natural Bridge Scenic Reserve**, 26km west of Waitomo, is a 5.5-hectare reserve with a giant natural limestone arch. It's a 20-minute round-trip walk to the arch on a wheelchair-accessible pathway. You can easily walk atop the arch. On the far side, big rocks full of oyster fossils jut up from the grass, and at night you'll see glow-worms.

About 4km further west is **Piripiri Caves Scenic Reserve**, where a five-minute walk along a track leads to a large cave containing fossils of giant oysters. Bring a torch and be prepared to get muddy after heavy rain.

The impressive three-tier **Marokopa Falls** are located 32km west of Waitomo. A short track (10 minutes return) from the road leads to the bottom of the falls.

The falls are near Te Anga, where you can stop for a drink at the pleasant **Te Anga Tavern** (☎ 07 876 7815; Te Anga Rd). From Te Anga you can turn north to Taharoa or Kawhia, 53km away, or southwest to **Marokopa**, a small village on the coast, 48km from Waitomo. The whole Te Anga-Marokopa area is riddled with caves.

The bitumen ends just past Marokopa at Kiritehere, but it is possible to continue 60km further south on a difficult but scenic road, until you meet SH3 at Awakino. About 20km south of Marokopa is the **Whareorino Forest**, which has forest walks. It pays to remember that there are no places to buy petrol in Marokopa.

The **Marokopa Camping Ground & Village Snack Bar** (☎ 07-876 7444; Rauparaha St; unpowered/powered sites per 2 people $20/22; dm $15) is close to the coast and has a snack bar and small shop that will cover the catering basics and supplies fishing gear, with a tennis court nearby.

There's also accommodation available in the Whareorino Forest at the backcountry and basic **Leitd's Hut** (☎ 07-878 1050; adult $5).

From Monday to Friday **Perry's bus** (☎ 07-876 7570) runs between Te Waitere, at the southern end of Kawhia Harbour, and Te Kuiti (adult/child $8/4), passing through Waitomo, Te Anga and the other scenic attractions along the Marokopa Rd. It leaves Te Waitere at 7.30am, arrives in Te Kuiti at 9.15am and makes the return journey at 1pm. Another weekday bus runs from Te Anga to Marokopa.

TE KUITI
pop 4540

This small, provincial town, south of Otorohanga, is the 'Shearing Capital of the World' and an OK base for visiting Waitomo, 19km away. The magnificently carved Te Tokanganui-o-noho Marae, overlooking the south end of Rora St, was Maori rebel leader Te Kooti's grateful gift to his hosts, the Ngati Maniapoto people, who looked after him once he had accepted the Maori king's creed of pacifism. As is only fitting, Te Kuiti hosts the annual NZ sheep-shearing championships and has a 'Big Shearer' statue as its most prominent feature.

Information
The useful **Te Kuiti visitor information centre** (☎ 07-878 8077; Rora St; ☑ 9am-5pm) can do transport and other bookings. There's Internet access at **Cabana** (☎ 07-878 8278; 129b Rora St; per 30min/hr $5/10). The **DOC office** (☎ 07-878 1050; 78

Taupiri St) can help with hiking information. The **post office** (123 Rora St) is on the main street.

Sights & Activities
The best time to visit is around the end of March or the beginning of April when the **Te Kuiti Muster** takes over the town. Sheep-shearing championships, sheep races, a parade, arts and crafts, Maori culture groups, live music, barbecues, *hangi* (a feast of Maori food) and lots of market stalls combine in this rural festival.

Near the Big Shearer statue is a **Japanese garden** and **Redwood Park**, which is full of dwarf conifers.

Te Kuitianga O Nga Whakaaro (Rora St) is an interesting pavilion that illustrates the town's history.

The Mangaokewa Stream winds through the town, with a pleasant walkway along it. Beside the stream, the **Mangaokewa Scenic Reserve** (SH30), 3km south of town, has picnic and barbecue areas and a waterhole for safe swimming. **Te Kuiti Lookout** (Awakino Rd), as the road climbs out of town heading south, provides a great view over the town, especially at night with the sparkling lights stretching out below.

On the northwestern boundary of Te Kuiti, the attractive **Brook Park** has a café (below) and a 40-minute walk leading up a hill to the site of the historic Matakiora Pa, which was constructed in the 17th century by Rora, son of Maniapoto.

Sleeping
Casara Mesa Backpackers (☎ 07-878 6697; casara@xtra.co.nz; Mangarino Rd; dm $17.50, d & tw with/without bathroom $45/40) North of town, this farmstay has great views from its veranda and will pick up guests from town.

Tapanui Country Home (☎ 07-877 8549; www.tapanui.co.nz; 1774 Oparure Rd; s/d/tw $185/195/195) This 770-hectare working farm is 20km northwest of Te Kuiti, with sheep, cattle and pet animals. Guests are asked to arrive after 4pm, and children under 16 are not allowed. Prices include breakfast. Dinner is by arrangement ($60, including NZ wine).

Eating & Drinking
Bosco Café (☎ 07-878 3633; 57 Te Kumi Rd; light meals around $7; ☑ breakfast & lunch) By Brook Park, this excellent industrial-chic café has

life-changing coffee and wonderful delights such as custard squares and savoury morsels that hit a lunchtime hunger.

BLT Café (King St; meals under $10; ✆ breakfast & lunch Mon-Fri) A small place with good pancakes, but you really must try the BLTs, which are thick and juicy.

Tiffany's (☎ 07-878 8872; 241 Rora St; mains $15-22; ✆ breakfast, lunch & dinner) Light meals at a good price are offered in this large, pleasant café, where you can happily wait for a bus to take you onto the next town while making bad jokes about breakfast at Tiffany's.

Riverside Lodge (☎ 07-878 8027; 1 Riverside La; ✆ lunch & dinner Tue-Sun) Off Sheridan St, this is a decent, friendly bar and bistro (mussel steamers $15 when available), with a deck that overlooks the stream.

Getting There & Away

InterCity buses arrive at and depart from Tiffany's restaurant at the south end of Rora St; book and buy your tickets at the visitor information centre. Long-distance buses stopping at Te Kuiti include those heading south to Taumarunui and New Plymouth and north to Hamilton and Auckland. Auckland–Wellington **Tranz Scenic** (☎ 0800 872 467, 04-495 4475) trains stop in Te Kuiti at the Rora St station.

Buses also operate in the local region. From Monday to Friday **Perry's bus** (☎ 07-876 7570) runs between Te Waitere, at the southern end of Kawhia Harbour, and Te Kuiti (adult/ child $8/4), passing through Waitomo, Te Anga and the other scenic attractions along the Marokopa Rd. It leaves Te Waitere at 7.30am, arrives in Te Kuiti at 9.15am, and makes the return journey at 1pm.

The road passes through the small town of **Piopio**, which has a small museum, and then tiny **Mahoenui**, from where the road follows the Awakino River, the most spectacular part of the route. Through a short road tunnel you enter the steep Awakino

TE KUITI TO MOKAU
☎ 06

From Te Kuiti, SH3 runs southwest to Awakino on the rugged west coast before continuing on to New Plymouth in Taranaki. The road runs through a lightly populated farming area and is very scenic in parts. Buses between Hamilton and New Plymouth take this route.

Gorge, lined with dense bush and giant ponga tree ferns.

The road follows the river to **Awakino**, a small settlement on the coast where boats shelter on the estuary, away from the wind-swept coast. The **Awakino Hotel** (☎ 06-752 9815; www.awakinohotel.co.nz; SH3; s without bathroom $40, d with/without bathroom $70/60) is a down-to-earth (and friendly) weatherboard pub on the river and near the beach. It has 10 straight-up rooms, a bar, pool table, garden, bistro meals and Sky TV. Awakino can also be reached via the Marokopa Rd from Waitomo.

Just south of Awakino is the **Manioroa Marae**, which contains the anchor stone of the *Tainui* canoe, whose descendants populated Waikato and the King Country. Ask at the organic farm opposite the *marae* on SH3 for permission to enter.

Five kilometres further south, the little fishing village of **Mokau** is at the border of the King Country and Taranaki. The town's **Tainui Museum** (☎ 06-752 9072; ✆ 10am-4pm) has a fascinating collection of old photographs from the time when this once-isolated outpost was a coal and lumber shipping port for pioneer Pakeha settlements along the Mokau River.

Mokau River Cruises (☎ 06-752 9775; adult/child $35/15) has three-hour trips up the river in the historic *Cygnet*. Reservations are essential.

Mokau has a fine stretch of black-sand beach and good surfing and fishing – the river mouth hides some of the best whitebait in the North Island. There's also a nine-hole golf course.

In Mokau township and a five-minute walk to the beach, **Palm House** (☎ 06-752 9081; www.taranaki-bakpak.co.nz/retreat/mokau; SH3; sites per 2 people $28, dm/s/d/tw $25/40/55/55) is a good 'get away from it all' backpackers that also has tent sites. Inquire at the house opposite if no-one is around. Also five minutes from the beach is **Mokau Motel** (☎/fax 06-752 9725; SH3; s/d/tw $70/80/80), where all units have bathrooms, cooking facilities and chipper management.

Just north of Mokau, **Seaview Holiday Park** (☎/fax 06-752 9708; SH3; unpowered/powered sites per 2 people $20/22, cabins $45-50, tourist flats $70) is right on the beach.

There are a couple of little stores in Mokau that do takeaways. The great **White-bait Inn** (☎ 06-752 9713; SH3) has takeaways and sit-down meals, with the area's famous whitebait on the menu in various forms.

The whitebait season runs from August until November.

TAUMARUNUI
pop 4500

A quiet little town, Taumarunui's main reason to stay is to kayak on the Whanganui River or as a cheaper alternative to staying in the tramping/skiing resorts at Tongariro National Park. See p284 for details of kayaking and jetboat trips on the Whanganui River. Taumarunui lies on SH4, 82km south of Te Kuiti and 43km north of the township of National Park.

Information
The helpful **Taumarunui visitor information centre** (☎ 07-895 7494; taumarunui@i-SITE.org; Hakiaha St; ☑ 9am-4.30pm Mon-Fri, 10am-4pm Sat & Sun) can book transport, accommodation and tours. It has a mighty working model of the Raurimu Spiral (50c).

DOC (☎ 07-895 8201; Cherry Grove Domain; ☑ 8am-5pm Mon-Fri) has information on Whanganui National Park and canoeing. The town has a **post office** (47 Miriama St), and the hospital is over the Ongarue River.

Sights & Activities
The **Hanaroa Whare** (hall) next to the police station has some beautiful carvings.

The **Raurimu Spiral** is a unique feat of railway engineering that was completed in 1908 after 10 years' work. Rail buffs can experience the spiral by taking the train to National Park township (adult/child return $32/22).

For details on the Stratford–Taumarunui **heritage trail** see p270, but note that 11km of it is unsealed.

You can walk along the Whanganui River from Cherry Grove Domain to the Taumarunui Holiday Park, 3km away, and continue further along the river through fine native bush. A shorter walk goes through native bush on the Domain and up the Incline, which provides good views over Rangaroa, the town, its rivers and mountains. Te Paka Lookout, across the Ongarue River on the western edge of town, is another good vantage point.

Sleeping
Accommodation here is well priced, as motels try to lure hikers and skiers away from Tongariro National Park.

Taumarunui Holiday Park (☎ 07-895 9345; www .taumarunuiholidaypark.co.nz; SH4; unpowered/powered sites per 2 people $20/22 cabins/tourist flats $30/50) On the banks of the Whanganui River, 3km east of town, the park has kayaks for hire and a range of classic NZ-style holiday-park sleeping options.

Kelly's Motel (☎ 07-895 8175; fax 07-895 9089; 10 River Rd; s/d/villas $55/75/95) Well-maintained and reasonably priced units with decent showers and can-do management.

Central Park Motor Inn (☎ 07-895 7132; www .central-park.co.nz; Maata St; r $65-120; 🖳) A wide range of good-quality units is available, and extensive renovations were under way when we visited, meaning that things can only get better. Book a studio suite if you fancy sleeping on a waterbed. Zeebers Restaurant (p256) is here.

Twin Rivers Motel (☎ 07-895 8063; twinriversmotel@ xtra.co.nz; 23 Marae St; d $70, 2-bedroom villa $155) In the midst of extensive refurbishment and renovation, these often-spacious units are a good choice and come complete with cooking facilities.

Fernleaf B&B (☎ 0800 337 653, 07-895 4847; www. babs.co.nz/fernleaf/index.htm; 58 Tunanui Rd, Owhango; s/d $75/100) This characterful villa offers spacious rooms with Sky TV and shared guest facilities inside the house. It's a third-generation working cattle-and-sheep farm and the kind hostess enjoys cooking so the generous breakfast and dinners (by arrangement) are labours of love. It's just off SH4, 15km southeast of Taumarunui.

Eating & Drinking
Flax (☎ 07-895 6611; 1 Hakiaha St; dinner mains $20-26; ☑ breakfast & lunch Tue, breakfast, lunch & dinner Wed-Sun) This very attractive spot is the nicest place to eat in town, with smart, stylish décor and an inventive, modern menu of such delights as supreme of salmon with bacon, or great green-lip mussels as a snack. Service is excellent too.

Trainspotters Café & Takeaways (☎ 07-895 8690; Hakiaha St; mains $19-21; ☑ lunch & dinner) The most interesting option in town is this cute converted train carriage, which has a long list of dining options, including hearty burgers, truckies meals, a kids menu and great dinner choices.

Copper Kettle (☎ 07-895 7541; Manuaute St; mains $15-21; ☑ breakfast, lunch & dinner) A huge range of interesting budget food can be found here, including such items as homemade soup, macaroni, cranberry meat loaf, roasts, homemade chocolate-chip cheesecake, all-day breakfasts and takeaways. It scores extra points for a sense of humour – the Mutton Dressed as Lamb burger is hard to resist.

Rock (☎ 07-895 8666; 111 Hakiaha St; dishes $7-16; ⏱ breakfast & lunch) This café boasts an unbeatable greasy confection called the Rock Breakfast ($14.50), and it's quite a challenge – you get two or two of everything. Batten the hatches.

Zeebers Restaurant (☎ 07-895 7133; Maata St; mains $17-28; ⏱ dinner Mon-Sat) This restaurant in Central Park Motor Inn (p255) has enjoyed a solid reputation for years and rolls out a good range of NZ staples and a few

more exotic items such as ostrich-based dishes in smart, businesslike surrounds.

Self-caterers can stroll the aisles of the **New World Supermarket** (10 Hakiaha St; ⏱ 8am-7pm Mon-Sat, 9am-7pm Sun).

Entertainment

Regent Cinema (Hakiaha St; adult $13; ⏱ Thu-Sun) Shows the latest releases. Check out the Art Deco interior.

Getting There & Away

Buses travelling between Auckland and Wellington all stop outside the train station in Taumarunui, which also houses the visitor information centre, where you can buy tickets.

Taranaki

The knuckle of land on the North Island's west coast, halfway between Auckland and Wellington, was known to the Maori as Taranaki (Peaks Without Vegetation). The large volcano that gives the region its name defines the region with an ever-visible cone and rich soil making the area a dairy heartland. Mt Taranaki's resemblance to Mt Fuji made it perfect for a star turn in *The Last Samurai* (2003), a film popular around these parts even if the rest of the world yawned. Mt Taranaki shrugged off the Mt Egmont title that Captain Cook had given it in an attempt to ingratiate himself with the Earl of Egmont, though you will still hear the older name.

But people in the 'naki (as locals call it) are proudly independent, with healthy dairy industries and off-shore mining creating enough prosperity for their own locally funded bank.

New Plymouth is the unofficial capital, and is a unique fusion of arts, café culture and surf coast. It's a short hop to Mt Egmont National Park, which boasts world-class walking or skiing, but fo' summer swells head down Surf Hwy 45 for some of the best chances to cut the curl in New Zealand. If you're keen to get off the beaten track try the Forgotten World Hwy, a swerving country drive through green hills that will lead you to another country, the Republic of Whangamomona.

HIGHLIGHTS

- Spotting sweet seals at **Sugar Loaf Islands Marine Park** (p261)

- Ascending the awe-inspiring **Mt Taranaki** (p268)

- Surfing the awesome breaks along **Surf Highway 45** (p268)

- Discovering the **Forgotten World Highway** (p270) and crossing the border into the **Republic of Whangamomona** (see the boxed text, p271)

- Getting experimental at New Plymouth's **Govett-Brewster Art Gallery** (p260)

- Hoeing down on the **Wheatly Downs farmstay** (p272) near Hawera

- Getting all shook up at the **Elvis Presley Memorial Record Room** (p272)

TELEPHONE CODE: 06

www.windwand.co.nz

as the west coast's only international deep-water port and handles cargo for much of the region. The city isn't all business though – it has a thriving arts scene and an outdoorsy focus, with awesome beaches and Egmont National Park a quick drive away.

History

The local Maori *iwi* (tribes) have long been contesting their land. In the 1820s they fled to the Cook Strait region to escape the Waikato tribes, who eventually took the area in 1832. A small group remained only at Okoki Pa (New Plymouth), where whalers also joined the fray. When European settlers arrived in 1841 the coast of Taranaki seemed deserted and there was little opposition to land claims. The New Zealand Company bought extensive tracts from the remaining Maori.

When other members of local tribes returned after years of exile, they fiercely objected to the land sale. Their claims were upheld when Governor Fitzroy ruled that the New Zealand Company was only allowed just over 10 sq km of the 250 sq km it had claimed around New Plymouth. The Crown slowly acquired more land from the Maori, who became increasingly reluctant to sell. Simultaneously the European settlers became increasingly greedy for the fertile land around Waitara.

The settlers forced the government to abandon negotiation, and war erupted in 1860. While the Maori engaged in guerrilla warfare and held the rest of the province, the settlers seized Waitara. Taranaki chiefs had refused to sign the Treaty of Waitangi,

Climate

Mt Taranaki is one of NZ's wettest spots, and frequently cops snowfalls. The moisture-laden winds coming in from the Tasman Sea are the climatic culprits as they are swept up to freezing heights by the mountain. Weather on the mountain is extremely changeable (see the boxed text, p269) and snow is common even in summer. Ironically, New Plymouth frequently tops the list of most sunshine hours on the North Island, emphasising the changeability of weather in the region.

November to April are the region's warmer months when temperatures hover around 20°C. From May to August, the temperatures drop to around 5°C to 14°C.

Getting There & Around

Air New Zealand Link and Origin Pacific have domestic flights and onward connections to/from New Plymouth. InterCity runs several bus services connecting to New Plymouth; Dalroy Express and White Star are smaller companies that run local services.

For comprehensive local timetable and fare information check online at www.wrc govt.nz/timetables. Getting to Mt Taranaki is easy as many shuttle services (p270) run between the mountain and New Plymouth.

NEW PLYMOUTH

pop 49,100

Dominated by Mt Taranaki and surrounded by lush agricultural land, New Plymouth acts

TARANAKI

so they were brutally treated as rebels by the Europeans. By 1870 over 500 hectares of their land had been confiscated with the remainder acquired through dubious transactions.

A relative peace meant that dairy farming created economic stability. Later the discovery of natural gas and oil in 1959 and more recently the creation of a natural gas field in the South Taranaki Bight have kept the province economically healthy.

Orientation & Information

Devon St (East and West) is the city's hub. For information about the region pick up the *Taranaki* guide or check online at www .windwand.co.nz and www.taranakinz.org.

BOOKSHOPS
Whitcoulls (☎ 06-758 4656; Centre City Shopping Centre, Gill St)

EMERGENCY
Ambulance, police & fire service (☎ 111)

INTERNET ACCESS
Internet access is available at the visitor information centre and at most of the backpackers.

MEDICAL SERVICES
Phoenix Urgent Doctors (☎ 06-759 4295; 95 Vivian St; ☑ 8am-10pm)
Southern Cross Hospital (☎ 06-758 2338; 205 St Aubyn St; ☑ 24hr)

MONEY

There are a number of banks along New Plymouth's main street and several foreign-exchange offices.

Bank of New Zealand (☎ 0800 275 269; 50-54 Devon St West)

Harvey World Travel Foreign Exchange (www.harveyworld.co.nz; 55-57 Devon St East)

TSB Foreign Exchange (www.tsb.co.nz; 87 Devon St West)

POST

Main post office (www.nzpost.co.nz; Currie St)

TOURIST INFORMATION

Automobile Association (AA; ☎ 06-759 4010; www.nzaa.co.nz; 49-55 Powderham St; ⏰ 8.30am-5pm Mon & Wed-Fri, 9am-5pm Tue)

Department of Conservation (DOC; ☎ 06-758 0433; www.doc.govt.nz; 220 Devon St West; ⏰ 8am-4.30pm Mon-Fri)

New Plymouth visitor information centre (☎ 06-759 6060; www.newplymouthnz.com; 1 Ariki St; ⏰ 9am-6pm Mon, Tue, Thu & Fri, 9am-9pm Wed, 9am-5pm Sat & Sun) In the Puke Ariki building.

Sights

GALLERIES

The **Govett-Brewster Art Gallery** (☎ 06-759 6060; www.govettbrewster.com; cnr Queen & King Sts; admission free; ⏰ 10.30am-5pm) is a fantastic contemporary art gallery renowned throughout NZ for its experimental, often international, shows. The work of New Zealand sculptor, film-maker, artist and overachiever Len Lye is well represented here, with showings of his 1930s animation and moves to create a wing to show his sculpture and kooky kinetic works.

For more modern artists, **Real Tart Gallery** (☎ 06-769 5717; www.virtualtart.co.nz; 62 Devon St West; admission free; ⏰ 11am-4pm) hosts shows every month by the province's newest artists and writers (some works are for sale).

Bone and wood carvings from local students are on display at the **Rangimarie Maori Arts & Crafts Centre** (☎ 06-751 2880; 80 Centennial Dr; admission free; ⏰ 9am-4pm Mon-Fri), 3km west of town at the foot of Paritutu Hill. Smaller pieces can be purchased as unique souvenirs.

PUKE ARIKI

The unmissable **Puke Ariki** (☎ 06-759 6060; www.pukeariki.com; 1 Ariki St; admission free; ⏰ 9am-6pm Mon & Tue, Thu & Fri, 9am-9pm Wed, 9am-5pm Sat & Sun) resembles silver strands of woven flax. The name means 'Hill of Chiefs', but these days the hill holds the visitor information centre, museum, library, Daily News Café and Arborio restaurant. The **museum** (admission free) has an extensive collection of Maori artefacts, wildlife and colonial exhibits. The half-hourly Taranaki Experience show features the history of the province while the audience sits in podlike seats that rumble and glow.

HISTORIC PLACES

The free *Heritage Walkway* leaflet, from the visitor information centre, outlines an interesting self-guided tour of around 30 historic sites.

Richmond Cottage (☎ 06-759 6060; www.pukeariki.com; cnr Ariki & Brougham Sts; admission free; ⏰ 11am-3.30pm) was built in 1853. Unlike most early cottages, which were made of timber, Rich-

---

MAORI NZ: TARANAKI

The Taranaki region has had a turbulent history ever since the eponymous mountain fled here to escape romantic difficulties elsewhere (p268). Since, the mountain has overlooked conflicts between local *iwi* (tribes) and invaders from the Waikato for centuries, followed by conflicts against the government in two separate wars (see p35): first in 1860–61, when traditional enemies the Waikato (p232) came to Taranaki's aid; and then again in 1865–69, where local forces were surprisingly successful under the remarkable general Titikowaru. Following the wars there were massive land confiscations and an extraordinary passive-resistance campaign at Parihaka (see the boxed text, p273).

Visitors to the region should visit Puke Ariki museum (above) in New Plymouth, and try to visit historic Parihaka (open on the 18th and 19th of each month) to see the place where passive resistance was born. Grab a copy of Maurice Shadbolt's very funny *Monday's Warriors* for an account of the Taranaki Land Wars.

For a good history of local tribes, check out Maori Tourism Taranaki (www.mtt.org.nz).

mond Cottage was sturdily built of stone. Nestled under Puke Ariki, the gardens are a fascinating fusion of old-world plants and rare NZ natives.

St Mary's Church (Vivian St), built in 1846, is the oldest stone church in NZ. Its graveyard has the headstones of early settlers and soldiers who died during the Taranaki Land Wars (1860–61 and 1865–69). Impressed by their bravery, the British also buried several Maori chiefs here.

On the eastern extreme of Devon St, the **Fitzroy Pole** was erected by the Maori in 1844 to limit settlers' land acquisition. At the base of the pole, a carving shows a sulking Pakeha (white person) topped by a triumphant Maori.

SUGAR LOAF ISLANDS MARINE PARK

The rugged islets, Back Beach on the west side of Paritutu, and the waters 1km offshore were made a marine park in 1991. The islands, which are eroded volcanic remnants, are a refuge for sea birds and over 400 NZ fur seals; most seals come here from June to October, but some stay all year round.

Boat trips to the islands are popular with **Happy Chaddy's Charters** (☎ 06-758 9133; www.windwand.co.nz/chaddescharters; adult/child $25/10), departing daily from Lee Breakwater, tide and weather permitting.

MARSLAND HILL & OBSERVATORY

The **New Plymouth Observatory** (☎ 06-753 2358; Marsland Hill; suggested donation adult/child $3/2; 7.30-9pm Tue Mar–Oct, 8-9.30pm Tue Nov–Feb) is off Robe St. Public nights include a planetarium programme and viewing through a 15cm refractor telescope, if the weather is clear.

PARITUTU

Above the power station is Paritutu, a steep hill with a magnificent view from the top. The name means 'Rising Precipice' and it's worth the tiring but quick scramble to the summit. Not only do you look down on the power station but also out over the city and the rocky Sugar Loaf Islands looming just offshore.

PARKS

New Plymouth has several picturesque parks. **Pukekura Park** (☎ 06-759 6060; www.newplymouthnz.com), a 10-minute stroll from the city centre, has 49 hectares of gardens, bush walks, streams, waterfalls, and ponds. **Display houses** (admission free; 8am-4pm) show off orchids and other exotic plants. **Row boats** (per 30min $5) make for a lazy exploration of the lake on weekends and summer evenings. The lights and decorations in Pukekura Park from late December to early February are worth making a special trip to see. The park also has a delightful cricket oval in the English tradition, with terrace seating cut into the surrounding hills.

Adjoining Pukekura is **Brooklands Park** and, between them, the **Bowl of Brooklands**, an outdoor sound-shell set amid bushland. Brooklands Park was once the grounds of a settler's home, which was destroyed by Maoris, though the fireplace and chimney survive today. Highlights include a 2000-year-old **puriri tree**, a **rhododendron dell** with over 300 varieties, a great children's **zoo** (admission free; 8.30am-5pm), which has a walk-through monkey enclosure, and the **Gables** (admission free; 1-4pm Sat & Sun), a former hospital, now an art gallery and medical museum.

On the waterfront is **Kawaroa Park**, with green areas, squash courts and the **New Plymouth Aquatic Centre** (☎ 06-759 6060; www.newplymouthnz.com; adult/child $3.60/2), which has a waterslide, an outdoor pool and an indoor pool (open year-round). Also on the waterfront in the central city area is **Puke Ariki Landing**, a historic area with sculptures, including the **Windwand**, a great phallic symbol and long pole designed by Len Lye as a kinetic sculpture that bends with the wind.

Activities

SURFING & WINDSURFING

The stunning Taranaki coastline is a world-class surfing and windsurfing area. Fitzroy and East End Beaches are both at the eastern end of New Plymouth. There's also decent surf at Back Beach, by Paritutu at the western end of the city, and at Oakura, about 15km west of New Plymouth. There are no buses to Oakura but hitching is easy. There are surf beaches all along Surf Hwy 45 (SH45). Fine volcanic sand is a real treat.

Vertigo (☎ 06-752 8283; vertigosurf@xtra.co.nz; 605 SH45, Oakura; hire per 30min/1hr $25/40, lessons $90) hires out surfboards and sailboards, and offers instruction. **Tangaroa Adventures** (☎ 021 701 904; tangaroa.adventure@xtra.co.nz; 25 Collins St, Hawera) and **Taranaki Coastal Surf Charters** (☎ 027 459 2306)

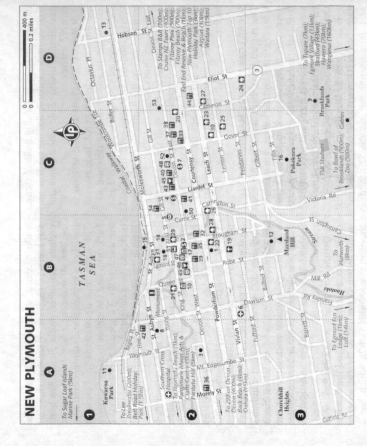

NEW PLYMOUTH

both provide guided surf tours of the area. The inexperienced can try **Tandem Surfing** (☎ 06-752 7734; www.hang20.com; 27 Maise Tce, Oakura; lesson & hire $80), who guarantee you'll stand up. **Carbon Art** (☎ 0508 946 376; carbonart@xtra.co.nz; Ngamotu Beach) specialises in windsurfing hire and lessons.

Learn to surf with **Surf Taranaki** (☎ 06-758 0400; 39 Beach St, Fitzroy; 1½hr one-on-one lesson $65) or try windsurfing with **Taranaki Windsurfing** (☎ 0508 946 376; Ngamotu Beach; per person from $35).

WALKING

The visitor information centre has leaflets about walks around New Plymouth, including coastal, local reserve and park walks, in addition to the Heritage Walkway. The 7km Coastal Walkway, from Lake Rotomanu to Port Taranaki makes for a scenic orientation of the town. Te Henui Walkway, extending from the coast at East End Reserve to the city's southern boundary, is one of the most interesting and varied walks. Huatoki Valley Walkway, following Huatoki Stream, makes an attractive walk to the city centre.

OTHER ACTIVITIES

Sugar Loaf Islands Marine Park offers activities such as boating, sailing, bird-watching, pole fishing, surfing, diving and beach walks.

Diving options on offer include **Blue Line Dive** (☎ 06-758 3100; 151 St Aubyn St; 2 dives $130) and **New Plymouth Underwater** (☎ 06-758 3348; www.newplymouthunderwater.co.nz; 16 Hobson St; equipment & dive from $95).

Tours

Beck Helicopters (☎ 0800 336 644; mountain flight $225) Can take you to the top of Taranaki and across to Tongariro, weather permitting.

Cruise NZ Tours (☎ 06-758 3222; kirstall@xtra.co.nz; adult/child full-day $90/60) Runs tours around the city and in the surrounding area.

Cycletours Taranaki (☎ 06-756 7727; www -cycle-taranaki.co.nz; 3-day tour ind bike hire & back-up service $300-350) Offers self-guided tours around the area.

Samurai Village Tours (☎ 06-752 6806; www .samuraivillagetours.com; adult/child $32/18; ☼) departs 10am Mon, Wed, Fri & Sun) Lets you pose like Tom Cruise on the sets of *The Last Samurai*.

INFORMATION
Automobile Association.....1 B2
Bank of New Zealand.....2 B2
Department of Conservation.....3 A2
Harvey World Travel Foreign
Exchange.....4 C2
Main Post Office.....5 B2
New Plymouth Visitor
Information Centre.....(see 14)
Phoenix Urgent Doctors.....6 B2
TSB Foreign Exchange.....7 C2
Whitcoulls.....(see 34)

SIGHTS & ACTIVITIES
Blue Line Dive.....8 A2
Brooklands Park.....9 D3
Govett-Brewster Art Gallery.....10 B2
Kawaroa Park.....11 A1
New Plymouth Aquatic
Centre.....(see 11)
New Plymouth Observatory.....12 B3
New Plymouth Underwater.....13 D1
Puke Ariki.....14 B2
Puke Ariki Landing.....15 B2
Pukekura Park.....16 C3
Real Tart Gallery.....17 B3
Richmond Cottage.....18 B2
St Mary's Church.....19 B2
Windwand.....(see 15)

SLEEPING
Abode on Courtney.....20 C2
Bella Vista.....21 B2
Brougham Heights
Motel.....22 B2
Central City
Lodge.....23 C2
Central Motel.....24 D2
Cottage Mews.....25 D2
Issey Manor.....26 C2
Landmark.....27 D2
Nice Hotel.....28 D2
Shoestring Budget
Backpackers.....(see 25)
Sunflower Lodge.....29 B2
Timata Ora.....30 C2
Waterfront.....31 B2

EATING
Andre's L'Escargot.....32 B2
Arborio.....(see 14)
Bella Vita.....33 C2
Centre City Shopping
Centre.....34 C2
Chaos.....35 B2
Daily News Café.....(see 14)
Down to Earth.....36 A2
El Condor.....37 C2
Empire.....(see 49)
Ly's Bakery.....38 C2
Mookai.....39 B2
Ozone Coffee Factory.....40 C2
Pak N Save.....(see 34)
Salt.....(see 31)
Sandwich Extreme.....41 C2
Simply Read Café & Bookshop.....42 A2
Ulta Lounge.....43 C2
Woolworths.....44 D2

DRINKING
Crowded House.....45 C2
Matinee.....(see 39)
Peggy Gordon's Celtic Bar.....46 B2
PowderRoom.....(see 49)

ENTERTAINMENT
Basement Bar.....(see 46)
Top Town Cinema 5.....48 C2
TSB Showplace.....49 B2

TRANSPORT
Air New Zealand Link.....50 C2
Bus Station for InterCity &
Dalroy Express.....51 B2
Cycle Inn Bike Hire.....52 C2
Rent-a-Dent.....53 D2
Travel Centre.....(see 34)

Sleeping

Sea views will edge up the price, but there are well-priced options, many close to the city.

BUDGET

Egmont Eco Lodge (06-753 5720; www.mttaranaki .co.nz; 12 Clawton St; sites per 2 people $22, dm/s/f $20/30/70, d & tw $50) This out-of-the-way lodge is set amid a bushy glade with chirping birds and babbling creek. Ten-bed mixed dorms are in the main lodge, but smaller pinewood cabins sleep a maximum of four. The kitchen is well set up, staff are cheerful and bonuses, such as nightly Egmont cake and morning eel feedings (look out for the large one called Conan), make good opportunities to meet fellow guests.

Shoestring Budget Backpackers (06-758 0404; shoestringbp@xtra.co.nz; 48 Lemon St; dm/s $19/27; d & tw $40-50) Set in a heritage building, Shoestring keeps its historical ties (such as gorgeous rimu timber interiors and a stained-glass window of the mountain) while being well maintained and sociable. Upstairs rooms are more secluded, but dorms downstairs are handy to the dining area, deck barbecues, small sauna and chilled-out sun room, which includes a massive map of New Plymouth. If you want to upgrade, Cottage Mews is next door.

Sunflower Lodge (06-759 0050; www.sunflower lodge.co.nz; 25 Ariki St; dm $20-22, s $40, d & tw $50-60;) This is as close as you can get to staying in Puke Ariki, with sea views from a sun-drenched balcony (in summer at least). Singles and doubles have good features, such as TVs. *The Last Samurai* is shown regularly in the cosy lounge, and the kitchen is well equipped.

Central Motel (06-758 6444; central.new.ply mouth@xtra.co.nz; 86 Eliot St; s/d $65/75) Up the hill on Eliot St, Central Motel is indeed central and has tidy studio units with a small kitchen and optional Sky TV. Excellent value.

Central City Lodge (06-758 0473; 104 Leach St; dm/s/d $20/30/50) Shhh, don't tell anyone we told you, but this little backpackers gets the advantages of next door's motel, such as Sky TV and pool, at backpacker prices. There are six bunks to a dorm in this older place, which could be a little soulless if not for the retro carpeting that's as funky as James Brown's shirt. There's a laundry and disabled access throughout.

Belt Road Holiday Park (0800 804 204, 06-758 0228; www.beltroac.co.nz; 2 Belt Rd; sites $24, cabins $35-80) This pohutukawa-covered Holiday Park is on a bluff overlooking the port, 1.5km west of the town centre. Cabin prices depend on facilities.

New Plymouth Top 10 Holiday Park (☎ 06-758 2566; www.nptop10.co.nz; 29 Princes St; sites/cabins $20/40, tourist flats $55-80, units $70-100; ☐) This park is in Fitzroy, 3.5km east of the centre, with pleasant cottages and family fittings, such as a life-sized chess set, trampoline, laundry and generous kitchen.

MIDRANGE

Issey Manor (☎ 06-758 2375; www.isseymanor.co.nz; 32 Carrington St; d $110-140) Staying at this slick and sophisticated spot combines the best of B&Bs and luxury motels. There are TVs and stereos in every room (borrow CDs from the collection downstairs), orange chairs and faux-fur throws. Pricier rooms have balconies that overlook the bush and feature designer bathrooms with spas.

Bella Vista (☎ 06-769 5932; www.bellavistamotels .co.nz; cnr King & Queens Sts; d $110; ☐ ☐) With a royal location, plenty of facilities and helpful staff, this new motel is perfect for those keen to explore the city. Extras include spa, Jetstream Internet and an ill-placed basketball hoop in the car park (hopefully portable).

Abode on Courtney (☎ 06-769 5465; 155 Courtenay St; d/f $110/165) Popular with a business crowd, this newer motel has spas, big TVs and interconnecting studios for holiday romances. Otherwise rooms are self-contained with kitchenettes and small dining areas.

Stamps B&B (☎ 06-757 4225; cnr Devon St East & Paynters Ave; d $130) Located in 'ye olde Fitzroy post office' this place keeps its 'periode charme' with quaint rooms and full English breakfasts, but makes considerate concessions to modernity with a hush glass against traffic noise and plenty of parking.

Loft (☎ 06-753 2950; www.taranakiloft.com; 729 Frankley Rd; d $110) A spot so secluded that the turn-off, 14km out of town, isn't even marked. This two-storey shack is deep in sheep country, and has a huge plant conservatory and plenty of room for a family.

Brougham Heights Motel (☎ 06-757 9954; www .broughamheights.co.nz; 54 Brougham St; d $115-130) A hilltop location and roomy bathrooms with spas make this an ideal retreat in the city. Sky TV and velour couches mean you can hide out here, and there's double glazing for quiet.

panelling and, in one room, a giant teddy, then you've found your B&B. The Totara suite is a luxury upstairs pad with four-poster bed, cavernous bathroom and sea views.

299 on Devon (☎ 0800 843 299; 299 Devon St; d/f $100/130; ☐ ☐) On the main thoroughfare through town, this place presents generously sized rooms with in-room broadband. Staff helpfully offer breakfast options and there's a small pool to soak in at day's end.

Cottage Mews (☎ 06-758 0403; shoestring@xtra .co.nz; 48 Lemon St; s/d $75/85) Check in at Shoestring Budget Backpackers for this modest motel. Well-kept rooms have smaller bathrooms, but feature antique furnishings and medium-sized TVs.

Landmark (☎ 06-769 9688; 72 Leach St; d $98-105) Under the shade of a massive tree, this modern place has kitchenettes and (in pricier rooms) spa baths.

TOP END

Waterfront (☎ 06-769 5301; www.waterfront.co.nz; 1 Egmont St; d $180-450) Few properties are placed to offer ocean, mountain and Windwand views, but this sleek motel exceeds expectations. Minimalist studios include super king beds and big-screen bay views, but the movie-star penthouses steal the show with DVDs, European-style laundries and balconies. The on-site Salt restaurant does excellent room service, though the restaurant itself has stunning views.

Nice Hotel (☎ 06-758 6423; www.nicehotel.co.nz; 71 Brougham St; d/ste $225/300) Truly a boutique hotel. Nice is an understatement to describe the six individual rooms, which include large bathrooms, DVDs and bold decoration. Each room is named for its view from St Mary's to the Windwand, with the exception of the ground-floor suite. This suite consists of several rooms and a grand piano, and can host a fully catered dinner party from the elegant in-house bistro.

Eating

New Plymouth is up to its *panini* in food: some pricey, some perfect.

RESTAURANTS

Bella Vita (☎ 06-758 3393; 37 Gover St; lunch $12-16, dinner $26-28; ☺ lunch Tue-Fri, dinner Mon-Sat) This fun, flirty Italian place does fine dining in the evenings offering innovative modern food, including the spicy Penne Diavolo

Timata Ora (☎ 06-757 9917; www.timatora.co.nz; 55 Gover St; s $90-100, d $120) If you're after homey touches like chocolates on your pillow, wood

with a snappy salami. Lunches are more casual and best enjoyed in the sunny courtyard; grab the steak sandwich (sorry, Bistecca Parino) for a flavoursome bite.

Salt (☎ 06-759 5304; 1 Egmont St; mains $13-30; ☑ breakfast, lunch & dinner) Some of the best views from the Waterfront hotel are at this snazzy restaurant, which offers a Pacific Rim menu and a Tasman aspect. Drinks at dusk in the sleek Pepper bar are an ideal way to ease into a divine meal.

Arborio (☎ 06-759 6060; 1 Ariki St; meals $5-10; ☑ breakfast, lunch & dinner) Similar to Salt, this sophisticated restaurant uses its seaside location to showcase the bay. The Mediterranean menu is complemented by a good Kiwi wine list and the location in Puke Ariki is another highlight.

CAFÉS

Mookai (☎ 06-759 2099; 67 Devon St West; snacks $9-18, mains $16-21; ☑ breakfast & lunch daily, dinner Mon-Sat) This joint is so hip it's in danger of dislocating itself with modish design and downbeat tunes. The tasting plate changes daily, but expect regular menu treats including Moroccan spiced fish or coconut-lemon grass curry.

Simply Read Cafe & Bookshop (☎ 06-757 8667; cnr Dawson & Hine Sts; meals $6-12; ☑ breakfast, lunch & dinner) Close to the beach, this popular café and New Agey bookshop is a good spot for browsing mums and the wave weary. The blackboard menu and deli display case have treats including *paninis*, egg-and-bacon pies, and some seriously tasty cakes and slices.

Empire (☎ 06-758 1148; 112 Devon St West; lunches $6-9; ☑ 9am-4pm Mor-Fri) These cute old-style tearooms do *quesadillas* (cheese folded between tortillas and fried or grilled), healthy salads, and less-healthy desserts. Beeline for the sunny courtyard in summer.

Daily News Cafe (☎ 06-759 6060; 1 Ariki St; meals $5-10; ☑ lunch) Want to feel like a foreign correspondent? At this library-café, you can plug into CNN or BBC news via headphones while swilling your coffee, enjoying current newspapers. Our favourite wall-decorating headline is right next to the moon landing and WWII ending: 'Taranaki wins shield'.

El Condor (☎ 06-757 5436; 170 Devon St East; meals $11-24; ☑ dinner Tue-Sat) The unique Argentinean take on tacos and calzones means there're hearty portions, but the signature dish is definitely double-layered pizza.

Andre's l'Escargot (☎ 06-758 4812; 37-39 Brougham St; mains $23-35; ☑ lunch & dinner Mon-Sat) A heritage building and a seasonal French menu make this one of the New Plymouth's best bites.

Ultra Lounge (☎ 06-758 8444; 75 Devon St East; lunch $5-14, dinner $25-30; ☑ lunch & dinner) At this modish place lunches are casual affairs with bagels and salads key to the menu, but dinner is an opulent experience with stylish Pacific rim fare. Booths are great for dining, but the balcony with its urban views is excellent in the evenings.

Ozone Coffee Factory (☎ 06-779 9020; 121 Devon St East; meals $6.50-13; ☑ lunch) For a jumper-lead brew of Ozone coffee (these guys supply most of New Plymouth), 'caffiends' head to this fashionable spot. Creative food runs to apple and snag rolls, *paninis* and sweet key-lime cupcakes. Fair-trade coffee is also offered.

QUICK EATS

Sandwich Extreme (☎ 06-759 6999; 52 Devon St East; dishes $5.50-7.50; ☑ lunch) A swift sandwich, toasty or baked spud are delivered at this snappy eatery.

Ly's Bakery (☎ 06-769 5087; 182 Devon St East; snacks $1-4; ☑ breakfast & lunch) This large place serves up old-style value with a range of pies, raspberry lamingtons and afghan biscuits; even 'fancy cake' is less than three bucks!

In the **Centre City Shopping Centre** (Gill St) there's a food hall with Chinese and Italian food, seafood, wholefood, sandwiches and desserts.

AUTHOR'S CHOICE

Chaos (☎ 06-759 8080; 36 Brougham St; slices $4-6, meals $10-16; ☑ breakfast & lunch) Slickly modern and throbbing with high-energy music, it's no wonder Chaos is popular with nearby radio DJs. The menu shows creative, but healthy (much of the produce is organic) flair, with smoked salmon and cream cheese challenging Ring of Fire Curry, and a 'grazing menu' for breakfast until 2pm (but get here early for comfy couches). We recommend the slices, especially sticky sweet Sludge.

SELF-CATERING

Pak N Save (Centre City Shopping Centre, Gill St) and **Woolworths** (btwn Leach & Courtenay Sts) supermarkets are both represented in town. **Down to Earth** (cnr Devon St West & Morley St) sells organic wholefoods.

Drinking

Ultra Lounge (☎ 06-758 8444; 75 Devon St East) Daytime coffees and late-night cocktails both suit this excellent venue that has good DJs spinning drum and bass, and old-school and underground house.

Peggy Gordon's Celtic Bar (☎ 06-758 8561; cnr Devon St West & Egmont St) Light on the blarney, this laid-back spot is a relaxed place to bend the arm with a Guinness.

Matinee (☎ 06-759 2088; 69 Devon St West) In a former theatre, this low-key bar maintains plush fittings and a luxury ambience ideal for sipping wines. A retro/indie soundtrack completes the scene.

Some other popular nightspots include **Crowded House** (☎ 06-759 4921; www.crowdedhouse .co.nz; Devon St East; mains $13-22; ⏲ 10am-late), which is popular with all ages, and **PowderRoom** (☎ 06-759 2089; 108 Devin St; ⏲ 4pm-late Tue-Sat), a smooth wine-cocktail bar that's popular with a smart after-work crowd.

Entertainment

Bowl of Brooklands (☎ 06-759 6080; www.bowl.co.nz; Brooklands Park) A large outdoor theatre. Check with the visitor information centre for current concert schedules and prices.

TSB Showplace (☎ 06-758 4947; tsbshowplace.new plymouth@xtra.co.nz; Devon St West) Formerly the Opera House, TSB stages a variety of big performances.

Top Town Cinema 5 (☎ 06-759 9077; www.cinema -5.co.nz; 119-125 Devon St East; adult/child $12/6.50) This cinema shows Hollywood's latest films.

Basement Bar (☎ 06-758 8561; cnr Devon St West & Egmont St; admission to see bands $10-20; ⏲ from 6pm Tue-Sat) This subterranean spot hosts local singer-songwriters, as well as a few good visiting rockers on weekends.

Getting There & Away

You can book tickets for InterCity, Tranz Scenic and the Interislander Wellington–

Picton ferry at **Travel Centre** (☎ /fax 06-759 9039; Level 2, Centre City Shopping Centre, Gill St).

AIR

Air New Zealand Link (☎ 06-737 3300; www.airnz .co.nz; 12-14 Devon St East) has daily direct flights to/from Auckland (45 minutes, three to four daily) and Wellington (55 minutes, four daily), with onward connections to Christchurch and Nelson. **Origin Pacific** (☎ 0800 302 302, 03-547 2020; www.originpacific.co.nz) also has direct flights to Wellington and Auckland with onward connections.

BUS

InterCity (☎ 06-759 9039; www.intercitycoach.co.nz; behind Centre City Shopping Centre on Gill St; runs buses to/from Hamilton (one way $44, four hours, two daily), Auckland (one way $68, six hours, two daily), and two buses daily (three on Friday and Sunday) to Wanganui (one way $33, three hours), Palmerston North (one way $43, four hours) and on to Wellington (one way $62, four hours).

Dalroy Express (☎ 0508 465 622; www.dalroytours .co.nz; 7 Erica Pl) operates a daily service between Auckland (one way $55, four hours) and Hawera (one way $13, four hours) via New Plymouth and Hamilton (one way $35, two hours). Buses depart from behind Centre City Shopping Centre.

White Star (☎ 06-758 3338; 25 Liardet St) has two daily buses during weekdays and one at weekends to/from Wanganui (one way $22, 2½ hours), Palmerston North (one way $30, 3¾ hours), Wellington (one way $45, 6¼ hours) and many small towns in between.

Getting Around

New Plymouth airport (☎ 06-755 2250) is 11km east of the centre. **Withers** (☎ 0800 751 177, 06-751 1777; www.withers.co.nz; adult $25) operates a door-to-door shuttle to/from the airport and offers online bookings.

Cycle Inn Bike Hire (☎ 06-758 7418; 133 Devon St; per day $20) rents out bicycles. For cheap car hire, head to **Rent-a-Dent** (☎ 0800 736 822; 191 Devon St East). To catch a taxi call **Energy City Cabs** (☎ 06-757 5580).

Okato Bus Lines (☎ 06-758 2799; okatobus@xtra .co.nz; timetables 50c) serves the city and its surrounding suburbs Monday to Saturday. The main bus stop is outside the Centre City Shopping Centre.

For details of shuttle services from New Plymouth to Mt Taranaki see p270.

AROUND NEW PLYMOUTH

Pukeiti Rhododendron Trust
This 4-sq-km garden (06-752 4141; www.pukeiti.org.nz; 2290 Carrington Rd; adult/child/senior $12/free/10; 9am-5pm Oct-Mar, 10am-3pm Apr-Sep) is the main drawcard, but there are other places of interest within 20km of New Plymouth.

This 4-sq-km garden is surrounded by bush land, and houses a renowned collection of rhododendrons and azaleas. Rhododendrons generally flower from September to November, although the garden is worth a visit at any time of year.

Pukeiti is 20km south of New Plymouth. The road passes between the Pouakai and Kaitake Ranges, both part of Egmont National Park, but separated by the trust.

Tupare
The Tudor-style Tupare (06-764 6544; 487 Mangorei Rd; admission by gold coin donation; garden 9am-5pm Sep-Mar), located 7km south of New Plymouth, is a genteel three-storey house surrounded by 3.6 hectares of traditional English gardens.

Hurworth
This 1856 homestead (06-759 6080, 753 3592; by appointment only), about 8km south of New Plymouth, was built by Harry Atkinson, who went on to be four-time NZ prime minister. The house is a survivor of the Taranaki Land Wars and features graffiti from the wars along with Atkinson's possessions.

Lake Mangamahoe & Taranaki Aviation, Transport & Technology Museum
If you're heading towards Stratford or North Egmont or State Hwy 3 (SH3), stop at Lake Mangamahoe, 9.5km south of New Plymouth, for great photographs of Mt Taranaki reflected in the lake.

Situated opposite the lake is the Taranaki Aviation, Transport & Technology Museum (Tatatm; 06-752 2845; www.nzmuseums.co.nz cnr SH3 & Kent Rd; adult/child $5/1; 10.30am-4pm Sun), which displays vehicles, railway and aviation exhibits, farm equipment and some household exhibits.

Inglewood
The small town of Inglewood has a butcher, fruit and veg shop, two pubs and a supermarket. It's a handy place for day-trippers to Egmont National Park. The visitor information centre is in the same spot as the Fun Ho! Toy Museum (06-756 7030; www.funho.com; adult/child $5/free), a charming museum of sand-cast toys of Kiwi yesteryear.

Forrestal Lodge (06-756 7242; forrestallodge@xtra.co.nz; 23 Rimu St; dm/s/tw/d $18/35/45/75), a large former convent, offers monkishly basic rooms and B&B rooms, with a St Francis statue keeping an eye on the trampoline.

Funkfish Grill (06-756 7287; 33 Matai St; snacks $4-12; lunch & dinner Tue-Sun), a hip fish and chippery, doubles as a bar at night and does excellent takeaway.

North via State Highway 3
Heading north towards Waikato from New Plymouth, SH3 is a scenic route. This is the route for Waitomo, and buses heading north go this way to Hamilton. Get the free Scenic 3 Highway brochure from the visitor information centres in Otorohanga (p247) or New Plymouth (p260).

Waitara is 13km northeast of New Plymouth on SH3. If you turn off SH3 at Brixton, just before Waitara, and head 7km south, you'll reach the site of the Pukerangiora Pa. It's beautifully situated on a high cliff by the Waitara River, but historically it was a particularly bloody battle site.

Heading north the highway follows the high sand dunes and surf beaches of the west coast. Urenui, 16km past Waitara, is a popular beach in summer.

About 5km past Urenui, you can sample organic beers at the White Cliffs Brewing Company (06-752 3676; www.brewing.co.nz/mikes.htm; Main Rd Ntn; 10am-6pm). The brewery is located near the turn-off to Pukearuhe and Whitecliffs, huge drops resembling their Dover namesake. The Whitecliffs Walkway leads from Pukearuhe to Tongaporutu River via a tunnel from the beach, accessible only at low tide. On clear days the eight-hour walk affords superb views of the coastline and Mts Taranaki and Ruapehu.

MT TARANAKI (MT EGMONT)
The massive cone of 2518m Taranaki, a dormant volcano that resembles Japan's Mt Fuji, dominates the province.

TARANAKI

Geologically, Mt Taranaki is the youngest of three large volcanoes, including Kaitake and Pouakai, on the same fault line. Mt Taranaki last erupted 350 years ago, so experts say it's long overdue for another eruption. The top 1400m is covered in lava flows from the last eruption; some descend to 800m above sea level.

History

Mt Taranaki was supremely sacred to the Maoris, both as a burial site for chiefs and as a hide-out in times of danger.

According to legend, Taranaki was once a part of the tribe of volcanoes at Tongariro, until he departed rather hurriedly when Tongariro caught him with the beautiful Pihanga, the volcano near Lake Taupo who was Tongariro's lover. The defeated Taranaki gouged out a wide scar (the Whanganui River) in the earth as he fled south in disgrace, moving west to his current position, where he's remained in majestic isolation ever since, hiding his face behind a cloud of tears.

The Maori did not settle the area between Taranaki and Pihanga very heavily, possibly fearing the reunification of the lovers in a spectacular eruption. Maori settlements in this district lined the coast between Mokau and Patea, concentrated around Urenui and Waitara.

Created in 1900, Egmont National Park is NZ's second-oldest national park.

Information

To tramp in Egmont National Park, it's *essential* that you get information about current track and weather conditions before you set off.

The best information is at New Plymouth DOC (p260) and **North Egmont visitor information centre** (☎ 06-756 0990; www.doc.govt .nz; ☒ 8am-4pm Oct-Apr, 9am-4pm May-Sep), which has the most current information. At the centre, there are interactive displays on the mountain, an informative video and a small café. **Dawson Falls visitor information centre** (☎ 027 443 0248; www.doc.govt.nz; Rd 29; ☒ 8am-4.30pm Wed-Sun, 8am-4.30pm Mon-Sun school summer holidays) is around the other side of the mountain. **Stratford DOC** (☎ 06-765 5144; www .doc.govt.nz; Pembroke Rd; ☒ 8am-4.30pm Mon-Fri) also offers advice. **Metphone** (☎ 0900 999 06) can also give climate updates.

Activities

WALKING & SKIING

Due to its accessibility, Mt Taranaki ranks as the 'most climbed' mountain in NZ. Nevertheless, tramping on this mountain is dangerous and should not be undertaken lightly (see the boxed text, opposite). It's *crucial* to get advice before departing and to fill out the intentions book at a DOC office or visitor information centre. If you intend to walk or climb for any distance or height be sure to have an appropriate map. All brochures mentioned here are available from DOC.

In winter the mountain is popular with skiers, while during the summer it can be climbed in a day. Some higher alpine tracks are suffering erosion and DOC is encouraging people to use the lower tracks, which are well maintained.

Trips to North Egmont, Dawson Falls and East Egmont are worthwhile for the views, and there are numerous long and short tracks and tramps as well; pick up a copy of *Short Walks in Egmont National Park* ($2.50). From North Egmont, the Ngatoro Loop Track (one hour return), Ram Track (four hours return) and Ambury Monument Walk (20 minutes return) are all recommended basic walks, while East Egmont has disabled access on Potaema Track (30 minutes return) and East Egmont Lookout (30 minutes return), with longer trails, such as the Enchanted Track (two to three hours return). Dawson Falls has the excellent, though challenging, Fanthams Peak Return (five hours return), which is snowed-in during winter.

Other walks include the York Loop Track, which follows part of a disused railway line (there is a free leaflet of this walk). York Rd, north of Stratford, provides access to the walk. The Pouakia Circuit (12 hours return) is a multiday walk that leaves from Dawson Falls and loops around the mountain and across Stony Creek. Buy a brochure ($1.50) at DOC.

The round-the-mountain track, accessible from all three mountain roads, goes 55km around the mountain and takes from three to five days to complete. You can start or finish this track at any park entrance and there are a number of huts en route. Purchase hut tickets (see Sleeping, opposite) and the handy *Around the Mountain Circuit* ($2.50) brochure from DOC.

DECEPTIVE MOUNTAIN

Mt Taranaki looks like an easy climb, but this scenic mountain has claimed more than 60 lives. The principal hazard is the weather, which changes from summery to white-out conditions unexpectedly and within a distance of 100m. You may leave New Plymouth in sun and, because of the higher altitude, find yourself in a snowfall. There are also precipitous bluffs and steep icy slopes.

In good conditions, tramping around the mountain is comfortable; January to March is the best time. You should have up-to-date maps and consult a DOC officer for current conditions before tramping. You must register your tramping intentions and emergency contact numbers with a DOC office. Pick up the brochure *Taranaki: The Mountain* from DOC offices or visitor information centres for more safety tips.

There is one main route to the summit, which starts at the North Egmont visitor information centre; it's a pole route and takes about six to eight hours for the return trip. This route on the mountain's north side loses its snow and ice earliest in the year – it's advisable not to make the climb in snow and ice conditions if you're inexperienced.

Guides

You can hike without a guide from February to March when snowfalls are low, but inexperienced climbers (or those looking for tramping companions) can check with DOC for contacts with local tramping clubs and guides. It generally costs around $200 per day to hire a guide. Reliable operators include the following:

MacAlpine Guides (☎ 0274 417 042, 06-765 6234; www.macalpineguides.com; 30 Celia St, Stratford)

Top Guides (☎ 0800 448 433, 021-833 513; www.top guides.co.nz)

Ski Passes

At the top of Pembroke Rd is Stratford Plateau, and from there it's a mere 1.5km walk to the small Manganui ski area. You can purchase ski passes for the day (adult/child $35/20), and skiing equipment can be hired at the **Mountain House Motor Lodge** (☎ 0800 668

682, 06-765 6100; www.mountainhouse.co.nz; Pembroke Rd) near Stratford. The Stratford visitor information centre has useful daily weather and snow reports and there's also a **snow phone service** (☎ 06-765 7669).

For more on skiing here, see p81.

Sleeping

BUDGET

There are many tramping huts scattered about the mountain, administered by DOC and accessed by trails. Most cost $10 a night (purchased from DOC offices), except Syme and Kahui huts, which cost $5. You need to bring your own cooking, eating and sleeping gear, and no bookings are necessary. It's all on a first-come, first-served basis, but you must purchase tickets before starting the walks. Camping is permitted in the park, though it is not encouraged; you're supposed to use the tramping huts.

Bookings are essential for the first two accommodation options and you must carry out *all* your rubbish.

Konini Lodge (☎ 027 443 0248; adult/child $20/10) Right by the Dawson Falls visitor information centre, this lodge offers bunkhouse accommodation.

Camp House (☎ 0800 688 2727; dm adult/child $25/15, d $65) This basic raw-pine lodge is located at North Egmont visitor information centre and offers bunkhouse-style accommodation. Double rooms are basic with shared amenities.

Eco Inn (☎ 06-752 2765; www.ecoinn.co.nz; 671 Kent Rd; s/tw/d $20/24/45) About 6.5km south of the Taranaki Aviation, Transport & Technology Museum, this ultra ecofriendly place is made from recycled timber, plus solar, wind and hydropower provide hot water and electricity. But there's no rationing of comforts, which include the spa and pool table. Eco Inn is close to Egmont National Park and offers transport to the mountain (at an extra cost).

Missing Leg (☎ 06-752 2570; missingleg@xtra.co.nz; 1082 Junction Rd, Egmont Village; unpowered/powered sites $20/24, dm/d/bach $16/40/45) This excellently ecocentric backpackers is easily spotted by the fence made out of bicycles and other odd sculptures. Upstairs has a basic loft with mattresses situated above the fire in winter. Out the back there are comfy little bachs (holiday homes) for doubles and a larger self-contained bach.

MIDRANGE & TOP END

Mountain House Motor Lodge (☎ 0800 668 682, 06-765 6100; www.mountainhouse.co.nz; Pembroke Rd; r from $115) This lodge, on the east side of the mountain, about 15km from Stratford, has rooms and chalets with kitchens. There's a restaurant, and you can hire skis in winter for use at the Manganui ski area.

Andersons Alpine Lodge (☎ 0800 668 682, 06-765 6620; www.mountainhouse.co.nz; 922 Pembroke Rd; r $150-190) The same management that runs Mountain House Motor Lodge also runs this place, further down the mountain, not far from the DOC office. It's a modern place in pleasant surroundings.

Rahiri Cottage (☎ 0800 688 2727; www.mttaranaki .co.nz; Egmont Rd, RD6; d $245) This enchanting clinker-brick cottage was once the tollgate into Egmont National Park and today it offers luxury B&B rooms in a bush setting.

Dawson Falls Mountain Lodge (☎ 0800 695 6344, 06-765 5457; www.dawson-falls.co.nz; Upper Manaia Rd; s/d $175/275) Just beside the visitor information centre, this Swiss-style lodge has alpine views, sitting rooms and a spacious dining room. All rooms have en suite and are individually decorated. Dinner and breakfast are included in the price.

Getting There & Away

There are several ways into the park, but three roads put lead to the best tracks. Closest to New Plymouth is Egmont Rd, turning off SH3 at Egmont Village, 12km south of New Plymouth, and heading another 14km up the mountain to the North Egmont visitor information centre. Pembroke Rd enters the park from Stratford and ascends 15km to East Egmont, Mountain House Motor Lodge, the Plateau car park and Manganui ski area. From the southeast, Upper Manaia Rd leads up to Dawson Falls, 23km from Stratford.

Public buses don't go to Egmont National Park, but shuttle buses (one way $30 to $40, return $40 to $50) to the mountain include the following:

Eastern Taranaki Experience (☎ 06-765 7482; www.eastern-taranaki.co.nz) Departs Stratford.
Withers (☎ 06-751 1777; www.withers.co.nz) Departs New Plymouth.

AROUND MT TARANAKI

Mt Taranaki is the main attraction of the region. There are two principal highways

around the mountain. SH3, on the inland side of the mountain, is the most travelled route, heading south from New Plymouth for 70km until it meets the coast at Hawera. The other route is the Surf Hwy 45 (see opposite). Get a *Taranaki Heritage Trails* booklet, free from visitor info centres and DOC offices.

Stratford

pop 9730

Stratford, 40km southeast of New Plymouth on SH3, plays up it's namesake Stratford-upon-Avon, Shakespeare's birthplace, by naming its streets after the bard's characters. It also claims NZ's first **Glockenspiel** (admission free; ☺ 10am, 1pm & 3pm). Thrice daily this clock doth chime out Shakespeare's greatest hits with some fairly wooden performances.

The town has a **visitor information centre** (☎ 0800 765 6708; www.stratfordnz.co.nz; Prospero Pl; ☺ 10.30am-4pm Mon-Fri, 10.30am-3pm Sat & Sun) that serves as the Automobile Association and houses the **Percy Thomson Gallery** (☎ 06-765 0917; www.percythomsongallery.org.nz; visitor information centre; ☺ 10.30am-4pm Mon-Fri, 10.30am-3pm Sat & Sun), a local gallery that has modern works. The main street is crowded with op shops and takeaway joints; **Urban Attitude** (☎ 06-7656534; 253 Broadway; light meals $6-12; ☺ 9am-4pm) is the better coffee and snack option.

On SH3, 1km south of the centre, the **Taranaki Pioneer Village** (☎ 06-765 5399; adult/child/family $10/5/20; ☺ 10am-4pm) is a 4-hectare outdoor museum housing 50 historic buildings. Littlies will love the historic re-creations, though some visitors find it more twee than traditional.

Top 10 Holiday Park (☎ 06-765 6440; 10 Page St; dm/sites/cabins/d $18/28/35/80) is a trim caravan park offering one-room cabins, motel-style units and backpackers bunks, plus barbecue and spa.

At Stratford is the turn-off for Pembroke Rd, heading up the mountain for 15km to East Egmont. (See p269 for more accommodation options.)

The Forgotten World Highway

The road between Stratford and Taumarunui (SH43) has become known as the Forgotten World Hwy. This Heritage Trail passes many historic sites, including Maori *pa* (fortified villages), waterfalls, abandoned coal mines and small museums. For details of interesting stops along the way pick up a free *Forgotten World Highway* booklet from visitor information centres or DOC offices in Stratford, Taumarunui or New Plymouth.

The meandering drive winds through hilly bush country with 12km of unsealed road, so allow five hours and plenty of stops. Fill up with petrol at Stratford or Taumarunui, as petrol stations are nonexistent.

A stop at **Whangamomona** is compulsory, mostly because of the border guard. This quirky village became an independent republic after disagreements with local councils (see the boxed text, right). The centre of the republic is the grand old **Whangamomona Hotel** (☎ 06-762 5823; 6016 Ohura Rd; meals $10-15; ⏰ 11am-late), an award-winning pub where you might share a glass with the president.

In the Tahora Saddle, **Kaieto Cafe** (☎/fax 06-762 5858; meals $14-20) has panoramic views of the surrounding countryside with Russian-influenced food and small but cosy bunkhouse cabins (dorms $28).

SURF HIGHWAY 45

Sweeping south from New Plymouth to Hawera, the 105km of State Hwy 45 has justifiably gained the title of the Surf Hwy. It has several good beaches dotted along the way.

Oakura

pop 1218

The first stop from New Plymouth, 15km southwest on SH45, is laid-back Oakura. Its beautiful **beach** is renowned to waxheads for its right-hander breaks, but also good for windsurfing or paddling. For gear hire head to **Vertigo** (☎ 06-752 8283; vertigosurf@xtra.co.nz; 605 SH45, Oakura; hire per 30min/1hr $25/40 lessons $90).

There're a few good craft shops worth pulling over for, including **Crafty Fox** (☎ 06-752 7291; Main Rd; ⏰ 10.30am-4.30pm), set in a 19th-century church, and **AlleyCat** (☎ 06-752 1001; Main Rd; ⏰ 10am-4pm Wed-Sun), next door, which sells innovative pottery.

SLEEPING & EATING

Oakura Beach Camp (☎ 06-752 7851; www.holiday parks.co.nz/oakurabeach; 2 Jans Tce; unpowered/powered sites $15/17, cabins $45) This simple park caters best to caravans, but has well-placed spots to pitch a tent and a few cabins, all with views back towards New Plymouth. There are family-friendly beaches nearby.

Reservation (☎ 06-752 7843; 021 100 9013; www .tekorutepees.co.nz; 304 Koru Rd; per person $40) For a real change, sleep out in a Sioux-style tepee (each sleeps up to five adults). Facilities are basic (you'll need a sleeping bag) and there are excellent mountain views. Reservation is off SH45.

Wave Haven (☎ 06-752 7800; www.thewavehaven .co.nz; Ahu Ahu & Main South Rds; dm/s/d $15/25/40) This surfers' paradise has a large deck to chill out on, a coffee machine and, most importantly, is close to the big breaks. It's a backpackers that feels like a holiday cottage.

Malaysian Carriage (☎ 06-752 1007; South Rd; mains $15-25; ⏰ lunch & dinner) This former railway carriage, behind the Crafty Fox, gets them streaming in from New Plymouth for traditional Malay dinners and Asian-fusion lunches.

Oakura to Opunake

The drive from Oakura veers inland, with detours to pleasant beaches along the way. **Stent Road**, less than 1km south of Warea, is legendary with experienced surfers for its shallow reef. Newbies prefer the gentler waves around **Komene Beach**, which at the mouth of Stony River attracts its fair share of interesting bird life, including black swans.

Another coastward turn at **Pungarehu** leads 20km to **Cape Egmont Lighthouse**, a picturesque cast-iron lighthouse that was shifted here in 1881 from just north of Wellington.

Opunake
pop 1500

Opunake is the surfie epicentre of the west coast, with a sheltered beach in Opunake Bay and plenty of more-challenging waves further out.

The **Opunake visitor information centre** (☎ 06-761 8663; opunake@stdc.govt.nz; Main Rd; ☻ 9am-4pm) is in the Egmont Public Library & Cultural Centre.

Opunake Beach Camp (☎ 0800 758 009, 06-761 7525; www.holidayparks.co.nz/opunake; Beach Rd; sites/cabins/cottages $23/35/60) is a mellow resort that's handy to the beach and has facilities.

Opunake Motel & Backpackers Lodge (☎ 06-761 8330; opunakemotel@xtra.co.nz; 36 Heaphy Rd; lodge r $25, d cottages/units $80/80) has a range of good accommodation options that should suit most travellers.

There are several pubs and takeaways in town, but the best bite (probably on the Surf Coast) is **Sugar Juice Café** (☎ 06-761 7062; 42 Tasman St; ☻ lunch Tue-Sun, dinner Wed-Sat), which serves up modern food and tip-top coffee.

Hawera
pop 8740

Hawera is not quite on the coast, 70km south of New Plymouth and 90km from Wanganui. It's the largest town on the southern coast of Taranaki.

INFORMATION
Automobile Association (☎ 06-278 5095; www.nzaa .co.nz; 121 Princes St)

Hawera visitor information centre (☎ 06-278 8599; visitorinfo@stdc.govt.nz; 55 High St; ☻ 8.30am-5pm Mon-Fri, 10am-3pm Sat & Sun)

SIGHTS & ACTIVITIES
Put on your blue suede shoes and jive down to the **Elvis Presley Memorial Record Room** (☎ 06-278 7624; www.digitalus.co.nz/elvis/; 51 Argyle St; admission by donation; ☻ by appointment only), which has a collection of Elvis records (over 5000), souvenirs and the King's own Cadillac.

The excellent **Tawhiti Museum** (☎ 06-278 6837; www.tawhitimuseum.co.nz; 401 Ohangai Rd; adult/child $10/2; ☻ 10am-4pm late-Dec-Jan, 10am-4pm Fri-Mon Feb-May & Sep-mid-Dec, 10am-4pm Sun Jun-Aug) houses a private collection of remarkable exhibits, models and dioramas. The creepily lifelike human figures were modelled on people around the region, while a large

collection of tractors pays homage to the province's rural heritage. It's near the corner of Tawhiti Rd, 4km from town. The cute *Wind in the Willows* dioramas in the café are an excuse to put grumpy Mr Badger in the fireplace.

Ohawe Beach makes for excellent swimming and nearby **Black Beach** is known for its eerie night-hued sands.

The most exciting activities around are dam dropping and white-water sledging with **Kaitiaki Adventures** (☎ /fax 06-278 4452, 025 249 9481; www.kaitiaki.co.nz; 3hr trips per person $80). The trips, which centre on the Waingongoro River, include sliding down a 7m dam on a board (more than once if you're game enough), then sledging a further 5km on the river (Grade II to III). This is one activity that rain can't spoil; in fact it can be more fun if it's rained hard the night before. Also included is a journey past **Okahutiti Pa**, birthplace of the Maori prophet Tohu Kakahi, an advocate of passive resistance following the Taranaki Land Wars of the 1860s (see the boxed text, opposite). All gear is provided. This group also does river trips in Rotorua (see p335 for details). Kaitiaki also offers night trips.

Two kilometres north of Hawera, on Turuturu Rd, are the remains of the pre-European **Turuturumokai Pa**. The name translates to 'stakes for dried heads', which were used to ward off potential attackers. Today the heads have well and truly dried up and there are a few remains of ramparts and storage pits still about. The reserve is open to the public daily. The Tawhiti Museum has a model of the *pa*.

SLEEPING & EATING
Hawera has a few standard motel offerings, but a farmstay is a really special stay.

Wheatly Downs (☎ 06-278 6523; www.mttaranaki.co.nz/hawera.htm; 46 Ararata Rd; sites/dm $14/25, d & tw $56) This well-kept farmstay backpackers lets you milk a cow for your morning cappuccino or chase cows (if you're into that kind of thing). The farm-style hospitality, well-kept rooms and the opportunity to see the agricultural life in action combine to make this place a real treat. To get to Wheatly Downs head past Tawhiti Museum and keep going straight on the Ararata Rd (the extension of Tawhiti Rd) for 5.5km beyond the museum. Sound too complicated?

PARIHAKA

The small village of Parihaka, east off Hwy 45 near Pungarehu, was, in the 1870s, the country's most prosperous Maori village, under the capable leadership of the remarkable prophets Te Whiti and Tohu. These two men led the people of Parihaka in a passive resistance campaign against the government's confiscation of land after the Taranaki Land Wars (see p35). Wearing the movement's iconic white feather in their hair, and in good humour, Parihaka's unarmed 'ploughmen' obstructed the surveying and development of confiscated land by ploughing troughs across roads, erecting random fences and pulling survey pegs. This was the first such civil-disobedience campaign anywhere – sixty-odd years before the same idea occurred to a chap called Gandhi in India.

Their settlement blended traditional Maori and Christian beliefs to form a peaceful, socialist community. For the government it was that socialism as much as the civil disobedience that rankled, so in 1881, around 1600 armed government troops marched in, burning crops, levelling the buildings and jailing many of the adult population (some for as long as 18 years). A judge, questioning the legality of the government's action at Parihaka, freed one prominent prisoner, the old general Titikowaru, prompting the government of the day to pass special legislation imprisoning Te Whiti and Tohu indefinitely without trial. (Even at the time this was seen as a bold move, sparking a minor constitutional crisis.)

In 2006 the NZ government issued a formal apology (and financial compensation) to the tribes affected by the invasion and confiscation of Parihaka lands.

Te Whiti's spirit lives on with annual meetings at Parihaka of his descendants and a public music-and-arts festival held early in the year (see www.parihaka.com for details), as well as in a ballad by Kiwi muso, Tim Finn, called 'Parihaka', about Te Whiti's life and philosophy. For more information, read Dick Scott's *Ask That Mountain*, or see http://history-nz.org/parihaka.html. Parihaka is open to the public on the 18th and 19th of each month.

There is also free pick-up available from Hawera.

Rembrandt Motel (06-278 5500; 219 South Rd; d $90) This motel has standard offerings (such as kitchenettes) on a pleasant if bland property.

For a light bite to eat try **Arabica** (06-278 9134; 227 High St; lunches $4-10; lunch), which is popular with locals for coffee, but for something harder try the **White Hart Hotel** (06-278 5704; 52 High St; lunch & dinner), which has good pub grub and country friendliness.

Wanganui & Palmerston North

The Wanganui and Manawatu districts form a hefty chunk of the North Island's southwest, running south from Tongariro National Park down towards Wellington. This is mellow, un-rushed pastoral country, dappled with curvaceous green hills, gently bent roads, socially significant cities and magical national parks, rivers and gorges.

The history-soaked Whanganui River curls lazily through Whanganui National Park down to Wanganui city. Ripe with outdoor opportunities, the splendorous Whanganui River Rd mimics the river's bows, while Wanganui itself – a 19th-century river town with an artful grace – has aged well, redefining its parameters after the grim demise of river traffic. Like any port there's an edgy transience about it, as if it's not sure what might come up or down the river next. Settle into Victoria Ave's top-notch restaurants and cool bars while you wait.

Palmerston North, Manawatu's main city, is a town of two peoples: laid-back country fast-foodies and caffeinated Massey University literati; coexisting with none of Cambridge's 'Town versus Gown' sabre-rattling. Easy-going and unaffected, 'Palmy' people walk around whistling and go barefoot on the grass. During the semester the cafés jump and pubs fill with students.

Beyond the city, the Manawatu blends rural grace with yesterday's pace, cut by the dramatic slice of Manawatu Gorge. A meandering Manawatu drive is the perfect antidote to NZ's tourism juggernaut – you might even find time for a little lethargy.

HIGHLIGHTS

- Kicking back under the summer leaves on Victoria Ave in **Wanganui** (p277)
- Blowing out the cobwebs with a jetboat ride on the **Whanganui River** (p284)
- Taking your time along the rainy **Whanganui River Road** (p283) to Jerusalem and Pipiriki
- Tramping the Matemateaonga and Mangapurua Tracks in the **Whanganui National Park** (p285)
- Recaffeinating on George St, the hip café strip in **Palmerston North** (p290)
- Connecting life, art and mind at **Te Manawa** (p288) museum in Palmerston North
- Flexing your All Blacks spirit at Palmerston North's **New Zealand Rugby Museum** (p288)
- Traversing the awesome **Manawatu Gorge** (p288), rich in Maori lore

TELEPHONE CODE: 06

■ www.wanganuinz.com ■ www.wanganuinz.com ■ www.manawatunz.co.nz

WANGANUI & PALMERSTON NORTH FACTS

Eat: Anything from Wanganui's hip new breed of eateries (p281)

Drink: A handle of Lion Red lager at a Palmerston North student bar (p291)

Read: *The Wanganui Chronicle*, NZ's oldest newspaper

Listen to: The self-titled EP by Palmerston North indie-melodists Reflector

Watch: The colonial epic *River Queen* (2006), filmed on the Whanganui River

Swim at: Palmerston North's Lido Aquatic Centre (p289), humming Boz Scaggs all the while

Festival: Swap tinned spaghetti for movie tickets at Wanganui's Cans Film Festival (p280)

Tackiest tourist attraction: Owlcatraz (p289) in Shannon (it's not the owls' fault)

Climate

Regional summer maximums range from 19°C to 24°C; 10°C to 14°C during winter. Wanganui winters are mild, but they're chillier on the plains around Palmerston North. There's buckets of sunshine – 2000 hours per year!

Wanganui and Palmerston North receive around 60mm of rain through summer and 95mm in winter. In February 2004 the monthly rainfall was six times the average causing incredible floods – a state of civil emergency was declared.

Getting There & Around

Palmerston North's airport is serviced internationally and domestically by Air New Zealand, Freedom Air (from Australia) and Origin Pacific. Air New Zealand also has flights between Wanganui and Auckland.

TOP ACTIVITIES

- Shatter the serenity of the Manawatu Gorge by jetboat (p288)
- See the majestic Whanganui River by canoe or paddle-steamer (p284)
- Explore the forest trails of the Whanganui National Park (p285)
- Get a bird's-eye view of the North Island on a scenic flight out of Wanganui (p280)
- Drive the winding, largely unsealed Whanganui River Rd – it's all about the journey, not how fast you get there (p283)

InterCity, Newmans and White Star City to City buses service both Wanganui and Palmerston North. Tranzit Coachlines and Tranz Scenic trains service Palmerston North. See the Getting There & Away sections for Wanganui (p282) and Palmerston North (p291) for details.

Driving north from Wanganui, take the scenic State Highway 4 (SH4) to the centre of the North Island via the Paraparas, an area of *papa* (large blue-grey mudstone) hills, Raukawa Falls and the Mangawhero River Gorge, or the winding Whanganui River Rd (p283). From the north, Whanganui River is road-accessible at Taumarunui, Ohinepane and Whakahoro.

Inside Whanganui National Park, the Rural Mail Coach Tour (p280), plies the Whanganui River Rd between Wanganui and Pipiriki. You can travel sections of the river itself by canoe, kayak, paddle-steamer or jetboat.

Manawatu Gorge is about 15km northeast of Palmerston North – take SH2.

WANGANUI REGION

History

The Wanganui region's liquid lifeblood is the Whanganui River in the Whanganui National Park. Despite the fact that there's more sitting down than walking involved, canoeing or kayaking the 'Whanganui Journey' is classed as one of NZ's Great Walks. Early Maoris named the river's estuary (over 30km long) Whanganui, meaning 'Great Harbour' or 'Great Wait'. The spelling difference between Whanganui and Wanganui causes global confusion – see the boxed text, p277.

In Maori legend the Whanganui River was formed when Mt Taranaki, after brawling

WANGANUI & PALMERSTON NORTH

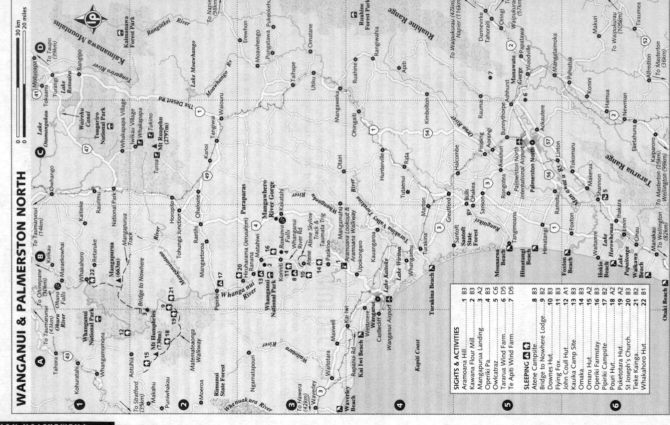

www.lonelyplanet.com

SIGHTS & ACTIVITIES	
Aramoana Hill	1 B3
Kawana Flour Mill	2 B3
Mangapurua Landing	3 A2
Operiki Pa	4 B3
Owlcatraz	5 C6
Tararua Wind Farm	6 D5
Te Apiti Wind Farm	7 D5

SLEEPING	
Atene Campsite	8 B3
Bridge to Nowhere Lodge	9 B2
Downes Hut	10 B3
Flying Fox	11 B3
John Coull Hut	12 A1
Kauika Camp Site	13 B3
Omaka	14 B3
Omaru Hut	15 A2
Operiki Farmstay	16 B3
Pipiriki Campsite	17 B2
Pouri Hut	18 A2
Puketotara Hut	19 A2
St Joseph's Church	20 B3
Tieke Kainga	21 B2
Whakahoro Hut	22 B1

with Mt Tongariro over the lovely Mt Pihanga, fled the central North Island for the sea, leaving a long gouge behind him. He turned west at the coast, finally stopping at his current address. Mt Tongariro sent cool water to heal the gouge – thus the Whanganui River was born.

Kupe, the great Polynesian explorer, is believed to have travelled 20km up the Whanganui around AD 800. Maoris were living here by 1100. When Europeans put down roots in the late 1830s, Maori settlements lined the river valley. Missionaries sailed upstream – their settlements at Hiruharama (Jerusalem), Ranana (London), Koriniti (Corirth) and Atene (Athens) have survived a dwindling river population.

Steamers first tackled the river in the mid-1860s, a dangerous time for Pakeha. Aligned with Taranaki Maoris, some river tribes joined the Hauhau Rebellion – a Maori movement seeking to expel settlers.

In 1886 a Wanganui company established the first commercial steamer transport service. Others soon followed, utilising the river between Wanganui and Taumarunui. Supplying river communities and linking the sea with the interior, the steamers' importance grew, especially after 1903 when the Auckland railway reached Taumarunui from the north.

New Zealand's contemporary tourism leviathan was seeded here. Internationally advertised trips on the 'Rhine of Maoriland' became so popular that by 1905, 12,000 tourists a year were making the trip upriver from Wanganui to Pipiriki, or downriver from Tauma-unui. The engineering feats and skippering ability required on the river became legendary.

From 1918, land upstream of Pipiriki was granted to returning WWI soldiers. Farming here was a major challenge, families struggling for years to make rugged land productive. By the early 1940s, only a few endured.

Standing in mute testimony to early settlers' optimism is the Bridge to Nowhere, built in 1936. The walking track from the Mangapurua Landing to the lonesome bridge was once part of a 4.5m-wide roadway from Raetihi to the river.

The completion of the railway from Auckland to Wellington and the improving roads ultimately signed river transport's death warrant; 1959 saw the last commercial river-boat voyages. Today, just one old-fleet vessel cruises the river: the *Waimarie* (p279).

WANGANUI

pop 40,700

With rafts of casual Huck Finn sensibility, Wanganui is a come-as-you-are, raggedy historic town on the banks of the wide Whanganui River. Despite the NZ-wide housing boom, cheap Wanganui real estate has somehow stayed cheap, much to the satisfaction of the thriving arts community. Old port buildings are being restored and the town centre rejuvenated – there are few more appealing places to while away a sunny afternoon than beneath Victoria Ave's leafy canopy.

History

Maori settlement here dates from around 1350. The first European on the river was Andrew Powers, in 1831, but Wanganui's European settlement didn't take off until 1840 when the New Zealand Co couldn't satisfy Wellington's land demands – settlers moved here instead. Initially called Petre, after a New Zealand Co director, the town's name was changed to Wanganui in 1844.

When the Maori understood that the gifts the Pakeha had given them were in permanent exchange for their land, they were understandably irate, seven years of conflict ensuing. Thousands of government troops occupied Queens Park, the Rutland

---

WHANGANUI OR WANGANUI?

Yeah, we know, it's very confusing. The river and national park have an 'h', but the city and region don't – the pronunciation is identical. Everything was originally spelled Wanganui, because in the local dialect *whanga* (harbour) is pronounced 'wan-ga', not (as in the rest of the country) 'fan-ga'. However, to indicate that the 'wan' sound is breathy and aspirated, the 'h' was officially inserted into the river and national park, but not the city or region. This was a culturally deferential decision – the Pakeha-dominated town and region retained the old spelling, while the river area – Maori territory – adopted the new. To allay mass befuddlement, moves are afoot for everything to adopt the querulous 'h'. Whanderful...

WANGANUI

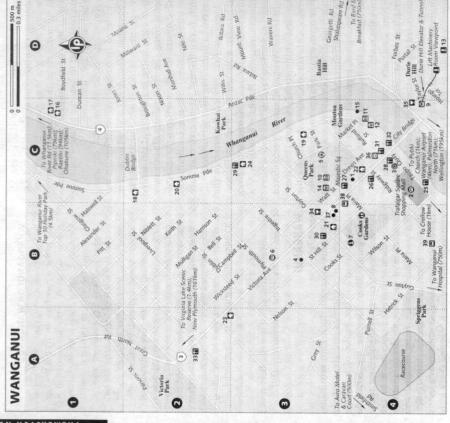

www.lonelyplanet.com

INFORMATION
Automobile Association (AA)...... 1 C4
Books & More New Zealand
  Post..................................... 2 C4
Catch 22................................. 3 C4
DOC Office.............................. 4 B3
Police Station.......................... 5 C4
Post Office.............................. 6 B3
Wanganui Visitor Information
  Centre................................... 7 B4
Whitcoulls............................... 8 B3

SIGHTS & ACTIVITIES
Durie Hill Elevator.................... 9 C4
Sarjeant Gallery....................... 10 C3
Te Wa................................... 11 C4
Waimarie Paddle-Steamer
  Tours................................... (see 15)
Wanganui Community Arts
  Centre................................. 12 C4

War Memorial Tower................ 13 D4
Wanganui Regional Museum..... 14 C4
Wanganui Riverboat Centre....... 15 C4

SLEEPING
Acacia Park Motel.................... 16 C1
Anndion Lodge........................ 17 C1
Astral Motel............................ 18 C2
Bradgate B&B......................... 19 C3
Braemar House YHA................. 20 B2
Grand Hotel........................... 21 B3
Rutland Arms Inn..................... 22 C4
Siena Motor Lodge................... 23 A2
Tamara Backpackers................ 24 C3

EATING
Amadeus Riverbank Café.......... 25 C4
Big Orange............................. 26 C4
Ceramic Wine Bar................... (see 26)
Indigo.................................... 27 C4

Kittya's Thai
  Restaurant............................ 28 C4
Legends................................. 29 C3
Red Eye Café.......................... 30 B3
Stellar................................... 31 C4
Vega..................................... 32 C4
Woolworths Supermarket.......... 33 A2

DRINKING
Bull 'n' Gate........................... 34 B3
Red....................................... 35 C4
Rosie O'Grady's...................... (see 21)

ENTERTAINMENT
Embassy 3 Cinemas................. 36 C4

TRANSPORT
Air New Zealand...................... 37 B3
Transit City Link Stop.............. 38 C4
Wanganui Travel Centre........... 39 B4

Stockade dominating the hill. Ultimately, the struggle was settled by arbitration; during the Taranaki Land Wars the Wanganui Maoris assisted the Pakeha.

Orientation

Wanganui is midway between Wellington and New Plymouth. The river slides lugubriously north-south past the city, the centre of which is on the west bank. Somme Pde and Taupo Quay trace the western shoreline; Anzac Pde parallels the east bank and leads to Whanganui National Park. Hanging baskets and deep verandas line Victoria Ave, Wanganui's main street.

Information

MAPS

Free town maps are available at the visitor information centre. You can also pick up maps at the visitor information centre and maps at the **Automobile Association** (AA; ☎ 06-348 9160; www.aatravel.co.nz; 78 Victoria Ave).

BOOKSHOPS

Whitcoulls (☎ 06-345 8747; www.whitcoulls.co.nz; 115 Victoria Ave)

EMERGENCY

Ambulance, fire service & police (☎ 111)
Police station (☎ 06-349 0600; Bell St)

INTERNET ACCESS

Aside from Catch 22, there's Internet access at the visitor information centre and the Big Orange (p282).
Catch 22 (☎ 06-348 7610; 62 Taupo Quay) Glowing screens and appalling high-school gamers.

MEDICAL SERVICES

Wanganui Hospital (☎ 06-348 1234; Heads Rd)

MONEY

Most major banks have branches and ATMs on Victoria Ave.

POST

Books & More New Zealand Post (Trafalgar Square Shopping Mall; Taupo Quay)
Post office (226 Victoria Ave)

TOURIST INFORMATION

DOC office (☎ 06-348 8475; www.doc.govt.nz; 74 Ingestre St)
Wanganui visitor information centre (☎ 06-349 0508; www.wanganui.nz; 101 Guyton St)

Sights & Activities

WHANGANUI RIVERBOAT CENTRE

Down by the river, the **Whanganui Riverboat Centre** (☎ 0800 783 2637, 06-347 1863; www.riverboat.co.nz; 1a Taupo Quay; admission free; ☺ 9am-4pm Mon-Sat, 10am-4pm Sun, closed Aug) has river history displays, but the crowds come for the *Waimarie*, the last of the Whanganui River's paddle steamers. In 1900 the *Waimarie* was shipped in a box from England then reassembled in Wanganui. After paddling up and down the Whanganui for 50 years, she sank ingloriously at her mooring in 1952. Miserably submerged for 41 years, she was finally raised, restored then relaunched on the first day of the 21st century. See p280 for tour details on the coal-fired dreamboat.

MUSEUMS, GALLERIES & CHURCHES

The **Wanganui Regional Museum** (☎ 06-349 1110; www.wanganui-museum.org.nz; Watt St, Queens Park; adult/child $5/free; ☺ 10am-4.30pm) is one of NZ's better natural-history museums. Maori exhibits include the astoundingly carved *Te Mata o Houroa* war canoe and some vicious-looking *mere* (greenstone clubs). The colonial and wildlife installations are first-rate, and there's plenty of button-pushing and drawer-opening to keep the kids engaged.

'Historical – Contemporary – Unique' – the elegantly neoclassical **Sarjeant Gallery** (☎ 06-349 0506; www.sarjeant.org.nz; Queens Park; admission free; ☺ 10.30am-4.30pm) covers all the bases in its extensive permanent art exhibition with frequent special exhibits.

Side-by-side on the river, **Te Wa** (☎ 06-348 7790; www.te-wa.com; 17 Taupo Quay; admission free; ☺ noon-4pm Tue-Sat) and the **Wanganui Community Arts Centre** (☎ 06-345 1551; 19 Taupo Quay; admission free; ☺ 10am-4pm Mon-Sat, 1-4pm Sun) exhibit mostly local artists (everyone's an artist in Wanganui...), mustering up a decidedly South Pacific vibe.

Across the Whanganui City Bridge from town and 1km towards the sea is the **Putiki Church**, aka St Paul's Memorial Church. It's nothing out of the ordinary externally, but just like the faithful pew-fillers, it's what's inside that counts. The interior is magnificent, completely covered in Maori carvings and *tukutuku* (wall panels). Unless it's a Sunday, the church will probably be closed, but the caretaker (☎ 06-345 4283) may lend you the key – call in advance for details.

PARKS & GARDENS

Wanganui has some grassy, stroll-worthy parks, including **Queens Park** (where the museum and gallery are) and **Cooks Gardens**. The visitors information centre has a *Walking for Fun* brochure, which maps out some walks through the city's parklands, and a couple of *Wanganui Heritage Walk* brochures directing amblers through the city.

The **Moutoa Gardens** are considered sacred Maori land and were occupied by Maoris for four months in 1995, an acrimonious land claim that strained local Maori-Pakeha relations. The city council, abandoned by Wellington, fought the claim in the High Court, while angry Pakeha counterdemonstrated under the banner of 'One New Zealand'. Police raids exacerbated the situation. When the claim was dismissed by the courts, the country expected violence, but the gardens were peacefully relinquished after a moving nightlong meeting addressed by Maori leaders.

The **Virginia Lake Scenic Reserve** (Rotokawau; winter gardens 9am–5pm, aviary 8.30am–5pm), about 1km north from the top end of Victoria Ave, is a rambling reserve with a lake, winter garden, walk-through aviary and the Higginbottom Fountain – possibly the world's only pay-per-view gusher (50c per eruption).

DURIE HILL

Across the Whanganui City Bridge from the town centre is the **Durie Hill Elevator** (☎ 06-345 8525; adult/child $1/50c; 7.30am–6pm Mon-Fri, 9am–5pm Sat, 10am–5pm Sun), built with grand visions for Durie Hill's residential future. A tunnel burrows 200m into the hillside, from where the elevator rattles 65m to the top.

There are two viewpoints at the summit: one on top of the lift machinery room, the other up the 176 steps of the **War Memorial Tower**. Assess the condition of Wanganui's roof-tiles, or scan the horizon for Mt Taranaki, Mt Ruapehu and even the South Island on a clear day.

Tours

See p284 for Whanganui River canoe, kayak and jetboat tours.

C the City Cycle Tours (☎ 06-343 7130; info@omakaholiday.co.nz; 1-3hr tours $20–60) Check out River City from a relaxed two-wheeled perspective; bikes and helmets provided.

Rural Mail Coach Tour (☎ 06-347 7534; www .whanganuitours.co.nz; tours $35; departs 7.30am, returns 3–4pm Mon-Fri) Join the mailman on his river valley run to Pipiriki, with lots of social and historical commentary. Tea and coffee supplied; BYO lunch. Ask about connecting jetboat trips from Pipiriki to the Bridge to Nowhere (Wednesday only).

Scenic Flights (☎ 06-345 0914; wanganui.aero.club@ xtra.co.nz; Wanganui Airport; 15min–1hr flights $87–325) Mile-high panoramas above Wanganui, Moutoua Island, Mt Ruapehu and Whanganui National Park.

Waimarie Paddle-Steamer Tours (☎ 0800 783 2637, 06-347 1863; www.wanganui.org.nz/riverboats; 1a Taupo Quay; adult/child/family $30/12/84; 2pm daily Nov–May, 1pm Sat & Sun Jun–Oct, closed Aug) Twohour tour weekdays; three hours with a one-hour stopover at weekends.

Whanganui River Road Tours (☎ 06-345 8488; www.whanganuiriverroad.com; 6hr tours $40) Smallgroup minibus tours up the river to Pipiriki, visiting Koriniti *marae* (meeting house) and Hiruharama (Jerusalem). BYO lunch.

Festivals & Events

Wanganui hosts a **Heritage Weekend** in March (riverboats, architectural adoration and markets), the **Blooming Artz** horticultural festa in September, and a pandemonic **Boxing Day Motorbike Race**. In November the Embassy 3 Cinema holds the **Cans Film Festival**, where you can swap a can of baked beans for a ticket.

Sleeping

BUDGET

Anndion Lodge (☎ 0800 343 056, 06-343 3593; www .anndionlodge.com; 143 Anzac Pde; dm/s $30/60, d $85–120;) Readers have been effervescing about this place since it opened in 2004. Hosts Ann and Dion (Anndion, get it?) have gone to enormous lengths to make things homey: stereo systems, big TVs, Playstation (!), spa, swimming pool, barbecue area, courtesy van etc. It's pricier than your average hostel, but everything's new, clean and thoroughly worth it.

Tamara Backpackers (☎ 06-347 6300; www.tama ralodge.com; 24 Somme Pde; dm/s/tw 21/35/46, d $46–56;) Tamara is a two-storey mazelike house with a wide balcony, kitchen, pool table, TV lounge, free bikes and a hammock-hung back garden. Ask for a double overlooking the rippling brown river-snake.

Braemar House YHA (☎ 06-3472529; www.braemar house.co.nz; 2 Plymouth St; unpowered sites per 2 people $24, dm $20, s/d cabin $35/50, guesthouse $55/90;)

There's a definite line drawn in the river mud here, segregating the Victorian guesthouse from the rambunctious backpackers. Centrally heated guesthouse rooms fill the main building. Out the back, airy dorms and no-frills cabins about limited tent space.

MIDRANGE

Grand Hotel (☎ 0800 843 472, 06-345 0955; www.the grandhotel.co.nz; cnr St Hill & Guyton Sts; d $70-85, ste $110-140) If you can't face another soulless motel room, rooms at this stately old-school Wanganui survivor have a bit more personality. Doubles are basic but good value; suites are spacious. The Irish pub, Rosie O'Grady's, and a restaurant are downstairs.

Rutland Arms Inn (☎ 0800 788 5263, 06-347 7677; www.rutland-arms.co.nz; 48 Ridgway St; ste $130-180, pub meals $14-27) Billed as a 'luxury heritage experience', this restored 1849 building has an old-fashioned pub downstairs with colonial-style accommodation above. Rooms have TV, phone, fax, plump pillows and spine-straightening beds. English hunting scenes adorn the bar's beer taps.

Crellow House (☎ 06-345 0740; 274 Taupo Quay; r $45-70) Staying at Crellow House is like staying with your grandma. Pam, the owner, cooks a mean breakfast and claims that 'Nobody leaves my house hungry'. Her cheese-dish collection (206 at last count) is a lifelong dedication. Rooms are cosy; the frieze in the queen-size room is another of Pam's efforts. Prices include breakfast.

Bradgate B&B (☎ 06-345 3634; vige@value.net.nz; 7 Somme Pde; s $40-50, d $80) This grand old river home has three comfortable rooms: one single, one double and one queen-size. The warm communal lounge has bay-window views upriver; breakfasts (included) arrive with 'We aim to please!' zeal.

Wanganui River Top 10 Holiday Park (☎ 0800 272 664, 06-343 8402; www.wrivertop10.co.nz; 460 Somme Pde; unpowered/powered sites per 2 people $32/36, cabins $45-55, units $78-98; ☐ ⚡) Pious and restrained, this park sits on the Wanganui's west bank, 6km north of Dublin Bridge. Facilities (including a 'jumping pillow' to exhaust the kids) are clean and prodigious.

Avro Motel & Caravan Court (☎ 06-345 5279; www .wanganuiaccommodation.co.nz; 36 Alma Rd; sites per 2 people $25, units $75-100; ⚡) Avro's yellow biplane heralds the closest camping to the city centre, 1.5km west. The motel units are OK, but camping facilities are a little weary. Unpowered/powered site prices are for two people.

Siena Motor Lodge (☎ 0800 888 802, 06-345 9009; www.siena.co.nz; 335 Victoria Ave; ste $120-145; ⚡) Aiming for Tuscany but hitting Taranaki, the rooms here are five star and spotless but surprisingly poky. The basket of free goodies, DVD player and Sky TV will ease your astonishment.

Astral Motel (☎ 0800 509 063, 06-347 9063; astral motel@clear.net.nz; 45 Somme Pde; s $75-80, d $80-100) Astrally aligned with the entirely terrestrial Dublin Bridge nearby, rooms here are a bit dated but have Sky TV and are well serviced. Good bang for your buck.

Acacia Park Motel (☎ 06-343 9993; www.acacia -park-motel.co.nz; 140 Anzac Pde; r $87; ⚡) The undisputed highlights of this riverside place are the roosting doves and the rotund cat, who apparently 'lives to eat' (doves?). The rooms have seen better days, and it's hard to know if those days were all that great, but you get what you pay for.

TOP END

Bard & Breakfast (☎ 06-343 2050; www.bardand breakfast.com; 56 Shakespeare Rd; r $120-180) East of the town centre, high above the *rive gauche*, the pithily named Bard has three plush B&B rooms – 'top-end' Wanganui without the price tag. Albert, your host, will whisk you up an Omelette Albert for breakfast as your eyes buzz from bloom to garden bloom.

Eating & Drinking

Vega (☎ 06-349 0078; 49 Taupo Quay; lunch $9-20, dinner $28-30; ⚡ lunch Tue-Sun, dinner daily) Vega's riverside building has been a merchant store and a brothel, but today it's 100% class. A packed house testifies to the virtuoso menu, professional service and meticulously constructed wine list. There's a separate seafood menu for the *poisson*-impassioned, and plenty of vegetarian and children's options. Open 'til the wee smalls, the back bar broods at the river through picture windows.

Red Eye Café (☎ 06-345 5646; 96 Guyton St; meals $6-20; ⚡ lunch Mon-Sat, till late Fri) With inexplicable familiarity (maybe it's the friendly staff), this funky urban café has colourful art (mostly for sale), tasty light snacks and more substantial meals drifting from curries to chicken burgers.

Indigo (☎ 06-348 7459; Majestic Sq; lunch $12-17, dinner $26-29; ⚡ breakfast & lunch Thu-Tue, dinner Thu-Sat)

Along with Vega, Indigo has dragged Wanganui dining into the new millennium. Its lofty interior and packed outdoor terrace swim with NZ wines and contemporary meat, pasta and fish dishes assembled with progressive flair.

Amadeus Riverbank Café (☎ 06-345 1538; 69 Taupo Quay; meals $8-17; ⓧ breakfast & lunch) Long, thin Amadeus looks like an average suburban takeaway joint from the outside, but inside it's a classically trained café. Grilled chicken sandwiches are the house special; outdoor riverside tables catch the morning rays. Dogs are welcome.

Stellar (☎ 06-345 2728; 2 Victoria Ave; meals $7-27; ⓧ breakfast, lunch & dinner) Stellar lives up to its name – a cavernous bar-cum-restaurant with a convivial family atmosphere, it's the town's pride and joy. Reclining contentedly in leather booths, locals and tourists sip premium lagers and feast on bar morsels, gourmet pizzas and surf 'n' turf fare.

Kittiya's Thai Restaurant (☎ 06-348 9089; 7 Victoria Ave; mains $10-22; ⓧ lunch Thu-Sat, dinner Tue-Sat) Kittiya's Thai classics zing across your palate in an elephant-gilded, chilli red room, punctuated with triangle cushions and *real* flowers.

Big Orange (☎ 06-348 4449; 51 Victoria Ave; meals $9-14; ⓧ breakfast & lunch; ⬚) The Big O (nothing to do with Roy Orbison) is a babbling espresso bar serving gourmet burgers, big breakfasts and sandwiches. The outdoor tables reportedly 'go off' in summer – we suspect this means they're popular, rather than mouldy.

Ceramic Wine Bar (☎ 06-348 4449; 51 Victoria Ave; mains $8-25) In a split-business arrangement with the Big Orange, Ceramic takes over for the dinner shift, serving upmarket café food and tapas in a lowlit blue-grey interior. Occasional DJs croon tunes across the tables to cocktail-sipping seducers.

Legends (☎ 06-345 7575; 25 Somme Pde; sandwiches $4-7, meals $20-30; ⓧ breakfast, lunch & dinner Tue-Sun) In a restored Victorian house, Legends' colourful, sunny rooms and riverside deck sustain an adventurous all-day menu and salacious sandwiches. Book for dinner.

Rosie O'Grady's (☎ 06-345 0955; cnr St Hill & Guyton Sts) Siphoning into NZ's insatiable (and, it has to be said, annoying) passion for Irish pubs, Rosie's, in the Grand Hotel, is as good a spot as any to elbow down a few pints of Guinness on a misty river afternoon.

Red (☎ 06-347 1157; 42 Anzac Pde) Across Whanganui City Bridge, the early-evening sun pours into the Red's noisy front bar, illuminating locals watching the races. New owners have tried to up the sophistication stakes, but nobody's seemed to notice.

Bull 'n' Gate (☎ 06-348 7922; 148 Victoria Ave) Keeping one of Wanganui's feet firmly on the ground, this low-brow big-screen bar sees tribute bands and DJs pumping up the punters on weekends.

The **Rutland Arms Inn** (p281) is a dependable place for a handle, and it serves thumping meals.

Self-caterers can swing into **Woolworths supermarket** (☎ 06-348 9470; Upper Victoria Ave).

Entertainment

Embassy 3 Cinemas (☎ 06-347 6774; www.embassy3 .co.nz; 34 Victoria Ave; tickets adult/child $11/6.50) The Embassy screens movies nightly, with new-release blockbusters selling out faster than you can say 'bored Wanganui teenagers'. November's Cans Film Festival is held here.

Getting There & Away

AIR

Wanganui Airport (☎ 06-345 5593) is 4km south of town, across the river towards the sea. **Air New Zealand** (☎ 06-348 3500; www.airnz.co.nz; 133 Victoria Ave) has direct flights from Wanganui to Auckland three to four times daily.

BUS

InterCity (www.intercitycoach.co.nz) and **Newmans** (www.newmanscoach.co.nz) buses operate from the **Wanganui Travel Centre** (☎ 06-345 4433; wag@tranzit.co.nz; 156 Ridgway St; ⓧ 8.15am-5.15pm Mon-Fri). Buses run to Auckland ($75, eight hours, two to four daily) via Taumarunui, and to New Plymouth ($32, 2½ hours, one to two daily). Heading south, buses go to Palmerston North ($20, 1¾ hours, one to four daily) continuing to Wellington ($36, four hours). For services north to Tongariro, Taupo and Rotorua, transfer at Bulls. For Napier, Hastings and Gisborne, change at Palmerston North.

White Star City to City (☎ 04-478 4734; fax 06-758 8878) has buses to Wellington ($27, three hours 20 minutes, one to two daily) and New Plymouth ($24, 2½ hours, one to two daily). Book at the visitors information centre.

For details about the mail-run bus to Pipiriki, see p280.

Getting Around

BUS

Transit City Link (☎ 06-343 5555; ticket $2.50) operates a limited weekday service, including a bus past the Wanganui River Top 10 Holiday Park, departing from the Maria Pl bus stop. **Leisure Travel** (☎ 06-343 5627; www.leisuretravelnz.com) can pick you up and shuttle you to the airport (around $10), bus station and other points in town.

TAXI

For a taxi, call **River City Cabs** (☎ 0800 345 3333).

CAR

The following companies have pick-up/drop off at Wanganui Airport:

Avis (☎ 06-358 7528; www.avis.com)

Budget (☎ 06-345 3122; www.budget.co.nz)

Hertz (☎ 06-348 7624; www.hertz.co.nz)

WHANGANUI NATIONAL PARK & RIVER ROAD

The Whanganui River in the Whanganui National Park curls its way 329km from its source on the flanks of Mt Tongariro (p315) to the Tasman Sea. It's the longest navigable river in the country, a fact that's been shaping its destiny for centuries. Historically functioning as a transport link between sea and interior, first for the Maori and then for the Pakeha, the route was eventually superseded by rail and road. Several of the landings along the Whanganui's banks were once riverboat landings. These days, a flotilla of canoes, kayaks and jetboats floats up and down the river's reaches, its waters shifting from deep mirror greens in summer to turbulent winter browns.

The native bush is thick podocarp broadleaved forest interspersed with ferns. Occasionally you'll see poplar and other introduced trees along the river, remnants of long-since-vanished settlements.

Traces of former Maori habitation also crop up along the river, with old *pa* (fortified village) and *kainga* (village) sites, and Hauhau *niu* poles (war and peace poles) at the confluence of the Whanganui and Ohura Rivers at Maraekowhai. The Ratakura, Reinga Kokiri and Te Rerehapa Falls, all near Maraekowhai on the Ohura, are where Maoris caught small *tuna riki* (freshwater eels).

The impossibly scenic Whanganui River Rd, a mostly unsealed river-hugging road from Wanganui to Pipiriki, makes a fabulous alternative to the faster but much less magical SH4.

Orientation & Information

For national park information, stroll into the affable Wanganui visitor information centre or DOC office (p279). There's also **Pipiriki DOC** (☎ 06-385 5022; Owairua Rd; www.doc.govt.co.nz; ☑ 8am–5pm Mon–Fri), and **Taumarunui DOC** (☎ 07-895 8201; Cherry Grove Domain; ☑ 8am–5pm Mon–Fri), though they're both field centres, not tourist facilities, and aren't always staffed. The Taumarunui visitor information centre (p255) is a safer bet.

Online, check out www.whanganuiriver.co.nz, or a more tangible river reference is the NZ Canoeing Association's *Guide to the Whanganui River* ($9). DOC's *In and Around Whanganui National Park* covers tramping territory, or collect a copy of the Wanganui Tramping Club's *Walking Opportunities in the Wanganui Area* ($5) from the Wanganui visitors information centre.

Sights

The main attraction along the Whanganui River Rd en route to Pipiriki is the cameraconducive scenery, with stark, wet mountain slopes plummeting down to the lazy brown stretches of the Whanganui River. A French Catholic mission led by Suzanne Aubert established the Daughters of Our Lady of Compassion in Jerusalem in 1892. Around a corner in the road, the picture-perfect St Joseph's Church (see p286) stands tall on a spur of land above a deep river bend – laying eyes on it makes it easy to believe that someone designed this planet.

Other sights include the restored **Kawana Flour Mill** (Map p276) near Matahiwi, **Operiki Pa** (Map p276) and other *pa* sites, and **Aramoana Hill**, from where there's a panoramic view. Visitors need to be invited to explore the Maori villages of **Atene**, **Koriniti**, **Ranana** and **Hiruharama** along the road.

Pipiriki is beside the river at the north end of Whanganui River Rd. It's a rainy river town without much going on (no shops or petrol), but was once a humming holiday hot spot serviced by river steamers and paddleboats. Seemingly cursed, the old **Pipiriki Hotel**, formerly a glamorous resort full of international tourists, burned to the ground twice. The latest attempt to rebuild it has stalled due to funding issues; it's been vandalised and stripped of anything of value, leaving a hollow brick husk riddled with potential. Pipiriki is the end point for canoe trips coming down the river, and the launching pad for jetboat rides.

Activities
CANOEING & KAYAKING
The most popular stretch of river for canoeing and kayaking is downstream from Taumarunui to Pipiriki. This has been added to the NZ Great Walks system (p87) and called the 'Whanganui Journey'. It's a Grade II river – easy enough for the inexperienced, with enough moiling rapids to keep things interesting. See the DOC leaflet *Whanganui Journey* for canoeing information.

Between 1 October and 30 April you'll need a **Great Walks Hut & Campsite Pass** (adult/child $60/30) for boat trips involving overnight stays between Taumarunui and Pipiriki. The rule applies only to this stretch of the river. The pass is valid for four nights and five days; you can stay overnight in the huts, camp sites beside the huts or in other designated camp sites along the river. If you're only doing the overnight journey from Taumarunui to Whakahoro, the pass costs $10/5 per adult/child; if you exclude Tieke Kainga (a *marae* meeting house) it's $50/25 per adult/child. If you're just paddling and not sleeping anywhere, there's no charge. People using huts must also have hut tickets or an annually valid **Backcountry Hut Pass** (adult/child $90/45). Passes and tickets are available at the Wanganui visitor information centre and regional DOC offices; some canoe operators also sell them. During summer, hut wardens are on duty and conservation officers patrol the river.

Taumarunui to Pipiriki is a five-day/four-night trip, Ohinepane to Pipiriki is a four-day/three-night trip, and Whakahoro to Pipiriki is a three-day/two-night trip. Taumarunui to Whakahoro is a popular overnight trip, especially for weekenders, or you can do a one-day trip from Taumarunui to Ohinepane or Ohinepane to Whakahoro.

From Whakahoro to Pipiriki, 88km downstream, there's no road access so you're wed to the river for a few days; this is the trip everyone clamours to do. Most canoeists stop at Pipiriki.

The season for canoe trips is usually from September to Easter. Up to 5000 people make the river trip each year, mostly between Christmas and the end of January. During winter the river is almost deserted – the winter currents run swift and deep, cold weather and short days deterring potential paddlers.

To hire a two-person Canadian canoe for one/three/five days costs around $80/220/300 including transport. A single-person kayak costs about $50 per day not including transport (around $50 per person). Operators provide you with everything you need for the journey, including life jackets and waterproof drums (essential if you go bottom-up).

You can also take guided canoe or kayak trips – prices start at $250 per person for a two-day guided trip and $780 per person for a five-day trip.

Operators include the following:

Blazing Paddles (☎ 0800 252 946; www.blazing paddles.co.nz; Pipiriki)

Bridge to Nowhere Tours (☎ 0800 480 308; www.bridgetonowheretours.co.nz; Pipiriki)

Canoe Safaris (☎ 0800 272 335, 06-385 9237; www.canoesafaris.co.nz; Ohakune)

Omaka (☎ 06-342 5595; www.omakaholiday.co.nz; Whanganui River Rd; ½-day unguided/guided tours $40/65)

Taumarunui Canoe Hire (☎ 0800 226 6348, 07-896 6507; www.taumarunuicanoehire.co.nz; Taumarunui)

Wades Landing Outdoors (☎ 0800 226 631, 07-895 5995; www.whanganui.co.nz; Whakahoro & Owhango)

Waka Tours (☎ 06-385 4811; wakatours@ihug.co.nz; Taumarunui)

Whanganui River Guides (☎ 07-896 6727; www .whanganuiriverguides.co.nz; Taumarunui)

Yeti Tours (☎ 0800 322 388, 06-385 8197; www.canoe .co.nz; Ohakune)

JETBOATING
Hold onto your hats: jetboat trips are a chance to quickly see parts of the river that would take you days to paddle through. Jetboats depart from Pipiriki and Wanganui, four-hour tours costing around $90 per person. The following operators can also provide transport to the river ends of the

Matemateaonga and Mangapurua Tracks (see Walking, following):

Bridge to Nowhere Tours (☎ 0800 480 308; www.bridgetonowheretours.co.nz; Pipiriki)
Scenic Experience Jet (☎ 06-342 5599; www.whanganuiriver.co.nz; Wanganui)
Whanganui River Adventures (☎ 0800 862 743, 06-385 3246; ken.pipiriki@xtra.co.nz; Pipiriki)

WALKING

The track seeing the most feet in Whanganui National Park is the 40-minute walk from the Mangapurua Landing (Map p276) to the Bridge to Nowhere, 30km upstream from Pipiriki by jetboat.

The Matemateaonga and Mangapurua Tracks are brilliant longer tramps (DOC booklets \$1). Both are one-way tracks beginning (or ending) at remote spots on the river, so you have to organise jetboat transport to or from the trailheads – ask any jetboat operator. To Pipiriki from the Matemateaonga Track is around \$45 per person; from the Mangapurua Track it's around \$80.

Three to four days end-to-end, the 42km **Matemateaonga Track** gets kudos as one of NZ's best walks. Probably due to its remoteness, it doesn't attract the hordes of trampers that amass on NZ's more famous tracks. Penetrating deep into wild bush and hill country, it traces an old Maori track and a disused settlers' dray road between the Wanganui and Taranaki regions. It follows the crest of the Matemateaonga Range along the route of the Whakaihuwaka Rd, started in 1911 to create a more direct link from Stratford to railway at Raetihi. WWI interrupted planning and the road was never finished.

On a clear day, a 1½-hour side-trip to the top of Mt Humphries (730m) rewards you with sigh-inducing views all the way to Mt Taranaki and the volcanoes of Tongariro. There's a steep section between the Whanganui River (75m above sea level) and the Puketotara Hut (Map p276; 427m above sea level), but mostly it's easy walking. There are three huts along the way: Omaru, Pouri and Puketotara (see Map p276).

The **Mangapurua Track** is a 40km trail between Whakahoro and the Mangapurua Landing, both on the Whanganui River. The track runs along the Mangapurua and Kaiwhakauka Streams (Whanganui River tributaries). Between these valleys a side track leads to the 663m Mangapurua Trig, the area's highest point, cloudless views from which run all the way to the Tongariro and Egmont National Park volcanoes.

The route passes the Bridge to Nowhere and abandoned farming land that settlers cleared early last century. Walking the track takes 20 hours. Unless you're some kind of insane tramping dynamo, allow three to four days. The Whakahoro Hut (Map p276) at the Whakahoro end of the track is the only hut, but there's plenty of good camping. There's road access to the track at the Whakahoro end and from a side track leading to the end of the Ruatiti Valley–Ohura Rd (from Raetihi).

There are a couple of shorter walks branching off the Whanganui River Rd that offer a glimpse of the national park's wilderness. The DOC booklet *In and Around Whanganui National Park* (\$2.50) details these walks.

The **Atene Skyline Track** begins at Atene on the Whanganui River Rd, about 22km north of the SH4 junction. The 18km track takes six to eight hours, taking in native forest, sandstone bluffs and the Taumata Trig (523m), with its broad views as far as Mt Ruapehu, Mt Taranaki and the Tasman Sea. The track ends back on the Whanganui River Rd, 2km downstream from the starting point.

From the Pipiriki DOC field centre a 1km track cuts its way through native bush to the top of Pukehinau, a hill with great valley vistas.

Sleeping

WHANGANUI NATIONAL PARK

The park has a sprinkling of huts, a lodge and numerous camping grounds. Along the Taumarunui–Pipiriki section are three Category 2 huts classified as Great Walks Huts during summer. Serviced Huts in the off-season: the Whakahoro Hut (Map p276) at Whakahoro, the John Coull Hut (Map p276) and Tieke Kainga (Map p276), which has been revived as a *marae*. You can stay here, but full *marae* protocol must be observed (see p57). On the lower part of the river, Downes Hut (Map p276) is on the west bank, opposite Atene.

Bridge to Nowhere Lodge (Map p276; ☎ 0800 480 308; www.bridgetonowheretours.co.nz; unpowered sites per 2 people \$20, s/d self-catering \$45/90, s/d incl breakfast &

dinner $125/250) Across the river from the Tieke Kainga *marae*, this remote lodge is deep in the national park, 21km upriver from Pipiriki near the Matemateaonga Track. The only way to get here is by river (jetboat from Pipiriki for $50) or on foot. It has a licensed bar, and meals are quality home-cooked affairs. The lodge also runs jetboat tours (p284) and canoe trips (p284).

WHANGANUI RIVER ROAD

Book the following places in advance – no-one's going to turn you away, but they appreciate a bit of warning! There's no mobile-phone coverage along the road, and no petrol or shops.

Omaka (Map p276; ☎ 06-342 5595; www.omaka holiday.co.nz; Whanganui River Rd; unpowered sites per 2 people $20, tw & d $70-90) A rural idyll: hill flanks fold into the river to the intermittent sound of sheep bleats. Friendly and farmy, it's about 12km north of Parikino, adjacent to the Atene Skyline Track. The lodge also runs short canoe trips (p284).

Flying Fox (Map p276; ☎ 06-342 8160; www.thefly ingfox.co.nz; Whanganui River Rd; sites per 2 people $20, tw & d $90-110) A superb, eco-attuned getaway on the riverbank across from Koriniti, this place is ace. You can self-cater in the Brew-house or the James K (self-contained cot-tages), opt for DB&B, or pitch a tent in a secluded bush clearing. Access is by jetboat, or you can drive then soar over the river on the flying fox.

Operiki Farmstay (Map p276; ☎ 06-342 8159; www .whanganuiriver.co.nz; Whanganui River Rd; d & tw incl 3 meals $110) On a steep hillside 1.5km north of Koriniti, this is a cheery in-with-the-family farmhouse. Your host Trissa loves a chat and loves to cook almost as much.

Koriniti Marae (☎ 06-348 0303, 021 365 176; Whanganui River Rd, Koriniti; dm $20) This *marae* on the east bank takes prebooked visitors; offer *koha* (a donation) plus the fee. It also runs a 24-hour 'cultural experience' for groups, in-cluding a *haka* (war dance), weaving, story-telling and three meals ($170 per person). Call Sunny Teki in Wanganui to make a reservation.

Kauika Camp Site (☎ /fax 06-342 8762; Morikau Rd, Ranana; sites per 2 people $20) In a tranquil spot beside the river, this privately owned site has hot showers, a kitchen and a laundry.

St Joseph's Church (☎ 06-342 8190; Whanganui River Rd, Jerusalem; dm $15) Taking in bedraggled

travellers, the Sisters at St Joe's await to issue your deliverance – book ahead for the privilege. Curtains divide the large room into cubicles.

There's an informal **camp site** with toilets and cold water at Pipiriki, and another one (even less formal) just north of Atene (see Map p276).

Getting There & Away

From the north, there's road access to the Whanganui River at Taumarunui, Ohine-pane and Whakahoro, though the latter is joining at Raetihi, 91km north of Wanganui. It takes about $1\frac{1}{2}$ to two hours to drive the 79km between Wanganui and Pipiriki. The full circle from Wanganui through Pipiriki and Raetihi and back along SH4 through the Paraparas and Mangawhero River Gorge takes about four hours. The Whanganui River Rd is unsealed between Matahiwi and Mangaetoroa; petrol is available at Raetihi and Upokongaro but nowhere in between. Despite the steep hills and gravel, the river road also lures a few cyclists.

Another option from Wanganui is the Rural Mail Coach Tour (p280) to Pipiriki.

PALMERSTON NORTH

pop 67,400

The rich sheep- and dairy-farming Mana-watu region embraces the districts of Ran-gitikei to the north and Horowhenua to the south. At the centre of it all on the banks of the Manawatu River is Palmerston North (as opposed to Palmerston on the South Island), its moderate high-rise attempts reaching up from the plains. Massey Uni-versity, the largest university in NZ, informs the town's cultural and social structures. As a result, 'Palmy' has an open-minded, rur-ally bookish vibe.

Orientation

The grassy expanse of The Square is the centre of city life. One block to the west,

George St is the main café and restaurant strip. Massey University is 3km south of town.

MAPS

Free town maps are available at the visitor information centre. You can also get maps at the **Automobile Association** (AA; ☎ 06-357 7039; www.aatravel.co.nz; 185 Broadway Ave).

Information

BOOKSHOPS

Bruce McKenzie Booksellers (☎ 06-356 9922; books@bmbooks.co.nz; 51 George St)

EMERGENCY

Ambulance, fire service & police (☎ 111)
Police station (☎ 06-351 3600; Church St)

INTERNET ACCESS

The Internet seems not to have caught on in food-focused cafés yet, but try the following options:
i Café (☎ 06-353 7899; cnr The Square & Fitzherbert Ave; ☑ 9am-11pm)
i Play (☎ 06-357 4578; 1st fl, 141 The Square; ☑ 9am-midnight)

MEDICAL SERVICES

Doctors (☎ 06-354 7737; www.thedoctors.co.nz; 27 Linton St; ☑ 8am-9pm) The chemist next door is open until 10pm.
Palmerston North Hospital (☎ 06-356 9169; 50 Ruahine St)

MONEY

There are plenty of banks and ATMs around The Square and Main St.

POST

Post office (388 Church St)

TOURIST INFORMATION

DoC office (☎ 06-350 9700; www.doc.govt.nz; 717 Tremaine Ave; ☑ 8am-4.30pm Mon-Fri) Three kilometres north of The Square.
Palmerston North visitor information centre (☎ 06-354 6593; www.manawatunz.co.nz, www.palmy.net.nz; The Square; ☑ 9am-5pm Mon-Fri, 10am-4pm Sat & Sun)

TRAVEL AGENCIES

House of Travel (☎ 06-356 7051; cnr Main St & The Square; www.stephenparsons.houseoftravel.co.nz; ☑ 8am-6pm Mon-Fri, 9.30am-12.30pm Sat)

Sights & Activities

Taking the English village green to a whole new level, The **Square** is Palmy's heart and soul. A clock tower, duck pond, Maori carvings, statues and trees of all shapes and seasonal dispositions dot the manicured lawns as locals eat lunch in the sunshine. The visitors information centre stocks the *Heritage Walk* brochure, an easy amble around The Square and surrounding streets.

Te Manawa (☎ 06-355 5000; www.temanawa.co.nz; 396 Main St; museum & gallery admission free, science centre adult/child/family $6/4/15; ☑ 10am-5pm) has merged a museum, art gallery and science centre into one complex. Vast collections (around 55,000 items) join the dots between 'life, art and mind'. The museum has a strong Maori focus; the gallery's emphasis is post-1960s NZ art. Kids will get a kick out of the hands-on exhibits at the Science Centre.

Rugby fans holler about the **New Zealand Rugby Museum** (☎ 06-358 6947; www.rugbymuseum.co.nz; 87 Cuba St; adult/child $5/2; ☑ 10am-noon & 1.30-4pm Mon-Sat, 1.30-4pm Sun). This amazing room overflows with rugby paraphernalia, from a 1905 All Blacks jumper to the actual whistle used to start the first game of every Rugby World Cup. NZ is hosting the 2011 World Cup – time to brush up on your *haka*.

Victoria Esplanade (☑ 8am-6pm Apr-Sep, to 9pm Oct-Mar) is a riverbank park. Mooch around the adventure playground, aviary, conservatory, bike trails, walkways, the **miniature railway** (☎ 06-357 3049; fax 06-357 3050; per ride $1.50; ☑ 1-4pm Sat & Sun), or just chill out on the lawns. The **Rose Garden**, voted among the world's top five prettiest gardens in 2003, brings tears of pride to Palmy's citizens.

About 15km northeast of Palmerston North, SH2 dips into **Manawatu Gorge**. Maoris named the gorge Te Apiti (the Narrow Passage), believing the big reddish rock near the centre of the gorge was its guardian spirit. The rock's colour is said to change intensity when a prominent Rangitane tribe member dies or sheds blood. It takes around 3½ hours to walk through the gorge from either end, or see it via jetboat (see Tours, opposite).

On the southeastern edge of the gorge, about 40 minutes drive from Palmerston North, is the **Tararua Wind Farm** (Map p276; ☎ 06-574 4800; www.trustpower.co.nz; Hall Block Rd), allegedly the largest wind farm in the southern hemisphere. From Hall Block Rd there are awesome views of the turbines and sometimes both oceans and the South Island. Spinning similarly north of the gorge is **Te Apiti Wind Farm** (Map p276; www.windpower.co.nz; Saddle Rd, Ashhurst). Ask at the visitors information centre for directions.

Our fine feathered friends at **Owlcatraz** (Map p276; ☎ 06-363 7872; www.owlcatraz.co.nz; Main Rd South, Shannon; adult/child $15.50/7; 9am-5pm) have obligingly adopted oh-so-droll names like Owlvis Presley and Owl MacPherson. It's a 40-minute drive south from Palmerston North, or pick-up package tours are available (see below).

When the summer plains bake, dive into the **Lido Aquatic Centre** (☎ 06-357 2684; www.lidoaquaticcentre.co.nz; Park Rd; adult/child $2.50/1.50; 6am-8pm Mon-Fri, 8am-9pm Sat & Sun). It's a long way from the beaches of Venice, but it has a 50m pool, waterslides, café and gym.

Palmy is, as the locals say, 'flat-as'. Grab a *Guide to Cycling in Palmerston North* brochure from the visitors information centre, which maps out **bike trails** around town. Adventure Backpackers hires out bikes (right).

Tours

Big Owlcatraz Experience (☎ 06-362 7872; www.owlcatraz.co.nz; Main Rd South, Shannon; tours $60; 9am-3pm) Includes pick-up/drop-off from your hotel or the visitor information centre, morning tea, lunch and afternoon tea.

Feilding Saleyards (☎ 06-323 3318; www.feilding.co.nz; 10 Manchester Sq, Feilding; tours $5; 11am) Local farmers instruct you in the gentle art of selling livestock.

Hiwinui Jet (☎ 06-329 2838, 0274 349 090; www.hiwinui.co.nz; 30min ride $55) Manawatu Gorge jetboat tours for groups of five or more, departing Balance Bridge, Ferry Reserve (or pick-up from the visitor information centre $25).

Festivals & Events

Summer in the Park is a series of concerts in Victoria Esplanade on summer weekends. The **Buskers Festival** in late February causes a ruckus in The Square, while the **George Street Fiesta** in early April circles around food, music and dance.

Sleeping

BUDGET

Pepper Tree Backpackers (☎ 06-355 4054; peppertreehostel@clearnet.nz; 121 Grey St; dm/s/d $23/42/54) Inexplicably strewn with green-painted boots, this enduring/endearing YHA is the best budget option. Mattresses are thick, the kitchen will never run out of spatulas, and the two cats make things feel downright homey. Doubles off the kitchen are a bit small – angle for one at the back.

Shamrock Inn (☎ 06-355 2130; www.shamrock.co.nz; 267 Main St; s/d $50/60) Three minutes' walk from The Square, the 'Shammy' is a friendly, old-fashioned boozer with surprisingly decent pub accommodation upstairs. Rooms have TVs; facilities are shared.

Adventure Backpackers (☎ 06-353 2418; www.adventure-backpackers.com; 95 King St; dm/s/d $19/35/52) Inside an old catering school, this place is central, large and clean (if a little thin on personality). The lounge and kitchen are school-sized – the rooms would benefit from some of this extra space. Mountain-bike rental is $20 per day.

Ann Keith's B&B (☎ 06-358 6928; www.grandmas-place.com; 123 Grey St; s/d $65/95) This B&B has five en suite rooms in an old-fangled house with TV, tea- and coffee-making accoutrements and electric blankets for cold plains nights. There's also a hostel at 146 Grey St, but the B&B is a better option.

Palmerston North Holiday Park (☎/fax 06-358 0349; 133 Dittmer Dr; sites per 2 people $24, cabins $25-48, units $60) About 2km from The Square, off Ruha St, this shady park has a wheezy boot-camp feel to it, but it's quiet and right beside Victoria Esplanade.

MIDRANGE

Cornwall (☎ 0800 170 000, 06-354 9010; www.cornwallmotorlodge.co.nz; 01 Fitzherbert Ave; ste $130-180) Cornwall has 27 enormous self-contained apartments on a bleak corner block. But forget about the block: rooms have spas, Sky TV, super king-size beds and balconies. Double-glazing culls the Fitzherbert Ave fracas.

Braemar (☎ 0800 355 805, 06-355 8053; www.braemarmotlodge.co.nz; 177 Ruahine St; ste $110-175) Braemar's studio units have king-size beds, TVs, spas, DVD players and stereos. With 50-plus titles in the DVD library, there should be something up your alley. Units on the street can be a bit noisy (it's a leaf-free zone), but the ones at the back are great.

Rose City (☎ 0508 356 538, 06-356 5388; www.rosecitymotel.co.nz; 120 Fitzherbert Ave; units $107-135) One for the postmodern aesthetes, Rose City's townhouse-style units are spacey and

AUTHOR'S CHOICE

Plum Trees Lodge (☎ 06-358 7813; www
.plumtreeslodge.co.nz; 97 Russell St; s/d $120/150)
In a flat-grid town with more motels than
seems plausible, this place comes as sweet
relief. Down a leafy driveway on a quiet
street, ascend past lead-lighting to the
secluded lodge. Brilliantly designed using
recycled native timbers from demolition
sites around Palmerston North, the raked
timber ceiling is punctuated with skylights,
the balcony set among swaying boughs.
Romantic nights beneath a mosquito net
slide lazily into breakfast – a sumptuous
hamper of fresh fruit, croissants, jams, eggs,
cheese, coffee and juice awaits.

shipshape but stylistically mired in the '80s.
Free videos, squash court and kids' play
room are bonuses.

Mid City Motel (☎ 06-357 2184; www.mid-city
.co.nz; 129 Broadway Ave; s/d from $75/85, f $120-150)
Slap-bang in the middle of town, this big
anonymous motel features bedspreads
from the Laura Ashley fantasy book and
inspiring paintings of tall ships and cavort-
ing steeds. Cooking facilities and Sky TV
compensate.

Empire Hotel (☎ 06-357 8002; www.trinitygroup.co
.nz; cnr Princess & Main Sts; s/d/f $70/80/135) With
slicker-than-average pub rooms upstairs,
the Empire is a solid central option. Rooms
have private bathrooms, TVs and fridges;
some open onto a wide veranda above the
street. The pub downstairs gets raucous –
steer for a room far from the beer cheer.

TOP END

Bentleys Motor Inn (☎ 0800 2368 5397; www.bentleys
motorinn.co.nz; cnr Linton & Chaytor Sts; ste $130-165)
The highest branch on Palmy's burgeon-
ing motel tree (as 'top-end' as it gets),
Bentleys' five-star apartments are worth
the investment. Inside are new appliances,
DVD players, spas, stereos, contemporary
furnishings and Sky TV; outside are a gym,
squash court and sauna.

Eating

Barista (☎ 06-357 2614; 77 George St; brunch $5-18,
dinner $20-30; breakfast, lunch & dinner) No mat-
ter what time you pass by, Barista seems
to always be open. It's a big, bustling café-

restaurant with professional staff shuffling
out plates of pasta, meat, seafood and salad.
The coffee will knock your socks off.

Moxies (☎ 06-355 4238; 81 George St; meals $6-16;
breakfast & lunch) This chipper corner café
is decked out in primary colours with big
windows. Staff members are equally upbeat,
the all-day menu is top value (stellar omelettes), and if you've got gluten issues, this
is the place for you.

Café Cuba (☎ 06-356 5750; cnr George & Cuba Sts;
all-day menu $7-16, dinner $19-25; breakfast, lunch
& dinner) On a sugar search? Proceed to Café
Cuba – the cakes here are for professional
chocoholics only. Supreme coffees and traditional café fare with flair also draw the
crowds.

IndiaToday (☎ 06-353 7400; 30 George St; mains
$14-19; lunch Wed-Fri, dinner daily) A million
miles from Bollywood schmaltz, this upmarket place won't break the bank. Behind
George St picture windows, today's northern Indian curries are served by immaculate black-clad waiting staff.

Vavasseur (☎ 06-359 3167; 201 Broadway Ave;
mains $29-32; dinner Tue-Sun) Elegant Vavas-
seur is decorated with vavoom: chocolate
brown walls, silk drapes and wooden floorboards. Tasty traditional food is prepared
with panache, and served with a smile.

Bathhouse (☎ 06-952 5570; 161 Broadway Ave; lunch
$15-28, dinner $29-32; lunch & dinner) A plush,
moody space, this long room is long on
style. Furnished with gilt mirrors, an open
fire and swanky couches, Bathhouse fills
with jazz swingers on Thursday and Friday
nights, snapping their fingers over upmarket
pub food. Families brunch on weekends.

Bella's Café (☎ 06-357 8616; 2 The Square; lunch
$12-18, dinner $28-30; lunch Tue-Sat, dinner Mon-Sat)
Romantically candlelit, Bella's warm red
walls create an inviting atmosphere for a
mature crowd. Windows fold open in summer revealing an Italian-Pacific menu – seafood, curries and pasta are the mainstays.

Stage Door Café (☎ 06-359 2233; Regent Arcade;
mains $9-14; breakfast & lunch) A low-key af-
fair with mellow tunes, spiky green plants,
orange plastic chairs and a retro red couch
area. Right across from a uni accommodation block, the Stage Door opens to students on the run from the books.

Self-caterers can fuel up on supplies at
Countdown supermarket (☎ 06-356 6066; cnr Ferguson & Ashley Sts).

Drinking

Flying Fish (☎ 06-359 3474; Regent Arcade) This cocktail bar is a world-class winner. Progressive, stylish and Pacifically hewn, the Flying Fish has got its finger firmly on the Palmy pulse. DJs smooth over the week's problems on Friday and Saturday nights as a sexy, urbane crew sips Manhattans and Tamarillo Mules (yes, they kick).

Celtic Inn (☎ 06-357 5571; Regent Arcade) The Celtic expertly offsets Flying Fish nearby with good old-fashioned pub stuff. Slow days build to pumping evenings, elbows, travellers and students bending elbows with a few tasty pints of the black stuff. Friendly staff, darts, pool table, red velvet chairs, kids darting around parents' legs – it's all here.

Mao Bar (☎ 06-354 8410; 76 George St; mains $8-28; breakfast, lunch & dinner) Coo, café by day, full-scale cocktail bar by night, serving East-meets-West fusion food. The interior is aptly bamboo-strewn, with tall screens, red lanterns and dark timbers. Mao Test-Tubes will lure any reds out from under the bed.

Fitz (☎ 06-350 0718; Ferguson St) This let-it-all-hang-out brawling beer-barn is usually full of pool-playing, jukeboxing students, unwinding after a hard day spent aspiring to adulthood.

Murphy's Law Brewery (☎ 06-355 2337; 481 Main St; meals $9-20) Another of NZ's ever-present Irish pubs (something to do with the weather perhaps?). Murphy's is replete with chesterfields, stone fireplace, weathered copper bar and wooden barrels. Business crowds flock for lunch; 20-somethings heave and lurch on Friday and Saturday nights. Live music Thursday to Saturday.

Highflyers (☎ 06-357 5155; cnr The Square & Main St; mains $10-25) 'Where everybody is somebody' – not quite as catchy as the *Cheers* strapline, but you get the picture. Inside it's impossible not to, with enormous pictures of Eastwood, Monroe, Dean, Ali etc inspiring punters to high-flying glories. Plenty of beer, pub grub and after-work booze hounds.

Entertainment

Downtown Cinemas (☎ 06-355 5655; www.dtcinemas .co.nz, Downtown Shopping Arcade, Broadway Ave; adult/child tickets $13/9.50) Incorporating the Rialto Cinema upstairs, the capacious Downtown Cinemas show mainstream new-release flicks.

Downtown Cinema Gold (☎ 06-353 1902; www .cinemagold.co.nz adult/child tickets $15/10) In the same complex as Downtown Cinemas, Cinema Gold has plush seats and a booze licence to enhance art-house classics and limited-release screenings.

There's a simmering theatre scene in Palmy. See what's playing at the following:

Abbey Theatre (☎ 06-355 0499; www.abbeymusical theatre.co.nz; 369-73 Church St) Airing a range of quality amateur performances, with a predilection for cheesy musicals.

Regent Theatre (☎ 06-484 2538, 06-350 2100; www.regent.co.nz; 63 Broadway Ave) A divinely detailed theatre hosting big-ticket international acts like the Russian Ballet and John Cleese.

Centrepoint Theatre (☎ 06-354 5740; www.centre point.co.nz; 280 Church St) Hosts bigger-name professional shows, theatre sports and seasonal plays.

Globe Theatre (☎ 06-358 9663; cnr Pitt & Main Sts) A large community theatre, home to the Manawatu Theatre Society.

Getting There & Away

AIR

Palmerston North International Airport (☎ 06-351 4415; www.pnairport.co.nz; Airport Dr), 4km north of town, is proud of its international status. International passengers pay a $25 departure tax; domestically there's a $5 development levy. The following airlines operate out of Palmy:

Air New Zealand (☎ 06-351 8800; www.airnz.co.nz; 366 Church St) Daily direct flights with onward connections to Auckland, Christchurch and Wellington; to Hamilton daily except Saturday.

Freedom Air (☎ 0800 600 500, 09-523 3686; www .freedomair.com) Direct flights one to four days per week to Sydney and Brisbane; usually the cheapest option to/from NZ.

Origin Pacific (☎ 0800 302 302; www.originpacific .co.nz) Daily direct flights to Auckland and Nelson with onward connections.

BUS

InterCity (www.intercitycoach.co.nz), **Newmans** (www .newmanscoach.co.nz) and **Tranzit Coachlines** (☎ 06-355 4955; cnr Main & Pitt Sts; ⊗ 8.30am-7pm Mon-Fri, 9am-3pm Sat & Sun). InterCity and Newmans run services from Palmerston North to most North Island destinations, including

Wellington ($31, 2¼ hours, six daily), Auckland ($76, nine hours, two daily), Napier ($38, two hours 40 minutes, two to three daily), New Plymouth ($43, four hours, three daily) and Wanganui ($20, 1¼ hours, three daily). Some direct services between Auckland and Wellington bypass Palmerston North, stopping instead at the nearby town of Bulls.

Tranzit Coachlines operates a Masterton service continuing to Wellington ($31, two hours 15 minutes, four daily).

White Star City to City (☎ 06-358 8777; fax 06-758 8878) operates from the Transit City Link bus stop on Main St near The Square, with daily services to Wellington ($22, 2¼ hours) and New Plymouth ($42, four hours, two daily Monday to Friday, one daily on weekends).

TRAIN
Palmerston North Train Station (☎ 0800 802 802; Mathews Ave) is off Tremaine Ave, about 2.5km north of The Square. It has no ticket sales.
Tranz Scenic (☎ 0800 872 467, 04-495 0775; www .tranzscenic.co.nz; ☼ 7am-7pm) runs long-distance trains between Wellington and Auckland, stopping at Palmerston North. From Palmy to Wellington, take the *Overlander* (adult/ child $29/25, 2½ hours, 5pm daily), or the *Capital Connection* (adult/child $20/10, two hours 10 minutes, 6.20am daily). Buy tickets from Tranz Scenic directly, either over the phone or via the website.

Getting Around
TO/FROM THE AIRPORT
There's no public transport between the city and airport, but taxis are plentiful. If you're driving into the CBD from the airport, take Ruahine St then turn right onto Main St.

If you're trucking through to Wellington, Main St becomes SH56 and continues to Wellington via Foxton, or turn left at The Square into Fitzherbert Ave, which leads to SH57 for Wellington via Shannon. It's a two- to three-hour drive either way.

BUS
Transit City Link (☎ 06-355 4955; www.horizons.govt .nz; to Massey $2) runs daytime minibuses departing from the Main St bus stop on the east side of The Square. Bus 12 goes to Massey University; none go to the airport.

CAR
The following companies have offices situated at the airport:
Avis (☎ 06-357 0168; www.avis.com)
Budget (☎ 06-356 8565; www.budget.co.nz)
Hertz (☎ 06-357 0921; www.hertz.co.nz)

TAXI
A city-to-airport taxi fare costs between $10 and $14.
Kiwi Cab Co (☎ 06-354 4111)
Manawatu Taxis (☎ 06-355 5111)
Taxis Palmerston North (☎ 06-355 5333)

SOUTH OF PALMERSTON NORTH
South of 'Student City' in the Horowhenua district, **Shannon** and **Foxton** are sleepy country towns en route to Wellington. **Foxton Beach** is one of a string of broad, shallow Tasman Sea beaches along this stretch of coast – brown sand, driftwood and holiday houses proliferate. Other beaches include Himatangi, Hokio and Waikawa. The town **Levin** is more sizable, but suffers from being too close to both Wellington and Palmerston North to warrant through-traffic making a stop.

Taupo & the Central Plateau

Plateaus are elevated flat landmasses, which may be (let's face it) a little dull sounding, but this central chunk of the North Island is anything but boring. Firstly, it's hardly flat, with Tongariro National Park's soaring peaks of Tongariro, Ruapehu and Ngauruhoe all at their photogenic best. Then there's New Zealand's largest body of water, Lake Taupo, a vast, water-filled crater that's a legacy of a volcanic blast that trashed the island and shook the world more than 26,500 years ago. And the area is still active, with Mt Ruapehu exploding in 1995. It's all part of the geothermal thrill of the Taupo Volcanic Zone, which stretches over to White Island and through Rotorua.

If all that isn't blowing your hair back, then there's the chance to catch a monster trout in the celebrated Tongariro River, jump aboard a jetboat to zoom up to Huka Falls or free fall in the skydiving capital of the world, Taupo. This once-sleepy lakeside township has woken up enough to rival Rotorua for daredevil activities such as parasailing on the bejewelled lake or bouncing on a bungy over the Waikato River, NZ's longest river. In winter the mountains are dusted with snow, which makes for top skiing at Turoa and Whakapapa ski fields.

There's also one of NZ's most achievable Great Walks, the Tongariro Northern Circuit, which winds around some spectacular 'volcanoscapes'. If you don't have a couple of days to spare there's the popular Tongariro Crossing, a day walk that packs in the best of the longer walk to make for one of the country's top short hikes. Still sounding plain to you?

HIGHLIGHTS

- Dodging and dripping your way up to **Huka Falls** (p307) on a jetboat
- Cutting the fresh powdery snow at **Turoa Ski Area** or **Whakapapa Ski Area** (p317)
- Snapping photos of smoking **Mt Ruapehu** (p314)
- Tramping the stunning **Tongariro Crossing** (p315)
- Bagging a monster trout on **Tongariro River** (p309)
- Cruising **Lake Taupo** (p301) to check out the modern Maori carvings
- Rediscovering the stunning 'lost valley' of **Orakei Korako** (p308)
- Taking the plunge by bungy jumping over the **Waikato River** (p298) in Taupo and maybe even taking a dunk
- Throwing yourself out of a plane in the world's skydiving capital, **Taupo** (p296)

TELEPHONE CCDE: 07

www.laketauponz.com

www.visitruapehu.com

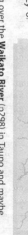

Map showing: Tongariro Crossing, Whakapapa Ski Area, Mt Ruapehu, Turoa Ski Area, Tongariro River, Huka Falls, Taupo, Lake Taupo, Waikato River, Orakei Korako

TAUPO & THE CENTRAL PLATEAU FACTS

Eat: Grilled trout from Tongariro River with a side of Ohakune carrots

Drink: A mouthful of water from the Waikato River as you bungy over it (p298)

Read: Peter Gossage's *The Battle of the Mountains*, retelling the troubled love of mythical Tongariro and Pihanga for kids

Listen to: Kooky 1980s three-piece, Normal Ambition, originally from Taupo

Watch: The starring role Mt Tongariro (p312) played as Mt Doom in the *Lord of the Rings* trilogy

Swim at: Tama Lakes (p317), a refreshing dip in the shadow of Mt Ruapehu

Festival: Ohakune's Carrot Festival, celebrating all that is orange and pointy (p322)

Tackiest tourist attraction: Ohakune's Big Carrot (p322)

Climate

Due to its altitude, the Central Plateau has a generally cool climate, with temperatures ranging from around 3°C in winter up to a maximum of around 24°C in summer. Above 2500m there is a small year-round snowfield, while July to October is the skiing season in Whakapapa and Turoa, and in some places snow can linger on into spring. On the mountains, storms and freezing temperatures can occur at any time.

Getting There & Around

Air New Zealand has flights from Taupo to Auckland and Wellington. There are also charter flights linking Auckland with the Whakapapa Ski Area, including those run by Mountain Air. Tranz Scenic trains on the Auckland–Wellington line stop at National Park. From Taupo, InterCity buses con-nect with most major destinations around NZ. There are several private shuttle-bus services operating around Tongariro National Park, and serving the snowfields in winter.

LAKE TAUPO REGION

NZ's largest lake, Lake Taupo, is the fiery heart of the North Island, lying in a caldera formed by one of the biggest volcanic eruptions ever. The eruption occurred more than 26,500 years ago, throwing out 800 cu km of ash and pumice, making Krakatoa (8 cu km) look like a pimple. The surrounding area is still volcanically active and, like Rotorua, has fascinating thermal areas.

Today the 606-sq-km lake and its tributaries are serene enough to be the world's trout-fishing capital. International trout-fishing tournaments are held on Lake Taupo annually on the Anzac Day long weekend (on or around 25 April) with much of the action centring around Turangi.

Well positioned by the lake, Taupo is a popular centre with visitors and has plenty of activities and facilities to cater for backpackers, families and independent travellers alike.

TAUPO
pop 21,040

Taupo rivals Rotorua as the North Island's capital of adrenalinised action, with plenty of skydiving, jetboating and bungy-jumping to set your heart racing like drum 'n' bass. Taupo is on the northeastern corner of Lake Taupo and has scenic views across the lake to the volcanic peaks of Tongariro National Park. There's a lot to do just outside of town, with attractions such as Huka Falls and the lost world of Orakei Korakei all within an hour's drive.

TOP ACTIVITIES

- Climb an active volcano…or three! (Ruapehu, p314; Ngauruhoe, p315; Tongariro, p315)
- Tease the Huka Falls by jetboat (p307)
- Ski the North Island's most popular ski fields (p317)
- Check out the lake and mountains from the air – as you plummet to earth (p296)
- Bungy over (or into!) the Waikato River (p298)

CENTRAL PLATEAU

Lake Taupo is the origin of NZ's longest river, the Waikato, which leaves the lake at the township, bashing its way through the Huka Falls and Aratiatia Rapids, before settling down for a sedate ramble through the North Island to climax on the west coast just south of Auckland.

The township lines the lake front where State Highway 1 (SH1; the main north–south artery) first touches the lake, making for an easy drive for most North Islanders on holiday.

History

When the Maori chief Tamatea-arikinui visited the area he thought the ground was hollow, making his footsteps reverberate,

so he dubbed it Tapuaeharuru (Resounding Footsteps). The modern name originates from the story of Tia, who discovered the lake and slept beside it draped in his cloak, so it became known as Taupo Nui a Tia (The Great Cloak of Tia).

Ironically, this leisure capital was originally a strategic military base, with Europeans first settling here in force during the East Coast Land War (1868–72), Colonel JM Roberts built a redoubt in 1869, and a garrison of mounted police remained until the defeat of the rebel warrior Te Kooti (see the boxed text, p378) later that year.

In the 1870s the government bought the land from the Maoris. In the 20th century the mass ownership of the motorcar saw

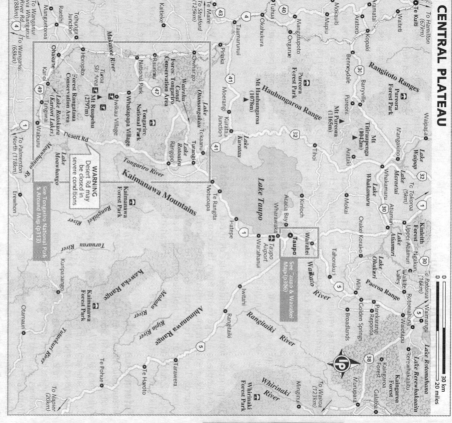

WARNING
Desert Rd may be closed in severe conditions

See Tongariro National Park & Around Map (p313)

See Taupo & Wairakei Map (p306)

0   30 km
0   20 miles

MAORI NZ: CENTRAL PLATEAU

The North Island's central region is home to a group of mountains that feature in several legends of lust and betrayal, ending in a few mountains fleeing to other parts of the island (for example, see Mt Taranaki's sad tale, p268).

Long after all that mountain-on-mountain action was over, the chief Ngatoro-i-rangi (see the boxed text, p312), fresh off the boat from Hawaiki, explored this region and named the mountains that remained. The most sacred was Tongariro, seen as the leader of all the other mountains.

The major *iwi* (tribe) of the region is the Tuwharetoa (www.tuwharetoa.iwi.nz), one of the few *iwi* in NZ that has retained an undisputed *ariki* (high chief). The current *ariki* is Tupu Te Heuheu, great-great-grandson of Te Heuheu Tukino, who gifted Tongariro to NZ as a national park in 1887 (p312), and a descendant of Ngatoro-i-rangi himself. The Tuwharetoa *ariki* holds a similar position in Maori regard as the leader of the Waikato-based King Movement (p233).

Admire carvings on meeting houses (Lake Taupo Museum & Art Gallery, below) and cliff faces (p301) from Taupo, or visit a local *marae* (meeting house; p300). Get up close and personal with the stately Tongariro on the Tongariro Crossing (p315).

Taupo grow from a lakeside village of about 750 people to a large resort town that could be driven to from most points in the North Island. Today the population still grows considerably at peak holiday times, when New Zealanders and international visitors alike flock to this lakeside town.

Information

Automobile Association (AA; Map p297; ☎ 07-378 6000; 93 Tongariro St) Centrally located.

Cybershed (Map p297; ☎ 07-377 4168; 115 Tongariro St; ☺ 9am-6pm) Has Internet access.

Experience Taupo (Map p297; ☎ 07-377 0704; 57 Tongariro St; ☺ 8.30am-6pm Apr-Sep, to 8.30pm Oct-Mar) Has Internet access and a good selection of brochures; also books tours.

House of Travel (Map p297; ☎ 07-378 2700; 37 Horomatangi St) For bus, train and plane tickets.

Internet Outpost (Map p297; 11 Tuwharetoa St) Has Internet access.

Log On (Map p297; ☎ 07-376 5901; 71 Tongariro St; ☺ 9am-9pm) Has Internet access and a good selection of brochures; also books tours.

Post office (cnr Horomatangi & Ruapehu Sts) Exchanges money.

Taupo Travel Centre (Map p297; ☎ 07-378 9032; 16 Gascoigne St) Sells tickets for trains and Interislander ferry.

Taupo visitor information centre (Map p297; ☎ 07-376 0027; www.laketauponz.com; Tongariro St) Handles bookings for all accommodation, transport and activities in the area; has a free town map as well as Department of Conservation (DOC) maps and information.

Travel Smart Taupo (Map p297; ☎ 07-378 9028; 28 Horomatangi St) For bus, train and plane tickets.

Sights

Taupo's main attractions, such as Wairakei Park and thermal regions, are north of town. In town, near the visitor information centre, the **Lake Taupo Museum & Art Gallery** (Map p297; ☎ 07-378 4167; Story Pl; adult/child $4/free; ☺ 10.30am-4.30pm) has many historical photos and mementos from around Lake Taupo. The centrepiece of the collection is a Maori meeting house, Te Aroha o Rongoheikume, which is adorned with elaborate carvings. Other exhibits include a moa skeleton, displays on the local forestry, nautical and trout-fishing industries, and a mock-up of a 19th-century shop. There are regular visiting art exhibitions.

In the middle of the Waikato River, off Spa Rd, a sweet footbridge will take you out to **Cherry Island** (Map p297; ☎ 07-378 9427; adult/child $8.50/3; ☺ 9am-5pm), which is a small trout and wildlife park with a café. The kid-friendly wildlife includes goats, pigs, pheasants and ducks, most of which are pattable.

The serene beaches of **Acacia Bay** are just 5km west of Taupo, perfect for a day trip when it's sunny.

Activities
SKYDIVING

There's no better place in the world to throw yourself out of a plane than Taupo – with more than 30,000 jumps per year, it's the skydiving capital of the world. The competitive market at the time of research meant that Taupo operators offered some of the cheapest rates in NZ, with even cheaper

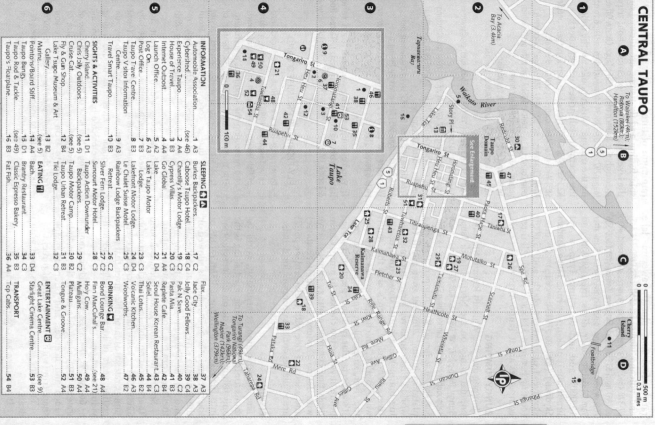

rates before 9am, plus the awesome lake and volcano views. **Freefall** (☎ 0800 373 335, 07-378 4662; www.freefly.co.nz; skydives ind ground video or DVD from $195) and **Skydive Taupo** (☎ 0800 586 766; www.skydivetaupo.co.nz; skydives before 9am/after 9am $135/150) offer dives from 9000ft and 12,000ft and include a limo (yup, a real limousine) pick-up, while **Taupo Tandem Skydiving** (☎ 0800 275 934; www.tts.net.nz) does skydives from between 6000ft and 15,000ft (costing between $145 and $299). All three companies are at Taupo Airport.

BUNGY JUMPING

Hanging over the Waikato River is the most popular bungy on the North Island: **Taupo Bungy** (Map p297; ☎ 0800 888 408, 07-377 1135; www.taupobungy.com; solo/tandem jump $100/160; ⏰ 8.30am-5pm Apr-Sep, to 7pm Oct-Mar). Jumpers leap off a platform jutting 20m out over a cliff (the world's first cantilever jump, for engineering boffins) and hurtle down towards the river, 47m below. There's also the 'touch water' option, which lets you take a dip into the river, an excellent antidote to hot days. It's a spectacular spot with plenty of vantage points if you're too chicken to jump. Cheap deals that combine a bungy jump, skydive with Taupo Tandem Skydiving (see above) and a jetboat ride with Huka Jet (see p307) are available; contact operators for details.

FISHING

The Taupo region is justifiably world famous for trout fly-fishing. Fly-fishing is the only fishing you can do on all rivers flowing into the lake, and within a 300m radius of the river mouths. Spin fishing is allowed on the Waikato River (flowing *out* of the lake) and on the Tokaanu tailrace, flowing into the lake from the Tokaanu Power Station.

Several fly-fishing guides operate around Taupo, most notably in Turangi. At roughly $200/400 per half-/full-day (including everything), rates are reasonable, given that you're getting years of local knowledge and individual attention.

Go Fish (☎ 07-378 9395; www.gofishtaupo.co.nz; 4hr share trip $150) is a guide outfit that includes lunch and licences, and offers a cheaper share trip (with a maximum of three).

Troutline (right) also offers good group deals.

If you take an organised trip, all equipment, plus licences, will be supplied, and a minimum of three hours is advised. Both spin fishing and fly-fishing are allowed on the lake. You can book organised boat trips through the **launch office** (Lake Taupo Charter Office; Map p297; ☎ 07-378 3444; www.fishcruisetaupo.co.nz) on the marina, which books for the following operators (all prices are per hour):

K2 (☎ 07-376 7452; www.k2charters.co.nz; per 4 people $85) With local Maori owner/operator Ed Tukaki.

Kiwi Charters (☎ 027 4957 744; www.kiwicharters taupo.co.nz; up to 6 people $85) A favourite outfit, which vacuum-packs fish for the flight home.

Te Moana (☎ 07-378 4839; www.gusgrace.orcon.net .nz; per 4 people $85) Scenic cruises (see p301) also available.

Top Cat Charters (☎ 07-378 5605; jumpers@wave .co.nz; up to 10 people $125)

Trout Catching (☎ 07-378 2736; www.troutcatching .com; per 4 people $90-130) Has several boat sizes available for different groups.

Troutline (☎ 0800 876 885; www.troutlinenz.com; fishing per hr from $75) Also offers fly-fishing.

Waimarie (☎ 025 776 279; www.fishlaketaupo.co.nz; up to 6 people $120)

If you're going fishing on your own (and haven't brought your own gear), **Taupo Rod & Tackle** (Map p297; ☎ 07-378 5337; 7 Tongariro St; gear

---

FLY-FISHING'S PROMISED LAND

Ever since fish were first introduced into Lake Taupo in 1898, there have been yarns of fish weighing more than a sack of spuds and measuring the length of a surfboard. The truth is that more than 28,000 fish of legal size are bagged yearly around Taupo, partly due to Tongariro National Trout Centre (see p309), which regularly restocks the famous Tongariro River with fingerlings.

Both rainbow and brown trout are hooked here, with rainbow trout especially prominent during spawning season (April to November), when 80,000 rainbows run the Tongariro River. This unique fishing area is protected by special conditions including a bag limit of three fish, no use of bait (except flies), and a minimum size of 30cm to 45cm (depending on where you fish; check your licence for details). If you're lucky enough to snag a Taupo whopper, remember the golden rule: no bragging until after dark.

hire $35; ⊙8.30am-5.30 Mon-Fri, to 4pm Sat, 9.30am-3pm Sun) and **Fly & Gun Shop** (Map p297; ☎07-378 4449; www.huntingandfishing.co.nz; 34 Heu Heu St; gear hire from $50; ⊙8am-5.30pm Mon-Thu, to 6pm Fri, to 4pm Sat, 9am-3pm Sun) hire and sell fishing tackle and gear.

Fishing licences are available from the visitor information centre or the launch office. Licences for fishing on Lake Taupo and the nearby rivers cost $15/33/73 per day/week/year. Make sure you always carry your fishing licence, as there are hefty fines for violations.

For more information on local spots, www.taupo.com is regularly updated by local fisherfolk, and includes weather and recent catches.

SWIMMING & BATHING

The **AC Baths** (Map p306; ☎07-376 0340; Spa Rd; adult/child $6.50/2.50, sauna/slide $3/3; ⊙8am-9pm) at the Taupo Events Centre, about 2km east of town, has a big, heated pool with a water-slide, indoor kids' pool, private mineral pools and sauna. There's also a world-class **climbing wall** (adult/child $13/11; ⊙5-9pm Mon-Fri, noon-9pm Sat & Sun).

Taupo Hot Springs & Health Spa (Map p306; ☎07-377 6502; www.taupohotsprings.com; Taupo-Napier Hwy (SH5); adult/child $10/4, massage per hr $89, body scrubs $85; ⊙7am-9.30pm) has a variety of mineral-rich indoor and outdoor thermal pools, freshwater pools and a giant dragon water-slide for the littlies (and not so littlies). While the kids are distracted parents can enjoy a wide choice of wellness treatments, including cleansing scrubs and massages. You can make a day of it with barbecue facilities available.

WATER SPORTS

With Lake Taupo, Waikato River and Tongariro River (plus the wild Rangitaiki and Wairoa Rivers not far away), there's plenty of chances to get wet and wild around Taupo. Whether it's parasailing, kayaking, waterskiing or jetskiing, there's no limit to the options for enjoying the waterways around town.

Kayaking is popular on both the lake and the rivers. **Kayak New Zealand** (☎0800 529 256) has two-hour guided trips ($40) on the Waikato River, while **Kayaking Kiwi** (☎080 0529 255; www.kayakingkiwi.co.nz; ⊙departs 8am & 1.30pm Oct-Mar, noon Apr-Sep) offers three-hour trips

Rapid Sensations (p310) runs trips to most of the big rivers.

Chris Jolly Outdoors (Map p297; ☎07-378 5596; www.chrisjolly.co.nz), located at the marina, offers a variety of activities, including zorb (waterskiing on an inflatable 'boat'; $75 per hour) and kayaking (single/double $15/20 per hour) and waterskiing ($150 per hour), and rents out self-drive boats ($50 to $65 per hour). The company also organises helicopter tours.

Purefun (☎0800 867 272; www.purefun.co.nz; ⊙summer only) runs more extreme sports on the lake including parasailing ($79) and jet-skiing ($75 for two).

The **Sailing Centre** (Map p306; ☎07-378 3299; www.sailingcentre.co.nz; 75 Kurupae Rd; at Two Mile Bay, south of Taupo, hires out kayaks ($25), canoes ($30), windsurfers ($30), catamarans ($50) and sailboats ($50) in summer. Rates are per hour.

($69) on the lake, including refreshments. It also does combination scenic launch cruises and kayak exploration ($129).

Kiwi River Safaris (☎0800 723 8577; www.krs.co.nz) offers two-hour, white-water rafting trips on the Rangitaiki, Wairoa and Tongariro Rivers ($95), including free pick-up from Taupo accommodation, and lunch. It also does kayak tours down the Waikato River (adult/child $40/25).

will pick you up in a helicopter and drop

For luxury rough-riding, **Heli-Biking** (☎07-384 2816; www.kaimanawahelibiking.co.nz; 4hr ride $345)

For self-propelled motion, Rainbow Lodge Backpackers Retreat (p302) and Go Global (p302) rent bikes for around $20 per day.

Lake Taupo Cycle Challenge (www.cyclechallenge.org.nz), held on the last Saturday in November each year, and October's 12-hour **Day-Night Thriller** (www.eventpromotion.co.nz), which regularly attracts more than 3000 mountain bikers. The visitor information centre produces an excellent free leaflet, *Cycling Around Lake Taupo*, which has suggested cycling and mountain-biking routes.

CYCLING

Seeing Taupo on two wheels is fun and easy, with dedicated cycle lanes along Lake Tce and Heu Heu St, and shared paths elsewhere. There are blue bike racks throughout town. Lake Taupo is also the location of two of NZ's biggest cycling events: the 160km

you on a remote mountain-bike track that you'll certainly have all to yourself.

WALKING

An enjoyable and easy all-day walk runs from Taupo to **Aratiatia** along the east bank of the Waikato River. The track follows the river to Huka Falls, crossing a hot stream. It's about a one- to 1½-hour walk from the centre of Taupo to Huka Falls. From the falls continue straight ahead along the 7km Taupo Walkway to Aratiatia (another two-plus hours). There are good views in town to get your gear, including **Pointons/Board** the river, Huka Falls and the power station across the river. To reach the start of the walk from the centre of town, head up Spa Rd, passing the Taupo Bungy site. Turn left at County Ave and continue through Spa Thermal Park till the end of the street. The path heads off to the left of the car park, up over a hill and down to the hot springs by the river. Alternatively, drive out to the falls and park, cross the bridge and walk out to Aratiatia.

Another walk goes to **Mt Tauhara**, which has magnificent views from the top. Take the Taupo–Napier Hwy (SH5) turn-off, 2km south of the Taupo town centre. About 6km along SH5, turn left into Mountain Rd. The start of the track is signposted on the right-hand side. It will take about two hours to the top, walking slowly.

A pleasant **walkway** goes from the Taupo lake front to Five Mile Bay. It's a flat, easy walk along public-access beaches. Heading south from Taupo, there's a hot-water beach on the way to Two Mile Bay. At Two Mile Bay the walkway connects with the Lions Walk, going from Two Mile Bay (4.2km south of Taupo) to Five Mile Bay (8km). Anywhere along here you can easily get back to SH1, the lakeside road.

There are plenty of other good walks and tramps in the area; the visitor information centre has the relevant Department of Conservation (DOC) pamphlets ($1).

Taupo can also be a good base for walking the Tongariro Crossing. See p319 for transport options.

GOLF

For a memorable round, **Taupo Golf Club** (Map p306; ☎ 07-378 6933; www.taupogolf.co.nz; 32 Centennial Dr; 9/18 holes $20/40) has two excellent, international-standard 18-hole courses. Al-

ternatively you could take on Killer Prawn Golf (see p307).

HORSE TREKKING

Running off-road treks, **Taupo Horse Treks** (Map p306; ☎ 07-378 0356; Karapiti Rd; 1hr/2hr rides $35/60) conducts treks through some fine forest with good views over the Craters of the Moon (p308).

SKIING

It's a little way to the fields, but there are plenty of affordable hire places in town to get your gear, including **Pointons/Board Stiff** (Map p297; ☎ 07-377 0087; 13 Tongariro St; snowboard hire $45, skis $20; ☒ 7am-7pm Apr-Sep, 9am-5pm Oct-Mar).

OTHER ACTIVITIES

Adrenaline junkies will leap at the vertiginous thrills of **Rock'n Ropes** (☎ 0800 244 508, 07-374 8111; www.rocknropes.co.nz; SH1; giant swing $15, adrenaline combo $40, half-day blast $60), a challenging obstacle course that includes balancing in teetering tree-tops, negotiating a two-wire bridge and scaling ropes. The 'adrenaline combo' includes the swing, high beam and trapeze. Rock'n Ropes is at **Taupo Adventure Park** (☎ 0800 462 7219; www.taupoadventurepark .co.nz; activities $6-30; ☒ 9am-4.30pm Apr-Sep, 9.30am-5pm Oct-Mar) on SH5, 13km north of Taupo, which also has plenty of petrol-head kicks including quad bikes ($18), sturdy off-road buggies ($40) and VW Beetle racing ($40). For littlies there's also minigolf, a maze and an animal park.

For more quad-biking adventures, **Taupo Quad Adventures** (☎ 07-377 6404; www.4x4quads .com; SH1 near Tutkau Rd; 1hr/full-day trips $70/250), 35km north of town, has fully guided off-road quad-bike trips.

For a more peaceful activity, **Taupo Gliding Club** (Map p306; ☎ 07-378 5627, 07-377 3162; Centennial Dr; flights from $70) goes gliding on Saturday, Sunday and Wednesday afternoons (weather permitting) at Centennial Park, about 5km up Spa Rd from the town centre.

Tours

Haka Trails (☎ 07-377 6016; www.hakatrails.co.nz; from $60) Offers guided trips to local marae (Maori meeting house), the birthplace of the haka (war dance), and walks further afield to Tongariro Crossing ($170 per person). Also offers courses in Maori culture including haka classes and flax weaving.

Paradise Tours (☎ 07-378 9955; www.paradisetours .co.nz; tours adult/child $60/30) Three-hour tours to the Aratiatia Rapids, Craters of the Moon and Huka Falls. Also offers tours to Tongariro National Park, Orakei Korako, Rotorua, Hawkes Bay and Waitomo Caves.

Taupo Tours (☎ 07-377 0774; www.taupotours.com; tours adult/child $5/2.50) Runs 20-minute sightseeing tours of Taupo in a refurbished 1950s British double-decker bus. Tours depart half-hourly from 10am to 4pm near the Superloo, not far from the visitor information centre.

Whirinaki Escape (☎ 07-377 2363; www.rainforest -treks.co.nz) Runs fascinating and educational 'ecocultural' guided walks in the Whirinaki Forest Park (one- to three-day trips between $155 and $745). Transport from Taupo, meals and accommodation are included in the price and there are reductions for children.

Wilderness Escapes (☎ 07-378 3413; www.wilder nessescapes.co.nz) Organises a wide variety of walks (from $60) and other outdoor activities, such as half-hour microlight flights ($120), kayaking (from $85), abseiling (from $60), rock climbing (from $80) and caving ($180). Also does a guided trip to Orakei Korako ($210).

AERIAL SIGHTSEEING

Air Charter Taupo (☎ 07-378 5467; www.aircharter taupo.co.nz; flights $50–180) Located at Taupo Airport, offers stunning scenic flights ranging from 15-minute flights to one-hour flights across Lake Taupo, Tongariro, Wairakei Park and Mt Ruapehu.

Chris Jolly Outdoors (Map p297; ☎ 07-378 5596; www.chrisjolly.cc.nz; flights $85–490) Also books tours, from 10 minutes around town (adult/child $85/60) to a more extensive flight that can be over Mt Tarawera ($560) or Tongariro National Park ($490). Located at the marina.

Helistar Helicopters (Map p306; ☎ 0800 435 478; www.helistar.co.nz; Huka Falls Rd; flights $75–945) About 3km northeast of town, offers a variety of scenic helicopter flights, ranging from five minutes to two hours. Also available is the Hukastar Combo, which is a helicopter flight followed by a spin on the Huka Jet (from $170).

Taupo's Floatplane (Map p297; ☎ 07-378 7500; www.taupofloatplane.co.nz; flights $70–425) Next to Taupo Boat Harbour, does a variety of trips, including quick flights over the lake and longer ones over Mt Ruapehu and as far afield as White Island. If you're looking for a full day out, try the Taupo Trifecta Combo (floatplane trip, followed by a jetboat trip and a walk through Orakei Korako; $260).

Volcanic Scenic Flights (☎ 0800 1376 7523; www .aeroplaneadventures.co.nz; flights from $225) Does good tours of Tongariro, Mt Tarawera and White Island with great MP3 commentary.

LAKE CRUISES & JETBOATING

The only way to see the impressive modern Maori carvings at Mine Bay is by taking a boat cruise of the lake. The carvings are on private land and so cannot be reached by foot, and trips take in other scenic spots along the way. Allow between 1½ and 2½ hours for trips, though some skippers will take longer if they're in the mood.

Several boats cruise the area and all are booked from the **launch office** (Lake Taupo Charter Office; Map p297; ☎ 07-378 3444; www.fishcruise .taupo.co.nz) on the marina, including these operators:

Alice (cruises adult/child $15/6; ☼ 11am, 12.30pm & 2pm Sat & Sun) A smaller steamboat working the lake and river.

Barbary (cruise $25–30) Originally built in 1926, and owned briefly by Errol Flynn according to skipper 'Barbary Bill', a real old-school character.

Ernest Kemp (cruises adult/child $28/10; ☼ 10.30am & 2pm Apr–Sep, 0.30am, 2pm & 5pm Oct–Mar) A reconstruction of a 1920s steamboat, which includes trip commentaries in various languages.

Te Moana (☎ 07-378 4839; www.gusgrace.orcon.net .nz; for 4 people $110)

For something with a little more zip, take the **Cruise Cat** (Map p297; tickets $28; ☼ 11.30am Mon–Sat & 10.30am Sun), a large, modern launch. Sunday brunches ($42) are especially worthwhile.

Sleeping

Taupo has a huge range of accommodation, with several hotels lining the busy Lake Tce and a competitive backpacker scene that includes central options.

BUDGET

Tiki Lodge (Map p297; ☎ 07-377 4545; www.tikilodge .co.nz; 104 Tuwharetoa St; dm from $24, d & tw from $60; ▣) This refreshing hostel appeals to backpackers who want that little bit more, like a pinball machine, snow and mountain views from balconies, and even an 'in-room' hangi (Maori cooking pit). Maori-tinged décor is complemented by modern touches such as the wall-mounted CD player in the kitchen, and a spa. It's new but instantly comfy.

Taupo Action Downunder Backpackers (Map p297; ☎ 07-378 3311; cnr Kaimanawa & Tamamutu Sts; sites per 2 people $24, dm $20-25, d/Internet Room $30/70; ▣) The local YHA pulls out all the stops to impress, with a barrel spa pool, expansive rainy-day video library, regular barbies on deck and even guitar hire. As well as the intimate video lounge, there are summer outdoor showings, especially of guests' own hair-raising skydiving DVDs. Kitchen space is a little limited, but double rooms are excellent value, particularly the Internet Room, which includes all-night web surfing on an in-room Mac.

Silver Fern Lodge (Map p297; ☎ 07-377 4929; www .silverfernlodges.co.nz; cnr Tamamutu & Kaimanawa Sts; dm d $28/85; ☐) What is a 'flashpackers'? According to this new place, it crosses a motel with a hostel, with plenty of idiosyncratic features like Internet in old arcade-game machines, shared kitchens with individual lockers, and TV in each room. It seems a little soulless if you're used to sardine-style dorms, but the good-sized rooms are clean and modern.

Rainbow Lodge Backpackers Retreat (Map p297; ☎ 07-378 5754; www.rainbowlodge.co.nz; 99 Titiraupenga St; dm from $20, d $50-58; ☐) Yet another solid hostel with clean, spacious rooms, including pricier doubles with their own en suites. The cottage next door is more secluded, with a large share TV (everyone is allotted time) and themed rooms including a totally *Jetsons* retro room and a soon-to-be-completed Jungle Room. Other great bonuses include bike and fishing-tackle hire, as well hairdryers and straighteners (!) in some bathrooms, plus the staff here are good at finding hospitality jobs for the cash-strapped.

De Bretts Thermal Resort (Map p306; ☎ 07-378 8559; www.debrettsresort.co.nz; SH5; sites per 2 people from $24, d/ste from $50/90; ☐) If you're keen to visit the Taupo Hot Springs, then this family-friendly park on Napier Rd is the go. Set in well-tended parkland, there's a good range of accommodation, from tent sites to motel-style units. De Bretts has plenty of kid-friendly features, such as a playground and safety trampoline.

Taupo Motor Camp (Map p297; ☎ /fax 07-377 3080; www.taupomotorcamp.co.nz; 15 Redoubt St; camp sites per 2 people from $26, cabins $48, caravans $50-60) Taupo's most central camping ground nestles by Waikato River in serene bushland, yet is only 200m from the town centre. There's a boat ramp (requires permit), an older shower block, kids' playground and affordable cabins, which one reader called 'bad-ass', in a good way.

Also recommended:

Burkes Backpackers (Map p297; ☎ 07-378 9292; www.burkesbp.co.nz; 20 Taniwha St; dm $21, d $46-50, f $70; ☐) Transitioning from motel to backpackers

means this place still has motel-style fittings such as pool tables, psychedelic art and pleasant green courtyard.

Go Global (Map p297; ☎ 0800 464 562, 07-377 0044; www.go-global.co.nz; cnr Tongariro & Tuwharetoa Sts; dm $22, s $35-45, d $48-55) A sociable backpackers; recent renovations have revitalised the bright common area and kitchens.

Taupo Urban Retreat (Map p297; ☎ 07-378 6124; www.taupourbanretreat.co.nz; 65 Heu Heu St; dm $21-25, d $56) A funky-styled party place with four- to six-bunk dorms that are popular with Kiwi Experience and Stray tour groups.

MIDRANGE

Taupo is packed with motels, most strung along Lake Tce.

Caboose Taupo Hotel (Map p297; ☎ 0800 222 667, 07-376 0116; www.cabooselodge.co.nz; 100 Lake Tce; d $99-159; ☐ ☒) This way-out-of-Africa hotel transports guests on a train trip through colonial Africa, including sloping hallways to mimic a train carriage, and a whole lotta leopard and zebra print. Rooms are either 'compartments' or 'sleepers', mixing tribal designs and hunting trophies, plus all rooms are set off the road so it's quiet enough to hear the springboks grazing.

Lake (Map p297; ☎ 07-378 4222; www.thelakeonline.co.nz; 63 Mere Rd; d $120-180) This retro motel pulls off classic 1960s style without getting too kitschy, with curvaceous couches and bedside lava lamps. The studio is tight, with the four other rooms better alternatives for larger groups. There's a pull-out sofa if necessary. This groovalicious pad is where Austin Powers would host intimate fondue love-ins when in Taupo.

Lake Taupo Motor Lodge (Map p297; ☎ 07-378 5401; 33 Kaimanawa St; d/f $120/140; ☒ ☐) This newer business-focussed spot is proving itself, with in-room broadband, voguish flatscreen TVs and balconies on the top storey. Some studios come with spas, but all rooms feature slick leather furnishings and filter coffee. The conference room is already popular with domestic and international visitors.

Chelmsford Motel (Map p306; ☎ 0800 238 238; 250 Lake Tce; d/f $80/140; ☒) This unpretentious place has simple studios, and larger family rooms with their own individual pools in a courtyard. Littlies can dip in the common pool or take play trucks for a hoon in the sand-pit. The motel also hires out some hotted-up mini motorbikes ($39 per hour).

Cypress Villas (Map p297; ☎ 07-378 4322; www .cypressvillas.co.nz; 37 Rifle Range Rd; d/ste $90/125) This contemporary, well-designed complex has six self-contained, serviced units in a sleepy lakeside part of town. Rooms range from studios to a plush 'honeymoon suite', with several featuring their own spa. The larger suites have full kitchens and huge bathrooms.

Le Chalet Suisse Motel (Map p297; ☎ 0800 178 378; www.lechaletsuisse.co.nz; cnr Titiraupenga & Northcroft Sts; ste from $89; ☒) This big motel has an overblown alpine theme, but offers a selection of self-contained 'chalet-style' units, which feature two levels (great for noisy kids and quiet-loving parents) and individual spas. The barbecue and children's play area also make for a good stay.

Suncourt Motor Hotel (Map p297; ☎ 0800 786 268; www.suncourt.co.nz; 14 Northcroft St; d/f $100/145; ☒) You can't miss the brightly coloured exterior of this rambling complex, which encloses a range of comfortable units with great facilities, including spa pool and kids' playground. Larger rooms with verandas and full kitchens are ideal for families, and though regular conferences can book the place out.

Oasis Resort Taupo (Map p306; ☎ 0800 555 378; www.oasistaupo.co.nz; d/ste $105/130; ☒) One of Taupo's oldest motels, this place has been slickly refurbished with big-screen TVs and a sandy-coloured exterior. Pleasant courtyards and the lakeside location make it a good spot for lovers of the shore front, though with a spa pool and indoor billiard area there's plenty to do just hanging around the motel.

Lakefront Motor Inn (Map p297; ☎ 0800 331 166; cnr Lake Tce & Taharepa Rd; d $89; ☒) Not quite on the lake, but far enough from the highway for peace, this older motel is well priced, plus there's the choice of several pools. Most rooms come with cute blue thermal pools, plus you can share two thermal outdoor pools (one at 40°C), and then there's a 'normal' swimming pool.

Chantilly's Motor Lodge (Map p297; ☎ 0800 160 700; www.chantillys.co.nz; 112 Tamamutu St; d from $135; ☒) Chantilly's is a slice of 1950s Americana, right down to its supersized units with large in-room spas and gold brocade bedspreads. Space is well used, with a small dining setting and DVD player, though some rooms curiously have a spa in the bedroom.

TOP END

Millennium (Map p306; ☎ 07-378 5110; www.millen niummanuels.taupo.co.nz; 243 Lake Tce; d & tw $170-220; ☒ ☒) With lake-frontage views from balcony rooms, this is one of the better placed motels in town. Millennium is particularly well-equipped for business travellers, with a business centre, wi-fi hot spot throughout, and two good in-house restaurants to entertain clients.

Outrigger Terraces Resort (Map p306; ☎ 07-378 7C80; SH5; d from $185; ☒) This revamped hotel has shared balconies with amazing views across the lake to the snowy mountains. Modern and tasteful decoration has kept the rooms pleasant, plus there's a Local Area Network (LAN) connection. At the time of research the hotel was expanding, so get there before the conference centre is completed or you'll be surrounded by suits.

Wairakei Resort (Map p306; ☎ 07-374 8021; www .wairakei.co.nz; Wairakei Park; d/ste from $155/225; ☒ ☒) This massive resort is well placed to enjoy the exclusive Wairakei International Golf Club. Standard rooms are modishly generic, but executive suites include huge TVs, full kitchens and laundries. Several rooms are interconnecting, a good option for larger families or groups.

Huka Lodge (Map p306; ☎ 07-378 5791; www.huka lodge.com; Huka Falls Rd; s/d/d cottages $1450/1950/3750; ☒) With former guests including the likes of Bill Gates and Joan Collins, Huka Lodge has a prestigious reputation for its expansive grounds right on the Huka River. Individual lodges are all close to the river with features such as gas fires, CD players and stunning window views. The recently revamped Owners Cottage is ideal for corporate retreats, with four double bedrooms and private courtyard. Rates include five-course dinner at one of 60 dining areas (our pick is the sunken cellar).

Eating

The dining scene in Taupo has developed a real sophistication in recent years, with many new cafés and restaurants appearing everywhere.

Replete Cafe (Map p297; ☎ 07-377 3011; www .replete.co.nz; 45 Heu Heu St; mains $5-12; ☒ breakfast & lunch) There's a warm-bread smell as soon as you enter this busy bakery-deli that excels at lighter meals like bacon and egg pie or miso soup. The kids' hamper is guaranteed to make car trips quiet.

Jolly Good Fellows (Map p297; ☎ 07-378 0457; 76-80 Lake Tce; meals $15-22; ☻ lunch & dinner) Corr, Guvnor! You ain't seen a pub like this since old Blighty, with lashings of cultural clichés and cheeky humour added to its pub grub, including the Highland Wing (a well-cooked chook) and Ooh arr! Park the Tractor (ploughman's platter to the rest of us). Wearing Corr Blimey trousers is not compulsory.

Flax (Map p297; ☎ 07-377 8052; 5 Horomatangi St; mains $5-13; ☻ 8am-4pm) At this modish nook you can choose innovative salads, tasty *panini* or light specials, all selected from the huge deli counter.

Volcanic Kitchen (Map p297; ☎ 07-377 1537; 113 Tongariro St; burgers & pizzas $7-17.50; ☻ 5-9pm) On a street ruled by an international burger monarch, this place does brilliant burgers and pizzas in a swanky location. Why whopper when you could have the Big Bird burger (including a whole chicken breast) or French Chic pizza topped with chicken, cranberry, Camembert and roasted pine nuts?

Soliel (Map p297; ☎ 07-376 5759; 43 Ruapehu St; mains $23-28; ☻ lunch & dinner Tue-Sun) The philosophy of new owners Nick and Ruby is simple enough: good wines, relaxed décor (think raffia chairs and couches) and refined modern dining with dishes such as duck confit on risotto.

Thai Lotus (Map p297; ☎ 07-376 9497; 137 Tongariro St; mains $15-20; ☻ lunch Wed-Fri, dinner Wed-Mon) With a warm ambience and friendly service, this Lotus opens to all. Dine in or take away affordable Thai standards in plentiful portions.

Brantry Restaurant (Map p297; ☎ 07-378 0484; www.thebrantry.co.nz; 45 Rifle Range Rd; mains $26-35; ☻ dinner) Set in a 1950s town house, the Brantry is one of Taupo's top tables with alfresco dining under the canopy or in the upper garden in summer. The menu samples NZ's finest, with dishes including roasted poussin, or the slightly pretentious 'study of lamb' (several different takes on NZ's favourite meat). The set menu (from $35) is an affordable sampler.

Fat Fish (Map p297; ☎ 07-377 0086; 10 Roberts St; mains $17-26; ☻ breakfast, lunch & dinner) This straight-up takeaway is a firm favourite with locals for its fish and chips, but also does pizzas and *panini*.

Tongue & Groove (Map p297; ☎ 07-378 3900; 11 Tuwharetoa St; ☻ 10am-3am) This snazzy upstairs bar doubles as a brasserie, with a solid lunch and dinner menu of local produce including venison and fish. Dancing and bands (see opposite) can make dining difficult later on weekend evenings.

Pasta Mia (Map p297; ☎ 07-377 2930; 26 Horomatangi St; mains from $8; ☻ breakfast, lunch & dinner) This classic Italian eatery does inexpensive pasta and risotto, best finished with a coffee.

Landing (Map p306; 213 Lake Tce; mains $14-27; ☻ breakfast, lunch & dinner) This waterfront restaurant, at the Cove Hotel, has awesome lake views and excellent fish, lamb and venison dishes. The wine list is a greatest hits of NZ's vineyards.

Seoul House Korean Restaurant (Map p297; ☎ 07-377 3344; 100 Roberts St; mains $15-25; ☻ lunch & dinner) This place has authentic barbecue-style Korean dishes, along with some Japanese specialities, including tempura and sushi.

Classic Espresso Bakery (Map p297; ☎ 07-378 8757; 15 Tamamutu St; light meals $2.50-5; ☻ 8am-5pm) Baking fresh pies and pastries every day is this budget diner's mission, with old-style treats like lamingtons, Eccles cake and definitively PC gingerbread people, all good with coffee.

Jade City (Map p297; ☎ 07-378 9554; 19 Tamamutu St; meals $5.50-9.50; ☻ lunch & dinner) For a no-fuss buffet bite there's plenty at this serve-yourself metropolis where, as the sign suggests, 'manners are appreciated'.

For self-caterers, **Pak N Save** (Map p297; Tamamutu St) and **Woolworths** (Map p297; Spa Rd) are both open until around 9pm.

Drinking

Most of the bars in town cater to the thriving backpacker scene, so you can expect a wild night out.

Holy Cow (Map p297; ☎ 07-378 7533; 11 Tongariro St) This upstairs bovine bar is a real Taupo institution, with cow portraits papering the walls and a central dance floor that gets crowded after 11pm. Before then it's a good spot for a Kiwi brew and a game of pool.

Tongue & Groove (Map p297; ☎ 07-378 3900; 11 Tuwharetoa St; ☑ 10am-3am) This cavernous upstairs bar has a balcony to enjoy the summer breeze. Occasional live bands and dancing make for a fun night out, or you can grab a meal here (opposite).

Finn MacCuhal's (Map p297; ☎ 07-378 6165; cnr Tongariro & Tuwharetoa Sts) With its fair share of Irish ephemera nailed to the walls and a backpackers next door, you can be sure that there will be plenty of *craic* here. There are soft-rock videos most nights and DJs on Saturdays.

Mulligans (Map p297; ☎ 07-376 9101; 15 Tongariro St) This Irish boozer aims its hearty meal and drink deals at backpackers, but it can be a good spot for a quiet Guinness.

Plateau (Map p297; ☎ 07-377-2425; 64 Tuwharetoa St; mains $25-30; ☑ lunch Mon-Fri & dinner daily) The gas fire and smooth leather chairs attract a more mature crowd, keen for a drink and a chat in the beer garden, all to a downbeat soundtrack.

Bond Lounge Bar (Map p297; ☎ 07-377 2434; 40 Tuwharetoa St; ☑ Thu-Sun) This swanky spot pulses to retro vinyl played earlier on, then cooks to bigger beats later in the evening. The international bar stars global cocktails and world beers (Duvel, Beck's, Kirin and then we lost track) with loungey DJs on Sundays.

Entertainment

Great Lake Centre (Map p297; ☎ 07-376 0340; Tongariro St) There's a theatre and hall for performances, exhibitions and conventions. The visitor information centre has the current schedule.

Starlight Cinema Centre (Map p297; ☎ 07-378 7515; Starlight Arcade, off Horomatangi St; tickets $7.50) Head here to catch the latest Hollywood films.

Bond Lounge Bar ($5 cover charge) and Finn MacCuhal's both have DJs, while there are weekend bands at Tongue & Groove.

Getting There & Away

AIR

Air New Zealand (☎ 0800 737 000) has daily direct flights to Auckland and Wellington, with onward connections.

BUS

InterCity (☎ 09-913 6100), **Newmans** (☎ 09-913 6200) and **Alpine Scenic Tours** (☎ 07-386 8918; www.alpinescenictours.co.nz) arrive at and depart from the Taupo Travel Centre (p296).

InterCity and Newmans have several daily buses to Turangi ($22, 45 minutes), Auckland ($57, 4½ hours), Hamilton ($37, 2¾ hours), Rotorua ($28, one hour), Tauranga ($50, 2¾ hours), Napier ($41, two hours), Palmerston North ($50, 4¾ hours) and Wellington ($75, 5¾ hours).

Shuttle services operate year-round between Taupo, Turangi, Tongariro National Park and the Whakapapa Ski Area (1½ hours). During winter, shuttles travel daily and can include package deals for lift tickets and ski hire. See p319 for details.

Getting Around

Taupo's Hotbus (☎ 07-377 1967; www.hotbus.co.nz; per hop $4; ☑ departs visitors centre hourly 10am-6pm Oct-Mar, 11am-5pm Apr-Sep) is a hop-on, hop-off bus that does an hourly circuit of all the major attractions in and around Taupo.

Taxi services in Taupo are provided by **Taupo Taxis** (☎ 07-378 5100), **Go Cabs** (☎ 07-378 5886) and **Top Cabs** (☎ 07-378 9250).

Taupo Scooters (Map p297; ☎ 07-378 1551; 1-day $40) delivers zippy motor scooters to most hostels and hotels. The Chelmsford Motel (p302) also hires out small motorbikes.

AROUND TAUPO
Wairakei Park

Crossing the river at Tongariro St and heading north from town on SH1, you'll arrive at the **Wairakei Park** (Map p306) area, also known as the Huka Falls Tourist Loop. Take the first right turn after you cross the river and you'll be on Huka Falls Rd, which passes along the river. When returning to Taupo, turn left back to the highway and you'll pass other interesting spots on your way back.

En route look out for **Honey Hive New Zealand** (Map p306; ☎ 07-374 8553; www.honey.co.nz; admission free; ☑ 9am-5pm Mon-Fri, to 5.30pm Sat & Sun), which has a glass-enclosed hive linked to the outside world, and honey and bee products including shampoos and beenut butter (peanuts and honey mashed together). At the **Meadery** (Map p306; ☎ 07-374 8525; www.nzfruitwines.co.nz; ❦ 9am–5pm), you can try wines or liqueurs made from kiwi fruit, blueberries and, of course, honey.

For another tipple, keep an eye out for **Wishart Huka Winery** (Map p306; ☎ 07-378 5426,

07-377 2326; www.wishartwinery.co.nz; 56 Huka Falls Rd; ❦ 10am–6pm), the local branch of the Hawkes Bay–based winery that does interesting varietals like syrah.

HUKA FALLS

At these stunning falls NZ's longest river, the Waikato, is slammed into a narrow

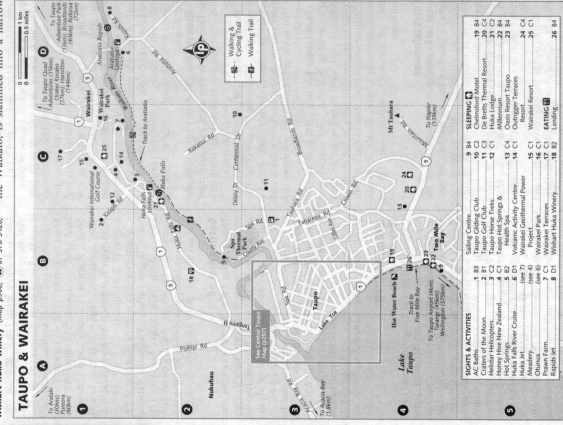

TAUPO & WAIRAKEI

SIGHTS & ACTIVITIES

AC Baths	1 B3
Craters of the Moon	2 B1
Helistar Helicopters	3 C2
Honey Hive New Zealand	4 C1
Hot Springs	5 B2
Huka Falls River Cruise	6 D1
Huka Jet	(see 7)
Meadery	(see 4)
Otunua	(see 6)
Prawn Farm	7 C1
Rapids Jet	8 D1
Sailing Centre	9 B4
Taupo Gliding Club	10 C2
Taupo Golf Club	11 C2
Taupo Horse Treks	12 C2
Taupo Hot Springs & Health Spa	13 C4
Volcanic Activity Centre	14 C1
Wairakei Geothermal Power Project	15 C1
Wairakei Park	16 C1
Wairakei Terraces	17 C1
Wishart Huka Winery	18 B2

SLEEPING

Chelmsford Motel	19 B4
De Bretts Thermal Resort	20 C4
Huka Lodge	21 C2
Millennium	22 B4
Oasis Resort Taupo	23 B4
Outrigger Terraces Resort	24 C4
Wairakei Resort	25 C1

EATING

Landing	26 B4

Walking & Cycling Trail
Walking Trail

chasm and then makes a spectacular 10m drop into a surging pool. As you cross the footbridge you can see the full force of this torrent that the Maori called Hukanui (Great Body of Spray), an apt description of NZ's Niagara Falls. On sunny days the water is crystal clear and you can take great photographs from the lookout on the other side of the footbridge.

You can also take a few short walks around the area or pick up the trail from Aratiatia Rapids into Taupo (see p300).

VOLCANIC ACTIVITY CENTRE

Wondering what the fuss is about with geothermal activity in the area? The **volcanic activity centre & bookshop** (Map p306; ☎ 07-374 8375; www.volcanoes.co.nz; Huka Falls Loop Rd; adult/child $6/3; ☑ 9am-5pm Mon-Fri, 10am-4pm Sat & Sun) has all the answers. This observatory monitors volcanic activity in the volatile Taupo Volcanic Zone, and the visitors centre has some excellent, if text-heavy, displays on NZ's geothermal and volcanic activity.

A favourite exhibit with kids is the Earthquake Simulator, a little boo∂h you can sit in to experience an earthquake, complete with teeth-chattering shudders and sudden shakes. You can also configure your own tornado then watch it wreak havoc, or see a simulated geyser above and below ground. Documentaries about the eruptions of Ngauruhoe and Ruapehu, which were the largest of the 20th century, are surprisingly uninspiring. Pick up a monitoring report to read about recent earthquakes or check if Ruapehu is about to erupt.

HUKA JET & PRAWN FARM

Further down the Waikato River is the launch for **Huka Jet** (Map p306; ☎ 0800 485 2538, 07-374 8572; www.hukajet.com; trips adult/child $79/49). You can take a 30-minute thrill ride up the river to cop the spray of Huka Falls or head down to see Aratiatia Dam, all the while doing acrobatic dodging and exciting 360-degree turns. Trips run all day (price includes transport from Taupo) and you can bundle it in with a helicopter ride with 'hukastar combo' ($170/110 per adult/child).

Just next door, the **Prawn Farm** (Map p306; ☎ 07-374 8474; www.prawnpark.com; mains $11-35; ☑ 9am-5pm) is the world's only geothermally heated freshwater prawn farm. There's a surprising array of activities here including

'fishing' for prawns and Killer Prawn Golf (balls $1 each, $10 for 20), which allows you to shoot balls over the prawn beds. For a more educational experience, tours leave hourly (between 11am and 4pm; adult/child $6/2.50). Best of all though is the restaurant where you can try prawns in various sauces or even cocktails.

ARATIATIA RAPIDS

Two kilometres off SH5, the Aratiatia Rapids were a spectacular part of the Waikato River until the government plonked a hydroelectric dam across the waterway, shutting off the spectacular flow. But the spectacle hasn't disappeared completely, with the floodgates opened from 1 October to 31 March at 10am, noon, 2pm and 4pm and from April to September at 10am, noon and 2pm. You can see the water crash through the dam from two good vantage points (entry is free) or even by standing on the dam itself (if you're brave enough).

Another good view is from **Rapids Jet** (Map p306; ☎ 0800 727 437, 07-378 5828; www.rapidsjet.com; Rapids Rd off SH5; adult/child $55/45), a jetboat that shoots along the lower part of the Aratiatia Rapids. It's a sensational 45-minute ride, rivalling the trip to Huka Falls. The boat departs from the end of the access road to the Aratiatia lookouts. Go down Rapids Rd; look for the signpost to the National Equestrian Centre. For a slower ride, try **Huka Falls River Cruise** (Map p306; ☎ 0800 278 336, 07-377 3454; dave.ang@paradise.net.nz; Aratiatia Dam; ☑ departs 10.30am, 12.30pm & 2.30pm), a relaxed trip from Aratiatia Dam to Huka Falls.

The paddle steamer **Otunua** (Map p306; ☎ 0800 278 336, 07-378 5828; cruises adult/child $35/25) makes cruises daily at 10.30am and 2.30pm to Huka Falls, from the Aratiatia Dam. The Moonlight Glowworm Cruise departs at 5.30pm from April to September and at 9pm from October to March.

WAIRAKEI TERRACES

This thermal valley is all that remains of what was once known as Geyser Valley. Before the geothermal power project started in 1958, it was one of the most active thermal areas in the world, with 22 geysers and 240 mud pools and springs.

It is now the site of **Wairakei Terraces** (Map p306; ☎ 07-378 0913; www.wairakeiterraces.co.nz; adult/child $18/9; ☑ tours 9am-4.30pm Apr-Sep, to 5pm

Oct-Mar), which are manmade silica terraces, pools and geysers, recreating, on a smaller scale, the fabled Pink and White Terraces. The **Maori Cultural Experience** (adult/child $75/37.50; ☉ 6.30pm) here, including a concert and *hangi*, gives an insight into how Maori people revere the geothermal areas and use them in cooking. There's loads of fun to be had with an animal buggy (including tui and some very lost emu), carriage rides, café and recreated Maori village.

WAIRAKEI GEOTHERMAL POWER PROJECT

The sci-fi looking silver pipes and squat powerhouses you've seen beside the road are all part of Wairakei Geothermal Power Project, which creates enough electricity to power Napier, Rotorua, Hamilton and Taupo; almost 5% of NZ's total power bill comes from this area.

Not far from the road, the **Wairakei Geothermal Power Project visitors centre** (Map p306; ☎ 07-378 0913; adult/child $2/1; ☉ 9am-5pm Oct-Mar, to 4.30pm Apr-Sep) can bring you up to speed on the world's second geothermal power station, including a video (shown from 9am to 4pm). You can drive up the road through the project and from a lookout see the long pipes, wreathed in steam.

Just south of here is the big Wairakei Resort and the Wairakei International Golf Club.

CRATERS OF THE MOON

This lesser-known geothermal area sprang to life as a result of the hydroelectric tinkering of the 1950s that created the power station (see above). When underground water levels fell and pressure shifted, the **Craters of the Moon** (Map p306; admission by donation; ☉ dawn-dusk) appeared with new steam vents and mud pools pocking the landscape. The bubbling mud and blasts of hot steam make it dangerous enough that only closed shoes are allowed. Don't miss the lookout just before the car park; it's the best place for photos. A small kiosk at the car park is staffed by volunteers, who also keep an eye on the car park.

Craters of the Moon is signposted on SH1, about 5km north of Taupo.

Orakei Korako

Between Taupo and Rotorua, **Orakei Korako** (☎ 07-378 3131; www.orakeikorako.co.nz; adult/child/family $23/8/54; ☉ 8am-4pm) gets fewer visitors

than other thermal areas because it's off the beaten track. But, since the destruction of the Pink and White Terraces by the Tarawera eruption in 1886, it has been possibly the best thermal area left in NZ. Although three-quarters of it now lies beneath the dam waters of Lake Ohakuri, the remaining quarter is the best part.

A sometimes steep walking track (allow 1½ hours) mostly follows a boardwalk around the colourful silica terraces for which the park is famous, as well as visiting geysers and **Ruatapu Cave**. This impressive natural cave has a jade-green pool, which is thought to have been used as a mirror by Maori women who prepared for rituals here (Orakei Korako means 'the place of adorning'). The **Emerald Terrace**, which sparkles like a jewel in the early morning light, is another stunning feature. Entry includes a boat ride across Lake Ohakuri.

Orakei Korako Geyserland Resort (☎ 07-378 3131; 0k@reap.org.nz; dm/d from $20/80) is right on the river at Orakei Korako. There's accommodation available in a self-contained flat (it sleeps up to seven people), or in a communal lodge (own linen required). Rates double on weekends and public holidays.

To get to Orakei Korako from Taupo, take SH1 towards Hamilton for 23km, and then travel for 14km from the signposted turn-off. From Rotorua the turn-off is on SH5, via Mihi. Alternatively, NZ River Jet (below) jets down the Waikato to get you here.

Broadlands

This beautiful and often-forgotten stretch of the mighty Waikato River is halfway between Rotorua and Taupo. To get here turn off SH5 onto Homestead Rd, just south of Reporoa.

For the impatient, the stunning scenery is best zoomed past on **NZ River Jet** (☎ 07-333 7111; www.riverjet.co.nz; Homestead Rd; 2½hr ride $125). You can travel downstream by jetboat to Orakei Korako thermal region, through some magnificent steamy gorges, or head upstream through the exciting Full James Rapids to Aratiatia.

Near the township of Reporoa is **Butcher's Pool** (admission free; ☉ daily), a natural thermal spring in the middle of a farmer's paddock that makes a soothing dip. It's equipped with a small parking area, changing sheds and wooden decking around the water's edge. To get here from Reporoa head south on Broadlands Rd for 2km and look for a row of trees lining a gravel driveway off to your left.

Pureora Forest Park

Fringing the western edge of Lake Taupo is the huge Pureora Forest. Logging was eventually stopped in the park in the 1980s after long campaigns by conservationists, and regrowth is impressive.

There are long and short forest treks, including tracks to the summits of Mt Pureora (1165m) and the rock pinnacle of Mt Titiraupenga (1042m).

The north section of the park is designated for recreational hunting, but you must obtain a permit from park headquarters. Pamphlets, maps and information on the park are available from the DOC offices in Taupo and Te Kuiti.

TURANGI

pop 3900

Once a service town for the nearby hydroelectric power station, Turangi has blossomed from Taupo's country cousin into a world-class trout-fishing destination. Turangi is 4km from Lake Taupo (accessed via nearby Tokaanu), but the Tongariro River is the important body of water for trout. For walkers there's also access to the northern trails of Tongariro National Park.

Information

The **Turangi visitor information centre** (☎ 07-386 8999; turangivc@laketauponz.com; ☑ 8.30am-5pm) has a detailed relief model of Tongariro National Park. It's a good stop for information on the national park, Kaimanawa Forest Park, trout fishing, and snow and road conditions. The office also issues hut tickets, InterCity bus tickets, ski passes and hunting and fishing licences.

The office of ever-helpful **DOC** (☎ 07-386 8607) is near the junction of SH1 and Ohuanga Rd. The nearest post office and Kiwibank branch is in **Naylor's Books** (Turangi Shopping Mall), opposite the visitor information centre. **Extreme Backpackers** (p311) has affordable Internet access.

Sights & Activities

TONGARIRO NATIONAL TROUT CENTRE

About 4km south of Turangi on SH1 is the last DOC-managed **trout hatchery & centre** (☎ 07-386 8085; admission by donation; ☑ 10am-4pm). Fishing fanatics worship this landscaped centre, which includes a self-guided 1½km walk to an underwater viewing chamber, keeping ponds and picnic area.

The information centre has excellent educational displays, including a huge collection of rods and reels, while the theatre shows a 14-minute film about the river's development. You can drop a line in to fish for trout in the Tongariro River, which runs close by.

TOKAANU THERMAL POOLS

The **Tokaanu Thermal Pools** (☎ 07-386 8575; Mangaroa St; public pools per visit adult/child $5/2.50, private pools 20min $7/3; ☑ public pools 10am-9pm, private pools till 9.30pm) is an interesting thermal area with hot baths, a trout stream, a barbecue area and displays. It's no Waiotapu (p347), but the 20-minute stroll along the boardwalk showcases the small mud pools and thermal springs. It is wheelchair accessible.

WALKING

There are several short walks around town that can be good warm-ups for the Tongariro Crossing. A favourite is **Tongariro River Walkway** (three hours return), which follows the sparkling river and is good for mountain biking.

Other good leg-stretchers include: the **Tongariro River Loop Track** (one hour loop; starts just north of the town centre); **Hinemihi's Track**, near the top of Te Ponanga Saddle, 8km south of Turangi (15 minutes return); and **Turangi-Taupo River Walk** (30 minutes), which heads to Lake Taupo.

Another great lake stroll is **Lake Rotopounamu**, with stunning bird life and serene little beaches, perfect for picnics and swimming (20 minutes to the lake from the car park, two hours around it).

The DOC *Turangi Walks* ($1) leaflet details most of these walks, along with a few further afield in Kaimanawa Forest.

TROUT FISHING

February and March are the best months for brown trout and June to September are the best for rainbow trout, but fishing is good year-round on the Tongariro River. Don't forget that you need a fishing licence.

If you're not sure where to start, a fishing guide will give you some local know-how,

www.lonelyplanet.com

INFORMATION
DOC....................................1 A3
Naylor's Books.......................2 A2
Turangi Shopping Mall.........(see 2)
Turangi Visitor Information Centre....3 B2

SIGHTS & ACTIVITIES
Barry Greig's Sporting World....4 B2
Rapid Sensations..................(see 7)
Vertical Assault Climbing Wall....(see 9)

SLEEPING
Anglers Paradise Resort Motel....5 A3
Bellbird Lodge......................6 B1
Club Habitat.........................7 A2
Creel Lodge..........................8 B3
Extreme Backpackers............9 B2
Judges Pool Motel...............10 B2
Tongariro River Motel..........11 B2
Turangi Leisure Lodge..........12 B2

EATING
Four Fish...............................13 B2
Grand Central Fry................14 B2
Mustard Seed Cafe..............15 B2
Red Crater Cafe..................(see 9)
River Rocks Cafe..................16 B2
Thyme for Food....................17 B2

TRANSPORT
Centre of Adventure............18 B2

TURANGI

as well as transport, gear, licence and possibly meals; guides generally charge around $70 per hour (minimum of three hours). Alternatively you can hire your own gear from sports stores around town such as **Barry Greig's Sporting World** (☎ 07-386 6911; www.greigsport.co.nz; 59 Town Centre; rods $15, waders $20; 9am-5pm Mon-Fri, to 2pm Sat). The shop also offer a good range of guides.

Boats can be hired for lake fishing. Aluminium dinghies cost around $25 per hour from **Motuoapa Marina** (☎ 07-386 7000), at Motuoapa, 10km east of Turangi.

OTHER ACTIVITIES

The Tongariro River has some superb grade III rapids for river rafting, as well as some

grade I stretches in the lower reaches during summer, suitable for beginners. **Tongariro River Rafting** (☎ 0800 101 024; Atirau Rd; rafting per person $90, raft fishing $300) can start you off with a three-hour trip on the grade II Tongariro or take you on a full day's raft fishing (summer only). The company also hire out bikes for $20 for two hours.

Rock 'n' River (☎ 0800 865 226; www.raftingnewzealand.com; 203 Puanga St, Tokaanu; 4hr/2-day trip $95/270, white-water kayaking full day $129) has a four-hour Tongariro River trip (grade III) topped off by a soak in a thermal pool, or a longer overnight trip on the Tongariro River. The company also offers white-water kayaking and various rafting outings on the Wairoa, Rangitikei and Mohaka Rivers. There's free pick up from Turangi.

Rapid Sensations (☎ 0800 353 435; www.rapids.co.nz; 25 Ohuanga Rd; 2hr/1-day trips $45/95) runs excursions on the Tongariro, Rangitaiki, Wairoa and Mangahao Rivers, and multiday trips on the Mohaka River. The company also runs mountain-bike tours to Craters of the Moon (p308; $65) and other locales.

For indoor fun, head to the **Vertical Assault Climbing Wall** (☎ 07-386 6558; 26 Ngawaka Pl; adult/child $15/11) to scale walls that challenge all skill levels.

Take a cruise of Tongariro River with **Great Lake Escapes** (☎ 021 251 5901; www.greatlake-escapes.co.nz; adult/child $40/25; ☼ departs 9.30am & 1pm), which takes in 48 bird species, the Waihi waterfall and Tongariro rivermouth.

Sleeping

BUDGET

Extreme Backpackers (☎ 07-386 8949; www.extreme backpackers.co.nz; 2E Ngawaka Pl; dm $20-26, d & tw $48-58; □) Crafted from pine and corrugated iron, this is the newest backpackers in town and has the bonus of a climbing wall. Cheaper dorms have eight bunks and skip the carpet, while pricier doubles have en suites, but all the rooms are clean and comfy. A lounge with an open fire, a sunny courtyard with hammocks and a barbecue make this a relaxing budget bet.

Bellbird Lodge (☎ 07-386 8281; www.bellbird.co.nz; 6 Rangipoia Pl; sites per 2 people $24, dm/d $20/46) This friendly, comfy lodge does its upmost to make for an easy stay, with log fires, piano, well-stocked kitchens and neat four- to six-bed dorms. Hosts provide transport to the Tongariro Crossing, as well as fishing licences and tackle. There's a freezer and you can arrange to have your catch smoked. At the time of research the backpacker rooms were being refurbished, so expect even better rooms!

Club Habitat (☎ 07-386 7492; clubhabitat@xtra.co.nz; 25 Ohuanga Rd; sites per 2 people $28, dm $19, d & tw $80, f $140) This is a huge pine-log complex (220 beds) with rooms and bunkhouses around the parklike grounds. Facilities such as a big restaurant-bar complex and adjoining rooms make it popular with larger groups. The sauna, spa and large playground make it attractive to families, plus activities are available through Rapid Sensations (opposite).

Sportmans Lodge (☎ 07-386 8150; 15 Taupahi Rd; d/f $55/80) Backing onto Tongariro River, this motel-style spot, with a sweet garden, is a hidden bargain for trout-fishing folk. The larger family room has its own balcony and all the rooms share the well-equipped kitchen.

MIDRANGE

Anglers Paradise Resort Motel (☎ 0800 500 039; anglers@reap.org.nz; cnr SH41 & Ohuanga Rd; d/ste from $95/155; □) In a leafy pocket of Turangi, this luxury place is a catch, with fishing guides available for keen trout chasers, and a smokehouse. Rooms are sumptuous dark wood, but have moved with the times to include new TVs, super-king beds and full kitchens. The restaurant (meals $16 to $28, open for lunch and dinner) has an intimate feel, with crackling fireplaces and a menu of good standards.

Judges Pool Motel (☎ 07-386 7892; www.judgespool motel.co.nz; 92 Taupahi Rd; s/d/f $70/80/111) Probably hoping to hook fishing lawyers, the Judges Pool has good rooms with kitchenettes, new bathrooms and a fish-cleaning area. Many rooms have outdoor decks for relaxing beers and talk of the one that got away.

Tongariro River Motel (☎ 07-386 8555; fax 07-386 0146; cnr SH-1 & Link Rd; s/d/units $75/95/165; ☼) A favourite with older fisherfolk, there's a 1970s vibe to this place, with pine panelling and some trippy layout to rooms (witness the microwave in the living room). Larger units sleep up to seven, and there's a spa and playground to amuse non-fisherfolk.

Creel Lodge (☎ /fax 07-386 8081; 183 Taupahi Rd; s/d $55/85; ☼) This peaceful lodge is in a picturesque setting, backing onto a fine stretch of the Tongariro River. All the ground-level suites have their own kitchen facilities and a balcony, overlooking a very attractive garden.

Turangi Leisure Lodge (☎ 07-386 8988; Ngawaka Pl; d/f $75/130; ☼) It can be difficult to find a room at this large timeshare place during busy periods, but with roomy units with TVs, stereos and full kitchens, it can be worth planning ahead to stay here. Larger units have an upstairs bedroom for privacy. The midsized pool and restaurant (for guests only) are real bonuses.

TOP END

Tongariro Lodge (☎ 07-386 7946; www.tongariro lodge.co.nz; Grace Rd; s/d $470/870) This luxury trout-fishing lodge handles everything, from hired guides (with helicopter drop-offs) to gourmet dining (including riverside hampers), leaving you to focus on fishing. Individual wooden chalets make this a private getaway, but there's plenty of socialising at the bar and on-site activities such as tennis or spa soaking. The week-long and conference packages are popular options.

Eating

River Rocks Cafe (☎ 07-386 8758; 55 Town Centre; meals $3-13; ☼ breakfast & lunch) Combine corrugated iron and stones from the river to create the rugged décor, serve up well-priced burgers, homemade pies and generous all-day brekkies, and it's easy to see why this place rocks.

Mustard Seed Cafe (☎ 07-386 7377; 0huanga Rd; mains $4-15; ☯ breakfast & lunch Wed-Mon) This modern café has old-style food like bacon and egg pie, vol-au-vents and whopping fish and chips.

Thyme for Food (☎ 07-386 0552; Town Centre; meals $6-16; ☯ breakfast & lunch) For a quick bite in an unfussy and laid-back setting, grab a pie, all-day brekkie or a burger at this timely spot.

Red Crater Cafe (☎ 07-386 6558; 26 Ngawaka Pl; mains $6-12; ☯ breakfast & lunch) Bright and new, this café inside Extreme Backpackers has light meals, snacks and drinks with a loungey outdoor area.

Four Fish (☎ 07-386 6340; cnr Pihanga & 0huanga Rds; pizzas $17, mains $9-15; ☯ breakfast, lunch & dinner) Inside a pub, this joint does good takeaway pizzas, but the sit-down bistro meals are less interesting ('soup of the moment' was pea and ham). Breakfasts are hearty.

Grand Central Fry (☎ 07-386 5344; 0huanga Rd; burgers $5; ☯ 11am-9pm) This local legend makes top fish and chips, plus burgers and anything else fryable.

Getting There & Away

Both **InterCity** (☎ 09-913 6100) and **Newmans** (☎ 09-913 6200) buses arrive at and depart from the **Centre of Adventure** (Tautahanga Rd). The Auckland–Wellington and Rotorua–Wellington buses that travel along the eastern side of the lake to and from Taupo all stop at Turangi.

Kiwi Traveller (☎ 0800 500 100; www.kiwitraveller.co.nz) runs to Wellington ($54) and Rotorua ($29).

Mountain Shuttle (☎ 0800 117 686) goes between Turangi ($30), Whakapapa ($25) and Tongariro Crossing twice a day.

Tongariro Expeditions (☎ 0800 828 763; www.tongariroexpeditions.com) runs shuttles from Turangi ($30), Taupo ($40) and Whakapapa ($20) for the Tongariro Crossing and the Northern Circuit. Shuttles depart at 6.20am and 7am. Bellbird Lodge and Extreme Backpackers also provide shuttles for the Tongariro Crossing ($25 return), and sometimes for the Whakapapa Ski Area.

Alpine Scenic Tours (☎ 07-386 8918; www.alpinescenictours.co.nz) runs a shuttle twice daily be-

tween Taupo ($35), Turangi ($30) and National Park township, stopping at the Ketetahi and Mangatepopo trail heads, and the Whakapapa Ski Area. Shuttles depart at 7am. This is an excellent service for skiers and trampers. It also has services to and from Taupo.

TONGARIRO & AROUND

TONGARIRO NATIONAL PARK

Established in 1887, Tongariro was NZ's first national park. The park's three peaks were a gift to NZ from the local Maori tribe, who saw it as the only way to preserve an area of spiritual significance. The name Tongariro originally covered the three mountains of the park (Tongariro, Ngauruhoe and Ruapehu) and comes from *tonga* (south wind) and *riro* (carried away).

With its towering active volcanoes, Tongariro is definitely one of NZ's most spectacular parks, best known for its cameo as Mordor's Mt Doom in Peter Jackson's *Lord of the Rings* trilogy. In summer it offers excellent walks and tramps, most notably the Tongariro Northern Circuit and the Tongariro Crossing. In winter it's a busy ski area.

Information

The **visitor information centre** (☎ 07-892 3729; fax 07-892 3814; AV display adult/child/family $5/1.50/12; -

TONGARIRO NATIONAL PARK & AROUND

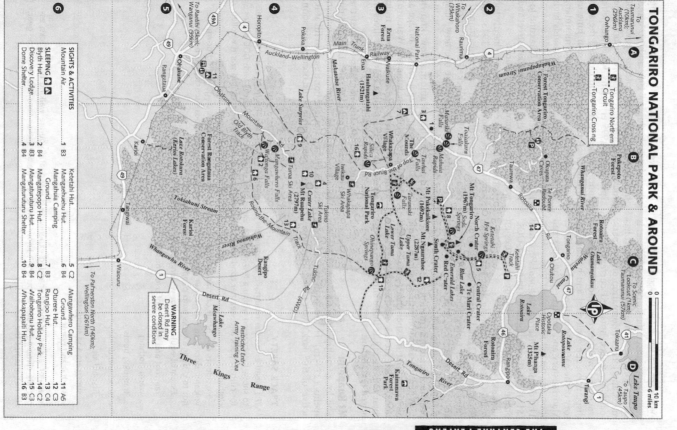

SIGHTS & ACTIVITIES

Mountain Air............................1 B3	

SLEEPING

Blyth Hut................................2 B4	
Discovery Lodge......................3 B3	
Dome Shelter...........................4 B4	
Ketetahi Hut............................5 C2	
Mangaehuehu Hut....................6 B4	
Mangatua Camping Ground........7 B3	
Mangatepopo Hut.....................8 B4	
Mangaturuturu Hut..................9 B4	
Mangaturuturu Shelter............10 B4	
Mangawhero Camping Ground...11 A5	
Oturere Hut............................12 C3	
Rangipo Hut...........................13 C4	
Tongariro Holiday Park.............14 C4	
Waihohonu Hut.......................15 C3	
Whakapapaiti Hut...................16 B3	

WARNING

Desert Rd may be closed in severe conditions

8am-5pm May-Nov, to 6pm Dec-Apr), in Whaka-papa (pronounced 'fa-ka-pa-pa') Village, is on the northwestern side of the park. It has maps and lots of information on the park, including walks, huts and current skiing, track and weather conditions. The many displays on the geological and human history of the park, the audiovisual show about Maori history and volcanoes, and the small shop, are perfect wet-weather time-wasters. The detailed *Tongariro National Park* map ($15) is worth buying before tramping. DOC produces a number of handy brochures on all walks in the park.

DOC centres serving the park are in Ohakune (p322) and Turangi (p309). From late December to late January DOC offers an excellent array of guided walks in and around the park; ask at park centres for brochures and information.

When visiting Tongariro National Park, be aware that it experiences alpine conditions, which means weather changes faster than you can say 'Is that a snowfall?'; see the boxed text, below.

Mt Ruapehu

The long, multipeaked summit of Mt Ruapehu (2797m) is the highest and most active of the park's volcanoes. The upper slopes were sprayed with hot mud during the volcanic hiccups of 1969 and 1975, and in December 1988 the volcano spewed hot rocks. These were just tame precursors to the spectacular 1995 eruptions, when Ruapehu spurted volcanic rock and cloaked the area in clouds of ash and steam. From June to September the following year the mountain rumbled, groaned and sent ash clouds high into the sky, writing off the 1996 ski season. Like patient parents, sanguine Ohakune locals set up deck chairs on the main street and watched the mountain's tantrums.

After all, these eruptions were hardly the worst of the century. Between 1945 and 1947 the level of Crater Lake rose dramatically when eruptions blocked the overflow. On Christmas Eve 1953 the overflow burst and the flood led to one of NZ's worst natural disasters. The volcanic mudflow (known as a lahar) swept away a railway bridge at Tangiwai (between Ohakune and Waiouru) moments before a crowded express train arrived, and 153 people lost their lives in the resulting derailment.

The 1995–96 eruption also blocked the overflow of Ruapehu's Crater Lake and the lake has begun to fill once more. Scientists predict that if the lake continues to fill at its current rate, a lahar could occur again soon.

TRACK SAFETY

The weather on the mountains is extremely changeable – it can change from warm sunshine to snow, hail or wind within a few minutes. Expect the unexpected and check with DOC offices for current track and weather conditions before setting out. Bring a raincoat and warm woollen clothing.

Accidents can occur on tracks when trampers misjudge loose rocks or go sliding down the volcanic slopes, so watch your step! On Ngauruhoe, watch out for loose scoria, and be careful not to dislodge rocks onto people coming up behind.

Essential equipment for walking in the park includes the following:

- raincoat and waterproof overtrousers
- warm clothing
- tramping boots
- food and drink
- first-aid kit
- suncream and sunglasses
- sunhat and warm hat

In winter, alpine or mountaineering experience is essential if you are walking many tracks, especially climbing peaks. If you don't know how to use ice axes, crampons and avalanche gear, do not attempt the summits.

A major lahar could be as catastrophic as previous eruptions, though Crater Lake may just leak through the dam and trickle away. DOC has set up alarm systems at Crater Lake's edge to monitor its build-up, so locals and emergency teams have plenty of warning should the angry mountain blow its top again.

Mt Tongariro

Another old, but still active, volcano is Mt Tongariro (1967m). Its Red Crater last erupted in 1926, it has a number of coloured lakes dotting its uneven summit as well as hot springs gushing out of its side at Ketetahi. The Tongariro Crossing (right), a magnificent walk, passes beside the lakes, right through several craters, and down through lush native forest.

Mt Ngauruhoe

Much younger than the other volcanoes in the park is Mt Ngauruhoe (2287m). It's estimated to have formed in the last 2500 years, and the slopes to its summit are still perfectly symmetrical. In contrast to Ruapehu and Tongariro, which have multiple vents, Ngauruhoe is a conical, single-vent volcano. It can be climbed in summer, but in winter (under snow) this steep but rewarding climb is definitely only for experienced mountaineers.

Both Ngauruhoe and Ruapehu were used in the *Lord of the Rings* films (2001–03), but as you'll easily see, it was Ngauruhoe that most resembled Mordor's Mt Doom.

Tongariro Northern Circuit

Classed as one of NZ's Great Walks, the Northern Circuit circumnavigates Mt Ngauruhoe and affords spectacular views of Mt Tongariro, and also has some well-maintained huts. As the walk is a circuit, there are several starting and finishing points, including Whakapapa Village, Ketetahi Rd, Desert Rd and even by continuing the Round the Mountain Track. Generally the walk is begun at Mangatepopo car park and concluded at Whakapapa Village and takes three to four days to complete. The walk also includes the Tongariro Crossing.

Highlights of the circuit include tramping through several volcanic craters, including the **South Crater**, **Central Crater** and **Red Crater**; brilliantly colourful volcanic lakes including the **Emerald Lakes**, **Blue Lake** and the **Upper** and **Lower Tama Lakes**; the cold **Soda Springs** and **Ohinepango Springs**; and various other volcanic formations including cones, lava flows and glacial valleys.

There are several possibilities for side trips that take from a few hours to overnight. The most popular side trip from the main track is to Ngauruhoe's summit (three hours), but it is also possible to climb Tongariro from Red Crater (two hours) or walk to Ohinepango Springs from Waihohonu Hut (30 minutes).

WALKING THE TRACK

The safest and most popular time to walk the track is from December to March. The track is served by four huts: Mangatepopo, Ketetahi, Oturere and Waihohonu. The huts have mattresses, gas heating (cookers in summer), toilets and water. Camping is allowed near all of the huts.

During the full summer season (from late October to early June) a Great Walks pass is required and must be bought in advance, whether you stay in the huts or camp beside them. Ordinary back-country hut tickets and annual passes (see p318) cannot be used during these months. All park visitor information centres sell passes (per night, camp sites per adult/child are $15/7.50, and huts are $20/10).

At other times, ordinary back-country hut passes or annual passes may be used (camp sites/huts $5/10 per adult per night; tickets available from DOC). However, this track is quite difficult in winter, when it is covered in snow, and becomes a tough alpine trek (requiring ice axes and crampons). Add at least another two hours to the estimated times here to allow for winter track conditions. Estimated walking times in summer:

Route	Time
Whakapapa Village to Mangatepopo Hut	3hr
Mangatepopo Hut to Emerald Lakes	3½hr
Emerald Lakes to Ketetahi Hut	2hr
Emerald Lakes to Oturere Hut	1½hr
Oturere Hut to Waihohonu Hut	3hr
Waihohonu Hut to Whakapapa Village	5½hr

Tongariro Crossing

Reputedly the best one-day walk in NZ, the Tongariro Crossing traverses spectacular

www.lonelyplanet.com

volcanic geography, from an active crater to steaming vents. And the views ain't bad either. It covers the most spectacular features of the Tongariro Northern Circuit between the Mangatepopo and Ketetahi Huts. Trampers tackling the Northern Circuit complete this section on their second day, with the extra walk along the Ketetahi track. Because of its popularity, shuttles are available to both ends of the track. The Tongariro Crossing can be reached from Mangatepopo Rd off SH47. There's plenty of track transport that can get you there (see p319).

A few steep spots will challenge you, but generally this day walk should be achievable, if exhausting. If you're not in top walking condition you may prefer to do it in two days, throwing in a few side trips to keep it interesting.

The track passes through vegetation zones ranging from alpine scrub and tussock, to places at higher altitudes where there is no vegetation at all, to the lush podocarp forest as you descend from Ketetahi Hut towards the end of the track.

Worthwhile side trips from the main track include ascents to the summits of Mt Ngauruhoe and Mt Tongariro. Mt Ngauruhoe can be ascended most easily from the Mangatepopo Saddle, reached near the beginning of the track after the first steep climb. The summit of Tongariro is reached by a poled route from Red Crater.

WALKING THE TRACK

The Mangatepopo Hut, reached via Mangatepopo Rd, is near the start of the track, and the Ketetahi Hut is a couple of hours before the end. In summer, to stay at or camp beside either hut you must have a Great Walks pass, purchased in advance and valid from the end of October until Queen's Birthday weekend (around 1 June).

The Ketetahi Hut is the most popular in the park. It has bunks to sleep 24 people, but regularly has 50 to 60 people trying to stay there on Saturday night and at the busiest times of year (summer and school holidays). As bunks are claimed on a first-come, first-served basis, it's not a bad idea to bring camping gear, just in case. Campers can use all of the hut facilities (except for bunks), which can make the kitchen crowded, especially at peak times.

Estimated walking times:

Route	Time
Mangatepopo Rd end to Mangatepopo Hut	15min
Mangatepopo Hut to Mangatepopo Saddle	1½hr
Mangatepopo Saddle to summit of Mt Ngauruhoe (side trip)	3hr return
Red Crater to Tongariro summit (side trip)	1½hr return
Mangatepopo Saddle to Emerald Lakes	1½–2hr
Emerald Lakes to Ketetahi Hut	2hr
Ketetahi Hut to road end	2hr

Round the Mountain

This off-the-beaten-track hike is a difficult hike, suitable for more experienced trampers, but is known as being a quieter alternative to the busy Tongariro Crossing. Looping around Mt Ruapehu, this trail takes in a diversity of country from glacial rivers to tussocky moors to majestic mountain views.

You should allow at least four days to complete this hike with six days a realistic estimate if you're including side trips to the remote Blyth Hut or Tama Lakes. This trail is particularly tough and not recommended for beginners or the underprepared.

WALKING THE TRACK

You can get to the Round the Mountain trail at a number of points depending on where you want to start and end; choose from Whakapapa Village, Waihohonu Track junction, Ohakune Mountain Rd or Whakapapaiti Hut. Most trampers start at Whakapapa Village and return there to finish the loop.

The track is safest from December to March when there is little or no snow, and less chance of avalanche. At other times of year, navigation and walking will be made difficult by snow, and full alpine gear (ice axe, crampons and specialised clothing) is a requirement. To take on the track you should prepare thoroughly with good quality maps (such as Parkmaps No 273-04), checks on the latest conditions and clothing and food for all climes. Be sure to notify DOC of your tramping plans and intended return date.

Sleeping in huts or camping is necessary on this multiday track, and costs $10/5 per adult/child for a bed in a hut and $5/2.50 camping. From the end of October to June, you'll need a Great Walks pass for part of the track; passes are available from DOC offices.

Estimated walking times:

Route

Route	Time
Whakapapa Village to Waihohonu Hut	5½hr
Waihohonu Hut to Rangipo Hut	5hr
Rangipo Hut to Mangaehuehu Hut	5½hr
Mangaehuehu Hut to Ohakune Mountain Rd	3hr
Ohakune Mountain Rd to Mangaturuturu Hut	5½hr
Whakapapaiti Hut to Whakapapa Village	4hr
Tama Lakes (side trip)	1½hr
Blyth Hut (side trip)	1hr

Other Walks

The visitor information centres at Whakapapa, Ohakune and Turangi have maps and information on interesting short and long walks in the park, as well as track and weather conditions.

The walk up to **Crater Lake** (seven hours return) is a good one, when Ruapehu is not volcanically active. You walk up into Ruapehu's crater and see the acidic lake up close, but it is strictly off limits if there's volcanic activity. The walk begins at Iwikau Village at the Top of the Bruce Rd and is a moderate to difficult walk. You can cut three hours off it by catching the **chairlift** (adult/child $61/9; 9am-4pm) from Whakapapa Ski Area. **Guided walks** (reservations 07-892 3738; adult/child incl lift pass $65/45) to Crater Lake leave daily at 9.30am from the chairlift. Like most of the walks in Tongariro, you'll need to check conditions before heading out and you can forget it in winter unless you're a mountaineer.

FROM WHAKAPAPA VILLAGE

A number of fine walks begin at or near the Whakapapa visitor information centre and from the road leading up to it. Several other good walks take off from the road leading from Ohakune to the Turoa Ski Area (see p322). *Whakapapa Walks* ($1), published by DOC, lists walks from the visitor information centre, including the following:

Ridge Track A 30-minute return walk, wh ch climbs through beech forest to alpine-shrub areas for views of Ruapehu and Ngauruhoe.

Silica Rapids A 2½-hour, 7km loop track to the Silica Rapids, named for the silica mineral deposits formed here by the rapids on Waikare Stream. The track passes interesting alpine features and, in the final 2.5km, passes down Top of the Bruce Rd above Whakapapa Village.

Tama Lakes A 17km track to the Tama Lakes (five to six hours return). On the Tama Lakes are great for a refreshing swim. The upper lake affords fine views of Ngauruhoe and Tongariro (beware of winds on the saddle).

Taranaki Falls A two-hour, 6km loop track to the 20m Taranaki Falls on Wairere Stream.

Whakapapa Nature Walk A 15-minute loop track suitable for wheelchairs, beginning about 200m above the visitor information centre and passing through beech forest and gardens typical of the park's vegetation zones.

NORTH OF WHAKAPAPA VILLAGE

Still more tracks take off from SH47, on the national park's north side, including the following:

Lake Rotoaira On the shores of Lake Rotoaira are excavations of a pre-European Maori village site.

Mahuia Rapids About 2km north of the turn-off leading to Whakapapa, SH47 crosses the Whakapapanui Stream jus; below the rapids.

Matariki Falls A 20-minute return track to the falls takes off from SH47 about 200m from the Mahuia Rapids car park.

Skiing

The two main ski areas are the **Whakapapa Ski Area** (1630m), above Whakapapa Village, and the **Turoa Ski Area**, to the south. The **Tukino Ski Area**, on the eastern side of Ruapehu, is only accessible by a 4WD road. You can check conditions and current lift rates at the Mt Ruapehu website (www.mtruapehu.com), which covers Whakapapa and Turoa. See also p79.

The only accommodation at the ski fields is in private lodges, so most skiers stay at Whakapapa Village, National Park township or Ohakune. One lift pass is valid for both Whakapapa and Turoa.

You can hire ski gear in Taupo, National Park or Whakapaka at stores such as **Edge to Edge** (0800 300754; www.edgetoedge.co.nz; Skotel Alpine Resort; 1-day full ski gear adult/chilc $55/39, 1-day snowboard gear $63/49). You can also hire skis on the mountain and organise for them to be ready when you arrive, which can be done online at www.mtruapehu.com.

Other Activities

The Bayview Chateau Tongariro in Whakapapa has a public nine-hole **golf course** and tennis courts, and hires out golf clubs and tennis rackets.

Mountain Air (☎ 0800 922 812; www.mountainair.co.nz; flights from $70), with an office on SH47 near the SH48 turn-off to Whakapapa, has flights over the volcanoes, eruptions permitting.

Plateau Outdoor Adventure Guides (☎/fax 07-892 2740) is based at Raurimu, 6km north of National Park township. It offers a wide variety of activities around Tongariro and the Whanganui River, including canoeing, kayaking, white-water rafting and tramping.

Outdoor Experiences (☎ 0800 806 369; www.tongarironz.com) runs guided four-day canoe trips (adult/child $595/360) down the Whanganui River, departing Thursday and Saturday.

Tours

Mountain Air (☎ 0800 922 812; SH47 opposite Whakapapa turn-off; flights from $90) offers 10-minute flights over Tongariro Crossing and a 30-minute tour of *Lord of the Rings* locations.

Tours of the Rings (☎ 07-895 4773; from $95) takes the whole thing more seriously, with trips that point out every orc footprint and hobbit hole.

Sleeping

Whakapapa Village has limited accommodation, most of which is run by DOC. Two DOC camping grounds are within the park (near National Park and Ohakune), as well as huts, accessible only by walking tracks. Prices quoted here are for summer; rates are much higher in winter. National Park (p320), Ohakune (p324) and Turangi (p311) offer a greater range of options close to the park.

BUDGET

Whakapapa Holiday Park (☎ 07-892 3897; whakapapaholpark@xtra.co.nz; sites per 2 people $28; dm/cabins/units $22/46/69) This well-maintained and popular park has a wide range of accommodation options, including a 32-bed backpackers' lodge, camp sites perched on the edge of beautiful bushland and self-contained units for couples.

Tongariro Holiday Park (☎ 07-386 8062; eivins@xtra.co.nz; SH47; camp sites per 2 people from $22, dm $20) Formerly Eivin's Lodge, this place is on SH47 about halfway between Turangi and Whakapapa (approximately 24km from either; see Map p313). It's basic but friendly with self-contained units, as well as tent and powered sites, a kitchen, lounge, spa pool, restaurant, dairy and postal agency. There's ski hire in winter.

There are two basic DOC camping grounds: **Mangahuia Camping Ground** (SH47; sites per 2 people $20) is between National Park and the SH48 turn-off heading to Whakapapa; and the **Mangawhero Camping Ground** (Ohakune Mountain Rd; sites per 2 people $20) is near Ohakune. Both have cold water and pit toilets.

Scattered around the park's tramping tracks are nine huts (Map p313; $10 per person). You can camp beside the huts for $5 per person. Back-country hut tickets and annual hut passes are both accepted.

In the summer season a Great Walks pass is required for the popular four Tongariro Northern Circuit huts: Ketetahi, Mangatepopo, Waihohonu and Oturere. Prebooked huts/camp sites cost $28/20, otherwise they cost $36/24.

All park visitor information centres sell hut tickets or Great Walks passes, as does Howard's Lodge (p320) at National Park.

MIDRANGE & TOP END

Skotel Alpine Resort (☎ 0800 756 835, 07-892 3719; www.skotel.co.nz; dm/d/chalets from $35/125/205; 🖳)

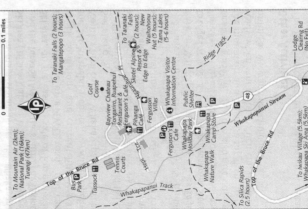

WHAKAPAPA VILLAGE

0 .... 100 m
0 .... 0.1 miles

To Mountain Air (2km);
National Park (16km);
Turangi (47km)

To Taranaki Falls (2 hours);
Mangatepopo (3 hours)

To Taranaki
Falls

Waihohonu
Hut (5 hours);
Edge to Edge
(5–6 hours)

New

Bayview Chateau
Tongariro, Ruapehu
Restaurant & Bar;
Ferguson's Café;
Pihanga
Café

Golf
Course

Skotel Alpine
Resort;
Edge to Edge

Whakapapa Visitor
Information Centre

Ferguson
Villas

Public
Shelter

Whakapapa
Camp Store

Whakapapa
Holiday Park

Ridge Track

Lodge
Clearing Rd
(No Exit)

Whakapapanui Stream

Bus
Park

Ferguson's
Café

Tennis
Courts

Top of the Bruce Rd

Tussock

Top of the Bruce Rd

Whakapapanui Track

Whakapapa
Nature Walk

To Iwikau Village (5.5km);
Whakapapa Ski Area (5.5km)

To Silica Rapids
(2.5 hours)

With timbered décor and a ski crowd, NZ's highest hotel) has an alpine feel with a few luxuries including sauna, spa pool, gym, ski shop, games room, licensed restaurant and, most importantly, bar. Chalets are great for groups, but the main lodge ;s known for a party crowd. Prices climb to rival Ruapehu's altitude in winter, with a $50 surcharge for Saturdays or single nights.

Bayview Chateau Tongariro (☎ 0800 242 832, 07-892 3809; www.chateau.co.nz; d/l/ste from $180/265/350; ☐ ☑) The majestic Chateau is the most eye-catching spot to stay, with a gorgeous view of the mountains. First opened in 1929, the building is a classic European mansion house. A recent refurbishment has ensured its place as one of NZ's finest hotels, with a cinema, tennis court, nine-hole golf course and several restaurants to sample. Package deals can make this a more affordable luxury.

Fergusson Villas (☎ 0800 242 832, 07-892 3809; www.chateau.co.nz; 1-2-bedroom chalets $185/225) These small self-contained chalets are good family options with kitchens, and small decks for relaxing on. Booking and check-in is through the Bayview Chateau Tongariro.

Eating

The Bayview Chateau Tongariro has a good range of dining options, including the elegant à la carte **Ruapehu Restaurant** (mains around $25; ☑ dinner); **Pihanga Café** (mains $15-20; ☑ lunch & dinner), with an innovative menu including chermoula chicken, and basil and ricotta ravioli; and the T-bar, which features seating in a former lift. **Ferguson's Café** (mains $4-8; ☑ 7am-3.30pm Mon-Fri, to 4.30pm Sat & Sun) is more casual with pies, sandwiches and coffee. **Tussock** (pizzas $8-12; ☑ lunch & dinner), on the main road, hosts occasional live entertainment in winter, and has a beer garden and awesome views. **Skotel Alpine Resort** (☎ 0800 756 835, 07-8923319; www.skotel.co.nz; mains around $15; ☑ dinner) also has a licensed restaurant and bar.

The Whakapapa Camp Store, in Whakapapa Holiday Park, sells basic groceries for self-catering, though it's pricier than the supermarket in Ohakune.

Getting There & Away

BUS & TRAIN

InterCity (☎ 09-913 6100) buses stop at National Park (p320), the primary gateway to Tongariro.

Tranz Scenic (☎ 0800 872 467; www.tranzscenic.co.nz) trains on the Auckland–Wellington line stop at National Park.

Alpine Scenic Tours (☎ 07-386 8918; www.alpine scenictours.co.nz) runs a shuttle twice daily between Taupo ($35), Turangi ($30) and National Park township ($20), stopping at the Ketetahi and Mangatepopo trail heads, and the Whakapapa Ski Area. The first shuttle departs from Taupo at 6.30am and from Turangi at 7am.

There are various shuttles running between Turangi, Whakapapa Village and National Park township during the day, and they go up to the ski area at Top of the Bruce Rd by request. Since seats are limited, book in advance to guarantee a spot.

Tongariro Expeditions (☎ 0800 828 763; www.tongariroexpeditions.com) runs two shuttles from Turangi ($30); Taupo ($40) and Whakapapa Northern Circuit. Shuttles depart Taupo at 5.40am and 6.20am and Turangi at 6.20am and 7am.

Tongariro Track Transport (☎ 07-892 3716, 021 563 109) is another option, specialising in the Tongariro Crossing (adult/child $25/15; departs 7.15am, 8am and 8.30am); it has buses departing from Whakapapa. The company also picks up from National Park to Whakapapa (adult/child/family $15/10/35, departs 7am on request and at 7.45am).

From National Park township other shuttles run to Whakapapa, Mangatepopo and Ketetahi for the Tongariro Crossing (see left). Transport is also available from Ohakune (see p326).

Book all shuttles in advance to avoid a cold morning waiting for a shuttle that might not know to pick you up.

CAR & MOTORCYCLE

The park is bounded by roads: SH1 (called the Desert Rd around here) to the east, SH4 to the west, SH46 and SH47 cross the northern side and SH49 along the south. The main road up into the park is SH48, which leads to Whakapapa Village, continuing further up the mountain to the Whakapapa Ski Area. Ohakune Mountain Rd leads up to the Turoa Ski Area from Ohakune.

For the Tongariro Crossing, access is from the end of Mangatepopo Rd off SH47, and SH46 from the end of Ketetahi Rd off

National Park Rd (between SH1 and SH47). Theft from parked vehicles is a problem at both ends: don't leave valuables in the car.

NATIONAL PARK
pop 460

Named for nearby Tongariro National Park, this tiny outpost at the junction of SH4 and SH47 is the gateway to Tongariro and just 15km from Whakapapa Village. In ski season accommodation is packed but in summer you can have the awesome views of Ruapehu to yourself.

The small township makes the perfect base for the walks around the park. Daily shuttles leave from here to the Tongariro Crossing and Whakapapa Village in summer, and the ski area in winter. If you can't decide between two ski fields, it's only a short drive further on to Ohakune and nearby Turoa. It is also a base for other ventures, such as canoe trips on the Whanganui River (see p284).

About 20km south on SH4 at Horopito is a monument to the Last Spike, the spike that marked the completion of the Main Trunk Railway Line between Auckland and Wellington in 1908.

Check out www.nationalpark.co.nz for more info.

Activities

Howard's Lodge, Pukenui Lodge, Pipers Lodge and Ski Haus (right) and Eivin's Café (opposite) hire out all necessary gear for the **Tongariro Crossing** and other treks. For a good soak, the **spa pools** at Ski Haus and Pukenui Lodge are available to nonguests.

Howard's Lodge takes **guided mountain-bike tours** (2hr from $20) and also provides transport and bike hire (from $20) for the **42nd Traverse**, an excellent 46km mountain-bike trail through the Tongariro Forest, classed among the best one-day rides in NZ; and the 21km downhill Fishers Track. For an easier ride, take a motorised quad bike with **Bushline Quads** (☎ 07-895 9489; 1½hr ride $90), which offers guided rides through the 42nd Traverse.

Adrift Guided Outdoor Adventures (☎ 0800 462 374, 07-892 2751; www.adriftnz.co.nz) runs canoe adventures (one-day trip per adult/child $175/145) and guided treks (from $135) up to Tongariro Crossing and Mt Ruapehu. **Tongariro River Rafting** (☎ 0800 101 024; www.tongariro-riverrafting.com) offers white-water rafting trips on the Tongariro River, as well as kayaking, fishing and mountain-biking excursions. Further out **Wade's Landing Outdoors** (☎ 07-895 5995; 1-day tour/hire $195/105) offers both guided trips and hire on the Whanganui River.

For those rainy days there's an 8m-high indoor **climbing wall** (☎ 07-892 2870; www.npbp.co.nz; Finlay St; adult/child $12/9, own gear $9/7; 9am-9pm) at National Park Backpackers, which offers 55 different climbs. Outdoor climbers with their own gear can find spots near Manataupo car park and Meads chairlifts in summer.

Most accommodation in town offers packages for lift passes and ski hire, which can save you lugging skis, and spare you the steeper prices further up the mountain.

Sleeping

Prices increase dramatically in the ski season, when accommodation is tight and bookings are essential (especially on weekends). The prices listed here are for summer. While there are no top-end options in National Park, in winter prices jump into that range, with increases of $80 not uncommon!

BUDGET

Ski Haus (☎ 07-892 2854; www.skihaus.co.nz; Carroll St; dm $25, sites per 2 people $30, d/3-bedroom cottages from $70/90; ☐) Ski Haus has superfriendly new owners who are keen to keep the cosy wood-cabin feel of this lodge-cum-backpackers. A large alpine-style lounge crackles with a log fire, while elsewhere there's a spa pool and billiards table for chilly evenings. The casual restaurant does burgers, roasts and soups (mains $7.50 to $15), with the bonus of a small bar. Rooms range from bunk dorms to a more private three-bedroom cottage.

Adventure Lodge & Motel (☎ 07-892 2991; www.adventurenationalpark.co.nz; Carroll St; dm $22, d $60-90; ☐) Thinking of taking on Tongariro? This friendly modern lodge has a great package to the Tongariro Crossing track that includes accommodation, transport, lunch and a T-shirt. If you're not heading out, there are great facilities right here, including spa pools, volleyball, *boules* and a barbecue. More expensive doubles come with en suites.

Howard's Lodge (☎ /fax 07-892 2827; www.howardslodge.co.nz; 11-13 Carroll St; dm $22-25, d $60-112, ste $110-140; ☐) Whoever Howard is, he knows how to lodge. This large place features a spa, comfortable lounge and spotless, well-equipped kitchens. Dorms are relatively roomy with only four bunks, while other rooms are smaller. For outdoor action, Howard also has plenty of skis, snowboards, tramping gear and mountain bikes available for hire.

National Park Backpackers (☎/fax 07-892 2870; www.npbp.co.nz; Finlay St; dm $21, sites per 2 people $24, d $52-75; ☐) Giant kiwi and moa statues peck the grounds of this family-owned YHA hostel, which has basic rooms, many including en suite facilities and toasty purple radiators. The big attraction is the 8m-high climbing wall (see opposite; discounted use for guests), but other facilities include a barbecue, spa and indoor badminton. They're a busy lot here with bike hire ($30 per day), a glow-worm tour ($15 at night) and their own track transport.

MIDRANGE

Pipers Lodge (☎ 09-415 5593; Millar St; d & tw $138) This massive place (around 150 beds) specialises in packages with lift passes and meals thrown in. The huge lounge area includes a bar, and free tea and coffee, and there's a games room with a pool table. Twin rooms can cram in up to four people, so you can get a smaller room if you're going to be out partying a lot. Ski hire is $25/18 per adult/child.

Pukenui Lodge (☎ 0800 785 368; www.tongariro.cc; Millar St; dm/d/chalets from $25/60/120; ☐) With breathtaking views across to the mountains and loads of extras including spa, restaurant, small kitchen, ski hire and the very pattable Barkly the dog, this well-kept spot is a brilliant option. The staff can also work out good packages including track transport ($20), bikes, skis or meals. Dorms are limited to four, and the large three-bedroom chalet can fit up to seven. Pukenui is very popular in winter and charges extra for weekends during the ski season.

Mountain Heights B&B and Motel (☎ 07-892 2833; www.mountainheights.co.nz; d from $95, d B&B from $130) This friendly Swiss chalet-style lodge on SH4, 2km south of National Park, has good-quality, self-contained motel units that sleep up to six people, and comfortable en suite rooms with TVs and tea-making facilities (breakfast included). Meals are available by arrangement, and mountain bikes can be hired (from $20 for two hours).

Tongariro Crossing Lodge (☎ 07-892 2688; www.tongarirocrossinglodge.com; 37 Caroll St; d/f $159/225; ☐) This white and baby-blue lodge offers high-quality B&B with optional dinner (by arrangement; from $40). Rooms range from a standard double to larger self-contained rooms that include a full kitchen. Don't miss the sun-soaked breakfast room that encourages idle mornings and lingering brunches. New owners are being experimental about prices so there are good deals to be had.

Discovery Lodge (☎ 0800 122 122; www.discovery.net.nz; cabins/d/chalets from $40/123/149; ☐) Handy to Whakapapa, this lodge is on SH47, between National Park and Whakapapa. The spa ($5) and restaurant both have excellent views of Ruapehu, plus there's a bar and comfy lounge. The blonde-wood lodge building has exposed rafters and a definite alpine feel. Cabins are basic, but large chalets are great getaways for up to four people.

Eating

Most accommodation in National Park provides meals or kitchens (or both) for guests, but there's plenty of great grub elsewhere in town.

Station (☎ 07-892 2881; cnr Station & Finlay Sts; cakes $2.5, mains $8-17; ⏲ 10am-11pm) This versatile little railway station serves up cakes (we're talking massive jam-crammed scones and old-style lamingtons), snacks and lunches before going all à la carte for an evening of surprisingly slick dining.

Basekamp (☎ 07-892 2872; Caroll St; mains $10-17; ⏲ lunch & dinner) Basekamp does a good wood-fired pizza, such as the kooky K2, a concoction of bananas, tandoori chicken and cashews. There's also a decent burger on the menu.

Eivin's Café (☎ 07-892 2844; cnr Caroll St & SH4; mains $15-28; ⏲ 4pm-late) Eivin's offers real alpine food such as gooey fondue, as well as tasty meals such as the pesto-encrusted lamb roasted on kumara. The café also hires ski and snowboarding gear.

Schnapps (☎ 07-892 2788; Finlay St; mains $7-20; ⏲ dinner) This popular pub does excellent pizzas, generous burgers, and better-than-average pub fare (think lamb shanks and a vegetarian dish of the day), and bands pack the place out on wintry Saturday nights.

Getting There & Away

BUS

InterCity (☎ 09-913 6100) buses arrive at and depart from outside Ski Haus on Carroll St daily except Saturday. Buy tickets at Ski Haus and Howard's Lodge. Journeys north to Auckland ($57) via Hamilton ($39) or south to Wellington ($57) via Palmerston North ($43) take about five hours.

Alpine Scenic Tours (☎ 07-386 8918; www.alpine scenictours.co.nz) has twice-daily shuttles that make a round trip between Turangi and National Park ($25), with stops at Whakapapa Village, Whakapapa Ski Area (by request), the Mangatepopo and Ketetahi car parks (for the Tongariro Crossing), and on from Turangi to Taupo. Make sure you arrange transport for the end of your tramp before you start out, as there are no phones at the trail heads.

Kiwi Traveller (☎ 0800 500 100; www.kiwitravel ler.co.nz) runs daily to and from Wellington ($49.50) and Rotorua ($44).

Tongariro Track Transport (☎ 07-892 3716, 021 563 109) operates a daily shuttle to Whakapapa (adult/child/family $15/10/35; departs at 7.45am daily and 7am by request), with buses to Mangatepopo car park or the ski fields.

TRAIN

Tranz Scenic (☎ 0800 872 467; www.tranzscenic.co.nz /services/overlander.aspx) runs the *Overlander* to and from Auckland ($78 one way) and Wellington ($77 one way) stopping at National Park and Ohakune ($20 one way). Train tickets are sold not from the train station but from Ski Haus or Howard's Lodge.

OHAKUNE

pop 1490

Because it's close to the Turoa Ski Area, on the southern side of Ruapehu, Ohakune leads a double life as the North Island's top ski destination and, strangely, NZ's Carrot Capital. Expect the orange vegetable to creep into burgers and appear on pizzas, especially during July's annual Carrot Festival (see the boxed text, right).

During winter skiers and snowboarders invade town for the big snowfalls. There's still plenty to do when dumps aren't big, including hiking, canoeing, white-water rafting and mountain biking.

Ohakune's commercial heart is south along the highway, but in winter the north-

ern end around the train station, known as the Junction, is the epicentre for skiers.

Information

The Ruapehu **visitor information centre** (☎ 0800 782 734, 06-385 8427; www.ruapehunz.com; 54 Clyde St; ☼ 9am-5pm Mon-Fri, to 3.30pm Sat & Sun) can make bookings for activities, transport and accommodation. During the ski season you can tune into SKI FM 96.6 for updates on all the slopes. The Turoa Ski Area operates an **information line** (☎ 0900 99 333), which regularly updates ski and road conditions.

The **Ohakune Field Centre** (☎ 06-385 0010; www.ohakune.info; Ohakune Mountain Rd; ☼ 8am-3pm, public holidays to 5pm) has maps, weather reports and advice about this side of the Tongariro National Park.

There's a post office at **Take Note** (5 Goldfinch St; ☼ 9am-5pm Mon-Fri, to 1pm Sat). Several places in town offer Internet access including Matai Lodge (p324) and **Ohakune Corner** (☎ 06-385 9512; cnr Ayr & Goldfinch Sts; ☼ 11am-9pm).

Activities

WALKING

There are several accessible, scenic walks around town, many heading off the Ohakune Mountain Rd, which stretches 17km from Ohakune to the Turoa Ski Area on Mt Ruapehu. Maps and information are available at Ohakune Field Centre,

Weather is highly changeable, so prepare for all temperatures and let someone know your itinerary.

Easy walks start from opposite the Field Centre, including the **Mangawhero Forest Walk** (one hour return, 3km), taking in native forest and the Mangawhero River. Popular tracks leading from Ohakune Mountain Rd include **Waitonga Falls** (1½ hours, 11km) with awe-inspiring views of Mt Ruapehu; **Old Blyth Track** (four to five hours, 7km), which steadily climbs Ruapehu; and **Lake Surprise** (five hours, 15km). You can continue on the Waitonga Falls track to join the Round the Mountain Track (p316).

In summer you can head out of the Turoa Ski Area on the **Crater Lake Climb** (eight hours), a challenging walk that takes you up into the volcano peak. The planned **Coach Rd Walk** will also kick off here, though at the time of research this walk was uncompleted.

Pick up the handy DOC brochure *Ohakune Coach Walks and Mountain Road* ($1) for information on these tracks. For transport details to these tracks see p319.

SKIING & SNOWBOARDING
The town really comes alive in winter with everyone keen to hurtle down the slopes as fast as possible on either skis or snowboards. Lift passes are available at the ski fields, with equipment available from various places around town including **Ski Shed**

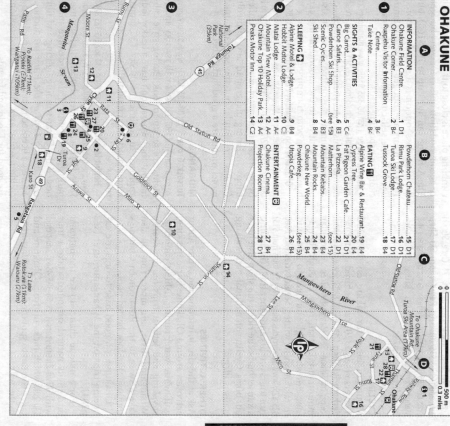

OHAKUNE

INFORMATION
Ohakune Field Centre.....................1 D1
Ohakune Corner...........................2 B2
Ruapehu Visitor Information
 Centre..................................3 B2
Take Note................................4 B2

SIGHTS & ACTIVITIES
Big Carrot...............................5 C4
Canoe Safaris..........................(see 5)
Powderhorn Ski Shop...................(see 15)
Scenic Cycles............................6 B3
Ski Shed.................................7 B3

SLEEPING
Alpine Motel & Lodge.....................8 B4
Hobbit Motor Lodge.......................9 C3
Matai Lodge.............................10 C3
Mountain View Motel.....................11 A4
Ohakune Top 10 Holiday Park............13 C1
Peaks Motor Inn........................14 C1

Powderhorn Chateau.....................15 D1
Rimu Park Lodge........................16 D1
Turoa Ski Lodge........................17 D1
Tussock Grove..........................18 B4

EATING
Alpine Wine Bar & Restaurant...........19 E4
Cypress Tree...........................20 E4
Fat Pigeon Garden Cafe.................21 D1
La Pizzeria............................22 D1
Matterhorn............................(see 15)
Mountain Kebabs........................23 B3
Mountain Rocks.........................24 B3
Ohakune New World......................25 B4
Powderkeg.............................(see 15)
Utopia Cafe............................26 B4

ENTERTAINMENT
Ohakune Cinema.........................27 B4
Projection Room........................28 D1

0   500 m
0   0.3 miles

(☎ 06-385 8887; www.skished.com; 71 Clyde St; ski hire adult/child $35/20) and **Powderhorn Ski Shop** (☎ 06-385 8888; www.powderhorn.co.nz; cnr Thames St & Mangawhero Tce). For more on skiing and snowboarding, see p79.

CYCLING

Mountain bikes for taking on the 42nd Traverse (see p320) can be hired from **Powderhorn Ski Shop** (☎ 06-385 8888; www.powderhorn.co.nz; cnr Thames St & Mangawhero Tce). A popular mountain-bike trail runs through Rangataua Forest, though you need to love mud to take it on in winter. **Scenic Cycles** (☎ 0800 825 825; www.sceniccycles.co.nz; 5 Tay St; tours from $15) run tours on this and other trails (including a sunset barbecue ride); the shop also hires out bikes. Cycling on national-park walking trails is illegal.

OTHER ACTIVITIES

Ask at the visitor information centre about activities around Ohakune: horse trekking, golf, white-water rafting, fishing, canoeing, kayaking and jetboat trips on the nearby Whanganui River, and more. You can also take a swim in the Powderhorn Chateau's (opposite) indoor heated pool.

Ohakune is a good base to organise canoeing trips on the Whanganui River (see p284).

For a unique chance to see the national bird in its natural surrounds, take a tour with **Kiwi Encounters** (☎ 06-385 4565; adult/child $40/20), which picks up from Ohakune and takes you out to spot the feathered favourite in the wild.

Sleeping

In summer the Junction is a bit of a ghost town, so stay near SH49. The prices listed here are for summer (October to March); expect to pay $20 to $50 more in winter and book ahead. Good savings can be made on winter rates by booking midweek.

BUDGET

Mountain View Motel (☎ 06-385 8675; 2 Moore St; dm $15-16, d $60-90) This older place has a new lease of life, with new owners and freshly painted backpacker rooms and large motel-style rooms. Rooms 1 to 4 especially live up to the name with great views across to Ruapehu.

Rimu Park Lodge (☎ 06-385 9023; www.rimupark.co.nz; 27 Rimu St; dm/d from $30/75) This massive, rambling place is close to the Junction, with an accommodation option for every budget. The A-frame can bunk up to 10 ($160), but the 'first class' option is a plushly restored 1934 train carriage. Budget-conscious families love the self-contained carriage, especially trainspotting dads.

Matai Lodge (☎ 06-385 9169; www.matailodge.co.nz; cnr Clyde & Rata Sts; dm/d from $22/50) With a fresh new look, this hostel sticks to top-notch accommodation at reasonable prices. It also provides shuttles to the mountain and can hook you up with tramping guides.

Ohakune Top 10 Holiday Park (☎/fax 06-385 8561; www.ohakune.net.nz; 5 Moore St; sites per 2 people $30, cabins/r from $42/75; ▢) This green family park by the river has plenty of extras to keep littlies happy including playground and minigolf. Cabins are simple, but the self-contained motel rooms are a good budget bet.

MIDRANGE

Tussock Grove (☎ 06-385 8771; www.tussockgrove.co.nz; 3 Karo St; d $90) These small swanky apartments are set up to look like log-style cabins, but the owners don't have a backwoods approach to facilities, with Sky TV, sauna, tennis courts, and mountain views in some rooms.

Hobbit Motor Lodge (☎ 0800 843 462, 06-385 8248; www.the-hobbit.co.nz; cnr Goldfinch & Wye Sts; dm/d/r from $20/95/120) Ever wondered where the Bagginses park their wagons? This gardenlike motel hosted the Oscar-winning lighting and film crew during *Lord of the Rings* production. There's a licensed restaurant, spa pool and a children's play area. Self-contained options are good for Frodo and friends.

Turoa Ski Lodge (☎ 06-385 8274; 10 Thames St; dm/d/f $25/85/140) Looking across at the mountains, this is the prime spot for skiers with rooms ranging from standard dorms to three-bedroom units with big TVs, full kitchens and large wardrobes for ski gear.

Peaks Motor Inn (☎ 06-385 9144; www.thepeaks.co.nz; cnr Mangawhero Tce & Shannon St; d from $80; ▢) This collection of pine motel rooms is well-kept, with basic gym, pool and large outdoor spa for apres-ski. Rooms are spacious, with bay windows, and baths generous enough for the tallest guests.

Alpine Motel & Lodge (☎/fax 06-385 8758; www.alpinemotel.co.nz; 7 Miro St; dm/d/town houses from $25/95/180; ▢) The motel rooms in the Alpine have a motor-lodge feel, with good extras like videos and spas in some rooms. The town house next door is a huge spot for a family or two, with three separate storeys to comfortably accommodate larger groups.

TOP END

Powderhorn Chateau (☎ 06-385 8888; www.powderhorn.co.nz; cnr Thames St & Mangawhero Tce; ste/apt $160/600; ☐ ☒ ☒) Looking for a pad fit for a Wellywood superstar? The Powderhorn has a traditional Swiss chalet-style feel with woody interiors, exposed rafters and a notorious reputation for après-ski. The grotto-like indoor pool is a more relaxed way to recover from the slopes before enjoying the bistro or restaurant, the very popular Matterhorn (right). *Lord of the Rings* fans will be thrilled that Peter Jackson bunked down in the split-level Mansion apartment while the hobbits kipped in other rooms.

Eating

The Junction is active during winter with the après-ski crowd, but little is open in summer. Many hotels open their restaurants during the ski season.

Utopia Café (☎ 06-385 9120; 47 Clyde St; mains $12-17; ☒ breakfast, lunch & dinner) With rootsy strumming for a soundtrack, this laid-back place offers decent café fare like bacon and egg pie and an affordable pasta of the day.

Cypress Tree (☎ 06-385 8857; 19a Goldfinch St; mains $18-29; ☒ breakfast, lunch & dinner Fri-Sun) During the days the vibe here can be a little Cypress Hill hip-hop, but in the evenings it's definitely a swanky diner with Mediterranean-influenced dishes like duck parpardelle and gourmet pizzas.

Mountain Kebabs (☎ 06-385 9047; www.mountainkebabs.com; 29 Clyde St; kebabs $7-9; ☒ lunch & dinner winter only) Any old kebabery can come up with the basic lamb, chicken or falafel variety, but seafood, Camembert or olives are rolled in here to make some great kebabs. Open in winter only.

Fat Pigeon Garden Cafe (☎ 06-385 9423; 2 Tyne St; mains $15-25; ☒ breakfast, lunch & dinner) Plump yourself down in this comfy garden setting for a breakfast of mushrooms on ciabatta and you'll find it stretching into a dinner of herb-encrusted lamb rump. Inside is bright with stained-glass windows and a good spot for a lazy coffee.

Mountain Rocks (☎ 07-385 9350; cnr Clyde & Goldfinch Sts; mains $8-25; ☒ breakfast, lunch & dinner) This barnlike place is popular with drinkers, and is known for excellent sandwiches, homemade burgers and heart-starting coffees.

La Pizzeria (☎ 06-385 8558; 6 Thames St; pizzas $12-28; ☒ lunch & dinner) For authentico pizza favourites and a few curveballs (try the smoked salmon with blue cheese), La Pizzeria is the place to head in town.

Alpine Wine Bar & Restaurant (☎ 06-385 9183; cnr Clyde & Miro Sts; starters $9-15, mains $17-24; ☒ dinner) Alpine's wine list is the envy of many places in town, while its cuisine is mainstream (think schnitzels and grilled salmon) with the odd surprise like the ostrich back fillet.

Powderkeg (☎ 06-385 8888; www.powderhorn.co.nz; cnr Thames St & Mangawhero Tce; mains $10-30; ☒ lunch & dinner) offers a versatile bistro menu of pizzas and risottos, while the **Matterhorn** (☎ 06-385 8883; www.powderhorn.co.nz; cnr Thames St & Mangawhero Tce; starters $10-13, mains $20-34; ☒ lunch & dinner) is an upmarket and upstairs dining experience; both are inside the Powderhorn Chateau (left).

Self-caterers should head for **Ohakune New World** (14 Goldfinch St; ☒ 8am-8pm), which is the last chance to stock up before heading for National Pa:k or Whakapapa.

Entertainment

Ohakune is known as a good-fun nightlife place during the ski season; the rest of the year it's quiet. Get hold of the gig guide, which is available from the visitor information centre and most lodges.

Powderkeg (☎ 06-385 8888; www.powderhorn.co.nz; cnr Thames St & Mangawhero Tce) The party bar of the Powderhorn Chateau, with bands in winter and regular dancing on the tables.

Projection Room (☎ 06-385 8864; 4 Thames St; ☒ 6pm-late Wed-Sun) This funky little spot has occasional films and a surprising roll call of international DJs who come to get on the piste.

Ohakune Cinema (☎ 06-385 8488; 17 Goldfinch Street; adults $8) This small cinema shows all the new-release films.

Getting There & Away

InterCity (☎ 09-913 6100) buses serve Ohakune daily except Saturday; buses arrive at and depart from outside Mountain Kebabs (left). The town is on the bus route from Auckland to Wellington via Taumarunui. **Kiwi Traveller** (☎ 0800 500 100; www.kiwitraveller.co.nz)

runs to Wellington and Rotorua from the same bus stop.

Auckland–Wellington **Tranz Scenic trains** (☎ 0800 872 467; www.tranzscenic.co.nz) stop at Ohakune and run via National Park. Buy tickets at the Ruapehu visitor information centre (p322), not at the station.

Getting Around

In winter several companies provide transport between Ohakune and the Turoa Ski Area, offering return door-to-door transport to accommodation.

Matai Shuttles (☎ 06-385 9169; return $15), **Snowliner Shuttle** (☎ 06-385 857; return adult/child $15/8) and **Snow Express** (☎ 06-385 4022; adult $15) offer transport to the slopes and walks along Ohakune Mountain Rd. Matai also offers drop-offs at most walks year-round.

Tongariro Crossing transport is available through Ohakune Top 10 Holiday Park (p324; return ticket $25) or the Ski Shed (p323; return ticket $25).

LAKE ROTOKURA

Just 12km southeast of Ohakune, on SH49, is Lake Rotokura, at Karioi in the Karioi Forest. There are actually two lakes here; locals call them the Karioi Lakes (*karioi* means 'places to linger'). The round-trip **walk** (one hour, 6km) takes you through ancient beech forest while spotting exotic waterfowl like dabchicks and paradise ducks. The top lake is *tapu* (sacred) to Maoris, which prohibits picnicking, fishing or swimming at the lake.

WAIOURU

pop 2600

At the junction of SH1 and SH49, 27km east of Ohakune, Waiouru is primarily an army base. In a large, grey concrete bunker with tanks out the front, the **Army Museum Waiouru** (☎ 06-387 6911; www.armymuseum.co.nz; adult/child $10/7; 9am-4.30pm) tells the history of the NZ army, with extensive collections of arms and uniforms from early colonial times to the present.

SH1 from Waiouru to Turangi is known as the Desert Rd and often closes in winter due to snow. It runs through the Rangipo Desert, east of Ruapehu. It's not a true desert, but was named for the desertlike appearance of this remote and windswept location.

Rotorua & the Bay of Plenty

When Captain Cook christened a place plentiful, he wasn't, oking. Just as when Cook hove into harbour in 1769, the Bay of Plenty remains blessed with a warm and sunny climate and stunning sandy beaches. Europeans may have taken up the many blessings of the Bay (as locals refer to it) to create thriving agriculture like the famous kiwi-fruit industry relatively recently, but Maori have been enjoying the region since the 14th century.

The Bay stretches from the vibrant city of Tauranga in the west all the way round to Opotiki. This is where New Zealanders come to holiday. Along the coast from Tauranga, the superb beaches of Mt Maunganui are a drawcard for surfers, but you can also find quieter stretches of sand to throw a towel over further eastwards. Take advantage of the water sports, including swimming with dolphins and whale-watching. Off Whakatane the moonscape island of New Zealand's most active volcano, Whakaari (White Island), is breathtaking.

Inland there are reminders that the lush landscape was once molten with rich volcanic soil and hills that could have oozed from a volcano just a few months ago. The 'Sulphur City' of Rotorua gives even more insight into what's happening beneath the earth's crust with its thermal springs, dynamic geysers and bubbling mud pools. Hold your nose, though, because the rich scent of sulphur has led some to call it Fartopolis.

Maori have remained close to this *tapu* (sacred) land and Rotorua is a good spot to catch up on Maori heritage. As you're chowing down at a *hangi* (earth oven–cooked meal) perhaps you'll even see the same flourishing villages of friendly Maoris that Cook found here.

HIGHLIGHTS

- Tucking into a Maori *hangi* and taking in a concert at **Tamaki** (p333) or **Mitai** (p333) Maori Villages

- Getting an eyeful and maybe even a mouthful of the world's biggest kiwi fruit at **Kiwi 360** (p359) in Te Puke

- Watching the kaleidoscopic colours swirling at **Waiotapu** (p347)

- Visiting the site of the **Buried Village of Te Wairoa** (p346)

- Taking a downhill tumble inside a zorb at **Zorb Rotorua** (p344) at Agrodome

- Surfing the brand-spanking-new artificial reef at Surf City, **Mt Maunganui** (p354)

- Visiting NZ's most active marine volcano, **Whakaari** (White Island, see p364)

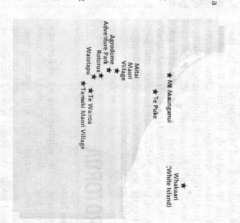

- Agrodome Adventure Park
- Mitai Maori Village
- Rotorua
- Waiotapu
- Te Wairoa
- Tamaki Maori Village
- Mt Maunganui
- Te Puke
- Whakaari (White Island)

TELEPHONE CODE: 07   www.rotoruanz.com   www.bayofplenty.co.nz

Today Maori cultural performances and traditional *hangi* are as big an attraction as the landscape itself.

Despite the ubiquitous rotten-egg odour, the 'Sulphur City' is one of the most touristed spots on the North Island and a perennial favourite with backpackers. Summer is definitely the busiest time of year with international and local visitors swarming to enjoy Lake Rotorua and the many attractions that lie just outside of town.

HISTORY

First settlement of the area was in the 14th century when the canoe *Te Arawa*, captained by Tamatekapua, arrived from Hawaiki at Maketu in the central Bay of Plenty. Settlers took the tribal name Te Arawa to commemorate the vessel that had brought them here. Tamatekapua's grandson, Ihenga, explored much of the inland forest, naming geographical features as he discovered them. Ihenga unimaginatively dubbed the lake Rotorua (or 'Second Lake') as it was the second lake he came across.

In the next few hundred years, subtribes spread and divided through the area with conflicts breaking out over limited territory. A flashpoint occurred in 1823 when the Arawa lands were invaded by tribes from the Northland in the so-called Musket Wars. After heavy losses by both the Arawa and the Northlanders, the Northlanders eventually withdrew.

During the Waikato Land War (1863-67) the Arawa tribe threw in its lot with the government against its traditional Waikato enemies, gaining troop support and pre-

---

ROTORUA & THE BAY OF PLENTY FACTS

Eat: Mint and lamb pie from Maketu (p360)

Drink: Pint of Swine lager, microbrewed at Rotorua's Pig & Whistle (p341)

Read: *Out of the Mist and Steam*, Alan Duff's perspective on childhood in Rotorua

Listen to: That old Maori wedding favourite, 'Pokarekare Ana'

Watch: The film *Crush*, a NZ drama set in Rotorua

Swim at: Ohope Beach (p364)

Festival: Tauranga's Arts Festival (p351)

Tackiest tourist attraction: Titan the Giant Sheep (p344)

Climate

The Bay of Plenty is one of the sunniest regions of NZ, with Whakatane and Eastern Bay recording the most hours of sunshine (2350 per year on average). In summer temperatures hover between 20°C and 27°C while winter sees the mercury fall to as low as 5°C, but it's slightly warmer on the coast. Rainfall is heavier inland in places such as Rotorua, which also experiences long dry spells in summer.

Getting There & Around

Air New Zealand has flights from Tauranga to Auckland and Wellington; from Whakatane to Auckland; and from Rotorua to Auckland, Wellington and Christchurch. Qantas flights connect Rotorua with Christchurch and Queenstown.

InterCity bus services connect Tauranga, Rotorua and Whakatane with most other main cities in NZ. Bay Coaster and Bay Hopper services run between Tauranga, Whakatane and Opotiki.

ROTORUA

pop 76,000

Breathe in the sulphur-rich air of Rotorua and you've already got a taste of NZ's most dynamic thermal area with spurting geysers, steaming hot springs and exploding mud pools. The Maori revered this unique topography, naming one of the most spectacular areas Waiotapu (Sacred Waters).

TOP ACTIVITIES

- Zorbing – the *only* way to travel (p344)
- Surf NZ's first artificial reef: Surf City (p354)
- Swim with dolphins at Tauranga (p349) or Whakatane (p361)
- Check out the riverside scenery while clinging to the side of an inflatable raft (p335)
- Pedal the paths of the Whakarewarewa and redwood forests (p336)

BAY OF PLENTY

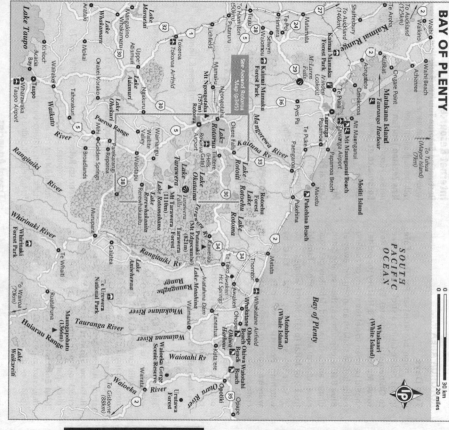

venting East Coast reinforcements getting through to support the Maori King Movement (see the boxed text, p233).

With peace in the early 1870s, European settlement around Rotorua really took off. The army and government personnel involved in the war had excited reports of scenic wonders and miraculous landscapes. People came to take the waters as cures for all manner of diseases, and Rotorua's tourist industry boomed. The town's main attraction was the fabulous Pink and White Terraces, formed by the sinter deposits of silica from volcanic activity. Touted at the time as the eighth natural wonder of the world, the terraces were destroyed in the 1886 Mt Tarawera eruption (see p346).

ORIENTATION

Tutanekai St is the central shopping area with plenty of parking and a pedestrian mall. Running parallel, Fenton St is the major through road and is lined with motels, particularly to the south.

Maps

Map & Track Shop (Map p332; ☎ 07-349 1845; www .mapandtrack.co.nz; 1183 Hinemoa St; ☻ 10am–4pm Mon–Fri) stocks one of the best ranges of maps in the country.

INFORMATION
Bookshops
Mcleods Booksellers (Map p332; ☎ 07-348 5388; 1269 Tutanekai St; ☻ 8.30am-5.30pm Mon-Thu, to 7pm

ROTORUA AREA IN...

Two Days

Grab a huge breakfast at **Fat Dog Café** (p341) before taking a stroll along the lake to **Ohinemutu** (opposite). By then the **Rotorua Museum of Art & History** (opposite) should be open so get the skinny on healing baths before soaking an afternoon away at **Blue Baths** (opposite). In the evening catch dinner and a show (and definitely get your nose rubbed) Maori-style at either **Tamaki** (p333) or **Mitai** (p333) Maori Villages.

Start the second day with a blast by watching **Pohutu** blow at **Te Whakarewarewa** (opposite) before watching Maori craftspeople at work on jade or wood at **Te Puia** (opposite). Get some perspective on the geothermal area with a **scenic flight** (p338) or a gondola ride at **Skyline Skyrides** (p344) before heading back into town for a meal on **Tutanekai St** (p341).

Four Days

Take the two-day itinerary, then use the extra days to explore further afield with a downhill tumble at **Zorb Rotorua** (p344), before dangling with a bungy at **Agrodome Adventures** (p346) or just watching a farm show at the **Agrodome** (p344). Stop in at **Rainbow Springs Nature Park** (p344) to check out a number of rare animals and birds, particularly the national bird at the **Kiwi Encounter Tour** (p344). On your last day, cram in out-of-town visits to **Waiotapu** (p347) or the **Buried Village** (p346).

Internet Resources

Destination Rotorua Tourism Marketing (www.rotoruanz.com/home.asp) Tourism marketing site with thorough information.

New Zealand Tourism (www.tourism.net.nz/region /rotorua) Good for accommodation and sights.

Rotorua.co.nz (www.rotorua.co.nz) Directory of local services.

Medical Services

Central Pharmacy (Map p332; ☎ 07-348 6028; 1245 Haupapa St)

Rotorua Hospital (Map p332; ☎ 07-348 1199; Rangiuru St; ⏱ 24hr)

Money

Most banks have a currency exchange, and there's another at Tourism Rotorua.

ANZ Bank (Map p332; cnr Hinemoa & Amohia Sts)

Bank of New Zealand (Map p332; cnr Fenton & Hinemoa Sts)

Thomas Cook (Map p332; cnr Fenton & Hinemoa Sts)

Post

Post office (Map p332; Hinemoa St) Between Tutanekai and Amohia Sts.

Tourist Information

Automobile Association (AA; Map p332; ☎ 07-348 3069; www.aatravel.co.nz; 1121 Eruera St) Get maps and other travel information here.

Tourism Rotorua (Map p332; ☎ 0800 768 678; www.rotoruanz.com; 1167 Fenton St) Books everything around Rotorua and elsewhere in NZ, with a travel agency. It also has an exchange bureau, a café and other services for travellers, including showers and lockers.

Travel Agencies

Galaxy United Travel (Map p332; ☎ 07-347 9444; cnr Amohau & Hinemoa Sts) Books buses and trains; is an American Express agent.

Travel Smart (Map p332; ☎ 07-349 2000; www.travel smart.co.nz; cnr Eruera & Tutanekai Sts; ⏱ 9am–5pm Mon–Fri, to 1pm Sat) Books flights.

SIGHTS

Lake Rotorua

Lake Rotorua is the largest of 16 lakes in the Rotorua district. It was formed by an eruption and subsequent subsidence of the area. Two cruises on the lake depart from the Rotorua lakefront jetty at the northern end of Tutanekai St.

The **Lakeland Queen paddle steamer** (Map p332; ☎ 0800 862 784; www.lakelandqueen.co.nz; Lakefront

Fri, 9am–4pm Sat, 10am–3pm Sun) Independent bookshop with extensive travel selection.

Whitcoulls (Map p332; ☎ 07-348 3699; 1238 Tutanekai St; ⏱ 8.30am–5pm)

Emergency

Ambulance, fire service & police (☎ 111)

Internet Access

There are plenty of Internet cafés around town including most hostels, all charging around $5 per hour.

Cyber World (Map p332; ☎ 07-348 0088; 1174 Haupapa St)

Cybershed (Map p332; ☎ 07-349 4965; 1176 Pukuatua St)

Fly'n'Net (Map p332; ☎ 07-350 2058; 1128 Hinemoa St)

Memorial Dr) offers one-hour breakfast (adult/child \$40/30), and longer cruises (lunch \$50/30, dinner \$85/50) with the option of seeing an authentic cultural performance on **Mokoia Island** (Map p345).

To explore the lake under your own steam, head for **Hamill Adventures** (Map p332; ☎ 07-348 4186; Lakefront; ☼ 9am-5.30pm wind permitting), which rents out pontoon boats (per hour \$95) and pedal boats (from \$8/5 per adult/child) and kayaks (\$10/35 per 30 minutes/half day). **Mana Adventures** (Map p332; ☎ 07-346 8595; www.manaadventures.co.nz; Lakefront) also has self-drive craft, from pedal boats (per hour adult/child \$8/5) to a small boat (per one/two hours \$80/95).

Ohinemutu

Ohinemutu is a charming lakeside Maori village, which traces the fusing of European and Maori cultures. The historic Maori **St Faith's Anglican Church** (Map p332; Memorial Dr; admission by donation; ☼ 8am-5pm) is intricately decorated with Maori carvings, tukutuku (woven panels), painted scrollwork and stained-glass windows. One window features an image of Christ wearing a Maori cloak as he appears to be walking on the waters of Lake Rotorua.

Opposite the church is **Tamatekapua Meeting House** (Map p332; Memorial Dr), built in 1887 and named for the captain of the Arawa canoe. This sacred meeting house for Arawa people is not open to visitors.

Rotorua Museum of Art & History

This impressive **museum** (Map p332; ☎ 07-349 4350; www.rotoruanz.com/rotorua_museum; Government Gardens; adult/child/family incl Blue Baths museum \$11/5/25; ☼ 9am-5pm Apr-Sep, tours 9.30am, 11am, 1pm, 2.30pm & 4pm) is in a grand mock-Tudor edifice originally constructed as an elegant spa retreat in 1908. Displays in the former shower rooms offer an insight into the eccentric therapies once practised here, including exposure to radium as a cure for gout and running an electrical current through baths as a treatment for 'nervous exhaustion'. You can wander into the basement (hard hats provided) for a glimpse of the complex piping system that became 'a maintenance nightmare' with so many corrosive and mineral-rich waters passing through it.

The museum collects the taonga (treasures) of the Arawa people, including traditional handicrafts such as woodcarving, flax weaving and jade. Other exhibitions relate the stories of the WWII 28 Maori Battalion, a military unit formed of local Arawa people, and the disastrous 1886 Mt Tarawera eruption, including survivors' stories. A gripping 20-minute film on the history of Rotorua, including the eruption (accompanied by shuddering seats), runs every 20 minutes in a small theatre just off reception. Other galleries host temporary exhibitions and there's also a pleasant café with picturesque garden views.

In the **Government Gardens** around the museum are typical English touches such as croquet lawns, bowling greens and rose beds, as well as steaming thermal pools. If you fancy a game of **bowls** (☎ 025 245 4433; 30min/1hr \$15/20; ☼ 4.30-6.30pm Mon-Wed, 9am-5.30pm Thu-Sun), reservations are essential, or you can take a whack at croquet (per half/full day \$3/6; inc Rotorua Museum of Art & History \$11/5/25; ☼ 10am-5pm) were opened in 1933 with gorgeous Spanish Mission–style baths and pools for holidaymakers. Today you can visit a small museum recalling the building's heyday, with recorded anecdotes and displays in the old changing rooms. If it all makes you feel like taking a dip yourself, there's a modern heated pool (adult/child \$7/4).

Nearby the **Blue Baths** (Map p332; adult/child/family

Te Whakarewarewa & Te Puia

Pronounced 'fa-ka-re-wa-re-wa' but mostly just called 'Whaka', Rotorua's largest and best-known thermal reserve doubles as a major Maori cultural area. If you're keen to stick with formalities, the area's full name is Te Whakarewarewatanga o te Ope Taua a Wahiao, meaning 'The Gathering Together of the War Party of Wahiao'.

Entry to Whaka's geyser area is through **Te Puia** (Map p345; ☎ 07-348 9047; www.tepuia.com; Hemo Rd; adult/child \$25/13, hangi \$80/45, hangi & tours \$95/52; ☼ 8.15am-5.15pm winter, 8am-6pm summer), an artist's workshop for many traditional Maori weavers, wood and greenstone carvers with tours detailing each process. You can observe some of their handiworks at the on-site Rotowhio Marae, which was built right here and is central to the daily Maori concerts and nightly hangi. The souvenir shop here has an excellent range of wood, paua shell and greenstone carvings, plus traditional clothing like korowai (cloak).

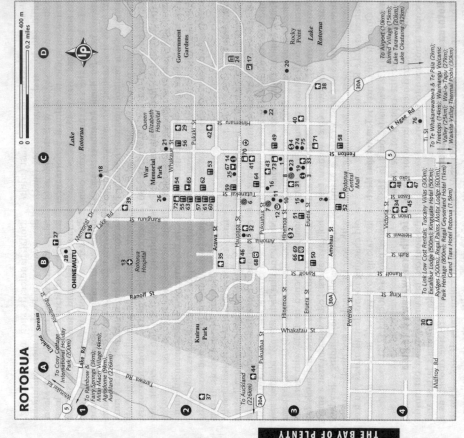

ROTORUA

www.lonelyplanet.com

But for many the main event is the spectacular geysers. The most famous is **Pohutu** ('Big Splash' or 'Explosion'), an active geyser that erupts between 10 and 20 times a day. Pohutu spurts hot water more than 20m into the air with an average eruption lasting about five to 10 minutes. You get a warning because the **Prince of Wales' Feathers** geyser always starts shortly before Pohutu.

Whakarewarewa Thermal Village (☎ 07-349 3463; www.whakarewarewa.com; Tryon St; adult/child incl tours & concerts $53/21/120; ☒ 8.30am-5pm, tours 9am-4pm, concerts 11.15am & 2pm) is on the eastern side of Whaka. The meeting house hosts concerts and there are guided tours through the smouldering village every hour. There's plenty of thermal activity in the village but

no access to the geysers. Whaka is 3km south of the city centre, straight down Fenton St. City buses drop you near Tryon St.

Want some cheap thermal thrills? Close to the centre of Rotorua is **Kuirau Park**, a volcanic area that you can wander around for free. Its most recent eruption in late 2003 covered much of the park (including the trees) in mud, drawing crowds of spectators hoping for more displays. It has a crater lake, pools of boiling mud, plenty of huffing steam and mineral baths for dipping.

Maori Concerts & Hangi

Maori culture is a major drawcard in Rotorua and, although some find it heavily commercialised, it's a great opportunity to

INFORMATION
Air New Zealand..........................1 C3
ANZ Bank..................................2 B3
Automobile Association...................3 C3
Bank of New Zealand......................4 C2
Central Pharmacy.........................5 B3
Cyber World..............................6 C3
Cybershed................................7 C3
DOC...................................(see 24)
Fly'n Net................................8 C3
Galaxy United Trave......................9 C2
Map & Track Shop........................10 C3
McLeods Booksellers.....................11 C3
Money Changing Bureau................(see 14)
Post Office.............................12 C3
Rotorua Hospital........................13 B1
Thomas Cook.............................14 C2
Tourism Rotorua......................(see 1)
Travel Agency........................(see 14)
Travel Smart............................15 C3
Whitcoulls..............................16 C3

SIGHTS & ACTIVITIES
Blue Baths..............................17 D3
Climbing Wall........................(see 31)
Hamill Adventures....................(see 18)
Kawarau Jet Boating..................(see 18)
Lady Jane's Ice Cream
  Parlour............................(see 54)
Lakeland Queen Paddle
  Steamer...............................18 C1
Mana Adventures......................(see 18)
Map & Track Shop.....................(see 10)
O'Keefe's...............................19 C3
Planet Bike..........................(see 31)
Polynesian Spa..........................20 D3
QE Health...............................21 C2
Realm of Tane...........................22 C3

Rotorua Cycle Centre....................23 C3
Rotorua Lakes Cruises................(see 18)
Rotorua Museum of Art &
  History...............................24 D2
Rotorua Public Library..................25 C2
Royal Lakes de Novotel Hotel............26 C2
St Faith's Anglican Church..............27 B1
Tamatekapua Meeting House...............28 B1

SLEEPING 🛏
Ambassador Thermal Motel................29 C2
Ann's Volcanic Rotorua..................30 A4
Base Backpackers Rotorua................31 C3
Cactus Jacks............................32 B3
Crash Palace............................33 C3
Funky Green Voyager.....................34 C4
Hot Rock................................35 B2
Jack & Di's Lake Rd Lodge...............36 B1
Kiwi Paka YHA...........................37 A2
Lake Plaza Rotorua......................38 D3
Ledwich Lodge Motel.....................39 C1
Millennium...........................(see 38)
Millennium..............................40 C2
Planet Nomad Backpackers................41 C2
Princes Gate Hotel......................42 C3
Rotorua Central Backpackers.............43 C3
Rotorua Top 10 Holiday Park.............44 A3
Six on Union............................45 C4
Treks Rotorua Backpackers...............46 B3
Tresco B&B..............................47 C4
Victoria Lodge..........................48 C2

EATING 🍴
Amazing Thai............................49 C3
Bistro 1284.............................50 B3
Capers Epicurean........................51 B3
Countdown...............................52 C2
Fat Dog Café............................53 C2
Lady Jane's Ice Cream
  Parlour...............................54 C2
Lewisham's Restaurant...................55 C2
Lime....................................56 C2
Lovely India............................57 C3
Nikau................................(see 40)
Pak N Save..............................58 C2
Pig & Whistle...........................59 C3
Relish..................................60 C2
River Monster...........................61 C2
Wellin's Noodle House...................62 C3
Zambique................................63 C3
Zippy Central...........................64 C3

DRINKING 🍸
Echo.................................(see 31)
Fuze....................................65 C3
Lava Bar.............................(see 35)
O'Malley's..............................66 B3
Pheasant Plucker........................67 C2

ENTERTAINMENT 🎭
Bar Barella.............................68 B3
Basement Cinema......................(see 31)
Princes Gate Hotel...................(see 42)
Reading Cinema..........................69 B3

SHOPPING 🛍
Best of Maori Tourism...................70 C3
Jade Factory............................71 C3
Madhouse Design.........................72 C3
Souvenir Centre.........................73 C3

TRANSPORT
Budget..................................74 C3
Bus Depot............................(see 14)
Link Low Cost Rentals...................75 C2
Rent-a-Dent.............................76 C4

learn more about Aotearoa's (Land of the Long White Cloud) original culture. The two big activities are concerts and *hangi*, with combinations that encourage audience participation and more than a few laughs.

By the end of the evening, you'll probably have been dragged up on stage, experienced a Maori *hongi* (nose-to-nose contact), and joined hands for a group sing-along. Other features of a Maori concert are *poi* dances (where women twirl balls of woven flax with impressive speed and agility) and dramatic *haka* (war dances) – expect tongue poking! These performances are described more thoroughly in the Maori Culture section (p59).

There are plenty of options to catch a concert and *hangi*. Whakarewarewa Thermal Village (see opposite) puts them on nightly, plus its year-round midday concert (included with admission) is great for busy people.

An established favourite is **Tamaki Maori Village** (Map p345; ☎ 07-346 2823; www.maoriculture .co.nz; SHS; adult/child $85/45; ☿ tours depart 5pm, 6pm & 7pm summer, 5pm & 7pm winter), which does an excellent Twilight Cultural Tour to a *marae* (meeting house) and Maori village complex 15km south of Rotorua. Buses collect from accommodation and feature a briefing on traditional protocol required to visit a *marae* by a Maori 'entertainer' (aka hilarious bus driver). The concert is followed by a meat-heavy *hangi*.

Buses also collect from the Tamaki building in town, which hosts the **Realm of Tane** (Map p332; ☎ 07-346 2823; 1220 Hinemaru St; admission $30; ☿ shows 4pm & 6pm), a theatre-video show that interactively recounts the Maori settlement story.

The newest *hangi* and concert is **Mitai Maori Village** (Map p345; ☎ 07-343 9132; www.mitai .co.nz; 196 Fairy Springs Rd; concert & *hangi* adult/child $75/35; ☿ concerts 6.30pm & 8.30pm, tours 8.30am-6pm) with guided bush walks that include Maori mythology, medicine and cuisine, plus a peek at the glow-worms. The *hangi* and concert are very popular. Pick-ups are available.

Another good outfit is **Rotoiti Tours** (☎ 07-348 8969; www.worldofmaori.co.nz; Rakeiao Marae; adult/child $80/40; ☻ 6.30pm). Based near Lake Rotoiti (Map p345), it will do pick-ups from most Rotorua hotels.

Many of the big hotels offer Maori concerts and *hangi*, making up for what they lack in ambience with convenience.

Some of the main venues:

Grand Tiara Hotel Rotorua (☎ 07-349 5200; Fenton St; concerts adult/child $26/13, incl hangi $52/26; ☻ 7pm)

Kingsgate Hotel (☎ 07-348 0199; Fenton St; concerts adult/child $21/10.50, incl hangi $42/21; ☻ 6.45pm)

Lake Plaza Rotorua (Map p332; ☎ 0800 801 440; www.lakeplazahotel.co.nz; 1000 Eruera St; concerts adult/child $24.75/12.40, incl hangi $55/27.50; ☻ 6.30pm)

Millennium (Map p332; ☎ 07-347 1234; cnr Eruera & Hinemaru Sts; concerts adult/child $30/15, incl hangi $60/30; ☻ 6.30pm)

Park Heritage (☎ 07-348 1189; cnr of Froude & Iryon St; concerts & hangi adult/child $65/32.50; ☻ 7pm)

Royal Lakeside Novotel Hotel (Map p332; ☎ 07-346 3888; Tutanekai St; concerts adult/child $25/12.50, incl hangi $52/26; ☻ 7pm)

ACTIVITIES
Thermal Pools & Massage
The popular **Polynesian Spa** (Map p332; ☎ 07-348 1328; www.polynesianspa.co.nz; off Hinemoa St; pools main adults only $15, private adult/child per 30min $12/4, massage & spa therapies from $70; ☻ 6.30am-11pm, last tickets 10.15pm, spa therapies 9am-9pm) is in the Government Gardens. A bathhouse was opened at these springs in 1886 and people have been swearing by the health-giving properties of the waters ever since.

Today the baths offer combinations of massage and beauty treatments including Aix massage (a hydrotherapy treatment) and mud spa treatments. The modern complex has several pools at the lake's edge that range in temperature from 36°C to 43°C, and a main pool at 38°C. Remember that silver instantly blackens on contact with the water, so be sure to remove silver jewellery.

For a more medicinal dip, **QE Health** (Map p332; ☎ 07-348 0189; www.qehealth.co.nz; cnr Whakaue & Lake Sts; massage 30 min/1hr from $50/70, mud bath $45; ☻ 8am-10pm Mon-Fri, 9am-10pm Sat & Sun) offers massages, cleansing and nourishing mud baths, or simple baths in spring water from nearby Rachel Spring.

There are two open-air natural pools with medicinal mineral waters (39°C plus) at the **Waikite Valley Thermal Pools** (Map p345; ☎ 07-333 1861; public pools adult/child $6/3, private pools per 40 min $10; ☻ 10am-10pm). To get there, go 30km south on State Highway 5 (SH5) to a signposted turn-off opposite the Waiotapu turn-off. The pools are another 6km down this road.

For a hot water dip visit **Kerosene Creek** (Map p345), 16km out on SH5. Turn left on the unsealed Old Waiotapu Rd and follow it for 2km. This is one of the few places where the public can bathe in natural thermal pools for free.

Walking
There are plenty of opportunities to stretch your legs around Rotorua, with fun day walks a speciality. Check in at the **Map & Track Shop** (Map p332; ☎ 07-349 1845; www.mapandtrack.co.nz; 1183 Hinemoa St; ☻ 10am-4pm Mon-Fri) for pamphlets and maps outlining walks in the area. The Department of Conservation (DOC) booklet *Walks in the Rotorua Lakes Area* ($2.50) was updated in 2005 and details the best walks in the area, while the Rotorua District Council's *Rotorua Walkways* leaflet showcases town walks including the popular lakefront stroll (20 minutes).

All these walks are shown on the map on p345.

The area around **Lake Okataina** offers some great walks, particularly the **Western Okataina Walkway** (seven hours, 22.5km), which takes in lake views and a dry crater known as the 'Bullring'. The track is not for beginners, and runs from Millar Rd at Lake Okareka to Ruato on Lake Rotoiti with public transport past the Ruato only end.

The **Eastern Okataina Walkway** (Map p345, three hours, 10.5km) goes along the eastern shoreline of Lake Okataina to Lake Tarawera and passes **Soundshell** (Map p345), a natural amphitheatre that has a *pa* (fortified Maori village) remains, and several swimming spots. The **Northern Tarawera Track** (Map p345, three hours one way, 6km) connects to the walkway creating a two-day walk from either Lake Okataina or Ruato to Lake Tarawera with an overnight camp at either **Humphries Bay** (Map p345; sites free) or **Tarawera Outlet** (Map p345; sites $10). From Tarawera Outlet you can walk on to Tarawera Falls (see p365).

The **Okere Falls** (Map p345) are about 16km northeast of Rotorua on SH33, with an easy

HINEMOA & TUTANEKAI

NZ's own Romeo and Juliet story is actually true, with descendants of Hinemoa and Tutanekai still living around Rotorua today.

Hinemoa was a young woman of a subtribe that lived on the western shore of Lake Rotorua. Tutanekai was a young man of the subtribe that lived on Mokoia Island. The pair met during a regular subtribe meeting, but although both were of high birth, Tutanekai was illegitimate and so, while Hinemoa's family thought he was a fine young man, they weren't in favour of them marrying.

At night Tutanekai would play his flute on the island, and sometimes the wind would carry his melody across the water to Hinemoa. In his music she could hear his declaration of love for her. Her people took to tying up canoes at night to ensure she wouldn't go to him.

Finally, Tutanekai's music won her over and Hinemoa undressed and swam the long distance from the shore to the island. When she arrived on Mokoia, Hinemoa was in a quandary. She had to shed her clothing in order to swim, but she could scarcely walk into the island's settlement naked! She sought refuge in a hot pool to figure out what to do next.

Eventually a man came to fetch water from a cold spring beside the hot pool. In a deep man's voice, Hinemoa called out, 'Who is it?' The man replied that he was Tutanekai's slave, come to get water. Hinemoa grabbed the slave's calabash gourd and smashed it. A few more slaves came only to have their gourds broken in the dark, until finally Tutanekai had to come out to the pool and demand that the interloper identify himself. He was amazed when it turned out to be Hinemoa.

Tutanekai stole Hinemoa into his hut. In the morning, when Tutanekai was sleeping very late, a slave came to wake him and returned with reports of someone else sleeping in Tutanekai's bed. The two lovers emerged, and when Hinemoa's superhuman efforts to reach Tutanekai had been revealed, their union was celebrated.

track (30 minutes, 1.2km) through native podocarp forest to the 7m falls, which are popular for rafting. Other walks continue up the Kaituna River to the lookout at **Hinemoa's Steps** (Map p345) and to some caves.

Just north of Waiotapu on SH5, the **Rainbow Mountain Track** (Map p345, 1½ hours, 2.5km) makes for a strenuous walk up to the summit of the peak known to Maori as Maungakaramea (or 'Mountain of coloured earth'). There are spectacular views from the summit with a panorama that takes in Lake Taupo, Tongariro National Park and the Paeroa Range.

White-Water Rafting & Sledging

Thrillseekers can find plenty of white-water action around Rotorua with the chance to take on the Grade V Kaituna River, with the 3m drop at Okere Falls a highlight. Most of these trips take a day, but times are often negotiable. Some companies head further out to the Rangitaiki (Grade V) and Wairoa River (Grade IV-V), which is only raftable when the dam is opened every second Sunday. Check visitors centres for dates.

You can also try the latest Kiwi craze in watersports: white-water sledging, where you zoom downriver on a sledge designed for manoeuvrability.

Good local companies:

Kaitiaki Adventures (☎ 0800 338 735, 07-357 2236; www.raft-it.com) Offers white-water rafting trips on the Kaituna ($115) and Wairoa ($80) with sledge-raft combos on the Kaituna ($170) as well as zorb and swoop packages ($99 each).

Kaituna Cascades (☎ 0800 524 8862; www.kaituna cascades.co.nz) Does rafting on the Kaituna ($68), Rangitiaki ($95) and Wairoa ($80) with longer trips to the Motu River (see p371).

Raftabout (☎ 0800 723 822; www.raftabout.co.nz) Does rafting on the Kaituna ($75) and Wairoa ($95) with sledging on the Kaituna ($99).

River Rats (☎ 0800 333 900; www.riverrats.co.nz) Takes on the Rangitaiki ($95) and Wairoa Rivers ($99), as well as the Kaituna ($85).

Wet 'n' Wild Rafting (☎ 0800 462 7238; www.wetn wildrafting.co.nz) Offers day trips to Kaituna ($79) as well as helicopter access trips to remote parts of the Motu (two days $590) and Mohaka (four days $700).

Whitewater Excitement Co (☎ 07-349 2858; www .raftnz.co.nz) Organises rafting trips on the Rangitaiki ($95) and Wairoa ($80).

Fishing

With so many lakes around Rotorua, there's always good fishing somewhere near town. You can hire guides to trout fish or go solo, but either way a licence (per day/week/season $18/34/90) is essential; they're available from **O'keefe's** (Map p332; ☎ 07-346 0178; 1113 Eruera St) and the **Map & Track Shop** (Map p332; ☎ 07-349 1845; 1183 Hinemoa St).

You can fish Rotorua's lakefront with a licence, though not all lakes can be fished year-round; check with Tourism Rotorua (see p330).

Some recommended guides:

Clark Gregor (☎ 07-347 1123; fish@troutnz.co.nz; per hr $95) Does boat fishing and trawling.

Gordon Randle (☎ 07-349 2555; troutfishing@xtra.co.nz; per day $500) Does river fishing with gear and lunch supplied.

Trout Connection (☎ 07-349 2385; glen@troutconnection.co.nz; per day $500) Specialises in boat-based fly-fishing.

Other Watersports

The waters are being plied in every imaginable way around Rotorua. **Adventure Kayaking** (☎ 07-348 9451; www.adventurekayaking.co.nz; hire per day $40, trips half/full day from $55/110) takes trips on Lakes Rotorua, Rotoiti, Tarawera and Okataina; and also rents kayaks. **Kaituna Kayaks** (☎ 0800 465 292; www.kaitunakayaks.com; lessons half/full day $130/240) offers kayaking lessons with locals on the Kaituna.

Speed it up jetboating with **Kawarau Jet Boating** (☎ 07-343 7600; www.kjet.co.nz; Lakefront Memorial Dr; 30min/2½hr $59/89), which tears around Lake Rotorua and includes tours of Mokoia in some packages. Around 41km away, **NZ River Jet** (☎ 07-333 7111; www.riverjet.co.nz; Homestead Rd; 2½hr $125) whips down the Waikato to Orakei Korako (see p308).

Mana Adventures (Map p332; ☎ 07-346 8595; Lakefront, Memorial Dr; www.manaadventures.co.nz) offers self-drive boating experiences on the lake from pedal boats (adult/child $8/5) to a small boat (per one/two hours $80/95). Its guided land and *waka* tour (adult/child $25/15, 45 minutes) lets you paddle a genuine Maori canoe followed by a guided tour.

Cycling

Whakarewarewa State Forest Park (see p346) has some of the best **mountain bike trails** in the country. There are 10 tracks within the nearby redwood forest that will keep mountain bikers of all skill levels happy. **Planet Bike** (Map p332; ☎ 07-348 9971; www.planetbike.co.nz; 1140 Hinemoa St; bikes per 2hr/day $30/50, guided rides 2hr/half day $60/100) hires out bikes with drop-offs and pick-ups, plus it organises guided rides. For more information about the forest contact the **Fletcher Challenge Forests Visitor Information Centre** (Map p345; ☎ 07-346 2082; 8.30am-6pm Mon-Fri, to 5pm Apr-Sep; 10am-4pm Sat & Sun) in the forest.

To explore Rotorua on two wheels you can hire a bike from **Lady Jane's Ice Cream Parlour** (Map p332; ☎ 07-347 9340; cnr Tutanekai & Whakaue Sts; per hr/day $10/25; noon-6.30pm) and the **Rotorua Cycle Centre** (Map p332; ☎ 07-348 6588; 1120 Hinemoa St; mountain bikes per hr/day $15/50; 9am-5pm Mon-Fri, to 4pm Sat & Sun). 'City bikes' (road bikes) cost around $25 a day.

Other Activities

Rotorua has still more ways to get your adrenaline pumping. For a bit of indoor exercise try the **climbing wall** (Map p332; ☎ 07-350 1400; thewall1140@hotmail.com; 1140 Hinemoa St; admission $14; noon-late Mon-Fri, 10am-late Sat, to 8pm Sun). It also organises full-day outdoor climbing trips ($100); bookings are essential.

There's no better birds-eye view of the lakes and volcanoes than from a tandem skydive with **NZOne** (☎ 0800 376 796; www.nzone.biz; dives $245-395), which takes dives from 9000ft or 12,000ft, leaving from Rotorua Airport.

The forests around Rotorua are made for idyllic horse trekking, with operators including **Farmhouse** (Map p345; ☎ 07-332 3771; per hr $30), northeast of Lake Rotorua, and **Peka** (Map p345; ☎ 07-346 1755; treks 30min/1hr $30/50) guiding riders through the Peka forest south of Rotorua.

Off Road NZ (Map p345; ☎ 07-332 5748; www.offroadnz.co.nz; 193 Amoore Rd) is the place for self-drive tours through bush, 20km north of Rotorua. You can zip through the bush in a 4WD ($80 per hour), or steer 'monster trucks' ($35) and sprint cars ($30) through purpose-built courses. It also offers clay-pigeon shooting ($18 for five shots) and archery ($15 for 10 arrows).

Mountain Action (Map p345; ☎ 0800 682 284; www.mountainaction.co.nz; Fairy Springs Rd) offers a wide range of activities including karts (two-seater dune buggy, per half-/one hour $55/90), horse treks (half-hour/hour $35/60), paintball ($40) and rides in the Argo, an eight-wheel, all-terrain amphibious vehicle (from $10). Kids are also well catered for, with a petting zoo. This is also home to **Dirtbike Tour** (☎ 027 2883 243; www.puredirttours.co.nz; hire from $280) which roars through the local scenery on 50cc to 160cc motorbikes.

Action New Zealand (Map p345; ☎ 07-348 3531; www.action-nz.co.nz; cnr Te Ngae Rd & Sala St) has a wacky array of activities, mostly aimed at the corporate 'team-building' market who would like to do physical harm to each other but instead try axe-and-knife throwing ($10), archery ($10 for 10 arrows), bull-whip-cracking ($10), pistol-shooting ($10) and electronic clay-target shooting ($10), and shooting a red laser at a disc. Less violent types can try the mechanical bull ($10).

WALKING TOUR

Start Rotorua Museum
Finish visitors centre
Distance 2.9km

Start out in the morning from **Rotorua Museum of Art & History** (1; p331), once a bathhouse for the rich and famous, which remains the town's most impressive building. Follow the road west through the exquisite Government Gardens, which conclude at Princes Gate Arches. Heading through the arch you'll see a grand structure on the right; **Princes Gate Hotel** (2; p340), which was moved here in the 1920s from Waihi.

Follow this street down to the roundabout before heading right down Lake St, towards (unsurprisingly) the lake. Head left before you hit the water and walk alongside black swans (which have been known to nip tourists) and the glittering lake. The road veers away from the water onto Memorial Dr, which in turn takes you to the old Maori village of Ohinemutu with its intricately carved **Tamatekapua Meeting House** (3; p331) and **St Faith's Anglican Church** (4; p331), which combines Christian and Maori traditions.

Double back to Lake Rd and head right up the hill for a stroll to Kuirau Park, the town centre volcanic area that simmers and

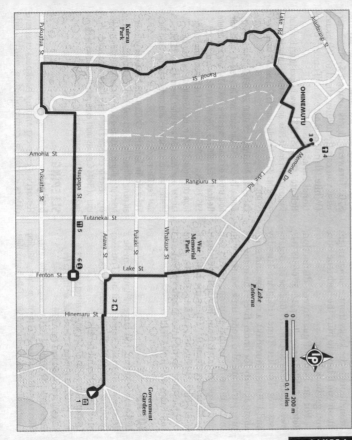

boils away. You'll really get a noseful of sulphur here! Once you're done exploring, turn left into Pukuatua St then left again to get you into Haupapa St. Head up this street passing the dining strip of Tutanekai, marked by the old police station, now the **Pig & Whistle (5;** p341) – have you earned yourself a drink yet? Keep on up Haupapa St to the mock-Tudor **visitors centre (6;** p330) and stock up on maps and pamphlets to explore further.

ROTORUA FOR CHILDREN

With all those activities and geothermal gimmicks, Rotorua is bound to be a hit with kids. Many of the geothermal areas like Waiotapu and Whaka have pram-able boardwalks, so bring the stroller for when little legs get tired.

You can save kids' feet with a gondola ride at **Skyline Skyrides** (p344), though teenagers will want to take on the luge. A unique and comfortable way to see the sites on land and water is to take a **DuckTour** (right), which will incite giggles from younger kids. **Maori concerts** (p332) with their sing-alongs and accompanying actions are made for children, though the kicks from a *hangi* might mean you'll have to bury the barbecue once you get back home.

For an hour of guaranteed distraction, **Rotorua Public Library** (Map p332; ☎ 07-348 4177; www.rotorualibrary.govt.nz; 1127 Haupapa St) organises free Toddler Time (10.30am Tuesday and 1.30pm Thursday), a reading and singalong activity for under-fives. The many nature parks are also good time wasters with many offering animal-patting, or you can rent a pedal boat from **Hammill Adventures** or **Mana Adventures** (p330) at the Lakefront. If all else fails you can threaten to strap troublesome teens into a **zorb** (p344) and roll them down the hill!

TOURS

If Rotorua seems too large, a tour can be a great way to make sense of it all. Tourism Rotorua (see p330) books most tours, as do most hostels and hotels.

Carlton Tours (☎ 07-544 4800; carltontours@xtra.co
nz; ☒ departs Rotorua 6.30am) Does ski trips to Mt
Ruapehu and Whakapapa (from $95).
Geyserlink (☎ 0800 000 4321; www.geyserlink.co.nz)
Offers excellent tours of most of the major sights, including
Waiotapu and Te Puia (adult/child $80/40, 4½ hours), Hells

Gate (adult/child $40/20, 2½ hours) and Rainbow Springs,
Agrodome, Skyline and Te Puia (per day adult/child
$145/70).
Jayzwayz Random Tours (☎ 0275 789 369;
www.randomadventures.co.nz; half/full day $40/65) Does
idiosyncratic walks up to Rainbow Mountain with a
swim in Kerosene Creek. Picks up from all the hostels.
Mt Tarawera New Zealand Ltd (☎ 07-349 3714;
www.mt-tarawera.co.nz) Organises guided half-day 4WD
tours to the top of Mt Tarawera ($121) as well as helicopter
landings on the summit ($415) and the Volcanic Eco Tour,
which combines the 4WD trip with Waiotapu and Waimangu ($210).

Newmans Coach Lines (☎ 07-343 1730; www
.newmanscoach.co.nz; adult/child from $96/68) Does
the rounds of the sights with hotel pick-up.
Rotorua Duck Tours (☎ 07-345 6522; www.rotorua
ducktours.co.nz; adult/child/family $58/35/139; ☒ 11am,
1pm & 3.30pm summer, 11am & 2.15pm winter) A unique
amphibious trip that departs from the visitors centre, taking
in the major sites of town then heads out onto the lake.

Scenic Flights

There's no better way to see the swirling colours of the thermal regions and the beauty of the lake than to fly over them. Flights over the city and the lake start at around $70, Tarawera flights around $150. Otherwise you can fly further afield to Whakaari (White Island) and across to Tongariro National Park.

Heli-pro (☎ 07-357 2512; www.helipro.co.nz) Based at
Rainbow Farm and Te Puia, does a variety of trips including
city flights ($85), Mokoia Island ($225) and Mt Tarawera
($300).
Lakeside Aviation (☎ 0800 535 363; Rotorua Airport;
30min/1hr $95/190) Can coast over Tarawera in a quick half-
hour trip or do a more extensive look at the lake and around.
Redcat (☎ 0800 733 228; www.redcat.co.nz; flights
$95-280) Is a 1950s Grumman Ag Cat biplane; trips range
from city flights ($100) to the 45-minute 'sulphur spec-
tacular' over Waiotapu and other thermal areas ($300).
Leather jackets, silk scarves and goggles are provided for
that Red Baron look.
Volcanic Air Safaris (☎ 0800 800 848; www.volcanic
air.co.nz; 10min/3hr flights $60/785) Has floatplane and
helicopter flights, including a combined flight and jetboat
experience or combined helicopter flight and guided
tour of Hell's Gate. Its most expensive flight takes in Mt
Tarawera and the crater lakes.

SLEEPING
Budget

Rotorua's ever-expanding backpacker scene offers cheap accommodation with loads of extras, mainly drink cards or meal vouchers.

Cactus Jacks (Map p332; ☎ 07-348 3121; www.cactusjackbackpackers.co.nz; 1210 Haupapa St; dm/s/d/tw $17/32/32/20) If you're looking for character, partner, then this Western-themed spot is just your gunfight. Rooms range from jail (dorms) to Madam Fifi's bordello (oddly two twins), and although older they're well kept. Sociable staff, a saloon, laundry and undercover thermal pool make it an ideal spot for weary cowpokes.

Treks Rotorua Backpackers (Map p332; ☎ 0508 487 357; www.treks.co.nz; 1278 Haupapa St; dm/tw $24/68, d $58-68; ☐ ☐) Bright and shinily new, this spotlessly clean and well-maintained hostel is a welcome addition to the RotoVegas hostelling scene. Outdoorsy owners specialise in organising off-the-beaten-track walks, plus there's storage for bikes and kayaks. Pricier rooms come with en suites.

KiwiPaka YHA (Map p332; ☎ 07-347 0931; www.kiwipaka-yha.co.nz; 60 Tarewa Rd; sites per 2 people $18, dm/s/d from $24/40/56; ☐ ☐) Away from the action (1km from town with a regular shuttle), this YHA hostel attracts older backpackers with its range of accommodation from a few tent sites to plain four-bed dorms to pine chalet-style doubles. It has the Twisted Pippie café and a bar with tastings of NZ beer, wine and cheese, as well as meals, which makes for a good deal.

Rotorua Central Backpackers (Map p332; ☎ 07-349 3285; 10 Pukuatua St; dm/d/tw $20/46/46; ☐) This heritage hostel was built in 1936 and retains historic features including dark-wood skirting boards and door frames, deep bathtubs and geothermal radiators. Dorms are no more than six beds, plus there's a spa pool and barbecue, all within strolling distance of the museum. The noticeboard is renowned as a place for getting work around town.

Base Backpackers Rotorua (Map p332; ☎ 07-350 2040; www.basebackpackers.com; 1140 Hinemoa St; dm/d from $24/54; ☐) Possibly the brightest star in the Base Backpackers universe, with generous rooms and communal areas. The female-only area, Sanctuary, and individual lockers under each bed show security smarts. Bonus facilities like bike hire, a bar and, unbelievably, a climbing wall-cum-cinema all make for a top stay.

Funky Green Voyager (Map p332; ☎ 07-346 1754; 4 Union St; dm/d from $20/46; ☐) Okay, so it's green because of the gardeny courtyard complete with rotunda, funky for little touches like music playing (and occasional jams with the owners) and lollies on your pillow when you arrive, but as one of Rotorua's best hostels this 'voyager' isn't leaving its residential neighbourhood anytime soon. The best doubles have bay windows and their own en suites, while dorms are roomy. Bike hire is a bonus.

Hot Rock (Map p332; ☎ 07-348 8636; hotrock@acb.co.nz; 1286 Arawa St; dm/s/d from $20/50/60; ☐ ☐) This huge hostel is ever popular with partying backpackers who love the Lava Bar ('Be a Lava not a fighter') which has drink vouchers and theme nights. Rooms can be tight, with eight bunks in some dorms, but extras like thermal pools, laundry and a café compensate.

Cosy Cottage International Holiday Park (☎ 0800 222 424; www.cosycottage.co.nz; 67 Whittaker Rd; unpowered/powered sites per 2 people $28/30, d units/cottages $65/85; ☐) With hedges between camp sites, you'll feel like you've got this green park on the Utuhina stream all to yourself. Thanks to the miracle of geothermal activity, sites are thermally heated, the beach is heated, a hangi cooker is heated with natural steam and hot mineral pools soothe at 40°C.

Rotorua Top 10 Holiday Park (Map p332; ☎ 07-348 1886; www.rotoruatop10.co.nz; 1495 Pukuatua St; sites per 2 people $32, d cabins/studio/motel $55/70/87) This newish park has cabins with well-preserved 1990s furniture and kitchens with bar fridges and microwaves. Powered sites are popular with Britz vans and there are young shrubs dividing each area and individual picnic benches.

Also recommended:

Crash Palace (Map p332; ☎ /fax 07-348 8842; www.crashpalace.co.nz; 1271 Hinemaru St; dm/d from $18/45; ☐) A sociable hostel with a small but well-stocked kitchen, a relaxing garden area, spa pool and lounge with pool table.

Planet Nomad Backpackers (Map p332; ☎ 07-346 2831; www.planetnomad.co.nz; 1193 Fenton St; dm/d from $21/47; ☐) Handily located and well set up, this friendly spot has bright rooms, a large lounge and plenty of activities on offer.

Midrange

Generic motels crowd Fenton St, but better and often more interesting rooms can be found away from the main drag.

Jack & Di's Lake Road Lodge (Map p332; ☎ 0800 522 526; www.jackanddis.co.nz; 21 Lake Rd; s/d/apt $99/117/250)

Lakeside views and a city-but-secluded location make this boutique hotel an excellent option. The upstairs penthouse is ideal for couples, while downstairs is better for families or groups. A spa pool, lazy lounge areas and help-yourself kitchens all add to the appeal.

Ann's Volcanic Rotorua (Map p332; ☎ 0800 768 683; www.rotoruamotel.co.nz; 107 Malfroy Rd; d/f $70/90) Ann's is a unique and affordable motel that has family charm (some rooms feature pictures of Ann's sons) and an ever-friendly host with loads of advice on daily itineraries. Larger rooms feature courtyard spas and disabled facilities, with a house available for big groups (price negotiable).

Six on Union (Map p332; ☎ 0800 100 062; www.six union.co.nz; 6 Union St; d $80-95, f $120-135) This modest place is a budget bonanza with pool, spa and small kitchenettes. Recently refurbished, the motel is well placed for the city or Waiotapu.

Sandi's B&B (Map p345; ☎ 07-348 0884; sandi .mark@xtra.co.nz; 103 Fairy Springs; d/f $85/150) Staying at this friendly family B&B is like staying with a friend; fortunately that friend is well-humoured Sandi who offers helpful tourist tips. The best bet is the A-frame chalet with video-TV and self-contained kitchen. Thoughtful extras including fresh fruit with brekky and sun deck ensure guests give rave reviews.

Ambassador Thermal Motel (Map p332; ☎ 0800 479 581; www.ambassrotorua.co.nz; cnr Whakau & Hinemaru Sts; d/f $90/110; ☒ ☟) Handily located in a forgotten central pocket, this motel boasts no fewer than four pools: two indoor mineral pools, an outdoor spa and a large figure-eight swimming pool. Tight but well-designed rooms can fit up to eight and feature new fittings and full kitchens.

Regal Geyserland Hotel (Map p332; ☎ 0800 881 882; www.silveroaks.co.nz; 424 Fenton St; d from $90; ☒ ☟) Overlooking Whakarewarewa, this large complex is popular with conferencing professionals, probably for its proximity to the golf course. Of the 68 rooms most are studios, but there are a few family rooms and plenty of facilities such as gym, spa, sauna and restaurant.

Tuscany Villas (☎ 0800 802 050; www.tuscanyvillas rotorua.co.nz; 280 Fenton St; d from $125) This neat new spot has vaguely Italianate décor including huge, deep silver spas in deluxe rooms and kitchenettes with plunger cof-

fee and microwaves. Business travellers stay here for the broadband access and central location.

Lake Plaza Rotorua (Map p332; ☎ 0800 801 440; www.lakeplazahotel.co.nz; 1000 Eruera St; d $599; ☟) As soon as you see this large yet rather plain building there's no doubt that it's the largest hotel in town. Although popular with big groups, it has plenty to offer independent travellers with lake-facing rooms, regular on-site *hangi*, and an impressive restaurant.

Troutbeck Cottage (Map p345; ☎ 0800 522 526; www.jackanddis.co.nz; 5 Arnold St; d/f $95/170) A lakeside position in a quiet, secluded spot makes this large house a good retreat from Rotorua. Multiple rooms cater for large families and high-end facilities such as dishwasher, spa and full kitchen make for pleasant stays.

Victoria Lodge (Map p332; ☎ 0800 100 039; www .victorialodge.co.nz; 10 Victoria St; d/apt $105/180) From small balconies in apartments for breakfasting to extra toiletries, this place excels at little luxuries. For example, you can enjoy a cheese platter and wine in the hot pools in each room. Apartments can squeeze in seven adults, though four would be very comfortable.

Top End

Treetops (☎ 07-333 2066; www.treetops.co.nz; 351 Kearoa Rd, Horohoro; s/d from $1037; ☟) Ever wondered what prizes Oscar winners get? In 2004, they scored a week at this luxury lodge set in bushland at the edge of an extinct volcano, with peacocks and pheasant wandering the grounds. Private individual lodges feature every comfort, from big-screen TVs to floor heating and super king beds. The dining room serves peerless cuisine, incorporating Maori food grown on the grounds and washed down with classic Kiwi drops.

Princes Gate Hotel (Map p332; ☎ 07-348 1179; www.princesgate.co.nz; 1057 Arawa St; d/ste from $165/300; ☟) Just because this grand 19th-century dame is a classic doesn't mean it skimps on modernisation with wi-fi throughout, plasma-screen TVs and cascading mineral baths with a private massage centre. Of the 50 custom-designed rooms a favourite is the richly decorated Marvelly suite – perhaps too pink for all but Barbara Cartland, but sink into the bottomless bath and all is forgiven.

Peppers (Map p345; ☎ 07-348 4868; www.pepper .co.nz; 214 Kawaha Point Rd; ste $1330-1550; ☒ ☟)

This newer player in the luxury market has seven suites, two cottages and a larger villa house that cater for visiting movie stars and high-end honeymooners. Rates include meals, access to the grounds, conservatory and even an on-site massage and wellness centre.

Regal Palms Motor Lodge (0800 743 000; www.regalpalmsml.co.nz; cnr Ward & Fenton Sts; d $155;) Dubbed by Qualmark as NZ's best self-contained and serviced motel in 2005, this place is packed with features you'd expect in pricier motels, including wi-fi throughout, huge spa baths and filter coffee. Families appreciate the spacious one-bedroom studios with chrome dishwashers, large fridges and DVDs.

Millennium (Map p332; 07-347 1234; www.millenniumrotorua.co.nz) The slick lobby's Maori-inspired ambience gives an impression of the accommodation available at this elegant motel. Wi-fi throughout and a small business centre cater to a conference crowd. Lakefront rooms afford excellent views as does the club room, a laid-back lounge available exclusively to guests. The poolside *hangi* is one of the better motel entertainments in town and Nikau (see right) is an excellent dining option.

EATING

It's not a town-planning type that has seen the northern end of Tutanekai St named the *Streat*, but other areas in town are equally good (and often cheaper) for dining out.

Restaurants

Bistro 1284 (Map p332; 07-346 1284; www.bistro1284.co.nz; 1284 Eruera St; entrees $15-16, mains $25-32; dinner) Definitely one of RotoVegas' hot date-dining spots in an intimate setting with inventive Pacific Rim cuisine. With fly rods and smoked trout pictures prominently displayed, it's an excellent place to sample trout, but leave room for gooily good desserts.

Zambique (Map p332; 07-349 2140; 1111 Tutanekai St; meals $20-35; breakfast, lunch & dinner Tue-Sun) An African theme runs through this eatery (see if you can spot the sunken hippo), especially the menu with ostrich steaks and Moroccan lamb. Breakfasts depart from the African theme with lamb's fry and waffles (though not in the same dish).

Lewisham's Restaurant (Map p332; 07-346 0976; 1099 Tutanekai St; breakfasts $15-20, lunch & dinner mains $23-32; breakfast, lunch & dinner) A real local stalwart, Lewisham's has an international meat-centric menu including steaks and other hearty fare.

Nikau (Map p332; 07-347 1234; cnr Eruera & Hinemaru Sts; mains $15-24; lunch & dinner) In Millennium, this is the pick of the hotel restaurants with a relaxed vibe and an internationally eclectic menu that includes pizzas for kids and some indulgent desserts.

Pig & Whistle (Map p332; 07-347 3025; cnr Haupapa & Tutanekai Sts; mains $12-23; 11.30am-late) This busy restaurant-bar-microbrewery in the former police station juggles its different patrons well, offering diners simple pub grub such as fish and chips, pizzas and steak sandwiches.

Amazing Thai (Map p332; 07-343 9494; 1246 Fenton St; mains $18-24; lunch & dinner) With an authentically Thai ambience (yep, there are portraits of the Thai King and Queen), friendly service and some tasty standards, there are plenty of reasons for this place to be called amazing.

Cafés

Lime (Map p332; 07-350 2033; cnr Fenton & Whakaue Sts; mains $16-2 ; Tue-Sun 8am-4pm) With a lime green colour scheme, this fashionable little place serves up hip food with great breakfasts, heart-starting coffee and top-notch cakes.

Zippy Central (Map p332; 07-348 8288; 1153 Pukuatua St; snacks $5-7, mains $12-17; breakfast, lunch & dinner) Expect a Smartie with your java at this snappy little café that does tasty

AUTHOR'S CHOICE

Fat Dog Café (Map p332; 07-347 7586; 1161 Arawa St; mains $12-22; breakfast, lunch & dinner) With frisky dog prints chasing themselves up the walls and across the ceiling and silly poems painted on every chair, this is the town's most fun eating experience. In the evening it's candlelit and packed with paunchy pooches sampling hefty portions of NZ lamb drizzled in 'blooberry' jus. By day the caffeinated canine grabs a coffee at the express shopfront next door or lazes with its playful puppies (kids love this place) in the sunny courtyard.

stir-fries, curries and BLEATs (add egg and avocado to a BLT and what else would you call it?) sandwiches. It's big with backpackers and alterna-kids who love the Laminex tables, fresh art, ultracool booths and specially decorated 'eight-ball' coffees.

Relish (Map p332; ☎ 07-343 9195; 1149 Tutanekai St; mains $12-29; ☻ Sun-Tue from 7am, Wed-Sat 7am-late) This fashionable spot does great brekkies, innovative pizzas (duck and cashew anyone?) and pastas for lunch and dinner, plus some excellent tapas for in between. The best seat in the house is a red couch above the door.

Lovely India (Map p332; ☎ 07-348 4008; 1123 Tutanekai St; mains $12-16; ☻ lunch Tue-Sat, dinner daily). This lovable little spot serves up generous portions of masala, korma and all your Indian favourites at affordable prices.

Capers Epicurean (Map p332; ☎ 07-348 8818; 1181 Eruera St; mains $15-27; ☻ breakfast, lunch & dinner) This slick deli is barnlike in size yet always busy with diners showing up for its delicious gourmet sandwiches, pastas and surprising salads.

River Monster (Map p332; ☎ 07-346 0792; 1139 Tutanekai St; mains $16-19) Serving up sushi, tempura, teriyaki and other Japanese favourites, this small spot is one of the better Asian options.

Quick Eats

Weilin's Noodle House (Map p332; ☎ 07-343 9998; 1148 Tutanekai St; mains $6-16; ☻ lunch & dinner Wed-Mon) Noodle soups and dishes that are as healthy as they are hearty, including the huge king prawn laksa.

Lady Jane's Ice Cream Parlour (Map p332; ☎ 07-347 9340; 1092 Tutanekai St) Grabbing a cone of the ingeniously created flavours at this ice creamery is almost compulsory on summer days or when strolling around the lake.

Self-catering

If you're whipping up your own meals there's the choice of **Countdown** (Map p332; 246 Fenton St; ☻ 24hr) or **Pak N Save** (Map p332; cnr Fenton & Amohau Sts; ☻ 8am-10pm).

DRINKING

There are a few good spots to slake your thirst.

The Anglo-Celtic pubs are well represented with the English **Pig & Whistle** (Map p332; ☎ 07-347 3025; cnr Haupapa & Tutanekai Sts;

☻ 11.30am-late) serving its own microbrewed Swine lager, while the **Pheasant Plucker** (Map p332; ☎ 07-343 7071; 1153 Arawa St; ☻ from 4pm) offers pints in a more traditionally British setting. **O'Malley's** (Map p332; ☎ 07-347 6410; 1287 Eruera St) is the best of the Irish boozers.

A younger backpacker crowd opts for **Lava Bar** (Map p332; ☎ 07-348 8616; 1286 Arawa St) at Hot Rock backpackers, which has theme nights and drink specials, or **Echo** (Map p332; 07-350 3291; 1140 Hinemoa St) in Base Backpackers (see p339), with a slightly quieter atmosphere but similar deals.

An older crowd hangs out at **Fuze** (Map p332; ☎ 07-349 6306; cnr Pukaki & Tutanekai Sts; ☻ 3pm-late Tue-Sat) for its cocktails and relaxed feel.

ENTERTAINMENT

Bar Barella (Map p332; ☎ 07-347 6776; 1263 Pukeuatua St) There are weekend DJs playing a mix of techno and harder house.

Princes Gate Hotel (Map p332; ☎ 07-348 1179, 1057 Arawa St; cabaret/opera $69/80) At the other end of town, this place hosts opera and 1930s-style cabaret with meals on weekend nights.

For films, **Reading Cinema** (Map p332; ☎ 07-349 0061; 1281 Eruera St; adult/child $13/7.50) shows big mainstream flicks, while **Basement Cinema** (Map p332; ☎ 07-350 1400; basement, 1140 Hinemoa St; adult/child $12/9.50) does arthouse and smaller films.

SHOPPING

Rotorua has heaps of tourist-oriented shops that sell a range of traditional woodcarvings, greenstone and thermal mud products, many more tacky than tiki. You can find several souvenir-shopping spots along Tutanekai and Fenton Sts, but you can snag yourself a bargain by wandering away from the main streets.

Maori Crafts

If you're looking for authentic reminders of your *hangi*, Rotorua has an abundance of souvenirs and gifts, particularly jade, woodwork and paua shell carvings, many made by local Maori .

Te Puia (Map p345; ☎ 07-348 9047; www.tepuia .co.nz; Hemo Rd; ☻ 8.15am-5.15pm winter, 8am-6pm summer) If you want to buy straight from the craftsperson then this is the spot to snap up paua-shell jewellery, woodcarvings and, of course, a jade tiki. Designs are individual

Souvenirs

Madhouse Design (Map p332; ☎ 07-347 6066; www .madhousedesign.co.nz; 1093 Tutanekai St) This funky place sells boutique art and homewares that would make a really special gift for that arty someone back home, especially pottery and paintings.

Souvenir Centre (Map p332; ☎ 07-348 9515; 1231 Fenton St) From T-shirts to tea towels, this shop has all the big souvenir items at reasonable prices. Thermal mud cosmetics are particularly affordable here.

Consider also picking up a unique bottle of blueberry liqueur from Mamuka Blue (p344) to bring home a special NZ drop.

and you can also buy traditional clothing such as *korowai* (cloak) here.

Jade Factory (Map p332; ☎ 07-349 3968; jadefact@ wave.co.nz; 1288 Fenton St) Specialises in high-end, handcrafted greenstone jewellery and carvings, from small, simple pieces up to elaborate items costing thousands of dollars. The separate store to the south of Eruera St stocks jewellery and sculpture.

Best of Maori Tourism (Map p332; ☎ 07-347 4226; www.natiyeartsnz.com; 1189 Fenton St) Has a wide assortment of Maori craftwork for sale, including woodcarvings, greenstone jewellery and clothing.

GETTING THERE & AWAY

Air

Air New Zealand (Map p332; ☎ 07-343 1100; cnr Fenton & Hinemoa Sts; ✈ 8.30am-5pm weekdays) offers daily direct flights to Auckland, Christchurch and Wellington, with onward connections to other destinations.

Qantas (www.qantas.com.au) flies direct to Auckland, Wellington, Christchurch and Queenstown, with onward connections.

At the time of research, extensions were being made to runways in preparation for direct international flights, which may begin in early 2007.

Bus

All the major bus companies stop at Tourism Rotorua (see p330), which handles bus bookings.

InterCity (☎ 07-348 0366) has daily buses to and from Auckland ($50, four hours), Wellington ($90, eight hours), Tauranga ($25, 1½ hours), Palmerston North ($60, 5½ hours) and Hamilton ($30, 1½ hours). On the East Coast routes, InterCity goes daily to Gisborne ($55, 4½ hours) via Opotiki ($30, 2¼ hours) and Whakatane ($30, 1½ hours), and to Napier ($60, three hours) via Taupo ($23, one hour).

Newmans (☎ 07-348 0099) services go daily from Rotorua to Auckland ($44, four hours), Palmerston North ($60, 5½ hours) and Hamilton ($23, 1½ hours).

Kiwi Traveller (☎ 0800 500 100; www.kiwitraveller .co.nz) runs to Wellington ($70, eight hours) and Taupo ($21, one hour).

GETTING AROUND

To/From the Airport

The airport is about 10km out of town, on the eastern side of the lake. **Super Shuttle** (☎ 07-349 3444; www.supershuttle.co.nz) offers door-to-door service to/from the airport for $12 for the first person and $3 for each additional passenger. A taxi from the city centre costs about $20.

Bus

Ritchies Coachlines (☎ 07-345 5694) operates shuttles to many of the attractions in and around Rotorua. An all-day pass costs $7; one stage costs $1.60. Ritchies also runs suburban buses to Whakarewarewa (route 3) and Rainbow Springs (route 2, Ngongotaha), departing/arriving Rotorua on Pukuatua St.

Several shuttles tour attractions outside of town with pick-ups at most hotels and hostels:

Dave's Shuttle (☎ 0272 467 451) To Waiotapu and Waimangu (both $20).

Geyserlink (☎ 0800 000 4321; www.geyserlink.co.nz) Goes to Waiotapu ($20) and Hell's Gate ($20).

Tim's Thermal Shuttle (☎ 0274 945 508) Goes to Waiotapu ($38) and Buried Village ($45).

Car

In Rotorua the car-rental competition is fierce so there are bargains to be had. Try the following:

Avis (☎ 07-345 7133; Rotorua Airport)

Budget (☎ 07-348 8127; 1230 Fenton St)

Link Low Cost Rentals (☎ 07-349 1629; 1222 Fenton St)

Rent-a-Dent (Map p332; ☎ 07-349 3993; 14 Ti St)

Taxi

You can grab a cab from either **Rotorua Taxis** (☎ 07-348 1111) or **Fast Taxis** (☎ 07-348 2444).

AROUND ROTORUA

NORTH OF ROTORUA

Nature Parks & Trout Springs

Surrounding Rotorua are several places devoted to native wildlife. **Rainbow Springs Nature Park** (Map p345; ☎ 0800 724 626, 07-350 0440; www.rainbowsprings.co.nz; Fairy Springs Rd; adult/child $24/14; ☼ 8am-5pm) has a number of springs (one with an underwater viewer) and an aviary featuring rare birds such as the tui and kaka. You can take a pleasant walk through the tree ferns and native bush or grab a bag of trout feed at the entrance to create a feeding frenzy. You can tour the springs with an MP3 audio tour and get an insight into the area's wildlife with eels, wallabies, deer, birds, sheep, wild pigs and other once-introduced, now-native fauna. The highlight is the conservation project **Kiwi Encounter Tour** (adult/child $26.50/16.50; ☼ tours on the hour 10am-4pm) with a peek into the lives of these nocturnal birds, including egg incubation and hatching.

Across the road, the **New Zealand Farm Show** (Map p345; ☎ 07-348 8683; www.nzfarmshow.co.nz; 171 Fairy Springs Rd; adult/child $19/10; ☼ shows 10.30am, 11.45am, 1pm, 2.30pm & 4pm) showcases NZ's rural life with sheep-shearing, lamb-feeding and sheepdog demonstrations.

Rainbow Springs is 4km north of central Rotorua, on the west side of Lake Rotorua – take SH5 towards Hamilton and Auckland.

Paradise Valley Springs (Map p345; ☎ 07-348 9667; www.paradisev.co.nz; adult/child $22/11; ☼ 8am-5pm) is set in a 6-hectare park with various animals, including trout, deer and a pride of lions (fed at 2.30pm). The springs, 13km west of Rotorua on Paradise Valley Rd, are at the foot of Mt Ngongotaha.

Mamaku Blue

If you want to bring home a really unique NZ wine, this **blueberry winery** (Map p345; ☎ 07-332 5840; www.mamakublue.co.nz; Mamaeroa Rd, Mamaku; tours adult/child $15/8, museum $2; ☼ 10am-5pm) is for you. There are daily tastings (strangely good, since you ask) and staff also make chutneys, liqueurs, bath salts and jams from blueberries and gooseberries grown on the farm. You can take a tour and find out more, but the museum upstairs is strictly for those interested in Mamaku's timber industry history.

Mamaku Blue is 20km northwest of Rotorua; take SH5 out of town and turn off onto Maraeroa Rd to head to Mamaku township. It's well signposted.

Skyline Skyrides

Near the Rainbow and Fairy Springs is **Skyline Skyrides** (Map p345; ☎ 07-347 0027; www.skylineskyrides.co.nz; Fairy Springs Rd; gondola adult/child $20/9, luge $7; ☼ 9am-11pm). You cruise up Mt Ngongotaha by gondola for panoramic views of the lake area, then fly back down the mountain on a luge (a sort of toboggan on wheels), coming back up again on a chairlift. There is a café and restaurant (adult gondola and dinner/lunch $55/43) on top of the mountain.

At the top there's also the 'sky swing' ($30), a great airborne ride that goes at speeds of up to 120km/h, as well as a restaurant and several walking tracks around the mountain.

Agrodome

To learn more about the biggest animal population in NZ, visit **Agrodome** (Map p345; ☎ 07-357 1050; www.agrodome.co.nz; Western Rd; adult/child/family tour $28/13/65, show $22/11/60, tour & show $45/20/90; ☼ shows 9.30am, 11am & 2.30pm), which has almost 20 different breeds of sheep. An educational one-hour show will tell you more, plus there are sheep auctions, sheep-shearing and sheepdog displays. If all that's not enough, it's recently unveiled Titan the Giant Sheep! There's also a dairy display, farmyard nursery, cow-milking demonstration, chocolate factory and woollen mill.

You can hire horses for a guided tour or else take a farm-buggy tour of the 120-hectare farm. Agrodome is 9km north of Rotorua on SH5. There are also helicopter trips over Mt Tarawera (see p338).

ZORB ROTORUA

Before you hit the Agrodome, a long track runs down the hill with several large spheres at the top. Look closely and people are being strapped into them and rolling down the course at **Zorb Rotorua** (Map p345; ☎ 0800 227 474; www.zorb.co.nz; adult/child $45/10; ☼ 9am-5pm Apr-Nov, to 8pm Dec-Mar). Zorbing is simple enough: climb into a plastic sphere, strap in and then roll downhill for 150m (or take a zigzag course 180m down). Some extreme fiends skip the tying in, throw in

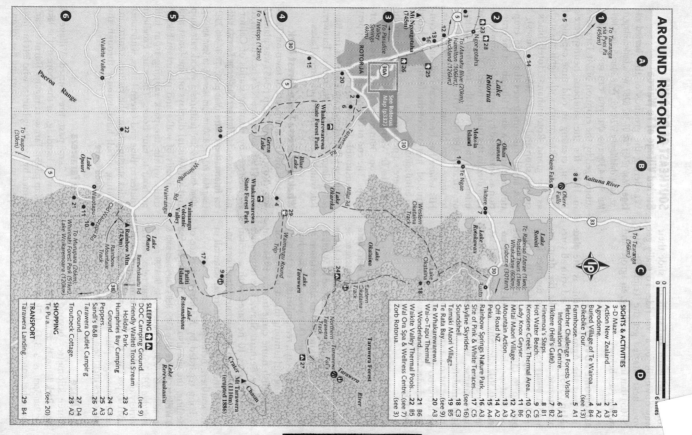

some cold water and slosh and slide their way downhill for a wet ride. To really get your heart started get the Triple By Pass ($105) that includes zorbing, an agrojet and swoop (see below).

AGRODOME ADVENTURES

Just past the Agrodome, this is the **place** (Map p345) to get adrenalised with all sorts of extreme activities: make the drop on a 43m **bungy** ($90), or join together for a tandem **swoop** (adult/child $40/30), which puts up to three people in a pouch to be swung at speeds of up to 130km/h. The **agrojet** ($40/30), allegedly NZ's fastest jetboat, speeds and splashes around a 1km man-made course, while **freefall xtreme** (adult $45) simulates skydiving by blasting you 5m into the air on a column of wind. You can get a combo with the Triple By Pass ($105) that includes the agrojet, swoop and zorbing (see p344).

NORTHEAST OF ROTORUA

Tikitere (Hell's Gate)

Known as Tikitere to the Maori, **Hell's Gate** (Map p345; ☎ 07-345 3151; www.hellsgate.co.nz; Te Ngae Rd; adult/child $25/10; �9am-8.30pm) is 16km northeast of Rotorua on the road to Whakatane (SH30). Tikitere is an abbreviation of *Taku tiki I tere nei* (My youngest daughter has floated away), remembering the tragedy of a young girl jumping into a thermal pool. The English name came from a 1934 visit by George Bernard Shaw. The impressive reserve covers 10 hectares, with a 2.5km walking track to the various attractions, including the largest hot thermal waterfall in the southern hemisphere.

Long regarded by Maoris as a place of healing, the site also houses the **Wai Ora Spa & Wellness Centre** (Map p345; Hell's Gate; mud bath & spa adult/child $70/30, 1hr massage $130, UltiMUD package adult/child $230/175) where you can relax with a variety of mud and spa treatments. The UltiMUD package includes bath, spa and one-hour massage, plus some manuka tea. All packages include a shuttle to/from Rotorua.

3-D Maze

Three kilometres beyond the airport, **Te Ngae Park** (Map p345; ☎ 07-345 5275; adult/child $6/3; �9am-5pm) is a 3-D, 1.7km-long wooden maze that entertains kids for an hour or two and makes a pleasant picnic spot.

SOUTHEAST OF ROTORUA

Buried Village of Te Wairoa

Wandering the grounds of this **buried village** (Map p345; ☎ 07-362 8287; www.buriedvillage.co.nz; adult/child/family $22/6/45; �8.30am-5.30pm Nov-Mar, 9am-4.30pm Apr-Oct) you can see buildings submerged by the eruption of Mt Tarawera in 1886. It's the southern hemisphere's Pompeii, creating an odd time capsule of NZ in the 19th century with highlights such as the grand Rotomahana Hotel, blacksmith's shop and several *whare* (houses).

A small museum traces the 1886 eruption, including a short film about the eruption as witnessed by a young English tourist who died in the village's hotel. Of particular interest is the story of the *tohunga* (priest or wizard) Tuhoto Ariki who, according to some, was blamed for the destruction. His *whare* has been excavated and reconstructed, just one of the features included in admission.

There's a peaceful bush walk through the valley to Te Wairoa Falls, where the Wairoa River drops 30m over a series of rocky outcrops. The end of the track is steep, slippery and unsuitable for young children.

Fifteen kilometres from Rotorua, the Buried Village is reached via scenic Tarawera Rd, which passes Blue and Green Lakes.

Whakarewarewa State Forest Park

Located on the southeast of town on Tarawera Rd, this **park** (Map p345) was planted early in 1901 to replace NZ's heavily logged native trees by planting stands of Californian redwoods. **Fletcher Challenge Forests Visitor Information Centre** (Map p345; ☎ 07-346 2082; Long Mile Rd; �8.30am-6pm Mon-Fri, to 5pm Apr-Sep; 10am-4pm Sat & Sun) features a woodcraft shop and audiovisual displays on the forest and has details of walks and mountain-biking trails within the park ranging from half an hour to four hours. There are excellent routes to Blue and Green Lakes, with most walks starting from the visitors centre, including a half-hour wander through the **Redwood Grove.**

Lake Tarawera

About 2km past the Buried Village is Tarawera Landing, on the shore of the lake (Map p345). Tarawera means 'Burnt Spear', named by a visiting hunter who left his bird spears in a hut and on returning the following season found both the spears and hut had been burnt.

Tarawera Launch Services (07-362 8595; adult/child $30/15) has a cruise at 11am crossing Lake Tarawera towards Lake Rotomahana. It stays on the other side for about 45 minutes, long enough for people to walk across to Lake Rotomahana, then returns to the landing. The trip takes 2½ hours.

A one-hour **cruise** (adult/child $18/10) on Lake Tarawera leaves at 1.30pm in winter and 1.30pm, 2.30pm and 3.30pm in summer. **Hotwater Beach** on Te Rata Bay has hot thermal waters and basic **camping** (sites $14) run by DOC. There's another DOC camping ground at **Tarawera Outlet** (sites $10).

SOUTH OF ROTORUA
Waimangu Volcanic Valley

The valley is another interesting **thermal area** (Map p345; 07-366 6137; www.waimangu.com; adult/child/family valley walk $25/7.50/55, boat trip $30/7.50/67.50, tour & cruise $55/15/120; 8.30am-5pm daily to 6pm Jan) created during the eruption of Mt Tarawera in 1886, making it young in geological terms. Taking the easy downhill stroll through the valley you'll pass many spectacular thermal and volcanic features, including Inferno Crater Lake, where overflowing water can reach 80°C, and Frying Pan Lake, the largest hot spring in the world. Waimangu (Black Water) refers to the dark, muddy colour of much of the water here.

The walk continues down to Lake Rotomahana (meaning 'Warm Lake'), from where you can either get a lift back up to where you started or take a half-hour boat trip on the lake, past steaming cliffs and the former site of the Pink and White Terraces.

Waimangu is approximately a 20-minute drive south from Rotorua, 19km along SH5 (towards Taupo) and then 5km to 6km from the marked turn-off. Last admission is at 3.45pm (4.45pm in January).

Waiotapu Thermal Wonderland

Also south of Rotorua, **Waiotapu** (Map p345; 07-366 6333; www.geyserland.co.nz; adult/child $23/8; 8.30am-5pm), meaning 'Sacred Waters', is perhaps the best-known thermal area, and is a compact area to visit. It has many interesting features, including the boiling, multihued **Champagne Pool**, bubbling mud, stunning mineral terraces and the **Lady Knox Geyser**, which spouts off (with a little

prompting from an organic soap) punctually at 10.15am and gushes for about an hour.

Waiotapu is 27km south of Rotorua on SH5 (towards Taupo), and a further 2km from the marked turn-off.

Whirinaki Forest Park

This exceptional park has majestic dense forests of native podocarp, with walking tracks, scenic drives, waterfalls, the Whirinaki River and some special areas, including Oriuwaka Ecological Reserve and Arahaki Lagoon. The DOC booklet *Tramping & Walking in Whirinaki Forest Park* gives details about walking and camping in the park.

The best source of information about the park is **DOC Rangitaiki Area Office** (07-366 1080) in Murupara.

For a shorter walk try the **Whirinaki Waterfall Track** (three to four hours), which loops to a waterfall and back. One of the longer walks is the **Whirinaki Track** (two days, 27km), which can be combined with **Te Hoe Loop Walk** (four days). The longer walk starts in some of NZ's finest podocarp forest, follows river valleys and takes in seven different huts.

Whirinaki Forest Park is 100km southeast of Rotorua, with access off SH38 on the way to Te Urewera National Park; take the turn-off at Te Whaiti to Minginui.

SLEEPING

There's an informal **camping area** (sites $12) at Mangamate Waterfall, with 10 **backcountry huts** (per night $10) throughout the forest; pay at the DOC office. Murupara has all types of accommodation as well as food outlets.

WESTERN BAY OF PLENTY

The western Bay of Plenty stretches from Katikati and Waihi Beach to Te Puke on the coast and south to the Kaimai Range. This is where New Zealanders come on holidays, shying away from busier Rotorua and lapping up the area's record for the highest proportion of sunny days in NZ, usually on one of the area's superb beaches.

TAURANGA
pop 100,000

With a real-estate boom since the 1990s, Tauranga is one of NZ's fastest-growing cities. It serves as a shipping hub for the surrounding agricultural area, making it one of the country's biggest export ports, but with a swell in holiday-home buyers the workhorse has become a show pony. Restaurants and bars line the attractive waterfront with its two marinas and excess of water sports. The expansion of Tauranga and Mt Maunganui, which is linked to Tauranga by a tombolo (thin strip of sand dunes), has blurred the border between the two towns.

Tauranga is the centre of NZ's principal kiwi-fruit region, with most work available during harvest (May and June) and odd jobs at other times (see the boxed text, p359).

Information

Tauranga visitor information centre (Map p348; ☎ 07-578 8103; ourcity.tauranga.govt.nz/; 95 Willow St; ☑ 7am-5.30pm Mon-Fri, 8am-4pm Sat & Sun) sells InterCity bus tickets. The public library, also located here, has Internet access, with other Internet options available at hostels. The local NZ post branch is at **Books & More** (Map p348; ☎ 07-577 9911; 17 Grey St).

The **DOC office** (☎ 07-578 7677; 253 Chadwick Rd W, Greerton) is about 10 minutes' drive south from the centre of Tauranga; follow Cameron Rd. You can pick up maps from the

CENTRAL TAURANGA

INFORMATION
Automobile Association (AA)...1 C4
Books & More/NZ Post...2 D2
Public Library...(see 3)
Tauranga Visitor Information Centre...3 C2

SIGHTS & ACTIVITIES
Brain-Watkins House...4 C3
Dive HQ...5 C2
Elms Mission Station House...6 C1
Monmouth Redoubt...7 D1
Robbins Park...8 D1
Te Awanui...9 C2

SLEEPING
Durham Motor Inn...10 C3
Harbour City Motor Inn...11 C3
Harbourside City Backpackers...12 D3
Hotel on Devonport...13 D3
Loft 109 Backpackers...14 D4
Puriri Park Boutique Hotel...15 C2
Roselands Motel...16 C1
Tauranga on the Waterfront...17 D4
Tauranga YHA...18 B3

EATING
Amphora...19 D2
Bravo...20 D3
Café Hasan Baba...21 C3
Collar & Thai...22 D3
Fresh Fish Market...23 D3
Kestrel...24 D3
Little India...25 D3
Mediterraneo Café...26 D3
Snackarama...27 D2
Turkish to Go...28 C4
Wharf Street Restaurant & Bar...29 D3

DRINKING
Cornerstone Pub...30 D2
Crown & Badger...31 D2
Grumpy Mole...32 D2

ENTERTAINMENT
Baycourt...33 C3
Buddha Lounge...34 D2
Cinema 8...35 C4
Home...36 D2
Rialto...(see 22)

TRANSPORT
Air New Zealand...37 D4
Avis...38 C4
Bay Hopper Bus Stop...39 D2
Bus Terminal...(see 3)
Ferry Service...40 D2

AA office (Map p348; ☎ 07-578 2222; cnr Devonport Rd & First Ave).

Sights

Founded in 1835, **Elms Mission Station House** (Map p348; ☎ 07-577 9772; Mission St; admission $5; ☑ 2-4pm Sun & public holidays) is the oldest building in the Bay of Plenty. The present house was completed in 1847 by the pioneering missionary Rev AN Brown and is furnished in period style, including the Mission Library.

Brain-Watkins House (Map p348; cnr Elizabeth & Cameron Sts; admission $2; ☑ 2-4pm Sun) was built in 1881 from native kauri wood and remains one of Tauranga's best-preserved Victorian colonial homes.

Te Awanui (Map p348), a replica of a *waka* (Maori canoe), is on display in an open-sided building at the top of The Strand. Further uphill, **Monmouth Redoubt** (Map p348; Monmouth St) was once a fortified site during the Maori Wars. **Robbins Park** (Map p348; Cliff Rd) is a verdant pocket with a rose garden, hothouse and excellent views across to Mt Maunganui.

Mills Reef Winery (☎ 0800 645 577; Moffat Rd, Bethlehem; mains $25-35; ☑ tastings 10am-5pm), 7km from the town centre at Bethlehem, has tastings of its award-winning wines and a restaurant (see p353).

Activities

All of the activities and operators listed are from Tauranga, but be aware that operators in Mt Maunganui, Te Puke and other surrounding areas are also available and may be just a short drive away.

WALKING

There are many walking options around Tauranga and Mt Maunganui. A number of these are outlined in the free *Walkways of Tauranga* pamphlet, including the fascinating **Waikareao estuary walkway** (Map p350) and the popular Mauao Base Track. For walks further afield pick up a copy of *Short Walks of the Western Bay of Plenty* ($1). Both are available from visitors centres.

The backdrop to the western Bay of Plenty is the rugged 70km-long **Kaimai Mamaku Forest Park**, 35km southwest of Tauranga on SH29, or 43km northwest of Rotorua, with tramps and basic camping (sites $6 to $20; check with DOC) for the more intrepid. More detailed information on walks in this area is provided in the DOC pamphlet *Kaimai Mamaku Forest Park Day Walks Long Walks* ($1).

McLaren Falls (admission free; ☑ 8am-5.30pm winter, 8am-7.30pm summer), found in the Wairoa River valley, 15km southwest of Tauranga just off SH29, is a 170-hectare lakeland park, with walking tracks, barbecues and a small animal park. There are three basic modern hostels (adult/child $15/10) and camp sites ($8). Contact **Tauranga District Council** (☎ 07-577 7000; www.tauranga.govt.nz) for bookings.

SEA ACTIVITIES

The waters around Tauranga are particularly blessed with dolphins and even the odd whale in summer. Other sea activities including diving, surfing, fishing and swimming are also great here. For more sea-based fun, see p354.

Dolphin Seafaris (☎ 0800 326 8747; www.nzdolphin.com; 90 Maunganui Rd, Mt Maunganui; adult/child $100/85; ☑ trps leave 8am summer, 9am winter) and **Butler's Swim with Dolphins** (☎ 0508 288 537; www.swimwithdolphins.co.nz; adult/child $100/85; ☑ leaves Tauranga 9am, Mt Maunganui 9.30am) run dolphin-swimming trips. Even without dolphins, the trips are always entertaining, particularly with Butler, a real old seadog who protested against Mururoa Atoll.

Tauranga Underwater Centre (Map p350; ☎ 07-571 5286; www.diveunderwater.com; 50 Cross Rd; courses from $450, trips $105; ☑ 8am-6pm Mon-Sat 10am Sun) and **Dive HQ** (Map p348; ☎ 07-578 4050; www.diveinqtauranga.co.nz; 213 Cameron St; courses from $450, trips $85) both offer PADI-qualifying courses or trips to local wrecks and reefs, plus gear rental.

WHITE-WATER RAFTING

White-water rafting is popular around Tauranga, particularly on the Wairoa River, which has some of the best falls and rafting in NZ. It's definitely a rafting trip for thrill-seekers, ranging from Grade II cascades to Grade V rapids. The Wairoa water level is controlled by a dam, so it can only be rafted on 26 days of the year; advance bookings are essential.

Operators in the area:

Kaituna Cascades (☎ 0800 524 862; www.kaitunacascades.co.nz) oes rafting on the Kaituna ($68), Rangitiaki ($95) and Wairoa ($80).

Raftabout (☎ 0800 723 822; www.raftabout.co.nz) Does rafting on the Kaituna ($75) and Wairoa ($95), with sledging on Kaituna ($99).

TAURANGA & MT MAUNGANUI

INFORMATION

Mt Maunganui Visitor Information Centre	1	E2

SIGHTS & ACTIVITIES

Assault	2	B2
Classic Flyers NZ	3	D4
Hot Saltwater Pools	4	A1
Island Style Surf Shop	5	B4
Kitesurfing New Zealand	6	B4
Mount Surf Shop	7	B2
Tauranga Underwater Centre	8	B4

SLEEPING

13th Ave Redwood Motel	9	B6
8A B&B	10	B4
Atrium	11	A1
Avenue 11 Motel	12	B5
Baywatch Motor Inn	13	C2
Bell Lodge Motel & Backpackers	14	A5
Calais Mount Resort	15	A1
Chalet Motel	16	E6
Cosy Corner Motor Camp	17	D3
Harbour View Motel	18	E5
Just The Ducks Nuts Backpackers	19	B4
Mission Belle Motel	20	A2
Mount Backpackers	21	B2
Mount Maunganui B&B	22	C3
Mt Maunganui Domain Motor Camp	23	A1
Oceanside Motor Lodge & Twin Towers	24	A1
Outrigger Motel	25	B2
Pacific Coast Lodge & Backpackers	26	C3
Pacific Motor Inn	27	B2
Reef	28	D2
Silver Birch Thermal Holiday Park	29	B6
Tauranga Tourist Park	30	B6
Westhaven	31	A2

EATING

Amphora	32	B2
Astrolabe	33	B2
Bardell's at the Mount	34	A2
Café Hasan Baba	35	A2
Gusto	36	B2
Kwang Chow	37	B2
Sand Rock Café & Bar	38	A2
Thai-Phoon	(see 20)	
Turkish to Go 2	39	A1
Two Small Fish	40	B2

ENTERTAINMENT

Barmuda	(see 34)	
Cinema 4	41	B2
Mount Mellick Hotel	42	B2

TRANSPORT

Budget	43	B4
Bus Depot	(see 1)	
Rent-a-Dent	44	B6

River Rats (☎ 0800 333 900; www.riverrats.co.nz) Takes on the Rangitaiki ($95) and Wairoa Rivers ($99), as well as the Kaituna ($85).

Wet 'n' Wild Rafting (☎ 0800 462 7238; www.wetnwildrafting.co.nz) Offers day trips to Kaituna ($79).

OTHER ACTIVITIES

Get the best of the wind and waves with **Kitesurfing New Zealand** (Map p350; ☎ 027 440 5517; www.kitesurfingnz.com; 90 Bureta Rd; per 1/4 lessons $80/250), which offers 1½-hour lessons in this thrilling new sport.

Tours

Seaspray Tours (☎ 07-574 6162; www.seaspraytours.co.nz; 1-day tours from $115) Does day tours to McLaren Falls, along the Eastern Bay of Plenty and inland to Rotorua with pick-ups from Mt Maunganui and Tauranga.

Tauranga Tasting Tours (☎ 07-544 1383, 021 122 4607; day tours $130) Does a whip around Mills Reef, Morton Estate and other wineries around the area.

SCENIC FLIGHTS

These can be arranged at the airport. Some operators:

Island Air Charter (☎ 07-575 5795; www.islandair.co.nz; flights 20min/2hr $40/120) Does flights over Whakaari (White Island), from $120; Rotorua thermal area ($120) and around town ($40).

Tauranga Aero Club (☎ 07-575 321C; 20min flights $40, White Island tours $120) Flies over White and Mayor Islands with a chance to grab the steering wheel on a trial flight ($94).

Volcanic Air Safaris (☎ 0800 800 848; www.volcanicair.co.nz; flights 10min/3hr $60/785) Does tours of town and a trip to White Island that includes going into the volcano itself.

Festivals & Events

Tauranga has become an arts mecca with several events celebrating culture.

National Jazz Festival (☎ 07-577 7188; www.jazz.org.nz or www.ticketdirect.co.nz) The cultural calendar kicks off at Easter, when the big blowers arrive for Dixieland, trad and all things in between, with plenty of concerts and food.

Tauranga Arts Festival (www.taurangafestival.co.nz) Kicking off on Labour Day weekend in October, showcasing dance, comedy, plays and everything arty.

Tauranga International Film Festival (www.nzff.telecom.co.nz) In late August/early September a touring movie festival arrives.

Sleeping

BUDGET

Backpackers have discovered Tauranga, with plenty of places catering for them.

Loft 109 Backpackers (Map p348; ☎ 07-579 5638; www.loft109.co.nz; 109 Devonport Rd; dm/d/tr $20/46/63; ▣) This central spot feels like a kooky group house complete with share kitchen, rooftop balconies in upper rooms, and a boat built into the roof. It's bright with skylights, plus on colder days there's a gas fire in the common area.

Tauranga YHA (Map p348; ☎ 07-578 5064; yha@yha.org.nz; 171 Elizabeth St; sites per 2 people $32, dm/d $19/58; ▣) This well-kept YHA features a sprawling back yard complete with hammocks for lazing or a nearby mangrove swamp to walk through on a boardwalk. It's a great spot to camp, though the immaculately clean dorms are equally tempting, with individual lockers.

Harbourside City Backpackers (Map p348; ☎ 07-5794066; www.backpacktauranga.co.nz; 105 The Strand; dm/tw/d $20/27/54; ☐) This smaller spot is a party place with handy access to The Strand's bars as well as an on-site bar and sea-view balcony. Rooms are small, but good for groups. A shuttle to Mt Maunganui's beaches makes this a safe bet for carless travellers.

Just the Ducks Nuts Backpackers (Map p350; ☎ 07-576 1366; www.justtheducksnuts.co.nz; 6 Vale St; dm/d $20/44) Set in a quieter area, this expanding hostel is a friendly place where you can be left to your own devices. Comfy rooms and a fulsome library make it a relaxed spot, with shuttles to the city and beaches. Quirky touches like flowers planted in the bathtub and duck-themed toilets are fun, but older couples might prefer the flats up the back, which are more private.

8A B&B (Map p350; ☎ 07-576 8895; 8A Vale St; s/d $50/80) Next door to the Ducks Nuts, this quaint place (we're talking doilies and frilly pillowcases here) is a good option if you're looking for a homey stay. Breakfasts are particularly generous.

Tauranga Tourist Park (Map p350; ☎ 07-578 3323; 9 Mayfair St; unpowered/powered sites per 2 people $20/44, cabins/flats $40/80) Well-placed for the beach, this place is popular with families who utilise the well-equipped kitchens and laundry to save their budget without sacrificing location.

MIDRANGE

Tauranga on the Waterfront (Map p348; ☎ 0800 109 007; www.taurangamotel.co.nz; 1 Second Ave; d/ste $115/130; ☒) This slick place has excellent harbour-view suites, many with spas making for perfect romantic getaways. Court-yard rooms are aimed at budget-conscious families with more room but less view. The recent addition of a conference centre and business facilities will bring in a working crowd.

Puriri Park Boutique Hotel (Map p348; ☎ 07-577 1480, 0800 4787 474; 32 Cameron Rd, d/ste $135/160) With large rooms, king-sized beds and LAN connections in rooms, this newish spot in town is making a play for the business traveller. Stress relievers like spas in suites and generous minibars are all appeals to the executive account.

Durham Motor Inn (Map p348; ☎ 07-577 9691; www.durham.co.nz; cnr Cameron Rd & Harington St; d/f from $115/155; ☒) This modern motor lodge is the pick with visiting salespeople, for its individual kitchens and well-kept rooms. The pool is slap-bang in the middle of the car park, making a quick dip after long drives convenient.

Avenue 11 Motel (Map p350; ☎ 07-577 1881; www avenue11.co.nz; 26 Eleventh Ave; d $99) This relaxed spot has only four self-contained, tastefully furnished rooms all with polished wood flooring and minikitchens. The well-tended garden and friendly hosts make it feel more like home than a motel.

Roselands Motel (Map p348; ☎ 07-578 2294; www .roselands.co.nz; 21 Brown St; d/ste from $95/105) This older-style place is a central yet quiet motel with roomy units that include kitchens, high-chairs and other family-friendly features. A spa pool and barbecue mean you could easily enjoy a few days at this affordable motel.

Harbour View Motel (Map p350; ☎ 07-578 8621; www.harbourviewmotel.co.nz; 7 Fifth Ave; s/d from $75/85) This large complex has a variety of units, the best with harbour views. Ground-floor rooms have less impressive vistas, but all rooms have full kitchens. Kayak rental is available.

Chalet Motel (Map p350; ☎ 07-578 4812; 84 15th Ave; tr $89, chalet $160-180; ☒) This old-style place is an excellent family option with trampolines, pool and A-frame chalets (sleeping up to eight) that have two storeys to separate parents and kids. All rooms are well equipped for self-catering.

13th Avenue Redwood Motel (Map p350; ☎ 07-578 9412; cnr Fraser St & 13th Ave; d $89-100) This well-kept older place has a limited number of units, all with bathtubs and full kitchens. The place regularly books out with groups and has a special 'team rate' for groups of more than 10.

TOP END

Hotel on Devonport (Map p348; ☎ 07-578 2668; www .hotelondevonport.net.nz; 72 Devonport Rd; d/ste $150/200; ☒) The Devonport is top of the town with rooms affording bayside views and hush glass for silence in the city centre, all of which appeals to business travellers and luxury weekenders. All rooms feature broadband and comfy couches so the rooms suit whether you're working or relaxing.

Harbour City Motor Inn (Map p348; ☎ 07-571 1435; www.taurangaharbourcity.co.nz; 50 Wharf St; d from $150; ☒) As one of the newest places in town, you'd expect all the mod cons such as a spa bath and pay TV in every room, and fashionable lounges. And Harbour City doesn't disappoint, but it also has friendly staff members who can give you straight-up advice on your itinerary.

Eating

Devonport St is the place to grab lunch, but places on The Strand excel at dinner and drinks to follow. You can pick up the useful free *Dine/nd* guide at the visitor information centre.

Kestrel (Map p348; 11am-11pm) The top table in town is actually on the water in this converted vessel, which affords waterfront views out to sea or back toward town. Sip an Australian or NZ wine at the downstairs bar, which offers a rusty peek into the old engine room, then enjoy outdoor dining from a modern Kiwi menu.

Collar & Thai (Map p348; 07-577 6655; Goddards Mall, Devonport Rd; mains $20-24; lunch Tue-Fri, dinner daily) No tie required at this upstairs, upper-end eatery that artfully elaborates on Thai standards and uses plenty of fresh seafood, with good value lunch specials.

Amphora (Map p348; 07-578 1616; 43 The Strand; mains $16-25; dinner) This Mediterranean-inspired eatery does creative pastas and risottos, plus some decadent desserts and well-chosen wines. No wonder it has a franchise over at Mt Maunganui.

Mills Reef Winery (Map p348; 0800 645 577; Moffat Rd, Bethlehem; mains $25-35; lunch & dinner) This bright and airy dining room makes the perfect adjunct to wine tasting (see p349) with a solid European-inspired menu and necessarily excellent wine list. The winery is 7km from town at Bethlehem.

Little India (Map p348; 07-579 0910; 113 The Strand; mains $10-15; lunch & dinner) This flavoursome curry house offers the best value on The Strand, especially with its lunch specials. Curries are slow-simmered in clay, making for tender meat and flavours suffused throughout the dish.

Snackarama (Map p348; 07-578 9228; cnr Harington St & The Strand; items $6-13; breakfast & lunch Mon-Sat) This simple takeaway does a roaring trade with an all-day brekky, huge cakes, burgers and sandwiches.

Bravo (Map p348; 07-578 4700; Red Square; mains $11-16; breakfast, lunch & dinner) This trendy, well-regarded restaurant and bar is a pleasant spot for inexpensive light meals, bagels, pizzas and drinks, with outdoor seating on the pedestrianised street.

Mediterraneo Café (Map p348; 07-577 0487; 62 Devonport St; mains $10-14; 7.30am-4.30pm Mon-Sat) Making some of the best coffee on the east coast, this café does great food to go with it, particularly sandwiches, flans and cakes. Lunchtime crowds can be frantic.

Turkish to Go (Map p348; 07-578 7296; 3/109 Devonport Rd; kebabs $6-9; lunch) Serving swift and swish kebabs, this place also enjoys a thriving lunchtime crowd with a branch at the Mount (Mt Maunganui).

Wharf Street Restaurant & Bar (Map p348; 07-578 8322; Upstairs, 8 Wharf St; mains $25-50; lunch & dinner) Swanky Wharf St specialises in fresh fish and seafood, with an extensive wine list and balcony views over the harbour. Embrace both with a balcony-side seafood platter, which samples the ocean's finest.

Café Hasan Baba (Map p348; 07-571 1480; 107 Grey St; mains $10-25; lunch & dinner) This modish noshery has Middle Eastern decor and menu, including couscous and sizzling lamb.

Fresh Fish Market (Map p348; lunch & dinner) Dive Cres; mains from $5; A local legend serving up top fish and chips within a seagull's cry of the water.

Cornerstone Pub (Map p348; 07-928 1120; 55 The Strand; lunch & dinner) This cheerful watering hole lifts the bar on pub grub by using game like ostrich and venison, to serve up hearty portions and some surprisingly good desserts.

Drinking

Crown & Badger (Map p348; 07-571 3038; cnr Strand & Wharf St) This Brit booze- does pukka pints of traditional beers in a laid-back environment.

Cornerstone Pub (Map p348; 07-928 1120; 55 The Strand; 10am-midnight Mon-Wed, 10am-3am Thu-Sun) This mature pub, usually with a crowd of over-25s, does tasty food (see above) and is good for watching National Provincial Cup (NPC) footy.

Grumpy Mole (Map p348; 07-571 1222; 41 The Strand; 3pm-3am Tue-Sat) Dig in your spurs for a wild night at this popular backpacker bar with a Western theme.

Entertainment

Baycourt (Map p348; 07-577 7189; www.baycourt.co.nz; cnr Durham & Wharf Sts) This big venue hosts an eclectic mix of theatre, visiting big bands, world-music concerts and music festivals.

Buddha Lounge (Map p348; ☎ 07-928 1515; 61b The Strand; visiting DJs $10; ☺ 5pm-late Thu, 4pm-3am Fri, 8pm-3am Sat) has local and visiting DJs on Friday and Saturday nights in an upstairs chilled spot with a breezy balcony. **Home** (Map p348; ☎ 07-578 6828; 15 Harington St; cover $10-15; ☺ 11am-11pm) has live music ranging from hip-hop to jazz most weekend nights.

Two cinemas in town offer Hollywood's latest flicks: the upstairs **Rialto** (Map p348; ☎ 07-577 0445; www.rialtotauranga.co.nz; Goddards Mall, Devonport Rd; adult/child $14/8) and **Cinema 8** (Map p348; ☎ 07-577 0800; www.movie.net.nz; Elizabeth St; adult/child $14/8).

Getting There & Away

AIR

Air New Zealand (Map p348; ☎ 07-577 7300; cnr Devonport Rd & Elizabeth St) has daily direct flights to Auckland and Wellington, with connections to other centres. Local outfit **Island Air** (☎ 0800 545 455; www.islandair.co.nz; Tauranga Airport) does charter flights to Great Barrier Island and most other NZ cities. Tauranga's airport is at Mt Maunganui.

BUS

InterCity (Map p348; ☎ 07-578 8103) tickets and timetables are provided by the Tauranga visitor information centre, where the bus terminal is located. InterCity connects Tauranga with Auckland ($40, 4½ hours), Hamilton ($28, two hours), Rotorua ($25, 1½ hours), Taupo ($50, 2½ hours) and Wellington ($90, nine hours).

Bay Hopper (☎ 0800 4229 287; www.baybus.co.nz) runs a morning and afternoon weekday bus to Rotorua ($10, 1½ hours) via Te Puke ($4, half hour). Daily buses go to Whakatane ($9, two hours), Ohope ($12, three hours) Opotiki ($12, three hours). Bay Hopper buses leave from Wharf St (Map p348).

Supa Travel (☎ 07-571 0583) is a local company that has buses on demand to Auckland Airport (one way $85), as does **Tauranga Airport Shuttles** (☎ 07-571 6177). **Coastline Shuttles** (☎ 07-541 0888; coastlineshuttle@xtra.co.nz) go daily by arrangement to airports in Auckland (adult/child $75/35), Hamilton (adult/child $50/25) and Rotorua (adult/child $50/25). Most bus lines continue to Mt Maunganui after stopping in Tauranga.

CAR

If you're heading to Hamilton, don't forget the toll road costs $1.

Getting Around

Tauranga's bright yellow **Bay Hopper** (☎ 0800 4229 287; www.baybus.co.nz) buses run Monday to Saturday to most locations around the area, including Mt Maunganui, Papamoa and Te Puke. There's a central stop at Wharf St. The timetable ($1) is available from the visitors centre.

Several car-rental agencies have offices in Tauranga:

Avis (Map p348; ☎ 07-578 4204; 325 Cameron Rd)
Budget (Map p350; ☎ 07-578 5156; Dive Cr)
Rent-a-Dent (Map p350; ☎ 07-578 1772; 19 Fifteenth Ave)

A taxi from Tauranga's centre to the airport costs around $11. Local taxi companies:

Citicabs (☎ 07-577 0999)
Mount Taxis (☎ 07-574 7555)
Tauranga Mount Taxis (☎ 07-578 6086)

MT MAUNGANUI

pop 16,800

Named for the massive 232m hill that dominates the township, Mt Maunganui (Large Mountain) is often just called 'the Mount', or Maumo. The Mount is the surfer-bum cousin just across the inlet from Tauranga, but lately the surfie has inherited a rich holidaymaking crowd that has created development along the shore and the mountain. Like any surfer kid with some cash, the Mount has pumped money into creating bigger waves by building a 250m artificial reef, which was completed at the time of research. With NZ's first artificial reef, the Mount's surfing reputation is stronger and will attract even more people to its beautiful beaches.

Information

The **Mt Maunganui visitor information centre** (☎ 07-575 5099; Salisbury Ave; ☺ 9am-5pm Mon-Fri, to 4pm Sat & Sun Oct-Easter) is excellent for local info.

Sights & Activities

The Mount can claim to be NZ's premier surf city, though there's top swimming on the beach between Moturiki and Maunganui. To hit the waves, head for the **Mount Surf Shop** (☎ 07-575 9133; 96 Maunganui Rd; rental per day wet suits/surfboards/body boards $15/30(20) or **New Zealand Surf School** (07-574 1666; www.nz surfschool.co.nz 1hr lessons incl all gear $90). You can cut through the macho surfer crap at **Hibiscus** (07-575 3792, 027 2799 687; lessons 1hr/2hr/6hr $50/80/230), a surfing course run by experienced 'chick surfer' Rebecca Taylor. Take on something more risky at **Assault** (07-575 7831; 24 Pacific Ave; info@assault.co.nz; 1hr lessons surfing/kiteboard $30/80, windsurfing from beginners to performance 1hr/1 day $40/80).

Mt Maunganui is the town's other unmissable feature with **walking trails** circumnavigating it and heading to the summit, where there are magnificent views. The walk takes about an hour and gets steeper near the summit. You can also climb around the rocks on **Moturiki Island**, which is joined to the peninsula; check out the *Walkways of Tauranga* pamphlet, available from the visitor information centre (opposite). The island and the base of the Mount also make up the Mauao Base Trail, offering spectacular views of the pohutukawa trees when they're blooming between November and January.

After all that walking you'll have earned a soak at the **hot saltwater pools** (07-575 0868; Adams Ave; adult/child $2.50/1.50; 6am-10pm Mon-Sat, 8am-10pm Sun & holidays) at the foot of the Mount.

A must-see for wing nuts is **Classic Flyers NZ** (07-572 4000; www.classicflyersnz.com; Tauranga Airport; adult/child $10/5; 10am-4pm), an aviation museum with several working aircraft including a working Spitfire replica.

For some kayaking with a local, check out **Oceanix** (07-572 2226; www.oceanix.co.nz; per half/full day $85/95), which goes up to McLaren Falls and takes on the waves on Pilot Bay.

There's a great chance to try a new extreme sport at **Blokart Heaven** (07-572 4256; www.blokart.com; Parton Rd, Papamoa; 15min $15; 10am-6pm summer, noon-5pm winter), NZ's only purpose-built course for land-based windsurfing on small carts.

Sleeping

Mt Maunganui is a hugely popular holiday destination with plenty of accommodation, particularly apartment style. Prices are higher than in Tauranga.

BUDGET

Mount Backpackers (/fax 07-575 0860; www.mount backpacker.co.nz; 87 Maunganui Rd; dm/d from $24;)

MIDRANGE

Atrium (07-572 3476; 23 Maunganui Rd; 2-bedroom apt $130) This modern self-serviced apartment suits visitors who want longer stays in the Mount with cheaper weekly rates. Full kitchens, separate lounge rooms and views from some rooms make you feel right at home.

Baywatch Motor Inn (07-574 7745; www.bay watchmotor-inn.co.nz; 349a Maunganui Rd d/ste $125/165;) An Art Deco charmer; family-run with modern, spacious units and no relationship to the David Hasselhoff TV series. Compact kitchenettes and a handy pool make suites good value for families, but Pamela Anderson doesn't lifeguard by the pool.

Mount Maunganui B&B (07-575 4013; www mountbedbreakfast.co.nz; 463 Maunganui Rd; s/d from $50/80) This five-room B&B is an affordable spot with presentable if tight rooms and cooked breakfast. Front rooms cop some traffic noise, but owners are convivial and friendly to visitors.

Westhaven (07-575 4753; www.westhavenmotel .co.nz; 27a The Mall; courtyard from $90) The 1970s style here pays homage to *Brady Bunch* architecture, with wooden shelving between

This well-run hostel is the party place in town within a drunken stagger of most of the restaurants and bars. Staff members are helpful and offer boogie boards and bikes for hire, plus there's deals on activities, including surf lessons.

Pacific Coast Lodge & Backpackers (0800 666 622; www.pacificcoastlodge.co.nz; 432 Maunganui Rd; dm/d from $20/50;) This efficiently clean hostel has great bunk rooms decorated throughout with jungle murals. Strict curfews (and the odd wake-up call) discourage wilder guests, but the place is well run.

Cosy Corner Motor Camp (07-575 5899; www .cosycorner.co.nz; 40 Ocean Beach Rd; sites per 2 people $26, cabins/d flats $55/70;) This family camping ground has a sociable feel with barbecues, trampolines for kids and a dedicated boat park. Cabins may prove too cosy for some guests, but the convenience of the beach more than compensates.

Mt Maunganui Domain Motor Camp (07-575 4471; 1 Adams Ave; sites per 2 people $24-26) With three different camping areas all nestled into the base of Mt Maunganui, this community-run park has spectacular camping with all the expected facilities, plus it's handy to the hot thermal baths.

kitchen and lounge and bathrooms sizable enough to retune your afro. Full kitchens are perfect for whipping up feasts, plus there are bayside views from the front rooms. Friendly hosts also offer fishing rods and dinghies for more family fun.

Mission Belle Motel (☎ 0800 202 434; www.mission bellemotel.co.nz; cnr Victoria Rd & Pacific Ave; d/f $105/135) A Spanish Mission–style exterior but modern interiors make this place affordable and comfortable. Two-storey family rooms feature large bathtubs and airy skylights.

Calais Mount Resort (☎ 0800 422 524; www.calais .co.nz; 6 Adams Ave; d/ste from $130/210) Styled in beachy sand and aqua tones, the Calais is an upper-end spot with DVDs and stereos in every room. Suites feature spas, but all guests receive a free pass to the nearby hot pools. The on-site restaurant (Sails) makes an excellent lazy dining option.

Outrigger Motel (☎ 0800 889 966; www.outrigger beach.co.nz; 48 Marine Parade; d/f from $95/135) This breezy motel has the chilled feel you'd expect from a place this close to the beach, including cane beds for your own tiki-hut décor. Sea views and spas make some rooms pricier, though most come with their own lockable garage: perfect for driving holidays.

TOP END

Oceanside Motor Lodge & Twin Towers (☎ 0800 466 868; www.oceanside.co.nz; 1 Maunganui Rd; d/ste from $165/250; ⊠) Rivalling the Mount itself in height, the high-rise Twin Towers and the attached motor lodge have some of the top beds in town. Rooms are subtly decorated in whites and creams with sea vistas framed by full bay windows. There's a two-night minimum stay here.

Reef (☎ 07-574 6220; cnr Marine Dr & Clyde St; www .thereef.co.nz; 2-/3-bedroom apts from $220/315; ⊠) This family-friendly spot has large apartments complete with kitchens and separate lounges tricked out with large TVs and DVDs. Sweeping balconies offer clear sea views and the secluded location means you might get the beach to yourself.

Eating & Drinking

Maunganui Rd has the biggest concentration of eateries in the area, though many are clones of Tauranga venues (see the boxed text, right).

Bardeli's at the Mount (☎ 07-572 0196; 19 Pacific Ave; mains $14-25; ⊠ breakfast & lunch daily, dinner Thu-Sun) Bardeli's remains a popular spot for its deli-style lunches, tasty breakfasts and fine coffee. Dinner is more sophisticated, with fish and pasta making appearances.

Astrolabe (☎ 07-574 8155; 82 Maunganui Rd; starters $14-17, mains $19-32; ⊠ breakfast, lunch & dinner) This swish restaurant caters to the Mount's hip crowd, with a menu packed with gourmet goodies like venison and oysters. You can also come in for a boutique beer on tap and a whack of pool.

Two Small Fish (☎ 07-575 0096; 107 Maunganui Rd; mains $10-35; ⊠ breakfast & lunch daily, dinner Thu-Sun) This fashionable little spot serves up great coffee and breakfasts, with plenty of creative lunch salads, sandwiches and quiches. Dinners include indulgent seafood and lamb dishes.

Gusto (☎ 07-575 5675; 200 Maunganui Rd; breakfast $5-12.50, lunch $9-13; ⊠ breakfast & lunch) This friendly spot keeps its menu affordable but interesting with Kiwi standards such as lamb and kumara (sweet potato) given a refreshing treatment.

Thai-Phoon (☎ 07-572 3545; 14a Pacific Ave; mains $13-17; ⊠ dinner) This relaxed place does artful Thai cuisine with attentive service and takeaways.

Sand Rock Café & Bar (☎ 07-574 7554; 4 Marine Parade; mains $21-34; ⊠ breakfast, lunch & dinner) This beachside place naturally does great fresh fish, but also has a menu that offers vegetarian options as well as well-cooked steaks.

Kwang Chow (☎ 07-575 5063; 241 Maunganui Rd; lunch $12, dinner adult $15-17, senior $13; ⊠ lunch & dinner) This all-you-can-eat Chinese place is a local favourite with a bargain bite that

A SNACK OF THE CLONES

Some places have been so successful in Tauranga that they've copied their venues into the Mount's busy dining scene. Their menus and opening hours are similar to those in Tauranga, so check those reviews for more details. Here are some of the copycat branches in the Mount:

Café Hasan Baba (☎ 07-574 8200; 16 Pacific Ave) See p353.

Amphora (☎ 07-574 1574; 91 Maunganui Rd) See p353.

Turkish to Go 2 (☎ 07-575 8090; 6 Adams Ave) See p353.

still maintains the flavour of individual dishes (rather than a *bain-marie* collage of tastes). Dinner prices are cheaper Monday to Wednesday.

Entertainment

There's a few bars in town that offer entertainment as well. **Barmuda** (☎ 07-575 8363; 19c Pacific Ave) is a laid-back bar above Bardelli's restaurant that has occasional jazz and acoustic performances. **Mount Mellick Hotel** (☎ 07-574 0047; 317 Maunganui Rd) is a blokey Irish pub with occasional live music and DJs on Friday nights.

Cinema 4 (☎ 07-572 3311; Maunganui Rd; adult/child $13.50/7.50) shows new-release films.

Getting There & Away

You can reach Mt Maunganui across the harbour bridge from Tauranga or from the south via Te Maunga on SH2. See p354 for public-transport details for the Mount. Tauranga airport is at Mt Maunganui.

Supa Travel, Coastline Shuttles, Tauranga Airport Shuttles and InterCity all serve Tauranga. Their buses stop at the bus depot at Mt Maunganui visitors centre. **Bay Hopper** (☎ 0800 422 9287) buses run from Wharf St in Tauranga to the Mount, stopping at visitors centre and hot pools.

AROUND TAURANGA

Tuhua (Mayor Island)

Commonly known as Mayor Island, this dormant volcano is located 40km north of Tauranga. The island is known for its black, glasslike obsidian rock and diverse bird life – there are plans to introduce kiwi here, because of the lack of predators. Walking tracks cut through the now-overgrown crater valley, and the northwest corner is a marine reserve. The area is managed by the Tuhua Trust Board and to land here you need permission from DOC, with a $5 landing fee.

There's limited **camping and lodge accommodation** (☎ 07-579 5655; sites per 2 people $24, dm from $12) with only a barbecue for cooking; bring your own food (there are no fridges either). You can charter a boat from Tauranga or Whangamata (see p223). A good ecotrip to Mayor Island is with Tauranga-based **Blue Ocean Charters** (☎ 07-578 9685; www.blueoceancharters.co.nz; 1-day tours $90), which can show you the best of the island.

Matakana Island

Just across the harbour from Tauranga, Matakana Island has 24km of secluded white-sand surf beach on its eastern shore and a relaxed island lifestyle. The best way to explore the island is to take a tour with **Matakana Island Tours** (☎ 080/ 276 391; tours from $35), which offers a unique crossing to the island on a Clydesdale-drawn wagon and does tours of the island's *marae* and beaches. Alternatively you can catch the **ferry** (☎ 035 927 251; one way $5; ☼ runs 7am, 2pm & 4pm) from Omokoroa, though you cannot visit the *marae* without permission.

Katikati

pop 2900

This small town was the only planned Ulster settlement in the world, and celebrates this history with bright *murals* on many of the town's buildings. Grab a free map from the **Mural Town Information Centre** (☎ 07-549 1658; www.katikati.co.nz; 36 Main Rd; ☼ 9am-4.30pm) and take a tour of the murals. From the information centre you can also take the **Haiku Pathway**, a pleasant walking route past boulders inscribed with haiku verses, which follows the Uretara River.

Katikati Heritage Museum (☎ 07-549 0651; cnr SH2 & Wharawhara Rd; adult/child $6/2, minigolf adult/child/family $4/3/15; ☼ 8.30am-3pm) traces local history with an eclectic mix of Maori artefacts and Ulster history, with some moa bones and reputedly the largest collection of bottles in the southern hemisphere all thrown in for good measure. You can also play a round of minigolf.

Morton Estate (☎ 07-552 0795; SH2; ☼ tastings 9.30am-5pm) has a branch of its Hawkes Bay–based empire here. One of NZ's bigger wineries, it's located on SH2, 8km south of Katikati. White wines are particularly good.

SLEEPING

Accommodation is scattered around the countryside surrounding Katikati, with several farmstays available.

Kingfisher (☎ 07-552 0388; www.kingfisher-backpack.co.nz; 122a Work Rd; dm/tw/d $20/23/30; ☐) Offering simple rooms in the middle of a working avocado farm, this new spot is a peaceful country getaway. To keep you busy there's a short walk through the gully and orchard, plus the new owners are eager to please. Small kitchens and bike storage garages make it a good option for independent travellers.

Colannade Backpackers (/fax 07-552 0902; colannade@actrix.co.nz; 122 Work Rd, Aongatete; dm $18) This basic bunkhouse 10km south of Katikati is set in the heart of the horticultural area, with discounts for stays longer than two nights.

Sapphire Springs Holiday Park (07-549 0768; sapphire.springs@xtra.co.nz; Hot Springs Rd; sites per 2 people $26, dm/d from $15/75) This popular park is perfect for families and large groups, with plenty of activities to keep everyone busy: barbecues, playgrounds, volleyball, minigolf and thermal pools that feature a slide for littlies. Units are a bit basic, but with short bush-walks around the area, there's plenty of chances to enjoy the outdoors.

Katikati Motel (07-549 0385; katikati@ihug.co.nz; cnr Main & Fairview Rds; d $70-80) This budget motel is one of the town's older places, but it's been well kept and remains a good cheap option.

Kaimai View Motel (07-549 0398; kaimaiview@xtra.co.nz; 78 Main Rd; d/tr $95/115;) This modern motel is opposite the Katikati Motel, offering neat rooms that include CD players and, in larger rooms, spas. Breakfast and dinner are also available.

Panorama Lodge (07-549 1882; www.panorama lodge.co.nz; 901 Pacific Coast Hwy; d $120;) This neat little B&B is set in a diverse orchard 10km north of town that grows kiwi fruit, tangelos and avocados, but most importantly it lives up to its name with sweeping views of the bay. It's a real farm experience, with quail and alpacas wandering the grounds. Luxury rooms have extras beyond brass beds and DVDs, including slippers and fresh coffee.

Matahui Lodge (07-571 8121; www.matahui -lodge.co.nz; 187 Matahui Rd; d $375) Luxurious but homey, this large place boasts a driving range and small personal gym. If all that sounds too active you can cosy-up around the roaring fireplaces and enjoy a glass of wine grown on the grounds, or relax in the patio spa.

EATING

Twickenham Homestead (07-549 0388; cnr SH2 & Mulgan St; panini $12-15, starters $12-18, mains $22-30; lunch & dinner) Set in elegant gardens and with a slightly chintzy feel inside (including a doll collection), Twickenham excels at

Devonshire teas. Its menu is sophisticated, from gourmet *panini* to mains such as pork cutlets stacked on apple-and-sage *roesti*.

Morton Estate (07-552 0795; 8km south on SH2; tastings 9.30am-5pm) This winery (see p357) has worked hard to build a menu using local food to complement its solid wine list, with excellent results. Sunday lunches feature live music.

One Wild Chook (07-549 3017; Main Rd; mains $10-12, cakes $6; 9am-5pm Mon-Fri, 9am-2pm Sat) This local favourite is good for coffee and cake, with lunches of deli-style sandwiches and other gourmet grub.

Omokoroa

Just 22km west of Tauranga, this popular summer destination affords views of the harbour and Matakana Island. There are a couple of campervan parks, including **Omokoroa Tourist Park** (07-578 0857; www.omo koroa.co.nz; 165 Omokoroa Rd; sites per 2 people $30, dm/cabins/units $20/60/80;), a family-oriented park with a wide range of accommodation and thermal hot pools. From Omokoroa you can visit Matakana on the regular ferry service.

Minden Lookout

From Minden Lookout, about 10km west of Tauranga, there's a superb view back over the Bay of Plenty. To get there, take SH2 to Te Puna and turn off south on Minden Rd; the lookout is about 4km up the road.

Papamoa
pop 7460

Papamoa is a pasture away from becoming a residential suburb of the Mount, and even that suburb is slated for development. Over the sheltering dune, the beaches are truly spectacular and it's easy to see why people move here for swimming and surfing.

Papamoa Beach Top 10 Holiday Resort (/fax 07-572 0816; www.papamoabeach.co.nz; 535 Papamoa Beach Rd; sites per 2 people $28, cabins/units/villas $50/80/160) is a modern park that has been hepped-up beyond its caravan-park origins, with an array of accommodation options, including self-contained villas.

The swanky **Pacific Palms Resort** (0800 808 835; www.pacificpalmsresort.co.nz; 21 Gravatt Rd; d $145-260;) has roomy, self-contained two- and three-bedroom apartments that cater to a family crowd. Facilities like tennis courts and a spa will ensure that the kids have plenty to do.

With its corrugated-iron exterior and tasteful caneware interior, **Beach House Motel** (☎ 0800 429 999; www.beachhousemotel.co.nz; 224 Papamoa Beach Rd; d $85-175; ▣) is the sophisticated beach bach that everyone would want to own. The handy beach and airy feel make it even more perfect.

Blue Biyou (☎ 07-572 2099; 559 Papamoa Beach Rd; mains from $7; ☼ 4pm-late) is known for fine meals and enormous Sunday brunches.

Navigator (☎ 07-542 2555; Cnr of Palm Springs Blvd & Papamoa Dr; starters $6.50-16.50, mains $18-27; ☼ dinner Tue-Sun, lunch Sun) is a tavern-style joint that does steaks, chicken and seafood plus a few surprises like Thai chicken curry and lamb shanks.

You can get takeaway food from places on Beach Rd, and **Palm Beach Plaza Shopping Centre** (cnr Domain & Gravatt Rds) is another popular spot for snacks and for stocking up on groceries.

Te Puke
pop 6775

Unchallenged as the 'Kiwi Fruit Capital of the World', Te Puke is busiest during the kiwi fruit-picking season when there's plenty of work (see the boxed text, below). The **Te Puke visitor information centre** (☎ 07-573 9172; 130 Jellicoe St; ☼ 8am-4.30pm Mon-Fri, 9am-noon Sat) is in the same building as the library.

ZESPRI, GOOSEBERRY OR KIWI FRUIT?

The humble brown-furred kiwi fruit annually pumps $2 billion into the Bay of Plenty, so it's no surprise that local people worship this fruit at shrines like Kiwi 360 (see above).

Originally the fruit was grown in China and called monkey peach, because people knew they were ripe when monkeys started eating them. When the fruit was brought to NZ they were referred to as Chinese gooseberries as they were small, grapelike fruits. Canny Kiwi invention saw the fruits grown to larger, more edible sizes and NZ began exporting them in the 1950s.

As recently as 2004 orchards of the golden variety of kiwi fruit in Italy have been chainsawed down after a court action to defend the furry fruit. The Zespri company grows two types of kiwi fruit: the common green and a new gold fruit, which the company calls the zespri. The company protects the intellectual property rights to the zespri in courts across the world. The green variety isn't protected and are grown as far afield as Turkey, Chile, Canada and Italy.

The fruit is fragile and can only be grown in temperate climates. As you drive around Te Puke, you'll see large screens of trees grown to protect the fruit from wind and the elements. Kiwi-fruit boffins believe that, much like grapes, you can only pick the fruit when they obtain a certain sugar level that makes for the best eating.

There's always work around the area in the kiwi fruit industry. You can check the noticeboard at the Te Puke visitor information centre (above) or for work in horticulture across NZ check out www.picknz.co.nz.

SIGHTS & ACTIVITIES

The Bay of Plenty is kiwi-fruit country and here you have the opportunity to learn a little more about the fruit that is so important to NZ's economy.

Formerly known as Kiwi Fruit Country, the rebranded **Kiwi 360** (☎ 07-573 6340; www.kiwi360.com; $4/2; adult/child $20/free; ☼ 9am-5pm) is a slicker insight into a kiwi-fruit orchard, at the turn-off for Maketu. An informative 35-minute 'Kiwi-kart' rides through the orchards which also grow nashi pears, citrus and avocados. The café serves up more than just kiwi fruit cuisine, including some great cakes and coffee, while the shop stocks all manner of kiwi-fruit products. You can also do helicopter tours with **Bay of Plenty Experience** (☎ 0800 864 354; www.aerius.co.nz; tours from 10min $95) from here. At the time of research there were plans to build a kiwi-fruit museum, which could be completed as soon as 2007.

Right next door is the **Vintage Auto Barn** (☎ 07-573 6547; www.vintagecars.nzhere.com; adult/child $8/2; ☼ 9am-5pm) with more than 100 vintage and classic cars on display, such as a 1906 Cadillac, 1923 Model T Ford and a Lamborghini suspended from the roof!

The **Comvita visitors centre** (☎ 0800 504 959; SH33, Paengaroa; admission free; ☼ 9am-5pm, tours 10am & 2pm) creates health-care treatments made from honey and other bee products. There's an educational gallery, shop and interesting tours that take you to the hive and let you spot the queen bee (she's the one with a green spot on her thorax).

Longridge Park (☎ 07-533 1515; www.longridge park.co.nz; Paengaroa; adult/child jetboat $75/35, farm tours $18/12, 4WD $75/35, rush combo $135; ☉9am-5pm summer, to 4pm winter) offers many different adventures from half-hour jetboat rides on the Kaituna River to cute tours of a kiwi-fruit farm, including sheep-milking demonstrations. Alternatively, you can jump into a 'wabbit' 4WD for a bit of hill-hopping. It also offers interesting packages such as Rush, a four-hour jetboating and rafting combo.

SLEEPING

The visitors centre has a list of home- and farmstays in the area.

Lindenhof Homestay (☎ 07-573 4592; 58 Dunlop Rd; s/d $80/100; ☒) Lindenhof has large comfy rooms in a lovely homestead with generous grounds that are perfect for getting away from it all. It's an affordable country house complete with tennis court and spa.

Lazy Days B&B (☎ 07-573 8188; 144 Boucher Ave $100) This unpretentious self-contained cottage offers rare privacy in a B&B with a pleasant garden to catch the sun in.

Beacon Motel (☎ 07-573 7825; 173 Jellicoe St; s/d $70/90; ☒) This well-presented motel is older in style, but suits passing businesspeople.

Maketu

pop 1000

By taking SH2 through Te Puke and turning left onto Maketu Rd, you'll find yourself at this lovely seaside town. The **visitors centre** (☎ 07-533 2343; Maketu Rd; ☉ 10am-1pm) has information on the town.

Maketu played a significant role in NZ's history as it was the landing site of *Te Arawa* canoe (see p328), which is commemorated today with an impressive stone monument on the foreshore. The **Maori Exhibition** (☎ 07-533 2176; cnr Waihi & Park Rds; ☉ by appointment) displays handicrafts and other Maori exhibits. There's a *pa* overlooking the water at Town Point not far from town.

Beach bums should head for **New Dick's Beach** (admission $2), a local hangout reached by following Town Point Rd to a small dirt track. It's on private property so you have to give a $2 donation at the gate. From this gorgeous little beach you can walk all the way to Waihi. You can ride on the beach with

Briars Seaside Ride Horse Trek (☎ 07-533 2582; www .briarshorsetrek.co.nz; Town Point Rd, 2hr rides $55).

You can stay at **Beach Holiday Park** (☎ 07-533 2165; www.maketubeach.co.nz; 3 Town Point Rd; unpowered/powered sites per 2 people $34/38, cabins/d from $45/85), a delightful spot on the beach with everything from log cabins to well-appointed motel rooms.

Don't forget to try Maketu's most famous pastries at **Maketu Pies** (☎ 07-533 2358; 6 Little Waihi Rd), which are baked fresh here daily; the lamb and mint is especially recommended.

EASTERN BAY OF PLENTY

Stretching from Maketu to Opotiki, the Eastern Bay of Plenty's main drawcard is long stretches of sandy beaches backed by cliffs covered in flowering pohutukawa trees. It's beautiful and often forgotten country; in fact between Whakatane and Opotiki you could find your own little patch of stunning coastline to lie back on.

WHAKATANE

pop 17,700

On a natural harbour at the mouth of the Whakatane (fa-ka-ta-ne) River lies this hub of the Rangitaiki agricultural district. But there's much more to Whakatane than

---

WHAKA LIKE A MAN

Whakatane's name originated some eight centuries ago, 200 years after the original Maori settlers arrived here. The warrior Toroa and his family sailed into the estuary in a huge ocean-going *waka* (canoe), the *Mataatua*. The men went to greet local leaders, leaving the women with the canoe, but as the tide turned, the *waka* drifted out to sea. Toroa's daughter, Wairaka, cried out '*E! Kia whakatane au i ahau!*' (Let me act as a man!) and, breaking the traditional Maori *tapu* that women never steer a *waka*, took the paddle and brought the boat safely to shore. A **statue of Wairaka** today stands proudly atop a rock in Whakatane's harbour in commemoration of her brave deed and for bestowing the town's name.

farming, with the chance to swim with dolphins or witness NZ's most active volcano, the smoking Whakaari (White Island) that lies just offshore. The beaches here and in neighbouring Ohope Beach are beautiful.

Information

Whakatane visitor information centre (☎ 0800 478 674; www.whakatane.com; Quay St; ☯ 8.30am-6.30pm Mon-Fri, 9am-5pm Sat & Sun summer, 8.30am-5pm Mon-Fri, 10am-3.30pm Sat & Sun winter) books tours and handles general inquiries for DOC. Nearby is a **New Zealand Post** (☎ 07-307 1155; Commerce St) outlet. For emergency medical treatment, visit **Whakatane Hospital** (07-306 0999; Stewart St). Most hostels offer Internet connection, but **Game House** (☎ 07-308 2211; 115 The Strand; per hr 5¢) has a good broadband connection.

Sights

Whakatane Museum (☎ 07-306 0505; www.whakatane museum.org.nz; 11 Boon St; admission by donation; ☯ 10am-4.30pm Mon-Fri, 11am-1pm Sat & Sun) is an impressive regional museum with artfully presented photo and artefact exhibits on early Maori and European settlers. Of particular interest are the *taonga* (treasures) of local Maori tribes tracing their lineage back to the *Mataatua waka* (see the boxed text, opposite). The adjacent art gallery features local artists.

Just to one side of the traffic circle is **Pohaturoa** (cnr The Strand & Commerce St), a large *tapu* (sacred) rock outcrop, where warriors were once tattooed. The Treaty of Waitangi was signed here by Ngati Awa chiefs in 1840. The coastline used to come right up to this point and there's a tunnel in the rock where baptisms and other rites were performed. Also here is a monument to the Ngati Awa chief Te Hurinui Apanui. Another Maori site is **Muriwai's Cave** (partially collapsed), which once provided shelter to Muriwai, Wairaka's aunt and famous seer. A ceremonial *waka* is caged in opposite the caves.

Whakatane Astronomical Observatory (☎ 07-308 6495; Hurinu Ave, Hillcrest; admission $5; ☯ dusk Tue) offers a great chance to star-spot when the sky is clear.

Activities

DOLPHIN SWIMMING

Dolphins Down Under (☎ 0800 354 7737; www.dolphinswim.co.nz; 2 The Strand; adult/child $100/75) and **Whales & Dolphin Watch** (☎ 07-308 2001; www.whalesanddolphinwatch.co.nz; 96 The Strand; trips adult/child $100/80; ☯ departs at 6am, 10.30am & 3pm) run dolphin-swimming trips year-round (subject to weather). Trips include all equipment and it's almost guaranteed you'll get your flippers near Flipper.

WALKING

The visitors centre sells *Discover the Walks Around Whakatane* ($2), a booklet detailing walks ranging from 30 minutes to half a day. Most of the walks are part of the **Nga Tapuwae o Toi** (Footsteps of Toi) walkway (13 hours, 18km), a large loop that takes in Ohope Beach and several sacred sites along the way. An easy section is the **River Walk** (three hours), a quick orientation to Whakatane passing Muriwai's Cave and Wairaka's statue.

MAORI NZ: BAY OF PLENTY

The Bay of Plenty's traditional name, Te Rohe o Mataatua, recalls the ancestral *Mataatua* canoe, which arrived here from Hawa ki to make an eventful landfall at Whakatane (see the boxed text, opposite). The region's history stretches back further than that, though, with the Polynesian settler Toi setting up what's claimed to be Aotearoa's first settlement in about AD 800.

Major tribal groups in the region are the Ngati Awa (www.ngatiawa.iwi.nz) of the Whakatane area, Whakatohea (www.whakatohea.co.nz) of Opotiki, Ngaiterangi (www.ngaiterangi.org.nz) of Tauranga, and Te Arawa (www.arawa.iwi.nz) of Rotorua. Tribes in this region were involved on both sides of the Land Wars of the late 19th century (see the boxed text, p35), with those fighting against the government suffering considerable land confiscations that have caused legal problems right up to the present day.

There's a significant Maori population in the Bay, and plenty to do for travellers looking to immerse themselves in Maori culture: Opotiki has the charming eyeball-eating scene in *Utu* (p365); Whakatane has Toi's Pa (perhaps NZ's oldest *pa* site, p362); and Rotorua has *hangi* meals, traditional villages (p333), Te Whakarewarewa (p331), and much, much, *much* more.

WHAKATANE

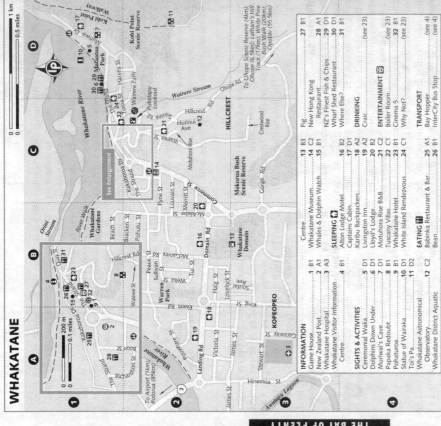

INFORMATION
Game House...........................1 B1
New Zealand Post...................2 A1
Whakatane Hospital...............3 A3
Whakatane Visitor Information
  Centre................................4 B1

SIGHTS & ACTIVITIES
Ceremonial Waka...................5 D1
Dolphins Down Under.............6 D1
Muriwai's Cave......................7 D1
Papaka Redoubt....................8 B1
Pohaturoa.............................9 B1
Statue of Wairaka................10 B1
Toi's Pa...............................11 D2
Whakatane Astronomical
  Observatory......................12 C2
Whakatane District Aquatic
  Centre...............................13 B3
Whakatane Museum...............14 C2
Whales & Dolphin Watch.......15 B1

SLEEPING
Alton Lodge Motel................16 B2
Captains Cabin.....................17 D1
Karibu Backpackers...............18 A2
Livingston Inn......................19 A2
Lloyd's Lodge......................20 B2
Motuhora Rise B&B...............21 C2
Tuscany Villas......................22 C1
Whakatane Hotel..................23 B1
White Island Rendezvous.......24 C1

EATING
Babinka Restaurant & Bar.......25 A1
Bean..................................26 B1
Fig....................................27 B1
New Hong Kong
  Restaurant........................28 A1
NZ's Finest Fish & Chips.......29 B1
Wharf Shed Restaurant.........30 D1
Where Else?........................31 B1

DRINKING
Crac..................................(see 23)

ENTERTAINMENT
Boiler Room.........................(see 23)
Cinema 5............................32 B1
Why Not?............................(see 23)

TRANSPORT
Bay Hopper.........................(see 4)
InterCity Bus Stop................(see 4)

Another popular stroll is **Kohi Point Walkway** (four hours, 5.5km), which extends through the Kohi Point Scenic Reserve, passing lookouts and **Toi's Pa** (Kapua te Rangi), reputedly the oldest *pa* site in NZ. Other walkways are the Ohope Scenic Reserve, the Mokorua Bush Scenic Reserve, Latham's Hill Track (17km out of town) and Puketapu Lookout and Papaka Redoubt. **White Pine Bush Walk** (30 minutes, 300m) starts 20km south of Whakatane and is designed for wheelchair and pram access.

OTHER ACTIVITIES

Most trips to Whakaari (White Island) leave from Whakatane (see p365). Ohope Beach also offers a range of activities.

Kiwi Jet Tours (0800 800 538; www.kiwijetboat tours.com; adult/child $65/55) rockets along Rangitaiki River from Matahina Dam to Aniwhenua Falls for a hell-raising ride.

Whakatane District Aquatic Centre (07-308 4192; Short St; adult/child $3.50/1.50; 6am-8pm Mon-Fri, 7am-6pm Sat & Sun) is a modern swimming complex with indoor and outdoor pools, spa pools and a waterslide.

To try fly-fishing, **Barnacles Guides** (07-308 7429; full day $450) knows the hidden spots. Prices include breakfast, lunch and dinner (hopefully a trout!).

Almost in Kawerau, **Tui Glen Farm** (07-323 6457, 07-322 1919; www.tuiglen.net.nz; 5H30, south of Kawerau; 1hr rides adult/child $35/25) offers horse treks through bush or, in summer, on the beach.

Sleeping

BUDGET

Cheaper accommodation in Whakatane is limited, but of a high standard.

Lloyd's Lodge (☎ 07-307 8005; lloyds.lodge@xtra .co.nz; 10 Domain Rd; dm $20, d $50-60; ☐) This friendly Maori-owned hostel is in a sprucely restored wooden house, offering fun in-house sing-alongs, sung welcomes and the odd *hangi*. Rooms are bright with large living spaces, making for a sociable hostel that's ideal for hooking up with other travellers.

Karibu Backpackers (☎ /fax 07-307 8276; 13 Landing Rd; sites per 2 people $24, dm $21-22; ☐) This converted house is a private hostel with a large garden and communal kitchen and good-sized dorms. Barbecues and free bikes are excellent extras for those after affordable fun.

Whakatane Hotel (☎ 07-307 1670; 79 The Strand; dm/s/d $16/30/55) This old Art Deco pub has basic rooms that suit partying backpackers who won't mind weekend bend noise, because they'll be in the thick of it downstairs at the Craic pub.

MIDRANGE

White Island Rendezvous (☎ 0800 242 299; www .whiteisland.co.nz; 15 The Strand East; c/f from $110/140) Immaculate White Island has decked rooms with raw timber floors and the vibe of a beach cottage. Deluxe rooms come with spas and there are disabled facilities. It also does deals for guests visiting White Island.

Tuscany Villas (☎ 0800 801 040; www.tuscanyvillas .co.nz; 57 The Strand; d/ste $125/165; ☐ ☑) This brand-spanking-new motel may be a long way from Florence, but still offers sophisticated accommodation. Facilities like broadband Internet, in-room spas and super king beds make stays here luxurious.

Livingston Inn (☎ 0800 770 77; www.livingston .co.nz; 42 Landing Rd; d/f $115/130) The Livingston has been refitted to remain one of the better motels in town, with spacious, well-kept units that are popular with business travellers. Full-sized spas in executive suites are a great fringe benefit.

Alton Lodge Motel (☎ 07-307 1003; 76 Domain Rd; s/d/f $80/90/145; ☑) This solid brick building has similarly solid rooms with full kitchens and disabled rooms. Two-level family rooms are like a home away from home, complete with laundry.

Captains Cabin (☎ 07-308 5719; 23 Muriwai Dr; r $75) In a serene part of town with breath-taking seaside views, this cheap and cheerful spot sleeps three, with breakfast extra. It's a homey self-contained room, perfect for longer stays.

TOP END

Motuhora Rise B&B (☎ 07-307 0224; 2 Motuhora Rise; s/d $190/205) At the top of the town in both senses, this hilltop spot affords great views across to White Island. You can expect a gourmet cheeseboard on arrival, along with other extras such as a DVD home theatre suite, outdoor spa pool on decking and fishing rods or golf clubs.

Eating

Babinka Restaurant & Bar (☎ 07-307 0009; 14 Kakahoroa Dr; mains $20-25; ☑ breakfast, lunch & dinner)

This innovative place isn't afraid to throw diverse ingredients like fetta, banana and bacon into a salad, in fact it does it with aplomb. The menu is a delicious fusion of Indian, Turkish and Moroccan.

Wharf Shed Restaurant (☎ 07-308 5698; The Strand; mains $28-35; ☑ lunch & dinner) The Wharf Shed is one of the hottest tables in town, with lashings of seafood, including mussels, and a tasty salmon timbale. Dining alfresco on balmy evenings here is a delight.

NZ's Finest Fish & Chips (☎ 07-308 1100; The Strand; meals $5-9; ☑ 10am-8pm) If you don't want to pay the big bucks at the Wharf Shed, then this little budget spot is the go. We recommend solid old-style chunky chips and a solid lump of local tarakihi, all best enjoyed while strolling past the pricier places.

Fig (☎ 07-308 6549; 93 The Strand; lunch $12-16, dinner $20-24; ☑ breakfast & lunch daily, dinner Thu-Sat) This is the posh place to grab a coffee or sip chai with tasty café-style food and cakes. The rear courtyard is best for a relaxed weekend breakfast.

Bean (☎ 07-307 0494; 54 The Strand; bagels $6-8; ☑ 8.30-4pm Mor-Fri, Sat 10am-2pm) Choose a chair to suit your mood (they range from retro leather to plush purple) and a brew (Guatemalan, Kenyan and Brazilian are all represented) to complement your hangover at this hip spot specialising in coffee and bagels.

Why Not? (☎ 07-308 8138; 79 The Strand; mains $14-25; ☑ lunch & dinner) This tavern-style spot attracts the hungry with whopping serves of pasta, salads, fish and steak.

Where Else? Inn (☎07-308 6721; 62 The Strand; mains $6-16; ☺lunch & dinner) The other interrogative restaurant in town is a log-cabin cantina with a Mexican menu of burritos, tacos and errr, burgers. It's affordable with filling meals in a fun atmosphere.

New Hong Kong Restaurant (☎07-308 5864; 12 Boon St; mains $6-10; ☺lunch & dinner Tue-Sun) This no-fuss takeaway does Sino-Kiwi grub like Egg Foo Young, chop sueys and, of course, chips. Lunch deals ($5) are a good bet.

Drinking & Entertainment

There are only a few nightspot options in town. The **Craic** (☎07-307 1670; 79 The Strand) is an affable Irish bar to enjoy a drink or watch a footy game in, while next door the **Boiler Room** (☎07-307 0176; 79 The Strand) has the occasional live band. Both venues are located in the Whakatane Hotel (see p363).

Why Not? (☎07-308 8138; 79 The Strand; mains $14-25; ☺lunch & dinner) has irregular live music best enjoyed over a few drinks.

Cinema 5 (☎07-308 7623; 100 The Strand; adult/child $13/8) is definitely the movie theatre in town, with a giant film reel projecting from its frontage.

Getting There & Around

Air New Zealand (☎07-308 8397; Whakatane airport) has daily flights linking Whakatane to Auckland, with connections to other centres.

InterCity buses stop outside the visitors centre and connect Whakatane with Rotorua ($25, 1½ hours) and Gisborne ($35, three hours), with connections to other places. All buses to Gisborne go via Opotiki. **Bay Hopper** (☎0800 422 9287) buses run to Tauranga and Opotiki, stopping at the visitors centre.

Taxis (☎0800 421 829) to/from the airport cost $20. There's no local bus service.

OHOPE BEACH

pop 3010

Just 7km over the hill from Whakatane, Ohope has great beaches, perfect for lazing or surfing, and is backed by sleepy Ohiwa Harbour. Just beyond the harbour is the small Sandspit Wildlife Refuge. If you want to take on the surf, get some lessons from local **Beaver** (☎07-312 4909; per day $100).

There's plenty of accommodation around the town including **Ohope Beach Top 10 Holiday Park & Adventure Complex** (☎/fax 07-312 4460; www.ohopebeach.co.nz; 367 Harbour Rd; unpowered/powered sites per 2 people $34/36, cabins/units/apts $70/100/135; ⚲), a family-friendly caravan park with activities like basketball and tennis court, minigolf and swimming. For a step up, **Beachpoint Resort** (☎0800 232 2476; 5 West End Rd; 1/2-bedroom apts $150/180; ⚲⚲) offers self-contained apartments with even better weekly rates.

There are several spots to eat in town, such as **Vanilla** (☎07-312 5292; 19 Pohutukawa Ave; mains $23-25; ☺dinner Tue-Sat), a hip place that serves fashionable ingredients like chermoula along with local faves like steaks and seafood; and **C'Vue** (☎0800 005 008; Bluett Rd; mains $16-22; ☺Wed-Sun) which specialises in complex fare.

For simpler grub, **Ohiwa Oyster Farm** (☎07-312 4565; Wainui Rd) on the highway towards Opotiki, is perfect for a fish and chip picnic, including some very fresh oysters.

MOTUHORA (WHALE ISLAND)

Nine kilometres off Whakatane is Motuhora or Whale Island, so-called because of its leviathan shape. This volcanic island follows the same volcanic trench as Whakaari, but is much less active. Along its shore are hot springs, which can reach 93°C. The summit is 353m high and the island has several historic sites, including an ancient *pa* site, quarry and camp.

Whale Island was settled by the Maori before the 1769 landing of Captain Cook. In 1829 there was a Maori massacre of sailors from the trading vessel *Haweis* while it was anchored at Sulphur Bay. In the 1840s the island passed into European ownership and remains privately owned, although since 1965 it has been a protected wildlife refuge administered by DOC.

Whale Island is a refuge for sea and shore birds, some of which are endangered. Some of the birds use the island only for nesting at certain times of the year, while others are present year-round.

The island's protected status means landing is restricted. There are only six trips to the island each year (adult/child $50/40) over the Christmas period; bookings can be made through the Whakatane DOC office or visitor information centre (see p361).

WHAKAARI (WHITE ISLAND)

NZ's most active volcano, 50km off Whakatane, is a small island formed by three separate volcanic cones, all of different ages.

You can expect to see a dynamic volcano complete with hissing and steaming. Erosion has worn down the two older cones and the youngest, which rose up between the two older ones, now occupies the centre of the island. Hot water and steam pour from vents over most of the crater floor and temperatures of 600°C to 800°C have been recorded. Mt Gisborne is the highest point on the island at 321m. Geologically, Whakaari is related to Motuhora (Whale Island) and Putauaki (Mt Edgecumbe), as all lie along the same volcanic trench.

The island is privately owned so you can only visit via a helicopter or boat tour that has prior permission. There's no jetty so boats land on the beach, which means landings aren't possible in rough seas.

Getting There & Away

Trips to Whakaari generally include a walking tour around the island. All trips (except for fixed-wing aerial sightseeing) incur a $20 landing fee, which should be included in the quoted price.

Operators include the following:

Dive White (☎ 0800 348 394; www.divewhite.co.nz; land tours $150, diving $220) Offers diving and snorkelling trips.

Vulcan Helicopters (☎ 0800 804 354; www.vulcanheli.co.nz; flights $430) Has 2½-hour helicopter flights (minimum of five people) with landing when safe.

White Island Tours (☎ 0800 733 523; tours $150) Offers a six-hour trip with dolphin-spotting en route and trip up to the crater.

WHAKATANE TO ROTORUA

Travelling along SH30 from Whakatane to Rotorua you'll come to the **Awakeri Hot Springs** (adult/child $5/1.50). Complete with springs, spa pools, picnic areas and **holiday park** (☎ 07-304 9117; RD2 off SH3?; sites per 2 people from $25, d/ste from $43/75), there's a bed available for every budget.

Just off SH30, the timber town of **Kawerau** is surrounded by pine forest that's regularly harvested by **Tasman Pulp & Paper Mill** (☎ 07-323 3456; Kawerau; ☑ tours by appintment). Kawerau's **visitors centre** (☎ 07-323 7550; Plunket St; ☑ 8.30am-4.30pm Mon-Fri, 10am-3pm Sat & Sun) has details of accommodation.

Tarawera Falls are a half-hour drive from Kawerau, along a well-graded road through pine forests (watch out for the logging trucks). From the car park, the **Tarawera Falls Track** (40 minutes return, 1.4km) tramps through native forest to the falls. The **Tarawera Outlet Track** (four hours return, 10km) continues on to Lake Tarawera with impressive views of Mt Tarawera. You can hike to **camping sites** (see p3-6). Visits require a permit ($2), obtainable from the visitors centre.

Dominating Kawerau is **Putauaki (Mt Edgecumbe)**, a volcanic cone with panoramic views of the entire Bay of Plenty. You need a permit for access ($2) but it closes during times of high fire risk; contact the visitors centre for permits and updates.

OPOTIKI
pop 7070

This sweet shy country kid of a town has several charms, such as an artsy centre, and is the last stop on the drive south. The beaches – Ohiwa and Waitahi – are worth the trip alone. Opotiki is the gateway to the East Cape and the rugged forests and river valleys of the Raukumara and nearby ranges. The town is a model of Maori tradition: the main street is lined with the works of master carvers.

The Opotiki area was settled from at least 1150, some 200 years before the larger 14th-century migration. In the mid-1800s Opotiki was a centre for Hauhauism, a Maori doctrine that was grounded in Judaeo-Christian beliefs and advocated, among other things, an end to the Maori oppression.

Information

The **Opotiki visitor information centre** (☎ 07-315 8484; www.opotikinz.com; cnr St John & Elliott Sts; ☑ 8am-5pm) and **DOC office** (☎ 07-315 1001) are in the same building. The centre takes bookings for a variety of activities and stocks the indispensable free booklet *Opotiki & East Cape*.

You can send mail at the **New Zealand Post Paper Plus** (☎ 07-315 6155; 106c Church St) outlet.

Sights & Activities

Known by the local Whakatohea tribe to have acted as a government spy, Rev Carl Volkner was murdered in 1865 in the **Church of St Stephen the Martyr** (Church St) – you can still see the bloodstains near the pulpit. You can pick up the key from **Kowhai Takeaways** (☎ 07-315 6112; 125 Church St; ☑ 9am-7pm), just opposite the church.

Just over 7km south of the town centre is the fascinating **Hukutaia Domain** (Woodlands Rd;

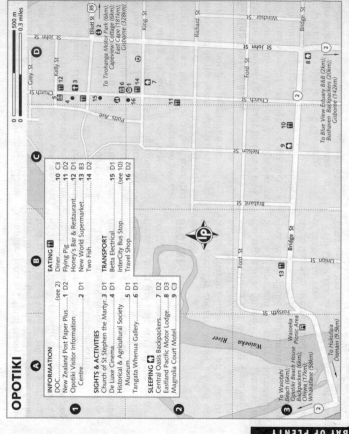

OPOTIKI

INFORMATION
DOC...(see 2)	
New Zealand Post Paper Plus......1 D2	
Opotiki Visitor Information	
Centre..................................2 D1	

SIGHTS & ACTIVITIES
Church of St Stephen the Martyr..3 D1	
De Luxe Cinema.........................4 D1	
Historical & Agricultural Society	
Museum..................................5 D1	
Tangata Whenua Gallery.............6 D1	

SLEEPING
Central Oasis Backpackers...........7 D2	
Eastland Pacific Motor Lodge.......8 D3	
Magnolia Court Motel.................9 C3	

EATING
Diner...................................10 C3	
Flying Pig.............................11 D2	
Honey's Bar & Restaurant.........12 D1	
New World Supermarket...........13 B3	
Two Fish..............................14 D2	

TRANSPORT
Betta Electrical......................15 D1	
InterCity Bus Stop.................(see 10)	
Travel Shop..........................16 D2	

daily), which has one of the finest collections of native plants in NZ, many rare or endangered. In the domain's centre is Taketakerau, a 21m puriri tree, estimated to be more than 2000 years old and a burial place for the distinguished dead of the Upokorere *hapu* (subtribe) of the Whakatohea tribe. The tree is no longer *tapu* as the remains have been reinterred elsewhere.

The **Historical & Agricultural Society Museum** (07-315 5193; 127 Church St; adult/child $2/1; 10am-3.30pm Mon-Sat) is currently in Shalfoon's old shop, an old general store. There are plans to re-create several retail shops from the 20th century in the space, but it currently displays an interesting collection of bric-a-brac.

Motu River Jet Boat Tours (07-325 2735; adult/ child $85/50) has as many as three 1½-hour trips daily on the Motu River. **Wet 'n' Wild** (0800 462 7238; www.wetnwildrafting.co.nz) offers two- to four-day rafting, camping and jetboating adventures on the Motu (from $640).

The charming old **De Luxe Cinema** (07-315 6110; 129 Church St) still shows the latest flicks plus a few arthouse favourites.

Also on the main street, **Tangata Whenua Gallery** (07-315 5558; 127b Church St; 9am-5pm Mon-Fri) stocks great crafts made by Maoris and Islanders, including cute bags, T-shirts and other authentic souvenirs.

Sleeping
Opotiki Beach House Backpackers (07-315 5117; Appleton Rd; dm $22, d & tw $48;) The large deck at this fun hostel offers good Pacific views of Waitahi Beach and plenty of opportunities to get in the water with free kayaks, body boards and surfboards. Dorm rooms are generous here, though the self-contained units are excellent value; for romance grab the couples caravan, aka the 'shaggin' wagon'.

Central Oasis Backpackers (07-315 5165; 30 King St; dm/tw/d $15/18/20;) This central backpackers is a snug spot with relatively spacious rooms with crackling fires and a rambling backyard to hang out in.

Tirohanga Motor Park (07-315 7942; East Coast Rd, Tirohanga; unpowered/powered sites per 2 people $22/24, dm $15, cabins $40-60) In the nearby town of Tirohanga, this spacious park has several camping options with cabins closer to the beach costing a little more.

Capeview Cottage (☎ 0800 227 384; www.capeview .co.nz; Tablelands Rd; d $130) Set amid chirruping birds and kiwi-fruit orchards, this serene cottage has two bedrooms, a spa and idyllic coast views. Weekly rates are available.

Eastland Pacific Motor Lodge (☎ 07-315 5524; www.eastlandpacific.co.nz; cnr Bridge & St John Sts; d $85-95) Eastland is a well-kept motel with 1980s bed linen and spa baths as standard, all of which prove popular with travelling sales representatives.

Magnolia Court Motel (☎ 0800 556 246; magnolia .crt.motel@xtra.co.nz; cnr Bridge & Nelson Sts; s/d/f $70/80/90; ☐) The mock-Tudor exterior of the Magnolia lets you know that this is an older place that has kept its rooms trim and neat.

Blue View Estuary B&B (☎ 07-315 4746; SH2; cottage $90) This self-contained cottage offers awe-inspiring hilltop views for those who want to get away from it all. The cottage sleeps up to four and comes with a kitchenette.

Eating

Opotiki has a scattering of reasonable eateries is available, but it isn't exactly a gourmet destination.

Two Fish (☎ 07-315 5548; 102 Church St; mains $8-14; ☑ 8am-11pm) Next door to the Royal pub, this funky eatery has the best coffee in town and hefty portions of burgers, sandwiches and innovative salads. The massive Beast burger has defeated many appetites.

Flying Pig (☎ 07-315 7618; 95 Church St; mains $6-12; ☑ breakfast & lunch) This licensed sow offers simple food with a great all-day breakfast and mysterious Flying Pig Surprise ($10). It's a fun spot to stick your snout in the trough.

Diner (☎ 07-315 5805; 77 Bridge St; mains $8-10; ☑ breakfast, lunch & dinner) This no-frills spot does hearty meals throughout the day, including burgers, fish and chips, and steaks. For in-between meals it has delicious cakes and paua (shellfish) fritters.

Honey's Bar & Restaurant (☎ 07-315 6078; Church St; mains $3.50-25; ☑ lunch & dinner) Honey's is an older place with a straight-up pub-grub menu.

Self-caterers should make a beeline for the **New World Supermarket** (19 Bridge St; ☑ 8am-8pm).

Getting There & Away

Travelling east from Opotiki there are two routes: SH2, crossing the spectacular Waioeka Gorge, or the SH35 around East Cape (see the East Coast chapter for this route). The SH2 route offers some scenic day walks in the **Waioeka Gorge Scenic Reserve**, with the gorge getting steeper and narrower as you travel inland, before the route crosses typically green, rolling hills, dotted with sheep, on the descent to Gisborne.

InterCity buses pick up/drop off at the Diner on Bridge St, though tickets and bookings are through **Betta Electrical** (☎ 07-315 8555; 115 Church St) or the **Travel Shop** (☎ 07-315 8881; 109 Church St; ☑ 9am-6pm Mon-Fri).

InterCity has daily buses connecting Opotiki with Whakatane ($18, 40 minutes), Rotorua ($29, two hours) and Auckland ($62, 6¾ hours). Heading south, the buses connect Opotiki with Gisborne ($30, two hours) by a daily service.

The Bay Hopper runs twice daily to Whakatane ($7, 1¼ hours).

The East Coast

The East Coast embraces some enticingly remote rural areas and increasingly sophisticated coastal towns. East Cape's Pacific Coast Highway (SH35) sees few tourists – the locals will tell you they're all down in Napier and Gisborne, two cultured, affluent cities with palpable sparkle and boom. Rich Hawkes Bay soils yield highly quaffable wines, while the primeval forests around Lake Waikaremoana in Te Urewera National Park count out the centuries far less indulgently.

From Opotiki in the eastern Bay of Plenty and arcing around to Gisborne, East Cape doesn't raise much of a blip on the tourist radar. As a result it's disarmingly charming: eye-popping coastlines rise to forest-steeped mountains; car bodies rust in the tall grass along the highway; farm outbuildings lean precariously. The Cape retains a vibrant Maori influence and rigorous community spirit.

Gisborne, New Zealand's most easterly city, is an easy-going but fast-developing, sunny surf Mecca. Further south on the broad sweep of Hawke Bay is civilised Napier with its well-preserved cache of Art Deco architecture.

Fertile inland plains support esteemed NZ wineries, most opening their cellar doors to visitors. The functional Hawkes Bay Wine Country towns of Hastings and Havelock North teem with fruity waves of international backpackers during harvest time.

HIGHLIGHTS

- Pursuing the secretly picturesque SH35 around **East Cape** (p374)
- Catching the sunrise at **East Cape Lighthouse** (p372), mainland NZ's most easterly point
- Getting gnarly in the surf at **Wainui Beach** (p379)
- Wobbling through the wineries around **Gisborne** (p378) and the **Hawkes Bay Wine Country** (p398)
- Exploring the unexpectedly beautiful **Mahia Peninsula** (p382)
- Tramping the **Lake Waikaremoana Track** (p384), one of NZ's Great Walks, in Te Urewera National Park
- Getting your decades confused in the Art Deco time warp of **Napier** (p386)
- Plotting out your wine-making empire from atop **Te Mata Peak** (p397), near Hastings and Havelock North

■ TELEPHONE CODE: 07 and 06   ■ www.hawkesbaynz.com   ■ www.gisbornenz.com

EAST CAPE

The East Cape is a gorgeous, detached, un-touristed slice of the North Island. Small Ngati Porou Maori communities seem to wash up along the coast, everyone seems to know everyone else, and life is rurally wound-down. The interior remains wild and woolly; the Raukumara Range is the Cape's jagged spine. The western side of the range hosts the Raukumara Forest Park, Urutawa Forest and Waioeka Gorge Scenic Reserve.

The Pacific Coast Hwy (SH35) hugs the coast, 330km of curvilinear asphalt that took decades to sculpt. The drive presents some stupendous views: bleak, postapoca-lyptic shores strewn with driftwood and punctured with tiny inlets that change as-pect with the weather. On sunny days the sea is shimmering turquoise; at other times clouds brood on craggy slopes and every-thing shifts to misty green. Clear mountain rivers surge through steep gorges, while the summer seashore turns crimson with pohutukawa blooms. Road signs warn of 'Wandering Stock' and that 'Drinking & Cooking Don't Mix'.

East Capers are passionate about their rugby team, Ngati Porou East Coast, based in Ruatoria, who manage to squeeze a few games in between beers each year. Their recent on-field form has been dismal, but don't miss an opportunity to catch the Sky Blues in action – the atmosphere is entirely raucous.

The **Maori Tourism Network** (☎ 06-864 4694; www.indigenousnewzealand.com) prints a leaflet on East Cape accommodation and activities, available at the Gisborne (p377) and Opo-tiki (p365) visitor information centres. Pick up a guide to basic *marae* (meeting house) protocol while you're there.

THE EAST COAST FACTS

Eat: A disgracefully greasy hamburger at Waikanae Beach (p381), Gisborne's city beach

Drink: A toasty chardonnay from the Hawkes Bay Wine Country (p398)

Read: Witi Ihimaera's *The Whale Rider*, set and filmed in Whangara (p374)

Listen to: Dame Kiri Te Kanawa cutting loose on *Songs of the Auvergne* (p379)

Watch: Mel Gibson's ponytail in *The Bounty* (1984), filmed in Gisborne

Swim at: Morere Hot Springs (p382)

Festival: Art Deco Weekend in Napier and Hastings (p390)

Tackiest tourist attraction: The unfailingly debonair Bertie, Napier's Art Deco ambassador (p390)

Climate

The East Coast basks in a warm, dry cli-mate. Summer temperatures around Napier and Gisborne nudge 25°C, rarely dipping below 5°C in winter. The Hawkes Bay region also suns itself in mild, dry grape-growing conditions, with an average annual rainfall of 800mm. Heavy downpours sometimes wash out sections of the Pacific Coast High-way (SH35) around the Cape.

Getting There & Around

Air New Zealand jets out of Gisborne and Napier to Auckland and Wellington; Origin Pacific flies from Napier to Auckland and Wellington. InterCity and/or Newmans run buses out of Gisborne, Wairoa, Napier and Hastings, linking up with the big cities, while Bay Xpress plies the highway between Napier and Wellington. East Cape has no public transport, but four private couri-ers operate between Gisborne and Opotiki (see p370).

TOP ACTIVITIES

- Circumnavigate Lake Waikaremoana in Te Urewera National Park by foot (p384)
- See the East Cape by horseback (p372)
- Explore the Motu (p373), Mohaka or Ngaruroro (p390) Rivers by jetboat or inflatable raft
- Swim or surf a city beach at Gisborne's Waikanae Beach (p379)
- Learn to hang-glide in Havelock North (p397)

Getting There & Around

Unless you're behind the wheel, transport around East Cape can be ponderous, especially on weekends, but these four operators regularly link Opotiki with Gisborne via Hicks Bay:

Cook's Couriers (☎ 06-864 4711)
Eastland Couriers (☎ 07-315 6350)
Hicks Bay Coastline Couriers (☎ 06-864 4654)
Polly's Passenger Couriers (☎ 06-864 4728)

Hicks Bay Coastline runs between Opotiki and Hicks Bay (one way $35, three hours, 2pm from Opotiki; 6.30am from Hicks Bay, Monday to Friday). Working in tandem, Eastland runs from Opotiki to Hicks Bay

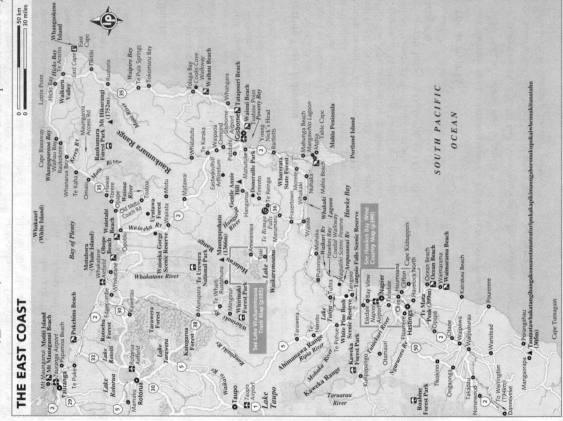

THE EAST COAST

then hands over to Polly's for the Gisborne leg the following morning ($60, eight hours, noon from Opotiki, 6.30am from Hicks Bay, Monday to Friday). The same price and duration apply in the opposite direction: Polly's leaving Gisborne for Hicks Bay at 1pm, Eastland rolling out of Hicks Bay for Opotiki at 6.30am the next day. Cook's Couriers runs from Gisborne to Hicks Bay ($35, three hours, 2pm Monday to Friday, 12.30pm Saturday), departing Hicks Bay for Gisborne at 8am. Hicks Bay Coastline and Eastland also run to and from Whakatane. Polly's offers an $80 unlimited-stops one-way ticket between Gisborne and Whakatane.

An East Cape alternative is the **Kiwi Experience** (☎ 09-366 9830; www.kiwiexperience.com; $340), which runs the four-day 'East As' backpacker bus leaving Taupo or Rotorua on Mondays, Wednesdays and Fridays. See p729 for more information on backpacker bus services.

OPOTIKI TO EAST CAPE

The drive north from Opotiki (see p365) to the East Cape is arguably the most picturesque part of SH35. Before you hit the road, collect the free *Pacific Coast Highway* booklet from the Opotiki visitor information centre (p365).

The first stretch from Opotiki offers hazy views across to the Whakaari (White Island) volcano, which only stopped coughing up smoke five years ago. At Waiaua River is the turn-off to Gisborne via Toatoa and the Old Motu Coach Rd; a route more suited to mountain bikes (or mountain goats) than cars. Check out the magnificent *whakairo* (carving) on the Torere school gateway, while the kids practice the *haka* (war dance) on the lawn.

The desolate beaches at **Torere**, **Hawai** and **Omaio** are steeply shelved and littered with ocean detritus. Hawai marks the boundary of the Whanau-a-Apanui tribe whose influence extends north to Cape Runaway. About 45km from Opotiki the road crosses the **Motu River**, famed for jetboating and white-water rafting (p373).

Some 25km further, the strung-out fishing town of **Te Kaha** once sounded the death knell for passing whales. There's a store here and good accommodation options. The local Tukaki *marae* could use a lick of paint but is sublimely carved. A succession of sleepy bays follows, including **Whanarua**, **Waihau** and **Whangaparaoa**, before **Cape Runaway** where kumara was first introduced to NZ. Between Whanarua and Waihau you'll pass the Raukokore Anglican Church at

Raukokore, an immaculately maintained beacon of belief on a lonely promontory. Cape Runaway can only be reached on foot; seek permission before crossing private land.

The road tracks inland from Whangaparaoa, hitting the coast again at **Hicks Bay**, named after a salty sea dog on Captain Cook's *Endeavour*. This is a real middle-of-nowhere town with a fabulous beach. Horse trekking is the way to get your kicks around here; see right.

Nearly 10km further is **Te Araroa**, a lonedog village with a **visitor information centre** (cnr Rata St & Moana Pde; ☼ Nov–Feb). The geology changes here from igneous outcrops to sandstone cliffs. More than 350 years old with 22 trunks and 40m boughs, Te-Waha-O-Rerekohu, allegedly NZ's largest pohutukawa tree, stands in the Te Araroa school yard. The progressive **East Cape Manuka Company** (☎ 0508 626 852; www.eastcapemanuka.co.nz; admission free; ☼ 9am–4.30pm daily Dec–Mar, Mon–Fri Apr–Nov) is also here, a well-managed oil distillery selling soaps, oils, creams and honey made from potent East Cape manuka. Stop for coffee and *kai* (food).

From Te Araroa, drive out to see the sunrise at the **East Cape Lighthouse**, the most easterly tip of mainland NZ. It's 21km (30 minutes) east of town along an unsealed road, with a 25-minute climb to the lighthouse.

HORSING AROUND

East Cape is tough on cars, so it's no surprise that equine appreciation is culturally ingrained. Getting a little saddle-sore is a small sacrifice for seeing the amazing beaches and forests that horses can take you to. Some reputable trekking operators:

Hicks Bay Horse Trekking (☎ 06-864 4634, 06-864 4859; jocebennett@paradice.net.nz; Onepoto Beach Rd, Hicks Bay; 1-3½hr beach, hill & station treks $30-80; ☼ Dec–Feb)

Maungaroa Station Horse Treks (☎ 07-325 2727; www.maungaroa.co.nz; Maungaroa Access Rd; 1-4hr bush treks $35-65) Off Copenhagen Rd.

Punruku Horse Treks (☎ 06-864 4993; SH35; Te Araroa; beach, riverbed & bush treks per hr $30; ☼ Dec–Feb)

Sleeping & Eating

Between Te Kaha and Te Araroa there are plenty of places to rest road-weary bones, but decent eating options are as rare as East Coast rugby victories. Stock up on supplies in Opotiki or Gisborne before you tackle the Cape. Listings below are sequential from Opotiki to Te Araroa.

Te Kaha Homestead Lodge (☎ /fax 07-325 2194; paoraobrien@hotmail.com; SH35; dm/d/f $25/45/80) Affable and big-hearted, this waterfront hostel perches amongst archaic pohutukawa trees with spa views to White Island. The enthusiastic owner organises fishing trips ($60 per hour) and bursts into choruses of 'Welcome to the Homestead at Te Kaha' (to the tune of 'Hotel California') given the slightest provocation. Crayfish and slimy kina (sea urchin) meals cost $25.

Tui Lodge (☎ /fax 07-325 2922; jorex@xtra.co.nz; Copenhagen Rd, Te Kaha; s/d $95/130) This capacious, modern guesthouse sits on three leafy acres irresistible to tui (parson birds). Roost in

an en suite room with ocean views. Dinner by arrangement, but breakfast is included; horse trekking, fishing and diving jaunts are also on the cards.

Te Kaha Holiday Park (☎ /fax 07-325 2894; www.tekahaholidaypark.co.nz; unpowered/powered sites per 2 people $23/25, dm $18, d $75-100; ☐) From tent patches to self-contained motels, this new megaplex is all-things-to-all-comers. Just 300m from the beach, there's a tumult of oceanic activities, a café and general store.

Maungaroa Station (☎ 07-325 2727; www.maungaroa.co.nz; Maungaroa Access Rd; s/d $20/40) This Raukumara Ranges lodge is 45 minutes up a dirt road, off Copenhagen Rd, with two river crossings, generator power, BYO food and a whole lotta wilderness. Bunk down in the self-contained lodge or camp outside; dunk yourself in the Kereu River, hug a tree or saddle-up for a horse trek (see above).

Waikawa B&B (☎ /fax 07-325 2070; www.waikawa.net; SH35; d $110-130) Towards Whanarua Bay, this magical B&B on a private rocky bay looks like manicured driftwood crossed with buried treasure, blending weathered timber, corrugated iron and paua inlay. The three-bedroom self-contained bach ($150) is perfect for groups.

Maraehako Bay Retreat (☎ 07-325 2648; maraehako@xtra.co.nz; SH35; dm/d $25/55; ☐) With absolute waterfront at Maraehako Bay (north of Whanarua Bay), this paradisaical hostel owes more than just a little to Robinson Crusoe. Seemingly cobbled together from flotsam and jetsam, it'll make you want to grow a beard and trace SOS messages in the sand. Fishing, snorkelling and kayaking complete your castaway days.

Oceanside Apartments (☎ 07-325 3699; www.wai haubay.co.nz; Onuaiti Beach, SH35; s/c $85/100) These apartments on a sandy stretch of Waihau Bay are comfortably familiar. Two self-contained units sleep four to seven slumberers, while the simpler bach next door sleeps eight ($120 per night). Fishing charters, cooked breakfasts and seafood dinners might tickle your fancy.

Lottin Point Motel (☎/fax 06-864 4455; Lottin Point Rd, ste $80) Midway between Whangaparaoa Bay and Hicks Bay but closer to 1985, this joint has more peach and turquoise than a Wham! video, yet insists it's 'the newest motel on the coast'. It's worth tackling the precipitous 4km driveway just to see the enormous snowdrift/jungle photographs behind the beds. The bar harbours the odd crusty fisherman and serves hearty dinners (mains $18 to $25).

Mel's Place (☎ 06-864 4694; www.eastcapefishing .co.nz; 88 Onepoto Bush Rd, Hicks Bay; unpowered sites per 2 people/dm $30/20) On an ancestral Maori pa (fortified village) site, Me. manages this busy hostel with aplomb. The camp sites have wicked bay views; two caravans are also available ($45 and $55). Maori cultural interpretation and fishing trips are a bonus.

Hicks Bay Motel Lodge (☎ 0800 200 077, 06-864 4880; www.hicksbaymotel.co.nz; SH35; d from $90; ☒) This sprawling, sternly managed motel above Hicks Bay has lofty opinions of itself, and equally lofty views. Dated, twee rooms are nothing flash; the restaurant, pool and glow-worm grotto are some compensation.

Te Araroa Holiday Park (☎ 06-864 4873; bill.mart in@xtra.co.nz; SH35; unpowered/powered sites per 2 people $20/24, dm/cabins/d $15/50/70) Over the rise from Hicks Bay, this sheltered park sustains mature Europeans and natives (trees and people), and resonates with children's laughter. The amenities blocks need an overhaul, but it's close to the beach and has the most easterly cinema in the world.

Sunrise Lodge (☎ 06-864 4854; sunriselodgeeasta pe@hotmail.com; SH35, Te Araroa; sites per 2 people $20, dm/s/d $22/30/54) With four bas.c rooms, this simple house doesn't offer much internally, but it faces due east and it's dead quiet at night (if you're a sunrise kind of person, you'll need a good night's sleep).

RAUKUMARA & WAIOEKA

The easiest way to explore this entirely undisciplined region is via SH2, the 144km ribbon linking Opotiki and Gisborne. The road follows Waioeka Gorge; fern crowns perforate steep, wooded hillsides while rapids rummage through shoals of grey stone below.

At 1752m, Mt Hikurangi is the highest peak in the Raukumara Range. Don't even think about tramping here if you're inexperienced; consult the Opotiki Department of Conservation (DOC) office (p365) or Gisborne visitor information centre (p377) first. The *Walks of the Eastland Region* brochure and DOC's *Walks in Waioeka and Urutawa* pamphlet detail some more realistic tramping options.

For white-water rafting on the Motu River, contact **Wet 'n' Wild Rafting** (☎ 0800 462 7238; www.wetnwildrafting.co.nz; 2- to 5-day trips $550-775). Jetboats also brave the Motu, the chief protagonists being **Eastern Bay Jet Boat Tours** (☎ 0800 668 853; fax 07-315 3892; 1½-2hr trips adult/child $75/50; ☒ daily) and **Motu River Jetboat Tours** (☎ 07-325 2735; motujet@xtra.co.nz; 1½hr trips adult/child $85/55; ☒ daily).

Rustic as hell, **The Quarters** (☎/fax 07-315 7763; wairata.forest.fam@xtra.co.nz; Wairata; lodge $40-50) is midway between Opotiki and Gisborne. It's a long way from luxurious, but just as far from pretence and snobbery. Chill out on the porch, read, draw on the walls; it's open fires and an open agenda. Sleeps eight. BYO food and linen.

Near The Quarters, **Wairata Station** (☎/fax 07-315 7761; www.wairatastation.co.nz; Wairata; dm/f $20/100; ☒) is a farmstay with a basic five-bunk cottage and a five-bed family B&B wing. Trout fishing in the Waioeka and bird-watching are the names of the games.

Refuel on pies and takeaways at the **Hard-drive Café** (☎ 06-862 4823; SH2; Matawai; 8am-6pm Mon-Fri, 9am-6pm Sat & Sun) – the hard drive to Gisborne or Opotiki awaits.

EAST CAPE TO GISBORNE

Moving into farming country south of Te Araroa, the first town you come to is **Tiki-tiki**. The spiffily painted St Mary's Anglican Church is the town's shining light.

A few kilometres off the road, **Ruatoria** is the Ngati Porou tribe's main centre. Inspiring politician Sir Apirana Ngata (Minister of Native Affairs in 1928) lived here, as did equally inspiring All Black George Nepia.

About 25km south is **Te Puia Springs**, a blink-and-you'll-miss-it hot-springs village. The **visitor information centre** (☎ 06-864 6727; SH35; ☺ 8.30am-12.30pm & 1-4.30pm Mon-Fri) will word you up on local homestays. Once a pumping wool port, with a cinema, hotel, butcher and blacksmith, nearby **Waipiro Bay** is an absolute stunner.

A further 11km south is **Tokomaru Bay**, a romantically crumbling town with sweeping cliffs and a famous surf break (Toko Point). When the local freezing works closed in the '50s, most of Toko's 5000 residents left too. Can't surf? Hiking, swimming, fishing and cycling will keep you out of trouble.

East Cape's largest community is **Tolaga Bay**, 36km further south. The beach here is deep and wide, with NZ's longest pier (660m) slowly disintegrating at its southern end; the heavy seas that hampered the pier's construction have exacted a rusty revenge. Nearby is **Cooks Cove Walkway** (2½ hours, 5.8km, closed August to October), an easy stroll through farmland and native bush to a cove where Captain Cook landed in 1769. South of Tolaga Bay beyond Waihau Beach is the photogenic Maori village **Whangara**, the setting for Witi Ihimaera's deeply human novel *The Whale Rider*, which will open your heart to local Maori culture and mythology. The much-awarded film was also shot here (see p49 for more on NZ cinema).

After passing Tatapouri and Wainui Beaches, you'll roll into Gisborne.

Sleeping & Eating

As on the Cape's western side, finding a bed here is easier than finding somewhere decent to eat. Supermarkets are saviours. Listings below are sequential from Tikitiki to Gisborne.

Eastender Farmstay (☎ 06-864 3042; eastender farmstay@xtra.co.nz; 836 Rangitukia Rd; dm $20) This unpretentious beachfront farm is 8km east of Tikitiki. The large dorms and four-bed solar-powered huts are clean and great value. It's a cheery, sit-around-the-campfire place, with horse rides ($50) and bone carving ($30) available. *Hangi* meals cost $10.

Footprints in the Sand (☎ 06-864 5858; backpack ers@footprintsinthesand.co.nz; 13 Potae St, Tokomaru Bay; unpowered sites per 2 people/dm/d $30/20/50) Just a block from the beach (footprints aplenty), this 100-year-old house is a cosy, owner-operated hostel. Bikes, kayaks, hammocks and haircuts help pass the time.

Brian's Place (☎ 06-864 5870; briansplace1@hotmail .com; 21 Potae St, Tokomaru Bay; unpowered sites per 2 people/dm/s/d $24/22/27/52) Elevated, ecofriendly Brian's balances atop a steep slope overlooking Toko Bay. The panoramic tent patch is worth every cent. Book a jaunty hillside cabin if tents aren't your bent.

Tolaga Bay Holiday Park (☎/fax 06-862 6716; tol agabayholidaypark@msn.com; 167 Wharf Rd; sites per 2 people $20, cabins $40) Aside from the redundant pier nearby, there's not a lot here, but this is a place where absence becomes substance. The stiff ocean breeze tousles Norfolk Islands Pines as open lawns mottle with sunshine – who needs anything more?

Tolaga Bay Motel (☎ 06-862 6888; fax 06-862 6526; cnr Cook & Monkhouse Sts, Tolaga Bay; s/d from $75/78) As close to the Uawa River as you can be without getting your feet wet, the six units at this old-school motel feature cooking facilities, TV and funky '60s brickwork.

Pickled Walnut (☎ 06-862 6691; 43 Cook St, Tolaga Bay; mains $12-25; ☺ lunch & dinner Tue-Sun) This restaurant drools over sweet pickled walnuts, industriously turning them into drizzles, sauces and condiments to accompany every meal. It sounds eccentric, but the results can be spectacular. Fine local wines will pickle you further.

Surf Café (☎ 06-864 5700; 5 Potae St; meals from $5, ☺ breakfast & lunch Mon-Fri) Head down the street from Footprints in the Sand (above) for a caffeine and Internet fix ($2 for 15 minutes).

TAKE THE LONG WAY HOME

State Highway 35 (SH35), the coastal route around East Cape, may look short on the map, but things aren't as they seem. It's a constantly crooked road with few chances to reach heady speeds, let alone overtake logging trucks and rust-bucket cars – cars that would *never* earn a Warrant of Fitness (WoF) anywhere except the Cape. Driving the length of SH35 in one day is an automotive marathon. It's a solid six hours, and that's without stopping to plunge into the surf, check out old *marae* or trudge into the forest. Take SH2 inland from Opotiki if you're time-poor, or allow at least two days to circumnavigate the Cape. (But beware – two days here can turn into three, or four, or five...)

POVERTY BAY

When Captain James Cook's 1769 expedition attempted to replenish its ship's supplies here, there were skirmishes with local Maoris, six of whom were killed. Irked, Cook decided the area had a lack of offerings, and the 'poverty' name stuck.

The actual bay is quite small, a half-moon stretching from Tuahine Point to Young Nick's Head. The wider Poverty Bay region runs from Tolaga Bay south to the Mahia Peninsula and west to the Huiarau Range, the soul of which is the otherworldly cauldron of Lake Waikaremoana.

Cook should have had a second look – he didn't know when he had it good. Poverty Bay's loamy soils and endless sunshine were perfect for settlement, but Gisborne didn't emerge for another 62 years. These days the town is a Poverty Bay highlight, with great food, wine, and plenty of time for snoozing in the sun.

GISBORNE

pop 32,700

With a dogged up-and-comer's approach, Gisborne has morphed itself from redneck backwater into progressive, ebullient town with sassy restaurants, classy motels, million-dollar Wainui Beach houses and an apartment-lined harbour bobbing with expensive yachts.

Nudging towards the International Date Line, this is NZ's most easterly city, the first in the country to see the dawn. The Maori name for the area, Tairawhiti, means 'the coast upon which the sun shines across the water'. And shine it does: Gisborne basks beneath more sunny skies than anywhere else in NZ. Surfing here is a mandatory indulgence, with some awesome breaks close to town.

Put your feet up and stay a few days. If you've emerged from East Cape isolation or the Lake Waikaremoana Track, you've earned a little civilisation.

History

The Gisborne region has been settled for more than 1000 years. A pact between two migratory waka (canoe) skippers, Paoa the Horo-uta and Kiwa the Takitimu, led to the founding of Turanganui a Kiwa (now Gis-

borne). Kumara flourished in the fertile soil and the Maori settlement blossomed.

Cook made landfall here in 1769, but European settlement didn't begin until 1831. Motivated self-starter John Williams Harris established a whaling base on the Turanganui River's west bank, and a farm near Manutuke. Whaling boomed, and missionaries followed. Father Baty and Rev William Colenso were the first Europeans to tramp into the dark heart of Te Urewera to Lake Waikaremoana. More Europeans moved to the area, but Maori resistance limited settlement. The 1840 Treaty of Waitangi (see p35) was ignored by the East Coast chiefs who refused to sign.

In the 1860s, battles between settlers and Maoris erupted. Beginning in Taranaki, the Hauhau insurrection spread to the East Coast, culminating in the battle of Waerenga-a-hika in 1865. The following year the government crushed all opposition and transported survivors, including the charismatic Te Kooti (see p378), to the Chatham Islands. Believing the coast was clear, European farmers flooded the coast, but in 1868 Te Kooti escaped, marauding Matawhero and inflicting heavy casualties.

A lot of local farmland is still leased from the Maori, much of it under their direct control. Enthusiastic but myopic pioneer farmers ripped out too many trees, massive erosion occurring where steeply sloping land can't hold the soil after heavy rains.

Orientation

'The city of bridges', Gisborne presides over the confluence of the Waimata and Taruheru Rivers, below which the Turanganui River runs to the sea. The main street in town is Gladstone Rd, the main beaches are south and north of town.

MAPS

Free town maps are available at the visitor information centre.

Automobile Association (AA; ☎ 0800 456 654, 06-868 1424; www.aatravel.co.nz; 363 Glastone Rd)

Information

BOOKSHOPS

Muirs Bookshop (☎ 06-869 0651; books@muirs bookshop.co.nz; 62 Gladstone Rd; mains $10-18; ☒ lunch Mon-Fri, breakfast & lunch Sat & Sun) The best bookshop in Gisborne (and probably the whole East Coast)

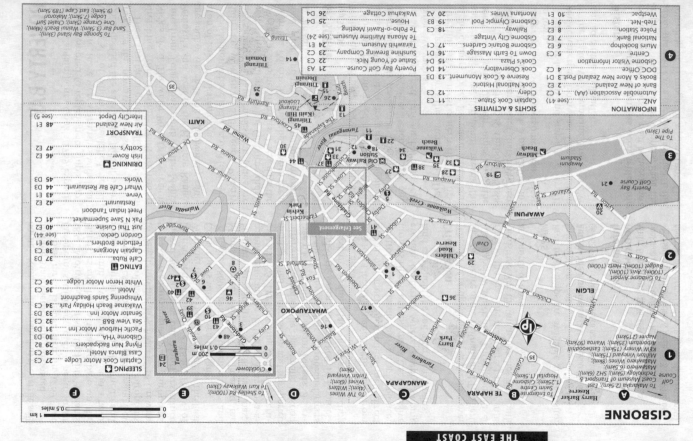

GISBORNE

INFORMATION
Automobile Association (AA)........1 C2
Bank of New Zealand...............2 E2
Books & More New Zealand Post.....3 D1
DOC Office........................4 C2
Gisborne Visitor Information
Centre............................5 C3
Muirs Bookshop....................6 E2
National Bank.....................7 E2
Police Station....................8 E1
Treb-Net..........................9 E1
Westpac..........................10 E1

SIGHTS & ACTIVITIES
ANZ.............................(see 41)
Captain Cook Statue..............11 C3
Cidery...........................12 C3
Cook National Historic
Reserve & Cook Monument..........13 D3
Cook Observatory.................14 D4
Cook's Plaza.....................15 D4
Down To Earth Massage............16 D1
Gisborne Botanic Gardens.........17 C1
Gisborne City Vintage............18 C3
Gisborne Olympic Pool............19 B3
Montana Wines....................20 A2
Poverty Bay Golf Course..........21 A3
Statue of Young Nick.............22 C3
Sunshine Brewing Company.........23 C2
Tairawhiti Museum................24 E1
Te Moana Maritime Museum......(see 24)
Te Poho-o-Rawiri Meeting
House............................25 D4
Waikahua Cottage.................26 D4

SLEEPING
Captain Cook Motor Lodge.........27 C3
Casa Blanca Motel................28 C3
Flying Nun Backpackers...........29 B2
Gisborne YHA.....................30 D3
Pacific Harbour Motor Inn........31 D3
Sea View B&B.....................32 E2
Senator Motor Inn................33 D3
Waikanae Beach Holiday Park......34 C3
Whispering Sands Beachfront
Motel............................35 C3
White Heron Motor Lodge..........36 C2

EATING
Café Ruba........................37 D3
Captain Morgans..................38 E3
Fettucine Brothers...............39 E1
Gordon Gecko..................(see 44)
Just Thai Cuisine................40 E2
Pak N Save Supermarket...........41 C2
Preet Indian Tandoori
Restaurant.......................42 E3
Verve............................43 E1
Wharf Café Bar Restaurant........44 D3
Works............................45 D3

DRINKING
Irish Rover......................46 E2
Scotty's.........................47 E2

TRANSPORT
Air New Zealand..................48 E1
InterCity Depot...............(see 5)

has been here since 1905. This is a red bookshop, a far cry from the usual small-town magazine-and-birthday-card barterers. The café upstairs is also a winner, with light summer lunches, hot winter soups, and good-looking staff year-round.

EMERGENCY

Ambulance, fire service & police (111)
Police station (06-869 0200; Peel St)

INTERNET ACCESS

Aside from Treb-Net, there's Internet access at the visitor information centre and Verve (p381).
Treb-Net (06-863 3928; Shop 7, Treble Court, 17 Peel St)

MEDICAL SERVICES

Gisborne Hospital (06-869 0500; Ormond Rd)

MONEY

The major banks (ANZ, Bank of New Zealand, National Bank and Westpac) tally their profits along Gladstone Rd.

POST

Books & More New Zealand Post (166 Gladstone Rd)

TOURIST INFORMATION

DOC (06-869 0460; www.doc.govt.nz; 63 Carnarvon St; 8am-4.30pm Mon-Fri)
Gisborne visitor information centre (0800 447 267, 06-868 6139; www.gisbornenz.com; 209 Grey St; 8.30am-5.15pm Mon-Fri, 10am-5pm Sat & Sun) Beside a doozey of a Canadian totem pole, this helpful centre stocks the thorough (and free) Eastland Region booklet. Seek regional outdoor info here before hassling DOC (which is more field office, less public facility).

Sights

MUSEUMS & MARAE

The **Tairawhiti Museum** (06-867 3832; www.tairawhitimuseum.org.nz; 18 Stout St; admission by donation; 10am-4pm Mon-Fri, 1.30-4pm Sat & Sun) is well considered, focusing on East Coast Maori and colonial history. Its gallery is Gisborne's arts hub, with rotating local, national and international exhibits. There's a fabulous café overlooking Kelvin Park, and outside is the reconstructed Wyllie Cottage (1872), Gisborne's oldest house.

The **Te Moana Maritime Museum** occupies a wing of the Tairawhiti complex. When the Star of Canada foundered on a Gisborne reef in 1912, the ship's bridge and captain's cabin were salvaged, installed in a local home then moved here for restoration. Displays on Maori canoes, whaling and Cook's Poverty Bay visit pale before the sensational vintage surfboard collection.

Te Poho-o-Rawiri meeting house (06-868 5364; cnr Ranfurly St & Queens Dr; admission free), is one of NZ's largest marae, its interior utterly decorated and framed by carved maihi (ornamental gable boards). The kneeling ancestral tekoteko (carved figure), challenges those entering the marae. It's often open, except when a function is in progress; call for permission before entering and observe marae protocol (see p57). The free visitor information centre leaflet Tairawhiti Heritage Trails: Gisborne District has information on other local Maori sites.

About 5km south of Gisborne, the **East Coast Museum of Technology & Transport** (ECMOT; 06-868 8254; SH2, Makaraka; adult/child $2/50c; 10am-4.30pm) is an improbable collation of rusty tractors, lawn mowers, engines, spanners, ploughs, ovens, chainsaws, trucks, pumps, harvesters, motorbikes and so on – a shrine to man's inventive capacity.

VIEWS & HISTORIC PLACES

Gisborne deifies Captain Cook. In a park by the river mouth there's a **statue of Young Nick** (Nicholas Young), Cook's cabin boy. Press-ganged into Cook's crew, his eagle-eyes were the first to spy NZ (the white cliffs at Young Nick's Head). There's a **Captain Cook statue** here too, erected on a globe etched with his roaming routes.

Across the river at the foot of Titirangi (Kaiti Hill) is the **Cook National Historic Reserve** (a glorified traffic island), with another **Cook monument**. This is where Cook first got NZ dirt on his boots (9 October 1769 according to Cook's journal, but actually the 8th). Nearby is the site of **Waikahua Cottage**, a refuge during the Hauhau unrest.

Titirangi has magical city views. Elbow your way past sweaty midlife-crisis victims on the steep track to the top, which starts near the Waikahua Cottage site. Near the summit is yet another Cook edifice, **Cook's Plaza**. Due to a cock-up of historic proportions, the Cook statue here isn't garbed in British naval uniform, nor does it bear any facial resemblance to Captain Jim. A plaque proclaims, 'Who was he? We have no idea!'.

TE KOOTI

Enigmatic prophet and warrior Te Kooti was born into the Poverty Bay Rongowhakaata tribe in the 1830s. Accused of assisting the Hauhau in Gisborne during a government siege, he was exiled to the Chatham Islands in 1865. Here, he received the visions that eventually led him to establish the Ringatu Church.

In 1867 Te Kooti led an astounding escape from the Chathams – more than 200 prisoners hijacked the supply ship *Rifleman* and sailed to Poverty Bay. During the welcome-home ceremony, Te Kooti's followers raised their right hands in homage to God rather than bowing submissively, the first time the Ringatu 'raised hand' was used.

The escapees headed inland, but Poverty Bay magistrate Reginald Biggs demanded they surrender their weapons. They refused. Skirmishes ensued, with government troops suffering humiliating defeats.

Te Kooti attacked Matawhero, killing Biggs then several chiefs, including his father-in-law. Hated and feared, he moved his forces through the Urewera region, plundering Poverty Bay and Bay of Plenty townships. In 1872, as government forces closed in on three sides, he retreated into the King Country, the Maori king's vast dominion where government troops feared to tread.

Safe in Te Kuiti, Te Kooti disarmed, dedicating his remaining days to pacifying enemies and developing the Ringatu Church creed. He made a series of predictions about his successor (Rua Kenana claimed this mantle in 1905), and his reputation as a prophet and healer spread.

After being pardoned, Te Kooti lived near Opotiki in the Bay of Plenty. He never returned to Poverty Bay, eventually dying at Ohiwa Harbour in 1893. His followers removed his body from its grave; no-one knows exactly where he was finally interred.

You can visit the *marae* Te Kooti built for his hosts in Te Kuiti (p253); the more intrepid might visit Ruatahuna/Maungapohatu (p383), Te Kooti and Rua Kenana's Urewera base.

Further around from the summit is the **Cook Observatory**, the world's easternmost star-gazing facility. The **Gisborne Astronomical Society** (☎ 06-867 7901; admission $2; ⏰ 8.30pm Tue) convenes here; all are welcome.

Matawhero is 6km south of Gisborne along SH2. The historic Presbyterian Church is the only building in town to have survived the 1868 conflict.

WINERIES

Gisborne is a major wine-producing area, famous for its cheeky whites. More than a third of NZ's chardonnay grapes are grown here (check out www.gisbornewine.co.nz). The visitor information centre (p377) has winery opening hours and tour details; your agenda might include the following:

KEW Winery (☎ 06-862 7722; www.kew.co.nz; 569 Wharekopae Rd)

Matawhero Wines (☎ 06-868 8366; www.matawhero wines.co.nz; 185 Riverpoint Rd)

Millton Vineyard (☎ 06-862 8680; www.millton.co.nz; 119 Papatu Rd, Manutuke)

Montana Wines (☎ 06-867 9819; www.montana wines.co.nz; Lytton Rd)

Tiritiri Vineyard (☎ 06-867 0372; www.tiritiriestate .com; 1646 Waimata Valley Rd)

TW Wines (☎ 021 864 818; www.twwines.co.nz; Back Ormond Rd)

Witters Wines (☎ 06-867 4670; www.gisborne wine.co.nz/wineries/WaiohikaEstate.asp; 75 Waimata Valley Rd)

OTHER ATTRACTIONS

The **Sunshine Brewing Company** (☎ 06-867 7777; gisbornegold@xtra.co.nz; 109 Disraeli St; ⏰ 9am–6pm Mon-Sat), Gisborne's own natural beer brewery, ships crates of 'Gisborne Gold' as fast as it can brew the stuff. Free tours and tastings by arrangement. Continuing the theme, the **Cidery** (☎ 06-868 8300; brian.shanks@fostersgroup.com; 91 Customhouse St; ⏰ 9am–5pm Mon-Fri, 10am–3pm Sat) is the apple-hued home of Bulmers Original, Scrumpy and Harvest ciders, with free tastings, sales and factory viewings on offer. Call for bookings.

Arboreal nirvana, **Eastwoodhill Arboretum** (Map p370; ☎ 06-863 9003; www.eastwoodhill.org.nz; 2392 Wharekopae Rd, Ngatapa; adult/child $10/free; ⏰ 9am–5pm) is 35km northwest of Gisborne along the Ngatapa-Rere Rd. Walking tracks ramble through NZ's largest collection of imported trees and shrubs. The less ambitious **Gisborne Botanic Gardens** (Aberdeen Rd) is beside the Taruheru River.

Gisborne City Vintage Railway (☎ 06-867 5083; www.gisborne.net.nz/wa165/index.htm; 2hr trip adult/child from $25/10; ☒ 9am-1pm Sat) runs steam-train excursions towards Wairoa three or four times annually (you might be lucky). If it's not running, you can still ogle the old WA165 engine.

Activities

SURFING

Surfing is mainstream in Gisborne, with the male teenage population looking appropriately shaggy. **Waikanae Beach** is good for learners and grommets; experienced surfers get tubed south of town at **The Pipe**, or north at **Sponge Bay Island**. North of town along SH35, **Wainui** and **Makorori** beaches also have quality breaks.

Surfing with Frank (☎ 06-867 0823; www.surfing withfrank.com; lesson $50) will get you in the green room with one-on-one surf lessons. Wet suits and boards are provided; rates are less for groups of two to four people.

SWIMMING

Pick your way through the driftwood for safe swimming at Waikanae Beach. Wainui Beach has a surf club where you can safely float between the flags. If the South Pacific is chilly, **Enterprise Swim Centre** (☎ 06-867 9244; 444 Nelson Rd; adult/child $4/2; ☒ 6am-3pm Mon-Fri) has a 25m heated indoor pool. Aquarobics classes are $4.

Get your lap times down at **Gisborne Olympic Pool** (☎ 06-867 6220; Centennial Marine Dr, Midway Beach; adult/child $3/2; ☒ 6am-8pm), a 50m indoor/outdoor pool with a 98m wormlike waterslide ($3). Aquafitness classes are $3.50.

OTHER ACTIVITIES

Through farmland and forest with commanding views, the **Te Kuri Walkway** (three hours, 5.6km, closed August to October) starts 4km north of town at the end of Shelley Rd.

Awaken your sense of mortality with a shark-cage dive from **Surfit Charters** (☎ 06-867 2970; www.surfit.co.nz; per person $250). Tamer fishing and snorkelling trips can also be arranged.

If you like your active more passive, head for **Down To Earth Massage** (☎ 0800 787 999, 06-867 0901; 131 Ormond Rd; ½hr/hr $25/40). Gary's hands are lethal chill-out weapons. Call for appointments.

Work the kinks out of your swing at **Poverty Bay Golf Club** (☎ 06-867 4405; povertybaygc@paradise.net.nz; cnr Lytton Rd & SH35; 9 holes $30; ☒ 8am-5pm Mon-Fri, 7am-5pm Sat & Sun).

Tours

Eastland Scenic Tours (☎ 027 441 3117; from $200) Full-day pay-by-group tours to Lake Waikaremoana (eight hours) and East Cape (12 hours) in a 10-seater bus.

Rose's Tiki Tours (☎ 06-867 1687; t.rose@actrix.co.nz; 4hr from $180) Small pay-by-group tours of East Cape, Mahia Peninsula and everywhere in between; wine tours a speciality.

Trev's Tours (☎ 06-863 9815; trevs.tours@xtra.co.nz; tours $50-100) Soaked in regional expertise, Trev runs tours of Gisborne and the surrounding area, including a wine trail.

Whale Rider Tours (☎ 06-868 6139; info@gisbornenz .com; per person $50, min 4 people) Guided tours around Whangara's *Whale Rider* film locations, focusing on Maori heritage. Book at the Gisborne visitor information centre (p377).

Festivals & Events

Leading up to the October Labour Weekend, local winemakers and foodies pool talents for the **Gisborne Wine Week** (☎ 0800 447

267; www.gisbornenz.com; tickets $15-35), seven days of wine, food and live music, culminating in the Wine & Food Festival shindig on the Sunday.

Sleeping

BUDGET

Flying Nun Backpackers (☎ 06-868 0461; yage@xtra.co.nz; 147 Roebuck Rd; unpowered sites per 2 people/dm/s/d $20/18/28/46; ☐) It's quite possible that Sally Field has never stayed here, but this historic former convent is where Dame Kiri Te Kanawa (see p379) toned her voice. Behind the incongruous façade there's stained glass, tight security, a chapel dorm and a lazy barbecue area.

Chalet Surf Lodge (☎ 06-868 9612; www.chaletsurf.co.nz; 62 Moana Rd, Wainui Beach; dm/d $25/60; ☐) In the peculiar mode of the modern surfer, this highway hostel manages to be laid-back and loud at the same time: big-screen surf videos blare while stoner beach-bums vegetate on the couches. Dorms can be a little sweaty, but the beach is situated right across the road; hire a board or take a lesson ($40).

Gisborne YHA (☎ 06-867 3269; yha.gisborne@dear.net.nz; 32 Harris St; dm/d/f $20/45/48) A short stroll across the river from town, this old-guard hostel fills a rambling mansion with colour and transience. It's a sociable place but big enough to be peaceful.

Waikanae Beach Holiday Park (☎ 06-867 5634; motorcamp@gdc.govt.nz; Grey St; unpowered/powered sites per 2 people $22/24, d/ste from $36/65; ☐) If the enviable beach position doesn't satisfy, this family-centric camp offers boogie-boards, bikes and tennis. The pseudowestern 'ranch' doubles look more Pizza Hut than Ponderosa, but they're good value.

MIDRANGE

Senator Motor Inn (☎ 06-868 8877; www.senatormotorinn.co.nz; 2 Childers Rd; ste $125-135) Fit for a senator, this stylish new motel overlooks the harbour. Sip a chardonnay on your private balcony and plot your political trajectory.

Pacific Harbour Motor Inn (☎ 06-867 8847; www.pacific-harbour.co.nz; 24 Reads Quay; ste $120-160) Next door to the Senator (once the same complex), Pacific Harbour bestows similar virtues.

Captain Cook Motor Lodge (☎ 0800 227 826, 06-867 7002; www.captaincook.co.nz; 31 Awapuni Rd; ste $99-180) Fresh as a Gisborne dawn, this top-shelf motel sparkles with the trappings of youth (including underdeveloped flora). How the owners managed to procure the motel's coveted website name in Cook-obsessed Gisborne is anyone's guess. Corporate guests schmooze between the bar and golf-driving booth.

White Heron Motor Lodge (☎ 0800 997 766, 06-867 1108; www.whml.co.nz; 474 Gladstone Rd; ste $115-125) Elevated standards and faceless anonymity define White Heron, another snazzy motel with modern, well-equipped units. Burn calories in the gym, or seduce them over a cooked breakfast.

Sea View B&B (☎ 06-867 3346; kerry.barry@xtra.co.nz; 68 Salisbury Rd; s/d $70/95) This contemporary waterfront homestay provides the opportunity to simply relax. Wade into the surf or soft-focus on the Norfolk Island Pines, it's all good for the soul. Family rates are available.

Whispering Sands Beachfront Motel (☎ 0800 405 030, 06-867 1319; whisperingsandsmotel@xtra.co.nz; 22 Salisbury Rd; ste $115) Can sand whisper? Something to ponder as Waikanae waves lull you to sleep. Book a top-floor room with Poverty Bay views.

Casa Blanca Motel (☎ 0800 172 000, 06-867 7107; casablancagisborne@yahoo.com; 61 Salisbury Rd; ste $80-115) This motel shouldn't be so ashamed of its unique nouveau-Spanish exterior, because inside the rooms it's a case of 'Play it again Sam'.

Eating

Wharf Café Bar Restaurant (☎ 06-868 4876; 60 The Esplanade; mains $24-33; ☒ breakfast, lunch & dinner) Overlooking fishing boats on the harbour, this is Gisborne dining for the new century. Smooth tunes waft through an elegant interior; excellent fish dishes swim through

---

AUTHOR'S CHOICE

One Orange (☎ 06-868 8062; www.oneorange.co.nz; Wairere Rd, Wainui Beach; from $200; ☒) Architecturally razor-sharp, this sumptuous B&B oozes affluence: voluminous wine glasses, Bose sound system, enormous beach towels, king-size beds and a salt-water swimming pool. Trout fishing trips and home-cooked dinners (passionately matched with local wines) by arrangement. Breakfast is included.

the menu. The outdoor concourse is perfect for a crisp morning coffee or a balmy evening beer.

Captain Morgans (☎ 06-867 7821; 285 Grey St; burgers $4-10; ☑ breakfast, lunch & dinner) Let's get one thing straight: there's nothing wrong with going downmarket on the coast. Burgers built this city, and Captain Morgans' are the biggest and best in town. Grab one and head for the beach.

Café Ruba (☎ 06-868 6516; 14 Childers Rd; mains $9-16; ☑ breakfast & lunch) This cool café was voted Gisborne's best in 2005. Progressive and urbane, Ruba's red and charcoal tones offset substantial breakfasts and adventurous lunches. Finish your palate with a good, strong coffee.

Works (☑ lunch & dinner; mains $10-26; ☑ lunch & dinner) Inside Gisborne's old freezing works, Works is a chic winery-restaurant serving imaginatively prepared meat, fish and vegetarian dishes. An extensive wine list proffers exceptional local vintages.

Gordon Gecko (☎ 06-863 1285; The Esplanade; mains $19-32; ☑ lunch & dinner) GG's successfully walks the line between restaurant and bar. Creative chicken, fish and beef dishes precede zingy desserts as a nightcap influx populates the bar. No sign of Michael Douglas.

Just Thai Cuisine (☎ 06-868 8028, 2 Lowe St; mains $14-17; ☑ lunch & dinner Mon-Sat) With fabulous feng shui, this bright, street-corner room overlooks the Taruheru River and serves traditional Thai classics (when was the last time you had chilli?).

Verve (☎ 06-868 9095; 121 Gladstone Rd; mains $8-20; ☑ breakfast, lunch & dinner; ☐) A slice of bohemia with Internet connections to a new age, Verve dishes up pastas, kebabs and Asian-influenced meals, an unpredictable array of homemade muffins and decent coffee.

Fettuccine Brothers (☎ 06-868 5700; 12 Peel St; mains $18-36; ☑ dinner Mon-Sat) Cheerfully colourful but retaining a certain intimacy, this pasta house is a Gisborne institution. We're not sure which of the staff are fraternal, but they're all friendly, and the well-stocked bar breeds brotherly love.

Preet Indian Tandoori Restaurant (☎ 06-863 0901; 55 Gladstone Rd; mains $13-25; ☑ lunch Mon-Sat, dinner daily) Get a curry fix at this remarkably un-Bollywood Indian eatery, dishing up

spicy standards from *rogan josh* to chicken *jal frazee*.

Self-caterers can fill the shopping trolley at **Pak N Save Supermarket** (☎ 06-868 9029; 274 Gladstone Rd).

Drinking & Entertainment

Sand Bar (☎ 06-868 6828; Oneroa Rd, Wainui) Hip bars aren't Gisborne's stock-in-trade, but Sand Bar makes the grade. A corrugated wave breaks over the bar as surfies shoot pool and down NZ beers. There's live weekend music, and a midnight shuttle back to town.

Irish Rover (☎ 06-867 1112; 99 Peel St) This Irish pub is packed on weekends, with occasional live music and inexpensive pub lunches and dinners. Signs subjectively declare, 'No hats, no undesirable tattoos'.

Scotty's (☎ 06-867 8173; 35 Gladstone Rd) Get a bit of grime under your fingernails at this grungy local watering hole, with ubiquitous pool table and regularly rockin' bands.

Getting There & Around

AIR

Air New Zealand (☎ 06-868 2700; www.airnz.co.nz; 37 Bright St) has daily direct flights to Auckland and Wellington, with onward connections. **Gisborne Airport** (☎ 06-867 1608; Aerodrome Rd) is 3km west of the city.

BUS

InterCity (☎ 06-868 6139; www.intercitycoach.co.nz) buses depart from the Gisborne visitor information centre for Wairoa ($24, 1½ hours, 9am daily), continuing to Napier ($39, four hours). The bus to Auckland ($74, nine hours, 7.55am daily) stops at Opotiki ($29, two hours). Whakatane ($39, three hours) and Rotorua ($55, 4½ hours).

For courier-service details from Gisborne to Opotiki travelling via East Cape's scenic SH35, see p370.

TAXI

A city-to-airport taxi fare costs between $12 and $15.

CAR HIRE

The following rental offices are at Gisborne Airport:

Avis (☎ 06-868 9084; www.avis.com)

Budget (☎ 06-867 9794; www.budget.co.nz)

Hertz (☎ 06-867 9343; www.hertz.co.nz)

Eastland Taxis (☎ 0800 868 294, 06-868 1133)
Gisborne Taxis (☎ 0800 505 555, 06-867 2222)
Link Taxis (☎ 06-868 8385)
Sun City Taxis (☎ 06-867 6767)

GISBORNE TO WAIROA

Heading south towards Napier you're confronted with a choice: follow SH2 along the coast, or take SH36 inland. Either way, you'll end up in Wairoa.

Coastal Route

The coastal road south from Gisborne actually runs a few kilometres inland, before entering the Whararata State Forest. Not quite out of the woods, 55km from Gisborne, Morere's famous hot springs burble up from a fault line. **Morere Hot Springs** (☎ 06-837 8856; morere.hot.springs@xtra.co.nz; SH2; adult/child $5/2.50; ☼ 10am-6pm Mon-Thu, 10am-7pm Fri-Sun) has hot and cold pools among lowland rainforest. Get osmotic with the water's minerals, or tackle the walking tracks (20 minutes to three hours).

Opposite the springs are the **Morere Tearooms & Camping Grounds** (☎ 06-837 8792; morere@xtra.co.nz; SH2; sites per 2 people $26, d $50-70). The campsites here are beautifully situated alongside a swimming hole in the babbling Tunanui Stream. The café serves homemade goodies and stocks basic provisions.

Moonlight Cottage (☎ 06-837 8824; moonlight lodge@xtra.co.nz; SH2; Morere; dm/d cabins $22/75; ☼ closed Jul-Aug) is a colonial farmhouse just off the highway. Clean and freshly painted among the deciduous boughs of a sheep-studded river valley, it's a hard-to-beat hostel. Guests contemplate staying put on the deep veranda. There's also a separate family cottage ($95 to $120).

SH2 continues south to Nuhaka at the northern end of Hawke Bay. From here it's west to Wairoa, or east to the marvellous **Mahia Peninsula**. Like Santorini crossed with Dover, Mahia's bald hills are interspersed with conifer stands, giving way to white sandstone cliffs and dark-brown beach sand, sighing beneath the lilting cadence of a vivid blue sea. Majestic in sun or storm, Mahia's strange atmospheres form the backdrop for surfing, diving, walking, fishing and bird-watching at Mangawhio Lagoon. You'll need your own transport to explore the peninsula, which was once an island before shifting sands latched onto the mainland.

Not far from the Nahuka junction, **East Land Aquaculture Ltd** (☎ 06-837 8880; www.paua nzabalone.co.nz; Waikokupu Rd, Nuhaka; tours $5; ☼ 8am-4pm daily Oct-Apr, 8am-4pm Mon-Fri, 8am-1.30pm Sat-Sun May-Sep) is a working paua farm. Take a tour or swoon over the gift shop's rainbow colour-scheme gleam.

Mahia Beach Motel & Holiday Park (☎ 06-837 5830; mahia.beach.motels@xtra.co.nz; 43 Moana Dr, Mahia Beach; unpowered/powered sites per 2 people $24/28, d $40-90) is your best (and pretty much only) bet for accommodation on the west side of Mahia. The beach seduces swimmers, and there's a café, shop and kayaks for hire.

Up a steep driveway on Mahia's east coast, **Mahia Café** (☎ 06-837 5094; 476 East Coast Rd; mains $7-25; ☼ breakfast, lunch & dinner; ☐) has 72 local jams and sauces at its disposal, with some tender paua dishes on the menu. Views are as wide as the day is long. Book for dinner.

East of the café, **Ellenayes Beach Accommodation** (☎ 06-837 5188; morrison@xtra.co.nz; 520 East Coast Rd; d $90) is a modern self-contained apartment sleeping two couples. Located right above the shoreline, there's not much between here and Chile except the sound of the surf and an Easter Island or two.

Inland Route

SH36, the inland road to Wairoa, is less spectacular than the Mahia route. We're not sure how she got her rep, but you can climb up **Gentle Annie Hill** for expansive views over Poverty Bay. **Doneraille Park**, 53km from Gisborne, is a peaceable bush reserve with a frigid mountain river to jump into.

The trout at the manmade **Tiniroto Lakes**, 61km from Gisborne, are hungry and fat. Get a good night's sleep before casting your morning flies at the quaintly country **Tiniroto Tavern** (☎ 06-863 7019; 2 School Rd, Tiniroto; dm/d $20/35), with basic but comfy rooms. About 10km further, the snow-white cascades of **Te Reinga Falls** are worth a detour off the main road.

HAWKES BAY

The Hawkes Bay region (confusingly, the body of water is called 'Hawke Bay') is a fertile agricultural area and hyperactive wine-producing region. Locals squint into familiar sunshine in a diverse landscape of fetching coastal scenery, fertile plains and the neighbouring but disparate cities of Napier and Hastings.

Rolling in wine money, Havelock North is Hastings' well-moneyed off-sider. Both towns make boozy bases for incursions into the Hawkes Bay Wine Country, or exploring Te Mata Peak and the Cape Kidnappers Gannet Colony.

WAIROA

pop 5228

SH2 and SH36 converge 98km south of Gisborne at Wairoa, a pit-stop river town a little thin on charisma. Wairoa is the gateway to Te Urewera National Park.

Information

DOC (☎ 06-838 8252; 272 Marine Pde) As in Gisborne, this isn't really a public facility.

Wairoa visitor information centre (☎ 06-838 7440; www.wairoanz.com; cnr SH2 & Queen St; ☼ 9am-5pm Mon-Fri, 10am-4pm Sat & Sun; ▯) Information on Te Urewera National Park, regional fishing and accommodation; also sells DOC passes.

Sights

Relocated to the Wairoa River, the **Portland Island Lighthouse**, built in 1877 of solid kauri, once shone off the Mahia Peninsula. **Whakaki Lagoon**, 10km east of town, is a flourishing wetland with quarrelsome bird populations.

A visit to the restored **Gaiety Cinema & Theatre** (☎ 06-838 3104; gaiety@xtra.co.nz; 142 Marine Pde) or the locally artefactual **Wairoa Museum** (☎ 06-838 3108; wairoamuseum@xtra.co.nz; 252 Marine Pde; admission by donation; ☼ 10am-4pm Mon-Fri, 10am-1pm Sat) might delay thoughts of moving on.

Sleeping & Eating

Three Oaks Motel (☎ 06-838 8204; cnr Campbell St & Clyde Rd; s/d $70/80; ▯) Restfully removed from the highway hum, Three Oaks has the usual motel comforts in ground-level units, plus a swimming pool. There are actually four oaks, but who's counting?

Vista Motor Lodge (☎ 0800 284 782, 06-838 8297; vistamotorlodge@xtra.co.nz; 2 Bridge St; ste $90-120; ▯) Vista has a cache of variously configured units by the river. Interior tones are a little dated (Rubik's Cube–inspired lino), but everything's in good shape, and the licensed restaurant is a hit with locals.

Mina Café & Restaurant (☎ 06-838 6289; 252 Marine Pde; mains $18-23; ☼ lunch & dinner Tue-Sun)

Mina is an island of Turkish flavour on burger row.

Oslers Bakery (☎ 06-838 8299; 116 Marine Pde; meals $4-12; ☼ breakfast & lunch) Much-awarded pie aficionados.

Getting There & Away

All **InterCity** (☎ 06-838 7440; www.intercitycoach .co.nz) buses that travel between Gisborne and Napier pass through Wairoa.

TE UREWERA NATIONAL PARK

Te Urewera protects part of the North Island's largest untouched native forest. Cloaked in dark-green woodland cut with lakes and rivers, it's a stunning area with walks ranging from 30 minutes to several days. There are 50-plus DOC huts in the park, and plenty of birds, trout and deer to restore your faith in the natural realm.

The jewel of Te Urewera is Lake Waikaremoana (Sea of Rippling Waters), a deep, mystic crucible of water encircled by the Lake Waikaremoana Track, one of NZ's Great Walks. Rugged bluffs drop away to reedy inlets, the lake's mirror surface disturbed only by mountain zephyrs and the occasional waterbird taking to the skies.

Home of the Tuhoe people, Te Urewera has a rich history. The army of Te Kooti (p378) took refuge here during running battles with government troops. Te Kooti's successor, Rua Kenana, led a thriving community beneath the sacred mountain Maungapohatu (1366m) from 1905 until his politically inspired 1916 arrest. Maungapohatu never recovered, and only a small settlement remains. Nearby Ruatahuna's extraordinary Mataatua Marae celebrates Te Kooti's exploits.

Information

Aniwaniwa visitor information centre (☎ 06-837 3900; fax 06-837 3722; urewerainfo@doc.govt.nz; SH38; ⏰ 8am-4.45pm) On the lakeshore, this is also the DOC office, with displays on the park's natural history, and tramping, weather and accommodation info. Get your hut or camping-ground passes for the Lake Waikaremoana Track here, or at the Gisborne, Wairoa, Whakatane or Napier DOC offices or visitor information centres.

Activities

LAKE WAIKAREMOANA TRACK

To say this three- to four-day tramp is hugely popular understates the situation. The 46km track scales the spectacular Panekiri Bluff, with open panoramas and jaw-dropping lake views interspersed with fern groves and beech and podocarp forest along the track. The walk is rated as moderate, the only difficult section being the Panekiri ascent. During summer and Easter the trail can resemble a queue for All Blacks tickets, but keep your eyes on the lake and you won't get annoyed.

It's a year-round track, but cold winter rain deters many people and makes conditions much more challenging. At this altitude, temperatures can drop quickly, even in summer. Walkers should take portable stoves and fuel as there are no cooking facilities en route. Parking your car at the trail heads isn't a great idea, as break-ins do occur.

There are five huts and camp sites spaced along the track, all of which must be pre-booked through DOC as far ahead as possible, regardless of the season. Huts cost $20/10 per adult/child per night; camp sites $10/5. To book, phone the Aniwaniwa visitor information centre (above).

Walking the Track

Propel yourself onto the trail either clockwise from just outside Onepoto in the south or anticlockwise from Hopuruahine Bridge

in the north. From Onepoto, all the steep climbing happens in the first few hours. Water on this section of the track is limited so fill your bottles before heading off. If you have a car, it is safest to leave it at the Waikaremoana Motor Camp (opposite) or Big Bush Holiday Park (opposite) then take a water taxi (see p386) to the trail heads.

Estimated walking times:

Route	Time
Onepoto to Panekiri Hut	5hr
Panekiri Hut to Waiopaoa Hut	3-4hr
Waiopaoa Hut to Marauiti Hut	5hr
Marauiti Hut to Waiharuru Hut	2hr
Waiharuru Hut to Whanganui Hut	2½hr
Whanganui Hut to Hopuruahine Bridge	2hr

Walking Legends (☎ 07-345 7363; www.walkinglegends.com) is an enthusiastic and experienced young company running three- to six-day guided walks around Lake Waikaremoana and through Te Urewera (walks from $850 all-inclusive).

OTHER WALKS

Another major walk in the park is the three- to five-day **Whakatane River Round Trip**, which starts at Ruatahuna on SH38, 45km from the Aniwaniwa visitor information centre towards Rotorua. The five-hut track follows the Whakatane River then loops back via Waikare River, Motumuka Stream and Whakatane Valley. You can continue north down the Whakatane River and out of the national park at Ruatoki, from where you'll probably have to hitch.

The **Manuoha–Waikareiti Track** is a three-day walk for experienced trampers, kicking off near Hopuruahine and heading up to Manuoha Hut, the park's highest point (1392m). It then follows a ridge down to Lake Waikareiti via Sandy Bay Hut, finishing at Aniwaniwa.

Shorter walks and day walks include the **Old Maori Trail** (four hours return), an old Maori route from Rosie Bay to Lake Kaitawa; the **Waikareiti Track** (two hours return, four hours to Sandy Bay Hut one way), through beech and rimu forest; and the **Ruapani Circuit** (six hours), including wetland wanderings. The DOC *Lake Waikaremoana Walks* booklet ($2) has the inside running on these and more.

LAKE WAIKAREMOANA TRACK

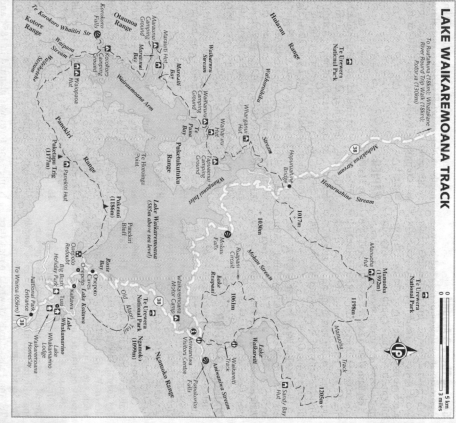

To Ruatahuna (18km); Whataroa
River Round Trip Walk (18km);
Rotorua (130km)

Sleeping & Eating

Waikaremoana Motor Camp (☎ 06-837 3826; www
.lake.co.nz; SH38; unpowered sites per 2 people/d/f from
$20/42/80) Right on Lake Waikaremoana's
rippling shore, this place has Swiss-looking
wooden chalets, fisherman's cabins and camp
sites, all with watery views. The on-site shop
fills with kids buying chocolate while trout-
engrossed parents are elsewhere. The camp
also runs water taxis to the trail heads.

Lake Whakamarino Lodge (☎ 06-837 3876; www
.lakelodge.co.nz; Tuai; s/d/ste $60/70/100) Trout equals
passion? Then this lodge on the fish-infested
hydroelectric Lake Whakamarino is your
destiny. Accommodation is in converted
hydro-housing; home-cooked meals by
request.

Big Bush Holiday Park (☎ 0800 525 392, 06-837
3777; www.lakewaikaremoana.co.nz; SH38; sites per 2
people/dm/d $20/25/75) Above a lake between
Lake Waikaremoana and Tuai and close to
the Onepoto trail head, Big Bush offers neat
cabins, acceptable backpacker rooms and a
roomy licensed café. Pick-ups, water taxis
and storage are available.

Waikaremoana Homestay (☎ 06-837 3701; www
.waikaremoanahomestay.co.nz; 9 Rotten Row, Tuai; s/d
$55/85) This homespun homestay occupies a
70-year-old cottage close to Lake Whakamarino. Hook yourself a trophy trout in the
morning then watch the shadows lengthen
across Lake Waikaremoana.

For camping and hut options on the Lake
Waikaremoana Track, see opposite.

0 5 km
0 3 miles

Getting There & Around

Approximately 105km of the road between Wairoa and Rotorua (on both sides of Lake Waikaremoana) remains unsealed, despite a recent million-dollar government contribution. It's a time-consuming drive, one that's less for tourists, more for travellers.

Big Bush Water Taxi (☎ 06-837 3777) will ship you to either Onepoto or Hopuruahine trail head ($30 return) or Hopuruahine trail head ($30 return), with hut-to-hut pack transfers for the less gung-ho. It also runs shuttles between Wairoa and Rotorua; call for prices and times.

The **Home Bay Water Taxi** (☎ 06-837 3826) operates from Waikaremoana Motor Camp (p385) to either trail head ($30 return). **Waikaremoana Guided Tours** (☎ 06-837 3729) provides a similar service.

WAIROA TO NAPIER

There's a string of historic nature reserves along this stretch of road to break the twisting drive, all accessible from SH2. The *Heritage Trails: Napier to Wairoa* brochure (from the Wairoa visitor info centre, p383) has the lowdown.

Occupied by early Maori, **Lake Tutira** has walkways and a bird sanctuary. The **Hawkes Bay Coastal Walkway** starts 12km from SH2 down Waikari Rd. The 16km trail connects the Waikari and Aropaoanui Rivers, involving boulder hopping, track and beach walking.

Off Waipatiki Rd 34km outside Napier is the 64-hectare **Waipatiki Scenic Reserve**, echoing with tui and native-pigeon calls. **Tangoio Falls Scenic Reserve**, 25km north of Napier, has Te Ana Falls, stands of wheki ponga (tree ferns), and native orchids. The **White Pine Bush Scenic Reserve**, 5km south of Tangoio, bristles with kahikatea and nikau palms. Between White Pine and Tangoio Reserves the **Tangoio Walkway** follows Kareaara Stream.

There's serene, rough-hewn backpacker accommodation at **Bushdale Farm** (☎ 06-838 6453; nicola.smale@xtra.co.nz; 438 Cricklewood Rd; dm/d $22/44; ⊠), 13km south of Wairoa. Birds, walks, horses, glow-worms and free eggs are what you're in for. It also runs **Napier Coastal Horse Treks Farm** (☎ 06-836 7626; nicola.smale@xtra .co.nz; 1760 Main Rd North, Tangoio; 1-2hr $45–70), 20km north of Napier.

Ancient convoluted pine trunks introduce **Glen-view Farm Hostel** (☎ 06-836 6232; glen viewhostel@xtra.co.nz; Arapaoanui Rd; dm/d $15/40), a

hill-country sheep and cattle station 31km north of Napier off SH2 (2km east along Arapaoanui Rd). The sunny reading room is as tempting as a horse ride ($40 for two hours).

NAPIER

pop 55,000

Shaken to the ground by an earthquake in 1931, Napier has emerged Phoenix-like from tragedy into a new era of prosperity. A dignified, sunny, composed city, there's the air of an affluent English seaside resort about the place. The focus rests squarely on Napier's urban virtues: its much-vaunted Art Deco architecture is milked for every tourist dollar, while good-looking middle-agers who've had too much sun glide between cool cafés. The less self-conscious expanses of Hawke Bay are just across Marine Pde.

Napier makes a good base for exploring the region's wineries, a cork's pop beyond the city limits.

History

Long before James Cook eyeballed the area in October 1769, Maoris knew this was a bountiful place. South of the city on Gloucester St, past the Eastern Institute of Technology, the Otatara Pa is authentically pre-European.

French explorer Jules Dumont d'Urville steered the *Astrolabe* into the bay in 1827. In the 1830s, whalers malingered around Ahuriri, establishing a trading base in 1839. Obsequiously named after the British general and colonial administrator Charles Napier, the town was planned in 1854 and soon flourished with commerce.

At 10.46am on February 3, 1931, the city was levelled by a catastrophic earthquake (7.9 on the Richter Scale). Fatalities in Napier and nearby Hastings numbered 258. Napier suddenly found itself 40 sq km larger, as the earthquake heaved sections of seabed 2m above sea level (Napier Airport was once more 'port', less 'air'). A fevered rebuilding programme ensued, constructing one of the world's most uniformly Art Deco cities.

Orientation

Bluff Hill looms ominously at the northern end of town dividing the CBD and Ahuriri, beyond which the cosmopolitan West Quay restaurant precinct prospers. Murmuring

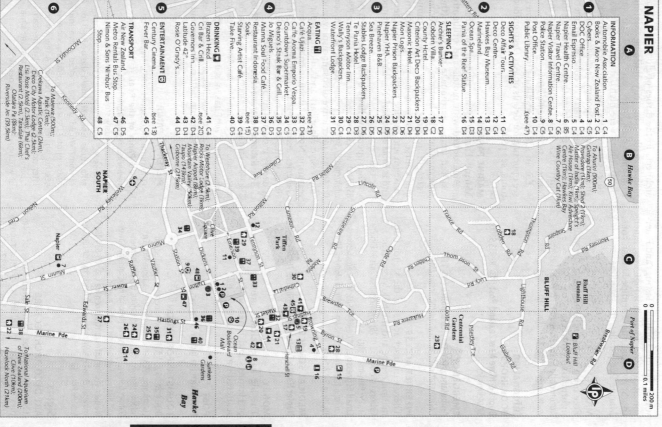

with economic hubbub, Hastings and Emerson Sts are the prime thoroughfares, Emerson St evolving into a semipedestrian zone. Marine Pde parallels the shoreline.

MAPS

Free town maps are available at the visitor information centre.

Automobile Association (AA; ☎ 06-834 2590; www.aatravel.co.nz; 87 Dickens St)

Information

BOOKSHOPS

Books & More New Zealand Post (☎ 06-835 9800; 57 Dickens St)

EMERGENCY

Ambulance, fire service & police (☎ 111)
Police station (☎ 06-831 0700; Station St)

INTERNET ACCESS

There's Internet access at the visitor information centre and the following cafés:

Cybers (☎ 06-835 0125; www.cybers.co.nz; 98 Dickens St; ☒ 9am–midnight)
Email Espresso (☎ 06-834 0963; www.emailespresso .co.nz; 6 Hastings St; ☒ 8am–10.30pm Mon–Fri, 10am–10.30pm Sat & Sun)

MEDICAL SERVICES

Napier Health Centre (☎ 06-878 8109; 76 Wellesley Rd)

MONEY

The big banks cluster around the corner of Hastings and Emerson Sts, with ATMs scattered throughout the CBD.

POST

Post office (cnr Dickens & Hastings Sts)

TOURIST INFORMATION

DOC (☎ 06-834 3111; www.doc.govt.nz; The Old Courthouse, 59 Marine Pde; ☒ 9am–4.15pm Mon–Fri) Information on walks around Napier, Cape Kidnappers Gannet Colony, Te Urewera National Park, and the Kaweka and Ruahine Forest Parks west of Napier.
Napier visitor information centre (☎ 06-834 1911; www.isitehawkesbaynz.com, www.hawkesbaynz.com; 100 Marine Pde; ☐)

Sights

ART DECO ARCHITECTURE

The 1931 quake demolished most of Napier's older brick buildings. Frantic reconstruction between 1931 and 1933 caught architects in the throes of global Art Deco mania, with many city buildings dating from these peak Deco years. Art Deco was cheap (debts were high), it was safe (two-storey concrete was more stable than brick), and it was contemporary (residents wanted to make a fresh start). A cohesive architectural vision grew from the ruins, putting the 'unity' back into the community and giving Napier a new *raison d'être*.

For an Art Deco walking tour of Napier, see opposite; for details on Art Deco guided tours, see p390.

MARINE PARADE

Marine Parade is an elegant pine-lined avenue dotted with motels and brilliantly restored timber earthquake survivors (the wise man built his house of wood?). Along its length are parks, sunken gardens, a mini-golf course, a swimming pool, aquarium, museum and marine park. At the northern end is **Pania of the Reef**, Napier's iconic statue (see below).

The superlative **Hawkes Bay Museum** (☎ 06-835 7781; www.hawkesbaymuseum.co.nz; 65 Marine Pde; adult/child $7.50/free; ☒ 9am–5pm May–Sep, 9am–6pm Oct–Apr) has interactive dinosaur displays and impressive Maori art and culture displays featuring Ngati Kahungunu tribal artefacts. Galleries accommodate temporary exhibitions, while the 35-minute earthquake film is deeply moving (no pun intended).

The **National Aquarium of New Zealand** (☎ 06-834 1404; www.nationalaquarium.co.nz; 546 Marine Pde; adult/child $13/7; ☒ 9am–7pm Jan, 9am–5pm Feb-Dec, feedings 10am & 2pm) has a stingray-inspired roof. Inside are crocodiles, piranhas, turtles, native eels, kiwis, prehistoric tuatara and a

---

PILFERING PANIA

One night in October 2005, Napier's beloved **Pania of the Reef** statue, a tragiromantic figure from local Maori folklore, was scurrilously stolen. Speculation raged across NZ: was this some kind of unforgivable student prank? Would she be held for ransom? Would she be melted down into brass ingots? Dear God, would anyone ever see her again? Oh the horror! A few weeks later, police found her disconsolate beneath a blanket in a Napier backyard. At the time of writing, charges were pending…

whole lotta fish. 'Behind the Scenes' tours cost adult/child $20/10 (leaving at 9am and 1pm). Qualified divers can swim with (or get married in the presence of) sharks. Non-nuptial dives are $50, plus $30 for gear.

Marineland (06-834 4027; 290 Marine Pde; adult/child $11/5.50; 10am-4.30pm) has seals and dolphins performing at 10.30am and 2pm (plus 4pm in summer). You can swim with dolphins ($45, wet-suit hire $10), touch and feed dolphins on a guided tour (adult/child $16/8), or investigate the penguin recovery workshop ($16). Bookings essential.

BLUFF HILL LOOKOUT

There are magnificent views over Hawke Bay from Bluff Hill, hulking 102m above Napier. There's a sheer cliff face down to the port, and a circuitous route to the top. It's open daily during daylight hours.

Walking Tour

Start AMP Building
Finish Hotel Central
Distance 1km
Duration 45 minutes

The Art Deco architectural style first made headlines at the 1925 Paris International Exposition of Modern Decorative and Industrial Arts. The Deco is in the detail: zigzags, lightning bolts, geometric shapes and rising suns are typical; ancient Egyptian and Mayan design was inspirational. Soft pastel colours (think Don Johnson's *Miami Vice* t-shirts) are another Deco giveaway, though many of Napier's buildings were originally monochrome plaster.

This walk shouldn't take more than 45 minutes, depending on coffee stops, and at just over 1km it won't raise much of a sweat (in decorous Deco style).

Start at the corner of Browning and Hastings Sts where the stylish **AMP Building (1)** promises providence to all. Shuffle along the west side of Hastings St to the corner of Tennyson St. Many of the shopfronts in this block have been modernised, so look up to the **second storeys (2)** for the Deco dazzle. Head west along Tennyson to the beautifully proportioned **Daily Telegraph Building (3)** with its superb electro-Egyptian aesthetic. Continue past the staunch élan of the **Scinde Building (4)**, the restored **Municipal Theatre (5)** and the impressive **Deco Centre (6; p390)**.

Turn left onto Clive Sq and trundle past the **Provincial Hotel (7;** now a beer hall), then left again into Emerson St. Kick back with a coffee, or continue below the stellar second storeys of the **Kidson's Building (8)**, **Hawkes Bay Chambers (9)** and **Criterion Hotel (10)**. The **ASB Bank (11)** on the Emerson-Hastings corner houses a Maori-meets-Deco interior. Above the Grosvenor Inn at the bottom of Emerson St is the A&B Building's **Deco clock tower (12)**, neon-lit by night. To the left is the grandiose **Masonic Hotel (13; p391)**; across Marine Pde the **Soundshell (14)** is classic Art Deco, as is the plaza's paving.

Back on Hastings St, hang a right onto Dickens St and the deluxe Moorish-Spanish spirals and stucco of the former **Gaiety de Luxe Cinema (15)**. Check out the fine scalloped window arches of the old **State Cinema (16)** on the corner of Dickens and Dalton Sts, then veer right onto Dalton to finish beneath the flamingo hues of the old **Hotel Central (17)**, all zigzag swagger and lead-light complexity. If you have time, cruise out for the magnificent National Tobacco Co façade on the corner of Bridge and Ossian Sts in Ahuriri, and the Deco-bedecked suburb of Marewa.

Activities

Napier beach is dubious for swimming, so head for **Ocean Spa** (06-835 8553; napier@h2omanagemen.co.nz; 42 Marine Pde; adult/child $6/4,

6am-10pm Mon-Sat, 8am-10pm Sun), a spiffy new waterfront pool complex. Get weightless in the spa (adult/child $8/6), or indulge in a half-hour massage ($35). There is a great café on site (p393).

Onekawa Aquatic Centre (06-834 4150; www .onekawaaquatic.co.nz; Maadi Rd; adult/child $3.50/2.50, waterslides $4 unlimited rides; 6am-9pm Mon-Fri, 11am-6pm Sat & Sun), south of town, has a 50m pool, waterslides, spas and a kids' pool.

See if you're any closer to challenging Spiderman on the climbing wall at the **Kiwi Adventure Centre** (06-834 3500; www.kiwi-adven ture.co.nz; 58 West Quay, Ahuriri; adult/child $15/12; 3-9pm Mon-Fri, 10am-6pm Sat & Sun). It also organises canyoning, caving and kayaking trips.

Mountain Valley (06-834 9756; www.mountain valley.co.nz; McVicar Rd, Te Pohue), 50km north of Napier on SH5, offers horse trekking ($50 to $120), white-water rafting (from $120), and horse/canoeing combos (prices on request). 'Fishing' is a word you'll hear spoken with reverent enthusiasm, and there's accommodation on site.

Feeling the need for speed? **Riverside Jet** (06-874 3841; www.riversidejet.co.nz; adult/child from $25/15) terrorises the Ngaruroro River's braided channels, 35 minutes from Napier. Call for bookings and times.

Feeling the onus of slowness? **Hawkes Bay Wine Country Cat** (0800 946 322, 06-877 7850; www.hbwinecountrycat.com; West Quay, Ahuriri; lunch/dinner cruise $50/55; 11am & 6.30pm) schmoozes out onto Hawke Bay on daily food cruises. Shorter cruises are also available.

Tours

The Napier Art Deco Trust promotes and protects the city's architectural heritage. Its one-hour Deco walk ($10) departs the visitor information centre daily at 10am; the two-hour walk ($15) leaves the **Deco Centre** (06-835 0022; www.artdeconapier.com; 163 Tennyson St; 9am-5pm) at 2pm daily. Walks include an introductory spiel, DVD screening and refreshments.

The Deco Centre shop stocks assorted Art Deco paraphernalia, including brochures for the self-guided *Art Deco Walk* ($4), *Art Deco Scenic Drive* ($4), and *Marewa Meander* ($2). Marewa is a Napier suburb, Deco through-and-through.

Trip the light fantastic in a cherry-red 1934 Buick with **Deco Affair Tours** (027-241 5279; www.decoaffair.com; 16/20 Midcity Plaza; tours 20min/2½hr $25/90), hosted by the endearingly eccentric Bertie, clad in full period regalia.

Less span-dangly, **Fairway Tours** (0800 428 687, 06-843 2264; www.fairwaytours.co.nz; tours $20) runs one-hour 'City Highlights' tours, departing the visitor information centre five times a day. Call for bookings and departure times.

For listings of Hawkes Bay winery tours, see p398.

Festivals & Events

In the third week of February, Napier and Hastings co-host the sensational **Art Deco Weekend** (06-835 1191; www.artdeconapier.com). Dinners, dances, drinks, balls, bands and Gatsby-esque fancy-dress fill the week with shenanigans. Bertie, Napier's Art Deco ambassador (see Deco Affair Tours, left), is omnipresent.

Also in February, Mission Estate Winery, NZ's oldest winery, holds an immensely popular **open-air concert** (Map p399; 06-845 9350; www.missionconcert.co.nz), importing a geriatric superstar (Kenny Rogers, Joe Cocker, The Doobie Brothers etc) to belt out some classics.

Napier, Hastings and Havelock North are the hubs of the Harvest Hawkes Bay festival in early February; see p397 for details.

Sleeping

BUDGET

Wally's Backpackers (06-833 7930; www.wallys backpackers.co.nz; 7 Cathedral Lane; dm/d/f $22/55/75;) Slick urban hostelling at its best, Wally's only opened in 2003 and it shows. Serious money has gone into spotless rooms, a restaurant-standard kitchen, single-person bathrooms, a landscaped barbecue area and luxurious TV lounge, belying the buildings' 85 years.

Criterion Art Deco Backpackers (06-835 2059; www.criterionartdeco.co.nz; 48 Emerson St; dm/s/d from $20/26/46;) Formerly the Criterion Hotel, this is arguably Napier's best Spanish Mission specimen (check out those fireplaces!). Vast kitchen and dining areas, free linen, heated rooms, double glazing, quiz nights, pool comps, drink vouchers... The trick in life is to know when you've got it good.

Stables Lodge Backpackers (06-835 6242; www .stableslodge.co.nz; 370 Hastings St; dm/d $19/48;) Sometimes the best plan is no plan: relinquish your destiny to the cosmos at Stables, an old house with horsey décor and low-altitude atmosphere. There's a barbecue courtyard, murals, hammocks, pizza nights, a couple of lazy dogs and free Internet.

Archie's Bunker (06-833 7990; www.archiesbunker.co.nz; 14 Herschell St; dm/s/d from $22/27/50;) One street back from the beach, Archie's is a modern, well-maintained hostel. It is indeed bunkerlike, with impressive security, engendering a sense of 'OK, I'm safe now'. There's a TV lounge, barbecue area, pool table, bike hire and disabled access.

Napier YHA (06-833 7039; yha.napier@yha.co.nz 277 Marine Pde; dm/s/d $21/25/50;) Napier's YHA fills a 110-year-old beachfront house with an endless ramble of rooms; try to book one back from the street. There's a fabulous overhanging reading nook and a sunny rear courtyard.

Waterfront Lodge (06-835 3429; www.napierwaterfront.co.nz; 217 Marine Pde, dm $20, s $28-36, d/f $56/84;) This hostel balances out the melange of Marine Pde accommodation options with its communal good-time atmosphere. It's an old, mazelike house with plenty of rooms. Any excuse is good enough for a soccer tournament or barbecue.

Napier Prison Backpackers (06-835 9933; www.napierprison.com; 55 Coote Rd; dm/s/d $22/35/54, tours adult/child $15/10,) Unavoidably macabre, this converted Victorian prison, only decommissioned in 1993, has creaking cell doors, high stone walls, gang graffiti and a hanging yard. Men have suffered here, but as a hostel it's entirely comfortable. Guided one-hour tours leave at 9.30am and 3pm (free for inmates).

Kennedy Park (0800 457 275, 06-843 9126; www.kennedypark.co.nz; Storkey St, Marewa; unpowered/powered sites per 2 people $30/32, d/units from $70/115;) This 'Top 10' park is top dog on the Napier camping scene. It's the closest camping ground to town (2.5km out), with the usual suspects: playground, games room, TV room and so on, plus a restaurant and reasonable winter rates.

MIDRANGE

Sea Breeze (06-835 8067; seabreeze.napier@xtra.co.nz; 281 Marine Pde; s/d $75/110) Inside this Victorian seafront villa are three richly coloured-themed rooms (Chinese, Indian and Turkish), decorated with a cornucopia of artefacts and exotic flair. The glazed veranda is perfectly sunny for breakfast, which is included in prices.

Pinehaven B&B (06-835 5575; www.pinehavenbnb.co.nz; 529 Marine Pde; s/d $80/100) Pinehaven is a travellers' favourite, with most of the eight cosy rooms looking out over the sea. Postsunrise breakfasts (included) feature organic coffee, free-range eggs, homemade jam and muesli.

Mon Logis (06-835 2125; monlogis@xtra.co.nz; 415 Marine Pde; s/d from $120) Run by a gregarious French monologist, Mon Logis was built in 1915 as a private hotel. Honeymooners sleep late in the en suite rooms; sea views from the balcony evoke Gallic reminiscences. Breakfast is included.

Lisa Rose Motel (0800 454 727, 06-843 4400; lisarose@clear.net.nz; 377 Marine Pde; ste from $90;) Private and personable, this welcoming out-of-town motel has been recommended by readers. Rooms are utterly immaculate and have full cooking facilities.

Masonic Hotel (06-835 8689; www.masonic.co.nz; cnr Herschell & Tennyson Sts; s/d/ste $80/95/120) Trading on its Deco heritage, the Masonic is right in the heart of town. In fact, it may well be the heart of town, with its accommodation, restaurants and pub taking up most of a city block. The atmosphere is intentionally '20s; rooms have dated without the intent.

Rocks Motorlodge (0800 835 9626, 06-835 9626; www.therocksmotel.co.nz; 27 Meeanee Quay, Westshore; ste from $115;) The Rocks' corrugated stylings have raised the bar on Westshore's otherwise grim motel row. TVs are massive, interiors are corporately comfy, and it's 80m from the beach. If the spa units are gone, go for a room with a claw-foot bath.

Deco City Motor Lodge (0800 536 6339, 06-843 4342; www.decocity.co.nz; 308 Kennedy Rd; ste from $110,) This upmarket Art Deco-inspired motel 2.5km from the CBD has an appropriately fashioned exterior. The Deco doesn't extend much past the front door, but hey, you're here to sleep, right? Rooms have spas and king-size beds.

Tennyson Motor Inn (0800 502 122, 06-835 3373; www.tennyson.co.nz; cnr Tennyson St & Clive Sq; d $120-130) Unspectacular but spectacularly anonymous, this motel monolith overlooks Clive Sq. A decent on-site restaurant serves breakfast and dinner.

TOP END

Cobden Villa (06-835 9065; www.cobdenvilla.com; 11 Cobden Rd; d $315-495) Wow! Amid meticulously maintained hillside gardens, this Art Deco home has been superbly renovated, the owners scouring NZ's antique shops and auctions to fill the four en suite rooms with period furniture. Everything's Deco: the mirrors, light fittings, door handles, stained glass, wall friezes, even the doormat.

Te Pania Hotel (☎ 06-833 7733; www.scenic-circle .co.nz; 45 Marine Pde; d from $245) The concave Te Pania takes its curvy design cues from the UN building in New York (on a more manageable scale). Most of the spacious rooms have floor-to-ceiling windows and sea views, and there's a restaurant and gym.

County Hotel (☎ 0800 843 468, 06-835 7800; www .countyhotel.co.nz; 12 Browning St; d/ste from $331/495) The County Hotel is an elegantly restored Edwardian building (a rare brick earthquake survivor), with 18 individually styled rooms. New owners have infused luxury between the masonry. Downstairs, Chambers restaurant breathes refined formality at dinner (mains $29 to $58).

Eating

Café Ujazi (☎ 06-835 1490; 28 Tennyson St; mains $8-15; ☻ breakfast & lunch) Ujazi feels like it's flown in from somewhere else, folding back its windows and letting the reggae vibes spill out onto surprised streets. Visiting celebrity waifs get their big-city café fix here, sipping espresso and nibbling the edges of wholesome vegetarian dishes.

Shed 2 (☎ 06-835 2202; West Quay, Ahuriri; mains $15-25; ☻ breakfast Sun, lunch Tue-Sun & dinner daily) Shed 2 heads the flotilla of new eateries and bars mushrooming up at West Quay. It's a cavernous barn-meets-booth kind of place, the menu scuttling between wood-fired pizzas, nachos and pasta dishes. DJs and occasional live bands take over after dinner on weekends.

Master of India (☎ 06-834 3440; cnr Routledge & Waghorne Sts, Ahuriri; mains $9-17; ☻ lunch Wed-Sat, dinner daily) Masterfully prepared curries and vegetarian delights are the staples here. The dimly lit interior is hushed with romantic mutterings and achingly polite service.

Restaurant Indonesia (☎ 06-835 8303; 409 Marine Pde; mains $24-26; ☻ dinner Wed-Sun) Crammed with Balinese artworks, batik prints and Indonesian curios, this intimate space smacks of authenticity. Lip-smacking Indo-Dutch *rijsttafel* smorgasbords are the house specialty (up to 19 dishes, $32 to $40 per person). Bookings essential.

Provedore (☎ 06-834 0189; West Quay, Ahuriri; mains $18-28, tapas $5-14; ☻ lunch Fri-Sun, dinner Tue-Sun) West Quay is, as they say, 'happening'. If you happen to happen here too, this sophisticated restaurant-bar serves fabulous tapas and eclectic meals. The celebrated wine and beer list will make you list sideways.

Gintrap (☎ 06-835 0199; West Quay, Ahuriri; mains $16-28; ☻ breakfast Sat & Sun, lunch & dinner daily) The good citizens of Napier people-watch from Gintrap's nautical deck, rigged with heaters for the times when even a stiff gin can't trap any warmth. The large open bar serves tasty snacks and seasonal seafood-centric meals.

Thai Chef's Restaurant (☎ 06-843 4595; 110 Taradale Rd; mains $14-19; ☻ lunch Wed-Fri, dinner daily) Thai foodies rave about this thronging place, 3km west of town. The unceasingly crimson interior offsets a lost-in-translation menu, featuring dishes like 'The 3 Alcoholics' and 'Sexy Little Duck'. Chilli warnings declare, 'Quest challenge for brave! HOT HOT HOT!'.

Take Five (☎ 06-835 4050; 189 Marine Pde; mains $23-32; ☻ dinner Tue-Sat) 'Wine-food-jazz-art-ambience' – the promo says it all. Organic beef, wild venison and fish dishes precede an indulgent dessert menu, with live jazz on weekends and monthly open-mic nights. Regular winemakers' dinners match five courses with local vino.

Acqua (☎ 06-835 8689; cnr Marine Pde & Emerson St; mains $17-33; ☻ dinner) Part of the Masonic Hotel's sprawl, Acqua's aqua shades cover most surfaces (with some respite on the ceiling), but don't let it put you off the sensational seafood. Scallops, oysters, monkfish and calamari are mainstays.

Caffe Aroma Emporio Vespa (☎ 06-835 3922; 20 Dalton St; bagels from $5; ☻ breakfast & lunch Thu-Tue) One of Napier's better cafés, tourists and locals alike flit through the door for a quick bagel and a strong coffee. Cooked breakfasts ($7.50 to $13) and Vespas ($2000 to $4500) are also on the menu.

Jo Miguels (☎ 06-835 8477; 193 Hastings St; meals $9-17; ☻ lunch Wed-Sun, dinner daily) Jo Miguels is a Mex-Iberian bar (complete with fat guitars, sombreros and matador posters), serving tapas and pizzas with plenty of cold Corona.

Manna Soul Food Café (☎ 06-834 1988; 180 Emerson St; meals $4-15; ☻ breakfast & lunch) Blending Maori *mana* (vitality) with manna from heaven, this place peddles gluten-free grain dishes and organic salads, juices, tea and coffee to a swanky jazz soundtrack.

Starving Artist Café (☎ 06-835 1646; 260 Emerson St; meals $4-9; ⓥ breakfast & lunch) This café conjures up (and then cures) an underfed dose of the *rive gauche* in downtown Napier. Coffee, salads and cakes compulsory; berets optional.

Soak (☎ 06-835 7888; mains $12-32; ⓥ breakfast, lunch & dinner) For a postswim lunch try the tastefully styled restaurant at Ocean Spa (p389).

Deano's Steak Bar & Grill (☎ 06-835 4944; 255 Marine Pde; mains $20-28; ⓥ lunch Tue-Sun, dinner daily) Unashamedly low-brow and old-fangled, Deano's serves iron-rich steak, chicken and fish dishes in king-size portions.

Self-caterers can stock up on supplies at **Countdown** (☎ 06-834 1401; cnr Munro & Dickens Sts) supermarket.

Drinking

Cri Bar & Grill (☎ 06-835 7162; 8 Market St) Pronounced 'Cry' (don't get it wrong or you'll never pick up the bar staff), this jostling backpackers bar has pool tables, big screens, occasional live bands (of which Napier has many) and cheap eats.

Brazen Head (☎ 06-834 3587; 21 Hastings St) Shamefully tucked into a nook, poker machines compromise the vibe here, but the beers are good and the outdoor deck is a brazen spot to get through a few.

Governors Inn (☎ 06-835 0088; cnr Emerson St & Marine Pde) The GI has a circular bar beneath an enormous copper 'cone of silence' (Don Adams would have loved it). The outdoor tables draw a mature, sedate crowd, surveying the menu and clinking glasses.

Rosie O'Grady's (☎ 06-835 8685; cnr Marine Pde & Tennyson St) Part of the Masonic megaplex, with access from Hastings St, Rosie's predictable Irishness fills in the gaps between dimly lit corners and intermittent live music. The not-unattractive Masonic staff call this place home.

Latitude 42° (☎ 06-835 5545; 53 Hastings St) A slice of the Wild West in the tame east, this L-shaped bar is heavy on the loud music and beery masses, light on the finer points of civilized behaviour.

Out on West Quay, **Provedore** (opposite) and **Gintrap** (opposite) restaurants have well-patronised bars, while **Speight's**

Ale House (☎ 06-834 1188; West Quay, Ahuri) pours cheery tankards of Dunedin's finest.

Entertainment

Fever Bar (☎ 06-834 0068; 35 Hastings St) Behind an improbably appealing Deco shopfront, live bands and DJs sweat it out with the city's just-legal drinking proletariat.

Century Cinema (☎ 06-835 9248; www.centurycin ema.co.nz; adult/child tickets $12/7) On the same site as the Hawkes Bay Museum is this cinema, screening art-house and international films and hosting plays and classical concerts.

Getting There & Away

AIR

Napier Airport (☎ 06-835 1130) is 8km north of the city.

Air New Zealand (☎ 06-833 5400; www.airnz.co.nz; cnr Hastings & Station Sts) Daily direct flights to Auckland, Christchurch and Wellington, with onward connections.

Origin Pacific (☎ 0800 302 302; www.originpacific .co.nz) Flies from Napier to Auckland on Sundays, and to Wellington daily from Monday to Saturday.

BUS

InterCity (www.intercitycoach.co.nz) and **Newmans** (www.newmanscoach.co.nz) operate from the **Napier Travel Centre** (☎ 06-834 2720; Munic St; ⓥ 8am-5pm Mon-Fri, 8-11.30am & 12.30-1.30pm Sat & Sun). InterCity runs to Auckland ($82, seven hours), Hamilton ($52, five hours), Rotorua ($56, three hours), Taupo ($38, two hours), Tauranga ($82, five hours), Gisborne ($39, four hours), Palmerston North ($33, 2¾ hours) and Wellington ($62, 4¾ hours). Newmans runs north to Taupo, Rotorua and Tauranga, and Wellington; fares and durations parallel those of InterCity.

BayXpress (☎ 0800 422 997; www.bayexpress.co.nz) runs to Wellington ($35, five hours, 8am daily), leaving from the visitor information centre.

Getting Around

BUS

Metro Rentals (☎ 06-835 0590; www.metrorentals .co.nz) Buses between Napier and Hastings following the Nimbus route on Saturdays ($5.70, 55 minutes), departing near the public library.

Nimon & Sons 'Nimbus' (☎ 06-877 8133; www.nim ons.co.nz) Regular buses between Napier and Hastings via Taradale ($5.70, 55 minutes, Monday to Friday), plus local services, departing Dalton St near the corner of Station St.

CAR

The following rental offices are at Napier Airport:

Avis (06-835 1828; www.avis.com)
Budget (06-835 5166; www.budget.co.nz)
Europcar (06-835 8818; www.europcar.co.nz)
Hertz (06-835 6169; www.hertz.co.nz)
Thrifty (06-835 8820; www.thrifty.co.nz)

TAXI

A city-to-airport taxi ride costs $12 to $13.
Napier Taxis (06-835 7777)
Super Shuttle (06-844 7333; www.supershuttle.co.nz)

HASTINGS

pop 50,200

Hastings is the fruit-picking kernel of the Hawkes Bay Wine Country. Just 20km south of Napier, it was similarly devastated by the 1931 earthquake, and its sturdy collation of Art Deco and Spanish Mission–style buildings emerged in the aftermath. Unlike Napier, where life revolves around tourism, café society and high times, Hastings is a utilitarian agricultural town with tractors on the streets and little of the chutzpah Napier manifests so readily.

A random scene: a shirtless young renegade drives his ember-red utility around and around Hastings' main block, The Doors' *Light My Fire* stuck on repeat, blaring from open windows, an unlit cigarette dangling from his lip… The question is, will Hastings light *your* fire?

Orientation

Hastings' flat grid centres on the railway line, with Heretaunga Sts East and West the main commercial strips on either side of the tracks.

Information

BOOKSHOPS

Books & More New Zealand Post (Map p395; 06-878 9425; K Mart Plaza, Karamu Rd)

EMERGENCY

Ambulance, fire service & police (111)
Police station (Map p395; 06-873 0500; Railway Rd)

INTERNET ACCESS

Hectic Netway (Map p395; 06-870 3772; 1st fl, 123 Heretaunga St E; 10am-10pm).

MEDICAL SERVICES

Hastings Health Centre (Map p395; 06-873 8999; 101 Queen St E)
Hawkes Bay Hospital (Map p395; 06-878 8109; Omahu Rd)

MONEY

The major banks have branches and ATMs on Heretaunga St and Central Plaza.

POST

Post office (Map p395; cnr Market St & Heretaunga St W)

TOURIST INFORMATION

Hastings visitor information centre (Map p395; 06-873 5526; www.hastings.co.nz; cnr Russell St & Heretaunga St E; 8.30am–5pm Mon-Fri, 9am–3pm Sat & Sun) In the Westerman's Building.

TRAVEL AGENCIES

Tremain Travel Café (Map p395; 06-878 4149; www.travelcafenz.com; 314 Heretaunga St W; mains $5-9; breakfast & lunch Mon-Sat;) An irresistibly popular café and travel agency full of travel magazines, coffee smells and dreams of elsewhere.

Sights & Activities

The legacy of the 1931 earthquake is an impressive collection of Art Deco and Spanish Mission–style buildings. The visitor information centre's *Heritage of Hastings* and *Spanish Mission Hastings* pamphlets have the nitty-gritty.

Top of the Deco deck are undoubtedly the **Westerman's Building**, with its intricate bronze and lead-light shopfront originality, and the Spanish Mission **Hawkes Bay Opera House** (Map p395; 06-870 9483; www.hawkesbayopera house.co.nz; Hastings St). Ballet, theatre, rock and opera grace the stage here. It was undergoing major refurbishments at the time of writing.

The marvellous, purpose-built **Hawkes Bay Exhibition Centre** (Map p395; 06-876 2077; www.hawkesbaymuseum.co.nz; 201 Eastbourne St, Civic Sq; admission $2-4; 10am-4.30pm) curates local and travelling exhibitions, from photography to ceramics to Maori arts.

Splash Planet Waterpark (Map p395; 06-876 9856; www.splashplanet.co.nz; Grove Rd, Windsor Park; adult/child $25/20; 9am-6pm), 2km southeast

MAPS

Free town maps are available at the visitor information centre.

Automobile Association (AA; Map p395; 06-878 4101; www.aatravel.co.nz; 337 Heretaunga St W)

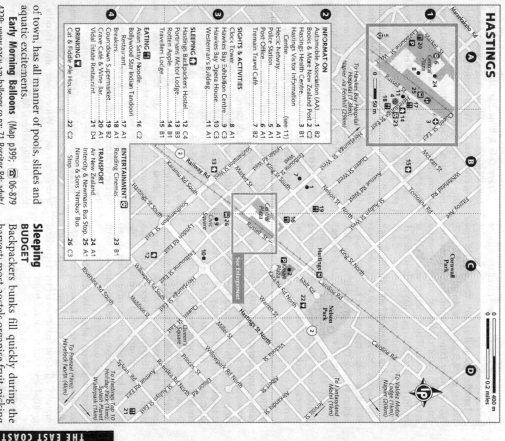

HASTINGS

INFORMATION
Automobile Association (AA).........1 B2
Books & More New Zealand Post.......2 C2
Hastings Health Centre..............3 B1
Hastings Visitor Information Centre.....(see 11)
Hectic Netway......................4 A1
Police Station......................5 A1
Post Office........................6 A1
Tremain Travel Café.................7 B2

SIGHTS & ACTIVITIES
Clock Tower........................8 A1
Hawkes Bay Exhibition Centre........9 C3
Hawkes Bay Opera House.............10 C3
Westerman's Building...............11 A1

SLEEPING
Hastings Backpackers Hostel........12 C4
Portmans Motor Lodge..............13 B3
Rotten Apple......................14 A1
Travellers Lodge..................15 B1

EATING
Asian Satay Noodle.................16 C2
Bollywood Star Indian Tandoori.....17 A1
Breakers Restaurant................18 A1
Countdown Supermarket.............19 B2
Crave Café & Wine Bar..............20 D4
Vidal Estate Restaurant............21 D4

DRINKING
Cat & Fiddle Ale House.............22 C2

ENTERTAINMENT
Reading Cinemas...................23 B1

TRANSPORT
Air New Zealand...................24 A1
Intercity & Newmans Bus Stop.......25 A1
Nimon & Sons 'Nimbus' Bus Stop....26 C3

of town, has all manner of pools, slides and aquatic excitements.

Early Morning Balloons (Map p399; ☎ 06-879 4229; www.early-am-balloons.co.nz; 71 Rossiter Rd; adult/child $270/200) provides inflated views across the grapey Hawkes Bay plains.

Festivals & Events

Hastings and Napier co-host the **Art Deco Weekend** (see p390) in the third week of February. The **Hastings Blossom Festival** (☎ 06-878 9447; www.blossomfestival.co.nz), a petalled spring fling, happens in the second half of September, with parades, arts, crafts and visiting artists. Napier, Hastings and Havelock North are the hubs of the Harvest Hawkes Bay festival in early February; see p397 for details.

Sleeping

BUDGET

Backpackers bunks fill quickly during the harvest; most hostels organise fruit-picking work.

Rotten Apple (Map p395; ☎ 06-878 4363; www.rottenapple.co.nz; 1st fl, 114 Heretaunga St E; dm/d $19/40; ☐) Rotten Apple is the pick of the crop, so to speak. The harvest air hangs thick with the funk of labour, but spacey communal areas, a big-screen TV, pool table, reading room and tidy dorms are saving graces.

Hastings Backpackers Hostel (Map p395; ☎ 06-876 5888; www.medasa.co.nz; 505 Lyndon Rd E; dm/s/d $19/25/46; ☐) This colourful 1920s villa has Mediterranean aspirations. Mandarin and lemon blossoms send divine scents drifting

THE EAST COAST

through the sun room as travellers snooze in caravans.

Travellers Lodge (Map p395; ☎ 06-878 7108; www .tlodge.co.nz; 606 St Aubyn St W; dm/s/d from $20/30/50; ☐) A busy family atmosphere pervades this complex of rooms, orbiting around a suburban house. Fruit-pickers watch DVDs or hire bikes ($25 per day) when they're sick of the sight of apples.

Hastings Top 10 Holiday Park (☎ 0508 427 846; www.hastingsholidaypark.co.nz; 610 Windsor Ave, Windsor Park; unpowered/powered sites per 2 people $26, d/ ste from $45/100) On the phone it's, 'Kia Ora, we're having a *lovely* day here at Hastings Top 10 Holiday Park! May we help you?' Things here are indeed lovely: sycamore groves, a duck pond, aviary and serenity to burn.

MIDRANGE

Fantasyland Motel (☎ 06-876 8159; fantasyland .motel@clear.net.nz; cnr Sylvan Rd & Jervois St; ste $80-150; ☐) A motel-in-the-round (well, octagon), this place is damn funky. With brushed aluminium light fittings, bright orange laminate and more teak veneer than your average forest, it's a '70s classic.

Valdez Motor Lodge (☎ 0800 825 339; www.valdez .co.nz; 1107 Karamu Rd N; ste $110-200; ☐) Optimistically Spanish-styled, Valdez is on the main road 1.5km from central Hastings, double glazing keeping the executive suites quiet. Some units have wheelchair access; most have private courtyards.

Portmans Motor Lodge (Map p395; ☎ 0800 767 862; www.portmans.co.nz; 401 Railway Rd; ste $100-120; ☐) Nothing to write home about, Portmans is a flat-roofed sprawler with spacious ground-level units not far from town.

TOP END

Greenhill The Lodge (Map p399; ☎ 06-879 9944; www .greenhill.co.nz; 103 Greenhill Rd; ste from $490; ☐) Confidently colonial, Greenhill is a high-Victorian mansion on a secluded hilltop 13km west of Hastings, off Raukawa Rd. The library, 14ft ceilings, full-sized billiard table and formal dining room will entice you from your luxury suite. Breakfast is included.

Eating & Drinking

In addition to the following options, the Tremain Travel Café (p394) serves up zingy sandwiches and salads.

Crave Café & Wine Bar (Map p395; ☎ 06-878 8596; 108 Market St S; meals $10-25; ☒ breakfast & lunch daily, dinner Wed-Sat) With minimal fuss, this low-lit contemporary bistro prepares simple quiches, salads, pastas, steaks and vegetarian dishes with nouveau-Italian flair. A wide wine list befits the wine-bar moniker.

Bollywood Star Indian Tandoori Restaurant (Map p395; ☎ 06-876 8196; 102-106 Heretaunga St E; mains $10-20; ☒ lunch & dinner) The menu at Bollywood Star shines with South Indian faves, and TV screens gyrate with smiling dance routines as you curry-down. All-you-can-eat weekend brunches are more than anyone can eat.

Vidal Estate Restaurant (Map p395; ☎ 06-876 8105; www.vidal.co.nz; 913 St Aubyn St E; mains $23-32; ☒ lunch & dinner) Frequently hailed as the best restaurant in Hawkes Bay, Vidal's crisply formal dining room serves high-quality lamb, beef, seafood and Vidal wine amid huge French Oak barrels.

Asian Satay Noodle (Map p395; ☎ 06-878 6778; 104 Market St N; mains $4-9; ☒ lunch & dinner) Soups, noodles, satays, curries and rice dishes, with influences spanning from Indonesia to China. Prices range from affordable to unbelievably cheap.

Sileni Estates (Map p399; ☎ 06-879 8768; www .sileni.co.nz; 2016 Maraekakaho Rd; mains $25-30; ☒ lunch daily, dinner Thu-Sat) Feeling decadent? Drive out to Sileni Estates, 10 minutes from Hastings, where creatively prepared seasonal Hawkes Bay produce rounds out the menu, accompanied, of course, by excellent wine.

Breakers (Map p395; ☎ 06-878 6701; cnr Heretaunga St E & Karamu Rd; mains $6-12; ☒ breakfast Sat & Sun, lunch & dinner daily) Wide open and friendly, Breakers breaks down the barriers between locals, backpackers, kids and oldies with affordable meals, plenty of beer and a main-stream main-street vibe.

Prenzel (Map p395; ☎ 06-870 8524; www.prenzel.com; 180 Havelock Rd; ☒ 10am-4.30pm Apr-Sep, to 5.30pm Oct-Mar) 'Get Schnapped' at Prenzel, a fruity distillery just out of Hastings on the road to Havelock North. Sample and buy liqueurs, schnapps and infused olive oils (the chilli oil is momentous).

Roosters Brewhouse (Map p399; ☎ 06-879 4127; 1470 Omahu Rd; ☒ 10am-7pm Mon-Sat) Ten minutes north of town with a randomly 'farmyard' aesthetic, Roosters has quality batch-brewed beers on tap (preservative-free for minimal hangovers).

Cat & Fiddle Ale House (Map p395; ☎ 06-878 4111; 502 Karamu Rd N; mains $8-20; ☒ lunch & dinner) A middle-of-the-road roadside pub festooned with English football scarves, this place has Anglo-style food and an Irish-style jam session on Wednesday nights.

Self-caterers can roam the aisles at **Countdown supermarket** (☎ 06-878 5099; cnr Queen St W & King St N).

Entertainment

Hawkes Bay Opera House (Map p395; ☎ 06-870 9483; www.hawkesbayoperahouse.co.nz; Hastings St) This old stager offers a regular programme of music and theatre.

Reading Cinemas (Map p395; ☎ 06-833 7766; www.readingcinemas.co.nz; 124 Heretaunga St E; tickets adult/child $12/8) When the lights go down over Hastings, make haste for the big screen.

Getting There & Around

AIR

Air New Zealand (☎ 06-837 2200; www.airnewzealand.co.nz; Westpac Bldg, Central Plaza) flies from Napier/Hastings to a number of destinations around NZ; check the website for details.

BUS

InterCity (www.intercitycoach.co.nz) and **Newmans** (www.newmanscoach.co.nz) buses to Napier continue to Hastings, with the bus stop (Map p395) near the visitor information centre. Book tickets at the information centre.

Nimon & Sons 'Nimbus' (☎ 06-877 8133; www.nimons.co.nz) operates frequent weekday buses from Hastings to Napier and Havelock North, departing from Hastings' at the bus stop in Civic Square (Map p395). **Metro Rentals** (☎ 06-835 0590; www.metrorental.co.nz) follows the Nimbus routes on Saturdays.

TAXI

To get around the town by taxi, contact **Hastings Taxis** (☎ 06-878 5055).

HAVELOCK NORTH

pop 8510

Five kilometres southeast of Hastings' rural toil, Havelock North is a different kettle of fish (or vat of wine) altogether. Range Rovers and BMWs cruise the streets as bleached-blonde 50-something wine wives sip lattes in a prosperous village atmosphere. The towering backdrop of Te Mata Peak keeps egos in check.

Information

Havelock North visitor information centre (☎ 06-877 9600; www.villageinfo.co.nz; www.havelocknorth.com; The roundabout; ☒ 10am-4pm) Maps and local lowdown.

Sights & Activities

The mellifluous **Arataki Honey Centre** (Map p399; ☎ 06-877 7300; www.aratakihoney.co.nz; 66 Arataki Rd; ☒ 9am-5pm), 3km east of Havelock North, has kid-conducive hands-on displays taking you through the whole sticky cycle from flower to slice of toast.

Kids also effervesce over the **Keirunga Park Miniature Railway** (☎ 06-877 8857; fax 06-876 5476; Puflett Rd; rides $1). All aboard the first and third Sundays of the month.

Spiking melodramatically from the Heretaunga Plains, **Te Mata Peak**, 16km south of Havelock North, is part of the 98-hectare Te Mata Trust Park. The road to the 399m summit passes lonesome sheep trails, rickety fences and vertiginous stone escarpments cowled in a bleak, lunar-meets-Scottish-Highland atmosphere. Clear-day views fall away to Hawke Bay, the Mahia Peninsula, Napier, Hastings, and all the way west to Mt Ruapehu. There are four official peak walkways; ask at the Havelock North visitor information centre.

Te Mata is a **hang-gliding** hotspot, with serious updraughts rampaging in from the South Pacific. Plunging into oblivion, **Airplay Paragliding** (☎ 027 451 2886; www.airplay.co.nz) has tandem paragliding ($140) and full-day beginners courses ($180).

Festivals & Events

Harvest Hawkes Bay in early February is the region's premier wine and food festival. Buses depart the Havelock North (and Napier) information centres, shunting increasingly bleary punters between dozens of vineyards. Check out www.harvesthawkesbay.co.nz for event details.

Sleeping

Peak Backpackers (☎ 06-877 1170; fax 06-877 1175; 33 Havelock Rd; dm/s/d from $18/27/40; ☒) Havelock's most central backpackers could use a bit of an airing. It used to be an old people's home, and it smells like it; but like we said, it's central, and it's also easy on the wallet. **Havelock North Motor Lodge** (☎ 06-877 8627; www.havelocknorthmotorlodge.co.nz; 7 Havelock Rd; ste

$105-180) Smack-bang in the middle of town, this motel is a cut above the rest. Tidy one- and two-bedroom units feature spas, Sky TV and cooking facilities.

Millar Road (Map p399; ☎ 06-875 1977; www.millar road.co.nz; 83 Millar Rd; cottages sleeping 2 couples $400-500; ☎) Set above a young vineyard in the Tuki Tuki Hills, off Tuki Tuki Rd, Millar Road is architecturally heaven-sent. Two seriously plush self-contained cottages (separated by a swimming pool with a bar) burgeon with NZ-made furniture and local artworks. Stylish, uncomplicated, perfect. Breakfast is included.

Diva (☎ 06-877 5149; Napier Rd; mains $30; ☎ dinner) An unexpected highlight of the Hawkes Bay contemporary food scene, Diva focuses on fresh, spontaneous cooking using local ingredients and suppliers. The urbane cocktail bar serves tapas, and usually closes down the town.

Eating & Drinking

Peak House Restaurant (Map p399; ☎ 06-877 8663; 357 Te Mata Peak Rd; mains $18-25; ☎ lunch & dinner Wed-Mon) The views here are unbelievable; the food is honest, unpretentious and full-flavoured in good-sized portions.

Georges Patisserie (☎ 06-877 8231; 12 Havelock Rd; snacks $5-15; ☎ breakfast & lunch) Georges' spread embraces cakes, quiches, pies and sausage rolls, and the best coffee in Havelock.

Strawberry Patch (☎ 06-877 1350; Havelock Rd; ice creams $3-4; ☎ breakfast & lunch Oct-Mar) This working strawberry farm morphs its red offspring into delicious ice creams. You can pick your own berries, or grab a coffee to go.

Loading Ramp (☎ 06-877 6820; 6 Treachers Lane; mains $22-27; ☎ lunch & dinner) This heady timber space pulls a mixed crowd of young'uns and seasoned drinkers, mutually appreciating boutique beers and local wines by the glass. The food is hearty, and an open fire blazes through winter.

Rose & Shamrock (☎ 06-877 2999; cnr Napier Rd & Porter Dr; mains $10-20; ☎ lunch & dinner) Irish tin-whistle hoopla resonates through this dark-wood beer hall, which serves big pub-grub plates. There's a monstrous array of tap beers, and live weekend music.

Getting There & Away

Nimon & Sons 'Nimbus' (☎ 06-877 8133; www.nim ons.co.nz) operates frequent weekday buses between Hastings and Havelock North.

Metro Rentals (☎ 06-835 0590; www.metrorentals.co .nz) runs the Nimbus route on Saturdays.

AROUND HAWKES BAY
Wine & Food
In case you hadn't noticed, Hawkes Bay is one of NZ's dominant wine-producing regions. The chardonnay is shouted about, but local cabernets and merlots are also lauded. Pick up the free *Hawkes Bay Wineries Guide* from visitor information centres; dedicated wine buffs can buy *The Complete Guide: Hawkes Bay Wine Country* ($25).

WINERIES
Some of the wineries offering tastings and/ or tours include the following:

Alpha Domus (☎ 06-879 6752; www.alphadomus.co.nz)
Brookfields (☎ 06-834 4615; www.brookfieldsvine yards.co.nz)
Church Road Winery (☎ 06-844 2053; www.church road.co.nz)
Crab Farm Winery (☎ 06-836 6678; www.crabfarm winery.co.nz)
Esk River Winery (☎ 06-836 6806; www.eskriver.co.nz)
Esk Valley Estate Winery (☎ 06-836 6411; www .eskvalley.co.nz)
Mission Estate Winery (☎ 06-845 9350; www .missionestate.co.nz)
Ngatarawa Wines (☎ 06-879 7603; www.ngatarawa .co.nz)
Sacred Hill Winery (☎ 06-844 0138; www.sacredhill .co.nz)
Sileni Estates (☎ 06-879 8768; www.sileni.co.nz)
Trinity Hill Winery (☎ 06-879 7778; www.trinityhill .com)
Vidal Estate (Map p395; ☎ 06-876 8105; www.vidal .co.nz)

Havelock North has a concentration of wineries, especially along Te Mata Rd. Well worth a visit are the following:

Akarangi Wines (☎ 06-877 8228; akarangi@paradise .net.nz)
Black Barn Vineyards (☎ 06-877 7985; www.black barn.com)
Craggy Range Winery (☎ 06-873 7126; www.craggy range.com)
Te Mata Estate Winery (☎ 06-877 4399; www.te mata.co.nz)

BIKE TOURS
Costing between $35 and $50 for a full day, a self-guided bicycle tour will temper your viticulture with a little exercise. The follow-

HAWKES BAY WINE COUNTRY

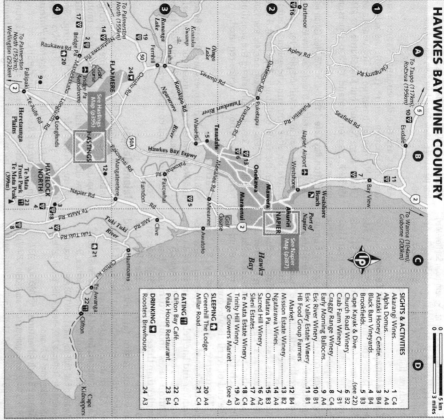

SIGHTS & ACTIVITIES	
Akarangi Wines	1 C4
Alpha Domus	2 A4
Arataki Honey Centre	3 A4
Black Barn Vineyards	4 B4
Brookfields	5 B3
Cape Kayak & Dive	(see 22)
Church Road Winery	6 B3
Crab Farm Winery	7 B1
Craggy Range Winery	8 B4
Early Morning Balloons	9 A4
Esk River Winery	10 B1
Esk Valley Estate Winery	11 B1
HB Food Group Farmers Market	12 B4
Mission Estate Winery	13 B2
Ngatarawa Wines	14 A4
Olatara Pa	15 B3
Sacred Hill Winery	16 A2
Sileni Estates	17 A4
Te Mata Estate Winery	18 C4
Trinity Hill Winery	19 A3
Village Growers Market	(see 4)

SLEEPING	
Greenhill The Lodge	20 A4
Millar Road	21 C4

EATING	
Clifton Bay Café	22 C4
Peak House Restaurant	23 B4

DRINKING	
Roosters Brewhouse	24 A3

ing folks equip you with a bike, helmet, water bottle, backpack and mobile phone if you get lost/tired/woozy:

Bike About Tours (☎ 06-845 9034; www.bikeabout tours.co.nz)

Bike D'Vine (☎ 06-833 6697; www.bikedevine.com)

On Yer Bike (☎ 06-879 8735; www.onyerbikehb.co.nz)

GUIDED TOURS

Motorised wine tours generally last around four hours and start at $40 per person, with four or five wineries on the agenda; full-day tours cost around $100. Operators pick up from Napier, Hastings or Havelock North.

Bay Tours (☎ 06-843 9034; www.baytours.co.nz)

Grape Escape (☎ 0800 100 489; www.grapescapenz .co.nz)

Odyssey NZ (☎ 0508 639 7739; www.odysseynz.com)

Toast The Bay (☎ 06-876 2849; www.toastthebay.co.nz)

Vicky's Wine Tours (☎ 06-843 9991; www.vickys winetours.co.nz)

Vince's Vineyard Tours (☎ 06-836 6705; vincestours@ hotmail.com)

FOOD MARKETS

Food is an integral part of the Hawkes Bay vineyard experience, with food markets drawing hordes of locals and tourists alike. Leading the way are the **HB Food Group Farmers Market** (☎ 06-876 5087; Hawkes Bay Showgrounds, Kenilworth Rd, Hastings; 8.30am-12.30pm Sun), which also happens in Napier behind the Daily Telegraph Building in Napier on Saturday mornings; and the **Village Growers Market** (☎ 06-877 7985;

Black Barn Rd, Havelock North; ⊙9am–noon Sat Nov–Mar) at Black Barn Vineyards, specialising in organic produce. The *Hawkes Bay Food Trail* brochure lists local produce growers.

Cape Kidnappers Gannet Colony

From late September to late April, Cape Kidnappers (named when local Maoris tried to kidnap Cook's Tahitian servant boy here) erupts with gaggling gannets. These big birds, completely unphased by human spectators, usually nest on remote islands, but here they settle for the mainland.

The gannets arrive in late July after winter storms cast nest-building driftwood onto the beach. Eggs arrive in October and November, taking about six weeks to hatch. In March the gannets start migration; by the end of April they're gone.

The reserve is administered by DOC, but you don't need a visitor's permit. Early November and late February are the best times to visit. The walk along the beach from Clifton takes about two hours. Leave no earlier than three hours after high tide; start back no later than 1½ hours after low tide. It's 20km return (at least five hours) and there are no refreshments beyond Clifton. Alternatively, take a tour:

Cape Kidnappers Guided Walks (☎06-875 0888; walks@gannetsafaris.co.nz; Summerlee Station, Te Awanga; half-/full-day walks $60/100) Amble around Summerlee Station, a 2000-hectare sheep-and-cattle run about 2km from Te Awanga.

Gannet Beach Adventures (☎0800 426 6387, 06-875 0809; www.gannets.com; adult/child $25/17) Ride along the beach on a tractor-pulled trailer, departing Clifton Beach car park, before a 20-minute guided walk through the bird boudoir. The return trip takes about four hours.

Gannet Safaris (☎0800 427 232, 06-875 0888; www.gannetsafaris.com; Summerlee Station, Te Awanga;

adult/child $48/24) 4WD overland trips across farmland into the gannet colony. Three-hour tours depart twice daily.

All trips are tide-dependent; Napier visitor information centre (p388) has schedules. No regular buses go to Te Awanga or Clifton from Napier, but **Kiwi Shuttle** (☎027-459 369) goes on demand ($28 per person one way).

Clifton Bay Café (☎06-875 0096; 468 Clifton Rd; mains $12-24; ⊙breakfast & lunch daily Nov–Mar, Wed–Sun Apr–Oct) is an airy, civilised place for a meal before or after you run the gannet gauntlet. In the same building is **Cape Kayak & Dive** (☎027 487 7898; www.capekayak.co.nz; 4hr tour $50), which runs kayak tours along the coastline to the gannets; no experience required.

Beaches

South of Cape Kidnappers are **Ocean Beach** and **Waimarama Beach**, famous for their surf. To get there, take Te Mata Rd out of Havelock North and continue east past Te Mata Peak.

Inland Ranges

Regional Hawkes Bay extends south and inland from the main Napier–Hastings population corridor. Inland are the remote Kaweka and Ruahine Ranges, with some of the North Island's best tramping. See the DOC pamphlets *Central Hawkes Bay*, *Southern Hawkes Bay*, *Maraetotara Plateau* and *Puketitiri Reserves* for details.

An ancient Maori track, now a road, runs inland from the bay, heading from Fernhill near Hastings to Taihape, via Omahu, Okawa, Otamauri, Blowhard Bush and Gentle Annie Rd. It's a three-hour return drive from Fernhill to the top of the Kaweka Ranges.

THE LONGEST PLACE NAME IN THE WORLD

Yes, it's longer than Llanfairpwllgwyngllgogerychwyrndrobwllllantysiliogogogoch in Wales. Take a deep breath and try this on for size:

Taumatawhakatangihangakoauauotamateaturipukakapikimaungahoronukupokaiwhenuakitanatahu.

Believe it or not, this is the abbreviated form of 'The Brow of a Hill Where Tamatea, the Man with the Big Knees, Who Slid, Climbed, and Swallowed Mountains, Known as Land Eater, Played his Flute to his Brother'. Tamatea Pokaiwhenua (Land Eater) was so famous for his epic North Island travels, people said he consumed the land with his strides. After his brother's demise in the Matanui battle, Tamatea sat on this hill with his flute and played a lament to his fallen bro.

Central Hawkes Bay

The two main towns in Central Hawkes Bay are Waipukurau (aka 'Wai-puk') and Waipawa. The **Waipukurau visitor information centre** (☎ 06-858 6488; www.centralhawkesbay.co.nz; Railway Esp; ⓥ 9am-5pm Mon-Fri, 9am-1pm Sat) brims with regional information.

The prestigious **Te Aute College**, 20km north of Waipukurau, schooled James Carroll, Apirana Ngata, Maui Pomare and Peter Buck, influential Young Maori Party leaders who lobbied the 1935 Labour government for equality.

Visiting the place with the longest name in the world (see opposite) is a Central Hawkes Bay essential. To get to the famous sign, fuel-up in Waipukurau and head

towards Porangahau on the coast. Drive 40km to the Mangaorapa junction, turn left and go 4km towards Porangahau. At the intersection with the signposts, turn right and continue 4.3km to the sign.

Contemplate the astronomic appellation then stay at **Lochlea Farmstay** (☎/fax 06-855 4816; lochlea.farm@xtra.co.nz; 344 Lake Rd, Wanstead; dm/s/d $18/30/40; ⓥ), an idyllic farm with breezy stands of poplar, pine and beech on green grazing slopes.

In Waipawa stop for lunch at the wedge-shaped **Hum n' Buzz Café** (☎ 06-857 7995; cnr Kenilworth & Ruataniwha Sts; meals $6-13; ⓥ breakfast & lunch). In Waipukurau your best bet is **Lily Pond** (☎ 06-858 7133; 119 Ruataniwha St; meals $4-12; ⓥ breakfast & lunch Mon-Sat).

Wellington Region

Despite its diminutive size (or perhaps because of it), Wellington feels like the perfect capital city. Compact and walkable, it is surprisingly scenic and full of institutions integral to the day-to-day running of the nation, but not too full of its own importance or overloaded with bureaucratic stuffed shirts. Instead, Welly is imbued with an easy, accessible blend of the political, the academic and the creative.

Wellington is only the third-largest city in the country and takes part in rivalry with larger Auckland, a friendly jibing that perhaps stems from the common misconception that Auckland is actually New Zealand's capital. Apart from Wellington's importance as the seat of government, it's a major travel crossroads between the North and South Islands. Government departments and good transport links aside, you won't need to spend much time in this hip, energetic city to appreciate its appeal. Steep hills and spectacular views, challenging walks, a thriving café and entertainment scene, and serious dedication to the arts make Wellington an enormously enjoyable place in which to spend a few days.

If, until now, your travels in NZ have been about small towns and the great outdoors, stop in Welly to dose up on big-city treats like art-house cinemas, designer clothes stores, sophisticated wine bars and late-night cafés. Alternatively, if you want to maintain the small-town-outdoors theme, there are great options less than an hour away by train or car. Along the Kapiti Coast are mystical Kapiti Island and relaxing beachside towns; in the Wairarapa you can delight your palate with the delicate flavours of a pinot noir (a regional speciality) and experience some fine country hospitality before checking out wild, remote coastline.

HIGHLIGHTS

- Getting acquainted with NZ at the country's finest museum, **Te Papa** (p409)
- Drinking in the views on a scenic drive to the wild and remote **Cape Palliser** (p434)
- Taking in a movie at the **Embassy Theatre** (p423) before cocktails in one of Wellington's slick **bars** (p421)
- Getting your feet wet at one of the beautiful, empty beaches along the **Kapiti Coast** (p427)
- Making like a local and brunching at the superbly situated **Chocolate Fish** (p420) café
- Practising your wine-speak while sampling a fine **Martinborough pinot** (p432)
- Catching the **cable car** (p409) from Lambton Quay to the manicured **Botanic Gardens** (p408)

TELEPHONE CODE: 04   ■ www.wellingtonnz.com   ■ www.wellingtonz.co.nz   ■ www.naturecoast.co.nz

WELLINGTON REGION FACTS

Eat: A Maori-fusion meal at Kai (see the boxed text, p420); boxed text, p420); chocolates from Greytown's Schoc Chocolate (p432)

Drink: Caffeine fixes at Welly's cool cafés (p420); pinot noir from Martinborough (p432) in the Wairarapa

Read: Katherine Mansfield's *The Garden Party & Other Stories*; the nutty *Tarzan Presley* by Nigel Cox

Listen to: *Based on a True Story* by the city's favourite groovers, Fat Freddy's Drop; the Mutton Bird's song 'Wellington'

Watch: Any film directed by revered local boy Peter Jackson

Swim at: Anywhere along the Kapiti Coast (p427)

Festival: See 'fashion as art (or is it art as fashion?) at the World of WearableArt (p416).

Tackiest tourist attraction: The Stonehenge replica in the Wairarapa

Climate

November to April are the warmer months and the best time to visit; average maximum temperatures during this time hover around 20°C. During the colder, wetter months, May to August, the daily temperature lurks around 12°C.

Wellington is renowned for being windy; the city's maritime climate catches the blustery, persistent and often chilly winds that whistle through the Cook Strait.

Getting There & Around

Wellington is an important transport hub; anyone going from one NZ island to the other (by sea) has to pass through here. There is also a busy airport serviced by several international and domestic airlines.

TOP ACTIVITIES

- Spend a day on untouched Kapiti Island (p430)
- Surf in the tiny footsteps of hobbits: take your board to Wellington's Lyall Bay (p413)
- Take advantage of Wellington's incessant wind: learn sailboarding or kitesurfing (p413)
- Avoid sea sickness: instead of crossing the Cook Strait by ferry, board a plane in Wellington and *skydive* into Picton! (see the boxed text, p424)
- Spend a day ripping up the trails of Makarara Peak Mountain Bike Park (p413)

Easy train and bus connections make commuting a viable option and many people travel to work (or party) in Wellington city. Approaching Welly from the north, you'll pass through either the Kapiti Coast on the western side of the island via State Highway 1 (SH1), or the Wairarapa on the eastern side via State Highway 2 (SH2), before entering the heavily populated Hutt Valley or the city itself.

InterCity is the main bus company that travels just about anywhere around the North Island. Commuter trains run to Palmerston North, the Kapiti Coast and the Wairarapa, and a long-distance train runs the length of the North Island to Auckland.

For more information on getting to and from Wellington, see p424.

WELLINGTON

pop 164,000 (city), 424,000 (region)

Bound by its magnificent harbour, with wooden Victorian buildings terraced up the steep hills, Wellington is home to the country's parliament and national treasures. The city prides itself as a cultural and artistic centre and, given the relatively small population, there is an astounding number of quality restaurants, cafés, bars, shops and theatres.

In recent times Wellington has stamped its place firmly on the world map as the home of NZ's growing film industry, earning itself the inevitable nickname 'Wellywood'. Acclaimed director Peter Jackson still calls Wellington home; the success of his *Lord of the Rings* productions, combined with the more recent *King Kong*, have made Jackson a powerful figure in Hollywood and bolstered NZ's reputation for international filmmaking. Jackson is quite

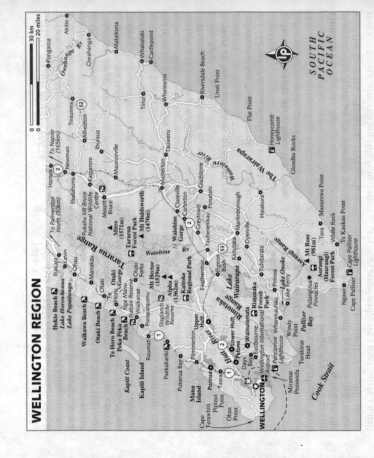

WELLINGTON REGION

the poster boy for Wellington's creativity and dynamism.

HISTORY

Maori legend has it that the explorer Kupe was the first person to discover Wellington harbour. The original Maori name was Te Whanga Nui a Tara, Tara being the son of a Maori chief named Whatonga who had settled on the Hawkes Bay coast. Whatonga sent Tara and his half-brother to explore the southern part of the North Island. When they returned over a year later, their reports were so favourable that Whatonga's followers moved there, founding the Ngati Tara tribe.

The first European settlers arrived in the New Zealand Company's ship *Aurora* on 22 January 1840, not long after Colonel William Wakefield arrived to buy land from the Maoris. The idea was to build two cities: one would be a commercial centre by the harbour (Port Nicholson) and the other, further north, would be the agricultural hub.

However, the Maoris denied they had sold the land at Port Nicholson, or Poneke, as they

called it. As it was founded on hasty and illegal buying by the NZ Company, land rights struggles followed – they were to plague the country for years, and still affect it today.

Wellington began as a settlement with very little flat land. Originally the waterfront was along Lambton Quay, but reclamation of parts of the harbour began in 1852 and it has continued ever since. In the 1850s Wellington was a thriving settlement of around 5000 people. In 1855 an earthquake razed part of Hutt Rd and the area from Te Aro flat to the Basin Reserve, which initiated the first major reclamation.

In 1865 the seat of government was moved from Auckland to Wellington, due to its central location in the country.

One blustery day back in 1968 the wind blew so hard it pushed the almost-new Wellington–Christchurch ferry *Wahine* onto Barrett's Reef just outside the harbour entrance. The disabled ship later broke loose from the reef, drifted into the harbour and slowly sank, causing the loss of 51 lives. The Museum of Wellington City & Sea (p409) has detailed information on this tragedy.

WELLINGTON REGION IN...

Two Days

Start by taking in the fresh air and city vistas at the **Botanic Gardens** (p408). Ride the cute **cable car** (p409) up, and walk back into town if you're feeling energetic. After lunch, give yourself an education in all things Kiwi at **Te Papa** (see the boxed text, p409), or get more Wellington-specific at the **Museum of Wellington City & Sea** (p409). Next day, depending on your interests, the city's **galleries** (p411) or **wildlife sanctuary** (p412) beckon, or you can take a snoop around **Parliament House** (p409). Try for a dinner table at **Kai** (p420) along Courtenay Pl and/or Cuba St. Late-night entertainment could be live music, a midnight snack at a late-closing café, or a movie at the gloriously restored **Embassy Theatre** (p423) – or all three.

Four Days

Shake and add water to the two-day itinerary and stir in the following: hightail it out of Wellington for some winery-touring in **Martinborough** (p432) followed by a seal-spotting safari along the wild **Wairarapa Coast** (p434). The next day, picnic in **Paraparaumu** (p429) before taking the plunge at one of the blissfully empty **Kapiti Coast beaches** (p427).

ORIENTATION

The city congregates on one side of the harbour but it's so cramped for space that many workers live in the two narrow valleys leading north between the steep, rugged hills – one is the Hutt Valley and the other follows SH1 through Tawa and Porirua.

Lambton Quay, the city's main business street, wriggles along almost parallel to the seafront (which it once was). The heart of the city stretches from the train station, at the northern end of Lambton Quay, south-east to Cambridge and Kent Tces. Thorndon, immediately north of the centre, is the historic area and embassy district.

The waterfront along Jervois Quay, Cable St and Oriental Pde is an increasingly revitalised area and houses the first-rate Te Papa museum, new Waitangi Park and a manmade beach. Queens Wharf has been redeveloped and has restaurants, museums and a gallery; Oriental Pde is Wellington's premier seafront boulevard.

Cuba St, Courtenay Pl, Manners St, Willis St and Queens Wharf, as well as Lambton Quay, are where the action is, be it for eating, drinking or shopping.

The airport is 8km southeast of the city centre. For information on getting to and from the airport, see p425.

Maps

Wellington's visitor information centre has free maps, and sells a wide range of maps and road atlases.

The **Map Shop** (Map p410; ☎ 04-385 1462; www.mapshop.co.nz; 193 Vivian St) carries a range of NZ city and regional maps, plus topographic maps for trampers.

MAORI NZ: WELLINGTON

In legend the mouth of Maui's fish (see p54), and traditionally known as Te Whanga-Nui-a-Tara, the Wellington area became known to Maori in the mid-19th century as 'Poneke' (a transliteration of Port Nicholas, its European name at the time).

The major *iwi* (tribes) of the region in traditional times were Te Ati Awa (www.whakarongotai .com) and Ngati Toa (www.ngatitoa.wi.nz); Ngati Toa was the *iwi* of Te Rauparaha, who composed the now famous *Ka Mate haka* (see p60). Like most urban areas the city is now home to Maori from many *iwi*, sometimes collectively known as Ngati Poneke.

Wellington is home to the country's finest museum, Te Papa (p409), where you'll find innumerable artefacts and displays on Maori culture, traditional and modern. History buffs can also see the Treaty of Waitangi (p35) at the National Archives (p410). For a really great Maori experience (and meal), check out Kai (see the boxed text, p420).

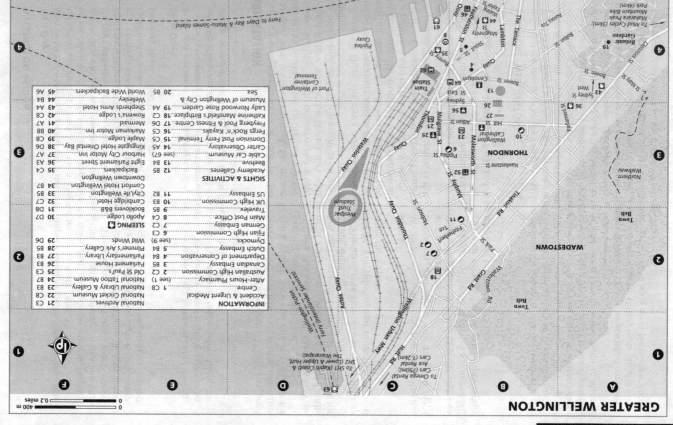

GREATER WELLINGTON

INFORMATION

Accident & Urgent Medical Centre	1	C8
After-Hours Pharmacy	(see 1)	
Australian High Commission	2	C2
Canadian Embassy	3	B5
Department of Conservation	4	B4
Dutch Embassy	5	B4
Dymocks	(see 6)	
Fijian High Commission	6	C3
German Embassy	7	C2
Main Post Office	8	C4
Travelex	9	B5
UK High Commission	10	B3
US Embassy	11	B2

SIGHTS & ACTIVITIES

Academy Galleries	12	B5
Beehive	13	B4
Cable Car Museum	(see 67)	
Carter Observatory	14	A5
Dominion Post Ferry Terminal	15	C5
Fergs Rock 'n' Kayaks	16	C5
Freyberg Pool & Fitness Centre	17	D6
Katherine Mansfield's Birthplace	18	C2
Lady Norwood Rose Garden	19	A4
Museum of Wellington City & Sea	20	B5

SLEEPING

National Archives	21	C3
National Cricket Museum	22	C8
National Library & Gallery	23	B3
National Tattoo Museum	24	B7
Old St Paul's	25	C3
Parliament House	26	B3
Parliamentary Library	27	B3
Plimmer's Ark Gallery	28	B5
Wild Winds	29	D6
Apollo Lodge	30	D7
Booklovers B&B	31	D8
Cambridge Hotel	32	C7
CityLife Wellington	33	B5
Comfort Hotel Wellington Downtown	34	B7
Backpackers	35	C4
Eight Parliament Street	36	A3
Harbour City Motor Inn	37	A7
Kingsgate Hotel Oriental Bay	38	D6
Maple Lodge	39	C8
Marksman Motor Inn	40	B8
Mermaid	41	A7
Rowena's Lodge	42	C8
Shepherds Arms Hotel	43	A4
Wellesley	44	B4
World Wide Backpackers	45	A6

WELLINGTON REGION

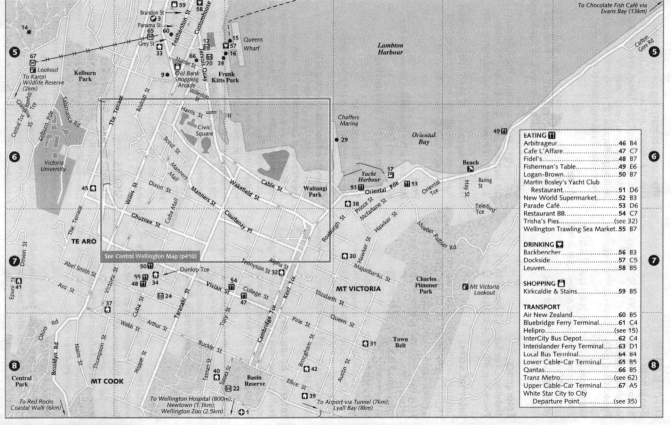

To Chocolate Fish Café via
Evans Bay (13km)

Lambton
Harbour

Queens
Wharf

Frank
Kitts Park

Kelburn
Park

Lookout
To Karori
Wildlife Reserve
(2km)

Victoria
University

Chaffers
Marina

Oriental
Bay

Beach

Yacht
Harbour

Oriental Pde

Waltangi
Park

Civic
Square

TE ARO

See Central Wellington Map (p410)

MT VICTORIA

Charles
Plimmer
Park

Mt Victoria
Lookout

Town
Belt

Basin
Reserve

MT COOK

Central
Park

To Red Rocks
Coastal Walk (6km)

To Wellington Hospital (800m);
Newtown (1.3km);
Wellington Zoo (2.5km)

To Airport via Tunnel (7km);
Lyall Bay (8km)

EATING
Arbitrageur..........................46 B4
Cafe L'Affare......................47 C7
Fidel's.................................48 B7
Fisherman's Table...............49 E6
Logan-Brown.......................50 B7
Martin Bosley's Yacht Club
Restaurant.........................51 D6
New World Supermarket.....52 B3
Parade Café........................53 D6
Restaurant 88......................54 C7
Trisha's Pies.................(see 32)
Wellington Trawling Sea Market..55 B7

DRINKING
Backbencher........................56 B3
Dockside.............................57 C5
Leuven.................................58 B5

SHOPPING
Kirkcaldie & Stains..............59 B5

TRANSPORT
Air New Zealand...................60 B5
Bluebridge Ferry Terminal.....61 C4
Helipro..........................(see 15)
InterCity Bus Depot.............62 C4
Interislander Ferry Terminal..63 D1
Local Bus Terminal...............64 B4
Lower Cable-Car Terminal......65 B5
Qantas................................66 B5
Tranz Metro....................(see 62)
Upper Cable-Car Terminal.....67 A5
White Star City to City
Departure Point............(see 35)

INFORMATION
Bookshops
Bellamy's (Map p410; ☎ 04-384 7770; 105 Cuba Mall) Secondhand bookshop.
Dymocks (Map pp406-7; ☎ 04-472 2080; 366 Lambton Quay)
Unity Books (Map p410; ☎ 04-499 4245; 57 Willis St) A Wellington institution, with an excellent fiction section, including NZ literature.
Whitcoulls (Map p410; ☎ 04-801 5240; Courtenay Central, Courtenay Pl)

Emergency
Ambulance, Fire Service & Police (☎ 111)
Police (Map p410; ☎ 04-381 2000; 39 Victoria St)

Internet Access
Internet facilities are plentiful; most places charge a minimum of $1 for 15 minutes, $4 per hour. Most backpackers have Net facilities. Central places with numerous terminals:
Cybernomad (Map p410; ☎ 04-801 5964; 43 Courtenay Pl)
Email Shop (Map p410; ☎ 04-802 4860; cnr Wakefield & Victoria Sts) Inside the visitor information centre.
Cyber City (Map p410; ☎ 04-384 3717; 97-99 Courtenay Pl)
iPlay (Map p410; ☎ 04-494 0088; upstairs, 49 Manners Mall; ☯ 24hr)

Internet Resources
Feeling Great (www.feelinggreat.co.nz) Events and activities, categorised under Arts & Entertainment; Recreation, Fitness & Outdoors; and Kids' Zone. Run by the city council.
Positively Wellington Tourism (www.wellingtonnz.com) Official tourism website for the city.
Wotzon.com (www.wotzon.com) Extensive listings of events, locations and services in Wellington and surrounds.

Media
Capital Times (www.captimes.co.nz) Free weekly newspaper full of happenings in the capital.
Dominion Post (www.stuff.co.nz) Wellington's newspaper, published Monday to Saturday.
Wellington Guide (www.theguide.co.nz) Glossy 'life-style magazine' ($6) published every three months, with good restaurant and bar listings.

Medical Services
Accident & Urgent Medical Centre (Map pp406-7; ☎ 04-384 4944; 17 Adelaide St, Newtown; ☯ 24hr) South of town; no appointment is necessary.

After-hours pharmacy (Map pp406-7; ☎ 04-385 8810; 17 Adelaide St, Newtown; ☯ 5-11pm Mon-Fri, 8am-11pm Sat, Sun & public holidays) Right next door to the Accident & Urgent Medical Centre.
Wellington Hospital (☎ 04-385 5999; Riddiford St, Newtown) About a kilometre south of the city centre.

Money
There are numerous banks and ATMs around Wellington; you'll find branches of major banks on Courtenay Pl, Willis St and Lambton Quay.

Moneychangers include the following:
City Stop (Map p410; ☎ 04-801 8669; 107 Manners St; ☯ 24hr) Convenience store that exchanges travellers cheques.
Travelex (Map p410; ☎ 04-472 2848; 358 Lambton Quay) Foreign-exchange office inside the Harvey World Travel branch. Also has a branch at the airport.

Post
Main post office (Map pp406-7; Ground fl, NZ Post House, Waterloo Quay)
Post office (Map p410; 43 Manners Mall)

Tourist Information
Airport information desk (1st fl, Main Terminal; ☯ 8am-7pm)
Automobile Association (AA; Map p410; ☎ 04-931 9999; 342-352 Lambton Quay)
Department of Conservation (DOC; Map pp406-7; ☎ 04-472 7356; www.doc.govt.nz; Government Bldgs Historic Reserve, Lambton Quay; ☯ 9am-4.30pm Mon-Fri, 10am-3pm Sat) Offers information about walks, parks, outdoor activities, camping in the region, and it's where you organise permits for Kapiti Island (p430).
Wellington visitor information centre (Map p410; ☎ 04-802 4860; www.WellingtonNZ.com; Civic Sq, cnr Wakefield & Victoria Sts; ☯ 8.30am-5pm Mon-Fri, to 6pm Dec-Apr, 9.30am-4.30pm Sat & Sun) The official tourist information centre. Its staff books almost everything, and provides the Official Visitor Guide to Wellington plus many useful brochures. There's a souvenir shop, the Email Shop and a café in the complex.

SIGHTS
Botanic Gardens & Cable Car
The tranquil, 25-hectare **Botanic Gardens** (Map pp406-7; ☎ 04-499 1400; www.wbg.co.nz; ☯ dawn-dusk) are easily visited in conjunction with a cable-car ride. The large gardens contain native bush and other gardens, including the Lady Norwood Rose Garden with over 100 rose species. There's also a teahouse, visitors centre and the NZ headquarters of

CARTER OBSERVATORY

In the gardens near the top cable-car terminal, **Carter Observatory** (Map pp406-7; ☎ 04-472 8167; www.carterobservatory.org; ☼ daytime hours 10am-5pm Nov-Feb, 11am-4pm Mar-Oct; also open Wed-Sat evening Nov-Feb, Fri & Sat evening Mar-Oct) has displays and videos about astronomy and you can view the night sky through the telescope (weather permitting). A look around the observatory plus solar viewing costs adult/

World Wide Fund for Nature, with information and displays. The gardens are also accessible from the Glenmore St entrance (bus 12).

One of Wellington's prime attractions, the red **cable car** (Map pp406-7; ☎ 04-472 2199; www.wellingtonnz.com/cablecar; one way/return adult $1.80/ 3.60, family return $10; ☼ every 10min, 7am-10pm Mon-Fri, 8.30am-10pm Sat, 9am-10pm Sun) chugs sweetly up the steep hill from Lambton Quay to Kelburn. At the top are photo opps galore, Wellington's Botanic Gardens, Carter Observatory (see following), Skyline Café and the small, well-presented **Cable Car Museum** (Map pp406-7; ☎ 04-475 3578; www.cablecarmuseum.co.nz; admission free; ☼ 9.30am-5.30pm Nov-Easter, to 5pm Mon-Fri, 10am-4.30pm Sat & Sun Easter-Oct), which tells the cable car's tale since it began in 1902.

Central Wellington is a stroll back down through the Botanic Gardens, or by a series of steps, which interconnect with roads (a 30- to 40-minute walk).

TREASURES OF TE PAPA

Te Papa (Map p410; ☎ 04-381 7000; www.tepapa.govt.nz; Cable St; admission free; ☼ 10am-6pm Mon-Wed & Fri-Sun, to 9pm Thu), the 'Museum of New Zealand', is an inspiring and interactive look at NZ's history and culture. Dominating the waterfront, the striking construction took five years to build (costing $317 million) and opened in 1998. Since its opening there have been over nine million visitors. Quickly gaining widespread praise for its innovation and approachability, the museum has become a national symbol, affectionately dubbed 'Our Place', as it celebrates the essence of NZ and its people.

Among Te Papa's treasures is a huge Maori collection, including its own *marae* (meeting house; dedicated hands-on 'discovery centres' for children; natural history and environment exhibits; a re-creation of a European settlement; contemporary art and culture, and more. Exhibits are presented in impressive gallery spaces with a touch o' high tech (eg a virtual bungee jump and a house shaking through an earthquake). Short-term changing exhibits require a small admission fee.

You could spend a day exploring but still not see it all. To target your areas of interest head to the information desk at level two. To get your bearings, the one-hour 'Introducing Te Papa' tour ($10) is a good idea; tours leave from the information desk at 10.15am and 2pm daily.
Two cafés ard an excellent gift shop round off this impressive complex.

child/family $6/2/15; planetarium shows and telescope sessions each cost $12/5/30 (which includes a look around the observatory and solar viewing). Some sessions are weather-dependent; call for times.

Museum of Wellington City & Sea

Professional exhibits in the three-storey **Museum of Wellington City & Sea** (Map pp406-7; ☎ 04-472 8904; www.museumofwellington.co.nz; Queens Wharf; admission free; ☼ 10am-5pm) offer an imaginative and interactive experience of Wellington's rich maritime history and social heritage since Maori settlement. There's a moving documentary about the tragedy of the *Wahine* (see p404), an impressive lighthouse lens, and ancient Maori legends are dramatically told using tiny hologram actors and excellent special effects.

Part of the museum, **Plimmer's Ark Gallery** (admission free) has solid chunks of the ship the *Inconstant* and an interesting historical overview of the 'Father of Wellington' John Plimmer.

Beehive & Parliament House

Three buildings on Bowen St form NZ's parliamentary complex. Office workers swarm around the distinctive and well-known modernist **Beehive** (Map pp406-7; Bowen St), which is exactly what it looks like. It was designed by British architect Sir Basil Spence and built between 1969 and 1980. Controversy surrounded its construction

CENTRAL WELLINGTON

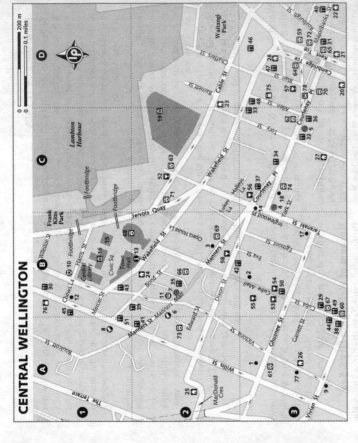

and, love it or loathe it, it's the architectural symbol of the country.

Next door to the Beehive is **Parliament House** (Map pp406-7; Bowen St), completed in 1922, and beside this is the 1899 neogothic Parliamentary Library building. The Parliament House **visitors centre** (☎ 04-471 9503; tour .desk@parliament.govt.nz; ☑ 9am-5pm Mon-Fri, 9.30am-4pm Sat, 11.30am-4pm Sun) is in the ground-floor foyer of Parliament House. This is where you can participate in free, one-hour **tours** (depart hourly 10am to 4pm Monday to Friday, to 3pm Saturday, noon to 3pm Sunday) of Parliament House.

National Library & Archives

Opposite the Beehive, the **National Library** (Map pp406-7; ☎ 04-474 3000; www.natlib.govt.nz; cnr Molesworth & Aitken Sts; admission free; ☑ 9am-5pm Mon-Fri, to 1pm Sat) houses the most comprehensive book collection in NZ. Also housed here is the Alexander Turnbull Library, an early colonial collection with many historical books, maps, newspapers and photographs. The library regularly hosts cultural events, and the **National Library Gallery** (ad-

mission free; ☑ 9am-5pm Mon-Fri, 9am-4.30pm Sat, 1-4.30pm Sun) has changing exhibits.

One block away, the **National Archives** (Map pp406-7; ☎ 04-499 5595, www.archives.govt.nz; 10 Mulgrave St; admission free; ☑ 9am-5pm Mon-Fri, to 1pm Sat) is the official guardian of NZ's heritage documents. It displays several significant national treasures, including the original Treaty of Waitangi (p35), NZ's founding document.

Historic Buildings

Completed in 1866, **Old St Paul's** (Map pp406-7; ☎ 04-473 6722; www.oldsaintpauls.co.nz; 34 Mulgrave St; admission free; ☑ 10am-5pm) looks quaint from the outside, while the striking interior is a good example of early English Gothic timber design. It features magnificent stained-glass windows and houses displays of Wellington's early history.

Opposite the Beehive building, at the northern end of Lambton Quay, stand the 1876 **Government Buildings** (Map pp406-7), among the world's largest all-wooden buildings. With their block corners and slab wooden planking, you have to look twice to realise that these aren't made of stone.

INFORMATION
Automobile Association (AA)...1 A3
Bellamy's...2 B3
City Stop...3 B2
Cyber City...4 C3
Cybernomad...5 C3
Email Shop...(see 13)
French Embassy...6 B2
iPlay...7 B2
Japanese Embassy...8 A1
Map Shop...9 A3
Police...10 B1
Post Office...11 B2
Unity Books...12 B1
Wellington Visitor Information Centre...13 B2
Whitcoulls...(see 34)

SIGHTS & ACTIVITIES
Bungy Rocket...14 C3
Capital E...15 B1
City Gallery Wellington...16 B1
Mediaplex & the Film Archive...17 B3
Penny Farthing Cycles...18 C3
Te Papa...19 C2

SLEEPING
Base Backpackers...20 D3
Halswell Lodge...21 D3
Majoribanks Apartments...22 D3
Museum Hotel de Wheels...23 D2
Nomads Capital...24 B2
Rosemere Backpackers...25 A2
Victoria Court Motor Lodge...26 A2
Wildlife House...27 C3

YHA Wellington City...28 D3

EATING
Aunty Mena's Vegetarian Café...29 B3
BNZ Centre...30 B1
Café Bastille...31 D3
Chow...32 C3
Commonsense Organics...33 C3
Courtenay Central...34 C3
Crêpes a Go-Go...35 C2
Eat...36 C2
Espressoholic...37 C3
Floriditas...38 A3
Flying Burrito Brothers...(see 29)
Hell...39 B2
Kai...40 D2
Kopi...41 A2
La Casa della Pasta...42 B2
Lido...43 B1
Midnight Espresso...44 A3
New World Metro...45 B1
New World Supermarket...46 B3
One Red Dog...47 D3
Pandora Panetteria...48 D3
Sushi takeaways...49 B3
Tulsi...50 B3
Wholly Bagels...51 A1

DRINKING
Basement...(see 20)
Brewery Bar & Restaurant...52 C2
Good Luck Bar...53 B3
JJ Murphy & Co...54 B3
Matterhorn...55 C3
Molly Malone's...56 C3

Ponderosa...57 D3
Red Square...(see 57)
Sovereign...58 B2
Tasting Room...(see 64)

ENTERTAINMENT
BATS Theatre...59 D3
Blue Note...60 B3
Bodega...61 A3
Cabaret...62 C3
Circa Theatre...63 C2
Downstage Theatre...64 C2
Embassy Theatre...65 D3
Hoyts Regent on Manners...66 B2
Indigo...67 B3
Michael Fowler Centre...68 B1
Opera House...69 B2
Paramount...70 D3
Pound...(see 58)
Reading Cinemas...(see 34)
Rialto...71 C2
Sandwiches...72 C3
Studio Nine...73 A2
Ticketek...(see 74)
Westpac Trust St James Theatre...74 C3

SHOPPING
Kura Gallery...75 D3
Mainly Tramping...76 B1
Ora Design & Art Space...(see 75)

TRANSPORT
Apex Car Rental...77 A3
Bus Stop...78 D3

The buildings have been restored and house various offices, including the DOC visitors centre.

Galleries

Wellington has a host of public, independent and dealer galleries. For a more comprehensive list pick up the *Arts Map* brochure from the visitor information centre.

City Gallery Wellington (Map p410; ☎ 04-801 3952; www.city-gallery.org.nz; Civic Sq, Wakefield St; admission by donation, charges may apply for major exhibits; ☎ 10am-5pm) has regularly changing contemporary exhibitions ranging from art to architecture and design. NZ artists feature prominently, but there are also international exhibitions. Also here is a popular lunch spot, the Nikau Gallery Café.

Part of the New Zealand Academy of Fine Arts, **Academy Galleries** (Map pp406-7; ☎ 04-499 8807; www.nzafa.com; 1 Queens Wharf; admission free; ☎ 10am-5pm) is a contemporary, international space for fine arts. When the gallery isn't exhibiting Academy graduates' work it's available for hire and may have artists' work from around the globe.

Museums

Highlighting Wellington's square-eye dedication to film and TV, **Mediaplex** (Map p410; ☎ 04-384 7647; www.filmarchive.org.nz; cnr Taranaki & Ghuznee Sts; admission free, movie $8) is part of the New Zealand Film Archive, an organisation charged with collecting, protecting and projecting NZ's moving-image heritage. The innovative Mediaplex combines a film archive, library, cinema and research centre under one roof and has an extensive collection with over 90,000 titles of NZ film, TV and video dating from 1895 to this year's sitcom. From Wednesday to Saturday, the cinema shows treasures from the vault; call ☎ 04-499 3456 for the week's screenings.

Cricket aficionados will be bowled over by the historical memorabilia at the **National Cricket Museum** (Map pp406-7; ☎ 04-385 6602; Basin Reserve, adult/child $5/2; ☎ 10.30am-3.30pm daily Nov-Apr, Sat & Sun May-Oct). There's an extensive range of videos, displays about cricket's arrival in the colonies, the first international test in 1894 and the original 1743 Addington bat.

The **National Tattoo Museum** (Map pp406-7; ☎ 04-385 6444; www.mokomuseum.org.nz; 42 Abel Smith

KATHERINE MANSFIELD

NZ's most distinguished author, Katherine Mansfield is known throughout the world for her short stories and often compared to Chekhov and Maupassant.

Born Kathleen Mansfield Beauchamp in 1888, she left Wellington at 19 for Europe, where she spent the rest of her short adult life. She mixed with Europe's most famous writers, such as DH Lawrence, TS Eliot and Virginia Woolf, and married the literary critic and author John Middleton Murry in 1918. In 1923, aged 34, she died of tuberculosis at Fontainebleau in France. It was not until 1945 that her five books of short stories (*In a German Pension*, *Bliss*, *The Garden Party*, *The Dove's Nest and Something Childish*) were combined into a single volume, *Collected Stories of Katherine Mansfield*. She spent five years of her childhood at 25 Tinakori Rd in Wellington; it's mentioned in her stories *The Aloe* (which in its final form became *Prelude*) and *A Birthday* (a fictionalised account of her own birth).

Katherine Mansfield's Birthplace (Map pp406-7; ☎ 04-473 7268; www.katherinemansfield.com; 25 Tinakori Rd; adult/child $5.50/2; ☻ 10am-4pm Tue-Sun) is a lovingly restored and maintained house with a restful heritage garden. The excellent video *A Portrait of Katherine Mansfield* screens here and the 'Sense of Living' exhibition displays photographs of the period alongside excerpts from her writing. A doll's house has been constructed from details in the short story of the same name. The 14 Wilton bus stops nearby.

St; admission $5; ☻ noon-5.30pm Tue-Sun) has thousands of examples of tattoo art on show, including Maori *moko* (facial tattoos), traditional and contemporary tools, and a tattoo studio in case the urge strikes. For dedicated ink-lovers only.

Scenic Lookout

The best view of the city, harbour and surrounding region is from the lookout at the top of 196m **Mt Victoria** (Map pp406–7), east of the city centre. You can take bus 20 (Monday to Friday) to the top or, if you're feeling particularly energetic, make the taxing walk. To drive, take Oriental Pde along the waterfront and then Carlton Gore St.

Ferry to Days Bay

Trips across the harbour to Days Bay are made on the **Dominion Post Ferry** (Map pp406-7; timetable ☎ 04-494 3339; www.eastbywest.co.nz; Queens Wharf, one-way tickets adult/child $7.50/4), departing from Queens Wharf 11 times daily weekdays and six times daily at weekends. It's a 30-minute trip to Days Bay, where there are beaches, a fine park and a boatshed offering canoes and rowboats for hire. A 10-minute walk from Days Bay brings you to the pretty settlement of Eastbourne, with appealing cafés and picnic spots.

At least three Days Bay ferries per day also call in at **Matiu-Somes Island** (return fare adult/child $16.50/9), a former prisoner-of-war camp and quarantine station. Now a re-

serve managed by DOC, it has walking trails, beaches and abundant bird life. Take a picnic lunch.

The Dominion Post ferry also operates a service between Queens Wharf and Petone Wharf, on the Esplanade in Lower Hutt (one way adult/child $7.50/4, three to six daily), also calling at Matiu-Somes Island, subject to demand.

Karori Wildlife Sanctuary

This unique, predator-free sanctuary (☎ 04-920 9200; www.sanctuary.org.nz; Waiapu Rd; ☻ 10am-5pm) is about 2km west of the city (buses 12, 18, 21, 22 and 23 pass nearby). It has an admirable programme of forest and wetland restoration, and the area is home to over 30 native bird species. There are plenty of walking tracks, roving guides, and a range of guided tours available.

Zoo

The well-maintained **Wellington Zoo** (☎ 04-381 6750; www.wellingtonzoo.com; 200 Daniel St; adult/child $12/6; ☻ 9.30am-5pm) has a commitment to conservation and research. There's a wide variety of native and non-native wildlife; outdoor lion and chimpanzee parks; and a nocturnal kiwi house, which also houses tuatara. Check the website for details of 'zoo encounters', which allow you to hand-feed giraffes or red pandas (for a fee). The zoo is 4km south of the city; catch bus 10 or 23.

ACTIVITIES

Mountain Biking

Makarara Peak Mountain Bike Park (www.makara peak.org.nz) is a council-run park in the hills of Karori, west of the city centre. The main entrance is on South Karori Rd (accessible on bus routes 12 and 18). The 200-hectare park has numerous tracks ranging from beginner to expert. **Mud Cycles** (☎ 04-476 4961; www.mudcycles.co.nz; 338 Karori Rd, Karori; ½-/full-day bike hire $25/40) has mountain bikes for rent, is close to the park, and offers free inner-city pick-up and drop-off (or can drop bikes at your accommodation). It also designs guided tours, catering for all levels. You can also hire Mud Cycles from Base Backpackers (p416).

Penny Farthing Cycles (Map pp410; ☎ 04-385 2279; www.pennyfarthing.co.nz; 89 Courtenay Pl; day/week bike hire $35/100) stocks a full range of bicycles, bicycle gear and clothing.

There are other good opportunities for mountain biking around town. The visitor information centre or any of the city's bike shops can give you specific information and maps.

Walking

If Wellington has a peak hour it's along Oriental Pde at lunchtime (BYO jogging shorts!), which is excellent for a stroll. The visitor information centre is a great source of information for walks, and for guided walks, see Tours (p414).

The easy **Red Rocks Coastal Walk** (two to three hours return), south of the city, follows the volcanic coast from Owhiro Bay to Red Rocks and Sinclair Head, where there's a seal colony. Take bus 1 or 4 to Island Bay, then 29 to Owhiro Bay Pde (or walk 2.5km along the Esplanade). From the start of Owhiro Bay Pde it's 1km to the quarry gate where the coastal walk starts.

Other Activities

With all this wind and water, Wellington is a great place for **sailboarding** and **kitesurfing** – choose from sheltered inlets, rough harbours and wave-beater coastal areas, all within a half-hour's drive of the city. **Wild Winds** (Map pp406–7; ☎ 04-384 1010; www.wildwinds.co.nz; Chaffers Marina, Oriental Bay; ☉ 10am-5:30pm Mon-Fri, to 3pm Sat, 11am-3pm Sun) has three-hour lessons for beginners from $120 (sailboarding) to $170 (kitesurfing); prices include all equipment.

At the long-running **Fergs Rock'n'Kayaks** (Map pp406-7; ☎ 04-449 8898; www.fergskayaks.co.nz; Shed 6, Queens Wharf; ☉ 10am-8pm Mon-Fri, 9am-6pm Sat & Sun) you can challenge your calf muscles with indoor rock climbing (adult/child $12/8), cruise the waterfront on a pair of inline skates ($15 for two hours) and see the sights from a kayak (from $15 for two hours). There's also a range of guided kayaking trips.

Gnarly surfing breaks are found at **Lyall Bay** near the airport, and **Palliser Bay**, south-east of Wellington. The visitor information centre can help you with fishing and diving charters.

Freyberg Pool & Fitness Centre (Map pp406-7; ☎ 04-384 3107; 139 Oriental Pde; adult/child $4/2; ☉ 6am-9pm) has a heated indoor pool for lap swimming plus a spa and sauna.

For something more dramatic try a reverse **bungy rocket** (Map p410; ☎ 0800 932 8669; cnr Taranaki St & Courtenay Pl per person $40), where you sit in a capsulelike device that's flung into the air at high speed (best attempted before a meal).

WALKING TOUR

Start Beehive
Finish Waitangi Park
Distance Approximately 1.5km
Duration One hour to one day, depending on stops

Start by admiring (or deploring, depending on your aesthetics) the modernist **Beehive** (1; p409) before heading east along Bowen St to Lambton Quay, known as the Golden Mile for all its retail revelry. With time up your sleeve, stop to browse at the elegant **Kirkcaldie & Stains** (2; p423) or at the Edwardian **Old Bank Shopping Arcade** (3). Purchases made, turn right onto Willis St then left at Mercer St, continuing along Wakefield St. Pause at Civic Sq to admire the public artworks, and check out whatever takes your fancy here: the **visitor information centre** (4; p408) to arrange tickets to one of to-night's theatre shows, **City Gallery Wellington** (5; p411) or, if you've got kids, **Capital E** (6; p414). Take a lunch break at the Nikau Gallery Café, inside City Gallery.

From Civic Square, take the City to Sea footbridge over to the waterfront path and wind your way past the boatsheds to the **Brewery Bar & Restaurant** (7; p421), a prime place to sit outdoors and watch the passing parade over a locally brewed Sassy Red or Wicked Blonde. Feeling suitably refreshed, it's time to tackle **Te Papa** (8; see the boxed text, p409). You could easily spend half a day here, but once you've reached your limit, you deserve some downtime – head for a patch of grass at the brand-new **Waitangi Park** (9).

WELLINGTON FOR CHILDREN

With ankle biters in tow, your best bet is a trip to colourful **Capital E** (Map p410; ☎ 04-913 3720; www.capitale.org.nz; Civic Sq), an educational entertainment centre designed especially for kids. It has interactive rotating exhibits, a children's theatre company and TV production studio. It's best to call or check the website for the events calendar and costs involved.

Te Papa (see the boxed text, p409) is not just a place for grown-ups; there are Discovery Centres loaded with interactive activities, and StoryPlace is designed for children

five and under. See the dedicated kids pages on its website for more details. Not far from Te Papa, waterfront places to exhaust energetic young things include **Frank Kitts Park** and the new **Waitangi Park**, both with playgrounds.

A lap around the **Botanic Gardens** (p408) gets fresh air into young lungs and when darkness falls head to **Carter Observatory** (p409), where kids can view the night sky. There's always plenty to see at the **Wellington Zoo** (p412).

Check out the website www.feelinggreat .co.nz, operated by the city council to keep locals and visitors up to date with what's going on in the city. Click on the Kids' Zone for a rundown on events and courses targeted to young 'uns.

TOURS

Wellington has a host of excellent tours – it's essential to book.

Flat Earth (☎ 0800 775 805; www.flatearth.co.nz; full-day tours $235–385) Offers an interesting array of themed small-group tours ('Wild Wellington', Martinborough wine tour, Middle Earth filming locations), but they come at a premium.

GAY & LESBIAN WELLINGTON

Wellington's gay scene is tiny, but friendly and inclusive. Sovereign bar and Pound nightclub are the main long-running contenders for best entertainment venues but there are loads of cafés and bars concentrated in the inner-city area, especially around Courtenay Pl, Lambton Quay and Cuba St, that are also gay-friendly.

Media such as **express** (www.gayexpress.co.nz; $3; every 2nd Wed) and **UP Newspaper** (www.upmag nz.com; $3.50; monthly) will keep you current with the latest happenings in the local gay scene. The publications are free from selected venues, or you can buy them from newsagents.

For phone information, or just to talk, contact **Wellington Gay Switchboard** (☎ 04-473 7878; gay.switchboard@xtra.co.nz; ☎ 7.30-10.30pm Tue, Thu & Sat) and **Lesbian Line** (☎ 04-499 5567; wgtnlesbianline@hotmail .com; ☎ 11pm-5am Fri & Sat), which sparks up at around 1am.

Excellent online resources include www.gaynz.com, which has comprehensive national coverage of all things queer; www.gayline.gen.nz and www.pound.co.nz; and www.wellington.lesbian.net.nz.

Sovereign (Map p410; ☎ 04-384 6024; www.pound.co.nz; Level 1, Oaks Complex, Dixon St; ☎ 4.30pm-late Wed-Fri, 8pm-late Sat, 5pm-late Sun) is a cosy, relaxed and retro bar with mixed gay and lesbian clientele; just look for the door with The straight route is often boring painted above it. Thursday night from 10pm is karaoke at Sovereign, but for disco and drag head to the adjacent **Pound** (Map p410; ☎ 11pm-5am Fri & Sat).

See also Gay & Lesbian Travellers, p711.

Hammond's Scenic Tours (☎ 04-472 0869; www .wellingtonsightseeingtours.com; adult/child city tour $45/22.50, Kapiti $75/37.50, Wairarapa $160/80; ☎ city tours depart 10am & 2pm, Kapiti 9am & 1.30pm, Wairarapa 8.30am) Runs a 2½-hour city highlights tour, four-hour tour of the Kapiti Coast, and a full-day Wairarapa experience, which includes Palliser Bay. Includes pick-up and drop-off at your accommodation.

Helipro (Map pp406-7; ☎ 04-472 1550; www.helipro .co.nz; Shed 1, Queens Wharf; 8/15/20/35min flights per person $95/150/210/350) Scenic helicopter flights that cover various routes.

Rover Ring Tour (☎ 021 426 211; www.wellington rover.co.nz; full day per person $150) Fantastic *Lord of the Rings* tour with an enthusiastic guide who manages to bring the scene locations, minus the props, to life. A stop at the Chocolate Fish café is included, as is a picnic lunch. Tours generally run daily (though there may be minimum numbers in the low season).

Walk Wellington (☎ 04-384 9590, 04-802 4860; www.wellington.nz.com/walkwellington; adult/child under 5/child $20/free/10; ☎ tours 10am Wed, Fri, Sat & Sun year-round, plus 5.30pm Mon, Tue, Thu Nov-Mar) Ninety-minute informative walking tours that focus on the city or waterfront, departing from the visitor information centre.

Wellington Rover (☎ 021 426 211; www.wellington rover.co.nz; adult day pass $40; ☎ departs visitor information centre 9am, 11.30am & 2.33pm) A popular 2½-hour tour that gives you the option of a hop-on, hop-off timetabled service and covers places that are tricky to reach without a car. Also offers an 'Adventure Wairarapa' tour (from $165).

FESTIVALS & EVENTS

Check at the visitor information centre or visit www.wellingtonnz.com/events for a comprehensive listing of festivals; tickets to most events can be booked through Ticketek (p422). Party-hardy regular events include the following:

January/February
Summer City Festival (☎ 04-499 4444; www.feeling great.co.nz) A two-month celebration of summer that begins on New Year's Eve and includes many free outdoor events.

February
International Sevens Tournament (☎ 04-389 0020; www.sevens.co.nz) The world's top seven-a-side rugby teams compete over the first weekend of February, and the fans descend.

Cuba St Carnival (☎ 04-499 0650; www.cubacarnival .org.nz) NZ's largest street carnival, held in late February every two years (odd-numbered years).

Late February/March
New Zealand Festival (☎ 04-473 0149; www.nzfes tival.telecom.co.nz) A month-long biennial event (held in even-numbered years) celebrating the arts, featuring theatre, dance, music and opera performances, with many top international artists involved.

Fringe NZ (☎ 04-382 8015; www.fringe.org.nz) More than three weeks of experimental visual arts, music, dance and theatre.

July/August

International Film Festival (04-385 0162; www .enzedff.co.nz) A two-week event showcasing the best of NZ and international cinema.

September

World of WearableArt Award Show (WOW; ☎ 0800 4969 746; www.worldofwearableart.com) Transplanted from Nelson to the capital in 2005 is this spectacular two-week event, where amazing garments take centre stage. Read more about WOW on p466.

November

Toast Martinborough Plenty of wine-loving Wellingtonians head to Martinborough for this day of indulgence. See p433.

SLEEPING

Typically, accommodation in Wellington is more expensive than in regional areas. Our price listings for the city fall into the following categories: Budget – doubles (with or without bathroom) for under $100; Midrange – doubles (with bathroom) between $101 and $200; Top End – over $201. The overall standard is generally high and there are many great places to stay right in, or within easy walking distance of, the city centre. One hassle is the lack of inner-city parking; if you have your own wheels, ask about where to park when you make a reservation (and be aware you'll probably have to pay for it).

Budget accommodation is predominantly in the form of multistorey hostels, although there is a handful of smaller, more personal hostels. Budget accommodation is scattered throughout the city, conglomerating around Courtenay Pl. There's no 'motel alley' in Wellington, rather they are scattered around the immediate city-centre fringe, but the city is awash with hotels and apartments. It's primarily a business destination and hotel rates drop dramatically (up to half-price) from Friday to Sunday.

During the peak holiday season (December to February), or during major festivals, it's advisable to book accommodation in advance.

Budget

HOSTELS

YHA Wellington City (Map p410; ☎ 04-801 7280; www.stayyha.com; cnr Cambridge Tce & Wakefield St; dm $26-29, tw/d without bathroom $66/70, with bathroom $90/90, f with bathroom $96;) These guys still know how to hostel. Despite the increased competition in town, this place wins points for the biggest and best communal areas: well-equipped kitchens, big dining area, games room, reading room and a dedicated TV-video room. Staff members are friendly and knowledgeable and can book anything you need with a minimum of fuss; group dinner nights are a big hit.

Base Backpackers (Map p410; ☎ 0800 227 369, 04-801 5666; www.basebackpackers.com; 21-23 Cambridge Tce; dm $25-28, d/tr with bathroom $75/85;) This slick chain of hostels aims squarely for young fun-seekers. The location here is top-notch (just metres from Courtenay Pl) and the rooms are fresh and modern (the female-only dorms are a nice touch). The sunny lobby is great, there are bikes for hire, and downstairs is the beer-happy Basement bar. The only gripe: the tiny kitchen and lounge area given the hostel's 290 beds.

Nomads Capital (Map p410; ☎ 0508 666 237, 04-978 7800; www.nomadscapital.com; 118 Wakefield St; dm $19-25, d with bathroom from $75;) The newest kid on the block in Welly (opened mid-2005) is in a central location opposite the visitor information centre. There's good security, shiny new rooms, an on-site café-bar called Blend (serving cheap meals), and discounts for longer stays. But as with Base, preceding, inadequate kitchen and lounge space.

World Wide Backpackers (Map pp406-7; ☎ 0508 888 555, 04-802 5590; www.worldwidenz.co.nz; 291 The Terrace; dm/tw/d $24/60/60;) The nicest small hostel in town. In an old house, this friendly, well-regarded backpackers is clean and homely and offers winning free extras like Internet, breakfast, and wine in the evening. It's down-to-earth and chilled.

Wildlife House (Map p410; ☎ 0508 005 858, 04-381 3899; www.wildlifehouse.co.nz; 58 Tory St; dm $25-27, tw & d with/without bathroom $75/65;) You can't miss this large zebra-striped building off Courtenay Pl. Rooms are spacious, although the furniture in some is looking dated. One level (of five) is dedicated to communal spaces, which are funkily designed with wood and corrugated iron, and include reading room, TV and video lounges, and a modern kitchen.

Maple Lodge (Map pp406-7; ☎ 04-385 3771; 52 Ellice St; dm/s/tw/d $23/35/50/52; P) In a residential neighbourhood, cosy Maple Lodge offers clean accommodation with small dorms and wee twins and doubles. There's no TV, instead there's chill-out music, board games and conversation. It's a popular option with solo travellers. From the train station, catch buses 1, 4, 12, 22 or 23 to Basin Reserve.

Rowena's Lodge (Map pp406-7; ☎ 0800 801 414, 04-385 7872; www.wellingtonbackpackers.co.nz; 115 Brougham St; sites per person $12.50, dm/s/d $20/30/50; 🖳 🖵) It's the views that have it at Rowena's. A women's hostel during WWII, this is a rambling, friendly place with an outdoor barbecue area and the only camping sites in town. There are free shuttle services to/from ferries, buses and trains.

If you prefer your NZ towns small and your hostels more personal than those listed earlier, consider two top-notch options within commuting distance of the capital: Moana Lodge (following) and Paekakariki Backpackers (p428).

Moana Lodge (☎ 04-233 2010; www.moanalodge.co.nz; 49 Moana Rd, Plimmerton; dm $24-27, tw & d $54-70; 🖵) This exceptional backpackers is on the beach in the village of Plimmerton, 25km from tow1 off SH1. It's immaculate and inviting, and the friendly owners are more than happy to share their local expertise and pick new arrivals up from the train station, 1km away (suburban trains between Wellington and Paraparaumu stop in Plimmerton). There's free use of kayaks and golf clubs; if you're lucky and the weather cooperates, the owner may take you over to Mana Island in his boat.

Also check out Cambridge Hotel, following, for high-quality backpacker accommodation. Other decent city options:

Rosemere Backpackers (Map p410; ☎ 04-384 3041; dm/s/tw/d incl breakfast $24/45/56/60; 🖵) Colourful option a short walk up-ill from the centre. Free Internet.

Downtown Wellington Backpackers (Map pp406-7; ☎ 0800 225 725, 04-473 8482; www.downtownback packers.co.nz; 1 Bunny St; dm/tw/d from $23/55/70; 🖵) Large, older backpackers opposite the train station.

HOTELS
Cambridge Hotel (Map pp406-7; ☎ 04-385 8829; www.cambridgehotel.co.nz; 28 Cambridge Tce; dm $23-25, s/d/tw $59/75/75, s/d/tw/tr/f with bathroom $85/95/99/115/125; 🖵) Top-quality pub accommodation at affordable prices in a restored heritage hotel. En suite rooms have Sky TV, phone and fridge (try for a room at the back if you're a light sleeper); the quiet backpacker wing

has a well-equipped kitchen and luxurious shared bathrooms. Cheap meal deals at the bar are another drawcard.

CAMPING
Camping grounds are scarce in Wellington. Rowena's Lodge (see earlier) can accommodate a few tents otherwise head to Hutt Valley (p427).

Midrange
GUESTHOUSES & B&BS
Booklovers B&B (Map pp406-7; ☎ 04-384 2714; www.bbnb.co.nz; 123 Pirie St; s/d $150/180) Booklovers is an elegant old home owned by award-winning NZ author Jane Tolerton. There are three charming rooms with sweeping views, TV, CDs and CD player, and the home is filled with books. From the front gate bus 2 runs to Courtenay Pl and the train station, and short bush walks begin right next door.

Mermaid (Map pp406-7; ☎ 04-384 4511; www.mermaid.co.nz; 1 Epuni St; s $80-125, d $90-140) In the cool Aro Valley neighbourhood, the Mermaid is a small women-only guesthouse in a wonderfully restored villa. Each room is individually themed with artistic flair (one room has its own bathroom, the other three rooms share facilities). White robes and fluffy towels make Mermaid a luxurious experience and there's a guest kitchen, lounge and deck area. The owners also have a nearby self-contained apartment ($160).

Eight Parliament Street (Map pp406-7; ☎ 04-499 0808; www.boutique-bb.co.nz; 8 Parliament St, Thorndon; r $120-185, house $270-370) In historic Thorndon, close to a villagelike strip of restaurants and boutiques, is this delightful house, stylishly renovated and run by a friendly German host. The three rooms (one with private bathroom) are comfortable and there's a great kitchen and decking area out in the country-cottage garden.

HOTELS
Shepherds Arms Hotel (Map pp406-7; ☎ 0800 393 782, 04-472 132C; www.shepherds.co.nz; 285 Tinakori Rd; s without bathroom $75-85, d with bathroom from $129; 🅿) Tinakori Rd is a real locals' spot, a good walking-browsing-eating strip with a village feel. This charming historic pub makes an excellent base, with character-filled rooms combining the old and the new (it's worth paying extra for a larger room). Nicely topped off by a fine restaurant downstairs.

Comfort Hotel Wellington (Map pp406-7; ☎ 0800 873 553, 04-385 2153; www.comfortwellington.com; 213 Cuba St; r $150; □) We stayed in this place back when it was a dingy backpackers – my, how things have changed. It's been renovated to within an inch of its life and now sports small, modern en suite rooms, well equipped with TV, phone, iron, hairdryer etc. Online deals can see prices drop below $100 – a good price for the heart-of-Cuba location.

Kingsgate Hotel Oriental Bay (Map pp406-7; ☎ 0800 782 548, 04-385 0279; www.kingsgateoriental bay.co.nz; 73 Roxburgh St; r weekdays/weekends from $150/110; P □ □) A large, well-sited but unremarkable hotel split into two wings: the Bay wing has larger rooms with harbour views, the Roxburgh wing has smaller rooms with street views – go for the upgrade.

MOTELS

Victoria Court Motor Lodge (Map p410; ☎ 04-472 4297; www.victoriacourt.co.nz; 201 Victoria St; r $135-190; P) Our top motel choice. Friendly owners offer spotless, stylish studios and apartments with spas and cooking facilities, right in the city centre, with plenty of parking.

Halswell Lodge (Map p410; ☎ 04-385 0196; www .halswell.co.nz; 21 Kent Tce; hotel r $89, units $135-160; P) Superhandy to all the central sights, Halswell has a few options, including small, affordable hotel rooms with TV, fridge and private bathroom. The upmarket lodge suite with spa is a better option for doubles looking to splurge, and families will appreciate the two-bedroom motel units.

Apollo Lodge (Map p410; ☎ 0800 361 645, 04-385 1849; www.apollo-lodge.co.nz; 49 Majoribanks St; d $100-140; P) Within easy striking distance of Courtenay Pl, Apollo Lodge has a range of accommodation, from older-style self-contained units or architecturally designed executive suites to Edwardian-style apartments.

Other options:

Majoribanks Apartments (Map p410; 38 Majoribanks St; weekly rates from around $600) The owners of Apollo Lodge also run Majoribanks Apartments, with self-contained ex-residential flats that sleep four. These flats are usually rented on a weekly basis.

Marksman Motor Inn (Map pp406-7; ☎ 04-385 2499; www.marksmanmotel.co.nz; 40-44 Sussex St; units $110-200; P) Clean, comfortable studios and apartments. Can be a little noisy, but well positioned for airport runs.

Harbour City Motor Inn (Map pp406-7; ☎ 0800 332 468, 04-384 9809; www.harbourcitymotorinn.co.nz; 92-96 Webb St; units $95-180; P) Studio units, most with kitchens.

Top End

CityLife Wellington (Map pp406-7; ☎ 0800 368 888, 04-922 2800; www.citylifewellington.nz-hotels.com; 300 Lambton Quay; r weekdays/weekends from $300/160; P □) Guest-spoiling serviced apartments in the city centre, ranging from studios to three-bedroom apartments. Features include broadband Internet, full kitchen, CD and video player, and in-room laundry facilities. Weekend rates are super value. The vehicle entrance is from Gilmer Tce, off Boulcott St.

Museum Hotel de Wheels (Map p410; ☎ 0800 944 335, 04-802 8900; www.museumhotel.co.nz; 90 Cable St; r & apt Mon-Thu $200-300, Fri-Sun $150-270; P □) We love this place for its boutique feel: the original artwork and warm, eclectic décor make a refreshing change from homogenised business hotels. Its history sets it apart too – the 'de Wheels' part of the hotel's name refers to its amazing relocation: it was moved 120m in 1993 to vacate the space needed for construction of Te Papa. Rooms here are elegant and spacious; consider a room with balcony and harbour view, or one of the brand-new apartments in the rear wing.

Wellesley (Map pp406-7; ☎ 04-474 1308; www.thewe llesley.co.nz; 2-8 Maginnity St; r weekdays/weekends from $250/175) A great CBD choice in this price bracket, with loads of charm and impeccable service. The Wellesley was formerly a gentlemen's club and still retains the refined, clubby feel and hushed tones. There are only 13 rooms, furnished with original art, antiques and claw-foot baths. First-rate guest facilities include a gym, sauna, billiards room, superb guest lounge and excellent restaurant.

EATING

Wellington has a comprehensive array of cuisines, scattered around the city. Cuba St is a popular hunting ground for a fine feed and Courtenay Pl also has plenty of cafés, bars and restaurants. Not surprisingly, most of the quality seafood restaurants can be found on the city's waterfront.

Restaurants

Café Bastille (Map p410; ☎ 04-382 9559; 16 Majoribanks St; mains $22-27; dinner Mon-Sat) Cuisine magazine gave its top gong (2005 restaurant of the year) to this charmingly unpretentious French restaurant, but it doesn't take bookings, so it's a good idea to arrive early or expect to wait for a table. There's an emphasis on local produce, an expansive wine list and knowledgeable staff. Try long-standing favourites such as *coq au vin* before finishing with orange-caramel crepes. If you don't love the French, you will after this meal.

Logan-Brown (Map pp406-7; 04-801 5114; 192 Cuba St; dinner mains $34-40; lunch Mon-Fri, dinner nightly) Despite the neighbouring sex shops, this place oozes class and makes a great setting for a fancy-pants dinner. It's set in a former 1920s bank chamber but you don't have to break the bank to participate: the weekday lunch and pretheatre set menus ($35, to be out by 7.30pm) are top value.

Chow (Map p410; 04-382 8585; 45 Tory St; meals $10-16; lunch & dinner) This stylish eatery-bar serves pan-Asian cuisine amid '70s decor: pots of spiky plants, retro chairs and orange low-hanging lamps. Head here for yum cha lunch or a weekend, $10 lunch deals, or choose from a menu loaded with temptation (Thai chicken wrapped in banana leaf, spicy mussel fritters, Cantonese roast duck). Motel is the fabulous adjacent lounge bar.

Martin Bosley's Yacht Club Restaurant (Map pp406-7; 04-920 8302; 103 Oriental Pde; mains $26-40; lunch Mon-Fri, dinner Tue-Sat) Swish fish. The prices (and most certainly the harbour views) should leave you in no doubt that this is one of Wellington's finest restaurants. Everything is top quality, from the elegant interior and polished service to the seafood-loaded menu.

Kopi (Map p410; 04-499 5570; 103 Willis St; mains $15-20; lunch & dinner) Malaysian for 'coffee', Kopi is consistently voted the city's best Malaysian eatery, the crowds attesting to its popularity. Choose from *roti chanai* (flat, flaky bread dipped in a creamy coconut curry); curries, such as beef rendang; and

Restaurant 88 (Map pp406-7; 04-385 9088; 88 Tory St; lunch $12-15, dinner mains $18-25; brunch Sat & Sun, lunch Tue-Fri, dinner Tue-Sun) There's a wonderfully mixed menu of Kiwi and Vietnamese dishes here, served in a tropical-flavoured space filled with wooden screens, plants and lanterns. Traditionalists can enjoy lamb or steak; the more adventurous can choose from fresh, spicy dishes such as lemongrass beef salad.

nasi kandar (coconut rice). For dessert, feijoa ice cream.

Tulsi (Map p410; 04-802 4144; 135 Cuba St; lunch $6-11, dinner mains $13-19; lunch & dinner) Big, bright and contemporary Indian place with the best butter chicken in Wellington. Ready for a taste test? Choose your spice level from mild, medium, 'Kiwi hot' or 'Indian hot'. Lunch deals are excellent. For more good-value Indian options, head to Allen St, off Courtenay P..

Floriditas (Map p410; 04-381 2212; 161 Cuba St; lunch $10-16, dinner mains $17-22; lunch & dinner) From the outside this is one of Cuba St's prettiest buildings, and the interior is just as lovely, with a charming old-world European feel helped along by white tiles, velvet drapes and leather banquettes. Quality bistro fare is the order of the day.

Arbitrageur (Map pp406-7; 04-499 5530; 125 Featherston St; mains $14-28; lunch & dinner Mon-Fri, dinner Sat) The hardest thing about the chi-chi Arbitrageur experience is pronouncing the name. Everything else is terribly polished. A clever colour-coding system will help you match your meal with a drop from the extensive wine selection, and there's a menu of well-priced nibbles and meals. Live jazz Friday and Saturday night rounds off a sophisticated experience.

Fisherman's Table (Map pp406-7; 04-801 7900; 245 Oriental Pde, Oriental Bay; mains $15-26; dinner) Built over the water in the old Oriental Bay Sea Baths and with good harbour views, this family-style eatery offers reasonably priced seafood and a menu full of daggy, old-fashioned (read crumbed and deep-fried) favourites.

La Casa della Pasta (Map p410; 04-385 9057; 37 Dixon St; mains $12-19; lunch Mon-Fri, dinner daily) Straight-up, home-style Italian food is what this welcoming, no-fuss place does well – food just like your *nonna* used to make. Options include comfort-food staples such as lasagne, ravioli, tortellini and gnocchi.

One Red Dog (Map p410; 04-384 9777; 9 Blair St; mains $15-26; lunch & dinner) A bustling, upmarket brewery pub, popular for late-night weekend drinks. On offer are gourmet pizzas, pastas, calzones and salads. Families take the early dinner sitting and young 20-somethings create a fun, upbeat atmosphere.

Flying Burrito Brothers (Map p4(); 04-385 8811; cnr Cuba & Vivian Sts; mains $17-27; dinner)

AUTHOR'S CHOICE

Kai (Map p410; ☎ 04-801 5006; 21 Majoribanks St; mains $20-28; ☻ dinner Tue-Sun) On our recent visit, Kai completely charmed us. The Maori family that owns and runs this tiny, 30-seater restaurant has created a warm, welcoming atmosphere, and the small kitchen churns out delicious Maori-fusion food. The menu features a helpful glossary for those who don't know their *heihei* (chicken) from their *kuku* (mussels), and you can make a meal of platters from the land or sea, *hangi* (oven made by digging a hole and steaming food in baskets over embers in the hole; a feast of Maori food) and spiced kumara pie, accompanied by Tohu Wines (NZ's first Maori-owned wine company). If you pick the right night (Friday and Saturday, but often other nights in the week), you'll be serenaded by the restaurant's owner, playing guitar and singing Maori songs. A truly memorable place. Bookings advised.

Cafés

Wellington prides itself on its cultural heart and no literati could flourish without a decent café scene. Per capita, the city boasts more cafés than New York City. Many offer breakfast all day and a brunch menu, are licensed and open late.

Chocolate Fish (☎ 04-388 2808; 497a Karaka Bay Rd, Scorching Bay; meals $8-16; ☻ breakfast & lunch) Much is made of this café being a favourite with film stars working in Wellywood, but it's good enough without such validation. It's a colourful, quirky place in Scorching Bay, east of the city (for the scenic route, take Oriental Pde and follow it all the way around Evans Bay, a total of 13km; shortcuts through Miramar are possible). Sit outside right on the beach (good for swimming) and tuck into a bumper breakfast, perfect *panini* or hunk of cake. Expect to wait for a table on sunny weekends.

Cafe L'Affare (Map pp406-7; ☎ 04-385 9748; 27 College St; meals $6-18; ☻ breakfast & lunch, closed Sun) Bustling L'Affare does everything right. It's a massive, atmospheric café with fast service, high communal tables, a disco ball and industrial stage lights. Kids can raid the toy box while Mum downs the perfect latte. Sensational giant toasties are a bargain.

Fidel's (Map pp406-7; ☎ 04-801 6868; 234 Cuba St; meals $5-18; ☻ breakfast, lunch & dinner) Fidel's is an institution for caffeine-craving, left-wing subversives, watched over by images of Castro. Terrific eggs (any way you want 'em) are miraculously pumped from the itsy kitchen, along with some of Welly's finest muffins. Pierced, tattooed staff are studiously vague, but friendly. Open until late.

Lido (Map p410; ☎ 04-499 6666; cnr Victoria & Wakefield Sts; lunch $8-15, dinner mains $15-25; ☻ breakfast, lunch & dinner) A popular corner café with a curved window frontage and sunny aspect. Dine on the likes of Japanese-style fish cakes or a salad combining roasted vegies with potato and *chorizo*. There's live jazz Sunday night.

Espressoholic (Map p410; ☎ 04-384 7790; 128 Courtenay Pl; meals $8-18; ☻ breakfast, lunch & dinner) A serious supporter of coffee addiction is this grungy café, with chipped black tables and colourful graffiti art. Espressoholic keeps late hours (midnight or later), keeping punters happy with a good veggie selection, cool music and courtyard.

Midnight Espresso (Map p410; ☎ 04-384 7014; 178 Cuba St; meals $8-15; ☻ breakfast, lunch & dinner) This local stalwart serves food till about 2am and is an institution for paper-reading, coffee-drinking and philosophising. Dine on primarily vegetarian and vegan food among the hessian-sack art and metal sculptures.

Aunty Mena's Vegetarian Café (Map p410; ☎ 04-382 8288; 167 Cuba St; meals $9-14; ☻ lunch Tue-Sat, dinner nightly) More joy for noncarnivores: this cheap 'n' cheerful stalwart serves up veggie and vegan Malaysian and Chinese dishes. There are loads more noodle houses along Cuba St, all offering shoestring travellers spice-loaded dishes for only a few bucks.

Parade Café (Map pp406-7; ☎ 04-939 3935; 148 Oriental Pde; meals $14-23; ☻ breakfast, lunch & dinner) The outdoor deck at Parade is the perfect place to unwind over brunch or a beer; it's just a pity there's no view of the nearby water. Still, it's a minor quibble, given the laid-back atmosphere and crowd-pleasing menu.

Quick Eats

Pandoro Panetteria (Map p410; ☎ 04-385 4478; 2 Allen St; meals $1.50-7; ☻ breakfast & lunch) An aromatic Italian bakery with smooth, flavoursome coffee, savoury and sweet muffins, stuffed breads, pastry scrolls, cakes, tarts and brownies.

Crêpes a Go-Go (Map p410; ☎ 04-801 5515; 32 Courtenay Pl; meals $3.50-9.50; ☒ breakfast & lunch daily, dinner Thu-Fri) From a tiny yellow stall in the Manners Mall, a Breton batter-master whips up cheap crepes with your choice of sweet or savoury fillings.

Wholly Bagels (Map p410; Manners Mall; crepes $3.50-9.50; ☒ breakfast & lunch daily, dinner Thu-Fri; Willis & Bond Sts; bagels $1.60-8; ☒ breakfast & lunch) Authentic boiled bagels, sold 'naked' or with a selection of flavoured cream cheeses and filled with the likes of tuna salad or pastrami.

Trisha's Pies (Map pp406-7; ☎ 04-472 2336; cnr Willis & Bond Sts; bagels $1.60-8; ☒ breakfast & lunch) Great pies filled with traditional manly flavours (steak and cheese/kidney/mushroom) or something different (chicken and apricot, vegies).

Eat (Map p410; ☎ 0800 847 847; 29 Courtenay Pl; meals $6-8; ☒ lunch & dinner) 'Gourmet takeout' offering a range of juicy burgers, plus salads and a few interesting vego options if you choose to take the healthy route.

Hell (Map p410; ☎ 04-473 5149; deliveries 0800 666 111; 14 Bond St; pizzas $7-15; ☒ lunch & dinner) Demon gourmet pizzas are themed after all things evil. Try the seven deadly sins range or the vegetarian 'purgatory'. Delivery available.

Sushi takeaways (Map p410; ☎ 04-385 0290; 189 Cuba St; meals $6-8; ☒ lunch) Has superfresh, ready-to-go Japanese treats that are cheap and tasty.

Wellington Trawling Sea Market (Map pp406-7; ☎ 04-384 8461; 220 Cuba St; meals $8-14; ☒ lunch & dinner) Sells caught-that-morning fish and lip-smacking fish dinners with chips and salad, or fat burgers for nonfish fans.

Good-value food courts can be found at **Courtenay Central** (Map p410; Courtenay Pl; meals $3.50-9; ☒ lunch & dinner) or the **BNZ Centre** (Map p410; Willis St; meals $4-10; ☒ lunch).

Self-Catering
New World supermarket (City (Map p410; 279 Wakefield St; ☒ 7am-midnight); Thorndon (Map pp406-7; Molesworth St; ☒ 7am-11pm) has two convenient branches. A smaller, central branch is **New World Metro** (Map p410; 68 Willis St; ☒ 7am-11pm Mon-Fri, 8am-11pm Sat & Sun).

Commonsense Organics (Map p410; ☎ 04-384 3314; 260 Wakefield St; ☒ 9am-7pm Mon-Fri, to 6pm Sat, 10am-6pm Sun) has a wide range of organic

produce and caters for those with food intolerances

DRINKING
Wellingtonians drink, but stylishly, in low-lit bars, or, more boisterously, in Irish and microbrewery pubs. Most places serve bar snacks and/or meals; in fact, it's tricky to determine whether many of the venues listed following sit best in Eating or Drinking sections – we'd happily recommend the Matterhorn and Tasting Room as much for a meal as for a pre- or post-dinner drink.

Courtenay Pl is the nightlife centre of Wellington. Blair and Allen Sts, running off Courtenay Pl, are fertile hunting grounds for booze and music, but here it's moody, upmarket lounge bars – wear your party frock. Cuba St has plenty to keep you entertained. The following are all open nightly, unless specified. See also Live Music, p423 and Nightclubs, p423.

Matterhorn (Map p410; ☎ 04-384 3359; 106 Cuba St) In an architecturally designed space with low lighting and polished concrete floors, Matterhorn is way cool. Three bars dispense drinks to 20-somethings (try the Backyard Bellini, which does wicked things with feijoa-flavoured vodka) and the leather-bound menu reveals an array of taste sensations (lunch and seriously good dinner options, plus bar snacks). DJs at weekends spin ambient funk, and there's occasional live music.

Tasting Room (Map p410; ☎ 04-384 1159; 2 Courtenay Pl) In the thick of the action, this Monteith's-sponsored gastropub features clubby décor and leather banquettes (think city-slicker hunting lodge), but it's the antler 'chandelier' that most impressed us. If you're brave, wild game is a feature on the menu.

Brewery Bar & Restaurant (Map p410; ☎ 04-381 2282; cnr Taranaki & Cable Sts) Occupying prime water frontage in a renovated warehouse near Te Papa, the Wellington Brewing Company takes beer seriously; those brewed on-site include Sassy Red, Sultry Dark or Wicked Blonde. Enjoy the outdoor seating or leather booths, diverse clientele and moreish bar food.

Leuven (Map pp406-7; ☎ 04-499 2939; 135 Featherston St) The menu at this 'beer café' is an ode to hearty Belgian cuisine: mussels come 10 different ways, the *frites* (fries) are cooked to perfection, and all the brewing big guns are present (including Hoegaarden, Leffe, Stella and Chimay), but there's a handy list of NZ wines by the glass too.

Dockside (Map pp406-7; ☎ 04-499 9900; Queens Wharf) An upmarket, nautically themed restaurant-bar, popular for after-work tie-loosening later in the week (it's nicknamed the 'dry cleaners' on a Friday night, as it's where you come to pick up a suit). Great indoor-outdoor venue with water frontage and quality seafood.

Basement (Map p410; ☎ 04-801 5666; 21-23 Cambridge Tce) Basement is at Base Backpackers, with a happy hour from 5pm to 8pm that includes $3 pints and $2 house spirits (happy indeed). There's free pool Monday night, plus regular live bands, DJs, quiz nights, and competitions to keep everyone in high spirits.

Molly Malone's (Map p410; ☎ 04-384 2896; cnr Courtenay Pl & Taranaki St) This rousing, popular pub has Guinness and Kilkenny on tap (of course) and live music nightly. Well-priced Irish fare is served upstairs in the slightly more refined Dubliner whiskey bar and restaurant.

Backbencher (Map pp406-7; ☎ 04-472 3065; cnr Molesworth St & Sydney St East) Opposite the Beehive is the Backbencher, where 3-D puppet heads of NZ pollies are mounted, trophy-room style, and there are clever satirical cartoons on the walls. Atmosphere is casual, fun and friendly.

JJ Murphy & Co (Map p410; ☎ 04-384 9090; 119 Cuba St) A popular bar in Cuba Mall with outdoor tables. Inside it's all dark-wood booths, big barrels and plenty of pool tables. The classic pub menu is Irish-themed and there's live music Wednesday to Sunday.

Red Square (Map p410; ☎ 04-802 4244; 24 Blair St; ☼ Wed-Sat) Opulent cocktail bar with seductive leather booths, red velvet drapes and lashings of chandeliers. Sample NZ vodkas in cocktails such as the delectable 'Kiwi pash' (kiwifruit vodka plus passionfruit pulp, lime and apple juice).

Ponderosa (Map p410; ☎ 04-384 1064; 28 Blair St; ☼ Tue-Sat) Nearby is Ponderosa, a fun, intimate, Wild West–themed cocktail bar (trust us, it's better than it sounds) with tree-stump tables, cowhide cushions and mounted animal heads. Ride 'em cowboy.

Good Luck Bar (Map p410; ☎ 04-801 9950; basement, 126 Cuba St) It seems every good Welly

bar needs a theme, and this one is retro Chinese opium den. Until recently, it was too cool to have a sign – now there's a small one to help guide you downstairs to the lantern bar and live music (Tuesday and Friday) or DJs.

ENTERTAINMENT

Wellington is undisputed king of NZ's nightlife with copious clubs, bars and other insomniac refuges. It also has a vibrant performing-arts scene. Purchase tickets from **Ticketek** (Map p410; ☎ 04-384 3840; www.ticketek.co.nz) at Westpac St James Theatre or the Michael Fowler Centre.

For gig guides pick up a copy of the free weekly brochure the **Package** (www.thepackage.co.nz), available at venues, cafés and record shops around town. Entertainment concentrates around Cuba St, Edwards St and Courtenay Pl, where it all starts to go rambunctiously wrong in the early hours of the morning.

Theatre

The most active place in NZ for live theatre, Wellington's accessible performing-arts scene supports a number of professional and quality amateur companies. Reduced-price, same-day theatre tickets for some productions are often available at the visitor information centre.

Circa Theatre (Map p410; ☎ 04-801 7992; www.circa.co.nz; 1 Taranaki St; adult/stand-by $35/18) Circa's main auditorium seats 250 people, its studio seats 100. Cheap tickets are available for preview shows (the night before opening night) and stand-by tickets one hour before a show.

Downstage Theatre (Map p410; ☎ 04-801 6946; www.downstage.co.nz; cnr Courtenay Pl & Cambridge Tce; tickets $35-40) A professional theatre company with a strong presence in the Wellington theatre scene, Downstage is NZ's longest-running theatre (established in 1964). Its 250-seat auditorium also shows contemporary dance.

BATS Theatre (Map p410; ☎ 04-802 4175; www.bats.co.nz; 1 Kent Tce; tickets $15-20) This alternative theatre (and home of the Fringe; p415) has a commitment to presenting the best of NZ's cutting-edge and experimental theatre, and remaining accessible to both audiences and artists.

Michael Fowler Centre (Map p410; ☎ 04-801 4231; www.wellingtonconventioncentre.com; 111 Wakefield St)

Live Music

Bodega (Map p410; cover charge varies; 4pm-3am) Welly's longest-running live-music venue, cool Bodega plays music every night from around 10pm. Expect to hear dirty rock, Latin, soul, DJs and reggae-mor. There are 17 beers on tap and the vibe here is rockin'.

Indigo (Map p410; 04-801 6797; www.indigobar .co.nz; 1st fl, 171 Cuba St; cover charge Fri & Sat; 3pm-3am Mon-Thu, to 6am Fri & Sat) A live-music

Rialto (Map p410; 04-385 1864; www.rialto.co.nz; cnr Jervois Quay & Cable St) This cinema screens independent productions.

Reading Cinemas (Map p410; 04-801 4600; www .readingcinemas.co.nz; Courtenay Central, Courtenay Pl) Screens mainstream new-release films.

Hoyts Regent on Manners (Map p410; 04-472 5182; www.hoyts.co.nz; 73 Manners St) Screens all the latest Hollywood blockbusters.

Paramount (Map p410; 04-384 4080; www.para mount.co.nz; 25 Courtenay Pl) Shows mainly art-house movies.

Cinemas

Show times for movies are listed in the local newspapers or at http://film.wellington.net .nz. Adult tickets cost around $14, children $8, and most cinemas have a cheap day early in the week.

Embassy Theatre (Map p410; 04-384 7657; www .deluxe.co.nz; 10 Kent Tce) This grand dame was built in the 1920s and underwent major restoration in 2003 (after which it hosted the world premiere of *LOTR: The Return of the King*). It now screens mainstream films; patrons can pay a few dollars extra for deluxe leather seats. The 1st floor of the theatre is home to Blondini's, a nicely chilled jazz bar.

Other cinemas:

A huge centre with 19 venues. It has great acoustics and hosts all sorts of performances, from popular bands to the New Zealand Symphony Orchestra.

Westpac Trust St James Theatre (Map p410; 04-802 4060; www.stjames.co.nz; 77 Courtenay Pl) is a grand old heritage building that, in conjunction with its sister venue, the nearby **Opera House** (Map p410; 111-113 Manners St), is used for opera, ballet and major musical shows, plus some high-profile musicians. It provides a permanent home for the **Royal New Zealand Ballet** (www.nzballet.org.nz).

haunt with local DJs spinning experimental techno, plus 'themed' nights (but in the best possible way): rock on Tuesday, drum'n'bass Wednesday, comedy nights Thursday. A prime place to kick back with a beer and in the passing parade from the balcony overlooking Cuba St.

Blue Note (Map p410; 04-801 5007; 191 Cuba St; cover charge varies; 4pm-6am) Punters from all walks of life – gay, straight, transgender – come to the slightly seedy Blue Note to sing; Monday, Wednesday and Sunday are dedicated karaoke nights, Tuesday is jam night, and Friday and Saturday feature live bands and DJs.

Cabaret (Map p410; 382 8585; www.chow.co.nz /cabaret.html; 45 Tory St; cover charge varies; from 7pm) If, after getting your hands dirty at the venues mentioned earlier, you're looking for a more grown-up night out, head along to Cabaret, brought to you by the groovin' folks behind Chow restaurant (p419). Enjoy jazz tunes, Latin grooves or songsmiths strutting their stuff, and dine from the Chow menu. Enter via the Chow restaurant.

Nightclubs

Studio Nine (Map p410; 04-384 9976; 9 Edward St; 8pm-late Wed-Sat) A cool dance club hosting international DJs and with a fab lounge area. This is the place to head for all-night doof – make sure you bring plenty of stamina.

Sandwiches (Map p410; 04-385 7698; www.sand wiches.co.nz; 8 Kent Tce; 3pm-late Tue-Sat) Funk it up at cool-man-cool Sandwiches, a lounge bar and nightclub with live performances (jazz, electronica, funky soul) and top DJs from Wednesday to Saturday.

See also Gay & Lesbian Wellington, p415.

SHOPPING

Keeping fashionistas in the loop is the *Fashion Map* – the guide to NZ and international designers and boutique clothes shops in Wellington, and a must-have for anyone about to indulge in serious retail therapy; pick it up at the visitor information centre.

Lambton Quay is known as the Golden Mile, for its designer boutiques, speciality stores and the chance to outlay plenty of cash. For secondhand records and books, plus retro clothing and funky off-beat furniture, take a stroll along Cuba St.

Kirkcaldie & Stains (Map pp406-7; 04-472 5899; 165-177 Lambton Quay) NZ's answer to

Bloomingdale's or Harrods, Kirkcaldie & Stains is an upmarket department store that's been running since 1863.

Mainly Tramping (Map p410; ☎ 04-473 5353; Grand Arcade, 16 Willis St) For all your specialist outdoor needs, be they tramping, kayaking or mountain climbing. Staff here are knowledgeable and helpful; rental of tramping gear is available. Other stores selling outdoor equipment are found on and around Mercer St.

If you're looking for something unique to NZ, try the excellent gift shop at Te Papa museum (see the boxed text, p409), or some of the galleries outlined in the *Arts Map* (p411). **Kura Gallery** (Map p410; ☎ 04-802 4934; 19 Allen St) and neighbouring **Ora Design & Art Space** (Map p410; ☎ 04-384 4157; 23 Allen St) are worth a browse. Both support NZ, Pacific and Maori art and display beautiful sculpture, weaving, jewellery and other art media.

GETTING THERE & AWAY

Air

Wellington is an international gateway to NZ. See p722 for information on international flights. At **Wellington airport** (☎ 04-385 5100; www.wellington-airport.co.nz; ⏰ terminal closed 1.30-4am) there's an **information desk** (☎ 04-385 5123; 1st fl, Main Terminal; ⏰ 7am-8pm) in the check-in hall. There's also a currency exchange office, ATMs, storage lockers, car-rental desks, cafés and shops. Those in transit or with early flights are not permitted to stay overnight inside the airport. Departure tax on international flights is adult/child $25/10. The prices listed following are for one-way flights.

Air New Zealand (Map pp406-7; ☎ 0800 737 000, 04-474 8950; www.airnz.co.nz; cnr Lambton Quay & Grey St) offers direct domestic flights to/from Wellington to most major centres, including Auckland (from $105, up to 20 per day), Christchurch (from $85, 14 daily), Dunedin (from $120, four daily), Rotorua (from $100, five daily) and Westport (from $100, one daily).

Origin Pacific (☎ 0800 302 302; www.originpacific.co.nz) has daily direct flights to Blenheim (from $70, three daily), Nelson (from $80, six daily) and Christchurch (from $85, one or two daily).

Qantas (Map pp406-7; ☎ 0800 808 767; www.qantas.co.nz; 2 Hunter St) runs connections to/from Wellington to Auckland (from $105, seven

daily) and Christchurch (from $85, two daily).

Soundsair (☎ 0800 505 005, 03-520 3080; www.soundsair.co.nz) runs a service between Wellington and Picton ($79, six to eight daily), Wellington and Kaikoura ($125, two daily), and Wellington and Nelson ($75, one daily) via Blenheim ($50). Holders of backpacker and student cards may be eligible for discounts; there are often reductions for online bookings on the main Wellington–Picton route.

Boat

On a clear day, sailing into Wellington Harbour or navigating the Marlborough Sounds is a memorable experience. Sailing can be rough in adverse weather but the ferries are large and have lounges, cafés, bars and an information desk (some even have a movie theatre). Note that the Lynx high-speed catamaran ceased operating in April 2005.

There are two options for crossing the strait between Wellington and Picton on the South Island by boat (note that sailing times are subject to change):

Bluebridge Ferries (Map pp406-7; ☎ 0800 844 844, 04-471 6188; www.bluebridge.co.nz; adult/child $45/25) Crossing takes three hours, 22 minutes. Departs Wellington at 3am and 7pm Sunday to Friday; returns from Picton at 8am and 7pm. On Saturday departs Wellington 10am and 7pm, returns from Picton 2.30pm and 11pm. Additional sailings in peak period (December to January). Car or

---

campervan up to 6m long $120, motorbike $50, bicycle or surfboard $10.

Interislander (Map pp406–7; ☎ 0800 802 802, 04-498 3302; www.interislander.co.nz; adult/child $63/30) crossing takes three hours. There are up to five sailings per day in each direction. Regular services depart Wellington at 1.55am (except Monday), 8.45am, 10.35am, 2pm and 6.15pm; and return from Picton at 5.45am (except Monday), 10am, 1.15pm, 2.25pm and 6pm. The most flexible (and expensive) fare for a car is $150, a motorbike costs $55, and for foot passengers to take a bicycle or surfboard you'll pay an extra $10. Discount fares are often available for advance bookings. Children under two travel free.

You can book ferries at many accommodation providers, by phone, online, at travel agents and directly at individual offices.

Bluebridge is based at Waterloo Quay, not far from the train station.

Interislander services arrive and depart from the Interislander terminal, northeast of the city centre. A free shuttle-bus service is provided; the shuttle to the terminal leaves from platform 9 of the Wellington train station (where long-distance buses also depart), departing 35 minutes before each sailing. A shuttle meets all arriving ferries and takes passengers to the train station. There is a taxi stand at the terminal.

Car-hire companies will pick-up and drop-off at the ferry terminal; if you arrive outside business hours, arrangements can be made to collect your hire vehicle from the terminal car park.

Bus

Wellington is an important junction for bus travel, with buses north to Auckland and all major towns in between. **InterCity** (☎ 04-385 0520; www.intercitycoach.co.nz) and **Newmans** (☎ 04-385 0521; www.newmanscoach.co.nz) buses depart from platform 9 at the train station. Tickets are sold at the travel centre in the train station (see under Train, following).

White Star City to City (☎ 06-758 3338) has one to two buses that depart daily from Bunny St, near Downtown Wellington Backpackers, and run along the west coast of the North Island to Palmerston North (one way $22, 2¼ hours), Wanganui ($27, 3½ hours) and New Plymouth ($45, 6½ hours). Connect at Palmerston North for services to Masterton, Hastings, Napier and Gisborne.

Kiwi Traveller (☎ 0800 500 100, 04-384 7031; www.kiwitraveller.co.nz) operates a daily service

through the heart of the North Island, from Wellington north to Palmerston North (one way $27.50, 2¼ hours), National Park ($50, 5½ hours), Taupo ($60, seven hours) and Rotorua ($70, eight hours). With a ticket to your final destination, you can hop on and off along the route.

Bay Xpress (☎ 0800 422 997; www.bayxpress.co.nz) has a daily service connecting the capital with Palmerston North (one way $20, 2¾ hours) en route to Hastings ($35, 4¾ hours) and Napier ($35, five hours).

Train

Wellington train station has a **travel centre** (☎ 498 3000, ext 44324; ☒ 6.45am–4pm Mon-Fri, to 12.15pm Sat & Sun) that books and sells tickets for Tranz Scenic trains, Intercity buses, Interislander ferries, tours and more. Luggage lockers are also available at the station.

Aside from the Tranz Metro (p426) suburban trains that leave from the city, there are long-distance services operated by **Tranz Scenic** (☎ 0800 872 467; www.tranzscenic.co.nz), namely the *Overlander* (standard adult one-way fare $170, 12 hours, departs Wellington 7.25am), operating daily between Wellington and Auckland. Discounted fares are available (as low as $79). There is also the *Capital Connection* (adult one way $20, two hours, departs Wellington 5.17pm), primarily a commuter service between Wellington and Palmerston North, operating Monday to Friday only.

GETTING AROUND
To/From the Airport

The airport is 8km southeast of the city centre.

Super Shuttle (☎ 0800 748 885; www.supershuttle .co.nz) provides a door-to-door minibus service at any hour between the city and the airport for $15 for one person, $4 for each additional person in the one travel party. Shuttles meet all arriving flights.

The **Stagecoach Flyer** (☎ 0800 801 700; www .stagecoach.co.nz/flyer; airport-city $5, StarPass $9) is a local bus running between the city and a local bus running between the city and the airport, via major stops. Buses run from the city to major stops. Wellington city and Lower Hutt, calling at major stops. Buses run from the city to the airport between 5.45am and 7.45pm weekdays, 6.15am to 8.15pm weekends; and from the airport, between 6.20am and 8.20pm weekdays, 6.5(?)am to 8.50pm weekends.

A taxi between the city centre and airport costs around $20.

Bus

Wellington has an efficient local bus system. **Stagecoach** (☎ 0800 801 700; www.stagecoach.co.nz /wellington) has frequent services from 7am to 11.30pm on most routes. Most depart from the Lambton Quay interchange (beside the train station) and from the major bus stop on Courtenay Pl at the intersection with Cambridge Tce. Useful colour-coded bus route maps and timetables are available at the visitor information centre and various convenience stores around town.

Bus fares are determined by zones: there are nine zones, and the cheapest fare is $1 for rides in zone one, $2 for two zones (the maximum fare is $3.50). A Single Daytripper ticket costs $5 and allows unlimited bus travel for one day (excluding the airport bus, After Midnight buses and services to Hutt Valley). An all-day StarPass for $9 allows unlimited rides on all bus services.

The **City Circular** (⏱ 10am-4.45pm) is the name given to the distinctive bright yellow buses that take in Wellington's prime inner-city locations, making it handy for travellers wishing to see the major sights. These buses loop the city every 15 minutes, and the fare is $3 (for once around the circuit, or any part of the circuit); turn this into a good-value hop-on, hop-off service by purchasing a $5 Single Daytripper ticket.

The **After Midnight Bus Service** (☎ 0800 801 700) has buses departing from the central entertainment district (Courtenay Pl or Cuba St) at 1am, 2am and 3am Saturday and Sunday on a number of routes to the outer suburbs. Fares range from $3.50 to $7, depending on distance travelled.

Car

Wellington has a number of hire-car operators that will negotiate cheap deals, es-

pecially for longer-term rental of a couple of weeks or more, but overall rates aren't as competitive as in Auckland. Rack rates range from around $39 to $79 per day; cars are usually a few years old and in excellent condition. Some of these companies:

Ace Rental Cars (☎ 0800 535 500, 04-471 1176; www.acerentalcars.co.nz; 150 Hutt Rd) Around 1.5km north of the centre.

Apex Car Rental (Map p410; ☎ 0800 939 597, 04-385 2163; www.apexrentals.co.nz; 186 Victoria St)

Omega Rental Cars (☎ 0800 667 722, 04-472 8465; www.omegarentals.com; 96 Hutt Rd) Around 1km north of the centre.

For details about major car-hire companies such as Avis and Budget, see the Transport chapter (p732).

If you plan on travelling to both the North and South Islands it's usually a much cheaper option to return your hire car to either Picton or Wellington and pick up another after crossing the strait. This is a common practice and car-hire companies make it a painless exercise.

There are often cheap deals on car relocation from Wellington to Auckland (most renters travel in the opposite direction). A few companies offer heavy discounts on this route, with the catch being that you may only have 24 or 48 hours to make the journey.

Turners Auctions (☎ 04-587 1400; www.turners.co .nz; 120 Hutt Park Rd, Lower Hutt), not far from the Top 10 Hutt Park Holiday Park (opposite), buys and sells used cars by auction. Also check noticeboards at backpackers for cheap deals.

Taxi

Taxi ranks are conveniently placed around town (eg Cambridge Tce, just near Courtenay Pl; outside Te Papa museum). Taxi companies include **Wellington Combined Taxis** (☎ 0800 384 444) and **Wellington City Cab** (☎ 0800 388 8000).

Train

Tranz Metro (☎ 0800 801 700; www.tranzmetro.co .nz) operates five suburban electric train routes. Trains run frequently from 6am to midnight, departing from Wellington train station. These routes are: Johnsonville, via Ngaio and Khandallah; Paraparaumu, via Porirua, Plimmerton and Paekakariki; Mel

METLINK

Metlink (☎ 0800 801 700; www.metlink .org.nz) is the new name for the Greater Wellington public transport network, covering all bus and train services in Wellington, Porirua, the Hutt Valley, Kapiti Coast and the Wairarapa. Phone the service centre for help with planning trips in the region, or check the website, which lists all relevant timetables and fares.

ling, via Petone; and the Hutt Valley, calling at Featherston, Carterton and Masterton. Timetables are available from many convenience stores, the train station, visitor information centre or online.

A useful online resource is www.visithutt city.org.nz.

HUTT VALLEY

pop 110,000

The Hutt River acts as the western boundary for land-starved Wellington's dormitory cities, Lower Hutt and Upper Hutt. Apart from some attractive forest parks for picnics and a few museums, they are fairly suburban. Both cities are easily reached by train or bus from Wellington.

Sights

Lower Hutt is home to the waterfront **Petone Settlers Museum** (☎ 04-568 8373; www.petoneset tlers.org.nz; The Esplanade; admission by donation; ✆ noon-4pm Tue-Fri, 1-5pm Sat & Sun), with stories of migration and settlement in the area. The **Dowse Art Museum** (☎ 04-570 6500; www.dowse.org .nz; 35 Laings Rd, Lower Hutt) is a showcase for NZ art, craft and design. At the time of research the Dowse was closed for major redevelopment; it's expected to reopen in February 2007 (call or check the website for opening hours).

The drive journeying from Upper Hutt to Waikanae (on the Kapiti Coast) along the windy, scenic Akatarawa Rd passes the 10-hectare **Staglands Wildlife Reserve** (☎ 04-526 7529; www.staglands.co.nz; adult/child $12/6; ✆ 10am-5pm) where the rare blue duck has been successfully bred. It's 17km from SH2, 20km from SH1.

Days Bay and **Eastbourne** are to the south of the Hutt Valley and make a great afternoon excursion (see p412).

Rimutaka Forest Park is 45 minutes' drive east of Wellington. Catchpool Valley, 14km south of Wainuiomata, is the most popular entrance to the park and there's a **DOC visitors centre** (☎ 04-564 8551), just off Coast Rd. Further on from the visitors centre is a **camping area** (adult/child $8/4) in a delightful setting.

Sleeping

Harcourt Holiday Park (☎ 04-526 7400; www.har courtholidaypark.co.nz; 45 Akatarawa Rd, Upper Hutt; unpowered/powered sites per 2 people $22/25, cabins & tourist flats $35-70, motel units $85) A well-designed park 35km northeast of Wellington, just off SH2 – from Wellington it's a 30-minute drive. The park is set in native bushland with a river nearby. Facilities aren't as numerous as the Top 10 Hutt Park, but the location is certainly prettier.

Top 10 Hutt Park Holiday Park (☎ 0800 488 872, 04-568 5913; www.huttpark.co.nz; 95 Hutt Park Rd, Seaview, Lower Hutt; sites per 2 people $33, cabins $52-64, units/motel $98/15; ☐) This busy park is 13km northeast of Wellington. Its family-friendly facilities are excellent, with three communal kitchens, games room, playground, spa etc, but its industrial and inconvenient location detracts. It's a 15-minute drive from the ferry (follow the signs off SH2 for Petone and Seaview), or take any bus bound for Eastbourne (81, 83 and 85).

KAPITI COAST

With striking, quiet beaches and water that begs to be swum in (depending on your constitution), the Kapiti Coast is a summer playground of the city, as well as a suburban extension of Wellington. The region takes its name from large Kapiti Island, a bird and marine sanctuary 5km offshore from Paraparaumu. Tararua Forest Park, in the Tararua Range, forms a stunning backdrop to the coastline along its length and also has some accessible day walks and longer tramps.

A visit to the Kapiti Coast is an easy and popular day trip from Wellington but if you're after a few restful days or are on your way further north, there are some quality accommodation options for stopovers. Pick up a copy of the *Kapiti Coast Arts Guide* from the visitor information centres if you're interested in visiting the region's many galleries, artists and studios.

Orientation & Information

The Kapiti Coast stretches 30km along the west coast from Paekakariki (41km north of Wellington) to Otaki (74km north of Wellington). Most towns have two settlements, one along the highway and another by the water. Paraparaumu is the most built-up town on the coast but still runs at a slow pace, especially by the beach.

The most comprehensive visitor information centres are at Otaki (p431) and Paraparaumu (opposite). Useful websites for the region are www.naturecoast.co.nz and www.kapiti.org.nz.

Getting There & Around

Getting to the west coast from Wellington is a breeze: it's on the major route (SH1) north from Wellington and regular use by commuters means that there are convenient transport options in place. By car, it's about 45 minutes from Wellington to Paraparaumu and an hour to Otaki, much of it by motorway.

For comprehensive timetable information, contact **Metlink** (☎ 0800 801 700; www.metlink.org.nz).

BUS

InterCity (☎ 04-385 0520; www.intercitycoach.co.nz) has buses between Wellington and Palmerston North (one way $31, 2¼ hours, five or six daily), stopping at Paekakariki ($20, 40 minutes), Paraparaumu ($21, 45 minutes) and Otaki ($24, 1¼ hours).

The daily services into/out of Wellington run by White Star City to City, Kiwi Traveller and Bay Express (see p425) also stop in major towns on the Kapiti Coast en route to points further north.

From the commercial heart of Paraparaumu (on SH1), local buses 71, 72 and 73 run down to the beach, and bus 70 heads to Otaki, calling at the highway settlement and the beach.

TRAIN

Tranz Metro (☎ 0800 801 700; www.tranzmetro.co.nz) commuter trains between Wellington and the coast are easier and more frequent than buses. There are services between Wellington and Paraparaumu (one way $8, 55 minutes, generally half-hourly between 6am and 11pm), stopping at Paekakariki ($7). Monday to Friday off-peak fares (9am to 3pm) are $2 cheaper.

Tranz Scenic's long-distance *Overlander* train connecting Wellington and Auckland stops at Paraparaumu, while the weekday-only, peak-hour *Capital Connection* travelling between Wellington and Palmerston North stops at Paraparaumu, Waikanae and Otaki. See p425 for details of these services.

PAEKAKARIKI

pop 1730

Paekakariki is a tiny, friendly seaside village spread along a lovely stretch of often-deserted black-sand beach, just two blocks from the train station and the highway. Paekakariki is well within striking distance of Wellington, 41km to the south, and is a relaxing place to chill out.

Queen Elizabeth Park (☼ 8am-dusk) is a popular 650-hectare area alongside the beach, with plenty of space for swimming, walking, cycling and picnicking.

About 5km north of Paekakariki at MacKay's Crossing, just off SH1, the **Tramway Museum** (☎ 04-292 8361; wellingtontrams.org.nz; Queen Elizabeth Park, MacKay's Crossing; admission free, tram rides adult/child/family $4/2/10; ☼ 11am-4.30pm Sat & Sun, daily 26 Dec-Jan) has restored wooden trams that ran in Wellington until its tram system was shut down in 1964. A 2km track runs from the museum through Queen Elizabeth Park and down to the beach.

Stables in the Park (☎ 04-292 8787; Queen Elizabeth Park, MacKay's Crossing) offers horse-riding opportunities from its base behind the Tramway Museum. Prices range from $10 for a 10-minute ride (perfect for children) to $45 for a one-hour ride through Queen Elizabeth Park and down to the beach. You'll generally find the stables staffed on weekends, but it's best to call ahead if you're interested in the one-hour tours (weekday trips can be arranged).

Sleeping & Eating

Paekakariki Backpackers (☎ 04-902 5967; www.wellingtonbeachbackpackers.co.nz; 11 Wellington Rd; dm $21, tw & d with/without bathroom $58/51; ☐) What a place! Set on a steep hill covered with a beautiful garden, dorms have sea and sunset views and there's a spa pool on the lower deck of the garden. It's a small, friendly and homey place and there's free use of boogie boards. Rooms with private bathroom and deck are backpacking luxury; ask the owners about their plans to develop yurts in the bush for travellers (really).

Paekakariki Holiday Park (☎ 04-292 8292; paekariki.holiday.park@xtra.co.nz; Wellington Rd; per 2 people sites $24, cabins & flats $42-64) A large and well-maintained park with individually hedged sites. It's roughly 1.6km north of the township at the southern entrance to Queen Elizabeth Park, a mere 200m from the beach.

Paekakariki Café (☎ 04-292 8860; 7 Beach Rd; brunch $5-16, dinner $19-27; ☑ breakfast & lunch Wed-Mon, dinner Tue-Sat) The perfect small-town café: a welcoming space with green-velvet and wrought-iron chairs and exhibitions of local artists. Early-risers can enjoy a fine caffeine fix; night-time visitors will dine on delicious, innovative Kiwi cuisine.

Salt-tea-Towers (☎ 04-292 8899; cnr Cecil & Tilley Rds; meals $3-13; ☑ dinner Tue-Sun, lunch Sat & Sun) An excellent fish 'n chipper with kumara chips, oysters, scallops and burgers.

PARAPARAUMU

pop 6835

Relaxing Paraparaumu is the principal town of the Kapiti Coast, forming a suburban satellite of Wellington, which is within commuting distance. The beautiful beach is the coast's most developed, and boat trips to Kapiti Island depart from here. (Note that you need to arrange permits for these trips in Wellington; see Kapiti Island, p430.)

The name Paraparaumu is rather a mouthful, so locally it's usually shortened to 'para-par-am', a corruption of the original. The correct pronunciation is 'pah-ra-pah-ra-oo-moo'; the name means 'Scraps from an Oven' and is said to have originated when a Maori war party attacked the settlement and found only scraps of food in the oven.

Orientation & Information

Coastlands Shoppingtown, the hub of Paraparaumu's highway settlement, is easily spotted on the main highway; left as you head into town from Wellington. Three kilometres west along Kapiti Rd (just past Coastlands) is Paraparaumu Beach; Seaview Rd is the main road for Paraparaumu's beach settlement. Sleeping and eating options are most atmospheric (and plentiful) by the beach.

Coastlands has all the services you'll need: banks with ATMs, post office, supermarkets, cinema. The small, helpful **visitor information centre** (☎ 04-298 8195; paraparaumu@naturecoast.co.nz; Coastlands Pde, SH1; ☑ 9am-5pm Mon-Fri, 10am-3pm Sat & Sun) is slap-bang in the middle of the Coastlands car park.

Sights & Activities

Paraparaumu Beach, with its beachside park, great swimming and other water activities, is the main attraction.

Paraparaumu Beach Golf Club (☎ 04-902 8200; www.paraparaumubeachgolfclub.co.nz; 376 Kapiti Rd; 9/18 holes $45/90) is ranked among NZ's best courses, and has played host to the NZ Golf Open on a number of occasions (most recently in 2002, when Tiger Woods competed). Visitors are welcome and you can book online; clubs, carts and shoes can be hired.

On SH1, 2km north of Paraparaumu, the **Lindale Centre** (☎ 04-297 0916; www.lindale.co.nz; farm walk adult/child/family $8/5/22; ☑ 9am-5pm) is a large tourist complex where you'll find the Lindale Farm Park, with Saturday and Sunday farm shows, farm walks and speciality food shops selling the region's renowned cheese, olive oil, honey and ice cream – definitely worth a taste. There's a farmers market held here on Saturday morning.

Another kilometre or so north, just off SH1, the **Southward Car Museum** (☎ 04-297 1221; www.southward.org.nz; Otaihanga Rd; adult/child $7/2.50; ☑ 9am-4.30pm) has one of the largest collections of antique and unusual cars in Australasia.

Kapiti Four x 4 Adventure (☎ 0800 368 794, 04-299 0020; www.kapitifourx4.co.nz; Maungakotukutuku Rd) can take you out trailblazing on quad bikes through 18,000 hectares of native wilderness. Prices range from $70 for one hour to $250 for a full day. The company is south of Paraparaumu, off SH1 (take Waterfall Rd); you can arrange transport to the site when you book.

Sleeping

Barnacles Seaside Inn (☎ 0800 555 856, 04-902 5856; www.seasideyha.co.nz; 3 Marine Pde; dm/s/tf $20/35/80; tw & d $44-54; ☐) Opposite the Paraparaumu Beach, Barnacles has wonderful YHA accommodation in a homely 1920s heritage building. Each cosy room is individually decorated with antique dressers and has a sink and heater; some have electric blankets and sea views.

Ocean Motel (☎ 0508 668 357, 04-902 6424; www.oceanmotel.co.nz; 42-44 Ocean Rd; r $70-130) There's no view here (the beach is a short walk away), but there is a range of spacious, no-surprises units, some with cooking facilities and/or spa. Top value on a quiet street.

Copperfield Seaside Motel (☎ 0800 666 414, 04-902 6414; www.seasidemotel.co.nz; 7-13 Seaview Rd; r $86-135) No spookily coiffed magicians here, just an attractively updated Best Western not far from the beach. Accommodation ranges from studios to two-bedroom apartments with full kitchen and balcony. Most units have a spa.

Eating

The beachside park is ideal for picnics, and takeaway outlets will oblige with perfect picnic fodder. Fashionable, latte-loaded cafés line Marine Pde, most offering pavement seating. The following options are in the beach area.

Maclean Street Fish Supply (☎ 04-298 5041; Maclean St; meals $7.50-14; ☯ lunch & dinner) Battering anything from tinned pineapple to fresh, plump scallops, Maclean's does a roaring trade. All meals come wrapped in paper and a serving of the fat, hand-cut chips is essential.

Burger Wisconsin (☎ 04-902 8743; 32 Marine Pde; burgers $7.50-11.50; ☯ dinner nightly, lunch Sat & Sun) A NZ chain whipping up burgers that satisfy the most deep-seated cravings. Buns are filled with traditional or gourmet fillings, including veggie options.

Ambrosia (☎ 04-298 9898; 10 Seaview Rd; lunch $9-24, dinner mains $25-30; ☯ breakfast & lunch Tue-Sun, dinner Tue-Sat) Some Wellingtonians thinks it's worth the drive to Paraparam for this place alone, and who are we to argue? Ambrosia offers superb food in a sleek, contemporary setting. The $20 lunch (Tuesday to Friday) is top value.

KAPITI ISLAND

About 10km long and 2km wide, Kapiti Island is the coastline's dominant feature. Since 1897 the island has been a protected reserve. It's a special place and many bird species that are now rare or extinct on the mainland still thrive on the island. All visitors receive an introductory talk; guided walks are also available ($15). You need to bring your own lunch with you.

Access is limited to 50 people per day and it's essential that you obtain a permit. Book a permit (adult/child $9/4.50) at Wellington's DOC (p408) up to three months in advance – in person, by phone or via email (kapiti.island@doc.govt.nz). During summer DOC recommends booking up to one month in advance for a weekday visit, two months for a weekend visit. You can also organise permits with the Paraparaumu visitor information centre (p429) but you must give at least a day's notice.

Transport is booked separately from the permit (arrange your permit before you book a boat trip). There are two commercial operators licensed to take visitors to the island. They both run to/from Paraparaumu Beach daily; departures are between 9am and 9.30am, returning between 3pm and 4pm (phone the local number in the morning to confirm weather and departure time). Both companies can arrange a local shuttle between Wellington and Paraparaumu Beach:

Kapiti Marine Charter (☎ 0800 433 779, 04-297 2585; www.kapitimarinecharter.co.nz; adult/child under 5/child $35/2/20)

Kapiti Tours (☎ 0800 527 484, 04-237 7965; www.kapititours.co.nz; adult/child under 5/child $35/2/20)

WAIKANAE
pop 6930

About 5km north of Paraparaumu at Waikanae is the turn-off to **Nga Manu Nature Reserve** (☎ 04-293 4131; www.ngamanu.co.nz; Ngarara Rd; adult/child/family $10/4/20; ☯ 10am-5pm), a great 15-hectare bird sanctuary featuring picnic areas, barbecues, bush walks and a nocturnal house with kiwi, owls and tuatara, eel feeding and guided tours. To reach the reserve, turn seawards from SH1 onto Te Moana Rd and then right down Ngarara Rd, following the signs; the sanctuary is 3.5km from the turn-off.

OTAKI
pop 5650

The sprawling, unremarkable town of Otaki is primarily a gateway to the Tararua Range. It has a strong Maori history and influence: the little town has nine *marae* (meeting houses) and a Maori college. The historic Rangiatea Church, built under the guidance of Ngati Toa chief Te Rauparaha nearly 150 years ago, was tragically burnt to the ground in 1995 but has been rebuilt. This was the original burial site of Te Rauparaha.

Orientation & Information

Most services, including the train station where buses stop, are on SH1. The main centre of Otaki, with the post office and other shops, is 2km seawards on Tasman Rd. Three kilometres further on the same road brings you to Otaki's windswept beach. Note that the telephone area code in Otaki is ☎ 06, not ☎ 04 like the rest of the Kapiti region.

The **visitor information centre** (☎ 06-364 7620; otaki@naturecoast.co.nz; Centennial Park, SH1; ☑ 9am-5pm Mon-Fri, 10am-4pm Sat & Sun) is just south of the main roundabout.

Activities

Two kilometres south of Otaki, scenic Otaki Gorge Rd heads inland from SH1 and leads 19km (5km unsealed) to **Otaki Forks**, the main western entrance to **Tararua Forest Park**. Otaki Forks has picnic, swimming and camping areas (sites per adult/child $4/2), and there are bush walks from 30 minutes to 3½ hours in the immediate area; longer tracks lead to huts. The visitor information centre sells detailed maps and knowledgeable staff can give information and advice about the walks. Ask at DOC in Wellington (p408) for advice on longer tracks in the park. You can walk across the Tararua Range, but must bring adequate clothing and be well equipped and prepared for adverse weather; be sure to sign the intentions book.

Sleeping & Eating

Otaki Oasis Backpackers (☎ 06-364 6860; www.otakioasis.co.nz; 33 Rahui Rd; dm $24, d $55-75; ☐ ☑) The Oasis is a friendly organic hobby farm on the inland side of the railway tracks. There's a small but adequate backpackers lodge next to the house; cooked breakfasts and dinners can be arranged, and you can help yourself to the produce of the plentiful fruit trees. Horse-riding lessons and treks are also available.

Byron's Resort (☎ 0800 800 122, 06-364 8121; www.byronsresort.co.nz; 20 Tasman Rd; unpowered/powered sites per 2 people $23/25, tourist flats & motels $75-105; ☐ ⓐ) An old-school family-focused resort by the beach. It's home to Byron Brown's restaurant and bar (meals $15 to $24, open nightly), a pool, spa, sauna, gym, tennis court and playgrounds.

Red House Café (☎ 06-364 3022; 385 SH1, Te Horo; meals $6-25; ☑ breakfast & lunch daily, dinner Thu-Sat) The pick of highway pit stops is this attention-grabbing café at Te Horo, about 5km south of Otaki – you'll know it by its fire engine red exterior. Inside it's all warm polished wood, with all-day breakfasts, a cabinet full of snacks and a blackboard menu on offer.

THE WAIRARAPA

The large region east and northeast of Wellington is known as the Wairarapa, named after Lake Wairarapa (Shimmering Waters), a shallow but vast 8000-hectare lake.

This region is principally a sheep-raising district – it boasts three million sheep within a 16km radius of Masterton, the region's main town. It also features the Pukaha Mt Bruce National Wildlife Centre, wineries at Martinborough and tramping tracks and camping areas in regional and forest parks. The Wairarapa region, particularly around Martinborough and Greytown, is popular with weekending Wellingtonians, and a strong foodie culture has sprung up alongside the countless restored cottages for rent.

The winding route through the Wairarapa, along SH2, is a mountainous, pleasant alternative to busy SH1 on the west coast.

See www.wairarapanz.com for info about the region. Note that the telephone area code over here on the east coast is ☎ 06, not ☎ 04 like the rest of the Wellington region.

Getting There & Away

From Wellington, **TranzMetro** (☎ 0800 801 700; www.tranzmetro.co.nz) has trains to Masterton (one way $13; 1½ hours, five to six on weekdays and two at weekends), calling at Featherston and Carterton. Without your own set of wheels, you then have to rely on local bus services to reach popular destinations such as Greytown and Martinborough. The number listed here can give information on train and bus links.

Tranzit Coachlines (☎ 0800 471 227, 06-377 1227) has a bus between Masterton and Palmerston North (one way $19, 1¾ hours, one daily), plus a few daily services (bus 200) between Featherston station and Masterton via Greytown and Carterton.

Wairarapa Coach Lines (☎ 0800 666 355, 06-308 9352; www.yellow.co.nz/site/wairarapacoachlinesandlimousines) operates buses between Featherston and Martinborough (one way $5, 15 minutes, three to five daily) and between Masterton and Martinborough ($6, 1½ hours, one to three daily).

Without your own wheels, it may be easier to take a tour out of Wellington. Hammond's Scenic Tours (p415) runs full-day tours that visit Cape Palliser and Martinborough; Wellington Rover (p415) offers tours taking in Patuna Farm, glow-worm caves, a local vineyard and Martinborough. **Tranzit Coachlines** (☎ 0800 471 227; www.tranzitcoachlines .co.nz) has two Wairarapa tour options; these can be joined from Wellington or from any of the main towns of the region. The Gourmet Wine Escape ($95/80 from Wellington/ Greytown) visits four Martinborough vineyards and includes tastings and lunch. The Natural Escape ($95/90 from Wellington/ Greytown) visits Pukaha Mt Bruce National Wildlife Centre plus various attractions in Masterton.

GREYTOWN

A number of rural communities line SH2, each with a minor attraction or two and varying degrees of appeal. Greytown has spruced itself up nicely over recent years and is the pick of the towns: Wellingtonians descend over the weekends, filling up its pretty rental cottages, high-quality eateries and numerous boutiques and galleries. Check out www .greytown.co.nz for more information.

Greytown was the country's first planned inland town and intact examples of Victorian architecture line the main street. The quaint **Cobblestones Village Museum** (☎ 06-304 9687; 169 Main St; www.cobblestonesmuseum.org.nz; adult/child $2.50/1; ☻ 9am-4pm Mon-Sat, 10am-4.30pm Sun) is an early settlers museum. Don't miss **Schoc Chocolate** (☎ 06-304 8960; www.chocolate therapy.com; Main St; ☻ 10am-5pm Mon-Fri, 10.30am-5pm Sat & Sun), in a 1920s cottage at the entrance to Cobblestones. Schoc produces heavenly choccies in intriguing flavours (it's bizarre how well lavender, Earl Grey tea and sweet basil flavours work in the hands of these choc-magicians).

Sleeping & Eating

Camping ground (☎ 06-304 9837; Kuratawhiti St; unpowered/powered sites per 2 people $13/15) This basic camping ground is scenically located in the park.

Greytown Hotel (☎ 06-304 9138; www.greytown -hotel.co.nz; 33 Main St; s/d $50/80) Purported to be the oldest pub in NZ, dating from 1860. In its favour are decent pub rooms (shared facilities) and a cooked breakfast in the morning. However, on our most recent visit, cleaning standards were sloppy at best.

Still, the place rates a mention as the cheapest lodgings in town. Simple bar meals ($3 to $12) are served Tuesday to Sunday.

Oak Estate Motor Lodge (☎ 06-304 8187; www .oakestate.co.nz; cnr SH2 & Hospital St; r $120-175) Has stylish self-contained units just south of town.

White Swan (☎ 06-304 8894; www.thewhiteswan .co.nz; Main St; r $139-259) Painted baby blue and easily the most elegant boutique accommodation in the region. Each of the seven rooms in the original building is individually decorated, and there are cheaper garden studios and suites. It's well worth popping in for a drink or meal, to unwind on the breezy veranda or in the lovely Lilac Dining Room (daytime menu $8.50 to $18.50, dinner mains $25 to $32).

Saluté (☎ 06-304 9825; 83 Main St; lunch $9-17, dinner mains $16-30; ☻ lunch Tue-Sun, dinner Tue-Sat, brunch Sat & Sun) Superpopular restaurant serving gourmet pizzas, *mezze* (small dishes) and other meals to an appreciative crowd. The menu is inspired by Middle Eastern and Mediterranean cuisines.

French Baker (☎ 06-304 8873; 81 Main St; ☻ 8am-4pm Tue-Sun) Stop in here for *tres* authentic pastries, gourmet breads and tarts, and kick-startin' espresso.

MARTINBOROUGH

Martinborough, with its many vineyards, is a prime 'minibreak' destination and the centre for tourism in the Wairarapa. At weekends, Gucci replaces gumboots as gourmands dine in the excellent restaurants, sniff the pinot, and lap up the luxurious boutique accommodation. It's best to time an overnight visit for midweek, when accommodation is cheaper (although many restaurants are closed Monday and Tuesday).

Orientation & Information

Martinborough is arrowed off the SH2 at both Featherston and Greytown, and is about 20km from each town. The helpful **visitor information centre** (☎ 06-306 9043; martin borough@wairarapanz.com; 18 Kitchener St; ☻ 9am-5pm Mon-Fri, 10am-4pm Sat & Sun) is full of brochures and information.

Sights & Activities

Nearly 40 small, often family-owned **wineries** are scattered around the town and are detailed in the free *Martinborough &*

Wairarapa Wine Trail brochure and map. Although the region is small in production terms, many of NZ's finest wines originate here and the region is particularly known for its pinot noir and sauvignon blanc. Read up on the wineries at www.winesfrom martinborough.com.

You can sample and purchase many wines under one gabled roof at the **Martinborough Wine Centre** (☎ 06-306 9040; www.martinborough winecentre.co.nz; 6 Kitchener St; ☒ 9am-5pm), which is also a food shop selling local produce. Its **Village Café** (meals $3.50-16.50; ☒ breakfast & lunch) serves light meals, cheese platters and wine by the glass. A local growers market is held here every Sunday.

A great way to tour the wineries is by bike, and the flat landscape makes for puff-free touring. **Christina Estate Vineyard** (☎ 06-306 8920; Puruatanga Rd; ☒ 8.30am-6pm) has bicycles for hire, costing for an hour/half day/full day $15/25/35.

Tours

Bookings are essential for all the following activities.

McLeods Quad Adventures (☎ 0800 494 335, 06-306 8846; www.mcleodsadventures.co.nz; 90min rides $100) Operates guided quad-bike rides around its hill-country farmland. Full training is provided, and kids are welcome to ride pillion.

Patuna Farm Adventures (☎ 06-306 9966; www.patunafarm.co.nz) Offers horse treks (from $30), a challenging pole-to-pole rope course (from $15), and a four-hour guided walk through native bush and a limestone gorge around the impressive Patuna Chasm Walkway ($15). The walkway is open late October until Easter; other activities operate year-round.

Wet N Wild (☎ 06-306 8252; www.wetnwild.co.nz) Can take you jetboating ($55), kayaking (from $45) and trout fishing ($250 for two people), with all gear supplied. It also offers vineyard tours ($60) and can tailor-make tours combining two or more of these activities.

Festivals & Events

Martinborough is famous for its **Toast Martinborough Wine, Food & Music Festival** (☎ 06-306 9183; www.toastmartinborough.co.nz), held annually on the third Sunday in November. This wine-tasting extravaganza sees Martinborough swell by around 11,000 wine-swillers. Local winemakers save vintages to be tasted specifically for the festival and around 8500L of wine is consumed over the day. Book well ahead if you want to participate.

Sleeping

The visitor information centre has a long list of B&Bs, farmstays and self-contained cottages in the area, and will book them for you. Cottages, in keeping with the weekend getaway theme, are available in town and the surrounding area; these average around $140 for two people. Budget-minded travellers take note: there is finally some accommodation joy in Martinborough.

Martinborough Village Camping (☎ 06-306 8919; www.martinboroughcamping.com; cnr Princess & Dublin St; sites per 2 people $25) A much-needed revamp has turned this campground, surrounded by grapevines, into an appealing patch of green. It boasts shady trees, a brand-new kitchen and amenities block, and the town pool as its neighbour. There are plans for cabins in the near future.

Kate's Place (☎ 06-306 9935; www.katesplace.co.nz; 7 Cologne St; dm $25-30, d $80; ☐) Kate's is a cosy, affordable homestay-backpackers, with a welcoming owner and a laid-back air. There are two dorms with new, solid bunks and extrawide mattresses; the airy double room has its own bathroom.

Claremont (☎ 0800 809 162, 06-306 9162; www.the claremont.co.nz; 38 Regent St; d $110-150, apt sleeping 4 $235) In a pretty, peaceful setting off Jellicoe St, the Claremont has older two-storey, self-contained units in great nick, plus sparkling new studios with spa, and stunning two-bedroom apartments, all at reasonable rates (specials often available for winter and/or midweek stays). Barbecues, bike hire and a babysitting service are bonuses.

Martinborough Hotel (☎ 06-305 9350; http://mar tinborough-hotel.co.nz; The Square; r incl breakfast $275-355) Grand old hotel on the main square that's been magnificently restored and is now home to 16 spacious, luxurious rooms, each individually decorated with style and flair. All open onto either a wide veranda or pretty courtyard garden. Downstairs the lively Settlers Bar (meals $5 to $18) serves posh pub grub and local wines by the glass, and the adjacent Bistro! (mains $29 to $32) has an innovative menu and terrific wine list.

Eating & Drinking

Eating and drinking is what Martinborough's all about, with award-winning restaurants and gourmet cafés, delicatessens and food shops. The unmissable Martinborough

Hotel (see earlier) is the best place to join the locals for a drink.

Est Wine Bar & Eatery (06-306 9665; The Square; lunch $9-15, dinner mains $23-28; dinner Wed-Sun, lunch Sat & Sun) A sophisticated option that wouldn't be at all out of place in the Big Smoke. Weekend lunches can be a selection of tapas or simple fish and chips; at night the kitchen struts its stuff.

Circus (06-306 9442; 34 Jellicoe St; meals $4-17; 3pm-late Wed-Sun) Take in an art-house flick in this boutique cinema (movie $14) before adjourning to the sleek café-bar, where you can critique the film over a bottle of something local.

Martinborough Beer & Ales (06-306 8310; New York St; noon-7pm Fri-Mon) If all that wine is giving you a headache, maybe beer is the answer? Join the locals bellying up to the bar at this boutique brewery, and be sure to sample the award-winning White Rock wheat beer.

WAIRARAPA COAST

The Wairarapa Coast from Palliser Bay to Castlepoint is one of the most remote and intriguing coasts in the North Island. The road to **Cape Palliser** is very scenic, hemmed in by the sea and the mountains of the Aorangi Range. It also offers grand views across to the South Island, a spectacular sight in winter when the far-off hills are cloaked in snow. On the way, you pass the Wairarapa wetlands and the Spit at Lake Onoke, both good bird-watching sites. This coast is also the best place around Wellington for surfing.

The **Putangirua Pinnacles**, formed by rain washing silt and sand away and exposing the underlying bedrock, stand like giant organ pipes. Accessible by a track near the car park on Cape Palliser Rd, it's a two-hour return walk along a streambed to the pinnacles, or take the three-hour loop track, which takes in the hills and coastal views.

Not far to the south is the archetypal fishing village of **Ngawi**. The first thing you'll notice is the old bulldozers pulling the fishing boats ashore. Continue on to the Cape Palliser **seal colony**, the North Island's largest breeding area. Whatever you do in your quest for a good photo, don't get between the seals and the sea. If you block off their escape route they're likely to have a go at you!

There are 250 steps up to the Cape Palliser **lighthouse**, from where there are even more breathtaking views of the South Island on a clear day.

Castlepoint, 68km from Masterton, with its reef and the lofty 162m-high Castle Rock, is an awesome place, with protected swimming and plenty of walking tracks. There is an easy 30-minute return walk across the reef to the lighthouse; over 70 species of fossil shells are in the rock. Another one-hour walk goes to a huge limestone cave (take a torch), or take the 1½-hour track from Deliverance Cove to Castle Rock. Keep well away from the lower reef when there are heavy seas.

The visitor information centre in Martinborough (p432) can help with accommodation options in the Lake Ferry and Cape Palliser area, which include camping grounds and holiday homes for rent.

MASTERTON
pop 19,500

The main town of the Wairarapa is Masterton but Martinborough is a nicer option to use as a base for exploring the region. Masterton's main claim to fame is the international **Golden Shears** (www.goldenshears.co.nz) competition, held annually during the first week of March. Over three days sheep-shearing is raised to the level of sport and spectators can experience a slice of rural life.

Orientation & Information

State Highway 2 runs through the centre of town. From the south SH2 is named High St, which is then named Chapel St. Queen St runs parallel to High/Chapel St, one block east. Another block east is Dixon St, home to the town's prime attractions.

The town's **visitor information centre** (06-370 0900; www.wairarapanz.com; 316 Queen St; 9am-5pm Mon-Fri, 10am-4pm Sat & Sun) is the place to head to for info on the Wairarapa.

Sights

The 32-hectare **Queen Elizabeth Park** (Dixon St) is the perfect place to stretch your legs, with its bird aviaries, small duck-filled lake, fabulous children's playgrounds and miniature railway. Opposite the park is **Aratoi – Wairarapa Museum of Art & History** (06-370 0001; http://aratoi.org.nz; cnr Bruce & Dixon Sts; admission free, donations welcome; ☺10am-4.30pm), displaying the art and cultural heritage of the region.

Next to Aratoi is the new **Shear Discovery** (☎05-378 8008; www.sheardiscovery.co.nz; Dixon St; adult/child/family $5/2/10; ☺10am-4pm), housed in two historic woolsheds and dedicated to the sheep-shearing and wool-production industries. No sheep-shagging jokes, OK?

Sleeping & Eating

Empire Lodge (☎06-377 1902; info@empirelodge.co.nz; 94 Queen St; backpackers dm/s/d $20/25/40, hotel s/d $60/70; ☐) A well-sited, old-school budget hotel and backpackers, complete with communal kitchen, TV room and views of the Tararua Range from the outdoor deck. Hotel rooms are good value, with bathroom and TV.

Discovery Motor Lodge (☎0800 188 515, 06-378 7745; www.discovery.co.nz; 210 Chapel St; r $99-165; ☐) Midrange motels line the highway, particularly in the southern part of town. Discovery is a cut above the rest with its modern, well-equipped studio, one- and two-bedroom units, plus swimming pool.

Café Strada (☎06-378 8450; 232 Queen St; meals $4.50-23; ☺breakfast, lunch & dinner) The best place in town for top-notch nosh, recommended for its friendly service and crowd-pleasing menu. Among the extensive all-day choices are several gluten- and wheat-free dishes, and vegos are embraced too. There's live music on Thursday night, or you can take in a postdinner movie next door at the Art Deco cinema.

Café Cecilie (☎06-370 1165; lunch $8.50-18.50, dinner $24-29; ☺lunch Tue-Sun, dinner Wed-Sat) In Queen Elizabeth Park is this intimate eatery, housed in an old cottage with lovely wide verandas. Cecilie lives a double life: café by day, restaurant and wine bar by night. Car-park access from Park Ave.

FOREST PARKS

Good opportunities for tramping in the Wairarapa are available in the Tararua, Rimutaka and Aorangi (Haurangi) Forest Parks. There are some fine coastal walks, too.

Maps and information are available from the DOC office in Wellington (p408) and visitor information centre in Masterton (opposite).

A favourite tramping spot is that known simply as Holdsworth, at the main eastern entrance to the Tararua Forest Park, where mountain streams run through beautiful virgin forest. The park entrance has swimming, picnic and **camping areas** (sites per adult/child $5/2.50), and fine walks including: short, easy family walks; excellent one- or two-day walks; and longer, challenging treks for the experienced, as far as the west coast, near Otaki. The resident **caretaker** (☎06-378 9163) has maps and information about the area, and an intentions book. Ask about the current weather and track conditions before setting off, and come prepared for all types of weather (the Tararua Forest Park has a notoriously changeable climate). The turnoff to Holdsworth is just south of Masterton on SH2; follow Norfolk Rd about 15km to the park entrance.

The **Kaitoke Regional Park**, 16km north of Upper Hutt on SH2, is good for swimming, camping, picnicking and walking; it has walks ranging from 15 minutes to six hours long. The park is home to *The Lord of the Rings'* site of Rivendell.

MT BRUCE

Pukaha Mt Bruce National Wildlife Centre (☎06-375 8004; www.mtbruce.org.nz; adult/child $8/free; ☺9am-4.30pm), 30km north of Masterton on SH2, is an important sanctuary for native NZ wildlife, mostly birds. Large aviaries and outdoor reserves have some of the country's rarest and most endangered species, as well as more common species. There's an impressive nocturnal house with kiwis (sightings aren't guaranteed), tuatara and other endangered reptiles. You can feed eels at 1.30pm and there are two guided tours of the park ($15, 10.30am and 2pm) on weekends.

Tranzit Coachlines runs buses between Masterton and Palmerston North and can pick up and drop off here on request (one way $10).

Marlborough & Nelson

Crossing Cook Strait from the North Island to the South Island is an exciting prospect – a bit like entering a new country, but one where everyone still says 'fush and chups' and takes 'wee Tiki tours'. New Zealand's South Island is less populated than the North and runs at a slower pace; the Maori influence is also less apparent.

The top of the South Island is stunning – and sometimes overlooked by travellers in their haste to head further south to fiords, lakes and ski fields. But the mild climate, magnificent coastline, superb national parks and laid-back seaside towns are definitely worth some hefty time on your itinerary – indeed, sunny Nelson and its surrounds is one of the top summertime holiday spots for Kiwis themselves. As clichéd as it sounds, there is something for everyone here – from the outdoorsy and active to the gourmands and alternative-lifestylers.

Gliding slowly past the scenic bays and inlets of Marlborough Sounds on the interisland ferries is a marvellous spectacle. In Marlborough, you'll find the popular Queen Charlotte Track (also ideal for mountain biking), famous wineries and gourmet restaurants around Blenheim, and the beautiful town of Kaikoura, lapped by wildlife-rich waters.

In the Nelson region there is some of the best tramping and kayaking in NZ in three diverse national parks. Nelson itself is a relaxing city with a thriving arts and crafts community and great café culture. Kaiteriteri has one of the country's loveliest beaches, and around Golden Bay there's the mellow town of Takaka and the haunting beauty of Farewell Spit.

HIGHLIGHTS

- Sighting your first **whale** (p457) off the shores of Kaikoura, followed by a **dolphin swim** (p457)
- Wending your way through the **Marlborough wine region** (p452) for a tipple of sauvignon blanc and a gourmet feast
- Luxuriating in a romantic boutique hideaway in an inlet of the **Marlborough Sounds** (p443)
- Drinking in the postcard-perfect beaches of **Abel Tasman National Park** (p478), by kayak or on foot
- Inspiring your creativity at Nelson's wonderful **World of WearableArt & Collectable Cars Museum** (p466)
- Taking in the sunshine while dining alfresco at one of Nelson's cool **cafés** (p469)
- Unwinding in the chilled-out, ecofriendly atmosphere of **Golden Bay** (p482)

■ TELEPHONE CODE: 03	■ www.destinationmarlborough.com	■ www.nelsonnz.com
	■ www.destinationmarlborough.com	

Golden Bay
Abel Tasman National Park
Nelson
Marlborough Sounds
Marlborough Wine Region
Kaikoura

MARLBOROUGH & NELSON FACTS

Eat: Seafood, and more seafood (especially local green-shell mussels and crayfish)

Drink: Sauvignon blanc in the wineries of Marlborough (p452); microbrewed beer in Nelson (p464)

Read: *The Wine Atlas of New Zealand* by Michael Cooper and John McDermott

Listen to: Some rootsy sounds from Salmonella Dub

Watch: Whales, seals, dolphins and seabirds in Kaikoura (p457)

Swim at: The gorgeous inlets of Abel Tasman National Park (p457)

Festival: Kaikoura Seafest (p460); Nelson Arts Festival (p466)

Tackiest tourist attraction: The dazzling collection of decorated bras on show at Nelson's World of WearableArt & Collectable Cars Museum (p466)

Climate

The forecast is good: both Marlborough and Nelson experience some of the sunniest weather in NZ. January and February are the warmest months, with temperatures averaging 22°C; July is the coldest month averaging 12°C. It's wetter and windier on the west coast, especially at the exposed Farewell Spit.

Getting There & Around

Soundsair is a local airline that connects Wellington with Picton, Blenheim, Nelson and Kaikoura. Air New Zealand offers domestic flights; Origin Pacific, based in Nelson, has flights to major NZ destinations.

Picton is the main starting point for explorations around the South Island as it's the entry/exit point for ferries crossing the Cook Strait. From Picton you can connect

to almost anywhere in the South Island by bus; InterCity is the major bus company but there are also local services and shuttle buses. Tranz Scenic operates the *Tranz-Coastal* train, which takes the scenic route from Picton to Christchurch, via Blenheim and Kaikoura.

Renting a car is easy and there are a host of car-hire companies at Picton ferry terminal. Water transport, kayaking or walking are the best ways to navigate large parts of this region, including the Marlborough Sounds and Abel Tasman National Park.

TOP ACTIVITIES

- Watch the whales (p457) and swim with the dolphins (p457) in Kaikoura
- Scuba dive to the sunken Russian cruise ship, the *Mikhail Lermontov* (p439)
- Go paragliding, skydiving or hang-gliding in the Nelson region (p464 and p474)
- Kayak and walk the famous Abel Tasman Track (see the boxed text, p481)
- Play Gollum in underground caves and caverns in Kaikoura (p458) and Golden Bay (p482, p485 and p487)

MARLBOROUGH REGION

The convoluted, sheltered waterways of the Marlborough Sounds are the first sight of the South Island for many visitors. Picton is the gateway to the island and a prime spot for walking, sailing, kayaking and exploring the many hideaways in the Sounds. A short drive south of Picton is Blenheim and the renowned Marlborough wine region.

History

The first European to visit the Marlborough district was Abel Tasman, who sheltered on the east coast of what is now called D'Urville Island in 1642 (more than 100 years before James Cook arrived in 1770). Cook named Queen Charlotte Sound, and Cook's detailed reports made the area the best-known haven in the southern hemisphere. In 1827 French navigator Jules Dumont d'Urville discovered the narrow strait now known as French Pass. His officers named the island just to the north in his honour. In the same year a whaling station was set up at Te Awaiti in Tory Channel, which brought about the first permanent European settlement in the district.

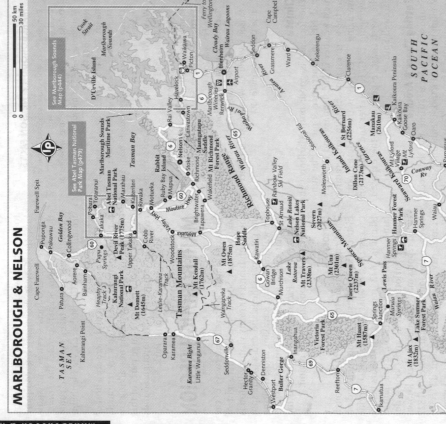

MARLBOROUGH & NELSON

PICTON

pop 4000

A pretty port at the head of Queen Charlotte Sound, Picton is the marine gateway to the South Island and also the best base from which to explore the Marlborough Sounds, particularly Queen Charlotte Track. Picton is a small town that is a hive of activity when the ferry docks and during the peak of summer, but slow and sleepy any other time.

Information

Picton visitor information centre (☎ 03-520 3113; www.destinationmarlborough.com; Foreshore; ☼ 8.30am-5pm Mon-Fri, 9am-4pm Sat & Sun) Pick up maps and information on walking in the Sounds. The DOC counter here is staffed during summer.

Post office (Mariners Mall, High St)
United Video (☎ 03-573 7466; 63 High St) For Internet access.

Sights & Activities

The *Edwin Fox* is purportedly the ninth-oldest wooden ship in the world (who counts these things?!). Built of teak in Bengal, the 48m, 760-ton vessel was launched in 1853. During its long and varied career it carried troops to the Crimean War, convicts to Australia and immigrants to NZ. The **Edwin Fox Maritime Centre** (☎ 03-573 6868; Dunbar Wharf; adult/child $8/2.50; ☼ 9am-5pm) has maritime exhibits and leads through to the vessel, which is gradually being restored.

Next door is the **Seahorse World Aquarium** (☎ 03-573 6030; www.seahorseworld.co.nz; Dunbar Wharf; adult/child/family $16/9/40; ☺ 9am-5pm). Its touch-pools and feeding times are a hit with kids, as is the nearby playground and minigolf.

The visitor information centre has a free map showing several walks in town. An easy 1km track runs along the eastern side of Picton Harbour to Bob's Bay. The **Snout Walkway** carries on along the ridge from the Bob's Bay path and has great views the length of Queen Charlotte Sound. Allow three hours for the return walk.

Diving opportunities around the Sounds include the wreck of the *Mikhail Lermontov*, a Russian cruise ship that sank in Port Gore in 1986 – it's said to be the world's biggest diveable cruise-ship wreck. **Diver's World** (☎ 03-573 7323; www.pictondiversworld.co.nz; London Quay; dive trips from $165) has dives to *Mikhail Lermontov* and to other wrecks in the Sounds. It also offers equipment hire and learn-to-dive courses.

Buzzy Boats & Bike Hire (☎ 03-573 7853; Town Wharf) hires mountain bikes (one/two days $40/75), kayaks (one day $40) and power boats (from $240 per day plus fuel). It also hires fishing rods ($10) and runs a water taxi. Other companies, including Marlborough Sounds Adventure Company and Endeavour Express (see right) offer rental of mountain bikes suitable for the Queen Charlotte Track; the average price is $50 per day.

Too tame? **Skydive the Sounds** (☎ 0800 373 264, 03-573 9101; www.skydivethesounds.co.nz; Picton airport; 12,000ft jump $295) offers tandem skydives that enjoy fantastic views.

Tours

There are loads of tours to choose from, most including a cruise-and-walk combination around Queen Charlotte Sound but there's also kayaking, wildlife-spotting, mountain biking or winery touring in the region.

Beachcomber Fun Cruises (☎ 0800 624 526, 03-573 6175; www.beachcombercruises.co.nz; Town Wharf; mail run $75, cruises $48-65) Scenic cruises from two to four hours, and you can be dropped at one of the resorts for lunch. Also has cruise-and-walk or cruise-and-mountain-bike options.

Charter Link (☎ 0800 862 427, 03-573 6591; www.charterlinksouth.co.nz; Waikawa Marina; day sailing $95) Put your feet up or help the skipper on a yacht tour of the Sounds. Also offers bareboat and skippered yacht charters and learn-to-sail courses.

Cougar Line (☎ 0800 504 090, 03-573 7925; www.cougarlinecruises.co.nz; Town Wharf; cruises adult/child $58/25) Offers three-hour cruises, cruise/walk deals, delivery to a resort for lunch, and a twilight cruise from mid-December to February.

Dolphin Watch Ecotours (☎ 0800 5453 5433, 03-573 8040; www.naturetours.co.nz; ecotours $65-75, bird-watching tour $50, dolphin swimming/viewing $115/75) Ecotours around Queen Charlotte Sound and Motuara Island bird sanctuary. Also cruise/walk options, plus popular trips where participants can swim with dusky dolphins.

Endeavour Express (☎ 03-573 5456 www.boatrides.co.nz; Town Wharf; one-day cruise/walk options all $55) Backpacker-friendly company offering a range of cruise/walk options. Has mountain bikes and camping gear for hire.

Marlborough Sounds Adventure Company (☎ 0800 283 283, 03-573 6078; www.marlborough sounds.co.nz; Town Wharf; 1-/2-/3-/4-day tours from $95/140/465/1120, twilight paddle $50, full-day kayak hire $45) Professional outfit organising a variety of sea-kayak trips and tramps. Kayaking ranges from a three-hour twilight paddle to a four-day guided tour. It also offers guided multiday walks or mountain biking on the track. Freedom rentals (of bikes and kayaks, plus camping gear) also available.

Myths & Legends Eco-tours (☎ 03-573 6901; www.eco-tours.co.nz; half-/full-day cruises $130/170) Spend a day on the Sound with a local Maori family – longtime locals, storytellers and environmentalists. There are different day trips to choose from (eg bird-watching, visiting Ship Cove) or evening barbecue cruises ($ 30).

Sounds Connection (☎ 0800 742 866, 03-573 8843; www.soundsconnection.co.nz; 16 Wellington St; half-day wine/fishing tour $55/69, full-day gourmet wine tour $149) Tours from wineries to waterways'.

Southern Wilderness (☎ 0800 266 266, 03-520 3095; www.southernwilderness.com; Railway Station, 30 Auckland St; Nydia Track half-/full-day trips from $90/130) An enthusiastic company with tours of the Marlborough and Nelson regions, including guided walks on the Nydia (two days $230) and Queen Charlotte Tracks (one/four days $150/1150). Also has lots of kayaking options and a full-day combo adventure (kayaking, walking or mountain biking, and a boat cruise back to Picton) for $110.

Sleeping

BUDGET

Villa (☎ 03-573 6598; www.thevilla.co.nz; 34 Auckland St; dm $23-27, d with/without bathroom $68/59; □) A very appealing place, from its blue-and-red exterior and blooming garden to its cheery staff, free spa and bikes for guest use. There are

www.lonelyplanet.com

PICTON

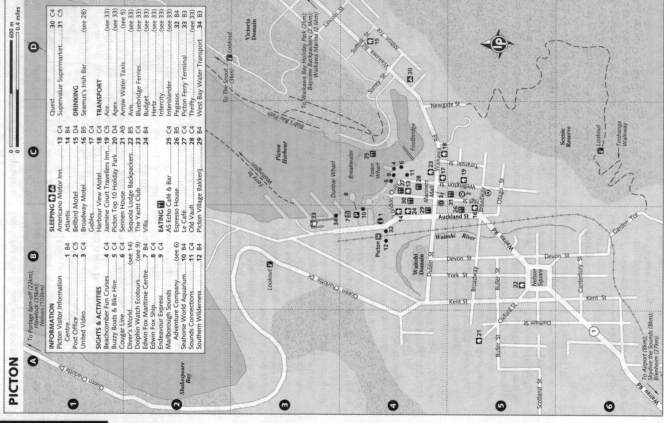

INFORMATION
Picton Visitor Information
Centre.....1 B4
Post Office.....2 C5
United Video.....3 C4

SIGHTS & ACTIVITIES
Beachcomber Fun Cruises.....4 C4
Buzzy Boats & Bike Hire.....5 C4
Cougar Line.....6 C4
Diver's World.....(see 14)
Dolphin Watch Ecotours.....7 B4
Edwin Fox Maritime Centre.....8 C4
Edwin Fox Ship.....9 C4
Endeavour Express.....(see 6)
Marlborough Sounds
  Adventure Company.....(see 6)
Seahorse World Aquarium.....10 B4
Sounds Connections.....11 C4
Southern Wilderness.....12 B4

SLEEPING
Americano Motor Inn.....13 C4
Atlantis.....14 B4
Bellbird Motel.....15 D4
Broadway Motel.....16 B5
Gables.....17 C4
Harbour View Motel.....18 C4
Jasmine Court Travellers Inn.....19 C5
Picton Top 10 Holiday Park.....20 D4
Sennen House.....21 A5
Sequoia Lodge Backpackers.....22 B5
The Yacht Club.....23 C4
Villa.....24 B4

EATING
AS Echo Café & Bar.....25 C4
Espresso House.....26 B5
Le Café.....27 C4
Old Vault.....28 C4
Picton Village Bakkerij.....29 B4

Quest.....30 C4
Supervalue Supermarket.....31 C5

DRINKING
Seamus's Irish Bar.....(see 28)

TRANSPORT
Ace.....(see 33)
Apex.....(see 33)
Arrow Water Taxis.....(see 5)
Avis.....(see 33)
Bluebridge Ferries.....(see 33)
Budget.....(see 33)
Hertz.....(see 33)
Intercity.....(see 33)
Interislander.....(see 33)
Pegasus.....32 B4
Picton Ferry Terminal.....33 B3
Thrifty.....(see 33)
West Bay Water Transport.....34 B3

0 600 m
0 0.4 miles

lots of indoor and outdoor lounge areas and in-demand en suite rooms. Fresh flowers and free night-time appie crumble (April to November) make this a great home-from-home.

Sequoia Lodge Backpackers (☎ 0800 222 257, 03-573 8399; www.sequoialodge.co.nz; 3a Nelson Sq; dm $22, d with/without bathroom $65/54; ☐) Another high-quality, well-run backpackers, a little out of the centre but a stone's throw from a locals' pub and general store. It's named after one of the enormous trees out the front and extras include a huge TV, videos, hammocks, barbecues and spa. In winter there are lures such as free breakfast and homemade bread.

Bayview Backpackers (☎ 03-573 7668; www.true nz.co.nz/bayviewbackpackers; 318 Waikawa Rd; d with/without bathroom $70/55; ☐) On Waikawa Bay, 4km from central Picton, and enjoying bay views, pleasant porch areas and a relaxed air. Friendly owners offer free pickup/drop-off in town; kayaks and bicycles are also free. There's a newer, fully equipped lodge next door with en suite doubles and balconies.

Bellbird Motel (☎ /fax 03-573 6912; 96 Waikawa Rd; d $60-75) Slightly out of town, the '70s-style Bellbird has six spacious self-contained units. The rooms are old school with daggy furnishings, but are more like staying in a house than a unit. Great value.

Atlantis (☎ 03-573 7390; www.atlantishostel.co.nz; cnr Auckland St & London Quay; dm $17-19, tw/d $46/48; ☐) Close to the ferry terminal, the basic rooms are cheap but dorms are large (up to 12 beds) and you'll pay $2 extra for a duvet. Good facilities include free breakfast, an indoor heated pool, pool table and hundreds of DVDs to keep your eyes square.

Camping

Picton Top 10 Holiday Park (☎ 0800 277 444, 03-573 7212; www.pictontop10.co.nz; 70-78 Waikawa Rd; sites per 2 people $32, cabins $48-65, self-contained units $75-110; ☐) About 1.5km from the town centre, this is a busy, well-kept park with a range of modern family-friendly facilities, including a playground and a recreation room stuffed with games.

Waikawa Bay Holiday Park (☎ 0800 924 529, 03-573 7434; www.waikawa.kiwiholidayparks.com; 302 Waikawa Rd; sites per 2 people $22, cabins $38-55, self-contained units $65-75; ☐) Considerably cheaper than the Top 10 but about 4km out of town. A pleasant spot with a range of well-priced accommodation, grassy sites and a courtesy van.

MIDRANGE

Jasmine Court Travellers' Inn (☎ 0800 421 999, 03-573 7110; www.jasminecourt.co.nz; 78 Wellington St; d $110-185; ☐) First-class accommodation at very reasonable rates. Warm, spacious self-contained studios and apartments are immaculate, with quality appliances, CD and DVD players and DVD libraries. Some rooms have a spa and upstairs balconies have views of the harbour; there's a new sauna as an extra treat.

Broadway Motel (☎ 0800 101 919, 03-573 6563; www.broadwaymotel.co.nz; 113 High St, d $95-175) More top-notch motel accommodation. Broadway is a newly refurbished, conveniently located opt on and features double-glazed windows, warm décor, DVDs and Sky TV. Some rooms have a balcony and a spa, and the different prices reflect size rather than standard.

Harbour View Motel (☎ 0800 101 133, 03-573 6259; www.harbourviewpicton.co.nz; 30 Waikawa Rd; d $110-140) A recent makeover has seen this ugly duckling become a swan. Harbour View has an elevated position that offers views of Picton's endearing harbour – the rates of the tastefully decorated, self-contained studios increase according to level (the higher you go, the better the views).

Americano Motor Inn (☎ 0800 104 104, 03-573 6398; www.americano.co.nz; 32 High St, d $95-115) Not in the same league as the other options listed here, but hard to beat for its central location and slightly retro feel. Clean, cheerful rooms are set around a garden; two-bedroom units have a living area and a balcony overlooking High St.

TOP END

Sennen House (☎ 03-573 5216; www.sennenhouse.co.nz; 9 Oxford St; d $225-375; ☐) This exquisitely restored colonial homestead dates from 1886 and now houses five delightfully plush apartments and suites, each with its own entrance, kitchen facilities and private

Gables (☎ 03-573 6772; www.tregables.co.nz; 20 Waikawa Rd; B&B c $110-135, cottage d $150-170) This bright B&B has three spacious, homely en suite rooms in the historic residence and lounge two cottages with kitchenettes and lounge at the back. Prices include breakfast.

lounge/dining area. Enjoy the surrounding greenery from the sunny private verandas while you tuck into the gourmet breakfast hampers. Good value given the attention to detail and luxuries included in the price.

The Yacht Club (☎ 0800 991 188, 03-573 7002; www .theyachtclub.co.nz; 25 Waikawa Rd; hotel d $155-195, apt d/q $300/380; ⊠) When we visited plans were underway for a complete overhaul to bring the dated, floral-heavy, hotel-room décor into line with the Yacht Club's sleek new image. As it stands, rooms are spacious and well-equipped but a revamp will make them a more attractive option. Already rejuvenated are the small, stylish restaurant, indoor/outdoor bar and pool area, and brand-new luxury apartments.

Eating & Drinking

Most of Picton's cafés and restaurants are on High St or facing the waterfront on London Quay.

Picton Village Bakkerij (☎ 03-573 7082; 46 Auckland St; snacks under $5; ⊠ 6am-3.30pm) Dutch owners bake a range of European treats here, including dense rye bread. The gourmet pies are scrumptious, as are the sandwiches, cakes and brownies.

Le Café (☎ 03-573 5588; London Quay; lunch mains $10-20, dinner mains $19-28; ⊠ lunch & dinner; ⬛) Le Café, all big windows and warm timber, is great for a lingering lunch or delicious dinner from the oft-changing blackboard menu. It's also a popular place for a drink, and there's occasional live music.

Espresso House (☎ 03-573 7112; 58 Auckland St; lunch mains $9-17, dinner mains $18-24; ⊠ lunch & dinner, closed Mon & Wed winter) In a converted house, this café-restaurant has a compact local wine list and a blackboard menu of sensational pasta and Pacific Rim fare. Food is fresh, nutritious and stylishly done.

Quest (☎ 03-573 6616; 31 High St; lunch mains $10-16, dinner mains $19-26; ⊠ breakfast, lunch & dinner) A cheery spot with sunny décor and classic black-and-white tiled floor. Despite the simple café interior the kitchen produces sophisticated fare, dominated by seafood dishes, plus good vegetarian options.

AS Echo Café & Bar (☎ 03-573 7498; Shelley Beach; meals $4-16; ⊠ breakfast, lunch & dinner, closed Mon & Tue May-mid-Oct) The deck of this old trading scow (built 1905) is the perfect place for drinks watching the comings and goings of the marina below. There's a menu

of solid, unpretentious home cooking at decent prices.

Old Vault (☎ 03-573 8210; 33 Wellington St; lunch mains $6-13, dinner mains $18-27; ⊠ lunch & dinner) One of the town's more interesting options is inside this striking purple building. There's a restaurant-bar downstairs, art gallery upstairs, and a Fijian-Indian chef concocting predominantly Indian dishes (but not exclusively so). Well worth a look.

Seamus's Irish Bar (☎ 03-573 8994; 25 Wellington St) Just down the road is this authentically snug drinking den. It gets packed to the rafters with thirsty locals who spill out into the wee courtyard, and Monday night sees everyone let their hair down for the jam session.

Self-caterers can head to **Supervalue supermarket** (Mariners Mall, High St; ⊠ 7.30am-7.30pm).

Getting There & Away

You can make bookings for trains, ferries and buses at Picton train station and at the Picton visitor information centre (p438).

AIR

Soundsair (☎ 0800 505 005, 03-520 3080; www.sounds air.co.nz) flies between Picton and Wellington (one way $79, six to eight daily). There are discounts for backpacker- and student-card holders, and often reductions for online bookings. A courtesy shuttle bus to/from the airstrip at Koromiko, 8km south, is included in the price of flights.

See p424 for details of a novel way of travelling between Wellington and Picton, courtesy of a tandem skydive.

BOAT

Ferries depart and arrive at the **Picton ferry terminal** (Auckland St), where both ferry services have booking desks. The terminal has conveniences such as public showers, phones and Internet access.

There are two options for crossing the strait between Picton and Wellington (note that timetables are subject to change).

Bluebridge Ferries (☎ 0800 844 844, 04-471 6188; www.bluebridge.co.nz; adult/child $45/25) Crossing takes three hours, 20 minutes. Departs Wellington at 3am and 1pm Sunday to Friday; returns from Picton at 8am and 7pm. On Saturday departs Wellington 10am and 7pm, returns from Picton 2.30pm and 11pm. Additional sailings in peak period (December to January). Car and campervans up to 6m long $120, motorbike $50, bicycle or surfboard $10.

Getting Around

Renting a car in Picton is easy and affordable – as low as $29 per day if you shop around the local companies (cheaper than the multinationals); most agencies allow drop-offs in Christchurch. If you're planning to drive in the North Island it's often cheaper to return your car in Picton and pick up another car in Wellington after crossing the strait.

Picton's car-hire companies include the following:

Ace (☎ 03-573 8939; www.acerentalcars.co.nz; Picton ferry terminal)

Apex (☎ 03-573 7009; www.apexrentals.co.nz)

Avis (☎ 03-5½0 3156; www.avis.com; Picton ferry terminal)

Budget (☎ 03-573 6081; www.budget.co.nz; Picton ferry terminal)

Hertz (☎ 03-520 3044; www.hertz.co.nz; Picton ferry terminal)

Pegasus (☎ 03-573 7733; www.rentalcars.co.nz; 1 Auckland St)

Thrifty (☎ 0½-573 7387; www.thrifty.co.nz; Picton ferry terminal)

See p447 for details of water taxis servicing the Sounds.

MARLBOROUGH SOUNDS

The Marlborough Sounds feature many delightful bays, islands, coves and waterways, formed by the sea flooding its deep valleys after the ice ages. Parts of the Sounds are now included in the Marlborough Sounds Maritime Park, which is actually many small reserves separated by private land. To get an idea of how convoluted the sounds are, Pelorus Sound is 42km long but has 379km of shoreline.

The Queen Charlotte Track is the main attraction for trampers, but there are other walks, such as the two-day Nydia Track (p448), and secluded accommodation is scattered throughout the Sounds.

With your own set of wheels, the 36km drive along Queen Charlotte Drive from Picton to Havelock, makes for leisurely cruising and lovely views, especially from Picton to The Grove.

Sleeping & Eating

Some sleeping options are accessible only by boat and are delightfully isolated. Most popular are those on or just off the Queen Charlotte Track (p446), and there are places to stay along Queen Charlotte Drive.

BUS

Buses serving Picton operate from the ferry terminal or the nearby visitor information centre.

InterCity (☎ 03-365 1113; www.intercitycoach.co.nz; Picton ferry terminal) runs services south to Christchurch (one way $50, 5½ hours, two daily), via Kaikoura ($31, two hours, two daily) with connections on to Dunedin, Queenstown and Invercargill. Services also run to/from Nelson ($31, two hours, three to four daily), with connections to Motueka and the West Coast, and to/from Blenheim ($12, 30 minutes, up to five daily). At least one bus daily on each of these routes connects with a Wellington ferry service. Keep an eye on the website for discounted fares – Picton was a supercheap $1C at the time of research, Christchurch–Picton was a supercheap $1C.

A handful of smaller shuttle buses head south to Christchurch, usually offering a door-to-door service. Companies include the following:

Atomic Shuttles (☎ 03-322 8883; www.atomictravel.co.nz)

KBus (☎ 0800 881 188, 03-548 4075; www.kbus.co.nz)

South Island Connections (☎ 0800 700 797; www.southislandconnections.co.nz)

TRAIN

Tranz Scenic (☎ 0800 872 467, 04-495 0775; www.tranzscenic.co.nz) runs the scenic *TranzCoastal* service daily each way between Picton and Christchurch via Blenheim and Kaikoura, departing from Christchurch at 7am, and from Picton at 1pm. The standard adult one-way Picton–Christchurch fare is $89, but discounted fares can be as low as $40. The service connects with the *Interislander* ferry.

Interislander (☎ 0800 802 802, 04-498 3302; www.interislander.co.nz; adult/child $63/30) Crossing takes three hours. There are up to five sailings per day in each direction. Regular services depart Wellington at 1.55am (except Monday), 8.45am, 10.35am, 2pm and 6.15pm; and return from Picton at 5.45am (except Monday), 10am, 1.15pm, 2.25pm and 6pm. The most flexible (and expensive) fare for a car is $150, a motorbike costs $55, and for foot passengers to take a bicycle or surfboard you'll pay an extra $10. Discount fares are often available for advance bookings. Children under two travel free.

MARLBOROUGH SOUNDS

0	10 km
0	6 miles

SLEEPING 🏠

Anakiwa Backpackers................1	B6	
Bay of Many Coves Camp Site.....2	D2	
Bay of Many Coves Resort...........3	D2	
Black Rock Camp Site..................4	C2	
Camp Bay Camp Site....................5	C5	
Cowshed Bay Camp Site..............6	C2	
Davies Bay Camp Site..................7	B6	
DOC Nydia Lodge........................8	A5	
Furneaux Lodge...........................9	C5	
Hopewell...................................10	B5	
Lazy Fish Retreat.......................11	D3	

Lochmara Lodge.........................12	C3	
Mahana Homestead Lodge..........13	C5	
Mistletoe Bay Camping &		
Accommodation....................14	C3	
Noeline's Homestay...............(see 13)		
Nydia Bay Camp Site.................15	A5	
Portage Bay Shop &		
Backpackers.....................(see 16)		
Portage Resort Hotel..................16	C2	
Punga Cove Resort.....................17	C5	
Queen Charlotte Wilderness		
Park....................................18	D4	

Resolution Bay Cabins...............19	C5	
Schoolhouse Bay Camp Site......20	D5	
Smiths Farm Holiday		
Park....................................21	B6	
Sunflower Units.........................22	B6	
Te Mahia Bay		
Resort..................................23	C2	
Te Mahoerangi...........................24	A5	
Tirimoana House........................25	B6	

EATING 🍴

Blist'd Foot Cafe...................(see 25)		

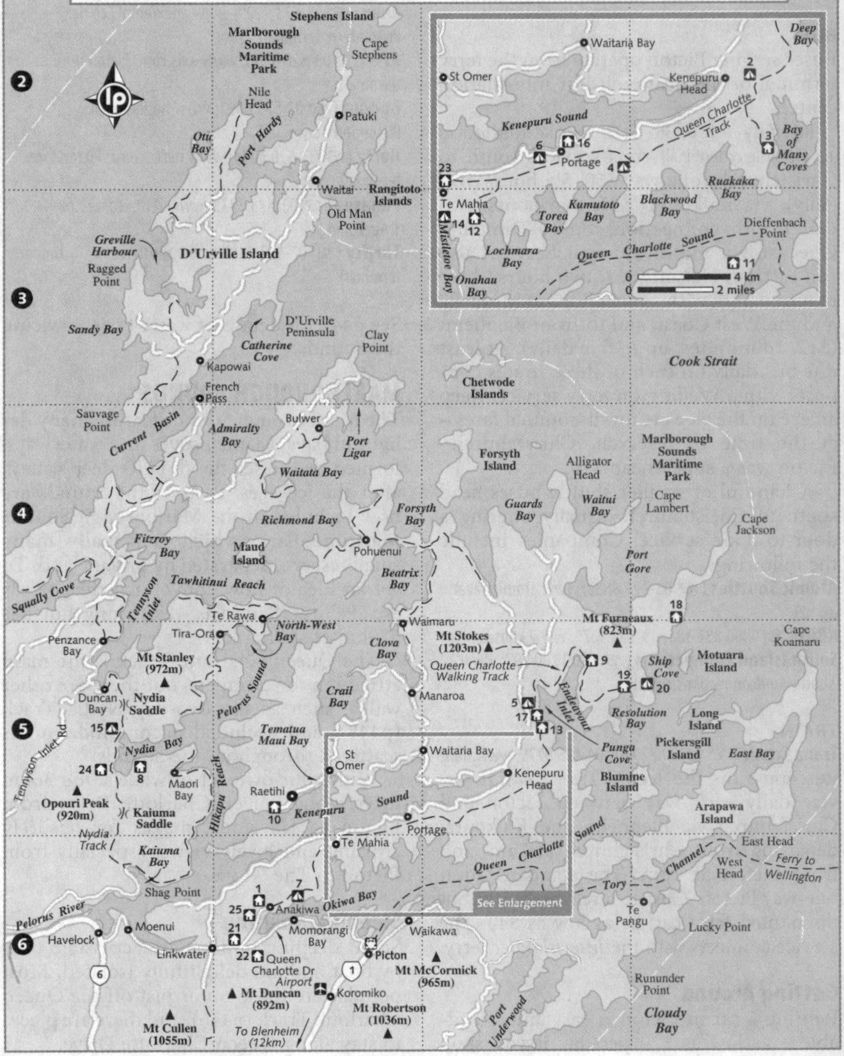

There are almost 30 DOC camping grounds throughout the Sounds, providing water and toilet facilities but not much else – none has cooking facilities. Unless you're carrying a tent it's wise to book accommodation in summer. Note that some places close over winter – call ahead to check.

If you're looking for your very own secluded retreat, **Sounds Great Holiday Homes** (☎ 03-574 1221; www.soundsgreat.co.nz) can arrange homes (from a humble bachelor pad to utter luxury).

QUEEN CHARLOTTE DRIVE

Sunflower Units (☎ 03-574 1074; www.sunflowerunits.co.nz; Queen Charlotte Dr; d $90) Just east of the turn-off to Anakiwa (about 20km from Picton) are these two cosy, affordable, self-contained units in a lovely setting. Free transport to/from Anakiwa is provided.

Smiths Farm Holiday Park (☎ 03-574 2806; www.smithsfarm.co.nz; Queen Charlotte Dr, Linkwater; unpowered/powered sites per 2 people $22/24, cabins $45, self-contained units $80-100) This is a cut above your average park with lush camping areas and comfy cabins and units. It's just east of the turn-off to Portage.

Accommodation at Anakiwa (p446) is easily accessed by the road off Queen Charlotte Drive.

QUEEN CHARLOTTE TRACK

See p446 for options along the track.

OUTER SOUNDS

Hopewell (☎ 03-573 4341; www.hopewell.co.nz; Kenepuru Sound; dm $28, d with/without bathroom $86/66, 4-person cottage $132; ☒ closed Jun-Aug; ☐) One of the country's best-loved backpackers, according to Budget Backpacker Hostels, and it's not hard to understand the appeal. Hopewell is on a remote part of Kenepuru Sound, surrounded by native bush and opening onto the sea. Access by road is possible but the long, bumpy drive makes water taxi from Te Mahia the best option. Once here, chill out with the roll call of facilities: books and games, outdoor spa, mountain bikes, kayaks, fishing equipment, gourmet pizzas and more.

Queen Charlotte Wilderness Park (☎ 03-579 9025; www.truenz.co.nz/wilderness; Cape Jackson; 2 nights & 3 days per person $300) North of Ship Cove and extending right up to Cape Jackson, this private nature reserve allows you to explore north of the Queen Charlotte Track. The package includes accommodation, meals and transfers from Picton. As well as opportunities for tramping on virtually deserted tracks, there's warm hospitality, wildlife-spotting, fishing and kayaking.

Lazy Fish Retreat (☎ 03-573 5291; www.lazyfish.co.nz; Queen Charlotte Sound; d $445-495) Magnificent boutique accommodation in secluded, peaceful surrounds. All meals are included and accommodation consists of bungalows or a sea-view apartment, each with veranda and hammocks or day beds (bungalows also have an outdoor bath). The retreat is accessible by boat only; there's a two-night minimum stay. Leave the kids at home.

Getting There & Around

The best way to get around the Sounds is by boat, although the road system has been extended. Scheduled and on-demand water taxis (see p447) service most points along the Queen Charlotte Track.

No buses service the Sounds, but much of the area is accessible by car. The road is sealed to the head of Kenepuru Sound but beyond that it's nothing but narrow, forever-winding gravel roads. To drive to Punga Cove from Picton takes at least two hours – or 45 minutes by boat.

Queen Charlotte Track

The Queen Charlotte Track has wonderful coastal scenery, beautiful coves and some 'great-escape' accommodation and some camping spots. The coastal forest is lush, and from the ridges you can look down on either side to Queen Charlotte and Kenepuru Sounds. The track is 71km long and connects historic Ship Cove with Anakiwa. It's not through national park but passes through privately owned land and DOC reserves – access depends on the cooperation of local landowners so it's important to respect their property by staying in designated camp sites and carrying out your rubbish.

Queen Charlotte is a well-defined track and suitable for people of average fitness. You can do the walk in sections using local boat transport, or walk the whole three- to five-day journey. Sleeping options are only half a day's walk apart; boat operators will transport your pack along the track for you. Though there aren't the hordes that walk the Abel Tasman Track, there's still some solid traffic. As with Abel Tasman, you can do part of the trip by sea kayak (see p439).

Mountain biking is also an option and it's possible to ride the track in two or three days, guided or self-guided – note that the section between Ship Cove and the Kenepuru Saddle is closed to cyclists December to February. At this time you can still get dropped by boat at the Saddle and ride to Anakiwa.

Ship Cove is the usual starting point, mainly because it's easier to arrange a boat from Picton to Ship Cove than vice versa, but the track can be started from Anakiwa. There's a public phone at Anakiwa but not at Ship Cove. Between Camp Bay and Torea Saddle you'll find the going toughest. About halfway along there's an excellent viewpoint, Eatwell's Lookout, about 20 minutes off the main track (45 minutes return). Estimated route times:

Route	Distance	Time
Ship Cove to Resolution Bay	4.5km	1½-2hr
Resolution Bay to head of Endeavour Inlet	10.5km	2-2¾hr
Endeavour Inlet to Camp Bay/Punga Cove	12km	3-4hr
Camp Bay/Punga Cove to Torea Saddle/Portage	24km	5½-7½hr
Torea Saddle/Portage to Mistletoe Bay	8km	2½-3hr
Mistletoe Bay to Anakiwa	13km	2½-3¾hr

INFORMATION
The Picton visitor information centre (p438) has copies of the *Queen Charlotte Track* brochure, and is the best spot for information. Online details are at www.qctrack.co.nz.

TOURS
Most of the tour companies based in Picton (p439) offer guided cruises around the Sounds and walks on Queen Charlotte Track, as well as mountain biking and kayaking in the area.

SLEEPING & EATING
It's strongly advised to book accommodation for the Queen Charlotte Track early, especially in summer, as the area can be solidly booked. There are **DOC camping grounds**

(adult/child $6/1.50) along the track, each with toilets and a water supply but no cooking facilities; there's no need to prebook or buy a pass. There's also a great variety of lodges and guesthouses; backpacker beds normally cost extra if you're not carrying your own linen.

The following listings are arranged in order heading south from Ship Cove (where camping is not permitted) – not all options on the track are covered in this book.

The first camp is the beautifully situated **Schoolhouse Bay camp** (Resolution Bay).

Resolution Bay Cabins (03-579 9411; reso@xtra .co.nz; Resolution Bay; sites per person $15, dm $30, self-contained cabins $160) A delightfully rustic place with backpacker beds and old-fashioned cabins with kitchen and bathroom. They have real character, with potbelly stoves and ageing furniture. It's incredibly peaceful; there's also a small café.

Furneaux Lodge (03-579 8259; www.furneaux.co .nz; Endeavour Inlet; dm $30-40, chalets/studios d $195/ 225;) A century-old place set amid lovely gardens, and a godsend for thirsty trampers. The basic backpacker section is located in an old stone cottage, plus there are self-contained two-bedroom chalets (sleeping up to seven) and swish waterfront studios. Meals are available in the bar and restaurant.

Camp Bay Camp Site (Punga Cove) On the western side of Endeavour Inlet.

Punga Cove Resort (03-579 8561; www.punga cove.co.nz; Endeavour Inlet; dm $35, lodge d $110-145, chalets $165-350;) A wonderful range of self-contained studio, family and luxury A-frame chalets, some with gorgeous sea views. For backpackers, there's a separate area of budget cabins. The resort has a pool, spa, shop, bar, café and an excellent fine-dining restaurant.

Mahana Homestead Lodge (03-579 8373; www .mahanahomestead.com; Endeavour Inlet; dm/d $30/65) Every room in this purpose-built lodge has sea views and it gets a huge rap from guests. It's also nicely intimate, with only 12 beds. Home-cooked meals are available; fishing gear and kayaks are free for guests' use.

Noeline's Homestay (03-579 8375; near Punga Cove; tw $50) Follow the pink arrows from Camp Bay to this relaxed homestay and be greeted by Noeline and her home-baked treats. It's a friendly place with a handful of beds, cooking facilities and great views.

Bay of Many Coves Camp Site (Bay of Many Coves) On a saddle above the track.

Bay of Many Coves Resort (☎ 0800 579 9771; www.bayofmanycovesresort.co.nz; studio $145, apt d/q $410/610; ☑) This exclusive retreat offers studios with shared bathrooms, plus a collection of luxurious self-contained apartments with private balconies and first-class views. There's also a shop and top-notch café and restaurant, plus the requisite outdoor pursuits. A steep track leads down to the resort from the walking track.

Black Rock Camp Site (Kumutoto Bay) Further along past Bay of Many Coves, above Kumutoto Bay.

Portage Resort Hotel (☎ 03-573 4309; www.portage.co.nz; Kenepuru Sound; dm $25-35, d $168-295; ☐ ☑) This large resort is a stalwart on Kenepuru Sound. It's flash with a restaurant, casual café and bar. The backpacker bunkhouse is pretty good, with small lounge and cooking facilities, plus there's a variety of upmarket accommodation. Even if you're not staying, drop in for a beer. The hotel has sailboats, fishing, spa, pool and tennis courts.

Portage Bay Shop & Backpackers (☎ 03-573 4445; www.portagecharters.co.nz; Kenepuru Sound; dm/ d $30/80, unit $120-150) Friendly owners offer a small, rather characterless backpacker lodge or a self-contained unit above the shop. The shop sells groceries, takeaways and fuel, plus hire out yachts, speedboats, dinghies, kayaks and bikes.

Cowshed Bay Camp Site (Cowshed Bay) Not far from the Portage Resort Hotel.

Lochmara Lodge (☎ 03-573 4554; www.lochmaralodge.co.nz; Lochmara Bay; dm $24, d $70-90, self-contained units & chalets $125-145; ☒ closed Jun-Sep) A superb retreat on Lochmara Bay, reached by a side track south of the Queen Charlotte Track, or by boat from Picton. Relaxation-inducing facilities include an outdoor spa, hammocks and barbecues; home-cooked meals are available. As well as a homely backpacker lodge, there are en suite rooms and units, all set in lush surroundings.

Mistletoe Bay Camping & Accommodation (☎ 03-573 4048; www.mistletoebaytrust.org.nz; Mistletoe Bay; sites adult/child $8/6, cottage $80-120) A former DOC campground, still with limited facilities (toilets and cold water) but also home to a bargain-priced self-contained cottage sleeping six.

Te Mahia Bay Resort (☎ 03-572 4089; www.temahia.co.nz; Kenepuru Sound; d $115-230) This sweetly low-key resort is north of the track, just off the main road, in a beautiful bay facing Kenepuru Sound. It has roomy, affordable self-contained units, plus brand-new luxury apartments. There's a small store selling precooked meals, plus dinghies and kayaks for hire.

Davies Bay camp (Umungata) Also a popular picnic spot, with barbecue facilities nearby.

Anakiwa Backpackers (☎ 03-574 1338; www.anakiwabackpackers.co.nz; Anakiwa Rd; dm/d $20/50; ☐) This small, homely place is right at the southern end of the trail and set in pretty gardens. A great place to recuperate from your walk.

Tirimoana House (☎ 03-574 2627; www.tirimoanahouse.com; Anakiwa Rd; d $110-150) About 1.5km down the road from the end of the track (near the pick-up point for water transport back to Picton) is this accommodating B&B. The wee Blist'd Foot Café is also here, where the B&B hosts serve up afternoon drinks and home-baked goodies to weary trampers.

GETTING AROUND

A number of boat operators service the track, allowing you to start and finish where you like. Prices usually include pack transfers, so your gear can wait for you at your chosen accommodation. Transport costs around $70 return, and $45 for a one-way drop-off. Bikes and kayaks can be transported.

Main operators in Picton are as follows (all except Arrow offer scenic cruises and cruise-and-walk options, see p439):

Arrow Water Taxis (☎ 03-573 8229; www.arrowwatertaxis.co.nz; Towr Wharf, Picton) Provides an on-demand service.

Beachcomber Fun Cruises (☎ 0800 624 526, 03-573 6175; www.beachcombercruises.co.nz; Town Wharf)

Cougar Line (☎ 0800 504 090, 03-573 7925; www.cougarlinecruises.co.nz; Town Wharf)

Endeavour Express (☎ 03-573 5456; www.boatrides.co.nz; Town Wharf)

West Bay Water Transport (☎ 03-573 5597; west_bay@xtra.co.nz; West Bay jetty, Picton ferry terminal) Covers the southern end of the track (Anakiwa, Lochmara Bay and Torea Bay), leaving from near the Picton ferry terminal. Can also organise transport to Kenepuru Sound.

HAVELOCK

pop 470

Tiny Havelock's thriving small-boat harbour and claim to fame as the 'green-shelled mussel capital of the world' pretty much sums it up. The town lies at the confluence of the Pelorus and Kaiuma Rivers 36km west of Picton, and is a base from which to explore the more remote parts of Marlborough Sounds, particularly Pelorus and Kenepuru Sounds.

The helpful staff at **Rutherford Travel** (☎ 0800 742 897, 03-574 2114; www.rutherfordtravel.co.nz; 46 Main Rd) book tours and offer regional advice. Rutherford Travel is also DOC and transport agents.

Good information is online at www.havelocknz.com.

Activities

The **Nydia Track** (27km, 9½ hours) starts at Kaiuma Bay and ends at Duncan Bay (or vice versa). Nydia Bay was originally the site of a Maori *pa* (fortified village) called Opouri, which means 'Place of Sadness', so named after a bloody battle between members of the same tribe. The walk passes through different bird habitats; it's also open to mountain bikers seeking a challenge.

There are **DOC camping grounds** (adult/child $6/1.50) at Nydia Bay and Duncan Bay, and the **DOC Nydia Lodge** (Map p444; ☎ 03-520 3002; Nydia Bay; dm $15), a 50-bed hut (bookings essential); about halfway along the track. **Te Mahoerangi** (Map p444; ☎ 03-579 8411; www.nydiatrack.org.nz; dm/d $25/50) is a small, peaceful backpackers right on Nydia Bay. Book all these options (and water-taxi transport to/from the track) through Rutherford Travel (above).

Tours

Water taxis, fishing charters, kayaking tours and scenic cruises operate out of Havelock.

All Season Cruises (☎ 03-574 1220; www.allseasoncruises.co.nz; lunch/dinner cruise $69/85) The popular 3½-hour lunch cruise, aboard the raunchy launch *Foxy Lady*, heads to a mussel farm (as does the sunset barbecue cruise). It also runs overnight options (from $180).

Havelock Adventure Company (☎ 021 236 0297; havelockadventureco@xtra.co.nz; kayak trips from $95, kayak hire for 1/3 days $65/169) Has guided sea-kayaking trips in the Sounds, specialising in Tennyson Inlet. Also offers freedom hires, and can help you combine the Nydia Track with kayaking.

Pelorus Mail Run (☎ 03-574 1088; www.mail-boat.co.nz; adult/child $105/free; ⏰ departs 9.30am Tue, Thu & Fri) This popular full-day boat cruise takes in the outer reaches of the Pelorus Sound on genuine NZ Post delivery services. Bookings essential; BYO lunch. A pick-up/drop-off bus from Picton can be arranged.

Pelorus Water Transport (☎ 027 239 0000, 03-577 6103; www.peloruswt.co.nz) Provides transport to all points in Pelorus and Kenepuru Sounds, as well as tailored scenic tours and fishing and diving charters.

Sleeping & Eating

Havelock Motor Camp (☎ 03-574 2339; Inglis St; unpowered/powered sites per 2 people $20/22, cabins $34) Near the marina, this park has cheerful managers, shady sites, basic cabins and spick-and-span facilities.

Rutherford YHA (☎ 03-574 2104; www.rutherfordtravel.co.nz/YHA.html; 46 Main Rd; sites per person $11, dm/d $22/52; ▯) This well-equipped (but TV-free) place is in an 1881 schoolhouse once attended by Lord Ernest Rutherford, who discovered the atomic nucleus. The enthusiastic manager has information about walks and activities and the rooms are simple but comfy (doubles are nicer than dorms).

Blue Moon (☎ 03-574 2212; www.bluemoonhavelock.co.nz; 48 Main St; dm/d $20/50) Another good budget option, the Blue Moon is a welcoming place in a cosy, homely main-street cottage. Spend leisurely afternoons on the barbecue-equipped, view-enriched back deck.

Havelock Garden Motel (☎ 03-574 2387; www.gardenmotels.com; 71 Main Rd; d $85-125) The beautiful garden aspect is a winning feature of this small, family-run motel. The lush grounds feature a hammock, pond and resident ducks, and the self-contained rooms (studios or two-bedroom options) are immaculate. The entrance is next door to Mussel Boys.

Mussel Boys (☎ 03-574 2824; 73 Main Rd; meals $10-25; ☐ lunch & dinner) Bright, cheery place specialising in fresh local mussels, especially 'steamers' (whole shell), 'flats' (grilled on the half shell) and chowders. You can't miss the 'mussel' team playing rugby on the roof.

Slip Inn (☎ 03-574 2345; Havelock marina; all-day menu $9-17, dinner mains $16-22; ☐ breakfast, lunch & dinner) Breakfast is a mussel-free zone at this great indoor-outdoor space down by the water, but at lunch or dinner you can't escape the bivalves – on pizzas, in chowders, or various other concoctions. There are plenty of nonmussel options too.

Getting There & Away

InterCity (☎ 03-365 1113; www.intercitycoach.co.nz) has a few daily Picton–Blenheim–Nelson buses that pass through Havelock. Several shuttlebus operators also ply this route, including

KBus (☎ 0800 881 188, 03-548 4075; www.kbus.co.nz) and **Atomic Shuttles** (☎ 03-322 8883; www.atomictravel.co.nz). There are no buses on the more direct 36km back road to Picton (Queen Charlotte Drive), but this is a recommended route if you're driving or cycling.

BLENHEIM

pop 26,500

Blenheim is the best place to access NZ's biggest wine-growing district. The town is 29km south of Picton on the flat Wairau Plain, a contrasting landscape to the Sounds.

Information

Automobile Association (AA; Map p449; ☎ 03-578 3399; cnr Seymour St & Maxwell Rd)

Blenheim visitor information centre (Map p449; ☎ 03-577 8080; www.destinationmarlborough.com; Railway Station, Sinclair St; ⏲ 8.30am-5pm Mon-Fri, 9am-4pm Sat & Sun) Friendly and efficient; dispenses information for all of the Marlborough area.

Post office (Map p449; cnr Scott & Main Sts)

Travel Stop Cyber Centre (Map p449; ☎ 03-579 1902; 3 Market St) For Internet access.

Sights & Activities

If you're not into wine (and aren't seeking seasonal work), there's not a great deal in town to hold your attention.

Opposite Seymour Sq, the **Millennium Art Gallery** (Map p449; ☎ 03-579 2001; Seymour Sq; admission by donation; ⏲ 10.30am-4.30pm Mon-Fri, 1-4pm Sat & Sun) is a contemporary gallery presenting

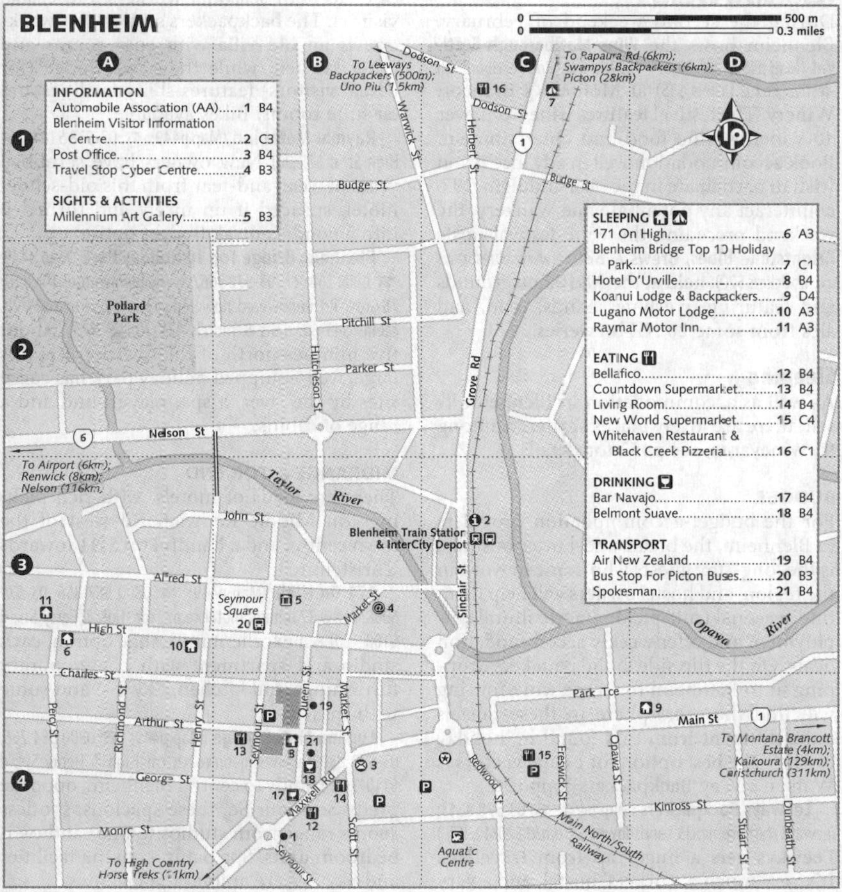
BLENHEIM
0 500 m
0 0.3 miles
INFORMATION
Automobile Association (AA)........1 B4
Blenheim Visitor Information Centre........2 C3
Post Office........3 B4
Travel Stop Cyber Centre........4 B3
SIGHTS & ACTIVITIES
Millennium Art Gallery........5 B3
SLEEPING
171 On High........6 A3
Blenheim Bridge Top 10 Holiday Park........7 C1
Hotel D'Urville........8 B4
Koanui Lodge & Backpackers........9 D4
Lugano Motor Lodge........10 A3
Raymar Motor Inn........11 A3
EATING
Bellafico........12 B4
Countdown Supermarket........13 B4
Living Room........14 B4
New World Supermarket........15 C4
Whitehaven Restaurant & Black Creek Pizzeria........16 C1
DRINKING
Bar Navajo........17 B4
Belmont Suave........18 B4
TRANSPORT
Air New Zealand........19 B4
Bus Stop For Picton Buses........20 B3
Spokesman........21 B4
To Leeways Backpackers (500m); Uno Piu (1.5km)
To Rapaura Rd (6km); Swampys Backpackers (6km); Picton (28km)
To Airport (6km); Renwick (8km); Nelson (116km)
To Montana Brancott Estate (4km); Kaikoura (129km); Christchurch (311km)
To High Country Horse Treks (11km)
Pollard Park
Blenheim Train Station & InterCity Depot
Seymour Square
Aquatic Centre
Taylor River
Opawa River
Main North/South Railway
Dodson St
Warwick St
Herbert St
Budge St
Pitchill St
Parker St
Hutcheson St
Nelson St
Grove Rd
John St
Alfred St
High St
Charles St
Market St
Sinclair St
Park Tce
Main St
Percy St
Richmond St
Henry St
Seymour St
Queen St
Arthur St
George St
Maxwell Rd
Scott St
Redwood St
Freswick St
Opawa St
Kinross St
Stuart St
Dunbeath St
Monro St

changing exhibitions by primarily local artists.

High Country Horse Treks (Map p449; ☎ 03-577 9429; www.high-horse.co.nz; Taylor Pass Rd; 1hr/4hr rides $40/110) has four-legged exploration from its base 11km southwest of town.

Tours

Molesworth Tour Company (☎ 03-5757525; www.molesworthtourco.com) offers pricey high-country farm trips to Molesworth cattle station via the Awatere valley ($270), day trips to Kaikoura ($180) and much more reasonable wine tours (half-/full-day $50/90).

See p452 for more operators offering winery tours.

Festivals & Events

During the second weekend of February, Blenheim hosts the **Wine Marlborough Festival** (Map p454; ☎ 03-577 9299; www.wine-marlborough-festival.co.nz; tickets $35) at Montana's Brancott Winery. The festival features wine from over 40 wineries, fine food and entertainment. Book accommodation well in advance if you wish to participate in the over-indulging. To counteract any potential wine-wankery, the weekend preceding the wine festival hosts **Brightstone Blues, Brews & BBQs** (www.bluesbrews.co.nz; tickets $20), held at the A&P showgrounds and featuring live blues bands, food, and ales from some 20 NZ breweries.

Sleeping

As well as accommodation in Blenheim itself, there are lovely places scattered among the vineyards; see p452 for details.

BUDGET

For the budget-accommodation providers in Blenheim, the bread-and-butter business is the long-stay guests who come to work in the region, and hostel owners will help them find seasonal fruit-picking/agricultural employment and offer weekly accommodation deals. On the flip side, holidaymakers dropping in to Blenheim for some wine-touring will find the atmosphere in these hostels quite different from that found in 'holiday towns.' The best option for casual visitors is Watson's Way Backpackers (opposite).

Leeways Backpackers (Map p454; ☎ 03-578 8843; leeway1@xtra.co.nz; 33 Landsdowne St; dm/d $20/40; □) Leeways gets a huge rap from travellers. It's very much a workers' hostel, and a very social one too, where the atmosphere is like a huge share-house. It's got good facilities for long-stayers and a shed well equipped for house parties. It's a couple of kilometres north of town.

Swampys Backpackers (Map p454; ☎ 03-570 2180; www.swampys.co.nz; 2 Ferry Rd, Spring Creek; dm/d $21/50; □) Another good social choice for long-termers, about 6km north of town (but with a pub and supermarket nice and close). There are great lounge areas, funky décor, two kitchens, nice bathrooms and a relaxing courtyard. Bikes and kayaks available.

Koanui Lodge & Backpackers (Map p449; ☎ 03-578 7487; www.koanui.co.nz; 33 Main St; dm $20-22, d with/without bathroom $62/50; □) Brownie points go to this big pink place for its attempts to cater to both seasonal workers and casual visitors. The backpackers section (for workers) is an old villa with cosy rooms and a big kitchen, while the newer lodge (for casual visitors) features shiny facilities and en suite rooms. Bikes available.

Raymar Motor Inn (Map p449; ☎ 03-578 5104; 164 High St; d $75-90) New owners have scrubbed years of wear-and-tear from this old-school motel, spruced it up nicely and turned it into a good, central, budget option.

Blenheim Bridge Top 10 Holiday Park (Map p449; ☎ 0800 268 666, 03-578 3667; www.blenheimtop10.co.nz; 78 Grove Rd; unpowered/powered sites per 2 people $24/28, cabins $45-60, units & motels $75-79; □ ☒) About five minutes north of the town centre, this large, well-equipped holiday park has camp sites by the river, a spa, playground and a range of cabins.

MIDRANGE & TOP END

There are loads of motels, with rich pickings on Middle Renwick Rd west of the town centre, and a handful on SH1 towards Christchurch.

171 On High (Map p449; ☎ 0800 587 856, 03-579 5098; www.171onhighmotel.co.nz; cnr High & Percy Sts; d $100-160) An excellent midrange option, each studio and apartment with contemporary furnishings, full kitchen, Sky TV and some with spas.

Lugano Motor Lodge (Map p449; ☎ 0800 584 266, 03-577 8808; www.lugano.co.nz; cnr High & Henry Sts; d $110-135) Handy to central Blenheim, opposite pretty Seymour Sq, these spacious, spotless rooms range from studios to one- and two-bedroom units. Spa baths, cooking facilities and Sky TV are among the facilities.

Hotel D'Urville (Map p449; ☎ 03-577 9945; www.durville.com; 52 Queen St; d $200-282) If you can afford a splurge, this is perfect. In the old public trust buildings, the 11 dazzling rooms in this boutique hotel are beautifully decorated and individually themed. Downstairs is the classy lounge bar and restaurant (mains $20 to $35, open for dinner nightly). Food here is highly rated and there's a wide selection of local wines; reservations advised.

Uno Più (Map p454; ☎ 03-578 2235; www.unopiu.co.nz; 75 Murphys Rd; d $240-380; ☒) This Kiwi-Italian-run boutique homestead is ideal for a romantic getaway, with two beautifully appointed in-house rooms or a separate self-contained cottage. Breakfasts are sumptuous; dinners available by arrangement. There's a pool, extensive gardens and an olive grove – *bellissimo*.

Eating & Drinking

Blenheim has a decent café and restaurant scene, but it's nicer to dine among the vines at the region's vineyards (see p452).

Living Room (Map p449; ☎ 03-579 4777; cnr Scott St & Maxwell Rd; meals $8-20; ☒ breakfast, lunch & dinner) The capacious Living Room is a chic café decorated in warm tones with artistic style. It's great for a cosy drink in the adjacent wine bar or for a quality breakfast.

Bellafico (Map p449; ☎ 03-577 6072; 17 Maxwell Rd; lunch mains $12-22, dinner mains $24-30; ☒ lunch & dinner Mon-Sat) The huge wine list here makes for great reading (as does the list of microbrewed beers). The menu has an emphasis on local produce with European influences and features the likes of local shellfish and cervena (venison).

Belmont Suave (Map p449; ☎ 03-577 8238; 67 Queen St; meals $12-20; ☒ lunch & dinner) A cool, funky, split-level bar that serves up a small menu of tasty dishes. Orange-and-green swivel chairs and mirrors create a retro feel, and DJs play at weekends.

Bar Navajo (Map p449; ☎ 03-577 7555; 70 Queen St; mains $15-30; ☒ breakfast, lunch & dinner) A bustling, American Indian–themed bar with a colourful totem (authenticity yet to be verified), booths and pool tables. The varied menu caters to most tastes and provides easy-drinking snacks. DJs on Thursday, Friday and Saturday.

For self-catering head to the supermarkets, **New World** (Map p449; Freswick St; ☒ 8am-9pm) or **Countdown** (Map p449; 51 Arthur St; ☒ 7am-10pm).

Getting There & Around

AIR

Blenheim airport is about 6km west of town on Middle Renwick Rd. **Air New Zealand** (Map p449; ☎ 0800 737 000, 03-577 2200; www.airnz.co.nz; 29 Queen St) has direct flights to/from Wellington (one way from $70, 12 daily), with connections to other centres.

BICYCLE

Spokesman (Map p449; ☎ 0800 422 453; 61 Queen St; half-/full-day $20/35) rents bikes; longer hire and delivery can be arranged.

BUS

Ritchies Transport (Map p449; ☎ 03-578 5467) has regular services between Blenheim and Picton ($8, 20 minutes, two to four daily), leaving from the bus stop on Seymour Sq.

InterCity (☎ 03-365 1113; www.intercitycoach.co.nz) buses run a few times daily from Blenheim to Picton ($12, 30 minutes) and on to Nelson ($26, 1¾ hours); two or three times a day buses head south to Christchurch ($49, five hours) via Kaikoura ($29, 1¾ hours). There's also a handful of shuttle buses that stop at Blenheim on the Nelson–Picton–Christchurch route (see p443).

TRAIN

Tranz Scenic (☎ 0800 872 467; www.tranzscenic.co.nz) runs the scenic *TranzCoastal* service between Picton (one way $24, 30 minutes, one daily) and Christchurch ($82, five hours, one daily), which stops at Blenheim in both directions. There are often decent discounts on the full fares listed here.

RENWICK

Renwick is a tiny town about 10 minutes west of Blenheim, with many of the region's wineries within walking distance (certainly within cycling distance.) A dedicated cycling path is being established around Renwick and through the surrounding vineyards. You can hire bikes and get more information from Watson's Way Backpackers.

Watson's Way Backpackers (Map p454; ☎ 03-572 8228; www.watsonswaybackpackers.co.nz; 56 High St; dm $22, d $50-65; ☒ closed Sep) is a superb place to stay. There's a purpose-built lodge at the back of the property, with small three- and four-bed dorms and cheery doubles (some with en suite). It's set in a delightfully leafy garden, and there are bikes for hire and lots

MARLBOROUGH WINE TRAIL

With more than 50 wineries and acres of vineyards dotted around Blenheim and Renwick, Marlborough is NZ's biggest wine-producing area. It's particularly famous for its floral sauvignon blancs, but aromatics such as gewürztraminer, rieslings and fashionable pinot gris have also gained recognition. Good information is at www.winemarlborough.net.nz.

Wine tours are the prime attraction and wineries have cellar-door sales and tastings. Tours also visit breweries, liqueur distilleries and cottage industries where you can sample preserves and olive oil.

Wineries are clustered around Renwick, 8km west of Blenheim, and along Rapaura Rd, north of Renwick – there are some 25 cellar doors in a 5km radius. It's perfect cycling distance, but due to the very busy nature of Rapaura Rd you'd do well to keep to the established tracks and back roads and heed the advice of in-the-know locals, until a planned cycling path through the heart of the area is finally developed. The Blenheim and Picton visitor information centres and various accommodation providers stock decent maps. For all the venues listed here see Map p454.

Montana Brancott Winery (☎ 03-578 2099; www.montana.co.nz; SH1; winery tours $10, meals $12-26; ☽ 9am-5pm), located away from the Rapaura Rd cluster of wineries on SH1 heading south from Blenheim, was the first to plant commercial vines in the region, in 1973, and is among NZ's largest wineries. It's also the host of the Wine Marlborough Festival (see p450). Tours of the winery run between 10am and 3pm.

Other wineries:

Cloudy Bay (☎ 03-520 9040; www.cloudybay.co.nz; Jacksons Rd; ☽ 10am-4.30pm) One of the most well-known wineries.

Forrest Estate (☎ 03-572 9084; www.forrest.co.nz; Blicks Rd; ☽ 10am-4.30pm) Award-winning crisp, delicate wines, plus picnic-friendly grounds and a sculptor-in-residence.

Grove Mill (☎ 03-572 8200; www.grovemill.co.nz; Waihopai Valley Rd; ☽ 11am-5pm) Knowledgeable staff, interesting displays and a bird-filled wetland sanctuary.

Huia (☎ 03-572 8326; www.huia.net.nz; Boyces Rd; ☽ 10.30am-5pm daily summer, Mon-Fri winter) A wee boutique company producing premium drops.

Matua Marlborough (☎ 03-572 8642; www.matua.co.nz; New Renwick Rd; ☽ 9am-5pm) A large, internationally renowned winery (big exporter).

Nautilus Estate (☎ 03-572 9374; www.nautilusestate.com; 12 Rapaura Rd; ☽ 10am-4.30pm) Another big exporting name, famed for its sauv blanc but continuing to expand into pinot noir.

Saint Clair Estate (☎ 03-570 5280; www.saintclair.co.nz; cnr Rapaura & Selmes Rds; ☽ 9am-5pm) Award-winning wines, country preserves and a café.

Te Whare Ra (☎ 03-572 8581; www.te-whare-ra.co.nz; 56 Anglesea St; ☽ 10am-4.30pm) An excellent boutique winery.

Villa Maria Estate (☎ 03-577 9530; www.villamaria.co.nz; cnr New Renwick & Paynters Rds; ☽ 10am-5pm) A big, highly regarded winemaker that consistently reels in major awards.

Tours

Wine Tours by Bike (☎ 03-572 9951; www.winetoursbybike.co.nz; 106 Jeffries Rd; half-/full-day bike hire $35/50) runs a pick-up/drop-off service from Blenheim to its Jeffries Rd base. Its hire fees include a winery map, pannier and support vehicle if you need to be picked up (if you get too tipsy or buy too many bottles to carry). It also offers guided cycling tours (price depends on numbers and length of tour), and Antares Homestay (see opposite).

There are several wine tours (by minibus) available from Blenheim and a couple from Picton. Pick-up from your accommodation is easily arranged.

Deluxe Wine Tour (☎ 0800 500 511, 03-578 5467; blenheim.depot@ritchies.co.nz; wine tours $40-55) A big operator with a six-hour option that includes a Montana tour (a four-hour option is also possible). Departures can be arranged from Picton.

Highlight Tours (☎ 03-577 9046; www.highlight-tours.co.nz; half-day tours $40-50) Offers personalised small-group tours.

Marlborough Wine Tours (☎ 03-578 9515; www.marlboroughwinetours.co.nz; 3-/5-/7hr tours $39/49/69) Has a range of tours from Blenheim and Picton.

Sounds Connection (☎ 0800 742 866, 03-573 8843; www.soundsconnection.co.nz; half-day tours $55, full-day gourmet tour $149) Has tours originating in Picton but can pick up in Blenheim. The gourmet tour includes a wine-matched four-course lunch.

Accommodation

Wine-lovers need somewhere stylish to lay their heads, and this area has plenty of cottages, B&Bs and boutique lodges perfect for a gourmet retreat. Budget travellers will be more than happy at Watson's Way Backpackers in Renwick (p451).

Antares Homestay (☎ 03-572 9951; www.antareshomestay.co.nz; 106 Jeffries Rd; s/d $120/150; □ ☒) Four-acre property with two en suite rooms, a log fire in the private sitting room, a hot tub and relaxing views. Bike hire included in the rates.

Chardonnay Lodge (☎ 03-570 5194; www.chardonnaylodge.co.nz; 104B Rapaura Rd; d $125-150; ☒) Set in a huge tree-filled garden, friendly owners offer two high-quality self-contained villas, or a B&B option in the main house.

Stonehaven (☎ 03-572 9730; www.stonehavenhomestay.co.nz; 414 Rapaura Rd; d $135-220; ☒) A lovely B&B with three guest rooms in a solid stone-and-cedar home. Rooms are comfy, with terrific views of the surrounding vineyard.

Strawlodge Vineyard Accommodation (☎ 03-572 9769; www.trailsofmarlborough.co.nz; Fareham Lane; d $225-295) Gorgeous suites set among the vines. Facilities include guest kitchen, spa, barbecue and free bikes. The owners offer a guiding service as well.

Vintners Retreat (☎ 03-572 7420; www.thevintnersretreat.co.nz; villas 55 Rapaura Rd, suites & restaurant 199 Rapaura Rd; d $120-340, q $230-370; ☒) Various types of large, self-contained villas (some sleeping up to six), all very roomy and luxuriously decorated. Down the road, at Vintness Retreat restaurant, are smaller one-bedroom suites. Prices vary according to size, season, number of guests and length of stay.

Food

With wine there must be food, and lunch at one of the vineyards is all part of the gourmet experience. Many vineyards have attached cafés or restaurants, usually with pretty outlooks, serving fresh local produce. Expect perfectly matured cheeses, plump scallops, herb-encrusted this and manuka-smoked that, so brush up on your gourmet-speak. Alternatively, pack a picnic basket – many w neries welcome picnickers enjoying their grounds. The following eateries serve delicious meals:

Herzog (☎ 03-572 8770; www.herzog.co.nz; 81 Jeffries Rd; set menus from $89; ☒ dinner Tue-Sun mid-Oct–mid-May, also lunch Sun mid-Dec–Mar) Acclaimed fine-dining experience from Michelin-starred European chefs. Also offers casual bistro lunches and cooking classes.

Makana Confections (☎ 03-570 5370; www.makana.co.nz; cnr Rapaura & O'Dwyer Rds; ☒ 10am–5pm) You won't get a full meal, but you'll want to stop here anyway for the chance to taste and buy divine hardmade chocolates.

Mud House Village (☎ 03-572 7170; www.mudhousevillage.co.nz; 197 Rapaura Rd; ☒ 10am–5pm) Family-friendly spot serving delicious platters, panini and cake. Has a lakeside garden, tasting of Le Grys and Mud House wines, an outlet for Prenzel liqueurs, an olive oil shop and quilters' barn.

Twelve Trees (☎ 03-572 9054; www.allanscott.com; Jacksons Rd; meals $15-22; ☒ lunch) Superb courtyard garden setting and an innovative menu.

Wairau River Wines (☎ 03-572 7950; www.wairauriverwines.com; Rapaura Rd; meals $13-20; ☒ lunch) Pretty, wisteria-covered mud-brick cottage and a blackboard menu of fresh, well-priced treats.

Whitehaven Restaurant & Black Creek Pizzeria (Map p449; ☎ 03-577 6634; www.whitehaven.co.nz; 1 Dodson St, Blenheim; ☒ lunch & dinner) A two-in-one deal close to Blenheim. Whitehaven is a more formal option, the adjacent p zzeria has a simple, casual feel, and both share a lovely garden.

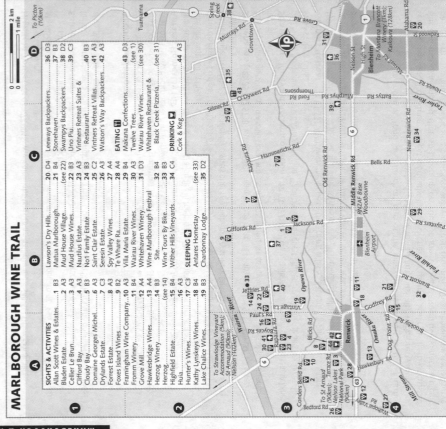

MARLBOROUGH WINE TRAIL

SIGHTS & ACTIVITIES
Allan Scott Wines & Estates....1 B3
Bladen Estate....................2 A3
Cellier Le Brun...................3 A3
Clifford Bay.......................4 A3
Cloudy Bay........................5 A3
Domaine Georges Michel........6 A3
Drylands Estate..................7 C3
Forrest Estate....................8 A3
Foxes Island Wines..............9 B2
Framingham Wine Company....10 A3
Fromm Winery...................11 B4
Grove Mill........................12 A4
Hawkesbridge Wines............13 A4
Herzog Winery...................14 B3
Herzog..........................(see 14)
Highfield Estate.................15 B4
Huia.............................16 A3
Hunter's Wines..................17 C3
Kathy Lynskeys Wines..........18 B4
Lake Chalice Wines.............19 B3

Lawson's Dry Hills...............20 D4
Matua Marlborough.............21 B4
Mud House Village.............(see 22)
Mud House Wines................22 B3
Nautilus Estate..................23 A3
No1 Family Estate...............24 A3
Saint Clair Estate...............25 C2
Seresin Estate...................26 A3
Spy Valley Wines.................27 A4
Te Whare Ra....................28 A4
Villa Maria Estate...............29 A4
Wairau River Wines..............30 A3
Whitehaven Winery.............31 D3
Wine Marlborough Festival
  Site..............................32 B4
Wine Tours By Bike..............33 B3
Wither Hills Vineyards...........34 C4

SLEEPING 🛏
Antares Homestay.............(see 33)
Chardomay Lodge...............35 D2

Leeways Backpackers............36 D3
Stonehaven.......................37 B3
Swampys Backpackers............38 D2
Uno Piu..........................39 C3
Vintners Retreat Suites &
  Restaurant......................40 B3
Vintners Retreat Villas...........41 A3
Watson's Way Backpackers......42 A3

EATING 🍴
Makana Confections..............43 D3
Twelve Trees...................(see 1)
Wairau River Wines...........(see 30)
Whitehaven Restaurant &
  Black Creek Pizzeria..........(see 31)

DRINKING 🍺
Cork & Keg.......................44 A3

of local information to tap into with the friendly hosts.

Cork & Keg (Map p454; ☎ 03-572 9328; Inkerman St) is an English-style country pub and a rip-roaring place for a night out after wine-touring. It brews its own draught beer and cider, plus there's a big open fire, beer garden and decent snacks.

KAIKOURA
pop 3850

Kaikoura is a stunning town with a superb setting, backed by the steeply rising foothills of the Seaward Kaikouras (snowcapped in winter). It's located 183km north of Christchurch on SH1, and a Mecca for wildlife enthusiasts.

Kaikoura was once just a sleepy little fishing town noted mainly for its crayfish, until Nature Watch Charters began whale-watching trips in 1987. The tours' fame escalated, putting Kaikoura on the tourist map. Thousands of international visitors come for the wildlife and during summer it pays to book the whale-watching and dolphin-swimming tours at least a few days ahead – and give yourself some leeway, as inclement weather may see tours cancelled.

The 'Big Five' most likely to be seen are the sperm whale, the endemic Hector's dolphin (the smallest and rarest of dolphins), the dusky dolphin (found only in the southern hemisphere), the New Zealand fur seal

AUTHOR'S CHOICE

The Store at Kekerengu (☎ 03-575 8600; SH1, Kekerengu; meals $9-33; ☺ breakfast & lunch) Don't be fooled by the name – this 'store' is an upmarket café where you can enjoy great slabs of cake and a cuppa, cafeteria-style, or choose chowder or half a cray from a seafood-loving menu. Dine by the fire in the shabby-chic interior, or out on wide sun decks, while taking in splendid sea views. The Store is halfway between Blenheim and Kaikoura – stop in even if you're not hungry.

and the bottlenose dolphin. Other animals frequently seen include orcas (killer whales), pilot whales and blue penguins. Sea birds include shearwaters, fulmars, petrels and royal and wandering albatross. Seals are readily seen on the rocks at the seal colony.

There's no guarantee of seeing any specific animal on any tour but something of interest will be seen. Sperm whales are most likely to be seen from October to August and orcas from December to March. Most other fauna is seen year-round.

Marine animals are abundant at Kaikoura because of the currents and continental-shelf formation. From land, the shelf slopes gradually to a depth of about 90m, then plunges to more than 800m. Warm and cold currents converge here, and when the southerly current hits the continental shelf it creates an upwelling current, bringing nutrients up from the ocean floor and into the light zone.

History

In Maori legend, the tiny Kaikoura Peninsula (Taumanu o te Waka o Maui) was the seat where the demigod Maui sat when he fished the North Island up from the depths of the sea. The area was heavily settled before Europeans came – at least 14 Maori pa sites have been identified.

Excavations near Fyffe House show that the area was a moa-hunter settlement about 800 to 1000 years ago. In 1857 George Fyffe came upon an early moa-hunter burial site near the present Fyffe House. He discovered the largest moa egg ever found (240mm long, 178mm in diameter).

James Cook sailed past the peninsula in 1770, but didn't land. His journal states that 57 Maoris in four double-hulled canoes came towards the Endeavour, but 'would not be prevail'd upon to put along side'. In 1828 the beachfront of Kaikoura, now the site of the Garden of Memories, was the scene of a tremendous battle. Here a Ngati Toa war party, led by chief Te Rauparaha, bore down on Kaikoura, killing or capturing several hundred of the Ngai Tahu tribe.

The first European to settle in Kaikoura was Robert Fyffe, who established a whaling station in 1842. Kaikoura was a whaling centre from 1843 until 1922, and sheep farming and agriculture flourished. After whaling ended, the sea and the farmland continued to support the community.

Information

Internet Outpost (☎ 03-319 7970; 19 West End)

Kaikoura visitor information centre (☎ 03-319 5641; www.kaikoura.co.nz; West End; ☺ 9am-5.30pm daily Sep-May, 9am-5pm Mon-Fri, to 4pm Sat & Sun Jun-Aug) By the car park (on the beach side). Staff are very helpful and can make tour and transport bookings. There's a DOC representative here during summer.

Post office (41 West End) Inside Take Note bookshop.

Sights & Activities

There's plenty of history among the wildlife. George Fyffe, cousin of Kaikoura's first European settler, Robert Fyffe, came to Kaikoura from Scotland in 1854 and built **Fyffe House** (☎ 03-319 5835; 62 Avoca St; adult/child $7/2; ☺ 10am-4pm Thu-Mon May-Oct, to 6pm daily Nov-Apr) around 186C. The house is the only survivor from the whaling days. Admission includes a 30-minute guided tour.

The 30-minute **Point Sheep Shearing Show** (☎ 03-319 5442; www.pointbnb.co.nz; Fyffe Quay; adult/child $10/5; ☺ shows 1.30pm & 4pm) is extremely entertaining.

Kaikoura Museum (☎ 03-319 7440; 14 Ludstone Rd; adult/child $3/50c; ☺ 12.30-4.30pm Mon-Fri, 2-4pm Sat & Sun) includes the old town jail (1910), historical photos, Maori and colonial artefacts, and an exhibit on the region's whaling era.

Just before Point Kean is a **seal colony**, with a nearby car park. From the shore, you can see seals lazing on the rocks wondering why everyone is looking at them.

For a taste of pinot, chardonnay and gewürztraminer with striking sea views, visit the **Kaikoura Wine Company** (☎ 03-319 7966;

KAIKOURA

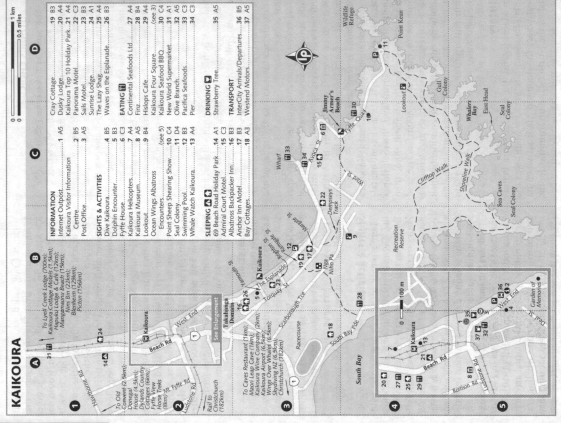

INFORMATION
Internet Outpost.....................1 A5
Kaikoura Visitor Information
Centre.................................2 B5
Post Office............................3 A5

SIGHTS & ACTIVITIES
Dive Kaikoura........................4 B5
Dolphin Encounter...................5 B3
Fyffe House..........................6 C3
Kaikoura Helicopters................7 A4
Kaikoura Museum....................8 A5
Lookout...............................9 B4
Ocean Wings Albatross
Encounters........................(see 5)
Point Sheep Shearing Show......10 C4
Seal Colony.........................11 D4
Swimming Pool.....................12 B3
Whale Watch Kaikoura.............13 A4

SLEEPING
69 Beach Road Holiday Park......14 A1
Admiral Court Motel................15 C3
Albatross Backpacker Inn..........16 B3
Anchor Inn Motel...................17 B3
Bay Cottages.......................18 A3

Cray Cottage........................19 B3
Dusky Lodge.........................20 A4
Kaikoura Top 10 Holiday Park....21 A4
Panorama Motel....................22 C3
Sails Motel...........................23 B3
Sunrise Lodge.......................24 A1
The Lazy Shag......................25 A4
Waves on the Esplanade..........26 B3

EATING
Continental Seafoods Ltd.........27 A4
Finz..................................28 B4
Hislops Cafe........................29 A4
Kaikoura Four Square...........(see 3)
Kaikoura Seafood BBQ...........30 C4
New World Supermarket..........31 A1
Olive Branch........................32 A5
Pacifica Seafoods..................33 C3
Pier..................................34 C3

DRINKING
Strawberry Tree....................35 A5

TRANSPORT
InterCity Arrivals/Departures.....36 B5
Westend Motors....................37 A5

0   1 km
0   0.5 miles

www.kaikourawines.co.nz; tours & tasting $8.50; ⌚ 10am-5.30pm), 2km south of town off SH1. Tours leave on the hour and take in the winery plus the amazing cellar. BYO your own picnic, or buy deli fodder here to be enjoyed on the outdoor terrace.

On the hill at the eastern end of town is a water tower with a **lookout**; you can see both sides of the peninsula and along the coast. Take the walking track up to the tower from Torquay St or drive up Scarborough Tce.

There's a safe swimming **beach** in front of the Esplanade and a **pool**. Other beaches are on the peninsula's northeast (eg Jimmy Armer's) and at South Bay. The whole coastline, with its rocky formations and abundant marine life, is good for snorkelling and diving. Dive Kaikoura (right) offers scuba-diving opportunities.

Mangamaunu Beach, about 15km north of Kaikoura, has good surfing; **Board Silly Adventures** (☎ 0800 787 352, 03-319 6464; surf lessons adult/child $75/65) can teach you to surf or, for those who know what they're doing, they offer wet suits and boards for hire.

For an aerial buzz, contact **SkydivingNZ** (☎ 0800 693 593, 03-319 7874; www.skydivingnz.com; Kaikoura airport, SH1; skydive $245-295) to arrange a tandem skydive from up to 12,000ft.

Dropping a line off the wharves is popular, particularly at the Kahutara River mouth or by surfcasting on the many beaches. For **fishing charters**, see p458.

In winter, nearby Mt Lyford has **skiing** opportunities (p84). When there's snow on the mountain, shuttle buses run from Kaikoura to the mountain.

WALKING

There are two **walkways** starting from the seashore and seal colony, one along the cliff top; a loop takes 2½ hours. If you go on the shoreline trail, check the tides with the visitor information centre beforehand (it's best to go within two hours of low tide). Both walks afford excellent views of the fur seal and red-billed seagull colonies. A trail from South Bay leads over farmland and back to the town (45 minutes).

Mt Fyffe (1602m) dominates the narrow Kaikoura Plain and the town. Information about history, vegetation, birds and walking tracks in the area is in the *Mt Fyffe and the Seaward Kaikoura Range* brochure.

Kaikoura Coast Track (☎ 03-319 2715; www.kaikouratrack.co.nz; package $150; Oct-Apr) is a three-day self-guided walk through private farmland and along the Amuri Coast, 50km south of Kaikoura. The 40km walk has spectacular coastal views and farm cottage nights' accommodation. The price includes three nights' accommodation and pack transport; BYO sleeping bag and food (some supplies and meals available). A two-day mountain-bike option is $70.

Kaikoura Wilderness Walkway (☎ 0800 945 337, 03-319 6966; www.kaikourawilderness.co.nz; package $695) offers more creature comforts than the walk listed above. This is a two-day, one-night guided walk (graded easy to moderate) through forests and alpine landscapes over 17km, with accommodation in a secluded lodge. Price includes pick-up and drop-off in Kaikoura; all meals and pack transport.

Tours

Tours are big business in Kaikoura. It's all about the marine mammals and there are some excellent opportunities to see these amazing creatures up close. For many, the main attraction is the sperm whale; other whales include orcas, minke, humpback and southern right. Dolphins and sea birds are also spotted.

WHALE-WATCHING

For most a whale-watch tour is a thrilling experience, but there's one hitch: the weather. Whale Watch Kaikoura depends on planes to spot whales from the air, which is extremely difficult in foggy or wet conditions. The Whale Watch office then cancels line after line of disappointed customers. If this trip is a *must* for you, allow a few days.

Aerial whale-watching companies give a guarantee that you see the whole whale (as opposed to possibly only viewing a tail or flipper from a boat) as you fly overhead.

Kaikoura Helicopters (☎ 0800 455 4354, 03-319 6609; www.worldofwhales.co.nz; Railway Station; 30-/40-/50-min flight $185/215/295)

Whale Watch Kaikoura (☎ 0800 655 121, 03-319 6767; www.whalewatch.co.nz; Whaleway Station, Whaleway Rd; tours adult/child $125/60) Based at the old train station. Tours (2½ hours, three to 16 trips daily) head out to sea in search of whales and other wildlife, in boats equipped with hydrophones (underwater microphones) to pick up whale sounds. Refund of 80% if no whales are sighted.

Wings over Whales (☎ 0800 226 629, 03-319 6580; www.whales.co.nz; Kaikoura airport; 30min flight adult/child $135/75; flights 9am, 11am, 1pm & 3pm) Flights in light planes, departing from the airfield about 7km south of town.

DOLPHIN & SEAL SWIMMING

Dive Kaikoura (☎ 0800 728 223, 03-319 6622; www.scubadive.cc.nz; 94 West End; seal swim adult/child $75/60, observation $60, dives from $85) Boat-based seal swimming, plus diving lessons and tours.

Dolphin Encounter (☎ 0800 733 365, 03-319 6777; www.dolphin.co.nz; 96 The Esplanade; swim adult/child $125/115, observation $60/30; trip 8.30am & 12.30pm year-round, plus 5.30am summer) The chance to swim with huge pods of dusky dolphins; wet suits, masks and snorkels provided. Limited numbers so book in advance; participants rave about this trip.

Seal Swim Kaikoura (☎ 03-319 6182; www.sealswimkaikoura.co.nz; shore-based tour adult/child $50/50, boat-based tour $70/60; ⊗ Oct-Apr) Two-hour guided snorkelling tours among NZ fur seals, either from the shore or a boat.

BIRD-WATCHING

Bird-watchers have the opportunity to see pelagic species, including albatross, shearwaters, shags, mollymawks and petrels, with **Ocean Wings Albatross Encounters** (☎ 0800 733 365, 03-319 6777; www.oceanwings.co.nz; 96 The Esplanade; adult/child $75/35).

OTHER TOURS

Fyffe View Horse Treks (☎ 03-319 5069; kaikourahorsetrekking.co.nz; Postmans Rd; treks from $45) Guided treks take in farmland, native bush and riverbeds; from October to March you can opt for a sunset trek ($75).

Glenstrae Farm 4 Wheeler Adventures (☎ 0800 004 009, 03-319 7021; www.4wheeladventures.co.nz; quad-bike tours $110, Argo tours adult/child $60/25) Get down and dirty on guided quad-bike tours (minimum age 16), or on family-friendly all-terrain vehicles.

Maori Leap Cave (☎ 03-319 5023; adult/child $12/5; ⊗ tours hourly 10.30am–3.30pm) A sea-formed limestone cave discovered in 1958. Six 40-minute tours a day depart from Caves Restaurant, 3km south of town. Book at the restaurant or the visitor information centre.

Maori Tours (☎ 0800 866 267, 03-319 5567; www.maoritours.co.nz; adult/child $85/45; ⊗ tours 9am & 1.30pm) Advance bookings are essential for this unique and fascinating half-day tour where you experience Maori hospitality and rituals.

Sea Kayak Kaikoura (☎ 0800 452 456, 03-319 7118; www.seakayakkaikoura.co.nz; seal tours adult/child $65/50) Guided sea-kayak tours to view fur seals and explore the peninsula's coastline. Kayaking lessons and freedom hire also available.

South Bay Fishing Charters (☎ 03-319 7517; 2hr charter per adult $65) Deep-sea fishing trips, or hire the boat and skipper for a half/full day ($450/650).

Top Catch Charters (☎ 03-319 6306; crayzeesmith@yahoo.com; 3hr trip adult/child $75/40) Three-hour fishing and crayfishing trips; fish is filleted and bagged, ready for you to take with you.

Sleeping

For such a small place, Kaikoura is wall-to-wall accommodation – book ahead in summer. There are some excellent B&Bs and guesthouses mostly on the outskirts of town, and plenty of motels to choose from, especially along The Esplanade.

BUDGET
Hostels

Intense competition keeps the budget accommodation standard high among the dozen or so backpackers in town.

The Lazy Shag (☎ 03-319 6662; 37 Beach Rd; dm/d $20/55; ▢) The name refers to the bird life around town, not the behaviour of visiting backpackers (but don't quote us on this). It's in a prime spot, with cafés on either side and a long outdoor deck taking in superlative mountain views. All rooms have bathrooms, the living area has a wood-fired stove and free Internet, and there are kayaks for guest use.

Dusky Lodge (☎ 03-319 5959; www.duskylodge.com; 67 Beach Rd; dm $22, d $50-75; ▢ ⊠) Easily Kaikoura's largest hostel, it's a busy, social place, with all the facilities to cope (including three lounge areas and three kitchens). The winning feature is the brilliant outdoor deck boasting heated pool and spa with mountain views. Feeling flush? Live it up in one of the new 'luxury doubles', complete with en suite and a flat-screen TV.

Sunrise Lodge (☎ 03-319 7444; 74 Beach Rd; dm $21-25, tw $54; ⊗ closed Jun-Aug; ▢) Lovely small lodge behind the owners' home, and the enthusiastic owners have built up quite a reputation for this place. However, the hostel was on the market when we visited, so there may be changes afoot. We've no doubt the bunk-free rooms will remain bright and comfortable, and fingers crossed extras such as free bike hire will continue.

Cray Cottage (☎ 03-319 5152; craycottage@hotmail.com; 190 The Esplanade; dm $22-24, tw $54; ▢) Like your hostels small and intimate, with an air of tranquillity thrown in? Look no further than this self-contained 12-bed cottage opposite the beach. It's about 1km east of the town centre and free pick-up/drop-off is available.

Albatross Backpacker Inn (☎ 03-319 6090; www.albatross-kaikoura.co.nz; 1 Torquay St; dm/s $25/48, d & tw $60; ▢) High-quality backpackers with a lovely large TV/living area, plus outdoor decks and verandas to chill out on. Some of the dorms have 'Turkish-theme' bunks – semi-enclosed beds with a unique design.

Lyell Creek Lodge (☎ 03-319 6277; www.lyellcreeklodge.co.nz; 193 Beach Rd; s/tw/d $40/50/54, d with bathroom $60) There'll be no fighting for cooking space behind the mock-Tudor walls of this small, friendly lodge. Guests can spread out over two kitchens and two lounges. And there'll be no fighting over the remote control either – all rooms have TV, some have private bathrooms. No bunks, free laundry and free pick-up/drop-off are added extras.

Camping

69 Beach Road Holiday Park (☎ 03-319 6275; www.holidayparks.co.nz/69beach; 69 Beach Rd; unpowered/powered sites per 2 people $26/28, cabins $50, units $85-95, motel $130) Excellent creek-side park, neat and well tended. It has friendly owners and ship-shape facilities, including a well-equipped communal kitchen.

Kaikoura Top 10 Holiday Park (☎ 0900 363 638, 03-319 5362; www.kaikouratop10.co.nz; 34 Beach Rd; unpowered/powered sites per 2 people $28/32, cabins $45-65, units $75-110, motel $100-110; ⊠) Tucked away behind a large hedge is this busy and well-maintained camping ground, offering family-friendly facilities (including a heated swimming pool) and a range of quality cabins on offer.

MIDRANGE

Prices vary dramatically from low to high season (low season lasts from May to September). The prices listed here are the maximum rates.

Bay Cottages (☎ 03-319 5506; baycottages@xtra.co.nz; 29 South Bay Pde; cottages $60-90) Highly recommended tourist flats (with kitchenette and bathroom) capable of sleeping four. They're on South Bay, a few kilometres south of town, close to swimming beaches and the excellent Finz restaurant. The friendly owner may take you out crayfishing and often puts on a coffee-and-cray brunch.

Sails Motel (☎ 03-319 6145; sails.motel@actrix.co.nz; 134 The Esplanade; d from $85) There are no sea views at this motel, so the owners have to impress by other means – and they manage this very successfully. This handful of secluded, tastefully appointed units is down a driveway in a garden setting (private outdoor areas abound).

Panorama Motel (☎ 0800 288 299, 03-319 5053; www.accommodation.co.nz/pages/panorama; 266 The Esplanade; d $90-150) In this price range, Panorama wins on the view front (we wish we could say the same about the décor, but alas it's all dated timber veneer and daggy bedspreads). Still, the units are clean, comfy and have cooking facilities. The bonus is

Anchor Inn Motel (☎ 0800 720 033, 03-319 5426; www.anchor-inn.co.nz; 208 The Esplanade; d $160-245) The top motel choice in town, home to helpful staff and spacious, immaculate units where every last detail has been taken care of. Extras include double-glazed tinted windows to enjoy the views without being seen, the sunny outdoor balconies from which to drink in those views.

Donegal House (☎ 0800 346 873, 03-319 5083; www.donegalhouse.co.nz; Mt Fyffe Rd; s/d $100/130) Be-gorrah! There is some fine Irish hospitality at this expanding B&B set in a huge garden. The en suite rooms are nothing fancy – the real reason to stay here is to be a short stumble from the wonderful old pub (p461).

Old Convent (☎ 0800 365603, 03-319 6603; www.theoldconvent.co.nz; Mt Fyffe Rd; s $85-95, d $120-185; ⊠) This memorable B&B retains many features of the rambling old buildings. The old chapel is now a guest lounge full of magazines, books and games and the rooms are decked out with old-fashioned furniture. Also in the flower-filled grounds is a café and chocolate shop.

Dylans Country Cottages (☎ 03-319 5473; www.dylanscottages.co.nz; Postmans Rd; cottages $150). Set on the fragrant 'Lavendyl' lavender farm, these two private, self-contained cottages make a great escape. They're set in pretty gardens; one cottage has a secluded outdoor bath and the other an indoor spa. Breakfast included.

Also recommended:

Admiral Court Motel (☎ 0800 555 525, 03-319 5525; www.kaikouramotel.co.nz; 16 Avoca St; d/q $125/180) Clean, self-contained units (studio and two-bedroom options) with Sky TV and a breezy aspect.

Kaikoura Cottage Motels (☎ 0800 526 882, 03-319 5599; www.kaikouracottages.co.nz; cnr Beach & Mill Rds; d $100) Enclave of comfy, well-priced tourist flats just north of town.

TOP END

Hapuku Lodge (☎ 03-319 6559; SH1 at Hapuku Rd; www.hapukulodge.com; d $350-520) Twelve kilometres north of Kaikoura is this fabulously indulgent place, perfect for a stylish retreat. It features warm contemporary décor and handcrafted furniture in its well-appointed guest rooms, self-contained apartment and new 'tree houses' (built at tree-top level to take advantage of the views). All this is on a deer stud and olive farm, complete with highly regarded café (p460).

plus there are cooking facilities, bikes for hire and a video library. Winter rates make this place more affordable; you'll pay more for full sea views.

Waves on the Esplanade (☎ 03-319 5890; www .kaikouraapartments.co.nz; 78 The Esplanade; apt $190-220) Can't do without the comforts of home? We're sure you'd be happy if your home had views such as those enjoyed by the guests of these luxury two-bedroom apartments. Each boasts a balcony overlooking the ocean, Sky TV and DVD player, plus two bathrooms, laundry facilities and full kitchen. Rates are for up to four people.

Eating

If you're not into seafood you might struggle for choice in Kaikoura, but if you love crustaceans and all things fishy you'll be in gastronomic heaven (if your wallet can take it).

Kaikoura Seafood BBQ (☎ 027 330 0511; Fyffe Quay; meals $3-6; ⏰ 10am-dark) A superb way to enjoy fresh fishy delicacies – by the sea, and with magical views – for a fraction of restaurant prices. At this roadside stall, en route to the seal colony, a chef casually barbecues choice seafood morsels – choose from garlic scallops or mussels, seafood chowder, or a delicious grilled fish sandwich, then hand over your loose change. Perfect.

Hislops Cafe (☎ 03-319 6971; 33 Beach Rd; lunch mains $7-17, dinner mains $17-30; ⏰ breakfast, lunch & dinner) This sunny, feel-good café has a reputation for fresh wholefood options. Start

the morning with fruit salad and toasted muesli and feel healthy and smug all day. Evening dining features organic meats plus good seafood, veg and vegan choices.

Hapuku Café (☎ 03-319 6558; SH1 at Hapuku Rd; meals $9-15; ⏰ breakfast & lunch, closed Tue & Wed winter) Worth a drive north, this café is at the luxury Hapuku Lodge (p459) and has made a name for itself churning out quality coffee, seafood and venison (not surprising, given it's located on a deer farm).

The Pier (☎ 03-319 5037; 1 Avoca St; meals $9-20) A smart makeover has turned this classic pub at the southern end of the beach into an upmarket eating option, with lunchtime treats including seafood chowder, tiger prawns or gin-cured salmon. Of an evening these dishes move up the ranks to become starters, joined by the likes of manuka-smoked lamb shanks or beef fillet.

Finz (☎ 03-319 6688; 103 South Bay Pde; mains $27-35; ⏰ dinner daily Oct-May, Wed-Sun Jun-Sep) At South Bay, Finz is widely regarded by locals as the best restaurant in town. Try the cray, or Finz's signature dish, seafood fettuccine. Meat-lovers will be tempted by venison, ribeye steak and lamb. Alternatively, share a vino at the adjacent bar (meals $10 to $20).

Olive Branch (☎ 03-319 6992; 54 West End; lunch mains $8-17, dinner mains $17-28; ⏰ lunch & dinner) The best main-street dining option is this warm, classy place. The menu features gourmet pizza, pasta dishes, local seafood and an interesting kids' menu.

For self-catering head to central **Kaikoura Four Square** (31-33 West End; ✆8am-7pm) or the new, large **New World supermarket** (124 Beach Rd; ✆8am-8pm), on the northern outskirts of town.

Drinking

Donegal House (☎ 03-319 5083; www.donegalhouse .co.nz;Mt Fyffe Rd) An unexpected little Irish pub in the country' and a real gem, with guaranteed good craic. Guinness and Kilkenny are available and there's regular live music and a huge outdoor area (all future beer gardens will pale in comparison). There's a simple menu offering well-prepared staples, including crayfish.

Strawberry Tree (☎ 03-319 6451; 21 West End) A fun, atmospheric pub with couches, pool table, beer garden and occasional live music – jamming sessions encouraged. All the furniture and décor has been taken from demolished historical buildings; check out the journalistic photos taken by the owner. Meals are available.

Getting There & Away

AIR

Soundsair (☎ 0800 505 005, 03-520 3080; www.sounds air.co.nz) has twice-daily flights between Wellington and Kaikoura (one way \$125).

BUS

There are **InterCity** (☎ 03-365 1113; www.inter citycoach.co.nz) services between Kaikoura and Nelson (one way \$55, 4½ hours, one or two daily), Picton (\$31, two hours, two daily) and Christchurch (\$27, 2½ hours, two daily). Buses arrive and depart from the car park on West End; tickets and information are available at the visitor information centre.

Atomic Shuttles (☎ 03-322 8883; www.atomic travel.co.nz) and **KBus** (☎ 0800 881 188, 03-578 4075; www.kbus.co.nz) also run services along SH1, south from Kaikoura to Christchurch, or north to Picton via Blenheim (and usually daily), with connections west to Nelson). These bus lines generally run once or twice daily in each direction.

Hanmer Connection (☎ 0800 242 5637) runs three times weekly between Hanmer Springs and Kaikoura (one way \$30, two hours).

TRAIN

Tranz Scenic (☎ 0800 872 467, 04-495 0775; www.tranz scenic.co.nz) runs the *TranzCoastal* service,

which stops at Kaikoura on its daily run between Picton (one way \$21 to \$49, two hours 20 minutes) and Christchurch (\$22 to \$51, three hours). The northbound train departs Kaikoura at 9.54am, and the southbound at 3.28pm.

Getting Around

The airport is 6.5km west of town. There is no public transport servicing the airport. Taxis can be reached on ☎ 03-319 6166.

You can hire bicycles from **Westend Motors** (☎ 03-319 5065; 48 West End; hr/half-day/full-day hire \$8/18/27), at the Shell service station.

NELSON REGION

The Nelson region is one of the top destinations for travellers to NZ – and for the locals too. It boasts an equable climate (more sunshine than any other part of NZ), top beaches, and some of the most popular national parks (Kahurangi, Nelson Lakes and Abel Tasman) in the country. It's also the home of an enthusiastic and progressive community of artists, craftspeople, winemakers and entrepreneurs.

NELSON

pop 43,500

One of NZ's most liveable cities, Nelson is a bright, active place and an obvious starting point for exploring the western coastal region. It's noted for its fruit-growing, wineries and breweries and its energetic arts and crafts community; there's no shortage of activities (sedate and thrilling) to keep you busy.

Information

BOOKSHOPS

Element Gallery & Books (Map p464; ☎ 03-539 1212; cnr Trafalgar & Halifax Sts) By the visitor information centre, selling NZ travel guides and pictorials.

Litter Arty (Map p464; ☎ 03-546 8005; 91 Hardy St) Quirky secondhand book exchange.

Page & Blackmore Booksellers (Map p464; ☎ 03-548 9992; 254 Trafalgar St)

INTERNET ACCESS

Aurora (Map p464; ☎ 03-546 6867; 16 Trafalgar St)

Boots Off (Map p464; ☎ 03-546 8789; 53 Bridge St)

KiwiNet (Map p464; ☎ 03-548 8095; 93 Hardy St)

GREATER NELSON

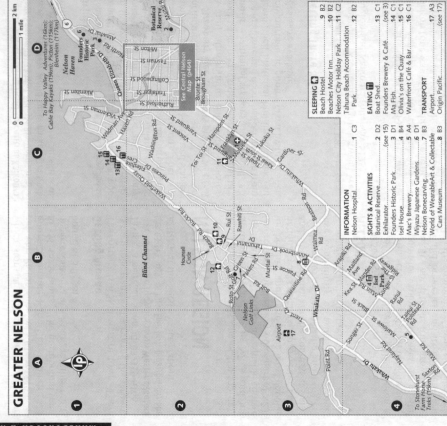

INFORMATION
Nelson Hospital.............................1 C3

SIGHTS & ACTIVITIES
Botanical Reserve..........................2 D2
Exhilarator...............................(see 15)
Founders Historic Park....................3 D1
Isel House................................4 B4
Mac's Brewery.............................5 A4
Miyazu Japanese Gardens...................6 D1
Nelson Bonecarving........................7 B3
World of WearableArt & Collectable
Cars Museum..............................8 B3

SLEEPING
Beach Hostel..............................9 B2
Beaches Motor Inn........................10 B2
Nelson City Holiday Park.................11 C2
Tahuna Beach Accommodation
Park....................................12 B2

EATING
Boat Shed................................13 C1
Founders Brewery & Café.............(see 3)
Ma Fish..................................15 C1
Olivia's on the Quay.....................16 C1
Waterfront Café & Bar....................16 C1

TRANSPORT
Airport..................................17 A3
Origin Pacific......................(see 17)

INTERNET RESOURCES
Backpack Nelson (www.backpacknelson.com)
Great source of information for the budget-minded.
Nelson Arts (www.nelsonarts.org.nz) Details the arts
and crafts produced in the region.
Nelson NZ (www.nelsonnz.com) Official tourism website
for the city.
Nelson Wines (www.nelsonwines.co.nz) Wineries and
galleries in the area.
The Taste (www.thetaste.co.nz) An excellent 'online
lifestyle magazine' covering the region.

MEDICAL SERVICES
City Care (Map p464; ☎ 03-546 8881; 202 Rutherford
St; ⏰ 8am-8pm) After-hours duty doctor available.
Nelson Hospital (Map p462; ☎ 03-546 1800; Waimea
Rd) Emergency doctor and dentist; enter from Franklyn St.

MONEY
Major banks can be found along the main
drag, Trafalgar St.

POST
Main post office (Map p464; cnr Trafalgar & Halifax Sts)

TOURIST INFORMATION
Automobile Association (AA; Map p464; ☎ 03-548
8339; 45 Halifax St)
Nelson visitor information centre (Map p464; ☎ 03-
548 2304; www.nelsonnz.com; cnr Trafalgar & Halifax Sts;
⏰ 8.30am-6pm Nov-Apr, 8.30am-5pm Mon-Fri 9am-4pm
Sat & Sun May-Oct) Pick up a copy of the useful *Nelson/
Tasman Region Visitor Guide* here, as well as countless brochures. The shiny new centre incorporates a DOC information
desk and displays on the region's national parks and walks.

Sights

HISTORIC BUILDINGS

The traditional symbol of Nelson is its Art Deco **Christ Church Cathedral** (Map p464; ☎ 03-548 1008; Trafalgar Sq; ☼ 8am-7pm), at the top of Trafalgar St. Work began in 1925 but was delayed, and arguments raged in the 1950s over whether the building should be completed according to its original design. Finally completed in 1965 to a modified design, it was consecrated in 1972, 47 years after the foundation stone was laid.

Close to the cathedral, South St is home to a row of restored workers' cottages, built between 1863 and 1867 and said to be the oldest preserved street in NZ. Some cottages are available as accommodation (p468).

South of town, the beautiful gardens of Isel Park are worth a wander. In the grounds you'll find the stately 1880s **Isel House** (Map p462; ☎ 03-547 1347; Hilliard St; admission by donation; ☼ 11am-4pm).

MUSEUMS & GALLERIES

Freshly opened in October 2005 is the shiny **Nelson Provincial Museum** (Map p464; ☎ 03-547 9740; www.museumnp.org.nz; cnr Hardy & Trafalgar Sts; admission free; ☼ 9am-5pm Mon-Fri, 10am-4.30pm Sat & Sun), in the centre of town. This modern space is filled with cultural heritage and natural history exhibits of regional interest and includes a roof-top garden. Charges may apply for major exhibits.

Adjacent to the Queen's Gardens, the **Suter** (Map p464; ☎ 03-548 4699; www.thesuter.org .nz; 208 Bridge St; adult/child $3/50c; ☼ 10.30am-4.30pm) is the city's main repository of high art, with changing exhibitions, musical and theatrical performances, films, a craft shop and café.

The visitor information centre has brochures detailing the numerous dealer galleries and craft outlets around town. Favourites include the following:

Flame Daisy (Map p464; ☎ 03-548 4475; 324 Trafalgar Sq) Boutique glass-blowing studio.

Höglund Art Glass Gallery (Map p464; ☎ 03-546 9850; Trafalgar Sq) Original, hand-blown glass, inside the Rutherford Hotel.

Jens Hansen (Map p464; ☎ 03-548 0640; www .jenshansen.com; 320 Trafalgar Sq) Gold and silversmith workshop producing contemporary jewellery.

Rutherford Gallery (Map p464; ☎ 03-548 1878; www.rutherfordgallery.co.nz; 42 Halifax St) Contemporary paintings by local and national artists.

CREATIVE TOURISM

If being surrounded by all this artistry has you yearning to exercise your own creative juices, contact Nelson-based **Creative Tourism** (☎ 0800 408 020; www.creativetourism.co.nz), which can put you in touch with individuals offering a variety of interactive workshops and creative experiences. The website outlines more detail – you can try your hand at artistic endeavours (wood-turning, bone-carving or felt-making, for example), Maori culture (learn basket-weaving, visit a marae or go food collecting), food and wine (bake a pavlova, have a lesson in NZ seafood from a restaurateur, talk to a brewer of organic beer) and nature (wilderness workshops).

The workshop offered by **Nelson Bone-carving** (Map p462; ☎ 03-546 4275; thebone carver@xtra.co.nz; 87 Green St, Tahunanui; day course $55) earns rave reviews from travellers. Here you obtain the instructions and materials to design and carve your own pendant out of bone. There's free pick-up and drop-off in town.

South St Gallery (Map p464; ☎ 03-548 8117; www .nelsonpottery.co.nz; 10 Nile St West) Noted for its extensive collection of pottery.

GARDENS

The **Botanical Reserve** (Map p462; Milton St) has walking tracks up to Botanical Hill, with a spire proclaiming it NZ's geographical centre. The interesting history of the reserve is outlined on information panels.

Just down the road from Founders Park are the beautifully serene **Miyazu Japanese Gardens** (Map p462; Atawhai Dr; admission free; ☼ 24hr), full of ponds and ducks.

FOUNDERS PARK

Founders Historic Park (Map p462; ☎ 03-548 2649; www.founderspark.co.nz; 87 Atawhai Dr; adult/child $5/2; ☼ 10am-4.30pm) is near the waterfront 1km from the city centre, and houses a replica historic village. It's also home to **Founders Brewery & Café** (Map p462; ☎ 03-548 4638; www.biobrew.co.nz; meals $7-15; ☼ lunch), NZ's first certified organic brewery, producing Tall Blonde, Red Head and Long Black brews. Sit outside and enjoy the beers and food. If you're only visiting the brewery, there's no admission charge.

www.lonelyplanet.com

CENTRAL NELSON

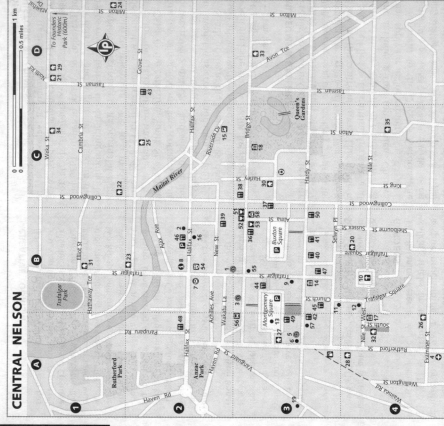

MAC'S BREWERY

Mac's Brewery (Map p464; ☎ 03-547 0526; www.macs .co.nz; 660 Main Rd, Stoke; tours $10; ☺ bar 10am-5pm Tue-Sat, tours 11am & 2pm Tue-Sat) is the source of the favourite beer for many discerning Nelsonites. Black Mac, a dark ale, is legendary but there are five varieties in all. Take a brewery tour or just turn up at the bar for a tasting. It's about 6km south of Nelson in Stoke.

NELSON MARKET

Don't miss the **Nelson Market** (Map p464; ☎ 03-546 6454; Montgomery Sq; ☺ 8am-1pm Sat), an excellent local market with lots of fresh produce, food stalls, fashion, and arts and crafts on offer. On Sundays the flea market, Mon-

ty's, is held at the same place from 9am to 1pm.

Activities

There are plenty of activities on offer in this region, and although most take place some way out of the city, most operators will pick up and drop off in Nelson.

Go paragliding with **Nelson Paragliding** (☎ 03-544 1182; www.nelsonparagliding.co.nz) or **Adventure Paragliding and Kiteboarding** (☎ 0800 111 611, 03-546 6863; www.skyout.co.nz). Both charge around $150 for a tandem flight and $180 for a full-day introductory course. The latter company can also get you airborne teaching you kiteboarding (aka kitesurfing); a fullday introduction costs $190.

INFORMATION
Aurora....1 B2
Automobile Association (AA)....2 B2
Boots Off....3 B3
City Care....4 A4
Element Gallery & Books....(see 8)
KiwiNet....5 A3
Litter Arty....6 A3
Main Post Office....7 B2
Nelson Visitor Information
Centre....8 B2
Page & Blackmore Booksellers....9 B3

SIGHTS & ACTIVITIES
Christ Church Cathedral....10 B4
Flame Daisy....11 B3
Höglund Art Glass
Gallery....12 B4
Jens Hansen....(see 11)
Nelson Market....13 A3
Nelson Provincial
Museum....14 B3
Riverside Pool....15 C2
Rutherford Gallery....16 B2
South St Gallery....17 A4
Suter....18 C3
Vertical Limits....19 A3

SLEEPING
Accents on the Park....20 B4
Apartments Paradiso....21 C1
California House Inn....22 C1
Cedar Grove....23 B2
Green Monkey....24 C1
Grove Villa B&B....25 C1
Lynton Lodge....26 A4
Nelson YHA....27 A4
Palace Backpackers....28 A4
Paradiso Backpackers....29 D1
Rosy Glow Cottage....30 C1
Shortbread Cottage....31 B1
South St Cottages....32 A4
Sussex House....33 C1
Tasman Bay Backpackers....34 C1
Trampers Rest....35 C4

EATING
Akbabas Kebabs....36 B3
Cut....37 C3
Diner....(see 36)
Fresh Choice....38 C1
Kafiene....39 B2
Lambretta's....40 B3
Morrison St Café....41 B3
My Piel....42 A3
Organic Greengrocer....43 D2
Penguino Gelato Café....44 B3
Rosy Glow Chocolates....(see 30)
Stingray Café & Bar....45 B2
Tozzetti Panetteria....46 B2
Victorian Rose....47 B3
Woolworths....48 A2
Yaza Cafe....49 A3
Zippy's....50 B3

DRINKING
Maen Fiddler....51 B3
Phat....52 B3
Shark Club....53 B3

ENTERTAINMENT
State Cinema 6....54 B2

TRANSPORT
Abel Tasman Coachlines....(see 56)
Air New Zealand....55 B3
Double Decker Experience....(see 56)
InterCity Depot....56 A3
Nelson Suburban
Bus Lines....(see 56)
Stewarts Cycle City....57 A3
Sun City Taxis....58 B3

Hang-gliding is another aerial possibility, arranged through one of two operators: **Nelson Hang Gliding Adventures** (☎ 03-548 9751; www.flynelson.co.nz; flight $140) and **Hang Gliding New Zealand** (☎ 0800 212 359, 03-540 2183; www.hanggliding.co.nz; flight $160).

If you prefer to stay on solid ground, there are plenty of ways to get your kicks. Of the many **walks** in and around town, the riverside footpath makes a pleasant stroll through the city.

Stonehurst Farm Horse Treks (☎ 0800 487 357, 03-542 4121; www.stonehurstfarm.co.nz; RD 1, Richmond; 1hr/half-day rides $35/89), about 22km south of town, offers kids' pony rides, one-hour farm rides, 2½-hour Sundowner treks and half-day exploration that involves a river crossing.

Rock climbing on the sheer limestone cliffs of the Golden Bay and Takaka area is popular with local outdoor enthusiasts. **Vertical Limits** (Map p464; ☎ 0506 837 842, 03-545 7511; www.verticallimits.co.nz; 34 Vanguard St; ✆ noon-9pm Mon-Thu, 10am-6pm Fri-Sun) has half-/full-day rock-climbing trips ($65/130), as well as an indoor climbing wall at its home base.

Another popular activity is the skywire and quad-bike tours at **Happy Valley Adventures** (☎ 0800 157 300, 03-545 0304; www.happyvalley adventures.co.nz; 194 Cable Bay Rd), a 20-minute drive northeast along SH6. The 3km-long Skywire is a cross between a chairlift and a flying fox, 150m above the native forest; a ride costs from $70/50 per adult/child, quad-bike tours start at $70/20 per driver/passenger for a one-hour ride through the forest.

Further down the road from Happy Valley Adventures is **Cable Bay Kayaks** (☎ 0508 222 532, 03-545 0332; nick.cablebaykayaks@clear.net.nz), offering half-/full-day guided sea-kayaking trips exploring the coastline and marine life from $50/80.

There are many opportunities to get out on the water of Tasman Bay.

The **Exhilarator** (Map p462; ☎ 0800 488 066, 03-548 8066; www.exhilarator.co.nz; Wakefield Quay; ✆ departs 9am, noon & 4pm) can take you speeding across the bay to Mapua or Marahau, as a sightseeing trip or as a means of transport to Abel Tasman National Park. One way to Marahau costs $25; a two-hour round-trip is $75.

To get out on a yacht, the best option is the Wednesday night races, run by **Cat Sailing & Launch Charters** (☎ 03-547 6666; www.sailingcharters.co.nz). You get two hours to help crew a boat around the harbour in racing conditions for only $40. This company also offers a number of very reasonably priced half-, full-day and multiday sailing trips through Abel Tasman National Park and/or the Marlborough Sounds. An evening sail, dinner barbecue, overnight on the boat and breakfast the next day costs $150 per person (the 'backpacker option' – BYO sleeping

WONDERFUL WORLD OF WEARABLEART & COLLECTABLE CARS MUSEUM

The Nelson and Golden Bay region exudes creativity. Artists, potters, weavers and fashion designers live and work here, so it's hardly surprising that NZ's most inspiring and successful art-meets-fashion show was born here.

It began humbly in 1987 when creator Suzie Moncrieff decided to hold an off-beat fashion show in a marquee in Wakefield, southwest of Nelson. The concept was not simply to design a dress, but to create a piece of art that could be worn and modelled. Local artists and audiences loved the idea and slowly the New Zealand WearableArt Award grew into an annual event, with traditional fabrics going out the window in favour of ever-more whacky and imaginative designs. Everything from wood, papier-mâché, paua shell, copper wire, soft-drink cans, wine bladders and foodstuffs have been used to create the garments. The show also features themed entries such as the illumination section, avant-garde and the popular Bizarre Bra Award. Entries are now received from around NZ and abroad, and a look at some of the past winners (and entries) shows that WOW creativity knows no limits. Many previous winners have gone on to work in costumes and props for the NZ film industry.

With ever-increasing popularity and attendances, the show in Nelson became a victim of its own success and needed to be moved to a bigger stage, both commercially and creatively. In 2005 the show, now called the Montana World of WearableArt Award Show (sponsored by one of NZ's largest winemakers, Montana), was transplanted to Wellington and in its first year in the capital drew an audience of around 30,000.

In Wellington each September, that year's entries will be showcased in a two-hour theatrical stage show featuring choreography, music, lighting and special effects. The show is performed over a two-week period in late September – if your visit to the capital coincides with these dates, it's well worth trying to obtain tickets to a performance, although these can be sold out well beforehand. Tickets start at $65; check out www.worldofwearableart.co.nz for all the ticketing details.

Even if you can't check out the show, be sure to get along to the eye-popping **World of WearableArt & Collectable Cars Museum** (Map p462; ☎ 03-547 4573; www.wowcars.co.nz; 95 Quarantine Rd; adult/child $18/7; ⏰ 10am–6pm late Dec–Easter, to 5pm rest of year). The WOW section showcases the bizarre and spellbinding 'garments' featured in the WearableArt Awards. The galleries are small but high-tech, with a carousel mimicking the usual catwalk models and an illumination room.

Equally enthralling is the display of 40 mint-condition classic cars found under the same architecturally designed roof. Exhibits change but may include a 1959 pink Cadillac, a 1908 Renault made famous as a Parisienne taxi, an E-type Jaguar and an Eldorado Cadillac convertible used by Eisenhower in the 1953 US presidential parade.

bag – is $100). **Sea Sense Sailing School** (☎ 03-539 4339; www.sailingschool.co.nz), as the name suggests, runs a number of learn-to-sail courses. The 15-hour 'sailing shoes' introduction costs $545.

For swimming, head to Tahunanui Beach or the **Riverside Pool** (Map p464; ☎ 03-546 3221; Riverside Dr; adult/child $3.10/1.60).

Tours

Popular tours around Nelson include wineries in the Richmond and Upper Moutere area, craft and scenic tours, and sightseeing flights.

Bay Tours (☎ 0800 229 868, 03-545 7114; www .baytoursnelson.co.nz; half-/full-day wine tour $65/198, half-day art tour $60; scenic tour $55–148) A variety of

tours, including combinations of wine and art. Full-day scenic-tour options include a cruise in Abel Tasman, visit to Golden Bay or trip to Nelson Lakes National Park.

JJ's Scenic Tours (☎ 0800 568 568; www.jjs.co.nz; tours from $60) Also offers scenic, wine-focused and craft-heavy tours, plus the half-day Natural Brewery Trail, visiting five boutique breweries.

Tasman Helicopters (☎ 03-528 8075; www.tasmanhel icopters.co.nz; tours from $110) A host of chopper flights and tours, including *Lord of the Rings* locations, D'Urville Island, trout fishing, helihiking, lunch tours and flights over Farewell Spit, and Kahurangi and Abel Tasman National Parks.

Festivals & Events

With its enthusiastic artistic flair, Nelson stages noteworthy events throughout the year, including:

Summer Festival (www.nelsonfestivals.co.nz) A two-month family-focused celebration of sunny weather, from mid-December to mid-February. There are buskers, outdoor cinema, theatre and concerts.

Arts Festival (03-546 0212; www.nelsonfestivals.co.nz) Held over 10 days in October; events include a masked parade, street carnival, exhibitions, cabaret, writers, theatre and music.

Sleeping

In summer Nelson swells with tourists. Book accommodation in advance or arrive early in the day.

Nelson is backpacker central, so accommodation is often purpose-built and high quality. Ye olde B&Bs, furnished in convincingly Victorian style, are popular and many of these are in beautiful heritage buildings.

Many of Nelson's motels are near the beach at Tahunanui, on Beach Rd and Muritai St. Others are on Waimea Rd (the extension of Rutherford St).

BUDGET

Hostels

Many of the 20 or so backpackers in Nelson offer free pick-up if required.

Accents on the Park (Map p464; 03-548 4335; www.accentsonthepark.com; 335 Trafalgar Sq; dm $20-28, d with/without bathroom $90/60;) A super new option that feels more like a guesthouse than a hostel. It's geared to the more discerning traveller, with lots of comfy communal areas, on-site café-bar, soundproofed rooms, quality linen, superclean bathrooms and bikes for hire. It may not attract the party crowd, but it will impress travellers looking for affordable luxury.

Green Monkey (Map p464; 03-545 7421; www.thegreenmonkey.co.nz; 129 Milton St; dm d $23/55;) Small, homely and exceedingly comfortable option, run by a friendly English couple. There are just two dorms and two double rooms (doubles with TV); enjoy your dinner outside among the fruit trees or inside by the toasty log fire.

Tasman Bay Backpackers (Map p464; 0800 222 257, 03-548 7950; www.tasmanbaybackpackers.co.nz; 10 Weka St; sites per person $12, dm/d $22/54;) This popular, well-designed option is light and airy, with colourful rooms, inviting living areas, a sunny outdoor deck and a well-used hammock. The kitchen is well organised and in winter the friendly owners offer free breakfast, as well as nightly specials

such as video and popcorn or homemade soup.

Trampers Rest (Map p464; /fax 03-545 7477; 31 Alton St; dm/d $24/58; closed Jun-Aug) With just a few beds (and no bunks), much-loved Trampers is hard to beat for a homely environment. The enthusiastic owner is a keen tramper and cyclist and provides comprehensive local information as well as free use of bikes. There's a small kitchen, book exchange, piano and music.

Nelson YHA (Map p464; 03-545 9988; www.stayha.com; 59 Rutherford St; d from $26/43/62, d with bathroom $78;) This spotless, central place is purpose-built with high-quality facilities such as a soundproof, vaultlike TV room and a well-organised modern kitchen opening onto an outdoor terrace.

Paradiso Backpackers (Map p464; 0800 269 667, 03-546 6703; www.backpackernelson.co.nz; 42 Weka St; sites per person $15, dm $23-25, tw & d $56;) Club Med for the impoverished, Paradiso is a sprawling place in spacious grounds popular with a younger crowd. There's plenty of pool-side action, watched over by the glassed-in main kitchen, a high-rotation hammock, volleyball court and sauna. Rooms are nothing special, dorms are four- and eight-bed, and there's heated A-frame tents.

Shortbread Cottage (Map p464; 03-546 6681; 33 Trafalgar St; dm/d $24/57;) A small, homely, 13-bed hostel, where some of the cosy rooms have en suites. There's a small kitchen, log fire and a great outdoor garden. You'll definitely get to sample the eponymous homemade shortbread biscuits.

Also recommended:

Beach Hostel (Map p462; 03-548 6817; www.nelsonbeachhostel.co.nz; 25 Muritai St; dm/d $20/50;) Chilled-out place close to Tahunanui Beach, about 4km from town. Free bikes.

Palace Backpackers (Map p464; 03-548 4691; www.thepalace.co.nz; 114 Rutherford St; dm/d $22/55;) Characterful old place set above the street, with free breakfast and spa. Entrance is via the driveway behind the Shell service station.

Camping

Nelson City Holiday Park (Map p462; 0800 778 898, 03-548 1445; www.nelsonholidaypark.co.nz; 230 Vanguard St; sites per 2 people $26-28, cabins $40-70;) The town's most central camping option, and new owners are giving it a welcome makeover, with new amenities blocks, landscaping and refurbished accommodation. There are good sites for tents at the park's rear.

Tahuna Beach Accommodation Park (Map p462; ☎ 03-548 5159; www.tahunabeachaccommodationpark .co.nz; 70 Beach Rd; sites per 2 people $28, cabins & units $55-90; ☐) This is a huge park accommodating thousands. It's really a mini-village, with its own supermarket, mini golf and playgrounds. It's near the beach, 5km from the city.

MIDRANGE

Cedar Grove (Map p464; ☎ 0800 233 274, 03-545 1133; www.cedargrove.co.nz; cnr Trafalgar & Grove Sts; studio $120-140, apt $140-170) A deservedly popular option – book ahead. Warm and spacious apartments feature elegant décor, with cooking facilities and all the business trimmings such as phone and fax. The spa, robes, CD player and DVD are for later.

Beaches Motor Inn (Map p462; ☎ 0800 332 232, 03-548 6008; www.beachesmotorinn.co.nz; 69 Tahunanui Dr; d $135-175) This fresh out-of-town option has a fun beachy-feel, with its crisp white walls brightened by splashes of colour. Extras include full kitchens, spas and Sky TV. Try for a ground-floor unit with courtyard.

Rosy Glow Cottage (Map p464; ☎ 03-548 3383; rosyglow@xtra.co.nz; 20 Harley St; d $125) Chocoholics might not sleep easy here, given what's downstairs... This well-priced modern unit sits above the chocolate shop (see opposite) and has a full kitchen, spa bath and lovely veranda on which to watch the town go by. A good choice; in summer there's a three-night minimum stay.

Apartments Paradiso (Map p464; ☎ 0800 269 667, 03-545 7128; www.paradisoapartments.co.nz; cnr Tasman & Weka Sts; d $75-140; ☐ ☑) Sink into a huge king-size bed at this attractive complex of motel-style units, each with small but well-equipped kitchenettes, spas, Sky TV and CD player. It's under the management of nearby Paradiso Backpackers (p467), and guests can use the swimming pool and other hostel facilities.

Sussex House (Map p464; ☎ 03-548 9972; www .sussex.co.nz; 238 Bridge St; s $110-140, d $130-160; ☐) In a historic riverside home, the Sussex has five lovely rooms, all named after famous composers (the Strauss room has the best views). There's a lush garden and verandas, and buffet breakfast is included.

Lynton Lodge (Map p464; ☎ 03-548 7112; www.hol idayguide.co.nz/Nelson/LyntonLodge.aspx; 25 Examiner St;

apt $95-100) High on the hill, with wonderful views of Nelson, Lynton Lodge has older-style self-contained apartments – try for one of the units with a balcony. In some instances the dated décor has become retro-cool. It looks and feels more like a guesthouse than a motel.

Grove Villa B&B (Map p464; ☎ 0800 488 900, 03-548 8895; www.grovevilla.co.nz; 36 Grove St; s/d $75/95, s/d with bathroom from $90/105; ☐) Reasonably priced B&B with six rooms in a gorgeous heritage home close to town. Rooms are furnished in period style with lots of natural light.

TOP END

South St Cottages (Map p464; ☎ 03-540 2769; www .cottageaccommodation.co.nz; 1, 3 & 12 South St; d $160-175) Stay on NZ's oldest preserved street in one of three charming, two-bedroom self-contained cottages built in the 1860s. Each has all the comforts of home, including kitchen, laundry, log fire and courtyard garden; breakfast provisions are supplied. The owners also have a modern two-bedroom villa on the waterfront for rent (double room $180 to $240).

California House Inn (Map p464; ☎ 03-548 4173; www.californiahouse.co.nz; 29 Collingwood St; r $210-295) An original manor home with six rooms immaculately furnished with Victorian-era furniture and grace. So as not to spoil the look, TVs, video and DVD players are available on request. Service is personalised and food is often organic and there are loads of vegetarian options.

Eating

The wealth of local produce, particularly seafood, makes dining out in Nelson an exciting prospect. Deep-sea fish, scallops from the bays, mussels and oysters are available, complemented by NZ wines and microbrewed beers. Food is often organic and there are loads of vegetarian options.

RESTAURANTS

Cut (Map p464; ☎ 03-548 9874; 94 Collingwood St; mains $29-35; ☑ dinner Tue-Sat) The prices alone indicate that this is one of Nelson's finest dining establishments, and the foodie reviews confirm it. Inside this unassuming cottage is a kitchen that specialises in local produce, and a cellar stocking plenty of local wine. Come to be impressed, but book first.

Boat Shed (Map p462; ☎ 03-546 9783; 350 Wakefield Quay; lunch mains $10-20, dinner mains $27-34; ☒ breakfast, lunch & dinner) A Nelson landmark sitting on stilts over the sea. As befits the setting, everything is fish themed – from the chairs to the water bottles, and especially the menu (but not exclusively so). Breakfast or lunch is easier on the wallet but still rich in experience.

Victorian Rose (Map p464; ☎ 03-548 7631; 281 Trafalgar St; mains $9-21; ☒ lunch & dinner) A pastiche of English/Irish pub styles in airy, high-ceilinged premises. Substantial counter meals include a traditional roast, the old pub classic surf 'n' turf, plus gourmet burgers and curries. There are backpacker specials available. (See also p470.)

Lambretta's (Map p464; ☎ 03-545 8555; 204 Hardy St; mains $14-30; ☒ breakfast, lunch & dinner) Named after the Italian scooter, this predominantly pizza-and-pasta restaurant is reasonably priced with a busy, casual atmosphere. There are no run-of-the-mill toppings here – all are interesting gourmet combinations. It's a big family-friendly place with Grecian columns.

There are other options by the water, all reliably good:

Ma Fish (Map p462; ☎ 03-539 1307; upstairs, 322 Wakefield Quay; mains $15-35; ☒ lunch & dinner)

Olivia's on the Quay (Map p462; ☎ 03-548 3361; 272 Wakefield Quay; lunch mains $13-19, dinner mains $20-28; ☒ lunch & dinner)

Waterfront Café & Bar (Map p462; ☎ 03-546 6685; 341 Wakefield Quay; lunch mains $10-15, dinner mains $26-30; ☒ lunch & dinner)

CAFÉS

Kafiene (Map p464; ☎ 03-545 6911; 22 New St; meals $7-14; ☒ breakfast & lunch Tue-Sun) Kid-friendly Kafiene is a chilled place, set in a pebble-covered courtyard that's dotted with well-loved couches, mirror mosaics, a dedicated

---

AUTHOR'S CHOICE

Stingray Café & Bar (Map p464; ☎ 03-545 8957; 8 Church St; dinner mains $14-21; ☒ breakfast, lunch & dinner) From its ecofriendly ethos to sunny courtyard, well-priced meals and smooth tunes, Stingray seems to capture the upbeat mood of Nelson. Drop by at any time of day to enjoy the relaxed atmosphere and snaffle a pizza or salad. Later, settle in with a cocktail to live music or a DJ.

---

play area, and established greenery. Feast on bagels, veggie burgers, nachos and thumpin' breakfasts.

Zippy's (Map p464; ☎ 03-546 6348; 276 Hardy St; meals $5-8; ☒ breakfast & lunch Mon-Sat) The décor here is a crazy combo of purple, teal and red and service is zippy. The vegetarian food includes burritos, salads and the 'locally famous' chocolate afghans. Drinks include ice-cream shakes, chai and heart-startlingly rich, full-flavoured coffee.

Yaza Cafe (Map p464; ☎ 03-548 2849; Montgomery Sq; meals $5-15; ☒ breakfast & lunch At the site of the weekend markets, Yaza is a cosy, kid-friendly café with all-day breakfast and live music most Fridays and Saturdays in summer, ranging from folk, acoustic blues and roots, punk, pop and reggae. The food is free-range and organic and patchouli lingers in the air – it's 'your lounge in town'. Opening hours are extended on the weekends over summer.

Morrison St Café (Map p464; ☎ 03-548 8110; 244 Hardy St; meals $8-16; ☒ breakfast & lunch) A polished operator compared with the arty cafés listed above. Down a hearty brekkie in the great outdoor area (inside the neighbouring garden shop), or pop by for an afternoon pick-me-up of coffee and cake.

QUICK EATS

Tozzetti Panetteria (Map p464; ☎ 03-546 8484; 41 Halifax St; snacks to $6; ☒ 7am-5pm Mon-Fri, to noon Sat) You'll smell fresh bread baking before you see Tozzetti. A tiny bakery serving beautiful breads, sandwiches and sweet treats (it also has a stall at the Saturday market).

Rosy Glow Chocolates (Map p464; ☎ 03-548 3383; 20 Harley St; per chocolate $1.50-3.50; ☒ 9am-5pm Mon-Fri, 10am-1pm Sat) Pretty as a picture with its baby-pink exterior. This is the sibling of the original Rosy Glow in Collingwood (p485), and a must on any chocoholic's itinerary. Try the homemade logs of rich, creamy chocolate such as conquistador (hazelnut praline in dark chocolate) and turtle (caramel with toasted walnuts).

My Pie! (Map p464; ☎ 03-546 7437; Rutherford Mews; pies $5; ☒ 10am-4pm Mon-Fri) Off Hardy St, My Pie! makes great gourmet snacks – try fillings such as wild venison and red wine or Thai coconut chicken. Mmm...look out for their stall at the Saturday market.

Penguino Gelato Café (Map p464; ☎ 03-545 6450; Montgomery Sq; ☒ 11am-6pm) Join the locals queuing for the superb gelato and sorbet, made daily on the premises.

A couple of options on Bridge St will quickly (and cheaply) fill a rumbling tum. **Akbabas Kebabs** (Map p464; ☎ 03-548 8825; 130 Bridge St; kebabs $6-9; ☺ lunch & dinner) is a tiny Turkish kebab house. Nearby, the **Diner** (Map p464; ☎ 03-548 4680; 142 Bridge St; meals $5-10; ☺ dinner Tue-Sat) pumps out burgers, fish and chips, and kebabs.

SELF-CATERING

Organic Greengrocer (Map p464; ☎ 03-546 9225; cnr Tasman & Grove Sts; ☺ 8.30am-6pm Mon-Fri, 9am-3pm Sat) This large organic food store stocks all things free of wheat/meat/dairy/gluten. You can also join up for Willing Workers on Organic Farms (WWOOF) memberships here (see p704).

Head to **Woolworths** (Map p464; cnr Paruparu Rd & Halifax St; ☺ 7am-10pm) and **Fresh Choice** (Map p464; 69 Collingwood St; ☺ 7am-9pm), which claims to stock more than 480 organic products.

Drinking

Nelson has a small but active nightlife scene. Most of the late-night pubs and bars cluster around Bridge St, where the action starts to build by around 10pm.

Maen Fiddler (Map p464; ☎ 03-546 8516; 145 Bridge St; ☺ 4pm-late Tue-Sat) A real bar, and a great one at that. This pub is traditionally Irish (owned by a Dubliner) but not obnoxiously so with leprechauns and shamrocks everywhere. It has the biggest range of whiskies in Nelson, a good range of local and imported beers, live music nightly and a cosy courtyard.

Victorian Rose (281 Trafalgar St) Backpackers (and locals) often start with a meal (see p469) and a few drinks at this popular spot. Try the full range of locally brewed Mac drops (p464). There's also live music Tuesday to Saturday, often with a jazz-groove leaning.

Shark Club (Map p464; ☎ 03-546 6630; 132-136 Bridge St; ☺ noon-late) If you're hankering for a game of stick with some of the fiercest white pointers around, head to this pool hall and pub. There's free pool from 5pm to 7pm, drinks deals for backpackers, regular pool comps, and bar snacks (nachos, wedges etc) for fuel.

Phat (Map p464; ☎ 03-548 3311; www.phatclub.co.nz; 137 Bridge St; cover from $5; ☺ 10pm-late Wed-Sat) DJs at this righteous club spin techno, dub, drum 'n' bass, breaks and hip-hop, and the club hosts big-name international acts. There's a cover charge every night, which those who worship the beats happily pay.

Entertainment

The theatre at the Suter (p463) often hosts drama, music and dance. **State Cinema 6** (Map p464; ☎ 03-548 8123; www.statecinema6.co.nz; 91 Trafalgar St) is the place to see mainstream, new-release flicks.

Getting There & Away

AIR

Air New Zealand (Map p464; ☎ 0800 737 000, 03-546 3100; www.airnz.co.nz; cnr Trafalgar & Bridge Sts) has direct flights to/from Wellington (one way from $80, 11 daily), Auckland (from $120, 10 daily) and Christchurch (from $85, eight daily), with connections to other cities.

Origin Pacific (☎ 0800 302 302, 03-547 2020; www.originpacific.co.nz) is based at Nelson airport and has direct connections to several major centres, including Auckland (one way from $115, two daily), Christchurch (from $85, up to four daily) and Wellington (from $80, six daily). There are also once-daily direct services to Hamilton, Palmerston North and New Plymouth, as well as Napier (via Wellington).

Soundsair (☎ 0800 505 005, 03-520 3080; www.soundsair.co.nz) offers a daily service between Nelson and Wellington (one way $75).

BUS

See p482 for details about services to/from Abel Tasman National Park. Note that services for many of these operators run on a reduced timetable from May to September. Prices given are for one-way fares.

Abel Tasman Coachlines (Map p464; ☎ 03-548 0285; www.abeltasmantravel.co.nz; 27 Bridge St) operates services to Motueka ($10, one hour, two to five daily), Takaka ($24, 2¾ hours, one or two daily), Kaiteriteri ($15, 1½ hours, one to three daily) and Marahau ($15, 1¾ hours, two to four daily). In summer it also runs to Totaranui and the Heaphy Track.

Atomic Shuttles (☎ 03-322 8883; www.atomictravel.co.nz) has a daily bus to/from Picton ($20, 2¼ hours, one daily) and to the West Coast, including Greymouth ($45, 5¼ hours, one daily) and Fox Glacier ($75, 8¾ hours, one daily). Services depart from the visitor information centre.

InterCity (Map p464; ☎ 03-365 1113, 03-548 1538; www.intercitycoach.co.nz; 27 Bridge St) runs services daily to Picton ($31, two hours, three to four buses daily), Christchurch ($69, 6½ hours, one daily) and Greymouth ($74, six hours, one daily) via Murchison and West-port, with onward connections to Franz Josef and Fox Glaciers.

KBus (☎ 0800 881 188, 03-578 4075; www.kbus.co.nz) has increased its services in recent times and now travels to various spots across the top of the island. From Nelson there are daily services to Picton ($22, 2½ hours), Kaikoura ($35, 3½ hours), Christchurch ($48, 6¼ hours), Motueka ($10, one hour), Marahau ($15, 1½ hours), Kaiteriteri ($15, 1¾ hours) and Takaka ($25, 2¾ hours). In summer there are also daily services to St Arnaud ($20, one hour), Westport ($35, 3¾ hours) and Greymouth ($45, 5¾ hours); this drops to four times a week in winter. In summer there are also services to the beginning of the Heaphy Track ($47, 3½ hours, one daily). KBus services arrive at and depart from Nelson's visitor information centre.

Southern Link Lazerline Coaches (☎ 03-546 8687; www.yellow.co.nz/site/southernlink) heads to Christchurch ($43, 7½ hours, one daily) via Murchison and the Lewis Pass (including a stop at Hanmer Springs if prebooked).

Getting Around

TO/FROM THE AIRPORT

Super Shuttle (☎ 0800 748 885, 03-547 5782; www .supershuttle.co.nz) offers 24-hour door-to-door service ($12/14 for one/two passengers travelling together) to and from the air-port, 6km southwest of town. A taxi to the airport costs about $15.

BICYCLE

If you want to nip from town to the beach or do some serious off-road touring, hire a bike from **Stewarts Cycle City** (Map p464; ☎ 03-548 1666; www.stewartscyclecity.com; 114 Hardy St; per day hire $35-95, per week from $140). It offers city and mountain bikes, plus touring bikes and equipment for long journeys.

BUS

Of most interest to travellers is the **Double Decker Experience** (Map p464; 27 Bridge St; one circuit $7.50; ☑ depart 11am & 1pm Sun-Thu Feb-mid-Dec, daily mid-Dec–Jan), which does two daily circuits of main attractions in and around Nelson,

including Founders Park, Isel Park, the World of WearableArt Museum, the Ta-hananui beach and the Nelson waterfront. For a good sightseeing trip around town, stay on for an entire circuit, or get off at one attraction and catch the later service; more information is available at the visitor information centre.

Nelson Suburban Bus Lines (SBL; Map p464; ☎ 03-548 3290; www.nelsoncoaches.co.nz; 27 Bridge St) oper-ates local services from its terminal out to Richmond via Tahunanui and Stoke until about 6pm weekdays, and until 4.30pm on weekends. These connect with two weekday-only loop services in Stoke, which will get you to Isel Park, Broadgreen House and Mac's Brewery.

The Bus (☎ 03-539 4107; www.lesuetravelnz.com /thebus.htm; adult $2) is a central bus service running every hour or so on four routes to outlying areas, all starting from the Inter-City depot.

TAXI

Sun City Taxis (Map p464; ☎ 0800 422 666, 03-548 2666; 140 Bridge St) has a convenient rank on Bridge St. Also try **Nelson City Taxis** (☎ 0800 108 855, 03-548 8225).

NELSON LAKES NATIONAL PARK

At the pristine Nelson Lakes National Park, two beautiful glacial lakes are fringed by beech forest and flax, with a backdrop of forested mountains. There's an unexpected hint of Fiordland about the place, but with-out the crowds – this serene area feels well off the tourist trail.

Part of the park, east of Lake Rotoiti, is classed as a 'mainland island' and is part of an aggressive conservation scheme to eradi-cate introduced pests such as possums and stoats, and recover native flora and fauna. There's excellent tramping, including short walks, lake scenery and also winter skiing at Rainbow Valley ski field (p84). Lakes Ro-toiti and Rotoroa are rich with bird life and famous for brown-trout fishing.

Orientation

The park is accessible from two different areas: Lakes Rotoiti and Rotoroa. St Arnaud village lies on the shore of Lake Rotoiti (on the highway between Murchison and Blen-heim) and, although tiny, is the main centre. Rotoroa, about 11km off the highway, has far fewer visitors (mainly trampers and fishing groups), although there is some accommodation down this way.

Information

The **DOC visitor information centre** (☎ 03-521 1806; starnauda@doc.govt.nz; View Rd, St Arnaud; ☒ 8.30am-4.30pm) has park information, including weather reports and hut tickets.

Excellent online information on the park can be found at www.nelsonlakesnational park.co.nz.

Activities

An excellent three-day tramp from St Arnaud takes you south along the eastern shore of Lake Rotoiti to Lake Head Hut, across the Travers River and up the Cascade Track to Angelus Hut on beautiful alpine Lake Angelus. The trip back to St Arnaud goes along Robert Ridge. The track descends steeply to the Mt Robert car park, from where it's a 7km road walk back to St Arnaud.

Other walks at Rotoiti, most starting from the car park and camping area at Kerr Bay, include the **Bellbird Walk** (15 minutes), **Honeydew Walk** (45 minutes), **Peninsula Nature Walk** (1½ hours), **Black Hill Walk** (1½ hours), **St Arnaud Range Track** (five hours), **Loop Track** (1½ hours) and **Lake Circuit** (seven hours).

Short walks around Lake Rotoroa include the **Short Loop Track** (25 minutes), a botanist's delight, while medium-length ones include **Porika Lookout Track** (one to three hours return) at the northern end of the lake, and **Braeburn Walk** (two hours return) on the western side. The arduous track along the eastern shore of the lake connects with the Travers-Sabine and Speargrass Tracks to Lake Rotoiti. The DOC visitor information centre has brochures about all these walks and can provide information about track conditions.

Sleeping

There are well-equipped **DOC camping grounds** (☎ 03-521 1806; unpowered/powered sites per 2 people Oct-May $20/24, winter $14/16) on the shore of Lake Rotoiti at West Bay and Kerr Bay (the former is open in summer only). Sites have toilets, hot showers, washing machines and a kitchen. Bookings are essential for the peak season (December to February).

St Arnaud has a few accommodation options, but it's a quiet place after 8pm.

Yellow House (☎ 03-521 1887; www.nelsonlakes.co.nz; Main St; sites per 2 people $26, dm/d $25/59; ☐) The cheerful Yellow House is spick-and-span and well equipped, with a big kitchen and relaxing sun deck, as well as a spa for bubbling away tramping aches and pains. You can hire tramping equipment and snowshoes, plus store luggage here. The helpful owners have extensive, all-season tramping experience in this neck of the woods and are happy to share their expertise.

Nelson Lakes Motels (☎ 03-521 1887; www.nelsonlakes.co.nz; Main St; d $99-129) Next door to the Yellow House (and run by the same people) are log cabins oozing rustic charm, but you certainly won't be roughing it here. The cabins are cosy and full of creature comforts, including full kitchens in the larger options.

Alpine Lodge (☎ 03-521 1869; www.alpinelodge.co.nz; Main St; d $135-160) Comfy rooms and apartments in a lodge that goes a long way to creating the alpine experience. There's a range of accommodation, beautifully finished with natural timbers. There's also the budget Chalet (dorm/double $23/61) next door, but it's a pretty sterile option and linen costs an additional $5.

Eating

Alpine Lodge (☎ 03-521 1869; www.alpinelodge.co.nz; Main St; restaurant mains $20-26; ☒ dinner) This place has the monopoly on eating out in St Arnaud, with a snug bar (meals $7 to $20, open lunch and dinner) serving casual, meaty meals, plus a more upmarket restaurant open nightly.

Elaine's Alpine Cafe (☎ 03-521 1979; lunch mains $4-13, dinner mains $20-25; ☒ lunch & dinner) Below the Alpine Chalet, this is a great place to warm up over soup and toasted sandwiches.

Top House (☎ 0800 967 468, 03-521 1848; www.top house.co.nz; B&B d $110, cottage d $100) Perched on a hill 9km from St Arnaud, the Top House dates from 1887, when it was a hotel. Now it's a lovely B&B with cosy fireplaces, rich history and superb views of the St Arnaud Range. As well as rooms in the historic house, there are self-contained two-bedroom units on the property. The Top House serves up delicious all-day devonshire teas ($5) to anyone who cares to pop in; dinner for guests is $25.

St Arnaud Village Store (☎ 03-521 1854; Main Rd; ☒ 7.30am-6.30pm) A general store selling fish and chips, pies and the like, as well as groceries and petrol, plus services such as snow-chain or mountain-bike hire.

Getting There & Around

KBus (☎ 0800 88 188, 03-578 4075; www.kbus.co.nz) passes through St Arnaud on its Greymouth to Nelson to Picton run, which operates four times a week in winter, daily from November to April; reservations are essential. Sample fares to/from St Arnaud include Greymouth ($40, 4½ hours), Nelson ($20, 1¼ hours) and Picton ($35, four hours).

Nelson Lakes Shuttles (☎ 03-521 1900; www.nels onlakeshuttles.co.nz) provides on-demand transport from St Arnaud to Mt Robert car park (per person $10), Lake Rotoroa (per person $25), Murchison (per person $30) and further afield, including services to various tracks and to Nelson, Picton and Blenheim. There's a minimum charge for longer trips, but the up-to-date website lists 'budget fares' on prebooked shuttles.

Water taxis (Lake Rotoiti ☎ 03-523 9199; Lake Rotoroa ☎ 03-521 1894, 021 702 278; Lake Rotoroa ☎ 03-521 1900) operate on both lakes. At Lake Rotoiti, the water-taxi company also offers kayak, canoe and row-boat hire, and can arrange fishing trips and scenic lake cruises.

NELSON TO MOTUEKA

From Richmond, south of Nelson, SH60 heads northwest to Motueka. This region fringing Tasman Bay is all the rage with local holidaymakers, so there's plenty of accommodation, art-and-craft outlets, vineyards, fishing and swimming. The area is rich with bird life, particularly Arctic migrant waders.

Sights

About 10km west of Richmond is the turnoff to **Rabbit Island**, a recreation reserve boasting unspoilt swimming beaches, boating, fishing and forest walks. The bridge to the island is closed at sunset and overnight stays are not allowed.

Further along, the picturesque Waimea Inlet and the twin villages of **Mapua** and **Ruby Bay** are at the mouth of the Waimea River. Mapua has numerous art-and-craft outlets, top-notch cafés and restaurants, and a small aquarium, **Touch the Sea** (☎ 03-540 3557; Mapua Wharf; adult/child/family $6.50/4/15; ☑ 10am-4.30pm).

WINERIES & CRAFTS

The Nelson region has a flourishing wine-making industry and although it doesn't rival the Marlborough region in size, there are enough wineries to keep you busy (more than 20 at last count), with chardonnay and sauvignon blanc the grapes of choice. Many vineyards on the **Nelson Wine Trail** (www.nel sonwines.co.nz) can be visited by doing a loop from Nelson through Richmond to Motueka, following the SH60 coast road in one direction and the inland Moutere Hwy in the other. Wineries are open for tastings and sales, and several have cafés and restaurants. There are loads of craft outlets along these routes – for more details pick up the *Nelson's Creative Pathways* brochure from the Nelson visitor information centre and various galleries and wineries in the area.

Other wineries worth a visit:

Grape Escape (☎ 03-544 4054; www.grapeescape.co .nz; cnr SH60 & McShane Rd, Richmond; ☑ 9am-4.30pm) is a complex housing two wineries, Richmond Plains (certified organic wine) and Te Mania, as well as a café-bar, liqueur distillery, kids' playground and a number of craft shops. It's on the wine-tour itineraries.

Neudorf Vineyards (☎ 03-543 2643; www.neudorf .co.nz; Neudorf Rd, Upper Moutere; ☑ 10.30am-4.30pm Sep-May)

Seifried Estate (☎ 03-544 1555; www.seifried.co.nz; cnr SH60 & Redwood Rd; ☑ 10am-5pm) One of the region's biggest wineries, at the turn-off to Rabbit Island, and home to an excellent restaurant.

Waimea Estates Winery (☎ 03-544 6385; www .waimeaestates.co.nz; SH60, Richmond; ☑ 10am-5pm Sep-Mar; 11am-4pm Wed-Sun Apr-Aug) Not far from the Grape Escape; has a great café on-site.

Tours

Mapua Adventures (☎ 03-540 3833; www.mapuaad ventures.co.nz; Mapua Wharf; boat/kayak tours from $35/49) offers an assortment of affordable boat, kayak and bird-watching tours around the Waimea Inlet and Rabbit Island, as well as bike hire (perfect for a day of winery touring). It also offers a shuttle service to Rabbit Island (one way $5). The company operates from mid-October to April.

See p466 for information about wine tours out of Nelson.

Sleeping & Eating

Consult staff at Nelson or Motueka visitor information centres for a host of out-of-the-way homestays, cottages and B&Bs in the area.

Mapua Leisure Park (☎ 03-540 2666; www.nelson holiday.co.nz; Toru St, Mapua; unpowered/powered sites per 2 people $26/30, cabins $42-75, motels $105-130; ☐ ☒) This park is 'NZ's only clothes-optional leisure park'. Don't let that scare you off – you don't *have* to bare all (many don't; the clothes-free option is only available February and March) and the position and facilities are superb – tennis and volleyball courts, kayak hire, pool, sauna, spa and a waterfront café.

Clayridge House (☎ 03-540 2548; www.dayridge .co.nz; 72 Pine Hill Rd, Ruby Bay; d $140-175) On a property in Ruby Bay with water views, surrounded by orchards and vineyards. It's the perfect place to unwind, with a choice of B&B guest rooms or two-bedroom self-contained cottages (two-night minimum stay for the cottages).

Smokehouse (☎ 03-540 2280; www.smokehouse .co.nz; Mapua Wharf; meals $10-29; ☑ lunch & dinner) This water's-edge eatery does delicious wood-smoked fish and a smorgasbord of seafood dishes (and nonfishy food too, including smoked vegies). Pull up a pew outside, feast on superb fish and chips, and revel in the fact you're on holiday.

Flax Restaurant & Bar (☎ 03-540 2028; Mapua Wharf; ☑ lunch & dinner Tue-Sun) Food-loving locals rave about this place. Just along from the Smokehouse, stylish Flax features stellar fresh-food creations in its retro-modern interior.

MOTUEKA
pop 6900

Motueka is usually used as a base or stop-over en route to Golden Bay and the Abel Tasman and Kahurangi National Parks, and in summer it's a bustling place. There's a solid community of craftspeople and some excellent cafés.

The town is the centre of a green-tea, hops and fruit-growing area. The main picking season for apples, grapes and kiwi fruit is March to June.

Information
Books & More (207 High St) This bookshop also moonlights as a post office.
Cyberworld (☎ 03-528 8090; 178 High St)
Motueka visitor information centre (☎ 03-528 6543; www.abeltasmangreenrush.co.nz; 20 Wallace St; ☑ 8am-5pm May-Oct, to 7pm Nov-Apr) Excellent resource, with helpful staff able to book hut passes and tours for the Abel Tasman Track. Check with staff here about all the different options for tackling the track. Luggage storage also available.

Sights & Activities
The small **Motueka District Museum** (☎ 03-528 7660; 140 High St; adult/child $2/50c; ☑ 10am-4pm Mon-Fri, to 2pm Sat, closed Mon in winter) has displays recreating the region's colonial past.

Take in outstanding views on the way up (and down, if you can concentrate on sightseeing!) on a tandem skydive with **Skydive Abel Tasman** (☎ 0800 422 899, 03-528 4091; www .skydive.co.nz; 16 College St, Motueka airstrip; jumps 9000ft/12,000ft $210/240). The price includes instruction and a certificate (video and photos of your exploits are additional); pick-up from Nelson can be arranged.

Motueka River Kayaks (☎ 03-528 6222; www.river kayak.co.nz; adult/child $95/45) operates journeys in inflatable kayaks on the Motueka River. Trips involve 2½ hours on the river sightseeing, swimming and navigating rapids, and can be geared for families. Free transport from Motueka to the river is provided.

If the weather won't allow you to get out and explore, the wee **Gecko Theatre** (☎ 03-528 4272; 78 High St; adult/child $12/7) shows interesting art-house movie selections.

Sleeping
BUDGET
There's some top-notch budget accommodation in town.

Laughing Kiwi (☎ 03-528 9229; www.laughingkiwi .co.nz; 310 High St; dm $21-23, d with/without bathroom $60/52; ☐) Readers rave about this place, and we certainly understand the appeal. Two homes (one old and cosy, the other modern and purpose-built) boast great attention to detail – TV-free lounge with CD player and board games, plus walls covered with inspiring photos of the owners' world travels. The en suite rooms are a bargain, and there's a free spa. Bliss.

Bakers Lodge (☎ 03-528 0102; www.bakerslodge .co.nz; 4 Poole St; dm $23-28, d with/without bathroom $66/56, f with/without bathroom $108/100; ☐) This YHA associate, in a carefully renovated former bakery, is another excellent choice. It's spacious, immaculate and has plenty of common areas, including a large kitchen and outdoor barbecue area.

MOTUEKA

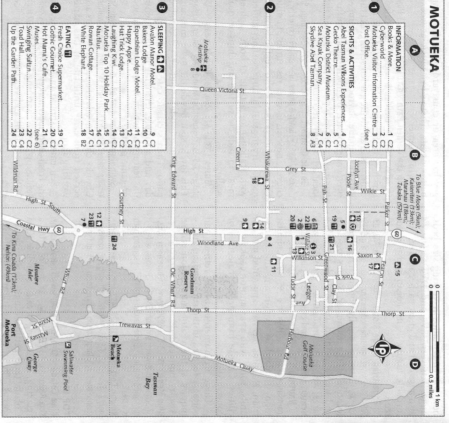

INFORMATION
Books & More..............................1 C2
Cyberworld.................................2 C2
Motueka Visitor Information Centre...3 C2
Post Office.............................(see 1)

SIGHTS & ACTIVITIES
Abel Tasman Wilsons Experiences.....4 C2
Gecko Theatre.............................5 C1
Motueka District Museum..............6 C1
Sea Kayak Company......................7 B2
Skydive Abel Tasman....................8 A3

SLEEPING 🏨
Avalon Manor Motel.....................9 C2
Bakers Lodge.............................10 C2
Equestrian Lodge Motel...............11 C4
Happy Apple..............................12 C4
Hat Trick Lodge.........................13 C2
Laughing Kiwi...........................14 C2
Motueka Top 10 Holiday Park........15 C1
Nautilus..................................16 C1
Rowan Cottage...........................17 C1
White Elephant..........................18 B2

EATING 🍴
Fresh Choice Supermarket............19 C1
Gothic Gourmet..........................20 C1
Hot Mama's Cafe.........................21 C1
Muses..................................(see 6)
Swinging Sultan.........................22 C4
Toad Hall.................................23 C4
Up the Garden Path.....................24 C4

Hat Trick Lodge (☎ 03-528 3353; www.hattricklodge.co.nz; 25 Wallace St; dm $22-25, d with/without bathroom from $62/52; ☐) This new backpackers gets big ticks for its location (opposite the visitor information centre), service and shiny new facilities (including rooms with en suite). It still needs some homely touches to overcome the sterility, but has great potential. Bike hire and shuttle services are offered.

Motueka Top 10 Holiday Park (☎ 0800 668 835, 03-528 7189; www.motuekatop10.co.nz; 10 Fearon St; sites per 2 people $28, cabins $40-60, units & motels $72-99; ☐ ☑) Busy, amenity-packed park at the northern end of town. There are grassy camp sites and plenty of options if you're after a roof over your head.

MIDRANGE
Avalon Manor Motel (☎ 0800 282 565, 03-528 8320; www.avalonmotels.co.nz; 314 High St; r $118-160) Terrific midrange accommodation in a prominent highway location close to town. Massive four-star rooms are modern with cooking facilities, Sky TV and free videos. Sumptuous

More quality hostel options:
Happy Apple (☎ 03-528 8652; www.happyapple backpackers.co.nz; 500 High St; dm/s/d $21/29/50; ☐) Bright, cheery and welcoming place, with some tent sites available.
White Elephant (☎ 03-528 6208; www.whiteelephant.co.nz; Whakarewa St; dm $23-24, d with/without bathroom $66/54; ☐) Gorgeous old villa in lovely grounds. Six new en suite doubles were being built when we visited.

new top-end studios have king-size beds, huge flatscreen TVs and DVDs. There's also a garden and guest barbecue area. 'Affordable luxury' is its slogan and it holds true.

Equestrian Lodge Motel (0800 668 782, 03-528 9369; www.equestrianlodge.co.nz; Tudor St; d/q $110/150;) Family-friendly option in a peaceful location off the main road. Rooms are clean and well-appointed and all look towards a large, well-manicured garden, complete with heated pool, spa and children's play area.

Nautilus (0800 628 845, 03-528 4558; www.nautiluslodge.co.nz; 67 High St; d $95-140) A similar high standard to Avalon and the Equestrian, Nautilus has well-appointed modern units, some with spas and/or cooking facilities. Choose from private balconies or courtyards.

There are numerous B&Bs, retreats and cottages located in the surrounding area – inquire at the visitor information centre. Also recommended:

Blue Moon (03-528 6996; www.thebluemoon.co.nz; 57 School Rd, Riwaka; s/d from $85/125) Private, self-contained unit in a serene garden setting. The sunken bath is a treat.

Rowan Cottage (03-528 6492; www.rowancottage .net; 27 Fearon St; d $110-140) B&B offering two rooms – choose the lovely large studio with outdoor deck and spa.

TOP END

Kina Colada (03-526 6700; www.kinacolada.co.nz; Kina Peninsula; d $195-490;) If you're after a relaxing, recharging break, you'll like Kina Colada (and getting caught in the rain... sorry). The turn-off is 10km south of Motueka at Tasman, and it's then a further 2km to the lodge and day spa. Four suites with balconies, great views and a lovely pool area make this a great getaway.

Eating & Drinking

High St, Motueka's seemingly endless main street, has some gems. There's an abundance of interesting daytime options; discerning locals head to Mapua if they're after something special of an evening.

Hot Mama's Cafe (03-528 7039; 195 High St; all-day menu $5-14, dinner $14-21; breakfast, lunch & dinner) A cool open-fronted place painted in vibrant colours, and the funkiest café in town. Start the day with a Hangover Brekkie (eggs, bacon and the works) or end it with a pizza before adjourning to the loun-

gey bar area or courtyard made for long balmy nights. There's live music at weekends in summer.

Up the Garden Path (03-528 9588; 473 High St; meals $7-22; breakfast & lunch) The perfect lunch or coffee spot, this licensed café and gallery is in an idyllic garden setting. Let the kids loose in the playroom so you can linger over your roasted pumpkin salad, stuffed panini or antipasto platter, then peruse the local art. Highly recommended.

Gothic Gourmet (03-528 6699; 208 High St; mains $27-29; lunch & dinner Tue-Sun) Formerly a church, now an elegant restaurant, Gothic Gourmet offers meat- and seafood-loaded meals – try the surf 'n' turf (eye fillet stuffed with scallops) for a taste of both. Lighter meals include classic fish and chips or local scallops.

Muses (03-528 8696; 140 High St; meals $6-15, platters $25-35; breakfast & lunch daily, dinner Thu-Sat) This lovely spot beside the town museum offers dining inside or out on the covered patio. There's classic café fare during the day and a simple, changing dinner menu, the feature of which is antipasto, seafood or game platters.

Swinging Sultan (03-528 8909; 172 High St; kebabs under $10; 8am-1am summer, to 9pm winter) Chunky chicken, falafel and beef kebabs are served from early until late at this hardworking shop.

Self-caterers should make a beeline for the **Fresh Choice supermarket** (108 High St; 7am-9pm). Stop by the charming **Toad Hall** (502 High St) for fresh fruit and veg (and yummy ice cream).

Getting There & Away

Abel Tasman Coachlines (03-528 8850; www.abeltasmantravel.co.nz) buses stop at the visitor information centre. There are services from Motueka to Nelson ($10, one hour, up to six daily), Marahau ($9, 30 minutes, three or four daily), Kaiteriteri ($9, 25 minutes, three or four daily) and Takaka ($17, one hour, two daily). Services run less frequently from May to September, but these destinations are serviced at least once a day to/from Motueka. From October to April there are daily services from Motueka to Totaranui and to the start of the Heaphy Track.

KBus (0800 881 188, 03-548 4075; www.kbus .co.nz) has buses to/from Takaka ($17, 1¼ hours, one daily) and Nelson ($10, 50 minutes, two to four daily); buses pick up at the visitor information centre. Buses also run to and from Kaiteriteri and Marahau. See p482 for more information on transport to and from the Abel Tasman Track.

MOTUEKA TO ABEL TASMAN

Kaiteriteri

This wee town (known just as Kaiteri to locals), 13km from Motueka on a sealed road (which continues on to Marahau), is one of the most popular resort beaches in the area. The town's safe swimming beaches have genuine golden sand and clear, green waters; there are also good short walks in the vicinity.

Launch and kayak trips run to the Abel Tasman National Park from Kaiteriteri, though Marahau is the usual base.

SLEEPING & EATING

Kaiteriteri Beach Motor Camp (03-527 8010; www.kaiteriteribeach.co.nz; Inlet Rd; sites per 2 people $22, cabins $30-55) This well-equipped, 400-site park is in pole position across from the beach and swells with summer holidaymakers, but is large enough to cope (and there's a general store on site). Book early for one of the 17 simple cabins. Showers are coin-operated.

Kaiteri Lodge (0508 524 8374, 03-527 8281; www.kaiterilodge.co.nz; Inlet Rd; dm $25-40, d $80-140, f $120-180;) Modern, purpose-built lodge with small, simple rooms — mainly en suite doubles. A nautical navy-and-white colour scheme has been used throughout, and communal facilities (kitchen, laundry, barbecue, bike hire) are excellent. The cheapest prices listed here apply from May to September.

Bellbird Lodge (03-527 8555; www.bellbirdlodge.com; Sandy Bay Rd; d $160-250) This option, 1.5km from the Kaiteri beachfront, offers all you'd expect from an upmarket B&B, and then some: great views, extensive gardens, gracious hosts, spectacular breakfasts, fluffy towels and impressive attention to detail. Dinner is by arrangement in the low season, given the erratic hours of the few restaurants in the area during this period. A real treat.

Beached Whale (03-527 8114; Inlet Rd; dinner mains $20-28; lunch & dinner, closed May-Nov) Adjacent to Kaiteri Lodge, the Beached Whale is a casual, family-friendly bar and restaurant with a menu featuring wood-fired pizzas, and live entertainment most evenings. Takeaway food available.

Shoreline (03-527 8507; Sandy Bay Rd; lunch mains $8-19, dinner mains $19-32; breakfast, lunch & dinner) A smart, modern café-bar-restaurant right on the beach. Punters relax on the sunny decking, linger over local seafood dishes and watch the day pass. Hours are erratic in winter.

Marahau

Further along the coast from Kaiteriteri, tiny Marahau, 18km north of Motueka, is the main gateway to the Abel Tasman National Park. From here you can book water taxis, hire kayaks, swim with seals or head on foot into the park. There are regular bus connections to/from Marahau (p482).

From Marahau you can also opt for nonpark activities such as horse riding and quad-biking. Pegasus Park (025 603 1992; Sandy Bay Rd; 2hr rides adult/child $60/45) offers four-legged exploration, while Marble Hills (0800 262 7253; www.marblehills4fun.co.nz; Moss Rd; 30min ride $55/85) prefers off-road adventures on four-wheel motorbikes. Kids mini-quads and karts (minimum age six) look like loads of fun.

SLEEPING & EATING

Marahau has quite a few accommodation possibilities (but considerably fewer eating options). The camping grounds fill up in summer.

Marahau Beach Camp (0800 808 018, 03-527 8176; www.abeltasmanmarahaucamp.co.nz; Franklin St; sites per 2 people $24, dm/d $20/45, cabins $50-60) A well-established camping ground on Marahau Beach with a range of options, from backpacker accommodation to 'comfy cabins'. There's a very good restaurant, Hooked on Marahau, and shop here, as well as kayak hire/tour and a water-taxi service.

The Barn (03-527 8043; Harvey Rd; sites per person $12, dm $20-26, tw & d $52-56) A rustic, tranquil place surrounded by gum and willow trees. There's a mix of comfy, homely accommodation, from an all-girls dorm, a big loft bunk room, appealing doubles, outdoor tepees and camp sites on the spacious lawn.

Old MacDonald's Farm (03-527 8288; www.old macs.co.nz; Harvey Rd; unpowered/powered sites per 2 people $24/30, dm $20, cabins $70, units from $120;) This ramshackle 100-acre property has llamas, alpacas, deer, pigs and cows, as well as backpacker huts, camping, self-contained units and the semi-open-air Gum Drop Café. There are swimming holes in the river running through the property, as well as bush walks – it's a relaxed place, perfect for families.

Ocean View Chalets (03-527 8232; www.accom modationabeltasman.co.nz; Franklin St; chalets d/q from $108/205) Beautiful, well-priced cypress chalets, 300m from the Abel Tasman Track and overlooking Sandy Bay. Placed for maximum privacy, the chalets are self-contained, some with wheelchair access.

Abel Tasman Marahau Lodge (03-527 8250; www.abeltasmanmarahaulodge.co.nz; Franklin St; d $130-200) On the main waterfront road, Marahau Lodge has modern, immaculate studios and self-contained units. They're lovely rooms with peaked roofs, fans, TVs, phone and microwave; there's also a large communal kitchen for self-catering guests, plus spa and sauna.

Park Café (03-527 8270; Harvey Rd; day menu $9-14; breakfast, lunch & dinner mid-Sep–Apr) Near the start of the Abel Tasman Track and the park information kiosk, the licensed Park Café is bright and breezy and the perfect place to rest weary feet. Options include seafood chowder, lasagne and vegie burgers; to finish, try the 'famous' blueberry crumble cake.

Hooked on Marahau (03-527 8576; Franklin St; dinner mains $23-28; dinner Oct–mid-May, also breakfast, lunch Dec-Mar) The top pick for dining in the area, so dinner reservations are a good idea. It's at Marahau Beach Camp and has a lovely art-bedecked interior (local art and weaving for sale), plus an outdoor area with meal-distracting views. Dinner mains include fresh fish, green-lipped mussels and scotch fillet steak, which you can wash down with local wine or Nelson-brewed Mac's beer.

ABEL TASMAN NATIONAL PARK

The coastal Abel Tasman National Park is an accessible and superpopular tramping area. The park is at the northern end of a range of marble and limestone hills extending from Kahurangi National Park, and the interior is honeycombed with caves and potholes. There are various tracks in the park, including an inland route, although the coastal track is by far the most popular.

Abel Tasman Coastal Track

This 51km, three- to five-day track is one of the most beautiful in the country, passing through native bush that overlooks beaches of golden sand lapped by gleaming blue-green water. The numerous bays, small and large, are like a travel brochure come to life. Visitors can walk into the park, catch water taxis to beaches along the track or kayak along the coast.

Once little-known outside the immediate area, this track has well and truly been 'discovered' and in summer hundreds of people may be on the track at any one time (far more than can be accommodated in the huts, so bring your tent). Track accommodation works on a booking system, similar to the Routeburn and Milford Tracks, and huts and camp sites must be prebooked year-round. There is no charge for day walks – if you're after a taster, the 2½ hour stretch from Torrent Bay to Bark Bay is regarded by many as the most beautiful part of the track.

Between Bark Bay and Awaroa Head, there is an area classified as the **Tonga Island Marine Reserve** that's home to a seal colony and visiting dolphins. Tonga Island itself is a small island out from Onetahuti Beach.

For a full description of the route, see Lonely Planet's *Tramping in New Zealand*.

INFORMATION

The track operates on a **Great Walks Pass** (per person sites/huts $10/25 Oct-Apr, $10/7 May-Sep) system. Children pay half price. The **Abel Tasman Coastal Track helpdesk** (03-546 8210; greatwalksbooking@doc.govt.nz) offers information and can make bookings. You can also book online (www.doc.govt.nz) or in person at the Nelson, Motueka and Takaka visitor information centres, where staff can offer suggestions to tailor the track to your needs and organise transport at each end. Try to plan your trip at least a couple of days beforehand (more if you're planning to walk from December to March).

WALKING THE TRACK

The Abel Tasman area has huge tides (up to 6m difference between low and high tide) and these will impact on your walking. Two sections of the main track are tidal, with no high-tide track around them: Awaroa Estuary can only be crossed 1½ hours before

ABEL TASMAN NATIONAL PARK

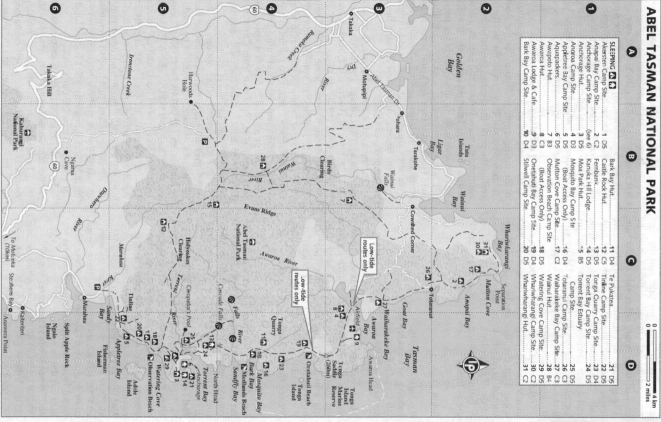

SLEEPING 🅰️ 🅱️
Akersten Camp Site............1 D5
Anapai Bay Camp Site..........2 C2
Anchorage Camp Site...........3 D5
Anchorage Hut............(see 6)
Anaroa Camp Site..............4 D3
Appletree Bay Camp Site.......5 D5
Aquapackers....................6 D5
Awapoto Hut...................7 B3
Awaroa Hut....................8 C3
Awaroa Lodge & Cafe...........9 D3
Bark Bay Camp Site............10 D4

Bark Bay Hut..................11 D4
Castle Rock Hut...............12 C5
Fernbank.....................13 C5
Kanuka Hill Lodge............14 D5
Moa Park Hut.................15 B5
Mosquito Bay Camp Site.......16 D4
  (Boat Access Only)
Mutton Cove Camp Site........17 C2
Observation Beach Camp Site..18 D5
Onetahuti Bay Camp Site......19 D4
  (Boat Access Only)
Stilwell Camp Site...........20 D5

Te Pukatea....................21 D5
Tinline Camp Site.............22 C5
Torga Quarry Camp Site........23 D4
Torrent Bay Camp Site.........24 D5
Torrent Bay Estuary
  Camp Site...................25 D5
Totaranui Camp Site...........26 C3
Waiharakeke Bay Camp Site.....27 C3
Wainui Hut....................28 B4
Watering Cove Camp Site.......29 D5
Whariwharangi Camp Site.......30 C2
Whariwharangi Hut.............31 C2

and two hours after low tide, and the narrow channel at Onetahuti Beach must be crossed three hours either side of low tide. The estuaries at Torrent and Bark Bay have tracks around them for use during high tide. Tide tables are posted along the track, and advice can be obtained from visitor information centres in the area. Many visitors combine walking and kayaking on the track – see opposite.

Take additional food so you have the inclination. Bays around all the huts are beautiful but you should definitely bring generous amounts of sandfly repellent.

Estimated walking times, south to north, are as follows:

Route	Time
Marahau to Anchorage Hut	4hr
Anchorage Hut to Bark Bay Hut	3hr
Bark Bay Hut to Awaroa Hut	4hr
Awaroa Hut to Totaranui	1½hr

Many walkers stop at Totaranui, the final stop for the boat services and a pick-up point for buses, but it is possible to keep walking around the headland from Totaranui to Whariwharangi Hut (three hours) and then on to Wainui (1½ hours), where buses service the car park.

TOURS

See also p482 for information about water taxis and flights into the park. These tour companies usually offer free pick-up in Motueka (pick up from Nelson is often available, at extra cost).

Abel Tasman Sailing Adventures (☎ 0800 467 245, 03-527 8375; www.sailingadventures.co.nz; half-day $55, full-day $55-145, overnight from $225) Has a fantastic range of well-priced sailing trips, plus yacht rentals and private skippered charters. Two hours of sailing plus a 45-minute walk costs only $55; a three-hour sunset cruise is $85.

Abel Tasman Seal Swim (☎ 0800 252 925, 03-527 8383; www.sealswim.com; Kaiteriteri Beach; seal swim adult/child $120/100, seal watch $60/40) Trips to the seal colony, departing from Kaiteriteri (operated by Kaiteriteri Kayaks). You can be dropped off in the park and walk or kayak back after the swim.

Abel Tasman Wilson's Experiences (Map p475; ☎ 0800 223 582, 03-528 7801; www.abeltasmannz.com; 265 High St, Motueka; half-day cruise $48, cruise & walk $48, kayak & walk $83-145) Large array of cruises, walks

and kayak (and combination) tours. Also has luxurious beachfront lodges at Awaroa and Torrent Bay.

Waka Tours (☎ 0800 925 227, 03-527 8160; www .wakatours.co.nz; Marahau; day trips $120-165) One of the few Maori cultural activities in the South Island. Experienced Maori guides run tours (from a half-day to overnight, with walking and kayaking possibilities), in which you get to paddle a traditionally carved Waka Tangata canoe and learn about indigenous culture.

Sleeping & Eating

At the southern edge of the park, Marahau is the main jumping-off point for the Abel Tasman National Park. From the northern end of the park, the nearest towns with accommodation are Pohara and Takaka. There is also the huge **Totaranui Camp Site** (☎ 03-528 8083; adult/child $12/6), in the north of the park, 32km from Takaka on a narrow, winding road (some of it unsealed), and serviced by buses from October to April. Bookings for Totaranui are essential (and hard to come by) from December to mid-February; there are no powered sites.

On the park's coastal track there are four huts – Anchorage (24 bunks), Bark Bay (28 bunks), Awaroa (22 bunks) and Whariwharangi (19 bunks) – as well as 21 designated camp sites. None of the huts has cooking facilities, so you should carry your own stove. Some of the camp sites have fireplaces but, again, you should carry cooking equipment. Hut and camp passes should be purchased before you enter the park (see p478). Note that from Christmas Day to late January these huts and camping grounds are usually full.

There are several other options in the park – the following are all accessible on foot or by kayak or water taxi, but not by road:

Aquapackers (☎ 0800 430 744, 025 510 882; www .aquapackers.co.nz; dm/d $60/175) The MV Parore (a former Navy patrol boat) and Catarac (a 13m catamaran), moored permanently in Anchorage Bay, are great options for backpackers, especially those who don't mind the drinking sessions that tend to eventuate on board. Rooms are basic but comfy; prices include dinner, breakfast and a packed lunch for you to take on the day's walk.

Fernbank (☎ 03-547 2357; www.abeltasmanaccom modation.co.nz; Torrent Bay; d $90-130, extra adult/child $10/5) Fernbank offers two classic holiday homes at Torrent Bay; each self-contained house can sleep up to seven and the houses are a surprising bargain (seven adults staying between May and October would pay a grand total of $140). BYO linen, or pay an additional charge. Of course, you'll need to bring all your food supplies too.

Kanuka Hill Lodge (☎ 03-548 2863; www.kanuk alodge.co.nz; Anchorage; s $205-300, d $345-500; ☷ closed May-Oct) When you really want to get away from it all, Kanuka Hill is a chilled place surrounded by native bush. Three double

PADDLING THE ABEL TASMAN

The Abel Tasman Coastal Track has long been famous among trampers, but its main attractions – the scenic beaches, coves and bays – make it an equally alluring spot for sea kayaking.

Many travellers choose to kayak around at least part of the park, cruising the relatively safe, sheltered waters and calling in at those impossibly pretty beaches. You can easily combine kayaking, walking and camping. It needn't necessarily be a matter of hiring a kayak and looking after yourself (although it is possible to do that) – a string of professional outfits can get you out on the water and the possibilities and permutations for guided or freedom trips are vast. You can kayak from half a day to three days, camping or staying in DOC huts, upmarket lodges or in Aquapackers (see opposite), choosing fully catered options or electing to self-cater. You can kayak one day, camp overnight and walk back, or walk further into the park and catch a water taxi back. A popular choice if your time is tight is a guided kayak trip to Anchorage, where you stay overnight, walk unguided to Onetahuti Beach and catch a water taxi back – it costs around $145 plus camping/hut fees or night at Aquapackers. Most companies offer a three-day trip where you get dropped at the northern end of the park and paddle back (or vice versa) for around $400 to $500 with food included. What you decide to do may depend on your own time (and financial) constraints – pick up the brochures, look at the options and talk to other travellers.

The peak season is from November to Easter but you can paddle year-round. December to February is by far the busiest time, so it's worth timing your visit earlier or later. Winter is a good time as you will see more bird life and the weather is surprisingly calm and mild.

Instruction is given to first-timers and double kayaks are used by all outfits unless you can demonstrate that you're competent enough to control and keep upright in a single kayak. If you're on your own you'll be matched with someone else in the group. Most companies have a minimum age of 14 for their tours. Camping gear is usually provided on overnight trips; if you're disappearing into the park for a few days, most operators offer safe car parking services for a few dollars per day.

Freedom rentals (kayak and equipment hire) are around $100 per person for two days; most companies require a minimum of two days' hire and do not allow solo hires.

Most of the sea-kayaking operators have plenty of experience and all offer similar-ish trips at similar prices. Marahau is the closest base but trips are also run out of Kaiteriteri. Some operators have their main office in Motueka; transport to the park from Motueka may be free, and some operators have shuttles doing pick-ups from Nelson for an additional charge.

Abel Tasman Sea Kayaks (☎ 0800 732 529, 03-527 8022; www.abeltasmankayaks.co.nz; Marahau Beach; full-day guided trips $75-350, 2-day kayak/walk & kayak from $260/240, 3-day guided tour incl meals $410)

Kaiteriteri Kayaks (☎ 0800 252 525, 03-527 8383; www.seakayak.co.nz; Kaiteriteri Beach; half-day & summer sunset paddle $70, full-day guided trips $95-210, 2-/3-day guided trip $315/510)

Kiwi Kayaks (☎ 0800 695 494, 03-528 7705; www.kiwikayaks.co.nz; Main Rd, Riwaka; one-day kayak & walk $79, full-day guided tour $99-175, 2-day tour $145-300, 3-day tour uncatered/catered $329/389)

Marahau Sea Kayaks (☎ 0800 529 257, 03-527 8176; www.msk.net.nz; Marahau Beach Camp, Marahau; 1-day catered trip $135-180, 2-day $203-299, 3-day $218-320)

Ocean River (☎ 0800 732 529; www.seakayaking.co.nz; Main Rd, Marahau; freedom rental 1/2/3 days per person $69/110/160) specialises in freedom rentals (with safety briefing), and hires out camping equipment.

Sea Kayak Company (Map p475; ☎ 0508 252 925, 03-528 7251; www.seakayaknz.co.nz; 506 High St, Motueka; 1-day tour $99-180, 2-day $190-320, 3-day $299-455; summer sunset tour $98-120)

Southern Exposure Sea Kayaking (☎ 0800 695 292, 03-527 8424; www.southern-exposure.co.nz; Moss Rd, Marahau; 1-day trip $95-170, 2-day $210-320, 3-day $400-510)

en suite rooms are available, and prices include all meals. There's a two-night minimum stay from December to March.

Awaroa Lodge & Café (☎ 03-528 8758; www.awaroalodge.co.nz; Awaroa Bay; d $255-400, f from $260; lunch mains $13-26, dinner mains $30-36) There's lots to love about this stunning luxury ecolodge at the northern end of the track. Rooms are beautifully furnished with artistic, contemporary touches, and the innovative café is open to all and produces delicious meals. Family units sleep up to eight, but there are no cooking facilities. Guided kayaking and other activities can be arranged, and there are private bush walks in the lovely grounds. Awaroa is also accessible by air.

Getting There & Away

Motueka is your best base for accessing the Abel Tasman Coastal Track.

AIR

If you're time-poor and funds-rich, consider a fly-in option – the following companies fly to/from Awaroa, as well as offering scenic flights:

Abel Tasman Air (☎ 0800 304 560, 03-528 8290; www.abeltasmanair.co.nz) Flies between Awaroa and Motueka or Nelson; Motueka–Awaroa one way is $105. Also offers a one-day 'cruise, dine & fly' option – take a coach to Marahau, water taxi to Awaroa, have lunch at Awaroa Lodge and then a scenic flight back to Motueka ($235).

Tasman Helicopters (☎ 03-528 8075; www.tasman helicopters.co.nz) Motueka–Awaroa by helicopter is around $150 one way, or there's a good deal including return helicopter flights and lunch at Awaroa Lodge for only $170 (minimum numbers apply).

BUS

Abel Tasman Coachlines (☎ 03-548 0285; www.abel tasmantravel.co.nz) operates buses between Motueka and Marahau ($9, 30 minutes, four daily), Takaka ($17, one hour, two daily), Totaranui ($25, 2¼ hours, one daily) and the Wainui car park at the northern end of the track ($30, 1¾ hours, one daily). These services all originate in Nelson, if you're based there.

KBus (☎ 0800 881 188, 03-548 4075; www.kbus.co.nz) services run between Motueka and Takaka ($17, 1¼ hours, one daily) and Marahau ($9, 30 minutes, three to five daily). There are daily summertime services from Totaranui and Wainui to Nelson via Motueka

and Takaka; services to these areas depart every morning from Takaka.

From October to April, **Nelson Bays Shuttles** (☎ 03-547 5321) offers twice-daily services from Nelson to Marahau and Kaiteriteri (one way/return $15/25).

Getting Around

The beauty of Abel Tasman is that it's easy to get to/from any point on the track by water taxi. General one-way prices from Marahau and Kaiteriteri include Anchorage and Torrent Bay ($23), Bark Bay ($27), Tonga ($29), Awaroa ($32) and Totaranui ($34). Operators include the following:

Abel Tasman Sea Shuttle (☎ 0800 732 748, 03-528 9759; www.abeltasmanseashuttles.co.nz; 415 High St, Motueka) Has its office in Motueka but operates its services from a kiosk on Kaiteriteri beach.

Abel Tasman Water Taxis (☎ 0800 423 397, 03-528 7497; www.abeltasman4u.co.nz; Kaiteriteri Beach)

Abel Tasman Wilson's Experiences (Map p475; ☎ 0800 223 582, 03-528 7801; www.abeltasmannz.com; 265 High St, Motueka) Offers a three-day explorer pass (adult/child $99/48) that covers three days of unlimited boat travel within a five-day period.

Aqua Taxi (☎ 0800 278 282, 03-527 8083; www.aqua taxis.co.nz; Marahau)

Marahau Water Taxis (☎ 0800 808 018, 03-527 8176; www.abeltasmanmarahaucamp.co.nz; Marahau Beach Camp, Franklin St, Marahau)

GOLDEN BAY

STATE HIGHWAY 60 TO TAKAKA

From Motueka, SH60 winds steadily up and over Takaka Hill with magnificent, dramatic scenery and onwards to Takaka and Collingwood. It's best to have your own transport to explore this region.

Takaka Hill (791m) separates Tasman Bay from Golden Bay. Near the summit are the **Ngarua Caves** (☎ 03-528 8093; adult/child $13/5; ⏰ 10am-4pm Sep-May) where you can see moa bones. You enter the caves on a 40-minute guided tour, leaving on the hour.

Also in the area is the biggest *tomo* (cave) in the southern hemisphere, **Harwood's Hole**. It's 400m deep and 70m wide (with a 183m vertical drop) and is a 30-minute walk from the car park at the end of the gravel Canaan Rd, off SH60. Exercise caution as you approach the lip of the hole – accidents have occurred; only *very* experienced cavers should attempt to explore the cave itself. The Canaan area was used as the location for Chetwood Forest in the *Lord of the Rings* movies.

Back on SH60, as you cross the crest of the hill, **Harwood Lookout** has fine views down the Takaka River Valley to Takaka and Golden Bay. From here you wind down through the beautiful Takaka Hill Scenic Reserve to the river valley.

TAKAKA

pop 1230

One of the most relaxed towns in NZ, Takaka is the centre for the Golden Bay area and the last town of any size as you head towards the northwestern corner of the South Island. It's a bustling place in summer, with a local community of 'Woodstock children' and artistic types.

Information

DOC (☎ 03-525 8026; www.doc.govt.nz; 62 Commercial St; ☑ 8.30am-4pm Mon-Fri) Information on Abel Tasman and Kahurangi National Parks, the Heaphy Track, Farewell Spit and Cobb Valley. Sells hut passes.

Golden Bay Internet Café (☎ 03-525 8355; 4 Commercial St)

Golden Bay Visitor Information Centre
(☎ 03-525 9136; gb.vin@nelsonnz.com; Willow St; ☑ 9am-5pm Mon-Fri, to 4pm Sat & Sun) Well stocked with information, maps and brochures.

Heart of the Parks (www.heartoftheparks.co.nz) Useful website for the region.

Sights

The **Golden Bay Museum** (☎ 03-525 6268; Commercial St; admission free; ☑ 10am-4.30pm, closed Sun winter) is a well-presented jumble of historical memorabilia, but the stand-out exhibit is the diorama depicting Abel Tasman's 1642 landing in Golden Bay. Entry is through the adjacent **Golden Bay Gallery** (☎ 03-525 9990; Commercial St; admission free; ☑ 10am-4.30pm, closed Sun winter), with three rooms full of local creations.

Many artists and craftspeople are based in the Golden Bay area, including painters, potters, screen printers, silversmiths and knitwear designers. The large **Artisans' Shop** (☑ 9am-5pm Mon-Fri, 10am-2pm Sat & Sun) displays and sells their wares. Pick up a copy of the *Guide to Artists in Golden Bay* leaflet for details and directions to all the galleries and workshops in the area, or visit www.virtualbay.co.nz for online info.

Sleeping

The nearby beach resort of Pohara is also popular and has the closest camping ground. Hostels are mainly found on Motupipi St – turn right at the Telegraph Hotel on the way into town.

Kiwiana (☎ 0800 805 494, 03-525 7676; 73 Motupipi St; dm/s/d $22/35/50) A friendly welcome awaits

Benari Nature Park & Café (☎ 03-525 8261; McCallums Rd; adult/child/family $12/6/35, meals $8-16; ☑ 10am-5pm daily school holidays, other times 10am-5pm Thu-Mon, closed May-mid-Sep), on the Anatoki River 6km south of town, has a variety of farm animals (including llamas and yaks), family activities and a café, but the prime attraction at this farm is feeding the fat, tame eels in the river.

Next door, you can fish for salmon at the **Anatoki Salmon Farm** (☎ 03-525 7251; www.anatokisalmon.co.nz; McCallums Rd; per kg catch $15), a relaxing venture in an idyllic setting. You can cook and/or smoke your catch on site; if you're not up for DIY, you can buy fresh or smoked fish.

TE WAIKOROPUPU SPRINGS

Simply called 'Pupu', these are the largest freshwater springs in NZ and reputedly the clearest in the world. About 14,000L of water a second is thrown up from a number of underground vents dotted around the Pupu Springs Scenic Reserve, including one with 'dancing sands' thrown upwards by the great volume of water emerging from the ground. Note that despite the enticing water, there is no swimming here.

Three short walks lead to the main springs (one suitable for wheelchairs) and take you to a tiny glassed-viewing area. To reach Pupu from Takaka, head 4km northwest on SH60, turn inland at Waitapu Bridge and continue for 3km.

Tours

Kahurangi Guided Walks (☎ 03-525 7177; www.kahurangiwalks.co.nz) specialises in taking small groups through the area's national parks, covering nearly every track option, including a five-day walk along the Heaphy Track or Abel Tasman Coast Track for $950. A day walk in the Golden Bay area will cost around $100.

See p487 for details of kayaking trips and ecotours out to Farewell Spit.

at this cottage dedicated to kiwiana – rooms are named after the jandal, gumboot, Buzzy Bee and tiki. There's a free outdoor spa and a converted garage full of treasures: wood-fired stove, pool table, CD player, books, games and bikes for guest use.

Barefoot Backpackers (☎ 0508 525 700, 03-525 7005; www.bare-foot.co.nz; 114 Commercial St; dm/s/d from $21/35/40; ☐) A small, cosy, renovated house with open lounge and kitchen areas and a barbecue-friendly garden out the back. More lures: homemade bread, and a spa to bubble in.

Annie's Nirvana Lodge (☎ 03-525 8766; www.nirvanalodge.co.nz; 25 Motupipi St; dm/d $20/50; ☐) Annie herself has moved on, but the name and atmosphere remain. Nirvana is a small, peaceful haven with a homely atmosphere. There's a separate shared room at the bottom of the garden, a spa, deck and bikes for hire.

Golden Bay Motel (☎ 0800 401 212, 03-525 9428; www.goldenbaymotel.co.nz; 132 Commercial St; d $95-115) Spacious self-contained units are clean and breezy and furnished with older-style fixtures. The rear decks overlook the lush green lawn.

Anatoki Lodge Motel (☎ 0800 262 333, 03-525 8047; anatoki@xtra.co.nz; 87 Commercial St; d from $105; ☐) Offers modern-ish studios and one- and two-bedroom units, all with cooking facilities, lounge/dining area, and private patio. The solar-heated pool's a bonus.

Eating & Drinking

Expect to see plenty of organic/free-range/wheat-free/meat-free/dairy-free labels on menus in the region.

Wholemeal Café (☎ 03-525 9426; www.wholemealcafe.co.nz; 60 Commercial St; meals $6-23; ☼ breakfast, lunch & dinner) A local institution and the stand-out place to eat in Takaka. It's a chilled café, restaurant and art gallery, and occasionally hosts live music. There's a dedicated curry menu, free-range eggs for breakfast, lots of veg-friendly options and smooth coffee. The noticeboard in the foyer gives a fascinating snapshot of the region.

Dangerous Kitchen (☎ 03-525 8686; 48 Commercial St; pizzas $10-24; ☼ breakfast, lunch & dinner) Dedicated to Frank Zappa, the Dangerous Kitchen specialises in whacky gourmet pizzas and serves strong coffee, hefty slabs of cake and bumper burritos. It's another mellow, laid-back place to hang.

The Brigand Café Bar (☎ 03-525 9636; 90 Commercial St; mains $20-28; ☼ dinner nightly, lunch in summer) Behind steel gates and a lush garden is this converted cottage, serving up fresh local produce in a relaxed atmosphere. Opt for the tapas platter or some local mussels, or just pop in for a drink (open-mic night on Thursday).

Eatery on the Rock (☎ 03-525 8096; 29 Main Rd; lunch mains $10-20, dinner mains $20-32; ☼ lunch & dinner, closed Mon-Tue in winter) Built atop a karst outcrop on the right as you head into town, and run by an accommodating bunch. The menu features local wine by the glass, plus local crab and various meat and seafood creations; walk it off with a stroll in the lovely gardens.

Golden Fries (☎ 03-525 9699; 7 Commercial St; meals $10-15; ☼ dinner, lunch in summer) Join salivating locals at this popular takeaway and choose between gourmet burgers, pan-fried scallops, fresh fish and whitebait fritters. Family options and kids' meals too.

The central **Supervalue supermarket** (27 Commercial St; ☼ 8am-7pm Mon-Sat, 9am-6pm Sun) is well stocked.

Telegraph Hotel (☎ 03-525 9308; cnr Commercial & Motupipi Sts) and the **Junction Hotel** (☎ 03-525 9207; 15 Commercial St) are old-fashioned pubs if you fancy a quiet lager or simple pub meal, but most people relax with a drink outside Wholemeal Café and Dangerous Kitchen. See also Mussel Inn (p486).

Entertainment

Catch a flick at Takaka's cinema, **Village Theatre** (☎ 03-525 8453; Commercial St; adult/child $10/5), which screens newish releases.

Getting There & Around

KBus (☎ 0800 881 188, 03-548 4075; www.kbus.co.nz) runs between Takaka and Collingwood ($14, 30 minutes, one daily), the beginning of the Heaphy Track ($23, 1¼ hours, one daily) and Nelson ($25, two hours, one daily). These daily services drop to four times a week from June to October.

Abel Tasman Coachlines (☎ 03-548 0285; www.abeltasmantravel.co.nz) also operates between Takaka and Nelson ($24, 2¾ hours, two daily), via Motueka. In summer, both this company and KBus have daily services to Totaranui at the northern end of Abel Tasman National Park.

Golden Bay Coachlines (☎ 03-525 8352; www.goldenbaycoachlines.co.nz) runs daily on the Takaka–

Motueka–Nelson route, and in summer has daily services to Collingwood, the Heaphy Track and Totaranui.

Quiet Revolution Cycle Shop (☎ 03-525 9955; 7 Commercial St; per day $15-33) hires town and mountain bikes, has local track information and also does repairs and servicing.

POHARA

Tiny Pohara is a popular summer resort 10km northeast of Takaka. It seems more 'yuppified' than other parts of Golden Bay, with large modern homes being built to take advantage of sea views. But there's still an agreeably relaxed air and some great accommodation.

The beach is on the way to the northern end of the Abel Tasman Coastal Track; the unsealed road to the park is scenic and passes by **Ligar Bay**, which has a lookout and a memorial to Abel Tasman, the first European to enter Golden Bay.

The **Rawhiti Cave**, en route to Pohara, has the largest entrance of any cave in NZ. It's well worth a look and is best seen on a guided tour as there's a rough track with limited markings. Kahurangi Guided Walks takes small groups through the cave on three-hour tours ($25).

Golden Bay Kayaks (☎ 03-525 9095; www.golden baykayaks.co.nz; Pohara beachfront) rents out kid-friendly kayaks for hour-long paddling or gear for multiday exploration, plus offers half-day guided tours (adult/child $55/25).

Sleeping & Eating

Pohara Beach Top 10 Holiday Park (☎ 03-525 9500; www.pohara.com/paradise; Abel Tasman Dr; sites per 2 people $28, cabins $45-75, motel units $105) Ideally situated on the beach in the middle of the village, this park has friendly managers and a fine range of cabins and self-contained units. Out front is the general store.

The Nook (☎ 0800 806 665, 03-525 8501; www.the nookguesthouse.co.nz; Abel Tasman Dr; dm/d $25/56, cottage $120-180) This cheery, casual backpackers is filled with artistic touches and is set in a fabulous garden. Behind the hostel is a lovely self-contained straw-bale cottage sleeping up to six. There's also limited camping spaces. Bikes are available.

Sandcastle (☎ 0800 433 909, 03-525 9087; www.gol denbayaccommodation.co.nz; Haile Lane; d $75-90) Delightful, ecofriendly place with a wood-fired sauna, outdoor spa pools, and an emphasis

on family fun. There are a handful of self-contained chalets set in tranquil native bush surrounds; look for the sign about 600m past the Penguin Café. Great value.

Penguin Café & Bar (☎ 03-525 6126; Abel Tasman Dr; dinner mains $23-25; ☒ breakfast, lunch & dinner summer, lunch & dinner Tue-Sun winter) A classy eating (and drinking) spot with open fire and pool table inside, and big outdoor area for sunny days. Choose from a day-time menu of brunch treats, gourmet pizzas or easy-drinking bar snacks.

Totally Roasted Café (☎ 03-525 9396; Abel Tasman Dr; meals $10-17; ☒ breakfast & lunch) This cool place embodies Golden Bay, with its walled garden full of art, organic fair-trade coffee, art-covered walls and funky tunes. It's at the entrance to the township and serves up café fare with flair.

COLLINGWOOD

pop 250

Tiny Collingwood is the last town in this part of the country and it certainly has that outpost feel. It's busy in summer, though for most people it's simply a jumping-off point for the Heaphy Track in Kahurangi National Park or a base for trips to the remarkable Farewell Spit.

No visit to Collingwood would be complete without dipping into the original **Rosy Glow Chocolate House** (☎ 03-524 8348; Beach Rd; ☒ 10am-5pm Sat-Thu). Chocoholics will go nuts here, where handmade chocolates are lovingly produced.

Barefoot Tours (03-524 8624; www.bare-foot.co.nz/tours; tours $55; tours depart 10am) operates out of Somerset House (see below) and aims to show you the natural highlights of Golden Bay. Great-value six- to seven-hour tours venture to the tip of the South Island and include a one-hour cliff-top walk. You can be picked up from Takaka ($5 extra).

Sleeping

There's accommodation in Collingwood itself and more places scattered along the road to Farewell Spit, including a couple of camping grounds.

Somerset House (03-524 8624; www.backpackerscollingwood.co.nz; Gibbs Rd; dm/s/d $22/35/50) Unwind at this small, low-key place, get local advice from the knowledgeable owners, and take in the great views from the outdoor area. The price includes breakfast; bikes can be hired, trampers transport can be arranged, and Barefoot Tours operates out of here.

Beachcomber Motel (0800 270 520, 03-524 8499; Tasman St; d $70-150) Clean and spacious self-contained units in excellent nick. The larger, family-sized units have a mezzanine floor and are good value.

The Innlet Guesthouse & Cottages (03-524 8040; www.goldenbayindex.co.nz/theinnlet.html; Main Rd; sites per person $18, dm/d $23/56, cottages $65-120;) The Innlet, on the way to Pakawau about 10km from Collingwood, is a great option. The main house is home to backpacker rooms, and there are various rustic huts around the property, from basic to self-contained. The environmentally conscious owners offer kayak and bike hire, as well as guided fishing and kayaking trips.

Eating & Drinking

There's a pub and simple takeaway options on the main street of Collingwood.

Courthouse Cafe & Gallery (03-525 8472; Haven Rd; meals $6-25; breakfast, lunch & dinner Thu-Sat, breakfast & lunch Sun & Mon) This historic café prepares delicious à la carte meals from locally grown organic produce and fresh seafood. There's an alfresco area where you can enjoy a lingering lunch.

Mussel Inn (03-525 9241; www.musselinn.co.nz; Onekaka; all-day menu $3-14, dinner mains $18-22; lunch & dinner, closed Aug) Halfway between

Takaka and Collingwood (not very well signed, so keep an eye out) is the wonderful Mussel Inn, a rustic tavern-café-brewery. There's music performed every week (twice a week in summer) and it brews its own ginger beer and lemonade. A big bowl of mussels has restorative properties, especially when washed down with a 'Captain Cooker', a brown beer brewed naturally with manuka. Check out the composting toilets too.

Getting There & Away

Abel Tasman Coachlines (03-528 8850; www.abeltasmantravel.co.nz) has services between Collingwood and Nelson ($35, 2¾ hours, one daily) via Takaka ($14, 30 minutes, one daily).

KBus (0800 881 188, 03-548 4075; www.kbus.co.nz) runs from Collingwood south to Takaka ($14, 30 minutes, one daily) and on to Motueka and Nelson. There's also a daily bus in summer travelling north to the Innlet and the Heaphy Track car park.

FAREWELL SPIT & AROUND

Farewell Spit visitor information centre (03-524 8454; Farewell Spit; 9am-5pm Nov-Apr, 10am-4pm May-Oct), 24km north of Collingwood, provides information about the region and can make bookings for tours out to the Spit. There's also a good café here, **Paddlecrab Kitchen** (03-524 8708; meals $8.50-16.50; breakfast & lunch), with superb views of Farewell Spit. On the track leading down from the centre is the assembled skeleton of a pilot whale, a species that often beaches here. You can walk down and look out over the eel grass flats and see many waders and sea birds.

Sights & Activities

FAREWELL SPIT

A wetland of international importance and a renowned bird sanctuary, Farewell Spit is the summer home of thousands of migratory waders from the Arctic tundra. On the 26km beach there are huge crescent-shaped sand dunes from where you get panoramic views of the Spit, Golden Bay and, at low tide, the vast salt marsh. It's bleak, unprotected and unusual country.

The crossing to the northern side of the Spit is made by tour companies (opposite), the only vehicles allowed to visit the Spit. The trucks grind up over the beach to about 1km from Cape Farewell. Down towards the start of the sand are a number of fossilized shellfish. Many species of birds are seen along the way and the normal trip ends at the old lighthouse compound.

Further east, up on the blown shell banks that comprise the far extremity of the Spit, are colonies of Caspian terns and Australasian gannets.

WHARARIKI BEACH

This isolated beach is a further 7km from Paddle Crab Kitchen along an unsealed road, and then a 20-minute walk from the car park over farmland (part of the Puponga Farm Park, administered by DOC). It's a wild introduction to the West Coast, with unusual dune formations, two looming rock islets just out from shore and a seal colony at its eastern end (keep an eye out for seals frolicking in the stream on the walk here). As inviting as a swim at this usually deserted spot may seem, there are strong undertows that make the sea very dangerous.

HORSE TREKS

As befits a frontier zone, this is a place where you can get a 'hoss': **Cape Farewell Horse Treks** (☎ 03-524 8031; www.horsetreknz.com) is en route to Whararik Beach. Treks in this wild country range from 1½ hours ($45) to three hours ($85, down to Wharariki Beach), or you can opt for an overnight coastal experience ($290) or 4½ day exploration of the West Coast ($950, all inclusive).

Tours

Scheduled tours leave daily but departure times are dependent on the tides (departure at low tide).

Farewell Spit Eco Tours (☎ 0830 808 257, 03-524 8257; www.farewellspit.co.nz; Tasman St, Collingwood; tours $80–105) A range of tour options (from three to 6½ hours), taking in the Spit, lighthouse and gannet colony. Tours depart Collingwood.

Kahurangi Nature Experiences (☎ 0800 250 500, 03-524 6044; www.naturetreks.co.nz; 37 Commercial St, Takaka; Spit tours $70-90) Tours of the Spit depart Farewell Spit Visitor Information Centre. Also has two-hour tours to Cape Farewell ($40) and summertime tours of the Te Anaroa caves ($25 to $45), about 9km west of Collingwood. Call into its Northwest Discovery Centre in Takaka for information and displays of the area.

KAHURANGI NATIONAL PARK

This is the second largest of NZ's national parks and undoubtedly one of the greatest.

Its 450,000 hectares comprise an ecological wonderland – more than 100 bird species, 50% of all NZ's plant species, 80% of its alpine plant species, a karst landscape and the largest known cave system in the southern hemisphere (explored by local caving groups, but only for the experienced). Kahurangi means 'treasured possession'.

Heaphy Track

One of the best-known tracks in NZ, the four- to six-day, 82km Heaphy Track doesn't have the spectacular scenery of the Routeburn or Milford Tracks, but it certainly has its own beauty.

The track lies almost entirely within Kahurangi National Park. Highlights include the view from the summit of Mt Perry (two-hour return walk from Perry Saddle Hut), and the coast, especially around Heaphy Hut. It's worth spending a day or two rest-ing at Heaphy Hut. It is possible to cross the Heaphy River at its mouth at low tide.

There are seven huts set up for around 20 or more people; all have gas stoves, except Brown and Gouland Downs, which need wood. There are nine camp sites available along the route, with limited capacity (as low as eight campers maximum near the Saxon Hut, as many as 40 by Heaphy Hut).

Huts/camp sites cost $10/7 per adult per night from May to September, $20/10 in the peak season from October to April; all must be prebooked.

INFORMATION

The best spot to pick up detailed information for the Heaphy Track is from the Nelson visitor information centre (p462).

All huts and camp sites on the track must be booked year-round. Bookings can be made in person at the DOC counter of the Nelson visitor information centre, or at the Takaka visitor information centre, online at www.doc.govt.nz or by post, email (greatwalksbooking@doc.govt.nz) or phone (☎ 03-546 8210).

WALKING THE TRACK

Most people travel southwest from the Collingwood end to Karamea. From Brown Hut the track passes through beech forest to Perry Saddle. The country opens up to the swampy Gouland Downs, then closes in with sparse bush all the way to MacKay

Hut. The bush becomes denser towards Heaphy Hut, with the beautiful nikau palm growing at lower levels.

The final section is along the coast through heavy bush and partly along the beach. Unfortunately, the sandflies can be unbearable along this, the most beautiful part. The climate here is surprisingly mild, but do not swim in the sea as the undertows and currents are vicious. The lagoon at Heaphy Hut is good for swimming, and fishing is possible in the Heaphy River.

The 82km Heaphy Track has kilometre markers; the zero marker is at the southern end of the track at the Kohaihai River near Karamea. Estimated walking times are as follows:

Route	Time
Brown Hut to Perry Saddle Hut	5hr
Perry Saddle Hut to Gouland Downs Hut	2hr
Gouland Downs Hut to Saxon Hut	1½hr
Saxon Hut to MacKay Hut	3hr
MacKay Hut to Lewis Hut	3½hr
Lewis Hut to Heaphy Hut	2½hr
Heaphy Hut to Kohaihai River	5hr

For a complete track description see Lonely Planet's *Tramping in New Zealand*. Also see the comprehensive online information on the website of the **Department of Conservation** (DOC; www.doc.govt.nz).

Wangapeka & Leslie-Karamea Tracks

After walking the Heaphy from north to south, you can return to the Nelson/Golden Bay region by the more scenic, though harder, Wangapeka Track. Although not as well known as the Heaphy, the Wangapeka is thought by many to be a more enjoyable walk. It starts 25km south of Karamea at Little Wanganui, runs 52km east to

the Rolling River near Tapawera and takes about five days. There is a chain of huts along the track.

The 91km Leslie-Karamea Track is a medium-to-hard tramp of five to seven days. It connects the Cobb Valley near Takaka with Little Wanganui, finishing on part of the Wangapeka Track.

Tours

See also p483 for details of Kahurangi Guided Walks.

Bush & Beyond (☎ 03-528 9054; www.naturetreks .co.nz) offers guided wilderness treks in Kahurangi National Park, designed to meet your abilities and interests (eg flora, fauna, photography). Day walks to Mt Arthur or the Cobb Valley cost $120 and include lunch and transport to/from Motueka. There's a range of multiday treks (backpacking or luxury options) – five days on the Heaphy Track costs from $1025, all inclusive.

Getting There & Away

From late October to April, both **Abel Tasman Coachlines** (☎ 03-528 8850, 03-548 0285) and **KBus** (☎ 0800 881 188, 03-578 4075; www.kbus.co.nz) run a daily scheduled bus service from Nelson to the Heaphy Track, via Motueka, Takaka and Collingwood. The cost of this 3½-hour journey is around $47 one way. In winter these services run on demand and are more expensive. There's also a number of on-demand shuttle services from various towns in the region.

There's a phone at the trailhead to call buses.

Wadsworths Motors (☎ 03-522 4248; Main Rd, Tapawera) services the eastern ends of the Wangapeka and Leslie-Karamea Track, on demand.

For details of transport at the Karamea end of all the tracks see p499.

The West Coast

Blessed with the photo gene, the West Coast (aka Westland) is a surf-battered stretch of craggy coastline soaring up to the summits of the Southern Alps. This is wild country, where the rain comes in sideways and the coast road is squeezed out away from the land. Caught between grinding grey ocean on one side of the highway and silent mountain whiteness on the other, you'll be forgiven for feeling insignificant.

Solitude is easy to find here. Turn off the highway and you're alone beneath a rainforest canopy or standing on a tumultuous shore – your face reflected in a mirror lake – or your feet kicking through the rusted waste of century-old mining abandon. This is a place where people aren't particularly important; where dreams aren't easily realised.

But solitude can be short-lived: tourists teem across land and sky like shoals of whitebait (the local delicacy) to see the West Coast's biggest drawcards – the monstrous icy fractures of the Franz Josef and Fox Glaciers.

Providing some competition in the scenery stakes are the earthquake-scarred Buller Gorge, the caves and limestone formations of Oparara Basin and the psychedelic geology of the Punakaiki Rocks. The West Coast is also a major source of *pounamu* (greenstone or jade); Hokitika is the jade-craft epicentre.

North to south or south to north – it's unrelentingly spectacular in both directions, but a few nights bunkered down in the West Coast's quirky townships will cure your 'view-fatigue'.

HIGHLIGHTS

- Standing dumbfounded before the gargantuan walls of **Franz Josef Glacier** (p516) and **Fox Glacier** (p519)
- Paddling through the shimmering channels of **Okarito Lagoon** (p514)
- Shooting the rapids in the **Buller Gorge** (p492)
- Salivating over nature's pancake stack at **Punakaiki** (p500; pass the maple syrup)
- Coming to grips with limestone in the **Oparara Basin** (p497)
- Bejewelling yourself with greenstone in **Hokitika** (p511)
- Contemplating (then deciding against) a leap into the flour-blue wate's of **Hokitika Gorge** (p512)
- Mooching around **Jackson Bay** (p524) in the rain, the rain, the endless rain....

TELEPHONE CODE: 03

www.west-coast.co.nz

www.westcoast.org.nz

★ Jackson Bay
★ Okarito Lagoon
★ Franz Josef Glacier/
★ Fox Glacier
★ Hokitika
★ Hokitika Gorge
★ Punakaiki
★ Buller Gorge
★ Oparara Basin

and Nelson. The major players are Atomic Shuttles and InterCity Coaches.

The *TranzAlpine*, one of the world's great train rides, links Greymouth and Christchurch; see p508.

MURCHISON

pop 850

Up-and-coming Murchison, 125km southwest of Nelson on the Buller Gorge Heritage Hwy/State Highway 6 (SH6), is the northern gateway to the West Coast. It's an Upper Buller Gorge service town and adventure base.

Information

The **Murchison visitor information centre** (☎ 03-523 9350; www.murchisonnz.com; 47 Waller St; ⏰ 10am-6pm, reduced winter hours) has bundles of info on local activities and transport. There are no banks in town; the postal agency is on Fairfax St. The **Commercial Hotel** (cnr Waller & Fairfax Sts) has Internet access.

Sights & Activities

Murchison is an outdoor activities hot spot with fishing, mountain biking, rafting and kayaking available. Floating fleets descend the Buller River in summer.

Ultimate Descents (☎ 0800 748 377, 03-523 9899; www.rivers.co.nz; 51 Fairfax St; half/full-day rafting $105/195) is a professional outfit offering white-water rafting and kayaking trips on the Buller, including half-day easy-going, family excursions (adult/child $95/75). Helirafting trips cost from $350.

The **New Zealand Kayak School** (☎ 03-523 9611; www.nzkayakschool.com; 22 Grey St; kayaks per day $45, 4-day intro course $695; ⏰ Sep-Apr) hires out kayaks and runs professional courses for all levels; price includes transport and accom-

---

Climate

During summer (December to February) the coast roads flood with campervans, but from May to September days can be warm and clear, with views of snow-dappled peaks, fewer crowds and cheaper accommodation. At around 5m annually, the West Coast has serious rainfall (Westland = Wetland) but Westland sees as much sunshine as Christchurch. When it's pouring in the east it's just as likely to be sunny here.

Getting There & Around

Air New Zealand will wing you into Westport from Wellington; into Hokitika from Christchurch.

Numerous coaches and shuttles traverse the coast, some of which connect to centres like Christchurch, Dunedin, Queenstown

---

TOP ACTIVITIES

- Walking to (or clambering over) the famous West Coast glaciers (p516 and p519)
- Watch the scenery fly past while jetboating or white-water rafting the rugged Buller Gorge (p492)
- Go subterranean in Westport (p494) or Karamea (p497)
- See the Coast by helicopter, departing from Karamea (p498) or Greymouth (p505) or take a chopper to the glaciers (p516 and p521)
- Do it all! Get really active in Murchison: fishing, mountain biking, white-water rafting, kayaking and gold panning (above)

THE WEST COAST

Southwest New Zealand World Heritage Area (Te Wahipounamu) Boundary

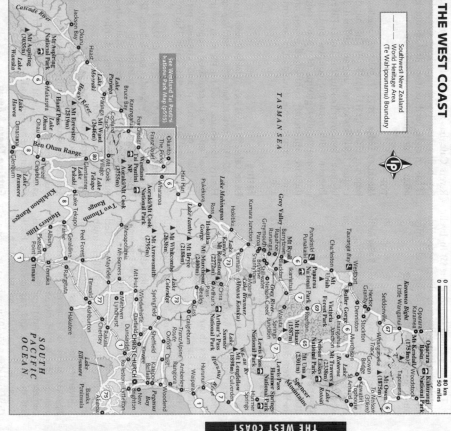

modation but BYO food. It also sells kayaking gear. Dorms ($20 per night) are usually full of course attendees.

White Water Action Rafting Tours (☎ 0800 582; 03-523 9581; www.whitewateraction.co.nz; Waller St; half-day rafting $105), right behind the visitor information centre, runs various half-day rafting trips that lunch.

If you don't want to get your feet wet, **Murchison 'Out There' Tours** (☎ 0800 888 003, 03-523 9958; murchbuses@xtra.co.nz; half/full-day tours $79/148) will bus (and boat) you around regional rivers, lakes and forests.

The area is threaded with **mountain-bike trails**. Tackle the west bank of the Matakitaki River (16km return) or the Maruia Saddle Trip (83km return). Hire bikes from **Riverview Holiday Park** (☎ 03-523 9591; riverview.hp@xtra .co.nz; Riverside Tce) or **Murchison Motels** (☎ 0800 166 500, 03-523 9026; murchison.motels@xtra.co.nz; 53 Fairfax St).

The barnlike **Murchison Museum** (☎ 03-523 9392; 60 Fairfax St; admission by donation; 10am-4pm) is a musty mishmash of Murchison memorabilia, with vintage farm equipment, antique telephonic gimmickry and photographs of the 1929 Murchison earthquake aftermath.

Murchison **trout fishing** is superb – full-day guided trips cost around $600; the visitor information centre has the lowdown. Back on dry land, the Tutaki Valley has great horse trekking; **Tiraumea Horse Treks** (☎ 03-523 9341; per hr $30) runs hour-long to full-day treks.

Try **gold panning** (equipment hire $5) in Lyell Creek, the Buller River or the Howard Valley – the visitor information centre hires out pans and shovels ($20 bond).

Festivals & Events

The year's crowning event is the **Buller Festival** (www.rivers.co.nz/bullerfestival), a kayaking and rafting extravaganza held over the first weekend in March.

Sleeping

BUDGET

Hu-Ha Bikepackers (☎ 03-548 2707; SH6; smidgley@ ihug.co.nz; unpowered sites per 2 people $28, dm/s/d $21/ 25/50) OK, so it's not actually *in* Murchison (45km north), but this laid-back, cyclist-loving farm is a cool place to relax en route. There are two dorms, one double, and plenty of goats, horses, pigs and lambs. The house sits above the road, 10km north of Kawatiri Junction.

Hampden Hotel (☎ 03-523 9008; cnr Waller & Fairfax Sts; s/d $30/50) Has no-frills pub rooms with shared facilities and scratches around key-holes from decades of fumbling drunks.

LazyCow (☎ 0800 5299269, 03-5239451; mdwright@ xtra.co.nz; 37 Waller St; dm/s/d $22/45/50) Affordable roadside accommodation with a sun deck to perch on. It's right in the middle of town, but attracts mixed reviews from travellers.

Riverview Holiday Park (☎ 03-523 9591; riverview .hp@xtra.co.nz; Riverside Tce; unpowered/powered sites per 2 people $16/18, d $36-80) Between the river and the cemetery (!), just north of town, this park has motel rooms and rustic cabins. Facilities are a bit weary, but mountain-bike hire (half/full day $15/30) weighs in its favour.

MIDRANGE

Commercial Hotel (☎ 03-523 9848; thecommercial hotel@xtra.co.nz; cnr Waller & Fairfax Sts; s/d $35/60; 💻) The recently renovated Commercial is great value for money – midrange quality if not price. Colourful rooms are simple and clean, with TVs and shared facilities.

Mataki Motel (☎ 0800 279 088, 03-523 9088; www .matakimotel.co.nz; 34 Hotham St; d $65-100; 💻) Quietly located a few blocks off the main street, Mataki has spotless rooms, big TVs, a rural river-valley backdrop, a kids playground and cooked/continental brekkies on request.

Murchison Motels (☎ 0800 166 500, 03-523 9026; murchison.motels@xtra.co.nz; 53 Fairfax St; d $100-150) This four-star motel complex, tucked behind

Rivers Cafe, has a bunch of spiffy one- and two-bedroom units with super king-size beds. It has an eight-berth cottage, and mountain bikes for hire (half/full day $15/30).

TOP END

Murchison Lodge (☎ 03-523 9196; www.murchison lodge.co.nz; 15 Grey St; s $115, d $145-175) This hand-crafted B&B sits on an untrammelled 1.2-hectare block overlooking the Buller River. Popular with romantic couples and (no less romantically) groups of up to nine, the three differently configured rooms are entirely comfortable. Breakfast is comfort-ably entire.

Eating

Rivers Cafe (☎ 03-523 9009; 51 Fairfax St; lunch $7-17, dinner $22-34; 🕑 breakfast, lunch & dinner, closed May-Sep) Hearty homemade food for the river-weary is served up here in generous proportions. Fab slabs of venison and chicken pies, quiches and lasagne take the cake. The coffee's good too.

Beechwoods Cafe (☎ 0800 114 211, 03-523 9571; 32 Waller St; meals $8-25; 🕑 breakfast, lunch & dinner; 💻) Coaches regularly belch into the car park at this roadhouse, which serves up sandwiches, burgers (including veggie), mixed grills and big breakfasts for ornery truckers.

Commercial Hotel (☎ 03-523 9696; cnr Waller & Fairfax Sts; lunch $9-18, dinner $17-28; 🕑 breakfast, lunch & dinner; 💻) Sink your choppers into seafood baskets, quiches, steaks, pork, chicken and salads as a '70s SoCal soundtrack trucks along in the background.

Getting There & Away

Buses pass through Murchison on the 'Coast-to-Boat' run from the West Coast to Picton. These include **Atomic Shuttles** (☎ 03-322 8883; www.atomictravel.co.nz) on its Picton–Fox Glacier service; **InterCity** (☎ 03-365 1113; www .intercitycoach.co.nz) on the Nelson–Fox Glacier run; and **K-Bus** (☎ 03-578 4075; www.kbus.co.nz) on its Greymouth–Picton and Greymouth–Nelson routes. Atomic stops at the visitor information centre, InterCity at Beechwoods Café, and K-Bus at the Midwest Café on Fairfax St.

BULLER GORGE

The road from Murchison to the coast was shaken up by the 1929 and 1968 earthquakes but still snakes through Buller Gorge. The gorge itself is a water-sports conduit; for white-water rafting and kayaking info, see p490.

About 14km west of Murchison is the **Buller Gorge Swingbridge** (☎ 03-523 9809; www.bullergorge.co.nz; SH6; bridge crossing adult/child $5/2; ⊗ 8am-7pm Oct-Apr, 9am-5.30pm May-Sep), New Zealand's longest swing bridge (110m). On the far side are some short walks, one to the White Creek Faultline, epicentre of the 1929 earthquake. Coming back, don your cape and put your underwear on the outside for the 160m **Comet Line flying fox** (seated adult/child $25/13; Supaman ride $35/20), either sitting in a harness or flying Superman-style. **Buller Experience Jet** (☎ 0800 802 023, 03-523 9880; www.murchison.co.nz/adult/child $65/45) runs 40-minute jetboat trips departing under the bridge.

Further west the road forks at Inangahua Junction – continue to the coast through Lower Buller Gorge on State Highway 6 (SH6), or head south to Greymouth via Reefton on SH69. SH6 is longer but has more to offer.

Inwood Farm Backpackers (☎/fax 03-789 0205; Inwoods Rd, Inangahua Junction; unpowered sites per 2 people/dm/tw $16/17/20; ⊗ closed Jun-Aug) is a friendly, sunny farmhouse with two small dorms and one twin. There's no TV, so you'll just have to commune with nature. There's also a **DOC camping ground** (adult/child $5/2.50) on SH6 at Lyell, Upper Buller Gorge, 10km northeast of Inangahua Junction.

On a murky day, Buller Gorge is dark and forbidding – primeval ferns and cabbage trees cling to steep cliffs; toi toi (tall native grass) flanks the road between gorge and river. Named after gold prospector Robert Hawks, the road at **Hawks Crag**, an overhang just high enough to fit a bus under, was handhacked out of the rock.

Berlins (☎ 0800 526 405, 03-789 0295; www.xtreme adventures.co.nz; SH6; dm/d $20/50) is a stylish café-meets-backpackers on the site of the old Berlins Hotel. Jetskiing is its particular bent – have a burl on the river ($145 to $165) then grab a meal and a beer at the all-day café (mains $10 to $25).

Buller Adventure Tours (☎ 0800 697 286, 03-789 7286; www.adventuretours.co.nz; SH6; about 4km from the coast, offers a hullabaloo of water- and land-based action in the Gorge: white-water rafting on Grade III to IV 'Earthquake Slip' rapids ($105); 1¾-hour jetboat rides

($75); two-hour riverbank horse treks ($65); and 1¾-hour quad-bike rides ($105).

WESTPORT

pop 4845

Westport made its fortune digging up coal, though the main mine is at Stockton, 38km north of town. A utilitarian port where the Buller River meets the Tasman Sea, there's little here to tickle the imagination, but it makes a good base for shenanigans in the Buller Gorge and Charleston ranges. It's also a logical stopover on the way to Karamea (for the Heaphy Track), and there's a seal colony (see p496) west of town.

Orientation

The town forms a basic grid on the east bank of the Buller River. Palmerston St is the main drag; Brougham St heads north-east to Karamea.

MAPS

Free town and regional maps are available at the visitor information centre.

Information

The major banks count their coins along Palmerston St.

Buller Hospital (☎ 03-788 9030; Cobden St)

Denniston Dog (☎ 03-789 5030; 18 Wakefield St) Internet access.

Department of Conservation office (DOC; ☎ 03-788 8008; 72 Russell St; ⊗ 8am-noon & 1-4.30pm Mon-Fri) Tickets for the Wangapeka Track and general tramping info.

Police station (☎ 03-788 8310; 13 Wakefield St)

Post office (cnr Brougham & Palmerston Sts)

Take Note (☎ 03-789 8731; 106 Palmerston St) Bookshop.

Web Shed (☎ 03-788 8002; 204 Palmerston St) Internet access.

Westport visitor information centre (☎ 03-789 6658; www.westport.org.nz; 1 Brougham St; ⊗ 9am-6pm Nov-Mar, to 4pm Apr-Oct) Information on local tracks, walkways, tours, accommodation, transport, and DOC hut tickets for the Heaphy Track.

Sights

The **Coaltown Museum** (☎ 03-789 8204; Queen St; coaltown@xtra.co.nz; adult/child $7/3; ⊗ 9am-4.30pm) is an authentic pastiche of mining life, including a walk-through faux mine with sound bites and videos. Rusty mining artefacts sit silently by brewery, photographic and

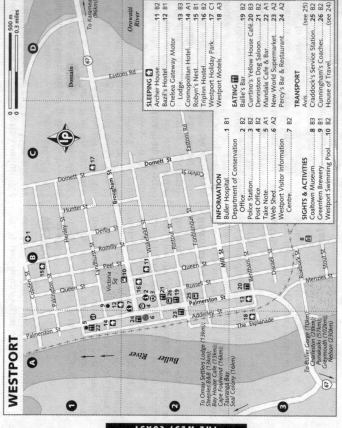

WESTPORT

INFORMATION	
Buller Hospital	1 B1
Department of Conservation	
Office	2 B2
Police Station	3 B2
Post Office	4 B2
Take Note	5 A1
Web Shed	6 A2
Westport Visitor Information	
Centre	7 B2

SIGHTS & ACTIVITIES	
Coaltown Museum	8 B3
Greenfern Brewery	9 B1
Westport Swimming Pool	10 B2

SLEEPING	
Archer House	11 B2
Bazil's Hostel	12 B1
Chelsea Gateway Motor	
Lodge	13 B3
Cosmopolitan Hotel	14 A1
Robyn's Nest	15 B1
TripInn Hostel	16 B2
Westport Holiday Park	17 C1
Westport Motels	18 A3

EATING	
Bailie's Bar	19 B2
Curtino's Yellow House Café	20 B3
Denniston Dog Saloon	21 B2
Mandala Cafe & Bar	22 A1
New World Supermarket	23 A2
Percy's Bar & Restaurant	24 A2

TRANSPORT	
Avis	(see 25)
Craddock's Service Station	25 B2
Cunningham's Coaches	26 B2
House of Travel	(see 24)

harbour-dredging displays, including a huge operational steam dredge (now electrical).

Established in 1993, the locally owned **Greenfern Brewery** (☎ 03-789 6201; www.greenfern .co.nz; 10 Lyndhurst St; ⏰ 10am-5.30pm Mon-Fri, 11am-5.30pm Sat) concocts seven different beers, including the organic Green Fern and the Good Bastards dark ale. Brewery tours have ceased, but you can still taste the product.

Activities

From Charleston, south of Westport, **Norwest Adventures** (☎ 0800 116 686, 03-789 6686; www .caverafting.com) runs 'Underworld Rafting' cave-rafting trips ($135, four hours) into the otherworldly, glow-worm-filled Nile River Caves (no, not *the* Nile). If you want the glow without the flow (no rafting), it's $75 per person. Both options start with a rainforest railway ride, available separately (adult/child $20/15, 1½ hours). The 'Adventure Caving' trip ($270, five hours) includes a 30m abseil into Te Tahi *tomo* (hole), rock squeezes, waterfalls, prehistoric fossils and trippy cave formations.

Submerge yourself in thoughts of 'Where will I go next?' at Westport's heated **swimming pool** (☎ 03-789 7236; Brougham St; adult/child $3/1.50; ⏰ 9am-6pm Mon-Fri, to 8pm Sat & Sun).

Tours

Outwest Tours (☎ 0800 688 937, 03-789 6883; www .outwest.co.nz) runs five- to eight-hour excursions in pugnacious 4WD vehicles to Stockton ($85), Denniston ($85), Denniston and Mackley ($125), and the coastal route to Charleston ($85), departing from the visitor information centre.

Festivals & Events

The **Buller Gorge Marathon** (www.bullermarathon .org.nz) collapses over the finish line in Westport on the second weekend in February. The **Cape Classic Surfing Contest** gets radical on the Labour Day weekend in October.

Sleeping

BUDGET

Robyn's Nest (☎ 03-789 6565; robyns.nest@xtra.co.nz; 42 Romilly St; dm/d $20/46; 🖳) The mural by the door overstates the scenery just a tad, but this 1910 house is as cosy as a bird's nest, with roomy rooms, monster TV, barbecue, pot-belly stove and plenty of natural light. Grab the upstairs balcony room if it's free.

Bazil's Hostel (03-789 6410; www.bazils.com; 54 Russell St; dm/tw/d $24/53/55;) Mr Fawlty is notably absent at the new bigger and better Bazil's, which has osmotically absorbed the Happy Wanderer hostel next door. This is high-quality hostelling, with a superb kitchen and split-level self-contained en suite dorms (No 7 out the back is wicked).

Tripinn Hostel (03-789 7367; tripinn@clear.net.nz; 72 Queen St; dm/s/d $21/36/50;) Set in a rambling, 64-bed, 140-year-old house on a quiet backstreet, this busy hostel has gas cooking, a wood heater, a separate video lounge, zestful owners, a magnificent rhododendron tree and an unhurried air.

Cosmopolitan Hotel (03-789 6305; coshotel@ihug.co.nz; 136 Palmerston St; s $35-42 d $68) Somewhat surprisingly, the rooms here are actually cosmopolitan. The $35 singles are a bit cramped and the north-facing rooms overlook a processing plant, but hey, you ain't here for the views. Downstairs the drinkers watch the dogs.

Westport Holiday Park (03-789 7043; www.westportholidaypark.co.nz; 31-37 Domett St; dm $19, unpowered/powered sites per 2 people $22/24, d $48-125) Five blocks from town, the A-frame 'chalets' in this bushy grove seem to have mushroomed up overnight. Bunk rooms, motel units and new self-contained studios are interspersed with decent amenities. Half-day kayak hire is $25.

MIDRANGE

Archer House (03-789 8778; www.archerhouse.co.nz; 75 Queen St; s/d $140/130) Archer House is Westport's top end at midrange prices. Tastefully old-world without being olde-worlde, this gorgeous Victorian villa has three rooms filled with antiques and lead lighting. Little extras like heated towel rails, hairdryers and complimentary glasses of wine seal the deal. Kids are most welcome.

Westport Motels (0800 805 909, 03-789 7575; www.westportmotels.co.nz; 32 the Esplanade; s/d from $65/75;) Westport is overrun with midrange motels. Surrounded by trees by the Buller River, this is one of the better ones, with thoroughly comfortable beds, outdoor tables, a spa and swimming pool. There are several family units to accommodate big broods.

Chelsea Gateway Motor Lodge (0800 660 033, 03-789 6835; www.chelseagateway.co.nz; 330 Palmerston St; ste $100-189) With an exterior a Chelsea Londoner might aptly describe as 'naff', this well-appointed motel scores points internally. As well as standard suites there are two- and three-bedroom family units. Spa units sometimes aren't much more expensive than standard rooms – if so, dive in.

Eating & Drinking

Currtino's Yellow House Café (03-789 8765; 243 Palmerston St; lunch $7-15, dinner $22-28; breakfast, lunch & dinner, reduced winter hours) Yep, it's yellow. The optimism continues inside where Currtino's single-handedly raises Westport out of the deep-fry-and-white-bread culinary quagmire. Beautifully prepared healthy food, homemade bread, lilting jazz and plenty of laughter from the kitchen – hard to beat.

Bailie's Bar (03-789 7289; 187 Palmerston St; mains $15-31; lunch Thu-Sat, dinner daily) This tentatively Irish beer parlour lets you cook your own steak for $11, or dumps 500g of rib eye on your plate for $31. With typical NZ democracy, the crowd ranges from hirsute Heaphy Track tramps to local businessmen, beers in one hand, burgers in the other.

Mandala Cafe & Bar (03-789 7931; 110 Palmerston St; mains $8-18; breakfast, lunch & dinner) Though the name hints at it, there are no mystic universal symbols here, just a standard café cooking up crumbed fish, pasta and burgers as the radio belts out forgotten '80s power ballads.

Percy's Bar & Restaurant (03-789 5030; 18 Wakefield St; mains $15-30; dinner;) Shamelessly stealing the American Greyhound Bus logo, Percy's is a cool little food nook on the main street. At the time of writing, it was about to be bought by Denniston Dog. We hope the coffee quality endures.

Denniston Dog Saloon (03-789 5648; 198 Palmerston St; meals $8-15; breakfast, lunch & dinner) Percy's is a rollicking local saloon, littered with pool tables and yesteryear photography. The bar serves snacks and more solid stuff on an anything-and-everything menu.

Self-caters should beat a path to **New World** (03-789 7669; 244 Palmerston St) supermarket without delay.

Getting There & Around

AIR

Air New Zealand (☎ 0800 737 000, 09-357 3000; www .airnz.co.nz) has direct flights to/from Wellington; book at the **House of Travel** (☎ 03-788 8120; www.houseoftravel.co.nz; 196 Palmerston St).

BUS

Inquire about bus tickets at the Westport visitor information centre or directly with operators.

InterCity (☎ 03-365 1113; www.intercitycoach.co .nz) buses depart from **Craddock's Service Station** (☎ 03-789 7819; 197 Palmerston St) to Nelson ($39 to $55, 3½ hours, 3.55pm daily), Greymouth ($22 to $31, two hours, 11am daily) and Franz Josef ($48 to $69, 6½ hours, 11am daily). Prices vary with season and advance purchase.

Atomic Shuttles (☎ 03-322 8883; www.atomictravel .co.nz) buses depart from the visitor information centre to Nelson ($35, 3½ hours, 1.30pm daily), Picton ($50, 4½ hours, 1.30pm daily), and Greymouth ($20, two hours, 1.45pm daily).

K-Bus (☎ 0800 881 188, 03-578 4075; www.kbus.co .nz) goes to Nelson ($35, 3½ hours, 10.30am daily), Motueka ($45, five hours, 10.30am daily), and Greymouth ($20, 1½ hours, 10.30am daily), departing from the visitor information centre (operates reduced days in winter).

East West Coach (☎ 0800 142 622, 03-789 6251; eastwestco@xtra.co.nz) operates a Christchurch service (adult/child $48/34, five hours, 8am daily) departing from Craddock's and returning from Christchurch at 2pm.

Karamea Express (☎ 03-782 6757; info@karamea -express.co.nz) links Westport and Karamea (adult/child $25/15, 1½ hours, 11.30am Monday to Friday May to October), plus Saturday from November and April), departing the visitor information centre. **Cunningham's Coaches** (☎ 03-789 7177; 179 Palmerston St) does this trip as a mail run ($16, three hours, 3pm weekdays), returning from Karamea at 6pm.

CAR HIRE

To hire a car head to **Avis** (☎ 03-789 6776; www .avis.com; Craddock's Service Station, 197 Palmerston St).

TAXI

A taxi from town to the airport costs around $15. Try **Buller Taxis** (☎ 03-789 6900).

AROUND WESTPORT

Depending on the season, anything from 20 to 200 grunting NZ fur seals dot rocks at the **Tauranga Bay Seal Colony**, 16km from Westport. Pups are born from late November to early December. For a month afterwards, land-bound mothers tend the young before swimming out on feeding forays.

The **Cape Foulwind Walkway** (1½ hours return) extends from the seal colony near it's southern end, 4km along the coast to Cape Foulwind, passing a replica of Abel Tasman's astrolabe (a navigational aid) and a lighthouse. The walk's northern end is car-accessible from Lighthouse Rd.

The Maori called the cape Tauranga, meaning 'Sheltered Anchorage'. The first European here was Abel Tasman, bobbing past in December 1642 and naming it Clyppygen Hoek (Rocky Point). When James Cook moored the *Endeavour* here in March 1770, a furious storm made it anything but a 'sheltered anchorage'. He left the cape's foul name in his wake.

From the Tauranga Bay car park it's a five-minute walk to the seal colony lookout, though seals often tumble around in the surf along the way. The cliffs are unstable, so stick to the path.

Sleeping & Eating

Steeples B&B (☎ 03-789 7876; steepleshomestay@xtra .co.nz; 48 Lighthouse Rd, Cape Foulwind; s $60-90, d $100-110) Close to the Cape, this home-style B&B has a private self-contained cottage as well as rooms inside the main house. Beautiful gardens feather away to sheer cliffs, with wide views of The Steeples rocks. Homemade muesli breakfasts will fuel you through the day.

Omau Settlers Lodge (☎ 0800 466 287, 03-789 5200; thecape@xtra.co.nz; 1054 Cape Rd, Cape Foulwind; s/d $90/125) Within convenient stumbling distance of the Cape Foulwind tavern, this new motel is built to weather many a malicious zephyr. Stylish corrugated units will protect you until it's time for the buffet breakfast (included in room price).

Bay House Cafe (☎ 03-789 7133; Tauranga Bay, Cape Foulwind; mains $28-32; ☑ breakfast, lunch & dinner) Bay House is one of the West Coast's (and NZ's) best restaurants, serving contemporary Pacific-fusion dishes in sophisticated but far from uptight surrounds. The deck, with views over the Tauranga Bay breakers,

WESTPORT TO KARAMEA

This drive north along SH67 is mighty fine, the road pressed against the rocky shoreline by hills smothered in vegetation. The first town beyond Westport is Waimangaroa, where there's a turn-off to **Denniston**, 9km inland and 600m above sea level. Denniston was once NZ's largest coal producer, with 1500 residents in 1911. By 1981 this had shrunk to eight; these days you're lucky if you see a sparrow. The **Denniston Bridle Track** follows sections of the fantastically steep **Denniston Incline**. The Incline was an engineering spectacular – empty coal trucks were hauled back up the 45-degree slope by the weight of descending loaded trucks. Ingenious, yes, but perhaps not quite the 'eighth wonder of the world' as a tourist leaflet claims. Four kilometres north of Waimangaroa is the **Britannia Track** (four hours return, 12km), winding towards the Britannia Battery's gold-mining detritus.

At Granity, 30km north of Westport, head 5km uphill to the semi-ghost town of **Millerton**, and a further 3km to **Stockton**, home of NZ's largest operational coal mine. The **Millerton Incline Walk** (20 minutes return) takes in parts of the old incline, a bridge and an old dam.

Further north at Ngakawau, just south of Hector, is the **Charming Creek Walk** (six hours return), an all-weather trail following an old coal line through the Ngakawau River Gorge. Alternatively, pursue the track 10km beyond the return point to **Seddonville**, a small bush town on the Mohikinui River. The short **Chasm Creek Walkway** links Seddonville with SH67.

At the Mohikinui River mouth, 3km off the highway, is the not-so-gentle **Gentle Annie Beach**, and the **Gentle Annie Coastal Enclave** (☎ 03-782 1826; www.gentleannie.co.nz; De Malmanche Rd, Mohikinui; unpowered sites per 2 people/dm $18/20, d $90-130). The surf hammers the coast, the wind whips the palms – this is the place to forget about whatever's been bugging you. There's a basic backpacker lodge, as well as a sensational three-bedroom cabin with driftwood doorhandles and two four-bedroom houses. Prices vary seasonally.

Between Mohikinui and Little Wanganui the road humps over **Karamea Bluff**, a slow,

meandering drive through rata and matai forest with snapshot views of the Tasman Sea below.

KARAMEA

pop 685

On a latitude north of Wellington, Karamea is literally the end of the road – the end of SH67 and near the southern ends of the Heaphy and Wangapeka Tracks. For 20 years debate has raged about continuing the road through to Nelson – local businesses are in favour; DOC adopts a 'when hell freezes over' stance. Town facilities cluster around Market Cross.

Information

Actively involved in promoting the region, the **Karamea visitor information centre** (☎ 03-782 6652; www.karameainfo.co.nz; Market Cross; 🕒 9am-5pm daily Jan-Apr, to 3pm Mon-Fri & to 1pm Sat May-Dec) has the local lowdown, maps and DOC hut tickets. The **DOC Office** (☎ 03-782 6852; 83 Waverley St; 🕒 8am-4:30pm Mon-Fri) is irregularly staffed.

Sights

OPARARA BASIN

North of Karamea in the **Oparara Basin** are some spectacular limestone arches and the unique Honeycomb Hill Caves (ancient home of the moa), the surrounding karst landscape blanketed by primitive rainforest. Moss-laden trees droop over the Oparara River, illuminated by light filtering through a dense forest canopy.

Ten kilometres along the road to the start of the Heaphy Track, turn off at McCallum's Mill Rd and go 15km past the sawmill along a winding gravel (sometimes rough) road to the arches. It's an easy walk (45 minutes return) through old-growth forest to the 200m-long, 37m-high **Oparara Arch**, spanning its namesake river. It's arch-rival is the archaic **Moria Gate Arch** (43m long, 19m high), accessed via a similar track (one hour return).

Other curious limey features are **Mirror Tarn** (an easy 20 minutes return), a tree-lined tarn full of reflections, and the **Crazy Paving & Box Canyon Caves** (10 minutes return, BYO torch), a cracked-up cave floor formation and a roomy cave system with fossils on the ceiling. Beyond these, in a protected area of Kahurangi National Park, are the superb **Honeycomb Hill Caves & Arch**, only accessible

---

is perfect for a long lunch on the days when foul winds blow elsewhere.

by a prebooked **guided tour** (☎ 03-782 6652; adult/child $70/35) – ask at the visitor information centre. These caves contain the bones of nine different moa species and the extinct giant Haast eagle, whose 4m wingspans spelt trouble for the moa.

Activities

The visitor information centre should be your first point of call for all activities.

The Karamea River has good swimming, fishing, whitebaiting and kayaking, but ask a local or use common sense before jumping in. Unguided kayak river trips are run by **Last Resort** (☎ 0800 505 042, 03-782 6617; www.lastresort.co.nz; 71 Waverley St; 2/3hr $20/30).

The Little Wanganui, Oparara and Kohaihai Rivers have good swimming holes. The only drawback to the awesome beaches around Karamea are the millions of sandflies; dousings of repellent (or wind) might save your sanity.

Longer walks around Karamea include the **Fenian Track** (four hours return) leading to **Cavern Creek Caves** and **Adams Flat**, where there's a replica gold-miners hut; a steep tramp for the reasonably fit to the 1084m **Mt Stormy** (eight hours return); and the first leg of the **Wangapeka Track** to Belltown Hut. Shorter walks include the **Lake Hanlon** (30 minutes return), **Big Remu** (45 minutes return), **Flagstaff** (one hour return) and **Zig Zag Track** (one hour return) walks.

If the prospect of walking the entire **Heaphy Track** makes you nauseous, you can walk as far as the **Heaphy Hut** (five hours, adult/child $20/10), stay overnight then head back. Heaphy Track huts must be booked in advance, regardless of season, through DOC or the Karamea visitor information centre (p497). Alternatively, walk as far as **Scotts Beach** (1½ hours return), passing nikau palm groves along the way, or continue to **Crayfish Point**. For detailed information on the Heaphy and Wangapeka Tracks, see p487 and p488.

The **K-Road** is a new mountain bike trail (27km return) kicking up dust along old Oparara Basin logging roads.

Helicopter Charter Karamea (☎ 03-782611; www .adventuresnz.co.nz; 79 Waverley St) will rotor you to anywhere in the area; phone for prices.

Sleeping & Eating

Rongo Backpackers (☎ 03-782 6667; www.livinginpeace.com; Waverley St; unpowered sites per 2 cosmic spirits $30, dm/tw/d $22/50/58; ☐) Karamea's only hostel is a peace-loving colour-pot of love. Blissed-out beings drift between the veggie and cactus gardens, beanbags, fire bath, rusty bikes, and the community radio station in the shed (107.5FM).

Karamea Holiday Park (☎ 03-782 6758; www.karamea.com; Maori Point Rd; unpowered/powered sites per 2 people $18/20, s $18-55, d $25-65) Set among native bush, 3km south of Market Cross, this is the place to perfect your whitebaiting skills and to otherwise wean yourself off urban rigmarole (in between visits to the TV room).

Last Resort (☎ 0800 505 042, 03-782 6617; www .lastresort.co.nz; 71 Waverley St; sites per 2 people $20, dm $24, d $69-140) This 30-room megaplex has sod-roof dorms with handmade beds, self-contained motel rooms and cottages. Spas and massage are available, or kayaking, fly-fishing, rafting and helisightseeing

WHITEBAIT SEASON

Whitebait are small, translucent fish – the imago (immature) stage of river smelt (salmonoid fish). They surge up West Coast rivers in dense schools and are caught in set seine-net traps or large, round scoop nets. During the whitebait season – usually from the start of September to mid-November, limited to allow declining whitebait stocks to regroup – fisherfolk line the riverbanks and estuaries and haul in their wriggling nets.

Fried up in batter, omelettes, sandwiches or burgers, these wee fish are damn tasty. During the season you won't find a West Coast menu without a whitebait special. A West Coast culinary doyenne provided this whitebait patties recipe:

Take a pint of whitebait (about 0.5L – yes, the fish are measured as a liquid rather than a solid, as they used to be sold in pint-size glass milk bottles) and pour into a bowl. For the batter take one egg, three tablespoons of flour, a pinch of salt and a little milk to make a smooth paste. Mix this and then pour over the whitebait. Cook patties in smoking-hot fat until golden brown; serve immediately with mint sauce, hot potato chips and pickled onions.

if you're feeling more industrious. The licensed restaurant (mains $15 to $26; open for breakfast and dinner from September to May, closed June to August) dishes up traditional Kiwi food; the café-bar (mains $7 to $22; open for lunch and dinner) serves less complex fare.

Karamea Beachfront Farmstay B&B (☎ 03-782 6762; www.westcoastbeachaccommodation.co.nz; SH67; d $90-150) This friendly farmstay has 2.5km of pristine beachfront, 16km south of Karamea. Your host Dianne loves to cook, and her cooking is loved (dinner $40 by arrangement). The three guest rooms are far from farmy.

Karamea Village Hotel (☎ 03-782 hotel@xtra.co.nz; Waverley St; d $95-120) The modern en suite motel units here have great hill views. Pub meals are heavy on the meat, the punters queuing up for whitebait sandwiches ($11).

Bridge Farm Motels (☎ 03-782 6955; www.karamea motels.co.nz; Bridge Rd; ste $90-130) Accommodation at this rural motel ranges from studios to two-bedroom units, which are bright, quiet and roomy. The pet alpacas will eyeball your continental breakfast, included in the tariff.

Getting There & Away

If you're driving from Westport to Karamea, fill up in Westport as there's no petrol until Karamea, 98km away.

Karamea Express (☎ 03-782 6757; info@karamea-express.co.nz) links Karamea and Westport (adult/child $25/15, 1½ hours, 7.50am Monday to Friday May to October, plus Saturday from November and April), departing the Last Resort. **Cunningham's Coaches** (☎ 03-789 7177; 179 Palmerston St, Westport) does this trip as a mail run ($16, three hours, 6pm weekdays), departing from Karamea Hardware.

Karamea Express also services Kohaihai at the southern end of the Heaphy Track, departing Kohaihai at 1pm and 2pm during summer – phone for prices and off-season times. It also services the Wangapeka Track on demand. There are phones at both trailheads to arrange transport out to Karamea.

You can also fly from Karamea to Takaka (around $150 per person) then walk back on the Heaphy Track – contact the visitor information centre for details.

WESTPORT TO GREYMOUTH

SH6 along the surf-pounded coastline proffers fine Tasman Sea views. Fill up in Westport if you're low on petrol – there's no fuel until Runanga, 92km away. Views aside, the main attraction along this stretch are the geologically brilliant Pancake Rocks at Punakaiki.

Jack's Gasthof (☎ 03-789 6501; jack.schuber@xtra.co.nz; SH6; sites per 2 people $10, d $50) is about 15km south of Westport on the Little Totara River. Wry-humoured Jack swapped his one-bedroom Berlin apartment for this place 20 years ago. There are two hippy doubles with colour-swirled walls, and a pizzeria (mains $15 to $27; open for breakfast, lunch and dinner) serving pizzas made with vegetables grown outside the door.

Between Westport and Punakaiki are several teensy towns (10 or so inhabitants), but it was a different story 140 years ago when gold fever gave people the sweats. For a taste of the hype, swing your shovel into **Mitchell's Gully Gold Mine** (☎ 03-789 6553; www.mitchellsgullygoldmine.8m.com; SH6; adult/child $5/1; ⏱ 9am-4pm), 22km south of Westport. It's an evocative site with a tumbledown water wheel, criss-crossed by old rail tracks, narrow forest paths and hillside tunnels (BYO torch).

Charleston, 28km south of Westport, boomed during the 1860s gold rush, with hundreds of shanties, gold-diggers staking claims along the Nile River and a beer-bellying 80 hotels and three breweries. The only pub left is the **Charleston European Tavern** (☎ 03-789 8862; SH6; mains $16-26; ⏱ breakfast, lunch & dinner), draped in international flags and with the usual small-town pub standards, including a Sunday roast.

Advertised by a fairly abstract rendering of a gold-mining scene, the **Charleston Motel** (☎ 03-789 7595; www.charlestonmotel.co.nz; SH6; d $75-85) comprises a quartet of recently renovated, comfortable units just off the highway.

The broken coastline from Fox River to Runanga will remind Californians of Big Sur. Woodpecker Bay, Tiromoana, Punakaiki, Barrytown, Fourteen Mile, Motukiekie, Ten Mile, Nine Mile and Seven Mile are **beaches** sculpted by relentless ocean fury.

Punakaiki & Paparoa National Park

Located midway between Westport and Greymouth is Punakaiki, a small settlement on the doorstep of the sensationally un-kempt, 38,000-hectare Paparoa National Park.

INFORMATION

The **Paparoa National Park visitor information centre** (☎ 03-731 1895; punakaikivc@doc.govt.nz; SH6; ⏰ 9am-9pm Oct-Dec, to 6pm Jan-May, to 4.30pm Jun-Sep) has info-laden displays on the park and details on local activities, accommodation and trail conditions.

SIGHTS

Punakaiki is famous for its splendiferous **Pancake Rocks** and **blowholes**. Through a layering-weathering process called stylo-bedding, the Dolomite Point limestone has formed into what looks like piles of thick pancakes. When the tide is right (ask at the visitor information centre), the sea surges into caverns below and booms in-timidatingly through blowholes. An easy 15-minute walk loops from the highway out to the rocks and blowholes.

Paparoa National Park offers more than just gritty flapjacks. The region is blessed with sea cliffs, toothy mountains (the Paparoa Range), rivers, diverse flora and a Westland petrel colony, the world's only nesting site of this rare sea bird.

ACTIVITIES

Walks in the national park are detailed in the DOC *Paparoa National Park* pamphlet ($1), and include the **Inland Pack Track** (27km, two to three days), a route established by miners in 1867 to dodge difficult coastal terrain. The **Croesus Track** (18km, one to two days), covered by another DOC leaflet (50c), is a tramp over the Paparoa Range from Black-ball to Barrytown, passing historic gold-mining areas. Talking walking? Register at the Greymouth or Paparoa visitor informa-tion centres first. Some inland walks are susceptible to river flooding – check condi-tions before you make happy trails.

Punakaiki Canoes (☎ 03-731 1870; www.riverkay aking.co.nz; SH6; canoe hire 2hr/full day $30/50) hires out canoes and kayaks near the Pororari River bridge. Guided tours start from $70.

Punakaiki Horse Treks (☎ 03-731 1839; www.pan cake-rocks.co.nz; SH6; 2½hr ride $95), based at Hy-drangea Cottages, conducts four-legged equine follies alongside the national park. Giddy-up.

TOURS

Green Kiwi Tours (☎ 0800 474 733; www.greenkiwi tours.co.nz; overland tours from $60, caving from $100) Locally based. Runs information-rich excursions throughout the region, including caving, bouldering, helihiking and history tours.

Kiwa Sea Adventures (☎ 03-768 7765; www.rcday .co.nz; 2hr tours adult/child $110/55) Takes you swimming with common and Hector's dolphins. Snorkelling equip-ment and pick-ups provided.

SLEEPING & EATING

Punakaiki Beach Camp (☎ 03-731 1894; beachcamp@ xtra.co.nz; 50 Owen St; unpowered/powered sites per 2 people $22/24, d $36-45) Cowering under a monolithic stone escarpment, this park is drenched with salty scents and studded with clean, old-style cabins. Amenities are ship-shape.

Beach Hostel Punakaiki (☎ 03-731 1852; www .punakaikibeachhostel.co.nz; 4 Webb St; dm/s/d $23/38/54; ▯) A sandy, beach-bumming hostel with a deep, sea-view veranda and an outdoor spa; a short trudge from Pancake Rocks, the beach and some trails. The 'house truck' double will drive your automotive dreamscapes.

Te Nikau Retreat (☎ 03-731 1111; www.tenikaure treat.co.nz; Hartmount Pl; dm $25, d $46-56, cabins $76-81, f $167; ▯) This magical place is a network of split-level dorms and asymmetrical huts in a dripping rainforest gully. Chilled-out travellers read/snooze/read in warm com-munal areas, wood-heaters smoulder and cheery kitchens careen with cookery. If the weather's clear (or even if it's not), the glass-roofed 'Stargazer' tent is unforgettable.

Rocks Homestay (☎ 0800 272 164; 03-731 1141; www.therockshomestay.com; 33 Hartmount Pl; s/d from $110/135) Three kilometres north of Punakaiki (100m north of the Truman Track), this view-endowed house looks over wild scrub to the sea. Tasty breakfasts are included; dinners by arrangement. Furnishings are a little twee, but the sunny reading room helps you forget.

Punakaiki Rocks Hotel & Villas (☎ 0800 786 252, 03-731 1168; www.punakaiki-resort.com; SH6; s/d from $110/135) Angling for fat tour-bus wal-lets, this complex reeks of capitalism, but if you're craving a little luxury you're in the right place. Ocean-facing rooms catch the sea spray; bush suites are very private. The restaurant serves breakfast ($7 to $17) and dinner ($24 to $32).

Hydrangea Cottages (☎ 03-731 1839; www.pan cake-rocks.co.nz; SH6; d $175-275) Perched on a hydrangea-sprouting hillside overlooking Pancake Rocks, these four, private, stand-alone cottages were built with timber recycled from submerged rimu logs. Puna-kaiki Horse Treks is based here.

Punakaiki Tavern (☎ 03-731 1188; punakaikitavern@xtra.co.nz; SH6; mains $14-29; ⏱ breakfast, lunch & dinner) Imbibe a glass or two of something cold in the beer garden or by the open fire when the drizzle settles in. Bountiful pub mains vie with bar snacks for your attention. There are nine double-glazed, soundproofed motel units (doubles $110) out the back.

Wild Coast Café (☎ 03-731 1873; SH6; lunch $10-16, dinner $20-30; ⏱ breakfast & lunch daily, dinner Dec-Feb) Beside the visitor information centre is this tourist-swollen café, (predictably) serving pancake stacks and whopping ice creams. We hope the 'blowhole breakfasts' aren't referring to the aftereffects.

GETTING THERE & AWAY

InterCity (☎ 03-365 1113; www.intercitycoach.co.nz), **Atomic Shuttles** (☎ 03-322 8383; www.atomictravel.co.nz) and **K-Bus** (☎ 0800 881 188, 03-578 4075; www.kbus.co.nz) services between Westport and Greymouth stop at Punakaiki, allowing enough time to check out Pancake Rocks. It's about $10 from Punakaiki to Westport or Greymouth.

The Coast Road

SH6 from Punakaiki to Greymouth is flanked by white-capped waves and calami-tous rocks on one side, and the steep, bushy Paparoa Ranges on the other.

Barrytown, 16km south of Punakaiki, is home to the low-slung **All Nations Hotel** (☎ 03-731 1812; allnations@xtra.co.nz; SH6, unpowered sites per 2 $25, d/s/d $22/32/64), and probably, once, someone called Barry. Its coaster-covered walls are opposite the western end of the Croesus Track, handy for trampers desper-ate for a bed and a beer (not necessarily in that order). Also serves pub meals.

For food, try the hip **Rata Cafe** (☎ 03-731 1151; SH6, Barrytown; mains $10-26; ⏱ lunch & dinner Oct-Apr, closed Mon & Tue May-Sep), a spacious food room perched above the road, blessed with a friendly atmosphere, an eclectic menu, rich aromas and occasional DJs.

GREY VALLEY

From Murchison, an alternative to the SH6 coast route is to turn off at Inangahua Junc-tion and travel inland via Reefton, over the mountains into the Grey Valley. Verdant slopes and spaghetti valley roads await.

Despite the efforts of a century of plun-derers, endless rains have regenerated the bush, abandoned paddocks fast returning to forest. Small towns are reminders of fu-tile farming attempts, and of the gold that saw diggers falling over themselves to get here in the 1860s.

Reefton

pop 1050

Reefton is an unconcerned little hamlet in the heart of superb tramping country, named after the region's gold-infested quartz reefs. As early as 1888, Reefton had its own electricity supply and street lighting, ahead of everywhere else in NZ. If you've crossed Lewis Pass from Christchurch, this is the first town of any size you come to.

INFORMATION

The **Reefton visitor information centre** (☎ 03-732 8391; www.reefton.co.nz; 67 Broadway; ⏱ 8.30am-6pm Nov-May, to 5pm Jun-Oct; ☐) has copies of in-formation, and sporadically well-informed staff. The one-room re-creation of the **Quartzopolis Mine** is worth the 50c.

SIGHTS & ACTIVITIES

Quite a few stops on Broadway date from the 1870s; check out the *Historic Reefton* leaflet ($1).

The community-run **Blacks Point Museum** (Franklin St, Blacks Point; adult/child $4/2; ⏱ 9am-noon & 1-4pm Wed-Fri & Sun, 1-4pm Sat Oct-Apr), 2km east of Reefton on the Christchurch road, is inside a former Methodist church that's crammed with prospecting paraphernalia. Next door is the still-functional **Golden Fleece Battery** (adult/child $1/free; ⏱ 1-4pm Wed & Sun Oct-Apr), used for crushing quartz to access the gold.

The Reefton area offers a bevy of walks – short trails around town including the **Pow-erhouse Walk** (40 minutes return) and **Reefton Heritage Walk** (30 minutes return). The **Mur-ray Creek Track** (two to seven hours return), from Blacks Point, takes you to a series of abandoned coal and gold mines along old mining trails.

There's also a wealth of walking in the 182,000-hectare **Victoria Forest Park** (NZ's largest forest park), overgrown by five dif-ferent species of beech tree. The three-day

Kirwans, Lake Christabel and **Robinson River Tracks** will fill you with fulfilment; the two-day **Big River Track** presents some tasty **mountain biking** opportunities. The visitor information centre has the requisite information and maps.

SLEEPING & EATING

Old Bread Shop (03-732 8420; reeftonbackpackers@ xtra.co.nz; 155 Buller Rd; dm $16-18, d & tw $40) This small, homely backpackers has a handful of doubles and a dorm inside a hypercoloured former bakery. The friendly owners next door are lifelong Reefton residents; ask them where to hook yourself a trout.

Reefton Motor Camp (03-732 8447; fax 03-732 8478; 1 Ross St; unpowered/powered sites per 2 people $16/20, d $35) On the audible Inangahua River at the eastern end of town, this birdsong-saturated park is encircled by ghostly Lawson's pines. The mess-hall kitchen is far from messy.

Reefton Autolodge (03-732 8406; reefton@xtra .co.nz; 74 Broadway; d/f $80/110) This central, no-fuss place has 16 serviceable units spangled with spray-painted fernscapes, huddled around a small rear courtyard.

Reef Cottage (0800 770 440, 03-732 8440; www .reefcottage.co.nz; 51-55 Broadway; d $85-140) This 1867 cottage, popular with couples and groups of up to eight, could have been transplanted from a Wild West movie set. Formerly a solicitor's office, one of the bathrooms is in the old vault (with original door). There's plenty of timber, warming the mood when the rain thrums on the tin roof. Adjoining the cottage, the thriving Reef Cottage Café (meals $5 to $20; open for breakfast and lunch) serves pies, cakes, quiches, pastas and salads with a vegetarian bias. There's a fair chance the coffee is the best in town.

Electric Light Restaurant (mains $13-25; breakfast & dinner) The ELR is under the Reefton Autolodge roof, with standard pub meals including a $13 daily roast with six (count 'em) veg. In a major marketing oversight, there's no ELO on the jukebox.

Alfresco Eatery & Accommodation (03-732 8513; paula.reefton@xtra.co.nz; 16 Broadway; mains $10-22; lunch & dinner) With a family bistro atmosphere on front and rear decks, Alfresco serves up meat and seafood grills and a half-dozen tasty pizzas. There are gas heaters or tables inside if the alfresco gets too

fresco. Next door the B&B (doubles $60 to $95 including breakfast) is a little suburban, but snug.

GETTING THERE & AWAY

East West Coach (0800 142 622, 03-789 6251; eastwestco@xtra.co.nz) is the only bus company servicing Reefton. Buses run daily to Westport ($20, 1¼ hours, 5.30pm) and Christchurch ($40, 3¾ hours, 9am).

State Highway 7 to Greymouth

At Hukarere, 21km south of Reefton, turn east and drive 14km to **Waiuta**, once a burgeoning ghost town, now a spectral collection of remnants. The Birthday Reef was unearthed here on King Edward VII's birthday in 1905. By 1906 the Blackwater Mine was booming, and the town's population swelled to 500. In 1951 the mine collapsed and Waiuta was abandoned virtually overnight.

Interpretive walks and the lonesomely ruinous atmosphere make Waiuta worth the trip – it's a leafy drive through beech forest, the last 7km a winding, narrow dirt road. If you feel like bedding down, **Waiuta Lodge** (adult/child $15/7.50, plus key deposit $10) is a 30-bunk building with full kitchen facilities. Book and collect the key at the **Reefton visitor information centre** (03-732 8391; www.reefton .co.nz; 67 Broadway).

BLACKBALL

Northeast of the Grey River, about 25km north of Greymouth, Blackball is a working town established in 1866 to service gold-diggers; coal mining kicked in between 1890 and 1964. The National Federation of Labour (a trade union) was conceived here, born from cataclysmic strikes in 1908 and 1931.

On the Roa Road 1km from Blackball is the trailhead of the **Croesus Track** (DOC leaflet 50c), tracking 18km across the Paparoa Range to Barrytown on the West Coast. Do it in a day if you're keen/mad, or stay overnight at DOC's **Ces Clark Hut** (adult/child $10/5), halfway along. Make sure you book the hut through the Greymouth visitor information centre (opposite) before you start walking.

The hub of Blackball society is the extroverted **Formerly the Blackball Hilton** (0800 4252 252 255, 03-732 4705; www.blackballhilton.co.nz; 26

Hart St; dm $22, d $110-180), designated a New Zealand Historic Place. The 'formerly' was added after a certain global hotel chain took umbrage. Accommodation-wise, there's a choice between B&B doubles and garishly funky dorms. The beer's cold, and there's an art gallery displaying local endeavours.

If you're hungry or phallically fixated, the **Blackball Salami Co** (☎ 03-732 4111; fax 03 732 4011; 11 Hilton St; ☻7am-5pm Mon-Fri, 9am-4pm Sat) sells lovingly produced (and entirely delicious) low-fat venison and beef salami.

LAKE BRUNNER

At Stillwater, detour to Lake Brunner, aka Moana Kotuku (Heron Sea). Lake Brunner and the Arnold River have the world's best **trout fishing** – not an uncommon boast in NZ. Hire a fishing guide in Moana (at the Moana Hotel) or corner a local for advice. **Lake Brunner Boat Hire** (☎ 03-738 029; 027 259 5927; koe66@ihug.co.nz; 66 Koe St) hires out fishing boats ($100 per day, plus fuel) and kayaks (single half/full day $30/40, double half/full day $40/60).

Local short walks include the **Velenski Walk** (20 minutes one way) from the motor camp through a stupendous tract of native forest; the **Arnold Dam Walk** (45 minutes return), which crosses a swing bridge over the Arnold River; and the **Rakaitane Track** (45 minutes return) through mixed podocarp forest with nocturnal kiwi rustlings and glow-worms.

Lake Brunner Motor Camp (☎ 03-738 0600; lake brunner@paradise.net.nz; Ahau St; sites per 2 people $20-25, s $20) has broad views across the lake. There's an array of sites, small four-berth cabins, an informative general store selling fishing gear and purportedly the West Coast's strongest showers.

The **Moana Hotel** (☎ 03-738 0083; moanahotel@clear.net.nz; 34 Ahau St; s $18, d $60-90), the local pub, has older hotel rooms and brand-spankin'-new hillside motel units. Its **bistro** (mains from $14; ☻lunch & dinner) has lake views and is the place to hook up with a fishing guide – elbow up to the bar and start winking.

The **Station House Cafe** (☎ 03-738 0158; 40 Koe St; lunch $10-15, dinner $20-25; ☻lunch & dinner) is on a hillside opposite the Moana Railway Station, where the *TranzAlpine* train pulls in. It's illegal for NZ restaurants to sell trout, but if you legally catch your own and bring it along, they'll cook it up for you.

GREYMOUTH

pop 13,500

Greymouth was once a Maori *pa* (fortified village), known as Mawhera (Widespread River Mouth). The Ngai Kahu people believe their ancestor Tuterakiwhanoa broke the side of Te Waka o Aoraki (Canoe of Aoraki) at Cobden Gap (north of town), releasing trapped rainwater to the sea.

Small-town in size and demeanour, Greymouth is nonetheless the West Coast's largest centre with gold-mining history as long as your arm. It's nested at the mouth of the Grey River (as logic would suggest), and despite a flood wall (Great Wall of Greymouth) the river still inundates the town occasionally.

At the western end of the East Coast–West Coast nexus (road and rail), Greymouth gets a fair slice of the tourist pie. The town's budget accommodation is outstanding, but aside from drinking Monteith's, there's not much to do. The Great Outdoors beckons...

Orientation

The town centre is on the Grey River's south bank, 1km from the river mouth. The intersection of Mackay and Tainui Sts is the centre of the known universe.

MAPS

Free town and regional maps are available at the visitor information centre. You can also pick up maps at the **Automobile Association** (AA; ☎ 03-768 4300; www.aatravel.co.nz; 84 Tainui St).

Information

The major banks and attendant ATMs loiter around Mackay and Tainui Sts. There's Internet access at the visitor information centre and at **DP:One Cafe** (108 Mawhera Quay).

Greymouth Hospital (☎ 03-768 0499; High St)
Greymouth visitor information centre (☎ 0800 473 966, 03-768 5101; cnr Herbert & Mackay Sts; ☻8.30am-7pm Mon-Fri, 9am-6pm Sat & Sun Oct-Apr, 8.30am-5pm Mon-Fri, 9am-5pm Sat & 10am-4pm Sun May-Sep); Also has DOC information.
Paper Plus (☎ 03-768 5175; 62 Mackay St) Bookshop.
Police station (☎ 03-768 1600; 45-47 Guinness St)
Post office (Tainui St)

Sights

History House Museum (☎ 03-768 4028; www.history-house.co.nz; Gresson St; adult/child $3/1; ☻10am-4pm

www.lonelyplanet.com

GREYMOUTH

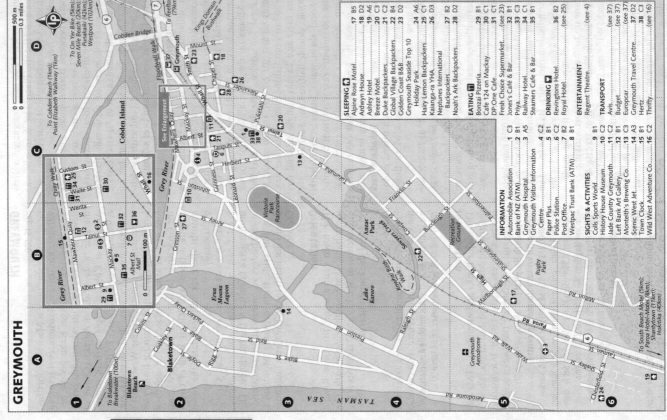

INFORMATION	
Automobile Association..............1	C3
Bank of NZ (ATM).......................2	B1
Greymouth Hospital....................3	A5
Greymouth Visitor Information	
Centre......................................4	C2
Paper Plus.................................5	B1
Police Station............................6	B2
Post Office.................................7	B2
Westpac Trust Bank (ATM).........8	B1

SIGHTS & ACTIVITIES	
Colls Sports World.....................9	B1
History House Museum............10	C2
Jade Country Greymouth..........11	C2
Left Bank Art Gallery................12	B1
Monteith's Brewing Co.............13	C3
Scenic West Jet.......................14	A3
Town Clock..............................15	C3
Wild West Adventure Co..........16	C2

SLEEPING	
Alpine Rose Motel...................17	B5
Ardwyn House.........................18	D2
Ashley Hotel............................19	A6
Breeze Motel...........................20	C3
Duke Backpackers....................21	C2
Global Village Backpackers......22	B4
Golden Coast B&B...................23	D2
Greymouth Seaside Top 10	
Holiday Park...........................24	A6
Hairy Lemon Backpackers........25	C1
Kaianga-ra YHA.......................26	D3
Neptunes International	
Backpackers..........................27	B2
Noah's Ark Backpackers..........28	D2

EATING	
Bonzai Pizzeria........................29	B1
Cafe 124 on Mackay................30	C1
DP-One Cafe............................31	C1
Fresh Choice Supermarket....(see 23)	
Jones's Café & Bar..................32	B1
Priya.......................................33	C1
Railway Hotel..........................34	C1
Steamers Cafe & Bar...............35	B1

DRINKING	
Revingtons Hotel.....................36	B2
Royal Hotel........................(see 25)	

ENTERTAINMENT	
Regent Theatre....................(see 4)	

TRANSPORT	
Avis....................................(see 37)	
Budget...............................(see 37)	
Europcar............................(see 37)	
Greymouth Travel Centre........37	D2
Hertz.....................................38	C3
Thrifty.................................(see 16)	

Mon–Fri) documents Greymouth's fascinating gold-prospecting past through photographs and historical accounts. There's gold in them thar hills!

The **Left Bank Art Gallery** (☎ 03-768 0038; www.leftbankart.co.nz; 1 Tainui St; adult/child $2/free; ☒ 10am-5pm Mon-Fri, to 3pm Sat & Sun Oct-Apr, to 4pm Mon-Fri & to 3pm Sat May-Sep) houses a small but esteemed collection of contemporary NZ jade carvings. Prints, paintings and photographs also get an airing.

Jade Country Greymouth (☎ 03-768 0700; 1 Guinness St; admission free; ☒ 8.30am-8pm Oct-Apr, to 5pm May-Sep) takes itself seriously, crafting original jade jewellery costing from $25 into the many thousands of dollars. There's a walk-through display on the precious *pounamu*, and a **café** (mains $9.50-18; ☒ breakfast & lunch) serving bagels, curries, whitebait and organic coffee.

Activities

The **Point Elizabeth Walkway** (three hours return, 8km) heads north of Greymouth into the Rapahoe Range Scenic Reserve. The **Floodwall Walk** from Cobden Bridge towards Blaketown is short and sweet (2km return, 30 minutes).

Mountain-bike trails include the appealingly (and appropriately) named Kumara Mud Plug. Hire a bike from **Colls Sports World** (☎ 03-768 4060; 53 Mackay St; per half/full day $15/20).

Sweet-As Adventures (☎ 0508 669 675; www.ecorafting.co.nz/raftingtrips $130-400) runs Grade II to IV ecorafting trips on the Arnold, Buller and upper Grey Rivers, plus helirafting further afield. Sweet-as, eh bro?

The **Wild West Adventure Co** (☎ 0800 147 483, 03-768 6649; www.nzholidayheaven.com; 8 Whall St) runs a frothy swath of rafting excursions (priced from $135 to $475), a three-hour river cruise ($125) aboard the *African Queen* (Bogart not included), and a 5½-hour 'Dragons Cave' expedition ($135), floating through a subterranean glow-worm gallery to a 30m hydro-slide.

On Yer Bike (☎ 0300 669 372, 03-762 7438; www.onyerbike.co.nz; SH6, Coa Creek; 2hr ride adult/child $120/100), 5km north of Greymouth, gets down 'n' dirty on quad-bikes. Take a two-hour 'Bush 'n Bog' ride or jump into the amphibious 8WD (one-hour trips $60).

The **surf** at Cobden Beach and Seven Mile Beach in Rapahoe is consistent, but dangerous for swimming.

Tours

Monteith's Brewing Co (☎ 03-768 4149; www.monteiths.co.nz; cnr Turumaha & Herbert Sts; admission $10; ☒ 1½hr tours 10am, 11.30am & 2pm Mon-Fri, 11.30am & 2pm Sat & Sun) Greymouth's pride ships its sumptuous beers worldwide. Its suite of eight beers includes a Golden Lager, Black Beer and Celtic Red, plus perky winter and summer drops. Observe, savour, revere.

Scenic West Jet (☎ 0800 2937 8538; Blaketown Boat Ramp; adult/child $60/40) Hurtles up the Grey River on 30-minute jetboat tours.

Festival & Events

The **Great Westland Half-Marathon** wheezes into town in the first week of December; motorcycles rev up for October's **Downtown Street Racing** petrol-fest.

Sleeping

BUDGET

Neptunes International Backpackers (☎ 0800 003 768 4868; www.neptunesbackpackers.co.nz; 43 Gresson St; dm/s/d $20/38/50; ☐) Travellers rave about this upmarket, spotless nautical hostel, formerly the Gilmor Hotel. There's not a bunk in sight, linen is provided, and the wrought-iron balcony is the perfect spot to introduce the afternoon to the sunset.

Duke Backpackers (☎ 03-768 9470; www.duke.co.nz; 27 Guinness St; dm $20, d $46-54; ☐) If you've stayed in lots of hostels, you'll know what to do when you open one. These guys know what to do: clean four-bed dorms, en suite doubles, heaters, Internet, new carpet, plenty of colour, big kitchen, free pool table, fourth night and first beer at the bar... The list goes on.

Noah's Ark Backpackers (☎ 0800 662 472, 03-768 4868; 16 Chapel St; unpowered sites per 2 people $28, dm/s/d $20/35/52; ☐) Originally a monastery, Noah's is now a zoologically obsessed hostel with eccentric animal-themed rooms. Take Millie the Malamute for a walk, or kick back on the balcony as the dusk reddens. Following Noah's lead, the camping price is for two people.

Global Village Backpackers (☎ 03-768 7272; globalvillage@miridata.co.nz; 42-54 Cowper St; dm/s $22/44, d $50-54; ☐) This highly rated riverside hostel wcos guests with great facilities, free bikes, kayaks, DVDs and outdoor spa indulgences. The 'global' theme continues throughout – prepare yourself for an Afro-Indo onslaught.

Kaianga-ra YHA (03-768 4951; yha.greymouth@yha.co.nz; 15 Alexander St; dm $20, s & d $52;) Built in 1938 as a Marist Brothers' residence, this hostel is big, clean, functional and pious – everything you'd expect from a YHA stalwart. The dorms have heaters, the video library has *Shrek*, and the guitar has three strings.

Hairy Lemon Backpackers (03-768 4022; 128 Mawhera Quay; www.thehairylemon.co.nz; dm/s/d $23/34/64;) Another of Greymouth's top-notch hostels demanding a mention, the Hairy Lemon is close to the train and bus station. It offers plentiful space, facilities and beer downstairs at the Royal Hotel.

Revingtons Hotel (03-768 7055; www.revingtons.co.nz; 46 Tainui St; dm/s/d $20/65/75;) Above this prominent two-storey pub are 31 large, well-kept rooms (some of which are vulnerable to ascending happy-hour hubbub).

Greymouth Seaside Top 10 Holiday Park (0800 867 104, 03-768 6618; www.top10greymouth.co.nz; 2 Chesterfield St; unpowered/powered sites per 2 people $26/28, d $45-100;) Another of NZ's unfathomably popular Top 10 parks (the comfort of a 'brand'?), this beachside park is 2.5km south of town. Facilities are serviceable, cabins sleep six, self-contained units sleep eight.

MIDRANGE

Alpine Rose Motel (0800 266 835, 03-768 7586; www.alpinerose.co.nz; 139 High St; d $95-145) Alpine Rose looks like it had neo-Tudor aspirations, but changed its mind midway through construction. Its large, comfortable units (some with spa) are the best of many this side of town. Free lollipops; breakfast on request.

Ardwyn House (03-768 6107; ardwynhouse@hotmail.com; 48 Chapel St; s $55, d $85-90) This old-fashioned homestay nestles amid steep gardens on a quiet, dead-end street – a tranquil respite from motel homogeneity. All the rooms have shared facilities; an extra $5 gets you a cooked breakfast.

Golden Coast B&B (03-768 7839; 10 Smith St; s $66, d $70-85) On a hillside above the train station, this guesthouse looks out over the Grey River. The house is cosy, the prices reasonable, and the electric blankets are saviours on grey Greymouth winter nights.

South Beach Motel (0800 101 222, 03-762 6768; www.southbeach.co.nz; 318 Main South Rd; s/d $85/100) This fuchsia-hued motel evokes tones of

Miami with a dozen reasonable units on Greymouth's southern outskirts, near a wild stony beach. There's a barbecue area, surf-fishing equipment for hire and facilities for travellers with disabilities.

Breeze Motel (0800 523 524, 03-768 5068; breeze motel@clear.net.nz; 125 Tainui St; s $95, d $100-125) Breeze has an older, low-riding cluster of one- and two-bedroom units, some with spa. Nothing out of the ordinary, its main selling point is its proximity to town.

TOP END

Ashley Hotel (03-768 5135; www.hotelashley.co.nz; 74 Tasman St; d $105-190;) Ashley has cornered the boutique corporate market with the kind of clinical ruthlessness Gordon Gecko would admire. The 60 variously sized rooms (one wheelchair-accessible) aren't far from the beach, but the heated indoor pool is far more 'money'.

Eating & Drinking

DP:One Cafe (03-768 4005; 108 Mawhera Quay; meals $3-10; breakfast & lunch;) This bohemian room plugs the grungy cred of a big-city café into the artsy vibe of a ramshackle garage sale. The menu features healthy pies, focaccias, salads and cakes, plus good coffee and fast Internet.

Priya (03-768 7377; 84 Tainui St; mains $12-15; lunch & dinner) An explosion of subcontinental spice on temperate West Coast tastebuds, this brisk, licensed pizzeria-café serves a plethora of pizzas, soups, pastas and steaks, all available takeaway and in kid-sized serves.

Bonzai Pizzeria (03-768 4170; 31 Mackay St; mains $14-24; breakfast, lunch & dinner Mon-Sat, lunch & dinner Sun) Ardently recommended by readers, this brisk, licensed pizzeria-café serves a plethora of pizzas, soups, pastas and steaks, all available takeaway and in kid-sized serves.

Cafe 124 on Mackay (03-768 7503; 124 Mackay St; lunch $3-16, dinner $18-24; breakfast, lunch & dinner) Jazzy Cafe 124 has some rare Greymouth commodities: outdoor tables and vegetarian options. There's daily fresh fish (seasonal whitebait), and a shop at the back selling local craftwork.

Jones's Café & Bar (03-768 6468; 37 Tainui St; lunch $8-15, dinner $17-29; breakfast, lunch & dinner) Jones's bills itself as a blues bar, but the vibe is more Elton John yawn than Stevie Ray

Vaughan. Still, the locals eat here habitually, and the trad meat and fish dishes are as dependable as the 12-bar blues in your blue suede shoes.

Steamers Cafe & Bar (☎ 03-768 4193; cnr Mackay St & Albert St Mall; mains $10-26; ☺ lunch & dinner) Committed vegetarians beware: this place is equally committed to fleshy feasts (Hawaiian ham steak to rib eye and schnitzels) served from a carvery counter.

Railway Hotel (☎ 03-768 7023; 120 Mawhera Quay; meals from $5; ☺ lunch & dinner) The Railway's iconic barbecue reasserts its status every night at 6pm – the $5 meat-fest draws impoverished backpackers and hungry residents towards the fatty flames... Wash it down with a few lagers at the bar.

Royal Hotel (☎ 03-768 4022; 128 Mawhera Quay) The Royal is an affable, old-fashioned pub, the jocular Brit owners welcoming all-comers with gusto. Grab a beer or three and get chatting.

Revingtons Hotel (☎ 03-768 7055; 46 Tainui St) This boozy old-timer has recently infused its warren of drinking spaces with Irishness, which despite the tackiness, seems to have raised the quality of drinkers at the bar.

Self-caterers should make a beeline for **Fresh Choice** (☎ 03-768 7545; 174b Mawhera Quay) supermarket near the train station.

Entertainment

The Art Deco **Regent Theatre** (☎ 03-768 0920; wct@minidata.co.nz; cnr Herbert & Mackay Sts; adult/child $10/8) is a good place to catch *Lord of the Rings* reruns, occasional dance performances and weathered rockers like Dave Dobbyn.

Getting There & Around

The **Greymouth Travel Centre** (☎ 0800 767 080, 03-768 7080; www.westcoasttravel.co.nz; 164 Mackay St; ☺ 9am-5pm Mon-Fri, 10am-3pm Sat & Sun) books all forms of transport, including buses, trains and interisland ferries, and has luggage-storage facilities. This is also the bus depot.

BUS

InterCity (☎ 03-365 1113; www.intercitycoach.co.nz) has daily 1.30pm buses north to Westport ($23 to $31, two hours) and Nelson ($56 to $74, six hours), and south to Franz Josef ($39 to $52, 3½ hours) and Fox Glaciers ($42 to $56, 4¼ hours). Prices vary depending on season and availability.

Atomic Shuttles (☎ 03-322 8883; www.atomictravel.co.nz) runs daily to Queenstown ($85, 10½ hours, 7.30am), and has separate daily services to Fox Glacier ($35, 4¼ hours, 3.30pm), Picton ($55, 7½ hours, 11.30am), Hokitika ($10, one hour, 11.30am) and Christchurch ($30, five hours, 1.45pm).

Coast to Coast (☎ 0800 800 847; www.coast2coast.co.nz) buses go to Christchurch ($35, five hours, 12.45pm daily) via Arthur's Pass ($20 from Greymouth, $25 from Christchurch), also running to Hokitika.

K-Bus (☎ 0300 881 188, 03-573 4075; www.kbus.co.nz) departs from, the visitor information centre for Westport ($20, 1½ hours, 9am daily) continuing to Nelson ($55, 6¼ hours) and Picton ($75, 8¼ hours) – reduced days in winter.

CAR HIRE

The Greymouth Travel Centre has the following branches:

Avis (☎ 03-768 9902; www.avis.com)
Budget (☎ 03-768 4343; www.budget.co.nz)
Europcar (☎ 03-768 9980; www.europcar.co.nz)

Also in town are **Hertz** (☎ 03-768 0196; www.hertz.co.nz; 92 Tainui St) and **Thrifty** (☎ 03-768 6649; www.thrifty.co.nz; 8 Whall St).

TAXI

For a taxi call **Greymouth Taxis** (☎ 03-768 7078).

TRAIN

TranzAlpine (☎ 0800 872 467, 03-768 7080; www.tranzscenic.co.nz; adult/child $81/70) runs a spectacular 224km, 4½-hour journey between Christchurch and Greymouth every day (see the boxed text, p508).

AROUND GREYMOUTH

The road from Greymouth to Hokitika crawls along the wild West Coast, a withering fray of surging waves and twisted driftwood masses.

Providing a tangible context for West Coast history, **Shantytown** (☎ 03-762 6634; www.shantytown.co.nz; Rutherglen Rd, Paroa; adult/child $14.50/8.50; ☺ 8.30am-5pm), 8km south of Greymouth and 3km inland from SH6, re-creates an 1860s gold-mining town, with post office, pub and 'Rosie's House of Ill Repute.' There's gold panning ($3.50 extra for adults) and trains to ride, with a storytelling focus. Map guides come in 14 different languages.

THE TRANZALPINE

One of the world's great rail journeys, the *TranzAlpine* traverses the Southern Alps between Christchurch and Greymouth, from the Pacific Ocean to the Tasman Sea. Until relatively recently, the comfortable carriages weren't much more than ramshackle railcars, the only link West Coasters had with the east during bad weather.

The *TranzAlpine* tracks through a sequence of unbelievable landscapes. Leaving Christchurch at 8.15am, it speeds across the flat, alluvial Canterbury Plains to the Alps' foothills. Here it enters a labyrinth of gorges and hills called the Staircase, a climb made possible by three large viaducts and a plethora of tunnels.

The train emerges into the broad Waimakariri and Bealey Valleys and (on a good day) the vista is stupendous. The beech-forested river valley gives way to the snowcapped peaks of Arthur's Pass National Park. At Arthur's Pass itself (a small alpine village), the train enters the longest tunnel, the 8.5km 'Otira', burrowing under the mountains to the West Coast.

The western side is just as stunning, with the Otira, Taramakau and Grey River valleys, patches of podocarp forest, and the trout-filled Lake Brunner (Moana Kotuku), fringed with cabbage trees. The train rolls into Greymouth at 12.45pm, heading back to Christchurch an hour later, arriving at 6.05pm.

This awesome journey is diminished only when the weather's bad, but if it's raining on one coast, it'll probably be fine on the other.

Popular with locals and highway blow-ins, the **Paroa Hotel-Motel** (☎ 0800 762 6860, 03-762 6860; www.paroa.co.nz; 508 Main South Rd; s $85, d from $95), located opposite the Shantytown turn-off, has had recent architectural rhinoplasty. Its spacious, garden-fronted units are situated 300m from the stone-strewn shore; its restaurant, **Ham's** (mains $14-19; ☺ lunch & dinner), plates up beefy roasts and schnitzels.

HOKITIKA

pop 4000

Hokitika ('Hoki' for short), 40km south of Greymouth, was a booming port during the 1860s gold rush. These days it's NZ's jade-craft centre, drawing the tourists like flies, but there's more to do around here than covet mass-produced greenstone. Hoki has a rich history and a wealth of waterways nearby.

Orientation

The town forms a simple grid at the mouth of the Hokitika River. Weld and Tancred Sts are the key commercial zones.

MAPS

Free town maps are available at the **Westland visitor information centre** (☎ 03-755 6166; hkkvin@xtra.co.nz; cnr Hamilton & Tancred Sts); regional maps at **Take Note** (☎ 03-755 8167; cnr Weld & Revell Sts).

Information

A handful of big banks huddles around Weld St.

Aim West Sports (☎ 03-755 8481; 20 Weld St) Internet access.

Bookworms 102 (☎ 03-755 8142; 102 Hampden St) Buy/sell/exchange secondhand reads.

DOC Office (☎ 03-756 8282; 10 Sewell St; ☺ 8am-4.45pm Mon-Fri)

Hokitika Travel Centre (☎ 03-755 8557; 60 Tancred St; ☺ 8.30am-5pm Mon-Fri) Books scenic flights and is where most buses stop.

Police station (☎ 03-756 8310; 50 Sewell St)

Post office (Revell St)

Take Note (☎ 03-755 8167; cnr Weld & Revell Sts) Maps, mags and West Coast books.

Tony's Computer Services (☎ 03-755 8475; 102 Revell St) Internet access.

Westland Medical Centre (☎ 03-755 8180; 54a Sewell St)

Westland visitor information centre (☎ 03-755 6166; hkkvin@xtra.co.nz; cnr Hamilton & Tancred Sts; ☺ 10am-6pm Mon-Fri, to 4pm Sat & Sun)

Sights

Hoki's premier attractions are its green-hued arts-and-crafts shops; see p511.

The **West Coast Historical Museum** (☎ 03-755 6898; hokimuseum@xtra.co.nz; cnr Hamilton & Tancred Sts; adult/child $5/1; ☺ 9.30am-5pm), behind the visitor information centre, has a thought-provoking parade of old photos, Maori artefacts, river and pub-life displays (with fetching barmaid), and the southern hemisphere's biggest Meccano set (a gold dredge replica).

Pick up the free *Hokitika Heritage Walk* leaflet from the visitor information centre and wander the **Gibson Quay Heritage Waterfront** – it's not hard to imagine the wharves here choked with old-time sailing ships.

Eco World (03-755 5251; kiwi.house@xtra.co.nz; 60 Tancred St; adult/child/family $13/7/33; 9am–5pm) has seen better days, but at least you'll see a kiwi – peer into the dimly lit enclosure and see what's rummaging about. There are also snake-necked and red-eared turtles, tuatara, crayfish and some sad-looking long-finned eels.

HOKITIKA

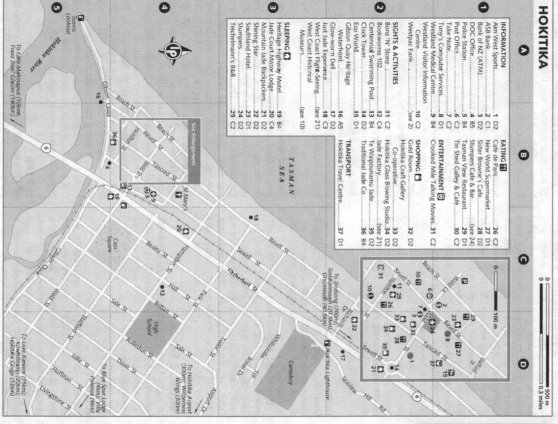

INFORMATION
Aim West Sports................1 D2
ASB Bank.............................2 C1
Bank of NZ (ATM)...............3 D2
DOC Office...........................4 B5
Police Station.......................5 B4
Post Office............................6 C2
Take Note..............................7 C2
Tony's Computer Services.....8 D1
Westland Medical Centre......9 B4
Westland Visitor Information
Centre.................................10 C2
Westpac Bank.............(see 2)

SIGHTS & ACTIVITIES
Bonz 'N' Stonz......................11 C2
Bookworms 102.....................12 C4
Centennial Swimming Pool...13 B4
Clock Tower..........................14 D2
Eco World..............................15 D1
Gibson Quay Heritage
Waterfront..........................16 A5
Glow-worm Dell....................17 D2
Just Jade Experience............(see 21)
West Coast Flight-Seeing.....(see 21)
West Coast Historical
Museum................................18 C2

SLEEPING
Heritage Highway Motel.......19 B4
Jade Court Motor Lodge.......20 C4
Mountain Jade Backpackers...21 D1
Shining Star..........................22 D2
Southland Hotel....................23 D1
Stumpers..............................24 D2
Teichelmann's B&B...............25 C2

EATING
Cafe de Paris........................26 D2
New World Supermarket.......27 D1
Sister Browne's Cafe.............28 D2
Stumpers Cafe & Bar......(see 24)
Tasman View Restaurant......29 D1
Tin Shed Galley & Café........30 C2

ENTERTAINMENT
Crooked Mile Talking Movies..31 C2

SHOPPING
Gold Room.............................32 D2
Hokitika Craft Gallery
Co-operative.........................33 D2
Hokitika Glass Blowing Studio..34 D2
Jade Factory...................(see 21)
Te Waipounamu Jade..........35 D2
Traditional Jade Co..............36 B4

TRANSPORT
Hokitika Travel Centre..........37 D1

See Enlargement

TASMAN
SEA

To Mahinapua (10km);
Franz Josef Glacier (140km)

Scenic
Lookout

Hokitika River

Beach St
Gibson Quay
Revell St
Tancred St
St Mary's
Sewell St
Cass
Square
Bealey St
Hamilton St
Fitzherbert St
Hall St
Park St
Sale St
Britain St
High
School
Rolleston St
Davie St
Stafford St
Jollie St
Hoffman St
Livingstone St

To Lake Kaniere (15km);
Kowhitirangi (20km);
Hokitika Gorge (33km)

To Blue Spur Lodge
(300m); Wilderness
Wings (300m)

To Hokitika Airport
(300m)

Cemetery

To Birdsong (700m);
Goldsborough (20.5km);
Greymouth (40.5km)

Hokitika Lighthouse
Seaview

Beach St
Revell St
Weld St
Tancred St
Sewell St

0   100 m
0   500 m
0   0.3 miles

A short stroll off the highway just north of town leads to a **glow-worm dell** (admission free; 24hr). Visit well after dark for the glow-show crescendo.

Activities

Dabble in a little **jade carving** at the utterly recommended **Bonz 'N' Stonz** (03-755 6504; www.bonz-n-stonz.co.nz; 16 Hamilton St; full-day workshop $80-150; Mon-Sat) where you design, carve and polish your own jade, bone or paua masterpiece. Prices vary with materials and design complexity. **Just Jade Experience** (03-755 7612; www.jadecountry.co.nz; 197 Revell St; full-day workshop $20-180; daily, closed Aug) is a similar workshop, but the carving is done by Gordon (the boss).

Due West Canoe Safaris (0800 383 9378, 03-755 6717; www.duewest.co.nz; half-day trip adult/child $85/40) takes you paddling on the gorgeous Lake Mahinapua, 10km south of Hokitika; no experience required. For even more leisurely water sports, splash around in the heated **Centennial Swimming Pool** (03-755 8119; 53 Weld St; adult/child $3.50/1.30; 9am-5pm Sep-May). Aquaerobics classes are $3.

Tours

Scenic Waterways (03-755 7239; www.paddleboatcruises.com; adult/child $25/15) runs 1½-hour paddleboat tours on Mahinapua Creek, 10km south of Hoki.

West Coast Flight-Seeing (0800 359 937; www.westcoastflightseeing.co.nz; 41 Weld St; flights from $280) wings you into the blue yonder with four-hour flights over Hokitika, Aoraki (Mt Cook) and the glaciers. **Wilderness Wings** (0800 755 8118; www.wildernesswings.co.nz; Hokitika Airport) offers similar flights and prices.

Festivals & Events

In mid-March Hokitika hosts the **Wildfoods Festival**, a bush cook-up attracting 20,000 salivating gourmands. Check out www.wildfoods.co.nz for details.

Sleeping

BUDGET

Birdsong (03-755 9179; www.birdsong.co.nz; SH6; dm/s/tw/d $25/40/60/60;) This relatively new Hoki hostel is just north of town. It feels like the beach house you always wished you owned, but never had the time/money/excuse – lazy living areas, sunset views, trashy novels, a pair of outdoor baths and a friendly dog.

Blue Spur Lodge (03-755445; bluespur@paradise.net.nz; dm/s $21/40, d $54-70) Follow the signs up Hampden St to this 37-hectare timber retreat, off Blue Spur Tourist Dr. The eight-bed dorm is warm, there's a wheelchair-accessible unit, wood fires in the main rooms and gumboots to borrow if you feel like stomping around in the bush.

Mountain Jade Backpackers (0800 838 301, 03-755 8007; mtjade@minidata.co.nz; 41 Weld St; dm/d $18/45) In the middle of Hoki, above the Jade Factory, this place can feel like Backpacker Factory in summer. Go for a double overlooking Sewell St, far from the madding crowds.

Shining Star (0800744646, 03-7558921; www.accommodationwestcoast.co.nz; 11 Richards Dr; unpowered/powered sites per 2 people $20/24, d $50-139) Strapping Tasman Sea breezes and surf sounds wash over Shining Star's jaunty log cabins and camp sites. Let your mind roam with the alpacas in the adjacent pastureland.

Stumpers (0800 788 673, 03-755 6154; www.stumpers.co.nz; 2 Weld St; dm/s/f $22/35/70, d $45-55;) Stumpers has clean, neat, reasonably priced rooms above its café-bar. Doubles have TVs; dorms have a maximum of three beds; most rooms have shared facilities (this was pub accommodation before Kerouac invented backpackers).

MIDRANGE

Southland Hotel (03-755 8344; www.southlandhotel.com; 111 Revell St; d $95-130) Southland's interior decorator sweated up a wood-panelling storm – planned renovations might tame the timber tempest. The best rooms have sea views; the rest are just as comfortable. Downstairs is the Tasman View Restaurant.

Jade Court Motor Lodge (0800 755 885, 03-755 8855; www.jadecourt.co.nz; 85 Fitzherbert St; d $85-140) This huge roadside place conducts itself with quiet professionalism, lacking the usual motel schmaltz. All units have full kitchens; winter rates are a steal.

Heritage Highway Motel (0800 465 484, 03-755 8098; www.heritagemotel.co.nz; 12 Fitzherbert St; d $85-130) An incurable case of the mock-Tudors is the only thing that might deter you from Hoki's most central motel. Otherwise, close the door and lose yourself in the faceless, nameless road movie that is your life.

TOP END

Villa Polenza (0800 241 801, 03-755 7801; www.villapolenza.co.nz; 143 Brickfield Rd; r from $400) This bou-

...tique, hilltop Italianate villa claims it's the West Coast's only five-star accommodation (minimum guest age is 13 years). Simmering sunsets pour through French doors into plush suites with huge beds and goose-down quilts. Slip into the outdoor baths and wonder what the poor plains people are doing below...

Teichelmann's B&B (☎ 0800 743 742, 03-755 8232; www.teichelmanns.co.nz; 20 Hamilton St; d $175-195) Once home to surgeon, mountaineer and beard-grower Ebenezer Teichelmann, now a luxurious B&B with amicable hosts. One unit has a spa, one is wheelchair accessible, all have en suites. Ebenezer wouldn't begrudge you a complimentary port on a wintry night.

Eating & Drinking

Tin Shed Gallery & Café (☎ 03-755 8444; 89 Revell St; lunch $8-14, dinner $21-24; ☺ breakfast, lunch & dinner) The Tin Shed is a bohemian bastion, expertly curating substantial vegetarian, fish and meat dishes in a funky, hippy gallery. Courtyard beach views come free with your morning coffee.

Stumpers Cafe & Bar (☎ 03-755 6154; 2 Weld St; mains $12-28; ☺ breakfast, lunch & dinner) For a pub in café clothing, Stumpers' menu achieves lofty heights – simply prepared, generous, internationally styled meals do more than the clientele demands. This corner room is also a great spot for a cold beer and some people-watching.

Sister Browne's Cafe (☎ 03-755 6993; 23 Weld St; meals $3-12; ☺ breakfast & lunch Mon-Sat) Sister Browne is a beloved pooch, but she adopts a paws-off management style and is rarely seen. Human staff members serve pasties, cakes, falafels, pies and quiches, made fresh on-site every day.

Cafe de Paris (☎ 03-755 8933; 19 Tancred St; mains $9-28; ☺ breakfast, lunch & dinner) This formal café aims Eiffel high and hits about three-quarters of the way up. Roasts, steaks, venison and whitebait are given the full Gallic treatment (usually involving butter). Outdoor tables woo cake-munching sun-seekers.

Tasman View Restaurant (☎ 03-755 8344; 111 Revell St; mains $20-21; ☺ dinner) The Southland Hotel's restaurant (accessed via Beach St) has the dry aesthetic of a late-'80s conference centre. Munificent ocean views and carefully prepared venison, pork and mandatory whitebait dishes to the rescue!

Self-caterers are able to satisfy their cravings at **New World** (☎) supermarket.

Entertainment

Crooked Mile Talking Movies (☎ 03-755 5309; www.crookedmile.co.nz; 36 Revell St; tickets adult/child $11/6; ☺ Wed-Sun) Assess art-house movies from leather couches in an old bank building on Revell St, once a far more bent thoroughfare than it is today.

Shopping

Most of Hoki's crafty shops are on Tancred St, where things of stone and wood (and glass, gold, bone and shell) are lovingly morphed into shape. Staff love to talk *pounamu*, and in some studios you can watch carvers carving it up.

Traditional Jade Co (☎ 03-755 5233; 2 Tancred St) This relatively small, family-run studio manages to distil the jade hype into something meaningful. Watch artists carving classic Maori greenstone designs.

Te Waipounamu Jade (☎ 03-755 8304; 19 Sewell St) Te Waipounamu is scrupulously authentic, selling only NZ *pounamu* meticulously crafted into beautiful, sensual designs.

Hokitika Craft Gallery Co-operative (☎ 03-755 8802; 25 Tancred St) Staffed by the artists themselves, this gallery displays and sells the realistically priced work of around 20 jade-carving, wood-turning, ever-weaving locals.

Jade Factory (☎ 03-755 8007; 41 Weld St) Resembling a megalithic jade menhir, this big-name chain's production line churns out everything from *koru* (spirals) to jade-faced golf putters and chunky sculptures.

Gold Room (☎ 03-755 8362; 37 Tancred St) This sparking room does a healthy jade trade but is best known for its nuggety auric

JADED TRADERS

Hokitika's streets are paved with *pounamu*, but before you adorn yourself, it's worth doing a little vendor research. Some shops are owned by overseas interests, or worse, sell jade that's imported from China or Europe. Buying from somewhere that lines the local coffers and trades in authentic NZ greenstone will help you (and us) sleep better at night.

jewellery, measured out in pennyweights and troy ounces.

Hokitika Glass Blowing Studio (03-755 7775; 28 Tancred St) From laughably cheesy to absolutely stunning, this glass studio opens itself up to subjective judgment. Things get toasty in here when the glass-blowers start puffing out their cheeks.

Getting There & Around

AIR

Hokitika Airport is on Airport Dr (off Tudor St), 1.5km east of the centre of town. **Air New Zealand** (0800 737 000, 09-357 3000; www .airnz.co.nz) has regular flights to/from Christchurch, with onward connections.

BUS

InterCity (03-365 1113; www.intercitycoach.co.nz) buses depart from the **Hokitika Travel Centre** (03-755 8557; 60 Tancred St) daily for Greymouth ($22, one hour, 12.30pm), Nelson ($75, seven hours, 12.30pm) and Fox Glacier ($45, 3½ hours, 2.50pm). **Atomic Shuttles** (03-322 8883; www.atomictravel.co.nz) departs the visitor information centre (bookings essential) to Fox Glacier ($30, 3½ hours, 8am and 4pm) and Greymouth ($10, one hour, 10.15am, 12.30pm and 5pm), Queenstown ($70, 10 hours, 8am) and Christchurch ($30, 6½ hours, 12.30pm). **Coast to Coast** (0800 800 847; www.coast2coast.co.nz) also runs daily to Christchurch ($29, 5½ hours, 12.30pm) from the Travel Centre.

CAR HIRE

These companies have branches at Hokitika Airport:
Avis (03-768 0902; www.avis.com)
Budget (03-768 4343; www.budget.co.nz)
Hertz (03-768 0196; www.hertz.co.nz)

TAXI

For a taxi call **Hokitika Taxis** (03-755 5075).

AROUND HOKITIKA

A 33km farmland drive or cycle gets you to **Hokitika Gorge**, a ravishing little ravine on the Hokitika River with improbably turquoise waters. Glacial flour (suspended rock particles) imbues the milky hues. Judder your knee joints across the swing bridge and launch into a couple of short forest walks. To get here, head up Stafford St past the Hoki dairy factory and follow the signs.

Kowhitirangi, en route to the gorge, was the scene of a massive 12-day manhunt involving the NZ army in 1941. Unhinged farmer Stanley Graham shot dead four Hokitika policemen, disappeared into the bush then returned to murder three others, eventually being killed himself. A grim roadside monument lines up the farmstead site through a stone gun shaft. The 1982 film *Bad Blood* re-enacts the awful incident.

A gravel forest road (lousy for big vehicles) circumnavigates **Lake Kaniere**, passing **Dorothy Falls**, **Kahikatea Forest** and **Canoe Cove**. The visitor or information centre and DOC have info on other local walks, including the **Lake Kaniere Walkway** (four hours one way, 13km), along the lake's western shore, and the **Mahinapua Walkway** (2½ hours one way, 5.5km), through the reserve on Lake Mahinapua's northeast side to a wildlife-engorged swamp.

There are **DOC camping grounds** (adult/child $6/3) at **Goldsborough**, 17km from Hoki on the 1876 'gold trail'; **Hans Bay**, 19km from Hoki on Lake Kaniere's eastern shore and 10km south of Hoki at **Lake Mahinapua**.

HOKITIKA TO WESTLAND TAI POUTINI NATIONAL PARK

From Hokitika it's 140km south to Franz Josef Glacier. Most travellers chew through the miles without stopping, but there are some interesting historic hot spots and walking, kayaking and bird-watching along the way. **InterCity** (03-365 1113; www.intercity coach.co.nz) and **Atomic Shuttles** (03-322 8883; www.atomictravel.co.nz) buses to the glaciers will stop anywhere along the highway.

Ross

Ross is a town of glories lost, 30km south of Hokitika, where the unearthing of NZ's largest gold nugget, the 2.772kg 'Honourable Roddy', caused a kerfuffle in 1907. The **Ross visitor information centre** (03-755 4077; www.ross .org.nz; 4 Aylmer St; 9am–5pm Dec-Feb, 9am-3pm Mar-Nov) features a scale model of the town in its golden years.

Opposite is the **Miner's Cottage Museum** (admission free; 9am–5pm), in an 1885 cottage containing two old Pianolas and a replica Roddy. The re-created **Ross Gaol** next door features a lame attempt at a 'prisoner' in a poor hygienic state.

The **Water Race Walk** (one hour return, 2.6km), starts near the museum, passing old gold-diggings, caves, tunnels and a cemetery. Behind the visitor information centre, the former **Birchfields Mine** is now a 90m-deep lake with imminent trout. Attempt to break the poverty cycle with some **gold panning** at the visitor information centre ($6.50), or hire a pan ($5) and head for Jones Creek.

The **Empire Hotel** (☎ 03-755 4005; empire_gold@paradise.net.nz; 19 Aylmer St; dm/s $18/35, d $55-65) has a row of threadbare four-bed backpacker dorms, while the grittily authentic pub rooms upstairs have seen a miner or two. Lunches and dinners (mains $15 to $25) revolve around good-sized nuggets of meat, fish and chicken.

Oozing rustic charm without overdoing the 'This is 1907' vibe, the **Roddy Nugget Cafe & Bar** (☎ 03-755 4245; 5 Moorhouse St; meals $4-12; ☒ breakfast & lunch) is a country café serving homemade meals. The bar in the back supplies liquid nutrients.

Ross to Okarito

South of Ross the rainforest closes in, sometimes looking like it would be easier to walk over the top of it than to find a way through.

About 16km south of Ross, the **Old Church** (☎ 03-755 4000; stay@theoldchurch.co.nz; SH6; unpowered sites per 2 people & dm $20, d $50-66) stands desolately on the Kakapotahi River like something out of *The Shining*. Bikes, kayaks, pool tables, fishing, a funky record collection and piety are on offer. The only problem is it's entirely isolated (as Jack Nicholson prefers), so BYO supplies.

PUKEKURA

Just north of Lake Ianthe is this tiny place, population two.

The tour buses purge into the **Bushmans Centre** (☎ 03-755 4144; www.pukekura.co.nz; SH6; admission free; ☒ 9am-5pm), a precariously rustic café-shop with an ingrained possum hatred. Inside is a souvenir shop and the **Bushmans Museum** (adult/family $4/10), laying on the blokey bush humour thick and fast with a 20-minute video on local industry, antipossum displays (including sad caged specimens) and some forlorn giant eels. Not really one for the kids.

Across the road is Puke Pub and integral **Wild Foods Restaurant** (☎ 03-755 4008; mains $7.50-11; ☒ lunch & dinner), specialising in 'road kill' dishes like 'wheel-tread possum' and 'head-light delight'. If you're nodding off at the wheel, **Pukekura Lodge** (☎ 03-755 4008; SH6; unpowered/powered sites per 2 people $20, s/d $20/45) has four rustic but decent rooms opposite the Bushmans Centre. Alternatively, there's a **DOC camping ground** (adult/child $6/3) beside Lake Ianthe, 6km south of Pukekura.

HARI HARI

About 22km south of Lake Ianthe, Hari Hari made headlines in 1931 when swashbuckling Australian aviator Guy Menzies completed the first solo trans-Tasman flight from Sydney. Menzies crash-landed his *Southern Cross Junior* in the La Fontaine swamp, the plane flipping over. When he undid his safety straps (swashbuckles?), he fell headfirst into the mud. Menzies flight took 11¾ hours, 2½ hours faster than fellow Australian Charles Kingsford Smith in 1928.

The **Hari Hari Coastal Walk** (2¾ hours return; aka Doughboy Walk or Coastal Pack Track) is a well-trodden low-tide loop passing the Poerua and Wanganui Rivers. The walk starts 20km from SH6, the last 8km unsealed – follow Wanganui Flats Rd then La Fontaine Dr. There's tidal info at the trailhead, or ask at the Ross visitor information centre.

Favoured by puffed-out cyclists, the '70s units at **Tomasi Motels** (☎/fax 03-753 3116; SH6; tw/d $40/80) are undergoing serious renovations. Ask about local fishing, or borrow some bikes and hoon around town.

The **Hari Hari Motor Inn** (☎ 0800 833 026, 03-753 3026; hhhi@xtra.co.nz; SH6; unpowered/powered sites per 2 people $16/19, dm/d $18/95) has serviceable doubles but doesn't have a camp-site kitchen, and the **bistro** (mains $10-26; ☒ lunch & dinner) is Hari Hari's only evening eatery (it's got you cornered). Wash down pizzas, steaks and roast dinners with a few forgiving lagers.

WHATAROA & THE KOTUKU SANCTUARY

Near Whataroa, 35km south of Hari Hari, is NZ's only nesting site for the *kotuku* (white heron), roosting here between November and February. The herons then fly off individually to muse over the perils of partnership all winter.

White Heron Sanctuary Tours (☎ 0800 523 456, 03-753 4120; SH6, Whataroa; www.whiteherontours.co.nz; adult/child $95/45, 4 tours daily Oct-Mar) has the only

DOC concession to see the herons, with 2½-hour 'jetboat ecotours' (the jetboat doesn't bug the birds). Next to the tours office is **Sanctuary Tours Motel** (d cabins $50, d $85-105), offering a choice between proletarian white-washed cabins with shared facilities ($8 extra for linen), or enthusiastically painted motel units in two different buildings.

Okarito

Another 15km south of Whataroa is The Forks and the turn-off to peaceful Okarito, 13km further on the coast. Keri Hulme's bestseller, *The Bone People*, is set in this unpeopled region (she's one of 30 permanent residents in the wee town). Okarito is sans commerce, so BYO food and supplies.

From the southern end of The Strand, there are a couple **coastal walks**: to **Three Mile Lagoon** (three hours return, 6km; low tide only) and to **Okarito Trig** (1½ hours return, 1.5km), from which there are sensational Southern Alps and Okarito Lagoon views.

Okarito Nature Tours (☎ 0800 524 666, 03-753 4014; www.okarito.co.nz; kayak rental per half/full day $45/55) hires out kayaks for thoroughly recommended paddles into the placid channels of **Okarito Lagoon**, a fishy smorgasbord for waterbirds. The lagoon is NZ's largest unmodified wetland, an intricate ecosystem of shallow water and tidal flats surrounded by rainforest. Guided tours are available (from $65); overnight camping trips ($80) take you to deserted North Beach or Lake Windemere.

Okarito Campground (off Russell St; adult/child $7.50/free) is a breezy patch of community-managed greenery near the sea, complete with barbecues, toilets, hot showers ($1) and a public telephone. Drop your dollars in the honesty box.

Falling asleep in class fully sanctioned: inside an 1892 school building owned by DOC, the community-run **Okarito YHA Hostel** (☎ 03-753 4151; thestrandhostel@yahoo.com; The Strand; dm $18) became a hostel in 1960. Bunk down in the classroom, and bring dollar coins for hot showers and buckets of insect repellent.

Popular with tour groups (book your bed ahead), the **Royal Okarito** (☎ 03-753 4080; www .okaritohostel.com; The Strand; dm $20, d $50-70; ▣) has semirustic hostel accommodation in two houses. The weathered, self-contained 'Hutel' ($70) is worth every cent. Crafty

touches like an enormous timber slab table top complete the royal treatment.

WESTLAND TAI POUTINI NATIONAL PARK

Literally the biggest highlights of the Westland Tai Poutini National Park are the Franz Josef and Fox Glaciers. Nowhere else at this latitude do glaciers come so close to the coast. These two frozen juggernauts are stereotypical cascades of ice, grinding unceasingly down valleys towards the sea.

The glaciers' staggering development is largely due to the West Coast's endless rain. Snow falling in the glaciers' broad accumulation zones fuses into clear ice at 20m depth, then surges down valleys. The glaciers are particularly steep, so the ice travels a long way before it finally melts.

The rate of descent is mind-blowing; wreckage of a plane that crashed into Franz Josef in 1943, 3.5km from the terminal face, made it down to the bottom 6½ years later – a speed of 1.5m per day. Big Franz usually advances about 1m per day, but sometimes ramps it up to 5m per day, over 10 times faster than the Swiss Alps' glaciers.

There's a whiff of 'glacier snobbery' in the air, some saying Franz Josef is the superior ice experience. While Franz may be the more visually impressive beast, the walk to Fox is shorter, more interesting and gets you closer to the ice (80m versus 200m).

Of course, the national park contains more than just glaciers. The park's lower reaches harbour deserted Tasman Sea beaches, rising up through colour-splashed podocarp forests to NZ's highest peaks. There are few world conservation areas where such diverse ecosystems bump up next to each other in interdependent ecological sequence. Seals jumble in the surf; deer sneak through the forests. The resident endangered bird species include *kowhiowhio* (blue duck), kaka, *kakariki* (a parrot) and *rowi* (Okarito brown kiwi), as well as kea, the South Island's native parrot. Kea are inquisitive and endearing, but feeding them threatens their health.

Heavy tourist traffic swamps the twin towns of Franz Josef and Fox Glacier, 23km apart, picture-postcard tourist villages providing accommodation and facilities at higher-than-average prices. Franz is the more action-packed of the two, but Fox has a more meadowy alpine charm.

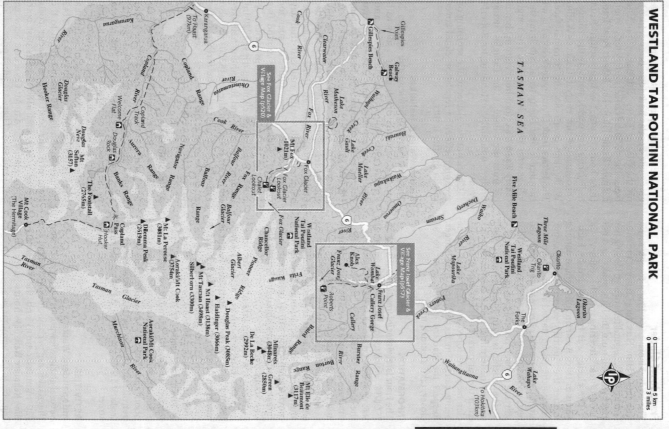

WESTLAND TAI POUTINI NATIONAL PARK

Franz Josef Glacier

The early Maori knew Franz Josef as Ka Roimata o Hine Hukatere (Tears of the Avalanche Girl). Legend tells of a girl losing her lover who fell from the local peaks, and her flood of tears freezing into the glacier.

The glacier was first explored by Europeans in 1865, Austrian Julius Haast naming it after the Austrian emperor. Easy come, easy go: the glacier started advancing in 1985 after a long period of retreat (see the boxed text, p519), progressing nearly 2km until it starting to back-pedal again in 1996.

The glacier is 5km from Franz Joseph village, the terminal face a 40-minute walk from the car park. Both Fox and Franz glacier faces are roped off to prevent people being caught in icefalls and river surges. Respect the glaciers – if you want to get closer, take a guided tour.

INFORMATION

The **Franz Josef visitor information centre** (☎ 03-752 0796; www.glaciercountry.co.nz, www.doc.govt.nz; SH6; ⊙ 8.30am–6pm Dec–Feb, to 4.30pm Mar–Nov), also the regional DOC office, has an excellent interpretive display, weather information and tramping-condition updates.

Alpine Adventure Centre (☎ 0800 800 793, 03-752 0793; SH6) is a major activities booking agent and screens the 20-minute *Flowing West* movie (adult/child $10/5) on a giant screen (great visuals, shame about the *Beverly Hills Cop* soundtrack).

When it's raining (about half the time), join the Internet queues at **Ferg's Kayaks** (☎ 03-752 0230; 20 Cron St), **Scott Base Tourist Information Centre** (☎ 03-752 0288; SH6), and at most hostels. Scott Base also has bike hire (per half/full day $10/20).

The **medical centre** (☎ 03-752 0700; SH6) is attended by a nurse Monday to Friday, and a doctor during summer on Monday afternoon and Thursday morning. The Mobil petrol station acts as the **postal agency** (cnr Condon St & SH6); there's an ATM on the main street.

ACTIVITIES

Independent Walks

Several glacier viewpoints are accessed from the glacier car park, including **Sentinel Rock** (20 minutes return) and the **Ka Roimata o Hine Hukatere Walk** (1½ hours return), leading you to the terminal face.

Other walks require a little more footslogging. The **Douglas Walk** (one hour return), off the Glacier Access Rd, passes moraine from the 1750 advance and Peter's Pool, a small 'kettle lake'. The **Roberts Point Track** (nine hours return, five hours return from the glacier car park), starts at the village, encompasses the rugged Callery–Waiho Walk, then overlooks the terminal face. The **Terrace Track** (30 minutes return) is an easy amble over bushy terraces behind the village with Waiho River views. The rough **Callery–Waiho Walk** (four hours return) heads off from the village to the Douglas Swing Bridge, optionally extending to Roberts Point.

Check out the glacier in the morning or evening, before the regulation cloud cover sets in or after it lifts.

Guided Walks & Helihikes

The best way to befriend the glaciers is to walk on them. Small group walks with experienced guides (boots, jackets and equipment supplied) are offered by two Franz Josef companies: the **Guiding Company** (☎ 0800 800 102, 03-752 0047; www.nzguides.com), based at the Alpine Adventure Centre, and the reader-recommended **Franz Josef Glacier Guides** (☎ 0800 484 337, 03-752 0763; www.franzjosef glacier.com). Both outfits run half-/full-day walks for $85/135 per adult (cheaper for children). Full-day trips have around five hours on the ice, half-day trips about two hours. Full-day ice-climbing trips ($220 including training) and three-hour helihikes with two hours on the ice ($320) are also available. Helihikes take you further up the glacier to explore blue-ice caves, séracs and pristine ice formations.

Aerial Sightseeing

As Julie Andrews might have observed, the hills are alive with the sound of buzzing helicopters and planes, winging past the glaciers and Aoraki (Mt Cook). Flying in close to the glacier face in a helicopter is a unique experience, while many flights include a snow landing. A 10-minute flight without a snow landing costs between $100 and $145 per person, while a 20-minute flight to the head of Franz Josef or Fox Glacier costs between $160 and $180. Flights past both of the glaciers and to Mt Cook cost between $310 and $345. These are adult prices; kids

FRANZ JOSEF GLACIER & VILLAGE

INFORMATION
Alpine Adventure Centre...............1 D1
Bank of ANZ (ATM)........................2 D2
Franz Josef Visitor Information
 Centre.......................................3 D2
Medical Centre..............................4 D2
Mobil Petrol Station.......................5 D2
Postal Agency............................(see 5)
Scott Base Tourist Information
 Centre.......................................6 D1

SIGHTS & ACTIVITIES
Air Safaris...................................7 D1
Ferg's Kayaks...............................8 D1
Fox & Franz Josef Heliservices....(see 8)
Franz Josef Glacier Guides.........(see 6)
Glacier Southern Lakes
 Helicopters...........................(see 7)
Guiding Company......................(see 1)
Helicopter Line.........................(see 1)
Mount Cook Ski Planes..............(see 2)
Mountain Helicopters................(see 2)

SLEEPING
Alpine Glacier Motor Lodge........10 D1
Chateau Franz............................11 D1
Franz Josef Glacier YHA..............12 D1
Glow Worm Cottages...................13 D1
Holly Homestead........................14 B1
Mountain View top 10.................15 B1
Punga Grove...............................16 D1
Rainforest Retreat & Forest
 Park..17 D1

EATING
Alice May...................................18 D1
Beeches.....................................19 D1
Blue Ice Café-Restaurant............20 D1
Guzzi Al Fresco..........................21 D1
Landing Cafe.............................22 D1

TRANSPORT
InterCity Bus Stop......................23 D1

---

under 15 pay between 50% and 70% of the adult price (it pays to shop around).

The recommended operators listed following are all situated on SH6 in Franz Josef Village:

Air Safaris (☎ 03-752 0716; www.airsafaris.co.nz)

Fox & Franz Josef Heliservices (☎ 03-752 0793; www.scenic-flights.co.nz)

Glacier Southern Lakes Helicopters (☎ 0800 800 732, 03-752 0755; www.glacierhelicopters.co.nz)

Helicopter Line (☎ 0800 807 767, 03-752 0767; www.helicopter.co.nz)

Mount Cook Ski Planes (☎ 0800 368 000, 03-752 0714; www.mtcookskiplanes.com)

Mountain Helicopters (☎ 0800 369 432, 03-752 0046; www.mountainhelicopters.co.nz)

Other Activities

For lower-altitude endeavours, take a laid-back guided kayak trip on Lake Mapourika (7km north of Franz) with **Ferg's Kayaks** (☎ 0800 423 262, 03-752 0230; www.glacierkayaks.co.nz; 20 Cron St; 3hr tours $65). Trips include ecological insights, mountain views and a serene channel detour. You can also hire kayaks ($50 for three hours).

Hire bikes from the **Scott Base Tourist Information Centre** (☎ 03-7520288; SH6) and **Glow Worm Cottages** (☎ 0800 151 027, 03-752 CI7Z; 27 Cron St).

South Westland Horse Treks (☎ 0800 187 357, 03-752 0223; www.horsetreknz.com; Waiho Flats Rd; treks $45-150), 5km south of town, runs one-hour to full-day equine excursions across farm-land and remote beaches.

SLEEPING
Budget

Glow Worm Cottages (☎ 0800 151 027, 03-752 0172; www.glowwormcottages.co.nz; 27 Cron St; dm from $22, s from $50, d $50-90; 🖥) The rooms and facilities here are pretty impressive, and the spa, video library, pool table, zany artefacts and free nightly vegetable soup will distract you when the rain descends. If it's dry, hire a bike ($10/20 per half/full day).

Franz Josef Glacier YHA (☎ 03-752 0754; yha.franz josef@yha.co.nz; 2-4 Cron St; dm $24-27, s $42, d $64-92; 🖥) A high-standard, internally gaudy place with over 100 beds (linen provided) in 36 heated rooms. There are three family rooms, a Kiwi sauna (non-nude) and the forest at the back door. The needs of travellers with disabilities are catered for throughout.

Chateau Franz (☎ 0800 728 372, 03-752 0738; www .chateaufranz.co.nz; 8 Cron St; dm $20-24, d $48-100; 🖥) The name has a ring of potential disappointment about it, but this place is surprisingly good. Heaps of different room options and free stuff (videos, popcorn, evening soup, hot spa and big-screen TV) make it easy to dispel rainy days (Franz has a submarine-like 7m annual rainfall).

Mountain View Top 10 Holiday Park (☎ 0800 467 897, 03-752 0735; www.mountainview.co.nz; SH6; unpowered/powered sites per 2 people $32, d $58-145; 🖥) Mountain View's one hectare is about to become five – even more room for the campervan contingent to rub shoulders (or rather, avoid rubbing shoulders). Amenities are consistently good, catering for singles through to families.

Midrange

Rainforest Retreat & Forest Park (☎ 0800 873 346, 03-752 0220; www.rainforestretreat.co.nz; 46 Cron St; unpowered/powered sites per 2 people $20/24, dm $20-25, d $65-190; 🖥) Nordic architecture in the rainforest? That's so crazy it just might work! Camp sites (gravel) and dorms share first-rate facilities (including sauna and spa), or there are tidy en suite cottages and elevated 'tree houses'.

Alpine Glacier Motor Lodge (☎ 0800 757 111, 03-752 0226; www.alpineglaciermotel.com; 14 Cron St; d $130-160) Standard motel offerings for the dorm-weary in a U-shaped configuration. Two units have spas; king-size units have cooking facilities. Warning: little bolted-on decks cause deck-envy.

Top End

Holly Homestead (☎ 03-752 0299; www.hollyhome stead.co.nz; SH6; s $170-230, d $200-280) This handsome, two-storey, 1920s B&B is draped in wisteria. The four tastefully furnished rooms (all with en suite, one with disabled access) will cradle you through to breakfast. Kids under 12 will have to sleep in the car.

Punga Grove (☎ 0800 437 269, 03-752 0001; www .pungagrove.co.nz; 40 Cron St; d $170-235) Priding itself on top-notch service, Punga is a quality motel on the rainforest verge. Split-level self-contained family units mix it up with spacious studios, or splurge on a luxury rainforest studio with leather couches and underfloor heating.

Glenfern Villas (☎ 0800 453 633, 03-752 0054; www.glenfern.co.nz; SH6; d $180-230) Easing upmarket without conceit, these self-contained architect-designed villas, 3km north of town, feature raked timber ceilings, satin-stainless light fittings and splashes of deep red paint. Check in, relax and raise a glass to the mountains.

EATING & DRINKING

Landing Cafe (☎ 03-752 0229; SH6; mains $10-28; 🕐 breakfast, lunch & dinner) More bar than café, this casual, sporty beer room is like a cricketing all-rounder – good at a bit of everything. Regularly changing soups, pastas and risottos prime you for the daily happy hour. Outdoor tables have individual gas heaters to warm nocturnal 18-to-35s.

Blue Ice Cafe-Restaurant (☎ 03-752 0707; SH6; mains $16-35; 🕐 dinner daily, lunch Dec-Feb) Blue Ice is a stylish eatery dressed up with white linen tablecloths, but it's still down-to-earth enough to serve pizza and warming, post-glacial comfort food. The upstairs bar has a pool table, regular DJs and keeps pouring 'til 3am.

Guzzi Al Fresco (☎ 03-752 0085; SH6; meals $8-12; 🕐 breakfast, lunch & dinner) Guzzi is a dose of budget, takeaway normality in the otherwise overheated Franz financial sector. Souvlakis, salads, falafels – all are good and good-to-go; double-shot coffees are standard.

Alice May (☎ 03-752 0740; cnr Cowan & Cron Sts; mains $17-29; 🕐 dinner) A faithful enough rendering of a Euro ski lodge (minus the snow bunnies and turtle-necked Norsemen), the Alice May has plenty of Monteith's on tap and serves middle-order food to a middle-aged crowd (expect pizzas, ribs, and fish and chips).

Beeches (☎ 03-752 0721; 5H6; mains $16-31; 🕐 breakfast, lunch & dinner) Beeches engages in the art of preparing NZ meats (beef, lamb, pork, venison and salmon), complemented by a 100% NZ wine list. The ambience dives into 'deep jade', but comes up a bit shallow.

GETTING THERE & AROUND

InterCity (☎ 03-365 1113; www.intercitycoach.co.nz) has daily buses south to Fox Glacier ($13, 40 minutes, 8am and 5.05pm) and Queenstown ($99, eight hours, 8am); and north to Nelson ($105, 10 hours, 9.15am). Book at the YHA or Scott Base Tourist Information Centre; buses depart across the road from the Mobil petrol station.

Atomic Shuttles (☎ 03-322 8883; www.atomictravel.co.nz) has daily services south to Queenstown ($50, 7½ hours, 10.15am) via Fox Glacier ($10, 30 minutes), and north to Greymouth ($30, 2½ hours, 3pm), departing from the Alpine Adventure Centre.

Glacier Valley Eco Tours (☎ 03-752 0699; www.glaciervalley.co.nz) runs shuttles to the glacier car park (return trip $10) and guided walks up the river valley to the terminal face ($50).

Fox Glacier

Not a bashful man, Sir William Fox, NZ's then prime minister, named this glacier when he visited in 1872. Even if you've already been to Franz Josef Glacier, 25km up the road, it's worth checking out Fox (you don't see a glacier every day of the week, do you?). At the very least, take the walk around beautiful Lake Matheson. Franz Josef's activities and attributes apply here too: glacier walks, flights, thermally wrapped humans, expensive accommodation etc.

INFORMATION

The **DOC South Westland Area Office** (☎ 03-751 0807; 5H6; 🕐 9am-noon & 1-4.30pm Mon-Fri) is no longer a general visitor information centre, but has the usual DOC information and weather/track updates.

GLACIER NOMENCLATURE

Like anything truly intimidating, a glacier always advances and never retreats. Sometimes ice melts at the bottom faster than it forms at the top – the glacier's terminal face moves back up the mountain, appearing to retreat, but internally it's still downwardly mobile, comin' atcha like Cleopatra.

During the last ice age (15,000 to 20,000 years ago) the Franz Josef and Fox Glaciers reached the sea; in the ensuing thaw they may have crawled back further than their current positions. In the 14th century a mini ice age descended and for centuries the glaciers advanced, reaching their greatest extent around 1750. The terminal moraines from this time are visible, but in the 250-odd years since, the glaciers have steadily ebbed, terminal faces now several kilometres further uphill.

If you want to impress/bore new friends with glaciology while you're ogling Fox and Franz, drop these into the conversation:

ablation zone – where the glacier melts
accumulation zone – where the snow collects
bergschrund – a large *crevasse* in the ice near the glacier's starting point
blue ice – as the accumulation zone (*névé*) snow is compressed by subsequent snowfalls, it becomes *firn* and then *blue ice*
crevasse – a crack in the glacial ice formed as it crosses obstacles while descending
dead ice – isolated chunks of ice left behind when a glacier retreats
firn – partly compressed snow en route to becoming *blue ice*
glacial flour – finely ground rock particles in the milky rivers flowing off glaciers
icefall – when a glacier descends so steeply that the upper ice breaks into a jumble of ice blocks
kettle lake – a lake formed by the melt of an area of isolated *dead ice*
moraine – walls of debris formed at the glacier's sides (*lateral moraine*) or end (*terminal moraine*)
névé – snowfield area where *firn* is formed
séracs – ice pinnacles formed, like *crevasses*, by the glacier rolling over obstacles
terminal – the final ice face at the bottom of the glacier

FOX GLACIER & VILLAGE

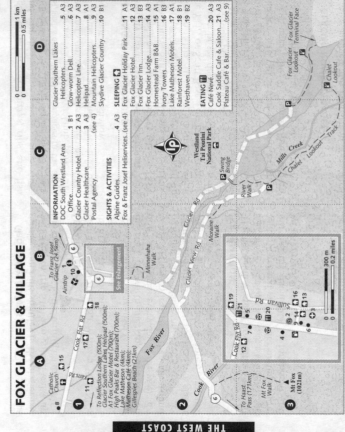

INFORMATION
DOC South Westland Area Office.....**1** B1
Glacier Country Hotel.....**2** A3
Glacier Healthcare.....**3** A1
Postal Agency.....(see 4)

SIGHTS & ACTIVITIES
Alpine Guides.....**4** A3
Fox & Franz Josef Heliservices.....(see 4)

Glacier Southern Lakes Helicopters.....**5** A3
Glow-worm Dell.....**6** A3
Helicopter Line.....**7** A3
Helipad.....**8** A1
Mountain Helicopters.....**9** A3
Skydive Glacier Country.....**10** B1

SLEEPING
Fox Glacier Holiday Park.....**11** A1
Fox Glacier Hotel.....**12** A3
Fox Glacier Inn.....**13** B3
Fox Glacier Lodge.....**14** A3
Ivory Towers.....**15** A1
Homestead Farm B&B.....**16** B3
Lake Matheson Motels.....**17** A1
Rainforest Motel.....**18** B1
Westhaven.....**19** B2

EATING
Café Nevé.....**20** A3
Cook Saddle Cafe & Saloon.....**21** A3
Plateau Café & Bar.....(see 9)

Alpine Guides (0800 111 600, 03-751 0825; www .foxguides.co.nz; SH6) books most activities and bus services. It's also the local postal agency and money exchange.

There's no dedicated town Internet facility, but you can get online at the **Fox Glacier Hotel** (0800 273 767, 03-751 0839; cnr SH6 & Cook Flat Rd) and at **Glacier Country Hotel** (03-751 0847; SH6).

The nurse at **Glacier Healthcare** (03-751 0836, after hours 027 464 1193; Sullivan Rd; 9-11.30am Mon-Fri) can patch you up on weekday mornings; there's a doctor here on Thursday afternoons – call for an appointment.

There are no banks or ATMs in town; the BP petrol station is the last fuel stop until Haast, 120km south.

ACTIVITIES
Independent Walks

It's 1.5km from Fox Village to the glacier turn-off, a further 2km to the car park. The terminal face is 30 to 40 minutes' walk from there, finishing 80m from the ice.

Short walks around the glacier include the **Moraine Walk** (over a major 18th-century advance) and **Minnehaha Walk**. The **River Walk** extends to the **Chalet Lookout Track** (1½ hours return) leading to a glacier lookout.

About 6km down Cook Flat Rd is the turn-off to **Lake Matheson**. It's an hour's walk around the lake, and at the far end (on a clear day) are impossibly photogenic views of Mt Tasman and Mt Cook reflected in the water. Visit during the early-morning calm; sun-low late afternoons are also 'choice', as they say.

Follow Cook Flat Rd for its full 21km (unsealed for the final 12km) to the remote black sand and rimu forest of **Gillespies Beach**, from where there's a dune track to **Galway Beach** (3½ hours return, 5km). Gillespies' bare-rooted driftwood and lullaby surf rhythms will bring you back to earth. The **Mt Fox Walk** (1021m above sea level; eight hours return), off the highway 3km south of town, makes for a challenging hike, only recommended for well-equipped trampers.

Behind the Mountain Helicopters building is a short path to a **glow-worm dell** (adult/ child $2/free; 24hr). Unlike Hokitika's free glow-show, this one costs a miserable $2.

We hope someone's made their fortune, as the site may be bulldozed soon to accommodate a new motel (RIP glow-worms). You can reportedly see glow-worms along the Minnehaha Walk at night – cross the bridge and turn off your torch.

Glacier Walks & Helihikes

Guided walks (equipment provided) are organised by **Alpine Guides** (☎ 0800 111 600, 03-751 0825; www.foxguides.co.nz; SH6). Half-day walks cost $60/43 per adult/child; full-day walks are $95 (over-13s only). If you're fighting fit, consider the full-day jaunt, which takes you further up the glacier; BYO lunch.

Helihikes cost $265/240 per adult/child, while a day-long introductory ice-climbing course costs $195 per adult. From October to April, Alpine Guides also conducts an easy-going two-hour interpretive walk to the glacier (adult/child $35/17). Longer guided helitrek adventures are also available – contact Alpine Guides to tailor a trip.

Skydiving & Aerial Sightseeing

With Fox Glacier's uncompromising backdrop of Southern Alps, rainforest and ocean, it's hard to imagine a better place to jump out of a plane. **Skydive Glacier Country** (☎ 0800 751 0080, 03-751 0080; www.skydiving.co.nz; Fox Glacier Airfield, SH6, Fox Glacier Village) is a professional outfit that toys with gravity from 12,000ft ($265) or 9000ft ($225). Video/photograph your terror for $175/25.

Aerial sightseeing costs at Fox parallel those at Franz Josef. Unless otherwise indicated, the following dependable operators are all on SH6 in Fox Glacier Village:

Fox & Franz Josef Heliservices (☎ 0800 800 793, 03-751 0866; www.scenic-flights.co.nz)

Glacier Southern Lakes Helicopters (☎ 0800 800 732, 03-751 0803; www.heli-flights.co.nz)

Helicopter Line (☎ 0800 807 767, 03-751 0767; www.helicopter.co.nz)

Mount Cook Ski Planes (☎ 0800 800 702, 03-752 0714; www.mtcookskiplanes.com; SH6, Franz Josef Village)

Mountain Helicopters (☎ 0800 369 423, 03-751 0045; www.mountainhelicopters.co.nz)

SLEEPING

Budget

Ivory Towers (☎ 03-751 0838; www.ivorytowerslodge.co.nz; Sullivan Rd; dm $21/38, tw & d $52-90; □) This place is more lemon than ivory and doesn't exactly tower, but inside it's a first-rate hostel: tidy, laid-back, colourful, draped in greenery and endowed with good facilities. The rainy-day 'cinema' has amazing old seats from a derelict Hokitika theatre.

Fox Glacier Holiday Park (☎ 0800 154 366, 03-751 082?; www.foxglacierholidaypark.co.nz; Kerrs Rd; unpowered/powered sites per 2 people $26/28, tw cabins $45, d $55-99; □) This practical park has a collaboration of different units in a rural setting. The cabins are bog-basic, but green-clad foothills rise up in the background (mountains too, behind the clouds).

Midrange

Rainforest Motel (☎ 0800 724 636, 03-751 0140; www.rainforestmotel.co.nz; Cook Flat Rd; d $105-130) Johnny B Goode wouldn't recognise the log cabins here: clean, bright, quiet and a long way from anything hillbilly. Four two-bedroom units sleep up to four (from $150).

Lake Matheson Motels (☎ 0800 452 2437, 03-751 0830; www.lakematheson.co.nz; Cook Flat Rd; s & d $75-120) This spick-and-span motel has 22 recently updated units, three with wheelchair access, all with hotplates to cook up antifreeze soups. A separate house, usually full of exhausted cyclists, sleeps up to seven (from $165, minimum of five slumberers).

Homestead Farm B&B (☎ 03-751 0835; foxhomst@xtra.co.nz; Cook Flat Rd; tw & d $135-155) An island in a sea of stream-furrowed pastureland, this was Fox Glacier's first farmhouse. Its three rooms are fittingly quaint and all have en suites. Continental breakfasts are included; cooked breakfasts cost an extra $7. Children under seven face an embargo.

Fox Glacier Inn (☎ 0508 369 466, 03-751 0022; www.foxglacierinn.co.nz; tw & d $75-110; □) The budget rooms here have shared facilities and are medically spartan, but they do have TVs and heaters with linen provided. The pricier en suite rooms have bed configurations to suit all-comers.

Fox Glacier Hotel (☎ 0800 273 767, 03-751 0839; www.resorts.co.nz; cnr SH6 & Cook Flat Rd; s $25-70, d $90-145; □) Builders managed to erect this two-storey hotel just in time for the Great Depression. Some of the budget rooms are greatly depressing, but a gracious old-world air nevertheless pervades. Rooms in the Sullivans wing (one of four wings) are the best of the bunch.

Some other recommended midrangers:

A1 Fox Glacier Motel (☎ 0800 187 900, 03-751 0804; www.a1foxglaciermotel.co.nz; Cook Flat Rd; d $95-125)

A little jaded, but good value in a hypertense accommodation market.

Fox Glacier Lodge (☎ 03-751 0888; www.foxglacier lodge.co.nz; Sullivan Rd; sites per 2 people $25, d $98-250) Well-proportioned timber buildings with mountain views; the B&B spa chalet is top of the heap. Bike hire $5 per hour.

Top End

Westhaven (☎ 03-751 0084; www.thewesthaven.co.nz; SH6; d $99-225) These architecturally precise suites are a textural melange of corrugated steel, local stone and lusty leather among burnt red and ivory walls. The deluxe king rooms have spas – you couldn't be further from Switzerland, but the mood is complicit.

Reflection Lodge (☎ 03-751 0707; www.reflection lodge.co.nz; Cook Flat Rd; d $150-180) A funky '60s ski lodge with a beach-stone hearth and faux-marble bathrooms. Where's Britt Ekland when you need her?

EATING & DRINKING

Plateau Café & Bar (☎ 03-751 0058; cnr Sullivan Rd & SH6; mains $19-25; ☺ lunch & dinner) Plateau roams a lonely plateau of flavours, few other places in Fox or Franz daring to extend to spicy curries and Asian stir-fries. Friendly service, good coffee, plenty of vegetarian options and NZ wines by the glass – you can't go wrong.

Café Nevé (☎ 03-751 0110; SH6; mains $14-30; ☺ breakfast, lunch & dinner) Nevé isn't new, realising that travellers want to eat NZ food when they're in NZ. Fresh local mussels, fish, venison, lamb and whitebait mix it up with Blackball Salami pizzas, washed down with Monteith's and Kiwi wines.

Matheson Café (☎ 03-751 0878; Lake Matheson Rd; mains $8-15; ☺ breakfast & lunch) Near the shores of Lake Matheson, this café does everything right: slick interior design, huge mountain views, outdoor deck with gas heaters, quality upmarket NZ fare, tasty cakes, strong coffee and sassy international staff.

High Peaks Bar & Restaurant (☎ 03-751 0131; Cooks Flat Rd; bar meals $14-23, restaurant mains $25-34; ☺ dinner) Angled towards Mt Cook, praying for the clouds to part, High Peaks has a back-corner restaurant and a front-of-house bar. Forget the calories, this is enjoyment food: steaks, pastas, fish and chips, roasts, chunky soups and stews.

Cook Saddle Cafe & Saloon (☎ 03-751 0700; SH6; meals $9-27; ☺ breakfast, lunch & dinner) Saddle up at the bar as Garth Brooks and Shania Twain twang away in the background, desperately trying to convince you that this is the *real* Wild West. Lasso some Finger Pickin' Chicken or a Howdy Doody Burger and gun down a few West Coast ales.

GETTING THERE & AROUND

Most buses stop outside the Alpine Guides building.

InterCity (☎ 03-365 1113; www.intercitycoach.co.nz) runs daily buses north to Franz Josef ($13, 40 minutes, 8.30am and 3.25pm), the morning bus continuing to Nelson ($106, 11 hours). Daily southbound services run to Queenstown ($94, 7½ hours, 8.45am).

Atomic Shuttles (☎ 03-322 8883; www.atomictravel .co.nz) runs daily to Franz Josef ($10, 45 minutes, 2.15pm), continuing to Greymouth ($30, 3¼ hours). Southbound buses run daily to Queenstown ($50, 6½ hours, 11am).

Fox Glacier Shuttle (☎ 0800 369 287) will drive you to Lake Matheson or Fox Glacier and allow you enough time for a stroll ($10 return, minimum four people).

SOUTH TO HAAST

About 26km south of Fox Glacier, along SH6, the **Copland Valley** is the western end of the **Copland Track** (three days one way). As challenging as it is spectacular, the walk is usually tackled east to west (starting from Mt Cook), but from SH6 you can still do a six- to seven-hour walk up Copland Valley to overnight at the **Welcome Flat DOC Hut** ($15), where thermal springs bubble. Annual DOC Hut Passes don't apply here, but you can buy tickets at any West Coast DOC office or visitor information centre.

Popular with Haast-to-Fox cyclists and Copland Track trampers, the **Pine Grove Motel** (☎ 03-751 0898; pine_grove@xtra.co.nz; SH6; unpowered/powered sites per 2 people $20, d $35-80) is 8km south of the trailhead. Despite a well-worn visage, units are affordable and in reasonable shape.

On stilts above fish ponds on the Paringa River, the **Salmon Farm Café & Shop** (☎ 0800 100 837, 03-751 0837; SH6; meals $8-26; ☺ breakfast & lunch) serves salmon-filled omelettes, platters, pastas and fresh pâté. It's $1 to feed the fish, but they don't look like they need it.

There's a basic **DOC camping ground** (adult/child $6/1.50) 70km south of Fox Glacier at **Lake Paringa**, a tranquil trout-filled lake surrounded by swaying forest boughs.

The historic **Haast-Paringa Cattle Track** hoofs off from SH6 (just south of Lake Paringa, 43km northeast of Haast) and emerges on the coast by the Waita River, just north of Haast. Before the road opened in 1965, this was the stock route between Haast and the Whataroa markets. The track's first leg to **Blowfly Hut** (four hours return) is an easy-going half-day hike. The full walk takes three days, stopping at **Maori Saddle Hut** and **Coppermine Creek Hut**. The track can get muddy – check conditions and pay hut fees ($5 per night) at the DOC Haast visitor information centre (right).

HAAST REGION

The Haast region is a major nature refuge, enormous stands of rainforest thriving alongside extensive wetlands. The area's kahikatea and flame-red rimu forests, swamps, sand dunes, seal and penguin colonies, bird life and sweeping beaches ensured its inclusion in the Southwest New Zealand (Te Wahipounamu) World Heritage Area. Bird nerds might see fantails, bellbirds, kereru (NZ pigeons), falcons, kaka, kiwi and morepork.

Lake Moeraki, 31km north of Haast, is another rippling fishing lake. An easy 40-minute walk from here brings you to **Monro Beach**, a west-facing gravel beach copping the full Tasman Sea force. There's a breeding colony of Fiordland crested penguins here (July to November) and fur seals.

Wilderness Lodge Lake Moeraki (☎ 03-750 0881; www.wildernesslodge.co.nz; SH6; d $400-900; ☐) is a pricey, private B&B lodge with plush rooms and cooked breakfasts. Sure, the breakfasts are good, but you're really paying for the waterside location and free guided walking, fishing and canoe trips.

About 5km south of Lake Moeraki is the much-photographed **Knights Point** (named after a surveyor's dog) where the Haast road was eventually opened in 1965. Deep waters just off shore and uninterrupted Antarctic swells make this a favoured eatery for seals, birds and sometimes whales.

Ship Creek, 15km north of Haast, has a lookout platform and two interpretive walks: the **Dune Lake Walk** (30 minutes return), and the **Kahikatea Swamp Forest Walk** (20 minutes return). The *Schomberg*, a clipper on its 1835 maiden voyage from Liverpool to Melbourne, was wrecked on the Australian coast; pieces of it washed up here some months later.

Haast

pop 295 'Haastafarians'

Some 120km south of Fox Glacier, Haast hunkers down around the mouth of the wide Haast River in three distinct pockets: Haast Junction, Haast Village, and Haast Beach. After the jaw-dropping scenery of the glaciers or Haast Pass, this modern service hub doesn't make a big splash, but in true West Coast fashion, wilderness is just a footstep away. Haast is also big on whitebaiting – see the boxed text, p498.

INFORMATION

The **DOC Haast visitor information centre** (☎ 03-750 0809; www.doc.govt.nz; cnr SH6 & Jackson Bay Rd; ☑ 9am-6pm Nov-Mar, to 4.30pm Apr-Oct) has wall-to-wall regional info and every half-hour it screens the all-too-brief Haast landscape film *Edge of Wilderness* (adult/child $3/free).

ACTIVITIES & TOURS

Take a hair-tousling two-hour 'sea to mountain' ecojetboat trip on the wild Waiatoto River with **Waiatoto River Safaris** (☎ 0800 538 723, 03-750 0780; www.riversafaris.co.nz; Jackson Bay Rd; adult/child $125/75; ☑ 10am, 1pm & 4pm), departing from the Waiatoto River Bridge 30km south of Haast. **Haast River Safari** (☎ 0800 865 382, 03-750 0101; www.haastriver.co.nz; adult/child $110/50; ☑ 9am & 2pm), based in the Red Barn between Haast Village and the visitor information centre, runs more leisurely covered-jetboat cruises on the Haast River.

Round About Haast (☎ 03-750 0890; www.round abouthaast.co.nz; tours $65-135) runs local boat and minibus tours. Out on Jackson Bay you'll see seals, dolphins and (seasonally) penguins, while the bus takes you to beaches, estuaries and forests, with walks and local folklore thrown in.

SLEEPING

Budget

Wilderness Accommodation (☎ 03-750 0029; www .west-coast.co.nz; Marks Rd; dm/s $24/40, d $55-90; ☐) A sprawling timber complex with hostel and motel wings, this place is the best value in town. Dorms aren't crowded, doubles even less crowded, there're free DVDs and a leafy covered courtyard for rainy-day jigsaws and chess.

Haast Lodge (☎ 0800 500 703, 03-750 0703; haast _lodge@xtra.co.nz; Marks Rd; sites per 2 people $24, dm $24, d $46-5; ☐) For the times you'd sell your soul for a clean shower, this YHA is spotless and meticulously managed, but rooms are squeezy and unceasingly lino and beige. Hire a bike for $10 per day.

Haast Beach Holiday Park (☎ 0800 843 226, 03-750 0860; haastpark@xtra.co.nz; Jackson Bay Rd; unpowered/powered sites per 2 people $24, dm $20, d $36-100) Close to the beach about 15km south of Haast, this caravan park has old but functional facilities. The Hapuka Estuary Walk (right) is right across the road.

Midrange

Haast World Heritage Hotel (☎ 0800 502 444, 03-750 0828; www.world-heritage-hotel.com; SH6; dm $30, s $30-55, d $79-159; 🖳) New management has poured reservoirs of cash into renovating this grandiosely titled place. Fifty centrally heated en suite rooms are coffee-and-cream colour schemed; the restaurant (mains $25 to $31) and café-bar (mains $9 to $30) open for lunch and dinner. The bar has new carpets, big screens and pool tables; occasional live bands kick out the jams.

Okuru Beach B&B (☎ 03-750 0719; www.okuru beach.co.nz; Cuttance Rd North; s $55, d $85-95) This low-key, beachy house, off Jackson Bay Rd, is a short stroll from sand and rainforest – turn right at the blue B&B sign 14km south of Haast. The main house has three B&B rooms, or there are two self-contained family units down the street.

McGuires Lodge (☎ 0800 624 847, 03-750 0020; www .mcguireslodge.co.nz; SH6; d $110-135, f $190) McGuires' en suite motel rooms walk the line between normal and unremarkable; family rooms sleep five. The restaurant-bar (mains $28 to $30; open for dinner) serves A-list venison, whitebait, lobster and lamb dishes, or there's a cheaper bar menu (mains $15 to $18).

Top End

Collyer House (☎ 03-750 0022; www.collyerhouse.co .nz; Jackson Bay Rd; s/d incl cooked breakfast $200/250) A roaring open fire, thick bathrobes, complimentary toiletries, luxuriant quilts, high-pressure showers, quality linen and beach views make Collyer House an indulgent choice. Dinner is $50 per person by arrangement. Follow the signs off SH6 for 12km down Jackson Bay Rd.

EATING

Smithy's Tavern (☎ 03-750 0034; Marks Rd; dinner $18-25; 🕓 lunch & dinner) Sounds like a hole-in-the-

wall bar, but it's actually a roomy bistro-pub with various soup, fish and roast offerings. Locals chow down under antler-festooned rafters.

Fantails Café (☎ 03-750 0055; Marks Rd; dinner $12-25; 🕓 breakfast, lunch & dinner) Forties crooner tunes swing through the cheery atmosphere at this licensed roadside eatery, serving everything from sandwiches to full steak dinners.

GETTING THERE & AWAY

InterCity (☎ 03-365 1113; www.intercitycoach.co.nz) and **Atomic Shuttles** (☎ 03-322 8883; www.atomic travel.co.nz) buses stop at the visitor information centre on their Fox-to-Wanaka runs.

Haast to Jackson Bay & Cascade River

From Haast Junction a sideroad heads to Jackson Bay with numerous wilderness walks along the way.

Near Okuru is the **Hapuka Estuary Walk** (20 minutes return), an information-packed boardwalk loop through a soporific whitebait sanctuary.

After crossing Arawhata Bridge, turn onto the narrow, unsealed road along the Jackson River to **Martyr Saddle**, with views of the Cascade River Valley and the incredible **Red Hills**. Their ruddy hues are due to high magnesium and iron concentrations in rocks forced up by colliding Australo and Pacific tectonic plates. Three kilometres beyond Martyr Saddle is an end-of-the-road lookout above the **Cascade River** – wilderness in the truest sense.

The main road continues west from Arawhata Bridge to the isolated fishing hamlet of **Jackson Bay**. Southern Alps views from here are unforgettable, and there are colonies of Fiordland crested penguins near the road. Migrants arrived here in 1875 under a doomed assisted-immigration scheme, their farming fantasies mercilessly shattered by never-ending rain and the lack of a wharf, not built until 1938. Today, fishing boats bob on the bay, gathering lobster, tuna, tarakihi and gurnard.

Walks at Jackson Bay include the **Smoothwater Bay Track** (three hours return) and the **Wharekai Te Kau Walk** (40 minutes return) to Ocean Beach, a secluded bay with curious rock formations.

HAAST PASS

Turning inland from Haast towards Wanaka (145km, 2½ hours), SH6 snakes alongside the Haast River, climbing up to Haast Pass and Mt Aspiring National Park. As you move inland the vegetation thins away until you reach the 563m pass – snow coun-

try covered in tussock and scrub. There are some stunning waterfalls en route (especially if it's been raining), tumbling down just minutes from the highway; **Fantail** and **Thunder Creek** falls are worth a look. There's also the **Bridle Track** (1½ hours one way) between the pass and Davis Flat. See the DCC booklet *Haast Pass/Tioripatea Highway: Walking Opportunities* ($1).

The Haast Pass road (Tioripatea, meaning 'Clear Path' in Maori) opened in 1965, before then Maoris walked this route bringing West Coast greenstone to the Makarora River in Otago. The pass (and river and township) take their European name from geologist Julius Haast, who passed through in 1863.

There are food and fuel stops at Makarora and Lake Hawea. If you're driving north, check your fuel gauge: Haast petrol station is the last one before Fox Glacier, 120km north.

Christchurch & Canterbury

Don't let the oh-so-English name of the region, or stories of its terribly Anglo main city, fool you into believing this area is merely a replica of something you might see in England. Canterbury offers a quintessential slice of New Zealand life and landscape – beyond the borders of Christchurch, the main city, is a living canvas of lush farmland, wildlife-rich coastline, turquoise blue lakes and breathtaking mountains.

Canterbury has a physical presence that slowly builds from the volcanically uplifted hills of Banks Peninsula and the expansive, well-farmed flatlands of Canterbury Plain to the mountaineer-calling pinnacles of the Southern Alps. It's the stuff of classic holiday snaps: emerald, sheep-strewn pastures backed by jagged, snow-tipped mountains.

The region's urban centre point (and the South Island's largest human enclave) is Christchurch, a city with puritan roots but an energetic enthusiasm for the trappings of modern life, where fulfilling distractions range from absorbing art galleries and Gothic rooflines to formal gardens and fashionable bars and restaurants. The region's environmental treats include the dolphin-cruised harbour just off the Francophile town of Akaroa, the sulphur pools and jetboat-happy canyons at Hanmer Springs, the popular, powdery ski slopes of Mt Hutt, the forested terraces lining Lewis Pass, the braided rivers of Arthur's Pass, and the vivid hues of Mackenzie Country lakes. And then there's *the* mountain – Mt Cook. You can walk around it, fly over it, even scale it if you're well and truly prepared, but there's no doubting that one of the country's most inspiring sights is of the highest peak in Aoraki/Mt Cook National Park on a bright, sunny day.

HIGHLIGHTS

- Strolling, punting and dining your way around charming **Christchurch** (opposite)
- Rambling through the gardens of the superb **Tree Crop Farm Park** (p561) in Akaroa, followed by an hour spent relaxing on the veranda
- Beholding quintessential NZ farmland and mountain landscapes on a **hot-air balloon trip** (p572) out of Methven
- Capturing the perfect photo of the Church of the Good Shepherd with gorgeous **Lake Tekapo** (p578) and the Southern Alps as the backdrop
- Getting wrinkly while taking a soothing soak in the **Hanmer Springs Thermal Reserve** (p565)
- Bar-hopping between quirky bars and drinking with the locals in **Lyttelton** (p558)
- Drinking in the views of the spectacular Cloud Piercer in **Aoraki/Mt Cook National Park** (p583)

TELEPHONE CODE: 03 ■ www.christchurchnz.net ■ www.mtcook.org.nz

CHRISTCHURCH & CANTERBURY FACTS

Eat: Anywhere with a view of Aoraki/Mt Cook (p588)

Drink: House-brewed beers alfresco at Christchurch's Dux de Lux (p553)

Read: *A Land of Two Halves* by Lyttelton local and well-known newspaper columnist Joe Bennett

Listen to: *Drive*, by silky-voiced Bic Runga; hip-hoppin' Scribe's *The Crusader*

Watch: *Heavenly Creatures*, for the crime that rocked 1950s Christchurch

Swim at: Akaroa, with the dolphins (p562), or soak at Hanmer Springs Thermal Reserve (p565)

Festival: Free street performances at Christchurch's World Buskers Festival (p539)

Tackiest tourist attraction: The Wizard (p531), now semiretired: tacky or treasure?

TOP ACTIVITIES

- Extreme punting? Just joking (p536)
- Go skiing! The closest fields are only an hour's drive from Christchurch (see p536)
- Head north to Hanmer Springs (p565), where you can ski, bike, bungy, ride and raft, before soothing your aching bones in the thermal hot springs
- Walk the trails and scale the slopes surrounding NZ's tallest peak – Mt Cook (p586) – or fly overhead in comfort (p587)
- See the Canterbury region from the saddle (Hanmer, p566; Methven, p572; Mt Cook region, p587; Mackenzie Country, p579)

Getting There & Around

Christchurch has a busy international airport serviced by several domestic airlines, with flights to numerous key destinations on the North and South Islands.

A long list of bus and shuttle operators scurries along the east coast, connecting settlements with northern destinations such as Picton and southern towns such as Dunedin. Some operators also connect Christchurch with points west such as Arthur's Pass, the West Coast and Mt Cook.

Rail options for east-coast and coast-to-coast travel are provided by Tranz Scenic: its *TranzAlpine* service connects Christchurch and Greymouth, while its *TranzCoastal* trains chug north to Picton, with connections to the North Island. For more information on getting to and from Christchurch, see p555.

CHRISTCHURCH

pop 344,100

Christchurch is often described as the most English of NZ's cities, a description bolstered by the punts gliding down the picturesque Avon River, a grand Anglican cathedral rising above the city's central square, and the trams rattling past streets with frightfully British names. Even the tranquil suburbia to the west, with its manicured gardens and crisply cut lawns with nary a blade of grass out of place, do little to challenge this.

But for all its self-consciously inherited charm, Christchurch is also a thoroughly modern NZ city, as exemplified by the Kiwi art that has pride of place in the city's modern gallery, the wildlife reserves teeming with native animals, and a multitude of great cafes, restaurants and bars.

HISTORY

Though it still has the Gothic architecture and wooden villas bequeathed by its

Climate

Canterbury is one of the driest regions of NZ. The moisture-laden westerlies from the Tasman Sea hit the Southern Alps and dump their rainfall on the West Coast well before reaching the eastern environs of the South Island. The statistics say it all: Canterbury has an annual rainfall of only 0.75m, compared with a soaking 5m on the West Coast.

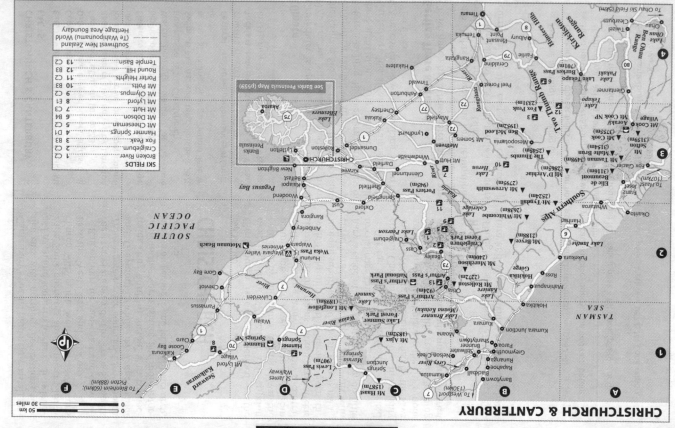

founders, Christchurch has strayed from the original urban vision. The settlement of Christchurch in 1850 was an ordered Church of England enterprise, and the fertile farming land was deliberately placed in the hands of the gentry. Christchurch was meant to be a model of class-structured England in the South Pacific, not just another scruffy colonial outpost. Churches were built rather than pubs, and wool made the elite of Christchurch wealthy. In 1862 it was incorporated as a very English city, but its character slowly changed as other migrants arrived, new industries followed, and the city followed its own aesthetic and cultural notions.

ORIENTATION

Cathedral Sq marks the centre of town and is itself marked by the spire of Christchurch Cathedral. The western half of the inner city is dominated by the Botanic Gardens.

Christchurch is compact and easy to walk around, although it's slightly complicated by the river twisting through the centre and constantly crossing your path.

Colombo St runs north–south past Cathedral Sq and is one of the main shopping strips. Oxford Tce is the prime dining boulevard, while the pedestrianised New Regent St is worth a look for its pastel-painted Spanish mission–style architecture.

CHRISTCHURCH IN...

Two Days

Start your touring with some church-admiring and people-watching at Cathedral Square (p531), then jump on the **tramway** (p535) for an inner-city tour. Disembark at the **Arts Centre** (p534) to browse the historic grounds, and enjoy lunch and a beer o° three at **Dux de Lux** (p551). Get back to nature in the **Botanic Gardens** (p531), walking down to the pretty **Antigua Boatsheds** (p536) for a late-afternoon **Avon punt** (p536). Finally, get acquainted with the prime eating and drinking spots on **Oxford Tce** (p551).

On day two, check out the **Canterbury Museum** (p535) and/or the **Christchurch Art Gallery** (p536) before heading out of town to ride the **gondola** (p536) and do some mountain-top walking. That evening, jump on a bus to **Lyttelton** (p558) fo° dinner and drinks at the town's character-filled eateries.

Four Days

Follow the two-day itinerary; then take a day trip to **Banks Peninsula** (p559) to explore Francophile **Akaroa** (p560) and its wildlife-rich harbour. On day four soak up more of Christchurch by **shopping** (p555) on High St, chilling at the **International Antarctic Centre** (pardon the pun; p536), visiting a **wildlife reserve** (p536), and joining an evening concert and feast at **Nga Hau e Wha** (p535).

Maps

Christchurch's visitor information centre distributes free tourist maps, and sells a wide range of maps and road atlases.

Map World (Map pp532-3; ☎ 03-374 5399; www .mapworld.co.nz; cnr Manchester & Gloucester Sts) carries a range of NZ city and regional maps, guidebooks, and topographic maps for trampers.

INFORMATION
Bookshops

Arts Centre Bookshop (Map pp532-3; ☎ 03-365 5277; www.bocksnz.com; Arts Centre, 2 Worcester St) Great range of NZ-oriented titles.

Scorpio Books (Map pp532-3; ☎ 03-379 2882; 79 Hereford St) Lots of travel, history and Maori culture, plus international periodicals.

Smith's Bookshop (Map pp532-3; ☎ 03-379 7976; 133 Manchester St) Excellent secondhand bookshop with shelves over three floors.

Whitcoulls (Map pp532-3; ☎ 03-379 4580; 111 Cashel St)

Emergency
Ambulance, Fire Service & Police (☎ 111)

Police station (Map pp532-3; ☎ 03-363 7400; cnr Hereford St & Cambridge Tce)

Internet Access

The going rate in Christchurch's many Internet cafés is around $3 an hour. Most hostels also have Internet available.

GREATER CHRISTCHURCH

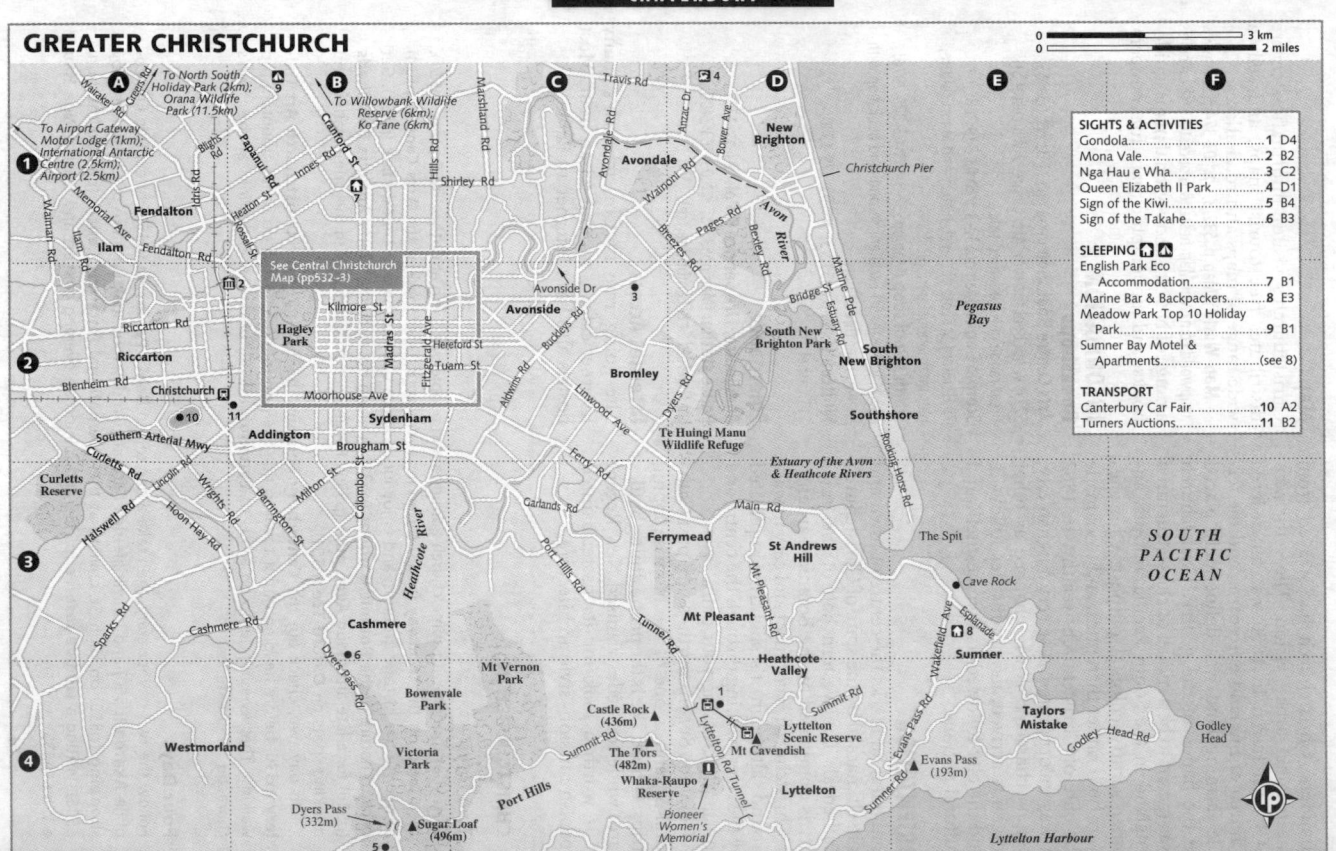

SIGHTS & ACTIVITIES

Gondola	1 D4
Mona Vale	2 B2
Nga Hau e Wha	3 C2
Queen Elizabeth II Park	4 D1
Sign of the Kiwi	5 B4
Sign of the Takahe	6 B3

SLEEPING

English Park Eco Accommodation	7 B1
Marine Bar & Backpackers	8 E3
Meadow Park Top 10 Holiday Park	9 B1
Sumner Bay Motel & Apartments	(see 8)

TRANSPORT

Canterbury Car Fair	10 A2
Turners Auctions	11 B2

0 — 3 km
0 — 2 miles

Internet Resources

Christchurch & Canterbury (www.christchurchnz.net) Official tourism website for the city and region.

Local Eye (www.localeye.info) Online gateway to the region.

Media

Press (www.stuff.co.nz) Christchurch's newspaper, published Monday to Saturday.

Tourist Times (www.touristtimes.co.nz) Free monthly newspaper for visitors to Canterbury.

Visitor Guide Christchurch & Canterbury (www .christchurchvisitorguide.co.nz) Useful free guide, published every three months.

Medical Services

24 Hour Surgery (Bealey Ave Medical Centre; Map pp532–3; ☎ 03-365 7777; cnr Bealey Ave & Colombo St; ☎ 24hr) North of town; no appointment is necessary.

After-hours pharmacy (Map pp532–3; ☎ 03-366 4439; 931 Colombo St; ☎ 6pm–11pm Mon-Thu, 9pm–11pm Fri, 9am–11pm Sat & Sun) Right next door to the 24 Hour Surgery.

Christchurch Hospital (Map pp532–3; ☎ 03-364 0640, emergency dept 03-364 0270; Riccarton Ave)

Money

The intersection of Hereford and Colombo Sts is home to major banks.

Travelex Cathedral Sq (Map pp532–3; ☎ 03-365 0235; visitor information centre, Cathedral Sq); Colombo St (Map pp532–3; ☎ 03-366 2087; Harvey World Travel, cnr Colombo & Armagh Sts)

Post

Post office (Map pp532–3 Cathedral Sq)

Christchurch Mail Centre (Map pp532–3; 53-59 Hereford St)

Tourist Information

Airport information desks (☎ 03-353 7774) At both terminals of the airport and open to meet all incoming flights; can book transport and accommodation.

Automobile Association (AA; Map pp532–3; ☎ 03-964 3650; 210 Hereford St)

Christchurch & Canterbury visitor information centre (Map pp532–3; ☎ 03-379 9629; www.christ churchnz.net; Cathedral Sq; ☎ 8.30am–5pm) Dispenses loads of information and books transport, activities and accommodation; also here is the Southern Encounter Aquarium & Kiwi House (see below). It is open later in peak periods.

Department of Conservation (DOC; Map pp532–3; ☎ 03-371 3706; www.doc.govt.nz; 133 Victoria St; ☎ 8.30am–5pm Mon-Fri) Has information on South Island national parks and walkways.

SIGHTS
Cathedral Square

Cathedral Sq, named after the building that dominates it, is where locals and tourists continually crisscross each other's paths, giving the city's flat centrepiece a lively bustle. In the centre of the square is the 18m-high *Metal Chalice sculpture*, created by Neil Dawson to acknowledge the new millennium.

In the past, a human landmark was provided by a local eccentric called the **Wizard**, who dressed like a Harry Potter film extra and harangued crowds with his soapbox philosophy. This pseudocelebrity is now semiretired although he makes occasional appearances (largely in summer; look out for him if you're nearby at 1pm).

Christchurch Cathedral (Map pp532–3; ☎ 03-366 0046; www.christchurchcathedral.co.nz; Cathedral Sq; admission free; ☎ 8.30am-7pm Mon-Fri, 5am-5pm Sat & Sun mid-Oct—mid-Mar, 9am-5pm daily mid-Mar—mid-Oct) was consecrated in 1881 and has an impressive rose window, wooden-ribbed ceiling and tile work emblazoned with the distinctive Fylfot Cross. You can also climb halfway up the Gothic church's 63m-high **spire** (adult/child/family $4/1.50/8). Administrators are keen to charge for whatever they can (eg a camera or video permit costs $2.50), but the proceeds help maintain the building.

Southern Encounter Aquarium & Kiwi House (Map pp532–3; ☎ 03-359 0581; www.southenencounter .co.nz; Cathedral Sq; adult/child/family $12/5/29; ☎ 9am–4.30pm), accessed through the visitor information centre, exposes you to disturbingly large eels, seahorses, turtles and other marine life. It also has a touch tank, feeding times and a small swaying bridge that kids will love. Don't expect much from the kiwi enclosure; these endangered birds don't like light and are hypersensitive to sound.

Banks of the Avon

The **Botanic Gardens** (Map pp532–3; ☎ 03-941 7590; www.ccc.govt.nz/parks/botanicgardens; Rolleston Ave; admission free; ☎ 7am–1hr before sunset) comprise 30 riverside hectares planted with 10,000-plus

---

E Blah Blah (Map pp532–3; ☎ 03-377 2381; 77 Cathedral Sq) Also offers mobile-phone rentals.

E-caf (Map pp532–3; ☎ 03-365 6480; 301 Montreal St)

Netopia (Map pp532–3; ☎ 03-365 2612; 728 Colombo St)

CENTRAL CHRISTCHURCH

www.lonelyplanet.com

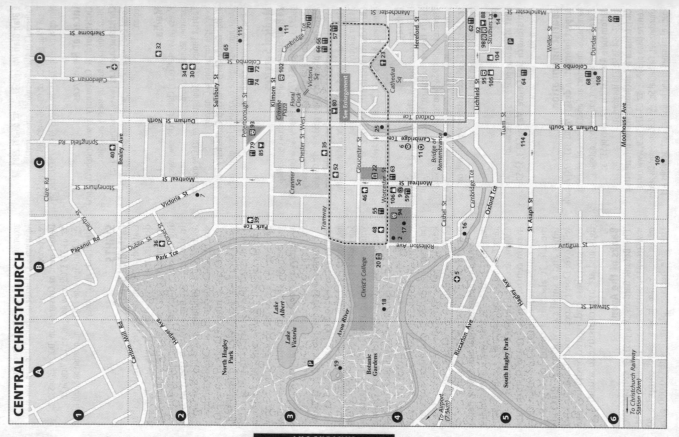

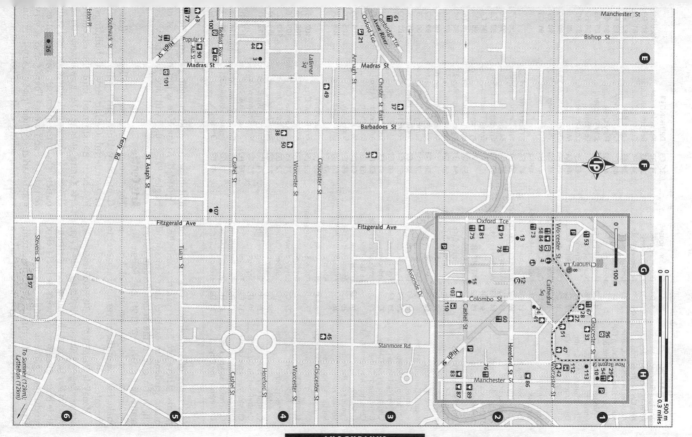

CHRISTCHURCH & CANTERBURY

INFORMATION

24 Hour Surgery	1	D1
After-Hours Pharmacy	(see 1)	
Arts Centre Bookshop	(see 17)	
Arts Centre Visitors Centre	2	B4
Automobile Association (AA)	3	E4
Christchurch & Canterbury Visitor Information Centre	4	G2
Christchurch Hospital	5	B5
Christchurch Mail Centre	6	C4
Department of Conservation	7	C2
E Blah Blah	8	G1
E-Caf	9	C4
Map World	10	H1
Netopia	(see 67)	
Police Station	11	C4
Post Office	12	G2
Scorpio Books	13	G2
Smith's Bookshop	14	D5
Travelex	(see 4)	
Whitcoulls	15	G2

SIGHTS & ACTIVITIES

Antigua Boatsheds	16	B5
Arts Centre	17	B4
Botanic Gardens	18	B4
Botanic Gardens Visitors Centre	19	A3
Canterbury Museum	20	B4
Centennial Leisure Centre	21	E3
Christchurch Art Gallery	22	C4
Christchurch Cathedral	23	D4
Christchurch Personal Guiding Service	24	G2
Punting on the Avon	25	C4
Science Alive!	26	E6
Southern Encounter Aquarium & Kiwi House	(see 4)	

SLEEPING

Base Backpackers	27	G1
Camelot Cathedral Square Hotel	28	G1
Central City YHA	29	H1
CentrePoint on Colombo	30	D2
Chester Street Backpackers	31	F3
City Centre Motel	32	D2
Coachman Backpackers	33	H1
Colombo in the City	34	D2
Croydon House	35	C3
Dorset House	36	B2
Foley Towers	37	E3
Frauenreisehaus	38	F4
George	39	B3
Hambledon	40	C1
Heritage	41	G2
Hotel off the Square	42	H1
New Excelsior	43	E5
Occidental Backpackers	44	E4
Old Countryhouse	45	H4
Orari B&B	46	C4
Quest Christchurch	47	H1
Rolleston House YHA	48	B4
Stonehurst	49	E4
Vagabond Backpackers	50	F4
Warners	51	H1
Windsor Hotel	52	C3

EATING

Caffe Roma	53	G1
City Fish & Chips	54	H1
Cook 'n' with Gas	55	C4
Copenhagen Bakery & Café	56	D3
Daily Grind	57	D3
Daily Grind	58	G2
Dux de Lux	59	C4
East in the City	60	G2
Indochine	61	E3
Java Coffee House	62	D5
Le Bon Bolli	63	C4
Lotus Heart	64	D5
Mainstreet Café	65	D2
Matsu Sushi	66	D3
Mum's	67	G1
New World Supermarket	68	D6
Pak N Save Supermarket	69	D6
Retour	70	D3
Savoy Brown	71	E5
Seafood Kitchen	72	D3
Sticky Fingers	73	G2
Strawberry Fare	74	D3
Tap Room	75	G2
Topkapi	76	H2
Two Fat Indians	77	E5
Vivace Espresso	78	G2
Zydeco	79	C3

DRINKING

Bailies Irish Bar	(see 51)	
Belgian Beer Café	80	D3
Coyote	81	G2
Foam Bar	82	E5
Grumpy Mole	83	H2
Holy Grail	84	G2
Jolly Poacher	85	C3
Le Plonk	86	H2
Loaded Hog	87	H2
Minx	88	H2
Shooters	89	H2
Twisted Hop	90	E5
Viaduct	91	G2

ENTERTAINMENT

Arts Centre Cinemas	(see 17)	
Base	92	D5
Christchurch Casino	93	C3
Court Theatre	94	C4
eye spy	95	D5
Hoyts Moorhouse	(see 26)	
Isaac Theatre Royal	96	H1
Jade Stadium	97	G6
Ministry/Propaganda	98	D5
Regent on Worcester	99	G2
Sammy's Jazz Review	100	E5
Southern Blues Bar	101	E5
Town Hall	102	D3

SHOPPING

Arts Centre Market	(see 17)	
Ballantynes	103	G2
Mountain Designs	104	D5
Snowgum	105	D5
Untouched World	106	C4

TRANSPORT

Ace Rental Cars	107	F5
Air New Zealand	108	D6
Backpackers Car Market	109	G6
City Bus Exchange	110	G2
First Choice	111	D3
InterCity Bus Depot	112	H1
New Zealand Motorcycle Rentals & Tours	113	H1
Omega Rental Cars	114	C5
Pegasus Rental Cars	115	D3
Qantas	(see 56)	

specimens of indigenous and introduced plants. There are conservatories and the-matic gardens to explore, lawns to sprawl on, and a café at the **Botanic Gardens visitors centre** (Map pp532-3; ☎ 03-941 7590; Rolleston Ave; ☉9am-4pm Mon-Fri, 10am-4pm Sat & Sun). Kids can make full use of the playground adjacent to the café.

MonaVale (Map p530; ☎ 03-348 9660; 63 Fendalton Rd; admission free; ☉9.30am-4pm daily Oct-Apr, 10am-3.30pm Wed-Sun May-Sep) is a charming Elizabethan-style homestead on 5.5-riverside hectares of landscaped gardens, ponds and fountains. Dine in the café inside the homestead, wander the gorgeous grounds, or take a half-hour Avon River **punt** (per person $16.50; ☉Oct-Apr). Mona Vale is just northwest of Hagley Park; bus 9 will take you there.

Arts Centre

The former Canterbury College site (later Canterbury University), with its enclave of wonderful Gothic Revival buildings, has been transformed into the excellent **Arts Centre** (Map pp532-3; www.artscentre.org.nz; 2 Worcester St; admission free), where arts and craft outlets share the premises with theatres, restaurants and cafés. There's also a very good **market** (☉10am-4pm Sat & Sun) here on weekends, selling craft and gourmet food items, often with live entertainment and plenty of cheap food stalls.

The **Arts Centre visitors centre** (Map pp532-3; ☎ 03-3632836; 2 Worcester St) found inside the clock tower on Worcester St, provides details of free guided tours of the complex.

Tramway

Trams were introduced to Christchurch streets in 1905 but were discontinued as a means of transport 50 years later. However, restored **trams** (☎ 03-366 7830; www.tram.co.nz; adult/child $12.50/free; ☑9am-9pm Nov-Mar, to 6pm Apr-Oct) now operate a 2.5km inner-city loop that takes in prime local features and shopping areas; tickets are valid for 48 hours and can be bought from the driver. One tram is fitted out as a **restaurant** (☎ 03-366 7511; dinner packages $54-115; ☑dinner), which means you can chew while you view.

Combo tickets (adult/chid/family $25/10/59) for the tram and gondola (p536) are also available (purchase from tram or gondola staff).

Canterbury Museum

(Map pp532-3; ☎ 03-366 5000; www.cantmus.govt.nz; Rolleston Ave; admission free; ☑9am-5pm Apr-Sep, to 5.30pm Oct-Mar)
The absorbing **Canterbury Museum** has amassed a wonderful collection of natural and artificial items of significance to New Zealand. Highlights include the Maori gallery, with some stunning *pounamu* (greenstone or jade) pieces on display; the coracle in the Antarctic Hall used by a group shipwrecked on Disappointment Island in 1907; and the child-oriented Discovery (admission $2), with interactive displays and living exhibits such as docile tarantulas. The 4th-floor café has views of botanic greenery.

MAORI NZ: CHRISTCHURCH & THE SOUTH ISLAND

NZ is a whole lot less brown in the south: the South Island was settled a few hundred years later than the north, with significant numbers coming south only after land became scarcer in the North Island. Before that, Maori mostly travelled to the south in search of moa, fishing and, of course, West Coast *pounamu* (greenstone). Even now, only 5% of NZ's Maoris live on the South Island.

The major *iwi* (tribe) of the South Island is Ngai Tahu (www.ngaitahu.iwi.nz), ironically now one of the country's wealthiest, because it is so much richer in land (per person) than the North Island tribes. In Christchurch, as in other cities, there are urban Maori of many other *iwi* as well.

Christchurch has more opportunities for travellers looking for a Maori experience than other South Island centres. The country's largest *marae*, **Nga Hau e Wha** (Marae of the Four Winds; Map p530; ☎ 03-388 7685; www.nationalmarae.co.nz; 250 Pages Rd; marae admission free, concert-tour-hangi package adult/child $65/36; ☑marae 9am-4.30pm Mon-Fri, concert 6.45pm daily) is here. This is a multicultural facility where you can see carvings, weavings and paintings in the *whare wananga* (house of learning). Tours (adult/child $30/19) must be booked in advance and are taken in conjunction with a nightly concert; an optional extra is a *hangi* (traditional feast).

There's another Maori cultural experience at Willowbank Wildlife Reserve (p536) called **Ko Tane** (☎ 03-359 6226; www.kotane.co.nz; Hussey Rd; dancing-tour-dinner package adult/child $82.50/47; ☑5.30pm & 6.30pm), featuring traditional dancing, a wildlife tour and buffet dinner. You can opt to forego the wildlife tour and/or dinner for a cheaper night out – the performance only is adult/child $36/20.

Elsewhere in the South Island, Maori experiences are harder to find. You can catch Maori performances or dine *hangi*-style in Queenstown (p637), Nelson (p463) or Kaikoura (p458), or travel in a traditional *waka* (canoe) in Abel Tasman National Park (p480).

As well as Christchurch's Canterbury Museum (above), you'll unearth Maori artefacts at museums in Akaroa (p560) and Okains Bay (Maori & Colonial Museum; p561), Dunedin (Otago Museum; p594), Invercargill (p674), Hokitika (p508) and Kaikoura (p455).

To polish your knowledge of *pounamu*, there's no better spot than the West Coast (Hokitika, p511; Greymouth, p505).

Enthusiasts could check out ancient rock art at Takiroa (p618) and Mt Somers (p573).

Christchurch Art Gallery

Set in an eye-catching metal-and-glass collage built in 2003, the city's **art gallery** (Map pp532-3; ☎ 03-941 7300; www.christchurchartgallery .org.nz; cnr Worcester & Montreal Sts; admission free; ⏰ 10am-5pm Thu-Tue, to 9pm Wed) has an engrossing permanent collection divided into historical, 20th-century and contemporary galleries, plus temporary exhibitions featuring NZ artists. Guided tours ($5) are held at 11am. Stop in at the spacious café-wine bar on-site, and browse the high-quality gift shop.

International Antarctic Centre

The **International Antarctic Centre** (☎ 0508 736 4846; www.iceberg.co.nz; Orchard Rd; adult/child/family $25/15/65, audioguide $6; ⏰ 9am-7pm Oct-Apr, to 5.30pm May-Sep) is part of a huge complex built for the administration of the NZ, US and Italian Antarctic programmes. Learn all about the icy continent via historical, geological and zoological exhibits, including videos of life on Scott Base, an aquarium of creatures gathered under the ice in McMurdo Sound, and an 'Antarctic Storm' chamber where you get a first-hand taste of -18°C wind chill (check at reception for 'storm' forecasts). The 15-minute **Hägglund Ride** (admission & ride adult/child/family $35/25/99) involves a zip around the centre's back blocks in an all-terrain vehicle. Visiting the centre is expensive, but worthwhile if you make the most of the Antarctic education on offer. You can reach it on the airport bus, as it's a short walk from the airport.

Science Alive!

Inside the city's old train station, **Science Alive!** (Map pp532-3; ☎ 03-365 5199; www.sciencealive .co.nz; 392 Moorhouse Ave; adult/child/family $10/7/25; ⏰ 10am-5pm) is crammed with ever-changing interactive exhibits – stuff with a scientific bent, from optical illusions to things that kiddies can push, pull and climb. There's even a glow-in-the-dark minigolf course, the **Black Hole** (entry plus minigolf adult/child/family $15/10/45). The city's free yellow Shuttle bus runs along Moorhouse Ave.

Wildlife Reserves

Orana Wildlife Park (☎ 03-359 7109; www.oranawild lifepark.co.nz; McLeans Island Rd; adult/child/family $16/ 6/38; ⏰ 10am-5pm) has an excellent walk-through native bird aviary, a nocturnal kiwi house, and a reptile exhibit featuring the wrinkly tuatara. But most of the grounds are devoted to Africana, including lions, rhinos, giraffes, zebras, lemurs, oryx and cheetahs. Animal feeding times are scheduled daily and there's a 'farmyard' area where children can pet the more domesticated animals.

Willowbank Wildlife Reserve (☎ 03-359 6226; www.willowbank.co.nz; Hussey Rd; adult/child/family $20/10/44; ⏰ 10am-dusk), about 6km north of the centre, is another good faunal reserve, with a focus on native NZ animals and hands-on enclosures that contain alpacas, wallabies and deer. Tours are held several times a day; evening Maori performances also take place here (see p535).

Gondola

The **gondola** (Map p530; ☎ 03-384 0700; www.gon dola.co.nz; 10 Bridle Path Rd; return adult/child/family $18/8/44; ⏰ 10am-9pm) takes 10 minutes to whisk you up from the Heathcote Valley terminal to the café-restaurant complex on Mt Cavendish (500m), which yields great views over Lyttelton Harbour and towards the Southern Alps. Paths lead to the Crater Rim Walkway, or you can take the gondola up and cycle down (see opposite). Lyttelton bus 28 travels here.

ACTIVITIES

The most popular activities around Christchurch are much gentler than the high-powered pursuits of places such as Wanaka and Queenstown. Punting down the Avon River is a good example, as are the inner-city walks and the trails further south at Lyttelton Harbour, plus the swimming off New Brighton and Sumner beaches. But there are a few up-tempo activities in the surrounding area too, such as skiing, sky-diving and jetboating the Waimakariri.

Boating

The photogenic green-and-white **Antigua Boatsheds** (Map pp532-3; ☎ 03-366 5885; www.boat sheds.co.nz; 2 Cambridge Tce; canoes per hr from $7, row-/paddleboats per 30 min $12/14; ⏰ from 9am) rents out) for independent Avon River exploration, and there's an appealing little café here too. Alternatively, the boatsheds are the starting point for **Punting in the Park** (☎ 03-366 0337; www.punting.co.nz; 30min trip adult/child $16.50/8; ⏰ 10am-dusk), where someone else does all the elbow work during a half-hour return trip in a flat-bottomed boat.

A similar experience is offered by **Punting on the Avon** (Map p532-3; [phone] 03-353 5994; [clock] 10am-4pm winter, 9am-dusk summer), leaving from the landing stage at the Worcester St bridge.

Cycling

City Cycle Hire ([phone] 03-339 4020; www.cyclehire-tours.co.nz; half/full day from $25/35) will deliver bikes to where you're staying; long-term rentals are available (one week from $140).

You can pedal downhill from the gondola terminal with the **Mountain Bike Adventure Company** ([phone] 03-339 4020; per ride $50. Price includes the gondola ride up the mountain; bookings are essential.

Outdoor Antics ([phone] 0800 692 584; outdoorantics@clear.net.nz; per day/week $55/280) offers mountain-bike rental (including delivery), or a day out mountain biking on purpose-built tracks in the Christchurch surrounds ($89, including pick-up and lunch).

See p539 for details of a two-wheeled guided tour around the city.

Walking

The visitor information centre has information on Christchurch walks. Within the city are the **Riverside Walk** and various historical strolls, while further afield is the excellent cliff-top walk to **Taylors Mistake** (2½ hours).

For great views of the city, take the walkway from the **Sign of the Takahe** (Map p530) on Dyers Pass Rd. The various 'Sign of the...' places in this area were originally roadhouses built during the Depression as rest stops. Now they vary from the impressive tearooms at the Sign of the Takahe to a simple shelter at the Sign of the Bellbird and are referred to primarily as landmarks. This walk leads up to the **Sign of the Kiwi** (Map p530) through Victoria Park and then along Summit Rd to Scotts Reserve, with several lookout points along the way.

You can walk to Lyttelton on the **Bridle Path** (1½ hours), which starts at Heathcote Valley (take bus 28). The **Godley Head Walkway** (two hours return) begins at Taylors Mistake, crossing and recrossing Summit Rd, and offers beautiful views on a clear day.

The **Crater Rim Walkway** (nine hours) around Lyttelton Harbour goes some 20km from Evans Pass to the Ahuriri Scenic Re-

---

WALKING TOUR

Start Cathedral Sq
Finish Cux de Lux
Distance About 4km
Duration Two hours to one day, depending on stops

Warm up by lapping **Cathedral Square** (1; p531), with a side trip into the Gothic ambience of **Christchurch Cathedral** (2; p531). Next, head north up Colombo St and turn right onto Gloucester St, then follow the restored tracks of the **Tramway** (3; p535) up pretty **New Regent Street** (4), full of pastel-coloured Spanish mission-style architecture.

Follow the tramline left down Armagh St, then turn right up Colombo St, and to your left is the greenery of **Victoria Square** (5). Head left down the path opposite Oxford Tce and cross the bridge over the gentle

---

serve. From the gondola terminal on Mt Cavendish, walk to **Cavendish Bluff Lookout** (30 minutes return) or the **Pioneer Women's Memorial** (one hour return).

Other Activities

Queen Elizabeth II Park (Map p530; [phone] 03-941 6849; www.qeiipark.org.nz; Travis Rd, New Brighton; pool adult/child/family $5/2/10; [clock] 6am-9pm Mon-Fri, 7am-8pm Sat & Sun) is a huge sports complex with indoor pools (including a wave pool), waterslides, a gym and squash courts; take bus 43. Closer to town is the **Centennial Leisure Centre** (Map pp532-3; [phone] 03-941 6853; www.centennial.org.nz; 181 Armagh St; adult/child/family $5/2/10; [clock] 6am-9pm Mon-Thu, 7am-7pm Fri-Sun), with a heated indoor pool.

The closest **beaches** to the city are Waimairi, North Beach, New Brighton and South Brighton; buses 5, 49 and 60 head here. Summer, to the city's southeast, is also popular (bus 3), while further east at Taylors Mistake are some good **surfing** breaks.

Several **skiing** areas lie within a two-hour drive of Christchurch (see p82). Other active options accessible from Christchurch include cruising on Lyttelton Harbour (p577), rafting on the Rangitata River (p558), tandem skydiving, tandem paragliding, hot-air ballooning, jetboating the Waimakariri River and horse trekking. Inquire at the visitor information centre, see also p539.

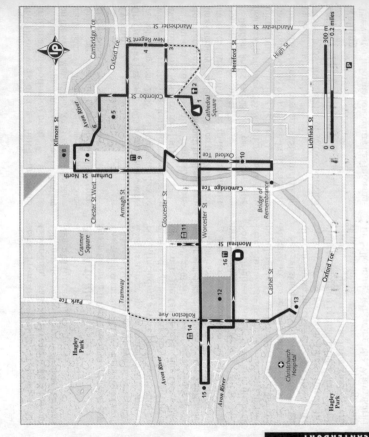

Avon River (6; p531) to smell the time at the **Floral Clock (7)**.

Ignore the looming ugliness of the Mayan temple-style **Crowne Plaza (8)** and turn left onto Durham St North. If you're in need of sustenance, pop into the riverside **Belgian Beer Café (9**; p553) for a pot of mussels or raspberry-flavoured beer. Rest break over, continue south along Durham St then turn left down Gloucester St and right along sociable **Oxford Terrace (10**; p551). Prowl the terrace to select a bar-restaurant for an evening of indulgence, then backtrack to Worcester St and head west, until you encounter the shining artistry of **Christchurch Art Gallery (11**; p536). The gallery, gift store and on-site wine bar make for fine distractions.

Continue west to the historic former-university confines of the **Arts Centre (12**; p534), with its inspired retail galleries, then turn left down Rolleston Ave to reach the candy-striped **Antigua Boatsheds (13**; p536), where a soporific punt down the Avon is on offer.

Head back to the corner of Rolleston Ave and Worcester St to the **Canterbury Museum**

(14; p535), then lose yourself in the **Botanic Gardens' (15**; p531) blooming beauty.

Now celebrate your high-stepping exploits by turning right on Rolleston Ave and then left on Hereford St to nab yourself an outdoor table at local favourite **Dux de Lux (16**; p553), the perfect place to while away the next few hours.

CHRISTCHURCH FOR CHILDREN

There's no shortage of kid-friendly sights and activities in Christchurch, some of them quite pricey but most with a low-level impact on your wallet. If family fun is a priority, consider planning your travels around NZ's biggest children's festival, **KidsFest** (www.kidsfest.org.nz). It's held in Christchurch every July, is aimed at under-12s and is chock-full of shows, workshops and parties.

For picnics and open-air frolicking, visit the **Botanic Gardens** (p531); there's a playground beside the café. Extend your nature-based experience with a **wildlife reserve** (p536) or a ride on the **gondola** (p536). At the engrossing **International Antarctic Centre** (p536), kids will love the storm chamber and the

Hägglund Ride. Educational and attention-getting factors are also high at the Discovery centre at **Canterbury Museum** (p535), and **Science Alive!** (p536); at the latter you can try your hand at minigolf on a glow-in-the-dark course.

If the weather's good and the kids are restless, head for the waterslides of **Queen Elizabeth II Park** (p537), or hit the **beaches** (p537) at Sumner or New Brighton.

TOURS

As the visitor information centre can inform you, numerous companies conduct tours of the city and will also trundle you out to nearby towns (Lyttelton, Akaroa) and sites further afield (Arthur's Pass, Hanmer Springs, the wineries of the Waipara).

Canterbury Leisure Tours (0800 484 485, 03-384 0999; www.leisuretours.co.nz; tours from $40) Offers a host of touring options in and around Christchurch. You can do everything from three-hour city tours to full-day Akaroa, Mt Cook, Arthur's Pass and Kaikoura outings (the day tours are fine if you're short on time, but otherwise try to spend longer in these fine places).

Canterbury Sightseeing (03-385 0982; www.christchurchsightseeing.co.nz) Offers a host of touring options in and around Christchurch. This company offers themed sightseeing tours around the region (mainly involving pleasuring one's palate), but also a new tour taking in Canterbury locations used in the filming of *The Chronicles of Narnia: The Lion, the Witch & the Wardrobe*.

Canterbury Vin de Pays (03-357 8262; www.vindepays.co.nz; tours from $65) Combines sightseeing with regional wine and cheese tasting, mainly around the outskirts of Christchurch and the Banks Peninsula but also offers a half-day reconnaissance of Waipara Valley wineries ($85).

Christchurch Bike Tours (03-366 0337; www.chchbiketours.co.nz; tours $25; 10am Nov-Mar) Pedal around the flat city on fun, informative, two-hour tours. Depart from visitor information centre.

Christchurch Personal Guiding Service (Map pp532-3; 03-379 9629; tours $10; tours 13am & 1pm Oct-Apr, 1pm May-Sep) Nonprofit organisation offering informative, two-hour city walks. Get tickets from the visitor information centre; tickets are also available from a red-and-black kiosk in the southeast of Cathedral Sq.

Christchurch Sightseeing Tours (0508 669 660, 03-366 9660; www.christchurchtours.co.nz; tours $35-39) Offers comprehensive half-day city tours year-round, a 3½-hour circuit of private gardens in spring and summer, and twice-weekly tours of heritage homes.

FESTIVALS & EVENTS

Check at the visitor information centre or online at www.bethere.org for a comprehensive listing of Christchurch's party-throwing. Some notable regular events:

December–March
SummerTimes (03-941 8999; www.summertimes.co.nz) Slip on your jandals and celebrate summer with a huge array of outdoor events (picnics, walks, theatre, brass bands and more).

January
World Buskers Festival (03-377 2365; www.worldbuskersfestival.com) National and international talent entertain the city streets for 10 days, concentrated around Cathedral Sq and the Arts Centre.

February
Flowers & Romance Festival (03-365 5403; www.festivalofflowers.co.nz) The city provides gardens in full bloom and a Valentine's Day dance, the romance is up to you.

May
Savour (03-377 0428; www.savournewzealand.com) A wicked weekend of waistline-expanding food and wine.

July
Christchurch Arts Festival (03-365 2223; www.artsfestival.co.nz) Biennial midwinter arts event (held in odd-numbered years).

November
NZ Cup & Show Week (03-941 8495; www.nzcup andshow.co.nz) Dominates the first half of November with major horse races such as the New Zealand Cup, 'fashion shows, fireworks and the centrepiece A&P Show (Agricultural & Pastoral Show; www.theshow.co.nz).

SLEEPING

Christchurch has a growing population of hostels, large and small, most of them within a 10-minute shuffle of Cathedral Sq. Several budget stalwarts are found around Latimer Sq, with some smaller, homelier options to the east of here. There are also several well-established options close to the foliage of the Botanic Gardens.

The city is overrun by motels, with their preferred habitats being Bealey Ave and Papanui Rd, north of the centre, and Riccarton Rd, west of town beyond Hagley Park. A number of top-end hotels are clustered on or around Cathedral Sq.

Christchurch is a little dearer than most regional areas so our prices fall into the following categories: budget – doubles (with or without bathroom) for under $100;

midrange – doubles (with bathroom) between $101 and $200; top end – over $201.

Budget

HOSTELS

There are approximately 25 hostels in Christchurch, so you shouldn't struggle to find a budget bed.

Stonehurst (Map pp532-3; ☎ 0508 786 633, 03-379 4620; www.stonehurst.co.nz; 241 Gloucester St; campervan sites per 2 people $26, dm $26, s from $60, d $70-90; P 🖳 🖭) This comprehensive complex has swallowed a city block. It's a well-managed, all-budget place where you can rent everything from a dorm bunk to a three-bedroom tourist flat (see p550). Then celebrate your arrival with a dip in the heated swimming pool or a drink and pizza at the bar. Decide in advance what you're after (eg don't get a poolside bunk room if you want peace and quiet) and book ahead at peak times.

Frauenreisehaus (Map pp532-3; ☎ 03-366 2585; jesse-sandra@quicksilver.net.nz; 272 Barbadoes St; dm/s/tw $23/35/56; 🖳) Sorry guys, this refreshing welcoming hostel is strictly women-only. It offers free bikes, free laundry, two well-equipped kitchens and the opportunity to plunder fresh herbs and spices from the garden. It's essential you reconfirm your booking before arrival.

Old Countryhouse (Map pp532-3; ☎ 03-381 5504; www.oldcountryhousenz.com; 437 Gloucester St; dm $21-23, d with/without bathroom $66/54; P 🖳) Well-loved for its cosiness and take-it-easy ambience, the Countryhouse has split itself into two separate villas featuring handmade timber furniture, reading lounge and lovely garden. It's a bit further out than other hostels, but still only 1km east of Latimer Sq; bus 21 stops opposite.

Foley Towers (Map pp532-3; ☎ 03-366 9720; www.backpack.co.nz/foley.html; 208 Kilmore St; dm $21-23, d with/without bathroom $58/52; P 🖳) Friendly Foley Towers provides lots of well-maintained rooms (some with bathroom) encircling quiet inner courtyards, and a warm welcome in dorms de-chilled by underfloor heating. It's a great spot to stay if you need a break from places specialising in mass off-the-bus arrivals.

Vagabond Backpackers (Map pp532-3; ☎ 03-379 9677; vagabondbackpackers@hotmail.com; 232 Worcester St; dm/s/d $20/34/50; P 🖳) Small, homely place reminiscent of a big share-house. There's an appealing garden that accentuates the

peaceful, unruffled air, and well-worn and comfy facilities. It's only a short walk from Cathedral Sq.

Chester Street Backpackers (Map pp532-3; ☎ 03-377 1897; chesterst@free.net.nz; 148 Chester St E; dm/d $23/50; 🖳) It has a suburban location but definitely not a suburban feel. Rather, this small and welcoming backpackers has an enticingly cosy atmosphere, and the barbecue set up in the boot of an old Anglia Deluxe is a nice touch.

Central City YHA (Map pp532-3; ☎ 03-379 9535; www.stayyha.com; 273 Manchester St; dm $27-30, d with/without bathroom $76/71; P 🖳) Comfortable bunks and beds, huge, spotless lounges and kitchens, a pool table and helpful staff are some of the characteristics of this well-equipped, efficiently run hostel. The notice boards are a font of information.

Base Backpackers (Map pp532-3; ☎ 0800 942 225, 03-300 9999; www.basebackpackers.com; 56 Cathedral Sq; dm $26-28, d with/without bathroom $80/60; 🖳) Slick, upbeat and busy hostel pitching itself to young travellers out for a good, social time (the name of the on-site bar, Saints & Sinners, should give you an idea of the market). It's in a prime location on Cathedral Sq, and offers a roll call of modern facilities, including plusher women-only dorms.

New Excelsior Backpackers (Map pp532-3; ☎ 0800 666 237, 03-366 7570; www.newexcelsior.co.nz; cnr Manchester & High Sts; dm $24-27, d with/without bathroom $70/57; 🖳) This revamped pub (which has a history as a hotel dating back to the 1880s) is a decent, central and well-equipped backpackers, with its own sports bar and great outdoor deck. It's well placed for restaurants and nightlife.

Dorset House (Map pp532-3; ☎ 03-366 8268; www.dorsethouse.co.nz; 1 Dorset St; dm/s/d from $25/50/60; P 🖳) Lovely 135-year-old weatherboard home with a grown-up atmosphere, large regal lounge with log fire, pool table and DVDs, and beds instead of bunks. It's only a short stroll from expansive parklands.

Coachman Backpackers (Map pp532-3; ☎ 0800 692 622, 03-377 0908; www.coachmanbackpackers.co.nz; 144 Gloucester St; dm/d $25/75; 🖳) Fresh-faced newcomer to the city, in a fine old central building with stained glass, timber panelling and a grand staircase. It's still establishing itself but has big potential. Most of the light-filled rooms come with private bathroom.

(Continued on page 549)

Nelson Lakes National Park (p471)

MARK PARKES

Abel Tasman National Park (p478)

MARK PARKES

Whale mural, Kaikoura (p454)

FERGUS BLAKISTON

Sea kayaking (p481), Abel Tasman National Park

DAVID WALL

542

GARETH MCCORMACK

Leslie-Karamea Track (p488), Kahurangi National Park, Nelson

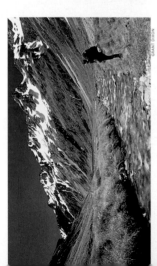

GRANT DIXON

Nelson Lakes National Park (p471)

MICHAEL GEBICKI

Sand dune, Farewell Spit (p486), Golden Bay

ANDERS BLOMQVIST

Sperm whale (p457), Kaikoura

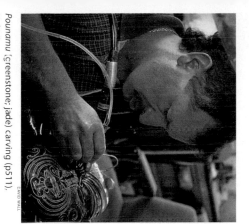

Pounamu ('greenstone; jade') carving (p511), Hokitika

DAVID WALL

Pancake Rocks (p500), Punakaiki, West Coast

JON DAVISON

Beech forest, Oparara Basin (p497), West Coast

OLIVER STREWE

Fox Glacier (p519), West Coast

OLIVER STREWE

International Antarctic Centre (p536),
Christchurch

DAVID WALL

Aoraki/Mt Cook National Park (p583)

FERGUS BLAKISTON

Chess game, Cathedral Square (p531), Christchurch

PETER BENNETTS

Christchurch's gondola (p536) to Mt Cavendish

DAVID WALL

St Clair Pool (p595), Dunedin

DAVID WALL

ower Stuart St, Dunedin (p590)

DAVID WALL

Taieri Gorge Railway (p593), near Dunedin

DAVID WALL

Te Kaihinaki boulders (p619), Moeraki, Otago

PAUL KENNEDY

River surfing (p627), Kawarau River, Queenstown

DAVID WALL

Treble Cone, near Wanaka (p646)

CHRISTIAN ASLUND

Autumn leaves, Lake Wanaka (p646)

OLIVER STREWE

The Luge (p629), Queenstown

DAVID WALL

SLOW DOWN

Jetboating (p625), Queerstown

RICHARD I'ANSON

Routeburn Track (p644), Mt Aspiring National Park

GRANT DIXON

Jetboating (p648), Wanaka

JOHN HAY

Bungy jumping (p625), Queenstown

CORINNE HUMPHREY

DAVID WALL

Matai Falls (p686), the Catlins

WES WALKER

Oban (p690), Stewart Island

CHRISTIAN ASLUND

Surfer and sea lion, Porpoise Bay (p684), the Catlins

CHRIS ME

Milford Sound (p666), Fiordland

(Continued from page 540)

Also recommended:

Rolleston House YHA (Map pp532-3; ☎ 03-366 6564; www.stayyha.com; 5 Worcester St; dm/d $27/66; P 🔲) Quiet, agreeable option with the Arts Centre and Botanic Gardens as neighbours.

Occidental Backpackers (Map pp532-3; ☎ 03-379 9234; www.occidental.co.nz; 208 Hereford St; dm $22-25, s/tw/d $45/55/60; P 🔲) Chief among the attractions here are free breakfast and $6 meals from the on-site bar.

CAMPING

If you want to be closer to the city than these options, Stonehurst (p540) offers powered campervan sites.

Meadow Park Top 10 Holiday Park (Map p530; ☎ 0800 396 323, 03-352 9176; www.meadowpark.co.nz; 39 Meadow St; sites per 2 people $33, cabins & units $58-113, motel $130; P 🔲 🔲) It's wall-to-wall campervars here, and accommodation with a roof ranges from old 'standard' cabins to motel units, with lots of options in-between. Also well equipped for leisure activities, with an indoor pool, spas, and games rooms and playground for the kids.

North South Holiday Park (☎ 0800 567 765, 03-359 5993; www.northsouth.co.nz; cnr Johns Rd/SH1 & Sawyers Arms Rd; unpowered/powered sites per 2 people $24/26, cabins & units $43-89; P 🔲) If you don't want to travel too far after picking up your campervan at the airport, consider driving here. The many facilities include a pool, sauna and playground. If you don't have your own transport, airport transfers can be arranged.

Midrange

GUESTHOUSES & B&BS

English Park Eco Accommodation (Map p530; ☎ 03-356 0228; www.englishpark.co.nz; 16 Sheppard Pl, St Albans; d $85-140) A first-rate B&B founded on ecologically sound principles, where the hospitable owners offer two modern guest rooms and varying levels of extras (you choose whether you want all the trimmings, according to your budget). Vegetarians, vegans and food intolerances catered for; dinner available by arrangement. It's directly north of the centre, next door to a park; take bus 14 or 16.

Orari B&B (Map pp532-3; ☎ 03-365 6569; www.orari.net.nz; 42 Gloucester St; r $160-198; P 🔲) Orari is a fine late-19th-century home that has been stylishly updated with light-filled, pastel-tored rooms, inviting guest areas and a

AUTHOR'S CHOICE

There's a laid-back village feel to the seaside suburb of Sumner, only 12km south-east of Christchurch and easily reached by bus 3 (one way $2.50). It makes for a wonderfully relaxing place to stay, especially in warmer weather. You can commute to Christchurch for sightseeing, or potter in the area's interesting stores and fine cafés. There's a supermarket here, cinema, and the beach almost at your doorstep.

Marine Bar & Backpackers (Map p530; ☎ 03-326 6609; www.themarine.co.nz; 26 Nayland St; dm/s/d $20/28/45, s/d with bathroom $40/55; P 🔲) A welcoming, social place with clean, comfy rooms, free breakfast and top-notch facilities. Try for a double that opens onto the large upstairs balcony. Downstairs is a bar with pool tables and sunny outdoor area.

Sumner Bay Motel & Apartments (Map p530; ☎ 0800 496 949, 03-326 5969; www.sumnermotel.co.nz; 26 Mariner St; d $138-188; P) Studios and one- and two-bedroom units are on offer at this sleek new development, all featuring balcony or courtyard, cooking facilities, polished floors and quality furnishings. The whole family is catered for: cots and toys are available, Sky TV and DVD players in units, bikes and surfboards available to rent, and a café out front.

front garden that is lovely in full bloom. Art connoisseurs note: it's right across the road from Christchurch Art Gallery.

In among the architectural mishmash of Armagh St are four character-filled old homes offering guesthouse accommodation, including the following:

Croydon House (Map pp532-3; ☎ 03-366 5111; www.croydon.co.nz; 63 Armagh St; d $140-180, apt from $220) Pretty as a picture with its flowerbeds and window boxes is this B&B in a charming 1920s building. Rooms have shared facilities or private bathroom; full cooked breakfast is included. The owner also rents out nearby self-contained apartments.

Windsor Hotel (Map pp532-3; ☎ 0800 366 1503, 03-366 1503; www.windsorhotel.co.nz; 52 Armagh St; s/d/tr/q $85/120/150/164; P 🔲) Another classic old abode, this one with several wings and around 40 sunny rooms is simple but exceedingly comfy. Note that all facilities here are shared (fluffy bathrobes provided); cooked breakfast is included.

HOTELS & APARTMENTS

Hotel off the Square (Map pp532-3; ☎ 0800 6338 4377, 03-374 9980; www.offthesquare.co.nz; 115 Worcester St; r $135-395; P ⬜) This recommended, 38-room boutique hotel provides a fabulous antidote to sterile business hotels and dated motels where every room's the same. No two rooms are alike (in either shape or décor), and the place radiates warmth with sensual colours and lots of original art, plants and comfy nooks.

Camelot Cathedral Square Hotel (Map pp532-3; ☎ 0800 258 858, 03-365 2898; www.thecamelot.co.nz; 66 Cathedral Sq; d $95-150; P) Camelot offers attractive rates for its rooms, considering its location is a mere pillow's toss from Christchurch Cathedral. The décor is nothing special but rooms are well equipped (Sky TV, fridge, kettle, iron, hairdryer); needless to say, try for a room with a view of the square.

Quest Christchurch (Map pp532-3; ☎ 0800 944 400, 03-964 6200; www.questchristchurch.co.nz; 113 Worcester St; d/q from $170/250; P) These brand-new serviced apartments are a shiny chink in the extensive Quest chain, just off Cathedral Square (with the tram running right next door). Studios are available, but it's worth opting for an apartment (one- or two-bedroom) with all the comforts of home, including full kitchen, living room and laundry facilities.

MOTELS

There is a mini motel 'alley' in Colombo St offering top-notch motels within walking distance of the heart of the city.

Stonehurst (Map pp532-3; ☎ 0508 786 633, 03-379 4620; www.stonehurst.co.nz; 241 Gloucester St; motel d $115-140, q $220, apt per week from $700; P ⬜ ⬛) The place to go for great deals on a variety of motel rooms (from studios to two-bedroom units) and fully self-contained flats sleeping up to six. The accommodation is central, modern and superbly equipped, staff members are exceedingly helpful, and reception is manned around the clock. It also has backpacking options; see p540.

Colombo in the City (Map pp532-3; ☎ 0800 265 662, 03-366 8775; www.motelcolombo.co.nz; 863 Colombo St; d $95-165; P) Has attractive near-new units luxuriously equipped (Sky TV, CD players, double glazing, spa baths). Don't fret if this place is booked out; it has a twin, under the same management, next door.

CentrePoint on Colombo (Map pp532-3; ☎ 0800 859 000, 03-377 0859; www.centrepointoncolombo.co.nz; 859 Colombo St; d $105-200; P) The sister establishment of Colombo in the City; it's the newer of the two and offers similarly stylish accommodation. Between them there are 24 units well suited for travellers on business or just touring. There are specially fitted rooms for wheelchair access.

City Centre Motel (Map pp532-3; ☎ 0800 240 101, 03-372 9294; www.citycentremotel.co.nz; 876 Colombo St; d from $95; P ⬜) Pretty flowerbeds soften the concrete here, and inside you'll find more high-standard motel accommodation in spacious, spotless units, all with kitchenette.

Airport Gateway Motor Lodge (☎ 0800 242 8392, 03-358 7093; www.airportgateway.co.nz; 45 Roydvale Ave; d/q from $135/175; P ⬜) One of a number of motels near the airport, handy for those early flights. Has a sizable arrangement of good-standard rooms and no lack of facilities.

Top End

George (Map pp532-3; ☎ 0800 100 220, 03-379 4560; www.thegeorge.com; 50 Park Tce; r from $400; P) The George's discreet finesse will impress. This boutique hotel, with 55 swanky rooms and suites, perches elegantly on the fringe of Christchurch's sweeping Hagley Park. Inside, staff will attend to your every need, the fine on-site restaurants will wine and dine you, and handsomely decorated rooms and suites will ensure a comfy night's sleep.

Heritage (Map pp532-3; ☎ 0800 368 888, 03-377 9722; www.heritagehotels.co.nz; 28-30 Cathedral Sq; d from $330; P ⬜ ⬛) The Heritage goes all out to impress with deluxe hotel rooms and plush self-contained suites installed in the restored innards of the adjacent Old Government Building. When you get tired of doing laps of your open-plan lounge, do laps of the heated pool instead.

Hambledon (Map pp532-3; ☎ 03-379 0723; www.hambledon.co.nz; 103 Bealey Ave; r from $250; P) Sumptuous antique-furnished heritage mansion with elegantly old-fashioned en suite rooms (some with four-poster beds) that will take your mind off modern-day worries. You can also rent out one of three garden-view cottages on the mansion's grounds.

Warners (Map pp532-3; ☎ 03-366 5159; www.warnershotel.co.nz; 50 Cathedral Sq; r $180-450; ⬜) This heritage hotel (established in 1863) has seen it all, no less the construction of the neighbouring cathedral. Warners' exceptional location, history and boutique size (23 rooms) keep it in distinguished company. Opt for a sumptuous corner suite for the best views in town of the Square.

EATING

Christchurch offers a pleasing variety of cuisines and eateries, and the quality is generally high. The largest concentration of cafés and restaurants is found along 'the Strip', the eastern side of Oxford Tce between Hereford and Cashel Sts. The common characteristics here are good vantage points, outdoor tables and seafood- and meat-enriched Mod-NZ dishes, not to mention the kind of intense rivalry that sees a fair bit of culinary innovation.

Restaurants

Cook 'n' with Gas (Map pp532-3; ☎ 03-377 9166; 23 Worcester St; mains $27-32; ☼ dinner Mon-Sat) A favourite of local foodies, this exuberant cottage restaurant serves up NZ produce with prize-winning flair and the help of a great wine (and beer) list. You can't go wrong with lamb or beef, though seafood dishes are equally tempting.

Dux de Lux (Map pp532-3; ☎ 03-366 6919; cnr Hereford & Montreal Sts; mains $16-24; ☼ lunch & dinner) We love the Dux. This vivacious place is a long-standing crowd favourite for its hearty veg and seafood menu, with veg-packed curries and Mediterranean pizza served up alongside local mussels or Cajun-flavoured calamari. It also scores highly for its outdoor courtyards, house-brewed beer and generally festive vibe.

Le Bon Bolli (Map pp532-3; ☎ 03-374 9444; cnr Worcester & Montreal Sts; mains $12-28; ☼ lunch & dinner) A French-leaning menu is served within this brasserie's inspired interior, with one room daubed with frescoes: upstairs is a more formal dining space (open for dinner, mains around $32). The Caesar salad here is excellent, as is the crème brûlée (even if they do say so themselves). You can stop by just for bubbly or coffee on the terrace as well.

Seafood Kitchen (Map pp532-3; ☎ 03-365 6543; 819 Colombo St; mains $25-35; ☼ dinner Tue-Sat) The small menu at this chic corner-store restaurant changes daily in order to present the freshest possible marine treats. You'll likely get to choose from sushi, shellfish, whole fish and other aquatic delights – choose a

local white wine to accompany and you've got yourself a memorable meal.

Mum's (Map pp532-3; ☎ 03-365 2211; cnr Colombo & Gloucester Sts; mains $10-18; ☼ lunch & dinner) Among Mum's happy diners is a steady stream of Japanese and Korean students, who surely appreciate the just-like-Mum-makes-at-home dishes and reasonable prices. Get a double hit of Asian flavours with options including sushi, sashimi and various noodle creations.

Indochine (Map pp532-3; ☎ 03-365 7323; 209 Cambridge Tce; meals $15-28; ☼ dinner Mon-Sat) Dripping in Sino-retro cool, Indochine makes for a gorgeous night out, and the hip Christchurch folk are flocking to the Asian-fusion dishes (available as dim sum for sharing, or all-to-yourself sizes) and fresh, interesting cocktails. The dim lighting, flocked wallpaper and lacquered screens create a rich, inviting interior.

Topkapi (Map pp532-3; ☎ 03-379 4447; 185 Manchester St; mains $10-23; ☼ lunch & dinner Mon-Sat) Grab yourself a cushioned, low-slung bench in the tapestry-draped interior and enjoy some great Turkish food, including a wide range of meat or veg kebabs and the all-important baklava finisher. The takeaway counter does brisk business.

Zydeco (Map pp532-3; ☎ 03-365 4556; 57 Victoria St; lunch $7-21, dinner mains $25-35; ☼ breakfast & lunch Mon-Fri, dinner nightly) For something a little different, Retour is an accomplished practitioner of modern NZ cooking. Eat your way through crab and crayfish ravioli, braised leg of wild hare or loin of venison.

Retour (Map pp532-3; ☎ 03-365 2888; Cambridge Tce; mains $27-33; ☼ dinner Tue-Sun) Raised splendidly above the banks of the Avon on a small, canopied rotunda, intimate Retour is an accomplished practitioner of modern NZ cooking. Eat your way through crab and crayfish ravioli, braised leg of wild hare or loin of venison.

Strawberry Fare (Map pp532-3; ☎ 03-365 4665; 114 Peterborough St; dinner mains $15-28; ☼ breakfast, lunch & dinner) Weight-watchers enter at your peril – this place has around 20 dessert options. It's a stylish daytime café that becomes a casual night-time restaurant, with a menu catering to all comers.

Tap Room (Map pp532-3; ☎ 03-365 0547; 124 Oxford Tce; dinner mains $20-33; ☼ breakfast, lunch & dinner) An accomplished member of the Oxford

Tce clan – a mixture of historic building (with industrial embellishments), upmarket café-restaurant and outdoor area where punters down Monteith's beer and dine out on pizzas, Canterbury lamb rack and an assortment of seafood dishes.

Sticky Fingers (Map pp532-3; ☎ 03-366 6451; Clarendon Towers, Oxford Tce; mains $15-30; ☺ breakfast, lunch & dinner) Carnivores can go crazy here on aged beef fillet, twice-cooked duck or on numerous pizzas and pastas. Follow your main course with 'Love Handles' (kiwi fruit pavlova with hokey pokey ice cream) for a slice of sweet kiwiana.

Two Fat Indians (Map pp532-3; ☎ 03-371 7273; 112-114 Manchester St; mains $15-20; ☺ dinner) Attracting backpackers and locals alike, this polished twin-room eatery lives by the tagline 'The art of pint and curry'. The extensive menu will please both carnivores and vegetarians, and includes *palak kofta* (spinach dumplings) and a reliable chicken tikka masala, all with matching beer recommendations.

Cafés

Vivace Espresso (Map pp532-3; ☎ 03-365 8248; 86 Hereford St; meals $5-16; ☺ breakfast & lunch) Long narrow space doling out seriously good coffee to loyal locals. Also serves hearty all-day breakfasts (how about crumpets with vanilla hazelnut honey?) and interesting lunch options.

Mainstreet Café (Map pp532-3; ☎ 03-365 0421; 840 Colombo St; meals $7-14; ☺ breakfast & lunch daily, dinner Tue-Sat) This bright, art-filled, upstairs-downstairs affair serves vegan and veg food with panache – cafeteria-style during the day, à la carte of an evening. It's good for breakfast with the works, a plate of wholesome salads or kumara balls (the house speciality) after a late night.

Savoy Brown (Map pp532-3; ☎ 03-365 7262; 143 High St; meals $5-16; ☺ breakfast & lunch) One of many fine, laid-back cafés on High St, in among the cool shops and galleries – well worth a wander. Excellent coffee, bumper brekkies and homemade cakes are a feature; peak hour is weekend brunchtime.

Java Coffee House (Map pp532-3; ☎ 03-366 0195; cnr High & Lichfield Sts; meals $5-15; ☺ breakfast & lunch) Funky, paint-splattered place with groovin' music, hungover staff and leaflets for upcoming dance events. It's a good place for a late-morning serve of eggs any way you like

them, and you can get your latte or chai tea in a cup or bowl. Open until late on Friday and Saturday.

Caffe Roma (Map pp532-3; ☎ 03-379 3879; 176 Oxford Tce; mains $9-19; ☺ breakfast & lunch) This European-style café has a refined persona – the kind of place you'd take your parents for brunch. The generously proportioned breakfasts include homemade muesli, lamb kidneys or corn fritters with bacon, avocado and eggs. It's not too grown-up, however – tea and coffee come with a chocolate fish.

Daily Grind (Map pp532-3; meals under $11; ☺ breakfast & lunch) City (☎ 03-377 4959; cnr New Regent & Armagh Sts); The Strip (☎ 03-377 6288; Worcester St & Oxford Tce) The perfect refuelling stop while out sightseeing, and in a number of city locations. Provides express delivery of coffee, juices and smoothies, plus fat bagels and rolls, salads and muffins.

Lotus Heart (Map pp532-3; ☎ 03-379 0324; 595 Colombo St; mains $7-13; ☺ breakfast & lunch Mon-Fri, dinner Fri, lunch Sat & Sun) Meditative meat-free eatery, where Buddhist chanting or ethereal melodies may accompany your red-lentil dhal, vege burger or Mexican red-bean chilli. Also has organic coffee, fresh juices and smoothies.

Quick Eats

A variety of food stalls set themselves up daily in Cathedral Sq, or you can accost one of the many food vans selling everything from Lebanese to Thai at the Arts Centre market (p534).

City Fish & Chips (Map pp532-3; ☎ 03-377 4483; 265 Manchester St; meals from $3; ☺ lunch & dinner) Handily situated for YHA-goers and offering the cheapest feed ($3 fush and chups) in town.

Matsu Sushi (Map pp532-3; ☎ 03-365 3822; 105 Armagh St; meals $5-8; ☺ lunch Mon-Fri) This no-frills little Japanese eatery doles out a sushi lunch box for $5, plus bargain-basement noodle soups and other hot dishes.

Copenhagen Bakery & Café (Map pp532-3; ☎ 03-379 3935; PricewaterhouseCoopers Centre, 119 Armagh St; ☺ breakfast & lunch) Snaffle some award-winning tarts, quiches, cakes and breads here, together with cheerful, old-fashioned service.

East in the City (Map pp532-3; ☎ 03-365 0168; 266 High St; ☺ lunch & dinner) Overlook the grungy interior and appreciate this place for what it is – a barnlike Asian food court where you can get your fix of cheap *pad Thai*, dim sum or *gado gado* from one of the 10 or so food outlets.

Self-Catering

Self-caterers should head to the large **Pak N Save supermarket** (Map pp532-3; 297 Moorhouse Ave; 8am-10pm) or the **New World supermarket** (Map pp532-3; South City Centre, Colombo St; 8am-8pm Mon-Wed, to 9pm Th-Fri, to 7pm Sat & Sun).

DRINKING

The chameleonic nature of the city's eating and drinking scene sees numerous restaurants and cafés packing away their dinner menus later in the evening and distributing cocktail, wine and beer lists. Predictably, the fashionable Oxford Tce is a prime area for after-dark bar-hopping, but there are plenty of other places.

Dux de Lux (Map pp532-3; 03-366 6919; cnr Hereford & Montreal Sts) You could easily settle in for a long, sunny afternoon drinking session at this Christchurch institution, sampling its home-brews. And you could feel somewhat virtuous too, as all meals are 'vegaquarian' (ie vegetarian and seafood, see p551). There's often live music; if you want to get away from the rabble, there's a lounge bar upstairs.

Belgian Beer Café (Map pp532-3; 03-377 1007; 88 Armagh St) Are Belgian beer cafés the new Irish pub? They seem to be springing up everywhere, with the cosy wood-heavy interiors, pots of mussels and fabulous array of beers. This is a fine example of the genre, with a suitably old-world exterior and a good-looking beer menu you'd be happy to work through.

Twisted Hop (Map pp532-3; Poplar St, Lichfield Lanes) In a revitalised part of town, two Englishmen have set up a 'real ale brewpub', where the beer is brewed in the traditional English manner. There are home-brews, including the wonderfully named Twisted Anke, plus a huge range of microbrewed beers from NZ and abroad. Good food too, including a kids menu. Brewery tours and tastings available.

Holy Grail (Map pp532-3; 03-365 9816; 88 Worcester St) Set in a converted Art Deco theatre, the Holy Grail is a multilevel complex that includes a 10m screen with its own set of padded bleachers, pool tables, balcony bars and a minimalist dance floor. Caters mainly to sport-lovers but there are also DJs most nights.

Bailies Irish Bar (Map pp532-3; 03-366 5159; 50 Cathedral sq) Convivial pub at Warners hotel (p550) with lovely large beer garden, pool tables, big-screen TVs, cheap food (particularly at lunchtime), a trivia night on Tuesday and live music later in the week.

Jolly Poacher (Map pp532-3; 03-379 5635; 31 Victoria St; noon-dawn) Keeps dangerously long hours and so what starts off as a casual lunch could become a gruelling liquid marathon. There may be some consolation in knowing that beer-sopping food is always available.

Indochine (Map pp532-3; 03-365 7323; 209 Cambridge Terrace; Mon-Sat) If you can't get a dinner reservation at this city hot spot (p551), drop in for one of the enticing cocktails. The signature drink, 'Kingofsnake', is vodka based, with fresh ginger, palm sugar, chilli, lemon and honey – full of bite.

Minx (Map pp532-3; 03-374 9944; 96 Lichfield St) Newly opened in 2005, this sleek minimalist restaurant continues to win praise from industry types, while the basement Rootes bar makes the most of its underground outlook. Prop on a neonlit cube, sip a cocktail and admire the commissioned graffiti in the car park.

Foam Bar (Map pp532-3; 03-365 2926; 30 Bedford Row; Wed-Sat) Sophisticated little back-alley bar, worth seeking out for its chilled-out crowd, art-bedecked walls and DJ-spun tunes. There's also the occasional live band, usually on Thursday night.

Le Plonk (Map pp532-3; 03-377 7724; 211 Manchester St; Mon-Sat) A cutely named wine bar, offering a grand selection of NZ tipples, lush leather lounges to sink into and regular live jazz. Very smooth.

Loaded Hog (Map pp532-3; 03-366 6674; cnr Manchester & Cashel Sts) Popular place with brewery equipment strewn along the walls (in testimony to its naturally brewed beers) and a fondness for major sports events, DJs, cover bands and, rather strangely, salsa nights (every Thursday).

The intersection of Manchester and Cashel Sts is fertile hunting ground for barrilike drinking-dancing dens, including **Shooters** (Map pp532-3; 03-365 1046; cnr Manchester & Cashel Sts; Tue-Sat), with pool tables, karaoke and DJs, and the **Grumpy Mole** (Map pp532-3; 03-371 9301; cnr Manchester & Cashel Sts; Mon-Sat), unapologetically hewn from all manner of Wild West kitsch.

There are numerous establishments on Oxford Tce that swap the knives and forks for wine glasses and beer goggles once mealtime is over, including **Coyote** (Map pp532-3; ☎ 03-366 6055; 126 Oxford Tce), ostensibly a Tex-Mex eatery but with well-established bar credentials with younger night owls; **Viaduct** (Map pp532-3; ☎ 03-366 6055; 126 Oxford Tce), popular for its food and bar service; and **Tap Room** (Map pp532-3; ☎ 03-365 0547; 124 Oxford Tce), where the long-lunch and after-work crowds like to hang out.

ENTERTAINMENT

Christchurch's vigorous bar-club scene is centred on Lichfield St (usually from 10pm Wednesday to Saturday), while many Oxford Tce restaurants transform into late-night watering holes with DJs and impromptu dance floors. Nightclub admission ranges from free to $10, though big-name DJ events can cost upwards of $20; live music in pubs, bars and cafés is mostly free. For information on clubbing events and live gigs, get the free fortnightly leaflet *JAGG* (www.jagg.co.nz) available from Java Coffee House (see p552) and other nightlife-conscious cafés, shops and venues. Also check out entertainment listings in the *Press* newspaper.

Christchurch is the hub of the South Island's performing-arts scene, with several excellent theatres; the major ticketing company is **Ticketek** (☎ 03-377 8899; www.ticketek.co.nz), with an outlet inside the Town Hall.

Performing Arts

Town Hall (Map pp532-3; ☎ 03-377 8899; www.convention.co.nz/information-whats-happening.html; 86 Kilmore St) The riverside town hall and its two main spaces (the Auditorium and the James Hay Theatre) are the main venues for local performing arts, where you can hear a chamber or symphony orchestra, choirs and bands, or catch some theatre and the odd visiting hypnotist.

Isaac Theatre Royal (Map pp532-3; ☎ 0800 205 050, 03-371 9452; 145 Gloucester St) Another stalwart of the local scene, where the Royal New Zealand Ballet might stage *The Nutcracker* before being upstaged the Canterbury Opera doing *La Traviata*.

Court Theatre (Map pp532-3; ☎ 0800 333 100, 03-963 0870; www.courttheatre.org.nz; 20 Worcester St) Found within the Arts Centre, the Court Theatre hosts year-round performances of

everything from Samuel Beckett to Shakespeare. The resident Court Jesters troupe stages its long-running improvised comedy show, *Scared Scriptless*, every Friday night at 11pm ($15).

Cinemas

Show times for movies are listed in the local newspapers. Adult tickets cost around $14, children $8, and most cinemas have a cheap day early in the week.

Arts Centre Cinemas (Map pp532-3; ☎ 03-366 0167; www.artfilms.co.nz; Arts Centre, Worcester St) Comprises two venues (the Academy and Cloisters) and, appropriately enough, they show art-house films.

Hoyts Moorhouse (Map pp532-3; ☎ 03-366 6367; www.hoyts.co.nz; 392 Moorhouse Ave) Screens the latest Hollywood blockbusters.

Regent on Worcester (Map pp532-3; ☎ 03-366 0140; www.hoyts.co.nz; 94 Worcester St) This classic old cinema favours middling films: not quite art house, but not blockbusters either.

Live Music

See listings under Drinking, p553, for pubs and bars offering regular live music.

Dux de Lux (Map pp532-3; ☎ 03-366 6919; www.thedux.co.nz; cnr Hereford & Montreal Sts) Invites ska, reggae, rock, pop and dub artists to cater to crowds at least four nights a week. It's also one of the city's busiest watering holes, particularly on a sunny day when the outdoor areas are a mass of raised glasses. See also p551.

Sammy's Jazz Review (Map pp532-3; ☎ 03-377 8618; www.sammys.co.nz; 14 Bedford Row; admission free; ☺ Tue-Sat) This great, brick-walled, wooden-floored jazz den is patronised by notable local singers and also accommodates the odd funk outfit. When the weather allows it, retreat to the outdoor courtyard for some alfresco listening. There may be an admission charge for big-name acts.

Southern Blues Bar (Map pp532-3; ☎ 03-365 1654; 198 Madras St; admission free) This divey blues bar has nightly gigs (starting around 10.30pm) and a dance floor for aficionados of good blues music. It pulls a mixed, loquacious crowd of musicians, office workers and the terminally fashionable.

Nightclubs

eye spy (Map pp532-3; ☎ 03-355 6500; 56 Lichfield St; ☺ from 8pm Wed-Sat) One of the better bar-club hybrids on the Lichfield St clubbing strip, infused with a chilled-out orange glow, cute little seats at the back and funky DJ sounds from around 11pm. Good place for early-evening cocktail slurping.

Base (Map pp532-3; ☎ 03-377 7149; www.thebase .co.nz; 92 Struthers Lane; ⏰ from 9pm Thu-Sat) Down a slightly s>edy side alley, as all good nightclubs should be (head down the alley next to Minx, p553, then turn right). Specialises in drum 'n' bass, house and trance nights, with some nights seeing up to half-a-dozen DJs sharing the turntables.

Ministry/Propaganda (Map pp532-3; ☎ 03-379 2910; 90 Lichfield St) Another long-standing favourite. Two venues in one big space, with all-star DJs often in attendance.

Sport

Jade Stadium (Map pp532-3; ☎ 0800 523 378, tickets 03-377 8899; www.jadestadium.co.nz; 30 Stevens St) This stadium has been known to host cricket internationals, but it's best known as Canterbury's rugby heartland, where you can see the Crusaders in action in the Super 14 competition.

Casino

Christchurch Casino (Map pp532-3; ☎ 03-365 9999; www.christchurchcasino.co.nz; 30 Victoria St; ⏰ 24hr) The country's oldest casino is actually only 12 years old, but has quickly come to grips with the rewards of round-the-clock gambling. Dress code is smart and neat; visitors must be aged 20 or over.

SHOPPING

Colombo St, High St and Cashel St (including its pedestrianised mall) are all crammed with cash- and credit-card-hungry places. If you've had your fill of woolly jerseys and assorted sheepskin/greenstone souvenirs and want to spend your dollars on something a bit funkier, head to High St (between Lichfield and St Asaph Sts) – this is where the creative output of young NZ designers is on display, in among galleries and great cafés. For a wider range of arts and crafts, visit the Arts Centre and the shops in the city's art galleries. A handy guide to retailers is the *Free Guide to Christchurch Fashion*, available from the visitor information centre.

Arts Centre (Map pp532-3; ☎ 03-363 2836; www .artscentre.org.nz; 2 Worcester St) This has dozens of craft shops and art galleries selling pottery, jewellery, woollen goods, Maori carvings, handmade toys and more; in some cases you can see the craftspeople at work.

Arts Centre market (Map pp532-3; ⏰ 10am-4pm Sat & Sun) Every weekend the Arts Centre also has a lively craft and produce market.

Untouched World (Map pp532-3; ☎ 03-962 6551; www.untouchedworld.com; 301 Montreal St) At the Arts Centre you can buy into the concept of this classy 'lifestyle store', where customers can procure quality NZ-made clothing and plant-extract skin care. Clothes may be made of 'mountainsilk' (machine-washable fine merino wool) or 'merinomink' (a blend of merino wool and possum fur). There's another, larger store with on-site restaurant and garden at 155 Roydvale Ave, near the airport.

Ballantynes (Map pp532-3; ☎ 03-379 7400; cnr Colombo St & City Mall) Venerable Christchurch department store with a respectful hushed atmosphere, selling everything from men's and women's fashions to cosmetics, travel goods and speciality NZ gifts.

For stores selling camping gear, hiking boots and other outdoors equipment, head to the intersection of Colombo and Lichfield Sts. **Snowgum** (Map pp532-3; ☎ 03-365 4336; 537 Colombo St) or **Mountain Designs** (Map pp532-3; ☎ 03-377 8522; 554 Colombo St) should stock what you need.

GETTING THERE & AWAY

Air

Christchurch airport (☎ 03-358 5029; www.christchurchairport.co.nz) is the main international gateway to the South Island; for details of international flights and the carriers which provide them, see p722. The airport has excellent facilities, including currency-exchange outlets, ATMs, baggage storage, car-rental desks, cafés and shops, plus travel and information centres (☎ 03-353 7774) in both the domestic terminal (open 6.30am until the last domestic flight arrives) and the international terminal (open for all international flight arrivals). Departure tax on international flights is adult/child $25/10.

Prices listed here are for one-way flights. ..n conjunction with small affiliated airlines under the collective banner of Air New Zealand Link, **Air New Zealand** (Map pp532-3; ☎ 0800 737 000, 03-363 0600; www.airnz.co.nz; 54 Colombo St) also offers numerous direct domestic flights with connections to other centres. There are direct flights to and from Auckland (from $110, 20 flights per day), Blenheim (from $105, three daily), Dunedin (from $85, nine daily), Hokitika (from $75, four daily), Invercargill (from $95, seven daily), Nelson (from $85, eight daily), Queenstown (from $100, six daily), Wanaka (from $115, one daily) and Wellington (from $85, 12 daily).

Qantas (Map pp532-3; ☎ 0800 808 767; www.qantas.co.nz; Price Waterhouse Centre, 119 Armagh St) offers direct flights to Auckland (from $110, eight daily), Queenstown (from $100, two daily), Rotorua (from $130, one daily) and Wellington (from $85, two daily).

Origin Pacific (☎ 0800 302 302; www.originpacific.co.nz) has direct flights to its hub at Nelson (from $85, four daily), with connections to a number of North Island cities. It also offers one or two direct flights a day to Wellington (from $85).

Bus

InterCity (☎ 03-365 1113; www.intercitycoach.co.nz; Worcester St; ☉7am-5.15pm Mon-Sat to 5.30pm Sun) buses depart from Worcester St, between the cathedral and Manchester St. Northbound buses go twice daily to Kaikoura ($27, 2¾ hours), Blenheim ($49, five hours) and Picton ($50, 5½ hours), with connections to Nelson ($69, eight hours). One daily bus also goes southwest to Queenstown direct ($65, 7½ hours), or to Queenstown ($148, 10½ hours) with a sightseeing stop in Mt Cook ($79, 5½ hours); there are also services to Wanaka ($62, seven hours) that involve a change in Tarras. Heading south, two buses run daily along the coast via the towns along SH1 to Dunedin ($45, 5¾ hours), with connections to Invercargill ($66, 9¾ hours) and Te Anau ($74, 10½ hours).

Myriad shuttle buses run to destinations such as Akaroa, Arthur's Pass, Dunedin, Greymouth, Hanmer Springs, Picton, Queenstown, Wanaka, Westport and points in-between, most of them bookable at the visitor information centre; see the sections on the respective towns for details.

For information on backpacker buses rumbling through Christchurch, see p729.

Train

Christchurch railway station (Map p530; ☎ 0800 872 467, 03-341 2588; Troup Dr, Addington; ☉ ticket office

6.30am-3.30pm Mon-Fri, to 3pm Sat & Sun) is serviced by a free shuttle that picks up from various accommodation; ring the visitor information centre to request pick-up.

The *TranzCoastal* runs daily each way between Christchurch and Picton via Kaikoura at 7am and arriving at Picton at 12.13pm; the standard adult one-way fare to Picton is $89, but discounted fares can be as low as $40.

The *TranzAlpine* runs daily between Christchurch and Greymouth via Arthur's Pass (see p508); the standard adult one-way fare is $116, but you may be able to get a fare as low as $55.

For more information on both these services and the various fares available, contact **Tranz Scenic** (☎ 0800 872 467; www.tranzscenic.co.nz).

GETTING AROUND
To/From the Airport

The airport is 12km from the city centre.

Super Shuttle (☎ 0800 748 885; www.supershuttle.co.nz) is one of several airport shuttles operating 24 hours and charging around $15 for one person between the city and the airport, plus $5 for each additional person in the one travel party. The cost is reduced for two or more people travelling together. Shuttles meet all arriving flights.

The airport is also serviced by public bus, the **City Flyer** (☎ 03-366 8855; www.redbus.co.nz/flyer.htm; adult/child $7/4), which runs from Cathedral Sq between 6am and 11pm Monday to Friday and 7.30am to 10.30pm Saturday and Sunday (from the airport 35 minutes later); it departs every 20 to 30 minutes up to 5pm or 6pm, then every hour. Note that there is a daily 12.55am bus meeting flights and running into town.

A taxi between the city centre and airport costs around $30.

Car & Motorcycle
HIRE

Major car- and campervan-rental companies all have offices in Christchurch, as do numerous smaller local companies; see the lengthy list in the *Yellow Pages*. Operators with national networks often want cars to be returned from Christchurch to Auckland because most renters travel in the opposite direction, so special rates may apply on this northbound route. For reliable national rental companies, see p733.

DRIVING IN CHRISTCHURCH

For drivers, Christchurch's network of one-way streets can create confusion, particularly for those whose sense of direction deserts them once they leave their own driveway. Be sure to equip yourself with a decent map. If you want to avoid the metered parking or car parks of the inner-city streets, check out the all-day parking a half-dozen blocks out of the centre (eg east of Latimer Sq).

Some smaller-scale rental companies:

Ace Rental Cars (Map pp532–3; ☎ 0800 202 029, 03-366 3222; www.acerentalcars.co.nz; 237 Lichfield St)

First Choice (Map pp532–3; ☎ 0800 736 822, 03-365 9261; www.firstchoice.co.nz; 132 Kilmore St)

New Zealand Motorcycle Rentals & Tours (Map pp532–3; ☎ 03-377 0663; www.nzbike.com; 166 Gloucester St) Also does guided motorbike tours; see p734.

Omega Rental Cars (Map pp532–3; ☎ 0800 112 121, 03-377 4558; www.omegarental.com; 227 Durham St S)

Pegasus Rental Cars (Map pp532–3; ☎ 0800 354 506, 03-365 1100; www.rentalcars.co.nz; 127 Peterborough St)

PURCHASE

If you want to buy or sell a car there are a few options, but be sure to do your homework and ask the right questions; Lonely Planet regularly receives letters from readers complaining of shonky practices from car sellers. Check out **Backpackers Car Market** (Map pp532–3; ☎ 03-377 3177; www.backpackerscarmarket.co.nz; 33 Battersea St), or the weekly **Canterbury Car Fair** (Map p530; 🕑 9am–noon Sun) held at Addington Raceway; sellers fee is $20. **Turners Auctions** (Map p530; ☎ 03-343 9850; www.turners.co.nz; 15 Lester La) buys and sells used cars by auction; vehicles priced under $6000 usually go under the hammer (metaphorically) at 6pm on Tuesday and Thursday.

Public Transport

The Christchurch **bus network** (Metro; ☎ 03-366 8855; www.metroinfo.org.nz; 🕑 6.30am–10.30pm Mon-Sat, 9am–9pm Sun) is inexpensive and efficient. Most buses run from the **City Bus Exchange** (also known as 'The Crossing'; Map pp532–3), with its pedestrian entrance on Colombo St opposite Ballantynes department store. The exchange has an information desk here; alternatively, get timetables

from the visitor information centre. A cash fare to anywhere in the city proper costs $2.50. Metrocards allow two-hour/full-day travel for $1.90/3.80, but the catch is that the cards must be loaded up with a minimum of $10 before you can use them.

For information on the following two services, contact **Red Bus** (☎ 0800 733 287; www .redbus.co.nz). The big yellow **Shuttle** (fare free; 🕑 7.30am–10.30pm Mon-Fri, 8am–10.30pm Sat, 10am–8pm Sun) is an inner-city service (as far north as Peterborough St, south to Moorhouse Ave) with about 20 pick-up points. The **After Midnight Express** (fare $5; 🕑 hourly midnight–4am Sat & Sun) operates on five suburban routes, most of them departing Oxford Tce.

The **Best Attractions Shuttle** (☎ 0800 484 485, 03-384 0099; 24-hr pass adult/child $15/10) links major attractions such as the International Antarctic Centre, the gondola and Willowbank Wildlife Reserve. It departs Cathedral Sq every ½ to two hours daily.

Taxi

Christchurch's main taxi companies:

Blue Star (☎ 0800 379 979)

First Direct (☎ 0800 505 555)

Gold Band (☎ 0800 379 5795)

AROUND CHRISTCHURCH

LYTTELTON
pop 3100

Southeast of Christchurch are the prominent Port Hills, which slope down to the city's port, Lyttelton Harbour. Christchurch's first European settlers landed here in 1850 to embark on their historic trek over the hills, and this is where you'll find the port of Lyttelton, only 12km from Christchurch. It's popular with weekend day-trippers because of its scenic setting, attractive old buildings and eclectic café-bars.

The helpful **Lyttelton visitor information centre** (☎ 03-328 9093; lyttinfo@ihg.co.nz; 20 Oxford St; 🕑 9am–5pm) has numerous leaflets on the town and surrounding area. Online information is at www.lyttelharbour.co.nz.

Sights

You can drive straight to Lyttelton via a **road tunnel**, an impressive piece of engineering with gleaming tiles reminiscent of a huge, elongated public toilet. But there's a much more scenic (and 10km longer) route along the narrow **Summit Road**, which has some breathtaking city, hill and harbour views, as well as vistas of the Southern Alps; see the *Lyttelton Port Hills Drive* pamphlet ($1).

Lyttelton Museum (☎ 03-328 8972; Gladstone Quay; admission by donation; ☼ 2-4pm Tue, Thu, Sat & Sun) has interesting maritime exhibits such as wreck-recovered artefacts and ship models (there's a 6ft version of the *Queen Mary*), plus Lyttelton historical paraphernalia such as a 19th-century pipe organ and an Antarctic gallery (both Scott and Shackleton used the port as a base).

The neogothic **Timeball Station** (☎ 03-328 7311; www.timeball.co.nz; 2 Reserve Tce; adult/child $7/2; ☼ 10am-5.30pm daily Oct-Apr, 10am-5.30pm Wed-Sun May-Sep), built in 1876, was where (for 58 years) a huge time ball was hoisted on a mast and then dropped at exactly 1pm, Greenwich Mean Time, allowing ships in the harbour to set their clocks and thereby accurately calculate longitude; the time ball is still dropped at 1pm on days when the station is open. Be aware that access requires a short, steep climb.

Tours

Black Cat (☎ 0800 436 574, 03-328 9078; www.blackcat .co.nz; 17 Norwich Quay; cruises adult/child $49/20; ☼ tour 1.30pm) operates two-hour 'Christchurch Wildlife Cruises' on Lyttelton Harbour, where you may (but may not) see rare Hector's dolphins, blue penguins and various seabirds. It operates free shuttle buses from Christchurch for tour participants.

Sleeping & Eating

Pubs down by the waterfront have a rough-around-the-edges charm and usually serve meat-heavy meals alongside plenty of beer. Most also have budget rooms available. There are a few B&Bs sprinkled around town and the surrounding hills; the visitor information centre can help with bookings.

Tunnel Vision Backpackers (☎ 03-328 7576; www .tunnelvision.co.nz; 44 London St; dm/tw/d $20/50/60) New owners recently took over this cheery, family-friendly place and it will now be open year-round. The inviting old former hotel has a colourful interior, filled with standard-issue bunks and beds and lots of plants, and there's a small deck off the kitchen.

Empire Hotel (☎ 03-328 8202; empire.hotel@clear .net.nz; 9 London St; r $50) On the main street this hotel has decent refurbished rooms (shared facilities) and a small, classy, downstairs bar.

Dockside Accommodation (☎ 03-328 7344; dock side@xtra.co.nz; 22 Sumner Rd; apt $80-100) Two homely self-contained apartments that each sleep up to four. They're a short, easy walk from town, or you can stay put and enjoy the harbour views from your private deck. A real bargain.

Volcano Cafe (☎ 03-328 7077; 42 London St; mains $20-28; ☼ dinner) Within popular Volcano's blinding yellow walls is a friendly, festive, Laminex-heavy café serving seafood risotto, enchiladas and variable but consistently delicious curries and pastas. The attached Lava Bar (see below) has a bar menu of cheaper options.

Satchmo (☎ 03-328 8348; 8 London St; mains $10-29; ☼ lunch & dinner) Mellow little place with small alcoves and a great leafy courtyard. Does a good trade in meaty meals and gourmet pizzas dedicated to music icons such as Billie Holiday, Ella Fitzgerald and Satchmo himself: Louis Armstrong. Stop by for live music on a lazy Sunday afternoon (not in winter), or for the Monday-night jam session.

Drinking & Entertainment

Wunderbar (☎ 03-328 8818; www.wunderbar.co.nz; 19 London St; ☼ 1pm-late) Head down the laneway off London St, walk behind the supermarket, clamber up the stairway and enter this decidedly uplifting place. Have a drink on the balcony, nurture a glass in a red-velvet booth surrounded by dolls heads, or have an eventful time in the fabulously eccentric upholstered backroom, which hosts everything from discos to trannie shows and live music.

Lava Bar (☎ 03-328 7077; 42 London St) Adjoining Volcano Cafe (naturally) and open for sociable boozing and snacking) nightly. Has an outdoor terrace and is crammed with quirky artistic touches, which seem less quirky the more you drink.

Harbour Light (☎ 03-3288615; www.harbourlight.co .nz; 24 London St) This wonderful old theatre (built in 1916) plays host to live music, mostly touring artists and one-off concert events, with a preference for jazz, Celtic and world music. Check the website for what's on – usually there's entertainment one or two nights a week. Ticket prices vary but normally range from $10 to $20. On show nights, there's a bar here and food is served.

Getting There & Away

Bus 28 runs regularly from Christchurch to Lyttelton. From Lyttelton by car you can continue around Lyttelton Harbour and eventually on to Akaroa. This is a very scenic, longer and occasionally trying route than via SH75, between Christchurch and Akaroa.

BANKS PENINSULA

Banks Peninsula and its hills were formed by two giant volcanic eruptions. Small harbours such as Le Bons, Pigeon and Little

Akaloa Bays radiate out from the peninsula's centre, giving it a cogwheel shape. The historic town of Akaroa is a highlight, as is the absurdly beautiful drive down the spine of the peninsula. Good information is at www.bankspeninsula.info.

History

James Cook sighted the peninsula in 1770 and thought it was an island, promptly naming it after naturalist Sir Joseph Banks. The Ngai Tahu tribe, who occupied the peninsula at the time, were attacked at the fortified Onawe *pa* (Maori village) by the Ngati Toa chief Te Rauparaha in 1831 and their population was dramatically reduced.

BANKS PENINSULA

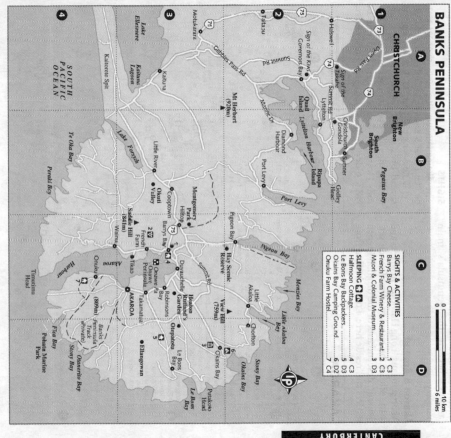

SIGHTS & ACTIVITIES	
Barys Bay Cheese........................	1 C3
French Farm Winery & Restaurant...	2 C3
Maori & Colonial Museum..............	3 D3
SLEEPING 🏠	
Halfmoon Cottage........................	4 C3
Le Bons Bay Backpackers..............	5 D3
Okains Bay Camping Ground..........	6 D2
Onuku Farm Hostel......................	7 C4

0   10 km
0   6 miles

In 1838 whaling captain Jean Langlois negotiated the purchase of Banks Peninsula from local Maoris and returned to France to form a trading company. With French-government backing, 63 settlers headed for the peninsula in 1840. But only days before they arrived, panicked British officials sent their own warship to raise the flag at Akaroa, claiming British sovereignty under the Treaty of Waitangi. Had the settlers arrived two years earlier, the South Island may well have become a French colony.

The French did settle at Akaroa, but in 1849 their land claim was sold to the New Zealand Company and the following year a large group of British settlers arrived. The heavily forested land was cleared and soon dairy farming (later supplanted by sheep farming) became the peninsula's main industry.

Akaroa & Around

Akaroa means 'Long Harbour' in Maori and is the site of the country's first French settlement; descendants of the original French settlers still reside here. Located 83km from Christchurch, this is a charming town that strives to re-create the feel of a French provincial village, down to the names of its streets (rues Lavaud, Balguerie, Jolie) and houses (Langlois-Eteveneaux), plus a few choice eateries.

INFORMATION

Akaroa visitor information centre (Map p560; ☎ 03-304 8600; www.akaroa.com; 80 Rue Lavaud; ☑ 9am–5pm) The information stockpiled here includes details of the peninsula's many tours, activities and farmstays.

Bank of New Zealand (Rue Lavaud) There's an ATM here, opposite the visitor information centre.

Bon-E-Mail (☎ 03-304 7447; 41 Rue Lavaud; ☑ 9am–8pm) Internet access.

SIGHTS

The **Akaroa Museum** (Map p560; ☎ 03-304 1013; cnr Rues Lavaud & Balguerie; adult/child/family $4/1/8; ☑ 10.30am–4.30pm Oct–Apr, to 4pm May–Sep) is spread over several historic buildings, including the old courthouse, the tiny Custom House by Daly's Wharf, and one of NZ's oldest houses, Langlois-Eteveneaux.

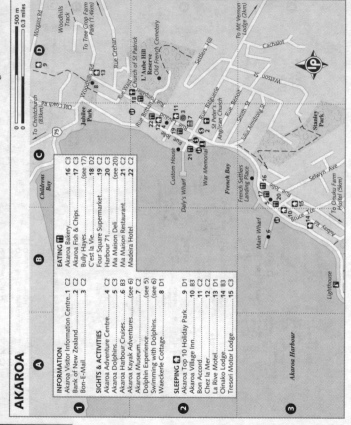

AKAROA

INFORMATION
Akaroa Visitor Information Centre	1 C2
Bank of New Zealand	2 C2
Bon-E-Mail	3 C2

SIGHTS & ACTIVITIES
Akaroa Adventure Centre	4 C2
Akaroa Dolphins	5 C3
Akaroa Harbour Cruises	6 B3
Akaroa Kayak Adventures	(see 6)
Akaroa Museum	7 C2
Dolphin Experience	(see 5)
Swimming with Dolphins	(see 6)
Waeckerle Cottage	8 D1

SLEEPING
Akaroa Top 10 Holiday Park	9 D1
Akaroa Village Inn	10 B3
Bon Accord	11 C2
Chez la Mer	12 C2
La Rive Motel	13 D1
Onaiko Lodge	14 B3
Tresori Motor Lodge	15 C3

EATING
Akaroa Bakery	16 C3
Akaroa Fish & Chips	17 C3
Bully Hayes	(see 17)
C'est La Vie	18 D2
Four Square Supermarket	19 C2
Harbour 71	20 C3
Ma Maison Deli	(see 20)
Ma Maison Restaurant	21 C2
Madeira Hotel	22 C2

It has modest displays on the peninsula's once-significant Maori population, a court-room diorama, a 20-minute audiovisual on peninsular history, and Akaroa community relics and archives (check out the weird timeline entwining major global events with NZ history).

Don't miss the fabulously quirky **Tree Crop Farm Park** (☎ 03-304 7158; www.treecropfarm.com; admission $10; ☼ 10am–5pm in good weather only), 1.8km off the main road through Akaroa (take Rue Grehan). This private, flower-filled wilderness garden is perfect for a wander on established tracks, or you can relax on the sheepskin-covered couches on the ramshackle veranda, flicking through magazines, playing a board game or simply reading the witticisms written all over the walls. A drink and snack is included in the admission price (the berry juice is divine); rustic, romantic accommodation ($285) is also available here.

At Barrys Bay, on the western side of Akaroa Harbour (12km from Akaroa), is **Barrys Bay Cheese** (Map p559; ☎ 03-304 5809; Barrys Bay; ☼ 9am–5pm), where you can taste and purchase fine cheddar, havarti and Gouda.

Just west of the cheese factory is the turn-off to **French Farm Winery & Restaurant** (Map p559; ☎ 03-304 5784; www.frenchfarm.co.nz; French Farm Valley Rd; ☼ 10am–4pm), set amid beautiful grounds. Inside, sample the winery's chardonnay and pinot noir ($1 per taste), or unwind with a cheese or antipasto platter over a bottle or two. In summer, pizzas are served alfresco from midday.

Maori & Colonial Museum (Map p559; ☎ 03-304 8611; Okains Bay; adult/child $6/2; ☼ 10am–5pm) at Okains Bay, northeast of Akaroa, started life as a private collection of indigenous and pioneer artefacts but went public 25 years ago. It features a reproduction Maori meeting house, a sacred 15th-century god stick and a war canoe.

ACTIVITIES

There's no shortage of activities to keep you occupied in Akaroa. See the visitor information centre if you like the sound of jetboating or sailing on Akaroa Harbour, fancy a tour of a working sheep farm, or prefer guided trips to nearby seal or penguin colonies.

The *Akaroa – an Historic Walk* booklet ($9.50) details an excellent walking tour around the town, starting at the 1876 **Waeckerle Cottage** (Map p559; Rue Lavaud) and finishing at the old Taylor's Emporium premises near the main wharf, along the way taking in all the wonderful old wooden buildings and churches that give the town its character.

To really break into stride, tackle the **Banks Peninsula Track** (Map p559; ☎ 03-304 7612; www.bankstrack.co.nz; per person $200), a 35km, four-day walk across private farmland and then around the dramatic coastline of Banks Peninsula; cost includes transport from Akaroa and hut accommodation. There's also a speedy two-day option ($125) covering the same ground.

The **Akaroa Adventure Centre** (Map p560; ☎ 03-304 8706; 64 Rue Lavaud; per hr/day sea kayaks 12/50, bikes $5/25) can help you get active. It rents out sea kayaks, bikes, golf clubs, fishing rods and windsurfing gear. For surfers, $52 will get you transport to and from a local surf beach, including board and wet-suit hire.

Akaroa Dolphins (Map p560; ☎ 0800 990 102, 03-304 7866; www.akaroadolphins.co.nz; 65 Beach Rd; boat rental per day not incl fuel $300) can set you up with daily or weekly rental of a motorboat (maximum six passengers), with fishing and water-skiing gear included.

TOURS

Akaroa Kayak Adventures (Map p560; ☎ 0800 436 574, 03-304 7641; www.blackcat.co.nz/kayak.asp; Main Wharf; tour $125; ☼ 8am Nov–Mar) Offers a full day exploring the bays and caves around Akaroa (about four hours of paddling is involved). Lunch and a *marae* (Maori meeting complex) visit is included.

Eastern Bays Scenic Mail Run (Map p560; ☎ 03-304 7873; www.easternbays tours.com; ☼ 9am Mon–Fri) A 120km, 4½-hour delivery service to remote parts of the peninsula, and visitors can travel along with the posties to visit isolated communities and bays (beachfront picnic included). The minibus departs the Akaroa visitor information centre; bookings are essential as there are only eight seats available.

Outer Bays Tours (☎ 0800 229 786; www.outerbays tours.com; tours $30–50) Can tour you briefly around Akaroa ($12 for one hour) or get you out to the remote parts of the peninsula.

Harbour Cruises

To go in search of Hector's dolphins and blue penguins, take a harbour cruise with one of two operators:
Akaroa Harbour Cruises (Map p560; ☎ 0800 436 574, 03-304 7641; www.blackcat.co.nz; Main Wharf; adult/child

SWIMMING WITH DOLPHINS

The waters around Akaroa are home to the world's smallest and rarest dolphin, the Hector's dolphin, found only in NZ waters. If merely viewing the dolphins on a harbour cruise isn't enough, two companies attempt to get you swimming alongside the dolphins, assuming they're feeling sociable. Both companies operate year-round and carry only 10 swimmers per trip, so book ahead. Wet suits and snorkelling gear are provided, plus hot showers back on dry land. A full refund is offered if no dolphins are seen. It's cheaper if you just like to watch:

Dolphin Experience (Map p560; ☎ 03-304 7726; www.dolphinsakaroa.co.nz; 61 Beach Rd; cruise & swim adult/child $92/70, cruise only $42/25) Two tours daily (9am and noon) May to October, four tours per day November to April.

Swimming with Dolphins (Map p560; ☎ 0800 436 574, 03-304 7641; www.blackcat.co.nz/dolphins.asp; Main Wharf; cruise & swim adult/child $99/79, cruise only $55/30) One tour daily (11.30am) May to September, minimum four tours per day October to April.

two cosy lounges and a garden to empty your mind in.

Mt Vernon Lodge (Map p560; ☎ 03-304 7180; www.mtvernon .co.nz; Purple Peak Rd; dm/d $28/59, cabins d $115-150) Off Rue Balguerie, Mt Vernon is a laid-back, family-friendly lodge 2km from town, set in the middle of extensive rural grounds roamed by chooks, ducks, dogs and even pigs. New owners have totally revamped the accommodation, and offer high-quality backpackers beds, a lodge sleeping 24 (perfect for groups), and self-contained cabins (some family-oriented and sleeping up to six, two decked out as romantic options for couples).

La Rive Motel (Map p560; ☎ 0800 247 651, 03-304 7651; www.holidayakaroa.com; 1 Rue Lavaud; d $75-140; ⌨) Old-style motel with big, light-filled rooms and good facilities; well priced considering each unit (studios, two- and three-bedroom options) is fully self-contained. There's good family distractions too, including barbecue, trampoline and Play Stations for hire.

Akaroa Village Inn (Map p560; ☎ 0800 695 2000, 03-304 7421; www.akaroavillageinn.co.nz; 81 Beach Rd; d $110-220; ⌨) Crop of modern lodgings (from motel-style units to luxury apartments) near the waterfront, many with harbour-view balconies and plenty of mod cons to take for granted while on holiday. Jacques Village units are the cheapest and come without a sea view. The website outlines all the options.

Tresori Motor Lodge (Map p560; ☎ 0800 273 747, 03-304 7500; www.tresori.co.nz; cnr Rue Jolie & Church St; d/q from $135/235) For designer-conscious lodgings try the nearby Tresori, with rich, colourful décor that's anything but bland.

$49/20; ☾ 1.30pm daily, plus 11am Nov-Mar) Two-hour cruises viewing wildlife, plus sea caves and volcanic cliffs.

Akaroa Dolphins (Map p560; ☎ 0800 990 102, 03-304 7866; www.akaroadolphins.co.nz; 65 Beach Rd; adult/child $52/25; ☾ 10.15am, 12.45pm & 3.15pm) Two-hour wildlife cruises, plus evening cruises and bird-watching trips by arrangement.

SLEEPING

Most Banks Peninsula accommodation is in or near Akaroa, but other possibilities are scattered around the various bays. The Banks Peninsula is blessed with some outstanding budget lodgings.

Akaroa

Akaroa Top 10 Holiday Park (Map p560; ☎ 03-304 7471; akaroa.holidaypark@xtra.co.nz; 96 Morgans Rd; sites per 2 people $26-30, on-site vans $36-50, cabins & units $50-85) On a terraced hillside above town and connected by a pathway to Woodhills Rd, this pleasant park has some good harbour views and options for every budget. Prices are for two people.

Chez la Mer (Map p560; ☎ 03-304 7024; www.chez lamer.co.nz; 50 Rue Lavaud; dm $23, d with/without bathroom $66/56; ⌨) Recommended backpackers with spotless, pretty rooms and a superb garden, complete with fish ponds, hammocks, barbecue and outdoor seating. Free bikes and fishing rods are available, as are boating trips. Note that it's a TV-free zone.

Bon Accord (Map p560; ☎ 03-304 7782; www.bon-accord.co.nz; 57 Rue Lavaud; dm/d $23/56; ⌨) Friendly, colourful backpackers with a sense of humour (note the doll 'bungy jumping' off the bridge out front, over a creek). It's a compact 150-year-old house, complete with

Oinako Lodge (Map p560; ☎ 03-304 8787; www.oinako.co.nz; 99 Beach Rd; d $180-220) Dignified old retreat built near the beach in 1865 for the then-British Magistrate, and still a place to kick back in style. Offers six individually themed rooms (most with spas), bay windows, garden/sea views, and a gourmet breakfast.

Around Akaroa

Halfmoon Cottage (Map p559; ☎ 03-304 5051; halfmoon.co@clear.net.nz; Barrys Bay; dm/s/d $22/40/60) This marvellous cottage at Barrys Bay (12km from Akaroa) is a blissful place to spend a few days, lazing on the big verandas or in the hammocks dotting the lush gardens. The rooms – mostly doubles – are warmly decorated, and there are free bikes and kayaks for guest use.

Onuku Farm Hostel (Map p559; ☎ 03-304 7066; www.onukufarm.co.nz; Onuku Rd; dm/d from $22/48; ☑ closed Jun-Aug) Another wonderful, eco-minded backpackers (with basic huts, tent sites and a comfy house) on a sheep farm near Onuku, 6km south of Akaroa. The owners also organise swimming-with-dolphins tours ($75) and kayaking trips ($30) for guests; they pick up from Akaroa.

Le Bons Bay Backpackers (Map p559; ☎ 03-304 8582; Le Bons Bay Rd; dm/d $21/52; ☑ closed Jun-Sep) Six kilometres before Le Bons Bay is this excellent restored farmhouse, wedged in a glorious valley. Besides bucolic splendour, you can also enjoy free breakfast, gourmet dinners ($12; including veg options) and two-hour wildlife-spotting bay tours ($25). The owners will pick up from Akaroa. Book ahead, as beds here are understandably in demand.

Okains Bay Camping Ground (Map p559; ☎ 03-304 8789; 1152 Okains Bay Rd; adult/child $7/4) Nice, pine tree-peppered ground right by the beach, with kitchen facilities and coin-operated hot showers. Pay your fees at the house at the camping ground's entrance, where you can also hire sea kayaks. There's a small general store a few hundred metres down the road.

EATING & DRINKING

You'll find some good options in Rue Lavaud in the north of town, or along Beach Rd.

Ma Maison Deli (Map p560; ☎ 03-304 8774; 67 Beach Rd; meals under $10; ☑ breakfast & lunch) Gourmet hot spot housing a cabinet full of tempting pastries, sandwiches and slices, plus soup and seafood chowder.

Ma Maison restaurant (Map p560; ☎ 03-304 7658; 6 Rue Balguerie; lunch $10-22, dinner mains $20-30; ☑ lunch & dinner) There's also this appealing restaurant with water views and a fine menu, behind the visitor information centre.

Madeira Hotel (Map p560; ☎ 03-304 7009; 48 Rue Lavaud; mains $15-20; ☑ lunch & dinner) Good NZ pub fare such as beer-battered blue cod or rib-eye steak is served in the Madeira's no-frills dining room. There's a sunny beer garden here and live bands often play on summer weekends.

C'est la Vie (Map p560; ☎ 03-304 7314; 33 Rue Lavaud; mains $29-33; ☑ dinner Tue-Sat) Diminutive place that welcomes diner 'reviews' in the form of comments scrawled over several walls (and now the ceiling!). Go classic French with escargot followed by duck à l'orange, or try the ever-popular fillet steak with spinach and blue cheese.

Bully Hayes (Map p560; ☎ 03-304 7533; 57 Beach Rd; lunch $10-18, dinner mains $15-29; ☑ breakfast, lunch & dinner) Casual, brasserie-style waterfront café-bar with a small outdoor terrace, larger courtyard and an easy menu consisting of pesto chicken, char-grilled beef salad, green-lipped mussels and breakfast pancakes.

Harbour 71 (Map p560; ☎ 03-304 7656; 71 Beach Rd; dinner mains $28-31; ☑ lunch & dinner Fri-Tue) The strip's classiest establishment, warm and inviting at night with candlelight, red wine-coloured walls and leather sofas. Meals utilise local produce (Akaroa salmon or groper) with mouth-watering side dishes such as macadamia and citrus potato. Lunch is more casual in both atmosphere and price.

Grab an all-day breakfast or sandwich at **Akaroa Bakery** (Map p560; ☎ 03-304 7663; 51 Beach Rd; meals $3-13.50; ☑ breakfast & lunch), or some marine takeaway at **Akaroa Fish & Chips** (Map p560; ☎ 03-304 7464; 59 Beach Rd; meals from $7; ☑ lunch & dinner).

The **Four Square supermarket** (Map p560; Rue Lavaud; ☑ 9am-6pm Mon-Sat) is good for picnickers and self-caterers.

GETTING THERE & AWAY

The **Akaroa Shuttle** (☎ 0800 500 929; www.akaroashuttle.co.nz; one way/return fare $15/20) departs from outside Christchurch visitor information centre at 8.30am year-round (with an additional 2pm service November to April), returning from Akaroa two to three times daily. It's advisable to book (especially in winter).

French Connection (☎ 0800 800 575; one way/ return fare $15/20) has a year-round departure from Christchurch visitor info centre at 8.45am, returning from Akaroa at 2.30pm or 4.30pm daily.

For those short on time, both these companies offer scenic tours out of Christchurch covering the prime sights of the Banks Peninsula, with prices starting at $35.

NORTH CANTERBURY

From Christchurch, SH1 heads north for 57km through Woodend and Amberley to Waipara. From here SH1 continues northeast to Kaikoura, while SH7 branches due north to Hurunui through flat farming country and itself splits a few kilometres north of Culverden – the northeastern route terminates at the whale-watching capital of Kaikoura, and the westerly path (the continuation of SH7) leads to the Lewis Pass, Maruia Springs and eventually either the West Coast or Nelson. About 27km from Culverden is the turn-off from SH7 to Hanmer Springs, a well-known thermal area and activity resort. *The Alpine Pacific Triangle Touring Guide*, free at visitor information centres, outlines things to see and do in this region, or check out www .hurunui.com.

The scenic **Waipara Valley** is NZ's fastest-expanding wine region and is home to over a dozen wineries, all outlined in the free *Waipara Valley Vineyards* brochure. Sample a Pegasus Bay pinot noir or Canterbury House sauvignon blanc, and stop for lunch at one of the lovely vineyard restaurants. **Waipara Springs** (☎ 03-314 6777; www.waipara springs.co.nz; SH1, north of Waipara), **Pegasus Bay** (☎ 03-314 6869; www.pegasusbay.com; Stockgrove Rd, south of Waipara) and **Canterbury House** (☎ 03-314 6900; www.canterburyhouse.com; SH1, south of Waipara) are open daily for wine tasting and sales, and are all home to restaurant-cafés; most other wineries are open by appointment.

The **Pegasus Bay restaurant** (mains $26-34; ☺ lunch) is particularly recommended – in 2005 *Cuisine* magazine voted this the best casual dining restaurant in the country. The gorgeous menu takes advantage of sensa-

See p539 for details of companies offering tours of the area.

tional local produce and suggests wines to complement your dish.

If you turn onto the SH7 at Waipara and then take the first right, you'll quickly find the novel **Waipara Sleepers** (☎ 03-314 6003; www.inet.net.nz/~waipara.sleepers; 12 Glenmark Dr; unpowered/powered sites per 2 people $20/24, dm/s/d from $20/27/40), where you can bunk down in converted train guards vans, camp among a small clutch of sites and cook meals in the 'station house', all of it on a pastoral plot conveniently close to the local pub and general store.

Where wine is produced, the gourmands will follow – and of course they need somewhere chic to stay. If you visit sometime after late 2006, you'll encounter the new **Waipara Wine Village** (www.waiparawinevillage.com) at the junction of SH1 and SH7, a development that will encompass an upmarket hotel, restaurant, wine bar and boutique ale house.

HANMER SPRINGS

pop 750

Hanmer Springs, the main thermal resort on the South Island, is 10km off SH7. Visitors swell the population year-round, as Hanmer is a favourite weekend destination for Christchurch folk. That's not surprising, given its broad appeal – you can treat the town as a retreat and indulge in pampering and fine dining, or there's an abundance of family-friendly outdoor activities that include forest walks, minigolf, horse treks and jetboating.

Information

Bank of New Zealand ATM (☺ 9am–9pm).

Hurunui visitor information centre (☎ 0800 442 663, 03-315 7128; www.hurunui.com; 42 Amuri Ave; ☺ 10am–5pm) Can book accommodation, transport and local activities.

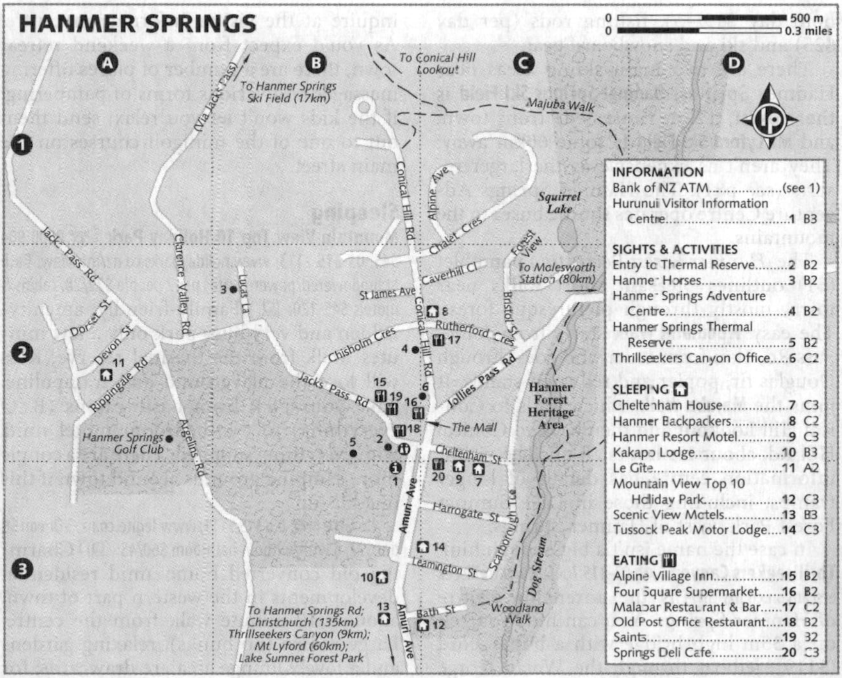
HANMER SPRINGS
0 500 m
0 0.3 miles
A
B
C
D
1
2
3
To Conical Hill Lookout
To Hanmer Springs Ski Field (17km)
(Via Jacks Pass)
Majuba Walk
Conical Hill Rd
Alpine Ave
Chalet Cres
Squirrel Lake
Forest View
To Molesworth Station (80km)
Caverhill Cl
St James Ave
Jack's Pass Rd
Clarence Valley Rd
Lucas La
Dorset St
Devon St
Rippingale Rd
Chisholm Cres
Rutherford Cres
Bristol St
Jacks Pass Rd
Jollies Pass Rd
Hanmer Forest Heritage Area
The Mall
Hanmer Springs Golf Club
Argelins Rd
Cheltenham St
Amuri Ave
Harrogate St
Scarborough Tce
Dog Stream
Leamington St
Bath St
Woodland Walk
To Hanmer Springs Rd; Christchurch (135km) Thrillseekers Canyon (9km); Mt Lyford (60km); Lake Sumner Forest Park
INFORMATION
Bank of NZ ATM..........(see 1)
Hurunui Visitor Information Centre..........1 B3
SIGHTS & ACTIVITIES
Entry to Thermal Reserve..........2 B2
Hanmer Horses..........3 B2
Hanmer Springs Adventure Centre..........4 B2
Hanmer Springs Thermal Reserve..........5 B2
Thrillseekers Canyon Office..........6 C2
SLEEPING
Cheltenham House..........7 C3
Hanmer Backpackers..........8 C2
Hanmer Resort Motel..........9 C3
Kakapo Lodge..........10 B3
Le Gîte..........11 A2
Mountain View Top 10 Holiday Park..........12 C3
Scenic View Motels..........13 B3
Tussock Peak Motor Lodge..........14 C3
EATING
Alpine Village Inn..........15 B2
Four Square Supermarket..........16 B2
Malabar Restaurant & Bar..........17 C2
Old Post Office Restaurant..........18 B2
Saints..........19 B2
Springs Deli Cafe..........20 C3

Sights

THERMAL RESERVE

Visitors have been soaking in the waters of **Hanmer Springs Thermal Reserve** (☎ 0800 442 663, 03-315 7511; www.hanmersprings.co.nz; entry on Jacks Pass Rd; adult/child $10/5; 🕑 10am-9pm) for over 100 years. Local legend has it that the thermal springs are a piece of the fires of Tamatea that dropped from the sky after an eruption of Mt Ngauruhoe on the North Island; Maoris call the springs Waitapu (Sacred Waters).

The hot spring water mixes with freshwater to produce pools of varying temperatures. In addition to the mineral pools, there are landscaped rock pools, sulphur pools, a freshwater 25m lap pool, private sauna/steam suites ($17 per half-hour), massage facilities, a restaurant, and a family activity area that includes a waterslide ($5).

MOLESWORTH STATION

Northeast of Hanmer Springs, Molesworth Station, at 180,500 hectares, is NZ's largest farm with the country's largest cattle herd (up to 10,000). Inquire at the visitor information centre about independent visits to Molesworth, newly under DOC control. These are usually only possible when the Acheron Rd through the station is open from late December to March, weather permitting. The drive from Hanmer Springs north to Blenheim on this narrow, unsealed backcountry road takes around six hours; note that the gates are only open from 7am to 7pm, and overnight **camping** (adult/child $6/1.50) is permitted in certain areas (no open fires allowed).

Alternatively, **Trailways Safaris** (☎ 03-315 7401; www.molesworth.co.nz; tours $99-249) offers 4WD tours of the station and the remote private land stretching north to St Arnaud. Tours operate from October to May. Day tours include a picnic lunch, while for those short on time there is a five-hour 'no frills' express tour.

Activities

Hanmer Springs Adventure Centre (☎ 03-315 7233; www.hanmeradventure.co.nz; 20 Conical Hill Rd; 🕑 9am-5pm) supplies information on (and handles bookings for) various activities, and rents equipment such as mountain bikes (per hour/day $19/45), fishing rods (per day $25) and ski and snowboard gear.

There are two main skiing areas near Hanmer Springs. **Hanmer Springs Ski Field** is the closest, 17km (unsealed) from town, and **Mt Lyford Ski Field** is some 60km away. They aren't as expensive as the larger resorts (see p81). The Hanmer Springs Adventure Centre operates shuttle buses to the mountains.

The *Hanmer Forest Recreation* pamphlet ($1) outlines pleasant short walks near town, mostly through picturesque forest. The easy **Woodland Walk** starts from Jollies Pass Rd, 1km from town, and goes through Douglas fir, poplar and redwood stands. It joins the **Majuba Walk**, which leads to Conical Hill Lookout and then back to Conical Hill Rd, about 1½ hours all up. The visitor information centre has details of longer tramps, including those in Lake Sumner Forest Park, west of Hanmer Springs.

In case the name isn't a big enough hint, **Thrillseekers Canyon** (☎ 03-315 7046; www.thrillseek erscanyon.co.nz; SH7) is the adrenaline centre of Hanmer Springs. You can hurl yourself off a 35m-high bridge with a bungy cord ($119), jetboat through the Waiau Gorge (adult/child $89/50) or go white-water rafting (grade II to III) down the Waiau River (adult/child $95/50). Book at the Thrillseekers Canyon centre, next to the bridge where the Hanmer Springs turn-off meets SH7. There's also an information/booking **office** (☎ 03-315 7346; The Mall) in town.

Hanmer Horses (☎ 0800 873 546, 03-315 7444; www .hanmerhorses.co.nz; Lucas La; 1hr rides adult/child $45/35) is walking distance from the town centre and offers one-hour scenic forest rides (adult/ child $45/35) or 2½-hour treks ($90/70). It'll even lead littlies on a 20-minute pony ride ($15).

BackTrax (☎ 0800 422 258, 027 419 4531; www .backtrax.co.nz; 2½hr trips $110) organises guided quad-bike trips up into the hills and along (and across) the Hanmer River; minimum age is 16. The region is also popular for mountain biking – the Hanmer Springs Adventure Centre (see p565) offers trail maps, advice and bike rental, and also does an organised ride ($79) up over Jacks and Jollies Passes (includes transport to the top of Jacks Pass).

Other activities are possible, including scenic flights, fishing trips and kayaking –

inquire at the visitor information centre. As you'd expect from a weekend retreat town, there are a number of places offering massages and various forms of pampering; if the kids won't let you relax, send them out to one of the minigolf courses on the main street.

Sleeping
Mountain View Top 10 Holiday Park (☎ 0800 904 545, 03-315 7113; www.holidayparks.co.nz/mtnview; Bath St; unpowered/powered sites per 2 people $22/28, cabins & motels $45-120; 🖳) Family-friendly, amenity-ridden and very busy park only a few minutes' walk from the thermal reserve. Kids will love the playground and trampoline. Take your pick from basic cabins (BYO everything) to two-bedroom motel units with everything supplied. There are a couple more camping grounds around town if this one fills up.

Le Gite (☎ 03-315 5111; www.legite.co.nz; 3 Devon St; dm $22, d with/without bathroom $60/45; 🖳) Charming old converted home amid residential developments in the western part of town, about a 10-minute walk from the centre. Large rooms (no bunks), relaxing gardens and a lovely lounge area are drawcards; for extra privacy, book a garden 'chalet' with private bathroom.

Kakapo Lodge (☎ 03-315 7472; stay-kakapo@xtra .co.nz; 14Amuri Ave; dm $24, d $50-80; 🖳) YHA-affiliated Kakapo has a simple, uncluttered aesthetic enhanced by a roomy kitchen and lounge, underfloor heating to banish winter chill, and an outdoor deck. Besides bunk-free standard-issue rooms (some with bathroom), there are also good-value motel-style units with TV and cooking facilities.

Hanmer Backpackers (☎ 03-315 7196; hanmer backpackers@xtra.co.nz; 41 Conical Hill Rd; dm/d $22/50; 🖳) The township's original backpackers is homely, inviting and comfortable, and has a barbecue area to hang about in summer and a log fire to huddle next to in winter. Linen for the dorms costs an additional $2.

Hanmer Resort Motel (☎ 0800 777 666, 03-315 7362; www.hanmerresortmotel.co.nz; 7 Cheltenham St; d/q $85/130) Super family option, and very affordable. Décor is somewhat dated but units are spotless and spacious. Two-bedroom units have full kitchen and private courtyard. There's a playground too.

Tussock Peak Motor Lodge (☎ 0800 8877 625, 03-315 5191; www.tussockpeak.co.nz; cnr Amuri Ave &

Leamington St; d $110-140, q $180) Motels line the main street but this, the newest place in town, is one of the best with its modern, well-appointed rooms decked out in warm golds and reds (well, it sure beats the florals of yesteryear). There are lots of choices: studio, one- or two-bedroom units, spas, courtyards or balconies.

Scenic View Motels (☎ 0800 843 9748, 03-315 7419; www.hanmerscenicviews.co.nz; 10Amuri Ave; d $109-180) An attractive timber-and-stone complex with modern, colourful studios and two- and three-bedroom apartments, with mountain views as an added extra.

Cheltenham House (☎ 03-315 7545; www.cheltenham.co.nz; 13 Cheltenham St; s $150-190, d $170-210) Superb B&B close to the thermal pools and with a half-dozen snooze-inducing suites, all with private bathroom and two of them in garden cottages. Gourmet cooked breakfasts can be delivered direct to your duvet and there's also a full-sized billiard table and grand piano to pose next to with aperitif in hand (there's complimentary predinner drinks). The fresh flowers in rooms are a lovely touch.

Eating

Springs Deli Cafe (☎ 03-315 7430; 47Amuri Ave; meals $9-15; ⏲ breakfast & lunch) Cruisy main-street café with cheery plant life, alfresco dining, pastries, focaccias, salads and sweet nibbles for lunch.

Alpine Village Inn (☎ 03-315 7005; 10 Jacks Pass Rd; mains $9-22; ⏲ lunch & dinner) Timber-clad place better known as the local boozer, but doing a sideline in reasonably priced bistro meals. There's no gastropub activity here, just classic old-school dishes like T-bone steak, chicken schnitzel and pavlova for dessert. Offers a kids menu too.

Malabar Restaurant & Bar (☎ 03-315 7745; 5 Conical Hill Rd; mains $25-33; ⏲ dinner) Swish restaurant offering a great range of Asian and Indian dishes – you can't go wrong with the house speciality, Malabar thali (four curries of the day served with rice and chutneys), but leave room for some of the amazing flavoured ice creams and sorbets. A limited takeaway menu is available, with easier-on-the-wallet prices of around $10 per dish.

Saints (☎ 03-315 5262; 6 Jacks Pass Rd; mains $15-25; ⏲ dinner) Make a night of it at this laid-back restaurant-bar, where you can indulge in gourmet pizzas, shoot some pool or just socialise over a few beers. In busier months it also opens for breakfast and lunch.

Old Post Office Restaurant (☎ 03-315 7461; 2 Jacks Pass Rd; mains $29-34; ⏲ dinner) Fine-dining restaurant much awarded for the way in which the chef wields beef and lamb. The drool-prompting desserts may include an intriguing hot liquorice pudding with butterscotch sauce.

Self-caterers should head to the **Four Square supermarket** (Conical Hill Rd; ⏲ 8.30am–6pm Mon-Fri, 9am–7pm Sat, 10am–5.30pm Sun).

Getting There & Away

Hanmer Connection (☎ 0800 242 663) runs from Hanmer Springs to Christchurch ($25, three daily) and Kaikoura ($30, three weekly).

Southern Link Lazerline Coaches (☎ 03-358 8355; www.yellow.co.nz/site/southernlink) operates a daily service between Christchurch and Nelson that travels via Lewis Pass and will stop at Hanmer Springs ($30 from Christchurch) on request.

East West Coach (☎ 0800 142 622, 03-789 6251) has a service that runs between Christchurch and Westport via Lewis Pass but, rather unhelpfully, doesn't go into Hanmer Springs itself – it can pick you up or set you down at the Hanmer Springs turn-off, 10km south of town.

LEWIS PASS HIGHWAY

The Lewis Pass Hwy (SH7) wiggles its way west from the Hanmer Springs turn-off to Lewis Pass, Maruia Springs and Springs Junction. This is a beautiful route, though as it lies at the northern end of the Southern Alps, the 907m-high **Lewis Pass** is not as steep or the forest as dense as on the routes through Arthur's and Haast Passes. The forest near Lewis Pass is mainly red and silver beech, and the kowhai trees that grow along the river terraces are spectacular in spring.

The Lewis Pass area has some interesting walks; pick up the DOC-produced pamphlet *Lae Summer/Lewis Pass Recreation* ($1). Most tracks pass through beech forest; snowcapped mountains form the backdrop and there are lakes, alpine tarns and mountain rivers. The most popular tramps are those around **Lake Sumner** in the Lake Sumner Forest Park and the **St James Walkway** (66km; three to five days) in the

Lewis Pass National Reserve. Subalpine conditions apply; sign the intentions book at the start of the St James Walkway and at Windy Point for the Lake Sumner area before heading off.

Maruia Springs (☎ 03-523 8840; www.maruia springs.co.nz; SH7; sites per adult/child $20/10, d $129-179, f $205-225; ▣) is a small, highway-side thermal resort on the banks of the Maruia River, 69km from the Hanmer turn-off and 15km east of Springs Junction. It has pricey, nondescript units (camping and room rates all include admission to the pools) and eateries, including a café-bar and Japanese restaurant. But the **thermal pools** (adult/child/family $10/5/25; ☉ 8am-9pm) are the main drawcard here – thermal water is pumped into a sex-segregated traditional Japanese bathhouse and outdoor rock pools that you can relax in no matter what the weather; magic in winter as snowflakes drift down. There are massages available and **private spa houses** (per person for 45min $15).

From the resort, SH7 continues to **Springs Junction**, where the Shenandoah Hwy (SH65) branches north to meet SH6 near Murchison, while SH7 continues west to Reefton and then down to Greymouth. At the junction of these two highways is a petrol station and café (the cooked-to-order food here is a better bet than some of the sorry-looking items in the display cabinet).

To the southwest of Christchurch (reached by SH73 and SH77) is the Mt Hutt ski resort and Methven.

CRAIGIEBURN FOREST PARK

Accessed from SH73, this forest park is 110km northwest of Christchurch and 42km south of Arthur's Pass. The park has a significant system of walking tracks, with longer tramps possible in the valleys west of the Craigieburn Range; see the DOC pamphlet *Craigieburn Forest Park: Day Walks* ($1). Some of the surrounding country is also suitable for skiing and rock climbing. Dominating the vegetation is beech, tussock, totara and turpentine scrub; if you're lucky, you may see patches of South Island edelweiss (*Leucogenes grandiceps*).

Craigieburn has a rise of 503m so is one of NZ's best skiing areas. Its wild-country slopes suit the advanced skier; see p83.

Located between the entrance to the forest park and the Broken River bridge to the south is **Cave Stream Scenic Reserve**, where you can explore a 594m-long cave with a small waterfall at one end; be sure to take all the necessary precautions (two light sources per person etc) if doing the one-hour walk through the pitch-black cave. For details, get the DOC brochure *Cave Stream Scenic Reserve* (50c). The reserve is in the **Castle Hill area**, a feature of which is prominent limestone outcrops much loved by the rock climbing and bouldering fraternity, and by location scouts – scenes from the *Lord of the Rings* trilogy and *Chronicles of Narnia: The Lion, the Witch & the Wardrobe* have been filmed in the vicinity. The latter movie set its climatic battle scene in the high country of Flock Hill station – see below. See also p539 for information on film-themed tours from Christchurch that visit the area.

Sleeping & Eating

Flock Hill Lodge (☎ 03-318 8196; www.flockhill.co.nz; SH73; dm/d $20/120) High-country sheep station 44km east of Arthur's Pass, adjacent to Lake Pearson and the Craigieburn Forest Park. Backpackers after a rustic experience can stay in old shearers' quarters, while large groups can opt for two-bedroom motel units or large cottages with kitchenette; one room is fully equipped for disabled travellers. When you're not out exploring the

CENTRAL CANTERBURY

It's about two hours west from Christchurch on SH73 to Arthur's Pass National Park. The trans-island crossing from Christchurch to Greymouth, over Arthur's Pass, is a scenic route covered by buses and the *TranzAlpine* train (see p508).

Nowhere else in NZ do you get a better picture of the climb from sea to mountains. From Christchurch, almost at sea level, the road heads over the flat Canterbury Plains, through rural towns such as Kirwee, Darfield, Sheffield and Springfield. It then winds up into the skiing areas of Porter Heights and Craigieburn before following the Waimakariri and Bealey Rivers to Arthur's Pass, passing good-looking lakes such as Pearson and Grasmere along the way.

station or participating in nearby activities, feed your hunger in the restaurant or bar.

Smylie's Accommodation (☎ 03-318 4740; www.smylies.co.nz; Main Rd, Springfield; dm $22, d $50-75; ▣) Welcoming YHA-associated hostel in the town of Springfield, around 30km southeast of Craigieburn. It's run by a Dutch-Japanese family and there's a strong Japanese influence here, most evident in the food (breakfast and dinner available), the popular Japanese bath, *kotatsu* (foot warmer) and some futon-equipped rooms. A handful of self-contained motel units is available. In winter, ski equipment and ski-field transport are provided. There are good year-round activities in the area too, including jetboating and horse treks.

Wilderness Lodge (☎ 03-3189246;www.wildernesslodge.co.nz; SH73; d $460-980) Luxurious 24-room lodge on a mountain beech-speckled sheep station (2400 hectares worth), 16km east of Arthur's Pass. Alpine views from the bedrooms and daily guided nature walks add to the great outdoors appeal of this stream-threaded property. Breakfast and a gourmet four-course dinner are included in the room price.

Bealey Hotel (☎ 03-318 9277; www.bealeyhotel.co.nz; dm $20, motel d $90-110) This hotel is 12km east of Arthur's Pass at Bealey, a tiny settlement famous for a hoax by the local publican in 1993, which led New Zealanders to believe that a live moa had been sighted in the area (hence the statue in front of the pub). There are self-contained motel units and the budget Moa Lodge with 10 double rooms, plus there's a decent restaurant and bar. In fine weather, drink in the sterling views from the outside deck.

ARTHUR'S PASS

pop 62

The settlement of Arthur's Pass is 4km from the pass of the same name and is the highest-altitude NZ town. The 924m pass was on the route used by Maoris to reach Westland, but its European discovery was made by Arthur Dobson in 1864, when the Westland gold rush created enormous pressure to find a crossing over the Southern Alps from Christchurch. A coach road was completed within a year of Dobson's discovery, but later on the coal and timber traffic demanded a railway, duly completed in 1923.

The town is a handy base for walks, climbs, views and winter-time skiing in Arthur's Pass National Park, and makes a good (though long) day trip from Greymouth or Christchurch.

Information

DOC Arthur's Pass visitor information centre (☎ 03-318 9211; arthurspassvc@doc.govt.nz; SH73; 🕐 8.30am-4.30pm) has information on all park walks, including route guides for longer hut-lined tramps. It doesn't make onward bookings or reservations, but can help with local accommodation and transport information. The centre also screens a 17-minute video (adult/child $1/free) on the history of Arthur's Pass and has excellent displays – check out the

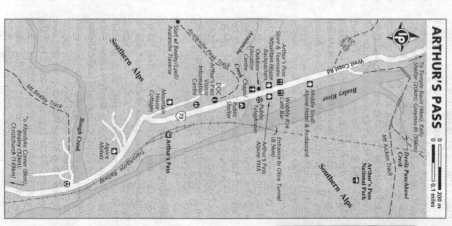

ARTHUR'S PASS

1888 Cobb & Co coach in a back room. For online information visit www.apinfo.co.nz.

Trampers can hire detailed topo maps ($1 per day, with $20 refundable deposit) from the visitor information centre, as well as locator beacons ($25). Staff members also offer invaluable advice on the park's often savagely changeable weather conditions. Check conditions here and fill out an intentions card before going on any walk; be sure to sign out again after returning, otherwise they'll send a search party to find you!

Sights & Activities

About 150m from the visitor information centre is the small interfaith chapel – pop in to admire the view above the altar (far nicer than a stained-glass window).

Day walks in this glorious national park offer some 360-degree views of snowcapped peaks, many of them over 2000m; the highest is Mt Murchison (2400m). There are huts on the tramping tracks and several areas suitable for camping. The best time to walk is in the drier months (January to April). The leaflet *Walks in Arthur's Pass National Park* ($1) details walks to scenic places including **Devils Punchbowl Waterfall** (one hour return), **Temple Basin** (three hours return) and **Avalanche Peak** (six to eight hours return). There's also skiing at Temple Basin; see p83.

Longer tramps with superb alpine backdrops include the **Goat Pass Track** (two days) and the longer and more difficult **Harman Pass** and **Harpers Pass Tracks**. Such tracks require previous tramping experience – flooding can make the rivers dangerous to cross and the weather is extremely changeable; seek advice from DOC first.

Sleeping & Eating

You can camp within Arthur's Pass township at the basic **public shelter** (adult/child $5/free), opposite the information centre, where there's stream water, a sink, tables and toilets. Camping is free at **Klondyke Corner**, 8km south of Arthur's Pass, and **Kelly Shelter**, 20km to the northwest; both have toilets and the water must be boiled before drinking.

Arthur's Pass Alpine YHA (03-318 9230; www .stayha.com; SH73; sites per person $15, dm/d $27/65;) Bright, friendly and well-maintained hostel, with a near-permanent log fire crackling away due to the Southern Alps chill.

Offers lots of advice on regional walks and there's plenty of room to stow your gear and bikes.

Mountain House Backpackers (03-318 9258; www.trampers.co.nz; SH73; dm $23-27, d $60, cottage sleeping up to 10 from $170;) This lodge gets a big thumbs-up from travellers for its cosy feel, good facilities and predisposition towards local walks and tramps. The owners also rent excellent, open fire-equipped cottages set well back from the roadside, which you can share with strangers on a backpacking basis, or rent out entirely for your family or group.

Alpine Motels (03-318 9233; alpine.motels@xtra .co.nz; SH73; d $85-120) Tucked away in the southern part of town is this small complex of comfortable motel units. Car storage is available ($3 per day) if you're going to disappear into the wilderness for a while.

Middle South Alpine Hotel (0800 676 884, 03-318 9236; www.middlesouth.co.nz; SH73; dm $25, d $100-120;) Formerly known as the Chalet, this is a large accommodation complex with decent, centrally heated rooms and an outdoor spa. There are also budget cabins available to backpackers. You can dine on the likes of venison casserole or Akaroa salmon in the hotel's à la carte restaurant (mains $19 to $29; open lunch and dinner), or snack on jacket potatoes or pizza from the bar (meals $9 to $20; open breakfast, lunch and dinner).

Other dining choices are limited. The **Arthur's Pass Store & Tearooms** (03-318 9235; SH73; 8am-8pm;) sells sandwiches, pies, other hot snacks, very limited groceries and expensive petrol. Your best bet is a spot by the fire at the **Wobbly Kea** (03-318 9101; SH73; meals $9-26; breakfast, lunch & dinner), a friendly café-bar serving a big menu of tasty meals, including kids options.

Getting There & Around

Arthur's Pass is on the main run for buses travelling between Christchurch ($20 to $25) and Greymouth ($20); **Atomic Shuttles** (03-322 8883; www.atomictravel.co.nz) and **Coast to Coast** (0800 800 847; www.coast2coast.co.nz) stop here. Bus tickets are sold at the **Arthur's Pass Store & Tearooms** (03-318 9235; SH73).

The *TranzAlpine* train operated by **Tranz Scenic** (0800 872 467; www.tranzscenic.co.nz) runs between Christchurch and Greymouth via Arthur's Pass. It leaves Arthur's Pass for

Greymouth (from $41) at 10.42am and for Christchurch (from $65) at 3.57pm.

The road over the pass was once winding and very steep – the most tortuous of all the passes – but a spectacular viaduct has removed many of the treacherous hairpin bends. It's slowly being extended to eliminate areas prone to rockfall.

Mountain House Shuttle (☎ 03-3189258), based at Mountain House Backpackers (opposite), offers a transport service to most of the walking tracks and ski fields.

METHVEN

pop 1140

Relatively quiet for most of the warmer months, Methven well and truly wakes up in winter, when it fills up with ski bunnies taking advantage of the excellent skiing at nearby Mt Hutt. But there are also nonwinter activities to draw travellers including excellent hot-air ballooning, fishing and golf.

Information

Bank of New Zealand (Main St) With ATM, not far from the visitor information centre.

E-mail Shop (☎ 03-302 8982; Forest Dr; 9am-9pm) Get online here.

Medical centre (☎ 03-302 8135; Main St) Can patch up skiing mishaps.

Methven visitor information centre (☎ 03-302 8955; www.methven.net.nz; 121 Main St; 8am-6pm daily May–Oct, 9am–5pm Mon–Fri & 11am–4pm Sat & Sun Nov–Apr) Can book accommodation, skiing packages, transport and activities.

Activities

It's skiing that keeps Methven busy. Nearby **Mount Hutt** (see p82) offers five months of skiing (June to October), often the longest ski season of any resort in NZ.

The place to go for ski rental and advice is **Big Al's Snow Sports** (☎ 03-302 8003; www.bigals.co.nz; cnr Main St & Forest Dr; golf clubs per day $12, mountain bikes per hr/day $12/39). It also rents out golf clubs and mountain bikes.

Methven Heliskiing (☎ 03-302 8108; www.heliskiing.co.nz/methven/about.htm; Main St; day trips $770) operates from July to September, offering trips that include five powder runs, guide service, safety equipment and lunch. Another

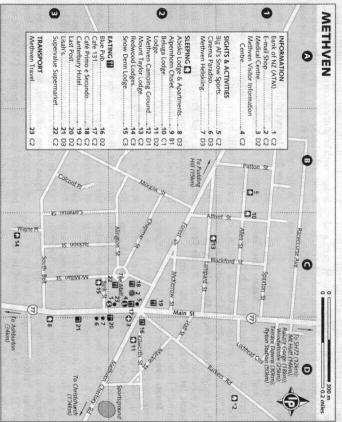

METHVEN

INFORMATION
Bank of NZ (ATM)..................1 C2
E-mail Shop..........................2 C2
Medical Centre......................3 C2
Methven Visitor Information Centre..............4 C2

SIGHTS & ACTIVITIES
Big Al's Snow Sports..............5 C2
Cinema Paradiso....................6 C3
Methven Heliskiing................7 C2

SLEEPING
Asisko Lodge & Apartments......8 D3
Alpenhorn Chalet...................9 B1
Beluga Lodge.......................10 C2
Lodge................................11 D1
Methven Camping Ground.......12 D1
Mount Taylor Lodge...............13 D2
Redwood Lodges...................14 A2
Snow Denn Lodge..................15 C2

EATING
Blue Pub............................16 D2
Cafe 131............................17 D2
Café Primo e Secundo............18 D2
Canterbury Hotel...................19 C2
Last Post............................20 D2
Lisah's...............................21 D2
Supavalue Supermarket...........22 C2

TRANSPORT
Methven Travel.....................23 C2

wintertime business getting you off the beaten slopes is **Black Diamond Safaris** (☎03-302 9696; www.blackdiamondsafaris.co.nz) takes you to the area's uncrowded club ski fields by 4WD. Prices start at $85 for 4WD transport only; $270 gets you transport, a lift pass, guiding and lunch.

Mt Hutt Bungy (☎0800 142 8649, 03-307 6659; bungy $89) provides the opportunity for an exhilarating 43m bungy jump from a cantilevered platform at Kea Rock. It even offers the chance for a unique 'powder touchdown' ($125) – bungy with your skis or snowboard off a specially designed jump ramp. It usually operates only over winter.

For a sedate aerial experience and the chance to view classic NZ landscapes of farmland backed by snowcapped mountains from on high, try a balloon flight with **Aoraki Balloon Safaris** (☎0800 256 837, 03-302 8172; www.nzballooning.co.nz; flights $245-295), which ends with a champagne breakfast.

The **Mount Hutt Forest** is predominantly mountain beech; it's 14km west of Methven. Adjoining it are the **Awa Awa Rata Reserve** and the **Pudding Hill Scenic Reserve**. There are two access roads: Pudding Hill Rd leads to foot access for Pudding Hill Stream, and McLennan's Bush Rd leads to both reserves. There are many walking trails, including the water-crossing **Pudding Hill Stream Route** (two hours).

There's a good, easy walk through farmland and the impressive **Rakaia River Gorge** (three to four hours return), beginning at the car park just south of the bridge on SH77. There are good picnic spots around the bridge. **Rakaia Gorge Alpine Jet** (☎03-318 6574; www.rivertours.co.nz; $68) and **Rakaia Gorge Scenic Jet** (☎03-318 6515; $65) both do 40-minute jetboat trips through the gorge.

Terrace Downs (☎0800 465 373, 03-318 6943; www.terracedowns.co.nz; SH72; green fees $90-115, club hire $35), 30km from Methven near Windwhistle, is a 'high-country resort' with a world-class 18-hole golf course. Also here is a very good restaurant and top-quality accommodation (from $350), for when you simply can't bear to sleep too far from the next 18 holes.

Call in to the visitor information centre for details of other walks and activities in the area, including horse riding, fishing, scenic helicopter flights, farm tours and 4WD tours to Mt Sunday, site of the Edoras in the *Lord of the Rings*.

Sleeping

Due to the influx of skiers in winter, many places have drying rooms and ski storage. Some are closed in summer, but the following are open year-round with the lower prices applicable outside the ski season.

Methven Camping Ground (☎03-302 8005; methvennz@hotmail.com; Barkers Rd; unpowered/powered sites per 2 people $22/24, cabins $34-50) Small park keeping to itself off Barkers Rd, close to the centre of town. It's in a scenic location, and the facilities (including a TV room) are serviceable. Tiny budget cabins offer the cheapest bed in town but it's worth spending a few dollars more for a bed at one of the backpackers.

Alpenhorn Chalet (☎03-302 8779; 44 Allen St; dm $20-25, d $50-70; □) Small, inviting budget chalet with a wonderful conservatory housing an indoor garden and spa pool, and other kindnesses such as free Internet, log fire and espresso coffee. Some rooms have private bathrooms.

Redwood Lodges (☎03-302 8964; www.methvennz.com; 5 Wayne Pl; dm $25, d $60, d with bathroom $75-85; □) Transformed from a one-time vicarage into two well-appointed travellers' lodges with brightly decorated rooms. Redwood is the backpacker option (but with no bunks). Skiered is quieter, with en suite and family rooms.

Snow Denn Lodge (☎03-302 8999; www.methvenaccommodation.co.nz; cnr McMillan & Bank Sts; dm/s/d $27/49/72, d with bathroom $84; □ ☺) This central YHA-associated lodge is a modern, purpose-built house with lots of room to lounge in and some appealing dining-living areas, a large kitchen and indoor and outdoor spa pool. Prices are higher than other hostels in town, but extras include free breakfast and equipment hire (bikes, golf clubs, fishing gear etc).

Beluga Lodge (☎03-302 8290; www.beluga.co.nz; 40 Allen St; r $190-220; □ ☺) Highly relaxing B&B is on offer here in the form of king-sized beds, fluffy bathrobes and a garden-sited hydrotherapy pool. Those in need of destressing should consider the garden suite, with its own patio and barbecue. A four-bedroom cottage is also available ($325; minimum three-night stay).

Ryton Station (☎0800 926 868, 03-318 5818; www.ryton.co.nz; sites $5, lodge per person $25-40, holiday house per person $25-50, chalet DB&B per person $140-160) Beautifully isolated 14,800-hectare sheep station,

60km northwest of Methven on the north shore of Lake Coleridge. The high-country accommodation ranges from a wilderness camping ground and 15-bed budget lodge (equipped with kitchen, but meals are available from the homestead) to self-contained holiday houses or DB&B (dinner, bed and breakfast) lake-view chalets. There are also great activities including 4WD tours, fishing, walking and ice-skating in winter.

Some friendly, hotel-style lodges:

Abisko Lodge & Apartments (☎ 03-302 8875; www.abisko.co.nz; 74 Main St; d/f $100/160, apt $240) A spa, sauna, pool table and bar enhance the enjoyment. Modern three-bedroom apartments sleep up to 10.

Lodge (☎ 03-303 2000; www.thelodgenz.com; 1 Methven Chertsey Rd; d $105-165;) New property, spa rooms available. Popular on-site restaurant and bar.

Mount Taylor Lodge (☎ 03-302 9699; www.mount taylorlodge.co.nz; 32 Lampard St; s $70-85, d $120-140;) Stylish 11-room lodge; breakfast included.

Eating & Drinking

In winter, most of Methven's eateries do a roaring trade but are often open only three to five nights a week in summer, some close down for the entire sunny season (finding it hard to employ a chef without the lure of skiing on days off).

Ask around during winter to find out special meal deals at various pubs and bars (eg $10 jug-and-curry nights) designed to lure hungry (and thirsty) skiers.

Café Primo e Secundo (☎ 03-302 9309; 38 McMillan St; meals $5-10; breakfast & lunch) Don't miss this wonderful café where everything is for sale. Breakfast on the homemade granola or stop by for a date scone with a cuppa, then browse the retro furniture, tea cosies, colourful fabrics and crockery, and just try to resist making a purchase.

Last Post (☎ 03-302 8259; Main St; mains $20-30; dinner winter, usually closed summer) We're not alone in ranking this place as Methven's finest restaurant-bar – crowds of regulars enjoy the soft orange-lit interior, snug fireplace and creative menu of local produce. Call in here for après ski straight off the slopes from 4.30pm to 6pm, for warming drinks and snacks.

Cafe 131 (☎ 03-302 9131; Main St; meals $6-15; breakfast & lunch) A warm space with polished timber, leadlight windows and a wood-fired stove. Serves up all-day breakfasts and the usual suspects in café fare (soup, pasta, sandwiches etc), plus fine cakes and muffins.

Canterbury Hotel (☎ 03-302 8045; cnr Main St & Forest Dr; mains $9-22; lunch & dinner) One of Methven's two pubs, known for obvious reasons as the Brown Pub. This is where locals tend to hang out, either conversing at the no-frills bar or downing one of the solid, blokey pub grills, including sausages, schnitzel and steak.

Blue Pub (☎ 03-302 8046; Main St; mains $12-23; lunch & dinner) The other of the town's pub options, a favourite of the visiting ski crowd for tall tales of the day's exploits on the mountain, and for listening to the occasional live band. Its café goes for more upmarket fare than its counterpart pub across the road.

Lisah's (☎ 03-302 8070; Main St; mains $15-25; dinner Tue-Sat) Mellow Lisah's is a good local choice. Slip into one of the red booths and warm up with the likes of a Canterbury lamb burger, venison hot pot or Cajun-flavoured fish. It's also a wine bar and cocktail lounge.

Self-caterers should head to the **Super-value supermarket** (cnr The Mall & MacMillan St; 7am-9pm).

Entertainment

If the weather won't cooperate, take in a movie at **Cinema Paradiso** (☎ 03-302 1957; www.cinemaparadiso.co.nz; Main St; adult/child $13/10), which screens mostly art-house releases.

Getting There & Around

Methven Travel (☎ 03-302 8106; Main St) picks up from Christchurch city and airport and delivers you to your accommodation (adult/child one way $30/15); a few other companies offer this service during the ski season.

InterCity (☎ 03-365 1113; www.intercitycoach.co.nz) has one daily bus between Methven and Christchurch ($32, one hour).

Many shuttles operate from Methven to Mt Hutt ski field (40 minutes away) in winter for around $25; inquiries and pick-ups are from the visitor information centre.

MT SOMERS

Mt Somers is a small settlement just off SH72, the main road between Geraldine and Mt Hutt. The **Mt Somers Subalpine Walkway** (17km, 10 hours) traverses the northern face of Mt Somers, linking the popular picnic spots of Sharplin Falls and Woolshed Creek. Trail highlights include volcanic formations, Maori rock drawings, deep river canyons and botanical diversity. There are two huts on the walk: **Pinnacles Hut** and **Mt Somers Hut** (each $5). Be warned that this route is subject to sudden changes in weather and all tramping precautions should be taken. Hut tickets and information are available at the well-stocked **Mt Somers General Store** (03-303 9831; Patons Rd). There are also several shorter walks in the area.

Based in the Mt Somers region is **Back of Beyond** (03-303 0888; www.mountainbiking.net .nz), offering small-group high-country mountain-bike tours from late November to early May. Options range from one day ($350) to four days (from $1800, including accommodation, meals and a support vehicle to carry luggage). Self-guided, self-catering tour options are available too, and include a support vehicle.

Campers and campervan pilots can stay at the small, well-kept **Mt Somers Holiday Park** (03-303 9719; www.mountsomers.co.nz; Hoods Rd; sites per 2 people $20, cabins $39-58).

At the highway turn-off to Mt Somers is **Stronechrubie** (03-303 9814; www.stronechrubie .co.nz; SH72; d $100-160), with studios and luxury chalets scattered across bird-filled gardens. Its intimate à la carte restaurant (mains $21 to $34, open for dinner Wednesday to Sunday and lunch Sunday) has a great reputation; if you stay here, consider one of the DB&B packages.

SOUTH CANTERBURY

The SH1 heading south from Christchurch along the coast passes through the port city of Timaru on its way to Dunedin and so carries a lot of traffic. But so does the inland SH8, which weaves towards the bright lanes (Tekapo, Pukaki, Ohau) of Mackenzie Country before veering south through Twizel – it's at this bend in the highway that SH80 branches off north up to the magnificent heights of Aoraki/Mt Cook National Park.

TIMARU
pop 26,750

Timaru, an important port city for the surrounding agricultural region, is also a con-

venient stopping point halfway between Christchurch and Dunedin, although many travellers prefer to press on to the smaller, more charming Oamaru, 85km further south. The town's moniker comes from the Maori name Te Maru, meaning 'The Place of Shelter'. However, no permanent settlement existed here when the first European arrivals, the Weller brothers of Sydney, set up a whaling station in 1839. The *Caroline*, a sailing ship that picked up whale oil, gave the picturesque bay its name.

Orientation

SH1 is known by many names as it passes through Timaru: the Hilton Hwy north of town, Evans St as it enters town and then Theodosia St and Craigie Ave as it bypasses the central business district around Stafford St. Continuing south, the highway becomes King St and then SH1 again after emerging from town.

Information

The **Timaru visitor information centre** (0800 484 6278, 03-688 6163; www.southisland.org.nz; 2 George St; 8.30am-5pm Mon-Fri, 10am-3pm Sat & Sun) is diagonally across from the train station (note that the trains in this area carry freight, not passengers). The centre has enthusiastic staff, street maps and information on local walks; it also handles transport bookings.

Sights

South Canterbury Museum (03-684 2212; www .timaru.govt.nz; Perth St; admission by donation; 10am-4.30pm Tue-Fri, 1.30-4.30pm Sat & Sun) has an interesting collection of historical and natural artefacts of the region. It's housed in a building with the interior look of a circus big top. Hanging from the ceiling à la trapeze is a replica of the aeroplane designed and flown by local pioneer aviator and inventor Richard Pearse. Many believe his mildly successful attempts at manned flight came before the Wright brothers first flew in 1903.

Aigantighe Art Gallery (03-688 4424; www.tim aru.govt.nz; 49 Wai-iti Rd; admission free; 10am-4pm Tue-Fri, noon-4pm Sat & Sun) is one of the South Island's largest public galleries, a 900-piece collection of NZ and European art from the previous four centuries set up in a 1908 mansion, and adorned externally by a sculpture garden (always open). The gallery's Gaelic name means 'at home'.

DB Mainland Brewery

DB Mainland Brewery (☎ 03-688 2059; Sheffield St; tours free; ⓨ tours 10.30am Mon-Fri), 6km north of town, offers free tours of its brewing and bottling plant. Enclosed footwear (no sandals or thongs) must be worn; bookings required.

The lovely **Botanic Gardens** (cnr King & Queen Sts; admission free; ⓨ 8am–dusk), established in 1864, have ponds, a conservatory and a notable collection of roses and native tree ferns. The gardens are south of town; enter from Queen St.

Activities

One of the few safe, sheltered beaches on the east coast is Caroline Bay – there's a fun, crowded **Christmas Carnival** (www.carolinebay.org .nz) here beginning 26 December and running for about 10 days. The beachside **park** has a walk-through aviary, a wading pool, rose garden, minigolf ($3), kids playground, skate park, a pleasant walkway and a landscaped 'piazza'.

A good one-hour **walk** heads north from town along Caroline Bay, past the Benvenue Cliffs and on to the Dashing Rocks

and rock pools at the end of the bay. Ask at the visitor information centre for the folder detailing walks in the area. There's good **surfing** in the south of town, east of the hospital at Patiti Point, where you might be lucky enough to spot sea lions.

In the past, operators have offered cruises taking in the marine wildlife around the port including Hector's dolphins and seals, but at the time of research these weren't operating. Check with the visitor information centre to see if they have started up again.

Sleeping

Timaru Top 10 Holiday Park (☎ 0800 242 121; 03-684 7690; www.timaruholidaypark.co.nz; 8 Glen St; unpowered/ powered sites per 2 people $24/26, cabins & motels d $45-90). Satisfyingly green parkland site with an excellent amenities block and a golf course next door where you can swing clubs without paying any green fees.

1873 Wanderer Backpackers (☎ 0800 187 392, 03-688 3795; 1873wandererbackpackers@xtra.co.nz; 24 Evans St; dm $18-22, d $45-50; ☐) Friendly, laidback spot with helpful owners offering free drop-off and pick-up from the bus station.

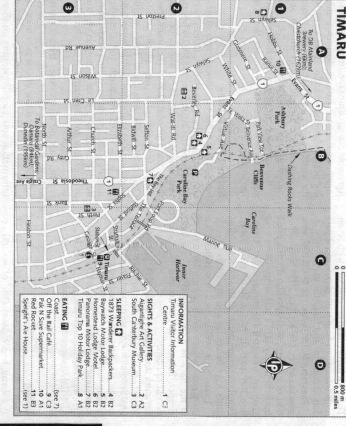

TIMARU

INFORMATION
Timaru Visitor Information Centre	1 C3

SIGHTS & ACTIVITIES
Aigantighe Art Gallery	2 A2
South Canterbury Museum	3 A2

SLEEPING 🛏
1873 Wanderer Backpackers	4 B2
Baywatch Motor Lodge	5 B2
Homestead Lodge Motel	6 B2
Panorama Motor Lodge	7 B2
Timaru Top 10 Holiday Park	8 A1

EATING 🍴
Coast	(see 7)
Off the Rail Café	9 C3
Pak N Save Supermarket	10 A1
Red Roccet	11 B3
Speight's Ale House	(see 1)

There's a barbecue to get culinary with (even a dishwasher to help with clean-up), a garden to relax in, and bikes for use.

Panorama Motor Lodge (☎ 03-688 0097; www.panorama.net.nz; 52 The Bay Hill; d $115-135) A selection of modern, well-appointed units piled up behind Bay Hill's café strip. There's no greenery to soften the concrete, but Caroline Bay park is just a short walk away. Family units are particularly spacious. Most units have balconies and bay views.

Evans St is wall-to-wall motels but it's a busy road, so it's worth asking for a room at the back of a property if you're a light sleeper. Rooms start at around $75. Some decent options:

Baywatch Motor Lodge (☎ 0800 929 828, 03-688 1886; 7 Evans St; d $110-140) Move beyond that disturbing David Hasselhoff imagery and check out this very well-appointed place. Front units have double-glazed windows to negate traffic noise.

Homestead Lodge Motel (☎ 0800 877 773, 03-684 5193; www.homesteadlodgemotel.co.nz; 28 Evans St; d $75-125) Accommodating owners and comfy, well-equipped, older-style units.

Eating

Coast (☎ 03-688 4367; 56 The Bay Hill; mains $10-28; breakfast, lunch & dinner) One of several refreshingly casual, well-patronised café-bars on the Bay Hill, newly named Coast (formerly known as Zanzibar) keeps the punters happy with a good breakfast menu from 7am, and food and drink served all day and well into the night.

Off the Rail Café (☎ 03-688 3594; Station St; meals $5-15; breakfast & lunch;) Drawing a diverse crowd (from hipsters to businessmen to grannies) is this funky licensed café at the train station, opposite the visitor information centre. Sate a rumbling tum with a wide array of baked goods and blackboard specials, including lots of veg options. Often open for drinks until late.

Red Rocket (☎ 03-688 8313; 4 Elizabeth St; mains $10-18; lunch & dinner) Simple pasta dishes and gourmet science fiction–styled pizzas (Supernova Satay Chicken, Meat-eorite Shower) served in a nicely converted old church. The attempted connection between pizzas, space travel and a house of worship is rather odd, but the food is great and the atmosphere fun. There's a play area and menu for little 'uns.

Speights Ale House (☎ 03-686 6030; 2 George St; lunch $7-16, dinner mains $14-27; lunch & dinner)

Agreeable casual choice for dining or drinking, housed in the historic former Landing Service bluestone building adjacent to the visitor information centre. The menu recommends a Speights drop to best accompany your dish of choice.

Self-caterers can shop at **Pak N Save supermarket** (cnr Ranui & Evans Sts; 8am-9pm Mon-Fri, to 7pm Sat & Sun).

Getting There & Away

InterCity (☎ 03-365 1113; www.intercitycoach.co.nz) stops outside the train station, from where buses head to Christchurch ($30, 2½ hours, two daily), Oamaru ($24, one hour, two daily) and Dunedin ($35, three hours, two daily); from Dunedin you can connect to Queenstown, Te Anau and Invercargill. There are also numerous shuttle buses running between Christchurch and Dunedin that stop at Timaru, including **Atomic Shuttles** (☎ 03-322 8883; www.atomictravel.co.nz); the average fare to Christchurch or Dunedin is $20 to $25.

There are no direct buses from Timaru to Lake Tekapo and Mt Cook – you'll need to first get to Geraldine or Oamaru to catch buses to the Mackenzie Country. Ask for information about local operators on these routes at the visitor information centre.

TO MACKENZIE COUNTRY

Those heading to Queenstown and the southern lakes from Christchurch will probably turn off SH1 onto SH79, along a scenic route towards the high country that signals the rise of Aoraki/Mt Cook National Park's eastern foothills. The road passes through the small towns of Geraldine and Fairlie before joining SH8, which heads over Burkes Pass to the blue intensity of Lake Tekapo.

Geraldine

pop 2210

Sweet Geraldine has an affable country-village atmosphere due in part to its pretty private gardens and active craft scene. The best website for the town is at www.geraldine.net.nz.

The **Geraldine visitor information centre** (☎ 03-693 1006; www.southisland.org.nz; cnr Talbot & Cox Sts; 8.30am-5pm Mon-Fri, 10am-4pm Sat & Sun) has brochures detailing the gardens to visit and the numerous galleries and craft stores in town, as well as rural B&Bs and farmstays. It's also surrounded by a worthy journey-breaker, the busy **Berry Barn Complex** (mr Talbot & Cox Sts; daily), catering to hungry blow-ins with a bakery, cafés and a cheese shop selling tasty Talbot Forest Cheeses. Also here is **Barker's** (03-693 9727), a fruit-products emporium selling fine juices, sauces, smoothies and jams.

The **Vintage Car & Machinery Museum** (03-693 8005; 178 Talbot St; adult/child $6/free; 10am-4pm daily Oct-Jun, to 4pm Sat & Sun Jul-Sep) has more than 30 vintage and veteran cars from as far back as 1907, while a massive shed at the back houses 100 tractors dating from 1912 onwards. There is also a rare 1929 Spartan Biplane and tonnes of heavy-duty farm equipment.

4x4 New Zealand (03-693 8847; www.4x4new zealand.co.nz) operates a range of 4WD tours in the surrounding high country, taking in sheep stations, braided rivers and *Lord of the Rings* film sites. Prices vary according to itinerary and length of tours.

SLEEPING & EATING

Geraldine Holiday Park (03-693 8147; www.geral dineholidaypark.co.nz; 39 Hislop St; unpowered/powered sites per 2 people $20/22, cabins $38-85) Neat, well-treed slice of greenery across the road from a large oval. Besides budget cabins and self-contained units, there's a TV room and playground.

Rawhiti Backpackers (03-693 8255; www.raw hitibackpackers.com; 27 Hewlings St; dm/s/d $24/30/55;) A well-travelled Dutch couple has transformed an old maternity hospital into this spacious, high-quality hostel with great extras – cooked breakfast for $10, dinner-time pizzas, bike hire. It's high above the town, off Peel St (grab a map before setting off).

Geraldine Motels (0800 400 404, 03-693 8501; gerald ne motels@actrix.co.nz; 97 Talbot St; d $70-110;) The most central motel option, with a range of large, old-style units and a couple of newish, nicely outfitted studios. There's also a spa pool, kids playground and a pleasant yard out back.

Totara Restaurant (03-693 8458; 31 Talbot St; mains $19-29; dinner) Inside the Crown Hotel, the Totara serves popular stone-grill meals, where lamb, venison, prawns and assorted protein are cooked over very hot rocks. If that sounds too swish head to the 'Crown jewels' bar out the back for basic pub meals priced around $10. Also under the pub's umbrella is the Village Inn complex next door, home to the appealing Red Red Wine Bar & Café.

The eateries at Berry Barn (opposite) are ideal for a quick bite. If you're after a quality sugar rush, visit **Chocolate Fellman** (03-693 9982; 10 Talbot St; 8.30am-6pm Mon-Fri, 9am-2pm Sat) for superb handmade choccies, plus coffee, hot chocolate and cake.

Peel Forest

The Peel Forest, 22km north of Geraldine (signposted off SH72), is among NZ's most important indigenous podocarp (conifer) forests. A road from nearby Mt Peel station leads to **Mesopotamia**, the run of English writer Samuel Butler (author of the satire *Erewhon*) in the 1860s.

Get information such as the *Peel Forest Park: Track Information* brochure ($1) at **Peel Forest Store** (03-696 3567; 9am-6pm), which stocks petrol, groceries and takeaway food, and has an on-site café-restaurant. The store also manages the very pleasant DOC **camping ground** (unpowered/powered sites per 2 people $16/20, cabins $32) beside the Rangitata River, about 3km beyond the store and equipped with very basic two- to four-berth cabins, showers, a kitchen, laundry and card phone.

The magnificent podocarp forest consists of totara, kahikatea and matai. One fine example of totara on the **Big Tree Walk** (30 minutes return) has a circumference of 9m and is over 1000 years old. Local bird life includes the rifleman, NZ pigeon (kereru), bellbird, fantail and grey warbler. There are also trails to several picturesque waterfalls: **Emily Falls** (1½ hours return), **Rata Falls** (two hours return) and **Acland Falls** (one hour return).

Rangitata Rafts (0800 251 251, 03-696 3534; www.raftg.co.nz; Sep-Apr) goes white-water rafting on the Rangitata River, which contains exhilarating grade V rapids. The company's base is at Mt Peel, 13km past the camping ground, where there's some budget lodge **accommodation** (dm/d $15/38). Rafting trips can be taken from either Peel Forest ($152) or Christchurch ($162, including return transport to Mt Peel) and include hot showers and a barbecue; time spent on the river is three hours.

CHRISTCHURCH & CANTERBURY

Fairlie

pop 725

Wee Fairlie is often described as 'the gateway to the Mackenzie' because west of here the landscape changes dramatically as the road mounts Burkes Pass to the open spaces of Mackenzie Country and the snowy mountain peaks come nicely into view.

The **Resource Centre** (☎ 03-685 8496; www.fairlie .co.nz; 64 Main St; ⏰ 10am-4pm Mon-Fri) is the local visitor information centre. Buses and shuttles pass through town on the Christchurch to Queenstown route.

There's skiing 29km northwest of here at **Fox Peak** in the Two Thumb Range. **Mt Dobson,** 26km northwest of Fairlie, is in a 3km-wide basin (see p82). The **Ski Shack** (☎ 03-685 8088; Allandale St) has information and gear rental.

SLEEPING & EATING

Both Main St pubs offer budget accommodation, or you can try one of the unassuming local motels, with room rates around the $80 mark.

Fairlie Gateway Top 10 Holiday Park (☎ 0800 324 754, 03-685 8375; www.fairlietop10.co.nz; 10 Allandale Rd; unpowered & powered sites per 2 people $26, cabins & units $42-75) Tranquil, creek-side park that's perfect for families, as it has a large playground for children to hurl themselves around and can also provide baby baths, cots and highchairs. Fishing rods and tackle are available for hire.

Rimuwhare Country Retreat (☎ 0800 723 723, 03-685 8058; rimuwhare@xtra.co.nz; 53 Mt Cook Rd; d $75-80) Old-fashioned but spacious units well off the main road amid a well-established garden, plus a licensed restaurant.

Pinewood Motels (☎ 0800 858 599, 03-685 8599; www.pinewoodmotels.co.nz; 25-27 Mt Cook Rd; d from $75) Reasonable self-contained units, including one that's wheelchair-accessible.

Old Library Café (☎ 03-685 8999; 6 Allandale Rd; dinner mains $25-27; ⏰ lunch & dinner) Has elegant touches like an old pressed-metal ceiling and serves fresh, tasty local food such as roasted rump of Mackenzie lamb or barbecued salmon steaks. There's also an all-day menu featuring meals such as pasta, chowder or warm chicken salad. A lovely spot to break your journey.

MACKENZIE COUNTRY

The expansive high ground from which the scenic peaks of Aoraki/Mt Cook National

Park grow is known as Mackenzie Country after the legendary James 'Jock' Mackenzie, who's said to have run his stolen flocks around 1843 in this then-uninhabited region. When he was finally caught, other settlers realised the potential of the land and followed in his footsteps. The first people to traverse the Mackenzie were Maoris, who used to trek from Banks Peninsula to Otago hundreds of years ago.

Good information is available online at www.mtcook.org.nz; for information on winter activities in the region, check out www.mackenziewinter.co.nz.

Lake Tekapo

pop 315

This small township at the southern end of its namesake lake has unobstructed views across turquoise water, with hills and snow-capped mountains as a backdrop. The town has boomed in recent times, with construction of plenty of residences (including B&Bs) and holiday homes – all taking advantage of those views. For an explanation of why this and other lakes in the region have such striking coats of blue, see the boxed text, above.

Lake Tekapo is a popular stop on tours of the Southern Alps, with Mt Cook and Queenstown buses chugging up to the cluster of main road tourist shops to create some short-lived retail chaos.

INFORMATION

Kiwi Treasures (☎ 03-680 6686; SH8; ⏰ 7.30am-8pm summer, shorter hours winter) acts as souvenir shop, post office and visitor information

---

LAKE TEKAPO

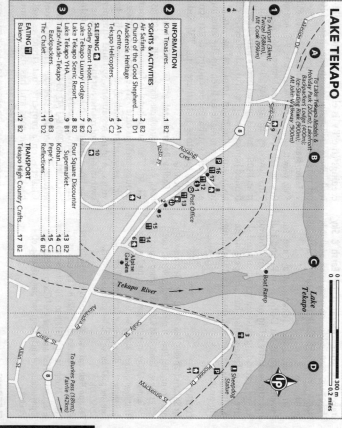

INFORMATION	
Kiwi Treasures............................1	B2

SIGHTS & ACTIVITIES	
Air Safaris....................................2	B2
Church of the Good Shepherd....3	D1
Mackenzie Heritage	
Centre.......................................4	A1
Tekapo Helicopters.....................5	C2

SLEEPING	
Godley Resort Hotel....................6	C2
Lake Tekapo Luxury Lodge..........7	B2
Lake Tekapo Scenic Resort..........8	B2
Lake Tekapo YHA.........................9	B1
Tailor-Made-Tekapo....................10	B3
The Chalet...................................11	D2

EATING	
Bakery..12	B2
Four Square Discounter..............13	B2
Kohan...14	C2
Pepe's..15	C2
Reflections..................................16	B2
Supermarket................................(see 13)	

TRANSPORT	
Tekapo High Country Crafts.........17	B2

centre. Here you can also book buses and hire fishing gear. For Web-based information visit www.laketekapountouched.co.nz and www.tekapotourism.co.nz.

There's **Internet access** (per 20min $2) at the Tekapo Helicopters office (p580); an ATM (no bank) is located out the front of the supermarket.

SIGHTS & ACTIVITIES

The diminutive, picturesque **Church of the Good Shepherd** beside the lake was built of stone and oak in 1935 and is a favourite for nuptials given its postcard-perfect setting. Further along is a **statue** of a collie dog, a tribute to the sheepdogs that helped develop the Mackenzie Country. This area is at its scenic best before or after the last bus group leaves, otherwise the place is swarming with rubberneckers, so come early morning or late afternoon.

Keep your eye out for the new **Mackenzie Heritage Centre** (www.inspiringnz.co.nz), a multi-million-dollar, multimedia museum on the highway just west of the township. This large, ambitious project (one local called

it 'Te Papa in Tekapo') will showcase the high country and its history and may open sometime in 2007 (but we suspect it may be later).

Popular walks include the track to the summit of **Mount John** (three hours return) from just beyond the camping ground. From there, continue on to Alexandrina and McGregor Lakes, making it an all-day walk. Other walks are detailed in the brochure *Lake Tekapo Walkway* ($1).

Lake Tekapo Adventures & Cruises (0800 528 624, 03-680 6629; www.laketekapo.co.nz; 90min cruise from $60) organises activities in the vicinity of the Godley Glacier ranging from 4WD safaris and mountain-bike runs to fishing and lake cruises.

Mackenzie Alpine Trekking Company (0800 628 269; www.matc.co.nz; 1/2hr ride $50/75, full-day ride $250) organises four-footed high-country exploration.

Thanks to clear skies and its distance from any main towns, the stargazing at Lake Tekapo is top-notch, and the University of Canterbury has a scientific observatory on Mt John. Join a 90-minute night-time stargazing tour operated by **Earth & Sky** (☎ 03-680 6960; www.earthandsky.co.nz; adult/child $48/24; ☼ Apr-Sep). Call for start times, as these vary.

In winter, Lake Tekapo is a base for **downhill skiing** at Mt Dobson or Round Hill Range, and **cross-country skiing** on the Two Thumb Range, providing ski-area transport and ski hire. Lake Tekapo also has an open-air **ice-skating rink** (☼ Jun-Sep), down past the camping ground.

TOURS

Air Safaris (☎ 0800 806 880, 03-680 6880; www.air safaris.co.nz; SH8) Does 50-minute flights over Mt Cook and its glaciers (adult/child $260/180), taking you up the Tasman Glacier, over the upper part of the Fox and Franz Josef Glaciers, and by Mts Cook, Tasman and Elie de Beaumont. It does a similar flight from Glentanner Park (see p587) but with higher prices (adult/child $295/200).

Tekapo Helicopters (☎ 0800 359 835, 03-680 6229; www.tekapohelicopters.co.nz; SH8) Has five options, from a 25-minute flight ($180) to a 70-minute trip taking in Mt Cook and Fox and Franz Josef Glaciers ($490). All flights include icefield landings and grand viewings of Mt Cook.

SLEEPING

There's been an explosion of B&Bs in the newer eastern part of town – Hamilton Drive is the epicentre.

Lake Tekapo Motels & Holiday Park (☎ 0800 853 853, 03-680 6825; www.laketekapo-accommodation .co.nz; Lakeside Dr; sites per 2 people $24, cabins $50, motel units $120) Has an exceptionally pretty and peaceful lakeside locale, plus everything from basic cabins to motel units with full kitchen and Sky TV.

Lakefront Backpackers Lodge (☎ 03-680 6227; www.laketekapo-accommodation.co.nz; Lakeside Dr; dm/d $26/60; ☐) An impressive lakeside place that opened in early 2005, not far from the holiday park (about 1km from the township). Relax by the open fire in the comfy lounge area or take in the sensational views from the front deck. Rooms are modern, bathrooms are top-notch, and canoes can be hired here. Highly recommended.

Lake Tekapo YHA (☎ 03-680 6857; www.stayha .com; 3 Simpson La; dm/d $24/54; ☐) Friendly, well-equipped little place, its living room adorned with open fireplaces, a piano and outstanding views across the lake to the mountains beyond, but with no TV to dominate pro-

ceedings (the TV is elsewhere in the building). There are limited camp sites here ($10 per person).

Tailor-Made-Tekapo Backpackers (☎ 03-680 6700; www.tailor-made-backpackers.co.nz; 9-11 Aorangi Cres; dm $21-23, d with/without bathroom $64/52; ☐) This low-key hostel favours beds rather than bunks and is spread over a pair of well-tended houses on a peaceful side street, well away from the main road traffic. An effort has been made to liven up the interior and there's a barbecue-equipped garden; couch potatoes note there's no TV. Kids welcome.

Godley Resort Hotel (☎ 0800 835 276, 03-680 6848; www.mountcookcollection.co.nz; SH8; d $90-165; ☐ 🏊) This large hotel is favoured by tour groups and has older-style budget rooms as well as smarter refurbished rooms with lake views. A gym, restaurant, spa and summer swimming pool round out the facilities, and the hotel also rents bikes and organises fishing and golfing excursions.

Chalet (☎ 0800 843 242, 03-680 6774; www.thecha let.co.nz; 14 Pioneer Dr; d $120-200) The lakefront Chalet is on a property that stretches well back from the road and has six bright and lovely, well-designed studios and one-/two-bedroom units with access to a lake garden. It also rents out local holiday houses. A good choice.

Lake Tekapo Scenic Resort (☎ 0800 118 666, 03-680 6808; www.laketekapo.com; SH8; dm $25, units d $160-230) Not so much a self-contained resort as a central complex of attractive, modern studio and family units, with only bare parkland separating it from the lake. Tough choice: opt for a spa or a balcony. There is also a budget wing offering backpacker accommodation.

Lake Tekapo Luxury Lodge (☎ 0800 525 383, 03-680 6566; www.laketekapolodge.co.nz; 24 Aorangi Cres; d $200-335) Luxurious hilltop B&B set in a youthful brick home with a monasterial entryway. Three of its four well-appointed rooms have direct access to the great views from the back deck; there's also a handy path that leads down to the village.

EATING

Disappointingly, Lake Tekapo is not exactly overflowing with dining options (quite the opposite of the accommodation scene). Lunchtime is perfect for grabbing supplies for a lakeside picnic.

Pepe's (☎ 03-680 6677; SH8; meals $14-26; ☻ dinner) Filled with large booths and its walls decorated with skiing paraphernalia, Pepe's is a cosy little place in which to attack various pastas and gourmet pizzas. Fancy a meal atop a doughy base? Try a pizza topped with pork, parsnip, apple sauce and crackling, or with marinated lamb, roast potato and mint sauce.

Reflections (☎ 03-680 6808; SH8; lunch $6-22, dinner mains $22-28; ☻ breakfast, lunch & dinner) First things first – bags an outdoor table with a view down to the lake, then select from a decent menu that may include roasted venison or baked Mt Cook salmon. Lunchtime offerings are more casual (burgers, souvlaki, salads); adjacent is the town's tavern for night-time imbibing.

Pick up supplies at the **Four Square supermarket** (SH8; ☻ 7am-9pm) and the nearby **bakery** (☎ 03-680 655; SH8; ☻ breakfast & lunch).

Kohan (☎ 03-680 6688; SH8; mains $10-25; ☻ lunch & dinner Mon-Sat, lunch Sun) You'll find the clinical décor of this Japanese restaurant down a path beside the Godley Resort Hotel. It caters mainly to transient tour groups, hence the lack of attention to interior niceties, but on the plus side it offers a full range of sushi treats and dishes such as teriyaki chicken, udon soups and tempura seafood; takeaway is an option.

GETTING THERE & AWAY

Southbound services to Mt Cook, Queenstown and Wanaka, and northbound services to Christchurch, are offered by a number of operators like **Atomic Shuttles** (☎ 03-322 8883; www.atomictravel.co.nz), **InterCity/Newmans** (☎ 03-365 1113; www.intercitycoach.co.nz), **Southern Link Lazerline Coaches** (☎ 03-358 8355; www.yellow.co.nz/site/southernlink) and **Wanaka Connexions** (☎ 03-443 9122; www.wanakaconnexions.co.nz). One-way fares range between $25 and $45.

Cook Connection (☎ 0800 266 526; www.cookconnect.co.nz) operates to Mt Cook (one way $25, one daily), Twizel (one way $20, one daily) or Oamaru (one way $40, four weekly).

Between them, **Kiwi Treasures** (☎ 03-680 6686; SH8) and **Tekapo High Country Crafts** (☎ 03-680 6905; SH8) handle bookings for visiting buses.

Mt Cook Salmon Farm

Some 15km west of Lake Tekapo along SH8 is the signposted turn-off to the **Mt Cook Salmon Farm** (☎ 021 370 038; www.mtcooksalmon.com; Canal Rd; adult/child $2/free; ☻ daylight hours). The farm operates in a hydroelectric canal system and is 12km from the turn-off – a scenic drive along a canal popular for fishing and enjoying great views of Mt Cook. Stop at the farm here to feed the fish, catch your own salmon (rods supplied) or pick up something for dinner. Continue on this stretch and you'll reach the southeastern shore of Lake Pukaki before the road rejoins SH8.

Lake Pukaki

On the southern shore of Lake Pukaki, 45km southwest of Lake Tekapo and 2km northeast of the turn-off to Mt Cook, is the **Lake Pukaki visitor information centre** (☎ 03-435 3280; info@mtcook.org.nz; SH8; ☻ 9am-6pm Oct-Apr, 10am-4pm May-Sep), with reams of information on Mackenzie Country. But the highlight here is the sterling **lookout** that on a clear day gives a picture-perfect view of Mt Cook and its surrounding peaks, with the ultra-blue lake in the foreground. For an explanation of the lake's colour, see the boxed text, p578.

Twizel

pop 1015

The oft-maligned town of Twizel, just south of Lake Pukaki, only came into existence in 1968 when it was built to service construction of the nearby hydroelectric power station. It was due to expire when the project was completed in 1984. The town's survival beyond the mid-'80s is thanks to the tenacity of residents and its handy proximity to Mt Cook (63km down the road). It makes a good base for visiting Mt Cook if the prices or availability of places closer to the mountain are prohibitive, and has its own quirky charm plus enough activities to keep you busy.

Right in town is the **Twizel visitor information centre** (☎ 03-435 3124; www.twizel.com; Market Pl; ☻ 9am-6pm daily Oct-Apr, 10am-4pm Mon-Sat May-Sep).

ACTIVITIES

Nearby **Lake Ruataniwha** is popular for rowing, boating and windsurfing. **Fishing** in local rivers, canals and lakes is also big business and there are a number of guides in the region; ask at the visitor information centre.

Discovery Tours ([a] 0800 213 868, 03-435 0114; www.discoverytours.co.nz) is based in Twizel and operates a number of guided, small-group tours around the Mackenzie Country, including walking, mountain biking and fishing, plus a popular 1½-hour tour ($65) taking in Ben Ohau Station, site of the Pelennor battlefield in the *Lord of the Rings* movies.

Helibike ([a] 0800 435 424, 03-435 0626; www.helibike.com) flies you by helicopter up a mountain, which you then descend on two wheels; one such trip is the 3½-hour Ben more descent ($215). There are also regular mountain-biking trips (no helicopters involved), such as a two-hour ride along farm tracks ($55), or if bikes aren't your thing, you can helihike (helicopter up and a guided walk down, $140). Minimum numbers apply.

The wading koki (black stilt bird) is found only in NZ and is one of the country's rarest birds. A breeding programme is now attempting to increase the population and the new Ahuriri Conservation Park is part of this effort. Just south of Twizel, the **Kaki Visitor Hide** ([a] 03-435 3124; adult/child $12.50/5; [Y] Oct-Apr) gives you a close-up look at these elusive fellows. Bookings are essential for the one-hour tour of the hide; for more info, visit the Twizel visitor information centre (note that you need your own transport to get to the hide).

Mt Cook Skydive ([a] 0800 2645 344; www.nzskydive.com; Pukaki Airport, SH8; tandem skydive $299) operates from a small airfield north of town, offering brave souls the chance to jump out of a plane at 12,000ft (the same height of Mt Cook) and enjoy spectacular views of five lakes (including the amazing hues of Pukaki and Tekapo), the Southern Alps and the big daddy, Mt Cook.

Helicopter Line ([a] 0800 650 652, 03-435 0370; www .helicopter.co.nz; Wairepo Rd) flies over the Mt Cook region from a helipad beside Mackenzie Country Inn. Sightseeing flights last from 25 minutes ($195) to 60 minutes ($495) and include a snow landing.

SLEEPING
Parklands Alpine Tourists Park ([a] 03-435 0507; parklands1@xtra.co.nz; 122 Mackenzie Dr; unpowered/powered sites per 2 people $20/22, cabins & cottages $40-85) Offering neat, green, flower-filled grounds and some quality accommodation in a

colourfully refurbished maternity hospital. The modern self-contained cottages are particularly good value. Prices are for two people.

High Country Holiday Lodge ([a] 03-435 0671; www.highcountrylodge.co.nz; Mackenzie Dr; dm $18, s/d $45/60, d with bathroom $70, motel from $95; [computer]) Cabins originally built for hydroscheme workers are now put to work accommodating out-of-towners. There's a large range of sturdy, decent-value but no-frills accommodation, beginning with two-bed dorms, plus games room and a nine-hole golf course opposite.

Mountain Chalet Motels ([a] 0800 629 999, 03-435 0785; www.mountainchalets.co.nz; Wairepo Rd; dm/d from $20/100) Recommended place with well-equipped, self-contained A-frame chalets. The cheapest units are studios, but there are a number of two-bedroom beasts for larger groups/families, too. There's also a small, laid-back lodge that's perfect for backpackers.

Lake Ruataniwha Homestays ([a] 03-435 0532; robinandlester@xtra.co.nz; 146 Max Smith Dr; d $120-150) En route to Lake Ruataniwha, about 4km from Twizel, is this striking, modern house with a curved roofline, taking in glorious views in all directions. The owners have three lovely ground-floor guest rooms (one with private bathroom, two sharing facilities) and offer cooked breakfasts served up with warm rural hospitality.

There are other good motel options in town:

Aspen Court Motel (☎ 0800 277 364, 033-435 0857; www.aspencourt.co.nz; 10 Mackenzie Dr; d $120-140)

Colonial Motel (☎ 0800 355 722, 03-435 0100; www.twizel.com/colonialmotel; 38 Mackenzie Dr; d $95-120)

EATING

Korner Kafe (☎ 03-435 0501; 1/20 Market Pl; lunch $8-15, dinner mains $15-26; ☺ breakfast, lunch & dinner Oct-Apr, shorter hours winter) Poor spelling aside, this is a locally recommended place with a rustic interior and a menu of simple meals done well. The cheaper end of the menu sees classic meaty dishes (bangers and mash, chicken Kiev, ham steak), but there's also a number of veg options.

Hunter's Cafe & Bar (☎ 03-435 0303; 2 Market Pl; meals $14-24; ☺ lunch & dinner Mon-Sat, lunch Sun) A light, open space that supplies generous mains of local produce (eg braised lamb shanks, hot smoked salmon on potato rösti) as well as cheaper bar snacks for small-stomached folk. There's a good selection of wine by the bottle or glass.

Shawty's Cafe (☎ 03-435 3155; 4 Market Pl; meals $14-24; ☺ breakfast, lunch & dinner) A welcome new addition to the local dining scene, with a warm interior, alfresco seating and a family-friendly menu of salads, pasta and gourmet pizzas.

Drop Zone Café (Pukaki Airport, SH8; snacks $3-7; ☺ breakfast & lunch) Well-situated pit stop en route from Christchurch to Queenstown. This sweet little café serves excellent coffee, toasted bagels and homebaked cakes. Sit outside and watch pumped-up skydivers on a high after landing, and try to work up the courage to jump yourself.

GETTING THERE & AWAY

InterCity (☎ 03-365 1113; www.intercitycoach.co.nz) buses stop at Twizel on the Christchurch–Queenstown/Wanaka route. Other bus companies ply the same route daily and also call in at Twizel; operators include **Atomic Shuttles** (☎ 03-322 8883; www.atomictravel.co.nz), **Southern Link** & **Lazerline Coaches** (☎ 03-358 8355; www.yellow.co.nz /site/southernlink) and **Wanaka Connexions** (☎ 03-443 9127; www.wanakaconnexions.co.nz).

The **Cook Connection** (☎ 0800 266 526; www .cookconnect.co.nz) is a useful shuttle for this region, operating services connecting Twizel with Mt Cook (one way $20, up to four per

day), Lake Tekapo (one way $20, once daily) and Oamaru (one way $25, four weekly).

Lake Ohau & Ohau Forests

Six forests in the Lake Ohau area (Dobson, Hopkins, Huxley, Temple, Ohau and Ahuriri) are administered by DOC. The numerous walks in this vast recreation grove are detailed in the DOC pamphlet *Ohau Conservation Area* ($1); huts and camping areas are also scattered throughout for adventurous trampers.

Lake Ohau Lodge (☎ 03-438 9885; www.ohau.co .nz; Lake Ohau Rd; s $50-135, d $60-150) is an idyllic setting on the western shore of the rower-friendly Lake Ohau, 42km west of Twizel, though its popularity means you can't expect to get it all to yourself. Prices listed here are for accommodation only (everything from backpacker-style to upmarket rooms with deck and mountain views); DB&B packages are worthwhile.

The lodge is the wintertime service centre for the **Ohau Ski Field** (see p82).

AORAKI/MT COOK NATIONAL PARK

The spectacular 700-sq-km Aoraki/Mt Cook National Park, along with Fiordland, Aspiring and Westland National Parks, has been incorporated into the Southwest New Zealand (Te Wahipounamu) World Heritage Area, which extends from Westland's Cook River down to the chilly toes of Fiordland. Fenced in by the Southern Alps and the Two Thumb, Liebig and Ben Ohau Ranges, more than one-third of the park has a blanket of permanent snow and glacial ice.

Of the 27 NZ mountains stretching over 3050m high, 22 are in this park. The peak that all the others look up to is the mighty Mt Cook – at 3755m it's the highest in Australas a. Known to Maoris as Aoraki (Cloud Piercer), after an ancestral deity in Maori mythology, the tent-shaped Mt Cook was named after James Cook by Captain Stokes of the survey ship HMS *Acheron*.

The Mt Cook region has always been the focus of climbing in NZ. On 2 March 1882, William Spotswood Green and two Swiss alpin sts failed to reach the summit of Cook after an epic 62-hour ascent. But two years later a trio of local climbers – Tom Fyfe, George Graham and Jack Clarke – were spurred into action by the news that two

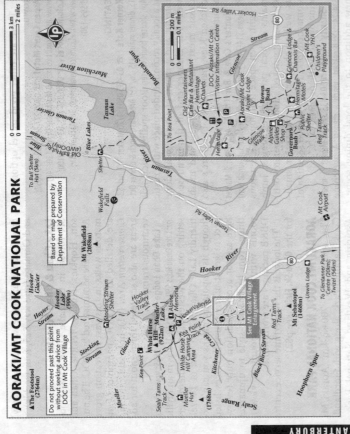

AORAKI/MT COOK NATIONAL PARK

Based on map prepared by Department of Conservation

Do not proceed past this point without seeking advice from DOC in Mt Cook Village

Mt Cook Village Enlargement

well-known European alpinists were coming to attempt Cook, and set off to climb it before the visitors. On Christmas Day 1884 they ascended the Hooker Glacier and north ridge, a brilliant climb in those days, and stood on the summit.

In 1913, Australian climber Freda du Faur became the first woman to reach the summit. In 1948 Edmund Hillary's party along with Tenzing Norgay climbed the south ridge – Hillary went on to become the first to reach the summit of Mt Everest. Since then, most of the daunting face routes have been climbed. Among the region's many

NOW *THAT'S* AN AVALANCHE

In the early hours of 14 December 1991, a substantial piece of Mt Cook's east face (around 14 million cu m) fell away in a massive landslide. Debris spewed out over the surrounding glaciers for 7.3km, cleaving a path down the Grand Plateau and Hochstetter Icefall and reaching as far as the Tasman Glacier.

great peaks are Sefton, the beguiling Tasman, Silberhorn, Elie de Beaumont, Malte Brun, Aiguilles Rouges, Nazomi, La Perouse, Hicks, De la Beche, Douglas and the Minarets. Many can be ascended from Westland National Park, and there's a system of climbers huts on both sides of the divide.

Mt Cook is a wonderful sight – assuming there's no cloud in the way. Most visitors arrive on tour buses, jump out at the Hermitage hotel for photos, and then zoom off back down SH80. Those who hang around should soak up this awesome peak and its glorious surrounding landscape by trying some of the excellent short walks. While on the trails, look out for the thar, a goatlike creature and excellent climber; the chamois, smaller and of lighter build than the thar but an agile climber; and red deer. In summer, you'll see the large mountain buttercup, often called the Mt Cook lily, as well as mountain daisies, gentians and edelweiss.

Information

The **DOC Aoraki/Mt Cook visitor information centre** (☎ 03-435 1186; mtcookvc@doc.govt.nz; Bowen Dr;

ⓘ 8.30am-6pm Oct-Apr, to 5pm May-Sep) is able to advise on weather conditions, guided tours and tramping routes, hires out beacons for trampers ($25), and screens a 20-minute audiovisual on the history and mountaineering of the Mt Cook region ($3). Online information is available at www.mount-cook.com.

The Hermitage's souvenir shop handles post. The hotel's coffee shop sells some food supplies, as does the YHA (see Sleeping p587), but you'd fare better by stocking up on groceries and petrol before turning off the SH8. And remember that Mt Cook has no banking facilities.

The **Alpine Guides shop** (ⓐ 03-435 1834; www .alpineguides.co.nz; Bowen Dr) sells skiing and mountaineering gear; you can also rent equipment such as ice axes, crampons, daypacks and sleeping bags.

Sights

TASMAN GLACIER

Higher up, the **Tasman Glacier** is a predictably spectacular sweep of ice, but further down it's downright ugly. Glaciers in NZ (and elsewhere in the world) have generally been retreating over the past century, although they are advancing now. Normally as a glacier retreats it melts back up the mountain, but the Tasman is unusual because its last few kilometres are almost horizontal. So in recent decades it has melted from the top down, exposing a jumble of stones, rocks and boulders. In other words, in its 'ablation zone' (where it melts) the Tasman is covered in a more or less solid mass of debris, which slows down its melting rate and makes it unsightly.

Despite this considerable melt, the ice by the site of the old Ball Hut is still estimated to be over 600m thick. In its last major advance (17,000 years ago), the glacier crept south far enough to carve out Lake Pukaki. A later advance did not reach out to the valley sides, so the Old Ball Hut Rd runs between the outer valley walls and the lateral moraines of this later advance.

Like the Fox and Franz Josef Glaciers on the other side of the divide, the Mt Cook glaciers move fast. The **Alpine Memorial**, near the old Hermitage site on the Hooker Valley Track and commemorating one of the mountain's first climbing disasters, illustrates the glaciers' speed. Three climbers were killed by an avalanche in 1914. Only one of the bodies was recovered at the time but 12 years later a second one melted out of the bottom of the Hochstetter Icefall, 2000m below where the party was buried.

HERMITAGE

This is arguably the most famous hotel in NZ, principally for its location and the fantastic views of Mt Cook. Originally constructed in 1884, when the trip up from Christchurch took several days, the first hotel was destroyed in a flash flood in 1913; you can see the foundations in Hooker Valley, 2km from the current Hermitage. Rebuilt, it survived until 1957, when it was completely burnt out; the present Hermitage was built on the same site and was given a new wing for the new millennium.

Even if you're not staying at the Hermitage, you can still sample the bar and restaurants here and look out the huge windows up at Mt Cook's indomitable face.

Activities

WALKING

Various easy walks from the Hermitage area are outlined in the brochure *Walks in Aoraki/Mt Cook National Park* ($1), available from the visitor information centre. Always be prepared for sudden weather changes.

The trail to **Kea Point** (two hours return from village) is lined with native plant life and kea, and ends at a platform with excellent views of Mt Cook, the Hooker Valley and the ice faces of Mt Sefton and the Footstool. The walk to **Sealy Tarns** (three to four hours return) branches off the Kea Point Track and continues up the ridge to **Mueller Hut** (4m $30-35; a new 28-bunk hut opened mid-2003, it is 300m south of the old hut and has its own gas.

The walk up the **Hooker Valley** (four hours return) crosses a couple of swing bridges to Stocking Stream and the terminus of the Hooker Glacier. After the second swing bridge Mt Cook totally dominates the valley.

The Tasman Valley walks are popular for their views of the Tasman Glacier. Walks start at the end of the unsealed Tasman Valley Rd, 8km from the village. The **Tasman Glacier View track** (40 minutes return) leads to a viewpoint on the moraine wall, passing the **Blue Lakes** (more green than blue these days) on the way. Views of Mt Cook and the surrounding area are spectacular, but the view of the glacier is limited mostly to the icy grey sludge of the terminal lake and the Tasman River. To approach the snub of the glacier, take the route to Ball Shelter (three to four hours one way) from the car park; you can stay here at **Ball Shelter hut** (dm $5).

If you intend staying at any of the park's huts, register your intentions at the visitor information centre and pay the hut fee; besides the aforementioned two, most huts cost $20 to $30 per night.

Longer Walks

Longer walks are only recommended for those with mountaineering experience, as conditions at higher altitudes are severe, the tracks dangerous and many people have died here; the majority of walkers shouldn't even consider tackling these trails.

Guided Walks

From November to March, **Aoraki Mt Cook Encounter** (0800 006 096, 03-680 6736; www.alpinerecreation.com), based in Lake Tekapo, organises high-altitude guided treks in the area, as well as mountaineering courses and ski touring. The challenging three-day Ball Pass Trek between the Tasman and Hooker Valleys costs $695.

Between October and May, **Cloud 9 Helihiking** (03-435 1077; www.glacierexplorers.com; helihike from $300) does trips to the 'Dark Side': you're flown to Mt Dark (approximately 2000m) and enjoy a guided walk back down.

MOUNTAINEERING

For the experienced, there's unlimited scope here for climbing. But regardless of your aptitude, take every precaution: over 200 people have died in climbing accidents in the park. These are recorded in the bleak 'In Memoriam' book in the visitor information centre, which begins with the first death on Mt Cook in 1907. Three deaths in March 2005 (including that of one of NZ's most experienced mountain guides), preceded by eight deaths in December 2003, show

just how terribly capricious the mountains can be.

The highly changeable weather is an important factor around here – Mt Cook is only 44km from the coast and bears the brunt of weather conditions blowing in over the Tasman Sea, which can mean sudden storms. Unless you know what you're doing in such conditions, don't attempt to climb anywhere without a guide.

It's important to check with the park rangers before attempting any climb, and to heed their advice. You must fill in a climber's intentions card before starting out, so rangers can check on you if you're overdue coming out. And make sure you sign out again when you return.

Alpine Guides (03-435 1834; www.alpineguides.co.nz; Bowen Dr) has guided climbs in summer, ranging from eight-day introductory courses ($2250) through to weeklong ascents of Mt Cook ($4750).

Alpine Recreation (0800 006 096, 03-680 6736; www.alpinerecreation.com) also has a summertime programme of climbing courses (a four-day introduction to climbing costs $960) and guided ascents of Mt Cook or Mt Tasman ($3600).

SKI TOURING & HELISKIING

Alpine Guides (03-435 1834; www.alpineguides.co.nz; Bowen Dr), over the winter months, does tailored ski-touring trips and ski-mountaineering and alpine snowboarding courses. One of its specialities is glacier heliskiing (www.heliskiing.co.nz) on the highest peaks in NZ – there are day trips on Tasman Glacier involving two ski runs (each up to 10km long) and three ski-plane flights ($685), plus a 'Wilderness Heliskiing' trip with four to five runs (runs average 750 to 1200 vertical metres) in the Liebig or Malte Brun Ranges ($770).

Southern Alps Guiding (03-435 1890; www.mtcook.com) offers a range of heliskiing and boarding options in the area, from a one-run heli lift ($140) to 10 runs ($1245) for those who can't get enough.

Alpine Recreation (0800 006 096, 03-680 6736; www.alpinerecreation.com) has a winter program involving two days touring in the high country around Lake Tekapo, wearing skis or snowshoes ($480), or a five-day option ($1500) in the Aoraki/Mount Cook and Westland National Parks.

AERIAL SIGHTSEEING

Mount Cook Ski Planes (☎ 0800 800 702, 03-430 8034; www.mtcookskiplanes.com), based at Mt Cook Airport, buzzes over this magnificent iced-in terrain during 40-minute (adult/child $310/230) and 55-minute flights (adult/child $410/310), both with snow landings. Flightseeing without a landing is considerably cheaper, such as the 25-minute 'Mini Tasman' trip ($210/170).

From Glentanner Park, the **Helicopter Line** (☎ 0800 650 651, 03-435 1801; www.helicopter.co.nz) does 20-minute 'Alpine Vista' flights ($190), an exhilarating 30-minute flight over the Ben Ohau Range ($280), and a 45-minute 'Mountains High' flight over the Tasman Glacier and by Mt Cook ($390). All flights feature snow landings.

Other airborne operators who fly around the region include **Air Safaris** (see p580) and the Twizel branch of the **Helicopter Line** (see p582).

OTHER ACTIVITIES

The visitor information centre, the Hermitage, the YHA and Glentanner Park provide information and make bookings for a multitude of activities and tours in the area, though be aware that most of them are weather-dependent.

The highly rated **Glacier Explorers** (☎ 03-435 1077; www.glacierexplorers.com; adult/child $105/50) heads out on the terminal lake of the Tasman Glacier. It starts with a half-hour walk to the shore of Lake Tasman, where you board a small motorised inflatable and get up close and personal with the ice for an hour.

The three-hour trips conducted by **Glacier Sea-kayaking** (☎ 03-435 1890; www.mtcook.com/trips $95) enable you to sea kayak across glacial bays, circumnavigating the odd iceberg as you paddle.

Glentanner Horse Trekking (☎ 03-435 1855; 1/2hr rides $50/70; ☼ Oct-mid-Apr) leads guided treks on a high-country sheep station, in the warmer months only. All levels of experience are welcomed.

Alan's 4WD Tours (☎ 03-435 0441; www.mount cooktours.co.nz; adult/child $100/50) operates 2½-hour 4WD trips up to Husky Flat, from where it is a 15-minute walk to a glacier viewpoint; there's plenty of interesting commentary and alpine flora to gaze at along the way.

Sleeping

Campers and walkers may like to make use of the handy public shelter (☼ 8am to 7pm October to April, 8am to 5pm May to September) in the village, which has running water, toilets and coin-operated showers.

White Horse Hill Camping Area (☎ 03-435 1186; Hooker Valley; per night adult/child $6/3) This basic DOC-run, self-registration camping ground is at the old Hermitage site and the starting point for the Hooker Valley Track, 2km from Aoraki/Mt Cook village. There's running water (boil before drinking) and toilets but no electricity, showers or cooking facilities.

Glentanner Park Centre (☎ 0800 453 682, 03-435 1855; www.glentanner.co.nz; unpowered/powered sites per 2 people $22/26, dm $22, cabins $60-95) On the northern shore of Lake Pukaki, this is the nearest facility-laden camping ground to the national park and has great views of Mt Cook, 25km to the north. It's well set up with various cabins, a dormitory (open October to April), a restaurant and a booking service for most of the activities outlined in the previous section.

Unwin Lodge (☎ 03-435 1100; unwin@alpineclub.org.nz; SH8C; dm $25; ▢) This lodge is about 3.5km before the village and belongs to the New Zealand Alpine Club (NZAC). Members get preference, but beds are usually available for climbing groupies. There are basic bunks and a big common room with a fireplace, kitchen and excellent views up the Tasman Glacier to the Minarets and Elie de Beaumont.

Mt Cook YHA (☎ 03-435 1820; www.stayyha.com; cnr Bowen & Kitchener Dr; dm/d $28/72; ▢) This excellent hostel comes equipped with a free sauna, drying room, a decent video collection and warming log fires. Rooms are clean and spacious, with new bunks recently installed; family rooms are available, as are disabled facilities. Book at least a few days in advance in high season.

Aoraki/Mt Cook Alpine Lodge (☎ 0800 680 580, 03-435 1860; www.aorakialpinelodge.co.nz; Bowen Dr; dm/f/d/tw $36/165/144/144; ▢) Finishing touches were going on when we visited this new addition to the visitor information centre. A young local couple has spied the gap in the midrange market and looks set to do well with this new lodge. All rooms feature private bathroom; the simple but comfortable doubles and twins also have TV, and family and disabled rooms are available. The excellent kitchen, lounge and deck on the upper level are bound to win over guests.

Hermitage (☎ 0800 686 800, 03-435 1809; www .mount-cook.com; Terrace Rd; r $220-880; 🖵) An enormous complex that has long had a monopoly on accommodation in the village. The least expensive beds are in well-equipped A-frame chalets (double/quad $220/240), which received a makeover in 2004 and are now very smartly furnished. Chalets sleep up to four and include kitchen. Priced up from these are the motel units (double/quad $260/295), the hotel-style rooms of Glencoe Lodge (for tour groups), and finally rooms (doubles $590 to $880) in various wings of the hotel proper. A luxurious upper-level room in the Aoraki Wing, built in 2001, comes with binoculars for taking in the magnificent Mt Cook views, plus breakfast and four-course dinners in the Panorama Restaurant (below). Winter (April to September) usually sees a reduction in accommodation prices.

Eating & Drinking

Old Mountaineers Café, Bar & Restaurant (☎ 03-435 1890; Bowen Dr; mains $16-35; 🕑 breakfast, lunch & dinner; 🖵) Stop by for happy hour between 5pm and 7pm and check out the wonderful old photographs of mountaineers lining the walls of this relaxed café-bar, right next to the visitor information centre. In a village that has been dominated by the high-priced Hermitage for more than a century, this place is a real breath of fresh, independent air, with its cosy interior, outdoor seating, extensive crowd-pleasing menu and views straight up the mountain.

The eating options at the Hermitage (p585) include the mezzanine-level **coffee shop** (meals $6-12.50; 🕑 breakfast & lunch), dispensing daytime snacks, and the extensive buffets of the **Alpine Restaurant** (breakfast $30, lunch $26, dinner $50). But the pride of place goes to the **Panorama Restaurant** (dinner mains $27-40; 🕑 dinner), a top-notch à la carte restaurant

with such fine Kiwi treats as grilled Mt Cook salmon, Canterbury lamb rack and slow-cooked venison. The view from here is outrageously good – you see Sefton to your left, Cook in the centre and the Ben Ohau Ranges, dark brown and forbidding, to your right. Adjacent to the Alpine Room is the Snowline Bar, with its well-upholstered lounges in which to woo a wine glass.

The smaller, less formal **Chamois Bar** (🕑 nightly Oct-Mar, Thu-Sat Apr-Sep) is upstairs in Glencoe Lodge, 500m from the main hotel near the YHA, where it entertains with a pool table and big-screen TV; beer-drinking food such as nachos, burgers and steak sandwiches is served here.

Getting There & Away

The village's small airport only serves aerial sightseeing companies. Some of these may be willing to combine transport to, say, the West Coast (ie Franz Josef) with a scenic flight, but flights are heavily dependent on weather.

If you book a one-way trip to/from Mt Cook with **InterCity** (☎ 03-365 1113; www.inter citycoach.co.nz), you'll end up on the morning departure of the Newmans Coach Lines service. Head to Mt Cook from Christchurch (one way $79), Queenstown (one way $63) and Wanaka (one way $46); buses stop at the YHA and the Hermitage, both of which handle bookings.

InterCity subsidiary **Newmans Coach Lines** (www.newmanscoach.co.nz) Christchurch (☎ 03-379 9020); Queenstown (☎ 03-4411344) runs the Mt Cook Wanderer, a Christchurch to Mt Cook to Queenstown (or reverse) sightseeing trip costing $148/99 per adult/child from Christchurch and $114/76 from Queenstown. Connections from Wanaka are available.

The **Cook Connection** (☎ 0800 266 526, 0274-583 211; www.cookconnect.co.nz) has shuttle services to Twizel (one way $20), Lake Tekapo (one way $25) and Oamaru (one way $40). In each of these towns you'll be able to connect with bus services on to major centres such as Christchurch, Queenstown, Wanaka or Dunedin.

If you're driving here, it's best to fill up at Lake Tekapo or Twizel. There is petrol at Mt Cook, but it's expensive and usually involves summoning an attendant from the Hermitage (for a $5 fee).

Dunedin & Otago

Punctuated with some of the South Island's more unusual natural wonders and its most accessible wildlife, the Dunedin and Otago area is a rolling, scenic chunk of land that's edged by the restless Pacific Ocean.

At its heart is the increasingly cosmopolitan city of Dunedin with its profusion of arts, cafés, music and student life, along with a couple of the country's top museums and some elegant Victorian architecture. From here you can catch the famous Taieri Gorge Railway, or escape inland to the charming historical towns of Clyde, St Bathans, Naseby and Lawrence – atmospheric locations that don't see a lot of tourist traffic. Outdoor enthusiasts can experience exhilarating scenery on foot or bike along the Otago Central Rail Trail, a multiday, mainly flat route that doesn't require the rigour of the treks in neighbouring regions.

If you're eager to spot some of the island's more aloof inhabitants, head to the Otago Peninsula, where penguins, albatross and seals are easily sighted amid stunning views. Or visit seaside Oamaru, with its pleasant historic district and resident penguin colonies.

Visitors with a penchant for rocks won't want to miss the perplexingly spherical Moeraki boulders or the enormous, otherworldly Elephant Rocks. You can also see early Maori cave paintings and unlikely 25 million-year-old fossils near Duntroon.

Unhurried, and rife with picturesque scenery, Otago is generous to explorers who are after something a little less than usual. The best part is, there'll be no crowds to share it with.

HIGHLIGHTS

- Nursing a latte or pint in the trendy cafés and bars of **Dunedin** (p600)
- Checking out the fascinating exhibits at the modern **Otago Museum** (p600)
- Gaping at the immense wingspan of the albatross on **Otago Peninsula** (p602)
- Taking in spellbinding scenery as you cycle the **Otago Central Rail Trail** (p612)
- Getting an eyeful of blue and yellow-eyed penguins in **Oamaru** (p615)
- Hanging on for dear life on the open platform of the snaking **Taieri Gorge Railway** (p593)
- Soaking up the historic atmosphere of quaint and peaceful **Clyde** (p607)
- Being perplexed by the utter roundness of the Te Ka hinaki (ancient boulders) at **Moeraki** (p619)

☎ TELEPHONE CODE: 03   ☐ www.cityofdunedin.com

Clyde ★
★ Otago Central Rail Trail
Taieri Gorge Railway
★ Oamaru
★ Moeraki
★ DUNEDIN
Otago Peninsula

DUNEDIN & THE OTAGO PENINSULA

Wedged at the southwestern end of the Otago Harbour, Dunedin is becoming increasingly popular as a mellow city nurturing a strong artsy side. If you can unglue yourself from the city's café scene, the raggedly shaped Otago Peninsula lies practically in Dunedin's backyard and is teeming with wildlife and outdoor activities.

DUNEDIN
pop 110,800

Dunedin's compact town centre is a comfortable blend of the historic and the contemporary, reflected in its alluring museums, tempting cafés, unique shops and excellent accommodation options. Wooden villas pepper its hilly suburbs and graceful stone Victorian buildings are dotted throughout the centre. Meanwhile, the country's longest-running university ensures an eclectic student vibe that drives a thriving arts and entertainment scene. The city also offers a surprising array of activities and tours, many of which can take you to the scenic wildlife haven of the nearby Otago Peninsula. All totalled, Dunedin is a wonderful place to park your bags for a few days.

History

The area's early Maori history was particularly bloody, involving a three-way feud between peninsular tribes that escalated in the early 19th century. This brutal warfare

InterCity, Atomic Shuttles, Wanaka Connexions, Catch-A-Bus and Bottom Bus.

For more information on getting to and from Dunedin, see p602.

Climate

With the Southern Alps as a natural blockade to the wet winds from the Tasman Sea, the east coast of Otago has a relatively dry climate. Summer days are generally warm to hot and rainfall is very low, while in winter temperatures can drop to well below freezing. This climatic spectrum is greatest in the tiny town of Ophir, which reputedly has the widest temperature range of any New Zealand town – from -20°C in winter to 35°C in summer.

Getting There & Around

Air New Zealand flies from Dunedin to the major centres of Christchurch, Wellington and Auckland.

Numerous bus and shuttle companies crisscross Otago and service most destinations within the region. These can also get you to neighbouring cities such as Christchurch, Queenstown, Wanaka, Te Anau and Invercargill, as well as to the west coast or through the Catlins. Major operators include

was closely followed by devastating diseases ushered in via coastal sealing and whaling; by 1848 the once considerable population of Otakau Pa was just over 100.

The first permanent European settlers arrived at Port Chalmers in March 1848. Its founders were Scottish ('Dunedin' is Celtic for 'Edinburgh'); a statue of the Scottish near-god, Robert Burns, remains watchful over the city centre today. Gold-rush wealth in the latter half of the 19th century produced a grand Victorian city, and the province quickly became the colony's richest, most influential entity. After such a heady start, Dunedin declined economically and much of its population drifted away. Recent decades have been more prosperous and, on the South Island, the city now ranks second only to Christchurch.

Information

BOOKSHOPS

Scribes (☎ 03-477 6874; cnr Great King & St David Sts) A mammoth collection of well-organised secondhand books.

University Book Shop (☎ 03-477 6976; www.unibooks.co.nz; 378 Great King St) A stock far outstretching its academic name, with an excellent selection of fiction, poetry, children's books and NZ titles as well as a Non-Stop Book Sale with great bargains.

EMERGENCY

Ambulance, fire service & police (☎ 111)
Dunedin Hospital (☎ 03-474 0999; 201 Great King St)

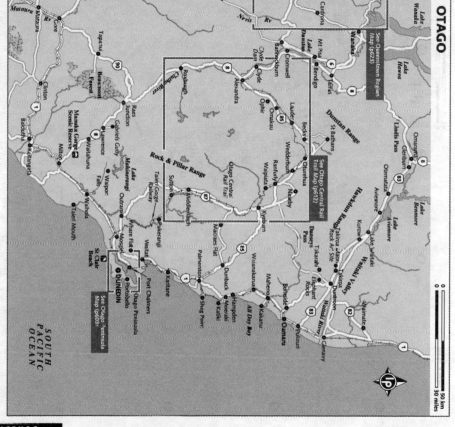

OTAGO

See Queenstown Region Map (p623)

See Otago Central Rail Trail Map (p612)

See Otago Peninsula Map (p603)

SOUTH PACIFIC OCEAN

0   50 km
0   30 miles

www.lonelyplanet.com

DUNEDIN

400 m
0.2 miles

See Enlargement

Otago Harbour

St Paul's Cathedral

The Octagon

Moray Pl

Upper Moray Pl

View St

Princes St

Moray Pl

The Octagon

Queens Gardens

Town Belt

Knox Church

Heriot Row

University of Otago

Water of Leith

Dunedin Botanic Gardens

To Dunedin Botanic Gardens (500m)
To Dunedin

To Baldwin St (1.5km);
Mt Cargill (8km)

To 858 George Street Motel (100m);
Leith Valley Touring Park (1.5km);
Mt Cargill-Bethunes Gully Walkway
(6km); Mt Cargill-Bethunes Gully Walkway;
Christchurch (361km)

To Aaron Lodge Top 10
Holiday Park (1.5km);
Corstophine House (2.5km);
Tunnel Beach (7.5km);
Flagstaff Walk; 5km)

To Carisbrook Stadium (1km);
Corstophine House (2.5km);
Tunnel Beach (6.5km); Airport
(27km); Balclutha (80km);
Invercargill (215km)

To Esplanade (2.5km);
St Clair Pool (2.5km);
Southern Coast Surf
Clinic (2.5km)

To Portobello Rd (1.5km; 4km);
Otago Peninsula

Kitchener St
Wharf St

Castle St North
Montgomery
Dundas St
Union St
Clyde St
Pitt St
Frederick St
Castle St
Cumberland St
St Andrew St
Hanover St
Filleul St
Moray Pl
Stuart St
Dowling St
Rattray St
Water St
Jetty St
Liverpool St
Crawford St
Vogel St
Bond St
Stafford St
High St
Manor Pl
Hope St
Carroll St
Clarke St
Arthur St
Canongate St
MacLaggan St
Graham St
Tennyson St
Elm Row
London St
Littlebourne Rd
Queens Dr
Royal Tce
Cobden St
Haddon Pl
Stuart St
Princes St
Anzac Ave
Ward St
Mason St
Willis St
Albany St
Leith St
Grange St
Harrow St
Pryor St
Duke St
Clyde St
Great King St
George St
Cumberland St
St David St

The Oval

DUNEDIN & OTAGO

INFORMATION

Automobile Association (AA)........1 D6
DOC......................................2 D6
Dunedin Hospital.....................3 C3
Dunedin Visitor Information
 Centre................................4 D5
Internet Depot........................5 D5
Monarch Wildlife Cruises &
 Tours.................................6 C5
Net Planet.............................7 C3
Post Office............................8 D5
Scribes................................9 D1
University Book Shop...............10 D5
Urgent Doctors & Accident
 Centre...............................11 C3
Web Runner..........................12 D5

SIGHTS & ACTIVITIES

Cadbury World.......................13 C4
Cycle Surgery......................(see 2)
Dive Otago..........................14 C5
Dunedin Public Art Gallery......15 C6
First Church of Otago.............16 D6
Moana Pool..........................17 A2
New Zealand Sports Hall of
 Fame................................18 C4
Olveston.............................19 E2
Otago Museum.....................20 D2
Otago Settlers Museum.........21 C4
Speight's Brewery.................22 B4
Taieri Gorge Railway.............23 C4

SLEEPING

526 George Street Boutique
 Hotel...............................24 C2
755 Regal Court Motel...........25 D1
Albatross Inn......................26 D1
Alexis Motor Lodge...............27 C2
Cargills Hotel......................28 D1
Central Backpackers..............29 D5
Chalet Backpackers...............30 A5
Dunedin City Hotel...............31 B4
Elm Lodge Backpackers........32 A4
Fletcher Lodge....................33 A5
Kiwis Nest..........................34 C1
Mandeno House...................35 C1
Manor Motel.......................36 A5
Mercure Hotel Dunedin.........37 B5
Motel Moray Place...............38 C6
On Top Backpackers.............39 C5
Stafford Gables YHA............40 A5

EATING

Arc Cafe..............................41 B4
Bell Pepper Blues.................42 A5
Countdown Supermarket........43 C3
Everyday Gourmet...............44 C1
Good Oil.............................45 C2
Hungry Frenchman..............(see 4)
Il Panificio.........................46 D6
Minami...............................47 D6
Modaks..............................48 C2
Nova Cafe.........................(see 15)
Potpourri............................49 D6
Reef.................................50 D6
Thai Over...........................51 D6
Tokyo Gardens....................52 C6

DRINKING

Barakah.............................53 D6
Benny's..............................54 C6
Captain Cook......................55 C2
Fix...................................56 C2
Mazagran Espresso Bar.........57 C6
Poolhouse.........................(see 39)
Woolshed...........................58 D6

ENTERTAINMENT

Bath St...............................59 D5
Fortune Theatre...................60 C6
Hoyts Cinema......................61 C6
Isis Lounge.........................62 C6
Metro Cinema......................63 C5
Ra Bar...............................64 D6
ReFuel...............................65 D2
Regent Theatre....................66 D5
Rialto Cinemas....................67 C3
Vatican NightClub................68 C3

SHOPPING

Adventure
 Outfitters.........................69 D5
Bivouac.............................70 D6
eco-nz...............................71 D6
Little Rock Shop..................72 C2
McKinlays..........................73 C2
Milford Galleries.................74 B4
Moray Gallery.....................75 C6
Records Records.................76 C6

TRANSPORT

Air New Zealand..................77 C5
City Bus Stop......................78 D6
InterCity Depot...................79 C3
Suburban Bus Stop..............80 C3

Dunedin visitor information centre (☎ 03-474 3300; www.cityofdunedin.com; 48 The Octagon; ☑ 8.30am-5.30pm Mon-Fri, 9am-5.30pm Sat & Sun)

Department of Conservation (DOC; ☎ 03-477 0677; 1st fl, 77 Stuart St; ☑ 8.30am-5pm Mon-Fri) Has info on regional walking tracks.

TOURIST INFORMATION

Automobile Association (AA; ☎ 03-477 5945; 450 Moray Pl; ☑ 8.30am-5pm Mon-Fri) For driving queries.

POST

Post office (233 Moray Pl) In the city centre, with poste restante.

INTERNET ACCESS

Internet access costs between $3 and $5 per hour and is available at several hostels and cafes. The following are all in the centre of town and open late:

Internet Depot (☎ 03-470 1730; 18 George St)
Net Planet (☎ 03-479 2424; 78 St Andrew St)
Web Runner (☎ 03-471 8182; 237 Moray Pl)

Urgent Doctors & Accident Centre (☎ 03-479 2900; 95 Hanover St) Deals with emergencies and has a pharmacy open outside normal business hours.

Housed in the restored and rather impressive municipal chambers, this centre has a decent selection of walking maps and a useful events listings board.

Sights

TAIERI GORGE RAILWAY

With narrow tunnels, deep gorges, winding tracks, rugged canyons and more than a dozen viaduct crossings (one of them 50m high), the scenic Taieri Gorge Railway (☎ 03-477 4449; www.taieri.co.nz; Dunedin Railway Station, Anzac Ave; ☑ 2.30pm Oct-Mar, 12.30pm Mon-Thu & Sat, 9.30am & 12.30pm Fri & Sun Apr-Sep, extra 9.30am holiday services) consistently rates highly with visitors. The four-hour return trip aboard 1920s heritage coaches travels to Pukerangi (single/return $45/65), 58km away. Some trips carry on to Middlemarch (single/return $50/75) or you can opt for a train-coach trip to Queenstown (single $115). You can also bring your bike along and cycle on to Clyde; see the boxed text, p612. For coastal scenery, take the less frequent train (from October to March it runs occasionally on Wednesday and Saturday) to Palmerston (single/return $36/55). All trains depart from the city's striking Edwardian station; check out the Royal Doulton mosaic-tile floors.

OTAGO MUSEUM

The fantastic **Otago Museum** (☎ 03-474 7474; www .otagomuseum.govt.nz; 419 Great King St; admission by donation, guided tour $10; ☽ 10am-5pm, guided tour 11.30am & 3.30pm) can easily fill your senses for a day. Bright and modern, its interactive exhibits give a thorough look into the area's cultural and physical past and present. Definitely worth a visit is the Tangata Whenua Gallery, which houses an amazingly long Maori war canoe, beautiful meeting-house carvings and a Kiribati warrior with a fierce looking shark-tooth sword. Fossil buffs will be gobsmacked by the museum's *plesiosaur* (NZ's sea serpent), moa skeletons and remains of the once-local crocodile. You'll also find NZ commissioned artworks, exhibits on the history of European settlement, a maritime gallery and an animal attic. Join a guided tour or a free gallery talk at 2pm, focusing on one item in the collection. Children are kept busy with a free activity book and can explore at the hands-on Discovery World (adult/child/family $6/3/14). You'll also find a decent shop and café.

DUNEDIN PUBLIC ART GALLERY

Explore NZ's art scene at Dunedin's top-notch **Public Art Gallery** (☎ 03-474 3240; www.dun edin.art.museum; 30 The Octagon; permanent exhibition free; ☽ 10am-5pm). With lots of light and excellent city views from the top floor, this is an excellent space to soak up three floors of mainly contemporary work. Recent temporary shows have included exhibits of Robin White, Ralph Hotere and Gordon Walters. Rotating exhibits that include some European works and Kiwi masters such as Frances Hodgkins are drawn from the museum's permanent collection.

OTHER MUSEUMS & GALLERIES

The eclectic collection at the **Otago Settlers Museum** (☎ 03-477 5052; 31 Queens Gardens; adult/child/concession $4/free/$3; ☽ 10am-5pm) will give you a look into the past of people in this region: what they drove, what they wore, where they came from and what they looked like. Kids and trainspotters will be all over the 1872-built steam engine; those with a thing for retro design will love the original Art Deco bus depot foyer; and it's difficult

not to be mesmerised by the thousand-plus photos of early settlers that cram the walls of the Smith Gallery. The museum also runs 90-minute walking tours for $8 per person, held at 2pm or 5.30pm, approximately twice a month; tour themes include Whalers, Jailers, Poets and More; Historic Hotels; and Women of Dunedin (call ☎ 03-474 2728 for details).

If you're a serious sports fan and into relics of the trade, you might enjoy a visit to the **New Zealand Sports Hall of Fame** (☎ 03-477 7775; www.nzhalloffame.co.nz; Dunedin Railway Station, Anzac Ave; adult/child/student $5/2/3; ☽ 10am-4pm). Fancy a gander at the kayak that Ferguson and MacDonald paddled to Olympic gold? How about a look at the arm guard that Colin Meads wore on his broken arm in a test match? It's all here, along with oodles of All Blacks memorabilia, trophies, uniforms and photos.

Once an impressive mark of modernity, **Olveston** (☎ 03-477 3320; www.olveston.co.nz; 42 Royal Tce; adult/concession/child $14/13/4; ☽ guided tours 9.30am-4pm) is now a trophy of the past. Designed by a London architect and built in 1904, it was the home of the ostentatious Theomin family. The 35 stately rooms are decorated and furnished as the family left them and have a lavish, if somewhat cluttered, feel about them. To look inside, you must book a place on a one-hour guided tour. The acre of formal garden (admission by donation; open 9.30am to 5pm) surrounding the house is also open for a wander.

DUNEDIN BOTANIC GARDENS

A lush oasis, the **Dunedin Botanic Gardens** (☎ 03-477 4000; cnr Great King St & Opoho Rd; admission free; ☽ gardens dawn-dusk, visitors centre 10am-4.30pm, café 9.30am-4.30pm) dates from 1868 and spreads across 28 scenic hectares. Its grounds include the impressive four-hectare rhododendron dell and an Edwardian winter garden. There's lots of well-tended grass to lounge on, a small children's playground and a fantastic café with views across the greenery.

OTHER SIGHTS

When Robert Lawson entered a design competition in the mid 1800s, little did he know that the resulting gothic edifice would be his masterpiece. Considered the 'Mother Church' by Kiwi Presbyterians, the limestone **First Church of Otago** (☎ 03-477

7150; 415 Moray Pl; admission free) was completed in 1873 and is towered over by a 56m-high spire. Inside are a beautiful rose window and illustrative tapestry. Watch for other Lawson designs in and around Dunedin.

If you're a chocolate-lover, follow your cravings to **Cadbury World** (☎ 0800 223 287, 03-467 7967; www.cadburyworld.co.nz; 280 Cumberland St; adult/child/student/family $15/8/12/38; ☺ tours every half hr 9am-3.15pm) for a 90-minute tour that includes a spiel on history and production, a look at a two-storey, liquid chocolate waterfall and a taste of the end product. In operation since the 1930s, this factory handles 85% of NZ's chocolate production.

You can also take an 90-minute, interactive tour of **Speight's Brewery** (☎ 03-477 7697; www.speights.co.nz; 200 Rattray St; adult/child/concession/family $15/5/12/35; ☺ tours 10am, 11.45am & 2pm daily, plus 7pm Mon-Thu & 4pm Sat & Sun), one of the last remaining 'gravity breweries' on the globe. The brewery has been churning out ale since the late 1800s. At the end, connoisseurs can sample (and the rest can guzzle) a taste of each of Speight's six beers. For $50, follow the tour with a three-course lunch or dinner at the adjacent Ale House.

The world's steepest street (or so says the *Guinness Book of Records*), **Baldwin St** has a clambering gradient of 1 in 1.266. From the city centre, head 2km north up Great King St to where the road branches left to Timaru, get in the right-hand lane and continue straight rather than taking the sharp right-hand turn. This becomes North Rd; Baldwin St will be on the right after 1km. If you've any doubts about your brakes, park at the bottom. The annual 'Gutbuster' race (February) sees the winner run up and back in around two minutes.

Activities

SWIMMING, SURFING & DIVING

Dive into the surf at either St Clair and St Kilda, both popular swimming beaches. The former is equipped with the heated, outdoor, saltwater **St Clair Pool** (☎ 03-455 6352; Esplanade, St Clair Beach; adult/child $4.50/2; ☺ late Oct-late Mar). It's also home to **Southern Coast Surf Clinic** (☎ 03-455 6007; www.surfoachnz.com), which teaches surfing to beginners (from $40 per hour), organises trips for the experienced (from $100), and rents out surfboards and wet suits ($20/50 per hour/half day). Take your board to the western end of St Clair Beach for decent surf-

ing. Alternatively, take your togs to **Moana Pool** (☎ 03-471 9780; 60 Littlebourne Rd; adult/child per swim $4.50/2.50, swim & waterslide $8.50/6), which has Olympic diving boards, waterslides, a spa and a superb children's pool.

Dive Otago (☎ 03-466 4370; www.diveotago.co.nz; 2 Wharf St) offers PADI courses from $395 and dive trips both locally and as far afield as Milford Sound or Stewart Island.

WALKING, TREKKING & CLIMBING

Short and spectacular, **Tunnel Beach Walkway** (45 minutes return; closed August to October for lambing) crosses farmland before descending the sea cliffs to Tunnel Beach. There you'll find sea stacks, arches and unusual rock shapes, all carved out by the wild Pacific. If you're lucky, you might also find a fossil or two in the impressive sandstone cliffs. Strong currents make swimming here dangerous but at low tide a sandy beach is exposed. It impressed John Cargill so much, he had a hand-hewn stone tunnel built to give his family access to secluded, beachside picnics. The walk is southwest of central Dunedin. Catch a Corstorphine bus from the Octagon to Stenhope Cres and walk 1.4km along Blackhead Rd to Tunnel Beach Rd, then 400m to the start of the walkway.

Catch a Normanby bus to the start of Norwood St, which leads to Cluny St and the **Mt Cargill-Bethunes Gully Walkway** (3½ hours return). The highlight is the view from Mt Cargill (also accessible by car). In Maori legend, the three peaks of Cargill (named after a leader of early Otago colonists) represent the petrified head and feet of an Otakau princess. From Mt Cargill, a trail continues to the 10-million-year-old lava-formed **Organ Pipes** and, after another half-hour, to Mt Cargill Rd on the other side of the mountain.

Northwest of Dunedin, the 5km-long **Pineapple-Flagstaff Walk** (two hours return) has great views of the harbour, coastline and inland ranges; look out for the signpost at Flagstaff-Whare Flat Rd, off Taieri Rd.

The **Walking Bus** (☎ 03-471 8571; single/multi trip $20/35) offers transport to many walks in the area; you can book at the visitor information centre. The **Otago Tramping & Mountaineering Club** (www.otmc.co.nz) organises full-day treks (usually on Sundays) and weekend tramping trips, often to the Silver Peaks Reserve north of Dunedin where the club maintains five huts. Nonmembers are welcome but must contact trip leaders beforehand (see website for details). Club meetings are held nearly every Thursday evening at 3 Young St, St Kilda at 7.30pm.

Traditional rock-climbing (nonbolted) is popular at **Long Beach** and **Mihiwaka**. Dave Brash, Dunedin's climbing guru, has written *Dunedin Rock*, which is packed with details on local climbs. You can pick it up at the visitor information centre or at Bivouac (p601).

OTHER ACTIVITIES

Hare Hill (0800 437 837, 03-472 8496; www.horserid-dunedin.co.nz; per half-/full-day $50/120) runs scenic horse treks that take in historic routes and wildlife-frequented beaches. **Bums 'n' Saddles** (03-488 0097) offers two-hour horse rides ($35) for all levels.

Cycle Surgery (03-477 7473; www.cyclesurgery .co.nz; 67 Stuart St; per day $25) rents out bikes and is a good source of mountain-biking info. Pick up the free brochure *Fat Tyre Trails* from the visitor information centre for mountain-bike routes around Dunedin.

Tours

For a DIY tour, pick up the *Heritage Walk* brochure from the visitor info centre and follow its one-hour city walks. Other tour options:

Arthur's Tours (0800 840 729, 03-474 3300; www.arthurstours.co.nz; tours 1/2/4 adults per person from $75/38/19) 'I am Dunedin', claims Arthur from beneath his plaid tam-o'-shanter. His small-group tours take in the city sights as well as the Otago Peninsula.

Dunedin City Explorer (0800 322 240; day ticket adult/child $15/7.50; buses depart the Octagon 9.45am, 11.30am, 1pm, 2.30pm & 4pm) One-hour bus tour that loops around the city's major sites and lets you hop on and off at as many places as you like. Stops include the Otago Museum, Olveston, Botanic Gardens and Baldwin St.

Hair Raiser (03-477 2258; $20; 6pm Wed & Fri) One of Dunedin's more unusual tours, Hair Raiser guarantees a spine-chilling time with its original Ghost Walk, departing from the visitor information centre. It also offers a pirate tour of Port Chalmers and Six Feet Down Under grave tours of Dunedin's Northern Cemetery.

Mainland Air (0800 284 284, 03-486 2200; www.mainlandair.com; per hr for 3 adults $350). Based at Dunedin airport, the company offers flight-seeing trips over the city or as far afield as Stewart Island.

Monarch Wildlife Cruises & Tours (03-477 4276; www.wildlife.co.nz; trips half-/full-day from $75/170) Half- and full-day tours to the Otago Peninsula. Tours visit breeding grounds for sea lions, penguins, albatross and seals.

Newton Tours (03-477 5577; www.transportplace .co.nz; adult/child $18/9) One-hour double-decker tours of Dunedin five times daily, taking in historic homes and buildings. Newton runs numerous other double-decker routes and peninsula wildlife tours.

Passion for Fashion (03-478 0164; tours $20; 9am Tue-Thu) For retail therapy, this tour gives the lowdown on the local shopping scene as well as on the city's fashionable past with a wander down George St.

Walk Dunedin (03-477 5052; walks $15; 11am Mon-Fri) A 90-minute history-themed stroll around the city, organised by the Otago Settlers Museum. Meet at the visitor information centre; bookings aren't necessary.

For tours that take in the nearby wildlife, see p605.

Sleeping

The real stand-out places to stay in Dunedin tend to fall into the budget or top-end price ranges. Midrange travellers will find a stream of motels at the northern end of George St. With few exceptions, the majority of places to stay are within easy walking distance of the city centre.

BUDGET

Leith Valley Touring Park (03-467 9936; lvtpdun@ southnet.co.nz; 103 Malvern St; sites per 2 people $26, d $40-85;) A short drive from the town centre, this excellent camping ground feels like it's in the wilds. You'll find two wilderness walks, glow-worm caves nearby and a creek next to the best camp sites. Doubles in the brand-new motel unit are spacious, well-equipped and relatively stylish. Timber tourist flats are smaller but have a more earthy feel.

Dunedin Holiday Park (Map p603; 0800 945 455, 03-455 4690; www.dunedinholidaypark.co.nz; 41 Victoria Rd; sites per 2 people $26, cabins from $39;) Over the hill from St Kilda Beach, this massive holiday complex has a kids' playgrounds, barbecue area, nearly 100 camp sites and a variety of well-equipped cabins. The en suite cabins are the most pleasant and can sleep up to five. This place gets packed out in the summer.

Aaron Lodge Top 10 Holiday Park (0800 879 227, 03-476 4725; www.aaronlodgetop10.co.nz; 162 Kaikorai Valley Rd; unpowered/powered sites per 2 people $26/28, cabins/d from $45/80;) Secluded camp sites are secreted away in a garden 2.5km northwest of the city. Cabins are cosy while motel rooms are dated. Kids will be amply entertained with an indoor heated pool, playroom for toddlers and an outdoor playground. There's good bus access (take a Bradford or Brockville bus from the Octagon).

Central Backpackers (☎ 03-477 7006; dunch_nz@yahoo.co.nz; 243 Moray Pl; dm $20-22, s/d $35/60; ☐) Located in the heart of town, this upstairs hostel is oh-so-modern with classy furnishings and soft lighting. Homey touches such as throws on the sofas and a wood stove in the lounge plus friendly, relaxed staff give it a cosy atmosphere. The kitchen is well equipped and the shared bathrooms are immaculate. Dorm rooms sleep two to 10 on bunks and private rooms are spacious. This place is more sleek and stylish than brimming with character but it's a real find.

Elm Lodge Backpackers (☎ 0800 356 563, 03-474 1872; www.elmwildlifetours.co.nz/elm_lodge.shtml; 74 Elm Row; dm/s/d from $24/33/55; ☐) A character-filled hostel is relaxed and well run. Staff are helpful, rooms are comfortable and the back garden is a great place to have a barbecue on a summer's eve. The owners have recently acquired a second, peaceful house up the road. The hostel is a short downhill walk into town; staff will map out the route that's easiest on your legs. The staff will also pick up new arrivals from the Octagon.

Chalet Backpackers (☎ 0800 242 538, 03-479 2075; kirsti@paradise.net.nz; 296 High St; dm/d $20/50; ☐) It's easy to make yourself at home in these sunny rooms complete with flowers and a hodgepodge of happy prints. Full of charm, this century-old house is well maintained. Dorm rooms have four or five beds each (no bunks) and doubles are roomy. The kitchen is big and the dining room has one long table so that you can get to know your neighbours. There's also a small garden out back, a cat, a piano and rumours of a ghost.

Manor Motel (☎ 0800 262 667, 03-477 6129; manormotel@earthlight.co.nz; 22 Manor Pl; studio $70, 1/2-bedroom units $80/85; ☐) It's a steal! The studio room is in the main house and has a splash of personality and a small kitchenette. Modern, one-bedroom units have a sitting room and kitchen; they're more like well-equipped flats than motel rooms. Two-bedroom units are a little dated but not tacky. The owners are friendly and have lots of local info and there's a small park across the road. Long-term deals are even cheaper.

Stafford Gables YHA (☎ 0800 600 100, 03-474 1919; www.yha.co.nz; 71 Stafford St; dm/d from $23/60; ☐ ☐) Somewhat sprawling, this late-19th-century former hospital has a comfortable air about it. Rooms are fairly big and each one is unique; those at the front have access to a deck. Try for the sunny Room 38, which has more character and its own tiny deck. Dorms sleep three to six people. The kitchen is big, the eating area not so big, and the front desk sells home-cooking essentials. Upstairs is a rooftop garden and there's also a peaceful sun room.

Other hostels worth a look-in:

On Top Backpackers (☎ 0800 668 672, 03-477 6121; www.ontopbackpackers.co.nz; cnr Filleul St & Moray Pl; dm $23, d $55-75; ☐ ☐) Brand-new, well-located hostel built atop a trendy pool hall.

Kiwis Nest (☎ 03-471 9540; kiwisnest@ihug.co.nz; 597 George St; dm/s $20/40, d $50-80) Popular, friendly hostel with two great self-contained double units.

MIDRANGE

858 George Street Motel (☎ 0800 858 999, 03-474 0047; www.858georgestreetmotel.co.nz; 858 George St; d $110-140; ☐) With a number of architectural awards under its belt, this modern motel's town-house-style units were built to resemble early Dunedin buildings. Little extras such as heavy wooden period doors and meticulous wooden trimmings lend a classy look and feel. One-bedroom units have a kitchenette, while the en suites in the studio flats are a little cramped. Furnishings are stylish and comfortable throughout and the owners are welcoming. For what you're getting, this is good value for money.

Albatross Inn (☎ 03-477 2727; www.albatross.inn.co.nz; 770 George St; high season $100-120, low season $125-140; ☐) While a little tumbledown on the outside, the inside of this characterful villa is brimming with atmosphere. Some quirky NZ knick-knacks and Victorian-style drapery give it a historic feel. Rooms are spacious and each unique with some period furnishings and en suites. Bigger rooms have small kitchenettes and king-sized beds. Try for sunny, corner Room 3. Staff are very accommodating, and the continental breakfast (included) features yummy baked goods.

526 George Street Boutique Hotel (☎ 0800 779 779, 03-477 1261; www.hotel526.co.nz; 526 George St; d $100-140; ☐) There's definitely a small, independent feel about this place although 'boutique' may be stretching it a bit far. Rooms are attractive, new and spacious with modern, classy décor but don't have a great deal of character. Executive rooms are even bigger and have spa baths. There's a breakfast restaurant, bar and small lounge.

Arcadian Motel (Map p603; ☎ 0508 272 234, 03-455 0992; www.dunedinmotel.co.nz; 85 Musselburgh Rise; high/low season d from $80/85, units $185; ℗) En route to the peninsula and not far from the beach, you'll find clean, well-priced rooms here. Studios are cheapest, a bit kitsch and definitely have the most character (especially the one next to the road with its big porthole window). There are also units that sleep up to six and all have decent cooking facilities. The neighbouring busy road quietens down at night.

Cargills Hotel (☎ 0800 737 378, 03-477 7983; www .cargills.co.nz; 678 George St; s/d $125/140; ℗) While something of a cement monster from the outside, the newly renovated rooms here are comfortable. The biggest selling point is the pleasant garden courtyard. Go for a room on the ground floor; you can hear the babbling fountains and the nearby foliage gives a nearly tropical feel. The more expensive suites are spacious but not worth the asking price ($165).

Other recommendations:

755 Regal Court Motel (☎ 0800 473 425, 03-477 7729; www.755regalcourtmotel.co.nz; 755 George St; d $125-155; ℗ 🖵) A relatively stylish, comfortable affair with enormous spa tubs.

Adrian Motel (Map p603; ☎ 0800 455 200, 03-455 2009; www.adrianmotel.co.nz; 101 Queens Dr; d $85-105; ℗) Dated but immaculate and very close to St Kilda Beach.

Alexis Motor Lodge (☎ 0800 425 394, 03-471 7268; www.alexis.co.nz; 475 George St; d $115-160; ℗ 🖵) Pricier rooms have gigantic spa baths, and there's a small play area for children.

Motel Moray Place (☎ 0800 909 797, 03-477 2050; info@97motel.co.nz; 97 Moray Pl; d $100-150; ℗) The standard rooms are good value and get lots of light. Pricier rooms are newer. The centre of town is only steps away.

TOP END

Fletcher Lodge (☎ 03-477 5552; www.fletcherlodge .co.nz; 276 High St; s $175-450, d $230-550; ℗ 🖵) Built in the 1920s, this charming period home has six unique rooms with antique furnishings and décor. The most lavish (and expensive) rooms have ultra-modern conveniences such as undertile heating and en suites and plasma TVs. Take the Edin-

Corstorphine House (☎ 03-487 1000; www .corstorphine.co.nz; Milburn St; d low/high season $400/550; ℗) Very grand and very plush, each of the eight opulent rooms in this 1863 mansion is decorated like a different corner of the world; sounds tacky but it couldn't be further from it. There's an ultra-chic Scandinavian room, one that's styled like a French country inn, and another that's very Rajasthani. Lounge in the big, period sitting rooms, breakfast in the conservatory, dine in the gourmet restaurant and wander the vast lawns. Staff are extremely accommodating. You'll find it a short drive south of the city in suburbia.

burgh room for its fantastic claw-foot tub or the gorgeous Craigard suite with its private city-view balcony. There's also a lovely guest lounge and beautiful breakfast room. The owners are friendly and pride themselves on discreet service.

Mandeno House (☎ 03-471 9595; www.mandeno house.com; 667 George St; s/d from $230/250) With only three rooms, this spot is for those who like to be pampered. Classy, fashionable décor is achieved through lots of white linen, wood floors and tasteful artwork, and colours are minimal. There's a very comfortable, private guest lounge and a full cooked breakfast (included) is served in the elegant dining room. Children are less than welcome.

For downtown hotels try the following:

Dunedin City Hotel (☎ 03-470 1470; www.scenic -circle.co.nz; cnr Princes & Dowling Sts; d from $200; ℗ 🖵) A flash, new baby on the block with designer-styled rooms, harbour views and top amenities.

Mercure Motel (Map p603; ☎ 03-477 1145; www .mercure.co.nz; 310 Princes St; d $275) Built in 1862 but renovated into sleek, modern rooms that are devoid of colour. Book online for half-price rates.

Eating

The streets surrounding the Octagon are overflowing with footpath tables and espresso machines. At many of these trendy cafés, you can plunk your coffee down next to hearty and well-priced meals. Fine dining is a little harder to come by in Dunedin but those mentioned in the following section are the city's long-standing favourites.

RESTAURANTS

Reef (☎ 03-471 7185; 333 George St; lunch mains $15, dinner mains $25; ☉ lunch & dinner Mon-Sat, dinner Sun) With fishing nets, filled aquariums and shell mobiles, the Reef makes a big effort to get you in the mood for something fishy. Whether you sink into calamari, crumbed sole, chilli crab or prawn curry, you won't be disappointed. Very tasty express lunches ($10) are ready in 15 minutes.

Thai Over (☎ 03-477 7815; 388 George St; mains $18; ☉ dinner) This tastefully decorated restaurant dishes up more than your standard Thai stir-fries, curries and salads.

Nova Cafe (☎ 03-479 0808; 29 The Octagon; mains $15; ☉ breakfast, lunch & dinner) Not surprisingly, this extension of the Public Art Gallery has a stylish look about it. A glass wall lets you check out the gallery-goers by day; at night it's curtained to create a cosier ambience. There's a much more restaurant than café feel about the place, with a menu of tasty items such as field mushrooms with pesto, daily risottos and seafood gumbo.

Bell Pepper Blues (☎ 03-474 0973; 474 Princes St; mains $32; ☉ dinner Mon-Sat) One of Dunedin's finer dining options, this restaurant has more than a decade of experience creating gourmet dishes such as prawn ravioli and cervena (farmed deer) noisettes. Extra niceties like freshly baked bread and roast-garlic jam ensure that you'll be duly awed. For dessert, try the frozen honey parfait. There's a corkage fee for BYO, and wheat-free diners will find a couple of options.

Hungry Frenchman (☎ 03-477 5748; 38 The Octagon; mains $26-30; ☉ lunch & dinner) Set in the basement of an Octagon heritage building, you'll feel anything but hungry when you leave this brasserie. Main courses such as a leg of duck with cranberry sauce, or portobello mushroom, brie and walnut tarts, almost don't leave room for the sumptuous desserts. But how can you refuse chocolate and orange Cointreau mousse?

Minami (☎ 03-477 9596; 126, 132 Stuart St; mains $12; ☉ lunch & dinner) This popular place will fulfil your fish and seaweed cravings. One room has bar stools and a takeaway menu. The other is classier with fountains and orchids.

Tokyo Gardens (☎ 03-474 5993; 351 George St; mains $15; ☉ lunch & dinner) For bigger pickings than Minami but less atmosphere, wade through the 150-item menu here.

CAFÉS

See p600 for cafés that serve espresso as the main course.

Arc Cafe (☎ 03-474 1135; www.arc.org.nz; 135 High St; mains $10-15; ☉ 10am-late Mon-Sat; ☐) High ceilings, well-worn couches and colourful lanterns make this funky, somewhat grungy place a pleasant spot to while away an afternoon. There are heaps of toys for kids, lots of nightlife flyers to peruse, yummy desserts and brunch (such as banana-berry pancakes) until midday. Coffee alternatives, including bowls of hot chocolate, and hot blackcurrant, line the menu board alongside bagels, pizza, and burgers. The café is also a popular music venue (see p600).

Good Oil (☎ 03-479 9900; 314 George St; mains $10; ☉ breakfast & lunch) Join in the well-heeled and sip your espresso beneath a chandelier. Stacks of magazines, chill-out music and minimalist design come together in a tranquil atmosphere. There isn't a huge amount of room inside but tables spill out onto the footpath for great people-watching. At the counter, fantastic baking rubs shoulders with filling salads, bagels and gourmet pot pies. There's also loose-leaf tea, smoothies and unpretentious staff.

QUICK EATS

Modaks (☎ 03-477 6563; 318 George St; mains $10; ☉ breakfast, lunch & dinner) With Formica tables and worn wooden floors, this funky little down-at-heel place is popular with students. Brick walls, reggae music and footpath tables add to the ambience. If sundaes, smoothies and giant cinnamon pinwheels won't fill you up, order some grilled, homemade focaccia bread with toppings such as brie, pesto, smoked salmon or bacon. Brunch sorts out omelettes, pancakes and a full veggie breakfast ($14).

Potpourri (☎ 03-477 9983; 97 Lower Stuart St; meals $6-9; ☉ breakfast & lunch) Funky, homey and kid-friendly, this colourful, vegetarian place serves up big portions of scrumptious quiche and pizza as well as flatbread melts and spicy samosas. Most of it's organic, much of it's vegan and it's all deliciously fresh.

Il Panificio (☎ 03-474 1255; 430 George St; mains $5-9; ☉ breakfast & lunch) This busy café churns out fantastically tasty focaccia (such as walnut or red onion), toasted *panini* and fresh pizza. Filling breakfasts include banana *panini*, smoked-salmon croissants or bagels Benedict. Be sure to leave room for the divine brownies.

SELF-CATERING

Everyday Gourmet (☎ 03-477 2045; 466 George St; mains $10; ☻lunch & dinner) In addition to the gourmet chutneys, pastas, sausages and salads, this deli sells take-home frozen dinners including lasagne and chicken casserole. The beef curry will feed two or three of you, especially if you add nan bread and rice. And grab a hot chocolate too; there's everything from amaretto to white mint.

Head to **Countdown supermarket** (309 Cumberland St) for 24-hour supplies.

Drinking

The Octagon is the heart of the city's bar scene, with the student crowd ensuring that things are kept lively until the wee hours. Dunedin also has particularly excellent coffee, most of which is sourced from Mazagran (below).

Fix (☎ 03-479 2660; 15 Frederick St; ☻early Mon-Thu, later Fri-Sun) Despite the orange walls, it's easy to relax at this hip café amidst magazines and an endless stream of uni students. Besides coffee, you'll find a great selection of teas, hot chocolate and juices. There's a footpath takeaway window if you're on the move and a sunny patio if you're not. The counter has lots of flyers to keep you up to date on Dunedin's nightlife. BYO food.

Mazagran Espresso Bar (☎ 03-477 9959; 36 Moray Pl; ☻8am-6pm Mon-Fri, 10am-2pm Sat) The mother of Dunedin's coffee scene, this tiny wood-and-brick coffee house is the source of beans for the majority of the city's restaurants and cafés. You'll feel dizzy from the aroma as you nibble on sweets, linger at one of the few tables or read magazines.

Barakah (☎ 03-477 3776; 12 The Octagon) Get settled on a big, round, cushy stool and soak in the ambience of this small, atmospheric Moroccan bar. Blue tiles, authentic lamps, a well-stocked bar and a tasty tapas menu will fill your senses.

Bennu's (☎ 03-474 5055; 12 Moray Pl) At night this lavish place is dominated by its large bar. It's usually propped up by a mellow, older crowd in for late-night glass-clinking.

Woolshed (☎ 03-477 3246; 318 Moray Pl) Looking very much like its name, this pub-style drinking hole often has a boisterous crowd

that keeps the beer flowing freely until the early hours. Worn and wooden, its finishing touches are a few pool tables and an unlikely disco ball.

Poolhouse (☎ 03-477 6121; 12 Filleul St; pool per hr $6-9) Stylish rather than seedy, this modern pool hall has top-notch 7ft and 9ft tables, plenty of local beers and funky break beats that you can dance to with the eight ball.

Captain Cook (☎ 03-474 1935; 354 Great King St) The 'Cook' was under maintenance when we visited but promised to soon resume services as a hang-out for procrastinating students. It features a beer garden, big-screen TV, cheap food and plenty of freshly filled glasses.

Entertainment

Pick up a free copy of *f*INK (www.fink.net .nz) from cafés and bars around the city for listings of music, films, theatre and dance. The *Otago Daily Times* also lists what's up and coming, and it's worth having a gander at the posters in the Fix and Arc cafés. A number of nightspots close on Sundays and Mondays and admission at most ranges from free to a tenner.

LIVE MUSIC & NIGHTCLUBS

Arc Cafe (☎ 03-474 1135; www.arc.org.nz; 135 High St; ☻10am-late Mon-Sat) The Arc Cafe has only one constant: it's always diverse, pumping out both the unusual and the current rage. Within the space of a week, you can catch acoustic gigs, funk, jazz, stand-up comedy and DJs as well as gay nights or poetry evenings. There's a laid-back crowd, and you can also eat at the funky café here (p599).

Isis Lounge (☎ 03-477 8001; 68 Princes St) This hip little place favours live acoustic lounge music, which you can enjoy from a comfortable sofa. If the music doesn't heat you up, head for the wood stove or the well-endowed wine list.

ReFuel (☎ 03-479 5334; Otago University, 640 Cumberland St) A campus-based venue, this intimate setting sees some big-name live acts and local DJs. One room is all bar, the other is all about getting down with the music.

Bath St (☎ 03-477 6750; www.bathst.com; 1 Bath St; ☻10pm-late Tue-Sat) Catering to students and backpackers, DJs spin hip-hop, drum 'n' bass and house music. The dance floor isn't huge but there's certainly enough room to shake your booty.

Other late night options:

Ra Bar (☎ 03-477 6080; 21 The Octagon) This is a big place with a small dance floor but if you're looking to wiggle to some Top 40 tunes, it's your best bet.

Vatican Nightclub (☎ 03-477 1637; 65 Hanover St) Hear the calling of funky house or drum 'n' bass at this Anglo-Saxon church.

Woolshed (☎ 03-477 3246; 318 Moray Pl) There's rustic live music (like bush bands) from midweek onwards at this pub (opposite).

CINEMAS

Blockbuster releases dominate the big screens at **Hoyts Cinema** (☎ 03-477 3250; info line 03-477 7019; 33 The Octagon; adult/child $14/8), while a fair mix of mainstream and independent releases is shown at the halcyon-era **Rialto Cinemas** (☎ 03-474 2200; www.rialto.co.nz; 11 Moray Pl; adult/child $14/8). Both have reduced weekday rates before 5pm and all day Tuesday. **Metro Cinema** (☎ 03-474 3350; www.metrocinema .co.nz; Moray Pl; tickets $10) resides in the Town Hall and prefers art-house titles.

SPORT
Carisbrook Stadium (☎ 03-455 1191; www.orfu.co .nz; Burns St; tickets adult $12-22, child $5, main stand $27) Want to see Kiwis get passionate? Attend a match at the 'home of NZ rugby' (aka the 'House of Pain'). The season runs from February to October, and tickets to low-key games are generally available at the ground.

Bottom Bus (☎ 03-434 7370; www.bottombus.co .nz) This outfit runs rugby trips combining meals, accommodation, drinks, face painting and transport for around $200. The Bottom Bus team really gets into the spirit of things. Really.

THEATRE
Fortune Theatre (☎ 03-477 8323; www.fortunetheatre .co.nz; 231 Stuart St; adult/child $25/18; ☑ box office 9am-5pm Mon-Fri, when shows running also 4.30-8.30pm Sat & 1.30-4pm) This local company pulls off daring theatrical feats with enough panache to have kept it in business for the past 25 years. The company turns out days-of-yore works (such as *Hamlet*) and contemporary NZ productions. Shows are performed in a graceful old church.

Regent Theatre (☎ 03-477 8597; The Octagon; ☑ box office 8.30am-5.30pm Mon-Fri, 10.30am-1pm Sat) The place to see mainstream big names in ballet, classical music and theatre.

Shopping
George St is *the* place to shop in Dunedin. And if you look hard, you'll find some unique options buried amidst the chain-store monotony.

ART, JEWELLERY & MUSIC
Records Records (☎ 03-474 0789; 213 Stuart St) This near-legend of a shop was about to change hands at the time of research. Keep your fingers crossed that it doesn't loose any of its *High Fidelity* ambience or its stacks of mainly secondhand incie vinyl and CDs.

Little Rock Shop (☎ 477-7657; 23 The Octagon) A tiny shop selling beautifully handcrafted jewellery at surprisingly reasonable prices. Settings include paua, and the necklaces are especially unusual.

Mo'ay Gallery (☎ 03-477 8060; 55 Princes St) This place has a small exhibition space as well as decently priced, quality pieces for sale such as contemporary pottery, blown glass and local paintings.

Milford Galleries (☎ 03-477 7727; 18 Dowling St) New, fresh stuff that's interesting to look at even if you're not in the market to buy. You'll find painting, sculpture, glass works and photography from regional artists.

CLOTHING & OUTDOOR EQUIPMENT
Bivouac (☎ 03-477 3679; 171 George St) The place to come for climbing, camping and trekking gear, with everything from boots to packs to camping stoves. You'll also find a good selection of maps and specialist guidebooks. The guys here have the last word in rock climbing.

Adventure Outfitters (☎ 03-479 2488; 106 George St) With more than 15 years under its belt, this company's range of clothing is both hard-wearing and fashionable in that out-doorsy way. Jackets, fleeces, pullovers and yoga gear all have a stylish edge. The shop itself is nothing special; apparently the focus is on the goods rather than the package.

3co-nz (☎ 03-479 2595; 3 The Octagon) Enough knitwear styles to please everyone from you to your granny. Especially soft are the ultra-thin tops made from merino possum (a blend of wool and fur). The majority of the stock is made locally with a few imports from far-flung Christchurch.

McKinlays (☎ 03-477 1839; 454 George St) A bit of a walk north on George Street, this shop will send you back in comfort. The shop has been crafting leather footwear since 1879 and continues to produce sturdy, durable boots and shoes. There are good options for kids as well as a made-to-measure service.

Getting There & Away

AIR

Direct, budget-priced flights between Dunedin and eastern Australia destinations are offered by **Freedom Air** (☎ 0800 600 500, 09-523 8686; www.freedomair.co.nz).

Air New Zealand (☎ 0800 737 000, 03-479 6594; www.airnz.co.nz; cnr Princes St & The Octagon) has direct flights to and from Auckland (from $125), Christchurch (from $85) and Wellington (from $120).

BUS

InterCity (☎ 03-474 9600, tickets 03-471 7143; www.intercitycoach.co.nz; 205 St Andrew St; ✆ ticket office 7am-5pm Mon-Thu, to 5.30pm Fri, 11am-3pm Sat & Sun, tickets by phone 7am-9pm daily) has direct services to Christchurch ($45), Queenstown ($40) and Invercargill ($40).

Several door-to-door shuttles service Dunedin, arriving and departing at Dunedin Railway Station on Anzac Ave; inquire at the visitor information centre. **Atomic Shuttles** (☎ 03-322 8883; www.atomictravel.co.nz) runs to and from Christchurch, Invercargill and Queenstown (all $30), and Wanaka ($35). **Knightrider** (☎ 03-342 8055; www.knightrider.co.nz) operates a night-time service to Invercargill ($36), Oamaru ($26) and Christchurch ($45). **Catch-A-Bus** (☎ 03-479 9960) operates daily between Dunedin and Te Anau ($50) and also has services to Christchurch ($50), Queenstown and Wanaka (both $45). **Wanaka Connexions** (☎ 03-443 9122; www.wanakaconnexions.co.nz) offers shuttles from Dunedin to Wanaka and on to Queenstown (both $40).

From Dunedin, **Bottom Bus** (☎ 03-434 7370; www.bottombus.co.nz) and **Catlins Coaster** (☎ 0800 304 333, 021 682 461; www.catlinscoaster.co.nz) do the scenic route through the Catlins; see p683.

TRAIN

The historic Taieri Gorge Railway chugs into the magnificent Dunedin Railway Station (Anzac Ave).

Getting Around

Dunedin Airport (☎ 03-486 2879; www.dnairport.co.nz) is 27km southwest of the city. The cheapest way to reach it is by a door-to-door shuttle,

which will set you back about $15 per adult. Try **Kiwi Shuttles** (☎ 03-473 7017; http://kiwishuttles.co.nz), **Super Shuttle** (☎ 0800 748 885; www.supershuttle.co.nz), **Dunedin Taxis** (☎ 03-477 7777) or **City Taxis** (☎ 03-477 1771). A standard taxi ride between the city and airport costs around $50 (or $60 in a limo). There is no public bus service to the airport.

City buses (☎ 0800 474 082; www.orc.govt.nz) leave from stops in the Octagon, while buses to districts around Dunedin depart a block away on Cumberland St. Buses run regularly during the week, but services are greatly reduced (or evaporate) on weekends and holidays. Pick up the *Dunedin Bus Timetable* from the visitor information centre. An average trip costs less than $2.

For details of the hop-on, hop-off Dunedin City Explorer, see p596.

OTAGO PENINSULA

With a reliable reputation for the most accessible wildlife on the South Island, Otago Peninsula makes it onto many travellers' itineraries. Albatross, yellow-eyed penguins, blue penguins, fur seals and sea lions all reside here, along with some stunning scenery, worthwhile historical sites, walkways and unique natural formations. Despite the multitude of tours and activities that have consequently made the peninsula their stomping ground, the area maintains a quiet pastoral feel. For an overview, pick up the *Otago Peninsula* brochure and map from Dunedin's visitor information centre and check out www.otago-peninsula.co.nz.

Sights

ROYAL ALBATROSS CENTRE

Taiaroa Head, at the peninsula's eastern end, has the world's only mainland royal albatross colony. The best time to see them is from December to February, when one parent is constantly guarding the young while the other delivers food throughout the day. You also get teenage birds cruising at speeds of up to 160km/h; at times there'll be close to 20 overhead. Sightings are most common in the afternoon when the winds pick up; calm days don't see much bird action.

The only public access to the colony is through the **Royal Albatross Centre** (☎ 03-478 0499; www.albatross.org.nz; Taiaroa Head; ✆ 9am-dusk Oct-Mar, 10am-4pm Apr-Sep, tours half-hourly in summer, on demand Apr-Sep) from where you can take

OTAGO PENINSULA

SOUTH PACIFIC OCEAN

DUNEDIN

See Dunedin Map (p592)

North East Valley

St Leonards

Portobello Rd

Highcliff Rd

Harington Point Rd

INFORMATION
Monarch Wildlife Cruises & Tours..1 D1

SIGHTS & ACTIVITIES
Fort Taiaroa..2 B3
Glenfalloch Woodland Garden....3 B2
Larnach Castle..................................4 C2
Marine Studies Centre....................5 D1
Royal Albatross Centre...................(see 5)
Yellow-Eyed Penguin Conservation
Reserve..6 D1

SLEEPING
Adrian Motel......................................7 A3
Arcadian Motel.................................8 A3
Bus Stop Backpackers.....................9 C2
Dunedin Holiday Park...................10 A3
Harington Point Village Motel......11 D1
Homestead......................................(see 6)
Larnach Lodge..............................(see 3)
McFarmers Backpackers..............12 C2
Penguin Place Lodge....................13 C2
Peninsula B&B...............................(see 14)
Portobello Motels.........................14 C2
Portobello Village Tourist Park...15 C2

EATING
190E Café..16 C2

0 ——— 5 km
0 ——— 3 miles

a one-hour, extremely informative 'Royal Albatross' tour (adult/child $30/15) that includes viewing from a glassed-in hut overlooking the nesting sites. From mid-September to the third week in November the birds are mating and tours (adult/child $18/9) are confined to the centre, with viewing restricted to live TV footage. From the end of November to December, the birds are generally plunked down on their eggs and there's little opportunity to see that magnificent wingspan. Blue penguins also nest here (often under the centre's walkways), meaning you can see the world's smallest penguin and largest flying seabird in one go.

Also on site is the now defunct **Fort Taiaroa** and its 1886 Armstrong Disappearing Gun

that was manned in somewhat overzealous anticipation of a Russian attack. If you are into big guns, check it out on the Fort Taiaroa tour (adult/child $15/7) or the **Taiaroa Experience** (adult/child $35/17), which includes the whole kit and caboodle. The centre also has some interesting exhibits on peninsular wildlife and a decent café (trains $8 to $13).

YELLOW-EYED PENGUIN CONSERVATION RESERVE

One of the world's rarest penguins, the hoiho (yellow-eyed penguin) faces an ongoing loss of habitat throughout Otago and Southland, perpetuated by farmers who allow cattle to trample the penguins' remaining patches of vegetation. The **Yellow-Eyed Penguin Conservation Reserve** (☎ 03-478 0286; McGrouther's Farm, Harrington Point Rd; tours adult/child/family $33/15/80; ☼ tours regularly 10am-7.45pm Oct-Mar, 3.45pm & 4.15pm Apr-Sep) has replanted this penguin's breeding habitat, built nesting sites, cared for sick and injured birds and trapped predators. The staff offer tours of the reserve, which include a talk on penguin conservation and close-up viewing from a system of trenches and hides. You can see the birds year-round but summer is best; these trips are very popular, so book ahead. For accommodation at the Penguin Place Lodge, see opposite.

Several other tours (see opposite) visit yellow-eyed penguin habitats on private farmland that's not accessible to the public. The birds also nest at a couple of public beaches, including **Sandfly Bay**, which has a DOC hide. If you go alone, stay on the trails, view penguins *only* from the hide and don't approach these shy creatures; even loud voices can disturb them. In recent years, the penguins have been badly distressed by selfish tourists using flash photography or traipsing through the nesting grounds. According to some locals, the birds are consequently moving further down the coast.

SEA LIONS

The New Zealand (or Hooker's) sea lions are most easily seen on a tour (see opposite) to a 'secret' beach where the first pup was born on the NZ mainland after a breeding absence of 700 years. Sea lions are also regularly present at **Allans** and **Victory** beaches where these predominantly bachelor males vacation from Campbell Island or the Auckland Islands. If you do see one, stay well back; they can move that bulk a lot faster than you'd guess.

LARNACH CASTLE

Standing proudly on the highest point of the peninsula, **Larnach Castle** (☎ 03-476 1616; www .larnachcastle.co.nz; Camp Rd; castle & grounds adult/child $20/10, grounds only $10/3; ☼ 9am-5pm) is the result of the excessive extravagance of William Larnach. Built in 1871 to impress his French nobility–descended wife, the ostentatious, gothic mansion is filled with exquisite, antique furnishings. Larnach, a merchant and politician, committed suicide in Parliament House in 1898 and the castle later fell into

disrepair. In 1967, it was bought and restored by the Barker family, who continue to reside in it today. An informative pamphlet guides you through the castle (with a children's version available). The **gardens** offer fantastic views of the peninsula and harbour; visit early to catch some impressive birdsong. There's also a café in the ballroom (open to those with a grounds-only ticket) and some unique accommodation (see opposite). You can reach the castle via the Portobello bus to Company Bay followed by a 4km walk uphill.

OTHER SIGHTS

Glenfalloch Woodland Garden (☎ 03-476 1775; 430 Portobello Rd; admission by donation; ☼ gardens 9.30am-dusk, café-wine bar 10am-4pm Mon-Fri, 1-4pm Sat & Sun summer) covers 12 hectares with a gorgeous profusion of colourful flowers, walking tracks and swaying, mature trees such as a 1000-year-old matai. You'll also catch some spectacular views over the harbour. The Portobello bus stops out the front.

The **Marine Studies Centre** (☎ 03-479 5826; www .otago.ac.nz/marine studies; Hatchery Rd; entry adult/child/family $8/4/16, entry & tour adult/child/family $16/8/30; ☼ noon-4.30pm) gives youngsters (and their folks) the chance to see octopus, seahorses, crayfish and sharks as well as get their hands salty in the touch tanks. You can join in with fish-feeding (Wednesday and Saturday 2pm to 3pm) or take a guided tour of the not-so-big facility at 10.30am. The centre showcases the work of the adjacent university-run marine laboratory.

Activities

The peninsula's coastal and farmland walkways offer stunning views and the chance to see wildlife on your own. Trailheads can be reached with your own transport or the Walking Bus (p595). Pick up a free copy of the detailed *Otago Peninsula Tracks* from Dunedin's visitor centre. A popular destination is the beautiful **Sandfly Bay**, reached from Seal Point Rd (moderate; 40 minutes) or Ridge Rd (difficult; 40 minutes). From the end of Sandymount Rd, you can follow a trail to the impressive **Chasm** (20 minutes). Most trails are closed during September and October for lambing.

Wild Earth Adventures (☎ 03-473 6535; www.wild earth.co.nz; trips from $80) offers two-hour trips in double sea kayaks, with wildlife often sighted en route. No previous experience is necessary and pick-up from Dunedin is included.

Tours

Elm Wildlife Tours (☎ 0800 356 563, 03-474 1872; www.elmwildlifetours.co.nz; standard tour $75) leads small groups on excellent, informative wildlife-spotting trips of up to six hours. Pick-up and drop-off from Dunedin is included. Other tours of a similar ilk included.

Twilight Wildlife Tour (☎ 03-474 3300; www.wild dunedin.co.nz; adult/student/child $60/50/40) and **Back to Nature Tours** (☎ 0800 477 0484, 03-477 0484; www.backtonaturetours.co.nz; adult/concession $65/55). The **Natures Wonders** (☎ 0800 246 446; www.natureswon dersnaturally.com; adult/child $40/35) tour includes a ride in an 8WD amphibious vehicle across a working sheep farm.

Monarch Wildlife Cruises & Tours (☎ 03-477 4276; www.wildlife.co.nz; trips hr/half day/full day from $32/75/170) runs one-hour boat trips from Wellers Rock, as well as half- and full-day tours from Dunedin (see p596). The tours visit breeding grounds for sea lions, penguins, albatross and seals, some of which are inaccessible by land.

Otago Nature Guides (☎ 03-454 5169; www.nz natureguides.com) offers small-group ecotours (maximum of four people) with walks, wildlife viewing, knowledgeable commentary, most food and the option of accommodation. Join the sunrise penguin walk ($60) or the day tour including Dunedin, the Otago Peninsula (and the albatross colony) and an hour-long boat cruise ($240).

Otago Explorer (☎ 0800 322 240, 03-474 3300; adult/child $40/20; castle tour 9am & 3pm, wildlife tour 5pm summer only) will unravel the tale of the Larnach family history on its guided tours inside Larnach Castle. The company also runs summertime wildlife tours. All include transport from Dunedin. **Citibus** (☎ 03-477 5577; www.transportplace.co.nz) offers a similar tour of the castle ($40/20 per adult/child, including castle entry) as well as various wildlife tours on and around Taiaroa Head (from $70/35 per adult/child).

Sleeping

BUDGET

McFarmers Backpackers (☎ 03-478 0389; mcfarmers backpackers@hotmail.com; 774 Portobello Rd; d $52, cottages $72) An absolutely top hostel, this rustic, timber place is steeped in cosy character.

Lounge on the window seat or deck for fabulous harbour views, barbecue out the back, rent a bike or get warm in front of the woodburning stove. With lots of colour and light, you'll almost forget that you came to visit the nearby albatross and penguins. The cottage is just as lovely, very private and well suited to families. Go on, chill with the chickens.

Bus Stop Backpackers (☎ 03-478 0330; www.bus-stop.co.nz; 252 Harington Point Rd; per person $23) One of peninsula's more atmospheric options, this enchanting little place feels much more like a home than a guesthouse. Enjoy great sea views from the '60s-style sitting rooms or buy muesli in the well-equipped kitchen. There's a triple and double in the house; outside you can opt for beds in the retro caravan or vintage bus. You'll find it just east of Portobello. Rent bikes for $20 a day and linen for $5.

Penguin Place Lodge (☎ 03-478 0286; Mc-Grouther's Farm, Harington Point Rd; per person $20) At the back of the farm with a well-equipped kitchen, homey lounge and basic rooms, you'll feel just like Old MacDonald. Beautiful views across the farm and harbour can be had from the deck, and you're close to the seals and albatross and neighbours with the penguins. Linen is $5 extra.

Portobello Village Tourist Park (☎ 03-478 0359; portoobellopark@xtra.co.nz; 27 Hereweka St, Portobello; unpowered/powered sites per 2 people $22/26, d $40-75) With enough trees and grass to make it feel like a park, this is a pleasant place to stake your tent. The owners are welcoming and offer useful amenities such as a barbecue area and bike hire. There's also a kids' play area, a baby bath, a modern kitchen and wheelchair-accessible facilities. Backpacker rooms are BYO everything; self-contained units are cosy and newly renovated.

MIDRANGE & TOP END

Larnach Lodge (☎ 03-476 1616; www.larnachcastle.co.nz; Camp Rd; lodge d $200 incl castle tour, coach house d incl castle entrance $98) Feeling like royalty? Stay in one of a dozen rooms in Larnach Castle's back-garden lodge. Rooms are individually decorated in period style; take the Rhododendron Room for spectacular harbour views, the White Room for a canopy bed or the Enchanted Forest Room for wallpaper designed in 1889. While they're fairly plush, rooms are also flirting with naffness. Much more atmospheric are the rustic rooms in the 125-year-old Coach House with Tudor, angular ceilings and a TV room in a cosied-up stable. Breakfast is included for all guests and dinner is available by arrangement.

Portobello Motels (☎ 03-478 0155; www.portobel lomotels.com; 10 Harington Point Rd, Portobello; d $110-130) New, sunny units just off the main road in Portobello. Blue and yellow rooms have a cabinlike feel with patios out front. Studio units are by far the best (and cheapest) with small decks overlooking the bay. One- and two-bedroom units are also available but viewless. Prices drop slightly in winter.

Harington Point Village Motel (☎ 03-478 0287; www.wildlifetours.co.nz; 932 Harington Point Rd; d $100-110) These spacious, charming self-contained units are set in a garden across from the sea. Appreciate the scenery from the deck or hike up the road to the nearby albatross centre.

Other options on the peninsula:

Peninsula B&B (☎ 0800 478 090; www.peninsula.co.nz; 4 Allans Beach Rd, Portobello; d $125-165; 🔲) Period home with lovely doubles, harbour views and a home-cooked breakfast. Rates drop from April to September.

Homestead (☎ 03-478 0384; thehomestead@clear.net .nz; 238 Harington Point Rd; d $100-120) Self-contained units that are huge and modern, with big views out to sea.

Eating

Dining is largely a self-catering affair on the peninsula. When you've had enough of wielding the frying pan, head to the **1908 Café** (☎ 03-478 0801; 7 Harington Point Rd; mains $12-35; 🕐 lunch & dinner), where traditional fare such as barbecue fish and steak are joined by gourmet blackboard specials. Kids have their own options and a box of toys. Walls are cheerful and embellished with local art.

Other dining options include the cafes at Larnach Castle, Glenfalloch Woodland Garden and the Royal Albatross Centre.

Getting There & Around

There are a half-dozen bus services each weekday between Dunedin's Cumberland St and Portobello Village ($4), with the odd one continuing on to Harington Point. Weekend services are more limited. Once you get to the peninsula, you'll find it's tough to get around without your own transport. Most tours will pick you up from your accommodation.

There's a petrol station in Portobello and one on Highcliff Rd at the western end of the peninsula but hours are unpredictable. It's wisest to fill up in Dunedin before driving out.

CENTRAL OTAGO

Lying in the shadow of the Southern Alps, this is gold-rush country. The shiny stuff was struck here in the late 19th century, bringing about 40 years of gold fever and creating a multitude of towns. While the miners (who came from as far as the Hebrides and China) have long since picked up sticks and left, they've left behind some of Otago's most charming towns and villages, complete with period architecture and lovely, riverside settings. Interpretative pamphlets including *Otago Goldfields: Heritage Trail* pinpoint areas where remnants of the gold-rush trade can be found; pick it up at any of the tourist information centres in the area. For good regional information, visit www.tco.org.nz.

CROMWELL

pop 2610

While Cromwell claims to be a town, it's hard to shake the impression of an outdoor shopping mall. This is because the town was purpose-built in 1993 when the Clyde Dam flooded the original Cromwell village. Cromwell leans heavily on its fruit production as a tourist drawcard (you can't miss the enormous Carmen Miranda hat-piece display) but the real attraction is the restored village on the banks of the river. It's not worth a trip in itself, but if you're passing through, it's a great place to stop for a wander and lunch.

Visit **Cromwell & Districts visitor information centre** (☎ 03-445 0212; cromwellvin@xtra.co.nz; 47 The Mall; 🕐 9am-5pm Mon-Fri, 10am-4pm Sat & Sun) for a plethora of local info.

Before Lake Dunstan swallowed up the village of Cromwell, concerned locals had the foresight to disassemble many of the historic buildings and move them uphill, where they're being painstakingly restored as **Old Cromwell Town**. There are currently a dozen 19th-century buildings rebuilt in a peaceful pedestrianised zone. Plaques detail their history, and you can pick up the *Old Cromwell Town Self-Guided Tour*. Many of the buildings are now home to artisans; see

Hullabaloo Art Space (☎ 03-445 0023; www.odelle.com) or **Stoop Gallery** (☎ 027 491 6125; www.stoop.co.nz). And don't miss the excellent Grain & Seed Café (below).

About 7km west (towards Queenstown) is the **Goldfields Mining Centre** (☎ 03-445 1038; www.goldfieldsmining.co.nz; S46; adult/child $15/7.50; ☑ 9am-5pm), a rather commercial operation with tours and the opportunity to pan for gold and shop. There are also a 40-minute jetboat rides from here along Kawarau River with **Goldfields Jet** (☎ 03-445 1038; hamish@goldfieldsjet.co.nz; adult/child $75/45).

Sleeping & Eating

Cromwell Top 10 Holiday Park (☎ 0800 107 275, 03-445 0164; www.cromwellholidaypark.co.nz; 1 Alpha St; sites per 2 people $26, cabins $45-95; ☑) Huge and filled with cabins of various descriptions, this isn't the place to get back to nature.

Golden Gate Lodge (☎ 0800 104 451, 03-445 1777; www.goldengate.co.nz; Barry Ave; r $115-120; ☑) Try here for somewhat dated rooms with a view.

Colonial Manor (☎ 03-445 0184; www.colonialmanor.co.nz; cnr Barry & Mead Aves; d $120) Fairly new and far enough from the highway to be peaceful, this pleasant motel has clean and comfortable rooms with small kitchens and shared patios or decks.

Grain & Seed Café (☎ 03-445 1007; mains $4-9; ☑ breakfast & lunch) Set in a beautiful stone building that was once Jolly's Grain Store, this excellent café is a perfect spot for lunch with its potbelly stove, home baking and picnic tables next to the river.

Big Picture (☎ 03-445 4052; cnr Sandflat Rd & SH6; mains $20-30; ☑ lunch & dinner) Sit in the director's chair as you dine on creative Mediterranean dishes. Also enjoy wine tasting and a wineology film in the adjoining room. It's 3km down the road heading to Queenstown.

Fusée Rouge Café (☎ 03-445 4014; 64b The Mall; mains $5-15; ☑ breakfast & lunch) Surprisingly stylish with excellent coffees and tasty meals.

Tin Goose (☎ 03-445 0217; The Mall; mains $4-13; ☑ breakfast & lunch) Vegetarians can take their appetite here, where there are great sandwiches and quiche.

Pick up some of Cromwell's famous fresh fruit at **Freeway Orchard** (☎ 03-445 1500; SH8).

Getting There & Away

Atomic Shuttles (☎ 03-471 4120), **InterCity** (☎ 03-474 9600) and **Catch-a-Bus** (☎ 03-322 8883), and **Wanaka Connexions** (☎ 03-443 9122) all run from Cromwell to Queenstown and Alexandra for about $20. Atomic Shuttles and InterCity have connections on to Dunedin, Christchurch and Invercargill, while Wanaka Connexions can get you to Wanaka.

CLYDE

pop 850

Once the centre of the Dunstan goldfields, this tiny historic town oozes atmosphere. With fabulous 19th-century architecture, some interesting walks, excellent dining and accommodation options and a friendly, small-town feel, it's a great place to chill out for a couple of days. Clyde is located beside the emerald green Clutha River, just south of Clyde Dam.

Sights & Activities

Pick up a copy of *Walk Around Our Historic Town: Clyde*, which leads you on an interesting self-guided walk through the town and its past. **Clyde Historical Museum** (☎ 03-449 2711; Blyth St; adult/child $3/1; ☑ 2-4pm Tue-Sun) contains the original exhibit of the 1879 museum as well as artefacts from the town's gold-dusty past. Up the road, the **Briar Herb Factory Complex** (☎ 03-449 2938; Fraser St; adult/child $3/1; ☑ 2-4pm Tue-Sun) displays exhibits on the lives of early settlers, including a herb factory, medicine dispensary and rabbiter's hut.

Nearby **Lookout Point** allows great views over the once-bustling gold diggings. The worthwhile **Cairnmuir Hill Track**, with a trailhead 4km from town on Clyde-Bannockburn Rd, is a 21km rough route with stunning views and altitudes of 1100m. It's accessible to mountain bikers and hikers but you'll need transport back from Bannockburn (near Cromwell). Also popular is the **Alexandra-Clyde 150th Anniversary Walk** (three hours one way), a riverside trail that's fairly flat and has ample resting spots and shade. **Trail Journeys** (☎ 0800 724 587; rail@trailjourneys.co.nz; Clyde Railhead; ☑ guided tours Sep-Apr) rents bikes (from $15 per day) and kayaks (from $35 per day) and offers cycling tours.

Sleeping & Eating

Hartley Arms Backpackers (☎ 03-449 2700; hartleyarms@xtra.co.nz; 25 Sunderland St; dm/d $20/50) Within a gorgeous garden setting, this 1869 stone guesthouse features a row of very quaint, lovingly restored rooms. It's somewhat rustic but homey touches add warmth, as do the electric heaters. The two dorms each sleep four and the sole double is especially atmospheric. The common kitchen/lounge is none too big, but tables in the garden under the cherry tree let you stretch out in summer. The owners are particularly congenial.

Dunstan Hotel (☎ 03-449 2817; 35 Sunderland St; s/d $30/55) With hand-stitched quilts in some rooms and psychedelic-touched carpet in others, rooms here are fairly basic. It's within staggering distance from the pub downstairs and has shared toilets and a common lounge with a toaster, kettle and fridge.

Dunstan House (☎ 03-449 2295; www.dunstanhouse.co.nz; 29 Sunderland St; d $100-140) This Victorian-aged inn has been restored with a fine-tooth comb. Rooms with en suites are a little pricier; most have claw-foot tubs and one room is wheelchair accessible.

Olivers (☎ 03-449 2860; www.olivers.co.nz; 34 Sunderland St; d $140-300) For the price, most of these 1860s rooms seem a little worn, but they've got character. Choose from converted stables, a lodge, barn and smokehouse, in order of ascending price. The romantic smokehouse is the most unique with a four-poster bed and sunken bath.

Olivers Restaurant (dinner mains $26-30; ☻ lunch & dinner) This somewhat cavernous restaurant has linen tablecloths that contrast nicely with the rough stone walls. The adjoining café serves gourmet pizzas and sandwiches on Turkish bread for lunch.

Post Office Cafe & Bar (☎ 03-449 2488; 2 Blyth St; mains $15; ☻ breakfast & lunch) The first post office was made of canvas and blew down. This one, built in 1899, has proven its durability and now houses a popular restaurant that serves filling, well-priced meals in a relaxed setting. Mains including gourmet sausages with red onion jam, and chilli fish keep locals coming back. On weekends, reservations are a good idea. The neighbouring Post Master's House (double rooms $90 to $120) has equally well-priced rooms with antique furnishings such as travelling trunks and bureaus. The king room has an en suite with a claw-foot tub.

Getting There & Away

Although none has a dedicated stop here, buses travelling between Cromwell and Al-exandra pick up and drop off in Clyde on request (it often incurs a small surcharge). See p607 for details.

ALEXANDRA

pop 4620

Unless you've come to Alexandra for September's **NZ Merino Shearing Championships** (an event that draws hundreds and leaves the entire town blurry-eyed), the reason to visit this rather nondescript service hub is for the nearby mountain biking. Once upon a time, the lure of gold brought thousands to the Dunstan goldfields, however the town owes its permanence to the dredging boom of the 1890s and its current prosperity to the orchardists who followed.

There's a **DOC office** (☎ 03-440 2040; 43 Dunstan Rd) on the town's outskirts and an informative **Central Otago visitor information centre** (☎ 03-448 9515; www.alexandra.co.nz; Pioneer Park, Centennial Ave; ☻ 9am-5pm).

Sights & Activities

At the time of research, the brand-new **Alexandra Museum** (☎ 03-448 6230; Dunorling St) was about to open its doors to show artefacts from gold panning and mining days. The town's other site is the 11m-diameter **Alexandra Clock** on the hill. You can reach it by walking track (one hour return) or by driving to a nearby viewpoint. Apparently Alexandrians like to be on time.

Mountain bikers will feel like they've found the route to cloud nine with excellent old gold trails weaving through the Old Man, Dunstan, Raggedy and Knobby Ranges. Highlights include the **Dunstan Trail** to Dunedin, **Thomson Gorge Road** and the **Otago Central Rail Trail** (see the boxed text, p612). Collect the relevant maps and bumph from the visitor info centre, along with a series of *Mountain Biking* pamphlets that detail many more exhilarating rides, from family to advanced. Always check track conditions first. **Altitude Adventures** (☎ 03-448 8917; www.altitudeadventures.co.nz; 88 Centennial Ave; half-/four-day tour $70/600) rents bikes, offers back-country cycling tours and provides transport to trailheads.

In winter, strap on skates and glide around **Iceinline** (☎ 03-448 8599; Molyneux Park; adult/child $7.50/5; ☻ 9am-4.45pm Tue-Fri, 10.30am-4.45pm Sat & Sun, 7-9.30pm Fri & Sat), NZ's only Olympic-sized, outdoor skating rink.

Sleeping

Alexandra Holiday Park (☎ 03-448 8297; alex.hol -park@xtra.co.nz; 44 Manuherikia Rd; sites per 2 people $20) Not particularly inspiring, but this big field offers some shade and backs onto a river where you can take a dip.

Almond Court Motel (☎ 0800 256 663, 03-448 7667; 53 Killarney St; d from $9ς;) Older but me-ticulously clean rooms are a great deal. You get a full kitchen, a lounge and an on-site pool.

Rocky Range (☎ 0800 153 293, 03-448 6150; www .rockyrange.co.nz; s/d $300/352;) This imposing house has magnificent views and very com-fortable rooms, complete with niceties such as comfy robes and slippers, cotton sateen linen and Juliet balconies. A home-baked bedtime snack and big breakfast (both in-cluded in the price) will make you like it even more.

Also consider the following:

Kiwi Motel (☎ 03-448 8258; 115 Centennial Ave; d $70-80) Welcoming and family-friendly.

Alexandra Heights (☎ 0800 862 539, 03-448 6366; 125 Centennial Ave; d $125) Spacious and new.

Alexandra Backpackers (☎ 03-448 7170; alexandra backpackers@hotmail.com; 8-12 Skird St; dm/d $20/48) A little sloppy but has cheap beds.

Eating

The Courthouse Café (☎ 03-448 7818; 8 Centennial Ave; mains $5-15; breakfast & lunch) Is this place guilty of great brunches, lunches and bak-ing? We think so, but you be the judge. The atmospheric gallery spills out onto the lawn and there's coffee, smoothies and wine to keep you quenched.

Craterscapes (☎ 03-448 7290; 12 Ennis St; mains $10-15; breakfast & lunch) The average-sounding menu doesn't prepare you for the gourmet dishes served up. Quiches, toasted sand-wiches, salads and baked potatoes are done with flare. Relax in the back garden amidst unusual sculptures and plants.

Grumpy's (☎ 03-448 9189; 26 Centennial Ave; mains $15-30; lunch & dinner) Across from the mu-seum, this 1892 period home is now a popu-lar family restaurant serving old favourites such as burgers and pasta.

Getting There & Away

The visitor information centre handles bookings for InterCity, Atomic, Wanaka Connexions and Catch-a-Bus, which all pass through Alexandra with connections to Wanaka, Queenstown and Dunedin.

ALEXANDRA TO PALMERSTON

Northeast of Alexandra, an irrigated strip of land tags alongside the highway like a running oasis of rolling pastures and tiny woods. The Dunstan and North Rough Ranges rise up on either side of the high-way. This is the Manuherikia Valley, which tumbles into the Maniototo plain as State Highway 85 (SH85) swings southeast at Blackstone Hill. From here to Palmerston and the sea, the scenic road is known as the 'Pig Foot' (alluding to its past condition).

Made up of half a handful of historic buildings, tiny **Ophir** lies on the eastern side of the Manuherikia River. Take the south-ern, gravel exit off SH85 to cross the 1870s wooden-planked Dan O'Connell Bridge; it's a rough, scenic ride.

The peaceful **Ophir Lodge Backpackers** (☎ 03-447 3339; blgaler@xtra.co.nz; 1 Macdonald St; dm $18, d $36; closed May-Aug;) has cement-block rooms that have been niced up with sheep-skin rugs, paint and wall art. The common kitchen/lounge has a potbelly stove. Linen costs extra. The tearoom-style **Old Bakery Café** (☎ 03-447 3704; 37 Swindon St; mains $15; breakfast & lunch) goes all out with the time-warp feel and scullery maids' caps. Corn hotcakes, salmon tarts, and lasagne all come with a 'scrummy' salad.

Back on SH85, **Omakau** seems nearly dead, but if you can make it past the un-appealing lobby and extremely pink halls, the **Omakau Commercial Hotel** (☎ 03-447 3715; omakaucommercial@xtra.xc.nz; 1 Harvey St; s/d $35/70) has sunny, quaint rooms. Look at a couple before you choose. You can also stay up the road in **Lauder** and **Becks**, where you'll find no-descript guesthouses.

Take the turn-off north into the foothills of the imposing Dunstan Range and on to spooky **St Bathans** (see the boxed text, p610), 17km from SH85. In a hollow at the foot of Mt St Bathans, this once-thriving gold-mining town of 2000 people is now home to a half-dozen permanent residents. Steps away is **Blue Lake**. Once a 120m hill, prolonged sluicing created the deep hole and abandoned workings nearby filled it with amazingly blue mineral water. This stunning result is otherworldly and makes for a peaceful picnic spot. Walk around the lake's edge to a lookout (one hour return).

The **Vulcan Hotel** (☎ 03-447 3629; Main Rd; dm/d $35/$90) dates from 1863. Rooms have pretty, white quilts but not as much character as you might hope. Some feel there's one guest too many (see the boxed text, below). Call ahead as wedding bookings often leave no room at the inn. Its **restaurant** (mains $20) serves bar meals and standard fare inside or on the grassy lawns.

Continuing on the SH85, the road turns southeast, passing through a few villages before reaching the turn-off for Naseby (right). From Naseby, you can continue 39km northeast to **Danseys Pass**. The scenery is spectacular but the narrow, gravel road has blind corners and is sometimes snowed in. **Danseys Pass Coach Inn** (☎ 03-444 9048; www.danseyspass.co.nz; d $125-145) is a characterful, 1860s stone building with big fireplaces and bigger views. Staff can set you up with activities including horse trekking and skiing. You'll find the inn 16km northeast of Naseby at Kyeburn Diggings.

After negotiating the fair-sized towns of Ranfurly (opposite) and Kyeburn, the SH85 runs 62km to Palmerston. Another option is to hop on the southbound SH87 directly to Dunedin. About 50km down this road is the tiny town of **Middlemarch**. With the Rock & Pillar Range as an impressive backdrop, this is a start or end-point of the Otago Central Rail Trail and also one end of the Taieri Gorge Railway (p593). **Blind Billy's Holiday Camp** (☎ 03-464 3355; blindbillys@xtra.co.nz; Mold St, Middlemarch; unpowered/powered sites per 2 people $20/22, dm $18, d $50-80) has a range of cheap accommodation, meals and excellent advice for bikers.

Naseby
pop 100

With more than its fair share of trees, Naseby is the quintessential small town, filled with friendly neighbours and pretty, 19th-century buildings. Situated east off SH85 towards the Hawkdun Range, there's not a lot to keep you here but it's a pleasant stopover. **Naseby Information & Crafts** (☎ 03-444 9961; Derwent St; ☼ 11am-2pm), in the old post office, is staffed with informative volunteers. Winter hours are sporadic. The **Early Settlers Museums** (☎ 03-444 9558; Earn & Leven Sts; admission $1; ☼ 10am-4pm, closed May-Oct) have displays on the area's gold-mining past.

Naseby's **Black Forest** was planted in 1900; visit **Naseby Forest Headquarters** (☎ 03-444 9995; Derwent St; ☼ 9am-noon & 1-4pm Mon-Fri) for maps of local walks. In winter, ice-skate at the small, outdoor **Maniototo Ice Rink** (☎ 03-444 9270; Channel Rd; adult/child $8/5; ☼ 10am-5pm Sun-Thu & 10am-9pm Fri & Sat Jun–mid-Aug). The admission price includes skate rental.

SLEEPING & EATING
Larchview Holiday Park (☎ 03-444 9904; johnsjoy naseby@paradise.net.nz; Swimming Dam Rd; sites per 2 people $22, cabins $30-60) Set in 17 acres of woods, these grounds have an alpine feel. There's a small on-site playground and swimming at the dam nearby. Timber cabins range from basic to chalet-style.

Mountain View Accommodation (☎ 03-444-9972; eileenherd@hotmail.com; 13a Channel Rd; d $80-100) Smallish, comfortable yellow rooms in the new, timber house have plush bedding and tea and toast facilities. Across the road, rooms in the quaint, period guesthouse offer a relaxed place to bunk down.

SPOOKY HOLLOW

If a trip to St Bathans leaves you with an eerie tingle down your spine, you're not the first. Set in a hollow in what feels close to the middle of nowhere, this tiny village is believed to be haunted. Ask the proprietor at the Vulcan Hotel (above) and you'll get an adamant nod followed by a quick look over her shoulder. Doors opening and closing, missing objects and books flying off the shelves are her frequent reminders of the nonpaying hotel guest.

While tales vary, the most commonly held story is that the ghost was once a lady of the night, resident in Room 1 at the hotel and murdered for her evening's earnings. There are embellishments about missing graves and many travellers believe they've caught the ghost on film in the local cemetery. Of course, it's all hearsay, but our own spooky experience wasn't. We dare you to go and have your own.

Ranfurly

pop 840

After a series of fires in the 1930s, rural Ranfurly was rebuilt in the architecture of the time. These days, it's trying a little too hard to cash in on its Art Deco past; while there are a few attractive buildings, the town itself is fairly bleak. Nevertheless, as part of the Otago Central Rail Trail (see the boxed text, p612), it does see its share of tourists and has a couple of unique accommodation options.

The friendly **Maniototo visitor information centre** (☎ 03-444 1005; Charlemont St; ☺ 10am-4pm Mon-Fri May-Sep, daily Oct-Apr; □) is in the old station and has an interesting exhibit on the town's old railway. Next door in the Centennial Milk Bar is the **Art Deco Exhibition** (☎ 03-444 9963; Charlemont St; admission by donation; ☺ 10.30am-4.30pm), with furniture, crockery and several random objects such as RJ Smiley's swimming shorts. Many of the items are antique but not Art Deco. For more Art Deco trappings, check out **Decollectables** (☎ 03-444 9010; 7 Charlemont St), a well-packed shop.

SLEEPING & EATING

Peter's Farm Hostel (☎ 03-444 9083; www.petersfarm.co.nz; Waipiata; dm/d $25/50) Built with mud bricks and oozing with character, this 1880s farmhouse is a fantastically relaxed place to stay. Catering largely to cyclists, the staff will pick you and your bike up in Ranfurly. If relaxing in the big, beautiful garden with a mountain view doesn't fill your day, you can kayak, gold-pan, fish or follow a walking trail. The hostel is 12km southeast of Ranfurly, signposted 3km from Waipiata. Ring first in winter, as it may be closed.

Moyola (☎ 03-444 9010; www.ruralartdeco.co.nz; 38 Charlemont St; d $140) This very cool three-bedroom house has been kitted out in Art Deco furnishings, art, crockery and linen. There's a barbecue in the backyard and lots of privacy.

E-central Café (☎ 03-444 8300; 14 Charlemont St; mains $7-15; ☺ breakfast & lunch) Yellow and warm with an open fire, local art and a Maniototo sports wall of fame, this is definitely the best option in town. There's nothing unexpected about the menu of *panini*, quiche and omelettes, but it's all yummy, as is the fresh baking.

Royal Hotel (☎ 03-444 9990; 1 Eame St; s $30, d $50-80, lunch mains $12, dinner mains $20; ☺ breakfast, lunch & dinner) If you're not feeling up to Hoffman's Loaded Hog or Raggedy Range Red Stag, you can fill up on bar snacks here. There are also burgers, fish and a salad or two at this historic pub and inn. Rooms are small but clean.

Cottage Garden Café (☎ 03-444 9820; 5 Derwent St; lunch mains $12, dinner mains $24; ☺ breakfast, lunch & dinner) Take your fresh baking and coffee in the warm, historic rooms or out into the garden. Tasty lunches and dinners, such as chicken breast in parmesan and ginger crumbs, go well with the wine list.

Also try the following:

Monkey Puzzle House B&B (☎ 03-444 9644; monkey.puzzle@xtra.co.nz; cnr Derwent & Oughter Sts; d $95) A restored mud-brick home in a pretty garden.

Turnstone B&B (☎ 03-444 9644; gifford@xtra.co.nz; 13 Carrowmore St; s/d $55/100) Antiquated and knick-knacky.

GETTING THERE & AWAY

If prebooked, **Catch-a-Bus** (☎ 03-479 9960) stops in Naseby on its Dunedin–Cromwell route. If you're driving, take the exit off SH85, just north of Ranfurly.

A daily **Catch-a-Bus** (☎ 03-479 9960) shuttle passes through Ranfurly on its way between Wanaka and Dunedin.

ALEXANDRA TO DUNEDIN

Heading south from Alexandra, the SH8 wanders through rough-hills scenery to Dunedin. En route lie a number of small towns that are products of the gold-rush days.

Only 13km from Alexandra, **Fruitlands** (☎ 03-449 2192; www.fruitlandscountrylodge.co.nz; SH8; d $95) is an atmospheric stone lodge with three not-quite-so-atmospheric units set on an acreage of garden. It's also home to a café and crafts shop. The staff can arrange lots of outdoor activities in the surrounding area.

Roxburgh township is surrounded by pretty hills in a productive fruit and farming area. **Villa Rose Backpackers** (☎ 03-446 8761; remarkableorchard@xtra.co.nz; 79 Scotland St; dm/d from $18/40) is an old-fashioned villa with high-ceilinged rooms. The manager can help sort out seasonal fruit-picking work. In the centre of town, try **Commercial Backpackers** (☎ 03-446 8160;

patroxx@hotmail.com; 106 Scotland St; dm/d $18/45; closed Jun-Sep), or **Lake Roxburgh Lodge** (☎ 03-46 8220; www.lakeroxburghlodge.co.nz; Lake Roxburgh Village; d $100), with views of the surrounding hills and a lakeside restaurant.

OTAGO CENTRAL RAIL TRAIL

Stretching from Dunedin to Clyde, the Central Otago rail branch was completed in 1907 and gave small, goldfield towns a reliable link to the big city. As cars gained popularity and roads were improved, use of the railway waned throughout the 20th century and, in 1990, the 150km of track from Middlemarch to Clyde was permanently closed. It landed in the able hands of DOC, who set about ripping up tracks and resurfacing to create a year-round trail that takes bikers, walkers and horseback riders along a historic route containing old rail bridges, viaducts and tunnels. With no steep hills, gob-smacking scenery and profound remoteness, the trail attracts well over 10,000 visitors annually.

The trail can be followed in either direction. A popular option is to travel from Dunedin on the scenic Taieri Gorge Railway (p593), cycle from Pukerangi to Middlemarch (19km by road) and begin the trail the following day. The entire trail takes approximately three to five days to complete; alternatively, many people choose to do a section of the trail as a day trip. The areas passed though include town-sized settlements such as Ranfurly, Alexandra and Clyde, and tiny villages such as Waipiata, Lauder and Ophir; almost all offer accommodation and dining of some sort. Mountain bikes can be rented in Alexandra and Dunedin.

Any of the area's major visitor information centres (Alexandra, Cromwell, Dunedin) can provide detailed information on the trail, or hop online at www.otagocentralrailtrail.co.nz.

From here, the road passes through Lawrence and the **Manuka Gorge Scenic Reserve**, a winding, scenic route through wooded hills and gullies. The SH8 joins SH1 in **Milton**, where it's well worth stopping for a stay at **Happy**

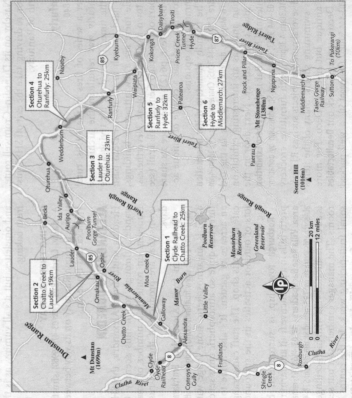

Lawrence
pop 475

A few tumble weeds blowing down main street would complete this tiny town's wild-west feel. An offspring of the gold rush that peaked here in 1862, Lawrence's sights and walks lean heavily on its interesting past.

The **Lawrence visitor information centre** (03-485 9222; Ross Pl; 10am-4.30pm Mon-Fri, 11am-3pm Sat & Sun, weekdays only Jun-Sep) is helpful and has a thick stash of brochures and maps as well as a small **museum**. Pick up the *Lawrence Districts Heritage Trail* brochure for local trails taking in old mining sights.

Nearby **Gabriels Gully** was the birthplace of the Otago gold rush and once home to 11,500 miners. It's now a quiet park with an interpretive walk (1½ hours return); details can be sought from the visitor centre. The original valley floor is buried below 50m of trailings waste, while a number of dams created for sluicing now offer good **fishing** for brown trout.

During the gold rush, local law prohibited Chinese immigrants from settling in existing towns, which led to settlements such as the **Lawrence Chinese Camp**. The area is currently in the throes of restoration; ask at the visitor information centre. You can also visit the site of **Wetherstones**, once the gold-rush centre for houses of ill repute and home to Hart Brewery, which continued churning out black beer during prohibition. These days, 10 hectares of daffodils fill the area in spring. **Gabriel's Junction** (03-485 9968; 34 Ross Pl; tours adult $15) offer tours here with Dusty, 'the lusty, busty, barmaid'.

Lawrence Markets (Main St; 11am Sun & holidays Oct-Apr) see local artwork take over the town's main street. Also visit the **Gateway Gallery** (03-485 9998; 27 Ross Pl; 10am-5pm Mon-Fri, closed Tue & Wed Jun-Oct) for functional pottery, jewellery, homemade soaps and paintings.

Inn Backpackers (03-417 4161; happyinn56@hotmail.com; 11 Shakespeare St; dm/d $20/52; closed May-Aug). Well run by the very personable Tony, this place has colourful rooms, fresh bread and a very cool sweat lodge that looks like a train. There's a barbecue in the garden and you can borrow bikes for an easy 18km ride to the beach. Bathrooms are immaculate and, while the kitchen is a tad small, Tony *insists* on doing the dishes. It's cosy, atmospheric and a wonderful place to just be.

SLEEPING & EATING

Oban House Backpackers (03-485 9259; oban house@xtra.co.nz; 10ban St; dm/s/d $17/20/40;). Stay in sunny rooms within the organised chaos of a local family home. Open fires and a barbecue area help to create a very relaxed atmosphere.

Marama lodge (03-485 9638; marama.k@xtra.co.nz; SH8; s/d $70/100, cottages $70-90) This lovely kauri home dates from 1875 and has a big guest lounge and country-style rooms. The comfortable cottage has a little less character but is a great deal. Huge lawns contain tennis courts and play gear for kids.

Jafa's Wine Bar & Café (03-485 9509; 21 Ross Pl; lunch mains $12, dinner mains $18; 11am-9pm Wed-Sun) Blue-cod cakes, beef and beer pie, Thai curry and grilled porterhouse steak are served in a casually classy atmosphere.

Jazzed on Java (03-485 9234; 26 Ross St; mains $8-20; lunch Thu-Tue, dinner Thu-Sun) With a garden, decent bar and good-looking chowders and sandwiches, this friendly café is a good spot for lunch.

CLUTHA DISTRICT

The mighty Clutha River is NZ's highest-volume river, and is dammed in several places to feed hydroelectric power stations. Balclutha is South Otago's largest town but is of little interest to tourists other than as a place to stock up on supplies before setting off into the Catlins. Drop into the **Clutha visitor information centre** (03-418 0388; balvin@azhost.com; 4 Clyde St; 8.30am-5pm Mon-Fri, 10am-2pm Sat & Sun) for local information and, if you must spend the night, park your bags at the bright, recently refurbished **Highway Lodge Motel** (03-418 2363; 165 Clyde St; d $90-95). **Naish Park Motor Camp** (03-418 0088; 56 Charlotte St; unpowered/powered sites per 2 people $20/24, d $45-50) has grassy, quiet sites, great facilities and comfortable doubles.

NORTH OTAGO

The broad Waitaki River rushes across the northern boundary of North Otago. South of it lies Oamaru, a penguin-packed town that's worthy of a day or two of your time. From there, you can follow the river east into the pretty Waitaki Valley which features the curious Elephant Rocks, Maori rock paintings and ancient fossils. Good sources of information on the area are www.tourismwaitaki.co.nz and www.waitaki.net.nz.

OAMARU

pop 12,000

At first glance, it might not look like there's a lot going on in Oamaru. Tourists saunter, locals languish and even the traffic seems mellow. But with countless penguins, gorgeous public gardens, a historic precinct and an excellent gallery – as well as some slightly less conventional sights such as a rustic jazz bar, upmarket cheese factory and penny-farthing races – this slightly eccentric, wonderfully friendly town will keep you engaged.

A questionably glamorous history of refrigerated-meat shipping made Oamaru prosperous enough in the 19th century to build a good number of imposing, limestone buildings. These continue to grace the town with doses of character. Oamaru also has an affinity with the arts that may well be rooted in its claim to Janet Frame (see the boxed text, opposite), but extends to a present-day entourage of artists and craftspeople.

Oamaru visitor information centre (03-434 1656; info@tourismwaitaki.co.nz; 1 Thames St; 9am-6pm Mon-Fri, 10am-5pm Sat & Sun), including lots of local walking tour maps. You can get online at Lagonda Tearooms (p617), where there is coin-operated Internet access. Send penguin-

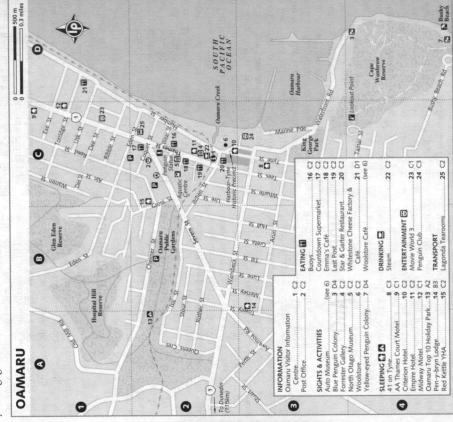

OAMARU

INFORMATION
Oamaru Visitor Information Centre 1	C2
Post Office 2	C2

SIGHTS & ACTIVITIES
Auto Museum .... (see 6)	
Blue Penguin Colony 3	D4
Forrester Gallery 4	C2
North Otago Museum 5	C2
Woolstore 6	C2
Yellow-eyed Penguin Colony 7	D4

SLEEPING
41 on Tyne 8	C3
AA Thames Court Motel 9	C1
Criterion Hotel 10	C2
Empire Hotel 11	C2
Midway Motel 12	C1
Oamaru Top 10 Holiday Park 13	A2
Pen-y-bryn Lodge 14	B3
Red Kettle YHA 15	C2

EATING
Buoys 16	C2
Countdown Supermarket 17	C2
Emma's Café 18	C2
Last Post 19	C2
Star & Garter Restaurant 20	C2
Whitestone Cheese Factory & Café .... (see 6)	
Woolstore Café .... (see 6)	

DRINKING
Steam 22	C2

ENTERTAINMENT
Movie World 3 23	C1
Penguin Club 24	C3

TRANSPORT
Lagonda Tearooms 25	C2

plastered postcards from the **post office** (on Coquet & Severn Sts) and get cash from ATMs on the main drag.

Sights

HARBOUR-TYNE HISTORIC PRECINCT

With the discovery of local limestone (known as whitestone), which was easily carved and moulded, Oamaru had solid, elaborate buildings from the early 19th century. Buildings were created in fashionable classic forms, from Gothic revival to neoclassical Italianate and Venetian palazzo. Today, Oamaru has some of NZ's best-preserved historic commercial buildings, particularly around the harbour and Tyne St, an area designated the Historic Precinct. Pick up the free *Historic Oamaru* pamphlet.

The area is now home to bookshops, antique stores, galleries and herbalists, and makes for an interesting afternoon's wander. The **Woolstore** (1 Tyne St) has a good café (see p616), souvenirs and the **Auto Museum** (03-434 1556; adult/child $4/free; 10am-4.30pm) for car buffs. Upstairs, there's a **craft market** (10am-4pm Sun) as well as a **farmers' market** (9am-1pm Sat & Sun) in summer.

PENGUINS

Oamaru is a fantastic place to get your fill of penguin sightings. At peak season, up to 200 blue penguins slip, slide and scuttle to shore in the town's **blue penguin colony** in the old limestone quarry. You can watch their amazingly laboured efforts from the **visitors centre** (03-433 1195; www.penguins.co.nz; Waterfront Rd; viewings adult/child/family $15/15/35, under 5yrs free; 9am-sunset), just before dark. You'll see the most penguins in December; in winter there are generally 15 or 20 birds. The conservation effort has increased the penguin population dramatically, transforming it from a local pest to the town's official mascot.

Oamaru is also home to hoiho (Maori for 'noisy'), more commonly known as yellow-eyed penguins and one of the world's rarest. DOC has recently opened larger hides and improved trails at the **Yellow-eyed Penguin Colony** at Bushy Beach, where the penguins come ashore in late afternoon to feed their young. They're extremely shy; if they see or hear you they'll head back into the water. The old trail that connected the blue and yellow-eyed colonies is closed; its continual

---

OAMARU IN FRAME

If you're an avid Janet Frame fan, you'll no doubt recognise 'Waimaru' as a town in her novels. This is, in fact, a pseudonym for Oamaru, the author's home throughout most of her early years. Frame was born in Dunedin in 1924 and first gained international recognition in 1957 with *Owls Do Cry*. Her other literary accomplishments include *Faces in the Water* (1961), *The Edge of the Alphabet* (1962), *Scented Gardens for the Blind* (1963), *A State of Siege* (1967) and *Intensive Care* (1970). Many of the settings for these novels can be found in Oamaru; pick up a free copy of *Heritage Trails of North Otago* from the visitor information centre and follow the 1½-hour Janet Frame Trail to take in the locations.

It was Jane Campion's film version of *An Angel at my Table*, based on the second volume of Janet Frame's autobiographical trilogy, that renewed interest in her works. Frame was short-listed for the Nobel Prize for literature in 2003. Sadly, she died on 29 January 2004, shortly after announcing that she was terminally ill with leukaemia.

---

slippage was proving dangerous for both visitors and penguins. Nevertheless, a new, scenic trail from the end of Waterfront Rd will take you up the hill from where you can walk to the yellow-eyed colony.

FORRESTER GALLERY

Housed in Oamaru's beautiful old bank, **Forrester Gallery** (03-434 1653; www.forrestergallery.com; 9 Thames St; admission free; 10.30am-4.30pm) has an excellent collection of regional art and hosts diverse temporary exhibits, including contemporary media. This really is a fantastic gallery, which is shockingly free. Check the website for current shows.

OTHER SIGHTS

The **Oamaru public gardens** (main entry on Severn St) was first opened in 1876 and remains one of NZ's best. Waterways, bridges, a children's playground, an aviary of bright birds and endless flowers and lawn make it a gorgeous place to lose yourself in.

In the old athenaeum (er...subscription library), the **North Otago Museum** (03-434 1652; www.northotagomuseum.co.nz; 60 Thames St;

admission free; ⏱ 10.30am-4.30pm Mon-Fri, 10am-1pm Sat, 1-4.30pm Sun) gives a historical perspective of the Waitaki district with displays on everything from architecture to war.

Oamaru livens up with locals wearing old-fashioned garb, penny-farthing races and other oddities during **Victorian Heritage Celebrations** in late November.

Tours

Penguin Express (☎ 03-434 7744; www.coastline -tours.co.nz; adult/child $20/5) Join a door-to-door 2½-hour tour taking in the blue and yellow-eyed colonies. The price includes admission to blue penguin colony. Times vary throughout the year.

Ralph's Rambles (tours adult/child $15/10; ⏱ 11am & 2pm) Ralph Sherwood will create a tour just for you, offering a personal introduction to the public gardens, Janet Frame literary sites, the penguins or historical buildings. Tours run from 90 minutes to two hours. Inquire at the visitor information centre.

Waitaki Air Services (☎ 03-431 3891; Oamaru airport; tours adult from $65) Get a bird's-eye perspective of the area, or venture as far as Mt Cook or Milford Sound.

Whitestone Walking Tour (adult/child/family $10/4/20; ⏱ tours 11am, noon, 2pm & 3pm) Delivering a close look at Oamaru's architectural past, these one-hour tours take in the Historic Precinct. Book at the visitor information centre and inquire about times.

Sleeping

BUDGET

Red Kettle YHA (☎ 0800 600 100, 03-434 5008; yha oamaru@yha.co.nz; cnr Reed & Cross Sts; dm/d $20/50) This small, red-roofed YHA is extremely snug. Room 5 has sheep to count on the pauashell mobiles or ceiling stars. It's got cosy sitting areas, a well-equipped kitchen, a barbecue in the garden and a log fire. It's on a quiet side street, a short walk from the town centre.

Empire Hotel (☎ 03-434 3446; empirehotel@hotmail .com; 13 Thames St; dm/s/d $18/30/45; 🖳) With recently renovated rooms, this 1867 family-run hotel is now a backpackers' haunt and a standing favourite. Rooms aren't huge but there are lots of common area to spread out in, such as two kitchens, a wood-stove-heated TV room, and a lounge with free Internet. Bathrooms are spotless, there's a book and video library to peruse and, located on the main drag, you're close to everything. Exceptionally friendly owners have a huge wealth of local info to share.

41 on Tyne (☎ 03-434 5066; Carolanda.DS@dear.net .nz; 41 Tyne St; d $65) With harbour views, these self-contained cabins are cosy, modern and a great deal. Continental breakfast with homemade bread is included, and you're a short stroll from the penguins.

Oamaru Top 10 Holiday Park (☎ 0800 280 202, 03-434 7666; Chelmer St; www.oamarutop10.co.nz; unpowered/powered sites per 2 people $25/26, cabins $70-90) Grassy and well maintained, with trees out the back and the fantastic public gardens next door.

MIDRANGE & TOP END

Pen-y-bryn Lodge (☎ 03-434 7939; www.penybryn.co .nz; 41 Towey St; s/d $500/800) Located in the suburbs, with views to the sea and mountains, this century-old timber mansion has lavish period rooms and an opulent, hushed air. Nestle in the beautiful, big sitting room with a fully licensed bar, show your skill in the billiards room or soak up the sun on the patio. Rates include a full breakfast, predinner drinks and a four-course, gourmet dinner.

Criterion Hotel (☎ 03-434 6247; www.criterion.net .nz; 3 Tyne St; d $120-160) Victorian right down to the wallpaper, the period rooms at this 1877 inn are small, in keeping with the style of the day. The owners have lovingly restored the building and give a warm welcome. Cooked brekkie is included and served in a homey dining room.

AA Thames Court Motel (☎ 0800 223 644, 03-434 6963; www.aathamescourt.com; 252 Thames St; d $85/105) Spacious, clean and functional, with lots of light, and small kitchenettes that are well-equipped for their size. This is a good option for families.

Midway Motel (☎ 0800 477 744, 03-434 5388; www.midwayoamaru.com; 289 Thames St; d $85-100) A friendly place with a kids' play area, small gym and a courtesy vehicle to ferry you to attractions.

Eating

Emma's Café (☎ 03-434 1165; 30 Thames St; meals $8-15; ⏱ breakfast & lunch) Unhurried and uncluttered, this friendly café serves fantastic, filling meals. Quiches, salads, great soups and all-day breakfasts are all scrumptious. Desserts are fab and you can buy treats for your picnic basket such as brandied apricots and chocolate-covered coffee beans.

Woolstore Café (☎ 03-434 8336; 1 Tyne St; lunch mains $10, dinner mains $26; ⏱ breakfast & lunch Tue, breakfast, lunch & dinner Thu-Sun) Sip coffee and savour desserts such as caramel poached pear with orange and pistachio ice cream. Better yet, order from the lunch or dinner menu for Moroccan lamb tagine, gourmet bagels or house-cured salmon. You really can't go wrong.

Whitestone Cheese Factory & Café (☎ 03-434 8098; 3 Torridge St; mains $10; ☒ lunch Mon-Sat) The home of tasty, award-winning organic cheeses, famous in these parts. Try the ultra-rich Mt Domet Double Cream, Moeraki Bay Blue and more. Factory viewing tours (adult/child $10/5; ☒ 9.30am Monday to Friday in summer) give you a chance to see how it's done. Buy reasonably priced cheese to take away, or munch pot pies, melts and *paninis*, all featuring cheese. The cheesecake is exquisite.

Star & Garter Restaurant (☎ 03-434 5246; 9 Itchen St; lunch mains $10, dinner mains $20; ☒ lunch & dinner) In operation for more than 125 years, Oamaru's oldest restaurant serves roasts, fish and chicken with tasty sauces such as sundried pesto and NZ wine. For lunch try the warm lamb salad or fish and chips. The open fire adds to the atmosphere.

Last Post (☎ 03-434 8080; 12 Thames St; mains $15-23; ☒ lunch & dinner) Begin with a starter such as crumbed Camembert or pork spare ribs, work your way through steamed mussels, baked salmon or gourmet pizza and finish off with a brandy. The old post office has a pub atmosphere, excellent service and a well-stocked bar. Just ignore the gaming room.

Buoys (☎ 03-434 8852; 39 Thames St; ☒ 9am-5.30pm Mon-Thu, 9am-9pm Fri) Whether you like it crumbed, curried, in sweet and sour sauce or as a chowder, your fresh seafood cravings will be well catered too. Bright and casual, this place also sells fresh fish to cook at home (as in, the hostel).

In the centre of town, **Countdown Supermarket** (cnr Thames & Coquet Sts; ☒ 7am-9pm) is well stocked for self-caterers.

Drinking & Entertainment

Steam (☎ 03-434 3344; 7 Thames St; ☒ 8.30am-4.30pm Mon-Fri, 10am-4.30pm Sat & Sun) These guys roast their own beans and offer caffeine-fix bliss amidst Italian-style paintings and jazzy music. And you can BYO food.

Penguin Club (☎ 03-434 1402; Emulsion Lane off Harbour St; admission free-$15) Next to the tracks in the Historic Precinct, acts at this inti-mate, tin-roofed venue take little competition from the roar of the neighbouring sea. Flyer-papered walls and a beer-soaked floor add to the fantastic ambience. Fridays are open-stage jam night with free admission, while other acts include comedy and local bands. Pick up a programme at the visitor centre.

Criterion Hotel (☎ 03-434 6247; 3 Tyne St) Hang out with weathered locals in this atmospheric, time-honoured pub. Sip wine and beer at long wooden tables and dig into some bangers and mash. There's also accommodation here (opposite).

Movie World 3 (☎ 03-434 1077; info line 03-434 1070; www.movieworld3.com; 239 Thames St; adult/child $12/6) A mix of older flicks and the latest blockbusters hit Oamaru's big-ish screen.

Getting There & Around

InterCity (☎ 03-474 9600; www.intercitycoach.co.nz) and **Atomic Shuttles** (☎ 03-322 8883; www.atomictravel.co.nz) and **South Island Connections** (☎ 03-366 6633; www.southislandconnections.co.nz) all stop off in Oamaru en route to Dunedin ($15) and Christchurch ($25). Hop on or off at **Lagonda Tearooms** (☎ 03-434 8716; 191 Thames St); bookings for all buses can be made through the visitor information centre.

Cook Connection (☎ 0800 266 526, 027 4583 211; www.cookconnect.co.nz) runs three times weekly from October to June between Oamaru and Mt Cook ($40), Tekapo ($40) and Omarama ($22).

WAITAKI VALLEY

The pastoral Waitaki Valley cradles some unique sights and scenery between the turn-offs at SH1 and Omarama. The road is pretty much a straight shot over rolling hills and farmland.

Sculpted by wind, rain and rivers, **Elephant Rocks** are giant boulders that look like beasts asleep in a field. They began as sand, hardened 25 million years ago, and eventually buried in a field. The rocks make for a peaceful, bizarre landscape and were used as the setting for the otherworldly Aslan's Camp in the blockbuster *Chronicles of Narnia: The Lion, the Witch & the Wardrobe* (2005). To find them, follow SH83 to the turning for Danseys Pass and follow signs for 6km.

Duntroon has an authentic blacksmith shop, nearby trout- and salmon-fishing and the **Vanished World Centre** (☎ 03-431 2024; www.vanishedworld.co.nz; 7 Campbell St; adult/family $5/10; ☼ 10am-4pm Mon-Fri winter, daily summer), with small but interesting displays of 25-million-year-old fossils of NZ's shark-toothed dolphins and 180cm penguins. Near here, you can see a **whale fossil** in its original site; veer to the east after the church in Duntroon and follow the gravel road 6km.

Just west of Duntroon is the **Takiroa Maori Rock Art Site**, with red ochre and charcoal drawings dating back many centuries. These relay history from early moa-hunting days to the arrival of Europeans. As limestone easily erodes, many of the drawings take a great deal of squinting to make out; the disheartening graffiti doesn't help.

Further west is **Windhaven** (☎ 03-431 2838; windhaven-accom@xtra.co.nz; 4208 SH85; dm/d $18/130), with a cosy, self-contained cottage for backpackers and a spacious, homey attic-style B&B room in the main house. It's surrounded by big open spaces and pretty views.

Tiny **Kurow** is at the junction of the Waitaki and Hakataramea Rivers. Mainly a collection of secondhand shops, it's home to a small **museum** (☎ 03-436 0950; SH83; admission by donation; ☼ 9am-5pm; 🖳) with relics such as farming machinery, sewing machines, and a 1925 Ford Model T.

Just west of Kurow is **Café Hydro** (☎ 03-436 0993; SH83; lunch mains $10, dinner mains $15; ☼ breakfast, lunch & dinner). Across from Waitaki Dam, its very blue water views make up for its lack of atmosphere, as does its surprisingly good food; try the pizza or the 'Dam-Buster' breakfast. This area was home to 3000 people when the dam was constructed in 1935; the restaurant is left over from that time, as are a number of houses out the back, which are being restored as guesthouses.

Instead of continuing west on SH83 to Otematata, take the scenic detour over the dam at Lake Aviemore, around the lake shore, then over the huge Benmore Dam earthworks; this 21km route brings you just north of Otematata. You'll find walking tracks and scenic spots to **camp** (per 2 people $10) at council-run sites on the northern edge of Lakes Aviemore and Benmore.

Omarama
pop 355

At the head of the Waitaki Valley, Omarama is more of a outpost than a town.

Surrounded by mountain ranges, this area hosts some fantastic sunsets. The **Omarama visitor information centre** (☎ 03-438 9816; Main Rd; ☼ 8.30am-5.30pm) is in the Glen Craig's souvenir shop.

The bizarre moonscape of the **Clay Cliffs** (admission $5) is the result of two million years of erosion on layers of silt and gravel that were exposed along the active Osler fault line. The cliffs are on private land; the turnoff is 3.5km north of Omarama.

A family-friendly strip-show? **Wrinkly Rams** (☎ 03-438 9751; www.thewrinklyrams.co.nz; SH8; adult/child $15/7.50; ☼ four shows daily 10.30am-4.30pm) offers stage shows of Merino sheep being shorn in modern and traditional methods, along with a film and a chance to 'touch a sheep'. It also has one of the area's better gift shops.

The area's northwest thermals allow for world-class gliding. **Southern Soaring** (☎ 03-438 9600; www.soaring.co.nz; 20min/1hr flights $235/395) will sail you over the Southern Alps.

SLEEPING & EATING
Buscot Station (☎ 03-438 9646; SH8; sites per 2 people $15, dm/d $18/50) Stay in a modern farmhouse on acres and acres of land with big, open views. Huge doubles in the main house and a new dormitory out back are all extremely comfortable. Tony shares his kitchen and beautiful garden as well as his interesting stories about NZ farming. You'll find Buscot's 10km north of Omarama.

Ahuriri Motels (☎ 03-438 9451; ahuririmotels@xtra.co.nz; SH83; sites per 2 people $24, dm/d $30/85) Older but well looked after self-contained cottages and dorms, with a common kitchen, laundry and lounge. Set up camp in powered or unpowered grassy sites.

Omarama Top 10 Holiday Park (☎ 03-438 9875; www.omaramatop10.co.nz; SH8; sites per 2 people $26, d from $40) You can also camp at this holiday park next to streamside greenery.

Clay Cliffs Estate (☎ 03-438 9654; SH8; mains $15-28; ☼ lunch & dinner summer only) The first winery to open in North Otago, this estate produces excellent Pinot Gris, Muscat and Pinot Blanc. Visit the Tuscan-style café for a cheese platter to accompany the wine.

Wrinkly Rams (☎ 03-438 9751; SH8; mains $10; ☼ breakfast & lunch) Home-style cooking and fresh baking make this reasonably priced café a great place to fill up, with comfortable couches, big windows and outdoor tables.

OAMARU TO DUNEDIN

The ocean-hugging road travelling south from Oamaru provides a peaceful break from SH1, with some gorgeous coastal views; take Wharfe St out of town (following the signs for Kakanui).

Situated on extensive beachside acreage 16km down this road is **Coastal Backpackers** (☎ 03-439 5411; coastalbackpacker@ihug.co.nz; All Day Bay; dm/s/d $22/24/50, self-contained d $75; ☒ closed Jun-Sep). With a big garden, swimming and homey pub dishing up grub, you may find yourself extending your stay. Choose from a slightly worn hostel, a small, basic cabin for two or the self-contained unit in the main house.

SH1 from Oamaru to Dunedin is a pleasant town-lined stretch of road. Stop for a wander through the **Te Kaihinaki** (ancient boulders) at **Moeraki**, 30km south of Oamaru. These spherical creations formed millions of years ago around lime crystals within the surrounding mudstone. They now rest on a stunning stretch of beach. Try to time your visit with low tide. There's a $2 honesty-box fee to visit the boulders. In addition, there's a **restaurant** (☎ 03-439 4827; mains $10; ☒ breakfast, lunch & dinner) with great views. You can also take the turning to Moeraki itself and head down to the beach just past the hedge (you'll know the one!) and walk along the sand to the boulders.

Moe'aki's **Memorial Lookout** was once home to a whaling station's signal mast. To reach it, head up Haverford St from town. The walkway from here leads back down to the town (45 minutes), passing a seal colony and a yellow-eyed penguin hide along the way.

From the outside, **Fleur's Place** (☎ 03-439 5980; Old Jetty, Moeraki; mains $20; ☒ breakfast, lunch & dinner) has a rumble-tumble look about it. Inside, this funky wooden hut serves up some of the South Island's best food. Not surprisingly, the speciality is fresh seafood in all its guises; Portions are big, and taste as good as they look, and draw herds of locals back again and again. Stained-glass windows and ocean-themed décor add to the boisterous atmosphere, or you can relax on the upstairs deck and enjoy views of the bay.

Moeraki Motel (☎ 03-439 4862; cnr Beach & Haven Sts; c $80) has two-storey, self-contained units with balconies. The décor crosses a number of decades but the units are comfortable and rates are extremely reasonable. Camp at **Moeraki Motor Camp** (☎ 03-439 4759; moerakimotorcamp@xtra.co.nz; 114 Haven St; sites per 2 people $22, d $38-85), where a small field has bay views.

Queenstown & Wanaka

The Queenstown and Wanaka region has been gifted with regal mountains that clamour up to the sky, lush rainforest, shimmering lakes and a popularity that has brought with it a strong tourism infrastructure. Continually outdoing itself with newer, faster and wilder adrenaline-charged activities, Queenstown is one of New Zealand's hottest destinations year-round. And neighbouring Wanaka isn't far behind.

Commercial bungy jumping was born here and spawned a plethora of other activities that defy gravity and common sense, from 200km/h freefalls to paragliding high over deep lakes or being dropped with your skis out of a helicopter on top of the Remarkables.

For the outdoorsy types who don't have the need for high-speed thrills, the Routeburn and Greenstone Tracks lead to remote wilderness and heart-stopping views. The area is also well known for its wine production, particularly its pinot noirs, and touring the region's many vineyards offers the opportunity to drink in the stunning scenery as well.

Quiet respites can also be found in Arrowtown, a historic gold-mining community that's strived to retain its 1900s appearance and charm, and in a number of smaller outposts throughout the region. In the region's north, Wanaka offers a slightly lazier, smaller version of Queenstown.

A bungy cord may be what draws you here, but you'll soon discover that it's the region's breathtaking beauty that is its most intense and enduring attraction.

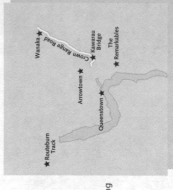

HIGHLIGHTS

- Being mesmerised by the sunset against the backdrop of the **Remarkables** (opposite)
- Careening along the twisting **Crown Range Road** (p655) and enjoying soaring views
- Hang-gliding, skiing, rafting or jetboating in **Queenstown** (p624), NZ's adrenaline-rush capital
- Delving deep into the rainforest and discovering sublime views along the gorgeous **Routeburn Track** (p644)
- Taking the plunge off **Kawarau Bridge** (p625), the world's original bungy site
- Wandering along the quaint streets of historic **Arrowtown** (p639)
- Kicking back on a sofa and watching your favourite flick at Wanaka's **Cinema Paradiso** (p652)
- Dining your way through Queenstown's tantalising **restaurant scene** (p635)

■ TELEPHONE CODE: 03   ■ www.queenstown-nz.co.nz

QUEENSTOWN REGION

With the mesmerising Remarkables and Eye Mountains stoically crowding the skyline, the kaleidoscopic Lake Wakatipu lapping at its heels and adrenaline pumping through its veins, Queenstown knows no rest. While its scenery will wow you, the majority of visitors are drawn here to indulge in the area's mammoth number of adventure pursuits. If you're not particularly keen to throw yourself off a bridge or mountainside, there are some spellbinding views that will give you a buzz nonetheless, and excellent vineyards in the area that will do the same. For those who are after a quieter base, head to historic Arrowtown or tiny Glenorchy.

Getting There & Around

Air New Zealand flies from Christchurch to Wanaka and Queenstown, from Auckland to Queenstown, and has connections to other major centres such as Wellington. Numerous bus and shuttle companies crisscross Otago, driving from Dunedin to Queenstown and Wanaka. Several also divert south to Te Anau and Invercargill, and others migrate north to Christchurch or wind through the Haast Pass and up the West Coast. The major operators include InterCity, Atomic Shuttles, Wanaka Connexions, Southern Link Shuttles and Catch-A-Bus.

to visit with relatively warm temperatures (15°C to 20°C), while spring (September to November) is slightly cooler.

QUEENSTOWN & WANAKA FACTS

Eat: Fresh fish – whether it be seared, sushi or battered – in one of Queenstown's classy eateries

Drink: Pinot noir

Read: *Walking the Routeburn Track* by Philip Holden for a wander through the history, flora and fauna of this tramp, along with a good dose of kiwi culture and some inspiring photos

Listen to: The Studio at 96.8FM for Queenstown's take on the hottest house, soul, drum 'n' bass, groove and funk as well as info on local gigs and events

Watch: *Willow* (1988), a near-classic mythical family adventure with trolls, giants, monsters and scenes from the region's snow-capped mountains

Swim: The northern arm of Lake Wakatipu with its blue waters and tranquil setting

Festival: Central Otago Wine Festival (p632) in Queenstown in late January/early February

Tackiest tourist attraction: Queenstown tours aboard the Duck (p632), an amphibious WWII vehicle

---

Climate

Summer (December to February) has long days with temperatures soaring as high as 30°C. January also sees the region's highest rainfall. Due to its elevation, this region gets crisp winters (June to August) with daytime temperatures hovering around 5°C to 10°C, dipping to freezing or below at night, and lots of snow dropping on the mountaintops. Autumn (March to May) is a pleasant time

TOP ACTIVITIES

- Take the plunge at the world's first commercial bungy site (p625)
- Throw yourself and your parachute from 12,000ft (p628 and p642)
- Soak up some calm in Mt Aspiring National Park (p647)
- Hurtle, bounce and splash through rough rivers by white-water raf: or jetboat (p625, p548 and p642)
- Ski amid NZ's most spectacular scenery at Coronet Peak or the Remarkables (p81 and p628)
- Take a day off the adrenaline frenzy: walk the trails and paths around Queenstown and admire the scenery without paying through the nose or tying a cord to your ankles (p628)

mainly young crowd that knows how to whoop it up. If you're adverse to crowds and bustle, you probably won't want to be here for long.

History

The region was deserted when the first Pakeha (white person) arrived in the mid-1850s, although there is evidence of previous Maori settlement. Sheep farmers came first, but after two shearers discovered gold on the banks of the Shotover River in 1862, a deluge of prospectors followed. Within a year, Queenstown was a mining town with streets, permanent buildings and a population of several thousand. It was declared 'fit for a queen' by the NZ government, hence Queenstown was born. Lake Wakatipu was the principal means of transport, and at the height of the boom there were four paddle-steamers and 30 other craft plying the waters.

By 1900 the gold had petered out and the population was a mere 190. It wasn't until the 1950s that Queenstown became a popular holiday destination. In recent years, Queenstown has wrestled with rising water levels in Lake Wakatipu and, in 1999, a third of the town was severely flooded. To thwart a repeat occurrence, there was an initial proposal to permanently lower lake levels. Instead, the town has decided to raise floor levels and put other flood-mitigation measures in place.

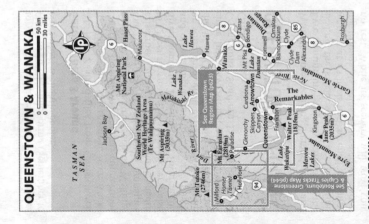

QUEENSTOWN

pop 8500

The size of a small town but with the restlessness of a city, Queenstown has mountains of things to do. As NZ's adrenaline-activity capital, there are countless bungy-jumping, caving, rafting, sledging, jetboating, skiing, skydiving and hang-gliding operations eager to give you the thrill of a lifetime. For those after more relaxed pursuits, Queenstown has atmospheric restaurants, laid-back cafés and excellent boutiques. And, of course, the scenery is magnificent. When the hype of the town gets to be too much, find a lakeside bench at sunrise or dusk and immerse yourself in one of NZ's most beautiful, calming mountain views.

Keep in mind that Queenstown is undeniably a big-budget resort town and draws more than a million visitors each year. This means great tourist facilities but also great big crowds. While early autumn is vaguely quieter, it's a popular destination all year round. Queenstown's streets are often paved with humanity and its restaurants and bars are regularly packed with a

Queenstown's town centre is compact and easily navigated on foot. Most tourist facilities are along Shotover St, Beach St and the pedestrianised Mall. The airport is 8km east of town; see p639 for info on how to reach it.

Information

Queenstown Medical Centre (Map p626; ☎ 03-441 0500; 9 Isle St; ☒ 8am–10pm) Emergency care, a pharmacy and lots of bones being bandaged.

INTERNET ACCESS

Many hostels offer Internet access, or you can head to one of the Internet cafés listed here. All are open late and most charge around 10c per minute:

Discovery Lodge (Map p626; ☎ 0800 462 396, 03-441 1185; 49 Shotover St; ☒ 24hr) Fast connections and cheap rates.

Orientation

QUEENSTOWN REGION

Efacé (Map p626; ☎ 03-442 9888; 50 Shotover St) Fast online connection.

Internet Laundry (Map p626; 1 Shotover St) While you do your laundry, plunk coins into online terminals.

Internet Outpost (Map p626; ☎ 03-441 3018; 27 Shotover St) Can put your digital photos onto CDs.

MONEY

ATMs and banks are scattered throughout town.

POST

Post office (Map p626; 15-19 Camp St) Offers poste restante facilities.

TOURIST INFORMATION

Department of Conservation (DOC) visitor information centre (Map p626; ☎ 03-442 7935; queenstownvc@doc.govt.nz; 37 Shotover St; 8.30am-5pm May-Nov, 8.30am-3pm Dec-Apr) Details and photos on the area's natural attractions and local tracks.

info & Track Centre (Map p626; ☎ 03-442 9703; www.infotrack.co.nz; 37 Shotover St) Info on tracks and transport.

Queenstown visitor information centre (Map p626; ☎ 0800 668 888, 03-442 4100; www.queenstown-vacation.com; Clocktower Centre, cnr Shotover & Camp Sts; 7am-7pm Dec-Apr, 7am-6pm May-Nov) The biggest booking agency in town. Helpful and often hectic but not always friendly.

TRAVEL AGENCIES

Kiwi Discovery (Map p625; ☎ 0800 505 504, 03-442 7340; www.kiwidiscovery.com; 37 Camp St) Walking track packages, ski transport and equipment hire.

Real Journeys (Map p626; ☎ 0800 656 503, 03-442 7500; www.realjourneys.co.nz; Steamer Wharf, Beach St) A prominent South Island travel firm that books and runs a huge range of lake trips and tours.

Sight Seeing Shop (Map p626; ☎ 03-442 7642; sight-seeing.shop@xtra.co.nz; cnr the Mall & Camp St) Another booking agency with computers to hop online.

Station (Map p626; ☎ 03-442 5252; www.thestation.co.nz; cnr Camp & Shotover Sts) Major activity-booking office housing AJ Hackett Bungy.

Sights

Hop on the **Skyline Gondola** (Map p626; ☎ 03-441 0101; www.skyline.co.nz; Brecon St; adult/child/family return $17/7/36; 9am-6.30pm) for fantastic views of Queenstown, the lake and mountains. The complex at the top of the hill has a café, restaurant and overpriced souvenir shops.

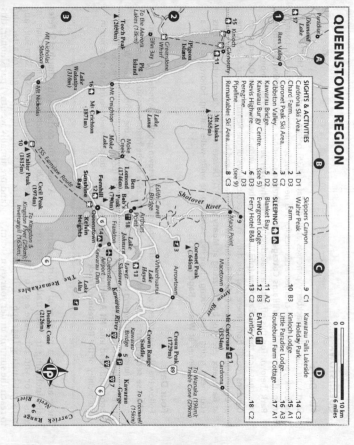

SIGHTS & ACTIVITIES	
Cardona Ski Area	1 D1
Charc Farm	2 C3
Coronet Peak Ski Area	3 C3
Gibbston Valley	4 D2
Kawarau Bridge	5 D2
Kawarau Burgy Centre	(see 5)
Nevis Highwire	6 D3
Peregrine	7 D3
Pipeline	8 C3
Remarkables Ski Area	(see 9)

SLEEPING	
Blanket Bay	9 C1
Evergreen Lodge	10 B3
Fery Hotel B&B	11 A2
Kawarau Falls Lakeside Holiday Park	12 B3
Kinloch Lodge	13 C2
Little Paradise Lodge	14 C3
Routeburn Farm Cottage	15 A1
	16 A3
	17 A1

EATING	
Gantley's	18 C2

QUEENSTOWN IN...

Two Days

Start your day with blackberry pancakes at **Vudu Cafe** (p636) before heading up Shotover St to book your adrenaline-charged activities for the next day. Spend the rest of the day taking in local sights, such as **Williams Cottage** (below), **Skyline Gondola** (p623) and **Kiwi & Birdlife Park** (below). Top this off with a mad dash on the **Shotover Jet** (opposite) or a more peaceful lake cruise on the **TSS Earnslaw** (p631). Wind up the day with a walk through **Queenstown Gardens** (p628) from where you can drink in gorgeous views of the Remarkables at dusk. Dine at **Coronation Bathhouse Cafe & Restaurant** (p635), and head back into town for wine sipping at **Bardeaux** (p636) or beer guzzling at **Monty's** (p637). Devote the next day to whatever gets your heart racing – be it bungy jumping, skydiving or white-water rafting. Follow this with a refuelling dinner at **Winnie Bagoes** (p635).

Four Days

Follow the two-day itinerary, then head to charming **Arrowtown** (p639) to wander the enigmatic **Chinese settlement** (p639), browse the local shops, take in the historic architecture and eat a gourmet lunch. The following day, take a leisurely, scenic drive along the shores of Lake Wakatipu to tiny **Glenorchy** (p642). Have lunch at **Glenorchy Café** (p643) and then strap on your hiking boots and head into **Mt Aspiring National Park** (p642) to do some wonderful short tramps in the vicinity of the **Routeburn Track** (p643).

There are also a number of short walking trials, including the **loop track** (30 minutes return) or you can have a go on the summit's gut-busting **Luge** (p629). If you prefer to reach the summit under your own steam, take the upper, left-hand gravel track from the trail head on Lomond Cres for an hour's uphill hike.

If you've high hopes of seeing a kiwi bird, the **Kiwi & Birdlife Park** (Map p626; ☎ 03-442 8059; www.kiwibird.co.nz; Brecon St; adult/child/family $16/6/33; ⏰ 9am-7pm Oct-Mar, 9am-6pm Apr-Sep, shows 11am, 1pm & 3pm) is your safest bet. Once a refuse site, it's now home to more than 10,000 native plants and umpteen birds, including the rare black stilt, kea, morepork and parakeets. Take a pleasant (though not spellbinding) stroll around the sanctuary, watch an info-packed conservation show and tiptoe into the darkened kiwi houses.

Williams Cottage (Map p626; cnr Marine Pde & Earl St; ⏰ 9am-5pm) is Queenstown's oldest home. An annex of the Lake District Museum & Gallery in Arrowtown, it was built in 1864 and remains very close to its original condition, with its 1930s wallpaper still hanging (and peeling) on the walls and the original kitchen table, Welsh dresser and coal range. The cottage and its 1920s garden are now home to the very cool Vesta shop and café and, all totalled, it's well worth a look-see.

Around the corner is the **Church of St Peter** (Map p626; www.stpeters.co.nz; cnr Church & Camp Sts; ⏰ service 10am Mon-Fri, 7.30am & 10.30am Sun), another oasis of calm. The gift of a faithful (and presumably wealthy) parishioner, this pretty little wood-beamed building has a beautiful organ and colourful stained glass. Also take a look at the cedar-wood lectern, which was carved by a Chinese immigrant in the 1870s.

Underwater World (Map p626; ☎ 03-442 8538; Queenstown Bay Jetty; adult/child/family $5/3/10; ⏰ 9am-5pm) has six giant windows that give you a glimpse of life under the lake. It won't give you an adrenaline rush but is interesting nonetheless, particularly if you've got kiddies along. A feeder attracts NZ long-finned eels and, if you pop a coin into a vendor, food pellets will bring huge brown and rainbow trout in droves. The highlights are the scaup (diving ducks), which swim by now and again.

Activities

You can buy combination tickets for a variety of Queenstown's more heart-stopping activities, giving you slightly cheaper rates. Tickets are available from **Queenstown Combos** (☎ 0800 423 836, 03-442 7318; www.combos.co.nz). Some activities operators have an office where you can book but for most, head to

Queenstown visitor centre or one of the many travel agents in town.

BUNGY JUMPING

Queenstown is famous for its bungy jumping, and the activity's local master of ceremonies is **AJ Hackett Bungy** (Map p626; ☎ 03-442 7100; www.ajhackett.com; Station, cnr Camp & Shotover Sts). Once you've done one AJ Hackett jump, you'll receive a 20% discount on subsequent jumps. Patrons over 65 years old jump free. Prices for the following options include transport out of town and gondola rides where relevant.

The historic 1880 **Kawarau Bridge** (Map p623), 23km from Queenstown, became the world's first commercial bungy site in 1988 and lets you leap 43m ($140). To gear you up, the **Kawarau Bungy Centre** (Map p623; ☎ 03-442 1177; SH6; adult/child $5/free; ☑ 8am-8pm) has a multimedia Bungy Dome theatre, bungy museum, café and bar.

At the top of Queenstown's gondola, the 47m-high **Ledge Bungy** (Map p626; per person $140) is scenic by day and fearsome by night.

If these just aren't high enough, try the dramatic 102m-high **Pipeline** (Map p623; per person $150; ☑ Oct-May only) off a suspension bridge and into Skippers Canyon (40 minutes from town). Dangling over the Shotover River, you'll get a rather close-up look at the site of some 1864 gold sluicing. You can also opt for a half-day trip ($280) to Skippers Canyon, which includes a gourmet lunch, mountain biking and the jump. Higher still is the truly terrifying 134m-high **Nevis High-wire** (Map p623; per person $200, where you jump from a pod suspended over the Nevis River. If you're a true masochist, you can do AJ Hackett's **Thrillogy** (per person $300), combining the Kawarau, Ledge and Nevis jumps.

BUNGY VARIATIONS

Who knew a swing could be so much fun? **Shotover Canyon Swing** (☎ 0800 279 464, 03-442 6990; www.canyonswing.co.nz; per person $110, additional swings $35) is touted as the world's highest rope swing (109m). If you can't force yourself to jump, it can 'launch' you. From there it's a 50m freefall and a wild swing across the canyon at 150km/h. On a similar theme, at AJ Hackett's Ledge Bungy site is the **Sky Swing** (Map p626; per person $85), where you go into free fall in a harness before soaring through the air on a huge arc.

JETBOATING

The Shotover and Kawarau are Queenstown's most popular rivers to hurtle along; the engthier and more scenic Dart River is less travelled (see p642). Trips depart from Queenstown or go via minibus to the river and awaiting jetboat.

Shotover Jet (☎ 0800 746 868; www.shotoverjet.co.nz; adult/child $105/60; does half-hour trips through the rocky Shotover Canyons, with lots of 360-degree spins that feel mad but are extremely safe. You'll laugh yourself sick. **Twin Rivers Jet** (☎ 03-442 3257; www.twinriversjet.co.nz; adult/child/family $85/45/220) and **Kawarau**

HYPER-ACTIVE

There is a bewildering array of activities in Queenstown, suitable for the old and the young, the timid and the true adrenaline junkie. Sifting through all the options can be a daunting task, but there are ways to make it easier. Pick up a free **Independent Traveller's Adventure Guide** (ITAG; www.itag.co.nz) for a handy overview, check the websites mentioned in this section to get the latest information and check out www.queenstownadventure.com. Also ask around; you'll find lots of travellers who have just jumped, dived or sped and who will be able to give you the lowdown.

Once in Queenstown you can book directly with activity companies, at your accommodation (most have a booking service) or at one of the town's many booking agencies, located mainly on Camp and Shotover Sts. Choose the most convenient, as prices won't vary from place to place. Also bear in mind that countless activity combinations (combos) are arranged between major operators, reducing the cost.

Be aware that adventure activities inherently involve a degree of risk. Most operators do everything possible to ensure that participants are safe and have a great time, but accidents do happen and Lonely Planet receives many letters from travellers with sad tales of broken bones and the like. Before you jump, read the fine print in your insurance to see if it'll cover any mishaps.

QUEENSTOWN

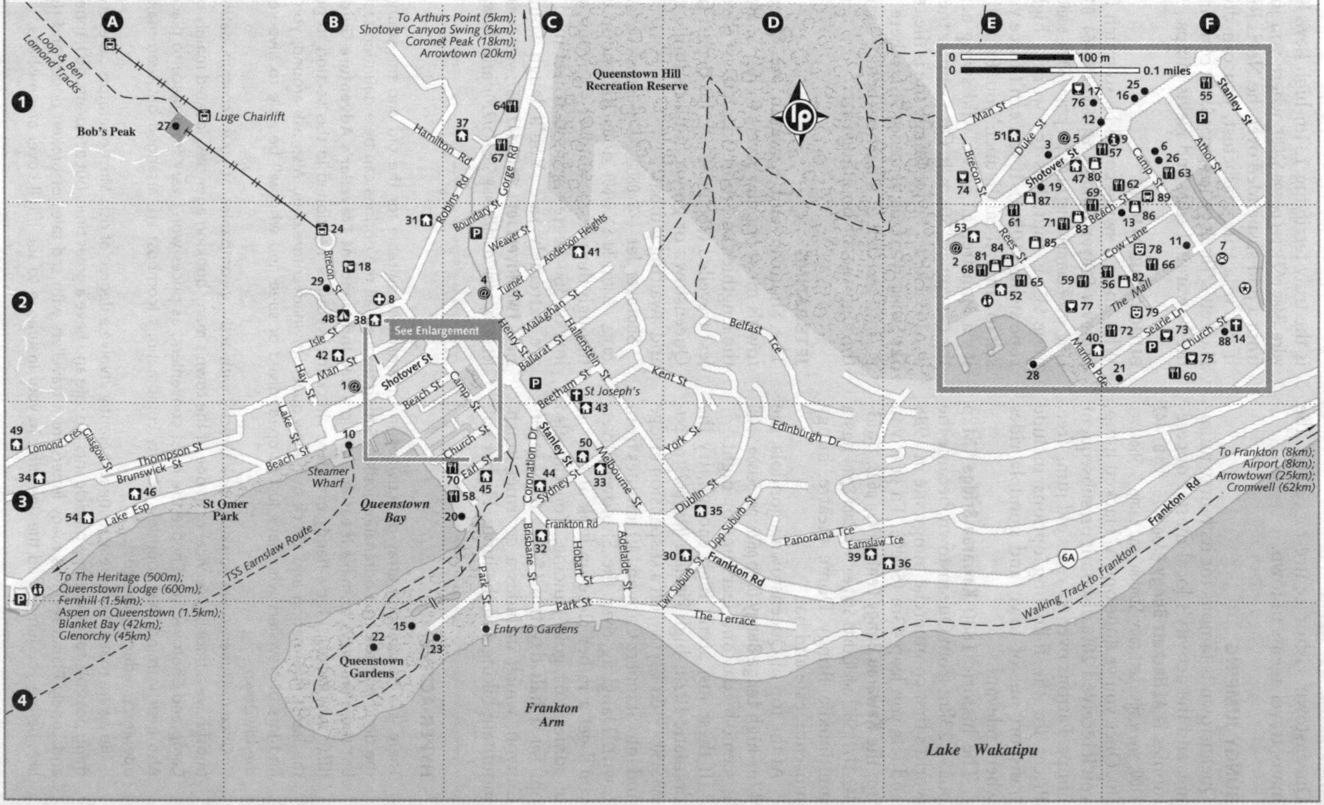
0 500 m
0 0.3 miles
To Arthurs Point (5km); Shotover Canyon Swing (5km); Coronet Peak (18km); Arrowtown (20km)
Loop & Ben Lomond Tracks
Luge Chairlift
Bob's Peak
Queenstown Hill Recreation Reserve
Hamilton Rd
Robins Rd
Gorge Rd
Boundary St
Weaver St
Anderson Heights
Turner St
Brecon St
Isle St
Man St
Hay St
Shotover St
Beach St
Camp St
Church St
Earl St
Henry St
Malaghan St
Ballarat St
Hallenstein St
Beetham St
St Joseph's
Belfast Tce
Kent St
York St
Edinburgh Dr
Stanley St
Coronation Dr
Sydney St
Melbourne St
Dublin St
Upp Suburb St
Lwr Suburb St
Panorama Tce
Earnslaw Tce
Frankton Rd
Brisbane St
Hobart St
Adelaide St
Park St
The Terrace
Entry to Gardens
Lake St
Lomond Cres
Glasgow St
Thompson St
Brunswick St
Beach St
Lake Esp
St Omer Park
Steamer Wharf
Queenstown Bay
TSS Earnslaw Route
To The Heritage (500m); Queenstown Lodge (600m); Fernhill (1.5km); Aspen on Queenstown (1.5km); Blanket Bay (42km); Glenorchy (45km)
Queenstown Gardens
Frankton Arm
Lake Wakatipu
Walking Track to Frankton
6A
To Frankton (8km); Airport (8km); Arrowtown (25km); Cromwell (62km)
See Enlargement
0 100 m
0 0.1 miles
Stanley St
Athol St
Duke St
Rees St
Cow Lane
The Mall
Searle Ln
Marine Pde

INFORMATION
Department of Conservation.....(see 3)
Discovery Lodge...................1 B2
Ecafé..............................2 E2
Info & Track Centre...............3 E1
Internet Laundry..................4 C2
Internet Outpost..................5 E1
Kiwi Discovery....................6 F1
Post Office.......................7 F2
Queenstown Medical Centre........8 B2
Queenstown Visitor Information
  Centre..........................9 F1
Real Journeys....................10 B3
Sight Seeing Shop................11 F2
Station..........................12 E1

SIGHTS & ACTIVITIES
AJ Hackett Bungy................(see 12)
Central Otago Wine
  Experience.....................13 F2
Church of St Peter..............14 F2
Frisbee Golf....................15 B4
Gravity Action..................16 F1
Green Toad.....................(see 67)
Hush Spa........................(see 6)
Kawarau Jet....................(see 28)
Kiwi & Birdlife Park............18 B2
Ledge Bungy....................(see 27)
Ledge Sky Swing................(see 27)
Luge...........................(see 27)
Outdoor Sports..................19 E1
Playground......................20 D3
Queenstown Bike Hire............21 F2
Queenstown Gardens..............22 B4
Queenstown Ice Arena............23 B4
Queenstown Paraflights.........(see 28)
Skyline Gondola.................24 D2
Small Planet Sports Co..........25 F1
Snowmentals.....................26 F1
Tandem Paragliding..............27 A1
TSS Earnslaw...................(see 10)
Underwater Word.................28 D2
Williams Cottage...............(see 70)
Zoom............................29 B2

SLEEPING
Alexis Motor Lodge &
  Apartments.....................30 D3
Bella Vista......................31 B2
Black Sheep Lodge................32 C3
Bungi Backpackers................33 C3
Butterfli Lodge..................34 A3
Chalet Queenstown B&B............35 D3
Colonial Village Motels..........36 D3
Creeksyde Top 10 Holiday Park....37 C1
Dairy............................38 B2
Earnslaw View Apartments.........39 D3
Eichardt's Private Hotel.........40 E2
Hippo Lodge......................41 D2
Lomond Lodge.....................42 B2
Melbourne Motor Lodge............43 C3
Mountvista.......................44 C3
Novotel Gardens Queenstown.......45 C3
Outrigger........................46 A3
Queenstown Accommodation
  Centre.........................47 E1
Queenstown Lakeview Holiday
  Park...........................48 B2
Scallywags Travellers
  Guesthouse.....................49 A3
Scenic Circle Aurum..............50 C3
Sofitel..........................51 E1
Thomas's Hotel...................52 E2
YHA Queenstown Central...........53 E2
YHA Queenstown Lakefront.........54 A3

EATING
Alpine Supermarket...............55 F1
Bunker...........................56 F2
Coco Espresso....................57 F1
Coronation Bathhouse Cafe &
  Restaurant.....................58 C3
Cow..............................59 E2
Dux de Lux.......................60 E2
Fergburger.......................61 E2
Fishbone Bar & Grill.............62 F2
Freya's..........................63 F1
Freshchoice......................64 C1
Habebes..........................65 E2
Kappa Sushi Cafe.................66 F2
Mediterranean Market.............67 C1
Minami Jujisei...................68 E2
Sombrero's.......................69 E2
Vesta............................70 C3
Vudu Cafe........................71 F2
Wai Waterfront Restaurant &
  Wine Bar......................(see 10)
Winnie Bagoes....................72 F2

DRINKING
Bardeaux.........................73 F2
Buffalo Club.....................74 E1
Eichardt's House Bar............(see 40)
Minus 5.........................(see 10)
Monty's..........................75 F2
Office Bar......................(see 76)
Red Rock Bar.....................76 F2
Surreal..........................77 E2

ENTERTAINMENT
Debajo...........................78 F2
Embassy Cinemas..................79 F2
Kiwi Haka.......................(see 27)
Subculture......................(see 75)
Tard's Bar......................(see 56)
Te Maori........................(see 18)

SHOPPING
Alpine Sports....................80 E1
Gallery Oceanic..................81 E2
Gift Centre.....................(see 69)
Goddess..........................82 F2
Hopscotch........................83 E2
Kathmandu........................84 E2
Out There Clothing...............85 E2
Play It Again....................86 F2
Wine Deli........................87 E1

TRANSPORT
Air New Zealand..................88 F2
Arrow Express...................(see 89)
InterCity.......................(see 9)
Shopper Bus......................89 F1

Jet (☎ 0800 529 272, 03-442 6142; www.kjet.co.nz; Queenstown Bay Jetty; adult/child $85/45) both do one-hour trips on the Kawarau and Lower Shotover Rivers.

WHITE-WATER RAFTING

The choppy Shotover and calmer Kawarau Rivers are both great for rafting. Trips typically take four to five hours; half of this is spent getting there and back by minibus. There's generally a minimum age of 13 years.

Rafting companies include **Queenstown Rafting** (☎ 0800 723 8464, 03-442 9792; www.rafting.co.nz), **Extreme Green Rafting** (☎ 03-442 8517; www.nzraft.com) and **Challenge Rafting** (☎ 0800 423 836, 03-442 7318; www.raft.co.nz); prices of trips with all three operators start from around $15C.

RIVER SURFING & WHITE-WATER SLEDGING

Hang onto a bodyboard and 'surf down the Kawarau River with **Serious Fun** (☎ 0800 737 468, 03-442 5262; www.riversurfing.co.nz) or **Mad Dog River Boarding** (☎ 03-442 7797; www.riverboarding.co.nz), racing over river waves, running rapids and riding whirlpools. Trips take about four hours (1½ hours in the water), cost around $140 and run from September to June.

Frogz Have More Fun (☎ 0800 338 738, 03-443 9130; www.ffogz.co.nz) lets you steer purpose-built, buoyant sledges down the challenging Kawarau River ($299) and through the more mellow Roaring Meg ($135).

CANYONING

Xll-Mile Delta Canyoning (☎ 03-441 4468; www.xiimile.co.nz; per person $145) runs half-day trips in the

12-Mile Delta Canyons that expose you to all the exciting stuff: waterslides, rock jumps, swimming through narrow channels and abseiling. Canyoning in the remote Routeburn Valley is possible with **Routeburn Canyoning** (☎ 0800 222 696, 03-441 4386; www.gycanyoning.co.nz; per person $210); the price includes transport from Queenstown.

FLYING, GLIDING & SKYDIVING

Tandem Paragliding (Map p626; ☎ 0800 759 688, 03-441 8581; www.paraglide.net.nz; per person $185) takes off from the top of the gondola for dreamy aerial cruises and views of Queenstown and Lake Wakatipu. **Flight Park Tandems** (☎ 0800 467 325; www.tandemparagliding.com; from 1140/1620m $170/210) does similar flights with spectacular views from Coronet Peak.

More relaxed paraflights take you up to 200m above the lake with **Queenstown Paraflights** (Map p626; ☎ 03-441 2242; www.paraflights.co.nz; Queenstown Bay Jetty; solo per adult/child $75/70, tandem $65/55). Soar with **Skytrek Hang Gliding** (☎ 03-442 6311; per person $165) from Coronet Peak or the Remarkables, and with **Antigravity** (☎ 0800 426 445, 03-441 8898; www.antigravity.co.nz; per person $165-185) from a plane over Cardrona Valley.

Fly by Wire (☎ 0800 359 299, 03-442 2116; www .flybywire.co.nz; per person $155) is a bizarre but exhilarating experience where you control a high-speed plane on a leash at speeds of up to 170km/h. It only lasts six minutes, but it'll feel like a lifetime.

The company's bumph tells you to embrace the fear – you'll certainly want to embrace something as you jump tandem-style out of an **NZONE** (☎ 0800 376 796, 03-442 5867; www.nzone .biz; from $245) plane and freefall up to 200km/h before remembering your parachute.

SKIING

In winter, the Remarkables (p81) and Coronet Peak ski fields (p81) are the region's key snow-sport centres (Map p623). You can hear snow reports on most local radio stations; try 99.2FM from 6.45am to 9am.

If you'd rather drive than slide, you can churn up the white stuff in the Garvie Mountains with **Nevis Snowmobile Adventure** (☎ 0800 442 250, 03-442 4250; www.snowmobilenz.com; adult/child $520/400); three-hour trips include a scenic helicopter flight over the Remarkables.

For serious skiers, heliskiing takes you to pristine, untouched terrain. Check out **Heli Ski Queenstown** (☎ 03-442 7733; from $745), **Har-**

ris Mountains Heli-Ski (☎ 03-442 6722; www.heliski .co.nz; from $695) or **Southern Lakes Heliski** (☎ 03-442 6222; www.southernlakesheliski.co.nz; from $560).

There are countless places in town to hire ski equipment. Wander into town or visit the Queenstown visitor information centre for more options:

Gravity Action (Map p626; ☎ 03-442 5277; 19 Shotover St)
Green Toad (Map p626; ☎ 03-442 5311; 48 Camp St)
Outdoor Sports (Map p626; ☎ 03-442 8883; Shotover St)
Snowrental (Map p626; ☎ 03-442 4187; 39 Camp St)

MOUNTAIN BIKING

There's some great mountain biking around Queenstown. **Fat Tyre Adventures** (☎ 0800 328 897; www.fat-tyre.co.nz; from $195) takes small tours off the main trails. Tours cater to different abilities with day tours, multiday tours, helibiking and single track riding. Bike hire and trail snacks are included.

If you're not keen on strenuous uphill pedalling, choose an operator who'll take you and your bike to a suitable high point. **Gravity Action** (Map p626; ☎ 03-442 5277; www.gravityaction .com; 19 Shotover St; adult/child from $130/110) does a trip into Skippers Canyon, while **Vertigo** (☎ 0800 837 8446, 03-442 8378; www.heli-adventures.co.nz) has guided downhill trips with tours geared to families (from $135) and a purpose-built track from the gondola ($125). Both operators also have helibiking options.

Places to hire bikes:

Gravity Action (Map p626; ☎ 03-442 5277; 19 Shotover St; per half/full day $40/50)
Queenstown Bike Hire (Map p626; ☎ 03-442 6039; cnr Marine Pde & Church St; per day from $25) Wide variety of bikes and suggestions on where to cycle.

WALKING & CLIMBING

Pick up a free copy of *Queenstown Walks and Trails* from DOC's **Info & Track Centre** (Map p626; ☎ 03-442 9708; www.infotrack.co.nz; 37 Shotover St) for local walking tracks ranging from easy one-hour strolls to tough eight-hour slogs.

Only footsteps from town, the lush and peaceful **Queenstown Gardens** (Map p626) has a number of walking trails to follow. You can also haul yourself up to **Bob's Peak**, where the gondola lands. It's not a particularly scenic walk but the views at the top are excellent. Another short local climb is up 900m **Queenstown Hill** (Map p626; two to three hours return); access is from Belfast Tce.

For a more spectacular view, climb 1746m **Ben Lomond** (Map p626; 6-8hr return), accessed from Lomond Cres. It's a difficult walk requiring high-level fitness and shouldn't be underestimated; consult DOC on this and the region's many other walks.

Guided Nature Walks (☎ 03-442 7126; www.nzwalks.com; from $95) offers excellent walks in the area, including a day walk along the Routeburn Trail ($195) and helihikes. **Encounter Guided Day Walks** (☎ 03-442 8200; www.ultimatehikes.co.nz; ☺ Oct-Apr) offers day walks on the Routeburn or Milford Tracks (adult/child $135/80) and Mt Cook (adult/child $95/65), as well as multiday tramps.

For climbers, **Rungway** (☎ 03-409 2308; www.rungway.co.nz; per person $150) has 12 routes of varying levels on Queenstown Hill. Each has permanent rungs, pegs, rails, ladders and cables. **Alpine Climb** (☎ 03-442 8883; www.independentmountainguides.co.nz) offers full-day instruction classes ($350), five-day trips up Mt Earnslaw ($2550) and rock-climbing day trips ($350).

If you're gear-needy, head to one of the following hire outfits:

Alpine Sports (Map p626; ☎ 03-442 7099; 28 Shotover St) Hires out packs, sleeping bags, tents, avalanche safety kits and more, all for reasonable rates.

Small Planet Sports Co (Map p626; ☎ 03-442 6393; 17 Shotover St) Sells new and used outdoor equipment.

HORSE TREKS

You can ride through stunning scenery on a 324-hectare working farm with **Moonlight Stables** (☎ 03-442 1229; adult/child $75/45). **Shotover Stables** (☎ 03-442 7486; adult/child $65/40) offers a fairly slow ride that includes bush trekking, a river crossing and an uphill canter home.

FISHING

The peaceful, remote rivers and lakes around Queenstown are home to huge brown and rainbow trout and, consequently, some excellent fly-fishing and trolling. All companies practise catch-and-release. Half-day guided trips start at around $400.

Some fishing companies:

Born to Fish (☎ 03-441 2000; www.borntofish.co.nz) Guided fly-fishing, lessons and multiday trips. Prices drop significantly for two or more patrons.

Fly Fishing (☎ 03-425363; www.wakatipu.co.nz) Helifishing, lake trolling, lure fishing and fly-fishing.

TC Charters (☎ 03-442 4462; www.tccharters.co.nz) Lake trolling and fly-fishing.

Walking Tour

From Beach St, start your walk with a wander around the bustling harbourfront, watching for the **TSS Earnslaw** (1; p631) chugging into the Queenstown Bay. Head out or the jetty to **Underwater World** (2; p624) to see what lies beneath, and then continue on to **Coronation Bathhouse Cafe & Restaurant** (3; p635) for a latte. From there, head into **Queenstown Gardens** (4; p628) where you can soak up the quiet or test your aim at **Frisbee Golf** (5; p629). Complete the garden's loop trail and return up Marine Pde to **Williams**

OTHER ACTIVITIES

If you want a little exhilaration on a tight budget, or don't have the audacity to jump out of a plane, hop into a three-wheeled **Luge** (Map p626; ☎ 03-441 0101; www.skyline.co.nz; Brecon St; 2/3/5 rides $10/13/20) at the top of the gondola. It looks much tamer than it feels. You have to do the 'scenic' run once before you're allowed on the advanced track with its banked corners, tunnel and sharp bends.

Frisbee Golf (Map p626) is gaining popularity and Queenstown has a marked course in Queenstown Gardens. Tees are indicated by numbered arrows on the ground and targets have numbered circles. Bring your own Frisbee and playmates. Also in Queenstown Gardens, **Queenstown Ice Arena** (Map p626; ☎ 03-441 8000; adult/child $13/8.50; ☺ 9am-5.30pm Mon-Thu, 9am-9pm Fri, 10.30am-5pm Sat & Sun) lets you show off your ice-bound disco moves on Friday night.

For a more leisurely pursuit, **Central Otago Wine Experience** (Map p626; ☎ 03-409 2226; www.winetastes.com; 14 Beach St; per taste 80c-$8, plus deposit $5; ☺ 10am-10pm) has more than 100 Otago wines to try with lots of local pinot noirs. There's also some ciabatta bread handy to taste-test local olive oil.

You can also golf, minigolf, quad bike, dive and more. See the Queenstown visitor information centre or any of the major booking agencies for details. When you've collapsed in an exhausted heap, visit **Hush Spa** (Map p626; ☎ 03-409 0901; www.hushspa.co.nz; cnr Gorge & Robins Rds; 30/60min massage from $60/95; ☺ 9am-late Mon-Sat, 11am-5pm Sun) for a relaxation or deep-tissue massage, aroma stone therapy or a deep bath soak. Or call the **Mobile Massage Co** (☎ 02-542 6161; ☺ 9am-9pm) for an in-room massage.

squint at those elusive balls of feathers and then hop on the **Skyline Gondola** (12; p623) for a peaceful (and steep) ride up Bob's Peak. At the top, you can laugh yourself silly on the **Luge** (13; p629) and brave souls can fly back down with **Tandem Paragliding** (14; p628). From the gondola's base, it's a straight tumble back into town for dinner at the **Bunker** (15; p635).

Queenstown for Children

While Queenstown is brimming with activities, many of them have age restrictions that may exclude the youngest in your group. Nevertheless, you shouldn't have any trouble keeping the youngsters busy.

For a high that'll make sugar rushes seems passé, take wilder kids on the **Shotover Jet** (p625). For older kids, consider a tamer variation on the classic bungy jump with the **Ledge Sky Swing** (p625) or go tandem with them on **Queenstown Paraflights** (p628). At **Kawarau Bungy Centre** (p625) kids can watch people plunging off the bridge and experience a virtual jump. For tiny tots who don't want to miss out on the fun, **Zoom** (Map p626; ☎ 0800 124 224; Brecon St Hill; child $10; ☉ 11am-5pm Wed-Sun) is a bungy trampoline that safely bounces them 8m into the air.

The **Skyline Gondola** (p623) offers a slow-moving activity from dizzying heights. At the top of the hill lies a fantastically zippy **Luge** (p629) suitable for ages three and up.

Kids who enjoy hanging out with the ducks will like the **Kiwi & Birdlife Park** (p624). Its conservation shows are especially geared to the younger crowd. **Queenstown Gardens** (p628) is a great place to let your children stretch their legs, and has a good beachside **playground** (Map p626) near the entrance on Marine Pde. Also in the park, **Queenstown Ice Arena** (p629) is great for a rainy day.

Several places in town hire out child-size **mountain bikes** (p628). **Queenstown Bike Hire** (p628) also hires out pogo sticks ($5 per day), foot scooters ($5 per day) and baby buggies ($15 per day), along with toboggans ($10 per day) in winter. **Hopscotch** (Map p626; ☎ 03-442 8153; 19 Beach St) hires out snowsuits for children aged one to 14 years, while most ski-hire shops (p628) have gear for tykes.

There are also a number of child-friendly tours available. Consider lake cruises on the **TSS Earnslaw** (opposite), steam train excur-

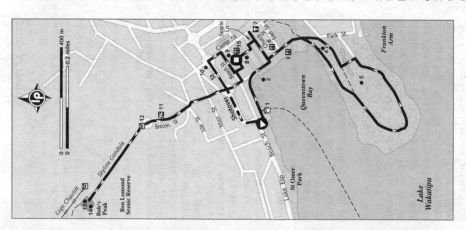

Start Beach St
Finish the Bunker

Cottage (6; p624) for a little history, retail therapy and lunch. Take a right on Church St to see the pretty **Church of St Peter** (7; p624), and then zigzag through the alleyways to the Mall to explore some local **boutiques** (8; p638). Next, visit the **Central Otago Wine Experience** (9; p629), as much to appreciate the local pinot as to steel your nerves for your visit to the **Station** (10; p623) to book your bungy jump for the next day. Make your way up to Brecon St and visit the **Kiwi & Birdlife Park** (11; p624) for your chance to

sions on the vintage **Kingston Flyer** (right) and 4WD tours of narrow, snaking **Skippers Canyon** (below). Most kids will also get a kick out of the wacky (or just plain weird) **Duck amphibious tour** (p632).

For more ideas and information (including a good list of baby-sitters) pick up a free copy of *Kidz Go!* from the visitor information centre.

Tours

AERIAL SIGHTSEEING

If you'd like to get a bird's-eye view but don't want to parachute out of a plane, join a flightseeing tour. **Over the Top Helicopters** (☎ 03-442 2233; www.flynz.co.nz; from $230) includes champagne picnics or the chance to land on a glacier; **Air Fiordland** (☎ 0800 103 404, 03-442 3404; www.airfiordland.com; from $290) includes wine tasting and lunch; and **Milford Sound Scenic Flights** (☎ 0800 207 206, 03-442 3065; www.milfordflights.co.nz adult/child from $300/175) will take you over the scound. To see the sights upside down, take a 15-minute aerobatic flight with **Actionflite** (☎ 03-442 9708; www.actionflite.co.nz; per person $290). Or hop in a hot-air balloon with **Sunrise Balloons** (☎ 0800 468 247, 03-442 0781; www.ballooningnz.com; adult/child $300/195).

FOUR-WHEEL-DRIVE TOURS

Skippers Canyon is reached by a narrow, winding road built by gold panners in the 1800s. This scenic but hair-raising 4WD route runs from Arthurs Point towards Coronet Peak and then above the Shotover River, passing gold-rush sights. To reach it, join **Skippers Canyon Heritage Tours** (☎ 03-442 5949; www.queenstown-heritage.co.nz; tours adult/child $120/60) for four-hour tours brimming with gold-mining stories and including a picnic set amid magnificent views. **Nomad Safaris** (☎ 03-442 6699; www.nomadsafaris.co.nz; adult/child $135/65) also runs four-hour tours, with the chance to gold pan and some home baking thrown in.

Nomad Saafaris (adult/child $130/65) can take you off-roading in the rugged foothills surrounding Queenstown, following wagon trails and offering you the chance to drive ($175). **Off Road Adventures** (☎ 03-442 7858; www.offroad.co.nz; adult/child $140/70) does similar tours, with a scenic photographic tour that gives professional hints at snapping the scenery. It also has a *Lord of the Rings* tour taking in nearby filming locations.

WINERY TOURS

A guided wine tour of the region's excellent vineyards means being able to enjoy a drink or three without having to get behind the wheel. **Queenstown Wine Trail** (☎ 03-442 3799; www.queenstownwinetrail.co.nz; adult/child from $95) offers

MILFORD SOUND

Day trips via Te Anau to Milford Sound take 12 to 13 hours and cost around $200/100 per adult/child, including a two-hour cruise on the sound. Bus-cruise-flight options are also available, as is pick-up from the Routeburn Track finish line. Operators include **Kiwi Experience** (☎ 03-442 9708; www.kiwiexperience.com), **Real Journeys** (Map p626; ☎ 0800 65 503, 03-442 7500; www.realjourneys.co.nz; Steamer Wharf, Beach St), **Great Sights** (☎ 0800 744 487; www.greatsights.co.nz), **Kiwi Discovery** (Map p626; ☎ 03-442 7340; www.kiwidiscovery.com) and **InterCity** (Map p626; ☎ 03-442 8238; www.intercitycoach.co.nz). The **BBQ Bus** (☎ 03-442 1045; www.milford.net.nz) takes groups of no more than 20 people; we'll let you guess what's included in the price.

To save on tour travel time and cost, consider visiting Milford from Te Anau (p657).

LAKE CRUISES

The stately, steam-powered **TSS Earnslaw** (Map p626) is more than a century old and continues to churn across Lake Wakatipu at 13 knots. Once the lake's major means of transport, it originally carried more than 800 passengers. Climb aboard for the standard 1½-hour Lake Wakatipu tour (adult/child $40/15), sing-along included. Or take a 3½-hour excursion to the high-country **Walter Peak Farm** (Map p623; adult/child $60/15) for sheep-shearing demonstrations and sheep-dog performances. Other tours include barbecue lunches, dinner or horse trekking. Book trips through **Real Journeys** (Map p626; ☎ 0800 656 503, 03-442 7500; www.realjourneys.co.nz; Steamer Wharf, Beach St).

KINGSTON FLYER

Board this heritage steam train in Kingston, 45km from Queenstown on the southern tip of Lake Wakatipu. Originally plying the tracks between Kingston and Gore from 1878 to the mid-1950s, the **Kingston Flyer** (☎ 0800 435 937, 03-248 8848; www.kingstonflyer.co.nz; return fare adult/child/family $90/45/200; ☼ twice daily Oct-May) now travels a 14km stretch to Fairlight.

BOOZE CRUISE

Even if you don't know your nose from your legs, exploring Central Otago's vineyards is a great day out. The earliest grapes were grown in the area in 1862, by a Frenchman named John Feraud. When the Dunstan gold rush dried up, so did Feraud's clientele and, following his departure, commercial wine making ceased until the 1980s. Today there are more than 70 vineyards in the region, with many open to the public for tours and tasting. Pinot noirs are the area's most celebrated wines, however, the chardonnays, sauvignons and rieslings are also great.

To avoid being the designated driver, join a tour from Wanaka (p650) or Queenstown (p631). If you do set out on your own, pick up a Central Otago Wine Map (free) from the Queenstown visitor information centre and check out www.otagowine.com. You can begin your taste test just outside Queenstown on State Highway 6 (SH6). Near the historic Kawarau Bridge and bungy jump, there are three excellent wineries. **Peregrine** (Map p623; ☎ 03-442 4000; ☘ 10am–5pm) is about 5km east of the bridge and produces excellent sauvignon blanc, pinot noir and pinot gris. The beautiful **Chard Farm** (Map p623; ☎ 03-442 6110; www.chardfarm.co.nz; ☘ 11am–5pm) is accessed by a scenic but hair-raising side road almost opposite the bridge; the wine at the end is well worth the effort. Finally, **Gibbston Valley** (Map p623; ☎ 03-442 6910; www .gvwines.co.nz), 700m from the Kawarau Bridge, is the region's largest wine producer and offers a multi-award-winning pinot noir, half-hour tours of the impressive wine cave, and a cheese factory and restaurant.

informative, unhurried tours; choose from a five-hour tour with tastings at four wineries or a shorter tour with lunch included. **Appellation Central Wine Tours** (☎ 03-442 0246; www.appellationcentral.co.nz; from $135) also runs palatable tours.

OTHER TOURS

Hop on a **Double-Decker Bus Tour** (☎ 03-441 4421; adult/child $35/15) to historic Arrowtown, taking in sights along the way. Queenstown's most bizarre tour must be aboard the **Duck** (☎ 03-441 2010; www.queenstownducks.co .nz; adult/child/family $70/30/160, 1 child free per adult; an amphibious WWII vehicle that takes you right into Lake Wakatipu as well as to regional sights.

Festivals & Events

If you're a real wine buff, try to time your visit to Queenstown with the annual **Central Otago Wine Festival** (☎ 03-442 4000; Queenstown Gardens), held in late January/early February. In early July, **Queenstown Winter Festival** (www.winterfestival.co.nz) encourages much joviality in the way of bizarre ski competitions, stage performances, live music and rugby. It draws huge numbers.

Sleeping

Queenstown has endless places to stay, but also countless visitors clamouring for a room. Midrange travellers won't find a

great deal of choice; consider treating yourself to a top-end place or go for one of the excellent budget options and spend the saved dosh on activities. Places book up and prices rocket during the peak summer and ski seasons; book well in advance at these times. Rooms with guaranteed lake views often have a surcharge.

The **Queenstown Accommodation Centre** (Map p626; ☎ 03-442 7518; www.qac.co.nz; 30 Shotover St) is a good place for families and groups to start their accommodation hunt. It has a range of holiday homes and apartments on its books (and its website) with prices ranging from around $180 to $850 per week. There is often a minimum-stay period.

BUDGET

Hostels & Lodges

Scallywags Travellers Guesthouse (Map p626; ☎ 03-442 7083; 27 Lomond Cres; dm/d $25/65) Feeling much more like a home than a hostel, this place has a fantastically relaxed atmosphere, an excellently equipped (if slightly small) kitchen and a conversation-inducing lounge. Rooms are comfortable and the shared bathrooms are tops. There's lots of local information to be had, especially from the longtime resident owner. It's up a steep hill but more than worth it for some of the best views in town. Besides, there's free pick-up on arrival.

YHA Queenstown Lakefront (Map p626; ☎ 03-442 8413; yha.queenstown@yha.org.nz; 88–90 Lake Esplanade; dm/d from $24/65;) This friendly alpine lodge has staff that are very well versed in Queenstown's activities. Rooms are basic but very clean; some rooms and the dining area have lake and mountain views. It's somewhat rambling but facilities are good with a well-equipped stainless-steel kitchen, a book exchange and stacks of board games and videos.

Butterfli Lodge (Map p626; 03-442 6367; www.butterfli.co.nz; 62 Thompson St; dm/d $25/60;) This modern house sits atop a hill and has a fantastic deck offering great views to barbecue before. Inside is a homey kitchen and sitting area. Rooms don't have a huge amount of character, but are modern and well maintained.

YHA Queenstown Central (Map p626; 03-442 7400; www.yha.org.nz; 48a Shotover St; dm/d $25/50) Newly under the flagship of YHA, this old standard still gives tribute to the '70s with carpet on the walls. Rooms have been freshened up with blue duvets and linen and each has an en suite and TV that lets you watch scheduled movies from bed. Some rooms have lake views, others have private patios. The hotel's crowning glories are the clean kitchen and lounge, which have panoramic views of the lake. The atmosphere is calm and family-friendly.

Black Sheep Lodge (Map p626; 03-442 7289; www.blacksheepbackpackers.co.nz; 13 Frankton Rd; dm/d $23/60;) This bunkhouse-style hostel is popular with young backpackers and keeps them happy with a spa, a fire-stoked lounge, complimentary breakfast and beer for sale at the 24-hour reception. Rooms are basic and characterless but it's a friendly affair.

Other budget options:

Hippo Lodge (Map p626; 03-442 5785; www.hippolodge.co.nz; 4 Anderson Heights; dm $24-26, s/d from $36/60;) Well maintained and relaxed with good views, cheerful pets and lots of stairs.

Thomas's Hotel (Map p626; 03-442 7180; www.thomashotel.co.nz; 50 Beach St; d $25, d $95-125) Basic rooms but deluxe lake views and extremely central.

Bungi Backpackers (Map p626; 03-442 8725; www.bungibackpackers.co.nz; 15 Sydney St; dm $18-22, d $43;) Grungy, comfy hostel feel with a spa and a volleyball field next door.

Camping

Creekside Top 10 Holiday Park (Map p626; 0800 786 222, 03-442 9447; www.camp.co.nz; 54 Robins Rd; sites per 2 people $32, d $60-155;) These sites are a little close together, but the pretty garden setting, with flowers, trees and a creek, makes it a lovely spot for camping. There's a gamut of other accommodation, from basic to self-contained, and some fancy facilities such as a sauna, hairdryers and a car wash. Tent sites can't be reserved.

Kawarau Falls Lakeside Holiday Park (Map p623; 0800 226 774, 03-442 3510; www.campsite.co.nz; SH6; dm $22, unpowered/powered sites per 2 people $24/28, cabins $55-160;) Terraced sites look out over the water and offer fine facilities, including a lounge warmed by a log fire. You'll also find a big kitchen, lots of videos, a playground and a small shop where you can rent fishing rods and mountain bikes. Cabins come in all shapes and sizes.

Queenstown Lakeview Holiday Park (Map p626; 03-442 7252; www.holidaypark.net.nz; Brecon St; sites per 2 people $28, d $82-100;) Only a short stroll from the gondola, this park has a big open field to camp in and great facilities. The modern 'luxury leisure lodges' are particularly nice, while the taller, flashier units behind have more of a motel feel.

MIDRANGE

Colonial Village Motels (Map p626; 03-442 7629; www.colonialvillage.co.nz; 136 Frankton Rd; s/d from $95; 105) This is a great deal. Yellow units climb the hillside and have a fair amount of character with tiered, beamed ceilings, balconies and excellent lake views across Frankton Arm. Each has a full kitchen and staff are welcoming.

Chalet Queenstown B&B (Map p626; 0800 222 457, 03-442 7117; www.chalet.co.nz; 1 Dublin St; d $135-185;) Looking like it's been lifted from the Swiss Alps, this tasteful, cosy alpine villa has lots of homey touches, such as patchwork blankets and homemade croissants for breakfast. All rooms have private bathrooms and good showers. While a few rooms have lake views, Room 5 has the lion's share. It all very relaxed with a resident holistic masseur to ensure a peaceful stay.

Lomond Lodge (Map p626; 03-442 8235; www.lomondlodge.com; 33 Man St; d $122-135;) A fairly standard but pleasant motel with very pleasant service and only 15 units. Rooms look like they've been recently refurbished with cranberry and yellow touches. Request a top-floor room with a balcony; they've got a bit more character. The garden area out back has a barbecue and there's a communal kitchen.

AUTHOR'S CHOICE

Little Paradise Lodge (Map p623; ☎ 03-442 6196; www.littleparadise.co.nz; Glenorchy-Queenstown Rd; s $45, d $100-120) You may well wonder if you've fallen down the rabbit hole when you step onto this property. Located opposite the lake, 28km from Queenstown, the thatched roof, babbling brook, aviary and flowerbeds are simply the icing on the cake. The true works of genius are the unique (and very cool) wooden furnishings and adornments that the owner has hand hewn, along with the beautifully painted patterns on the walls. Fur rugs keep your toes warm and the kitchen stove is straight out of *Hansel and Gretel*. It's eccentric, it's peaceful and it's a fabulous place to stay rather than just being somewhere to sleep. Breakfast can be had for $10, as can boat hire. It's on the Queenstown-Glenorchy bus route; see p643 for bus info.

Novotel Gardens Queenstown (Map p626; ☎ 03-442 7750; www.novotel.co.nz; cnr Earl St & Marine Pde; d from $140) Recently acquired by a worldwide chain, this lakeside hotel's rooms have been spiffed up. In some rooms, the new, classy look is marred by older, standard-style furnishings, but generally it's got a fashionable feel about it. Views of the lake are excellent; some rooms have only partial views and no lake-view surcharge. Enjoy nightly music at the bar and an aromatic wander through the rose garden.

Other worthwhile midrange options:

Melbourne Motor Lodge (Map p626; ☎ 03-442 8431; stay@mmlodge.co.nz; 35 Melbourne St; d $120) Standard, older rooms but nice patios and amiable staff.

Alexis Motor Lodge & Apartments (Map p626; ☎ 03-409 0052; www.alexisqueenstown.co.nz; 69 Frankton Rd; d $150) Views of the lake, particularly from the better end units.

Bella Vista (Map p626; ☎ 03-442 4468; www.bellavista motels.co.nz; 36 Robins Rd; d $110-135) Chain feel but clean, friendly and with views of paragliders landing in the field next door.

TOP END

Eichardt's Private Hotel (Map p626; ☎ 03-441 0450; www.eichardtshotel.co.nz; cnr Marine Pde & Church St; d $1100-1600) Truly gorgeous. Originally opened in the 1860s, this hotel has been recently refurbished into an oasis of opulence. Each of the five giant suites has a fireplace, lake views and a beautiful blend of antique and modern décor. Sink into a super king bed amid warm, earthy tones and a fur throw. With heated floors and deep tubs, the bathrooms are so luxurious you'll want to sleep in them.

Mountvista (Map p626; ☎ 03-442 8832; www .mountvista.com; 4 Sydney St; d $500-600) With a Mediterranean feel, this classy boutique hotel is the perfect place to be pampered. With only 14 rooms, you get personal yet discreet service. Large rooms have white linen, heavy wood furnishings, wool carpets and mohair throws. Luxurious bathrooms come with a two-person tub and underfloor heating. In addition to breakfast, there're cookies and fudge to fill your tum.

Dairy (Map p626; ☎ 0800 333 393, 03-442 5164; www .thedairy.co.nz; 10 Isle St; s $230-360, d $360-390; ☐) This luxurious, top-end guesthouse has fabulous rooms with classy, colourful touches, dark wooden furnishings and a pile of silk cushions on a cloudlike bed. Get cosy in the antique library or the outdoor spa. The country-style breakfast room was a corner store in the 1920s, hence the hotel's name.

Evergreen Lodge (Map p626; ☎ 03-442 6636; www .evergreenlodge.co.nz; 28 Evergreen Pl, Sunshine Bay; d $545; ☐) Handcrafted timber furnishings outfit these four elegant, enormous rooms, and local, contemporary art adorns the walls. Each has a private en suite and commanding lake views. Predinner drinks are meted out in the plush lounge while a gourmet breakfast is served at the long oak dining table. The lodge has a gym, sauna and back courtyard where you can relax beneath a canopy of blossoms.

Sofitel (Map p626; ☎ 03-450 0045; reservations@ sofitelzqn.co.nz; 8 Duke St; d from $620) This giant, five-star joint is just a baby on Queenstown's hotel scene. Subtle browns and beiges make a cosy nest, and rooms include an espresso maker, fur throws, an extra-soft mattress and a deliciously deep tub that's got a flat-screen TV at its foot. The '70s-style wood panelling is truly unfortunate but head up to the wine-tasting bar and you'll forget all about it. Rooms sometimes go for as low as $250, especially if you book online.

Ferry Hotel (Map p626; ☎ 03-442 2194; www.ferry .co.nz; Spence Rd; d $155-220) An extremely comfortable, old-fashioned house with unusual antique knick-knacks lining the shelves and flora, bedroom décor. The homey lounge features a wood stove and black-and-white photos of the nearby wooden bridge that once carried hotel guests over the mighty Shotover. Whip up a home-cooked meal in the well-equipped kitchen and enjoy the lush flowerbeds out front. It's 11km east of town.

For posh, excellently equipped apartments with top service and outstanding views, try the following:

Scenic Circle Aurum (Map p626; ☎ 03-442 7700; www .scenic-circle.co.nz; 27 Stanley St; d $200-300, apt $250-360)

Earnslaw View Apartments (Map p626; ☎ 03-442 7650; www.earnslawviewapartments.co.nz; 21 Earnslaw Tce; d from $270)

Outrigger (Map p626; ☎ 03-441 0890; www.outrigger .com; 33 Lake Esplanade; d $145-290, apt $165-330)

Eating

Queenstown's town centre is peppered with busy eateries. While many of these carry a chain feel or are hot on the tourist dollar, there are some real finds offering international and local fare and plenty of atmosphere. At the more popular places, it's smart to make a reservation for weekend dining.

RESTAURANTS

Winnie Bagoes (Map p626; ☎ 03-442 8635; 1st fl, 7 the Mall; mains $15-25; ☼ lunch & dinner) Winnie's is a Queenstown institution. Get settled in a comfy booth beneath the retractable ceiling, in front of the log fire or on the outside balcony, and dig into gourmet pizzas, such as chicken, cranberry and brie or Moroccan lamb. It's also got old stand-bys, such as Hawaiian, and handmade pastas at dinnertime. And if pizza ain't your thing, steak and burgers are on offer.

Bunker (Map p626; ☎ 03-441 8030; Cow Lane; mains $40; ☼ dinner) Feeling very exclusive, this low-lit, sophisticated place is secreted away behind an unmarked door down Cow Lane. There's a roaring log fire, big leather couches to enjoy your apéritif on and a handful of tables for dining on classy mains such as caramelised duck or pan-fried salmon. The wine list is as heady as the atmosphere. Definitely reserve ahead. You can also drop in for after-dinner drinks.

Fishbone Bar & Grill (Map p626; ☎ 03-442 6768; 7 Beach St; mains $23-28; ☼ dinner) A boat's hull floats above you, on the wall hangs a life-ring and in front of you sits an excellent dinner of warm, marinated calamari salad, crumbled blue cod or wine-steamed mussels. Bright and cheerful with booths and a kids' menu.

Freiya's (Map p626; ☎ 03-442 7979; 33 Camp St; mains $6-18; ☼ lunch & dinner) Vindaloos, tandoors and kormas, all bursting with flavour. This Indian restaurant has lots of veggie dishes and a banquet option ($28) that brings on a feast of different dishes. Purple and orange walls brighten up this semiclassy joint.

Minami Jujisei (Map p626; ☎ 03-442 9854; 45 Beach St; mains $14-28; ☼ lunch Mon-Sat, dinner daily) Authentic Japanese restaurant with pictures of sumo wrestlers watching over your dining experience. The menu is in Japanese with English subtitles; try *nabe mono* (hotpot), king prawns, tuna steak or crayfish ($80). Standards, such as tempura and noodle soup, are also offered.

Cow (Map p626; ☎ 03-442 8588; Cow Lane; mains $18-30; ☼ lunch & dinner; open until 11pm) Wood rafters, stone walls and an open fire make this intimate restaurant feel like an age-old cottage. It's well known for its pizzas and is a popular local hang-out. Wondering about the name? Cows from nearby paddocks were milked along this lane during the 1860s gold rush.

Coronation Bathhouse Cafe & Restaurant (Map p626; ☎ 03-442 5625; 28 Marine Pde; lunch $15-21, dinner $27-38; ☼ lunch & dinner Tue-Sat) Looking like a giant crown, this restored 1911 bathhouse is set alongside Queenstown Gardens and the harbour. Inside it's classy, with a cushion-filled sun room to relax in and an exceptionally diverse menu. Next to the children's playground, it's also a handy place for coffee; you can pick up kids' picnic baskets for $8.50.

Wai Waterfront Restaurant & Wine Bar (Map p626; ☎ 03-442 5969; Steamer Wharf, Beach St; mains $30-40; ☼ lunch & dinner) Small, intimate and acclaimed in many a cuisine magazine, Wai (meaning 'water' in Maori) is white-linen classy and has views of TSS *Earnslaw* steaming into harbour. It's known for its gourmet seafood, but also serves venison rack, wild pork and twice-cooked duck. The seven-course degustation menu ($100) and wine list will keep connoisseurs impressed. There's even a kids' menu.

Sombrero's (Map p626; ☎ 03-442 8240; 1st fl, Beech Tree Arcade, Beach St; mains $12-25; ☼ dinner) Tacky chairs but yummy smells. The walls of this happy place are hung with giant Mexican hats and blankets. Dine on fajitas, enchiladas and burritos, all washed down with margaritas or a bottle of Corona. Set meals for two or more people give you a chance to sample lots of different dishes. BYO wine ($5 corkage fee).

Gantley's (Map p623; ☎ 03-442 8999; Arthurs Point Rd; mains $23-39; ⏰ dinner) An atmospheric dining experience in a historic 1863 stone-and-timber house at Arthurs Point. The contemporary NZ cuisine and highly regarded (and award-collecting) wine list are essential; a courtesy bus is run to and from town for à la carte diners.

Dux de Lux (Map p626; ☎ 03-442 9688; 14 Church St; mains $15-25; ⏰ lunch & dinner) A classier sister of the Christchurch original, this popular restaurant spotlights vegetarian and seafood dishes. If you're looking for something a little less chic, try the attached pub for pizza and buffalo chips.

CAFÉS & QUICK EATS

Vudu Cafe (Map p626; ☎ 03-442 5357; 23 Beach St; breakfast $4-14, lunch & dinner $7-23; ⏰ breakfast, lunch & dinner; 🖥) Casual and funky, Vudu is home to gut-filling breakfasts, including blackberry pancakes with honeycomb and lemon butter, and equally tasty lunches and dinners. And don't even try to resist the baking. Little'uns will be happy with the toy box, small playroom and highchair, and you can hop online for free (15 minute maximum).

Coco Espresso (Map p626; ☎ 03-442 8542; Clocktower Bldg, Shotover St; mains $6-14; ⏰ breakfast & lunch) Funky little café with local art on the walls and big doors that open out to the pavement. Dive into fresh baking, overstuffed sandwiches (a bargain!), all-day brunch, noodles, quiche and the like. Not that many veggie options but those that exist are scrumptious.

Kappa Sushi Cafe (Map p626; ☎ 03-441 1423; Lvl 1, 36a the Mall; sushi $4-9, mains $10-24; ⏰ lunch Mon-Fri, dinner Mon-Sat) A casual Japanese diner with sashimi, tempura, noodles and teriyaki – all the best Japanese standards. Sushi plates come with four to eight pieces. People-watch over the Mall from the weatherproofed balcony.

Habebes (Map p626; ☎ 03-442 9861; Wakatipu Arcade; meals $6-11; ⏰ lunch) A bright Lebanese takeaway with a huge selection of impressive salads (such as pumpkin, tabbouleh or beetroot), fresh pies and packed pita rolls.

Fergburger (Map p626; ☎ 03-441 1232; 42 Shotover St; burgers $9-15; ⏰ lunch & dinner, open until 5am) Fergburger's not joking when it says that it's serious about burgers. There's very functional décor but a creative menu with choices including the Cockadoodle, Oink, Little Lamby, Bun Laden (falafel) and classic Fergburger. Delicious, but you need three hands to eat them.

AUTHOR'S CHOICE

Vesta (Map p626; ☎ 03-442 5687; cnr Marine Pde & Earl St; light mains $5-8; ⏰ breakfast & lunch) Flip through contemporary design magazines as you relax into the comfy sofas in Queenstown's oldest home. Set within Williams Cottage, itself both a museum and a shop, this atmospheric café has excellent light fare, such as couscous salad, deliciously stuffed bagels or ciabatta, soups and baked goods. Wallpaper from the 1930s is peeling from the walls, and chilled out tunes flow from the stereo set atop the original coal range. If the sun's on your side, you can take your coffee (or make it a hot honey, lemon and fresh ginger) out into the 1920s-style garden. And when you're all filled up, there's fantastic shopping to be done inside.

SELF-CATERING

Mediterranean Market (Map p626; cnr Gorge & Robins Rds; ⏰ 8am-7pm Mon-Sat, 10am-6pm Sun) is the place to fill a picnic basket. There are fresh pastas, sauces, Asian cuisine, good local produce and a fantastic deli and bakery. Around the corner, the well-stocked **Freshchoice** (64 Gorge Rd; ⏰ 7am-midnight) is Queenstown's big supermarket. In town, the **Alpine Supermarket** (Map p626; cnr Stanley & Shotover Sts; ⏰ 8am-9pm Mon-Fri, 9am-9pm Sat & Sun) has most staples.

Drinking

Drinking is a hearty pastime in Queenstown and there are more than enough bars and pubs to keep you well watered.

Bardeaux (Map p626; ☎ 03-442 8284; Eureka Arcade, 11 the Mall) Down a narrow alleyway, this small, low-key wine bar is all class. Under a low ceiling await plush leather armchairs, a rock fireplace, a well-stocked bar and sleek ambience. No beanies, rugby jerseys or work boots allowed.

Eichardt's House Bar (Map p626; Marine Pde) Get a taste of this flash hotel from its chic yet cosy bar. Its got an excellent cocktail and wine menu, hazy mountain views and five-star service. Treat yourself.

Bunker (Map p626; ☎ 03-441 8030; Cow Lane) After the dinner dishes are cleared away, the Bunker becomes a sophisticated bar space with a club lounge, open fire and a secretive, just-discovered feel, especially in the wee hours (it closes at 5am).

Minus 5 (Map p626; admission $25; ☑10.30am-10.30pm) Steamer Wharf, Beach St; admission $25; With top marks for the unusual, this small place is made entirely from 18 tonnes of ice: an ice bar, ice chairs, ice carvings, even ice glasses. You can only enter via a half-hour tour (parkas and boots provided). Along with your one free vodka cocktail, you can order up to two more; apparently carbon-dioxide levels give one drink the same strength as three so expect to emerge not only cold, but wobbly too.

Monty's (Map p626; ☎ 03-441 1081; Church St) A rustic stone building with a popular patio. Fur trappers, miners and loggers will feel right at home slugging back the house favourite, Monteith's.

Dux de Lux (Map p626; ☎ 03-442 9688; 14 Church St) Housed in an old stone building, this cottage brewery concocts tasty potions including lager, pale ale and alcoholic ginger beer. It's very popular, especially for its live music.

Surreal (Map p626; ☎ 03-441 8492; 7 Rees St) Funky music, low lighting, red-velvet booths, disco balls and DJs make this a comfortable and stylish place to order your pleasure – be it beer or cocktails.

Winnie Bagoes (Map p626; ☎ 03-442 8635; 1st fl, 7 the Mall) A deservedly popular place for a beer, with a laid-back ambience, retractable roof, pool table and patio. Also a popular dining spot.

Buffalo Club (Map p626; ☎ 03-442 4144; 8 Brecon St) Lit by candles and an enormous campfire in the middle of the room, this is a popular after-work hang-out for young locals. Maybe it's the pool tables and sports-dedicated TV screen that make it such a hit, or maybe it's the potent drinks like Green Demons or French Fantasies.

Red Rock Bar (Map p626; ☎ 03-442 6850; 48 Camp St) Join a young crowd in an alcove-riddled interior with wooden barrels to rest your beer on. Outside are some picnic tables, and upstairs is the tiny but much classier Office Bar (open Thursday to Saturday).

Entertainment

Pick up the **Source** (www.thesourceonline.com), a free weekly flyer with a gig guide and events listings. Also check the flyers and posters at **Play It Again** (Map p626; ☎ 03-442 8940; O'Connells Shopping Centre, Beach St) for local events. Live music and clubbing are a nightly affair in Queenstown and most venues stay open until the wee hours on weekends and during the high seasons. Most DJ and live-music gigs are free, though you will encounter inexpensive cover charges in some nightclubs, mainly postmidnight from Thursday to Saturday.

LIVE MUSIC

Several bars have live music and DJs:

Bunker (Map p626; ☎ 03-441 8030; Cow Lane) DJs spinning ambient beats in the upstairs bar.

Surreal (Map p626; ☎ 03-441 8492; 7 Rees St) DJs, retro, dub 'n' bass and open mic.

Dux de Lux (Map p626; ☎ 03-442 9688; 14 Church St) Lots of live bands, both locals and out-of-towners.

Buffalo Club (Map p626; ☎ 03-442 4144; 8 Brecon St) DJs and live bands.

Winnie Bagoes (Map p626; ☎ 03-442 8635; 1st fl, 7 the Mall) Acoustic shows and DJs.

NIGHTCLUBS

Subculture (Map p626; ☎ 03-442 7685; downstairs, 12-14 Church St) Friendly, underground Subculture has some skilful locals and out-of-towners toying with the turntable to make drum 'n' bass, hip-hop, dub and reggae noises that get the crowds moving.

Debajo (Map p626; ☎ 03-442 6099; Cow Lane) Smallish downstairs affair with a tentative Latin décor and a solid reputation for house beats and decent cocktails.

Tardis Bar (Map p626; ☎ 03-441 8397; Skyline Arcade) A good dance bar with a foot-weathered floor and regular DJs playing hip-hop, dancehall, drum 'n' bass and dub.

HAKA

To see traditional Maori dancing and singing, take in **Kiwi Haka** (Map p626; ☎ 03-441 0085; www.skyline.co.nz Brecon St; adult/child/family $30/18/30; ☑ from 5.30pm) at the top of the gondola.

There are a number of shows each evening but bookings are essential. Interested in traditional Maori dining as well? **Te Maori** (Map p626; ☎ 03-442 8059; www.kiwibird.co.nz; Brecon St; tickets $90; ☉ 6pm Apr-Sep, 7pm Oct-Mar) serves up song, dance, chants and food within the Kiwi & Birdlife Park. A traditional dinner is cooked in *hangi* (ovens made by digging a hole and steaming food in baskets over embers) in a reconstructed 16th-century hunting village; one is left to wonder when pavlova become an age-old Maori dish.

CINEMA

Embassy Cinemas (Map p626; ☎ 03-442 9994; info 03-442 9990; www.embassymovies.co.nz; 11 the Mall; adult/child/student $13/6.50/9) Mainly a Hollywood blockbuster line-up, spiced up with Kiwi productions now and again. Shows before 5pm on weekdays are cheaper.

Shopping

With lots of stores in a small area, Queenstown is a good place to shop for souvenirs and gifts. It's also got its fair share of boutiques; a brief wander is likely to unearth some unusual and lovely goods. And, of course, there are lots of shops specialising in outdoor and adventure gear; prices are relatively competitive. Begin your shopping spree along the Mall, Shotover St and Beach St.

CLOTHING

Goddess (Map p626; ☎ 03-442 6696; 18 the Mall) Kiwis are funkier than we thought. Goddess stocks original designer clothing for women with everything from hats to frocks to accessories. It's very hip and has mainly party wear.

Out There Clothing (Map p626; ☎ 03-441 3029; 27 Beach St) A fairly new NZ label with functional clothing that leaves you looking outdoorsy *and* stylish. Who'd of thought? The logo is either an angel or a bat – depends on your mood.

Hopscotch (Map p626; ☎ 03-442 8153; 19 Beach St) If you forgot the kids' snowsuits or weren't prepared for just how cold it can get in the mountains, Hopscotch has the goods to keep them cosy.

OUTDOOR GEAR

Alpine Sports (Map p626; ☎ 03-442 7099; 28 Shotover St) Long-standing outdoor outfitters with plenty of gear to get you out camping, hiking, skiing or climbing.

Kathmandu (Map p626; ☎ 03-409 0880; 45 Beach St) A well-known but not particularly exciting NZ chain. If you're in need of outdoor gear, its regular sales bring some good bargains to town. And the quality is tops.

SOUVENIRS, GIFTS & MUSIC

Vesta (Map p626; ☎ 03-442 5687; cnr Marine Pde & Earl St) In total contrast to its historic surroundings within Williams Cottage, this shop has a fantastic collection of contemporary housewares, jewellery, gift cards, baby clothes, perfumes and accessories. With few exceptions, everything is crafted in NZ. It's a shopping experience.

Gallery Oceanic (Map p626; ☎ 03-442 6076; 43b Beach St) Some beautiful and unusual jewellery, tie clips and framed photographs of local scenery, as well as a few unique items like a paua-shell curtain. You'll also find hand-blown glass and functional pottery. And its all Kiwi made.

Gift Centre (Map p626; ☎ 03-442 8528; Upper Beach St) Touted as the Jade and Paua Superstore, this shop is jam-packed with handcrafted souvenirs, made from jade, paua, glass and local wood. Not sure what to take home for mum? Shop here.

Play It Again (Map p626; ☎ 03-442 8940; O'Connells Shopping Centre, Beach St) If your music collection needs some freshening up, you'll find a good range of CDs here.

Wine Deli (Map p626; ☎ 03-442 4482; 40 Shotover St) You'll find lots of local Otago wines here as well as a small deli. But let's be honest: the real draw is the divine De Spa chocolate.

For even more wine choices, head to **Central Otago Wine Experience** (Map p626; ☎ 03-409 2226; www.winetastes.com; 14 Beach St).

Getting There & Away

AIR

Direct daily flights are offered by **Air New Zealand** (Map p626; ☎ 0800 737 000, 03-441 1900; www.airnz.co.nz; 8 Church St) between Queenstown and Christchurch (from $150), Christchurch (from $100) with connections to other major centres like Wellington. **Qantas** (☎ 0800 808 767, 03-379 6504; www.qantas.co.nz) also has direct flights to Christchurch (from $100), with connections to Auckland and Rotorua.

BUS

You can book seats for **InterCity** (Map p626; ☎ 03-442 8238; www.intercitycoach.co.nz) trips in the Queenstown visitor information centre. It offers daily bus services from Queenstown to Christchurch ($65), Te Anau ($45), Milford Sound ($70), Dunedin ($40) and Invercargill ($50), plus a daily West Coast service to the glaciers ($95) via Wanaka ($30) and Haast Pass.

'Alternative' bus tours, such as Kiwi Experience, Magic Bus or the Flying Kiwi, also go up the West Coast to Nelson; see p729.

The **Bottom Bus** (www.bottombus.co.nz) does a loop service around the south of the South Island (see p683). Book tickets at the **Info & Track Centre** (Map p626; 03-442 9708; 37 Shotover St).

Endless shuttle buses can also be booked at the Queenstown visitor info centre. Shuttles charge around $20 or $25 to Wanaka, $30 to Dunedin, $30 to Te Anau and $45 to Christchurch. Providers:

Atomic Shuttles (03-322 8883; www.atomictravel .co.nz) Travels to Christchurch, Dunedin, Te Anau and Invercargill.

Catch-a-Bus (03-479 9960) Heads to Dunedin.

Southern Link Shuttles (03-358 8355; www .southernlinkcoaches.co.nz) Services to Dunedin, Christchurch and Wanaka.

Wanaka Connexions (03-443 9122; www.wanaka connexions.co.nz) Offers regular services to Wanaka.

TRAMPERS' & SKIERS' TRANSPORT

Both the **Info & Track Centre** (Map p626; 03-442 9708; www.infotrack.co.nz; 37 Shotover St) and **Kiwi Discovery** (Map p626; 0800 505 504, 03-442 7340; www .kiwidiscovery.com; 37 Camp St) can arrange transport to the tracks. **Backpacker Express** (Map p626; 03-442 9939; www.glenorchyinfocentre.co.nz; 2 0ban St) runs to and from the Routeburn, Greenstone, Caples and Rees-Dart Tracks, all via Glenorchy. It costs $15 per ride (so $15 to Glenorchy and another $15 to the Routeburn trai head) or $20 if you don't prebook.

Bus services between Queenstown and Milford Sound via Te Anau can be used for track transport. See p664 for information on the tramper-servicing company TrackNet.

If you're looking for a lift to the ski slopes, you can catch a return shuttle to Coronet Peak or the Remarkables for about $25 and to Cardrona and Treble Cone for around $40. The following will all give you a lift. Most offer transport and lift deals and kids' rates:

Gravity Action (Map p626; 03-442 5277; 13 Shotover St)

Info & Track Centre (Map p626; 03-442 9708; www .infotrack.co.nz; 37 Shotover St) Travels to Cardrona only.

Kiwi Discovery (Map p626; 0800 505 504, 03-442 7340; www.kiwidiscovery.com; 37 Camp St)

Snowrental (Map p626; 03-442 4187; Camp St)

Getting Around

TO/FROM THE AIRPORT

Queenstown Airport (Map p623; 03-442 3505; www .queenstownairport.co.nz; Frankton) is 8km east of town. **Super Shuttle** (0800 748 8853, 03-442 3639; www.supershuttle.co.nz) picks up and drops off in Queenstown (from $8). The **Shopper Bus** (03-442 6647) runs to the airport ($5) hourly from 8.15am to 11.15pm. **Alpine Taxis** (03-442 6666) or **Queenstown Taxis** (03-442 7788) charge around $20.

PUBLIC TRANSPORT

The **Shopper Bus** (03-442 6647) has services to Fernhill and Frankton accommodation ($4).

ARROWTOWN

pop 1700

Excessively quaint Arrowtown sprang up in the 1860s following the discovery of gold in the Arrow River. Today the town retains more than 60 of its original wooden and stone buildings, and has pretty, tree-lined avenues and a contemporary artsy side. With the gold panning done and dusted, the town now depends heavily on tourism, but some find its historic slant a little too contrived. Only a half-hour drive from Queenstown, it's a popular day-trip destination, yet remains a quieter and cheaper place to base yourself.

The helpful **Arrowtown visitor information centre** (03-442 1824; www.arrowtown.com; 49 Buckingham St; 8.30am-7pm) shares its premises (and phone line) with the **Lake District Museum & Gallery** (www.museumqueenstown.com; adult/child $5/50c; 8.30am-5pm), which has exhibits on the region's early history and gold-rush era. Younger visitors might enjoy the Museum Fun Pack ($5) which includes activity sheets, museum treasure hunts, stickers and a few flecks of gold.

Arrowtown has the best example of a gold-era **Chinese settlement** (admission by gold coin donation; 24hr) in NZ. Interpretive signs explain the lives of Chinese 'diggers' during and after the gold rush, while several restored huts fill out the picture. Subjected to much racism, the Chinese often had little choice but to rework old tailings rather than seek new claims, searching for fine gold missed by earlier miners. The Chinese settlement is off Buckingham St.

If you feel yourself succumbing to gold fever, you can try your luck **gold panning** on the Arrow River. Rent pans from the visitor information centre ($5 to $15) and head to the northern edge of town. This is also a good spot for a picnic and there are trail heads for local **walks** nearby. Pick up *Arrowtown Walks* ($1) from the visitor information centre; you'll find routes and history on walks to Macetown (seven hours) and **Tobins Track** (one hour). Also pick up *Historic Buildings of Arrowtown* ($3) for self-guided walks in the township.

Arrowtown Golf Course (☎ 03-442 1719; www .arrowtown.nzgolf.net; green fees $40, club hire $20) is picturesque and challenging, with narrow defiles and rock obstacles. Fancy-pants golfers can head to the Sir Bob Charles–designed championship course at **Millbrook** (☎ 03-441 7010; www.millbrook.co.nz; Malaghans Rd;

green fees $85-125, club hire $40), surrounded by mountain scenery.

Sleeping

Arrowtown has some comfortable accommodation options to keep midrange travellers happy. Folks on a tighter budget have few pickings. Try **Poplar Lodge** (☎ 03-442 1466; www.poplarlodge.co.nz; 4 Merioneth St; s/d55/70) or **Riverdown Guesthouse** (☎ 03-409 8499; 7 Bedford St; s/d 45/55; ☒ closed May-Oct), two small but popular backpacker haunts.

Arrowtown Holiday Park (☎ 03-442 1876; 11 Suffolk St; unpowered/powered sites per 2 people $20/21, d $45-80) An array of cabins on well-trimmed lawns and camping in an open field, surrounded by magnificent mountain views.

New Orleans Hotel (☎ 03-442 1745; neworleans hotel@xtra.co.nz; 27 Buckingham St; d $70-95) It's exterior looks straight out of the Wild West, however rooms are disappointingly average. Nevertheless, newly refurbished units overlook the river and are good value for money.

Viking Lodge (☎ 03-442 1765; www.vikinglodge.co .nz; 21 Inverness Cres; d $90-125; ☒) These A-frame

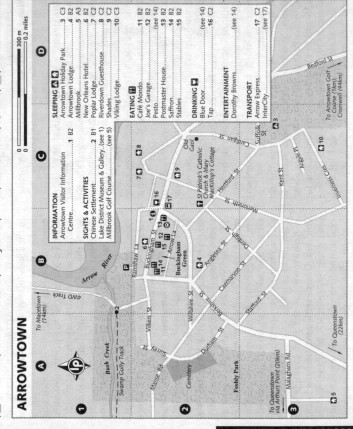

units are older but comfortable and very family-friendly. Kids will be chuffed with the outdoor pool, a playground and a loft to call their bedroom. Affable owners are bursting with local knowledge. Winter and weekly rates are lower.

Shades (☎ 03-442 1613; www.shadesofarrowtown .co.nz; cnr Buckingham & Merioneth Sts; d $100-140) The bungalow-style cottages on a grassy lawn are very well maintained. The newer suites are homiest; choose from studios, one-bedrooms or family units.

Arrowtown Lodge (☎ 0800 258 802, 03-442 1101; www.arrowtownlodge.co.nz; 7 Anglesea St; d $185) Each of these four rooms has a unique shape, lots of light and a patio with views to the hills. From the outside they look like old-fashioned cottages; inside they're cosy and modern. Owners are very friendly and breakfast is included.

Millbrook (☎ 0800 800 604, 03-441 7000; www.mill brook.co.nz; Malaghans Rd; d $300-510; 🖵) Just outside Arrowtown, this enormous resort is a town unto itself. You can cocoon yourself in plush accommodation with a top health spa, champion golf course and decent restaurants close at hand. Expect gorgeous views but not much character.

Eating

For its size, Arrowtown has an excellent choice of unique eateries offering some mighty tasty fare. You'll certainly get more joy from your soup bowl than your gold pan.

Joe's Garage (☎ 03-442 1116; Arrow Lane; mains $10; ☽ breakfast & lunch) This casual, friendly upstairs diner has an extremely popular deck. It's not big but keeps the crowds happy with hugely stuffed baguettes, *panini* and equally filling breakfasts. The coffee is excellent, too.

Café Mondo (☎ 03-442 0227; Ballarat Arcade, Buckingham St; breakfast $15-15, lunch & dinner $10-25; ☽ breakfast & lunch daily, dinner Wed-Sun; 🖵) Located in a courtyard, this relaxed place has plants, couches and a pleasant atmosphere. Popular for its excellent breakfasts and scrumptious baking, it's a great place to fill up at or just have coffee and a light bite. It's fully licensed and there's a great kids' menu.

Pesto (☎ 03-442 0885; 18 Buckingham St; mains $17-20; ☽ dinner) Down a short alley, this candlelit, benches-and-booths restaurant serves Italian food with a contemporary slant. Dig into asparagus risotto, mussel fettuccine or pizzas with telling names like the Gamekeeper, Happy Hippie or Taj Mahal. It's all fantastico.

Postmaster House (☎ 03-442 0991; cnr Buckingham & Wiltshire Sts; mains $35; ☽ dinner) You can guess the origin of this early-1900s villa. All creams, beiges and blacks, it's like stepping into a black-and-white photograph, brightened up with pictures of local scenery. Fancy (and award-winning) dinners should give your tastebuds an adventure, and there's a seven-course degustation menu with matched wines ($140).

Saffron (☎ 03-442 0131; 18 Buckingham St; lunch $10-28, dinner $26-45; ☽ lunch & dinner) Classy and chic (for Arrowtown). Sit yourself down in a high-backed leather chair and dine on fine food, such as Bendigo pheasant with chestnut stuffing or steamed blue cod with ginger, shiitake and shallots. The curries are popular, as is the dessert wine.

Stables (☎ 03-442 1818; 28 Buckingham St; lunch $13-25, dinner $20-32; ☽ lunch & dinner) Courtyard tables set next to a grassy square offer a great spot for lunch (try the caramelised pear, rocket and blue-cheese salad) or step inside the 1860s stone building for an atmospheric, intimate dinner (such as mint-infused lamb shank). The original guests here were the horses of patrons at the New Orleans Hotel.

Drinking & Entertainment

Blue Door (☎ 03-442 0415; 18 Buckingham St) Low ceilings, stone-layered walls and candlelight make this an intimate place for a pint.

Tap (☎ 03-442 1860; 51 Buckingham St) Like most Arrowtown buildings, the Tap dates back to the gold rush. Inside you'll find wines, a pool table, pub grub and – you guessed it – golden liquid on tap.

Dorothy Browns (☎ 03-442 1968; www.dorothy browns.com; Ballarat Arcade, Buckingham St; adult/child/ student $15/5/10) A theatre, bar and bookshop all rolled into one, this is as good a place to pick up some great reading material as it is to see new and classic films. Buy a tub of gourmet ice cream, a glass of mulled wine or a coffee and head into the cinema. It's down an alley and upstairs.

Getting There & Away

From Queenstown, the **Double-Decker Bus Tour** (☎ 03-441 4471; adult/child $35/15) does a three-hour round trip to Arrowtown twice daily.

Arrow Express (☎ 03-442 1900; www.arrowtownbus.co.nz) has three services daily (adult/child $10/6, return $18/10) stopping opposite the museum in Arrowtown and on Camp St in Queenstown.

InterCity (☎ 03-442 8238; www.intercitycoach.co.nz) buses running to Dunedin or Christchurch can stop at Arrowtown (opposite the museum) for prebooked passengers.

AROUND ARROWTOWN

Fourteen kilometres north of Arrowtown lies **Macetown**, a ghost town reached via a long, unimproved and flood-prone road (the original miners' wagon track), which crosses the Arrow River more than 25 times. Four-hour trips are made from Queenstown by 4WD vehicle, with gold panning included. The main operator is **Nomad Safaris** (☎ 03-442 6699; www.nomadsafaris.co.nz; adult/child from $130/65), which picks up from Arrowtown.

GLENORCHY

pop 215

Set in dazzlingly gorgeous surroundings, there's not much to tiny Glenorchy. Home to a number of adventure-activity operators and the trail heads for some excellent walks, it's a peaceful place to call home for those tempted by the outdoors. Glenorchy lies at the head of Lake Wakatipu, a scenic 40-minute (68km) drive northwest from Queenstown.

The **DOC visitor information centre** (☎ 03-442 9937; glenorchyvc@doc.govt.nz; cnr Mull & Oban Sts; ☼ 8.30am-4pm Nov-May) has the latest walking-track conditions and hut tickets; get camping gear and supplies in Queenstown and, in winter, buy hut passes at **Glenorchy visitor information centre** (☎ 0800 109 939, 03-441 0303; www.glenorchyinfocentre.co.nz; Oban St). Located in the General Store as you enter town, this place is well stocked with activities information.

There is a petrol station in Glenorchy but you'd be wise to fill up before you leave Queenstown.

Activities

Almost all organised activities offer shuttles to and from Queenstown for a small surcharge.

WALKING & SCENIC DRIVING

The DOC leaflet *Glenorchy Walkway* (free) details an easy waterside walk around the

outskirts of town that's pretty but not thrilling. If you're after something slightly more demanding, pick up *Great Wilderness Walks* (free) from the visitor information centre. It's got walks ranging from two hours to two days, and taking in Routeburn Valley, Lake Sylvan, Dart River and Lake Rere (a walk much gushed about by travellers). For track snacks or meals, be sure to stock up on groceries in Queenstown.

Those with sturdy wheels can explore the superb valleys north of Glenorchy. **Paradise** lies 15km northwest of town, just before the start of the Dart Track. Keep your expectations low: Paradise is just a paddock, but the gravel road there runs through beautiful farmland surrounded by majestic mountains. You can also explore the Rees Valley or take the road to Routeburn, which goes via the Dart River Bridge. Near the start of the Routeburn Track, in Mt Aspiring National Park, is a day hut and the short **Double Barrel** and **Lake Sylvan** walks.

If you'd rather be a passenger, visit Rees Valley with **Mountainland Rovers** (☎ 0800 246 494, 03-441 1323; www.mountainlandrovers.co.nz; 3½hr 4WD trip $140/60), which runs 4WD tours into the remote wilderness. It also picks up from Queenstown.

JETBOATING & KAYAKING

Dart River Safaris (☎ 0800 327 853, 03-442 9992; www.dartriver.co.nz; Mull St; adult/child $180/90) journeys by jetboat into the heart of the glorious Dart River wilderness, followed by a 4WD trip down a back road to Paradise. The round trip from Glenorchy takes three hours. Or try the 75-minute jetboat ride up the Dart, with a river descent in an inflatable three-seater canoe called a '**funyak**' (www.funyaks.co.nz; adult/child $255/195); from Glenorchy it's seven hours return.

Dart Wilderness Adventures (☎ 0800 109 939, 03-442 9939; www.glenorchyinfocentre.co.nz; Oban St; adult/child $160/80) also jetboats along the Dart River from Glenorchy, giving a three-hour, 70km round trip that includes historical commentary, a nature walk and a barbecue lunch. Shuttles are available from Queenstown.

OTHER ACTIVITIES

An extreme way to take in the local scenery is from a 45-second freefall, 3600m up. **Vertical Descent** (☎ 03-409 0363; www.verticaldescent.co.nz; 2700/3600m $250/300) gives you the heart-stopping chance to jump out of plane and soar into Glenorchy. Book at the Glenorchy visitor information centre.

You can also take in the views from horseback. **Dart Stables** (☎ 0800 474 3464, 03-442 5688; www.dartstables.com; Coll St) offers a two-hour ride ($85), a full-day hoof ($160) or an overnight trek with a sleep over in Paradise ($380). **High Country Horses** (☎ 03-442 9915; www.high-country-horse.co.nz) also runs two-hour rides ($95), full-day rides ($200) and overnighters ($525).

Sleeping & Eating

Glenorchy Holiday Park (☎ 03-442 7171; www.glen orchyinfocentre.co.nz; 2 Oban St; unpowered/powered sites per 2 people $18/20, cabins $32-80) Set up camp in a field surrounded by basic cabins, for which you need to BYO everything. Out front is a small shop and the handy Glenorchy visitor information centre.

Glenorchy Hotel & Backpackers (☎ 03-442 9902; relax@glenorchynz.com; Mull St; dm $20, d $75-100) Attached to a pub, yellow rooms here are surprisingly homey. The backpacker unit is bright and basic and a popular base for returning trampers.

Routeburn Farm Cottage (Map p623; ☎ 03-442 9901; elfinbay@queenstown.co.nz; Routeburn Rd; d $85) The rural Routeburn Farm is 6km from the start of the Routeburn Track, 21km from Glenorchy. The comfortable three-bedroom self-contained cottage is often let out to farm hands so reservations are essential.

Mt Earnslaw Motels (Map p623; ☎ 03-442 6993; www.earns law.bizland.com; Mull St; d $100) This cute row of units is older from the outside but redone inside, creating cosy, well-priced rooms with big, comfy recliners, a small kitchen and an enormous bed.

Glen-Roydon Lodge (Map p623; ☎ 03-442 9968; www.glen roydon.com; Argyle St; c $110) Upstairs rooms at this alpine lodge have wood-beamed ceilings, view-filled balconies and private (though separate) en suites. There's a grassy lawn to relax on, as well as in-house dining and friendly hosts.

Kinloch Lodge (Map p623; ☎ 03-442 4900; www.kin lochlodge.co.nz; Kinloch Rd; dm/d $28/70, d heritage r $165-185; 🖵) Across Lake Wakatipu from Glenorchy, this excellent retreat is a great place to unwind or prepare for a tramp. Rooms in the bunkhouse are comfy, with an outdoor hot tub in which to soak up the starlight. The 19th-century Heritage Rooms are small but plusher. A café, bar and ex-

cellent restaurant (mains $15) are on site. Kinloch is a 26km drive from Glenorchy; you can organise a five-minute boat ride ($5) to Glenorchy and track transfers.

Blanket Bay (Map p623; ☎ 03-442 9442; www.blan ketbay.com; Glenorchy Rd; r $1290-2390; 🖵 🌐) Excessive/discreet world-class resort that's a home away from home to the rich and famous. With a stunning view, this alpine lodge is all native timber and local schist stone, and plush rooms have loads of privacy.

Glenorchy Café (☎ 03-442 9958; Mull St; meals $7-15; 🕒 breakfast & lunch year-round, dinner Oct-May) Funky music, happy paintings and tables spilling out onto the lawn make this a popular spot to dine on hearty soups, sandwiches and all-day breakfasts. There's a small bar that comes to life in the evening and cats that purr all day long.

Getting There & Away

With sweeping vistas and gem-coloured water views, the sealed Glenorchy to Queenstown Rd is wonderfully scenic. Its constant hills are a killer for cyclists. Pick up the Queenstown to Glenorchy Road leaflet from the Queenstown visitor information centre for points of interest along the way.

Between November and April, **Backpacker Express** (☎ 03-442 9939; www.glenorchyinfocentre.co nz; 2 Oban St), based at the Glenorchy visitor information centre, travels this road daily, continuing on (or with connections) to the Routeburn, Rees-Dart, Greenstone and Caples Tracks. Each segment costs $15, with a $5 surcharge if you don't prebook. In winter, you can arrange similar transport for a minimum of three people.

LAKE WAKATIPU REGION TRAMPS

The mountainous region at the northern head of Lake Wakatipu has some gorgeous, remote scenery, best viewed while tramping along the famous Routeburn and lesser-known Greenstone, Caples, and Rees-Dart Tracks. For shorter tracks, see the DOC brochure Lake Wakatipu Walks and Trails ($1). Glenorchy is a convenient base for all these tramps.

Routeburn Walk Ltd (☎ 03-442 8200; www.route burn.co.nz) has a three-day guided walk on the Routeburn ($950/1090 low/high season); a six-day 'Grand Traverse' ($1330/1480), combining walks on the Routeburn and Greenstone Tracks; and a one-day 'Routeburn

ROUTEBURN, GREENSTONE & CAPLES TRACKS

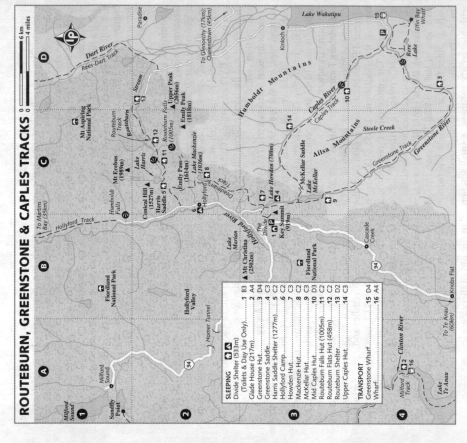

SLEEPING
Divide Shelter (533m) (Toilets & Day Use Only)......	1 B3
Glade House (217m)......	2 A4
Greenstone Hut......	3 D4
Greenstone Saddle......	4 C3
Harris Saddle Shelter (1277m)......	5 C2
Hollyford Camp......	6 C2
Howden Hut......	7 C3
Mackenzie Hut......	8 C2
McKellar Hut......	9 C3
Mid Caples Hut......	10 D3
Routeburn Falls Hut (1005m)......	11 C2
Routeburn Flats Hut (458m)......	12 D2
Routeburn Shelter......	13 D2
Upper Caples Hut......	14 C3

TRANSPORT
Greenstone Wharf......	15 D4
Wharf......	16 A4

Encounter' ($130), which is available from mid-October to May. Prices include return transport, accommodation and all meals.

Track Information

For details of accommodation, transport to and from all trail heads and DOC visitor information centres, see Queenstown (p623), Glenorchy (p642) and Te Anau (p658).

DOC staff advise on maps and sell hut and Great Walks passes; before setting out, it's essential that you contact them for up-to-date track conditions. It's also advised to book your intentions but be sure to let DOC know when you return. For more details on all these tracks see Lonely Planet's *Tramping in New Zealand*.

Routeburn Track

Passing through a huge variety of landscapes and affording fantastic views, the three- to four-day Routeburn Track is one of the most popular rainforest/subalpine tracks in NZ. Increased pressure on the track has necessitated the introduction of a booking system; reservations are required throughout the main season (October to April), either through DOC visitor information centres or by emailing greatwalksbooking@doc.govt.nz. The **Great Walks huts pass** (per night adult/child $40/20) allows you to stay at Routeburn Flats Hut, Routeburn Falls Hut, Mackenzie Hut and Howden Hut; various 'family' passes are also available. A **camping pass** (per night adult/

child$15/7.50) allows you to pitch a tent only at Routeburn Flats and Lake Mackenzie.

Outside the main season, passes are still required (huts cost $10/5 per adult/child per night; camping costs $5/2.50 per adult/child). Note that the Routeburn Track is often closed by snow in winter and stretches of the track are very exposed and dangerous in bad weather; always check conditions with DOC.

There are car parks at the Divide and Glenorchy ends of the Routeburn; they're unattended, so don't leave valuables in your car.

The track can be started from either end. Many people travelling from Queenstown try to reach the Divide in time to catch the bus to Milford and connect with a cruise on the sound. En route, you'll take in breathtaking views from Harris Saddle and the top of nearby Conical Hill from where you can see waves breaking at Martins Bay. When you feel like you've reached the top of the world, you're likely to be at Key Summit, with a panoramic view of Hollyford Valley and the Eglinton and Greenstone River valleys.

Estimated walking times:

Route	Time
Routeburn Shelter to Flats Hut	3hr
Flats Hut to Falls Hut	1-1½hr
Falls Hut to Mackenzie Hut	4½-6hr
Mackenzie Hut to Howden Hut	3-4hr
Howden Hut to the Divide	1-1½hr

Greenstone & Caples Tracks

Following meandering rivers through lush, peaceful valleys, these two tracks form a loop that many trampers stretch out into a moderate four- or five-day tramp. Basic huts en route are Mid Caples, Upper Caples, McKellar and Greenstone (all $10 per person per night). You can camp (free) but not on private land; check with DOC for where not to pitch your tent. Both tracks meet up with the Routeburn Track; you can either follow its tail end to the Divide or (if you've prebooked) pursue it back to Glenorchy.

From McKellar Hut you can walk two or three hours to Howden Hut on the Routeburn Track (you'll need to book this hut from October to April), which is an hour from the Divide.

Access to the Greenstone and Caples tracks is from Greenstone Wharf; nearby you'll find unattended parking. The road from Kinloch to Greenstone Wharf is unsealed and rough; in summer, **Backpacker Express** (03-442 9939) usually runs a boat across the lake from Glenorchy.

Estimated walking times:

Route	Time
Greenstone Wharf to Mid Caples Hut	3hr
Mid Caples Hut to Upper Caples Hut	2-3hr
Upper Caples Hut to McKellar Hut	5-8hr
McKellar Hut to Greenstone Hut	5-7hr
Greenstone Hut to Greenstone Wharf	4-6hr

Rees-Dart Track

This is a difficult, demanding four- to five-day circular route from the head of Lake Wakatipu, taking you through valleys and over an alpine pass, with the possibility of a side trip to the Dart Glacier if you're suitably equipped and experienced. Access by vehicle is possible as far as Muddy Creek on the Rees side, from where it's two hours to 25-Mile Hut.

Park your car at Muddy Creek or arrange transport with Queenstown's **Info & Track Centre** (Map p626; 03-442 9708; www.infotrack.co.nz; 37 Shotover St). Most people go up the Rees track first and come back down the Dart. The three basic DOC huts (Shelter Rock, Daleys Flat and the brand new Dart) cost $10 per person.

Estimated walking times:

Route	Time
Muddy Creek to Shelter Rock Hut	6hr
Shelter Rock Hut to Dart Hut	5-7hr
Dart Hut to Daleys Flat Hut	6-8hr
Daleys Flat Hut to Paradise	6-8hr

WANAKA REGION

With overgrown valleys, unspoiled rivers and tumbling glaciers, the Wanaka region is crowned with the colossal Mt Aspiring (Tititea), the highest peak outside the Mt Cook region. If you enter this area from the north via Haast Pass, you'll encounter the region's centrepiece lakes, Wanaka and Hawea, a grand freshwater pairing wedged among some awesome hills and cliffs. If you arrive from the south, via Cardrona, you'll take in stunning valley views and mountain vistas. While the Wanaka region, and particularly the activity-filled town of Wanaka itself, is making it onto the itineraries of more and more travellers, it remains a quieter neighbour to overambitious Queenstown. And the gorgeous Mt Aspiring National Park lets you wander even further into the remote beyond.

WANAKA

pop 3500

Beautiful scenery, nearby tramping and skiing opportunities, and a growing list of adrenaline-inducing activities have turned the lakeside town of Wanaka into a year-round tourist destination. Many travellers

come here as an alternative to hyped-up Queenstown and, while some locals fear Wanaka is following too closely in that 'big city's' footsteps, it manages to retain its relaxed, small-town feel. Take note: Wanaka wakes up in a big way for New Year.

Wanaka is situated just over 100km northeast of Queenstown via Cromwell, and is located at the southern end of Lake Wanaka. It's the gateway to Mt Aspiring National Park and to the Treble Cone, Cardrona, Harris Mountains and Pisa Range Ski Areas.

Information

Lake Wanaka visitor information centre (☎ 03-443 1233; www.lakewanaka.co.nz; ☼ 8.30am–5pm), off

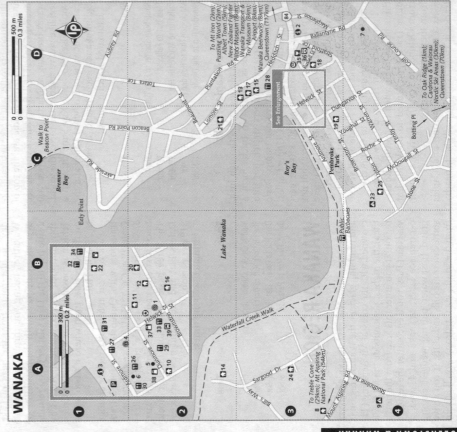

WANAKA

Ardmore St, is in a conspicuous log cabin on the waterfront. In an A-framed building on the edge of town, **DOC Wanaka visitor information centre** (☎ 03-443 7660; Ardmore St; ☒8am-4.45pm Mon-Fri year-round, 9.30am-4.45pm Sat May-Oct, 8am-4.45pm Sat & Sun Nov-Apr) is the place to inquire about all walks and tramps. You'll also find a small **museum** (admission free) on Wanaka wildlife, geology and plants to watch for while you're tramping.

Wanakaweb (☎ 03-443 7429; 1st fl, 3 Helwick St) is a very funky place to get online, with a notice board loaded with skis and cars for sale. Alternatively, email from **Bits & Bytes** (☎ 03-443 7073; 48 Helwick St). Both are open late.

Sights

More of a scenic and activity-minded place, Wanaka isn't brimming with conventional sights. Nevertheless, there's enough to keep you busy on a rainy day.

For a bit of the bizarre, visit **Puzzling World** (☎ 03-443 7489; www.puzzlingworld.com; adult/child $10/7; ☒8am-5.30pm) with its 3-D 'Great Maze' that's more difficult than you'd imagine. There are lots of illusional treats to keep kids (and adults) bewildered. It's en route to Cromwell, 2km from town.

New Zealand Fighter Pilots Museum (☎ 03-443 7010; www.nzfpm.co.nz; Wanaka Airport; adult/child/family $8/4/20; ☒9am-4pm Feb-Dec, 9am-6pm Jan) is dedicated to NZ combat pilots and the aircraft they flew, and has a well-preserved collection of Hawker Hurricanes, de Havilland Vampires and the odd-sounding Chipmunk.

The museum is due to move into a bigger new building in 2007 with an interactive theatre and kids' area.

For something a little more light-hearted, visit the neighbouring **Wanaka Transport & Toy Museum** (☎ 03-443 8765; SH6; adult/child/family $6/2/15; ☒8.30am-5pm), the end result of one man's obsessive collecting that will make your attic seem remarkably uncluttered. Among the 30,000 items, watch for a Cadillac Coupe de Ville, a mysteriously acquired MiG jet fighter and toys that bring nostalgic moments for just about everyone.

If this all sounds a little too dry, head to **Wanaka Beerworks** (☎ 03-443 1865; www.wanakabeerworks.co.nz; SH6; ☒9.30am-6pm, tours 2pm) where you can taste this small brewery's three carefully brewed, award-winning products – a malt lager, a dark ale and the tasty, bitter 'Brewski' – for a total cost of around $5.

Activities

Wide valleys, alpine meadows, more than 100 glaciers and sheer mountains make **Mt Aspiring National Park** an outdoor enthusiast's paradise where many of the following activities are possible. Protected as a national park in 1964 and later included in the Southwest New Zealand (Te Wahipounamu) World Heritage Area, the park now blankets more than 3500 sq km along the Southern Alps, from the Haast River in the north to its border with Fiordland National Park in the south.

INFORMATION
Bits & Bytes.....................1 B2
DOC Wanaka Visitor Information Centre.....................2 D3
Lake Wanaka Visitor Information Centre.....................3 A1
Wanakaweb.....................4 A1

SIGHTS & ACTIVITIES
Good Sports.....................5 A2
Green Toad.....................6 A2
Lakeland Adventures.....................(see 3)
Wanaka Golf Club.....................7 D4

SLEEPING
Altamont Lodge.....................8 A3
Aspiring Campervan Park.....................9 A4
Aspiring Lodge.....................10 A2
Bay View Motel.....................(see 9)
Bella Vista Motel.....................11 B2
Brook Vale.....................12 B2
Drury Hill Motel.....................13 B2
Edgewater Resort.....................14 A2
Lakeside Serviced Apartments.....................15 D3
Matterhorn South.....................16 B2
Moorings.....................17 D3
Mountain View Backpackers.....................18 D3
Purple Cow Backpackers.....................19 C3
Te Wanaka Lodge.....................20 B2
Wanaka Bakpaka.....................21 C2
Wanaka Hotel.....................22 B1
Wanaka Lakeview Holiday Park.....................23 C4
Wanaka Stonehouse.....................24 A3
Wanaka YHA.....................25 C4

EATING
Bombay Palace.....................26 A2
Café Gusto.....................(see 28)
Kai Whakapai.....................27 D3
Missy's Kitchen.....................28 D3
New World Supermarket.....................29 A2
Reef.....................30 A2
Relishes.....................31 A1
Soulfood Store & Cafe.....................32 B1
Thai Toko.....................33 A2
Tuatara Pizza.....................34 B1

DRINKING
Barluga.....................35 D3
Red Rock.....................(see 34)
Shooters.....................(see 30)

ENTERTAINMENT
Cinema Paradiso.....................36 D3

SHOPPING
Gallery Thirty Three.....................37 D3
Mainly Tramping.....................38 A2
Originz.....................(see 26)
True.....................(see 26)

TRANSPORT
Alpine Coachlines.....................(see 5)
Edgewater Adventures.....................(see 39)
InterCity.....................39 A2

WALKING

While the southern end of Mt Aspiring National Park is well trafficked by visitors and includes popular tramps such as the Routeburn Track (p644), there are great short walks and more demanding, multi-day tramps in the Matukituki Valley, close to Wanaka; see the DOC leaflet *Matukituki Valley Tracks* ($1). The dramatic **Rob Roy Valley Track** (three to four hours return) takes in glaciers, waterfalls and a swing bridge, yet is a fairly easy route. The **West Matukituki Valley** track goes on to Aspiring Hut (four to five hours return), a scenic, more difficult walk over mostly grassy flats. For overnight or multiday tramps, continue up the valley to **Liverpool Hut** for great views of Mt Aspiring, or over the very difficult **Cascade Saddle** to link up with the Rees-Dart Track (p645), north of Glenorchy.

Many of these walks are subject to snow and avalanches and can be treacherous. Be sure to register intentions and seek advice from DOC in Wanaka before heading off. You'll also need to purchase hut passes. Tracks are reached from Raspberry Creek at the end of Mt Aspiring Rd, 54km from Wanaka; for details of shuttle services, see p653.

For walks closer to town, pick up the DOC brochure *Wanaka Walks and Trails* ($1). This includes the easy lakeside stroll to **Eely Point** (20 minutes) and on to **Beacon Point** (30 minutes), as well as the **Waterfall Creek Walk** (one hour return), which heads east along the lakeshore.

The fairly gentle climb to the top of **Mt Iron** (549m, 1½ hours return) reveals panoramic views. Fit folks after a view can undertake the taxing, winding 8km tramp up **Mt Roy** (1578m, five to six hours return), starting 6km from Wanaka on the Mt Aspiring Rd. The high track crosses private land and is closed from October to mid-November for the lambing season. From Roys Peak, you can continue along the **Skyline Track** (five to six hours) to Cardrona Rd, 10km south of Wanaka. Don't do this one in winter; low cloud eliminates views and makes it treacherous.

The following outfits offer guided walking tours around Wanaka, many into Mt Aspiring National Park:

Alpine Coachlines (☎ 03-443 7966; www.alpinecoachlines.co.nz; full day $180; ☯ Oct-Jun) Full-day walks to Rob Roy Glacier.

Alpinism & Ski Wanaka (☎ 03-442 6593; www.alpinismski.co.nz; half/full day $100/185) Day walks.
Mount Aspiring Express (☎ 03-443 8422; www.adventure.net.nz; half/full day from $85/195) Day, half-day and multiday trips.
Wild Walks (☎ 03-442 4476; www.wildwalks.co.nz; 3 days from $690) Multiday tramps.

JETBOATING, RAFTING & RIVER SLEDGING

Lakeland Adventures (☎ 03-443 7495; www.lakelandadventures.co.nz; adult/child $75/35), at the Lake Wanaka visitor information centre, does one-hour jetboat trips that zip across the lake and up the Clutha River at scream-inducing speeds. **Pioneer Rafting** (☎ 03-443 1246; ecoraft@xtra.co.nz; half-day rafts per adult/child $115/75, full-day $165/95) has ecorafting on the high-volume Clutha with grade II to III rapids, gold panning, bird-watching and boiling up the billy for tea. If you'd prefer to get right in the water, try white-water sledging with **Frogz Have More Fun** (☎ 03-443 9130; www.frogz.co.nz; from $135; ☯ Oct-May) where you steer a hydrospeed sledge through the currents. Trips range from relaxed on the Clutha to challenging on the Kawarau.

CANYONING & KAYAKING

Adventurous souls will love canyoning, a summertime-only activity staged by **Deep Canyon** (☎ 03-443 7922; www.deepcanyon.co.nz; trips from $195; ☯ mid-Nov-Apr) and involving climbing, swimming and waterfall-abseiling through confined, steep and wild gorges. Transport to the canyon, lunch, instruction and equipment are included.

Alpine Kayak Guides (☎ 03-443 9023; www.alpinekayaks.co.nz; half day $125; ☯ Nov-May) paddles down the Hawea, Clutha and Matukituki Rivers and runs float trips (adult/child $75/55) that are great for kids. You can also hire kayaks from **Lakeland Adventures** (☎ 03-443 7495; www.lakelandadventures.co.nz) for $10 per hour.

SKYDIVING & PARAGLIDING

Skydive Lake Wanaka (☎ 03-443 7207; www.skydivenz.com; adult $250-400) does jumps from 2700m, 3600m and a bracing 4500m; the latter lets you soar for a full 60 seconds. **Wanaka Paragliding** (☎ 03-443 9193; www.wanakaparagliding.co.nz; adult $170) will take you on tandem flights at 800m from Treble Cone, while **Lucky Montana's Flying Circus** (☎ 0800 247 287; adult $170) tow-launches you by boat before releasing you at 700m, from where you can opt for a scenic soar or an aerobatic adventure. It also offers paragliding trips off mountains ($170), some of which are reached via helicopter ($285).

ROCK CLIMBING & MOUNTAINEERING

Mt Aspiring National Park is a fave haunt of mountaineers and alpine-climbing companies. **Aspiring Guides** (☎ 03-443 9422; www.aspiringguides.com 5 days from $2300), **Adventure Consultants** (☎ 03-443 8711; www.adventure.co.nz; 4 days from $1350) and **Alpinism & Ski** (☎ 03-443 6593; www.alpinismski.co.nz; 6 days from $2200) all offer beginners courses and multiday guided ascents of Mts Aspiring, Tasman and Tutoko.

Wanaka Rock Climbing & Abseil Adventures (☎ 03-443 6411; www.wanakarock.co.nz) has an introductory one-day rock-climbing course ($185), a half-day abseiling intro ($95), and bouldering and multipitch climbs for the experienced.

MOUNTAIN BIKING

Many tracks and trails in the region are open to cyclists. DOC produces *Mountain-Biking Around Wanaka* (50c), describing mountain-bike rides ranging from 2km (the steep Mt Iron track) to 20km (West Matukituki Valley). For high-altitude, guided mountain biking, contact **Alpine & Heli Mountain Biking** (☎ 03-443 8943; www.mountainbiking.co.nz), which does helibiking trips at Treble Cone and Mt Pisa ($320), and alpine biking tours of the Pisa Range (half/full day $150/195). You can also rent bikes from **Lakeland Adventures** (☎ 03-443 7495; www.lakelandadventures.co.nz; half/full day $25/35).

FISHING

Lakes Wanaka and Hawea (16km away) have excellent trout fishing. Numerous guides are based in Wanaka, including **Hatch** (☎ 03-443 8446; www.hatchfishing.co.nz; full day $330/530) and **Lakeland Adventures** (☎ 03-443 7495; www.lakelandadventures.co.nz; 3 adults $250). Alternatively, you can hire a motorised dinghy (per hour/day $20/100) and rod ($20 per day) from Lakeland Adventures and pick up a 24-hour/weekly licence ($20/35). The governmental Fish & Game department puts out *Lake Wanaka* (free), a handy brochure of what and where to catch; pick it up at the Lake Wanaka visitor information centre.

OTHER ACTIVITIES

For skiers after untouched powder and exclusive views, there are a number of companies offering heliskiing in the area (p84). More easily reached slopes include **Treble Cone** (p81), **Cardrona** (p82), **Wairau Snow Farm** (for cross-country skiing, p82). For gear hire, head to **Green Toad** (☎ 03-443 4315; 6 Pembroke Mall, Ardmore St).

Wanaka Golf Club (☎ 03-443 7888; www.wanakagolf.co.nz; Ballantyne Rd; green fees $50, club hire from $15) has a view-filled 18-hole course with a bar and café to lounge in afterwards.

Good Sports (☎ 03-443 7966; www.good-sports.co.nz Dunmore St) hires out a vast array of sports equipment, including bikes, camping and hiking accessories, fishing rods and watersports gear.

Tours

AERIAL SIGHTSEEING

The following companies are all based at Wanaka Airport. Book trips through the Lake Wanaka visitor information centre.

Aspiring Air (☎ 0800 100 943, 03-443 7943; www.nz-flights.com) Has a range of scenic flights, including a 50-minute flight over Mt Aspiring (adult/child $185/115), a Milford Sound fly-past and landing ($340/200) and a buzz around Mt Cook and the glaciers ($365/225).

Wanaka Flightseeing (☎ 0800 105 105, 03-443 8787; www.flightseeing.co.nz) Offers similar flights at similar prices, with an early bird discount of $35 for early-morning departures.

All the following chopper outfits offer 20-minute flights around Wanaka for about $150 and 45-minute tours of Mt Aspiring and the glaciers for about $390.

Alpine Helicopters (☎ 03-443 4000; www.alpineheli.co.nz)

Aspiring Helicopters (☎ 03-443 1454; www.aspiringhelicopters.co.nz)

Wanaka Helicopters (☎ 03-443 1085; www.heliflights.co.nz)

OTHER TOURS

The following can all be booked from the Lake Wanaka visitor information centre.

Lake Wanaka Cruises (☎ 03-443 1230; www.wanakacruises.co.nz; from $55) Does similar tours to Lakeland Adventures aboard a catamaran, with overnight options.

Lakeland Adventures (☎ 03-443 7495; www.lakelandadventures.co.nz) Has one-hour lake cruises (adult/child $50/25) and a three-hour trip with a guided walk on Mou Waho ($90/45).

NZ Natural (☎ 0800 696 868; www.nzntours.co.nz) Runs wine tours (adult/child $125/65) as well as day tours around town (adult/child $125/65).

Wanaka Sightseeing (☎ 03-443 1855; www.wanaka sightseeing.co.nz; full-day winery tour $280; Lord of the Rings tour from $280) Will bus you out on various Central Otago tours, including a full-day winery excursion with lunch provided. For lingering Lord of the Rings fans, it offers exhaustive tours of filming sights where you can dress up like a hobbit and hang out with Ian Brodie, author-cum-guru of the The Lord of the Rings: Location Guidebook.

Festivals & Events

Wanaka Fest (www.wanakafest.co.nz) is held mid-September and is a five-day event that has the feel of a small-town fair. Street parades, live music, unusual competitions (such as build-a-thons) and kiddies' dance troupes bring Wanakians out in droves.

Every second Easter (even-numbered years), Wanaka hosts the incredibly popular **Warbirds Over Wanaka** (☎ 0800 496 920, 03-443 8619; www.warbirdsoverwanaka.com; Wanaka Airport; 3-day admission adult/child $125/25, first day only $35/10, each of last 2 days $55/10), a huge international air show that can attract more than 100,000 people to the town.

Sleeping

Much like Queenstown, Wanaka is bursting with hostels and luxury accommodation but doesn't have a great deal to offer those in the middle. We challenge you to help us pinpoint some dazzling midrange options!

BUDGET
Hostels & Lodges

Matterhorn South (☎ 03-443 1119; www.matterhorn south.co.nz; 56 Brownston St; dm $22, d $50-85; □) The dorm building here is relaxed and extremely homey. Many rooms open onto decks and there's a kitchen and lounge fitted with window seats and peppered with cushions. Rooms in the lodge next door are nothing special but are comfortable and very well priced. There's a separate country-style, communal kitchen.

Wanaka YHA (☎ 03-443 7405; yha.wanaka@yha.org.nz; 181 Upton St; sites per 2 people $20, dm d $25/55; □) Friendly and cosy, this relatively small YHA has a number of small buildings connected by boardwalks. The open-plan kitchen and lounge is very comfortable and holds lots of games, videos and local info. Rooms are spick-and-span clean, and there's good storage for skis, too.

Altamont Lodge (☎ 03-443 8864; altamontlodge@xtra.co.nz; 121 Mt Aspiring Rd; s/d $40/60) This excellent, laid-back lodge has timber rooms whose walls are a little thin but which are nevertheless popular with skiers. The lodge offers a great lounge with a big fire, tennis courts, a spa pool, drying room and ski storage. It often gets booked out by big groups so reserve ahead. Linen costs $5 per bed, per stay.

Purple Cow Backpackers (☎ 03-443 1880; www.purplecow.co.nz; 94 Brownston St; dm/d $22/65; □) Warmed by a wood stove, the lounge at this ever-popular hostel holds commanding views of the lake and mountains beyond. Dorms are rather drab with six bunks and older en suites. Doubles are much more pleasant; try for Room 2 with its awesome views. At the time of research, the clientele had outgrown the kitchen and plans were underway to expand. Other niceties include outdoor patios, a pool table, a TV lounge and bike hire.

Other hostels worth giving a bell:

Mountain View Backpackers (☎ 03-443 9050; www.mtnview.co.nz; 7 Russell St; dm/d $23/30) A characterful house with a relaxed lounge, big lawn and warm, comfortable rooms.

Wanaka Bakpaka (☎ 03-443 7837; wanaka bakpaka@xtra.co.nz; 117 Lakeside Rd; dm/d $23/60) A short, lakeside walk out of town but popular and busy; this place was up for sale at the time of research.

Camping

Aspiring Campervan Park (☎ 0800 229 8439, 03-443 6603; www.campervanpark.co.nz; Studholme Rd; sites per 2 people $35) Gravel sites surrounded by trimmed grass, trees and pretty views. Great facilities include a barbecue area, lounge, kitchen and spa. Campervans only; no tents welcome.

Wanaka Lakeview Holiday Park (☎ 03-443 7883; www.wanakalakeview.kiwiholidayparks.com; 212 Brownston St; sites per 2 people/cabins $24/38/70) Open your tent flaps to views of the lake. The park also has a playground, a scattering of trees and lots of space to set up camp. Rooms range from basic cabins to en suite flats.

MIDRANGE

Brook Vale (☎ 0800 438 333, 03-443 8333; www.brookvale.co.nz; 35 Brownston St; d $95-125; □) These 10 older, self-contained studio and family units are an excellent option. The rooms have got a few new, classy touches and patios opening onto a grassy lawn complete with a babbling creek. You'll also find a barbecue and spa.

TOP END

Te Wanaka Lodge (☎ 0800 926 252, 03-443 9224; www .tewanaka.co.nz; 23 Brownston St; d $190-210; ▢) With the look and feel of an alpine chalet, this intimate lodge is both classy and homey. With two cosy lounges, a small house bar, lots of books, a rock garden and a hot tub, you'll be tempted to skip the slopes and sprawl here. Upper-level rooms have slightly higher ceilings and better views than their ground-floor siblings.

Wanaka Stonehouse (☎ 03-443 1933; www.wanaka stonehouse.co.nz; 21 Sargood Dr; d $350-400) Yes, it's fake Tudor. But it's nice fake Tudor. Lots of timber and big beams give this wonderful B&B an earthy feel. Each room is individually designed with sitting nooks and solid furniture; the king room has a claw-foot tub. A cosy library and big lounge with an open fire make this place a home away from home. And then there are the thick robes, spa and fancy chocolates….

Edgewater Resort (☎ 0800 108 311, 03-443 8311; www.edgewater.co.nz; Sargood Dr; d from $150) At first glance it's an '80s eyesore but step inside for

Aspiring Lodge (☎ 03-443 7816; www.aspiringlodge .co.nz; cnr Dunmore & Dungarvon Sts; d $120-130) Older but well-maintained motel units with a patio or balcony, a small kitchenette and lots of light. The owners are friendly, and it's located a short stroll to the main drag or the lakefront.

Some slightly less inspired midrange options include the following:

Bella Vista Motel (☎ 0800 201 420, 03-443 6066; www.bellavistamotels.co.nz; 2 Dunmore St; d from $100-115) A link in the chain but well located with good facilities.

Bay View Motel (☎ 0800 229 843, 03-443 7766; www.bayviewwanaka.co.nz; Studholme Rd; r $140-155; ▢) Decks, views and spacious one-bedroom units run by friendly folks. Spa and mountain bikes on site.

Durry Hill Motel (☎ 03-443 8139; Lakeside Rd; d $120-150) Enormous, newish two-bedroom units with no character but set next to the lake.

Wanaka Hotel (☎ 03-443 7826; wanakahotel@xtra .co.nz; 71 Ardmore St; d $105; ▢) Old-school, slightly stale rooms take you back to the '60s, but rooms have a deck with views and in-house movies.

rooms renovated in classic design with lots of windows and light. Decks and patios are view-friendly and the peaceful lawns hold quiet ponds. Look online for deals.

Wanaka has lots more high-end accommodation. Try the following:

Moorings (☎ 03-443 8479; www.themoorings.co.nz; Lakeside Rd; d $175) Overlooking the lake, these apartments are stylish and new but slightly cramped.

Lakeside Serviced Apartments (☎ 0800 002 211, 03-443 0188; www.lakesidewanaka.co.nz; 9 Lakeside Rd; r $300-800; ☒) Luxury! This is a plush affair with a heated pool to bob in.

Eating

No matter what your budget, you'll have no problem finding worthwhile places to brandish cutlery in Wanaka.

RESTAURANTS

Thai Toko (☎ 03-443 4061; 43 Helwick St; mains $12-20; ☒ dinner) Very classy with silk-covered booth seats, carved wooden panels and a central fireplace. The Thai half includes curries, sweet-and-sours and lip-smacking soups; the Toko half is sushi, sashimi, tempura and noodles.

Reef (☎ 03-443 1188; 145 Ardmore St; mains $20-25; ☒ lunch & dinner) With multilevel seating so that everyone gets a view, this bright restaurant lives up to its name with nautical décor and excellent seafood. There's a kids' menu and an excellent $10 express lunch deal. In warmer months, dine on the sheltered deck.

Missy's Kitchen (☎ 03-443 5099; Lvl 1, 80 Ardmore St; mains $15-30) An upstairs, classy joint with a chilled-out atmosphere, top views and an oft-changing menu that has included goat's cheese and beetroot ravioli, feijoa-vodka-cured salmon, and confit of pork belly.

Relishes (☎ 03-443 9018; 99 Ardmore St; mains $17-27; ☒ breakfast, lunch & dinner) A café by day, this place whips out the white tablecloths at night and serves creative Asian-inspired dishes alongside a good wine list. Locals rave about it.

Bombay Palace (☎ 03-443 6086; Lvl 1, Pembroke Mall, Ardmore St; mains $ 6-20; ☒ dinner) Eat large, satisfying portions of Indian food from wooden booths with views, or take them away for a spicy, lakefront picnic. Wednesday nights equal curry specials.

Tuatara Pizza (☎ 03-443 8186; 72 Ardmore St; pizzas $17-30; ☒ dinner) Interesting gourmet pizzas (along with more standard, recognisable options) are served within this casual, yellow restaurant.

CAFÉS & QUICK EATS

Soulfood Store & Cafe (☎ 03-443 7885; 74 Ardmore St; mains $7-10; ☺ breakfast & lunch) This tiny, slightly rough-around-the-edges café serves up delicious food that will please your tastebuds and your wholesome side. Soups, omelettes, pastas and pizza, along with excellent smoothies and some mouth-watering baked goods, are served by some of Wanaka's friendliest staff. You'll also find a decently priced organic food store where you can stock up your picnic basket.

Kai Whakapai (☎ 03-443 7795; cnr Helwick & Ardmore Sts; meals $10-30; ☺ breakfast, lunch & dinner) Towering eggs Benedict and fabulous, homemade croissants for brekkie, salads and creative pastas for lunch, and curries and daily fish specials for dinner. It's no wonder that this little two-storied café is continually jammed with patrons spilling out onto the pavement.

Café Gusto (☎ 03-443 6639; 1 Lakeside Dr; mains $7-18; ☺ breakfast & lunch) Buttermilk hotcakes and sweet-corn fritters will fill you up at breakfast, while hot smoked Aoraki salmon salad will tempt you at lunch. With red walls and warm lighting, this stylish place is tucked in the bottom of a lakeside complex.

Hula Café (☎ 03-443 9220; Pembroke Mall, Ardmore St; meals $10-15; ☺ breakfast & lunch) Funky and orange, with high ceilings that make it nearly as tall as it is wide, this trendy café serves popular pizzas, salads, quiche and all-day breakfasts.

SELF-CATERING

The **New World supermarket** (Dunmore St; ☺ 8am-8pm) is well stocked for self-caterers.

Drinking & Entertainment

Barluga (☎ 03-442 5400; Post Office Lane) Cocooned beneath a petrol station, off Ardmore St, this small, very stylish bar has leather chairs to sink into while you enjoy cocktails and cheese platters. Funky music, fashionable wallpaper and walls of wine cabinets act like a beacon to Wanaka's chicest residents. It ain't cheap but it's loaded with atmosphere.

Red Rock (☎ 03-443 5545; Lvl 1, 68 Ardmore St) With terracotta-red walls, decks to admire the moon from and weekend DJs from around 10pm, this is a friendly place to shuffle your feet or get cosy in cowhide-covered booths.

Shooters (☎ 03-443 4345; 145 Ardmore St) Picnic tables outside and an alcohol-flushed, barn-sized tavern inside, this is the place to be... or at least drink at. There are sofas by a fire, pool tables and a dance floor where DJs usually spin something from 10pm on Friday and Saturday (admission free).

Cinema Paradiso (☎ 03-443 1505; www.paradiso.net.nz; 1 Ardmore St; adult/child $12/8) One of Wanaka's biggest attractions. Sit yourself down in an old lounge chair or sofa in this eccentric cinema. Doors open one hour before film screenings, giving you time to order your coffees, homemade ice cream or savouries (such as blue cheese artichoke dip). Dinner can also be preordered and is served during intermission. Shows include blockbusters as well as artsy flicks and, now and again, live performances.

Shopping

For its size, Wanaka has a good number of interesting shops. Have a wander through the malls and along the main drags (Ardmore and Helwick Sts) and see what you can unearth.

Originz (☎ 03-443 4488; Pembroke Mall, off Ardmore St) This fantastic gift shop is filled with local crafts including cards, soaps, clocks, candles, paintings and pottery. You'll find unique, reasonably priced objects. Either the tacky stuff is all sold out or they just don't stock it.

True (☎ 03-443 8297; Pembroke Mall, off Ardmore St) If winter has snuck up on you, come here for custom-made down jackets that are soft, cosy and even classy. Buy off the rack ($420) or pick your colours, zips and style ($450). It also carries some great casual clothes from small NZ labels.

Gallery Thirty Three (☎ 03-443 4330; 33 Helwick St) Exhibitions of pottery, glass and jewellery. It's pricey, but even if you're not planning to buy, it's an interesting look at what local artists are up to.

Mainly Tramping (☎ 03-443 2888; Spencer House, Dunmore St) Upstairs in the mall, this shop is filled with clothes, boots, tents, skis and everything else you need to get out and about.

Good Sports (☎ 03-443 7966; www.good-sports.co.nz; Dunmore St) Similar items to hire and buy.

Getting There & Away

AIR

Air New Zealand (☎ 0800 737 000; www.airnz.co.nz) has daily flights between Wanaka and Christchurch ($115). **Aspiring Air** (☎ 0800 100 943, 03-443 7943; www.aspiringair.com) has daily flights between Queenstown and Wanaka ($140, 20 minutes) in small, twin-engine planes.

BUS

The bus stop for **InterCity** (☎ 03-443 7885; www.intercitycoach.co.nz) is on Brownston St, near the corner of Helwick St. Wanaka receives daily buses from Queenstown ($30), which motor on to Franz Josef ($75) via Haast Pass. You can also catch a daily bus to Christchurch (from $65) via Mt Cook ($50), and a daily bus to Cromwell ($10) to connect to Dunedin ($70).

The town is well serviced by door-to-door shuttles, nearly all of which can be booked at the Lake Wanaka visitor information centre. **Southern Link** (☎ 03-443 9122) and **Atomic Shuttles** (☎ 03-322 8883) all service Christchurch ($50 to $60) and Queenstown ($20 to $30). Wanaka Connexions and **Catch-a-Bus** (☎ 03-479 9960) head to Dunedin ($40 to $50); Atomic Shuttles goes to Fox ($40) and Franz Josef ($45) Glaciers and on to Greymouth ($75); and Wanaka Connexions and Atomic Shuttles service Te Anau ($45). The majority pick up at or near the Lake Wanaka visitor information centre; inquire when you book.

Getting Around

Alpine Coachlines (☎ 03-443 7966; www.good-sports
.co.nz; Dunmore St), operating from Good Sports, meets and greets flights at Wanaka Airport ($10). Or you can cover the 8km via **WanaCab** (☎ 03-443 5555) or **Wanaka Taxis** (☎ 03-443 7999).

Alpine Coachlines and **Edgewater Adventures** (☎ 0800 731 731; www.adventure.net.nz; 59 Brownston St) have daily services to the ski fields of Cardrona, Snow Farm and Treble Cone (adult/child return $30/20). **Flying Bus** (☎ 03-443 9193) does door-to-door trips to the slopes ($25).

Alpine Coachlines and **Mount Aspiring Express** (☎ 03-443 8422; www.adventure.net.nz) have daily services to Raspberry Creek at Mt Aspiring National Park ($25, return $45) from October to May. Mount Aspiring Ex-

press will also drop you at the Mt Roy trail head ($5).

MAKARORA

pop 40

When you reach Makarora you've left the West Coast behind and entered Otago, however the township still has a West Coast frontier feel. Visit the **DOC visitor information centre** (☎ 03-443 8365; www.makarora.co.nz; SH6; ⊗ 8am-4.45pm daily Nov-Apr, 8am-4.45pm Mon-Fri May-Oct) for conditions and routes before undertaking any regional tramps.

Activities

WALKING

Short walks in this secluded area include the **Bridal Track** (1½ hours one way, 5km), from the top of Haast Pass to Davis Flat, and the **Blue Pools Walk** (30 minutes return), where you can see huge rainbow trout.

Longer tramps go through magnificent countryside but shouldn't be undertaken lightly. Alpine conditions, flooding and the possibility of avalanches mean you must be well prepared; consult with DOC before heading off. DOC's *Tramping Guide to the Makarora Region* ($5) is a good investment.

The three-day **Gillespie Pass** tramp goes via the Young, Siberia and Wilkin Rivers; this is a high pass with avalanche danger. With a jetboat ride down the Wilkin to complete it, this rates alongside the Milford Track as one of the great tramps. The **Wilkin Valley Track** heads off from Kerin Forks Hut, at the top of the Wilkin River, and on to Top Forks Hut and the picturesque **Lakes Diana, Lucidus** and **Castalia** (one hour, 1½ hours and three to four hours respectively from Top Forks Hut).

Jetboats go to Kerin Forks, and a service goes across the Young River mouth when the Makarora floods; inquire at **Wilkin River Jets** (☎ 0800 538 945, 03-443 8351; www.wilkinriverjets.co.nz; adult/child $80/37) or the visitor information centre.

OTHER ACTIVITIES

The lush Siberia Valley was named by an (obviously short-sighted) early traveller, who as an encore called some nearby peaks Dreadful and Awful. One of NZ's great outdoor adventures, the **Siberia Experience** (☎ 0800 345 666, 03-443 8666; www.siberiaexperience.co.nz; adult $240) is a thrill-seeking extravaganza combining a half-hour scenic small-plane flight, a three-hour bush walk through a remote mountain valley and a half-hour jetboat trip down the Wilkin and Makarora Rivers in Mt Aspiring National Park. To avoid getting lost, keep your eye on the markers as you descend from Siberia Valley.

Wilkin River Jets does a superb 50km, one-hour jetboating trip into Mt Aspiring National Park, following the Makarora and Wilkin Rivers. It's a fair bit cheaper than Queenstown options, and also offers trips that include helicopter rides or tramping.

Southern Alps Air (☎ 0800 345 666, 03-443 4385; www.southernalpsair.co.nz) does trips to Mt Cook and the glaciers ($350/170) and landings at Milford Sound ($350/180).

Sleeping & Eating

Makarora Wilderness Resort (☎ 0800 800 443, 03-443 8372; www.makarora.co.nz; SH6; dm $24, d $60-125; ⌂ ⌂) Set amid forest and bush are self-contained chalets, basic cabins and

backpacker doubles and dorms. They've all got a snug, alpine feel, and the resort has a café, outdoor pool, grocery store and petrol station.

Larrivee Homestay (☎ 03-443 9177; www.larrivee homestay.co.nz; off SH6; s $80, d $120-150) Made of stone and hand-split cedar, this unusual octagonal house offers comfortable accommodation in a peaceful setting. Full breakfast is included in the house; continental breakfast is provided in the two-bedroom self-contained cottage. Dinners can also be arranged. Larrivee is situated down a side road between DOC and the tourist centre.

The nearest DOC camping grounds are on SH6 at **Cameron Flat**, 10km north of Makarora, and at **Boundary Creek Reserve**, 18km south of Makarora on the shores of Lake Wanaka; both charge $5/2.50 per adult/child.

Getting There & Away

InterCity (☎ 03-442 8238; www.intercitycoach.co.nz) has one northbound bus (to the glaciers)

STORM IN A D-CUP

Travelling around NZ, you'll more than likely encounter stretches of roadside fence strung with various (and often vast) assortments of shoes. Created by passers-by, shoe fences aren't entirely unusual; similar practices exist in the US (you'll find shoe trees in the Midwest), Scotland and parts of Asia, and star in the Kiwi film *Price of Milk* and the American *Big Fish*. However, take Crown Range Road between Arrowtown and Wanaka and, just outside Cardrona, you'll find a slightly more flamboyant fence.

Around the turn of the latest millennium, four women strung their bras from the fence under the cover of night. Within two months, around 60 women had followed suit and these days there are more than you can count. The object of more than 100 interviews and a German documentary, and starring in photographic journals and international press, the Bra Fence (as it's now commonly known) has brought a great deal of attention to the area. Proper roadside lay-bys are planned and a shelter has been built to ease the weather's wear and tear on the flimsy garments. Radio stations have used the fence as a fundraiser for charity, donating dollars for every bra exhibited, and husbands have posted bras, requesting they be hung up in memory of deceased wives.

However, not everyone looks so light-heartedly on the fence. Ask about it at Wanaka's visitor information centre and at least one member of staff will respond with an emphatic 'vulgar'. On a number of occasions, offended vandals have cut the bras off and damaged the fence. After each incident, the media attention brought by the vandals has simply increased the flow of bestowed bras.

In April 2006, the local council declared that the fence was on public property and unlicensed. They told the farmer he could keep the fence but that the bras were an eyesore and a traffic hazard and had to go. Despite further bra burning and thieving that followed the ruling, the farmer is not stripping the fence without a fight.

A rainbow of strung-up bras blowing in the wind – it may be a rather brazen way of saying 'I was here', but then Kiwis aren't generally ones to do things by halves. If it doesn't bring you a laugh, you'll at least have to concede that it's one of the world's more unusual tourist attractions.

and one southbound bus (to Hawea, Wanaka and Queenstown) per day.

HAWEA

The small town of Hawea, 15km north of Wanaka, is mostly a collection of holiday and retiree homes, which are afforded some spectacular lake and mountain views. From **Lake Hawea** you can look across to the indomitable Corner Peak on the western shore and out to the distant Barrier Range. Separated from Lake Wanaka by a narrow isthmus called the Neck, Lake Hawea is 35km long and 410m deep, and home to trout and landlocked salmon. The lake was raised 20m in 1958 to facilitate the power stations downriver.

Lake Hawea Motor Inn (0800 429 324, 03-443 1224; www.lakehawea.co.nz; 1 Capell Ave; dm $25, d from $100) has unbeatable views across the lake and an on-site restaurant. On the lakeshore is the spacious and relatively peaceful **Lake Hawea Holiday Park** (03-443 1767; www.lake hawea.web-nz.com; SH6; sites per 2 people $20, d $35-75), a favourite of fishing and boating enthusiasts; standard cabins are nothing flash but an all-right deal.

CARDRONA

Although the sealed **Crown Range Road** from Wanaka to Queenstown via Cardrona is much shorter than the route via Cromwell, it's actually a narrow, twisting-and-turning mountain road that needs to be tackled with care, especially in poor weather. It's certainly not advisable at night. That said, this is one of the South Island's most scenic drives, with picturesque views of the lush valleys, foothills and countless snowy peaks. The road passes through tall, swaying tussock grass in the **Pisa Conservation Area**, with a number of short walking trails en route. You'll also find a number of **rest stops** to drink in the view; particularly good ones are at the Queenstown end of the road, as you switchback down towards Arrowtown. And keep your eyes open for the Bra Fence (see opposite), just outside Cardrona.

The unpretentious looking **Cardrona Hotel** (03-443 8153; www.cardronahotel.co.nz; Crown Range Rd; d $135-185) first opened its doors in 1863. Today you'll find lovingly restored, peaceful rooms with snug, country-style furnishings and patios opening onto a garden. There's also an entirely cosy and deservedly popular pub and a good **restaurant** (mains $15-20; lunch & dinner).

The hotel is located near the turn-off for the **Waiorau Snow Farm**. From December to April you can ride mountain bikes or hike along these trails; bikes can be hired for $35/45 per half/full day, plus a $10 trail-use fee for bikers, $5 for hikers. Also situated nearby is **Backcountry Saddle** (03-443 1712; backcountry.saddle.expedition@xtra.co.nz; Crown Range Rd; adult/child from $65/45), which runs horse treks through Cardrona Valley on Appaloosa horses.

Fiordland & Southland

The south of the South Island is all about scenery. Mountains are covered in lush forest and snuggle up to one another like sleeping giants. Between them plunge undisturbed fiords that harbour treasure-troves of sea life. Windswept beaches stretch lazily across a coastline that snakes into countless bays.

To the west lies Fiordland National Park, with misty peaks, glistening lakes and utter remoteness. The park is accessible by the highly prized Milford Track, which meanders its way through spellbinding landscape. It's also home to Milford and Doubtful Sounds, popular for their soaring cliffs and tranquil waters as well as for their gorgeous approaches, either by road or boat.

In Southland's eastern reaches, the peaceful, rolling hills of the Catlins sit in contradiction to the rugged coastline that they butt up against. Sleepy villages, secluded guesthouses and countless roadside attractions such as raging waterfalls and dramatic caves create a road trip for the intrepid. It's a route where one eye should always be on the water in search of visiting whales, the other on the dunes for resident penguins.

Southland is the New Zealand many of us dream of; expect to wear holes in your boots, go through countless rolls of film and capture vistas in your memory that will stay with you for a lifetime.

HIGHLIGHTS

- Kayaking between lush cliff walls at **Milford Sound** (p668)
- Exploring the side roads and natural sights in the peaceful, windswept **Catlins** (p681)
- Stretching your legs along the stunning **Milford Track** (p666) and **Kepler Track** (p660)
- Sailing through the vast, remote **Doubtful Sound** (p671)
- Watching for dolphins, whales and penguins at **Porpoise Bay** (p684)
- Being inspired by art and gardens at Invercargill's **Anderson Park Art Gallery** (p675)
- Travelling **Milford Road** (p664) with its magnificent views and maundering keas
- Wandering among 160-million-year-old petrified trees in the fossil forest at **Curio Bay** (p684)
- Soaking up some culture at Gore's impressive **Eastern Southland Gallery** (p680)

■ TELEPHONE CODE: 03   ■ www.southland.org.nz   ■ www.fiordland.org.nz

Milford Sound ★
Milford Track ★
★ Milford Road
Doubtful Sound ★
★ Kepler Track
Invercargill ★
★ Gore
★ Catlins
Porpoise Bay & Curio Bay

FIORDLAND & SOUTHLAND FACTS

Eat: Bluff oysters, breaded or raw

Drink: A bottle of Pitch Black, Wasp or IBS, all from Invercargill Brewery (p676)

Read: *Country Road & Other Poems*, Ruth Dallas' works from 1947–52, which invoke a strong sense of Southland

Listen to: *Pipin' Hot*, an album by the Invercargill Caledonian Band, NZ's oldest pipe band

Watch: *The World's Fastest Indian* (2005), the story of Burt Munroe, an Invercargillite who broke land-speed records in the 1960s with his pride and joy, a 1920s Indian motorcycle

Swim at: Porpoise Bay (p684), where you may be joined by wildlife

Festival: New Zealand Gold Guitar Awards (p681) in Gore

Tackiest tourist attraction: Paua Shell House (p679) in Bluff

Climate

Southland has a temperamental climate; you'll find that even in the height of summer, downpours are not uncommon. This is something you should resign yourself to while preparing for a cruise on one of the sounds (where the average annual rainfall is 6m), a bush walk, road trip or any other type of activity in or through the great outdoors.

The upside is that the reverse is also true; colder months can yield crisp, sunny days. One constant is that it's generally a few degrees cooler here than areas to the north.

Getting There & Around

Air New Zealand connects Invercargill with Christchurch, while Stewart Island Flights connects Invercargill with Oban.

Major bus operators shuttle to Te Anau and Invercargill from Queenstown or Dun-

edin, and some also ply the Southern Scenic Route and take in Milford Sound. These include InterCity, Topline Tours, Atomic Shuttles and Bottom Bus. Companies confining themselves more or less to Southland include TrackNet and Scenic Shuttle.

TOP ACTIVITIES

- Glide a kayak over the glistening waters of the lush Milford Sound (p668)
- Trek through the gorgeous Milford (p666), Kepler (p660) or Hump Ridge (p672) Tracks
- Watch for whales, dolphins and penguins along windswept beaches in the Catlins (p683)
- Be wowed by the unreal fossil forest at Curio Bay (p684)
- Sail through the vast scenery of Doubtful Sound (p671)

FIORDLAND

Spectacular Fiordland is a raw wilderness area sliced by numerous deeply recessed sounds that reach like crooked fingers into the Tasman Sea. Part of the Southwest New Zealand (Te Wahipounamu) World Heritage Area, it remains, for the most part, fantastically remote. Milford and Doubtful Sounds and a half a handful of urban centres receive the bulk of the region's guests. The World Heritage Area's longest-term residents are remarkable animals and plants that were once found on the ancient supercontinent of Gondwanaland (see p64).

Milford Track makes tentative inroads into the wilds, as do kayaking and boat trips along the sounds, and it's through such excursions that you come to appreciate the true immensity and beauty of Fiordland.

TE ANAU
pop 1785

Te Anau sits peacefully on the edge of NZ's second largest lake. Mainly a base for trekkers and visitors travelling to Milford Sound, it's a pleasant, small town and a good place to recharge your batteries. There's not a great deal to do or see, but lake-side strolls and cafés offer subdued treats.

Lake Te Anau was gouged out by a huge glacier, and has several arms that penetrate into the mountainous forested shore. Its deepest point is 417m and it stretches 53km long. The lake takes its name from the caves called Te Ana-au (Cave with a Current of

FIORDLAND & SOUTHLAND

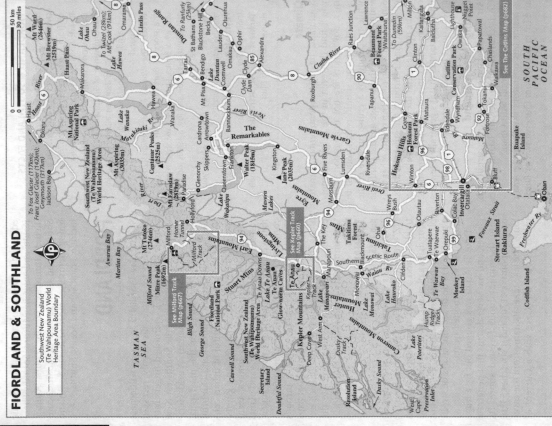

Southwest New Zealand
(Te Wahipounamu) World
Heritage Area Boundary

Swirling Water), which lie on its western shore.

Information

Te Anau's main shopping strip is referred to as 'Town Centre'. You'll find lots of information centres along Lakefront Dr and the Town Centre; when booking tours and activities, the majority will offer identical prices.

Department of Conservation (DOC) Fiordland National Park visitor information centre (☎ 03-249 7924; fiordlandvc@doc.govt.nz; Lakefront Dr; 8.30am-4.30pm May–Oct, to 6pm Nov–Apr) An excellent resource centre for the area, with museum-style exhibits including a 17-minute multimedia display ($3) on the park.

E-Stop (50 Town Centre) Coin-operated computers to get you online.

Great Walks counter (☎ 03-249 8514; greatwalksbooking@doc.govt.nz; DOC visitor information centre, Lakefront Dr; ☑ 8.30am-6pm Nov-Apr) Bookings for the Milford, Routeburn and Kepler Tracks.

Medical Centre (☎ 03-249 7007; Luxmore Dr; ☑ 24hr) When you need more than a sticking plaster.

Photocentre.com (☎ 03-249 7620; 62 Town Centre; 10 min $1) Terminals to get online and a digital-photo print kiosk.

Post Office (102 Town Centre) Find it inside the newsagency.

Te Anau visitor information centre (☎ 03-249 8900; iSite@realjourneys.co.nz; Real Journeys, Lakefront Dr; ☑ 8.30am-5.30pm) Brochures and info galore along with Milford Road conditions.

Tick-It-Centre (☎ 03-249 7505; www.airfiordland.com; 7) Town Centre) A good place to book activities and transport; it's also the InterCity bus depot and Air Fiordland's headquarters.

Sights

TE ANAU GLOW-WORM CAVES

Once present only in Maori legends, these impressive caves were rediscovered on the lake's western shore in 1948. Accessible only by boat, the 200m cave system is a magical place with waterfalls, whirlpools and a glow-worm grotto in its inner reaches. (Who'd have guessed those pretty lights are actually the larvae of fungus gnats?) **Real Journeys** (☎ 0800 656 501, 03-249 7416; Lakefront Dr; ☑ tours 2pm & 6.45pm; tours per adult/child from $50/15;

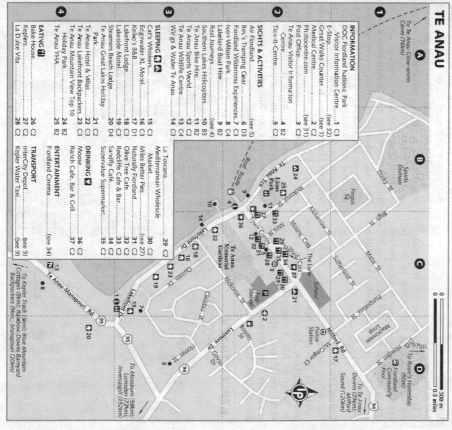

TE ANAU

INFORMATION

DOC Fiordland National Park	
Visitor Information Centre......1 C3	
E-Stop......(see 32)	
Great Walks Counter......(see 1)	
Medical Centre......2 C3	
Photocentre.com......(see 31)	
Post Office......3 C2	
Te Anau Visitor Information	
Centre......4 B2	
Tick-It-Centre......5 C2	

SIGHTS & ACTIVITIES

Air Fiordland......6 C3	
Bev's Tramping Gear......(see 5)	
Fiordland Wilderness Experiences.7 C3	
Ivon Wilson Park......8 C4	
Lakeland Boat Hire......9 B2	
Real Journeys......(see 4)	
Southern Lakes Helicopters......10 B3	
Te Anau Bike Hire......11 C2	
Te Anau Sports World......12 C3	
Te Anau Wildlife Centre......13 C4	
Wings & Water Te Anau......14 C4	

SLEEPING ☑

Cat's Whiskers......15 C2	
Edgewater XL Motel......16 C2	
Keiko's B&B......17 D1	
Lakefront Lodge......18 C3	
Lakeside Motel......19 C2	
Steamers Beach Lodge......20 D4	
Te Anau Great Lakes Holiday	
Park......21 C3	
Te Anau Hotel & Villas......22 C2	
Te Anau Lakefront Backpackers.23 C3	
Te Anau Mountain View Top 10	
Holiday Park......24 B2	
Te Anau YHA......25 B2	

EATING ☑

Bake House......26 C2	
Keplers......27 C2	
La Dolce Vita......28 C2	

La Toscana......29 C3	
Mediterranean Wholesale	
Market......30 C2	
Miles Better Pies......(see 27)	
Naturally Fiordland......31 C2	
Olive Tree Cafe......32 C3	
Redcliffe Cafe & Bar......33 C2	
Sandfly Cafe......34 C3	
Supervalue Supermarket......35 C3	

DRINKING ☑

Moose......36 C2	
Ranch Cafe, Bar & Grill......37 C2	

ENTERTAINMENT

Fiordland Cinema......(see 34)	

TRANSPORT

InterCity Depot......(see 5)	
Kepler Water Taxi......(see 9)	

plus 5pm Nov-Mar & 8.15pm Oct-mid-May) conducts 2½-hour trips to this mysterious place, reaching the heart of the caves by a walkway and a shallow boat.

TE ANAU WILDLIFE CENTRE

The DOC-run **Te Anau Wildlife Centre** (☎ 03-249 7924; Te Anau-Manapouri Rd; admission by donation; ☺ dawn-dusk) harbours a large array of native bird species, including the rare flightless takahe, NZ pigeons, tui, kaka, weka, the diminutive orange-fronted parakeet and various waterfowl. It's a boisterous group, belting out a mixed bag of song. Across the road is the landscaped **Ivon Wilson Park**, within which Lake Henry has been developed as a children's fishery.

Activities
WALKING

If you're planning to do any tramping in the area (such as the Dusky or Milford Tracks), pick up your information and brochures and register at the DOC office in Te Anau. There is no DOC office in Milford or Manapouri.

Kepler Track

This 60km circular Great Walk starts just outside Te Anau and heads west to the Kepler Mountains. Like any Fiordland track, the weather has a major impact on the walk; you should expect at least one day of rain and be prepared for *very* wet conditions (like 1m to 2m deep!). The alpine

sections of the track require a good level of fitness and may be closed in winter due to bad weather conditions; other sections are considered moderate with climbs and descents of up to 1000m and unbridged stream crossings.

During the main walking season (late October to April), advance bookings must be made by all trampers through the Te Anau DOC office. Over this period, a **Great Walks huts pass** (per night adult/child $40/20) buys you accommodation in the track's three well-maintained huts, Luxmore, Iris Burn and Moturau, each with heating and cooking facilities. A **camping pass** (per night adult/child $10/5) permits you to camp only at the designated sites at Brod Bay and adjacent to Iris Burn Hut. Outside this main season, hut passes still need to be prepurchased (per night adult/child $10/5) but no heating, cooking or radio is on offer. Off-season camping is free.

The walk can be done over four days, or three if you opt to exit at Rainbow Reach. The trail takes in the lake, rivers, gorges, glacier-carved valleys and beech forest. On the first day you reach the tree line, giving panoramic views. The alpine stretch between Luxmore and Iris Burn Huts goes along a high ridge, well above the bush and offers fantastic views when it's clear; in poor weather it can be treacherous. It's recommended that the track be done in the Luxmore–Iris Burn–Moturau direction. Estimated walking times:

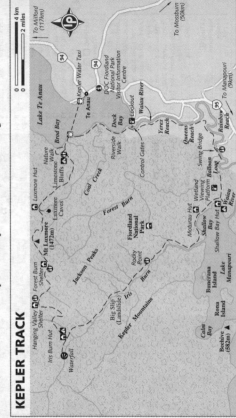

KEPLER TRACK

Route	Time
DOC Fiordland visitor information centre to control gates	50min
control gates to Brod Bay	1½hr
Brod Bay to Luxmore Hut	3½-4½hr
Luxmore Hut to Iris Burn Hut	5-6hr
Iris Burn Hut to Moturau Hut	5-6hr
Moturau Hut to Rainbow Reach	1½-2hr
Rainbow Reach to control gates	2½-3½hr

See p664 for details of services to Rainbow Reach and Brod Bay.

Short Walks

You can set out along the Kepler Track on day walks; there is no charge, but you do need to inform the DOC office of your plans. **Kepler Water Taxi** (☎ 03-249 8364; stevsaunders@xtra.co.nz; one way/return $20/35; ☒ Nov-Apr 8.30am & 9.30am, by reservation winter) will scoot you over to Brod Bay from where you can walk to Mt Luxmore? (seven to eight hours) or along the lakeshore to Te Anau (two to three hours). There are also many short walks off Milford Road (see p664).

Trips 'n 'Tramps (☎ 03-249 7081; www.milfordtours walks.co.nz; ☒ Oct-May) offers small-group guided hikes, including a Milford Track day walk (adult/child $140/90) and a 2½-hour Milford Sound cruise followed by a walk in the Hollyford Valley or along the Routeburn Track to Key Summit (adult/child $150/95). Real Journeys (p659) also runs day hikes along Milford Track (adult/child $150/95; November to April), including a cruise on Lake Te Anau.

Equipment

Make sure you're well equipped before starting out on any tracks, particularly with rain gear.

Bev's Tramping Gear (☎ 03-249 7389; 16 Homer St; ☒ 9am-noon & 6-8pm) Topographical maps for sale and tramping and camping equipment for hire at decent rates.

Te Anau Sports World (☎ 03-249 8195; Town Centre; ☒ 8.30am-9pm) Lots of (name-brand) equipment for sale or hire.

KAYAKING & JETBOATING

Kayaking in the pristine waterways of the World Heritage Area is unbeatable. **Fiordland Wilderness Experiences** (☎ 0800 200 434, 03-249 7700; www.fiordlandseakayak.co.nz; 66 Quintin Dr) runs guided day paddles on Milford Sound

(including transport to and from Te Anau), costing $125, or $95 if you meet at Milford. The company also runs trips for trampers coming off the Routeburn Track, various overnight trips, and rents out kayaks ($50 per day) for independent paddling. Rosco's Milford Sound Sea Kayaks (see p668) offers similar trips year round.

Luxmore Jet (☎ 0300 253 826, 03-249 6951; www .luxmorejet.co.nz; adult/child/family $75/40/19) sets off on a one-hour ride on Waiau River to Lake Manapouri; its bus will pick you up at your door.

OTHER ACTIVITIES

If walking is just way too slow for you, consider the **Kepler Challenge** (www.fairydown.co .nz; a December mountain run where 400 competitors race around the entire 60km loop. A shorter option is the 27km Luxmore Grunt, held at the same time.

The visitor information centre provides information on the abundance of guided trout fishing (fly, trolling or spinning). River and stream fishing takes place roughly from October to May, while lake fishing occurs year-round. You'll need to pick up a licence from the DOC visitor information centre.

From a lakeside caravan, **Lakeland Boat Hire** (☎ 03-249 8364; Te Anau Tce; per hr $10-25) rents out pedal boats, canoes, and dinghies with an outboard motor, from around December to March.

Te Anau Bike Hire (☎ 03-249 8166; 7 Mokonu St; bike hire per hr/day from $10/25; ☒ 10am-late summer) hires mountain bikes, quadricycles, baby capsules, kids' bikes and tandems. **High Ride Adventures** (☎ 03-249 8591; www.highride.co.nz; quad-bike trips $120) offers three-hour back-country trips on quad bikes, with great views over the lakes. This outfit also runs 3½-hour horseback trips along Whitestone River ($80).

Tours
AERIAL SIGHTSEEING

Flying overhead offers impressive views of the massive wilderness. Consequently, there are a number of flightseeing tours departing from Te Anau. **Wings & Water Te Anau** (Water .co.nz; Te Anau Tce) has seaplane flights trip around Te Anau area (adult/child $65/40), a 20-minute Kepler Track overfly (adult/child

$125/75) and one-hour flights over Milford Sound (adult/child $320/190). **Air Fiordland** (☎ 03-249 7505; www.airfiordland.co.nz; 70 Town Centre) offers similar flights.

Southern Lakes Helicopters (☎ 03-249 7167; www .southernlakeshelicopters.co.nz; Lakefront Dr) buzzes over Te Anau for 25 minutes ($150) and does trips over Milford, Dusky and Doubtful Sounds (from $600) and 'Triple Buzz Heli-Hike' tours ($140) on the Kepler Trail.

CRUISES

Cruises on Lake Te Anau are popular. As well as Te Anau glow-worm cave trips (p659), **Real Journeys** (☎ 0800 656 501, 03-249 7416; Lakefront Dr) runs boat transfers from November to March from Te Anau Downs to Glade Wharf, the Milford Track's starting point. You can do the trip one way (adult/child $60/15) if you're walking the track, or opt for the return cruise (adult/child $90/30).

Sinbad Cruises (☎ 03-249 7593; www.sinbadcruises .co.nz) runs a number of lake tours in the gorgeous 36ft Manuska sail-boat. Take the Discovery Cruise ($60), including an easy nature walk, or a twilight sail under the stars ($60).

Sleeping

Te Anau has plenty to offer budget travellers, and some of the midrange options have a definite top-end feel. The majority of accommodation is in easy walking distance of the centre of town.

BUDGET

Te Anau YHA (☎ 03-249 7847; yhatanau@yha.org.nz; 29 Mokonui St; dm/d $25/70; □) Exceptionally friendly, bright and modern, this large but homey hostel offers great facilities. Lounge in the hammock, barbecue in the grassy backyard, get cosy by the wood fire or check out the excellent video selection. There's a book exchange, games and laundry, and the staff are great at giving the lowdown on activities and booking them too.

Rainbow Downs Barnyard Backpackers (☎ 03-249 8006; rainbow.downs@xtra.co.nz; Rainbow Downs, 80 Mt York Rd; dm from $22, s & d $50; □) This tranquil backpackers, on a deer farm 9km south of Te Anau, has a row of comfortable log cabins with fantastic valley and mountain views. The main building has a big, open fire in its relaxed, rustic lounge, along with a functional kitchen and mezzanine with pool tables. You can store your stuff here and get a lift to the Kepler trail head.

Rosie's Homestay (☎ 03-249 8431; backpack@paradise.net.nz; 23 Tom Plato Dr; dm/d $23/50) This family welcomes you into their home for as much a cultural experience as accommodation. A short walk north of the town centre, you'll find comfortable rooms, use of the kitchen, and lake and mountain views. It's closed June and July.

Steamers Beach Lodge (☎ 0800 483 2628, 03-249 7457; www.destinationnz.com/steamers_beach_lodge .htm; 1 Te Anau-Manapouri Rd; dm/d $23/55; □) Rooms here are characterless but new and clean. The kitchen and lounge are in a steamboat-shaped (well...sort of) building with a good kitchen, lounge and sun-catching deck. It's modern but not homey.

Te Anau Lakefront Backpackers (☎ 03-249 7713; www.teanaubackpackers.co.nz; 48-50 Lakefront Dr; dm from $23, d from $55; □) It's luck of the draw in this random collection of buildings; some are sunny and relatively spacious while others are worn. It's nonetheless popular for its lakeside location, attentive staff, spa pool and barbecue area. There's a tiny shop selling essentials like Tim Tams and fresh eggs.

Te Anau Mountain View Top 10 Holiday Park (☎ 0800 249 746, 03-249 7462; www.teanautop10.co.nz; Te Anau Tce; sites per 2 people from $32, d $55-145; □) This classic holiday park has excellent facilities with small but private sites, a playground, sauna, bike hire, barbecue area and kitchen. There's also a huge array of cabins, from fancy to basic but all are well maintained. You'll also find lots of local information and efficient staff.

Te Anau Great Lakes Holiday Park (☎ 03-249 8538; www.teanaugreatlakes.co.nz; cnr Luxmore Dr & Milford Rd; sites per 2 people $25-29, d $50-170; □) This holiday park has good facilities and grassy camp sites.

MIDRANGE & TOP END

Keiko's B&B (☎ 03-249 9248; www.keikos.co.nz; 228 Milford Rd; d $120-190) Lovely cottages set within a phenomenal flower garden and run by friendly, relaxed hosts. Each plush cottage has a full en suite and privacy created by bamboo screens. Start your day with a full Kiwi or Japanese breakfast (included) and finish it in the bamboo-bordered hot tub next to a babbling fish pond. Keiko's is closed in the dead of winter; out of the peak season, you can get some amazing walk-in rates.

Lakefront Lodge (☎ 0800 525 337, 03-249 7728; www.lakefrontlodgeteanau.com; cnr Lakefront Dr & Mokonui St, low season ste $95-140, high season $120-190) With double bedroom doors and stripes and checks in reds and blues, there's something vaguely French about this classy motel. There are good kitchenettes, outside patios, lots of other niceties (such as spa baths and plunger coffee) and very friendly owners. The only drawback is that units face Mokoroa St rather than the lake.

Blue Mountain Cottages (☎ 03-249 9030; Hwy 95; cabins $250) With a double room, a twin and a pull-out sofa in the lounge, you can comfortably sleep six in these modern, very plush cabins, making them a pretty good deal. Inside are low-key colours, very tasteful décor and a full kitchen. Outside there's a barbecue on the veranda, beautiful views and a working farm. It's located 8km south of town; the very welcoming owners are likely to cut you a deal in the winter.

Lakeside Motel (☎ 0800 452 537, 03-249 7435; www.lakesideteanau.com; 36 Lakefront Dr; d $100-150) Ignore the 1980s exterior. Inside, these rooms are newly renovated and snug, if a little over-stuffed with furniture. Excellent lake views across a large lawn are the big draw.

Edgewater XL Motel (☎ 0800 433 439, 03-249 7258; edgewaterxl.motel@xtra.co.nz; 52 Lakefront Dr; d $85-120) Although it doesn't look like much from the outside, this lakeside motel is a steal. Rooms have a great 1960s look about them with big windows, lots of light, a cute kitchen and a shared veranda. It's meticulously clean.

Cat's Whiskers (☎ 03-249 8112; www.catswhiskers .co.nz; 2 Lakefront Dr; s/d $135/150) Set in a family home, this B&B is slightly flouncy by not tacky. Some rooms have lake views and all four have big en suites. The spacious family room sleeps four. A full cooked breakfast is included.

Te Anau Hotel & Villas (☎ 03-249 9700; www.te anauhotel.co.nz; Lakefront Dr; d $115-150; ▯) This site has been home to a hotel since 1890. The latest version is getting on in years but has recently been spruced up with a few modern touches, creating comfortable rooms at decent rates. Garden-view rooms just look out the back; pay the few extra dollars for lake views. Good walk-in rates are sometimes available.

Eating

RESTAURANTS & CAFÉS

Redcliffe Cafe & Bar (☎ 03-249 7431; 12 Mokonui St; mains $18-30; ☻ dinner) Looking and feeling like an old settler's cottage, this restaurant greets you with big wagon wheels on the front patio, wood stove ablazin', old photos, and mains such as wild venison, fresh fish and seafood. Desserts are fantastic: try Montieths lager ice cream or chocolate fondant with berry coulis.

Olive Tree Cafe (☎ 03-249 8496; 52 Town Centre; mains $6-18; ☻ breakfast, lunch & dinner) Tucked down an arcade, the licensed Olive Tree is warm and funky with an excellent courtyard to sip coffee in the sun. There are big brekkies such as pancakes, omelettes, muesli or eggs Benedict, and great salads, sandwiches and pastas for later in the day.

La Dulce Vita (☎ 03-249 8895; 90 Town Centre; lunch mains $8-15, dinner mains $23-45; ☻ lunch & dinner) Run by familia Lombardi, this very stylish and ultramodern restaurant has stretched its Italian menu to include many dishes with an Asian slant alongside lamb, pork and seafood platters. Even so, the pasta, antipasto and *tiramisu* aren't yet displaced.

La Toscana (☎ 03-249 7756; Town Centre; mains $10-20; ☻ dinner) Exactly what you'd expect of an Italian eatery; complete with empty wine bottles lining the shelves, cosy booths and huge portions of rich pastas and pizza. It's a long-standing favourite with locals.

Keplers (☎ 03-249 909; Town Centre; mains $22-29; ☻ dinner) A fairly standard family restaurant serving up Kiwi favourites with fries alongside more interesting options such as tandoori prawns and magic mushrooms (but not really). There's a kids' menu too.

QUICK EATS & SELF-CATERING

Sandfly Café (☎ 03-249 9529; 9 The Lane; mains $5-13; ☻ breakfast & lunch) The perfect place to linger over a coffee, all-day breakfast or yummy baking. Or you can take it out on the lawn.

Naturally Fiordland (☎ 03-249 7111; Town Centre; mains $4-9; ☻ breakfast & lunch Mon-Sat, dinner Fri & Sat; ▯) A relaxed, trendy café with a happy hippy look about it, and great salads, calzone and bagels to be scoffed with smoothies and coffee. Toddlers are welcomed with high chair and toy basket, and there are outdoor tables to catch the sun. Book your activities here and get a free coffee.

Miles Better Pies (☎ 03-249 9044; cnr Town Centre & Mokonui St; pies $4; ☺ breakfast & lunch) If you've put off trying the ubiquitous NZ pie, the star of roadside greasy spoons, this is the place to have a go. Choose from freshly made, nearly gourmet versions such as venison, Thai curry, satay chicken or apricot. There are a few outdoor tables, but the pies make a good snack for the road.

Bake House ($4; ☺ breakfast, lunch & dinner Mon-Sat; 1 Milford Cres; light meals $4; This glasshouse churns out fresh breads such as walnut, cheese, rye or multigrain. You can also stock up on cheese, sausages and desserts galore, or plunk yourself at a window seat and eat sandwiches and quiche.

Supervalue Supermarket (1 The Lane) and the **Mediterranean Wholesale Market** (cnr Town Centre & Luxmore Dr; ☺ 8.30am-5.30pm Mon-Fri, to 1.30pm Sat) are good place to stock up for home cooking, the latter having lots of bulk goods and a well-stocked cheese counter.

Drinking & Entertainment

For after-dinner drinks, Redcliffe Cafe & Bar (p663) is the relaxed, atmospheric option. For something a little more rambunctious, try **Ranch Cafe, Bar & Grill** (☎ 03-249 8801; Town centre), where Te Anau's youth slugs beer, plays pool and listens to cowboy tunes. Otherwise the cavernous **Moose** (☎ 03-249 7100; Lakefront Dr) has big-screen sports and a sunny patio.

Fiordland Cinema (☎ 03-249 8844, info line 03-249 8812; www.fiordlandcinema.co.nz; The Lane) screens slightly older flicks in comfortable surroundings, with ice cream, and wine, beer and coffee to sip during the film.

Getting There & Away

InterCity (☎ 03-249 7559; www.intercitycoach.co.nz) has daily bus services between Queenstown and Te Anau ($35) and on to Milford ($35), plus daily runs to Invercargill ($40) and to Dunedin ($45), continuing to Christchurch ($73). The InterCity depot is on Town Centre.

Topline Tours (☎ 03-249 8059; www.toplinetours.co.nz) operates a daily door-to-door shuttle between Te Anau and Queenstown, departing Te Anau at 10am and Queenstown at 2pm (adult/child $35/23). **TrackNet** (☎ 0800 483 2628, 03-249 7777; www.tracknet.net) also operates

on this route (adult/child $35/25), as well as offering trips from Te Anau to Milford (adult/child $40/27), Invercargill (adult/child $40/30) and Bluff (adult/child $50/35). **Catch-A-Bus** (☎ 03-249 8900) leaves the InterCity depot for Dunedin ($45) at 1pm and from Dunedin for Te Anau at 8.15am; bookings are essential.

Fill up with petrol in Te Anau before setting off for Milford Sound. Chains should be carried in winter and can be hired from most service stations.

TRAMPERS' TRANSPORT

A shuttle operated by **TrackNet** (☎ 0800 483 2628, 03-249 7777; www.tracknet.net) has daily shuttles to the Kepler, Routeburn, Milford and Hollyford Tracks from October to April. The shuttle to Milford passes the Divide at the start/end of the Routeburn and Greenstone Tracks.

The **Kepler Water Taxi** (☎ 03-249 8364) runs regularly to Brod Bay ($20) in summer. **Wings & Water Te Anau** (Waterwings Airways; ☎ 03-249 7405) provides transport to Supper Cove ($240 per person, minimum two passengers) for Dusky Sound trampers.

TE ANAU TO MILFORD

If you don't have the opportunity to hike into Fiordland's wilderness, the 119km road from Te Anau to Milford will give you a small taste of its vastness and beauty. Even if you don't do a cruise at the other end, this is a top road trip for sheer scenic wonder. If travelling in summer, head out superearly (8am) or later in the morning (11am) to avoid tour-bus congestion. The trip takes two hours if you drive straight through but take time to explore the many viewpoints and nature walks en route. A few are listed in the following section, but with a copy of *The Milford Road World Heritage Highway Guide* (free from Te Anau's visitor information centre) you're well equipped to discover your own. Make sure your car is filled with petrol, check road conditions and, in winter, carry chains and obey avalanche warnings.

The first part of the road meanders through rolling farmland atop the lateral moraine of the glacier that gouged out Lake Te Anau. The road passes **Te Anau Downs** after 29km and heads towards the entrance of Fiordland National Park, passing patches of beech (red, silver and mountain), alluvial flats and meadows.

There are lookout points en route, including **McKay Creek** (at 51km), which looks over Eglinton Valley, and **Mirror Lakes** (at 58km), for shimmering views on clear days. **Knobs Flat** (at 63km) has an unmanned visitor centre with toilets, a telephone and water; if the road is too treacherous, there are details on how to arrange for a bus to pick you up.

At the 77km mark is the area referred to as O Tapara, or more commonly as **Cascade Creek**. O Tapara is the original name of nearby Lake Gunn, and was a stopover for Maori parties heading to Anita Bay in search of greenstone. A walking track (45 minutes) passes through tall red beech forest that shelters a variety of bird life. Paradise ducks and NZ scaup are often afloat on the lake. In Cascade Creek you may see long-tail bats, which are NZ's only native land mammals.

The vegetation alters significantly on the approach to the **Divide**, with prominent ribbonwood and fuchsia. The Divide is the lowest east-west pass in the Southern Alps, and there's a shelter here for walkers either finishing or starting the Routeburn, Greenstone or Caples Tracks. A walk along the Routeburn to **Key Summit** (two hours return) offers tarns and patches of alpine bog. Three river systems (the Hollyford, the Greenstone/Clutha and the Eglinton/Waiau) start from the sides of this summit and radiate to the island's west, east and south coasts.

From the Divide, the road falls into the beech forest of the **Hollyford Valley** and there's an interesting turn-off to **Gunns Camp & Museum** along an unsealed road. At the end is a walk to the high **Humboldt Falls** (30 minutes return) and the start of the Hollyford Track (right).

Back on the route to Milford, the road climbs to the **Homer Tunnel**, 101km from Te Anau and preceded by a spectacular, high-walled, ice-carved amphitheatre. Construction on the tunnel began in 1935, providing much-needed employment during the Depression, and wasn't finished until 1953. Rough-hewn, the 1207m tunnel has a steep east-west gradient and emerges into the spectacular **Cleddau Canyon** on its Milford side. At the western end, you're likely to see plenty of cheeky kea on the roadside; this brown and green parrot lures inquis-

tive tourists from their cars and then chases them back in.

About 10km before Milford, the **Chasm Walk** (20 minutes return and accessible by wheel-chair) is well worth a stop. The forest-cloaked Cleddau River plunges through beautifully eroded boulders in a narrow chasm, creating deep falls and a natural rock bridge. From here, watch for views of **Mt Tutoko** (2746m), Fiordland's highest peak, which are glimpsed above the beech forest just before Milford.

Hollyford Track

This track follows the broad Hollyford Valley through rainforest, passing lakes and views of the Darren Mountains and with seals and penguins often greeting hikers on their arrival to the Tasman Sea. Its low altitude means it's open year-round. While graded as a moderate hike, its 56km-length means four days of walking one way. The track also suffers frequent, extreme flash floods, that quite literally leave trekkers swimming for their lives and waiting it out en route for several days until the trail becomes passable. DOC officials are not stationed along the track; it's therefore imperative that you check with DOC in Te Anau for the latest track and weather conditions and for detailed maps. From Long Reef at Martins Bay, the trail becomes the ill-defined **Pyke–Big Bayroute**, to be followed by experienced, equipped hikers only.

Hollyford Track Guided Walks (☎ 0800 832 226, 03-442 3760; www.hollyfordtrack.com; 3-day trip adult/child $1860/1400) offers trips that include a flight to Milford Sound, a jetboat trip on Lake McKerrow and avoidance of the most difficult part of the walk. **TrackNet** (☎ 0800 483 2628, 03-249 7777; www.greatwalksnz.com) has shuttles from October to May from Te Anau to the Hollyford Rd turn-off ($30) and the start of the trail ($40) or you can charter **Air Fiordland** (☎ 03-249 7505; www.airfiordland.com) to fly between Te Anau and Martins Bay ($500) or between Te Anau and Martins Bay ($830). The charge is per load; four people can be transported. You can shorten the return journey by taking a jetboat from Martins Bay Lodge to Pyke Lodge with Hollyford Track Guided Walks for $75.

Sleeping & Eating

Along State Highway 94 (SH94) are many basic **DOC camping grounds** (sites $10), which operate on an honesty system. You'll find them in the *Milford Road World Heritage Highway Guide* (free from Te Anau's visitor information centre), with the majority situated between 45km and 81km from Te Anau.

Clumped together at Te Anau Downs are three accommodation options (www.teanau-milfordsound.co.nz). Located 27km along Milford Road, they're a pack's throw from Glade Wharf where boats depart for Milford Track. **Grumpy's Backpackers** (☎ 0800 478 6797, 03-249 8133; dm/d $25/65) is basic but has lake and mountain views, a wood stove and rooms with en suites and heaters. **Fiordland National Park B&B & Hotel** (☎ 0800 500 706, 03-249 7510; SH94; d $120; 🖳) has a big fire in the lobby and standard rooms with awesome views. The price includes breakfast and there's a restaurant serving dinner daily. **Te Anau Downs Motor Inn** (☎ 0800 500 805, 03-249 7811; SH94; d $140; 🖳) has 1980s units with pink and grey décor and kitchenettes. Rooms are comfortable enough but don't offer such great views.

Gunn's Camp (Hollyford Rd; sites/d $14/38), also known as Hollyford Camp, is 8km down Hollyford Rd from the highway. Cabins are ultrarustic: you need your own linen (not available for hire), and cooking and heating is via a coal/wood-fired stove (fuel provided). A generator supplies limited electricity each night. There's also a small shop and a **museum** (admission adult/child $1/30c; guests free) with pioneering memorabilia.

MILFORD SOUND
pop 170

Gliding over calm waters between sheer, weather-scuffed cliffs, and catching sight of the spectacular 1692m-high Mitre Peak in the distance, is a captivating experience that drives home the uniqueness of this corner of the world. Milford Sound offers an easily accessible trip into the heart of Fiordland, complete with seals, dolphins and an almost guaranteed downpour of rain (an average of 6m per year!) that creates a spectacular deluge of cascading waterfalls and adds a ghostly mist to the scene.

One of NZ's biggest tourist attractions, Milford Sound receives tens of thousands of visitors each year. Some 14,000 arrive annually on the Milford Track, which ends at the sound, but most hitch a ride on the

SOUTHWEST NEW ZEALAND (TE WAHIPOUNAMU) WORLD HERITAGE AREA

In the southwest corner of NZ, the combination of four huge national parks make up the Southwest New Zealand (Te Wahipounamu) World Heritage Area. Known in Maori as Te Wahipounamu (The Place of Greenstone), the region covers 2.6 million hectares and is recognised internationally for its cultural significance as well as the unique vegetation and wildlife of the area. Te Wahipounamu incorporates the following:

- Aoraki/Mt Cook National Park (p583)
- Westland National Park Tai Poutini (p514)
- Fiordland National Park (p657)
- Mt Aspiring National Park (p647)

buses that pull into the cruise wharf. At peak times, the **Milford Sound visitor information centre** (☎ 03-249 7735) resembles a busy international air terminal. Nevertheless, when you get out on the water, all of this humanity seems tiny in the face of nature's vastness.

The wharf area is also regularly swarming with ferocious sandflies with a bite far bigger than their buzz. Thankfully they stay behind on land.

Milford Track

The justifiably famous Milford Track is a 53.5km walk often described as one of the finest in the world. The number of walkers is limited each year; accommodation is only in huts (camping isn't allowed) and you must follow a four-day set itinerary. Some walkers resent these restrictions, but the benefits far outweigh the inconvenience: keeping numbers down protects the environment and, though it's a hassle to book, you're guaranteed the track won't be overcrowded. Expect lots of rain, in the wake of which water will cascade *everywhere* and small streams will become raging torrents within minutes. Remember to bring wet-weather gear and pack belongings in an extra plastic bag or two.

In the off-season, experienced trekkers can walk the track without bookings (hut

MILFORD TRACK

Map labels: Milford Sound; Mackay Falls; Giant Gate Falls; Sutherland Falls; Sutherland Falls; Arthur River; Boatshed; Dumpling Hut (DOC); Quintin Hut; Mackinnon Pass (1073m); Mt Balloon (1853m); Pompolona Hut; Mintaro Hut; Mt Hart (1782m); Fiordland National Park; Lake Quill; Hirere Falls; Clinton Hut (DOC); Clinton River; Lake Te Anau; Lake Ada; Mt Ada (1891m); Sandfly Point; Bowen Falls; Milford; Lake Te Anau; Neale Burn; Glade House; Glade Wharf; To Te Anau (65km); To Te Anau (10km); Homer Tunnel; Launch route from Te Anau Downs; 94; 0 5 km / 0 3 miles

tickets must be purchased). There's limited trail transport, the huts aren't staffed, some of the bridges are removed and, in the height of winter, snow and avalanches make it unwise.

BOOKINGS

You can walk the track independently or with a guided tour. For independent bookings contact DOC's Great Walks counter (p659) in Te Anau. The track can only be done in one direction (Lake Te Anau to Milford) and you must begin on the date specified on your DOC permit. The track must be booked from October to April; it pays to book as far ahead as possible (bookings commence on 1 July for the following season). A Great Walks pass (adult/child $120/60) allows you three nights in the huts.

Milford Track Guided Walk (☎ 03-441 1138; www .milfordtrack.co.nz; low season adult/child $1490/1050, high season adult/child $1750/1050) has five-day guided walks that include everything from packs to snacks to raincoats and stays at a plusher chain of huts to those used by independent walkers. The final night is spent at Mitre Peak Lodge at Milford Sound.

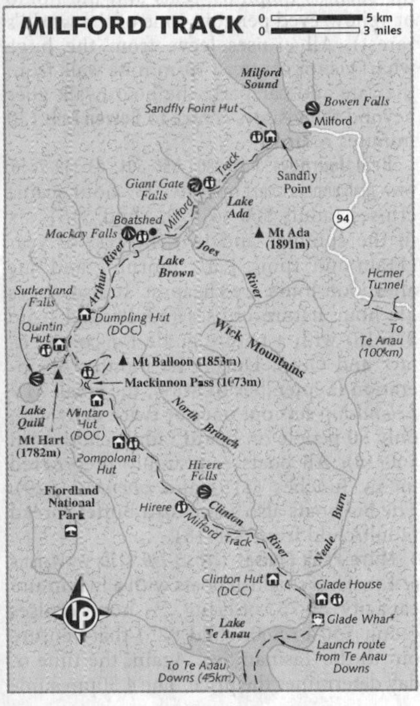

WALKING THE TRACK

The trail starts at Glade House, at the northern end of Lake Te Anau and accessed by boat from Te Anau Downs or Te Anau. The track follows the fairly flat Clinton River Valley up to Mintaro Hut, passing through rainforest and crystal-clear streams. From Mintaro it crosses the scenic **Mackinnon Pass** from where a long, wooden staircase leads you down alongside the rapids. The trail then continues down to Quintin and Dumpling Huts and through the rainforest in the Arthur River Valley to Milford Sound. You can leave your pack at the Quintin public shelter while you make the return walk to 630m-high **Sutherland Falls**, NZ's highest. If the pass appears clear when you arrive at Mintaro Hut, make the effort to climb it, as it may not be clear the next day. Estimated walking times:

Route	Time
Glade House to Clinton Hut	1–1½hr
Clinton Hut to Mintaro Hut	6hr
Mintaro Hut to Dumpling Hut	6–7hr
side-trip to Sutherland Falls	1½hr return
Dumpling Hut to Sandfly Point	5½–6hr

TRANSPORT TO GLADE WHARF

Buses operated by **TrackNet** (☎ 03-249 7777; www.tracknet.net) drive the half hour from Te Anau to Te Anau Downs (adult/child $17/11) at 9.45am and 1.15pm. **Real Journeys** (☎ 0800 656 501, 03-249 7416; www.realjourneys.co.nz) runs boat transfers from November to March from Te Anau Downs to Glade Wharf (adult/child $55/15) at 10.30am and 2pm; the trip takes 1½ hours. Both of these can be booked at Te Anau's Great Walks counter. Alternatively, **Sinbad Cruises** (☎ 03-249 7106; www.sinbadcruises.co.nz) sails the length of Lake Te Anau, from Te Anau to Glade Wharf ($70).

TRANSPORT FROM SANDFLY POINT

There are ferries leaving Sandfly Point at 2pm and 3.15pm for the Milford Sound cruise wharf (adult/child $29/17). From there you can bus back to Te Anau (adult/child $40/27). These can both be booked from Te Anau's Great Walks counter.

Activities

SEA KAYAKING

One of the most tremendous perspectives you can have on Milford Sound is at water level in the sound's awesome natural amphitheatre. The company **Rosco's Milford Sound Sea Kayaks** (0800 476 726, 03-249 8500; www .kayakmilford.co.nz) has various tours that take in the sound's most breathtaking sights; with/without return transport to Te Anau the cost is $135/105. Another tour includes a short paddle to Sandfly Point and a walk on the Milford Track ($60).

Fiordland Wilderness Experiences also offers excellent, guided trips on the sound; see p661.

UNDERWATER EXPLORATION

Unique environmental circumstances have allowed the sound to become home to some rarely glimpsed marine life. Heavy rainfall creates a permanent tannin-stained freshwater layer above the warmer sea water. This layer filters out much of the sunlight and, coupled with the sound's calm, protected waters, replicates deep-ocean conditions. The result is that deep-water species thrive not far below the surface. A similar situation exists at Doubtful Sound.

Milford Deep Underwater Observatory (03-249 9442; www.milforddeep.co.nz) dangles from a system of interlinked pontoons attached to Milford's rock face. Here, four storeys below the surface, you can check out the resident corals, tube anemones, large horse mussels, bottom-dwelling sea perch and other diverse creatures. The half-hour observatory visits are informative and highly recommended, even though the accompanying tour groups may dilute the experience. Various cruise operators stop here (adult/child from $25/13) or catch the **observatory shuttle** (0800 326 969; ind observatory adult/child $50/free) from Milford wharf.

Tawaki Dive (03-249 9006; www.tawakidive.co .nz) explores the depths of the sound. Trips include a five-hour boat cruise on the sound and two guided dives ($200); it's an extra $60 for gear hire. If you don't dive you can

join the boat trip ($100) and strap on some snorkelling gear ($30). The cost is $35 less if you find your own way to Milford.

Tours

AERIAL SIGHTSEEING

Milford Helicopters (03-249 8384; milford.helicop ters@xtra.co.nz) can take you over Mitre Peak ($125), glaciers ($200) and Sutherland Falls ($220). You can also fly in to the sound with Real Journeys (see opposite).

MILFORD SOUND CRUISES

There are a number of cruises on Milford Sound; each claims to be quieter, smaller, bigger or in some way better than the rest. In the end, what really makes a difference is the timing of the cruise; most bus tours aim for 1pm sailings so, unless you're desperate for crowds, it's best to avoid that time of day. All cruises are hugely popular so it's wise to book ahead; you generally need to arrive 20 minutes before departure.

On all trips you can expect to see Bowen Falls, Mitre Peak, Anita Bay and Stirling Falls, with the possibility of glimpsing wildlife such as dolphins, seals and the hoiho or yellow-eyed penguin (one of the world's rarest). All cruises leave from the huge wharf visitor centre, a 10-minute walk from the café and car park; the boardwalk goes beyond the visitors centre to **Bowen Falls** (30 minutes return).

Real Journeys (0800 656 501, 03-249 7416; www.realjourneys.co.nz) operates 1½-hour scenic cruises (adult $60 to $75, child $15); six in the summer and two the rest of year (11am and 1pm). Early morning and late afternoon tours are cheapest. It also stages 2½-hour nature cruises (adult/child from $75/15) with a nature guide for commentary and Q&A. During its months of operation (September to May), the small MV *Friendship* sets out once or twice daily with only 60 people on board (adult/child from $60/15). All boats can supply preordered picnic lunches ($15) and *obentos* ($29). The big boats also serve up a buffet spread (adult/child from $28/18).

Mitre Peak Cruises (03-249 8110; www.mitre peak.com) has smallish boats with a maximum capacity of 75, offering 2½-hour cruises (adult $50 to $60, child $25) that venture out to the Tasman Sea. Again, the time of day determines the price. The 4.30pm sum-

Fiordland Wilderness Experiences (Map p659; 0800 200 434, 03-249 7700; www.fiordlandseakayak.co .nz; 66 Quintin Dr, Te Anau) has guided kayaking from Sandfly Point to Milford ($70), including transport back to Te Anau.

mer cruise is an excellent choice as many of the larger boats are heading back at this time.

Red Boat Cruises (☎ 0800 264 536, 03-441 1137; www.redboats.co.nz) offers trips lasting 1¾ hours (adult/child $50/12) in a fancy catamaran and other red-bottomed boats. The noon cruise is slightly shorter and slightly more expensive. You can also opt for tours that take in the observatory (adult/child $70/22). Picnics ($14 to $26), *obentos* ($26) and buffet lunches (adult/child $26/15) are available on some trips.

OVERNIGHT CRUISES

Three boats operated by **Real Journeys** (☎ 0800 656 501, 03-249 7416; www.realjourneys.co.nz) offer overnight cruises, letting you appreciate the fiord when all other traffic has ceased. You can kayak and take nature tours in tender crafts en route. Trips include all meals and you can tack on transport from Te Anau or Queenstown. All depart around 4pm and return around 9.30am the following day. Cheaper prices apply on the cusp of the season, in May, September and October. Cruises don't operate from June to August.

The budget-oriented *Milford Wanderer*, modelled on an old trading scow, carries 61 passengers overnight from October to April. Accommodation in tiny four-bunk cabins (with shared bathrooms) costs $210/105 per adult/child. The *Wanderer* is YHA-affiliated, so 10% member discounts apply.

The *Milford Mariner* sleeps 60 in more upmarket, en suite, twin-share cabins and runs between September and May. The cost in a twin room is $350/175 per adult/child. The *MV Friendship* departs between November and March and sleeps only 12 in a share bunk cabin for $210/105 per adult/child.

Sleeping & Eating

If you're seeking a little luxury after finishing the Milford Track, hightail it to Te Anau or Queenstown; Milton's upmarket Mitre Peak Lodge caters only to those doing

Cruising Milford Sound (☎ 0800 500 121, 03-441 3913; www.cruisings.co.nz) calls itself Milford's boutique cruise line. This might be pushing it, but it does offer 1½-hour trips (adult $40 to $60, child $15) on a small boat with lots of deck space.

Real Journeys (☎ 0800 656 501, 03-249 7416; www.realjourneys.co.nz) has a coach-cruise-coach excursion that leaves Te Anau at 8am and returns at 4.30pm, costing from $130/65 per adult/child for the scenic cruise and from $145/75 for the nature cruise (October to April). There are also coach-cruise-fly ($305) and fly-cruise-fly ($375) options. **InterCity** (☎ 03-249 7559; www.intercitycoach.co.nz) has basically the same trip for a similar price, except the cruise is with Red Boat Cruises (left). **Trips'n'Tramps** (☎ 03-249 7081; www.milfordtourswalks.co.nz) also has a coach-and-cruise option out of Te Anau (adult/child $135/75) as does the BBQ Bus (p631) out of Queenstown.

Getting There & Away

You can reach Milford Sound by foot, flight, bus or car. If you're driving to Milford, see p664.

There is a dizzying array of bus trips that include a boat cruise on the sound; most are around $110/70 per adult/child from Te Anau or $160/90 per adult/child from Queenstown (but it's a very long 13-hour day). Book at any visitor information centre or booking agency in those towns. **InterCity** (☎ 03-249 7559; www.intercitycoach.co.nz) runs daily bus services from Queenstown ($70) and Te Anau ($50). Trampers' buses also operate from Te Anau (p664) and Queenstown (p639) and will pick up at the Milford Sound Lodge. All these buses pass the Divide and the start/end of the Routeburn, Greenstone and Caples Tracks.

the guided walk. Also see for details of floating accommodation options.

Milford Sound Lodge (☎ 03-249 8071; www.milfordlodge.com; SH94; unpowered/powered sites per 2 people $30/34, dm/d $30/70; ☐) Beside the Cleddau River and surrounded by forest, this basic lodge offers hot showers and quiet for weary trampers. It was still 'about' to be plugged into the region's mains supply at the time of research; until then the generator kicks in for power between 6.30am and 11.30pm. There's a tiny shop, and continental breakfast is available.

Milford Café (☎ 03-249 7931; SH94; ⏰lunch) is on the edge of the car park and sells a basic menu of overpriced sandwiches, pies and packaged snacks. Next door is the **Blue Duck** (☎ 03-249 7427; SH94; mains $12-25; ⏰lunch & dinner) with standard meals, beer and a smattering of local workers.

MANAPOURI

pop 210

The jumping-off point for cruises to the sublime Doubtful Sound, Manapouri is mainly a base for those about to set out on cruises or walking expeditions. Situated beside the pretty and very deep Lake Manapouri and surrounded by mountains, the town itself is little more than a handful of hotels, with a glut of sandflies to keep you hopping. On the shoreline near town is the picturesque Frasers Beach.

In 1969, Manapouri was the site of NZ's first major environmental campaign; a struggle to stop the building of a hydroelectric dam that would have raised Lake Manapouri's water levels by 30m. The campaign led to a petition with a staggering 265,000 signatures and the election of a new federal government.

The Real Journeys visitors centre (☎ 0800 656 502, 03-249 6602; www.realjourneys.co.nz; Pearl Harbour; ⏱ 7.30am-8pm Oct-Apr, 8.30am-5.30pm May-Sep) organises west Arm Power Station and Doubtful Sound trips. Basic supplies and the post office can be found in Manapouri Stores (☎ 03-249 6619).

Activities

Adventure Kayak & Cruise (☎ 03-249 6626; www.fiordlandadventure.co.nz), beside the garage in Manapouri, rents kayaks (from $45 per person per day, minimum two people) for paddles on Lake Manapouri. It also has Doubtful Sound day trips combining a cruise and kayaking (from $210). You can rent row boats from Manapouri Stores (☎ 03-249 6619; per day $20).

With a kayak, dinghy or water taxi (see FishFiordland, right), you can cross the Waiau River for some low-altitude day walks, detailed in the DOC brochure Manapouri Tracks ($1). A walk along the Circle Track (three hours return) can be extended to Hope Arm (five to six hours return), crossing the uninvitingly named Stinking Creek. Although Te Anau is the usual access point for the Kepler Track (p660), the trail touches the northern end of Lake Manapouri and part of it can be done as a day walk from Manapouri; access is via the swing bridge at Rainbow Reach, 10km north of town. From Pearl Harbour there's also a walk along the river to Frasers Beach (1½ hours

return), from where you can gaze across the beautiful lake.

Manapouri is also a staging point for the remote 84km Dusky Track, a walk that takes eight days if you tramp between Lakes Manapouri and Hauroko, with a two-day detour possible from Loch Maree Hut to Supper Cove on Dusky Sound. With regular tree falls, deep mud, river crossings, delaying floods and 21 three-wire bridges, this is an extremely challenging wilderness walk, suitable only for well-equipped, very experienced trampers. Contact DOC and read Lonely Planet's Tramping in New Zealand for more details.

For fishing tours contact FishFiordland (☎ 03-249 8070; www.fishfiordland.co.nz; per hr/day $70/ 550), which also offers dinghy hire, scenic trips on Lake Manapouri and guided nature walks.

Sleeping

Manapouri Lakeview Chalets & Motor Park (☎ 03-249 6624; manapouri@xtra.co.nz; 50 SH95; unpowered/ powered sites per 2 people $22/24, d $38-105) This slightly bizarre motor park has a collection of Morris Minors, pinball machines and eclectic cabins, ranging from basic budget shacks to enlarged doll houses with kitchens, en suites and views. There's also a playground and good communal kitchen.

Freestone Backpackers (☎ 03-249 6893; freestone@ xtra.co.nz; Manapouri-Hillside Rd; dm/d $20/50) Fantastically peaceful four-bunk cabins nestled on a view-blessed hill, some 3km east of town. Each cabin is fitted with a small kitchen, veranda and potbelly stove; toilets, showers and fridge are communal. Electricity is solar-powered; bring a torch. The friendly owner will book activities and has created a number of trails on his 4-hectare property.

Possum Lodge (☎ 03-249 6623; 13 Murrell Ave; sites per 2 people $24, dm $23, d $55-85) Rooms here are basic and dated, with shared kitchens and lounge. Camp sites sit up above the river and are pleasant if you can deter the sandflies.

Manapouri Lakeview Motor Inn (☎ 03-249 6652; www.manapouri.com; 68 Cathedral Dr; dm from $28, d $95-110; 🖳) Somewhat worn rooms but great views and friendly proprietors. Dorms are bunk-free and the self-contained two-bedroom units are a great deal.

Cottage (☎ 03-249 6838; www.thecottagefiordland .co.nz; Waiau St; d $120) Very cosy and very granny with lace and floral patterns in spades. The snug lounge has a fireplace and the flower-covered garden has lovely views of the mountains and water. The two en suite rooms are very comfy and the owners welcoming.

Eating

You're certainly not plagued with dining options in Manapouri. The visitor information centre café (☎ 03-249 6602; light mains $3; ☑ breakfast & lunch) has a bright outlook over Pearl Harbour and sells fresh juices, pies, pastries and quiche. The Motor Inn's Beehive Café (☎ 03-249 6652; 68 Cathedral Dr, mains $12-30; ☑ lunch & dinner) serves unsurprising but substantial meals before a lake view and the tiny Cathedral Cafe (☎ 03-249 6619; Waiau St; meals $5-20; ☑ breakfast, lunch & dinner) upholds the roadside diner tradition with schnitzels, pies and chips.

Getting There & Away

Scenic Shuttle (☎ 0800 277 483, 03-249 7654; reservation@scenicshuttle.com) drives between Manapouri and both Te Anau ($17) and Invercargill ($37). Alternatively, ask Real Journeys (☎ 0800 656 502, 03-249 6602; Pearl Harbour) if there are spare seats on coaches to Te Anau.

DOUBTFUL SOUND

The absolutely massive Doubtful Sound is a magnificent wilderness area of rugged peaks, dense forest and thundering post-rain waterfalls. Fur seals and bottlenose and dusky dolphins can be glimpsed in its waters, and Fiordland crested penguins nest in October and November. Black coral and other deep-sea life exist at unusually shallow levels. At the sound's mouth is the Tasman Sea lies Nee Island, inhabited by seals.

Until relatively recently, only the most intrepid tramper or sailor entered Doubtful Sound's inner reaches. Even Captain Cook only observed it from off the coast in 1770, saying he was 'doubtful' whether the winds in the sound would be sufficient to blow the ship back out to sea. In 1793 the Spanish sailed in, naming Malaspina Reach and Bauza Island after the expedition's leaders.

Doubtful Sound became more accessible when the road over Wilmot Pass opened in 1959 to facilitate construction of the West Arm Power Station, built to provide electricity for the aluminium smelter near Bluff. A tunnel was dug through the mountain from Lake Manapouri to Doubtful, and the massive flow of water from lake to sound drives the power station's turbines. Today Doubtful Sound is most readily accessible via tours from Manapouri.

Fortunately, Doubtful Sound remains exquisitely peaceful and still feels entirely remote. While a continual debate rages amongst travellers as to which sound is better, cliff-hemmed Milford or the larger, less-trafficked Doubtful, it's like comparing kea with kaka.

Tours

Doubtful Sound is only accessible by tour. The easiest place to base yourself is Manapouri, although some tours do pick up in Te Anau and Queenstown.

Real Journeys (☎ 0800 656 502, 03-249 6602; www.realjourneys.co.nz; Pearl Harbour, Manapouri) has a 'Wilderness Cruise', beginning with a half-hour boat ride across Lake Manapouri, followed by a bus ride that ventures 2km underground (by road) for a tour of the West Arm Power Station. The bus then travels over Wilmot Pass to the sound, which you explore on a three-hour cruise. The eight-hour trip costs $225/$5 per adult/child from Manapouri or $235/55 from Te Anau; picnic lunches can be preordered ($22).

From October to mid-May, Real Journeys also runs a Doubtful Sound overnight cruise, departing Manapouri at 12.30pm and returning at noon the next day. The Fiordland Navigator sleeps 70 and offers twin-share, en suite cabins (adult/child $500/250) and quad-share bunk rooms (adult/child $325/165); 10% YHA discounts and transport to and from Te Anau and Queenstown are available. Fares include meals and kayaking.

Fiordland Ecology Holidays (☎ 03-249 6600; www.fiordland.gen.nz; 5 Waiau St, Manapouri) has small-group boat tours (maximum 12 guests) led by people with a passion for the area's flora and fauna, and a sense of humour. The superbly equipped yacht sails into remote parts of the World Heritage Area, along Doubtful and Dusky Sounds. Rates are about $850 for a three-day trip and $1500 for six days. Snorkelling, diving and swimming are all possible. Other voyages take in Stewart Island and even NZ's Subantarctic Islands. Book all trips well in advance.

Adventure Kayak & Cruise (opposite) runs day trips to the Doubtful Sound. Other cruising options for the sound include the following:

Deep Cove Charters (☎ 03-249 6828; www.deep covecharters.co.nz; cruises adult/child $300/200) Overnight cruises with a maximum of six people.

Fiordland Explorer Charters (☎ 0800 434 673, 03-249 6616; www.fiordland.org.nz; Pearl Harbour; cruises adult/ child $160/80) A maximum of 15 people on day cruises.

Sleeping

If you'd like to spend the night on the sound, it generally means joining an overnight cruise. The only other option is **Deep Cove Hostel** (☎ 03-216 1340, 03-249 6602; dm/d $22/ 50), a remote hostel situated right on Doubtful Sound with a number of bush walks radiating from it. It's predominantly used by school groups, but, if booked well in advance, independent travellers can stay here from mid-December to mid-February. Real Journeys can sometimes book you in here for a night or two in conjunction with the company's tours. BYO food and linen.

SOUTHERN SCENIC ROUTE

The unhurried and vista-blessed Southern Scenic Route begins in Te Anau and heads south to Tuatapere via Manapouri, from where it wraps itself around the coast to Riverton and Invercargill. For more detailed information, see www.southernscenic route.co.nz and pick up *Southern Scenic Route* (free) from any visitor information centre; both of these sources cover the route from Te Anau, all the way along the coast to Dunedin. Public transport along the route is limited, however **Bottom Bus** (☎ 03-442 9708; www.bottombus.co.nz) and **Scenic Shuttle** (☎ 0800 277 483, 03-249 7654; reservations@scenicshuttle.com) offer regular shuttles.

South of Manapouri, the road follows the Waiau River between the forested Takitimu and Hunter Mountains, with the very blue, snowcapped Kepler Mountains disappearing in the rear-view mirror. Near Clifden is the **Clifden Suspension Bridge**, built in 1899 and visible from the road. **Clifden (Waiau) Caves** are signposted on Otautau Rd, 2km from the Clifden Rd corner. The caves offer an exhilarating underground scramble over rocks, through crawl spaces and up ladders. These are undeveloped caves, so bring a friend, spare torch batteries and lots of caution, and visit Tuatapere visitor information centre (right) for conditions and a map beforehand.

Just south of the suspension bridge is a turn-off to a walking track through **Dean Forest**, a reserve of 1000-year-old totara trees (23km off the main road). From Clifden you can also drive 30km of mostly unsealed road to **Lake Hauroko**, the deepest lake in NZ and surrounded by lush, precipitous slopes. The lake's Mary Island holds an interesting example of a Maori cave burial, with a woman of high rank buried in about 1660 sitting upright. The area has many other ancient *urupa* (burial sites) so be respectful and keep to trails. The Dusky Track (p670) also ends (or begins) here. **Lake Hauroko Tours** (☎ 03-226 6681; www.duskytrack.co.nz; tours adult/child $80/40; ☉ tours Mon & Thu Nov-May) has five-hour return tours from Tuatapere, including light lunch.

Tuatapere
pop 740

Once a timber-milling town, Tuatapere is now a very sleepy farming centre on the banks of the Waiau River. Early woodcutters were so determined that only a small remnant of a once large tract of native podocarp forest remains. At one time Tuatapere was known as NZ's 'sausage capital'; today it's mainly used as a base for trips to Lake Hauroko or the Hump Ridge Track.

Tuatapere visitor information centre (☎ 03-226 6399; www.atoz-nz.com/tuatapere.asp; Orama Rd; ☉ 8.30am-6pm Oct-Apr, 9.30am-4.30pm May-Sep) is extremely helpful when it comes to Clifden Caves, Hump Ridge hut passes and transport, and details of local activities.

HUMP RIDGE TRACK

The excellent 53km Hump Ridge Track passes along rugged coastline and through forests of podocarp and beech, subalpine settings and sandstone outcrops. En route you'll cross Percy Burn Viaduct, built in 1920 and the largest surviving wooden viaduct in the world. Beginning and ending at Bluecliffs Beach on Te Waewae Bay, 20km from Tuatapere, the track was only inaugurated late in 2001. It takes three days to complete; estimated walking times:

Route	Time
Bluecliffs Beach Car Park to Okaka Hut	5-7hr
Okaka Hut to Port Craig Village	7-9hr
Port Craig Village to Bluecliffs Beach Car Park	3-5hr

It's essential to book for this track, which is administered by a local trust rather than DOC. Contact the **Tuatapere Hump Ridge Track Trust** (☎ 0800 486 774, 03-226 6739; www.humpridgetrack.co.nz).

JETBOATING

Jetboat rides typically cross Lake Hauroko and go up the Wairaurahiri River, the ride lasting two or three hours. Operators include **W-Jet** (☎ 0800 376 174, 03-226 6845; www.wjet.co.nz; rides adult/child $190/90) and **Humpridge Jet** (☎ 0800 270 556, 03-225 8174; www.humpridgejet.com; rides adult/child $160/70). **Waiau Jet Tours** (☎ 03-226 6996) can take you from Tuatapere Bridge to Clifden Bridge ($40, one hour) or Dean Forest ($90, 3½ hours).

SLEEPING & EATING

Check with the visitor information centre for a current list of B&Bs and farmstays.

Peace Street Camping (☎ 03-226 6626; 23 Peace St; unpowered/powered sites per 2 people $12/15) A small field enclosed by a big hedge and butting up to farmland, this place offers just what it says – peace. Facilities are basic.

Hump Track Backpackers & Motel (☎ 03-226 6250; 6 Clifden Rd; unpowered/powered sites per 2 people $20/30, dm $24, d $50-90) Set next to the high-way, this newish backpackers has a spacious kitchen with a wood stove, a big deck with a barbecue and uninspired but clean rooms. Motel rooms are nothing flash but comfort-able and self-contained. Camping is on a stretch of green lawn.

Waiau Hotel (☎ 03-226 6409; www.waiauhotel.co.nz; 47 Main St; s/d from $45/90) Very average rooms, some with en suite. Its bistro (mains $3 to $10; open for lunch and dinner) serves surprisingly tasty, homemade fare in unat-mospheric surroundings.

And what would a visit to Tuatapere be without a taste of its 'world famous' sau-sages? Head to **Tuatapere Butchery** (☎ 03-226 6596; 75 Main St).

Tuatapere to Riverton

About 10km south of Tuatapere, the scenic route reaches the cliffs above **Te Waewae Bay**, where Hector's dolphins and southern right whales are sometimes seen. At the eastern end of the bay is tiny **Monkey Island**, or Te Poka a Takatimu (Anchor Stone of the *Taka-tima* Canoe). Once a Maori whale lookout, the island is accessible at low tide when you can climb to the viewing platform.

Detour off the highway to check out **Cosy Nook**, a handful of holiday homes set next to a rugged coastline with waves smashing against outcrops of rocks. On clear days you can see the Solander Islands on the southwest horizon. It's a good spot for a picnic though you'll quickly understand why the surrounding macrocarpa trees lean dramatically away from the shore; the coast is regularly bombarded by strong southwesterlies.

Colac Bay, an ancient Maori settlement, is now a popular Southlander holiday and surfing spot. Surf at the eastern end of the beach (BYO gear) or ask locally about **Por-ridge**, a top surfing spot that involves cross-ing a private paddock.

Dusetz Bak Paka's & Camping Ground (☎ 03-234 8399; dusetz@xtra.co.nz; 15 Colac Bay Rd; sites per 2 people $20, dm $25, d $45-55) has basic rooms open-ing onto a covered courtyard, and camp-sites in a grassy field, surrounded by hedge on one side and a pen of chickens on the other. The owner apparently has a thing for garden and lawn knick-knacks. If you find the attached tavern (slightly obscured by an enormous surfing dude) you can enjoy some home-cooked food.

Riverton

pop 1850

This small, slow-paced town was one of NZ's first European settlements, dating from the sealing and whaling days. With uncrowded swimming beaches and decent accommoda-tion, it's a good place to break your journey, just 38km west of Invercargill.

The **Riverton Rocks** area is a popular 'if cold' local beach. **Taramea Bay** is a safe place to swim but don't venture past the point. Visit the lookout at **Mores Reserve** to see the wind-sheared canopy of coastal southern rata and views to Stewart Island.

Riverton visitor information centre (☎ 03-234 9991; www.riverton-aparima.co.nz; 127 Palmerston St; ✆ 10am-4pm) takes bookings for the **Bottom Bus** (www.bottombus.co.nz), which overnights in Riverton. The centre is temporarily resident in Something Special Gift Shop while its home (the old courthouse) is being restored to house it and the **Wallace Early Settlers**

Museum (03-234 8520; 172 Palmerston St); swing by to see if it has reopened.

If you're itching to shop, Palmerston St is lined with arts-and-crafts gift shops and boutiques.

SLEEPING & EATING

Riverton Caravan Park & Holiday Homes (03-234 8526; Hamlet St; sites per 2 people $16, dm $10, d $30-50) Very basic facilities and sites with obstructed sea views. Cabins have better lookouts.

Globe Backpackers (03-234 8527; www.theglobe.co.nz; 144 Palmerston St; dm/d $19/45) Nicely decorated in warm autumnal colours, this central place has friendly owners and good facilities but tends to get major backpacker-bus traffic in summer. Avoid the two downstairs dorms and opt for a smaller, quieter one upstairs.

Riverton Beach Motel (03-234 8181; 4 Marne St; d $85) A guesthouse. Two cute one-bedroom units with sea views. They're small and rather mint green but extremely well-equipped and just across the road from Taramea Beach. Pull out the couch in the front room and sleep four.

Riverton Rock (03-234 8886; www.riverton.co.nz; 136 Palmerston St; d $95-145) A guesthouse since 1863, this classy place has been renovated once again to create very comfortable rooms with lots of character. All but one have shared bathrooms. A bright, cushy lounge has a wood stove, and there's a fantastic yellow kitchen for guest use. The garden has a small fountain and outdoor fireplace.

Beach House (03-234 8274; 126 Rocks Hwy; lunch mains $10-19, dinner $20-28; breakfast, lunch & dinner summer, breakfast & lunch daily, dinner Thu-Sun winter) A good place for coffee and scrumptious baking with a view over the water. This place is also well known for its inventive seafood, meat and veggie mains. Inside it's stylish and open; outside there's a heated patio. To find it, follow signs along the coast to the lookout.

CENTRAL SOUTHLAND

Central Southland is home to the majority of the region's population, sandwiched between the coast and the surging Hokonui Hills, which are but a precursor to the Garvie and Remarkable Mountains to the north.

Southland's biggest city, Invercargill, stands proudly to the south, footed by the port town of Bluff. SH1 stretches to the northeast, through farmland and rural communities. Central Southland doesn't hold a great deal for visitors, however it's a jumping off point for Stewart Island, the Catlins and the Southern Scenic Route.

INVERCARGILL

pop 49,300

Invercargill rarely scores high marks with travellers, something that the city is working hard to rectify. Boy racers in souped-up cars and girls with souped-up hair-dos hint at the fact that there's not much to do around here. Nevertheless, most travellers in Southland will find themselves in Invercargill at some point and, if you're willing to explore a little, there are a few gems in the way of architecture, museums, parks and galleries that are worth calling on. The city is a little rough around the edges but it certainly won't be swamped with other tourists. It's also a good place to stock up on supplies and equipment before setting off into the Catlins or trekking on Stewart Island.

Information

Automobile Association (AA; 03-218 9033; 47 Gala St; 8.30am-5pm Mon-Fri)

Comzone.net (03-214 0007; 45 Dee St) Get online.

DOC (03-214 4589; 7th fl, State Insurance Bldg, 33 Don St; 9am-5pm Mon-Fri) For info on tracks around Stewart Island and Lake Manapouri.

Global Byte Cafe (03-214 4724; 150 Dee St) Coin-operated computers to hop online between coffees.

Invercargill visitor information centre (03-214 6243; www.invercargill.org.nz; Victoria Ave, Queens Park; 8am-7pm Oct-Apr, to 5pm May-Sep) Handily located in same building as the Southland Museum & Art Gallery.

Library (03-218 7025; 50 Dee St) Head upstairs for Internet access.

Post office (Don St)

Sights

SOUTHLAND MUSEUM & ART GALLERY

On the edge of Queens Park, this **museum & gallery** (03-218 9753; www.southlandmuseum.com; Victoria Ave, Queens Park; admission by gold-coin donation; 9am-5pm Mon-Fri, 10am-5pm Sat & Sun) is worth a wee wander. Permanent museum exhibits include a Maori gallery with a 16th-century *tauihu* (canoe prow) found on Stewart Island's coast in 1995; a history gallery with colonial artefacts such as an impressive printing press; a Roaring Forties exhibit on NZ's Subantarctic Islands; and a natural-history gallery with the skeleton of a rather alarming 'giant spider crab'. The art gallery hosts visiting exhibits that often included contemporary Maori and other local artists, as well as international shows and pieces from the gallery's own collections.

The star of the building is Henry, a centurion tuatara who, weighing in at 1.2kg, is possibly the heaviest in the world. You'll find him in the tuatara enclosure, along with some of his fellow living fossils.

ANDERSON PARK ART GALLERY

Housed in a 1925 Georgian-style home, this wonderful **gallery** (03-215 7432; parkgallery@xtra.co.nz; McIvor Rd; admission by donation; gallery 10.30am-5pm, gardens 10.30am-dusk) contains diverse works from a huge array of NZ artists. Absorbing landscapes, impressive block prints, pottery and a beautiful flock of sculpted birds hovering over the staircase will keep your eyes on the prowl. You'll also find short biographies on the artists, or-iginal antique furnishings, and a free tea-room with black and white photos of the building's early days. Outside, 24 hectares of landscaped gardens are a lovely place to linger, with trees and trails, a children's playground and a *wharepuni* (sleeping house).

INVERCARGILL

INFORMATION	
Automobile Association (AA).....	1 B3
Comzone.net.....	2 C4
DOC.....	3 C4
Global Byte Cafe.....	4 A3
Invercargill Visitor Information Centre.....	5 B3
Library.....	6 B3
Post Office.....	7 D4

SIGHTS & ACTIVITIES	
City Gallery.....	8 C4
First Presbyterian Church.....	9 B4
Observatory.....	(see 9)
Queens Park Golf Course.....	10 B3
Shearing South.....	(see 22)
Southland Museum & Art Gallery.....	11 C4
Splash Palace.....	12 B4
Water Tower.....	13 B4
Wensley's Cycles.....	14 C4

SLEEPING	
Balmoral Lodge.....	14 B4
Burrowood B&B.....	15 B3
Living Space.....	16 C4
Queens Park Motel.....	17 B2
Southern Comfort Backpackers.....	18 A3
Tower Lodge Motel.....	19 B3

EATING	
Bensal.....	20 C4
Cafe Amici.....	21 C4
Cod Pot.....	(see 26)
Countdown.....	(see 28)
Fat Indian.....	(see 28)
In A Pickle.....	22 C4
Louie's.....	25 A3
Mevlana Kebabs.....	26 C4
Picadly Capers Cafe & Bar.....	27 C4
Sassy's Café.....	28 C4
Thai Dee.....	29 C4
Vinnie's Pizza & Pasta Bar.....	30 C4
Zookeepers Cafe.....	31 C4

DRINKING	
Frog 'n' Firkin.....	32 C4

ENTERTAINMENT	
Embassy Theatre.....	33 C4
Globe.....	34 A3
Reading Cinemas.....	35 B3
Stadium Southland.....	36 C3

SHOPPING	
H&J's Outdoor World.....	(see 37)
Southern Adventure.....	37 C4

TRANSPORT	
Air New Zealand.....	38 C4

The gallery is located 7km north of the city centre; follow North Rd and turn right on McIvor Rd.

OTHER SIGHTS

Wander around the half-wild, half-tamed **Queens Park**, with its aviary, duck ponds, children's playground, huge trees and fitness track. The nearby **observatory** (03-218 9753; Victoria Ave, Queens Park; adult $1; 7pm–9pm Wed Apr–Oct) gives you a skyward view, while climbing the curious, pepper pot–style **water tower** (Leet St; adult/child $2/50c; 1.30–4.30pm Sun & holidays) gives a bird's-eye look over town.

In the centre of town, **City Gallery** (03-214 1319; 28 Don St; citygallery@ihug.co.nz; admission free; 11am–4pm Mon-Fri, 10am–2pm Sat) showcases talent from NZ's south, including handcrafted silver, pottery, photography, woodwork and paintings (most of which are for sale). Exhibits are changed every third week and art classes are sometimes available with local or visiting artists for around $120 for two days; call for more details.

The unusual **First Presbyterian Church** (03-218 2560; 181 Tay St) is of Italian Romanesque design, similar to the distinctive buildings of Italy's Lombardy plains and a rather unlikely sight in NZ. Completed in 1915, it's made of more than a million bricks. Its interior isn't as impressive as its exterior.

For a different kind of holy water, head to **Invercargill Brewery** (027 493 2056; www.invercargillbrewery.co.nz; 155 Oteramika Rd; 11am–3pm Sat), east of town, for tastings of natural ciders and beers. Tours are often possible; call ahead. Try the Pitch Black, described as 'chocolate cake, roast coffee with cream…it shouts stout'.

Shearing South (03-214 9177; www.shearingsouth.co.nz; 55 Dee St; adult/child/family $12/5/20; 9am–5pm Mon-Sat, 10am–4pm Sun) is an odd experience, with a film that looks at the 'sport' of shearing; shearing stories, shearing memorabilia, a shearers' Hall of Fame and even a shearing art gallery. Huh?

Activities

For a one-hour self-guided walk, pick up the *Invercargill City Spirit Walk* brochure (free) from the visitor information centre. In **Thomson's Bush**, 1km north along Queen's Dr, you can follow a one-hour loop beneath the ancient kahikatea and matai trees that once covered Invercargill. **Sandy Point Rec-**

reation Reserve, 7km south of the city, has 13.5km of trails taking in forest and estuary along Oreti River and Daffodil and Whalers Bays. Trails range from five minutes to 1½ hours; arm yourself with a *Sandy Point* map and brochure from the visitor information centre. Sweeping **Oreti Beach** is 10km west of the city; warm currents make the water milder than expected. (As in, it's not quite freezing cold, just cold.)

For family fun, **Splash Palace** (03-217 3838; www.splashpalace.co.nz; Elles Rd; adult/child/family $4/2/10) has an Olympic-sized pool, wave pool, waterslide, kids' pool, spa and steam room. **Queens Park Golf Course** (03-218 8371; 215 Kelvin St; green fees $15, club rental $15; 9am–4.30pm) is a flat, tree-lined 18-holer in the heart of town. **Wensley's Cycles** (03-218 6206; cnr Tay & Nith Sts) rents mountains bikes for $25 per day.

Sleeping

If you were hoping to splash out, you've come to the wrong place; top-end accommodation in Invercargill is very thin on the ground. You'll find countless midrange motels along Hwy 1 East (Tay St) and Hwy 6 North (North Rd). Many places will store luggage for guests heading to Stewart Island; ask when you make your booking.

BUDGET

Southern Comfort Backpackers (03-218 3838; 30 Thomson St; dm/s/d $21/45/50) An excellent choice, this vintage villa has very comfortable, colourful rooms, a big sitting room, well-equipped kitchen and good showers. Doubles are spacious, or opt for the very wee, very basic playhouse (ie shed) for a cut rate. There's a front and back garden, laundry facilities and little extras like electric blankets and cut flowers in the kitchen. The owners have heaps of local knowledge to share. Payments must be in cash and bedding is extra ($3/5 per single/double).

Tuatara Lodge YHA (0800 4882 8272, 03-214 0954; tuataralodge@xtra.co.nz; 30-32 Dee St; dm/d from $24/60;) Sunny rooms are basic and a little worn, with doubles on the small side. Facilities are modern, and the staff are friendly and downstairs is a great café.

Invercargill Top 10 Holiday Park (0800 486 873, 03-215 9032; gumtreefarmMP@xtra.co.nz; 77 McIvor Rd; sites per 2 people $24, cabins $75-85) Across from parkland, this place is a 6km drive north of town but peaceful, small and well maintained. Sites have trees and fencing for privacy and there's a basic but new communal kitchen and TV lounge, along with a sheltered barbecue area. The new, comfortable studio and self-contained cabins have en suites.

MIDRANGE

Lorneville Holiday Park (☎ 03-235 8031; www.lorneville.kiwiholidayparks.co.nz; SH98; sites per 2 people $20, on-site caravan $36, d $40-70) Located on a small, working farm, this well-maintained camping ground has lots of good amenities, a shearing shed converted into a TV room, and lambs and calves to feed in spring. From town, head north along SH6 for 8km, then turn right on SH98 and travel a further 3.5km.

MIDRANGE

Victorian Railway Hotel (☎ 0800 777 557, 03-218 1281; www.vrhotel.info; cnr Leven & Esk Sts; d $95-135) Built in 1896, this hotel has recently been returned to an elegant state and feels more top end than midrange. Rooms are each uniquely decorated with period furnishings, extra-warm duvets and big en suites; one is wheelchair accessible. The classy bar is extremely cosy and there's a breakfast room that granny would die for (breakfast is not included in the price). This doesn't feel like the best part of town but it's around the corner from the centre. Staff are attentive and security is tops.

Living Space (☎ 0508 454 846, 03-211 3801; www.livingspace.net; 15 Tay St; d $75-140) In the heart of the city, this ultrasleek, supermodern place is decorated in vibrant colours and has fantastic common kitchens, lounges and an excellent, comfy cinema that you can book (BYO video). Doubles are a little small and lacking – or is it industrial minimalism? Two- and three-bedroom apartments are fab. All rooms have a TV and multitude of channels, en suite and kitchenette. Longer stays get cheaper rates.

Queens Park Motel (☎ 0800 800 504, 03-214 4504; www.queensparkmotels.co.nz; 85 Alice St; d $95-110) On a quiet side street tucked into the northwestern corner of Queens Park, these newly refurbished, self-contained units are a good deal. Run by friendly hosts, and it's a short stroll through the park to the city centre.

Tower Lodge Motel (☎ 03-217 6729; timotel@es.co.nz; 119 Queens Dr, d $95-110, ste $125-135) Across from the water tower, the newer doubles are very comfortable with fancy TVs, and

tubs to soak in. Older doubles are nothing special. Suites sleep two to four; the one at the front was part of an old house and has lots more character than the rest.

Burtonwood B&B (☎ 03-218 8884; www.burtonwood.co.nz; 177 Gala St; s $75, d $100-125;) This Edwardian-style house has a single and twin rooms with shared bathrooms, and two queen rooms with en suites. It's not sumptuous, but it is very comfortable and well priced, and Queens Park is across the road. Continental breakfast is included, or ask for a full cooked version ($10), and there's a laundry and bikes for guest use.

Balmoral Lodge (☎ 03-217 6109; www.ilt.co.nz/bal moral.htm; 265 Tay St; d $92-110) Older units here are dated but spacious; opt instead for the much nicer newer ones that go for the same price. In the one-bedrooms you sleep in the loft and have a spa bath, while smaller studios have showers only.

Eating

Invercargill has a surprisingly diverse restaurant scene.

RESTAURANTS

Vinnie's Pizza & Pasta Bar (☎ 0800 484 6643; 16 Don St; mains $14-17; lunch Tue-Fri, dinner Tue-Sat) With original brickwork showing through the yellow walls, big wooden tables, candles and a roaring fire, this place is cosy and atmospheric. Pizzas, pastas and authentic antipasto will have you crying *eccellente!*

Bonsai (☎ 03-218 1292; 35 Esk St; lunch mains $8-13, dinner mains $10-28; lunch & dinner Mon-Sat) Adorned with Japanese parasols, kimonos and fans, this is a casual, agreeable place to dig into sushi, tempera, curry or noodles. Or you can pick up an *obento* to go.

Fat Indian (☎ 03-218 9933; laneway off 38 Dee St; mains $15-20; lunch & dinner) Tucked down an alleyway, this restaurant has wooden floors and brick walls that give it a somewhat basic but snug interior. The food comes highly recommended. Try flavourful vindaloos, kormas and baltis or, if you can't decide, go for the 'tandoori sampler'.

Thai Dee (☎ 03-214 5112; 9 Dee St; mains $10-16; lunch Mon-Fri, dinner daily) Orange, yellow and red walls with big pictures of Thailand will get you in the mood for well-spiced Thai salads, soups, noodles and curry dishes.

Mevlana Kebabs (☎ 03-218 6468; 61 Tay St; mains $8-19; lunch & dinner) Casual but comfortable, this place whips up authentic Turkish cuisine like shish kebabs and doner kebabs with chilli or yoghurt and garlic. Finish it off with baklava and excellent, strong coffee. There are a few outdoor tables, a sofa by the fireplace and a takeaway menu. Vegetarians are well catered for.

Zookeepers Cafe (☎ 03-218 3373; 50 Tay St; meals $8-28; ☺ breakfast, lunch & dinner) Dine with at-least-life-sized apes, cheetahs and elephants in this bright eatery serving up hearty breakfasts, seafood, pastas and diverse sandwiches. If it starts to feel a bit too much like a zoo, escape to outside tables. Kids will be more than pleased with a teddy bear picnic.

Cabbage Tree (☎ 03-213 1443; 379 Dunns Rd, Otatara; light meals $7-20, mains $18-40; ☺ lunch & dinner Tue-Sun) Different rooms here have different themes; sit on couches around a fire, movie seats in front of a big-screen TV, or in a formal dining room. Food ranges from bangers and mash to porterhouse steak. You'll find this much-awarded restaurant a short drive away at Otatara (past the airport).

CAFÉS & QUICK EATS

Picadilly Capers Cafe & Bar (☎ 03-218 1044; 38 Dee St; lunch mains $7-17, dinner mains $13-26; ☺ lunch & dinner) Big and colourful with a mezzanine, couches and lots of cushions, this is a comfortable spot for a coffee or meal. The menu overflows with standard fish, pastas and meat but the specials are far more interesting.

Sassy's Café (☎ 03-218 8836; 45 Esk St; mains $5-14; ☺ breakfast & lunch Mon-Sat) In the city centre, this tiny café is vaguely stylish and definitely popular. Sassy makes interesting sandwiches (such as asparagus and ham or chicken, mango, chilli and lime), all-day breakfast, salads and burgers, and has pavement tables with a prime people-watching vantage point.

In a Pickle (☎ 03-218 7340; 16 Don St; meals $4-12; ☺ breakfast Mon-Fri, lunch Mon-Sat; ☐) The atmosphere (or lack thereof) gears you to expect white-bread sandwiches and day-old pies, but you'll be pleasantly surprised by excellent (and cheap) quiche, bagels, panini, pancakes and the like. The smoothies are fantastic; try autumn pear and maple or blueberry buttermilk.

Other options:

Louie's (☎ 03-214 2913; 142 Dee St; mains $15-26; ☺ lunch Tue-Sat, dinner Tue-Sun) Intimate, fashionable café-cum-tapas-bar that's open late.

Cafe Amici (☎ 03-214 1914; 73 Dee St; light mains $5; ☺ breakfast & lunch Mon-Sat) Soups, savoury muffins, panini and cakes go down well in the company of magazines and local art.

Cod Pot (☎ 03-218 2354; 136 Dee St; meals $6-30; ☺ lunch & dinner) Pre-dates café culture with a few booths, a good takeaway menu, battered oysters and hearty portions of fish and chips.

SELF-CATERING

To create your own one-pot-wonder, head to **Countdown** (cnr Doon & Tay Sts).

Drinking

The **Frog 'n' Firkin** (☎ 03-214 4001; 31 Dee St) is an atmospheric pub with exposed brickwork, an uncluttered interior and couches to while away the hours. Another good option is hip **Louie's** (☎ 03-214 2913; 142 Dee St), also a café, where you can settle yourself at the bar or in one of the booths. The **Zookeepers Cafe** (☎ 03-218 3373; 50 Tay St) is a restaurant that also has a well-stocked bar.

Entertainment

Frog 'n' Firkin (☎ 03-214 4001; 31 Dee St) As a background to clinking pint glasses, this pub has a small stage and hosts free DJ events on end-of-week nights.

Globe (☎ 03-214 3366; www.theglobe.net.nz; 25 Tay St; free-$10) One of the biggest clubs in town, capturing crowds from Thursday to Saturday nights in the DJ-attended main space and live bands in the upstairs Thirsty Kiwi bar.

Embassy Theatre (☎ 03-214 0050; 112 Dee St) Open as a club-bar on roughly the same nights as the Globe, and also doubling on occasion as a large live-music, comedy and thespian venue.

Reading Cinemas (☎ 03-211 1555; www.reading cinemas.co.nz; 29 Dee St; adult/child $12/7) Offers big-screen entertainment, showing first-run films.

Stadium Southland (☎ 03-217 1200; www.stadiumsouth.co.nz; Surrey Park, Isabella St) Home to Invercargill's extremely popular Southern Sting women's netball team (www.sting.co.nz). In 2005 they lost the national title that they'd held for six consecutive years. The season runs late March to late May.

Shopping

Invercargill certainly won't give shoppers a buzz. However, if you're looking to outfit yourself with gear for Southland's trails, you're in luck. Check out **Southern Adventure** (☎ 03-218 3239; 31 Tay St) and **H&J's Outdoor World** (☎ 03-214 2052; 21 Tay St), conveniently located next door to each other, and stocked with everything from maps to boots to sleeping bags to dried food.

Getting There & Away

AIR

Catch a daily flight to Christchurch (from $95) via **Air New Zealand** (☎ 0800 737 000, 03-215 0000; www.airnz.co.nz; 46 Esk St), with connections to other major centres. **Stewart Island Flights** (☎ 03-218 9129; www.stewartislandflights.com) flies to Oban from Invercargill (adult/child one way $90/55, return $155/85) three times daily.

BUS

Buses leave from the visitor information centre where you can also book your tickets. **InterCity** (☎ 03-214 6243; www.intercitycoach.co.nz) heads to Dunedin ($31) twice daily via Gore ($15), with connections on to Christchurch ($54). **Atomic Shuttles** (☎ 03-214 6243; www.atomictravel.co.nz) also has daily runs to Dunedin ($30, three hours) via Gore ($20, one hour) and to Queenstown (three hours) via Te Anau ($40, 2½ hours). You can connect on to Christchurch ($60) from Dunedin and to Wanaka ($50) from Queenstown.

Catch-A-Bus (☎ 03-249 8900) also heads daily to Dunedin ($37) while **Knightrider** (☎ 03-342 8055) operates a night-time service on the Christchurch–Dunedin–Invercargill route.

Wanaka Connexions (☎ 03-443 9122; www.wanakaconnexions.co.nz) has daily buses to Queenstown ($45) and Wanaka ($60). **Scenic Shuttle** (☎ 0300 277 483, 03-249 7654; reservations@scenicshuttle.com) offers a door-to-door daily shuttle to Te Anau (adult/child $40/32).

Stewart Island Experience (☎ 0800 000 511, 03-212 7660; www.stewartislandexperience.co.nz) runs a door-to-door shuttle to Bluff (adult/child $15/7.50) connecting with the Stewart Island ferry. Catlins Coaster and Bottom Bus pass through Invercargill; see p683.

Getting Around

Invercargill Airport (☎ 03-218 6920; 106 Airport Ave) is 2km west of central Invercargill. **Spitfire Shuttle** (☎ 03-214 1851) will take you door-to-door from $6 (depending where you are or where you're going in Invercargill). By taxi

it's around $15; try **Blue Star Taxis** (☎ 03-218 6079) or **Taxi Co** (☎ 03-214 4478).

It's difficult to miss Invercargill's bright-pink Express Freebie, a free bus service around the town centre departing every 15 minutes from 10am to 4.30pm week-days, and 10am to 2.30pm Saturday. Stops include the visitor information centre and Dee, Tay, Esk, Kelvin and Gala Sts. Other-wise, regular **city buses** (☎ 03-218 7108; single trip adult/child $1/80c, day pass adult/child $3.50/2; 7am-6pm Mon-Fri, 9am-3pm Sat) run to the suburbs; these buses are free from 9am to 2.30pm weekdays and from 9am to 3pm Saturday.

BLUFF

pop 2100

Shabby little Bluff is Invercargill's port, 27km south of the city. The only reason to come here is to catch the ferry to Stew-art Island. That said, there is some decent accommodation should you need to stay overnight. For information, visit the vis-itor information centre in Invercargill, a visitors desk at the ferry terminal or www.bluff.co.nz.

While Bluff isn't actually the South Is-land's southernmost point (this claim to fame belongs to Slope Point in the Catlins), 'from Cape Reinga to Bluff' is oft-quoted to signify the entire length of NZ. The coun-try's main highway, SH1, runs between the two and terminates near Bluff at the **Stirling Point signpost**, which indicates distances to far-flung cities around the world.

The small **Bluff Maritime Museum** (☎ 03-212 7534; 241 Foreshore Rd; adult/child $2/free; ☑ 10am-4.30pm Mon-Fri, 1-5pm Sat & Sun) is packed to the gills with exhibits on local history and in-dustry, including whaling, mutton-birding and Bluff's shipwreck-littered bay.

Paua Shell House (258 Marine Pde; admission $5; ☑ 9am-5pm) is nearly impossible to miss, with its giant emu and dinghy-sized fake paua shell crowding the lawn. Inside are shells from around the world (includ-ing more than 1000 wall-decorating paua shells) along with kitsch statuary. Odd.

If you've got some time to kill, tackle **Foveaux Walk** (2½ hours return; 6.6km), a coastal walkway from the signpost to Ocean Beach; alternatively, follow it for 1km and return, by the 1.5km **Glory Track**. Drive or walk the 3km to the observation point on top of 265m-high **Bluff Hill** (accessed off Lee

St) for unobstructed views of surrounding flatlands and Stewart Island. Pick up *Bluff Walking Tracks* (free) from the visitors desk.

The **Bluff Oyster & Southland Seafood Festival** celebrates Bluff's famous delicacy and is held annually in either late April or early May. The oysters are in season from late March to late August; brave folks let them slide down to their belly raw.

Sleeping & Eating

Bluff Camping Ground (☎ 03-212 7106; unpowered/powered sites per 2 people $16/28, cabins $24) Ultrabasic everything, with gravel or grass sites and simple cabins. Use of the kitchen or showers costs $2 extra. Sites have views out to the bay...and factories.

Bluff Lodge (☎ 03-212 7106; 120 Gore St; dm $15, d $32-45; □) Dated and basic, but doubles are somewhat homey and there's a big kitchen. Dorm beds are lined up in a large room.

Lazy Fish (☎ 03-212 7245; www.thelazyfish.co.nz; 35 Burrows St; d $100-120) This gorgeous period villa has a sunny deck and garden with two nice big rooms that are tastefully decorated (if you can ignore the '70s carpet). The self-contained room is out the back; the other room is smaller, with old-fashioned nautical touches. Both have private entrances, and it's close to the ferry terminal.

Land's End (☎ 03-212 7575; www.landsend.net.nz; Stirling Point; d $125-140) Opposite the Stirling Point signpost, this prominent house has old-fashioned rooms. The more expensive ones offer great water views, and breakfast is included, but the price is still somewhat steep. There's also a country-style restaurant (lunch mains $10 to $17) with fresh seafood; dinner is available by reservation.

Drunken Sailor Cafe & Bar (☎ 03-212 8855; Stirling Point; lunch mains $7-20, dinner mains $17-30; ☺ lunch daily, dinner Tue-Sun) A slightly dated interior is instantly forgotten as you take in the superb sea views that this Land's End eatery has to offer. Unsurprisingly, it specialises in seafood. In summer, book ahead for Saturday nights.

Big Oyster Seafood Restaurant (☎ 03-212 8180; Ocean Beach Rd; mains $15-25; ☺ lunch & dinner Tue-Sun) Adjacent to Fowler's Oysters company, the oysters here are as fresh as they come. Other fresh catch and some token nonseafood mains are available. You'll find it on the edge of town, en route to Invercargill.

Getting There & Away

Stewart Island Experience (☎ 0800 000 511, 03-212 7660; www.stewartislandexperience.co.nz) runs a door-to-door shuttle between Bluff and Invercargill (adult/child $15/7.50) connecting with the Stewart Island ferry. It also offers secure vehicle storage by the ferry terminal ($5 per day).

INVERCARGILL TO DUNEDIN

Following SH1 across interior farmland is the somewhat faster, most direct route from Invercargill to Dunedin. While the scenery is pretty in a pastoral way, it's certainly not as dramatic as the route via the Catlins (p684); if you have the time, opt for the latter. En route, decently sized Gore is a good place to stop to refuel yourself and your car and to take in a little culture via its superb gallery.

Gore

pop 8500

Unpack your cowboy boots and stomp into town. Relaxed Gore is Southland's second largest town and the hub for all of that surrounding farmland. Spanning the brown trout-laden Mataura River, with the Hokonui Hills as a pretty, though distant, backdrop, Gore has some good spots for lunch. And despite appearances, the town's folk don't bite.

Inside **Hokonui Heritage Centre** is the **Gore visitor information centre** (☎ 03-208 9908; gorvin@nzhost.co.nz; Norfolk St; ☺ 8.30am-5pm Mon-Fri year-round, 10am-4pm Sat & Sun Nov-May, 1-4pm Sat & Sun Jun-Oct); the **Gore Historical Museum** (admission by donation), with some well-executed exhibits; and the **Hokonui Moonshine Museum** (admission $5), which explores a history of insobriety and prohibition in the area.

The outstanding **Eastern Southland Gallery** (☎ 03-208 9907; cnr Hokonui Dr & Norfolk St; admission free; ☺ 10am-5pm Mon-Fri, 2-4.30pm Sun) is set in Gore's gorgeous old public library, with a repurposed interior that houses a hefty collection of NZ art. Expect diverse, contemporary exhibits along with a Ralph Hotere Gallery and the amazing, local and global John Money collection. Art lovers will find bliss.

Croydon Aircraft Company (☎ 03-208 9755; www.croydonaircraft.com; SH94, Mandeville), 16km down the road to Queenstown, restores vintage aircraft and offers flights in a two-seater

Tiger Moth ($65 for 10 minutes), five-seater Dragonfly (from $45 per person for 10 minutes) or other tiny 1930s planes.

To stretch your legs, visit **Dolamore Park**, 95 hectares of podocarp forest, lawns and gardens on the edge of the Hokonui Hills. Lots of bird life, 500-year-old rimu and totara trees and, in spring, 500 rhododendrons make for a colourful escape. Trails lead into **Croydon Bush Scenic Reserve**, with 10-minute to four-hour routes and views of the Mataura Valley. You'll find the park 11km west of Gore, signposted off SH94.

If you've already passed the enormous fish statue in town, you won't be surprised to learn that Gore lays claim as the 'World Capital of Brown Trout Fishing'. Often described as 'gin clear', the Mataura River and other local waterways offer popular fly-fishing. Pick up a *Fishing Guide* brochure (free) from the visitor information centre for listings of local guides or try **Daniel Agar** (☎ 025 223 2007; www.mataura-flyfishing.com; per day $625).

Gore has an unusual array of annual events. In February, the **Moonshiners Festival** celebrates food and lots of whiskey. Early June brings the amazingly popular **New Zealand Gold Guitar Awards**, a 10-day country-music festival during which the town is booked out. And it comes less than a month after the **NZ Line Dancing Championships!**

SLEEPING

You can also camp at Dolamore Park (above; sites $10) where there are basic facilities and lots of nature.

Gore Motor Camp (☎ 03-208 4919; gorecamp@xtra .co.nz; 35 Broughton St; unpowered/powered sites per 2 people $22/24, on-site caravans from $32, cabins $36-70) With a small playground, trees and lots of lawn, this is a pleasant place to camp despite its proximity to the highway. If you haven't brought your own house on wheels, settle into a kitsch '70s caravan. Cabins range from basic and clean to recently renovated comfort.

Old Fire Station Backpackers (☎ 03-208 1925; oldfirestation@ispnz.co.nz; 19 Hokonui Dr; dm/d $20/50) Very clean and homey, with friendly caretakers, this stylishly renovated hostel only sleeps 12. Rooms have skylights and dorms have sturdy, wooden bunks with lots of head room. There's a good kitchen, laundry and a pleasant patio with a barbecue and lots of potted flowers. Facilities are wheel-chair accessible. I's located opposite the visitor information centre.

There are a number of nondescript but well-maintained motels in Gore. Try the older **Charlton Motel** (☎ 0508 202 780, 03-208 3130; charlton.motel@xtra.co.nz; 9 Charlton Rd; d $95) or the more contemporary **Riverlea Motel** (☎ 0508 202 780, 03-208 3130; www.nzmotels.co.nz/riverlea; 46-48 Hokonui Dr; d $90-120). The visitor information centre can hook you up with local B&Bs or farmstays.

EATING

Café De Paz (☎ 03-208 5888; 51 Main St; lunch mains $7-12, dinner mains $14-28; ☯ lunch & dinner Wed-Sun) A colourful café serving feisty Mexican fare (as hot as you require) amid sombreros, maracas and bright blankets. Try a Mexican-style gourmet pizza (with names like sweet senorita or veggie virgin). Kids have an excellent menu. For dessert, dare to try the chilli chocolate ice cream or mango pudding. This is also a great place for coffee.

Green Room Café (☎ 03-208 1005; 59 Irk St; mains $5-10; ☯ lunch; ▯) A sunlight-dappled café with wooden floors, old-fashioned movie seats and excellent coffee. The cakes are yummy and it's exceptionally child-friendly, with an area for tykes to hang out.

Howl at the Moon (☎ 03-208 3851; 2 Main St; mains from $15-25; ☯ lunch & dinner; ▯) Catering to the cowboys, this ranch-themed restaurant serves typical, hearty mains as well as a 'wine and food experience menu' with dishes like ostrich hotpot. There's a children's menu but, not surprisingly, not much for vegetarians.

THE CATLINS

The winding coastal route between Invercargill and Dunedin passes through the enchanting Catlins, a region of beautifully isolated forests and wildlife-filled bays, stretching from Waipapa Point in Southland to Nugget Point in South Otago. With endless natural sights, beaches, side roads and gorgeous vistas, it's well worth spending a couple of days exploring. You won't find much in the way of facilities but there is wonderful accommodation where you can kick back and watch the coast for whales. Though recently sealed, SH92 through the Catlins has lots of twists, turns and narrow

THE CATLINS

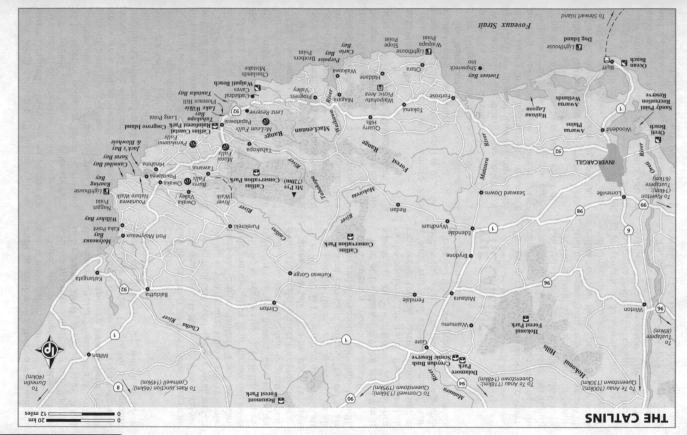

History

The Catlins was once inhabited by moa hunters and evidence of their camp sites and middens has been found at Papatowai. Between AD 1600 and 1800 the Maori population thinned out because of the decline of the moa, the lack of kumara cultivation, and a fear of wild, legendary, yeti-like creatures called *maeroero* (wild men of the forest), who were believed to live in the area (see the boxed text, p684). Later, whalers occupied sites along the shore line, including Waikawa Harbour, Tautuku Peninsula and Port Molyneaux. Next, timber millers moved into the dense stands of beech forest in the 1860s (at the height of logging there we're about 30 mills in the area), followed by a wave of settling pastoralists.

Flora & Fauna

Podocarp forests still exist in the Catlins, with tall kahikatea, totara, rimu and miro trees. Behind the sand dunes of Tahakopa and Tautuku Bays, native forest extends several kilometres inland, with vegetation zones most clearly visible at Tautuku. Watch for sand-dune plants (marram, lupin, flax) near the beach; low trees like rata, kamahi and five-finger just beyond the sands behind the dunes; and mature forest beyond. A good example of young forest is found near Lake Wilkie, where growth has occurred on the sediments that have gradually filled in the lagoon.

The Catlins is a wonderful place for independent wildlife-watching. There are lots of New Zealand fur seals and Hooker's sea lions lazing along the coast, while elephant seals breed at Nugget Point (p686). In spring, keep your eyes peeled for southern right whales, which are occasionally spotted offshore. There are also many sea estuary and forest birds, plus the endangered hoiho (yellow-eyed penguin), blue ducks and the rare mohua (yellowhead).

Information

Contact the main Owaka-based **Catlins visitor or information centre** (03-415 8371; info@catlins-nz.com; 20 Ryley St; 9am-5pm Mon-Fri), also the home of **DOC** (03-419 1000). Or try the smaller **Waikawa visitors centre** (03-246 8444; dolphinmagic@xtra.co.nz; Main Rd, Waikawa; 10am-5pm summer only). All centres stock the free *Catlins Highway Guide* map, listing sights and walks. Both www.catlins.org.nz and www.catlins-nz.com are well-maintained websites on the region. *Stay a While in the Catlins* ($3), written by local wildlife ranger, K Widdowson, has details on spotting wildlife and a little on walking tracks.

The Catlins has no banks, few petrol stations and limited options for eating out or grocery shopping. If you plan to spend some time here, stock up before you arrive.

Tours

Bottom Bus (Dunedin 03-434 7370, Queenstown 03-442 9708; www.bottombus.co.nz) motors along a regular loop that visits Queenstown, Dunedin, Te Anau and Milford Sound via the Catlins, Invercargill and the Southern Scenic Route. It stops at all main points of interest, where you can hop off and catch the next bus coming through. The Southlander pass ($375) lets you to start anywhere and includes a Milford Sound cruise. There are also lots of other pass options.

Catlins Coaster (0800 304 333, 021 682 461; www.catlinscoaster.co.nz; Sep-May), run by Bottom Bus, offers a day tour through the Catlins from Dunedin (adult/child $140/85), a tour from Dunedin to Invercargill (adult/child $130/30) and multiday options including farmstays and Stewart Island flights.

Papatowai-based **Catlins Wildlife Trackers** (0800 228 567, 03-415 8613; www.catlins-ecotours .co.nz) offers ecofriendly guided walks (two nights for $380) and tours (two/four nights $300/590) of the region with food, accommodation and transport (from Balclutha if necessary). The conservation-guru guides have been running the tours for 15 years and also manage **Top Track**, a 26km self-guided walk through beaches and a private forest. It costs $15 if you walk it in a day or $35 if you do it in two, including accommodation in a converted bus.

Catlins Natural Wonders (0800 353 941; www .catlinsnatural.co.nz) also offers first-rate guided trips focusing on wildlife. One-day trips cost $130/85 out of Dunedin/Balclutha, or there's an overnight trip ($200/150, plus accommodation).

In Owaka, **Catlins Adventures** (03-415 8488; www.catlinsadventuress.co.nz; Nov-Apr) runs day

sections; it's similar in distance but slower going than the inland route along SH1.

trips to Cathedral Caves ($85) including time on foot, in a kayak and in a 4WD. The company also rents kayaks ($30) and mountain bikes ($30), and runs yellow-eyed penguin tours ($40). **Catlinger Adventure Centre** (☎ 03-415 8835; www.catlinger.co.nz) runs similar tours and blokart trips ($30).

If you're short on time, **Catlins Tours** (☎ 03-230 4576; www.nzcountry.co.nz/catlinstours; tours $100) runs day tours from Invercargill to the region's major sites like Curio Bay and Cathedral Caves.

INVERCARGILL TO PAPATOWAI

Heading southeast from Invercargill, SH92 passes close to the 14,000-hectare **Awarua Wetlands**, which is waddled in by various wading bird species. The SH92 then arrives at Fortrose, from where the **Shipwreck Inn** is visible at low tide, across the sandy harbour.

From Fortrose, take the turn-off to **Waipapa Point**. The lighthouse here was built in 1884, three years after NZ's second-worst maritime disaster, where SS *Tararua* struck the Otara Reef 1km offshore, leaving only 20 survivors from 151 passengers and crew. From here, it's well worth continuing on the backroads via Haldane, Waikawa and Niagara (where you can rejoin SH92), not only for the sights but for the reflective inlets and wind-blown, rolling hills.

Slope Point, off Waipapa Point, is the South Island's most southerly point. A walk across private land (20 minutes) leads to a small beacon atop a spectacular spur of rock. If anyone is about, ask permission first; the track is closed in September and October for lambing. Take the turn-off at Tokanui for the 13km drive to Slope Point.

Continuing east, clamour down to **Curio Bay** within four hours either side of low tide, to see a 160-million-year-old fossil forest left over from the Jurassic period. The petrified stumps, fallen-log fossils and plant species identified here show NZ's one-time connection to the ancient supercontinent Gondwanaland. This is one of the world's oldest such sites and fascinating to explore.

Neighbouring **Porpoise Bay** has excellent accommodation and a gorgeously sandy, windswept beach that's safe for swimming. Blue penguins nest here and, in summer, you may see Hector's dolphins, which come here to rear their young; please give them

a wide berth as human harassment has been encouraging them to find alternative nurseries. Fur seals and sea lions also live here. Join a one-hour **Progress Valley Downhill** (☎ 03-246 8781; niagarafallscafe@xtra.co.nz; Main Rd, Niagara; tours $25) for a 4WD trip to a knoll with gorgeous views over Porpoise Bay and a mountain-bike ride down to Niagara Falls Café.

Inside the old church in **Waikawa** is **Porpoise Bay Wildlife Cruises** (☎ 03-246 8444; dolphin magic@xtra.co.nz; St Mary's Church, Main Rd), which runs sea-bound tours in the area and acts as an information centre and store.

The tall, arched **Cathedral Caves** (www.cathedralcaves.co.nz; admission per car $5, per cyclist or tramper $2) are big and open, tempting even the claustrophobic inside for a look-see. Located on Waipati Beach, the caves are only accessible for two hours either side of low tide; bring your wellies and check the tide timetables posted on the website, at the highway turn-off and at visitor information centres. The caves are sometimes closed due to weather conditions; pay heed. From the highway it's 2km to the car park, a 15-minute walk to the beach and a further 25 minutes to the caves. The turn-off to pretty **Mclean Falls** (40 minutes return) is just before Cathedral's car park; the trail is 3.5km up a dirt road.

From here, the road passes through forest that's a collage of greens. **Lenz Reserve** has a bird lodge and the remains of the old Tautuku sawmill just a short walk from the road. At **Tautuku Bay**, walk 15 minutes to the stunning, sandy beach punctuated by drifts of seaweed, and at **Lake Wilkie** wander among unique plant life. Past Tautuku is a great lookout over sandy beach and sea, at **Florence Hill**.

Further east, at the mouth of the Tahakopa River, is tiny **Papatowai**. A base for forays into the nearby forests, it has a few facilities but not many. From here, stretch your legs in the **Catlins Coastal Rainforest Park** along Tahakopa Bay.

Sleeping & Eating

WAIPAPA & SLOPE POINTS

Slope Point Backpackers (☎ 03-246 8420; justherb@ xtra.co.nz; Slope Point Rd; cm/d $18/40) Basic dorms and doubles on a 140-hectare sheep and cattle station where you can join in with farming activities.

Nadir Outpost (☎ 03-246 8544; nadir.outpost@ihug .co.nz; 174 Slope Point Rd; dm/d $18/36) Next door to Slope Point Backpackers, this is a '70s-style cottage with tiny, slightly stale dorms, a small shop selling basic supplies and a pleasant garden where you can pitch a tent.

Waipapa Point (☎ 03-246 8493; www.waipapa point.co.nz; 59 Waipapa Point Rd; d $120) Just up the road from the lighthouse, settle into a spacious, modern, self-contained cottage with lots of light and ocean views, or a comfortable double in the main house. The hosts are friendly and relaxed, and you can walk across their working farm to the coast where sea lions lounge.

CURIO BAY

Curio Bay Camping Ground (☎ 03-246 8897; 601 Curio Bay Rd; unpowered/powered sites per 2 people $30/50) A whaling station once upon a time, this is a beautiful spot to camp with tall grass making for private sites, some with sea views. There's beach access, a small shop and a penguin hide.

Dolphin Lodge (☎ 03-246 8577; niagarafallscafe@ xtra.co.nz; 529 Curio Bay Rd; dm/d $22/62) An older, '70s-style house with nothing-special rooms but magnificent views from the lounge and deck. There's a big kitchen, and when we visited, there were two southern right whales showing off in the harbour. For an extra $3 you get breakfast and a duvet.

Curio Bay Boutique Accommodation (☎ 03-246 8797; accommodation@curiobay.com; Curio Bay Rd; d $150-220) With a big deck and even bigger sea views, these two plush units are well equipped and have giant, timber-framed beds to watch the surf from.

WAIKAWA & NIAGARA

Waikawa Holiday Lodge (☎ 03-246 8552; niagara fallscafe@xtra.co.nz; Main Rd, Waikawa; d$50) Quaint but fairly basic with doubles and twins in an older, green house. There's a small kitchen, fireplace, a big grassy lawn and you're across the street from the Waikawa visitors centre (p683), where you can get sandwiches, cakes and the like in summer.

Niagara Falls Café (☎ 03-246 8577; Main Rd, Niagara; lunch mains $8-15, dinner mains $19-22; ☯ breakfast & lunch Sep-May, dinner Nov-Mar) An excellent, atmospheric eatery with fantastic, fresh soups, *panini*, all-day breakfasts, and pastas, catering well to carnivores and herbivores. Enjoy scrumptious cakes on the patio or have a browse through the small gift shop with crafts from local and South African artists.

PAPATOWAI

Papatowai Motor Camp (☎ 03-415 8500; pest@es.co.nz; unpowered/powered sites per 2 people $14/16) Behind

AUTHOR'S CHOICE

Curio Bay Backpackers (☎ 03-246 8797; accommodation@curiobay.com; Curio Bay Rd; dm $22, d $55-75) Disguised as a Portakabin from the outside, this amazing place will beg you to stay for weeks. Opening onto a grassy lawn that slopes down to the sandy beach, you get views of dolphins and orcas jumping in the bay. The cosy front room has a wood stove and the modern kitchen is spacious. Two doubles (one with en suite and view) and a room of bunks means a top capacity of nine – unless you count the blue penguins waddling by at night.

the Papatowai Scenic Highway Store is this field, with little foliage for privacy.

Hilltop (☎ 03-415 8028; www.catlins-nz.com/hilltop .html; 77 Tahakopa Valley Rd; dm $22, d $60-70) With parkland at its doorstep, this exceptional backpackers is surrounded by rolling green hills and has amazing sunset views over the bay. The two beautifully furnished farmhouses seem far too upmarket to be a backpackers. It's truly a home away from home.

Papatowai Scenic Highway Motels & Store (☎ 03-415 8147; b.bevin@paradise.net.nz; Main Rd; d $80) A rare chance to stock up on essentials, basic takeaways and petrol. Also offers spacious, well-appointed motel units.

Southern Secrets Motel (☎ 03-415 8600; southern secret@xtra.co.nz; Main Rd; d $95) Four comfortable, newly renovated units, two with happy nautical décor and each with a balcony; DVD player and full kitchen; one is wheelchair accessible. The owner was talking about turning the neighbouring house into a boutique backpackers. Worth checking out.

Erehwon (☎ 03-415 8877; southernsecret@xtra.co.nz; 5 Alexandra St; d $130) A three-bedroom holiday home with a wood stove, wood furnishings and vaguely granny-esque décor, but entirely homey nonetheless.

PAPATOWAI TO BALCLUTHA

From Papatowai, follow the highway north to **Matai Falls** (10 minutes) on the Maclennan River, then head southeast on the signposted road to the tiered **Purakaunui Falls** (10 minutes). Both are reached via pleasant forest walks and are much more impressive after heavy rain.

You can continue along the gravel road from Purakaunui Falls to the 55m-deep **Jack's Blowhole** (⊗ closed for lambing Sep & Oct). In the middle of paddocks on the southern side of the Catlins River's mouth, it's 200m from the sea but connected by a subterranean cavern. It was named after Chief Tuhawaiki, nicknamed Bloody Jack for his frequent use of the English expression. On the river mouth's northern side is the **Pounawea Nature Walk** (45 minutes return), looping through kahikatea, ferns, kamahi, rimu, totara and southern rata. On the northern side of SH92 lies Owaka Valley and the **Catlins Conservation Park** with the **Catlins River Walk** (five hours one way) through silver beech forest. At each end there's a DOC camping ground.

Owaka is the Catlins' main town (although its population is only 395), with a visitor information centre and DOC office (see p683), grocery store and petrol station. A number of tours and activities base themselves here and there's some decent accommodation. However, it's not the most welcoming place. Once you're stocked up, it's worth venturing off into the more remote Catlins.

East of Owaka, **Cannibal Bay** was named by a geologist who discovered human bones in the dunes. Today it's the breeding ground of Hooker's sea lions, which are visible along the walk (30 minutes) between here and Surat Bay.

Heading north from Owaka, detour off SH92 to **Nugget Point**, stopping for a short walk (15 minutes) to view wave-thumped rocky outcrops off the lighthouse-topped promontory. If you get there when the sunlight is hitting the rocks just so, you'll understand how they came by their name. Fur seals, sea lions and elephant seals occasionally bask together on the rocks, a very rare coexistence. Yellow-eyed and blue penguins, gannets, shags and sooty shearwaters all breed here. On your way to the 1869 lighthouse, you'll pass **Roaring Bay**, where there's a well-placed hide to see yellow-eyed penguins coming ashore (usually two hours before sunset).

From Nugget Point the road loops back through **Kaka Point**, with its sandy, quiet beach, and on through Port Molyneux towards Balclutha.

Sleeping & Eating
OWAKA & PURAKAUNUI

There's a DOC camping ground (camp sites $4) down on the water at Purakaunui Bay.

Falls Backpackers (☎ 03-415 8724; spar@es.co .nz; Purakaunui Falls Rd; dm/d $22/55) Five minutes east of Purakaunui Falls, this lovely farmhouse has country-style rooms with homey touches and peaceful views of rolling, sheep-dotted hills.

Catlins Backpackers (☎ 03-412 8111; www.catlin backpackers.co.nz; 24 Main Rd, Owaka; dm/d $23/60) Two beautifully renovated houses with warm colours, characterful rooms and a big grassy yard. Originally Blowhole Backpackers, new owners are maintaining this hostel's charm, and have upped security and heating. A great place to stay.

PJ's B&B (☎ 03-415 8711; jennyandpeter@xtra.co.nz; 32 Waikawa Rd, Owaka; s/d $50/100) A warm retreat in a period homey guest rooms and breakfast is included. You'll find it on the eastern edge of town.

Catlins Area Motel (☎ 03-415 8821; www.nzmotels .co.nz/catlins; Clark St, Owaka; d $105) A new and very tasteful row of spacious, self-contained units. Each has a small deck with patio furniture to laze on.

Lumberjack Bar & Café (☎ 03-415 8747; 3 Saunders St; mains $9-25; ☒ lunch & dinner Thu-Sun, daily summer) With a rustic, log-cabin feel, big open fire and a timber bar made from a 6m-long piece of macrocarpa, this is Owaka's best bet for meals. The menu is unsurprising but diverse.

Catlins Diner (☎ 03-415 8392; Main Rd; mains $4-12; ☒ breakfast, lunch & dinner) Standard takeaway along with a funked up eat-in area with leather sofas, wobbly modern art and chill-out music.

Catlins Inn (☎ 03-415 8350; 21 Ryley St) Hang out with the locals (if you dare) and have a drink here while filling up with 'bar baskets' of food ($4 to $6).

Other accommodation options:
Owaka Lodge Motel (☎ 03-415 8728; owakalodge motel@xtra.co.nz; 12 Ryley St, Owaka; d $80) Across from the visitor information centre, these units are dated but comfy and clean.
Catlins Retreat Guesthouse (☎ 03-415 8830; www .catlins-nz.com/retreat.htm; 27 Main Rd, Owaka; d $120-130) An atmospheric, century-old home with brand-new owners who whip up a fabulous breakfast (included).

SURAT BAY & POUNAWEA
Pounawea Motor Camp (☎ 03-415 8483; pounawea .moto.camp@xtra.co.nz; Park Lane, Pounawea; sites per 2 people $20, cabins & caravans s/d $19/45) Wooded tent sites sandwiched between the gorgeous beach and bird-friendly Pounawea Scenic Reserve. An ace place to camp. From Owaka, follow the signs to Pounawea.

Surat Bay Lodge (☎ 03-415 8099; www.suratbay.co .nz; Surat Bay Rd, Surat Bay; dm $25/65, cabins s/d $30/50; ☒) This dated hostel has some excellent views of the sea (particularly the back twin room) and is neighbours with the Hooker's sea lions. There are also some new, basic cabins with a communal kitchen.

Kepplestone-by-the-sea (☎ 03-415 8134; kepple stone@xtra.co.nz; 9 Surat Bay Rd, Surat Bay; tw/d $75/120) A spacious twin or snug double, both with en suite and situated in a lovely, flower-speckled garden. The décor is a little old-fashioned but the hosts are as sweet as can be.

NUGGET & KAKA POINTS
Fernlea Backpackers (☎ 03-412 8834; Moana St, Kaka Point; dm/d $18/36) Perched atop a view-blessed hill, this tiny bungalow is ultrasnug with excellent sea views and basic facilities. There's one wee double with views all of its own. Head up the garden trail from Moana St.

Cardno's (☎ 03-412 8181; www.cardnosaccommo dat on.co.nz; 8 Marine Tce, Kaka Point; d $90-130) Furnished with a contemporary Scandinavian design look, these airy, plush units have huge views out to sea. There's a small guest bar, continental breakfast available ($10), a walkway down to the beach and very personable hosts. Choose between a studio unit with kitchenette or a self-contained unit. Multinight stays earn you a discount.

Lazy Daisy (☎ 0800 478 752; www.lazydaisy.co.nz; Main Rd, Kaka Point; d $120) An 1893 cottage across the street from the beach with two doubles, a bunk room, comfortable furnishings, a small garden and great views. Kids are catered to with books, DVDs and treats. The owners live off-site.

Nugget Lodge (☎ 03-412 8783; www.nuggetlodge .co.nz; Nugget Rd, Nugget Point; d $140-150) Flanked on either side by quiet sandy beaches, you can listen to the pounding surf from these two rooms. The upstairs pad has a private deck overlooking the sea and more character than the downstairs unit. Both are tastefully furnished, peaceful retreats. Breakfast is $15. One of the owners is the local wildlife ranger and can provide a wealth of local naturalist information. It's about 5km down a side road from Kaka Point.

Point (☎ 03-412 880C; 58 Esplanade, Kaka Point; mains $9-24; ☒ lunch & dinner) An average menu, with a fresh 'daily catch', sea views and a driftwood bar.

Stewart Island & Outer Islands

From tiny, balmy, tropical atolls to subantarctic bird-haven islets, New Zealand's island life stretches far from the shores of its North and South landmasses. Many of the country's extended family of islands are not easily reached and getting to them is truly half of the adventure, taking you on seafaring voyages into the frozen south or into the Pacific's earthquake-riddled 'ring of fire'. That said, both Stewart Island and the Chatham Islands are accessible, tourist-friendly destinations that are well worth the effort.

Take the relatively short jaunt to relaxed Stewart Island and you will be rewarded with a warm welcome from the kiwis – well, not quite, but this is one of the few places where you can spot these shy birds in the wild. NZ's largest outer island, Stewart Island is only 40km from the underside of the South Island, and is brimming with native birds, sandy coves and long, scenic tramping tracks.

Lying 850km east of NZ's main islands, the Chatham Islands offer diverse, lush landscape with flocks of endemic bird life, the chance to experience unique Moriori culture and ample opportunity to dine on crayfish.

Head to the Subantarctic Islands to see deep-south nature reserves, or travel 1000km northeast of NZ to the volcanic Kermadec Islands, the site of the country's biggest marine reserve. Even further north are the lagoon-surrounded atolls of Tokelau, sitting halfway to Hawai'i and under threat of rising sea levels.

If you've got a sense of adventure, even a vague interest in bird life and appreciate a good seafood dinner, your efforts to reach NZ's most remote shores will not go unrewarded.

HIGHLIGHTS

- Discovering sheltered bays and sandy coves along Stewart Island's **Rakiura Track** (p693)
- Wandering the lush, bird-laden trails of **Ulva Island** (p692)
- Taking in the dramatic scenery, including 200-year-old Moriori tree carvings, in the **Chatham Islands** (p696)
- Being serenaded by the multiplicity of birds on **Stewart Island** (p691)
- Sailing to the **Subantarctic Islands** (p700) with a scientific expedition
- Swimming with the spotted black groper in the **Kermadecs** (p701)
- Filling up on succulent crayfish in **Waitangi** (p699)
- Visiting tiny **Tokelau** (p701) where tourists are rare but culture rife

■ TELEPHONE CODE: 03 ■ www.stewartisland.co.nz

★ Tokelau

★ Kermadec Islands

Stewart & Ulva Islands ★
Subantarctic ★ ★ Chatham Islands & Waitangi
Islands

STEWART ISLAND & OUTER ISLANDS FACTS

Eat: Fresh crayfish

Drink: Anything on tap at the South Sea Hotel (p695), NZ's southernmost bar

Read: *Hand Guide to the Birds of NZ* by Hugh Robertson

Listen to: The cacophony of birdsong

Watch: *The Feathers of Peace* (2000), a moving, brutal account of the history of the Moriori

Swim at: Remote Mason Bay on Stewart Island, where the water's cold but the sand is frequented by kiwis

Climate

The incredibly changeable weather on Stewart Island can bring four seasons in one day. Frequent downpours create a misty, mysterious air and lots of mud, making boots and waterproof clothing your new best friends. Nevertheless, the temperature is milder than you'd expect: the winter average is around 10°C; summer is 16.5°C.

The Chatham Islands are very exposed but have a temperate climate. Average daily temperatures vary from 12°C to 18°C in February and 6°C to 10°C in July. The best time to visit is in December and January, when temperatures often reach 23°C.

Tokelau has a tropical climate, with an average temperature of 28°C and heavy but irregular rainfall. Tropical storms are rare, but do occasionally wreak havoc.

Climatic forecasts for the utterly remote islands are a little harder to come by but can be summed up as tropical for the Ker-

madecs and wet, cold and windy for the Subantarctic Islands.

TOP ACTIVITIES

- Hike Stewart Island's boardwalked Rakiura Track (p693)
- Spot shy kiwis in the wild (p693)
- Take in lush scenery and bird mania on tiny Ulva Island (p692)
- Hop on a vast vessel to the Subantarctic (p700) or a two-person kayak through Stewart Island's Paterson Inlet (p693)
- Check out what's under the warm waters around the Kermadecs (p701)

STEWART ISLAND & OUTER ISLANDS

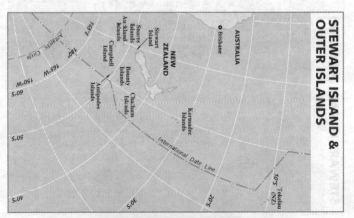

STEWART ISLAND

pop 420

Due south of Invercargill, Stewart Island's Maori name is Rakiura or Glowing Skies; stay for a spectacular blood-red sunset or catch a glimpse of the *aurora australis* and you'll quickly know why. This is NZ's third-largest island, home to an unspoilt wilderness that stretches across its triangular mass and is filled with an unbelievable cacophony of birdsong. Rakiura National Park protects 85% of the island, creating an oasis for trampers and birdwatchers. It's also surrounded by countless sandy, isolated coves, many of which are good for swimming if you're willing to brave the chilly water.

Stewart Island's small, easy-going population is primarily settled in the fishing village of Oban in Halfmoon Bay. The atmosphere here is remote and rugged and friendly. It's a wonderful place to just chill.

www.lonelyplanet.com

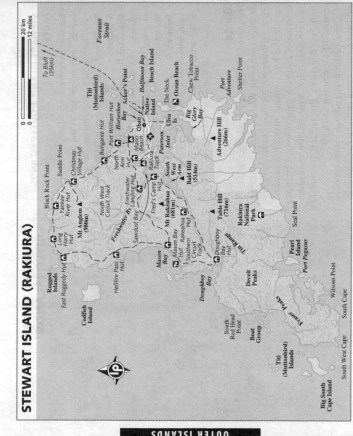

STEWART ISLAND (RAKIURA)

History

According to myth, NZ was hauled up from the ocean by Maui (p54), who said, 'Let us go out of sight of land, far out in the open sea, and when we have quite lost sight of land, then let the anchor be dropped'. The North Island was the fish that Maui caught, the South Island his canoe, and Rakiura was the anchor – 'Te Punga o te Waka o Maui'.

There is evidence that parts of Rakiura were occupied by moa hunters as early as the 13th century. The *titi* (mutton bird or sooty shearwater) on adjacent islands were an important seasonal food source for the southern Maoris.

The first European visitor was Captain Cook, who sailed around the eastern, southern and western coasts in 1770 but somehow couldn't figure out if it was an island or a peninsula. Deciding it was attached to the South Island, he called it South Cape. In 1809 the sealing vessel *Pegasus* circumnavigated Rakiura and named it after its first officer, William Stewart.

In June 1864, Stewart and the adjacent islets were bought from the Maoris for £6000. Early industries were sealing, timber milling, fish curing and shipbuilding, with a mini, short-lived gold rush towards the end of the 19th century. Today the island's economy is dependent on tourism and fishing – crayfish (lobster), paua (abalone), salmon, mussels and cod, with plenty of opportunities for you to test the wares.

Orientation

Stewart Island is roughly 65km long and 40km across at its widest point. It has less than 20km of roads and a rocky coastline incised by numerous inlets, the largest of which is Paterson. The highest point on the island is Mt Anglem (980m).

Set in Halfmoon Bay, Oban, the main settlement, is a tiny village and easily traversed on foot. Bring a torch (flashlight) for nightfall in lieu of street lights.

Information

On the ferry from Bluff there's a folder stuffed with information on the island, including lists and photos of accommodation. There are no banks on Stewart Island. In a squeeze, the visitor information centre can offer Eftpos services, but certainly don't count on it. Credit-card payment is accepted for many services, but it's wise to bring a supply of cash to last the duration of your stay.

You can access the Internet at Justcafé and South Sea Hotel.

DOC Stewart Island visitor information centre (☎ 03-219 0009; stewartislandfc@doc.govt.nz; Main Rd; ☑ 8.30am-7pm Mon-Fri & 9am-7pm Sat & Sun summer, 8.30am-5pm Mon-Fri & 10am-noon Sat & Sun winter) A wealth of information on all things related to the island along with an interesting permanent exhibition (free) and exceedingly helpful staff.

Oban visitor information centre (☎ 03-219 0056; Main Rd) Stewart Is and Experience (the ferry folk) takes bookings for activities, organises sightseeing tours and rents scooters, cars, fishing rods, dive gear and even golf clubs.

Post office (Elgin Tce) Located at the office of Stewart Island Flights.

Stewart Island Health Centre (☎ 03-219 1098; Argyle St; ☑ 10.30am-12.30pm) For medical assistance, has 24-hour on-call service.

Stewart Island Visitor Terminal (☎ 03-219 0034; Main Wharf) Booking agency for local activities, the Bluff ferry and water taxis.

Sights
FLORA & FAUNA

You don't have to step off your balcony to experience the island's lush flora and fauna, yet the more you explore, the more you'll encounter. Nature has cranked the birdsong up to full volume here; it's impossible not

---

---

to notice the abundance of tui, parakeets, kaka, bellbirds, fernbirds, robins and dotterels that continually flap overhead, perch in the garden and sing to you on the patio. With a little more effort, you can also see kiwis (below) as well as Fiordland crested, yellow-eyed and blue penguins.

Two species of deer, the red and the Virginia (whitetail), were introduced to the island in the early 20th century, as were brush-tailed possums, which are numerous in the northern half of the island and highly destructive to the native bush. Stewart Island has lots of NZ fur seals, which sometimes beach themselves right up in Halfmoon Harbour.

Unlike NZ's North and South Islands, there is no beech forest on Stewart Island. The predominant lowland vegetation is hardwood but there are also lots of tree ferns, ground ferns and several types of orchid. Along the coast there's mutton bird scrub, grass tree, tree daisies, supplejack and leatherwood. Around the shores are clusters of bull kelp, fine red weeds, delicate green thallus and bladder ferns of all shapes and sizes.

Kiwi Spotting

The search for *Apteryx australis lawryi* is a highly rewarding ecoactivity, particularly when you know where to look. The Stewart Island kiwi is a distinct subspecies, with a larger beak and longer legs than its northern cousins. Kiwis are common over much of Stewart Island, particularly around beaches where they forage for sandhoppers

INFORMATION
DOC Stewart Island Visitor Information Centre....1 A2
Oban Visitor Information Centre................2 A2
Post Office...3 B2
Stewart Island Health Centre..................4 B2
Stewart Island Visitor Terminal...............5 B2

SIGHTS & ACTIVITIES
Community Centre..................................6 B2
Observation Rock...................................7 A3
Presbyterian Church Hall........................8 B2
Rakiura Museum....................................9 B2
Seabuzz Tours.....................................10 B2

SLEEPING
Bay Motel...11 A2
Bellbird Cottage..................................12 B3
Jo & Andy's B&B..................................13 A2
Joy's...14 A2
Kaka Cottages.....................................15 B1
Latt 47° Cottage..................................16 B2
Michael's..17 B3
Pilgrim Cottage....................................18 B1
South Sea Hotel...................................19 B2
Stewart Island Backpackers...................20 B2
Stewart Island Lodge............................21 B3

EATING
Bush Honey...22 A3
Charliez Pizzeria..................................23 B2
Church Hill Cafe, Bar & Restaurant.........24 B1
Fishermen's Co-op.........................(see 31)
Justcafé...25 B2
Kai Kart...26 B2
Ship to Shore......................................27 B2
Wharfside Café.............................(see 5)

ENTERTAINMENT
Rakira Theatre..............................(see 23)

SHOPPING
Fernery..28 A3
Island Outdoors...................................29 B2
Rakiura Gallery............................(see 23)

TRANSPORT
Golden Bay Wharf.................................30 A3
Stewart Island Experience Ferry..............31 B2
Stewart Island Flights.....................(see 3)

STEWART ISLAND & OUTER ISLANDS

under washed-up kelp. Unusually, Stewart Island's kiwis are active during the day as well as at night – the birds are forced to forage for longer to attain breeding condition. Many trampers on the North West Circuit Track spot them. For a helping hand with sightings, see Tours (p691). Also see the boxed text, p694.

ULVA ISLAND

Ulva Island is a tiny paradise, covering only 250 hectares but packed with natural splendour. An early naturalist, Charles Traill, was honorary postmaster here. He would hoist a flag to signal that mail had arrived and hopefuls would paddle in from surrounding islands. His postal service fell out of favour in 1921 and was replaced by one at Oban. A year later, Ulva Island was declared a bird sanctuary.

Bird-watchers go all woozy here. As soon as you get off the launch the air is alive with the song of tui and bellbirds, and you'll see kaka, weka, kakariki and kereru (NZ pigeon). The abundance of bird life is due mainly to the absence of predators.

Good walking tracks have been developed in the island's northwest and are detailed in *Ulva: Self-Guided Tour* ($2), available from DOC. Popular routes include **Flagstaff Point Lookout** (20 minutes return) and **Boulder Beach** (1½ hours return). The forest has a mossy floor and many paths intersect beautiful stands of rimu, miro, totara and rata.

You can get to Ulva by water taxi for a return fare of about $20 to $25 (see p696).

OTHER SIGHTS

Rakiura Museum (Ayr St; adult/child $2/50c; ☼ 10am-noon Mon-Sat, noon-2pm Sun) is compact and worthwhile. See the various boats used to ferry folk to the island over the years, a small but sobering exhibit on whaling, Maori artefacts, and old photos, maps and objects from early European settlements. One has to wonder at the willpower needed to bring an organ all the way from Britain.

The wooden **Presbyterian Church Hall**, relocated from a whaling base in Paterson Inlet in 1937, is worth a look. At Harrold Bay, about 2.5km southwest of town, is a **stone house** built by Lewis Acker around 1835. It's one of the oldest stone buildings in NZ.

Activities

WALKING

Even if you're not a gung-ho hiker, Stewart Island is a wonderful place to stretch your legs and immerse yourself in wilderness on a short walk. For more serious trampers, there are excellent, multiday, DOC-maintained trails to sink your boots into. The **DOC Stewart Island visitor information centre** (for DOC-specific inquiries ☎ 03-219 0002; Main Rd) sells hut passes and has detailed pamphlets on local tramps. Gear can be stored here in small/large lockers for $2.50/5 per day.

In the northern part of the island, there's a good network of tracks with huts occupied on a first-come, first-served basis. Each hut has foam mattresses, wood stoves for heating, running water and toilets; you need to carry a stove, food, sleeping bags, eating and cooking utensils and first-aid equipment. A tent can be very useful over the summer holidays and at Easter, when the huts tend to fill up. The southern part of the island is undeveloped and desolate. You're strongly advised not to go off on your own, particularly from the established walks.

Day Walks

There are a number of short walks, ranging from half an hour to seven hours, and the majority are easily accessed from Halfmoon Bay. Pick up *Day Walks* ($1) from the visitor information centre for route details and maps. The walk to **Observation Rock** (30 minutes return) has good views over Paterson Inlet. Continue past the old stone house at Harrold Bay to **Acker's Point Lighthouse** (three hours return), where there are good views of Foveaux Strait and the chance to see blue penguins and a colony of shearwaters (muttonbirds).

Multiday Walks

The 29km, three-day **Rakiura Track** is one of NZ's Great Walks (p87), a well-defined, easy circuit starting and ending at Oban with copious bird life, beaches and lush bush en route. Extensively boardwalked, this scenic track gets very crowded in summer. Besides the shelter of huts at Port William and North Arm (both with room for 30 trampers), there are camping grounds at Sawdust Bay, Maori Beach and Port William. Overnight trampers need to buy either a Gate-stamped **Great Walks hut pass** (adult/child per night $10/5) or **camping pass** (adult/child per night $6/3); there's a limit of two consecutive nights in any one hut. For more info, see the DOC pamphlet *Rakiura Track* ($1).

Following the island's northern coast is the **North West Circuit Track**, a 125km trail that takes between 10 and 12 days to complete and is often plagued with deep, thick mud. This walk is only suitable for well-equipped and experienced trampers, as is the 56km **Southern Circuit Track** that branches off it, adding a further four days. A **North West Circuit Pass** ($38) gives you a night in each of these tracks' huts. Alternatively, you can use **Back Country Hut tickets** (per night $5) or an **Annual Hut Pass** ($65) to stay in huts on either circuit track, but you'll still have to buy a **Great Walks huts pass** (per night adult/child $10/5) for use at Port William and North Arm. See the DOC brochure *North West & Southern Circuit Tracks* ($1) for full details.

Both the Rakiura and North West Circuit Tracks are detailed in Lonely Planet's *Tramping in New Zealand*.

OTHER ACTIVITIES

Paterson Inlet consists of 100 sq km of sheltered, kayak-friendly waterways, with 20 islands, DOC huts and two navigable rivers. A popular trip is a paddle to Freshwater Landing (7km upriver from the inlet) followed by a three- to four-hour walk to Mason Bay to see kiwis in the wild. **Rakiura Kayaks** (☎ 03-219 1160; www.rakiura.co.nz) rents kayaks from $40 a day, and also runs guided trips around the inlet (half-/full-day trip $50/75). **Stewart Island Sea Kayaks** (☎ 03-219 1080) also rents kayaks for similar rates and runs guided trips (one-/two-day trip $85/215). **Oban visitor information centre** (☎ 03-219 0056; Main Rd) rents mountain bikes/motor scooters (per half day $25/45). The island's **Community Centre** (☎ 03-219 1477; 10 Ayr St; nonmembers $5) houses a gym, a coin-operated sauna, netball and squash courts, all of which are open to visitors.

Tours

Book tours at the DOC visitor information centre or Stewart Island Visitor Terminal.

Ruggedy Range Wilderness Experience (☎ 03-219 1066; www.ruggedyrange.com) takes small groups on guided walks, kayaking or kiwi spotting, with an ecofriendly, conservation angle and lots of local knowledge. Excursions range from a full-day trip to Ulva Island ($145) to a five-day tramp around Stewart Island ($2550).

Ulva's Guided Walks (☎ 03-219 1216; www.ulva.co.nz) offers just that, but with Maori history and conservation included in the interpretation. Three-hour tours are $85, with transport included.

Coast to Coast (☎ 03-218 9129; www.stewartisland flights.com; adult/child $155/105) can give you an adventure-packed day with a flight from Oban and beach landing at Mason Bay, a four-hour independent bush walk and a one-hour boat ride through Paterson Inlet to Golden Bay. You can extend the trip by staying overnight on the track and can also do it in the reverse order.

Stewart Island Experience (☎ 03-219 1134; www .stewartislandexperience.co.nz; Stewart Island Visitor Terminal), a branch of Real Journeys, not only operates the ferry but runs 2½-hour Paterson Inlet cruises (adult/child $70/18; daily Oct to April) via Ulva Island; daily 1½-hour minibus tours of Oban and the surrounding bays (adult/child $32/15); and daily, 45-minute semisubmersible cruises (adult/child $37/15) for a chance to see what lies below.

If you're keen to see a kiwi in the wild, **Bravo Adventure Cruises** (☎ 03-219 1144; philldi smith@xtra.co.nz) and Ruggedy Range Wilderness Experience (above) run night-time tours to spot these flightless marvels. Numbers are limited, for protection of the kiwi, so make sure you book *well* ahead.

There are a number of charter companies all vying for your company on their boat. The companies offer fishing trips, wildlife cruises and trips up Paterson Inlet. Prices are dependent on the number in your party, but a half day at sea usually goes for

around $75 per person. Contact the visitor information centre for a full list or try the following:

Aurora Charters (☎ 03-219 1126; www.auroracharters .co.nz)

Bravo Adventure Cruises (☎ 03-219 1144; philldi smith@xtra.co.nz)

Seabuzz Tours (☎ 03-219 1282; www.seabuzz.co.nz; Argyle St) Runs two-hour glass-bottom boat tours (adult/child $60/30).

Talisker Charters (☎ 03-219 1151; www.talisker charter.co.nz) Also runs dive charters and 'live aboard' charters along the Fiordland.

Thorfinn Charters (☎ 03-219 1210; www.thorfinn .co.nz) Half- and full-day tours.

Sleeping

Despite Oban's surprisingly high number of motels, hostels, holiday homes and B&Bs, finding accommodation can be difficult, even in the off-season when many places shut down. It's very wise to book ahead; otherwise, head to the visitor information centre pronto for help finding and booking a room.

Keep in mind that self-contained flats or holiday homes often offer very good value. Basic backpacker-style accommodation is available in some homes (often only in summer); it's often impossible to prebook these and for most you'll need your own sleeping bag.

BUDGET

Jo & Andy's B&B (☎ 03-219 1230; jariksem@clear.net .nz; cnr Morris St & Main Rd; s/d/tw $40/60/60) An excellent option for budget travellers, this cosy blue home somehow manages to have a twin, double and single room in it. A big breakfast of muesli, porridge, fruit and homemade bread is included and dinner is available for $18. One of the hosts is a massage therapist – handy knowledge if you're coming off a long tramp.

Stewart Island Backpackers (☎ 03-219 1114; back packers@stewart-island.co.nz; cnr Dundee & Ayr Sts; dm/d $20/45; 🖳) Rooms are basic but clean, some are brightly painted and many open onto a courtyard. There are only three beds per dorm (with the exception of one with bunks) and the common kitchen and lounge are spacious. There's also table tennis, coin-operated Internet, books and a barbecue.

For basic accommodation also try **Michael's** (☎ 03-219 1425; Golden Bay Rd; dm $20) or **Joy's** (☎ 03-

219 1376; Main Rd; dm $20). Both are open in summer only.

MIDRANGE

Pilgrim Cottage (☎ 03-219 1144; 8 Horseshoe Bay Rd; d $95) This very quaint, weatherboard cottage is approached along a short forest trail, making for a wooded oasis just steps from the centre of town. Lots of warm wooden furnishings, a potbelly stove, a well-equipped kitchen and small TV and radio will keep you snug. The many windows and patio give a small view of the harbour.

Lerwick (☎ 03-219 1552; Butterfield Beach; d $95) Located a 20-minute walk north of town, this open-plan, self-contained house has two bedrooms and a sleep-out. Water views and some lovely wooden furnishings make it very homey and it's about as private as you can get.

Rakiura Retreat Motel (☎ 03-219 1096; www.rakiuraretreat.co.nz; Horseshoe Bay Rd; d $140) Surrounded by native bush, this row of motel units isn't fancy but the rooms are comfortable and peaceful. Situated northeast of Oban, the rooms capture good views over Halfmoon Bay. Mountain bikes are available for guest use and meals can be prearranged.

Kaka Cottages (☎ 03-219 1252; 7 & 9 Miro Cres; d $100-120) At the back of town, these studio units and self-contained cottages have wooden interiors and verandas facing the bay. They're not flash but have a pleasant cabin feel. Courtesy transfers and baby furnishings (cot and highchair) are available.

Bellbird Cottage (☎ 03-219 1330; Excelsior Rd; d $95) It's nothing fancy but this three-bedroom house has a veranda with gorgeous views of the bay and surrounding hills and a tranquil garden inviting countless birds.

South Sea Hotel (☎ 03-219 1059; www.stewartislandlodge.co.nz; 26 Elgin Ter; s $40-80, d $80-120; ▢) Built in 1890, this harbourside hotel has slightly worn, floral rooms with a big deck and excellent sea views. There's a basket of earplugs in the hall, alluding to the fact that the downstairs pub often overpowers the sound of the surf on weekends. Out the back, sunny motel units manage a South Pacific look with high ceilings, a small kitchenette and veranda.

TOP END

Port of Call B&B (☎ 03-219 1394; www.portofcall.co.nz; Leask Bay Rd; s/d $210/290) With only one guest room, you'll be very well catered for in this comfortable home. Relax in the library, soak up views over the bay and strait, get cosy before the big open fire or head down to the isolated beach. Your hosts are a sixth-generation Stewart Island family; you'll find them 1.5km southwest of Oban, on the way to Acker's Point. The owners also rent out a nearby, modern studio unit called the Bach ($220 to $250), which is equally comfortable.

Bay Motel (☎ 03-219 1119; www.baymotel.co.nz; Dundee St; d $140-160) Modern, comfortable units with lots of light and views over Oban and the harbour. One- and two-bedroom units have big spa tubs, all rooms have full kitchens and two are wheelchair-accessible. Free transfers to and from town and cots and highchairs are also available.

Latt 47° Cottage (☎ 03-219 1330; 12A Excelsior Rd; d $170) A newly built, spacious, very central guesthouse with a wood-beamed ceiling, nautical colours and modern furnishings. The front room opens onto the patio, with harbour views. Inside, there are two double bedrooms and a big bath. Kids aren't welcome.

Greenvale B&B (☎ 03-219 1357; www.greenvalestewartisland.co.nz; Elgin Ter; s/d $200/250) Only 50m from the sea, this modern home has stunning views over Foveaux Strait. Each of the two rooms is plush with en suite, pure-cotton linen, contemporary furnishings and splashes of red. It's a five-minute walk into town.

Stewart Island Lodge (☎ 03-219 1085; www.stewartislandlodge.co.nz; Nichol Rd; per person $220-300) Upmarket retreat with six en suite rooms, each opening onto a shared deck. The gorgeous garden is a magnet for birds. Situated up a steep hill or the edge of town, the lodge commands magnificent views. Prices include just breakfast, or breakfast and a gourmet seafood dinner.

Eating & Drinking

Justcafé (☎ 03-219 1567; Main Rd; meals $7-9; ☑ lunch; ▢) Warm little place with wooden-bench tables, lots of magazines, and funky crafts for sale. Fill up on soups, tasty sandwiches and baking and nurse a good coffee.

South Sea Hotel (☎ 03-219 1059; 26 Elgin Ter; mains $14-28; ☑ breakfast, lunch & dinner) With old B&W photos and a café-style interior, this hotel is a comfortable place to dine with

up basic tramping gear like tents, rain gear and torches.

The visitor information centre has a great selection of books on island history and wildlife, with lots aimed at children. It also sells CDs of bird calls in case you've become used to Stewart Island's outdoor soundtrack.

Getting There & Away

AIR

Stewart Island Flights (03-218 9129; www.stewart islandflights.co.nz; Elgin Tce) flies between the island and Invercargill (adult/child one way $90/55, return $155/85). Flights depart three times daily year-round. Phone ahead for occasional discount fares. The bus trip from the island's Ryan's Creek airstrip to Oban is included in the air fare.

BOAT

The passenger-only **Stewart Island Experience Ferry** (03-212 7660; www.stewartislandexperience .co.nz) runs between Bluff and Oban (adult/child $50/25), three times daily. Definitely book a few days ahead in summer. The strait crossing takes one hour and is often a rough ride. The company also runs a shuttle between Bluff and Invercargill (adult/child $13/6.50), with pick-up and drop-off at many Invercargill motels and the visitor information centre.

Getting Around

There are many sea taxis offering pick-ups and drop-offs to remote parts of the island, which is a handy service to trampers. The taxis also service Ulva Island; return fares are about $20. Try **Stewart Island Water Taxi & Eco Guiding** (03-219 1394), **Seabuzz Tours** (03-219 1282) or **Kaian Water Taxi** (03-219 1013). Several operators are based at Golden Bay Wharf, about a 10-minute walk from the township.

CHATHAM ISLANDS

pop 770

Named Rekohu (Misty Sun) by the Moriori, the Chathams lie way out in the South Pacific Ocean, 850km due east of Christchurch. This remote group of 10 islands comprises the first human habitation over the international dateline. Apart from the 50 or so people on Pitt Island, only Chatham Island is significantly populated.

AUTHOR'S CHOICE

Church Hill Cafe, Bar & Restaurant (03-219 1323; 36 Kamahi Rd; lunch mains $10-22, dinner mains $16-38; lunch & dinner) Walk up a wooded trail to this excellent eatery, which has an intimate interior and tables on the deck and lawn. The hilltop perch offers excellent sea views, particularly at sunset. Seafood is the speciality but there's also stone-grilled meat, huge salads and mutton bird. Reservations are highly recommended for dinner.

---

the locals, digging into tasty seafood and interesting vegetarian dishes (like gnocchi). The attached pub is the town's main drinking hole, graced by an occasional weekend band.

Kai Kart (03-219 1225; Ayr St; meals $5-15; lunch & dinner Oct-Apr) Squid rings, mussel chowder and blue cod and chips are dished up from this blue van outside the Rakiura Museum. There are a couple of booths inside and picnic tables on the lawn.

Wharfside Café (03-219 0070; Wharf) At the time of writing, this eatery was being taken over by Stewart Island Experience (the ferry folk), who promised to have it open year-round with warm food and coffee to preempt your journey.

Charliez Pizzeria (03-219 1429; Main Rd) was also due to open, serving gourmet pizzas and wine in close proximity to the brand new Rakiura Theatre, home to art-house and mainstream films.

Self-caterers can get groceries from Oban's general store, **Ship to Shore** (03-219 1069; Elgin Tce; 7.30am-6.30pm Mon-Fri). The Fishermen's Co-op at the main wharf often has fresh fish and crayfish for sale and you can pick up some fresh, organic bush honey at a roadside stand at 5 Golden Bay Rd.

Shopping

You certainly don't come to Stewart Island for the shopping, but the **Fernery** (03-219 1453; 29 Golden Bay Rd) is a gallery well worth a visit. In a beautiful bush setting, it sells unique crafts, island-themed books, paintings and etchings. **Rakiura Gallery** (03-219 1429; Main St) sells pottery, paua jewellery and other local crafts, while **Island Outdoors** (03-219 1437; Elgin Tce) is the place to pick

CHATHAM ISLANDS

The islands' geographical contrasts are striking: rugged coastlines and towering cliffs, volcanic peaks, lagoons and peat bogs, sweeping beaches, isolated farms and dense patches of forest. The main industry, besides farming and tourism (particularly ecotourism) is crayfish processing, and there are plants at Waitangi, Kaingaroa, Owenga and Port Hutt. These four towns have strong communities and what you might call a dilapidated charm.

History

The Chatham Islands were formed aeons ago by volcanic upthrust and were first inhabited by the Moriori tribe, which arrived between 500 and 1100 years ago. Its distinctive Polynesian culture was mainly peaceful but the situation changed for the worse with the arrival of Europeans in 1791 and groups of mainland Maoris in the mid-1800s. By the beginning of the 20th century there were just 12 full-blooded Moriori left and, in 1933, the last full-blood Moriori died. See the boxed text, p698.

Information

Information on the islands is available from the **Te Iwi Moriori Trust Board** (☎ 03-305 0466; info@chathams.govt.nz; Waitangi Wharf, Oweng Rd, Waitangi), **Air Chathams** (☎ 03-305 0209; chatsoffice@xtra.co.nz), or the local **council** (☎ 03-305 0033; www.cic.govt.nz; Tuku Rd, Waitangi). Once you're on the Chatham Islands, the best way to get

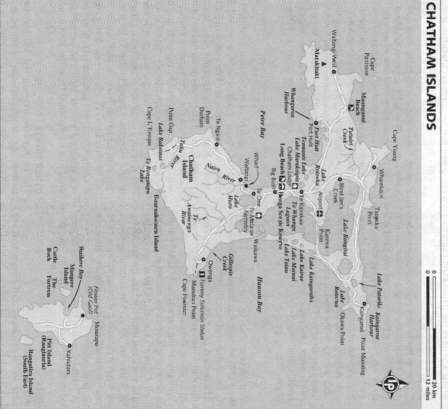

THE SURVIVAL OF THE MORIORI

Some time between AD 900 and AD 1500, a group of Polynesians landed on the isolated Chatham Islands. Over time, they became the Moriori, a people with a distinct culture and language. While historians have long claimed that the Moriori were originally Maori who sailed from NZ, more recent finds strongly argue that the Moriori arrived directly at the Chathams. They lived in a society without rigid social divisions, they forbade tribal warfare and settled disputes on a one-to-one basis with hand-to-hand combat. Today you can still see the fascinating symbols they carved into trees (dendroglyphs) and rocks (petroglyphs) fringing Te Whanga Lagoon (opposite).

When the HMS *Chatham* arrived in 1791 and claimed the islands for Britain, there were believed to be about 2000 Moriori on the islands. But the establishment of whaling and sealing industries, and the consequent depletion of two of the Moriori's main sources of food, soon took its toll on the local population.

Hard times got worse in 1835, when groups of mainland Maoris began to arrive in the Chathams. The 900 new residents began to occupy the land in a process known as *takahi*, killing about 300 resisting Moriori and enslaving others. By 1841 there were believed to be only 160 Moriori and over 400 Maoris, and it wasn't until two years later that the last of the Moriori slaves were released. In 1870 the Native Land Court Hearings recognised that the mainland tribes had sovereignty over 97% of the Chathams by right of conquest, and small reserves were created for the 90 surviving Moriori.

In time, the Moriori intermarried and slowly their unique culture and identity faded. Their language died with the last great Moriori scholar, Hirawanu Tapu, in 1900. In 1933 the last full-blood Moriori, Tommy Solomon, died. His passing was seen, at the time, as the extinction of the race, but it was far from that. His three sons and two daughters were identified as Moriori and there were many other families on the island who claimed Moriori ancestry. There are now believed, with a revival of Moriori consciousness, to be over 300 Moriori descendants in the Chathams.

In August 2001, the Waitangi Tribunal decided that the ancestral rights to the Chatham Islands belong to the Moriori and concluded that Moriori should receive compensation for the lasting impact of the Crown's failure to intervene after the 1835 mainland Maori invasion. Moriori descendants have begun to negotiate their redress with the NZ government and, while justice is still a long time coming, they have won recognition to claim a share of the resources in the islands' fishing grounds.

informed is to talk to the locals. The **DOC office** (☎ 03-305 0098; amckillop@doc.govt.nz; Te One) may be unattended, so call before you visit.

The book *A Land Apart*, by Michael King and Robin Morrison, has a wealth of information about the islands.

Waitangi is the islands' only sizable town and has a couple of shops, a hotel and a small hospital. There's also an **ANZ bank**, which also doubles as a **post office** (⏰ 10am–2pm Mon, Tue, Thu & Fri). There are no ATMs; some businesses accept credit cards but it's wise to bring cash. Time on the islands is 45 minutes ahead of mainland NZ time.

All visitors need to have confirmed accommodation before they arrive on the islands.

Sights

BIRDS & SEALS

There are 18 species of bird unique to these islands and, because of their isolation, there is a large degree of endemism, as with the local tui, pigeon and mollyhawk. While entry to sanctuaries on Pitt and Rangatira (South East) Islands is prohibited, many species can still be seen outside; DOC staff can outline the best viewing spots for twitchers. Endangered birds include the black robin, once perilously close to extinction in its last refuge, Mangere Island. The very rare Chatham Island taiko (*Pterodroma magentae*) nests in the Tuku River region of Chatham Island's south coast.

There's a fur seal colony near Kaingaroa in the northeast of Chatham Island, but access is across private land and permission must first be obtained from the landowner.

OTHER SIGHTS

The mysterious 200-year-old Moriori **tree carvings** (dendroglyphs) can be found in a grove adjacent to the old Te Hapupu aerodrome, in a signposted and fenced-off area open to the public. **Rock engravings** (petroglyphs) survive on the shores of Te Whanga Lagoon, not far from the airstrip.

Fossilised sharks teeth can be seen at Blind Jim's Creek, also on the shores of Te Whanga Lagoon. These teeth are about 40 million years old and an extremely important part of local heritage; please leave them where you see them. Their appearance here, pushed up by the waves of the lagoon, has not yet been fully explained.

At Manukau Point near Owenga, there's **a statue** of the 'last Moriori', Tommy Solomon; see the boxed text, opposite. There's also a small **museum** (☎ 03-305 0033; admission free; ☒ 8.30am-4.30pm Mon-Fri) of Moriori artefacts in the council offices in Waitangi.

Activities & Tours

The islands have plenty of fine beaches where you can fish and catch crayfish. Crays are a major industry in the Chatham Islands and are exported to North America and Japan. There are daily per-person quotas for cray and paua hauls; be sure to check with DOC. Divers can explore shipwrecks in the clear waters around the islands. **Chatham Fish & Dive Charters** (☎ 03-305 0575; chathamadventures@xtra.co.nz) and **Starkeys Fishing Tours** (☎ 03-305 0424; www.starkeys.co.nz) both offer fishing and diving tours. Hotel Chathams and Chatham Lodge (see Sleeping, following) can also organise tours.

Trampers can strike out on the **walking tracks** in DOC-established reserves. **Liz & Bruce Tuanui** (☎ 03-305 0351; listuanui@xtra.co.nz) offer guided tours into the Tuku Reserve.

For tour operators visiting local sights, check with the Te Iwi Moriori Trust Board.

Sleeping

All visitors are required to have confirmed accommodation before arriving on the islands. Over summer, the hotel and the lodge are often filled by tour groups, and this means other accommodation subsequently gets booked out too, sometimes for months at a time. Book as far ahead as possible in peak season.

Beach House Backpackers (☎ 03-305 0048; www.beachhousebackpackers.co.nz; Waitangi; dm $35) Centrally located with a kitchen, laundry, bike hire (per day $20) and airport transfers ($10). There's also a camping area.

Chatham Motels (☎ 03-305 0003; www.chathammc.co.nz; Waitangi; dm/d $50/100) Basic accommodation in a bunkhouse as well as self-contained units. Unit three is right in the centre of town and has two bedrooms and extras like a barbecue and deck with a harbour view. There's also a more remote farmhouse for rent ($70 per person).

Te Matarae Farmstay (☎ 03-305 0144; s/d $85/100, ☒) This family farmstay near the shores of Te Whanga Lagoon, 11km from Waitangi, is built of wood and surrounded by natural bush. You'll find good kayaking and swimming opportunities, free airport transfers, breakfast included and meals available. The three bedrooms are separated from the home by an indoor pool and there's a guest dining room if you're after privacy.

Hotel Chathams (☎ 03-305 0048; www.hotelchatham.co.nz; Waitangi; s/d $75/120) Waitangi's social focal point, with good rooms – most with balconies and sea views. Singles have shared facilities.

Chatham Lodge (☎ 0800 424 2842, 03-305 0291; www.chathamlodge.net.nz; s/d from $100/125) With rolling farmland out the front door and the lush Henga Scenic Reserve out the back, this is a peaceful place to bunk down. Rooms are quiet and comfortable and activities include boating and hiking through the reserve to the coastline. Decently priced meals are available as are package tours from Wellington. You'll find the lodge north of the Kaingaroa and Airport Rds junction.

Eating

Most places to stay offer meals. Central eating options include the **Hotel Chathams** (☎ 03-305 0048; Waitangi; ☒ lunch & dinner), with a restaurant specialising in seafood, and **Petre Bay Takeaways** (☎ 03-305 0132; Waitangi). Self-caterers can head to **Waitangi General Store** (☎ 03-305 0041; Wharf Rd, Waitangi).

You can buy crayfish and blue cod at the packaging factory in Waitangi. Flounder and whitebait can be caught in the lagoon, and paua and kina gathered just offshore.

Getting There & Away

Air Chathams (☎ 03-305 0209; chatsoffice@xtra.co.nz) flies directly to Chatham Island from Wellington, Christchurch and Auckland (one way adult/child from $325/225). You can book these through **Air New Zealand** (☎ 0800 737 000, 03-363 0600; www.airnz.co.nz). The flight takes two hours and it's wise to book well ahead as seats are limited.

Getting Around

The airport is 21km north of Waitangi on Chatham Island and isn't serviced by any regular transport. Accommodation owners do prearranged airport pick-ups, usually for a fee of $10 to $20.

Air Chathams (☎ 03-305 0209; chatsoffice@xtra.co .nz) operates a light aircraft for aerial sightseeing ($380 per hour) and transport to Pitt Island ($70 per person), 19km from Chatham Island.

Beyond Waitangi most roads are unsealed and there's no public transport. **Chatham Motors** (☎ 03-305 0093; chathammotors@xtra.co.nz; Reserve Rd, Waitangi) hires cars and 4WD vehicles, as do Chatham Lodge, Te Matarae Farmstay, Hotel Chathams and Beach House Backpackers. Expect to pay from $80/100 per day for a car/4WD.

land.gen.nz), based in Manapouri, occasionally runs tours to the Subantarctic Islands aboard a small sailing vessel. The company also runs scientific trips that sometimes have room for casual explorers. Spaces are limited and there's often a long waiting list; email or call them about upcoming possibilities.

Heritage Expeditions NZ (☎ 0800 262 8873, 03-338 9944; www.heritage-expeditions.com) runs upmarket, small but lengthy cruises to the Subantarctic and Chatham Islands.

Snares Islands

The Snares Islands are famous for their incredible number of *titi*. It's been estimated that on any one evening during the breeding season (November to April), there will be five million birds in the air. Other birds found here are the Snares crested penguin, cape pigeon and Buller's mollymawks. Landings are not permitted on the islands.

OTHER ISLANDS

NZ fully or partially administers a number of far-flung islands: the Subantarctic Islands to the south, and the Kermadecs and Tokelau in the northern Pacific Ocean.

SUBANTARCTIC ISLANDS

With a spectacularly unrewarding human history of sealing, shipwrecks and forlorn attempts at farming, NZ's remote and windswept Subantarctic Islands have since discovered their true calling as a reserve. The Snares, Auckland, Bounty and Antipodes Islands are all established nature reserves, protecting the lush, diverse vegetation and breeding grounds for sea birds, penguins and mammals such as the elephant seal. The remarkable wealth of bird life found here led to the archipelago's recognition by Unesco as a World Heritage Site in 1998.

The reserves are run and strictly controlled by the Invercargill office of **DOC** (☎ 03-214 4589; www.doc.govt.nz) and can be visited only by permit. To get some idea of this wild environment, visit the Roaring 40s exhibit at Invercargill's Southland Museum & Art Gallery (p674).

You can visit the islands via expensive, well-managed ecotourism boat trips. **Fiordland Ecology Holidays** (☎ 03-249 6600; www.fiord

Auckland Islands

Discovered in 1806, the Auckland Islands posed a shipwreck risk in the 19th century. Settlement was once attempted in Erebus Cove, and it wasn't until 1992 that the last of the introduced cattle were destroyed.

Many species of birds make Enderby Island their temporary or permanent home, including endemic shags, the flightless teal and the royal albatross. Skuas (gull-like birds) are ever-present in the skies above the Hookers sea lion colony. On Disappointment Island there are over 60,000 whitecapped mollymawks and Derrycastle Reef often attracts the turnstone and bartailed godwit waders. With the appropriate permits and guide, landings are permitted on the islands at designated locations.

Campbell Island

Campbell Island is the true domain of pelagic bird species. It's estimated there are over 7500 pairs of southern royal albatross based here, not to mention sizable colonies of greyheaded and blackbrowed mollymawks. The Campbell Island teal is one of NZ's rarest birds, with perhaps only 50 to 100 remaining. Rats found their way to Campbell Island with early explorers and have had detrimental effects on smaller birds. Campbell Island can be visited with the appropriate permits and guide.

Antipodes Islands

These islands get their name from the fact that their position at latitude 180 degrees puts them opposite latitude 0 degrees at Greenwich, England. The real treat here is the endemic Antipodes Island parakeet, which is found with (but does not breed with) the red-crowned parakeet. Wandering albatross nest in the short grass on the islands' higher ground. You cannot land on the Antipodes.

Bounty Islands

Landing is not permitted on any of the 13 Bounty Islands – there's a good chance that you would step on wildlife, as the 135 hectares of these granite islands is soaked in mammals and birds. There are literally thousands of erect crested penguins, fulmar prions and salvins mollymawks clustered in crevices near the lower slopes.

THE KERMADECS

Known in Polynesian as Rangitahua, these subtropical, volcanic islands lie 1000km northeast of NZ. Annexed to NZ in 1887, the group lies in the Pacific's 'ring of fire', where earthquakes and volcanic eruptions regularly occur. The area is home to NZ's largest marine reserve.

Raoul Island is the largest of the archipelago and was settled periodically, most notably in the early 19th century by whalers. Today it has a number of protected archaeological and historical sites as well as a tiny resident population of scientists, rangers and weather-station personnel. Other islands include McCauley and Curtis Islands, L'Esperance Rock and a number of stony outcrops. Most of the islands have boulder-strewn beaches and steep, rocky cliffs.

The Kermadecs perch on the edge of the enormously deep **Kermadec Trench**, and are in the transitional zone between temperate and tropical waters. The unique marine ecosystem has made diving popular, with sighting the elusive spotted black groper the goal.

The islands can't usually be reached without great difficulty and permits aren't readily granted. **New Zealand Seabird Expeditions** (www.nzseabirds.com) has multiday boat journeys from Tauranga to the Kermadecs, including bird-watching and diving. **Heritage Expeditions NZ** (☎ 0800 262 8873, 03-338 9944; www.heritage-expeditions.com; per person from $4000) also runs cruises, with diving, hiking and bird-watching.

TOKELAU

pop 1500

About halfway between NZ and Hawaii, Tokelau is made up of a trio of tiny atolls – Atafu, Nukunonu and Fakaofo. Each has a ribbon of tiny islets surrounding a central lagoon and, together, they total 12.2 sq km of dry land and measure only 5m at their highest point. Tokelau is at extreme risk from the effects of global warming, with rising sea levels, increased severity of storms and the death of coral reefs all frighteningly predicted for the not-too-distant future. UN study teams do not expect Tokelau to be inhabitable beyond the 21st century.

While Tokelau has been governed by NZ since 1925 and, in more recent times administered partially by Samoa, the islands have steadily moved towards self-government, but a referendum in February 2006 failed to result in independence.

Not surprisingly, Tokelau can't support a large population and there has been a steady stream of emigrating Tokelauans for many years – there are now many more Tokelauans living in NZ than on the atolls.

It's tough to visit Tokelau as there's no airport and only one cargo/passenger ship per month. The MV Tokelau departs from Samoa for the 36-hour journey to Tokelau and is usually fully booked with locals. There's no tourism to speak of and almost no established facilities for visitors, although there are a couple of places to stay and a fortnightly interatoll catamaran called the Tu Tolu. Once there, you can snorkel the amazing coral reefs, fish, laze or join in a local batting game of kilikiti.

The **Tokelau Apia Liaison Office** (TALO; ☎ 685-20822; zak-p@lesamoa.net; PO Box 865, Apia), based in Samoa, deals with inquiries and issues visitors permits (NZ$30 for one month), stipulating that consent to visit must be given by village elders, accommodation must be arranged prior to departure, and a return ticket to Samoa must be booked. On Nukunonu, you can stay at the basic **Luanaliki Hotel** (☎ 690-4116; per person $50), with meals included. On Fakaofo and Atafu, homestays can be arranged through TALO.

Read about Tokelau online at www.tokelau.org.nz, www.nukunonu.tk and www.fakaofo.tk, and also check out Lonely Planet's South Pacific & Micronesia guide, which has a chapter on Tokelau.

Directory

CONTENTS

Accommodation	702
Activities	706
Business Hours	706
Children	706
Climate Charts	707
Customs	708
Dangers & Annoyances	708
Disabled Travellers	709
Discount Cards	709
Embassies & Consulates	709
Festivals & Events	710
Food	710
Gay & Lesbian Travellers	711
Holidays	711
Insurance	712
Internet Access	712
Legal Matters	713
Maps	713
Money	714
Post	715
Shopping	716
Telephone	717
Time	718
Tourist Information	719
Visas	719
Women Travellers	720
Work	720

ACCOMMODATION

Across New Zealand, you can tuck yourself in at night in guesthouses that creak with history, facility-laden hotels, comfortably uniform motel units, beautifully situated camp sites, and hostels that range in character from refreshingly relaxed to tirelessly extroverted.

The listings in this guidebook's accommodation sections are ordered from budget to midrange to top-end options. We generally designate a place as budget accommodation if it charges up to $65 per single or $80 per double. Accommodation qualifies as midrange if it costs roughly between $80 and $150 per double, while we've given the top-end tag to any double room costing over $150. These categories differ slightly

in the nation's largest cities (Auckland, Wellington and Christchurch). Here, budget accommodation is up to $100 per double, midrange is between $100 and $200, and top end applies to rooms costing above $200.

If you're travelling during peak tourist seasons, you'll need to book a bed well in advance. The periods when accommodation is most in demand (and at its priciest) include the summer holidays from Christmas to the end of January, Easter, and winter in snowy resort towns such as Queenstown and Wanaka. At other times of the year, you might find that weekday rates are cheaper than weekend rates (except in business-style hotels in larger cities, where the reverse applies), and you'll certainly discover that low-season rates abound. When they're not run off their

PRACTICALITIES

- For weights and measures, the metric system is used.

- Videos you buy or watch will be based on the PAL system (the same system used in Australia, the UK and most of Europe; Japan and the US use the NTSC system).

- Use a three-pin adaptor (the same as in Australia; different to British three-pin adaptors) to plug yourself into the electricity supply (230V AC, 50Hz).

- For news, leaf through Auckland's *New Zealand Herald*, Wellington's *Dominion Post* or Christchurch's *Press* newspapers, or check out www.stuff.co.nz.

- Tune in to National Radio for current affairs and Concert FM for classical and jazz (see www.radionz.co.nz for frequencies), or one of the many commercial stations crowding the airwaves. Kiwi FM (www.kiwifm.co.nz) is a 'choice' choice – it plays only NZ music.

- Watch one of the four national commercial TV stations (not all are available in all regions) or the subscriber TV service Sky TV.

BOOK ACCOMMODATION ONLINE

For more accommodation reviews and recommendations by Lonely Planet authors, check out the online booking service at www.lonelyplanet.com. You'll find the true, insider lowdown on the best places to stay. Reviews are thorough and independent. Best of all, you can book online.

feet, many accommodation providers offer walk-in rates that are significantly reduced from their advertised rates. Walk-in rates are best queried late in the day; travellers should also check websites such as www.wotif.com for last-minute deals.

Visitor information centres usually have reams of information in their areas, often in the form of folders detailing facilities and up-to-date prices; many can also make bookings on your behalf. Alternatively, flick through one of NZ's free, widely available and often-hefty accommodation directories, including the annual *New Zealand Accommodation* guide published by the **Automobile Association** (AA; www.aatravel.co.nz), and the *Holiday Parks & Campgrounds* and *Motels, Motor Lodges & Apartments* directories produced by **Jasons** (www.jasons.com).

B&Bs & Guesthouses

Bed and breakfast (B&B) accommodation in private homes is a growth industry in NZ, with rooms on offer in everything from suburban bungalows and weatherboard cottages to stately manors that have been owned by generations of one family. B&Bs are ubiquitous, popping up in the middle of cities, in rural hamlets and on stretches of isolated coastline. We found that some hosts are getting cheeky though, charging hefty prices for what is, in essence, a room in their home.

Guesthouses are usually spartan, cheap, 'private' (unlicensed) hotels, mostly low-key places patronised by people who eschew the impersonal atmosphere of many motels. However, some are quite fancy and offer self-contained rooms.

Although breakfast is part of the deal at genuine B&B places, it may or may not feature at guesthouses. Your morning meal may be 'continental' (cereal, toast, tea or coffee), 'hearty continental' (add yoghurt, fruit, home-baked bread or muffins), or a stomach-loading cooked meal that includes eggs, bacon and sausages. Some B&B hosts, especially in isolated locations or in small towns where restaurants are limited, may cook dinner for guests, hence places with dinner, bed and breakfast (DB&B) packages.

Tariffs are typically in the $120 to $180 (per double) bracket, though some places charge upwards of $300 per double. Many upmarket B&Bs demand bookings and deposits at least a month in advance, and enforce strict and expensive cancellation policies – ie cancel within a week of your arrival date and you'll forfeit your deposit plus the balance of the room rate. Check such conditions before making a booking.

The B&B Directory of New Zealand (www.bed-and-breakfast.co.nz) is available online and at bookshops and visitor information centres.

Camping & Campervan Parks

Campers and campervan drivers alike are thrown together in 'holiday parks' (previously known as motor camps) that provide powered and unpowered sites, as well as cheap bunk rooms (dorm rooms), a range of cabins, and self-contained units that are often called tourist flats. They also have well-equipped communal kitchens and dining areas, and often games and TV rooms too. In cities, such parks are usually located away from the centre, but in smaller townships they can be very central or near lakes, beaches, rivers and forests.

The nightly cost of holiday-park camping is usually between $10 and $15 per adult, with children charged half-price; powered sites are slightly more expensive. Sheltered accommodation normally ranges from $40 to $90 per double. Prices given for camp sites, campervan sites, huts and cabins in this book are generally for two people.

If you'll gladly swap facilities for wilder, less-developed locations such as national parks, head for one of the 250-plus, vehicle-accessible camping grounds managed by the **Department of Conservation** (DOC; www.doc.govt.nz). DOC also looks after hundreds of back-country huts, most of which can only be reached on foot. For more information, see Tramping (p85).

Farmstays

Farmstays enable you to learn about the agricultural side of NZ life, with guests encouraged to 'have a go' at typical activities on dairy, sheep, high-country, cattle or mixed-farming spreads, as well as orchards. Costs vary widely, with B&B generally around $80 to $120. Some farms have separate cottages where you fix your own food, while others have low-cost, shared, backpacker-style accommodation.

Farm Helpers in NZ (FHINZ; www.fhinz.co.nz) produces a booklet ($25) that lists around 190 farms throughout NZ providing lodging in exchange for four to six hours work per day. **Rural Holidays NZ** (☎ 03-355 6218; www.rural holidays.co.nz) lists farmstays and homestays throughout the country on its website.

Hostels

NZ overflows with backpacker hostels, ranging from small, homestay-style affairs with a handful of beds to refurbished hotels with

scuffed façades and the towering modern structures you'll find in the big cities. The prices given for hostel beds throughout this guidebook are the nonmembership rates.

HOSTEL ORGANISATIONS

The biggest hostel group (and growing all the time) is **Budget Backpacker Hostels** (BBH; ☎ 03-379 3014; www.bbh.co.nz), which has more than 360 hostels on its books, including homestays and farmstays. Membership costs $40 (the membership card doubles as a phonecard with $20 worth of calls) and entitles you to stay at any of the member hostels at a cost no greater than the rates advertised in the annual (free) *BBH Backpacker Accommodation* booklet. Nonmembers pay an extra fee of between $2 and $4, though not all hostel owners charge the difference. The membership card can be bought at any member hostel, or you can have it sent overseas for $45 (including postage; see the website for details). BBH rates each hostel according to traveller feedback, using a percentage figure that supposedly tells you how good (or at least how popular) each hostel is. While the system is generally pretty accurate, our experience is that some highly rated hostels are not that great, and some low-rated places are not that bad.

NZ has 62 Youth Hostels Association (YHA) hostels. The **YHA** (☎ 0800 278 299, 03-379 9970; www.stayyha.com) is part of the International Youth Hostel Federation (IYHF; also known as Hostelling International or HI), so if you're already a member of that organisation in your own country, your membership entitles you to use NZ hostels. Hostels also take non-YHA members, but you'll pay an extra $3 per night. Visitors to NZ should preferably purchase an HI card in their country of residence, but can also buy one at major local YHA hostels at a cost of $40 for 12 months; see the HI website for further details (www.hihostels.com).

YHA hostels provide basic accommodation for individuals, families and groups in small dorms (bunk rooms, usually with four to six beds) and most also have a limited supply of singles, twins, doubles and rooms with bathroom. They have 24-hour access, cooking facilities, a communal area with a TV, laundry facilities and, in larger hostels, travel offices. There's often a maximum-stay period (usually five to seven days). NZ YHA hostels supply all bed linen; you don't need to bring a sleeping bag. Nightly charges are between $19 and $35 per person for members ($3 extra for nonmembers).

The annual *YHA New Zealand Hostel & Discount Guide* booklet details all Kiwi hostels and the discounts (transport, activities etc) members are entitled to.

VIP Backpackers (www.vip.co.nz) represents around 70 NZ hostels, particularly in the cities and major tourist spots. An advantage with VIP is that it's international, with a large network of hostels in Australia, southern Africa, Europe, America and some in Fiji. For around $38 you'll receive a 12-month membership, entitling you to a $1 discount on accommodation. You can join online (www.vipbackpackers.com), at VIP hostels or at larger agencies dealing in backpacker travel.

Nomads Backpackers (www.nomadsworld.com) has only a handful of franchisees in NZ. Membership costs A$39 for 12 months and like VIP results in NZ$1 off the cost of nightly accommodation. You can join at participating hostels, backpacker travel agencies or online.

All of the aforementioned membership cards also entitle the user to sundry discounts on transport, tours, activities and dining.

INDEPENDENT HOSTELS

NZ is an incubator for independent hostels, hatching them across both islands at an impressive rate. With so many places vying for the overnight attention of backpackers and other travellers, it's no surprise that these businesses try hard to differentiate themselves from their competitors. Some promote themselves purely on low-key ambience, lazy gardens, personable owners and managers, and avoidance of noisy bus groups of backpackers, while others bury you in extras such as free breakfasts, free videos, spa pools, use of bikes and kayaks, shuttle buses, theme nights and tour bookings. If possible, check out your chosen place to stay before committing to a night there, to make sure the atmosphere and facilities correspond at least roughly to your expectations. If travelling with your family, note that a number of hostels designate themselves 'unsuitable for children'.

Independent backpacker establishments typically charge $19 to $25 for a dorm bed, $38 to $50 for a single and $50 to $70 for a twin or double room (usually without bathroom), with a small discount if you're a member of BBH, VIP or Nomads (see opposite). Some also have space for a few tents.

If you're a Kiwi travelling in your own country, be warned that some hostels only admit overseas travellers, typically inner-city places that cite problems they've had with locals bothering their guests. If you encounter such discrimination, either try another hostel or insist that you're a genuine traveller and not a bedless neighbour.

Hotels & Motels

The least-expensive form of hotel accommodation is the humble pub, which gets its name from the term 'public house'. These are older-style establishments that purvey beer and assorted social moments, but do a sideline in relatively cheap beds upstairs. Some old pubs are full of character and local characters, while others are grotty, ramshackle places that are best avoided, especially by solo women travellers. If you're considering renting a room above a pub's bar towards the end of the week, always check whether live music is scheduled for that night, or you could find yourself listening to the muted thump of a sound system until the early hours. In the cheapest pubs, singles/doubles might cost as little as $30/50 (with a shared bathroom, that's probably a long trek down the hall), though $40/60 is more common.

At the other end of the hotel scale are five-star international chains, resort complexes and boutique heritage places, all of which charge a hefty premium for their mod cons, snappy service and/or historic opulence. We quote 'rack rates' (official advertised rates) for such places throughout this book, but regular discounts and special deals mean you rarely have to pay such high prices.

There are plenty of midrange hotels around the country that charge between $80 and $150 for their double rooms, but they face stiff competition from NZ's glut of nondescript low-rise motels and 'motor lodges'. These tend to be squat structures that congregate just outside the CBD or on the highways at the edge of town. Most are modern-ish (though the décor in many seems stuck in a 1970s time warp) and have similar facilities (tea- and coffee-making, fridge, TV) but the price will indicate the standard.

Rental Accommodation

The basic Kiwi holiday home is called a 'bach', short for 'bachelor' (and pronounced 'batch') as they were often used by single men as hunting and fishing retreats; in Otago and Southland they're known as 'cribs'. These are simple self-contained cottages that can be rented in rural and coastal areas, often in a soothingly private location. They can be good for longer stays in a region, although some are only available for one or two nights at a time. Prices are typically $80 to $130, which isn't bad for a whole house or self-contained bungalow.

For more-upmarket holiday houses, the current trend is to throw rusticity to the wind and erect luxury-filled cottages on beautiful nature-surrounded plots. Expect to pay anything from $120 to $400 a double.

A good website to help you find the perfect holiday rental is www.holidayhomes .co.nz. A selection of swanky self-contained apartments around the country can be found at www.newzealand-apartments.co.nz.

If it's a longer, more permanent stay you're thinking about, check out www.nz flats.co.nz.

ACTIVITIES

See the New Zealand Outdoors chapter, p69, for details of the activity smorgasbord on offer in NZ.

BUSINESS HOURS

Most shops and businesses open their doors at 9am and close at 5.30pm Monday to Friday and either 12.30pm or 5pm on Saturday. Late-night shopping (until 9pm) occurs in a number of cities on Thursday and/or Friday nights; Sunday trading is the norm in most large towns and cities. Supermarkets are usually open from 8am until at least 7pm, often until 9pm or later in cities. Dairies (corner stores) and superettes (small supermarkets) close later than most other shops.

Banks normally open from 9.30am to 4.30pm Monday to Friday (some city branches also open on Saturday mornings).

Post offices are open 8.30am to 5pm Monday to Friday, with main branches also open 9.30am to 1pm Saturday; postal outlets situated in other businesses such as newsagencies may be open longer than these hours.

Restaurants typically open until at least 9pm but tend to serve food until 11pm or later on Friday and Saturday night; the main restaurant strips in large cities keep longer hours throughout the week. Cafés can open as early as 7.30am and close around 5pm, though café-bar hybrids tend to their patrons until well into the night. Pubs usually serve food from noon to 2pm and from 6pm to 8pm. Pubs and bars often start pouring drinks at noon and stay open until late, particularly from Thursday to Saturday.

Don't count on any attractions being open on Christmas Day.

CHILDREN

All cities and most major towns should have centrally located public rooms where mothers (and sometimes fathers) can go to nurse their baby or change its nappy (diaper); check with the local visitor information centre or city council for details.

Many motels and most holiday parks have playgrounds, games and video equipment, and occasionally fenced swimming pools. Cots, highchairs and baby baths aren't always easy to obtain at budget and midrange accommodation, but the majority of top-end hotels will be able to supply them, and the plushest places have child-minding services. B&Bs are not usually amenable to families, as many of these businesses promote themselves as grown-up getaways where peace and quiet is valued above all else. Hostels that want to concentrate on the young backpacker demographic don't welcome kids either, but there are plenty of other hostels (including YHA affiliates) that do.

There are lots of so-called family restaurants in NZ where highchairs are provided for toddlers and kids can choose from their own menus. Pubs often serve kids' meals, and most cafés and restaurants (with the exception of adult-focused upmarket eateries) can handle the idea of child-sized portions.

For specialised childcare, look under 'Baby Sitters' and 'Child Care Centres' in the *Yellow Pages* directory, or try phoning the local council.

Child concessions (and family rates) are often available for such things as accommodation, tours, attraction entry fees and air, bus and train transport, with some discounts as high as 50% of the adult rate. However, the definition of 'child' can vary from under 12 to under 18 years; toddlers (under four years old) usually get free admission and transport.

Medical services and facilities in NZ are of a high standard, and goods such as formula and disposable nappies are widely available in urban centres. Many hire-car companies struggle with the concept of baby seats – double-check that the company you choose can supply the right size of seat for your offspring, and that the seat will be properly fitted before you pick up the vehicle.

For more helpful general tips, see Lonely Planet's *Travel with Children*. In NZ, some regions are the subject of free, family-oriented information booklets, with one example being *Kidz Go!* (www.kidzgo.co.nz), detailing child-friendly activities and restaurants in Queenstown, Wanaka and the Te Anau region; pick it up at local visitor information centres. Another handy site presenting information for city-bound families is www.kidsnewzealand.com – it covers Auckland, Wellington, Christchurch, Dunedin and Nelson in detail. The people behind this website produce a *Kids New Zealand Directory*; available online or from newsagents for around $7. Finally, www.kidsfriendlynz.com is a well-maintained site with extensive links to various facets of kiddy culture.

CLIMATE CHARTS

NZ's location within the Roaring Forties means it gets freshened (and sometimes blasted) by relatively warm, damp winds blowing in from the Tasman Sea – Wellington is the Chicago of the southern hemisphere, getting slapped by the winds whistling through Cook Strait.

In the South Island, the Southern Alps act as a barrier for these moisture-laden easterlies, creating a wet climate on the western side of the mountains (more than 7500mm of rain annually) and a dry climate on the eastern side (about 330mm). After losing their moisture, the now-dry winds continue east, gathering heat and speed as they blow downhill and across the Canterbury

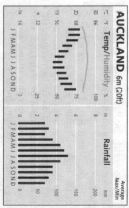

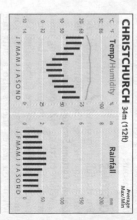

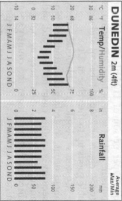

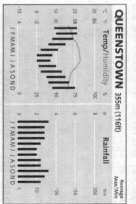

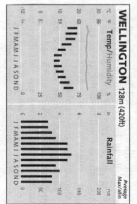

Plains towards the Pacific coast; in summer this katabatic or föhn wind can be hot and fierce.

In the North Island, the western sides of the high volcanoes get a lot more rain than the eastern sides but the rain shadow isn't as pronounced, as the barrier here isn't as formidable as the Alps. Rainfall is more evenly distributed over this island, averaging around 1300mm annually.

Also see p20 for further information on the seasons.

CUSTOMS

For the full story on what you can and can't bring into NZ, see the website of the **New Zealand Customs Service** (www.customs.govt.nz).

When entering NZ you can bring most articles in free of duty provided that customs is satisfied they are for personal use and that you'll be taking them with you when you leave. There's also a duty-free quota per person of 1125mL of spirits or liqueur, 4.5L of wine or beer, 200 cigarettes (or 50 cigars or 250g of tobacco) and dutiable goods up to the value of $700.

Customs people are obviously fussy about drugs, so declare all medicines. Biosecurity is another customs buzzword, with authorities serious about keeping out any diseases that may harm the country's significant agricultural industry. Tramping gear such as boots and tents will be checked and may need to be cleaned before being allowed in; ditto golf clubs and bicycles. You must declare any plant or animal products (including anything made of wood), and food of any kind. You'll also come in for extra scrutiny if you've arrived via Africa, Southeast Asia or South America. Weapons and firearms are either prohibited or require a permit and safety testing.

DANGERS & ANNOYANCES

Though often reported in loud and salacious detail by headline-hungry broadsheets, violent crime is not common in NZ. Auckland is considered the 'crime capital' of the country, but it's very safe by most international city standards.

Theft, primarily from cars, is a major problem, and travellers are viewed as easy targets. Avoid leaving any valuables in a vehicle no matter where it's parked; the worst places to tempt fate are tourist park-

ing areas and the car parks at the start of walks. If the crown jewels simply must be left behind, pack them out of sight in the boot (trunk) of the car – but carry your passport with you, just in case.

Don't underestimate the risks posed by NZ's unpredictable, ever-changing maritime climate in high-altitude areas; see p85 for more information.

NZ has thankfully been spared from the proliferation of venomous creatures found in neighbouring Australia (poisonous spiders, snakes, jellyfish etc). Sharks exist in NZ waters but are well fed by the abundant marine life and rarely pose a threat to humans; that said, attacks on humans do occasionally occur. Much greater hazards in the ocean, however, are the rips or undertows that haunt some beaches and are capable of dragging swimmers right out to sea. Take notice of any local warnings when swimming, surfing or diving.

The islands' byways are often made hazardous by speeding locals, wide-cornering campervans and traffic-ignorant sheep. Set yourself a reasonable itinerary instead of careering around the country at top speed, and try to stay alert on the road despite the distractingly beautiful scenery.

SANDFLIES *Sir Ian McKellen*

As an unpaid but enthusiastic proselytiser on behalf of all things Kiwi, including the New Zealand tourist industry, I hesitate to mention the well-kept secret of sandflies. I first met them en masse at the glorious Milford Sound, where visitors (after the most beautiful drive in the world) are met, at least during the summer, by crowds of the little buggers. There are patent unctions that cope, and tobacco repels them too, but I would hope that travellers find them an insignificant pest compared with the glory of their habitat.

Oddly, when actually filming scenes for *Lord of the Rings*, I don't recall being bothered by sandflies at all. Honestly. Had there been, we would have set the Orcs on them.

Sir Ian is a UK-based actor who spent several years in NZ filming and has become something of an unofficial ambassador for NZ tourism.

In the annoyances category, it's hard to top a sandfly visitation (see the boxed text, opposite). Equip yourself with insect repellent in coastal areas.

DISABLED TRAVELLERS

Kiwi accommodation generally caters fairly well for disabled travellers, with a significant number of hostels, hotels, motels and B&Bs equipped with wheelchair-accessible rooms and disabled bathrooms. Many tourist attractions similarly provide wheelchair access, with wheelchairs often available at key attractions with advance notice.

Tour operators with accessible vehicles operate from most major centres. Key cities are also serviced by kneeling buses and taxi companies with wheelchair-accessible vans. Large car-hire firms such as Avis and Hertz provide cars with hand controls at no extra charge; advance notice is required. Mobility parking permits are available from branches of **New Zealand CCS** (☎ 0800 227 200, 04-801 0854; www.ccs.org.nz), which is in all the main centres.

There's good general information on NZ's **disability information website** (www.weka.net.nz); click on Living with a Disability, then check out the contents of categories including Transport, Recreation, and Travel and Tourism. The latter lists NZ tour operators catering specifically to disabled travellers.

Disabled travellers need not miss out on NZ's great outdoors. If you'd like to take to wilderness pathways, pick up a copy of *Accessible Walks* by Anna and Andrew Jameson, which offers first-hand descriptions of more than 100 South Island walks. It's available online at www.accessiblewalks.co.nz. If cold-weather activity is more your thing, see the website of **Disabled Snowsports New Zealand** (www.disabledsnowsports.org.nz).

DISCOUNT CARDS

The **International Student Travel Confederation** (ISTC; www.istc.org) is an international collective of specialist student travel organisations, and the body behind the internationally recognised International Student Identity Card (ISIC), issued to full-time students aged 12 years and over, and giving discounts on accommodation, transport and admission to various attractions. The ISTC also produces the International Youth Travel Card (IYTC or Go25), which is issued to people who are between 12 and 26 years of age and not full-time students, and gives equivalent benefits to the ISIC. A similar ISTC brainchild is the International Teacher Identity Card (ITIC), available to teaching professionals. All three cards are chiefly available from student travel companies.

For details of hostel organisations that issue membership cards entitling the user to numerous discounts on travel, tours, accommodation, food and shopping, see p704.

Senior and disabled travellers who live overseas will find that the cards issued by their respective countries are not always officially recognised in NZ, but that most places will still acknowledge such a card and grant a concession where one applies.

EMBASSIES & CONSULATES
New Zealand Embassies & Consulates

There's a full listing of all NZ diplomatic missions overseas at www.nzembassy.com. The list includes the following:

Australia Canberra (☎ 02-6270 4211; nzhccba@iimetro.com.au; Commonwealth Ave, Canberra, ACT 2600); Sydney (☎ 02-9225 2300; nzcgsydney@bigpond.com; Lvl 10, 55 Hunter St, Sydney, NSW 2000)

Canada Ottawa (☎ 613-238 5991; info@nzhcottawa.org; Suite 727, 99 Bank St, Ottawa, Ontario K1P 6G3) Also in Vancouver and Toronto.

Fiji Suva (☎ 679-311 422; nzhc@is.com.fj; Reserve Bank of Fiji Building, Pratt St, Suva)

France Paris (☎ 01 45 01 43 43; nzembassy.paris@oleane.com; 7ter, rue Léonard de Vinci, 75116 Paris)

Germany Berlin (☎ 030-206 210, visa section 030-206 2121; nzembassy.berlin@t-online.de; Friedrichstrasse 60, 10117 Berlin) Also in Hamburg.

Ireland Dublin (☎ 01-660 4233; nzconsul@indigo.ie; 37 Leeson Park, Dublin 6) Also in Belfast.

Japan Tokyo (☎ 03-3467 2271, visa section 03-3467 2270; nzemb.tky@mail.com; 20-40 Kamiyama-cho, Shibuya-ku, Tokyo 150-0047)

Netherlands The Hague (☎ 070-346 93 24; nzemb@xs4all.nl; Carnegielaan 10, 2517 KH The Hague)

UK London (☎ 020-7930 8422; aboutnz@newzealandhc.org.uk; New Zealand House, 80 Haymarket, London SW1Y 4TQ)

USA Los Angeles (☎ 310-566 6555; www.nzcgla.com; Suite 600e, 2425 Olympic Blvd, Santa Monica, CA 90404); Washington DC (☎ 202-328 4800; nz@nzemb.org; 37 Observatory Circle NW, Washington DC 20008) Also in New York.

Embassies & Consulates in New Zealand

Most principal diplomatic representations to NZ are in Wellington. Addresses of major offices include the following. Check the *Yellow Pages* directories of main Kiwi cities for a more extensive listing.

Australia (Map pp406-7; ☎ 04-473 6411; www .australia.org.nz; 72-76 Hobson St, Thorndon, Wellington)

Canada (Map pp406-7; ☎ 04-473 9577; www .dfait-maeci.gc.ca/newzealand; Lvl 11, 125 The Terrace, Wellington)

Fiji (Map pp406-7; ☎ 04-473 5401; www.fiji.org.nz; 31 Pipitea St, Thorndon, Wellington)

France (Map p410; ☎ 04-384 2555; www.amba france-nz.org; 12th fl, 34-42 Manners St, Wellington)

Germany (Map pp406-7; ☎ 04-473 6063; www.wel lington.diplo.de; 90-92 Hobson St, Thorndon, Wellington)

Ireland (Map p106; ☎ 09-977 2252; www.ireland.co.nz /diplomatic_rep.asp; Lvl 6, 18 Shortland St, Auckland)

Japan (Map p410; ☎ 04-473 1540; www.emb -japan.go.jp; Lvl 18 & 19, The Majestic Centre, 100 Willis St, Wellington)

Netherlands (Map pp406-7; ☎ 04-471 6390; www .netherlandsembassy.co.nz; 10th fl, Investment Centre, cnr Featherston & Ballance Sts, Wellington)

UK (Map pp406-7; ☎ 04-924 2888; www.britain.org.nz; 44 Hill St, Thorndon, Wellington)

USA (Map pp406-7; ☎ 04-462 6000; http://wellington .usembassy.gov; 29 Fitzherbert Tce, Thorndon, Wellington)

It's important to realise what your own embassy – the embassy of the country of which you are a citizen – can and can't do to help you if you get into trouble. Generally speaking, it won't be much help in emergencies if the trouble you're in is even remotely your own fault. Remember that while in NZ you are bound by NZ laws. Your embassy will not be sympathetic if you end up in jail after committing a crime locally, even if such actions are legal in your own country.

In genuine emergencies you might get some assistance, but only if other channels have been exhausted. For example, if you need to get home urgently, a free ticket is exceedingly unlikely – the embassy would expect you to have insurance. If you have all your money and documents stolen, it might assist with getting a new passport, but a loan for onward travel is out of the question.

FESTIVALS & EVENTS

Want to plan your travels around the various food and wine, sporting or arts festivals

staged throughout the country? A useful planning resource can be found on the website of **Tourism New Zealand** (www.newzealand .com/travel); click on Sights & Activities, then Events Calendar.

Details of major festivals and events that take place in a single city or town are provided throughout the destination chapters of this book. The following events, however, are pursued across several cities, throughout a particular region or even around the country.

February

Harvest Hawkes Bay (www.harvesthawkesbay.co.nz) Appropriately indulgent wine and food celebration, with participating wineries scattered around Napier and Hastings.
NZ Masters Games (www.nzmg.com) The country's biggest multisport event, held in Dunedin (even-numbered years) and Wanganui (odd-numbered years).
Waitangi Day Commemorates the signing of the Treaty of Waitangi on 6 February 1840 with various services and functions around the country.

May

New Zealand International Comedy Festival (www .comedyfestival.co.nz) Three-week laugh-fest in venues across Auckland, Wellington and assorted regional centres.

July

New Zealand International Film Festivals (www .enzedff.co.nz) After separate film festivals in Wellington, Auckland, Dunedin and Christchurch, a selection of flicks takes to the road to be screened in major provincial towns over the next four months.

FOOD

The preparation of food in NZ was once ruled by strict adherence to the *Edmond's Cookery Book*, a slavish reflection of Anglo-Saxon stodge. But nowadays the country's restaurants and cafés are adept at throwing together local staples such as lamb, beef, venison, green-lipped mussels and many other island-harvested meats, and adding a dash of Asian, European and pan-Pacific culinary innovation; the end result is often referred to as Pacific Rim, a term as broad in its definition as Mediterranean or Asian.

The eateries themselves are represented by everything from no-frills fish and chip shops and pub bistros to cafés drowned in faux-European style or artsy decoration, restaurant-bars that do full à la carte before toasting themselves with numerous late-night drinks, and fine-dining establishments where the linen is so crisp you're afraid of leaning on it in case it shatters. The website www.dinecut.co.nz is worth browsing for customers' comments on NZ restaurants. Reading menus on www.menus.co.nz will certainly have your mouth watering, but the website only covers restaurants in Auckland and Wellington.

Vegetarian offerings – particularly in cities and towns with a resident food-infatuated bourgeoisie – have become quite creative, a world apart from the salad or roasted-vegetable mains that used to be the norm. Urban centres and tourist-popular towns usually have at least one (often several) dedicated vegetarian cafés or restaurants, a number of them catering to vegans and those with dietary requirements such as coeliac-sufferers. A recommended source of info is the Wellington branch of the **New Zealand Vegetarian Society** (www.vegsoc.org.nz) – its website has a restaurant guide covering veg and veg-friendly options around the country.

When it comes to cities, the eating recommendations provided in this book are ordered from restaurants to cafés to quick eats. The best value is often found in the cafés, where you can get a good meal in casual surroundings for under $20. Some city pubs call themselves 'gastropubs' and offer upmarket restaurant-style fare, but most pubs serve standard bistro meals, usually under $20. Midrange restaurants can charge as high as $30 for a main meal, and don't be surprised to see mains priced at $30 to $40 at fancy-pants top-end options.

Smoking is now banned in all restaurants, pubs and bars, and many establishments have set up outdoor areas (often heated) for puffers. Tipping in restaurants and cafés is not expected. See the boxed text, p712, for a warning about nasty surcharges for eating out on public holidays.

Also refer to the Food & Drink chapter (p93).

GAY & LESBIAN TRAVELLERS

The gay and lesbian tourism industry in NZ is not as high-profile as in that other country across the Tasman Sea, but homosexual communities are prominent in the main cities of Auckland and Wellington, and there is a multitude of organisations throughout both islands. NZ has progressive laws protecting the rights of gays and lesbians; the legal minimum age for sex between consenting persons is 16. Generally speaking, Kiwis are fairly relaxed and accepting about homosexuality, but that's not to say that homophobia doesn't exist.

There are loads of websites dedicated to this topic. **Gay Tourism New Zealand** (http://gaytourismnewzealand.com) is a good starting point, with links to various sites. Other worthwhile queer websites include www.gaynz.com, www.gaynz.net.nz and www.lesbian.net.nz. Visitors to Queenstown should check out www.gayqueenstown.com.

The biggest excuse for a party is the huge **HERO Festival** (www.hero.org.nz), held every February in the Ponsonby district of Auckland. **Our Takes** (www.outtakes.org.nz) is a gay and lesbian film festival staged in Auckland, Wellington and Christchurch in June, while Queenstown stages the annual winter **Gay Ski Week** (www.gayskiweeknz.com).

For more information, see Gay & Lesbian Auckland (p138) and Gay & Lesbian Wellington (p415).

HOLIDAYS

Public Holidays

The following is a list of NZ's main public holidays.

New Year 1 & 2 January
Waitangi Day 6 February
Easter Good Friday & Easter Monday, March/April
Anzac Day 25 April
Queen's Birthday First Monday in June
Labour Day Fourth Monday in October
Christmas Day 25 December
Boxing Day 26 December

In addition, each province in NZ has its own anniversary-day holiday; a hangover from the old days when each was separately administered. The dates of provincial holidays can vary – when these holidays fall between Friday and Sunday, they are usually observed on the following Monday; if they fall between Tuesday and Thursday, they are held on the preceding Monday; enabling the great Kiwi tradition of the 'long weekend' to continue.

These holidays include the following:

Southland 17 January
Wellington 22 January
Auckland 29 January

PUBLIC HOLIDAY SURCHARGES

If you dine out on a NZ public holiday, be aware that the bill will have a sting in its tail. The vast majority of restaurants and cafés recently introduced a policy whereby diners pay a 15% to 20% surcharge on top of their bill on public holidays, to cover staff costs (others simply don't open on these days).

If this sounds a bit cheeky to you (after all, supermarkets can't simply hike up their prices on public holidays), plan ahead and enjoy a picnic. Bear in mind, too, that most eateries are closed on Christmas Day.

Northland 29 January
Nelson 1 February
Otago 23 March
Taranaki 31 March
South Canterbury 25 September
Hawkes Bay 1 November
Marlborough 1 November
Chatham Islands 30 November
Westland 1 December
Canterbury 16 December

School Holidays

The Christmas holiday season, from mid-December to late January, is part of the summer school vacation. It's the time you are most likely to find transport and accommodation booked out, and long, restless queues at tourist attractions. There are three shorter school-holiday periods during the year, falling roughly from mid- to late April, early to mid-July, and mid-September to early October. Exact dates are given on the website of NZ's **Ministry of Education** (www.minedu.govt.nz).

INSURANCE

Don't underestimate the importance of a good travel-insurance policy covering theft, loss and medical problems; nothing will ruin your holiday plans quicker than an accident or having that new digital camera stolen. Most policies offer lower and higher medical-expense options; the higher ones are chiefly for countries that have extremely high medical costs, such as the USA. There is a wide variety of policies available, so compare the small print.

Some policies specifically exclude designated 'dangerous activities' such as scuba diving, parasailing, bungy jumping, white-water rafting, motorcycling, skiing and even bushwalking. If you plan on doing any of these things (a distinct possibility in NZ), make absolutely sure that the policy you choose covers you fully.

You may prefer a policy that pays doctors or hospitals direct rather than you having to pay on the spot and claim later. If you have to claim later make sure you keep all documentation. Some policies ask you to call back (reverse charges) to a centre in your home country where an immediate assessment of your problem is made. Check that the policy covers ambulances and emergency medical evacuations by air.

It's worth mentioning that under NZ law, you cannot sue for personal injury (other than exemplary damages). Rather, the country's **Accident Compensation Corporation** (ACC; www.acc.co.nz) administers an accident compensation scheme that provides accident insurance for NZ residents and temporary visitors to the country, regardless of who is at fault.

While some people cry foul of this arrangement, others point to the hugely expensive litigation 'industries' in other countries and raise a silent cheer. This scheme does not, however, cancel out the necessity for your own comprehensive travel-insurance policy, as it doesn't cover you for such things as loss of income or treatment in your home country, as well as other possible eventualities such as illness.

Also see p737 for notes about medical insurance. For information on car insurance, see p734.

Worldwide cover for travellers from over 44 countries is available online at www.lonelyplanet.com/travel_services.

INTERNET ACCESS

Getting connected in NZ is relatively simple in all but the most remote locales.

Hooking Up

If you've brought your palmtop or notebook computer and want to get connected to a local Internet Service Provider (ISP), there are plenty of options, though some limit their dial-up areas to major cities or particular regions. Whatever enticements a particular ISP offers, make sure it has local dial-up numbers for the places where you intend to use it – the last thing you want is to be making timed long-distance calls every time you connect to the Internet. If you're based in a large city there's no problem. Major ISPs:

Clear.Net (0508 888 800; www.clear.net.nz)

Earthlight (03-479 0303; www.earthlight.co.nz) Has a page on its website detailing prepaid Internet access for travellers to NZ.

Telecom Xtra (0800 289 987; http://xtra.co.nz /products)

The country's main telecommunications company is **Telecom New Zealand** (www.telecom .co.nz), with a growing number of wireless hotspots around the country. If you have a wi-fi-enabled device, you can purchase a Telecom wireless prepaid card from participating wireless hotspot venues, or get a prepaid number (from the log-in page at any wireless hotspot, you can purchase an online number using a credit card). The cost is $10 per hour. Loads more information, together with a list of hotspots, is on Telecom's website – go to Product Finder, then Internet & Data.

Otherwise, NZ uses British BT431A and RJ-11 telephone plugs, but neither are universal: local electronics shops should be able to help. You'll also need a plug adaptor, and a universal AC adaptor will enable you to plug in without frying the innards of your machine. A lot of mid-range accommodation and nearly all top-end hotels will have sockets, but you'll be hit with expensive call charges. In most cheaper places you'll probably find that phones are hardwired into the wall.

Keep in mind that your PC-card modem may not work in NZ. The safest option is to buy a reputable 'global' modem before you leave home or buy a local PC-card modem once you get to NZ.

For a list of useful NZ websites, see p23.

Internet Cafés

Internet cafés are usually brimming with terminals, high-speed connections and a bit of independent character in the bigger urban centres or other places where tourists sweep through in numbers. But facilities are a lot more haphazard in small, out-of-the-way towns, where a so-called Internet café could turn out to be a single terminal in the corner of a video store.

Most hostels also make an effort to hook you up, with the Internet sometimes thrown in as a freebie for guests. Many public libraries have Internet access too, but generally there are a limited number of terminals, and these are provided for research needs, not for travellers to check their email, so head for a Internet café first.

The cost of access ranges anywhere from $3 to $8 per hour, with the lowest rates found in cities where competition and travellers generate dirt-cheap prices. There's often a minimum period of access, usually in the vicinity of 10 minutes.

If you don't already have one, it's worth setting up a travelling address with one of the many free Web-based email services; these include **Yahoo** (www.yahoo.com), **MSN Hotmail** (www.hotmail.com) and **Excite** (www.excite.com).

LEGAL MATTERS

Marijuana (aka 'New Zealand Green', 'electric puha' or 'dac') is widely indulged in but illegal, and anyone caught carrying this or other illicit drugs faces stiff penalties. Even if the amount of drugs is small and the fine not too onerous, a conviction will still be recorded against your name and this may affect your visa status.

Always carry your licence when driving; for more info, see p731. Drink-driving is a serious offence and remains a significant problem in NZ despite widespread campaigns and an increase in the severity of penalties. The legal blood alcohol limit is 80mg per 100mL of blood (0.08%).

If you are arrested, it's your right to consult a lawyer before any formal questioning begins.

MAPS

Good-quality maps are widely available throughout NZ, everything from street maps and road atlases to detailed topographical cartography.

The **AA** (www.aatravel.co.nz) produces excellent city, town, regional, island and highway maps, available from any of their local offices; members of affiliated overseas automobile associations will be able to obtain free maps and discounts on presentation of a membership card. The AA also produces a detailed *New Zealand Road Atlas*. Other reliable countrywide atlases, available from visitor information centres and from bookshops, are produced by Hema, KiwiMaps and Wises.

Land Information New Zealand (www.linz.govt .nz) publishes several exhaustive map series, including street, country and holiday maps, maps of national parks and forest parks, and handy topographical maps for trampers. You can find some of these publications in bookshops; for the topo maps (a good idea for serious tramping), try the nearest DOC office or visitor information centre.

A nifty new online resource for travellers is the **AA SmartMap** (www.aamaps.co.nz), which can be used to obtain a customised street map or driving directions, or to locate sights or places to stay or eat in a specific destination.

MONEY

The NZ dollar has gained considerable ground against other currencies in recent years (particularly against the US dollar), making NZ less of a bargain destination than it once was. See the Quick Reference section on the inside front cover for a list of exchange rates that were current just before publication.

ATMs & EFTPOS

The country's major banks, including the Bank of New Zealand, ANZ, Westpac and ASB, have 24-hour ATMs attached to various branches, which accept cards from other banks and provide access to overseas accounts. You won't find ATMs everywhere, but they're widespread across both islands.

Many NZ businesses use Electronic Funds Transfer At Point Of Sale (EFTPOS), a convenient service that allows you to use your bank card (credit or debit) to pay for services or purchases direct, and often withdraw cash as well. EFTPOS is available practically everywhere these days, even in places where it's a long way between banks. Just like an ATM, you need to know your Personal Identification Number (PIN) to use it.

Bank Accounts

We've heard mixed reports on how easy it is for nonresidents to open a bank account in NZ. Some sources say it's as simple as flashing a few pieces of identification, providing a temporary postal address (or your permanent address) and then waiting a few days while your request is processed. Other

sources say that many banks won't allow visitors to open an account with them unless they're planning to stay in NZ for at least six months, or unless the application is accompanied by some proof of employment. The websites of the banks in question are also rather vague on the services offered to short-term visitors. Needless to say, if you think you'll need to open an account, do your homework before you arrive in the country. Also be prepared to shop around to get the best banking deal; avoid banks that attempt to charge you for every imaginable transaction.

Credit & Debit Cards

Perhaps the best way to carry most of your money is within the electronic imprint of a plastic card. Credit cards such as Visa and MasterCard are widely accepted for everything from a hostel bed or a restaurant meal to a bungy jump or a bus ticket, and such cards are pretty much essential (in lieu of a large deposit) if you want to hire a car. They can also be used to get cash advances over the counter at banks and from ATMs, depending on the card, but be aware that such transactions incur immediate interest. Charge cards such as Diners Club and AmEx are not as widely accepted.

Apart from losing them, the obvious danger with credit cards is maxing out your limit and going home to a steaming pile of debt and interest charges. A safer option is a debit card with which you can draw money directly from your home bank account using ATMs, banks or EFTPOS machines around the country. Any card connected to the international banking network (Cirrus, Maestro, Plus and Eurocard) should work, provided you know your PIN. Fees for using your card at a foreign bank or ATM vary depending on your home bank; ask before you leave.

The most flexible option is to carry both a credit and a debit card.

Currency

NZ's currency is the NZ dollar, made up of 100 cents. There are 10c, 20c and 50c, $1 and $2 coins, and $5, $10, $20, $50 and $100 notes. In July 2006, a new design for smaller, lighter silver coins (10c, 20c and 50c) was introduced, and the poor wee 5c coin was withdrawn from circulation, deemed to have little value. Prices are often still marked in single cents and then rounded to the nearest 10c when you come to pay.

Unless otherwise noted, all prices quoted in this book are in NZ dollars. For an idea of the costs associated with travelling around the country, see p21.

There are no notable restrictions on importing or exporting travellers cheques. Though not prohibited, cash amounts equal to or in excess of the equivalent of NZ$10,000 (in any currency) must be declared on arrival or departure – you'll need to fill out a Border Cash Report.

Moneychangers

Changing foreign currency or travellers cheques is usually no problem at banks throughout NZ or at licensed money-changers such as Travelex (formerly Thomas Cook) in the major cities. Money-changers can be found in all major tourist areas, cities and airports, and conveniently tend to stay open beyond normal business hours during the week (often until 9pm).

Taxes & Refunds

The Goods and Services Tax (GST) is a flat 12.5% tax on all domestic goods and services. Prices in this book almost invariably include GST, but look out for any small-print announcing that the price is GST-exclusive. There is no refund of GST paid when you leave NZ.

Tipping

Tipping is completely optional in NZ, and staff do not depend on tips for income – the total at the bottom of a restaurant bill is all you need to pay (note that this figure does not include a service charge). That said, it's totally acceptable to reward good service, and the tip you leave is at your discretion; a gratuity of between 5% and 10% of the bill is the norm.

Travellers Cheques

The ubiquity of debit- and credit-card access in NZ tends to make travellers cheques seem rather clumsy. Nevertheless, AmEx, Thomas Cook and other well-known international brands of travellers cheques are easily exchanged. You need to present your passport for identification when cashing them. Fees per transaction for changing foreign-currency travellers cheques vary from bank to bank, while AmEx or Travelex perform the task commission-free if you use their cheques. Private moneychangers found in the larger cities are sometimes commission free, but shop around for the best rates.

POST

Letters

The services offered by **New Zealand Post** (www.nzpost.co.nz) are reliable and reasonably inexpensive. Within NZ, standard post costs 45c for standard letters and postcards, and 90c for larger letters.

International destinations are divided into five zones:

Zone	Region	Postcard/ letter	Approx delivery time
A	Australia	$1.50/$1.50	3-6 days
B	South Pacific	$1.50/$1.50	3-10 days
C	East Asia & North America	$1.50/$2	4-10 days
D	UK & Europe	$1.50/$2	4-10 days
E	Rest of world	$1.50/$2	5-10 days

Parcels

International parcel zones are the same as for letters; pricing depends on weight and whether you send the parcel 'economy' (three to five weeks), 'air' (one to two weeks) or 'express' (within a matter of days). You can send a parcel weighing 1/2/5kg by 'economy' to Australia for $11/19/35, to North America and East Asia and to the UK and the rest of Europe for $23/42/83, and to the UK and the rest of Europe for $25/47/92. To send such parcels by 'air' is roughly 20% more expensive, and by 'express' at least 50% more.

Sending & Receiving Mail

NZ post offices are generally called 'post shops' now, as most have been removed from their traditional old buildings and set up in modern shop-style premises, but we still stubbornly refer to them as post offices throughout this guidebook. For standard post office opening hours, see p706. Stamps can usually also be purchased at supermarkets and bookshops.

You can have mail addressed to you care of 'Poste Restante, Main Post Shop' in whichever town you require. Mail is usually held for 30 days and you need to provide some form of identification (such as a passport) to collect it.

SHOPPING

NZ isn't one of those countries where it's necessary to buy some sort of souvenir in order to remember where you've just been; the spectacular island landscapes are mementoes in themselves, to later be plucked out of the depths of memory or the innards of a camera. But there are numerous locally crafted items you can purchase for their own unique qualities.

Clothing

The main cities of Auckland (p140), Wellington (p423) and Christchurch (p555) boast fashion-conscious boutiques filled with the sartorial flair of young and well-established NZ designers. Check out www.fashionz.co.nz for up-to-date information on the hottest designers and labels, and where to buy them. Be on the lookout for labels such as Zambesi, Kate Sylvester, Karen Walker, Trelise Cooper, Nom.D and Little Brother.

In Auckland, head to places such as Newmarket, Ponsonby Rd and High St, while Wellington offers some retrospective mix-and-match style along Cuba St and high fashion in the Lambton Quarter. In Christchurch, pick up new duds on Colombo, High or Cashel Sts and then show them off on self-important Oxford Tce. To see just how far New Zealanders are prepared to push the boundaries of fashionable creativity, visit the wonderful World of WearableArt museum (see the boxed text, p466) in Nelson, or attend the festival of the same name in Wellington (p416).

A spin-off from the backs of NZ sheep are sheepskin products (particularly cosy footwear, including the much-loved ugg boot) and beautiful woollen gear, particularly jumpers (jerseys or sweaters) made from hand-spun, hand-dyed wool. Hand-knitted jumpers are something of a rural art form in NZ and are of the highest quality, as are other knitted goods such as hats, gloves and scarves. Look out for garments made from a lovely soft yarn that's a combination of merino wool and possum fur (at least they've found a use for the national pest!).

Woollen Swanndri jackets, shirts and pullovers are so well made that they're just about the national garment in the countryside. Most common are the red-and-black or blue-and-black plaid ones. You can buy long-lasting Swanndri products (colloquially called 'Swannies') in outdoor-gear shops.

Crafts

The fine wares of NZ craftspeople can be purchased in almost every sizable town. It appears that few (if any) places in this country are devoid of someone who's been inspired to hand-shape items for sale to passing visitors. In Christchurch head to the Arts Centre (p534), where you'll find dozens of shops and galleries selling locally designed and crafted jewellery, ceramics, glassware and accessories. The Nelson region (p461) is another very crafty place, heavily populated by galleries and with the odd market to wander around. Ditto Devonport (p113), within striking distance of downtown Auckland and replete with galleries, and Arrowtown (p639), an artistic enclave near Queenstown.

Maori Arts

For some fine examples of Maori *whakairo rakau* (woodcarving), check out the efforts of artisans at Te Whakarewarewa cultural area in Rotorua (p331), then browse the town's large collection of Maori craft and souvenir shops; in some cases you may be able to buy direct from the artists. Carvers produce tremendous forms such as leaping dolphins, as well as the sometimes highly intricate traditional Maori carvings. Expect to pay a small fortune for high-quality work; unfortunately, you may also unwittingly pay top dollar for the poor examples of the craft that are turned out for the tourist trade and end up lining souvenir shops in Auckland.

Maori bone carvings are another fine art form undergoing something of a renaissance. Maori artisans have always made bone carvings in the shape of humans and animals, but nowadays they feed the tourist industry. Bone fish-hook pendants, carved in traditional Maori and modernised styles, are most common and are worn on a thong or a chain around the neck.

One way of confirming the authenticity of any Maori-made piece is to see if it's accompanied by the trademark **toiiho** (www.toiiho.com), represented by a symbol created by a Maori arts board to identify the output of individual artists or groups of artists of Maori descent. There are also modified versions of the trademark, which identify items produced by groups of 'mainly Maori' artists and via 'coproductions' between Maori and non-Maori artists. Note, though, that not all Maori artists are registered with this scheme.

Paua

Abalone shell, called paua in NZ, is carved into some beautiful ornaments and jewellery, and is used as an inlay in many Maori carvings. Lovers of kitsch and general tackiness will find that it's also incorporated into generic souvenirs, often in the most unattractive ways. Shells are used as ashtrays in places where paua is plentiful, but it's illegal to take natural paua shells out of the country; only processed ornaments can be taken with you.

Pounamu

Maoris consider *pounamu* (greenstone, or jade or nephrite) to be a culturally invaluable raw material. It's found predominantly on the West Coast of the South Island – Maoris called the island Te Wahi Pounamu (The Place of Greenstone) or Te Wai Pounamu (The Water of Greenstone).

You're unlikely to come across any *mere* (war clubs) in contemporary greenstone studios or souvenir shops, but you will find lots of stony green incarnations of Maori motifs. One of the most popular is the *hei tiki*, the name of which literally means 'hanging human form', as Tiki was the first man created and *hei* is 'to hang'. They are tiny, stylised Maori figures, usually depicted with their tongue stuck out in a warlike challenge, worn on a thong or chain around the neck. They've got great *mana* or power, but they also serve as fertility symbols. Other popular motifs are the *tentiwha* (monster), and the *marakihau* (sea monster).

The best place to buy greenstone items is Hokitika (p511), which is strewn with jade workshops and gift shops. Rotorua (p342) also has its fair share of greenstone crafts. To see impressive collections of both ancient and modern pieces, visit the Otago Museum (p594) in Dunedin, Te Papa museum (see the boxed text, p409) in Wellington, Auckland Museum (p109), and Canterbury Museum (p535) in Christchurch. Traditionally, greenstone is bought as a gift for another person, not for yourself.

TELEPHONE

Telecom New Zealand (www.telecom.co.nz) is the country's key domestic player and also has a stake in the local mobile (cell) market. The other mobile network option is **Vodafone** (www.vodafone.co.nz).

Domestic & International Calls

INFORMATION & TOLL-FREE CALLS

Numbers starting with ☎ 0900 are usually recorded information services, charging upwards of $1 per minute (more from mobiles); these numbers cannot be dialled from payphones.

Toll-free numbers in NZ have the prefix ☎ 0800 or ☎ 0508 and can be called free of charge from anywhere in the country, though they may not be accessible from certain areas or from mobile phones. Telephone numbers beginning with ☎ 0508, ☎ 0800 or ☎ 0900 cannot be dialled from outside NZ.

INTERNATIONAL CALLS

Payphones allow international calls, but the cost and international dialling code for calls will vary depending on which provider you're using. International calls from NZ are relatively inexpensive and subject to specials that reduce the rates even more, so it's worth shopping around – look in the *Yellow Pages* for a list of providers.

The toll-free Country Direct service connects callers in NZ with overseas operators to make reverse-charge (collect) or credit-card calls. Details, including Country Direct numbers, are listed in the front of telephone directories or are available from the NZ international operator. The access number varies, depending on the number of phone companies in the country you call, but is usually ☎ 000-9 (followed by the country code).

To make international calls from NZ you need to dial the international access code (☎ 00), the country code and the area code (without the initial 0). So for a London number you'd dial ☎ 00-44-20, then the number. Certain operators will have you dial a special code to access their service.

Following is a list of some country codes:

Country	International country code
Australia	☎ 61
Canada	☎ 1
Fiji	☎ 679
France	☎ 33
Germany	☎ 49
Ireland	☎ 353
Netherlands	☎ 31
UK	☎ 44
USA	☎ 1

If dialling NZ from overseas, the country code is ☎ 64 and you need to drop the zero in the area codes.

LOCAL CALLS

Local calls from private phones are free, while local calls from payphones cost 50c; both involve unlimited talk time. Calls to mobile phones attract higher rates and are timed.

LONG-DISTANCE CALLS & AREA CODES

For long-distance calls, NZ uses regional area codes. National calls can be made from any payphone. The main area codes:

Region	Area code
Auckland	☎ 09
Bay of Plenty	☎ 07
Central Plateau	☎ 07
Coromandel	☎ 07
East Coast	☎ 06
Hawkes Bay	☎ 06
King Country	☎ 07
Manawatu	☎ 06
Northland	☎ 09
South Island	☎ 03
Taranaki	☎ 06
Waikato	☎ 07
Wanganui	☎ 06
Wellington Region	☎ 04

If you're making a local call (ie to someone else in the same town), you don't need to dial the area code. But if you're dialling within a region (even if it's to a nearby town) you do have to dial the area code, regardless of the fact that the place you're

calling has the same code as the place you're dialling from. All the numbers in this book are listed with their relevant area codes.

Mobile Phones

Local mobile phone numbers are preceded by the prefix ☎ 021, ☎ 025 or ☎ 027. Mobile phone coverage is good in cities and towns and most parts of the North Island, but can be patchy away from urban centres on the South Island.

Having a mobile phone is extremely useful on your travels, especially for booking accommodation, tours, restaurants etc as you go. If you want to bring your own phone and go on a prepaid service using a local SIM card, **Vodafone** (www.vodafone.co.nz) is the one. Any Vodafone shop (found in most major towns) will set you up with a SIM card and phone number (about $35, including $10 worth of calls), and top-ups can be purchased at newsagencies, post offices and shops practically anywhere. Telecom also has a prepaid system, but you must buy one of its phones to get on the network (there are no separate SIM cards).

Alternatively, if you don't bring your own phone from home, you can rent a handset from **Vodafone Rental** (www.vodarent.co.nz) priced from $5/25 per day/week, with pick-up and drop-off outlets at NZ's major airports. You can arrange this in advance via the website.

Phonecards

NZ has a wide range of phonecards available, and these can be bought at hostels, newsagencies and post offices for a fixed dollar value (usually $5, $10, $20 and $50), to be used with any public or private phone by dialling a toll-free access number and then the PIN number on the card. It's worth shopping around, as call rates vary from company to company.

TIME

Being close to the international date line, NZ is one of the first places in the world to start the new day (Pitt Island in the Chatham Islands gets the first sunrise each new year). NZ is 12 hours ahead of GMT/UTC and two hours ahead of Australian Eastern Standard Time.

In summer NZ observes daylight-saving time, where clocks are put forward by one hour on the first Sunday in October; clocks are wound back on the third Sunday of the following March.

So (excluding the effects of daylight saving), when it's noon in NZ it's 10am in Sydney, 8am in Singapore, midnight in London and 5pm the previous day in San Francisco. The Chathams are 45 minutes ahead of NZ's main islands. For more on international timing, see the map of world time zones (pp770–1).

TOURIST INFORMATION

Even before the success of recent international marketing campaigns and the country's new-found cult status as a pseudo-Middle-earth, NZ had a highly developed tourism infrastructure busily generating mountains of brochures and booklets, plus information-packed Internet pages.

Local Tourist Offices

Almost every Kiwi city or town – whether it has any worthwhile attractions or not – seems to have a visitor information centre. The bigger centres stand united within the i-SITE network, which is affiliated with Tourism New Zealand (the official national tourism body), and have trained staff, abundant information on local activities and attractions, and free brochures and maps. Staff in such centres can also act as travel agents, booking most activities, transport and accommodation. Not to be outdone, staff at smaller centres are often overwhelmingly helpful.

Bear in mind, though, that many information centres only promote accommodation and tour operators who are paying members of the local tourist association, while others are ironically hamstrung by the demands of local operators that they be represented equally. In other words, sometimes information centre staff aren't supposed to recommend one activity or accommodation provider over another, a curious situation that exists in highly competitive environments.

Contact details for local visitor information centres are given in the relevant city and town sections.

Tourist Offices Abroad

Tourism New Zealand (☎ 04-917 5400; www.newzealand.com; Lvl 16, 80 The Terrace, Wellington) has representatives in various countries around the world. A good place to start some pretrip research is the official website, which has information in several languages (including German and Japanese). Overseas offices include the following;

Australia (☎ 02-8220 9000; Suite 3, Lvl 24, 1 Alfred St, Sydney, NSW 2000)

UK & Europe (☎ 020-7930 1662; New Zealand House, 80 Haymarket, London SW1Y 4TQ)

USA & Canada (☎ 310-395-7480; Suite 300, 501 Santa Monica Blvd, Santa Monica, CA 90401)

VISAS

Visa application forms are available from NZ diplomatic missions overseas, travel agents or the website of the **New Zealand Immigration Service** (NZIS; ☎ 0508 558 855, 09-914 4100; www.immigration.govt.nz). The NZIS also has over a dozen offices overseas; see the website for details.

Visitor's Visa

A visitor's visa is an endorsement in your passport allowing you to visit NZ, where (unless there's a major problem) you'll be granted a visitor's permit confirming your ability to stay in the country. These visas come with a standard validity of three months and cost around NZ$85 if processed in Australia or certain South Pacific countries such as Samoa and Fiji, and NZ$120 if processed elsewhere in the world.

Citizens of Australia do not need a visa or permit to visit NZ and can stay indefinitely (if they don't have any criminal convictions). UK citizens don't need a visa either and can stay in the country for up to six months.

Citizens of another 47 countries that have visa-waiver agreements with NZ do not require a visa for stays of up to three months, provided they can show an onward ticket to a country they have the right to enter, sufficient funds to support their stay (NZ$1000 per month, or NZ$400 per month if accommodation has been prepaid), and a passport valid for three months beyond the date of their planned departure from NZ. Nations in this group include Canada, France, Germany, Ireland, Japan, the Netherlands and the USA.

VISA EXTENSIONS

Visitors' visas can be extended for stays of up to nine months within one 18-month period. Some visitors, however, may be eligible for an extension allowing a maximum of 12 months in the country. Visitors will need to meet criteria such as proof of ongoing financial self-support. Apply for extensions at any NZIS office, or online via www.e-immigration.govt.nz/onlineservices.

Work Visa & Working Holiday Scheme

It's illegal for foreign nationals to work in NZ on a visitor's visa, except for Australians who can legally gain work without a visa or permit. If your primary reason for visiting NZ is to seek work (you need to be a 'bona fide applicant'), or you already have an offer of employment, you'll need to apply for a work visa, which paves the way for the granting of a work permit once you arrive – this will be valid for up to three years from the date of arrival. You can still apply for a work permit once you're in NZ, but the validity will be backdated to when you entered the country. The fee for a work visa ranges from NZ$150 to NZ$290 depending on where it's processed and the type of application.

Travellers only interested in short-term employment to supplement their travels should, if they're eligible, take part in one of NZ's Working Holiday Schemes (WHS). Under these schemes, citizens aged 18 to 30 years from 25 countries – including Canada, France, Germany, Ireland, Japan, Malaysia, the Netherlands, the Scandinavian countries, the UK and the USA – can apply for a visa. For most nationalities the visa is valid for 12 months. It's only issued to those seeking a genuine working holiday, not for permanent work, so you're not supposed to work for one employer for more than three months.

Most eligible nationals must apply for this visa from within their own country, and residents of some participating countries can apply online. Applicants must be able to show an onward ticket, a passport valid for at least another three months from the date they will leave NZ, and evidence of at least NZ$4200 in accessible funds. The application fee is NZ$120 regardless of where you apply (and isn't refunded if your application is declined).

The rules differ somewhat for different nationalities (including whether you need to be resident in your home country to apply,

the length of stay allowed and how long you can work for one employer), so it's best to read up on the specifics of your country's agreement with NZ on the relevant section of the NZIS website (www.immigration.govt.nz/migrant/stream/work/workingholiday). This website also has general information on work opportunities; see also below.

WOMEN TRAVELLERS

Rugby scrums aside, NZ is generally a very safe place for women travellers, although the usual sensible precautions apply. It's best to avoid walking alone late at night in any of the major cities and towns. And if you're out on the town, always keep enough money aside for a taxi back to your accommodation. The same applies in rural towns where there may be a lot of unlit, semi-deserted streets between you and your temporary home. When the pubs and bars close and there are inebriated people tottering around, it's not a great time to be out and about. Lone women should also be wary of staying in basic pub accommodation unless it looks safe and well managed.

Sexual harassment is not a widely reported problem in NZ, but it does happen. Don't presume that male chauvinism or downright aggressive attitudes are the preserve of so-called rural backwaters – urban/suburban males can also be adept at making fools of themselves.

Check out www.womentravel.co.nz for more information.

WORK

If you arrive in NZ on a visitor's visa, then you're not allowed to work for pay. If you're caught breaching this (or another) visa condition, you could be expelled from the country.

If you've been approved for a WHS (see left), you can begin to check out the possibilities for temporary employment. There's usually quite a bit of casual or temp work around, mainly in the fields of agriculture (fruit picking, farming etc), hospitality, ski resorts and, in Auckland and Wellington at least, office-based work in IT, banking and finance, and telemarketing. Registering with an agency is your best bet for inner-city office work.

Seasonal fruit picking, thinning, pruning and harvesting is readily available short-term work for visitors. Apples, kiwi fruit and other types of fruit and vegetables are picked in summer and early autumn. Pay rates are low (you can usually expect to earn $10 to $15 an hour) and the work is hard, so the demand for workers is usually high; you're usually paid by how much you pick (per bin, bucket or kilogram). The main picking season is from December to May, though there's some form of agricultural work in the country year-round. Places where you may find picking work include the Bay of Islands (Kerikeri and Paihia), rural Auckland, Tauranga, Gisborne and Hawkes Bay (Napier and Hastings) in the North Island; Nelson (Tapawera and Golden Bay), Marlborough (around Blenheim) and Central Otago (Alexandra and Roxburgh) in the South Island. Approach prospective employers directly where you can, or stay at hostels or holiday parks in the picking areas that specialise in helping travellers to find work.

The winter work available at ski resorts, or in the towns that service them, includes bartending, waiting tables, cleaning, working on ski tows and, if you're properly qualified, ski or snowboard instructing. Have a look at the website for each resort (p79) for signs of prospective work.

There are certainly many possibilities for picking up short-term work in NZ, but finding something suitable will not always be easy, regardless of how straightforward it may look from afar on work-touting websites. Be prepared to hunt around for worthwhile opportunities, and to make your own wellbeing the priority if you find yourself coping with unsatisfactory conditions such as exploitative pay.

Information

Backpacker publications, hostel owners or managers, and other travellers on the road are all great sources of information for local work possibilities.

Kiwi Careers (www.kiwicareers.govt.nz) features a helpful directory of websites in various job-search fields (agriculture, creative, health, recruitment agencies, teaching, volunteer work).

Seasonal Work NZ (www.seasonalwork.co.nz) has a database of thousands of casual jobs. It gives the contact details of employers looking for workers. Rates of pay and nearby accommodation. **Pick NZ** (www.picknz.co.nz) provides a similar service, focusing on seasonal horticultural work.

New Zealand Job Search (www.nzjs.co.nz) is a handy employment service run out of Auckland and Central Backpackers (p120). **NZ Jobfind** (www.nzjobfind.com) operates out of Wellington's Wildlife House backpackers (p416). The website of the latter has interesting details on pay rates and average annual earnings in NZ by industry.

The website of the **Budget Backpacker Hostels** (BBH; www.bbhnet.co.nz/billboard_home.asp) network has a noticeboard listing current job vacancies in BBH hostels, as well as a few other possibilities.

IRD Number

Travellers undertaking paid work in NZ are required to get an Inland Revenue Department (IRD) number. Download the form from the website of the **Inland Revenue Department** (www.ird.govt.nz); use the search function to find document No IR595. The issuing of an IRD number normally takes eight to 10 working days.

Paying Tax

There is no escaping it! For the vast majority of travellers, any money they earn while working in NZ will have income tax deducted from it by their employer, a process called Pay As You Earn (PAYE). Standard NZ income tax rates are 19.5% for annual salaries up to $38,000 ($730 gross per week), then 33% up to $60,000 and 39% for all higher amounts. A NZ accident compensation scheme levy (1.2%) will also be deducted from your pay packet.

If you visit NZ and work for a short period of time (eg on a working holiday scheme), you may qualify for a tax refund when you leave. You must complete a Refund Application – People Leaving New Zealand (document No IR50) form and send it in with your tax return, along with proof of your departure (eg copies of your air tickets) to the IRD. Further information is available on the IRD website, or contact the **Inland Revenue Non-Resident Centre** (☎ 03-467 7020; nonres@ird.govt.nz; Private Bag 1932, Dunedin).

Transport

CONTENTS

Getting There & Away   **722**
Entering the Country   722
Air   722
Sea   725
Getting Around   **726**
Air   726
Bicycle   726
Boat   728
Bus   728
Car & Motorcycle   731
Hitching   735
Local Transport   736
Train   736

> ### THINGS CHANGE...
>
> The information in this chapter is particularly vulnerable to change. Check directly with the airline or a travel agent to make sure you understand how a fare (and ticket you may buy) works and be aware of the security requirements for international travel. Shop carefully. The details given in this chapter should be regarded as pointers and are not a substitute for your own careful, up-to-date research.

New Zealand's peaceably isolated location in a distant patch of the South Pacific Ocean is one of its drawcards, but it also means that unless you travel from Australia, you have to contend with a long-haul flight to get there. As NZ is serviced by good airline and bus networks, travelling around the country is a much less taxing endeavour.

Flights, tours and rail tickets can be booked online at www.lonelyplanet.com /travel_services.

GETTING THERE & AWAY

ENTERING THE COUNTRY

Disembarkation in NZ is generally a straightforward affair, with only the usual customs declarations to endure (see Customs, p708) and the inevitable scramble to get to the luggage carousel first. Recent global instability has resulted in conspicuously increased security in NZ airports, both in domestic and international terminals, and you may find that customs procedures are now more time-consuming. One procedure has the Orwellian title 'Advance Passenger Screening', a system whereby documents that used to be checked after you touched down in NZ (passport, visa etc) are now checked before you board the flight that will transport you there – make sure all your documentation is in order so that your check-in is as smooth as possible.

Passport

There are no restrictions when it comes to foreign citizens entering NZ. If you have a visa (see p719), you should be fine.

AIR

There's a number of competing airlines servicing NZ and thus a wide variety of air fares to choose from if you're flying in from Asia, Europe or North America, though ultimately you'll still pay a lot for a flight unless you jet in from Australia. NZ's inordinate popularity and abundance of year-round activities means that almost any time of year can prove to be busy for inbound tourists – if you want to fly at a particularly popular time of year (eg Christmas), make your arrangements well in advance.

The high season for flights into NZ is roughly during the country's summer (December to February), with slightly less of a premium on fares over the shoulder months (October/November and March/April). The low season generally tallies with the winter months (June to August), though this is still a busy time for airlines ferrying skiing enthusiasts.

Airports & Airlines

Seven NZ airports handle international flights, with Auckland receiving most of the overseas traffic. The airports:

Auckland (airport code AKL; ☎ 0800 247 767, 09-275 0789; www.auckland-airport.co.nz)

Christchurch (airport code CHC; ☎ 03-358 5029; www.christchurch-airport.co.nz)

Dunedin (airport code DUD; ☎ 03-486 2879; www.dnairport.co.nz)

Hamilton (airport code HLZ; ☎ 07-848 9027; www.hamiltonairport.co.nz)

Palmerston North (airport code PMR; ☎ 06-351 4415; www.pnairport.co.nz)

Queenstown (airport code ZQN; ☎ 03-442 3505; www.queenstownairport.co.nz)

Wellington (airport code WLG; ☎ 04-385 5100; www.wellington-airport.co.nz)

AIRLINES FLYING TO & FROM NEW ZEALAND

NZ's own overseas carrier is Air New Zealand, which flies to runways across Europe, North America, eastern Asia and the Pacific. Airlines that connect NZ with international destinations include the following (note that 0800 phone numbers mentioned here are for dialling from within NZ only):

Aerolíneas Argentinas (airline code AR; ☎ 09-379 3675; www.aerolineas.com.ar; hub Buenos Aires Ezeiza International Airport)

Air New Zealand (airline code NZ; ☎ 0800 737 000; www.airnz.co.nz; hub Auckland International Airport)

Air Pacific (airline code FJ; ☎ 0800 800 178; www.airpacific.com; hub Nadi Airport, Fiji)

Cathay Pacific (airline code CX; ☎ 0800 800 454; www.cathaypacific.com; hub Hong Kong International Airport)

Emirates (airline code EK; ☎ 0508 364 728; www.emirates.com; hub Dubai International Airport)

Freedom Air (airline code SJ; ☎ 0800 600 500; www.freedomair.com; hub Auckland International Airport)

Garuda Indonesia (airline code GA; ☎ 09-366 1862; www.garuda-indonesia.com; hub Soekarno-Hatta International Airport, Jakarta)

Jetstar (airline code JQ; ☎ 0800 800 995; www.jetstar.co.nz; hub Melbourne International Airport)

Korean Air (airline code KE; ☎ 09-914 2000; www.koreanair.com; hub Incheon International Airport, Seoul)

Malaysia Airlines (airline code MH; ☎ 0800 777 747; www.malaysiaairlines.com; hub Kuala Lumpur International Airport)

Pacific Blue (airline code DJ; ☎ 0800 670 000; www.flypacificblue.com; hub Brisbane Airport)

Polynesian Blue (airline code DJ; ☎ 0800 670 000; www.polynesianblue.com; hub Brisbane Airport)

Qantas (airline code QF; ☎ 0800 808 767; www.qantas.com.au; hub Kingsford-Smith Airport, Sydney)

Royal Brunei Airlines (airline code BI; ☎ 09-302 1524; www.bruneiair.com; hub Bandar Seri Begawan Airport)

Singapore Airlines (airline code SQ; ☎ 09-303 2129; www.singaporeair.com; hub Changi International Airport)

Thai Airways International (airline code TG; ☎ 09-377 3886; www.thaiairways.com; hub Bangkok International Airport)

DEPARTURE TAX

There is an international departure tax of NZ$25 when leaving NZ, payable by anyone aged 12 and over (NZ$10 for children aged two to 11, free for those under two years of age). This tax is not included in the price of airline tickets, but must be paid separately at the airport before you board your flight.

Tickets

Automated online ticket sales work well if you're doing a simple one-way or return trip on specified dates, but are no substitute for a travel agent with the lowdown on special deals, strategies for avoiding layovers and other useful advice.

INTERCONTINENTAL (RTW) TICKETS

If you're flying to NZ from the other side of the world, round-the-world (RTW) tickets can be real bargains. They are generally put together by the three biggest airline alliances, **Star Alliance** (www.staralliance.com), **Oneworld** (www.oneworldalliance.com) and **Skyteam** (www.skyteam.com), and give you a limited period (usually a year) in which to circumnavigate the globe. You can go anywhere the participating airlines go, as long as you stay within the prescribed kilometre extents or number of stops and don't backtrack when flying between continents. Backtracking is generally permitted within a single continent, though with certain restrictions; see the relevant websites for details.

An alternative type of RTW ticket is one put together by a travel agent. These are usually more expensive than airline RTW fares but allow you to devise your own itinerary. RTW tickets start from around UK£850 from the UK and around US$1850 from the USA.

CIRCLE PACIFIC TICKETS

A Circle Pacific ticket is similar to a RTW ticket but covers a more limited region, using a combination of airlines to connect

Australia, NZ, North America and Asia, with stopover options in the Pacific Islands. As with RTW tickets, there are restrictions on how many stopovers you can take.

ONLINE TICKET SITES

For online ticket bookings, including RTW fares, start with the following websites:

Air Brokers (www.airbrokers.com) This US company specialises in cheaper tickets. To fly LA–Tahiti–Auckland–Sydney–Bali–Singapore–Bangkok–Hong Kong–LA costs around US$2100 (excluding taxes).

Cheap Flights (www.cheapflights.com) Informative site with specials, airline information and flight searches from the USA and other regions.

Cheapest Flights (www.cheapestflights.co.uk) Cheap worldwide flights from the UK; get in early for the bargains.

Expedia (www.expedia.msn.com) Microsoft's travel site, mainly USA-related.

Flight Centre International (www.flightcentre.com) Respected operator handling direct flights, with sites for NZ, Australia, the UK, the USA, Canada and South Africa.

Flights.com (www.flights.com) International site for flights; cheap fares and an easy-to-search database.

Roundtheworldflights.com (www.roundtheworld flights.com) This excellent site allows you to build your own trips from the UK with up to six stops. A four-stop trip including Asia, Australia, NZ and the USA costs from UK£900.

STA Travel (www.statravel.com) Prominent in international student travel but you don't have to be a student; site linked to worldwide STA sites.

Travel Online (www.travelonline.co.nz) Good place to check worldwide flights from NZ.

Travel.com.au (www.travel.com.au) Good Australian site; look up fares and flights to/from the country.

Travelocity (www.travelocity.com) US site that allows you to search fares (in US dollars) from/to practically anywhere.

Asia

Most Asian countries offer fairly competitive air fare deals, with Bangkok, Singapore and Hong Kong being the best places to shop around for discount tickets.

Common one-way fares to Auckland cost approximately US$600 from Singapore, US$800 from Kuala Lumpur, Bangkok and Hong Kong, and US$750 from Tokyo. Going the other way, return fares from Auckland to Singapore cost around NZ$1300, and around NZ$1500 to Kuala Lumpur, Bangkok, Hong Kong and Tokyo, depending on the airline.

Hong Kong's travel market can be unpredictable, but excellent bargains are some-times available. **Phoenix Services** (☎ 2722 7378) is recommended.

STA Travel Bangkok (☎ 02-236 0262; www.statravel .co.th); Singapore (☎ 6737 7188; www.statravel.com.sg); Tokyo (☎ 03-5391 2922; www.statravel.co.jp) has offices in many major cities of the region.

Australia

Air New Zealand and Qantas operate a network of flights linking key NZ cities with most major Australian gateway cities, while quite a few other international airlines include NZ and Australia on their Asia-Pacific routes.

Another trans-Tasman option is the no-frills budget airline Freedom Air, an Air New Zealand subsidiary that offers direct flights between destinations on Australia's east coast (Brisbane, Sydney and especially the Gold Coast, a popular holiday destination for Kiwis) and the NZ centres of Auckland, Christchurch, Dunedin, Wellington, Palmerston North and Hamilton.

Pacific Blue, a subsidiary of budget airline Virgin Blue, offers direct flights between Auckland, Wellington and Christchurch and east-coast capitals, with connections on the domestic Virgin Blue network to many other Australian cities.

In December 2005 Qantas' budget subsidiary, Jetstar, commenced flights between Christchurch and Sydney, Melbourne, Brisbane and the Gold Coast.

This newest addition to the skies above the Tasman means increased competition and hopefully the regular outbreak of pricing wars between the budget airlines (a potential boon for travellers in search of a bargain!).

If you book early, shop around and have the gods smiling upon you, you may pay under $200 for a one-way fare on a budget carrier from either Sydney or Melbourne to Auckland, Christchurch or Wellington. More common prices are from $260 to $300 one way. You can fly into Auckland and out of Christchurch to save backtracking, but you may not get the cheapest fares with this itinerary.

From key NZ cities, you'll pay between NZ$250 and NZ$300 for a one-way ticket to an Australian east-coast city.

There's usually not a significant difference in price between seasons, as this is a popular route year-round. The intense competition, however, inevitably results in some attractive discounting.

For reasonably priced fares, try one of the numerous Australian capital-city branches of **STA Travel** (☎ 1300 733 035; www.statravel.com .au). Another good option, also with dozens of offices around the country, is **Flight Centre** (☎ 133 133; www.flightcentre.com.au).

Canada

The air routes flown from Canada are similar to those from mainland USA, with most Toronto and Vancouver flights stopping in a US city such as Los Angeles or Honolulu before heading on to NZ.

The air fares sold by Canadian discount air-ticket sellers (consolidators) tend to be about 10% higher than those sold in the USA. **Travel CUTS** (☎ 866-246-9762; www.travelcuts .com) is Canada's national student travel agency and has offices in all major cities.

Return fares out of Vancouver to Auckland cost between C$1500 and C$1900 via the US west coast. From Toronto, fares cost around C$2000. One-way fares from NZ start at around NZ$1500 to Toronto and NZ$1400 to Vancouver.

Continental Europe

Frankfurt and London are the major arrival and departure points for flights to and from NZ, both with extensive connections to other European cities. From these two launching pads, most flights to NZ travel via one of the Asian capitals.

A good option in the Dutch travel industry is **Holland International** (☎ 0900-8858; www .hollandinternational.nl). From Amsterdam, return fares start at around €1600.

In Germany, good travel agencies include the Berlin branch of **STA Travel** (☎ 030-2859 8264; www.statravel.de). Return fares from Frankfurt start at around €1200.

In France, try **Usit Connect Voyages** (☎ 01 43 29 69 50; www.usitconnections.fr) or **OTU Voyages** (☎ 01 40 29 12 22; www.otu.fr) – both companies are student/youth specialists and have offices in many French cities. Other recommendations include **Voyageurs du Monde** (☎ 08 92 23 56 56; www.vdm.com/vdm) and **Nouvelles Frontières** (☎ 08 25 00 08 25; www.nouvelles-frontieres.fr/nf). Return fares from Paris start from €1200.

Return air fares from NZ to key European hubs such as Paris and Frankfurt usually cost between NZ$1800 and NZ$2400.

UK & Ireland

Depending on which airline you travel with from the UK, flights to NZ go via Asia or the USA. If you fly via Asia you can often make stopovers in countries such as India, Thailand, Singapore and Australia; in the other direction, stopover possibilities include New York, Los Angeles, Honolulu or a variety of Pacific islands.

Discount air travel is big business in London. Advertisements for many travel agencies appear in the travel pages of the weekend broadsheet newspapers, in *Time Out*, the *Evening Standard* and in the free magazine *TNT*.

Typical one-way/return fares from London to Auckland start at around £450/650; note that June–July and mid-December fares can go up by as much as 30%. From NZ you can expect to pay between NZ$1800 and NZ$2200 for return fares to London.

Popular agencies in the UK include the ubiquitous **STA Travel** (☎ 0870 160 0599; www.sta travel.co.uk), **Trailfinders** (☎ 020-7628 7628; www.trail finders.co.uk) and **Flight Centre** (☎ 0870 499 0040; www.flightcentre.co.uk).

USA

Most flights between the North American mainland and NZ are to/from the USA's west coast, with the bulk routed through Los Angeles but some going through San Francisco. Some airlines offer flights via various Pacific islands.

San Francisco is the ticket consolidator capital of America, although some good deals can be found in Los Angeles, New York and other big cities. **STA Travel** (☎ 800-777 0112; www.statravel.com) has offices all over the USA.

Typically a return ticket to NZ from the US west coast will start around US$1100/1400 in the low/high season; fares from the east coast start at US$1400/1700. Return fares from NZ to the US west coast are around NZ$1300, and to New York NZ$1800.

SEA

It's possible (though by no means easy or safe) to make your way between NZ and Australia, and some smaller Pacific islands, by hitching rides or crewing on yachts. Try asking around at harbours, marinas and yacht and sailing clubs. Popular yachting harbours in NZ include the Bay of Islands and Whangarei (both in Northland), Auckland and Wellington. March and April are the best months to look for boats heading to Australia. From Fiji, October to November is a peak departure season as cyclones are on their way.

There are no passenger liners operating to/from NZ and finding a berth on a cargo ship (much less enjoying the experience) is no easy task.

GETTING AROUND

AIR

Those who have limited time to get between NZ's attractions can make the most of a widespread network of intra- and inter-island flights.

Airlines in New Zealand

The country's major domestic carrier, Air New Zealand, has an aerial network covering most of the country. The next biggest carrier is regional airline Origin Pacific, which has services to many major centres (although it doesn't travel further south than Christchurch). Australia-based Qantas also maintains routes between main urban areas, mostly using other airlines' planes.

Providing essential transport services to the small outlying islands such as Great Barrier Island in Hauraki Gulf, Stewart Island and the Chathams are several small-scale outfits.

The list of NZ regional airlines includes the following:

Air Chathams (☎ 03-305 0209; www.airchathams.com) Provides services to the remote Chatham Islands from Wellington, Christchurch and Auckland.

Air New Zealand (☎ 0800 737 000; www.airnz.co.nz) Offers flights between 25 domestic destinations in conjunction with a couple of small affiliated airlines under the banner Air New Zealand Link.

Air West Coast (☎ 03-738 0524; www.airwestcoast.co.nz) Flies between Greymouth and Wellington (via Westport).

Air2there.com (☎ 0800 777 000; www.air2there.com) Connects destinations across Cook Strait, including Wanganui, Palmerston North, Wellington and Blenheim.

Great Barrier Airlines (☎ 0800 900 600, 09-275 9120; www.greatbarrierairlines.co.nz) Connects Great Barrier Island with Auckland, Whangarei and the Coromandel Peninsula; also flies direct between Auckland and the Coromandel (Whitianga and Matarangi).

Mountain Air (☎ 0800 222 123, 09-256 7025; www.mountainair.co.nz) Flies regularly between Auckland, Whangarei and Great Barrier Island.

Origin Pacific (☎ 0800 302 302, 03-547 2020; www.originpacific.co.nz) Flies between 10 major locations across both islands from its hub in Nelson.

Qantas (☎ 0800 808 767; www.qantas.co.nz) Joins the dots between five key tourism centres: Auckland, Rotorua, Wellington, Christchurch and Queenstown.

Soundsair (☎ 0800 505 005; www.soundsair.co.nz) Hops across Cook Strait between Wellington and Picton up to 16 times per day; also flies between Wellington and Kaikoura, and offers a new Wellington–Blenheim–Nelson–Wellington route.

Stewart Island Flights (☎ 03-218 9129; www.stewartislandflights.com) Flies between Invercargill and Stewart Island.

Air Passes

With discounting being the norm these days, and a number of budget airlines now serving the trans-Tasman route as well as various Pacific islands, air passes do not generally represent great value.

Air New Zealand offers the **South Pacific Airpass** (www.airnewzealand.com), valid for selected journeys within NZ, and between NZ, Australia and a number of Pacific islands. The pass is only available to nonresidents of these countries, and must be issued outside NZ. Passes are issued in conjunction with an international ticket (with any airline) and are valid for the life of that ticket.

The pass involves purchasing coupons for domestic flights (one way from NZ$120 to NZ$408, depending on distance), or flights to/from major Australian cities or Pacific islands including Fiji, New Caledonia and Tonga, and as far afield as the Cook Islands and Samoa (one way from NZ$400 to NZ$834).

BICYCLE

Touring cyclists in NZ are so numerous, particularly over summer, that it's as if the Kiwis have some secret breeding program for creatures with brightly coloured plumage and aerodynamic heads. The country is popular with bikers because it's clean, green, relatively uncrowded, and has lots of cheap accommodation (including camping) and easily accessible freshwater. The roads are also good and the climate generally not too hot or too cold, except on the rain-loving west coast (particularly on the South Island).

TRANSPORT FARES

Air Fares

From	To	One way (from NZ$)
Auckland	Christchurch	90
Auckland	Dunedin	125
Auckland	Great Barrier Island	85
Auckland	Hamilton	65
Auckland	Kaitaia	85
Auckland	Kerikeri	85
Auckland	Napier	95
Auckland	Nelson	120
Auckland	New Plymouth	95
Auckland	Palmerston North	85
Auckland	Rotorua	85
Auckland	Queenstown	150
Auckland	Taupo	85
Auckland	Wellington	85
Auckland	Whakatane	90
Auckland	Whangarei	85
Christchurch	Chatham Islands	360
Christchurch	Dunedin	85
Christchurch	Hamilton	150
Christchurch	Hokitika	75
Christchurch	Invercargill	95
Christchurch	Napier	150
Christchurch	Nelson	85
Christchurch	New Plymouth	140
Christchurch	Queenstown	75
Christchurch	Rotorua	130
Wellington	Blenheim	70
Wellington	Chatham Islands	360
Wellington	Christchurch	70
Wellington	Dunedin	120
Wellington	Gisborne	100
Wellington	Hamilton	100
Wellington	Nelson	80
Wellington	Napier	90
Wellington	Palmerston North	80
Wellington	Rotorua	100
Wellington	Westport	100
Wellington	Whakatane	140

Bus Fares

From	To	One way (from NZ$)
Auckland	Hamilton	25
Auckland	New Plymouth	70
Auckland	Paihia	50
Auckland	Rotorua	50
Auckland	Taupo	55
Auckland	Tauranga	40
Auckland	Thames	25
Auckland	Wellington	95
Christchurch	Dunedin	45
Christchurch	Greymouth	35
Christchurch	Kaikoura	30
Christchurch	Nelson	70
Christchurch	Picton	50
Christchurch	Queenstown	65
Dunedin	Invercargill	40
Nelson	Wellington	75
New Plymouth	Wanganui	35
Paihia	Kaitaia	35
Picton	Kaikoura	35
Picton	Nelson	35
Rotorua	Gisborne	55
Queenstown	Dunedin	40
Queenstown	Greymouth	85
Queenstown	Invercargill	50
Queenstown	Milford Sound	70
Queenstown	Mt Cook	65
Queenstown	Te Anau	45
Queenstown	Waraka	30

Train Fares

From	To	One way (from NZ$)
Auckland	Hamilton	45
Auckland	Palmerston North	125
Auckland	Wellington	145
Christchurch	Greymouth	100
Kaikoura	Christchurch	50
Picton	Blenheim	25
Picton	Kaikoura	45
Picton	Christchurch	80
Wellington	Palmerston North	35

The many hills make for hard going at times, but there are plenty of flats and lows to accompany the highs. Bikes and cycling gear (to rent or buy) are readily available in the main centres, as are bicycle repair services.

The choice of itineraries is limited only by your imagination. Cycling along the extensive coastline is an obvious highlight, but the inland routes have their share of devotees. One increasingly popular expedition is to follow an upgraded path along an old railway line into the former gold-mining heartland of Otago – for details, see the boxed text, p612.

By law you must wear an approved safety helmet (or risk a fine) and it's also good to have reflective gear for cycling at night or on dull days. Cyclists who use public transport will find that major bus lines and trains only take bicycles on a 'space available' basis (meaning bikes may not be allowed on) and charge up to $10. Some of the shuttle or backpackers buses, on the other hand, make sure they have storage space for bikes, which they carry for a surcharge.

If importing your own bike or transporting it by plane within NZ, check with the relevant airline for costs and the degree of dismantling and packing required.

Hire

The rates charged by most outfits for renting road or mountain bikes – not including the discounted fees or freebies offered by accommodation places to their guests – are anywhere from $10 to $20 per hour and $30 to $45 per day.

Purchase

Bicycles can be readily bought in NZ's larger cities, but prices for newer models are high. For a decent hybrid bike or rigid mountain bike you'll pay anywhere from $700 to $1500, though you can get a cheap one for around $400 to $500 – however, then you still need to get panniers, a helmet and other essential touring gear, and the cost quickly climbs. Arguably you're better off buying a used bike (assuming you can't bring your own over), but finding something that's in good enough shape for a long road trip is not always as easy as it sounds. Other options include the post-Christmas sales and midyear stocktakes, when newish cycles can be heavily discounted.

BOAT

NZ may be an island nation but there's virtually no long-distance water transport around the country. Obvious exceptions include the boat services between Auckland and various islands in Hauraki Gulf (see p147), the interisland ferries that chug over Cook Strait between the North and South Islands – see under Wellington (p424) or Picton (p442) – and the passenger ferry that negotiates the width of Foveaux Strait between Bluff and the town of Oban on Stewart Island (see p696).

BUS

Bus travel in NZ is relatively easy and well organised, with services transporting you to the far reaches of both islands (including the start/end of various walking tracks), but it can be expensive, tedious and time-consuming. The bus 'terminals' in smaller places usually comprise a parking spot outside a prominent local business.

The dominant bus company is **Inter-City Coachlines** (www.intercitycoach.co.nz; Auckland [tel] 09-623 1503; Wellington [tel] 04-385 0520; Christchurch [tel] 03-365 1113; Dunedin [tel] 03-471 7743), which also has an extracomfort travel and sightseeing arm called **Newmans Coach Lines** (www.newmanscoach.co.nz). InterCity can drive you to just about anywhere on the North and South Islands, from Invercargill and Milford Sound in the south to Paihia and Kaitaia in the north.

Smaller regional operators running key routes or covering a lot of ground on the North Island include the following:

Alpine Scenic Tours ([tel] 07-386 8918; www.alpinescenictours.co.nz) Has services between Turangi and National Park, with useful stops for trampers in Tongariro National Park and extension services up to Taupo.

Bay Xpress ([tel] 0800 422 997; www.bayxpress.co.nz) Connects Wellington with Hastings and Napier.

Dalroy Express ([tel] 0508 465 622; www.dalroytours.co.nz) Operates a daily service between Auckland and Hawera via New Plymouth and Hamilton.

Go Kiwi Shuttles ([tel] 0800 446 549, 07-866 0336; www.go-kiwi.co.nz) Links places like Auckland, Rotorua and Hamilton with various towns across the Coromandel Peninsula.

Kiwi Traveller ([tel] 0800 500 100, 04-384 7031; www.kiwitraveller.co.nz) Operates a service between Wellington and Rotorua, via National Park and Taupo.

Northliner ([tel] 09-307 5873; www.northliner.co.nz) Runs from Auckland north to Paihia in the Bay of Islands.

Waitomo Wanderer (☎ 0508 926 333; www.waitomotours.co.nz) Does a loop from Rotorua to Waitomo.

White Star City to City (☎ 06-758 3338) Shuttles between Wellington, Palmerston North, Wanganui and New Plymouth.

South Island shuttle bus companies include the following:

Abel Tasman Coachlines (☎ 03-548 0285; www.abeltasmantravel.co.nz) Runs services between Nelson, Golden Bay and the national parks of Kahurangi and Abel Tasman.

Atomic Shuttles (☎ 03-322 8883; www.atomictravel.co.nz) Has services throughout the South Island, including to Christchurch, Dunedin, Invercargill, Picton, Nelson, Greymouth/Hokitika, Te Anau and Queenstown/Wanaka.

Coast to Coast (☎ 0800 800 847; www.coast2coast.co.nz) Travels from Christchurch to Hokitika/Greymouth via Arthur's Pass.

Cook Connection (☎ 0800 266 526; www.cookconnect.co.nz) Runs between Mt Cook and Twizel, Lake Tekapo and Oamaru.

East West Coach (☎ 0800 142 622, 03-789 6251; eastwestco@xtra.co.nz) Offers a service between Christchurch and Westport, running via Hanmer Springs turn-off, Maruia Springs and Reefton.

Hanmer Connection (☎ 0800 242 6637; info@atsnz.com) Provides services between Hanmer Springs and Christchurch, and three weekly services between Hanmer and Kaikoura.

KBus (☎ 0800 881 188, 03-578 4075; www.kbus.co.nz) Roams across the top of the South Island, taking in Christchurch, Nelson, Picton, Blenheim and Greymouth, among others.

Knightrider (☎ 03-342 8055; www.knightrider.co.nz) Runs a night-time service from Christchurch to Invercargill via Dunedin.

Scenic Shuttle (☎ 0800 277 483, 03-249 7654; reservation@scenicshuttle.com) Drives between Te Anau and Invercargill via Manapouri.

South Island Connections (☎ 0800 700 797; www.southislandconnections.co.nz) Operates shuttles between Dunedin, Christchurch and Picton.

Southern Link Lazerline Coaches (☎ 03-358 8355; www.yellow.co.nz/site/southernlink) Heads from Christchurch to Nelson via Lewis Pass (with connections to Westport); also runs from Christchurch to Queenstown and Wanaka, and from Queenstown and Wanaka to Dunedin.

Topline Tours (☎ 03-249 8059; www.toplinetours.co.nz) Connects Te Anau and Queenstown.

Wanaka Connexions (☎ 03-443 9122; www.wanakaconnexions.co.nz) Links Wanaka, Queenstown, Christchurch, Invercargill and Dunedin.

Backpacker Buses

While the bus companies offering transport options for budget travellers can almost be classified as organised tours, they do also get you from A to B (usually with hop-on, hop-off services) and so can be a cost-effective alternative to the big bus companies. The buses are usually smaller, you'll meet lots of other travellers, and the drivers sometimes double as tour guides; conversely, some travellers find the tour-group mentality (which sometimes includes being stuck in party mode) and inherent limitations don't suit them. Discounts for card-carrying students and members of hostel organisations are regularly available.

We get lots of feedback about such companies, a real mixed bag of rave reviews and lengthy criticisms. It's a good idea to compare party outfits and the deals they offer when you arrive in NZ, particularly by talking to other travellers – you're bound to see them piling out of such buses at hostels.

Prominent operators:

Bottom Bus (☎ www.bottombus.co.nz) Dunedin (☎ 03-434 7370); Queenstown (☎ 03-442 9708) Affiliated with Kiwi Experience (see following), this hop-on, hop-off service runs a deep-south loop taking in Queenstown, Te Anau and Milford Sound, Dunedin and Invercargill via the Catlins and the Southern Scenic Route. Subroutes include Dunedin to Te Anau ($260 including Milford Sound), Dunedin to Queenstown ($410 including Milford and Stewart Island) and the 'In a Stew' route ($499 including a Milford Sound cruise, plus visits to Stewart Island and either Otago Peninsula or Te Anau Caves).

Flying Kiwi (☎ 0800 693 296, 03-547 0171; www.flyingkiwi.com) The Flying Kiwi is a tour rather than a bus service (although there is a top-on, hop-off element available), of which we've heard good reports. With an emphasis on outdoor activities, this company's 'rolling travellers' home' includes a kitchen and carries mountain bikes, Canadian canoes, boogie boards and more. Accommodation is camping (an additional $12 per night) – you can bring you own tent or hire one. There's an additional food fund and the group takes turns at cooking. South Island excursions include eight-day ($525) and 16-day ($1115) trips. North Island options include nine-day comprehensive ($585) and two-day 'Northern Express' ($140) trips. The 27-day, trans-NZ 'Ultimate Explorer' costs $1495.

Kiwi Experience (☎ 09-366 9830; www.kiwiexperience.com) The biggest of the hop-on, hop-off backpacker/tour buses, Kiwi Experience's familiar pea-green buses operate a comprehensive service around the North and South Islands. There are over 20 pass options, and most passes are valid for one year. Trips include: 'Northern

Roundup' ($425); 'Southern Roundup' ($500); all-NZ tours ($895 to $1790); and the 'Full Monty' trip ($1790). Useful small loops where other services are limited include the 'Awesome & Top Bit' route around Northland, the 'Southlander' (run by Bottom Bus) through the Catlins and along the Southern Scenic Route, 'East As', from Taupo around the East Cape, and 'Milford Overland'.

Magic Travellers Network (☎ 09-358 5600; www.magicbus.co.nz) Magic Bus is another hop-on, hop-off bus operating an extensive network on the North and South Islands, with 19 main trips, and passes lasting one year. Trips range from the basic 'Top of the North' ($190) or 'Top of the South' ($260) to the countrywide 'Spirit of NZ' (minimum 23 days) for $1120.

Stray Travel (www.straytravel.co.nz) Christchurch (☎ 03-377 6192) Stray promotes itself as getting further off the beaten track, and has more than 20 hop-on, hop-off passes to choose from, including the Jill (all North Island, $410), the Ron (round South Island, $710) and the Max (a comprehensive all-NZ pass, $1115). All passes are valid for 12 months. At the time of research the company was engaging in good PR with free city orientation tours in Auckland and Christchurch (see the website for details).

Bus Passes

InterCity offers numerous bus passes, either covering the whole country, or the North and South Islands separately. If you're planning to cover a lot of ground, the passes can work out cheaper than paying as you go, but they lock you into using InterCity buses (rather than, say, the convenient shuttle buses that cover much of the country). There's a 15% discount for members of YHA and VIP. Northliner offers discount backpackers passes for Northland.

INTERCITY

The appropriately named **Flexi-Pass** (www.flexipass.co.nz) is valid for one year and allows you to travel pretty much anywhere (and in any direction) on the InterCity network; you can get on and off wherever you like and can change bookings up to two hours before departure without penalty. The pass is purchased in five-hour blocks of travel time, from a minimum of 15 hours ($164) up to a maximum of 60 hours ($585) – the average cost of each block becomes cheaper the more hours you buy. You can top up the pass if you need more time.

InterCity offers a range of other passes tailored to travel on each island and across the country, each with a maximum life of one year. All passes can be done in reverse.

There may be a reservation charge of $3 per sector (depending on the agent), additional to the cost of the pass.

There are two North Island passes, both offering travel between Auckland and Wellington. The 'North Island Value Pass' (adult/child $150/100) goes via the Central Plateau and Taupo; the 'Pacific Coast Hwy Pass' (adult/child $200/135) takes in the Coromandel Peninsula and the East Coast.

South Island passes include: 'West Coast Passport' (adult/child $165/110), which allows travel from Picton to Queenstown via the West Coast; 'Milford Bound Adventurer' (adult/child $225/150), running between Christchurch and Queenstown via Milford Sound and Mt Cook; and 'Southern Discovery' (adult/child $340/230), travelling between Christchurch and Greymouth via Queenstown, Milford Sound and the West Coast.

Dual-island passes include: 'Pathfinder' (adult/child $540/360), taking you from Auckland to Christchurch or vice versa, including along the South Island's West Coast and to Milford Sound; 'Trail Blazer' (adult/child $560/380), describing a loop that starts/finishes at Auckland; and 'Total New Zealand Experience' (adult/child $700/470), the kitchen sink of coach passes.

TRAVELPASS

The nationwide 'multitransport' **Travelpass** (☎ 0800 339 966; www.travelpass.co.nz) combines bus travel with a ferry crossing, plus train or air travel if desired. Passes are purchased for 'days' of travel, which you can use over a 12-month period:

- Two-in-one pass: InterCity bus travel, plus one Interislander ferry crossing (Wellington–Picton or vice versa); the pass costs for five/10/15 travel days $370/575/810.

- Three-in-one pass: as above for bus and ferry, plus one train journey (choose from the TranzAlpine, TranzCoastal or Overlander); the pass costs for five/10/15 travel days $460/690/850.

- Four-in-one pass: as above for bus, ferry and train, plus a one-way domestic flight; the pass costs for five/10/15 travel days from $625/850/1005.

NORTHLINER

Northliner offers card-carrying backpackers (YHA, VIP, BBH and Nomads; for details of these organisations see p704) various passes enabling unlimited travel on different routes. The 'Bay of Islands' ($60), 'Loop' ($90) and 'Northland Freedom' ($120) passes are all valid for one month from date of purchase, while the 'Top Half' ($92) pass is valid for two months.

Classes

There are no separate classes on buses and smoking is not permitted.

Reservations

Over summer, school holidays and public holidays, you should book well ahead on the more popular routes. At other times you should have few problems getting on to your preferred service, but if your long-term travel plans rely on catching a particular bus, book at least a day or two ahead just to be safe.

Intercity fares vary widely according to how far ahead they're booked and their availability, and the best prices are generally obtained a few weeks in advance.

CAR & MOTORCYCLE

The best way to explore NZ in depth is to have your own transport, as it allows you to create your own (leisurely) flexible itinerary. Good-value car- and campervan-hire rates are not hard to track down; alternatively, consider buying your own set of wheels.

Automobile Association (AA)

NZ's **Automobile Association** (AA; 24hr road service ☎ 0800 500 222; www.aa.co.nz) provides emergency breakdown services, excellent touring maps and detailed guides to accommodation (from holiday parks to motels and B&Bs). Members of foreign automobile associations should bring their membership cards, as many of these bodies have reciprocal agreements with NZ's AA.

Driving Licence

International visitors to NZ can use their home country's driving licence – if your licence isn't in English, it's a good idea to

NORTH ISLAND ROAD DISTANCES (KM)

	Auckland	Cape Reinga	Dargaville	Gisborne	Hamilton	Hicks Bay	Kaitaia	Napier	New Plymouth	Paihia	Palmerston North	Rotorua	Taupo	Tauranga	Thames	Waitomo Caves	Wanganui	Wellington	Whakatane	Whangarei
Auckland	---																			
Cape Reinga	440	---																		
Dargaville	185	285	---																	
Gisborne	511	943	690	---																
Hamilton	127	566	312	399	---															
Hicks Bay	513	546	691	180	400	---														
Kaitaia	325	114	169	831	450	833	---													
Napier	421	851	606	215	252	395	743	---												
New Plymouth	371	789	554	585	242	590	699	413	---											
Paihia	241	220	130	750	368	748	109	664	597	---										
Palmerston North	531	959	541	390	402	574	853	176	236	773	---									
Rotorua	235	672	420	292	109	290	560	229	259	475	341	---								
Taupo	280	730	466	333	153	373	604	147	300	520	259	82	---							
Tauranga	210	645	390	300	108	302	537	300	306	447	424	83	165	---						
Thames	115	555	300	413	106	416	440	349	348	356	470	166	211	151	---					
Waitomo Caves	198	640	390	437	75	441	521	307	163	708	341	167	225	114	182	---				
Wanganui	454	853	640	466	329	644	780	250	166	708	74	307	211	440	479	268	---			
Wellington	666	1095	845	534	521	720	970	319	356	896	143	460	378	543	591	463	193	---		
Whakatane	301	740	487	206	155	204	630	315	554	705	421	86	168	94	236	239	358	545	---	
Whangarei	170	270	58	668	295	678	154	597	526	71	697	406	450	381	268	372	625	820	476	---

TRANSPORT

SOUTH ISLAND ROAD DISTANCES (KM)

	Aoraki/Mt Cook	Arthur's Pass	Blenheim	Christchurch	Dunedin	Franz Josef Glacier	Greymouth	Hanmer Springs	Hokitika	Invercargill	Kaikoura	Milford Sound	Nelson	Oamaru	Picton	Queenstown	Te Anau	Timaru	Wanaka	Westport
Aoraki/Mt Cook	...																			
Arthur's Pass	408	...																		
Blenheim	640	420	...																	
Christchurch	330	149	308	...																
Dunedin	331	478	674	360	...															
Franz Josef Glacier	493	248	486	395	562	...														
Greymouth	510	99	333	258	551	181	...													
Hanmer Springs	466	264	260	135	495	395	214	...												
Hokitika	530	104	370	260	570	140	41	256	...											
Invercargill	449	694	888	578	217	575	769	714	690	...										
Kaikoura	518	337	132	187	545	550	338	133	420	767	...									
Milford Sound	550	922	1075	768	410	678	860	910	810	280	960	...								
Nelson	744	384	117	418	786	470	290	305	334	1018	250	1145	...							
Oamaru	215	334	556	247	114	506	448	380	456	330	436	524	671	...						
Picton	667	458	29	336	701	531	360	300	400	918	160	1121	114	583	...					
Queenstown	271	645	794	489	280	404	583	620	513	190	676	291	693	321	822	...				
Te Anau	434	798	960	650	289	560	732	785	690	158	840	122	1025	410	988	168	...			
Timaru	212	250	470	162	200	492	352	300	365	417	351	610	588	85	499	336	486	...		
Wanaka	214	528	745	424	276	285	469	560	426	285	612	394	588	234	774	119	273	280	...	
Westport	666	200	266	334	695	102	218	145	869	340	958	230	580	292	659	828		497	592	...

carry a certified translation with you. Alternatively, use an International Driving Permit (IDP), which will usually be issued on the spot (valid for 12 months) by your home country's automobile association.

Fuel

Fuel is available from service stations with the well-known international brand names. LPG (gas) is not always stocked by rural suppliers; if you're on gas it's safer to have dual fuel capability. Prices vary from place to place, but basically petrol (gasoline) isn't pumped cheaply in NZ, with per-litre costs averaging around $1.40. More remote destinations may charge a smallish fortune to fill your tank and you're better off getting fuel before you reach them – places in this category include Milford Sound (fill up at Te Anau) and Mt Cook (buy fuel at Twizel or Lake Tekapo).

Hire

CAMPERVAN

Campervans (also known as mobile homes, motor homes or RVs) are an enormously popular form of transport for those doing slow-paced tours of NZ, so popular that in well-trafficked parts of the South Island during peak tourist season you can feel socially inadequate if you're driving anything else.

You can hire campervans from an assortment of companies for an assortment of prices, depending on the time of year, how big you want your home-on-wheels to be, and how long you plan to rent the vehicle. **Maui** (☎ 0800 651 080, 09-275 3013; www.maui.co.nz), **Britz** (☎ 0800 831 900, 09-275 9090; www.britz.co.nz) and **Kea Campers** (☎ 0800 520 052, 09-441 7833; www.keacampers.com/newzealand) are three of the biggest operators.

A small van suitable for two people typically has a minikitchen and fold-out dining table, the latter transforms into a double bed when meal time is over. Larger 'superior' two-berth vans include shower and toilet. Four- to six-berth campervans are the size of light trucks (and similarly sluggish) and, besides the extra space, usually contain a toilet and shower.

Over summer, rates offered by the main rental firms for two-/four-/six-berth vans

BACKPACKER VAN RENTALS

There are a number of new players in the campervan industry, offering slick deals and funky, well-kitted-out vehicles to attract young, independent travellers (the kind that would shun the larger, more traditional box-on-wheels). All companies offer living, sleeping and cooking equipment, 24-hour roadside assistance, and maps and travel tips. Rates are competitive (between $40 and $50 a day from May to September, $90 to $110 in the peak season); check out the following:

Backpacker Sleeper Vans (☎ 0800 32 939, 03-359 4731; www.sleepervans.co.nz)

Escape Rentals (☎ 0800 216 171; www.escaperentals.co.nz) With its tongue-in-cheek slogan – 'the freedom to sleep around' – and loud, original artwork on each van's exterior, this company is pitching squarely for young travellers after something different. DVDs, TVs and outdoor barbecues are available for rent.

Spaceships (☎ 0800 772 2374, 09-309 8777; www.spaceships.tv) From the people behind Stray Travel (p730) come these more understated, converted 'people-movers', with extras including DVD and CD players. Accessories for rent include roof rack and solar shower.

Wicked Campers (☎ 0800 246 870; www.wickedcampers.com.au/nz) Also offers cool spray-painted vans.

are usually around $190/280/300 per day, dropping to as low as $45/90/110 in winter; industry in-fighting often sees even lower rates.

CAR

Competition between car-rental companies in NZ is fierce, so rates tend to be variable and lots of special deals come and go (we've heard of discounted rates as low as $19 per day, so shop around); car rental is most competitive in Auckland, Christchurch, Wellington and Picton. The main thing to remember when assessing your options is distance – if you want to travel far, you need unlimited kilometres. You need to be at least 21 years old to hire a vehicle.

Sizable multinational companies include **Budget** (☎ 0800 283 438, 09-595 7784; www.budget.co.nz), **Thrifty** (☎ 0800 737 070, 03-359 2721; www.thrifty.co.nz), **Hertz** (☎ 0800 654 321; www.hertz.co.nz)

and **Avis** (☎ 0800 655 111, 09-526 2847; www.avis.com), which all have offices or agents in most major cities, towns and larger airports.

There's a vast number of local firms, or firms with outlets in a limited number of locations, which we detail throughout this guide. These are almost always cheaper than the big operators – sometimes half the price – but the cheapest car hire may come with serious restrictions. Some less expensive operators have national networks, including the recommended **Omega Rental Cars** (☎ 0800 525 210, 09-377 5573; www.omegarentalcars.com), as well as **Pegasus** (☎ 0800 803 580, 03-548 2852; www.rentalcars.co.nz) and **Ezy** (☎ 0800 399 107; www.ezy.co.nz). Note that these companies all have free-call numbers from various international locations – see the websites for details.

The big firms sometimes offer one-way rentals (eg pick up a car in Auckland and leave it in Christchurch) but there are a variety of restrictions and sometimes a substantial drop-off fee may apply if you're not returning the car to the city of hire; however, for rentals of a month or more this should be waived between Auckland and Wellington or Christchurch. On the other hand, an operator in Christchurch may need to get a vehicle back to Auckland and will offer an amazing one-way deal (Budget and Thrifty list relocation specials on their website, under 'Hot Deals').

Some car-hire firms will not allow you to take their vehicles on the ferries that cross Cook Strait. Instead, you drop your car off at either the Wellington or Picton terminal and pick up another car once you've crossed the strait (this also saves you a decent amount by not having to pay to transport a vehicle on the ferries).

The major companies offer a choice of either unlimited kilometres, or 100km or so a day free plus so many cents per kilometre over this. Daily rates in main cities typically start around $70 per day for a compact late-model, Japanese car, and around $90 for medium-sized cars (including GST, unlimited kilometres and insurance). Local firms start around $40 per day for the smallest option. It's obviously cheaper if you rent for a week or more and there are often low-season and weekend discounts. Credit cards are the usual payment method.

MOTORCYCLE

NZ has great terrain for motorcycle touring, despite the changeable weather in parts of the islands. If you're tempted to bring your own motorcycle into the country, be aware that this will entail an expensive shipping exercise, valid registration in the country of origin and a *Carnet De Passages en Douanes*.

Most of the country's motorcycle-hire shops are in Auckland and Christchurch, where you can hire anything from a little 50cc moped (nifty-fifty) for zipping around town to a big 750cc touring motorcycle and beyond.

New Zealand Motorcycle Rentals & Tours (www .nzbike.com; Auckland ☎ 09-360 7940; Christchurch ☎ 03-377 0663) rents out Yamahas, BMWs, touring and enduro bikes from $55 to $355 a day (rates vary according to size of bike, length of rental period and time of year). You can climb on a Harley 1450cc from $235 per day. The company can also arrange fully booked, customised tours, or fully guided tours.

Insurance

When it comes to renting a vehicle, know exactly what your liability is in the event of an accident. Rather than risk paying out a large amount of cash if you do have an accident (minor bingles are common in NZ), you can take out your own comprehensive insurance policy, or (the usual option) pay an additional daily amount to the rental company for an 'insurance excess reduction' policy. This brings the amount of excess you must pay in the event of an accident down from around $1500 or $2000 to around $150 or $200. Smaller operators offering cheap rates often have a compulsory insurance excess, taken as a credit-card bond, of around $900.

Most insurance agreements won't cover the cost of damage to glass (including the windscreen) or tyres, and insurance coverage is often invalidated on beaches and certain rough (4WD) unsealed roads, so always read the small print.

Purchase

For a longer stay and/or for groups, buying a car and then selling it at the end of your travels can be one of the cheapest and best ways to see NZ. You can often pick up a

car as cheap as (or cheaper than) a one- or two-month rental, and you should be able to get back most of your money when you sell it. The danger, of course, is that you'll buy a lemon and it will break down every five minutes.

Auckland is the easiest place for travellers to buy a car, followed by Christchurch. An easy option for a cheap car is to scour the notice boards of backpacker places, where other travellers sell their cars before moving on; you can pick up an old car for only a few hundred dollars. Some backpackers specials are so cheap it may be worth taking the risk that they will finally die on you. Besides, these vehicles often come complete with water containers, tools, road maps and even camping gear.

Car markets and car auctions are also worth investigating – check out information on car markets in the Auckland (p142) and Christchurch (p557) sections. At auctions you can pick up cheap cars from around $1000 to $6000 – **Turners Auctions** (☎ 0800 282 8466; www.turners.co.nz) is the country's largest such outfit with 11 locations.

Make sure any car you buy has a WoF (Warrant of Fitness) and that the registration lasts for a reasonable period. A WoF certificate, proving that the car is roadworthy, is valid for six months but must be less than 28 days old when you buy a car. To transfer registration, both you and the seller fill out a Change of Ownership form which can be filed at any post office. Papers are sent by mail within 10 days. If needed, registration can be purchased for three months ($56), six months ($104) or a year ($200). Third-party insurance, covering the cost of repairs to another vehicle in an accident that is your fault, is also a wise investment.

Car inspections are highly recommended as they'll protect you against any dodgy WoFs (such scams have been reported in the past) and may well save you a lot of money in repair bills later. Various car-inspection services will check any car you intend to buy for less than $130. They stand by at car fairs and auctions for on-the-spot inspections, or will come to you. The AA also offers a mobile inspection service – it's slightly cheaper if you bring the car to an AA-approved mechanic. AA checks are thorough, but most garages will look over the car for less.

Before you buy it's wise to confirm the ownership of the vehicle, and find out if there's anything dodgy about the car in question (eg any outstanding debts on it). A number of companies offer this service, including the AA's LemonCheck (☎ 0800 536 602; www.lemoncheck.co.nz): a search costs $25 and is done using the Vehicle Identification Number (VIN; found on a plate near the engine block) or licence plate.

If you don't have your own motorcycle but do have a little bit of time up your sleeve, getting mobile on two wheels in NZ is quite feasible. The beginning of winter (June) is quite a good time to start looking. Regional newspapers and the local bike press have classified advertisement sections. The main drawback of buying a bike is obviously that you'll have to try to sell it again afterwards.

BUY-BACK DEALS

One way of getting around the hassles of buying and selling a vehicle privately is to enter into a buy-back arrangement with a car or motorcycle dealer. However, dealers may find ways of knocking down the price when you return the vehicle (even if it was agreed to in writing, often by pointing out expensive repairs that allegedly will be required to gain the WoF certificate needed to transfer the registration. The buy-back amount varies, but may be 50% less than the purchase price – in a strictly financial sense, hiring or buying and selling the vehicle yourself (if you have the time) is usually much better value.

Road Hazards

The full spectrum of drivers and driving habits is represented on NZ roads, from the no-fuss motorist who doesn't mind pulling over to let you past, to back-roads tailgaters who believe they know a particular stretch of bitumen so well that they can go as fast as they like – and this despite narrow, twisting roads. Traffic is usually pretty light, but it's easy to get stuck behind a slow-moving truck or campervan on uphill climbs, so bring plenty of patience. There are also lots of gravel or dirt roads to explore, which require a very different driving approach from sealed roads.

Road Rules

Kiwis drive on the left-hand side of the road and all cars are right-hand drive. A 'give way to the right' rule applies and is interpreted to a rather strange extreme here – if you're turning left and an oncoming vehicle is turning right into the same street, you have to give way to it.

Speed limits on the open road are generally 100km/h; in built-up areas the limit is usually 50km/h. An 'LSZ' sign stands for 'Limited Speed Zone,' which means that the speed limit is 50km/h (although the speed limit in that zone is normally 100km/h) when conditions are unsafe due to bad weather, limited visibility, pedestrians, cyclists or animals on the road, excessive traffic, or poor road conditions. Speed cameras and radars are used extensively. At single-lane bridges (of which there are a surprisingly large number), a smaller red arrow pointing in your direction of travel means that you give way, so slow down as you approach and pull a little to the side if you see a car approaching the bridge from the other end.

All new cars in NZ have seat belts back and front and it's the law to wear yours – you're risking a fine if you don't. Small children must be belted into an approved safety seat.

Drivers might want to buy a copy of the New Zealand Road Code, which will tell you all you need to know about life on the road. Versions applicable to both cars and motorcycles are available at AA offices and bookshops, or check the online rundown of road rules on the website of the **Land Transport Safety Authority** (www.ltsa.govt.nz/roadcode).

HITCHING

If there's anywhere in the world where you can still hitch a ride, NZ is it (but wrap up warm in winter and keep a raincoat handy). It's not unusual to see hitchhikers by the side of country roads (signalling with a thumbs-up or a downward-pointed finger), although extensive bus networks and cheap car-rental rates mean that this mode of transport is not as common among travellers as it once was. Still, hitching is not totally without danger, and those who decide to do it should understand that they are taking a small but potentially serious risk. People who do choose to hitch will be safer if they travel in pairs and let someone know where they are planning to go.

Before you start warming up your hitching thumb, get an idea of the challenges ahead by reading Joe Bennett's *A Land of Two Halves* (see p23), an entertaining account of one man's hitching adventure through NZ.

Ride-Shares

People looking for travelling companions for car journeys around the country often leave notices on boards in backpacker accommodation. The website www.carshare.co.nz is an excellent resource for people seeking or offering a lift.

LOCAL TRANSPORT
Bus, Train & Tram

Most of NZ's urban buses have been privatised. Larger cities have fairly extensive bus services but, with a few honourable exceptions, they are mainly daytime, weekday operations; on weekends, particularly on Sunday, bus services can be hard to find or may stop altogether. Negotiating the inner-city area in Auckland is made easier by the Link and City Circuit buses, and in Christchurch by the Shuttle bus service and the historic tramway. Most main cities have a late-night bus service roaming central entertainment districts on social, end-of-week nights.

The only city with a decent train service is Wellington, comprising four suburban routes.

Taxi

The main cities have plenty of taxis and even small towns may have a local service. Taxis cruise the busy areas in Auckland, Wellington and Christchurch, but elsewhere you usually either have to phone for one or go to a taxi rank.

TRAIN

In NZ you travel on the train for the journey, not in order to get anywhere (with the ex-

ception of the single commuter service detailed following). The company **Tranz Scenic** (☎ 0800 872 467, 04-495 0775; www.tranzscenic.co.nz) operates several visually stunning routes, namely the *Overlander* between Auckland and Wellington, the *TranzCoastal* between Christchurch and Picton, and the *TranzAlpine* which rattles over the Southern Alps between Christchurch and Greymouth (all routes run in both directions daily). It also operates the weekday *Capital Connection* commuter service between Palmerston North and Wellington.

Reservations can be made by contacting Tranz Scenic and at most train stations, travel agents and visitor information centres, where you can also pick up booklets detailing timetables. It pays to ask about discounted fares – children, seniors and students are eligible for reduced fares, as are holders of hostel membership cards (YHA, BBH, VIP). There is also a sizable discount (up to 60% off the standard adult fare) for a seat in a 'backpacker carriage', which has smaller viewing windows than other carriages.

Train Passes

Given NZ's limited rail network, buying a train pass doesn't represent particularly good value.

Tranz Scenic's **Scenic Rail Pass** (www.tranzscenic.co.nz/services/ScenicPass.aspx) allows unlimited travel on all of its rail services (with the exception of the *Capital Connection*) and includes passage on the Interislander ferry between Wellington and Picton. A pass lasting a week/month costs $299/499 for an adult, $179/299 for a child.

For details of a pass combining travel on InterCity coaches, Tranz Scenic trains and Interislander ferries (as well as the option of a domestic flight), see the boxed text, p730.

Health Dr David Millar

CONTENTS

Before You Go 737
Insurance 737
Recommended Vaccinations 737
Medical Checklist 737
Internet Resources 738

In Transit **738**
Deep Vein Thrombosis (DVT) 738

In New Zealand **738**
Jet Lag & Motion Sickness 738
Availability & Cost of Health Care 738
Infectious Diseases 739
Travellers' Diarrhoea 739
Environmental Hazards 739

New Zealand is one of the healthiest countries in which to travel. The risk of diseases such as malaria and typhoid are unheard of, and thanks to NZ's quarantine standards, even some animal diseases such as rabies have yet to be recorded. The absence of poisonous snakes and dangerous animals makes this a very safe region to get off the beaten track and out into the lovely countryside.

BEFORE YOU GO

Since most vaccines don't produce immunity until at least two weeks after they're given, visit a physician four to eight weeks before departure. Ask your doctor for an International Certificate of Vaccination (otherwise known as 'the yellow booklet'), which will list all the vaccinations you've received. This is mandatory for countries that require proof of yellow fever vaccination upon entry, but it's a good idea to carry it wherever you travel.

Bring medications in their original, clearly labelled containers. A signed and dated letter from your physician describing your medical conditions and medications, including generic names, is also a good idea. If carrying syringes or needles, be sure to have a physician's letter documenting their medical necessity.

INSURANCE

If your health insurance doesn't cover you for medical expenses abroad, you should consider getting extra insurance – check www.lonelyplanet.com for more information. Find out in advance if your insurance plan will make payments directly to providers or if it will reimburse you later for overseas health expenditures. (In many countries doctors expect payment in cash.)

RECOMMENDED VACCINATIONS

NZ has no vaccination requirements for any traveller. The World Health Organization recommends that all travellers should be covered for diphtheria, tetanus, measles, mumps, rubella, chickenpox and polio, as well as hepatitis B, regardless of their destination. Planning to travel is a great time to ensure that all routine vaccination cover is complete. The consequences of these diseases can be severe, and while NZ has high levels of childhood vaccination coverage, outbreaks of these diseases do occur.

MEDICAL CHECKLIST

- acetaminophen (paracetamol) or aspirin
- adhesive or paper tape
- antibacterial ointment (for cuts and abrasions)
- antibiotics
- antidiarrhoeal drugs (eg loperamide)
- antihistamines (for hay fever and allergic reactions)
- anti-inflammatory drugs (eg ibuprofen)
- bandages, gauze, gauze rolls
- DEET-containing insect repellent for the skin
- iodine tablets or water filter (for water purification)
- oral rehydration salts
- permethrin-containing insect spray for clothing, tents and bed nets
- pocket knife
- scissors, safety pins, tweezers
- steroid cream or cortisone (for poison ivy and other allergic rashes)
- sun block
- thermometer

INTERNET RESOURCES

You'll find that there's a wealth of travel health advice on the Internet. For further information on health, **Lonely Planet** (www .lonelyplanet.com) is a good place to start. The **World Health Organization** (www.who.int/ith) publishes an excellent book called *International Travel and Health*, which is revised annually and is available online at no cost. Another good website of general interest is **MD Travel Health** (www.mdtravelhealth.com), which provides complete travel health recommendations for every country and is updated daily.

IN TRANSIT

DEEP VEIN THROMBOSIS (DVT)

Blood clots may form in the legs during plane flights, chiefly because of a prolonged period of immobility. The longer the flight, the greater the risk. The chief symptom of DVT is swelling or pain of the foot, ankle or calf, usually – but not always – on just one side. When a blood clot travels to the lungs, it may cause chest pain and breathing difficulties. Travellers with any of these symptoms should seek medical attention immediately.

To prevent the development of DVT on long flights, you should walk about the cabin, perform compressions of the leg muscles (ie flex the leg muscles while sitting), drink plenty of fluids and avoid alcohol and tobacco.

JET LAG & MOTION SICKNESS

Jet lag is commonly experienced when a traveller crosses more than five time zones, and can result in insomnia, fatigue, malaise or nausea. To avoid or minimise the unpleasant effects of jet lag, try drinking plenty of nonalcoholic fluids and eating light meals. Upon arrival to your destination, get exposure to natural sunlight and readjust your schedule (for meals, sleep etc) as soon as possible.

Antihistamines such as dimenhydrinate and meclizine are usually the first choice for treating motion sickness. Their main side effect is drowsiness. A herbal alternative is ginger, which works like a charm for some people.

IN NEW ZEALAND

AVAILABILITY & COST OF HEALTH CARE

Health insurance is essential for all travellers. While health care in NZ is of a high standard and not overly expensive by international standards, considerable costs can be built up and repatriation can be extremely expensive. See p737 for insurance information.

Health Care in New Zealand

NZ does not have a government-funded system of public hospitals. All travellers are, however, covered for medical care resulting from accidents that occur while in NZ (eg motor vehicle accidents, adventure activity accidents) by the Accident Compensation Corporation (ACC). Costs incurred by treatment of a medical illness that occurs while in NZ will only be covered by travel insurance. For more details see www.moh .govt.nz. and www.acc.co.nz.

NZ has excellent specialised public health facilities for women and children in the major centres. No specific health concerns exist for women but greater care for children is recommended to avoid environmental hazards such as heat, sunburn, cold and marine hazards.

The 24-hour, free-call **Healthline** (☎ 0800 611 116) offers health advice throughout NZ.

Self-care in New Zealand

In NZ it is possible to find yourself in a remote location where there may well be a significant delay in emergency services getting to you in the event of a serious accident or illness. This is usually the result of weather and rugged terrain, particularly on the South Island. Therefore, an increased level of self-reliance and preparation is essential. Consider taking a wilderness first-aid course (such as the one from the Wilderness Medicine Institute). In addition, you should carry a comprehensive first-aid kit that is appropriate for the activities planned. To be really safe, ensure that you have adequate means of communication. (NZ has extensive mobile-phone coverage, but additional radio communication equipment is important for remote areas, and can usually be hired from Department of Conservation visitor centres in popular tramping areas.

Pharmaceutical Supplies

Over-the-counter medications are widely available in NZ through private chemists. These include painkillers, antihistamines for allergies, and skin care products.

Some medications that are available over the counter in other countries are only available by a prescription obtained from a general practitioner. These include the oral contraceptive pill, most medications for asthma and all antibiotics. If you take a medication on a regular basis, bring an adequate supply and ensure you have details of the generic name as brand names differ between countries. The majority of medications in use outside of the region are available.

INFECTIOUS DISEASES
Amoebic Meningitis

There is a small risk of developing amoebic meningitis as a result of bathing or swimming in geothermal pools in NZ – mostly in regions such as Rotorua and Taupo. In such pools, keeping the head above water to prevent movement of the organism up the nasal passage reduces the risk (which is pretty low to start with). Symptoms usually start three to seven days after swimming in a geothermal pool and early symptoms of this serious disease include headache, fever and vomiting. Urgent medical care is essential to differentiate the disease from other causes of meningitis and for appropriate treatment.

Giardiasis

The giardia parasite is widespread in NZ waterways. Drinking untreated water from streams and lakes is not recommended. Using water filters and boiling or treating water with iodine are effective ways of preventing the disease occurring. The symptoms consist of intermittent bad-smelling diarrhoea, abdominal bloating and wind. Effective treatment is available (tinidazole or metronidazole).

Hepatitis C

This disease is still a growing problem among intravenous drug users. Blood-transfusion services fully screen all blood before use.

HIV

The country's HIV rates have stabilised after major media campaigns, and levels are similar to other Western countries. Clean needles and syringes are widely available.

Meningococcal Disease

This occurs worldwide and is a risk if you have prolonged stays in dormitory-style accommodation. A vaccine exists for some types of the disease (meningococcal A, C, Y and W).

Sexually Transmitted Diseases (STDs)

In NZ STDs (including gonorrhoea, chlamydia and herpes) occur at rates similar to most Western countries. The most common symptoms are pain on passing urine and a discharge. Infection can be present without symptoms, so seek medical screening after any unprotected sex with a new partner. Sexual health clinics are run as part of major hospitals.

TRAVELLERS' DIARRHOEA

If you develop diarrhoea, be sure to drink plenty of fluids, preferably an oral rehydration solution containing lots of salt and sugar. A few loose stools don't require treatment but if you start having more than four or five stools a day, you should start taking an antibiotic (usually a quinolone drug) and an antidiarrhoeal agent (such as loperamide). If diarrhoea is bloody, persists for more than 72 hours and/or is accompanied by fever, shaking chills or severe abdominal pain, you should seek medical attention.

ENVIRONMENTAL HAZARDS
Hypothermia

This is a significant risk, especially during the winter months, or year-round in the mountains of the North Island and all of the South Island. Mountain ranges and/or strong winds produce a high chill factor that can result in hypothermia even in moderately cool temperatures. Early signs include the inability to perform fine movements (such as doing up buttons), shivering and a bad case of the 'umbles' (fumbles, mumbles, grumbles, stumbles). The key elements of treatment are changing the environment to one where heat loss is minimised, changing out of any wet clothing, adding dry clothes with windproof and waterproof layers, adding insulation and providing fuel (water and carbohydrate) to allow shivering to build the internal temperature. In severe hypothermia, shivering actually stops; this is a medical emergency requiring rapid evacuation in addition to the preceding measures.

Spider Bites

NZ has two poisonous spiders, the native katipo (not very poisonous and uncommon to the point of being endangered) and the introduced (thanks, Australia) white-tailed spider (also uncommon). White-tailed spider bites have been known to cause ulcers that are very difficult to heal. Clean the wound thoroughly and seek medical assistance if an ulcer develops.

Surf Beaches & Drowning

NZ has exceptional surf beaches, particularly on the western, southern and eastern coasts. The power of the surf can fluctuate as a result of the varying slope of the seabed at many beaches. Check with local surf life-saving organisations before entering the surf and be aware of your own limitations and expertise.

Ultraviolet Light Exposure

NZ has one of the highest rates of skin cancer in the world, so you should monitor UV exposure closely. UV exposure is greatest between 10am and 4pm, so avoid skin exposure during these times. Always use 30+ sunscreen, making sure you apply it 30 minutes before exposure and that you reapply regularly to minimise sun damage.

Water

Tap water is universally safe in NZ. Growing numbers of streams, rivers and lakes, however, are being contaminated by bugs that cause diarrhoea, making water purification when tramping essential. The simplest way of purifying water is to boil it thoroughly. You should also consider buying a water filter. It's important to read the specifications so that you know exactly what it removes from the water and what it doesn't. Simple filtering will not remove all dangerous organisms, so if you cannot boil water it should be treated chemically. Chlorine tablets will kill many pathogens, but not parasites such as giardia or amoebic cysts. Iodine is more effective in purifying water. Follow the directions carefully and remember that too much iodine can be harmful.

Language

New Zealand has two official languages: English and Maori. English is the language you'll usually hear spoken, but Maori, long on the decline, is making a comeback. You can use English to speak to anyone in NZ – all Maori people speak English. There are some occasions, though, when knowing a little Maori would be useful, such as visiting a marae, where often only Maori is spoken. Maori is also useful to know since many places in NZ have Maori names.

KIWI ENGLISH

Like the people of other countries in the world who speak English, New Zealanders have a unique way of speaking the language. The flattening (some would call it slaughtering) of vowels is the most distinctive feature of Kiwi pronunciation. The NZ treatment of 'fish and chips' – 'fush and chups' – is an endless source of delight for Australians. In the North Island sentences often have 'eh!' attached to the end. In the far south a rolled 'r' is practised widely, a holdover from that region's Scottish heritage – it's especially noticeable in Southland. See the Glossary on p744 for an explanation of Kiwi English words and phrases.

A Personal Kiwi-Yankee Dictionary by Louis S. Leland Jr is a fine and often hilarious book of translations and explanations of the quirks that distinguish Kiwi and American ways of speaking English. Yanks will love it.

MAORI

The Maori have a vividly chronicled history, recorded in songs and chants which dramatically recall the migration to NZ from Polynesian Hawaiki and other important events. Early missionaries were the first to record the language in a written form, and achieved this with only 15 letters of the English alphabet.

Maori is closely related to other Polynesian languages (including Hawaiian, Tahitian and Cook Islands Maori). In fact, NZ Maori and Hawaiian have the same degree of lexical similarity as Spanish and French,

even though over 7000km separates Honolulu and Auckland.

The Maori language was never dead – it was always used in Maori ceremonies – but over time familiarity with it was definitely on the decline. Fortunately, recent years have seen a revival of interest in it, and this forms an integral part of the renaissance of Maoritanga (Maori culture). Many Maori people who had heard the language spoken on the marae for years but had not used it in their day-to-day lives are now studying it and speaking it fluently. Maori is now taught in schools throughout NZ, some TV programs and news reports are broadcast in it and many English place names are being renamed in Maori. Even government departments have been rechristened with Maori names: for example the Inland Revenue Department is also known as Te Tari Taake (the last word is actually *take*, which means 'levy', but the department has chosen to stress the long 'a' by spelling it 'aa').

In many places, Maori people have come together to provide instruction in their language and culture to young children; the idea is for them to grow up speaking both Maori and English, and to develop a familiarity with Maori tradition. It's a matter of some pride to have fluency in the language. On some marae only Maori can be spoken, encouraging everyone to speak it and emphasising the distinct Maori character of the marae.

Pronunciation

Maori is a fluid, poetic language and surprisingly easy to pronounce once you remember to split each word (and some can be amazingly long) into separate syllables.

Most consonants in Maori – **h**, **k**, **m**, **n**, **p**, **t** and **w** – are pronounced much the same as in English. The Maori **r** is a flapped sound (not rolled) with the tongue near the front of the mouth. It's closer to the English 'l' in pronunciation.

The two combinations of consonants **ng** and **wh** require special attention. The **ng** is

MAORI GEOGRAPHICAL TERMS

The following words form part of many place names in NZ:

a – of
ana – cave
ara – way, path, road
awa – river or valley
heke – descend
hiku – end, tail
hine – girl, daughter
ika – fish
iti – small
kahurangi – treasured possession; special greenstone
kai – food
kainga – village
kaka – parrot
kare – rippling
kati – shut or close
koura – crayfish
makariri – cold
manga – stream or tributary
manu – bird
maunga – mountain
moana – sea or lake
moko – tattoo
motu – island
mutu – finished, ended, over
nga – the (plural)
noa – ordinary; not tapu
nui – big, great
nuku – distance
o – of, place of ...
one – beach, sand or mud
pa – fortified village
papa – flat land, broad slab
pipi – shellfish
pohatu – stone
poto – short

pouri – sad, dark, gloomy
puke – hill
puna – spring, hole, fountain
rangi – sky, heavens
raro – north
rei – cherished possesion
roa – long
roto – lake
rua – hole in the ground; two
runga – above
tahuna – beach, sandbank
tane – man
tangata – people
tapu – sacred, forbidden, taboo
tata – close to; dash against; twin islands
tawaha – entrance, opening
tawahi – the other side (of a river or lake)
te – the (singular)
tonga – south
ure – male genitals
uru – west
wahine – woman
wai – water
waingaro – lost; waters that disappear in certain seasons
waha – broken
waka – canoe
wera – burnt or warm; floating
wero – challenge
whaka... – to act as ...
whanau – extended family
whanga – harbour, bay or inlet
whare – house
whenua – land or country
whiti – east

Knowledge of just a few such words can help you make sense of many Maori place names. For example: Waikaremoana is the Sea (moana) of Rippling (kare) Waters (wai); Rotorua means the Second (rua) Lake (roto); and Taumatawhakatangihangakoauauotamateaturipukakapikimaunga-horonukupokaiwhenuakitanatahu means ... well ... perhaps you'd better read The Longest Place Name in the World in the East Coast chapter (p400) for that translation. Some easier place names composed of words in this list:

Aramoana – Sea (moana) Path (ara)
Awaroa – Long (roa) River (awa)
Kaitangata – Eat (kai) People (tangata)
Maunganui – Great (nui) Mountain (maunga)
Opouri – Place of (o) Sadness (pouri)
Te Araroa – The (te) Long (roa) Path (ara)

Te Puke – The (te) Hill (puke)
Urewera – Burnt (wera) Penis (ure)
Waimakariri – Cold (makariri) Water (wai)
Wainui – Great (nui) Waters (wai)
Whakatane – To Act (whaka) As A Man (tane)
Whangarei – Cherished (rei) Harbour (whanga)

(Note that the adjective comes after the noun in Maori constructions. Thus 'cold water' is wai makariri not makariri wai.)

pronounced as in the English words 'sing-ing' or 'running', and can be used at the beginning of words as well as at the end. To practise, just say 'ing' over and over, isolate the 'ng' part of it and then practise using it to begin a word rather than end one.

The **wh** also has a unique pronunciation in Maori – generally as a soft English 'f'. This pronunciation is used in many place names in NZ, eg Whakatane, Whangaroa and Whakapapa (all pronounced as if they begin with a soft 'f'). There is some local variation, however: in the region around the Whanganui River, for example, the **wh** is pronounced as in the English words 'when' and 'why'.

When learning to speak Maori the correct pronunciation of the vowels is very important. The examples below are only a rough guideline – to really get it right you'll have to listen carefully to someone who knows how to pronounce the language correctly. Each vowel has both a long and a short sound with long vowels often denoted in text by a macron (a line over the letter) or a double vowel. We have not indicated long/short vowel forms in this book.

VOWELS

a	as in 'large', with no 'r' sound
e	as in 'get'
i	as in 'marine'
o	as in 'pork'
u	as in the 'oo' in 'moon'

DIPHTHONGS

ae, ai	as the 'y' in 'sky'
ao, au	as the 'ow' in 'how'
ea	as in 'bear'
ei	as in 'vein'
eo	as 'eh-oh'
eu	as 'eh-oo'
ia	as in the name 'Ian'
ie	as the 'ye' in 'yet'
io	as the 'ye o' in 'ye old'
iu	as the 'ue' in 'cue'
oa	as in 'roar'
oe	as in 'toe'
oi	as in 'toil'
ou	as the 'ow' in 'sow'
ua	as the 'ewe' in 'fewer'

Each syllable ends in a vowel and there is never more than one vowel in a syllable. There are no silent letters.

There are many Maori phrasebooks, grammar books and Maori-English diction-aries if you want to take a closer look at the language. Learning a few basic greetings is an excellent thing to do, especially if you plan to go onto a marae, where you'll be greeted in Maori.

The *Collins Maori Phrase Book* by Patricia Tauroa is an excellent book for starting to speak the language, with sections on every-day conversation and also on how the lan-guage is used in a cultural context (such as on a marae). Lonely Planet's *South Pacific Phrase-book* has a section on the Maori language and several Pacific languages (Tongan, Samoan, Cook Island Maori) that you may hear spo-ken around Wellington or South Auckland. Other English-Maori dictionaries include the *English-Maori Maori-English Dictionary* by Bruce Biggs, and the *Reed Dictionary of Modern Maori* by PM Ryan, which is one of the most authoritative.

Greetings & Small Talk

Maori greetings are finding increased popularity; don't be surprised if you're greeted with *Kia ora*. Try these:

Haere mai!	Welcome!
Kia ora.	Hello/Good luck/ Good health.
Tena koe.	Hello, (to one person)
Tena korua.	Hello, (to two people)
Tena koutou.	Hello, (to three or more people)
E noho ra.	Goodbye. (to person staying)
Haere ra.	Goodbye. (to person going)
Kei te pehea koe?	How are you? (to one person)
Kei te pehea korua?	How are you? (to two people)
Kei te pehea koutou?	How are you? (to three or more)
Kei te pai.	Very well, thanks/That's fine.

Glossary

This glossary is a list of abbreviations, 'Kiwi English' and Maori terms and phrases you may come across in New Zealand. Also see the Maori Geographical Terms boxed text (p742) in the Language chapter for Maori words that pop up again and again in NZ place names.

AA – New Zealand's Automobile Association, which provides road information and roadside assistance

across the ditch – referring to Australia, across the Tasman Sea

afghan – popular homemade chocolate biscuit (origin of recipe unknown, but unlikely to be Afghanistan)

All Blacks – NZ's revered national rugby union team (the name comes from 'All Backs', which is what the press called the NZ rugby team on an early visit to England); this moniker has started a trend for many national sporting teams to be similarly nicknamed (including the Tall Blacks for the basketball team, the Black Caps for the cricket team, and – being debated at the time of research – the Black Cocks for the badminton team)

Aoraki – Maori name for Mt Cook, meaning 'Cloud Piercer'

Aotearoa – Maori name for NZ, most often translated as 'Land of the Long White Cloud'

atua – spirits or gods

awa – river

B&B – 'bed and breakfast' accommodation

bach – holiday home, usually a wooden cottage (pronounced 'batch'); see also *crib*

backpackers – independent travellers to NZ, often (but not always) travelling the country on a budget; the term also refers to hostels, the accommodation catering to these travellers

Barrier, the – local name for Great Barrier Island in the Hauraki Gulf

baths – swimming pool, often referred to as municipal baths

Beehive – Parliament House in Wellington, so-called because of its distinctive shape

black-water rafting – rafting or tubing underground in a cave or *tomo*

boozer – public bar

box of birds – an expression meaning 'on top of the world', usually uttered in response to 'How are you?'

bro – literally 'brother'; usually meaning mate, as in 'just off to see the *bros*'

bush – heavily forested areas

Buzzy Bee – a uniquely *Kiwi* child's toy; a wooden bee dragged along by a string to produce a whirring noise

BYO – 'bring your own' (usually applies to alcohol at a restaurant or café)

BYOW – 'bring your own wine'

cervena – farmed deer

CHE – not the revolutionary but Crown Health Enterprise (regional, privatised health authorities)

chillie bin – cooler; esky; large insulated box for keeping food and drink cold

choice – fantastic; great

ciggies – cigarettes

crib – the name for a *bach* in Otago and Southland

cuzzie, cuz – cousin; relative or mate; see also *bro*

dairy – small corner store that sells milk, bread, newspapers, ice cream and pretty much everything else

DB&B – 'dinner, bed and breakfast' accommodation

DOC – Department of Conservation (or *Te Papa Atawhai*); government department which administers national parks and thus all tracks and huts

domain – open grassed area in a town or city, often the focus of civic amenities such as gardens, picnic areas and bowling clubs (and sometimes camping grounds)

dropkick – a certain method of kicking a rugby ball; a personal insult

eh – roughly translates as 'don't you agree?' and is commonly added to the end of many *Kiwi* sentences, usually followed by *bro* (as in '*Choice jandals eh bro?*')

farmstay – accommodation on a *Kiwi* farm where you're encouraged to join in the typical day-to-day activities

football – rugby, either union or league

freezing works – slaughterhouse or abattoir for sheep and/or cattle

Gilbert – the most popular brand of rugby football

Godzone – New Zealand (from Richard Seddon who referred to NZ as 'God's own country')

good as gold, good as – very good; no problem

greenstone – jade; *pounamu*

haka – any dance, but usually refers to the traditional challenge; war dance

hakari – feast

handle – beer glass with a handle

hangi – oven made by digging a hole and steaming food in baskets over embers in the hole; a feast of Maori food

hapu – subtribe or smaller tribal grouping

hard case – unusual or strong-willed character

Hawaiki – Polynesian homeland from where the Maori tribes migrated by canoe (probably Ra'iatea in the Society Is ands); also a name for the Afterworld

het tiki – carved, stylised human figure worn around the neck, often a carved representation of an ancestor; also called a *tiki*

hikoi – march

hoa – friend; usually pronounced 'e hoa'

hokey pokey – delicious variety of ice cream with butterscotch chips

hoki – type of fish common in fish and chip shops

homestay – accommodation in a family house where you're treated as one of the family

hongi – Maori greeting; the pressing of noses and sharing of life breath

hui – gathering; meeting

Instant Kiwi – state-run lottery

Interislander – large ferries crossing Cook Strait between Wellington and Picton

'Is it what?' – strong affirmation or agreement; 'Yes isn't it!'

iwi – large tribal grouping with common lineage back to the original migration from *Hawaiki*; people; tribe

jandals – sandals; flip-flops; thongs; usually rubber footwear

jersey – jumper, usually woollen; the shirt worn by rugby players

jiff – short measurement of time (as in 'I'll be back in a *jiff*'); see also *two ticks*

judder bars – bumps in the road to make you drive slowly; speed humps

K Rd – Karangahape Rd in Auckland

ka pai – good; excellent

kai – food; almost any word with *kai* in it has a connection with food

kainga – village; pre-European unfortified Maori village

kapa haka – Traditional Maori group singing and dancing

karakia – prayer

kaumatua – highly respected members of a tribe; the people you would ask for permission to enter a *marae*

kina – sea urchins; a Maori delicacy

kiwi – the flightless, nocturnal brown bird with a long beak that is the national symbol; a New Zealander; an adjective to mean a nything relating to NZ

kiwiana – the collective term for anything uniquely connected to NZ life and culture, especially from years gone by, and likely to bring on waves of nostalgia in any expat Kiwi (examples include the *Buzzy Bee*, *hokey pokey*, *jandals* ard the *pavlova*)

kiwi fruit – small, succulent fruit with fuzzy brown skin and juicy green flesh; a Chinese gooseberry

koha – donation

kohanga reo – schools where Maori language and culture are at the forefront of the education process; also called language nest schools

kumara – Polynesian sweet potato, a Maori staple food

kunekune – type of wild pig introduced by Chinese gold diggers in the 19th century

Kupe – early Polynesian navigator from *Hawaiki*, credited w th the discovery of the islands that are now NZ

league – rugby league football

lounge bar – more upmarket bar than a public bar; called a 'ladies bar' in some countries

mana – spiritual quality of a person or object; prestige; authority of a chief or priest

manaia – traditional carving design; literally means 'b rd-headed man'

manuhiri – visitor; guest

Maori – indigenous people of NZ

Maoritanga – Maori culture

marae – literally refers to the sacred ground in front of the Maori meeting house, more commonly used to refer to the entire complex of buildings

marakihau – sea monster

Maui – a figure in Maori (Polynesian) mythology

maunga – mountain

mere – flat, *greenstone* war club

metal/metalled road – gravel (unsealed) road

MMP – Mixed Member P'oportional; a cumbersome electoral system used in NZ and Germany; a limited form of proportional voting

moa – large, extinct flightless bird

moko – tattoo; usually refers to facial tattoos

Moriori – isolated Polynesian group, inhabitants of the Chatham Islands

motorway – freeway or expressway

naiad – rigid-hull inflatable boat (used for dolphin swimming, whale-watching etc)

nga – the (plural); see also *te*

ngai – literally, 'the people of' or 'the descendants of'; see also *te*

NZ – the universal term for New Zealand; pronounced 'enzed'

OE – Overseas Experience: a working holiday abroad, traditionally to the UK (the young *Kiwi*'s near-mandatory 'tour of duty')

pa – fortified Maori village, usually on a hill top

Pacific Rim – term used to describe modern NZ cuisine; cuisine with an innovative use of local produce, especially seafood, with imported styles

Pakeha – Maori for a white or European person; once derogatory, and still considered so by some, this term is now widely used for white New Zealanders

pakihi – unproductive and often swampy land on the South Island's west coast; pronounced 'par-kee'

papa – large blue-grey mudstones; the word comes from the Maori for Earth Mother

parapenting – paragliding

paua – abalone; tough shellfish pounded, minced, then made into patties (fritters), which are available in almost every NZ fish and chip shop; the beautiful, iridescent *paua* shell is often used in decoration and jewellery

pavlova – meringue cake, usually topped with cream and *kiwi fruit*; the quintessential *Kiwi* dessert

pig islander – derogatory term used by a person from one island for someone from the other island

pillocking – 'surfing' across mud flats on a rubbish-bin lid

poi – ball of woven flax

poi dance – women's formation dance that involves singing and manipulating a *poi*

polly – politician

ponga – the *silver fern*; called a bungy (pronounced 'bungee', with a soft 'g', in parts of the South Island)

pounamu – Maori name for *greenstone*

powhiri – traditional Maori welcome onto a *marae*

quad bikes – four-wheel farm bikes

Rakiura – literally 'Land of Glowing Skies'; Maori name for Stewart Island, which is important in Maori mythology as the anchor of *Maui's* canoe

rap jump – face-down abseil

raupo – bulrush

Rheiny – affectionate term for Rheineck beer

rigger – a refillable half-gallon plastic bottle for holding draught beer

riptide – dangerously strong current running away from the shore at a beach

Roaring Forties – the ocean between 40° and 50° south, known for very strong winds

scrap – a fight

section – small block of land

silver fern – the symbol worn by the *All Blacks* and other national sportsfolk on their jerseys, representative of the underside of a *ponga* leaf; the national netball team are called the Silver Ferns

Steinie – affectionate term for Steinlager beer

superette – grocery store or small supermarket open outside normal business hours

sweet, sweet as – all-purpose term like *choice*: fantastic, great

Tamaki Makaurau – Maori name for Auckland

tane – man

tangata – people

tangata whenua – people of the land; local people

taniwha – fear-inspiring water spirit

taonga – something of great value; a treasure

tapu – a strong force in Maori life, with numerous meanings; in its simplest form it means sacred, forbidden, taboo

tauihu – canoe prow

te – the (singular); see also *nga*

Te Kooti – prominent East Coast Maori prophet and rebellion leader

Te Papa – literally 'our place', the name of the national museum in Wellington

Te Papa Atawhai – Maori name for *DOC*

tiki – short for *hei tiki*

tiki tour – scenic tour; roundabout way

toheroa – large clam

tohunga – priest; wizard; general expert

toi toi – tall native grass

tomo – hole; entrance to a cave

tramp – bush walk; trek; hike

tua tua – type of shellfish

tuatara – prehistoric reptile dating back to the age of dinosaurs (perhaps 260 million years)

tukutuku – Maori wall panellings in *marae* and churches

tuna – eel

two ticks – short measurement of time (as in 'I'll be there in *two ticks*'); see also *jiff*

umu – earth oven

urupa – burial site

varsity – university

wahine – woman

wai – water

waiata – song

Waikikamukau – mythical NZ town; somewhere in the *wopwops* (and pronounced along the lines of 'Why-kick-a-moo-cow')

Waitangi – short way of referring to the Treaty of Waitangi

waka – canoe

Watties – the NZ food and canning giant; NZ's answer to Heinz (until Heinz took over the company)

whakairo rakau – Maori woodcarving

whakapapa – genealogy

whanau – family

whare – house

wharepuni – sleeping house

whare runanga – meeting house

whare whakairo – carved meeting house

whenua – land

whitebait – translucent fish that is scooped up in nets and eaten whole (head, eyes and all!) or made into patties

wopwops – remote; 'out in the *wopwops*' is out in the middle of nowhere

Behind the Scenes

THIS BOOK

Our first edition of the *New Zealand* guide was written by Lonely Planet's cofounder Tony Wheeler in 1977. Since then a horde of LP authors have scoured the roads and trails of Aotearoa putting together ever-better *New Zealand* guidebooks. The previous edition, the first in Lonely Planet's new format, was coordinated by Paul Smitz.

This edition was coordinated by Carolyn Bain. Carolyn was joined on the road by a star troupe: Charles Rawlings-Way, Sally O'Brien, Korina Miller and George Dunford. Other material was supplied by the cultured Russell Brown, the historical Prof James Belich, the earthy Vaughan Yarwood and the culinary Julie Biuso. The special section on Maori Culture was written by Errol Hunt using some material by Jeff Williams.

This guidebook was commissioned in Lonely Planet's Melbourne office, and produced by the following:

Commissioning Editors Errol Hunt, Jessa Boanas-Dewes

Coordinating Editor Sasha Baskett

Coordinating Cartographer Jacqueline Nguyen

Coordinating Layout Designer Vicki Beale

Managing Editor Bruce Evans

Managing Cartographer Corinne Waddell

Assisting Editors Kim Noble, Helen Christinis, Jackey Coyle, Liz Heynes, Charlotte Orr, Katie Lynch, Charlotte Harrison

Assisting Cartographers Marion Byass, Andrew Smith, Csanad Csutoros, Hunor Csutoros, Dane Balodis

Cover Designer Daniel New

THE LONELY PLANET STORY

The story begins with a classic travel adventure: Tony and Maureen Wheeler's 1972 journey across Europe and Asia to Australia. There was no useful information about the overland trail then, so Tony and Maureen published the first Lonely Planet guidebook to meet a growing need.

From a kitchen table, Lonely Planet has grown to become the largest independent travel publisher in the world, with offices in Melbourne (Australia), Oakland (USA) and London (UK). Today Lonely Planet guidebooks cover the globe. There is an ever-growing list of books and information in a variety of media. Some things haven't changed. The main aim is still to make it possible for adventurous travellers to get out there – to explore and better understand the world.

At Lonely Planet we believe travellers can make a positive contribution to the countries they visit – if they respect their host communities and spend their money wisely. Every year 5% of company profit is donated to charities around the world.

Project Managers John Shippick, Nancy Ianni

Language Content Coordinator Quentin Frayne

Thanks to Darren O'Connell, Marg Toohey, Diana Duggan, James Ellis, Wendy Wright, Lisa Tuckwell, Karen Emmerson, Meagan Williams, Michael Lynden-Bell, Meg Worby, Nicole Hansen, Jane Thompson, Kate McDonald, Cela Wood, Sally Darmody

THANKS
CAROLYN BAIN

First, and most importantly, huge bouquets to Team NZ – George, Korina, Sally and Charles – for their outstanding work on this tome. It's been a pleasure working with such a fine bunch. Special thanks to George for sanity-checking coffees and lakšas in the 'hood during write-up, and to my great friend Sally for the restorative phone calls while on the road (and writing up) and everything else besides. Kudos, too, to fellow LP scribe Simone Egger for borrowed Swag words of wisdom, and to Errol for his duties as boss hog.

Researching Wellington often felt more like a holiday than work, thanks largely to Kelvin Adams, Niki Bern, David Whittaker and Amanda Denise and Peter, and John and Helen Chipper. Big cheers to you all. Elsewhere, boundless gratitude to Melissa and the skydiving team in Motueka for a top day (despite the terror), Anthea and Brian in Kaiteriteri, Graeme and Jan in Kaikoura, Don and Helen in Twizel, and a cast of thousands (well, maybe hundreds) who answered questions, gave directions, offered opinions or just generally helped out. Sweet as.

GEORGE DUNFORD

Thanks first-up to my excellent travelling companions, Simon Hall and Beryl May Dunford, who kept me cheery and listened to my on-the-road whining above and beyond the call of their duty. Big shouts also to fellow authors Sally O'Brien and Carolyn Bain for their tips, wisdom and great gags. Many thanks to the hard yards of previous authors who let present authors stand on the shoulders of giants. Thanks also to LP's token Kiwi, Errol Hunt, who commissioned the little package you hold in your hands.

In Wellington supreme gratitude to Kylie Mary-Margaret McQuellin ('What are your plans, McQ?'), Richard 'Ricardo' Foy, Laura (thanks for letting me borrow your bunk) and young William, for all their chats, tender care and valued friendship. Big cheers to Tommy-boy, Amanda and Rodry in Auckland for the good grub and hot tips. Thanks to all the good folks in visitor information centres across the country (you know who you are) for all their tips, maps and frank advice. Special thanks to Ann in Rotorua for her sage advice and to the Powderhorn Chateau for the special tour of Peter Jackson's apartment.

KORINA MILLER

Many thanks to the Kiwis I met en route for sharing their gorgeous country with me and to fellow travellers for sharing their tales of wonder and woe. Thanks to Errol for inviting me to join this project and ensuring it operated with a healthy dose of humour; to coordinating author, Carolyn, for her fantastic support; and to Corinne at LP for getting the maps to me wonder-woman-style. Thanks and love to Paul for driving, baby-sitting and being my much needed pillar and big hugs to Simone for being such an amazing traveller and for helping Mummy to keep it all in perspective.

SALLY O'BRIEN

Snaps to coordinating author Carolyn Bain for empathy, phone calls and a lot of laughs about a lot of crap, plus George Dunford for the soup and chuckles. Stella Kinsella was a marvellous companion throughout a rain-soaked trip to the Coromandel, while Niki Bern was a great hostess in Wellington. Many Kiwis are owed a debt of gratitude, among them Mike and Sharon in Auckland, John, Jo and Angela on Waiheke Island, Kate and Bruce on Great Barrier Island, Bev and Julian in Titirangi, Helen and Wendy in Waitomo, Jeremy and Lynda in Raglan, John and Dorothy in Rawene, Sally, David and Brad in Russell, and Inge in Paihia. Thanks to Errol Hunt

for the job – a nice 'swansong' gig, and to everyone in-house at LP who worked on the book.

CHARLES RAWLINGS-WAY

Thanks to the many generous, knowledgeable and quietly self-assured Kiwis I met on the road, especially the staff at the Westport, Wanganui and Palmerston North visitors centres who flew through my questions with the greatest of ease. Thanks to Errol Hunt for signing me up, and the in-house LP staff who nurtured this book through production (the fence between us is a myth – tear it down). Thanks also to the very coordinated Carolyn Bain, Pablo Smitz for the sturdy West Coast springboard, Warren Jones for infectious enthusiasm (choice gig, eh bro?), and I wouldn't be doing this if it weren't for Kevin Bailey, who handed me a dog-eared copy of Kerouac's The Dharma Bums in 1989. Undermining my inner monk with hamburgers and bowls of soup were Paul Dawson and Jimmy Laksa.

When it comes to fumbling around inside yourself looking for what really matters, it helps to have someone by your side who sees you more clearly than you do. Thank you Megan, my sweetheart, always.

OUR READERS

Many thanks to the travellers who used the last edition and wrote to us with helpful hints, useful advice and interesting anecdotes:

A Gep Aadriaanse, Hannah Aagaard-Jensen, Lucy Abbott, Mark Aberkrom, Niels Ackerman, Claire Adams, Heather Adams, Leah Adams, Natalie Adams, Tadzrul Adha, Sharon Agar, Deeanne Akerson, Friederike Albrecht, Tim Alexander, Nick Allen, Chris Allitt, Roger Almond, Adrian Altenhoff, Ginny Amaya, Carla Ambrose, Pam Amos, Heath Anderson, Jamie Anderson, Nicole Anderson, Maria Andersson, Richard Anthony, Nan Arens, Mark Armstrong, Stephen Armstrong, David Arnby, David Arnold, Belen Arranz, Phyllis Arthu, Michael Arthur, Jason Ashwell, James Aslanis, Gill Aslett, Louise Atkin, Elizabeth Ayarra, Matthew Ayre, Robert Ayres **B** Ken Bailey, Tanya Bailey, Ana Bailey-Brown, Chris Bain, Nicol Baird, David Baker, Karen Baker, Jessica Ball, Lyndon & Sarah Banbury, Austin Barber, Simon Barnett, Rebecca Barnshaw, Brad Barr, Janet Barrett, Claire Bartlett, Geoff Barton, Cris Bastianello, Stefan Baum, Cornelia Baumermann, Nadine Baxter-Smallwood, Leslie Beard, Alyson Bee, Eric Beeby, Michael Beech, Pamela Beeler, Andrew Bell, Charlotte Bell, Claire Bell, Graeme Bell, Gordon Bennett, Lene 3erge, Pamela Berghegen, Andreas Bertram, David Bertram, Kim Bestic, Simon & Joanne Betney, Liz & Neil Beverley, Tanya Beynon, Marc Biedermann, Merve Bigden, Shaun Bigg, Douglas B:ggar, Itai Birger, Brenda & Dave Birss, Kate Black, Joanne Blackburn, David Blakemore, Richard Blakey, Danielle Blanchard, Jeannine Blarer, Alexander

SEND US YOUR FEEDBACK

We love to hear from travellers – your comments keep us on our toes and help make our books better. Our well-travelled team reads every word on what you loved or loathed about this book. Although we cannot reply individually to postal submissions, we always guarantee that your feedback goes straight to the appropriate authors, in time for the next edition. Each person who sends us information is thanked in the next edition – and the most useful submissions are rewarded with a free book.

To send us your updates – and find out about Lonely Planet events, newsletters and travel news – visit our award-winning website: **www.lonelyplanet.com/feedback**.

Note: We may edit, reproduce and incorporate your comments in Lonely Planet products such as guidebooks, websites and digital products, so let us know if you don't want your comments reproduced or your name acknowledged. For a copy of our privacy policy visit www.lonelyplanet.com/privacy.

Bleha, Charlotte Blixt, Iris Blok, Mendy Blok, Henk Boerrigter, Marijn Bogers, Hugh Bolt, Joseph Bolt, Alex Bond, Sue & Tony Borer, Nick Borg, Don Borin, Katharina & Daniel Borszik, Adam Bourreau, Mireille Boucin, Christine Bourgeois, Benedicte Boushek, Sharn Bowley, Vicki Bowman, Louise Bowsher, Harriet Boyce, Kieran Boyde, Tammy Boyer, D Braam, Charles Bradley, Julie & Glenn Bradley, Chris Brady, Lee Braem, Ralf Brand, Silvia Brandl, Alys Brazendale, Jaz Breitlow, Davide Brero, Bob & Nancy Breslin, Sarah & Tim Brasseleers, Jayne Bretherton, Shona Brethouwer, Andy & Claire Brice, Eleanor Bridger, Pat Bridges, Neil Brigder, James Brooks, Carolyn Brown, David Brown, Sue Brightr, Helen Bright, Robin Britten, Mary Britton, Ben Brock, Browniey, Jens Brueggemann, Brenda Brugts, Carola Bruhn, Rachel Brooker, Peter Buchanan, Angela & Jason Buckley, Helen Burton, Dan Bugajski, Claire Bullock, Con Bullot, Andrew Bunbury, Mischa Brus, Leila Buni, Scott Burcher, Desmond Burdon, Miranda Burger, Belinda Burgmann, Mary Burrows, Clare Burton, Warren Burton, Jason Calvert, Kirsty Cambridge, Rachel Cameron, Puhl & James Damiar Bush, John Byrne **C** Aurelie Gaillebotte, Keith Calder, Campbell, Mandy Cantle, Tm & Liz Capon, Marie Capuccio, Jean Carder, Gavin Carey, Diane Carr, Fiona Carruthers, Nicholas Carson, Shelly Carter, Tommy Carter, Katrina Casey, Ross Cashmore, Robert Catto, Johan Cauwels, Xavier Cazauran, Sumana Chadalavada, Pierre Chalfajew, Brook Chambers, Nila Chambers, Anthony Chant, Ben Chapman, David C Chang, Mathew Channon, Doreen Charlton, Cressida Chatfield, Joelle Chaubeau, Alison Chick, Andrew Chinn, Na Choo, Ivar Christensen, Charlotte Christensen

Jillian Christoff, Maria Christoff, Stephanie Chua, Chan Wai Chung, Fred & Darla Clark, William Clarke, Bjorn Clasen, Gea Classen, Jodi & Rob Clayson, Caroline Clear, Jim Clemmer, Colin Cloudesley, Chris Coffey, Mary Colbeck, Les Colbourne-Creak, Ka Colby, Rich & Sally Coleman, Berna Collier, Kendall Collier, Conrad Collinge, Becca Collins, Carol Collins, Marie Collins, Tarla Collins, Furio Collins, Temra & Damien Coman, Anna Compton, Salvatore Consalvi, Roger Cooke, Clare Cooper, Paul Coopersmith, E Copping, Paul Corbett, Tony Corcoran, Claire Cordell, Terry Cormier, Steve Cotter, John Cotton, Linda Cotton, Lynda Cotton, Francis Cousin, Katrina Cowen, Eileen Coyne, Jo Coyne, Erin Crampton, Ian Crawford, Paul Crofskey, Richard Cross, Andy Crossley, Alan Crosswell, Brian Crowley, Joann Crowley, Sarah Cruickshank, Michael Cuming, John Cummings, Jena Curtis, Rebecca Curtis, William Cymbalsky **D** Luisa D'Accione, Paul Dale, Jerry & Cobi Daley, Ryan Daly, Angela Danyluk, Lisa Darby, Jenny Darragh, Felix Daschek, Arjan Dasselaar, Anthony Davenport, Christine Davey, Barry Davidson, Dorothy Davies, Laura Davies, Alice Davis, Ben Davison, Lee Dawson, Phil Day, Tim Day, Robert de Bruyn, Ton de Bruyn, Martine de Flander, Fedor de Koning, Fedor & Diana de Koning, Anton & Kathy de Luc, Jean & Bernadette de Maulmin, Kaye de Ross, Brenda de Ruiter, Pieter de Wilde, Steve Deadman, Bronwen Dean, John & Trudy Dean, Louise Dean, Sheldon Dean, Marilyn Deasy, Sarsha Deeley, Eddie Deevy, RoseMarie Deevy, Rangimarie Delamere, Kim Dellaca, Ka'in Demidoff, Ali Dent, Peter Deuart, Danielle D Fonzo, Beverly & Michael Diggins, Nicole Dijkstra, Derek Distin, Sebastian Dittrich, Loretta Dixon, Carolin Doderer, David Doff, Juanita Doherty, Matthew Doidge, Tina Domitek, Nerida Donelan, Julie Donlon, Shannon Donovan, Mike Dooran, W F Doran, Bill & Julie Dormandy, Stephen Doughty, Richard Downey, Murray Downs, Karen Doyle, Jason Drake, Roger Drake, Steve Drury, Steven Drury, Erik Duerr, Elizabeth Duffield, Ruth Dumaboc, Jodi Dunbar, Graeme Dunn, Ray Dunn, Terry Dunn, Wayne Cunning, Fred Duprat, Helen & Chris Dussling, Bruce Dyer **E** Helen & Paul Eagles, Sarah Eales, Christina Echols, Richard Eckman, David Edgar, Chad Edison, Roger Edmonds, Susan Edwards, Dorit Efrat, Johan Eikelboom, James Elvers, Samantha Elliott, Nicola Elliottson, George Ellis, James Ettringham, Joan Enright, Moritz Euchner, April Evans, Jan Evans, Sarah Evers, Jane Everex, Alwin Evers, Stephen Eyer **F** Jesper Fahlen, Hagar Fainberg, Michael Falk, Paula Fallows, Jim Farquhar, Ken Farrance, Julie Farrell, Jean Farrelly, Paul Farrelly, Vonny Fast, Simon Fathers, Michelle & Jason Fayers, Christiane Federlin, Jurjen Feikens, Martin Feldmann, Frank Felten, Aishim Fernor, Carol Ferris, Nicolas Fevrier, David Fields, Antoinette Figliola-Kaderli, Callum Finlay, Jennifer Fisher, Nick Fisher, Bette Flagler, Chris Fleming, Nic Fletcher, Hilary Ford, Jean Ford, Clive Fortune, Nigel Foster, Marc Frank, Louise Franklin, Paul Freeman, Sarah Freeth, Reto & Sancra Frei, Kip Freytag, Peter Fries, Flair Friesen, Nicolas Friman, Allison Fritsch, Karla Fryer, Patrick Fuglister, Gareth Fullerton, Holger Funk, Erika Furger **G** Daniele Galli, Anne Garber, Chris Gardner, Louise Gardner, Jean Garelick, Sandra Gasson, Dorothy Gay, John Gay, David & Barbara Geary, Linde Geenen, John Geisen-Kisch, Carsten Geuer, Graham Gibson, Erik & Anja Gielen-abaay, Cynthia & Norman Gierke, Julie &

Maurice Gilligan, Ronnie Gillman, Bernadette Girlich, Mark Given, Jan Glas, Sandra Glasglow, Christian Glossner, Val Goddard, Ralph Goldstein, Rosalie Goldsworthy, Virginia Gonzalez, Julian Gonzalez, Sergio & Pinol Gonzalez, David & Adele Goodall, Nicola Goodanew, Sam Goodenough, Andria Goodkin, Karen Goodlet, Hattie Goodman, Kate Goodrich, Robyn Goods, Annemarie Gordon, Leisa Gordon, Matthew & Adrian Gough, Fredrik Graffner, Lisa Grant, Sala'am Grant, Peter Grattan, Nikki Graves, Joanna Gray, Wendy Gray, Lyn Green, Mark Green, Robert Green, Ronalie Green, Andrew Greenhill, David Gregory, Angela Griffiths, Myles Griffiths, Amy Griggs, James Grigg, Scott Grossman, Edwin Grovenstein, Andrea Gryak, Annette & Marc Guerin, Antoinette Gussenhoven **H** Sue & Bob Haddow, Caroline Hager, Yutaka Hagino, Mary Hall, Mike & Diana Hall, Richard Hall, Carole & Geoff Hamer, Lexy Hamilton-Smith, Jane Hammet, Katrina Hammond, Alan Harding, Kelly Harlen, Dorie & Lee Harmon, Lynn Harris, Rebecca Harrison, Robert Hart, Ed Harte, Frans Hartman, Beate Hartmann, Marina Hartwel, Paul Harvey, Ryley Hatchard, Geoff Hawthorn, Gillian & Jim & Ji Hay, Wendy Haycock, William Hayducsko, Richard Hayton, Christopher Hayward, Gareth Heal, Marjorie Heasman, Gemma Hebertson, Kelly Hedstrom, Carol & Dennis Hegarty, Heidi Heidi, Nancy Heinz-Sader, Anna Heiro, Paul Hellyer, S K Hendy, Elaine Heney, Jenny Henman, Patrick Hennessy, Mark & Emma Herbert, Floortje Herder, Judith Hereford, Ira & Stefan Hervel, Joelle Hervy, Rob Herwson, Bill Hetzel, Joy Hewgill, Alex Hewlett, Anna Higgins, Sarah Higgins, Alyson Higgs, Timothy Hildebrandt, Andy Hill, Belinda Hill, Brian Hill, L J Hill, Neryl Hill, Tom Hill, Eva Himmelberg, Duncan & Natalie Hind, John Hinde, Norman Hinds, Catia Hirsch, Rob Hocking, Dagmar Hoehr, Werner Hoelzl, Ingrid Hoffman, Rita & Gerd Hofmann-Credner, Grainne Hogan, Kay & Glenn Hogg, Zoe Hogg, Chris Holland, Adrian Holliday, Jason Hollinger, Malcolm Holmes, Craig Holz, Dorothea Holzapfel, Christiane Holzenbecher, Michael Hopkins, Robbins Hopkins, Andy Hopko, Nathan Hopper, Kate Horsley, Mark Hoskins, Jennifer Hough, Linda House, Alan Howarth, Graeme Howie, Jenny Howson, Hao-Ching Hsiao, Gerhard Hucke, Rachel Hucknall, Sherrie Hudson, Cate Hughes, Janet Hughes, Marina Hughes, Emma Humphreys, Trevor Humphreys, Jodie Humphries, Chris Hunt, Kathrin Hunziker, Edward Hurley, Warren Hurley, Trudi Hurren, Stuart Hutchings, Nadine Huwe **I** Kelly Iacono, Fermin Iglesias, Barbara Ingendae, Stephen Ireland, Steve Isaacs, Lucy Isherwood, Anja Issbruecker **J** Gemma Jackson, Mike Jackson, Kristina Jacob, Rosie Jaffer, Kristina Jakobsen, Gareth James, Libby James, Keith & Trish Janes, Alienke Jansen, Patrick Jansen, Simon Jay, Neil Jebb, Mike Jeffcoat, Tony Jenkins, Robby Jennings, Davide Jermini, Evelyne Jessop, Joan Jewett, Angie Jezard, Ingela Johansson, Dave Johnson, Michele Johnson, Rachel Johnson, Peggy Jonckheere, Cerys Jones, Giff & Mary Jones, Greg Jones, Kelly Jones, Louise Jones, Rowan & Anna Jones, Ilma Joukes, Gary Joynes, Ulf Juergensen, Bernd Juhre, Tim Julou **K** William Kaderli, Joanne Kaijen, Gerard & Jeanette Kamberg, Timon Kampschulte, Hayden Kantor, Farah Karim, Sue Karutz, Richard Kay, Liza Kee, Shannon Keenan, Marina Kelly, Margot Kennedy, Jenny Kerr, Carla Kersten, Esther Killat, John King, Melissa King, Sarah Jane King, Trish King, Ken Kirkman, Lucas Klamert, Andrea Kleemann, Anne-Marie Kleijberg, Maureen

Kljin, Henry Klos, Jeremy Knight, Kati Knuttila, Antonella Koenig, Megan Konar, Silke Korbl, Laura & Steve Koulish, Nir & Michal Kraiem, Joe Krampel, Tatiana Krause, Karin Krone, Christopher Kruzel, Judy Kullberg, Kathrin Kuske **L** Nicole la Juett, Suzanne LaBarre, Bernadette Lahme, Peter Laight, Michaela Lambauer, Malcolm Lambert, Marty Lampard, Carsten Lampe, Markus Landvogt, Louise Langhorn, Martin Langsch, Dennis Langsdorf, Phil Langsford, Tony Lansdowne, Ben Lapsley, Chris LaRoche, Tony Laskey, Joanna Lau, Michael Laufersweiler, Nick Laugier, Lars Lauridsen, Markus Laux, Glen Lawrence, Rob Lawrence, Ian Leak, Diane Lee, Gloria Lee, Lai Yin Lee, Vivian Lee, Jane Lehmann, Peter Leichliter, Dennis Lennie, Christoph Leon, Vanessa & Lucas Leonardi, Meredith Lepore, Elizabeth Leppman, Katharine Lequesne, Martin Lerner, Jeannie-Marie Leroi, Sarah Leslie, Andrea Lewis, Janet Lewis, Wayne Lewis, Ulrich Lichtenhaler, Marina Lieber, Daniel Lilienstein, Kim Lim, Willie Lim, Sean Limpens, Sylvia Lin, Ola Lindberg, Gunilla Lindblad, Desiree & Niklas Linden, Sidsel Lindgaard, Elizabeth & David Lindsey, Paul Lintott, Lindsay Lipson, Jessica Lischka, Russell Lloyd, Elizabeth Loeff, Gill Logan, Jo Logan, M K Loh, Lorraine Lohan, Ditte Lokon, Mette Loland, Roberto Longi, Margaret Longsbrough, Inge Loo, Lai Kit Looi, Sarah Lopez, Melanie Loriz, Nick Lott, Lars Lounds, Graham Love, Debbie Lovell, Nicky Lovf, Jeffrey Lowe, Connie Lowry, Katherine Lubar, William Lucas, Cristin Luey, Bas Lugtigheid, Kelsi Luhnow, Fleur Luijten, Thomas Lynnerup **M** John MacDonald, Nick Mace, Andrea Macfarlane, James Macguill, Lisa Macguill, Julian Maclaren, Bob Maclennan, Ceri Macleod, Helen Macmullins, Andrew Madden, Bernhard Maenner, Abbey Magargee, William & T Maguire, Jane Maher, Claude Malet, Leane Malone, Alison Maloney, Chalin Malz, Evy Mandikos, Orlaith Mannion, Gabriel Manrique, J Marcovecchio, Lilee Marer, Anne Margrethe, Raymond Mark, Peter Marko, Michelle Maro, Harry Marotto, Michael Marsh, Mike Marshall, Daniel Martin, Lee Martin, Linsey Martin, Christian Massett, Scott Mather, Alisdair Matheson, Fionnuala Matthews, Valerie Matthews, Michael Mayfield, Mary Maynard, Peter Maz, Jillian Mazzagetti, Trevor Mazzucchelli, David Mccambridge, Dai Mcclurg, Jamie McCormack, Eron Mccormick, Tom Mcdermott, Grant Mcdonnell, Steve McFadyen, Magnus McGillivray, Pamela McGinn, Callum Mcglinchy, Fraser McInnes, Tanya Mckay, Alan McKinnon, Lynne Mclaren, Diane Mclean, Cathryn McNamara, Neil McRae, Philip Meehan, Nick Meeten, Ralph & Janneke Meijer, Mark Melman, Martijn Mennen, Lucy Menzies, Keith & Sandra Menzies, Shane Merchant, Jonathan Merrett, Kimberly Merris, Brenda Merz, Karen Metcalf, Katja Mewes, Keld Mex-Jorgensen, Bjoern Meyburg, Rita Mezel, Gaspard Michardiere, Marco Miersemann, Yann Mihoubt, Kristian Mikkelsen, Robert Miley, Danielle Miller, Harris Miller, Michael Milligan, Janet Mills, William & Rebecca Minchin, Helen Minogue, Nicki Miquel, Barry Mitchell, Craig Mitchell, Steve Mitchell, Sue Mobley, Knut Moen, Paul Mohme, Marjolijn Molenaar, Roos Molenaar, Helena Molloy, Norman Monshall, Bob & Sandra Mooney, Tom Mooney, Tom Moore, Mary Morehouse, Nonie Morish, Anne Lloyd Morris, Edward Morris, Sallie Morris, Ted & Wendy Morris, Joanna Morrison, Hugh & Eileen Morton, Friedi Moschner, Wolfgang Moser, Tim Mowat, Arjun Mukerjee, Sanjukta

Mukherjee, Sebastian? Mulder, James Mulhern, Ronaldo Müller, Amanda Mulley, George G Mulligan, Andrew Multenan, Ole Munk, Vicki Munro, Dan Murphy, Heather Murphy, Cathy Murray, Tim Musclow, Naomi Musoline N Elad Nachman, Ralph Nafziger, Christina Nagel, Chris Nash, Regina Natsch, Pauline Neal Corinne Nedelec, Frank Neff, Ai-Ling Neo, Leni Neoptolemos, Elke Neumann, F Newbery, Emma Newton, Simon Niblett, Martin & Helen Nicholas, Eva Nichols, Geoff Nichols, Louisa Nichols, Steven Nicholson, Nina Nick, Hanne Nielsen, Petra Niesel, Joseph Nigro, Erwin & Hennie Nijkeuter, Birgitte Nikolajsen, Andy Nilsson, Shohei Nimomiya, Chuck Nip, Elvi Rohde Nissen, Helen Noakes, Bethan Nolan, Per Nordqvist, Kelly Norfolk, Deirdre Norris, Gisela Nurahyanti O Nicola O'Brien, Hilary Oakley, Philip Obergfell, Jane O'Brien, Christopher O'Brien, Malcolm O'Brien, Mark O'Connell, Mel O'Connell, Lynda O'Dea, Mr & Mrs KL O'Dea, Julie Odell, Maureen O'Driscoll, Cindy Oehmig, Kartini Oei, Sebastian Oergel, Karin Ohlin, Stewart Oliver, Liz Oldham, Lars Olesen, Janet Oliver, Jenny O'Neill, Sarah & Adrian Orchard, Michelle O'Riordan, Sarah Orr, Stacy Orr, Jack & Nancy Ostheimer, Dennis O'Sullivan, Brian O'Sullivan, Lynn O'Sullivan, Sara Owen, Suzanne Owen, Bill Czanne P Maria Pacheco, Alexis Packer, Melissa Paddrick, Stu Padget, Kaye & Trevor Painter, Claudia Palko, James Palmer, Pau Panichelli, W R Pankhurst, Shannon Pantages, Diana Par?, Leisyka Parrott, Emma Parsons, Nathan Parsons, Julie Pattie, Mary Jane & Walter Pawlowski, Virginia Pawlyn, Stephanie Payen, Matthew Fayne, Olivia Payne, Paul Pelczar, Ben Peled, Rolf Pentzlin, Jane Fensho, Edwin Perkins, Omer Peristein, Joe & Patti Perna, Patricia Ferry, Theo Perry, Katie Pervan, James Peskett, Stephanie Fettigrew, Jo Petty, Hans Pezold, Rosemarie Pforter, Abby Philips, Fachel Phillips, Sue Picard, Adi Pieper, Stephanie Pietruszynski, Sandra Pijl, Roger Pike, Sarah Pike, C Pillemer, Bob Piper, Sheila Firie, Barry & Sarah Pitt, Judy Pittman, Stafford Pitts, Heike Platz, Cathie Plowman, Jen-Eric Plusingrand, Anne Pohl, Judith Pohl, Colette Polk? Jan Poker, Essi Pölhö, Anna Poller, Kerstin Pomplun, Maggie Ponder, Stephanie & Randall Popelka, Dianne Pornish, S Poteet, Arne Poulsen, Zoe Poulton, Dawn Powers, Maggie Pressley, Anouk Prins, Sarah Pritchard, Michael Prys-William, Victoria Purdie, Phyllis Purdy Q Paul Quenby, Katy Quévillon, Rohan Quinby, Brian & Cate Quinn, John Quinn R Nicole Radermacher, Michael Raffaele, Amir Rahimzadeh, Poorani Ramalingam, Riju Ramrakha, Emma Ramsay, Amina Rand, Gamal Rasmy, Thomas Rau, Nigel Rayner, Susie Reale, Joy Rebello, Susie Reddick, Janice Redford, Janis Redmond, Bruce Reed, Peter Reeder, Caroline Rees, Andy & Becky Reeves, Martin Reindl, Peter Reisinger, Alenka Remec, Jean-Daniel Renevey, Charlotte Renner, Marisa Reynaldi, Frank & Louise Richards, Laurie Richards, Jennifer Rickett, Michael Riggs, Kim Riedel, Mary Riemens, Matthew Rifkin, Michael Riggs, Luke Riley, Rory Riley-Gillespie, Anne Rimmer, Thorsten Rinner, Mary Rios, Tamara Rios, Lutz Ritter, Janet Roach, Bridget Roberts, Grahame Roberts, Victoria Roberts, Neil & Sarah Robertson, James & Tanie Roberts-Thomson, Christie Robinson, Connie Robinson, Anne Roche, Jesus Rodriguez, Bob & Marie Roger, Gillian Rogers, James Rogers, Kerrie Rogers, Andrea Rogge, MacKinzie Rogge, William Ro!o, Susan Rolph, Elizabeth Romhild, Fiona Roscoe, Judith Rosendahl, Petra

Rossback, Clive Rowe, Elizabeth Rowe, Phillip Rowe, Zoe Rowe, Marie Royd, Gil Rozen, Ken Rubin, Jim Rucker, Margot Rudolf, Jackie Rumble, Jochen Rundholz, Sandy Rushing, Carol Russell, D'ster Ruth, Jonathan Ryan, Peter Ryan, Sue Ryan S Eva Sabate, Kate Sabey, Martin Sackert, Keith Safey, Amy Sagan, Ayumi Sakurai, Darren Salter, Thomas Saluz, Natalie Salway, Michelle Sampson, Torres San Juan, Mark Sander, Mischa Sarder, Sarah Sanders, Brenda Sandilands, Peter Sapper, Alex Sas, Chiko Sato, Yoshiki Sato, Barry Sayer, Ian Scales, Laura Schaefer, Sandra Scheidmann, Jacques Schildknecht, Hans Schiltrars, John Schindler, Matt Schiltz, Ursula Schmidt, Axel Schmickte, David Schneider, Rainer Schmidt-Renner, Jutta Schneider, Luree Schneider, Ursula Schober, Timm Schoening, Ann Schofield, Holger Schonherr, Apollonia Schreiber, Ingrid Schulz, Frieder Schurr, Edwin Schuurman, Ann-Christin Schwab, Tobias Schwabold, Carol Scott, Emilie Scott, Janette Seal, Mike & Claire Sealey, Kerstin Seja, Sanjib Sen, Kim Senini, Dan Senior, Maarian Senior, Lorenza Saveri, Jeff Sewell, Sandra Sewell, Nitzan Shadmi, Eyal Shaman, Richard Sirell, Gregory Skipper, Michael Skully, Kristoffer Sletten, Rod Shapland, Andrew Sharp, Allison Shaw, Geoff Shaw, Jodie Snaw, Jon Shaw, Eyleen Shed, Lizzie Shelley, Trent Shepard, Michael Siefert, Simone Siemons, Ingrid Siemonsma, Anne Sikanen, Arend & Lous Sijpestein, D P Siliss, Alisha Simpson, Kenneth Simpson, Ritchie Sims, Vicki Sinclair, Debbie Snger, Heidi Singleton, James Sington, Patrick Sinke, Anneke Sips, Brian Sisk, Julie Smellie, Caroline Sm?t, Casey Smith, Danny Smith, Roger Smith, G H Smith, Jayne Smith, John Smith, Moira Smith, Peter Smolka, Chris Smullen, Bel a & Peter Snook, Adam & Lora Snow, Lynne Snow, Trina So, Markus Sodergren, Brenda So?oman, Iain Sommerville, Yaara Sorek, Maria Sotiropoulos, Sally Sparkes, Claire Speedy, Jo Spencer, John Spencer, Claudia Spiegel, David Spielvogel, Freek Spits, Catherine Spratt, Abi Stafford, Michae Staider, Nicole Stamsnieder, Clare Stanley, John Stansberry, Karen Stark, Jane Stearns, Sarah Steegar, Stuart Steel, Care Steele, Fnnelies Steen, Karen Stefkova, Jorrit Steinz, Margrethe Stendahl, Fay Stenhouse, Judith Stettner, Andrew Stevenson, Andrew & Emmeline Stevenson, Jonny Stevenson, Rebecca Stevenson, Stacey Stevenson, Rik Stewart, William Steyn, Jo & Tim & Thomas Stokes, Laurie & Daph Stokes, Peter Stone, Bill & Ann Stoughton, Shane Straiko, Sarah Street, Karen Strehlow, Nick Strickland, The Strosbergs, Greg Sullivan, Mandy Sutyak, Rinko Suzuki, Troud Svendsen, Caroline Swain, Bonar Swale, Petra Swa?ue, Felicity Swift, Mary & William Swing, Kathrine Switzer, Kath Swolinzky, Caro Syddall, Lucy & Bev Sydney, Eileen Synnott, Christian Szeglat, Queenie Szeto T Konia Tack, Jed Tai, Julie Talbot, Guy Talmor, Brenda Tan, Larissa Tandy, Donna Tang, Mariann Tang, Brian Tanner, Chas Tanner, Anne Tapp, Kelly Tarbuck, Vanessa Tasker, David Taylor, Mary Taylor, Steve Taylor, James Teare, Garry Telford, Stuart Templeton, Philip Tew, Ray & Leahn Theedam Parry, Rebecca Thiessen, A Thomas, Liz Thomas, Paul Thomas, Sally Thomas, Wayne & Monica Thomas, Carl Thompson, Stephen Thompson, William Thompson, Jo Thomson, Romua d Thoraval, Michael Thorn, Noppon Thurmanond, Nathan Tidridge, Patricia Tierney, Kevin Timmins, Edmund Ting, Maarten Tip, Noel Titter, Luke Tolson, Louise Tong, Jochen Topf, Karen Towns, Sophie

Trembath, Gillian Trotter, Morena Trottolini, Paul Tuckwell, Mark Turner, Toni & Rick Tuttle, Rob Twamley, Tom Tweddell, Rachel Tyler **U** Cal Ulberg, Andy Ulery, Giora Unger, Harkiran Uppal **V** Ivan Valencic, Koosje van Bergen, Mariska van den Akker, Stefan van den Bos, Tiny van den Brink, Suzanne van der Kolk, Dennis van der Voort, Charlotte van der Wiel, Bart van Dongen, Karen van Druten, Leondra van Hattum, Teun van Metelen, Chris van Namen, Johann van Niekerk, Len van Rossum, Peter Vanbussel, Luke Vanguns, Liz Vaughan, Peter Vaughan, Amy Veasey, Zoe Veater, Lorien Vecellio, Gerben Veneman, Frans Verhoef, Clem Vetters, Brice Villion, Nate Vinatelli, Michael & C Vink, Erna Jansen Vledder, H Plenter Vledder, Jacqueline Vlotman, Shayne Volk, Christine Volpert, Fiona Vorrink, Ilse Vossen, Caspar Vroonland **W** Parani Waaka, Reto Wagner, Patrick Wainwright, Ollie Waite, Jim & Jill Waits, Catriona Walker, Steve Walker, Anna Walkington, Emma Walmsley, Hannah Walters, Katharina Wandt, Lek Warawut, Andy Ward, Lucille Warlow, Diana Warr, Adrian Warren, Beth Wasgatt, Etsuko Watanabe, David Watkin, Natalie Watson, Rebekah Watts, Chris Webb, Lesley Webb, Angelika Weber, Christine Weber, M Weber, Graham Webster, Mary Weeder, Harald Wegele, Charles Weir, Ben & Adriana Wensink, Helmut & Karin Wermbter, Karen West, John Wester, Bastiaan Westerhout, Peter Westhofen, Laura Weston, Zoe Whamsby, Susie Wheatley, David Wheeler, David Whelan, Georgina Whetham, Elva & Peter Whitaker, Heather White, Matt Whitehead, Lorna Whitfield, David Whiting, Naomi Whitney, Laura Whittle, Allan Wicker, Jennifer Widom, Julie Wilchins, Fred Wilde, Anna Wilkinson, Louise Wilkinson, Tanya Wilkinson, Anna Willets, Catrin Williams, Hannah & Metua Williams, Katie Williams, Lynne Willimott, Lee Wills, Andy Wilson, Ann Wilson, Keith Winders, Marilynn Windust, Jennie Winroth, Mandy Winter, Leonie Wise, Eugene Wojcinski, Alison Wolf, Will Woodall, Caroline Woodruff, Donald Woods, John Wormington, Valerie Wotton, Craig Wright, Maureen Wright, Mandy Wuendsch **Y** Genine Yallop, Lesley Yamauchi, Kaori Yasukochi, Barbara Yates, Emma Yates, Johnnie Yates, Man Yau, Chee Keong Yeoh, Kristen Yong, Terry Yoshimura, D C Young, E M Young, John Young, Peter Young, Jacqueline Yurneaux **Z** Junaid Zaman, Marc Zangwill, William Zasoba, Rene Zenden, Oliver Zoellner, Amy Zuber

ACKNOWLEDGMENTS

Many thanks to the following for the use of their content:

Globe on back cover ©Mountain High Maps 1993 Digital Wisdom, Inc.

Alexander Turnbull Library, Wellington, NZ for use of images.

Richard von Sturmer (lyrics) and Don McGlashan (music) for 'There is No Depression in New Zealand' lyrics (p42).

Index

42nd Traverse 320, 324
309 Road 216-17, **128**

A
abalone 95, 717
Abbey Caves 203
Abel Tasman Coastal Track 478-80, 481, **87**
Abel Tasman National Park 67, 478-82, **479**, 7, 541
abseiling
   Lake Taupo region 301
   Waitomo 250, 76
   Wanaka 649
   Wharepapa South 243
Acacia Bay 296
accommodation 702-6, see also individual locations
Acker's Point Lighthouse 693
activities 69-92, see also individual activities
adventure & amusement parks
Agrodome Adventures 346
Happy Valley Adventures 465
Kiwi Adventure Centre 390
Longridge Park 360
Parakai Aquatic Park 147
Rainbow's End Adventure Park 117
Splash Planet Waterpark 394
Taupo Adventure Park 300
Thrillseekers Canyon 566
Waiau Waterworks 216
Waterworld 235
aerial sightseeing, see scenic flights
Agrodome 344
Agrodome Adventures 346
Ahipara 178-9
Aigantighe Art Gallery 574
air travel 722-5
   air fares 723-5, 726, 727
   airlines 722-3, 726
   airports 722-3
   departure tax 723
   to/from New Zealand 722-5
   within New Zealand 726
Akaroa 560-4, **560**

000 Map pages
000 Photograph pages

albatross 602-3, 700
Aldermen Islands 222
Alexandra 608-9
Allans Beach 604
amoebic meningitis 739
amusement parks, see adventure & amusement parks
Ancient Kauri Kingdom 179
Anderson Park Art Gallery 675-6
Angora rabbits 250
animals 64-6, see also individual animals
Antipodes Islands 701
Aoraki/Mt Cook National Park 62, 67, 583-8, **584**, 6, 544
Aorangi 200
Aranui Cave 248, 249
Aratiatia Dam 307
area codes 718
Arnold River 503
Aroha Island 197-8
Arrowtown 639-42, **640**
Arrowtown Golf Course 640
Art Deco 389, 390, 394, 463, 611
Arthur's Pass 83, 90, 569-71, **569**
arts 48-53, see also individual arts
ASB Classic 119, 139
Athenree Hot Springs 225
Atkinson, Harry 267
ATMs 714
Auckland 101-43, **104**, **106**, 2, **125**, **126**
   accommodation 119-33
   activities 102, 115-17
   city centre 120, 122, 124, 133-4, 137
   Devonport 113-14, 121, 123-4, 133, 137, 138, **111**
   drinking 137-8
   emergency services 105
   entertainment 138-40
   festivals 119
   food 99, 133-7
   history 102-3
   Internet access 105
   itineraries 103
   K Rd 114, 135
   medical services 105
   Mt Eden 114, 121, 123, 135-6, **109**

Newmarket 135-6, **109**
Parnell 121, 122-3, 124, 135, 138, **108**
Ponsonby 114, 121, 123, 124, 133, 136-7, 138, **110**
Princes Wharf 134-5, 137-8
shopping 140-1
sights 108-15
surrounding region 144-7, **144**
tourist offices 107-8
tours 118-19
travel to/from 102, 141-2
travel within 102, 142-3
Viaduct Harbour 134-5, 137-8
walking tour 117-18, **118**
Auckland Anniversary Day Regatta 119
Auckland Art Gallery 112, **126**
Auckland Cup 119
Auckland Domain 114, **125**
Auckland Islands 700
Auckland Museum 109-10, **125**
Auckland Zoo 112
Aupouri Forest 180
Aupouri Peninsula 179-80
Australasian gannets 71, 146-7
Automobile Association 731
avocado oil 96
Awakeri Hot Springs 365
Awakino 254
Awarua Wetlands 684

B
B&Bs 703
back-country huts 91
backpacker buses 729-30
backpacker vans 733
Bad Blood (movie) 512
Balclutha 613
Baldwin St 595
bank accounts 714
Banks Peninsula 559-64, **559**
Banks Peninsula Track 90, 561
barbecues 98
Barrytown 501
bar-tailed godwits 226
Batten, Jean 47
Bay of Islands 160, 185-205, **185**, 8, **127**
Bay of Plenty 327-67, **329**, **130**

B
..lys Beach 171
b
..ches
Ahipara 178-9
Allans Beach 604
Auckland region 116
Bay of Islands 187
Baylys Beach 171
Bethells Beach 146
Black Beach 272
Colac Bay 673
Coopers Beach 182
Foxton Beach 292
Frasers Beach 670
Gentle Annie Beach 497
Goat Island 166-7, *9*
Great Barrier Island 154-6
Hawai 371
Hicks Bay 372
Himatangi 292, *8*
Kaiteriteri 477
Karekare Beach 145-6
Komene Beach 271
Long Beach 195
Mangamaunu Beach 457
Mangawhai 167-8
Manu Bay 240, *9*
Matai Bay 181
Mokau 254
Monro Beach 523
Mt. Maunganui 354-5
Muriwai Beach 146-7
New Chum's Beach 216
New Dick's Beach 360
Ngarunui Beach 240
Ninety Mile Beach 177, 178-81
Ockura 271
Ocean Beach 400
Ohawe Beach 272
Ohiwa 365
Ohope Beach 364
Omaha 166
Opito Bay 216
Opoutere Beach 223
Opunake 272
Otama Beach 216
Pekiri 167
Peraparaumu Beach 429
Piha Beach 145-6, *126*
Pohara 485
Porpoise Bay 684, 548
Puheke Beach 181
Raglan 238
Rangipu Beach 240
Rangiputa 181
Rapahoe 505

Ripiro Ocean Beach 171
Riverton Rocks 673
Ruapuke Beach 240
St Clair Beach 595, *3, 545*
St Kilda Beach 595
Sandy Bay 200
Taipa 182
Tarama Bay 673
Taranaki 261-2
Tauranga 349
Taylors Mistake 537
Te Henga Beach 146
Tokomaru Bay 374
Tolaga Bay 374
Victory Beach 604, *9*
Waihi Beach 225
Waiheke Island 151
Waikanae Beach 379
Wairarama Beach 400
Waipu 168
Wairarapa Coast 434
Waitahi 365
Whale Bay 240
Whiariki Beach 487
Whatipu Beach 146
Beehive 409-10
beer 97, *see also* breweries
bellbirds 65
Bennett, Joe 23, 66
Bethells Beach 146
bicycle travel, *see cycling*
Big Carrot 322
Big River Track 502
birds 65-6, *see also individual birds*
bird-watching 65, 71, *see also kiwi*
Awarua Wetlands 684
books 65, 71
Cape Kidnappers Gannet Colony
400
Catlins 683
Chatham Islands 698
Farewell Spit 486-7
Haast region 523
Howarth Wetlands Reserve 227
Kaikoura 458
Kapiti Island 430
Karaka Bird Hide 239
Little Barrier Island 159
Miranda 225
Nga Manu Nature Reserve 430
Okarito 514
Otorohanga Kiwi House 3..
Native Bird Park 247
Rabbit Island 473
Rainbow Springs Nature Park 344

Stewart Island 691
Tiritiri Matangi Island 159
Tongariro River 311
Jiva Island 692
Waimea Inlet 473
Whakaki Lagoon 383
Black Beach 272
Blackball 502-3
Blenheim 449-51, **449**
blokarting 70, 178, 179, 355
Blue Baths 331
Blue Lake 610
Bluff 679-80
Bluff Oyster & Southland Seafood
Festival 680
boat travel 725-6, 728, *see also*
jetboating
boat trips
Akaroa 561-2
Aratiatia Dam 307
Auckland 115
Bay of Islands 186-7
Cathedral Cove 217, 220
Doubtful Sound 671-2
Goat Island 167
Greymouth 505
Havelock 448
Kawhia 241
Lake Rotorua 330-1
Lake Tarawera 347
Lake Taupo 301
Lake Te Anau 662
Lyttelton 558
Milford Sound 631, 668-9
Nelson region 465-6
Pelorus Sound 448
Queen Charlotte Sound 439
Stewart Island 694
Sugar Loaf Islands Marine Park 261
Tongariro River 311
Waipu 168
Wanaka 649
Wellington 412
Whitianga 217
Bone People (book) 514
bone-carving, *see carving*
books 22, 23, 48
bird-watching 65, 71
fishing 73
history 36
Maori culture 58
plants 66
walking 87
Bounty Islands 701

bra fence 654
breweries
  Founders Brewery 463
  Greenfern Brewery 494
  Invercargill Brewery 676
  Lion Breweries 112
  Mac's Brewery 464
  Monteith's Brewing Co 505
  Speight's Brewing 595
  Sunshine Brewing Company 378
  Wanaka Beerworks 647
  White Cliffs Brewing Company 267
Bridal Veil Falls 240-1
Brightside Blues, Brews & BBQs 450
broTown (TV show) 46
Broadlands 308-9
Broken Hills gold-mine workings 223
brush-tailed possums 66
Buller Gorge 490-1, 492-3, 91, 92
Buller Gorge Marathon 494
Buller Gorge Swingbridge 493
bungy jumping 70, 71
  Auckland 116
  Hanmer Springs 566
  Mt Hutt 572
  Queenstown 625, 71, 547
  Rotorua 346
  Taupo 298
bungy rocket rides 413
Buried Village of Te Wairoa 346
bus travel 727-31
bushwalking, see walking
business hours 706
Butcher's Pool 308-9
BYO 97

C
Cadbury World 595
cafés 98-9
Cambridge 243-5
Campbell Island 700
campervan travel 703, 732-3
camping 91, 703
Cannibal Bay 686, 72
canoeing & kayaking 72, 91-2
Abel Tasman Coastal Track 481, 87
Abel Tasman National Park 480
Ahipara 179
Akaroa 561
Aoraki/Mt Cook National Park 587

Auckland 116-17
Bay of Islands 187, 188
Buller River 490-1, 91, 92
Cape Reinga 180
Cathedral Cove 220
Dart River 642
Doubtful Sound 670, 73
Fiordland 661
Golden Bay 485
Hokitika 510
Kaikoura 458
Lake Karapiro 245
Lake Mapourika 517
Lake Rotorua 331
Lake Taupo region 299, 301
Marlborough Sounds 439, 448
Martinborough 433
Milford Sound 668
Motueka 474
Mt Maunganui 355
Nelson region 465
Paterson Inlet 693
Puhoi 164
Punakaiki 500
Rabbit Island 473
Raglan 239
Rawene 175
Rotorua 336
Tauranga Bay 185
Tongariro National Park 318
Tongariro River 310, 320
Turangi 310
Waiheke Island 151
Waimea Inlet 473
Waitomo 251
Wanaka 648
Wellington 413
Whanganui National Park 284
Cans Film Festival 280
Canterbury region 526-88, 528
Canterbury House 564
Canterbury Museum 535
canyon swinging 70, 625
canyoning
  Auckland 116
  Queenstown 627-8
Waitakere Ranges 145
  Wanaka 648
Cape Brett 200
Cape Classic Surfing Contest 494
Cape Egmont Lighthouse 271
Cape Foulwind 496-7
Cape Foulwind Walkway 496
Cape Kidnappers Gannet Colony 400

Cape Maria van Diemen 179
Cape Palliser 434
Cape Reinga 179-81, 188, 127
Cape Runaway 371-2
Caples Track 90, 645, 644
car travel 731-5
  backpacker vans 733
  driving licence 731-2
  hire 732-4
  insurance 734
  organisations 731
  purchase 734-5
  road distance charts 731, 732
Cardrona 82, 655, 79
Caro, Niki 50
carrots 322
Carter Observatory 409
carving 61, 10, 128, 543
Cascade Creek 665
Cascade Saddle 648, 90
Castle Hill area 568
Castle Pamela 246
Castlepoint 434
Cathedral Caves 684
Cathedral Cove 217, 220
Cathedral Square 531, 544
Catlins Coastal Rainforest Park 685
Catlins Conservation Park 686
Catlins 681-7, 682, 548
Cavalli Islands 184
cave rafting 70
caving 72
cell phones 718
Central Otago Wine Experience 629
Central Otago Wine Festival 632
Central Plateau 293-326, 295
cervena 96
Champagne Pool 347
Charleston 499
Chatham Islands 688, 689, 696-700, 697
cheese 95
Cherry Island 296
Chidgey, Catherine 48
children, travel with 706-7
  Auckland 118
  Bay of Islands 188
  Christchurch 538-9
  food 99-100
  Queenstown 630-1
  Rotorua 338
  Wellington 414
Christ Church 194-5
Christ Church Cathedral 463

000 Map pages
000 Photograph pages

Christchurch 526-57, **528**, **530**, **532-3**, **544**
 accommodation 539-51
 activities 536-7
 drinking 553-4
 emergency services 529
 entertainment 554-5
 festivals 539
 food 551-3
 internet access 529, 531
 itineraries 529
 medical services 531
 shopping 555
 sights 531-6
 surrounding region 557-64
 tourist offices 531
 tours 539
 travel to/from 555-6
 travel within 556-7
 walking tour 537-8, **538**
Christchurch Art Gallery 536
Christchurch Arts Centre 534-5
Christchurch Botanic Gardens 531, 534
Christchurch Cathedral 531
Christchurch tramway 535
Chronicles of Narnia (movie) 30, 50
 Aslan's Camp 590, 617
 Flock Hill Station 568
cinema 22, 30, 47-8, 49-50
City Gallery Wellington 411
Clark, Helen 29, 39
Clay Cliffs 618
Clifden (Waiau) Caves 672
Clyde 672
climate 20-1, 64, 707-8
Climate District 613
Clutha 607-8
Coast to Coast Walkway, 115
coffee 97
Cockle Bay 673
Collingwood 485-6
colonialism 38
Colville 215-16
consulates 709-10
Cook, James 33, 34
Cook Observatory 378
Coopers Beach 182
Copland Track 522
Coromandel Coastal Walkway 216
Coromandel Forest Park 212
Coromandel Peninsula 206-25
Coromandel region 206-28, **208**
Coromandel Town 213-15, **214**
Coronet Peak 81

costs 21-3, see also inside front cover
Cosy Nook 673
crafts 716
Craigieburn 83
Craigieburn Forest Park 568-9
Craters of the Moon 308
crayfish 684
Crazy Paving & Box Canyon Caves 497
credit cards 714
cricket 46
Croesus Track 500, 502
Cromwell 606-7
Crowded House 242
Crown Range Road 655
culture 40-61
Curio Bay 684
customs regulations 708
cycling 75, 726-8
 42nd Traverse 320, 324
 Ahipara 179
 Auckland 117, 143
 Christchurch 537
 Great Barrier Island 156
 Greymouth 505
 Hanmer Springs 566
 Hawkes Bay region 398-9
 Lake Taupo region 299
 Mt Somers 574
 Murchison 491
 National Park 320
 Ohakune 324
 Otago Central Rail Trail 612
 Queenstown 628
 Rotorua 336
 Twizel 582
 Wanaka 649
 Wellington 413
 Wharepapa South 243

D
dam dropping 272
dangers 708-9
Danseys Pass 610
Dargaville 169-71, **170**
Dart River 642
Darwin, Charles 34
Dean Forest 672
deep vein thrombosis 738
deer 96, 246, 691
dendroglyphs 698
Denniston 497
Devonport 113-14, 119, 121, 123-4, 133, 137, 138, **117**
Devonport Food & Wine Festival 119
diarrhoea 739

disabled travellers 709
diving 77-8, **77**, 69
 Auckland 117
 Bay of Islands 187
 Cathedral Cove 217, 220
 Chatham Islands 699
 Gemstone Bay 220
 Gisborne 379
 Goat Island 166, 167
 Great Barrier Island 156
 Manu Bay 240
 Mikhail Lermontov 439
 Whangarei 203
 Tauranga 349
 Tairua 222
 Sugar Loaf Islands Marine Park 262
 St Kilda Beach 595
 St Clair Beach 595
 Raglan 238
 Poor Knights Islands 200-1
 Milford Sound 668
 Whangaroa Harbour 183
dolphin swimming 75
 Akaroa 562
 Auckland 116
 Bay of Islands 187
 Kaikoura 454-5, 457-8
 Tauranga 349
 Whakatane 361
Dome Forest 165
dotterels 71, 146, 223, 226, 691
Doubtful Sound 670, 671-2, 6, 73
Doubtless Bay 181-3
drinks 96-7
driving, see car travel
Driving Creek Railway 213
du 'aur, Freda 584
Dunedin 589, 590-602, **592**, 545
 accommodation 596-8
 drinking 600
 emergency services 591-3
 entertainment 600-1
 food 598-600
 Internet access 593
 shopping 601-2
 sights 593-5
 tourist information 593
 tours 596
 travel to/from 602
 travel within 602
Dunedin Botanic Gardens 594
Dunedin Public Art Gallery 594
Duntroon 617-18
Durie Hill 280
Dusky Track 670

E

Eagles Nest 196
earthquakes 64
East Cape 369-74
East Cape Lighthouse 372
East Coast 368-401, **370**
East Coast war 35
Eastern Bay of Plenty 360-7
Eastern Southland Gallery 680
Eastwoodhill Arboretum 378
economy 29-30, 39, 41, 43, 44
Edwin Fox 438
Egmont National Park 268-9
electricity 702
Elephant Rocks 617
Elvis Presley Memorial Record Room 272
email services 713
embassies 709-10
Emerald Lakes 315
emergencies, *see inside front cover*
Endless Summer (movie) 237
energy consumption 63
environmental issues 63, 67
exchange rates, *see inside front cover*
extreme sports 70, *see also* blokarting, bungy jumping, canyon swinging, canyoning, sky jumping, skydiving, sledging, zorbing

F

Fairlie 578
Fairy Pools 198
falcons 247, 523
fantails 65, 197
Farewell Spit 486-7, 542
farmstays 704
fashion 716
ferns 66
Ferry Landing 219
festivals 22, 710, *see also* food & wine festivals, music festivals, sporting events
Cans Film Festival 280
HERO Festival 711
New Zealand Festival 415
New Zealand International Comedy Festival 710
New Zealand International Film Festivals 710
Pasifika Festival 119

film, *see* cinema
Finn brothers 242
Fiordland 656-74, **658**
Fiordland National Park 67, *6, 73*
First Taranaki war 35
Firth Tower 245-6
fish & chips 99
fishing 67, 72-3
Ahipara 178
Akaroa 561
Arnold River 503
Bay of Islands 187
Cape Reinga 180
Cathedral Cove 217
Coromandel Town 213
Gabriels Gully 613
Gore 681
Great Barrier Island 156
Kaikoura 457, 458
Karamea 498
Lake Brunner 503
Lake Moeraki 523
Lake Ruataniwha 581
Lake Taupo region 298-9
Martinborough 433
Mokau 254
Mountain Valley 390
Murchison 491
Poor Knights Islands 200-1
Pukenui 181
Queenstown 629
Rotorua 336
Ruapuke Beach 240
Tairua 222
Tauranga 349
Te Anau 661
Tiniroto Lakes 382
Tongariro River 298, 320
Turangi 309-10
Waihi 225
Waipu 168
Wanaka 649
Whakatane 362
Whangaroa Harbour 183
Whitianga 217
Fletcher Bay 216
food 93-6, 97-100, 710-11
    cafés 98-9
    customs 100
    restaurants 98-9
    vegetarian travellers 99
food & wine festivals
    Bluff Oyster & Southland Seafood Festival 680

Brightstone Blues, Brews & BBQs 450
Carrot Festival 322
Central Otago Wine Festival 632
Devonport Food & Wine Festival 119
Gisborne Wine Week 379-80
Harvest Hawkes Bay 397
Kumara Festival 169
Moonshiners Festival 681
Savour festival 539
Toast Martinborough Wine, Food & Music Festival 433
Wildfoods Festival 98, 510, *12*
Wine Marlborough Festival 450
Forgotten World Highway 270-1
Forrester Gallery 615
Founders Brewery 463
Four Brothers Scenic Reserve 240
Four Sisters 173
Fox Glacier 514, 519-22, **520**, *543*
Fox Peak 578
Foxton Beach 292
Frame, Janet 615, 616
Franz Josef Glacier 514, 516-19, **517**
Frasers Beach 670
French Farm Winery 561
frisbee golf 629
Froggate Edge 243
Frying Pan Lake 347

G

Gabriels Gully 613
galleries
    Aigantighe Art Gallery 574
    Anderson Park Art Gallery 675-6
    Auckland Art Gallery 112, *126*
    Christchurch Art Gallery 536
    City Gallery Wellington 411
    Dunedin Public Art Gallery 594
    Eastern Southland Gallery 680
    Forrester Gallery 615
    Govett-Brewster Art Gallery 260
    Lake Taupo Museum & Art Gallery 296
    Millennium Art Gallery 449-50
    Southland Museum & Art Gallery 674-5
    Suter 463
    Tairawhiti Museum 377
    Te Manawa 288
    World of WearableArt & Collectable Cars Museum 466
gannets 400

000 Map pages
000 Photograph pages

gae ens
hristchurch Botanic Gardens 531, 534
nuredin Botanic Gardens 594
astwoodhill Arboretum 378
ienfalloch Woodland Garden 604
amilton Gardens 233
ree Crop Farm Park 561
Wellington Botanic Gardens 408-9
ga travellers 711
uckland 138
Wellington 415
ge-os 213
Ge-nstone Bay 220
ce-tic engineering 63
Ge-tte Annie Beach 497
ge-graphy 62-4
ge-logy 62-4
G-alcine 576-7
ge-ses 64
Lady Knox Geyser 347
Mokena Geyser 227
Pohutu 332
Prince of Wales' Feathers geyser 332, **131**
Te Puia 331-2
Wairakei 308
g-rdiasis 739
Gi-lespie Pass 653, 91
Gi-borne 375-82, **376**
Gi-borne City Vintage Railway 379
Gi-borne Wine Week 379-80
G-ciers 519
Fox Glacier 514, 519-22, **520**, 543
Franz Josef Glacier 514, 516-19, **517**
Tasman Glacier 585, 586
G-ade Wharf 667
Gi-enbrook Vintage Railway 230
Gi-en-lloch Woodland Garden 604
Gi-enorchy 642
Gi-ow-worms 249
Go-at Island 166-7, 9
Go-at Island Marine Reserve 167
Go-ds 54-5
Go-ld panning 492, 640
Go-ldblatt, David 40
Go-lden Bay 485
Go-lden Shears 434
Go-ldfields Vintage Train 224
Go-ldie, Charles Frederick 52
Go-lf 73
Arrowtown Golf Course 640
Killer Prawn Golf 307
Millbrook 640

Paraparaumu Beach Golf Club 429
Poverty Bay Golf Club 379
Queens Park Golf Course 676
Taupo 300
Terrace Downs 572
Wanaka Golf Club 649
Whakapapa 317-18
Gore 680-1
government 29
Govett-Brewster Art Gallery 260
Grace, Patricia 48
Great Barrier Island 154-9, **155**
Great Walks 87-9, see also walks
Greenfern Brewery 494
greenstone 343, 717, 543
Greenstone Track 90, 645, **644**
Grey Valley 501-3
Greymouth 503-7, **504**
Greytown 431, 432
guesthouses 703
Gumdiggers Park 179

H
Haast Pass 525
Haast region 523-5
Hahei 220-1, **128**
haka 59-61
Hamilton 230, 232-7, **334**
Hamilton Gardens 233
Hamilton Zoo 233-4
hangi 98
Hanmer Springs 84, 564-7, **565**
Hanmer Springs Thermal Reserve 565
Happy Valley Adventures 465
Haruru Falls 191
Hari Hari 513
Harvest Hawkes Bay 397
Harwood's Hole 482-3
Hastings 394-7, **395**
Haumia-tike-tike 54
Hauraki Gulf Islands 147-59
Hauraki Gulf Maritime Park 147
Hauraki region 225-8
Havelock 447-9
Havelock North 397-8
Hawai 371
Hawea 655
Hawkes Bay 382-401, **399**
Hawkes Bay Museum 388
Hawks Crag 493
health 737-40
insurance 737
websites 738
Heaphy Track 487-8

Hector's dolphins 562, *see also* dolphin swimming
Heineken Open 119, 139
Heke, Hone 36, 176, 193, 195
Helensville 147
helibiking 299, 582
helihiking 500, 516, 521, 582, 586
helirafting 505
heliskiing 84, 346, 571, 586, 628, **83**
hepatitis C 739
Heritage 585-6, 588
Hermitage 711
HERO Festival 711
Hicks Bay 372
hiking, *see* walking
Himatangi 292, **8**
Hinemoa 335
Hine-titama 54
Hirakimata 156
history 31-9
books 36
colonialism 38
European settlement 32-4
immigration 36, 37, 38
Musket Wars 34
Polynesian settlement 31-2
hitching 735-6
HIV 739
Hobbiton 245
Hokianga 173-6
Hokianga-Waipoua Coastal Track 174
Hokitika 508-12, **509**
Hokitika Gorge 512
holidays 21, 711-12
Ho Jyford Track 665
Honey Hive New Zealand 305
Honeycomb Hill Caves & Arch 497-8
hongi 58
Honourable Roddy 512
horse riding 74
hostels 704-5
hot springs 62-4
Athenree Hot Springs 225
Awakeri Hot Springs 365
Butcher's Pool 308-9
Champagne Pool 347
Frying Pan Lake 347
Great Barrier Island 156
Hanmer Springs Thermal Reserve
565
Hotwater Beach 347
Inferno Crater Lake 347
Kerosene Creek 334
Maruia Springs 568
Miranda Hot Springs 226
Morere Hot Springs 382

hot springs continued
Mt Maunganui 355
Opal Hot Springs 246
Rotorua 334
Taupo Hot Springs & Health Spa 299
Te Aroha 227
Te Puia Hot Springs 241
Te Puia Springs 374
Tokaanu Thermal Pools 309
Waikite Valley Thermal Pools 334
Waingaro Hot Springs 237
Waiwera Thermal Resort 164
Hot Water Beach 221
hot-air ballooning 70
hotels 705–6
Hotere, Ralph 53
Hotwater Beach 347
Houhora Heads 181
Howarth Wetlands Reserve 227
Huka Falls 306–7
Hukutaia Domain 365–6
Hulme, Keri 514
Hump Ridge Track 90, 672–3
Hundertwasser, Friedensreich 199
hunting 67
Huntly 232
Hutt Valley 427
hypothermia 739–40

I
immigration 36, 37, 38, 44–5, 168
regulations 722
Inferno Crater Lake 347
Inglewood 267
Inland Pack Track 90, 500
insurance
health 737
travel 712
vehicle 734
International Antarctic Centre 536, 544
International Sevens Tournament 415
Internet access 712–13
Internet resources 23
air tickets 724
health 738
walking 85
inventions 42
Invercargill 674–9, 675
Invercargill Brewery 676

itineraries 24–8
Auckland 103
coordinating author's favourite trip 17, 17
Christchurch 529
North Island 26, 26
Queenstown 624
Rotorua 330
South Island 25, 25
Wellington 405
wineries 28, 28

J
Jack's Blowhole 686
Jackson Bay 524–5
Jackson, Peter 30, 49–50, 403–4
jade 343, 717, 543
jetboating 74, 74, see also boat trips
Aratiatia 307
Bay of Islands 186
Buller Gorge 493
Dart River 642
Fiordland 661
Greymouth 505
Haast 523
Hanmer Springs 566
Huka Falls 307
Kawarau Gorge 625, 546
Lake Taupo 301
Manawatu Gorge 289
Martinborough 433
Motu River 366, 373
Mt Aspiring National Park 654
Ngaruroro River 390
Orakei Korako 308
Queenstown 625–7
Rakaia River Gorge 572
Rangitaiki River 362
Rotorua 336, 346
Tuatapere 673
Waiatoto River 523
Waitomo 251
Wanaka 648, 547
Whanganui National Park 284–5

K
K Rd 114, 135
Kahurangi National Park 487–8, 542
Kai Iwi Lakes 172, 174
Kaikohe 176
Kaikoura 454–61, 564, 456, 541, 542
Kaikoura Coast Track 90, 457
Kaikoura Wilderness Walkway 457
Kaikoura Wine Company 455–6
Kaipara Lighthouse 171–2

Kaitaia 177–8
Kaiteriteri 477
Kaka Point 686, 687
Kapiti Coast 427–31, 132
Kapiti Island 430
Karaka Bird Hide 209
Karamea 497–9
Karangahake Gorge 226–7
Karangahake Gorge Historic Walkway 226
Karapiro 245
Karekare Beach 145–6
Karikari Peninsula 181
Karioi Lakes 326
Karori Wildlife Sanctuary 412
Katikati 357–8
kauri 66
Kauri Coast 168–73
Kawarau Gorge 625, 546
Kawau Island 165–6
Kawerau 365
Kawhia 241–2
kayaking, see canoeing & kayaking
kea 65, 247, 514
Kelly Tarlton's Antarctic Encounter & Underwater World 111–12
Kepler Challenge 661
Kepler Track 660–1, 660
Kerikeri 186, 196–9, 197
Kermadec Islands 688, 689, 701
Kerosene Creek 334
Killer Prawn Golf 307
King Country 229, 230, 246–56, 231
Kingston Flyer 631
kiteboarding 92
kiwi 64, 65, 71
Aroha Island 197
Hokitika 509
Kiwi & Birdlife Park 624
National Aquarium of New Zealand 388–9
Ohakune 324
Orana Wildlife Park 536
Otorohanga Kiwi House & Native Bird Park 247
Pukaha Mt Bruce National Wildlife Centre 435
Rainbow Springs Nature Park 344
Southern Encounter Aquarium & Kiwi House 531
Stewart Island 691–2
Tiritiri Matangi Island 159
Trounson Kauri Park 172

000 Map pages
000 Photograph pages

Wellington Zoo 412
Whangarei 203
Willowbank Wildlife Reserve 536
Kiri Adventure Centre 390
Kiwi fruit 96, 359, 130
Knights Point 523
Kobbs Flat 665
Tane 535
nukohu 176
...ako 176
...nene Beach 271
...initi marae 280, 286
Koripo Pa 198
...uku 513-14
...whai 66
...whitirangi 512
...sotunu 216
...rau Park 332
...mara 168, 169
...mara Festival 169
KCpe 217

L

...y Knox Geyser 347
L.e Brunner 503
L.e Hakanoa 232
L.e Hauroko 672
L.e Hawea 655
L.e Kai Iwi 172
L.e Karapiro 245
L.e Mangamahoe 267
L.e Mapourika 517
L.e Matheson 519
L.e Moeraki 523
L.e Ohau 583
L.e Paringa 522
L.e Pukaki 581
...e Rotoiti 471
...e Rotokura 326, 331
...e Rotopounamu 309
...e Rotorua 330-1
...e Ruataniwha 581
...e Summer Forest Park 567-8
...e Taharoa 172
...e Tarawera 346-7
...e Taupo 294-312, 129
...e Taupo Cycle Challenge 299
...e Taupo Museum & Art Gallery 296
...e Tekapo 578-81, **579**
...e Te Anau 657-8
...e Waikaremoana 333
...e Waikaremoana Track 384, **385**
...e Waikere 172
...e Wakatipu 643-5, 69
...e Wanaka 645, 546

Lake Willkie 685
lamb 93-4
Lange, David 41
language 741-3
Larnach Castle 604
Lost Samurai (movie) 257, 262
Lawrence 613
legal matters 713
Leigh 166
Lenz Reserve 685
lesbian travellers 711
  Auckland 138
  Wellington 415
Leslie-Karamea Track 88, 542
Lewis Pass 567-8
Ligar Bay 485
Lion Breweries 112
literature, *see* books
Little Barrier Island 159
Long Beach 195
longest place name in the world 400, 401
Longridge Park 360
long-tail bats 665
Lord of the Rings (movie) 30, 49
  Castle Hill area 568
  Chetwood Forest 433
  Geraldine 577
  Hobbiton 245
  Mt Doom 312
  Nelson 466
  Pelennor battlefield 582
  Powderhorn Chateau 325
  Queenstown 631
  Rivendell 435
  Torgariro National Park 318
  Wanaka 650
  Wellington 415
Lost World Cave 250
Lower Hutt 427
Luge 629, 546
Lyttelton 557-9

M

Macetown 642
Mackenzie Country 578-83
Mac's Brewery 464
maerero 684
magazines 46
Mahamudra Centre 216
Makarora 653-5
Maketu 360
Maketu *marae* 241
Mamaku Blue 344
mamaku 66

mana 55-6
Mania Lodge 176
Manapouri 670-1
Manawatu Gorge 288, 289
Mangamaunu Beach 457
Manganui 81
Mangapohue Natural Bridge Scenic Reserve 252
Mangapurua Track 285
Mangawhai 167-8
Mangonui 182-3
Manhire, Bill 48
Maniapoto, Rewi 36
Manioroa *marae* 254
Mansfield, Katherine 412
Manu Bay 240, 9
Manuoha-Waikareiti Track 384
Maori
  cooking 96
  crafts 716-17
  culture 54-61, *see also marae*
  geographical terms 742
  history 31-9
  language 741-3
  population 45
  radio 47
  spirituality 32, 47
Maori King Movement 230, 233, 246-7
Maori Leap Cave 458
Maori Party 41, 56
Maori regional highlights
  Auckland 103
  Bay of Plenty 361
  Central Plateau 296
  Christchurch & the South Island 535
  East Cape 371
  Northland 191
  Taranaki 260
  Waikato 232
  Wellington 405
maps 713-14
Mapua 473
marae 57-9
  Korinti 280, 286
  Maketu 241
  Manaia Lodge 176
  Manioroa 254
  Matakana Island 357
  Nga Hau e Wha 535
  Rawhiti 200
  Rotowhio 331
  Tamaki Maori Village 333
  Tamatekapua Meeting House 331

marae continued
  Te Poho-o-Rawiri meeting house
    377
  Te Tokanganui-o-noho 253
  Tukaki 371
  Turangawaewae 232
  Whakarewarewa Thermal Village
    332
Marahau 477-8
Marine Studies Centre 604
Marineland 389
Marlborough region 436-61, **438**
Marlborough Sounds 439, 443-7, **444**
Marlborough Wine Trail 452-3, **454**
Marmite 96
Marokopa 253
Marokopa Falls 252
Marokopa Rd 252-3
Martinborough 431, 432-4
Martyr Saddle 524
Maruia Springs 568
Masterton 431, 434-5
Matai Bay 181
Matai Falls 686, 548
Matakana Island 357
Matakohe 169
Matamata 245-6
Matauri Bay 184-5
Matawhero 378
Matemateaonga Track 285
Matiu-Somes Island 412
Matukituki Valley Walks 90
Maui 54-5, 180, 690, 55
Mayor Island 357
McCahon, Colin 42, 52
McLaren Falls 349
measures 702, see also inside front
  cover
Mediaplex 411
medical services 738-9
meningococcal disease 739
Mesopotamia 577
Methven 571-3, **571**
metric conversions see inside front
  cover
Middlemarch 610
Mikhail Lermontov 439
Milford Deep Underwater Observatory
  668
Milford Sound 631, 666-9, 88, 548
Milford Track 666-8, **667**, 88

Millbrook 640
Millennium Art Gallery 449-50
Millerton 497
Mills Reef Winery 349
Mimiwhangata Coastal Park 205
Minden Lookout 358
Miranda 226
Miranda Hot Springs 226
Mirror Tarn 497
Mission House 197
Mitai Maori Village 333
Mitchell's Gully Gold Mine 499
Mitimiti 176
moa 64-5
Moana Kotuku 503
mobile phones 718
Moeraki 619, 545
mohua 683
Mokau 254
Mokena Geyser 227
moko 61, 11
Moncrieff, Suzie 466
money 21-3, 714-15, see also inside
  front cover
  discount cards 709
  public holiday surcharges 712
Monkey Island 673
Monro Beach 523
Monteith's Brewing Co 505
Moonshiners Festival 681
Morere Hot Springs 382
Moria Gate Arch 497
Moriori people 31, 698
Motat (Museum of Transport &
  Technology) 112
motels 705-6
motorcycle travel 731-5
Motu River 366, 371, 373
Motueka 474-7, **475**
Motuhora 364
Motuihe Island 159
Motuora Island 159
Moturiki Island 355
Motutapu Island 147-9, **148**
Mt Aspiring National Park 647, 649,
  654, 7, 87, 90, 91, 547
Mt Bledisloe 191
Mt Bruce 435
Mt Cook Salmon Farm 581
Mt Cook, see Aoraki/Mt Cook
  National Park
Mt Dobson 578, 580
Mt Doom 312
Mt Eden 114, 121, 123, 135-6, **109**
Mt Edgecumbe 365

Mt Egmont, see Mt Taranaki
Mt Holdsworth Circuit 90
Mt Humphries 285
Mt Hutt 82, 571, 572
Mt Hutt Forest 572
Mt Iron 648
Mt Karioi 240
Mt Lyford Ski Field 457, 566
Mt Mania 205
Mt Maunganui 354-7, **350**, 131
Mt Murchison 570
Mt Ngauruhoe 315
Mt Pirongia 243
Mt Potts 82-3
Mt Pureora 309
Mt Roy 648
Mt Ruapehu 314-15, 129
Mt Somers 573-4
Mt Somers Subalpine Walkway 573-4
Mt Taranaki 258, 267-70
Mt Tarawera 346, 347
Mt Tauhara 300
Mt Te Aroha 227
Mt Titiraupenga 309
Mt Tongariro 312, 315
Mt Tutoko 665
Mt Victoria 113
Mt Whiria 174
mountain biking, see cycling
Mountain Valley 390
mountaineering 75-6,
  see also walking
Moutoa Gardens 280
movies, see cinema
Murchison 490-2
Muriwai Beach 146-7
Muriwai Regional Park 146
Muriwai's Cave 361
museums
  Auckland Museum 109-10, 125
  Canterbury Museum 535
  Hawkes Bay Museum 388
  International Antarctic Centre
    536, **544**
  Lake Taupo Museum & Art Gallery
    296
  Mediaplex 411
  Motat (Museum of Transport &
    Technology) 112
  Museum of Wellington City &
    Sea 409
  National Cricket Museum 411
  National Maritime Museum 110
  National Tattoo Museum 411-12
  New Zealand Rugby Museum 288

000 Map pages
000 Photograph pages

Ytago Museum 594
'uke Ariki 260
totorua Museum of Art & History 331, 131
science Alive! 536
southland Museum & Art Gallery 674-5
Taiarawhiti Museum 377
'awhiti Museum 272
'e Manawa 288
Te Papa 409, 132
Waikato Museum of Art & History 233
Wanganui Regional Museum 279
World of WearableArt & Collectable Cars Museum 466
n sic 50-2
n sic festivals
Ao Tearoa Hip Hop Summit 119
Mission Bay Jazz & B ues Streetfest 119
National Jazz Festiva 351
New Zealand Gold Guitar Awards 681
Toast Martinborough Wine, Food & Music Festival 433
Waiheke Jazz Festival 119, 149
World Buskers Festival 539
W sket Wars 34, 328
n ssels 95

pier 386-94, **387**, 10
walking tour 389, **389**
N seby 610-11
N tional Aquarium of New Zealand 368-9
National Archives 410
tional Cricket Museum 411
tional Library 410
tional Maritime Museum 110
tional Park 320-2
tional parks, see parks & reserves
tional Tattoo Museum 411-12
utilus 186
sen 461-71, **462**, **464**
sen Lakes National Park 471-3, 541, 542
lson region 84, 436, 437, 461-82, **438**
tball 46
w Chum's Beach 216
w Dick's Beach 360
w Plymouth 257-67, **262**
w Plymouth Observatory 261

New Zealand Cup & Show Week 539
New Zealand Farm Show 344
New Zealand Festival 415
New Zealand Gold Guitar Awards 681
New Zealand International Comedy Festival 710
New Zealand International Film Festivals 710
New Zealand Line Dancing Championships 681
New Zealand Masters Games 710
New Zealand Merino Shearing Championships 608
New Zealand Rugby Museum 288
New Zealand Sports Hall of Fame 594
Newmarket 135-6, **109**
newspapers 46, 702
Nga Hau e Wha 535
Nga Manu Nature Reserve 430
Ngaiotonga Scenic Reserve 200
Ngakawau 497
Ngarua Caves 482
Ngaruawahia 232, 6, 10
Ngarurui Beach 240
Ngaruroro River 390
Ngata, Apirana 56, 373, 401, 60
Ngatoro-i-rangi 312
Ngawi 434
Niagara 685
Nikau Cave 232
Nile River Caves 494
Ninety Mile Beach 177, 178-81
Ninety Mile Beach-Cape Reinga Walkway 90
North Head 114
North West Circuit Track 693
Northland 160-205, **162**, **177**
Northland Land War 35, 176
Nugget Point 686, 687
Nydia Track 448

O
O Tapara 665
Oakura 271
Oamaru 614-17, **614**
Oban 589-96, **692**, 548
Ocean Beach 400
Ohakune 322-6, **323**
Ohau Forest 583
Ohawe Beach 272
Ohinemutu 331
Ohiwa 365
Ohope Beach 364
Okahutiti Pa 272
Okarito 514

Olveston 594
Omaha 166
Omahuta Forest 176
Omakau 609
Omapere 174-5
Omarama 618
Omokoroa 358
One Tree Hill 114
Opal Hot Springs 246
Oparara Arch 497
Oparara Basin 497-8, 543
Ophir 609
Opito Bay 215
Opo oni 174-5
Opoiki 365-7, **366**
Opoitere Beach 223
Opua Forest 191
Opunake 272
Oraka Deer Park 246
Orakei Korako 301, 308
Orana Wildlife Park 536
orcas 455
Orewa 163-4
Otago 589-619, **591**, **612**, 92
Otago Central Rail Trail 612
Otago Museum 594
Otago Peninsula 590-605, **603**
Otaki 430-1
Otama Beach 216
Otorohanga 247
Otorohanga Kiwi House & Native Bird Park 247
Otunua 307
Owaka 686-7
Owlcatraz 239
oysters 95

P
Pacific Ring of Fire 62
Paekakariki 428-9
Paihia 186, 189-93, **190**
Pakiri 167
Paku 222
Palmerston North 274, 275, 286-92, **276**, **287**
Pancake Rocks 500, 543
Pania of the Reef 388
Papamoa 358-9
Paparoa National Park 499-500
Papatowai 585-6
Papatuanuku 54
Paradise 642
paragliding 76, 76
Parakai 147
Paraparaumu 429-30

Paraparaumu Beach Golf Club 429
parasailing 188
Parihaka 273
parks & reserves 67-8, **68**, see also gardens
Abel Tasman National Park 67, 478-82, **479**, 7, 541
Aoraki/Mt Cook National Park 62, 67, 583-8, **584**, 6, 544
Auckland region 144
Catlins Coastal Rainforest Park 685
Catlins Conservation Park 686
Coromandel Forest Park 212
Craigieburn Forest Park 568-9
Dome Forest 165
Egmont National Park 268-9
Fiordland National Park 67, 6, 73
Four Brothers Scenic Reserve 240
Goat Island Marine Reserve 167
Hauraki Gulf Maritime Park 147
Howarth Wetlands Reserve 227
Kahurangi National Park 487-8, **542**
Kapiti Island 430
Lake Sumner Forest Park 567-8
Mangapohue Natural Bridge Scenic Reserve 252
Mimiwhangata Coastal Park 205
Mt Aspiring National Park 647, 649, 654, 7, 87, 90, 91, 547
Nelson Lakes National Park 471-3, 541, 542
Ngaiotonga Scenic Reserve 200
Paparoa National Park 499-500
Parry Kauri Park 164
Pewhairangi 189
Pirongia Forest Park 243
Pureora Forest Park 309
Rakiura National Park 689
Rapaura Water Gardens 213
Shakespear Regional Park 162
Southwest New Zealand (Te Wahipounamu) World Heritage Area 666
Sugar Loaf Islands Marine Park 261, 262
Tangoio Falls Scenic Reserve 386
Tawaroa Forest 252
Te Urewera National Park 67, 383-6

Tongariro National Park 67, 312-20, **313**, 7, 85, 129
Trounson Kauri Park 172
Victoria Forest Park 501-2
Waipatiki Scenic Reserve 386
Waipoua Kauri Forest 172-3, **173**, 127
Waitakere Ranges Regional Park 144-5
Wenderholme Regional Park 164
Westland Tai Poutini National Park 514-22, **515**, 6
Whakarewarewa State Forest Park 346
Whangamumu Scenic Reserve 200
Whanganui National Park 283-6
Whangaruru North Head Scenic Reserve 200
Whirinaki Forest Park 347
White Pine Bush Scenic Reserve 386
Parliament House 409-10
Parnell 121, 122-3, 124, 135, 138, **108**
Parry Kauri Park 164
Pasifika Festival 119
passports 722
Pataua 205
Paterson Inlet 693
paua 95, 717
Paua Shell House 679
Pauanui 221
pavlova 96
Peel Forest 577
Pegasus Bay 564
Pelorus Sound 448
Peters, Winston 29, 56
petroglyphs 699
Pewhairangi 189
Picton 424, 438-43, **440**
pigeon-grams 154
Piha Beach 145-6, 126
Pinnacles 212
Piopio 254
Pipiriki 283-4
Pirongia Forest Park 243
planning 20-3, see also itineraries
discount cards 709
plants 64-5, 66, see also individual plants
books 66
podocarp forests 683
Pohara 485
Pohaturoa 361
Pohutu 332

pohutukawa 66, 179, 212, 372
poi 61
politics 29, 39, 56
Pompallier 195
ponga 66
Ponsonby 114, 121, 123, 124, 133, 136-7, 138, **110**
Poor Knights Islands 77, 200-1
population 29, 39, 44-5
Porpoise Bay 684, 548
Porridge 673
Port Charles 215
Porter Heights 83
Portland Island Lighthouse 383
postal services 715-16
pounamu 343, 717, 543
Pounawea 687
Pouto 171-2
Poverty Bay 375-82
Poverty Bay Golf Club 379
Prawn Farm 307
Presley, Elvis 272
Prince of Wales' Feathers geyser 332, 131
Princes Wharf 134-5, 137-8, 125
puha 96
Puheke Beach 181
Puhoi 164
Pukaha Mt Bruce National Wildlife Centre 435
Puke Ariki 260
Pukeiti Rhododendron Trust 267
pukeko 65
Pukekura 513
Pukenui 181
Pukerangiora Pa 267
Puketi Forest 176
Puketui Valley 223
Punakaiki 499-501, 543
Purakaunui 686-7
Pureora Forest Park 309
puriri 261, 366
Putangirua Pinnacles 434
Putauaki 365

Q
quad biking 70
Queen Charlotte Sound 439
Queen Charlotte Track 90, 445-7
Queens Park Golf Course 676
Queenstown 620-39, **622**, **626**, 71, 546, 547
accommodation 632-5
activities 624-9
drinking 636-7

000 Map pages
000 Photograph pages

emergency services 632
entertainment 637-8
festivals 632
internet access 622-3
itineraries 624
shopping 638
sights 623-4
tourist offices 623
travel to/from 638-9
travel within 639
walking tour 629-30, 630

R

Rabbit Island 473
rafting 46-7, 702
rafting, 91-2, see also cave rafting,
helirafting
Buller Gorge 490-1, 493
Greymouth 505
Hanmer Springs 566
Lake Taupo region 299
Motu River 373
Mountain Valley 390
Queenstown 627
Rangitata River 577
Rotorua 335
Tauranga 349-51
Tongariro National Park 318
Tongariro River 310, 320
Waitomo 250-1
Wanaka 648
Raglan 237-9, 238, 128
Rainbow Falls 198
Rainbow Mountain Track 335
Rainbow Springs Nature Park 344
Rainbow Warrior 39, 170, 184, 187
Rangaia River Gorge 572
Rangiriri 230-2
Rangitaiki River 362
Rangitata National Park 689
Rakiura Track 693
Rakiura, see Stewart Island
Ranfurly 611
Rangikapiti Pa Historic Reserve 182
Ranginui 54
Rangipu Beach 240
Rangiputa 181
Rangiriri 230-2
Rangitaiki River 362
Rangitoto Island 147-9, 148
Ranapahoe 505
Rapaura Water Gardens 213
Raukokore 372
Raukumara 373
Raurimu 54
Rawene 175-6
Rawhiti 200
Rawhiti Cave 485

Rayner, Eddie 42
real estate 29-30
recycling 63
Red Hills 524
Reefton 501-2
Rees-Dart Track 90, 645
religion 42, 47
Remarkables 81
Remuera 81
rental accommodation 706
Renwick 451-4
reserves, see parks & reserves
responsible travel 63, 67, 86
restaurants 98-9
rhododendrons 267
rimu 145
Ripiro Ocean Beach 171
Riverton 673-4
Riverton Rocks 673
road distance charts 731, 732
Roaring Bay 686
rock climbing 76
Castle Hill area 568
Froggatt Edge 243
Lake Taupo region 301
Mt Aspiring National Park 649
Nelson 465
Wanaka 649
Wharepapa South 243
rock flour 578
Rongo-matane 54
Ross 512-13
Rotorua 327-43, 332, 130, 131
accommodation 338-41
activities 334-7
drinking 342
emergency services 330
entertainment 342
food 341-2
Internet access 330
medical services 330
shopping 342-3
sights 330-4
surrounding region 344-7, 345
tourist offices 330
tours 338
travel to/from 343
travel within 343
walking tour 334-5
Rotorua Museum of Art & History
331, 131
Rotowhio marae 331
Round Hill 580
Round the Mountain 90, 316-17
Routeburn Track 644-5, 644, 87, 547

Roxburgh 611-12
Royal Albatross Centre 602-3
Ruakuri Cave 251
Ruapuke Beach 240
Ruatapu Cave 308
Ruatoria 373
Ruby Bay 473
rugby 30, 45-6
Russell 186, 193-6, 194
Russell Road 200

S

saddlebacks 159
safe travel
beaches 221, 708, 740
hitching 735-6
Mt Taranaki 269
roads 708, 735
Tongariro National Park 314
walking 86, 87
sailing 76
Abel Tasman National Park 480
Auckland 115
Bay of Islands 186-7
Doubtless Bay 182
Nelson region 465-6
Waiheke Island 151
St Bathans 609-10
St Clair Beach 595, 8, 545
St Kilda Beach 595
St Mary's Church 261
sandflies 708
Sandfly Bay 604
Sandfly Point 667
Sandy Bay 200
Savour festival 539
scenic flights 70
Aoraki/Mt Cook National Park
582, 587
Bay of Islands 188
Fox Glacier 521
Franz Josef Glacier 516-17
Hokitika 510
Lake Tekapo 580
Oamaru 616
Queenstown 628, 631
Rotorua 338
Taupo 301
Tauranga 351
Te Anau 661-2
Tongariro National Park 318
Wanaka 649
Wanganui 280
Whakaari Island 351

Science Alive! 536
sea kayaking, see canoeing & kayaking
sea lions 604, 683, 548
Seahorse World Aquarium 439
seals & seal swimming 75
  Abel Tasman National Park 480
  Cape Palliser Seal Colony 434
  Kaikoura 457-8
  Sugar Loaf Islands Marine Park 261
  Tauranga Bay Seal Colony 496
Second Taranaki war 35
Seddon, Richard John 37
Seddonville 497
Shakespear Regional Park 162
Shantytown 507
sharks 75
Shaw, George Bernard 40
sheep farming 93
sheep-shearing 253
Sheepworld 165
Ship Creek 523
shoe fences 654
shopping 716-17
Shortland Street (TV show) 46
Siberia Experience 653
skiing 79-84, **79**
  Aoraki/Mt Cook National Park 586
  Arthur's Pass 83
  Cardrona 82
  Coronet Peak 81
  Craigieburn 83
  Fox Peak 578
  Hanmer Springs 84, 566
  Lake Taupo region 300
  Manganui 81
  Mt Dobson 578, 580
  Mt Hutt 82, 571
  Mt Lyford 457, 566
  Mt Potts 82-3
  Mt Taranaki 268-9
  Nelson region 84
  Ohakune 323-4
  Porter Heights 83
  Queenstown 628, 82
  Remarkables 81
  Round Hill 580
  South Canterbury 82
  Tasman Glacier 586
  Treble Cone 81, 546, 81
  Tukino 80, 317
  Turoa 80, 317
  Waiorau 82
  Wanaka 649
  Whakapapa 80, 317, 80
sky jumping 70, 116
Sky Tower 108-9, 116, 125
skydiving 84
  Auckland 116
  Bay of Islands 187-8
  Fox Glacier 521
  Kaikoura 457
  Matamata 245
  Motueka 474
  Picton 424, 439
  Queenstown 628
  Rotorua 336
  Taupo 296-8
  Twizel 582
  Wanaka 648-9
  Wellington 424
Skyline Gondola 623
Skyline Skyrides 344
Skyline Track 648
sledging 70
  Queenstown 627
  Rotorua 335
  Waingongoro River 272
  Wanaka 648
Slipper Island 223
Slope Point 684, 685
Snares Islands 700
snowboarding 79-84, 323-4, **79**
South Canterbury 82
Southern Alps 64
Southern Encounter Aquarium & Kiwi House 531
Southern Scenic Route 672-4
Southland 656, 657, 674-81, **658**
Southland Museum & Art Gallery 674-5
Southwest New Zealand (Te Wahipounamu) World Heritage Area 666
Speight's Brewery 595
spider bites 740
Splash Planet Waterpark 394
Split Enz 242
sporting events
  ASB Classic 119, 139
  Auckland Anniversary Day Regatta 119
  Auckland Cup 119
  Buller Festival 492
  Buller Gorge Marathon 494
  Cape Classic Surfing Contest 494
  Golden Shears 434
  Heineken Open 119, 139
  International Sevens Tournament 415
  Kepler Challenge 661
  Lake Taupo Cycle Challenge 299
  NZ Cup & Show Week 539
  NZ Masters Games 710
  NZ Merino Shearing Championships 608
  Te Houtawea Challenge 177
sports 45-6, see also individual sports
Springbok tour 40-1
SS Rangiriri 235
Staglands Wildlife Reserve 427
Stardome Observatory 112
State Highway 35 374
Stent Road 271
Stewart Island 688-96, **689, 690, 692,** 548
Stirling Point signpost 679
Stockton 497
Stone Store 196
Stony Bay 215-16
Stratford 270
Subantarctic Islands 688, 689, 700
Sugar Loaf Islands Marine Park 261, 262
Sulphur City 328
Summit Road 558
sun exposure 740
Sunshine Brewing Company 378
Surat Bay 687
Surf Highway 45 271-3
surfing 77, 78, see also beaches
Suter 463
Sutherland Falls 667

T
Taieri Gorge Railway 593-4, 545
Tainui canoe 241, 254
Taipa 182
Tairawhiti Museum 377
Tairua 221-3
takahe 65, 159, 660
Takaka 483-5
Takaka Hill 482
Taketakerau 366
Takiroa Maori Rock Art Site 618
Tamaki Maori Village 331
Tamatekapua Meeting House 331
Tane-mahuta 54
Tangaroa 54
Tangoio Falls Scenic Reserve 386
Tapotupotu Bay 179
tapu 55-6
Taramea Bay 673

000 Map pages
000 Photograph pages

Tamaki 257-73, **259**
Tamaki Land Wars 35, 273
Tamua Wind Farm 288-9
Tasman, Abel 32
Tasman Glacier 585, 586
tattoos 61, 11
Taranaki 255-6
Ta piri Mountain 232
Ta oo 393-305, **297, 306**
Ta oo Adventure Park 300
Ta oo Hot Springs & Health Spa 299
Ta oo Volcanic Zone 62
Tauranga 348-54, **348, 350**
Tauranga Bay 184-5
Tauranga Bay Seal Colony 496
Tautulu Bay 685
Tararau Forest 252
Tawhiti-matea 54
Tawhiti Museum 272
Tawhiti Rahi 200
taxes 715, 721, 723
taxis 736
Taylor, Chad 48
Taylors Mistake 537
Te Anau 657-64, **659**
Te Anau Glow-worm Caves 659-60
Te Anau Wildlife Centre 660
Te Apiti Wind Farm 289
Te Araroa 372
Te Arewa 328
Te Arawa canoe 360
Te Aroha 227-8
Te Aute College 401
Te Awamutu 242-3
Te Henga Beach 146
Te Houtawea Challenge 177
Te Kaha 371
Te Kaihinaki 619
Te Kanawa, Dame Kiri 379
Te Kooti 253, 378
Te Kuiti 253-4
Te Manawa 288
Te Mata Peak 397
Te Matua Ngahere 173
Te Papa 409, **132**
Te Pare Point 220
Te Pcho-o-Rawiri meeting house 377
Te Puia 331-2, 10
Te Puia Hot Springs 241
Te Puia Springs 374
Te Puke 359-60, **130**
Te Reinga Falls 382
Te Rerenga-Wairua 57, 179
Te Tai Tokerau, see Northland
Te Tokanganui-o-noho marae 253

Te Urewera National Park 67, 383-6
Te Waewae Bay 673
Te Waikcropupu Springs 483
Te Wairoa 62, 346
Te Whakarewarewa 331-2, 131
Te Whiti 273
telephone services 717-18
Terrace Downs 572
Te-Waha-O-Rerekohu 372
Thames 209-12, **210**
theft 703
thermal pools & springs,
   see hot springs
Thrillseekers Canyon 566
Tiki 61
Tikitere 346
Tikitiki 373
time 718-19
Timaru 574-6, **575**
Timeball Station 558
Tiniroto Lakes 382
tipping 715
Tirau 246
Tiritiri Matangi Island 159
Titan the Giant Sheep 344
Toast Martinborough Wine, Food &
   Music Festival 433
toheroa 95
Tohu 273
Tokaanu Thermal Pools 309
Tokelau 688, 689, 701
Tokomaru Bay 374
Tolaga Bay 374
Tongariro Crossing 90 315-16
Tongariro National Park 67, 90,
   312-20, **313**, 7, 85, 129
Tongariro National Trout Centre 309
Tongariro Northern Circuit 315
Tongariro River 298, 310, 311, 320
totara 60
tourist information 719
train travel 727, 736
tramping, see walking
Tranz Scenic 736
TranzAlpine 508
travellers cheques 715
Treaty of Waitangi 35, 41, 102, 186,
   191, 241, 361
Treble Cone 81, 81, 546
Tree Crop Farm Park 561
trekking, see walking
Trounson Kauri Park 172
trout 95, 298, 309, 344
Tryphena 154
TSS Earnslaw 631

Tuatapere 672-3
tuatara 64, 430
Tuhua 357
tui 65, 197, 344, 660, 691
Tukaki marae 371
Tukino 80, 317
Tu-matauenga 54
Turanga marae 232
Turangawaewae marae 232
Turangi 309-12, **310**
Turoa 80, 317
Turururumokai Pa 272
Tutaekai 335
Tutanekai Pa 272
Tutu 200
Tutukaka Coast 200-1
TV 46, 702
Twizel 581-3

U
ugg boots 716
Ulster history 357
Ulva Island 692
Upper Hutt 427
Urenui 267
Urupukapuka Island 189

V
vacations 21, 711-12
Vegemite 96
vegetarian travellers 99, 711
Viaduct Harbour 134-5, 137-8
Victoria Forest Park 501-2
Victory Beach 604, 9
video systems 702
visas 719-20, see also passports
visual arts 52-3
Volcanic Activity Centre 307
vo canoes 62-4,
   Auckland region 114, 119
   Kuirau Park 332
   Lake Taupo region 294
   Mayor Island 357
   Motuhora 364
   Motutapu Island 147-9, **148**
   Mt Edgecumbe 365
   Mt Ngaurunoe 315
   Mt Ruapehu 314-15, **129**
   Mt Taranaki 258, 267-70
   Mt Tarawera 346, 347
   Mt Tongariro 312, 315
   Putauaki 365
   Rangitoto Island 147-9, **148**
   Tuhua 357
   Whale Island 364
   Whakaari Island 364-5, **130**
Volkner, Rev Carl 365

W

Wai Ora Spa & Wellness Centre 346
Waiatoto River 523
Waiau Waterworks 216
Waiheke Island 149-54, **150,** 126
Waihi 224-5
Waikanae 430
Waikanae Beach 379
Waikato 229-46, **231**
Waikato Land War 230, 246-7, 328-9
Waikato Museum of Art & History 233
Waikato River 295
Waikato war 35
Waikawa 684, 685
Waikite Valley Thermal Pools 334
Waimangu Volcanic Valley 347
Waimarama Beach 400
Waimarie 279
Waimea Inlet 473
Waingaro Hot Springs 237
Wainui Beach 379
Waioeka 373
Waiorau 82
Waiotapu Thermal Wonderland 347, **130**
Waiouru 326
Waipapa Point 684, 685
Waipara Springs 564
Waipara Valley 564
Waipatiki Scenic Reserve 386
Waipawa 401
Waipoua Kauri Forest 172-3, **173,** 127
Waipu 168
Waipukurau 401
Wairaka 360
Wairakei 305-8
Wairarapa 431-5
Wairoa 383-401
Waitahi 365
Waitakere Ranges Regional Park 144-5
Waitaki Valley 617-18
Waitangi 189-93, **190,** 127
Waitangi Day 188
Waitiki Landing 180
Waitomo 248-52, **248**
Waitomo Cave 248-9, 250, **128**
Waiuta 502
Waiwera Thermal Resort 164
Wake, Nancy 38

Wakefield, Edward Gibbon 36
walking 85-91
books 87
equipment 85, 141
Great Walks 87-9, **89**
Internet resources 85
maps 87
responsible tramping 86
track classification 87
track safety 87
walks
Abel Tasman Coastal Track 478-80, 481, 87
Arthur's Pass 570
Banks Peninsula Track 90, 561
Big River Track 502
Cape Foulwind Walkway 496
Caples Track 90, 645, **644**
Cascade Saddle 648, **90**
Coast to Coast Walkway 115
Copland Track 522
Coromandel Coastal Walkway 216
Croesus Track 500, 502
Dusky Track 670
Gillespie Pass 653, 91
Great Walks 87-9, **89**
Greenstone Track 90, 645, **644**
Heaphy Track 487-8
Hokianga-Waipoua Coastal Track 174
Hollyford Track 665
Hump Ridge Track 90, 672-3
Inland Pack Track 90, 500
Kaikoura Coast Track 90, 457
Kaikoura Wilderness Walkway 457
Karangahake Gorge Historic Walkway 226
Kepler Track 660-1, **660**
Lake Waikaremoana Track 384, **385**
Lake Wakatipu region 643-5
Leslie-Karamea Track 488, 542
Mangapurua Track 285
Mangawhai Cliffs Walkway 167
Manuoha-Waikareiti Track 384
Matemateaonga Track 285
Milford Track 666-8, **667,** 88
Mt Somers Subalpine Walkway 573-4
Mt Taranaki 268-9
Ninety Mile Beach-Cape Reinga Walkway 90
Nydia Track 448
Queen Charlotte Track 90, 445-7
Rainbow Mountain Track 335

Rakiura 693
Rees-Dart Track 90, 645
Round the Mountain 316-17
Routeburn Track 644-5, **644,** 87, 547
Skyline Track 648
Taupiri Mountain 232
Tongariro Crossing 90, 315-16
Tongariro National Park 312-17, 85
Tongariro Northern Circuit 315
Wangapeka Track 488
Whakatane River Round Trip 384
Whanganui National Park 284, 285
Wanaka 646-53 **622, 646**
Wanaka Beerworks 647
Wanaka Golf Club 649
Wanaka region 620, 621, 645-55
Wanganui 274, 275, 277-83, **276, 278**
Wanganui region 274-86
Wanganui Regional Museum 279
Wangapeka & Leslie-Karamea Tracks 91
Wangapeka Track 488
Warawara Forest 176
warfare 34, 37-8
Warkworth 164-5
water 740
Waterworld 235
weather 20-1, 707-8
websites, see Internet resources
weights 702
weka 247, 660, 692
Wellington 402-27, **404, 406-7, 410,** 11, 132
accommodation 416-18
activities 413
drinking 421-2
emergency services 408
entertainment 422-3
festivals 415-16
food 418-21
Internet access 408
itineraries 405
medical services 408
shopping 423-4
sights 408-12
tourist offices 408
tours 414-15
travel to/from 424-5
travel within 425-7
walking tour 413-14, **414**
Wellington Botanic Gardens 408-9
Wellington Zoo 412
Wenderholme Regional Park 164

000 Map pages
000 Photograph pages

We... Coast 489-525, **491**
We...rn Bay of Plenty 347-60
We... and Tai Poutini National Park 4-22, **515,** 6
We...port 493-6, **494**
we... 54
Wh...aari Island 351, 364-5, 130
Wh...aki Lagoon 383
Wh...apapa 80, 314, 317-20, **318,** ?, 129
Wh...arewarewa Thermal Village 6
Wh...arewarewa State Forest Park
2
Wh...atane 360-4, 364-5, **362**
Wh...atane Astronomical Observatory
31
Wh...atane River Round Trip 384
Wh...e Bay 240
Wh...e Island 364
Wh...e Rider (movie) 50, 374, 379
wh... watching 75, 187, 454-5, 57, 542
Wh...ngamata 223-4
Wh...ngamumu Scenic Reserve 200
Wh...nganui National Park 283-6
Wh...nganui River Road 283, 286
Wh...nganui Riverboat Centre 279
Wh...ngaparaoa Peninsula 162-3
Wh...ngapoua 216
Wh...ngara 374
Wh...ngarei 201-5, **202**
Wh...ngaroa Harbour 183-5
Wh...ngaruru North Head Scenic eserve 200
Wh...rariki Beach 437
Wh...rekawa Wildlife Refuge 223
Wh...repapa South 243
Wh...taroa 513-14
Wh...tipu Beach 145
Wh...rinaki Forest Park 347
Wh...e Cliffs Brewing Company 267

White Island, see Whakaari Island
White Pine Bush Scenic Reserve 386
white heron 513-14
whitebait 95, 498
white-water rafting, see rafting
Whitianga 217-19, **218**
Wildfoods Festival 98, 510, 12
wildlife parks & zoos
  Agrodome 344
  Auckland Zoo 112
  Cherry Island 296
  Hamilton Zoo 233-4
  Karori Wildlife Sanctuary 412
  Kiwi & Birdlife Park 624
  Nga Manu Nature Reserve 430
  Orana Wildlife Park 536
  Owlcatraz 289
  Paradise Valley Springs 344
  Pukaha Mt Bruce National Wildlife Centre 435
  Rainbow Springs Nature Park 344
  Royal Albatross Centre 602-3
  Staglands Wildlife Reserve 427
  Te Anau Wildlife Centre 560
  Wellington Zoo 412
  Wharekawa Wildlife Refuge 223
  Willowbank Wildlife Reserve 536
  Yellow-eyed Penguin Conservation Reserve 603-4
Willing Workers on Organic Farms 704
Willowbank Wildlife Reserve 536
windsurfing 92, **92**
wine 96-7, 97-8
Wine Marlborough Festival 450
wineries 97
  Auckland region 119, 144-5
  Canterbury House 564
  Castle Rock Winery 216
  Central Otago 629, 532
  Cooks Landing 230
  French Farm Winery 561
  Gisborne 378

Hawkes Bay 398-400, **399**
itineraries 28
Kaikoura Wine Company 455-6
Kerikeri 198
Mamaku Blue 344
Marlborough region 452-3, **454**
Martinborough 432-3
Mills Reef Winery 349
Nelson region 466, 473
Ohinemuri Estate 227
Okahu Estate Winery 178
Pegasus Bay 564
Purangi Winery 221
Queenstown 631-2, 12
Te Rerenga 216
Waiheke Island 149-51
Waipara Springs 564
Warkworth area 166
Vishart Huka Winery 306
Wizard 531
women travellers 720
women in New Zealand 47-8
woodcarving, see carving
Woollaston, Toss 52
work 720-1
Word of Heritage areas 67
World of WearableArt & Collectable Cars Museum 466
World of WearableArt Award Show 416
Wrinkly Rams 618
wrybill 226
WWI 37-8
WWII 38

Y
Yellow-eyed Penguin Conservation Reserve 603-4

Z
zoos, see wildlife parks & zoos
zorbing 70, 344-6, 130

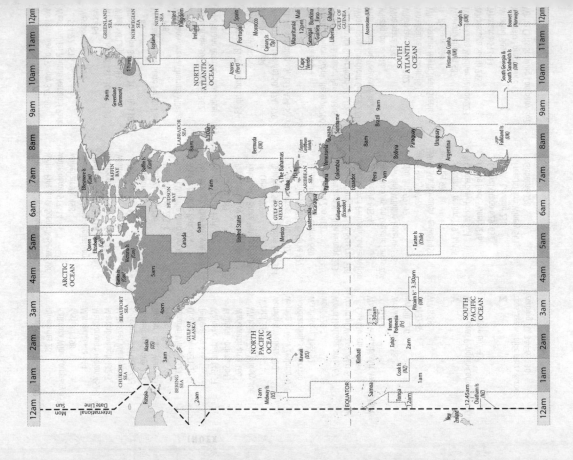

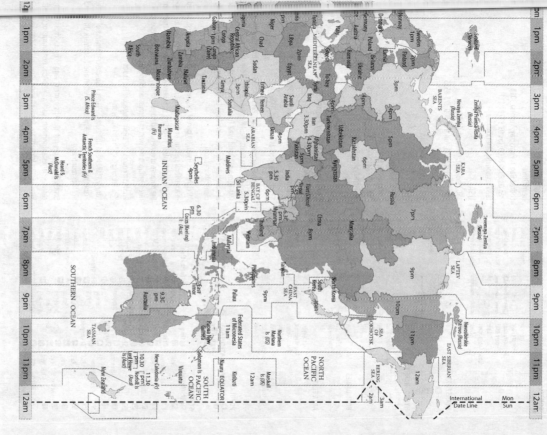

1pm · 2pm · 3pm · 4pm · 5pm · 6pm · 7pm · 8pm · 9pm · 10pm · 11pm · 12am

Iceland (Norway)

Sweden 1pm · Norway · Denmark · Finland

Germany · Poland, Belarus · Austria · Italy · Greece · Romania · Ukraine

MEDITERRANEAN SEA · Malta · 2pm · Turkey · Libya · Egypt · Iraq 3pm · Saudi Arabia · Iran 3.30pm · Turkmenistan

Tunisia · Niger · Chad · Sudan · Eritrea · Yemen · Oman · Afghanistan 4.30pm · Pakistan 5pm

Nigeria 2pm · Central African Republic · Ethiopia 3pm · Somalia · ARABIAN SEA · India 5.30pm

Gabon 1pm · Congo · Congo (Zaire) · Kenya · Tanzania · Maldives · Sri Lanka · 5.30pm · BAY OF BENGAL

Angola · Zambia · Malawi · Madagascar · Seychelles 4pm · INDIAN OCEAN · 6pm · Myanmar · 6.30pm

Namibia · Zimbabwe · Mozambique · Mauritius · Reunion (Fr) · 6.30pm · Cocos (Keeling) Is (Aust) · Thailand · Vietnam

Botswana · South Africa

BARENTS SEA · Zemlya Frantsa-Iosifa (Russia) · Novaya Zemlya (Russia)

Uzbekistan · Kazakhstan · KARA SEA

Kyrgyzstan · 6pm

Nepal 5.45pm · China 8pm · Russia 7pm · Mongolia

Prince Edward Is (S. Africa) · French Southern & Antarctic Territories (Fr) · Heard & McDonald Is (Aust)

SOUTHERN OCEAN

TASMAN SEA · New Zealand

9.30 pm Australia

EAST CHINA SEA · Taiwan · Philippines · Palau · East Timor · Indonesia · Malaysia

LAPTEV SEA · Severnaya Zemlya (Russia)

EAST SIBERIAN SEA

SEA OF OKHOTSK · Novosibirskie Ostrova (Russia)

South Korea · North Korea · Japan 9pm · 10pm · 11pm · 12am

BERING SEA

NORTH PACIFIC OCEAN · 12am · Marshall Is (US) · Northern Mariana Is (US)

Papua New Guinea 11am · Federated States of Micronesia 11am · Nauru · Kiribati · Solomon Is · Vanuatu · New Caledonia (Fr) 11.30 · Norfolk Is (Aust) · Lord Howe Is (Aust) 10.30 pm · Fiji · EQUATOR

SOUTH PACIFIC OCEAN

1pm · 2pm · 3pm · 4pm · 5pm · 6pm · 7pm · 8pm · 9pm · 10pm · 11pm · 12am · 1am

2am · 3am · International Date Line · Mon Sun

MAP LEGEND

ROUTES

Tollway	One-Way Street
Freeway	Street Mall/Steps
Primary Road	Tunnel
Secondary Road	Walking Tour
Tertiary Road	Walking Tour Detour
Lane	Walking Trail
Under Construction	Walking Path
Track	Pedestrian Overpass
Unsealed Road	

TRANSPORT

Ferry	Rail
Metro	Rail (Underground)
Bus Route	Tram

HYDROGRAPHY

River, Creek	Canal
Intermittent River	Water
Swamp	Lake (Dry)
Mangrove	Lake (Salt)
Reef	Mudflats

BOUNDARIES

State, Provincial	Regional, Suburb
Marine Park	Cliff

AREA FEATURES

Airport	Mall
Area of Interest	Market
Beach, Desert	Park
Building	Reservation
Campus	Rocks
Cemetery, Christian	Sports
	Urban
Forest	
Land	

POPULATION

CAPITAL (NATIONAL)	CAPITAL (STATE)
Large City	Medium City
Small City	Town, Village

SYMBOLS

Sights/Activities
Beach, Castle, Fortress, Christian, Diving, Snorkelling, Islamic, Jewish, Monument, Museum, Gallery, Point of Interest, Pool, Ruin, Skiing, Surfing, Surf Beach, Trail Head, Winery, Vineyard, Zoo, Bird Sanctuary

Eating
Eating

Drinking
Drinking, Café

Entertainment
Entertainment

Shopping
Shopping

Sleeping
Sleeping, Camping

Transport
Airport, Airfield, Bus Station, Cycling, Bicycle Path, General Transport, Parking Area, Petrol Station, Taxi Rank

Information
Bank, ATM, Embassy/Consulate, Hospital, Medical, Information, Internet Facilities, Police Station, Post Office, GPO, Telephone, Toilets

Geographic
Lighthouse, Lookout, Mountain, Volcano, National Park, Pass, Canyon, Picnic Area, River, Flow, Waterfall

---

LONELY PLANET OFFICES

Australia

Head Office
Locked Bag 1, Footscray, Victoria 3011
☎ 03 8379 8000, fax 03 8379 8111
talk2us@lonelyplanet.com.au

USA

150 Linden St, Oakland, CA 94607
☎ 510 893 8555, toll free 800 275 8555
fax 510 893 8572
info@lonelyplanet.com

UK

72–82 Rosebery Ave,
Clerkenwell, London EC1R 4RW
☎ 020 7841 9000, fax 020 7841 9001
go@lonelyplanet.co.uk

Published by Lonely Planet Publications Pty Ltd

ABN 36 005 607 983